J. M. and M. J. Cohen

The New Penguin Dictionary of

Quotations

VIKING

VIKING

Published by the Penguin Group
Penguin Books Ltd, 27 Wrights Lane, London W8 5TZ, England
Penguin Books USA Inc., 375 Hudson Street, New York, New York 10014, USA
Penguin Books Australia Ltd, Ringwood, Victoria, Australia
Penguin Books Canada Ltd, 2801 John Street, Markham, Ontario, Canada L3R 1B4
Penguin Books (NZ) Ltd, 182–190 Wairau Road, Auckland 10, New Zealand

Penguin Books Ltd, Registered Offices: Harmondsworth, Middlesex, England

The Penguin Dictionary of Quotations first published in Penguin 1960
This revised and expanded edition first published 1992
10 9 8 7 6 5 4 3 2 1

The Penguin Dictionary of Quotations copyright © J. M. and M. J. Cohen, 1960
The New Penguin Dictionary of Quotations copyright © M. J. Cohen and
the Estate of the late J. M. Cohen, 1992

Printed in England by Clays Ltd, St Ives plc
Set in 8/10 pt Lasercomp Photina

A CIP catalogue record for this book is available from the British Library

ISBN 0–670–82952–8

To fill up a work with these scraps may, indeed be considered as a downright cheat on the learned world, who are by such means imposed upon to buy a second time in fragments and by retail, what they already have in gross, if not in their memories, upon their shelves.

HENRY FIELDING: *Tom Jones*

I might repeat to myself, slowly and soothingly, a list of quotations beautiful from minds profound; if I can remember any of the damn things.

DOROTHY PARKER: *The Little Hours*

Foreword to the New Edition

The opportunity to prepare a new edition of *The Penguin Dictionary of Quotations* a generation later than our first has allowed great expansion of the entries drawn from the twentieth century but the loss of only a handful of lines that now seem to us to have rolled over the edge of memorability. This has meant that where Winston Churchill, G. K. Chesterton, W. H. Auden and a number of other highly quotable contributors found themselves uncomfortably straddled between this dictionary and its sister volume, *The Penguin Dictionary of Modern Quotations*, we have now been able to include all the most memorable and best-remembered lines from such writers in this dictionary. Yet *The Penguin Dictionary of Modern Quotations* – since it is devoted solely to the twentieth century – can serve up not only all these classic lines but also a generous helping of the less familiar phrases from the same writers. Then, too, our first edition was published in mid-century and was sound and middle-aged in its quotationary choice. But, now the century is so elderly, people's memories have become less literary and more quirky. So television, the cinema, advertising, graffiti rightly have their say. In the foreword to our first edition we were doubtful that there would be phrase-making politicians in the future. Westminster and Washington cannot be said to reverberate with oratory, but along with one of our new entrants we have needed to do a U-turn, even if it would be an exaggeration to say that Margaret Thatcher and President Reagan rub shoulders with Edmund Burke and Franklin D. Roosevelt as phrase-makers. So while the book continues to provide, we hope, an unrivalled feast of the classical quotations that form the staple of our literary and popular culture, it has been enriched by a new range of flavours. Not surprisingly, it has put on a good deal of weight in the process, and we are grateful for having been allowed to let out its jacket accordingly.

J.M.C. M.J.C.
1991

Foreword to the First Edition

A dictionary of quotations must serve at least three purposes. Its owners must be able to find, with the aid of the index, the speaker or writer responsible for a phrase that has stuck – or half-stuck – in their heads, or for a reference found during their reading. The dictionary must guide them to the context, giving them, where possible, line and page references to some easily available edition. By use of the index too, they must be able to see what has been said on a particular subject by a variety of men; to turn up such key-words as *God*, *life*, *love*, *money*, *peace*, *war*, *word* and *world* is to discover a babel of opinions, with one or more of which they may care to embellish their own writing or conversation at the proper moment. Direct use of the first section, moreover, arranged under alphabetical order of authors, will give them some of the outstanding statements made by the great, or by the not-so-great who have for some reason been remembered.

It is remarkable that it is not always those who are most read or respected who have left the greatest number of sayings in the popular memory. Samuel Butler the elder, for example, can have few readers today, yet his once universally quoted political satire *Hudibras* has enriched the language with a great number of almost proverbial maxims, many of which are included in the present book. Wilde and Shaw coined ready-made quotations as they wrote; Henry James and D. H. Lawrence, though at present even more widely read, have left few phrases that are remembered. Single observations of theirs can seldom be detached from their context.

A large proportion of the quotations to be found here are necessary inclusions in any dictionary of quotations. The Bible, Shakespeare, *Paradise Lost* and Boswell's *Life of Johnson* inevitably contribute a great number of pages. The compilers' free choice is limited to modern authors; and here they have to decide what will be read and quoted during the lifetime of their book. What to take from W. H. Auden, Christopher Fry, John Osborne and Dylan Thomas; which, if any, of our present-day politicians will be remembered for anything at all; what newspaper, broadcasting or advertising catchwords will last longer than the customary few months: these are problems which force them to take risks, possibly at the price of proving bad prophets.

Not only in the choice of modern authors, but also in the selection from writings in foreign languages, the present compilers have taken their own line. With the decline in the study of the Classics, it has seemed sensible to dispense with all quotations in the original Greek, and severely to limit the representation of Latin authors. On the other hand French is more adequately covered in this book than in most other dictionaries, and quite a few entries have been admitted in German. All foreign quotations are followed by a prose translation; and often, where the original does not stick in the English memory, the translation only is given. It would be pedantic, for instance, to print the very well-known sayings from *Don Quixote* in Spanish, since the book is invariably read in English.

Quotations are taken from the most readily available source; those from the Bible are, except when otherwise described, taken from the Authorized Version; those from Shakespeare from the one-volume Oxford edition edited by

W. J. Craig; those from the English poets from the Oxford Editions of Standard Authors; and those from the Latin from the Oxford Classical Texts. Line numbering invariably differs from edition to edition, particularly in Shakespeare, on account of the interpolated prose passages. Those possessing other editions therefore may have to glance up and down the page.

The compilers hope that the book will prove easy to use. The index acts as a guide not only to the page on which the quotation is given, but to the number of that quotation on the page; and the indexing is, we hope, so thorough that users will find the saying they want by turning up any of the more striking words in it, that stick in their minds. Finally we hope that, in addition to its use as a reader's and writer's companion – and occasional aid in the solution of crossword puzzles – *The Penguin Dictionary of Quotations* will give some pleasure to those who browse in it.

J.M.C.   M.J.C.
1960

Note

In order to save space, lines of verse are run on and the divisions between lines are indicated by oblique strokes.

A

LUCIUS ACCIUS 170–c. 85 BC

1 *Oderint, dum metuant.* – Let them hate so long as they fear. [Quoted in Cicero's *Philippic, I. 14]*

LORD ACTON 1834–1902

2 Power tends to corrupt, and absolute power corrupts absolutely. Great men are almost always bad men. [*Historical Essays and Studies,* Appendix]

CHARLES FOLLEN ADAMS 1842–1918

3 I haf von funny leedle poy / Vot gomes schust to mine knee: / Der queerest schap, der createst rogue / As efer you dit see. [*Yawcob Strauss*]

F. P. ADAMS 1881–1960

4 The rich man has his motor car, / His country and his town estate. / He smokes a fifty-cent cigar / And jeers at Fate. [*The Rich Man*]

5 Yet though my lamp burns low and dim, / Though I must slave for livelihood – / Think you that I would change with him? / You bet I would!

JOHN QUINCY ADAMS 1767–1848

6 Think of your forefathers! Think of your posterity! [Speech, 22 Dec. 1802]

SAMUEL ADAMS 1722–1803

7 A nation of shopkeepers are very seldom so disinterested. [Speech said to have been made at Philadelphia, 1 Aug. 1776 (see 291:21, 398:17)]

SARAH FLOWER ADAMS 1805–1848

8 Nearer, my God, to Thee. [Hymn title]

JOSEPH ADDISON 1672–1719

9 And, pleased the Almighty's orders to perform, / Rides in the whirlwind, and directs the storm. [*The Campaign,* 291]

10 'Tis not in mortals to command success, / But we'll do more, Sempronius; we'll deserve it. [*Cato,* I. ii. 43]

11 And if, the following day, he chance to find / A new repast, or an untasted spring. / Blesses his stars, and thinks it luxury. [I. iv. 68]

12 When love once pleads admission to our hearts, / In spite of all the virtue we can boast, / The woman that deliberates is lost. [IV. i. 29]

13 It must be so – Plato, thou reason'st well! – / Else whence this pleasing hope, this fond desire, / This longing after immortality? [V. i. 1]

14 'Tis heaven itself, that points out an hereafter, / And intimates eternity to man. / Eternity! thou pleasing, dreadful thought! [8]

15 From hence, let fierce contending nations know / What dire effects from civil discord flow. [iv. 111]

16 For wheresoe'er I turn my ravished eyes, / Gay gilded scenes and shining prospects rise, / Poetic fields encompass me around, / And still I seem to tread on classic ground. [*Letter from Italy*]

17 Music, the greatest good that mortals know,

/ And all of heaven we have below. [*Song for St Cecilia's Day*]

1 Pray consider what a figure a man would make in the republic of letters. [*Ancient Medals*, i]

2 Thus I live in the world rather as a spectator of mankind than as one of the species. [*The Spectator*, 1]

3 Nothing is capable of being well set to music that is not nonsense. [18]

4 A perfect tragedy is the noblest production of human nature. [39]

5 In all thy humours, whether grave or mellow, / Thou'rt such a touchy, testy, pleasant fellow; / Hast so much wit, and mirth, and spleen about thee, / There is no living with thee nor without thee. [68, adapted from Martial, xii. 47]

6 The infusion of a China plant sweetened with the pith of an Indian cane. [69]

7 Sunday clears away the rust of the whole week. [112]

8 Sir Roger told them, with the air of a man who would not give his judgement rashly, that much might be said on both sides. [122]

9 I have often thought, says Sir Roger, it happens very well that Christmas should fall out in the middle of winter. [269]

10 These widows, sir, are the most perverse creatures in the world. [335]

11 This Mr Dryden calls 'the fairy way of writing'. [419]

12 Through all Eternity to Thee / A joyful song I'll raise, / For oh! Eternity's too short / To utter all Thy praise. [453]

13 We have in England a particular bashfulness in everything that regards religion. [458]

14 The spacious firmament on high, / And all the blue ethereal sky, / And spangled heavens, a shining frame, / Their great Original proclaim. [465, Ode]

15 Soon as the evening shades prevail, / The moon takes up the wondrous tale, / And nightly to the listening earth / Repeats the story of her birth:

Whilst all the stars that round her burn, / And all the planets, in their turn, / Confirm the tidings as they roll, / And spread the truth from pole to pole.

16 The Hand that made us is divine.

17 A woman seldom asks advice before she has bought her wedding clothes. [475]

18 Our disputants put me in mind of the skuttle fish, that when he is unable to extricate himself, blackens all the water about him, till he becomes invisible. [476]

19 I value my garden more for being full of blackbirds than of cherries, and very frankly give them fruit for their songs. [477]

20 'We are always doing', says he, 'something for Posterity, but I would fain see Posterity doing something for us.' [583]

21 I remember when our whole island was shaken with an earthquake some years ago, there was an impudent mountebank who sold pills which (as he told the country people) were very good against an earthquake. [*The Tatler*, 240]

22 I have but ninepence in ready money, but I can draw for a thousand pounds. [Contrasting his powers of conversation and writing. Quoted in Boswell, *Life of Johnson*, 7 May 1773]

23 See in what peace a Christian can die. [Dying words. Quoted in Young, *Conjectures on Original Composition*]

MAX ADELER 1847–1915

24 We have lost our little Hanner in a very painful manner. [*Little Hanner*]

25 Willie had a purple monkey climbing on a yellow stick, / And when he sucked the paint all off, it made him deathly sick. [*The Purple Monkey*]

ADVERTISEMENTS

26 Beanz Meanz Heinz. [Ascr. to Ruth Watson of Young & Rubicam agency]

27 Body Odour. [Advertising slogan for Lifebuoy soap]

28 Born 1820 – Still Going Strong [Advertisement for Johnny Walker whisky]

29 Dr Williams' pink pills for pale people.

30 Drinka pinta milka day.

31 Even your best friends won't tell you. [American advertisement for Listerine mouthwash]

32 Every picture tells a story. [Advertisement for Sloane's Backache and Kidney Pills, *c.* 1907]

1 Go to work on an egg. [Ascr. to Fay Weldon in the *Sunday Times*, 12 Jan. 1975]

2 Guinness is Good For You. [Ascr. to O. Greene of S. H. Benson agency, 1929]

3 Heineken. Refreshes the parts other beers cannot reach. [Ascr. to Terry Lovelock *et al.* of Collett, Dickenson, Pearce & Partners in E. Booth-Clibborn (ed.), *Design and Art Direction '78*]

4 Is your journey really necessary? [Railway poster of 1939–45 War]

5 The man from the Pru. [Used from 1950, but phrase of far earlier origin]

6 My Goodness, My Guinness. [Ascr. to John Gilroy of S. H. Benson agency, 1935]

7 Penny plain, twopence coloured. [Slogan for Pollock's Toy Theatres]

8 Put a Tiger in Your Tank [Esso petrol, from 1964]

9 That schoolgirl complexion. [For Palmolive soap. Ascr. to C. S. Pearce]

10 That's Shell, that was. [Current in 1930s]

11 They come as a boon and a blessing to men, / The Pickwick, the Owl, and the Waverley pen.

12 We're number two. We try harder. [Avis car rental slogan. Ascr. to Doyle, Dane & Bernbach agency]

13 What did you do in the Great War, daddy? [Recruiting poster, 1914–18 War]

14 Whiter than white. [Detergent advertisement]

15 Worth a guinea a box. [For Beecham's Pills]

THOMAS ADY 17 Cent.

16 Matthew, Mark, Luke, and John, / The bed be blest that I lie on. / Four angels to my bed, / Four angels round my head, / One to watch, and one to pray, / And two to bear my soul away. [*A Candle in the Dark* (1655)]

AESOP *fl. c.* 550 BC

17 Beware that you do not lose the substance by grasping at the shadow. [*Fables*, 'The Dog and the Shadow']

18 The Dog in the Manger. [Title of fable]

19 I am sure the grapes are sour. ['The Fox and the Grapes']

20 Thinking to get at once all the gold that the goose could give, he killed it, and opened it only to find – nothing. ['The Goose with the Golden Eggs']

21 The gods help them that help themselves. ['Hercules and the Waggoner']

22 It is not only fine feathers that make fine birds. ['The Jay and the Peacock']

23 While I see many hoof-marks going in, I see none coming out. ['The Lion, the Fox, and the Beasts']

24 I will have nothing to do with a man who can blow hot and cold with the same breath. ['The Man and the Satyr']

25 Don't count your chickens before they are hatched. ['The Milkmaid and her Pail']

26 The boy cried 'Wolf, wolf!' and the villagers came out to help him. ['The Shepherd's Boy']

27 Only cowards insult dying majesty. ['The Sick Lion']

28 The Wolf in Sheep's Clothing. [Title of fable]

AGATHON 447?–401 BC

29 Even God cannot change the past. [Quoted in Aristotle's *Nicomachean Ethics*, 6]

A. C. AINGER 1841–1919

30 God is working His purpose out as year succeeds to year, / God is working His purpose out and the time is drawing near; / Nearer and nearer draws the time, the time that shall surely be, / When the earth shall be filled with the glory of God as the waters cover the sea. [Hymn]

THOMAS À KEMPIS *see* KEMPIS, THOMAS À

MARK AKENSIDE 1721–1770

31 Such and so various are the tastes of men. [*The Pleasures of the Imagination*, iii. 567]

EDWARD ALBEE 1928–

32 Who's Afraid of Virginia Woolf? [Title of play]

ALCUIN 735–804

33 *Nec audiendi sunt qui solent docere, 'Vox*

populi, vox dei'; cum tumultuositas vulgi semper insaniae proxima est. – Nor should we listen to those who say, 'The voice of the people is the voice of God', for the turbulence of the mob is always close to insanity. [*Epistolae*, 166. §9]

HENRY ALDRICH 1647–1710

1 If all be true that I do think, / There are five reasons we should drink; / Good wine, a friend, or being dry, / Or lest we should be by and by; / Or any other reason why. [*A Catch*]

ALEXANDER THE GREAT 356–323 BC

2 I am dying with the help of too many physicians. [Quoted in Evan Esar (ed.), *Treasury of Humorous Quotations*]

MRS C. F. ALEXANDER 1818–1895

3 All things bright and beautiful, / All creatures great and small, / All things wise and wonderful, / The Lord God made them all. [Hymn]

4 The rich man in his castle, / The poor man at his gate, / God made them, high or lowly, / And ordered their estate.

5 Jesus calls us; o'er the tumult / Of our life's wild, restless sea. [Hymn]

6 Once in royal David's city / Stood a lowly cattle shed, / Where a Mother laid her Baby / In a manger for His bed: / Mary was that Mother mild, / Jesus Christ her little Child. [Hymn]

7 There is a green hill far away, / Without a city wall, / Where the dear Lord was crucified, / Who died to save us all. [Hymn]

WILLIAM ALEXANDER, EARL OF STIRLING 1567?–1640

8 The weaker sex, to piety more prone. [*Doomsday*, Hour V. 45]

ALFONSO THE WISE, KING OF CASTILE 1221–1284

9 If I had been present at the creation, I would have given some useful hints for the better arrangement of the Universe. [Attr.]

RICHARD ALISON *fl. c.* 1606

10 There is a garden in her face, / Where roses and white lilies grow. [*An Hour's Recreation in Music*]

11 There cherries grow, that none can buy / Till cherry-ripe themselves do cry.

ABBÉ D'ALLAINVAL 1700–1753

12 *L'embarras des richesses.* – Too much to choose from. [Title of play]

GRANT ALLEN 1848–1899

13 The Woman who Did. [Title of novel]

WOODY ALLEN 1935–

14 Is sex dirty? Only if it's done right. [From film *All You've Ever Wanted to Know About Sex*]

15 It was the most fun I ever had without laughing. [On sex. From film *Annie Hall*, scripted with Marshall Brickman]

16 Don't knock it, it's sex with someone you love. [Of masturbation]

17 It's not that I'm afraid to die. I just don't want to be there when it happens. [*Without Feathers*, 'Death (A Play)']

18 I am at two with nature. [Quoted in Adler and Feinman, *Woody Allen: Clown Prince*, Ch. 3]

WILLIAM ALLINGHAM 1828–1889

19 Up the airy mountain, / Down the rushy glen, / We daren't go a-hunting, / For fear of little men. [*The Fairies*]

20 Four ducks on a pond, / A grass-bank beyond, / A blue sky of spring, / White clouds on the wing: / What a little thing / To remember for years – / To remember with tears! [*A Memory*]

ST AMBROSE 337–397

21 *Si fueris Romae, Romano vivito more: / Si fueris alibi, vivito sicut ibi.* – When in Rome, live as the Romans do; when elsewhere, live as they live elsewhere. [Advice to St Augustine, quoted by Jeremy Taylor, *Ductor Dubitantium*, I. i. 5]

LEO AMERY 1873–1955

22 Speak for England. [Said to Arthur Greenwood, spokesman for the Labour Party, in the House of Commons, 2 Sept. 1939, but Harold Nicolson, in his diary, attributes the words to Robert Boothby]

23 You have sat too long here for any good

you have been doing. Depart, I say, and let us have done with you. In the name of God, *go!* [Speech, repeating Cromwell's words (see 129:16), addressed to Neville Chamberlain's government, House of Commons, 7 May 1940]

HENRI-FRÉDERIC AMIEL 1821–1881

1 *Un paysage quelconque est un état de l'âme.* – Any landscape is a condition of the spirit. [*Fragments d'un journal intime*]

KINGSLEY AMIS 1922–

2 Lucky Jim. [Title of novel]

3 Feeling a tremendous rakehell, and not liking myself much for it, and feeling rather a good chap for not liking myself much for it, and not liking myself at all for feeling rather a good chap. [*That Uncertain Feeling*, Ch. 7]

4 More will mean worse. [Of the expansion of higher education. Article in *Encounter*, July 1960]

HANS CHRISTIAN ANDERSEN 1805–1875

5 'But the Emperor has nothing on at all!' said a little child. [*The Emperor's New Clothes*]

6 The Ugly Duckling. [Title of story]

LANCELOT ANDREWES 1555–1626

7 The nearer the Church the further from God. [*Sermon on the Nativity* (1622)]

NORMAN ANGELL 1874–1967

8 The Great Illusion. [Title of book which proved that war could not pay]

ANONYMOUS

Play

9 Everyman, I will go with thee and be thy guide, / In thy most need to go by thy side. [*Everyman* (morality play)]

Poems

10 From alle wymmen my love is lent. / And lyht on Alysoun. [*Alysoun*, 13 Cent.]

11 Lenten ys come with love to toune, with blosmen and with briddes roune. [*Lenten is Come with Love to Town*, 13 Cent.]

12 Nou sprinkes the sprai, / al for love icche am to seeke / that slepen i ne mai. [*Now Springs the Spray*, 13 Cent.]

13 Sumer is icumen in. / Lhude sing cuccu! / Groweth sed and bloweth med / And springth the wude nu. [*Sumer is Icumen In*, 13 Cent.]

14 Maiden in the mor lay – / in the mor lay – / sevenyst fulle, sevenist fulle. [*Maiden of the Moor*, 14 Cent.]

15 Adam lay I-bowndyn, bowndyn in a bond, / Fowre thowsand wynter thowt he not to long; / And al was for an appil, an appil that he tok, / As clerkis fyndin wretyn in here book. [*Bless the Time the Apple was Taken!* 15 Cent.]

16 Western Wind, when wilt thou blow, / The small rain down can rain? / Christ if my love were in my arms / And I in my bed again! [16 Cent.]

17 From the hag and hungry goblin / That into rage would rend ye, / And the spirit that stands by the naked man / In the book of Moons defend ye! [*Tom o' Bedlam*, 17 Cent.]

18 The Gipsy snap and Pedro / Are none of Tom's comradoes. / The punk I scorn and the cutpurse sworn / And the roaring boys' bravado.

19 With an host of furious fancies / Whereof I am commander, / With a burning spear, and a horse of air, / To the wilderness I wander. / By a knight of ghosts and shadows / I summoned am to tourney / Ten leagues beyond the wide world's end, / Methinks it is no journey.

20 If all the world were paper, / And all the sea were ink, / And all the trees were bread and cheese, / What should we do for drink? [*If All the World were Paper*, 17 Cent.]

21 In his chamber, weak and dying, / While the Norman Baron lay, / Loud, without, his men were crying, / 'Shorter hours and better pay'. [*A Strike among the Poets*, 19 Cent.]

22 When he kill the Mudjokivis, / Of the skin he made him mittens, / Made them with the fur side inside, / Made them with the skin side outside. [*The Modern Hiawatha*, 19 Cent.]

Rhymes, Catches and Epigrams

23 An Austrian army, awfully arrayed, / Boldly by battery besieged Belgrade. ['Siege of Belgrade', *The Trifler* (1817)]

24 Great Chatham with his sabre drawn / Stood waiting for Sir Richard Strachan; / Sir Richard, longing to be at 'em, / Stood waiting for the Earl of Chatham. [*At Walcheren* (1809). Sometimes ascr. to George Canning]

Anonymous

1 He that fights and runs away / May live to fight another day. [*Musarum Deliciae*, 17 Cent.]

2 Here lies Fred, / Who was alive and is dead: / Had it been his father, / I had much rather; / Had it been his brother, / Still better than another; / Had it been his sister, / No one would have missed her; / Had it been the whole generation, / Still better for the nation: / But since 'tis only Fred, / Who was alive and is dead, – / There's no more to be said. [Horace Walpole, *Memoirs of George II*]

3 Here we come gathering nuts in May, / Nuts in May, On a cold and frosty morning. [*Here We Come Gathering Nuts in May*]

4 I know two things about the horse, / And one of them is rather coarse. [*The Weekend Book*]

5 I slept and dreamed that life was beauty; / I woke and found that life was duty. [*Duty*, 19 Cent. Some sources ascr. to Ellen Sturgis Hooper]

6 King Charles the First walked and talked / Half an hour after his head was cut off. [Peter Puzzlewell, *A Choice Collection of Riddles, Charades, and Rebuses*, 18 Cent.]

7 The law doth punish man or woman / That steels the goose from off the common, / But lets the greater felon loose, / That steels the common from the goose. [On enclosures, 18 Cent.]

8 Little Willie from his mirror / Licked the mercury right off, / Thinking in his childish error, / It would cure the whooping cough. / At the funeral his mother / Smartly said to Mrs Brown: / ''Twas a chilly day for Willie / When the mercury went down'. [*Willie's Epitaph*]

9 Lizzie Borden took an axe / And gave her mother forty whacks; / When she saw what she had done, / She gave her father forty-one! [On an American trial of the 1890s]

10 Miss Buss and Miss Beale / Cupid's darts do not feel. / How different from us, / Miss Beale and Miss Buss. [On two Victorian headmistresses]

11 Multiplication is vexation, / Division is as bad; / The Rule of three doth puzzle me, / And Practice drives me mad. [Elizabethan MS (1570)]

12 The noble Duke of York, / He had ten thousand men, / He marched them up to the top of the hill, / And he marched them down again. / And when they were up, they were up, / And when they were down, they were down, / And when they were only half way up, / They were neither up nor down. [*The Noble Duke of York*, 18 Cent.]

13 Now I lay me down to sleep; / I pray the Lord my soul to keep. / If I should die before I wake, / I pray the Lord my soul to take. [Prayer. 18 Cent.]

14 Please to remember the Fifth of November, / Gunpowder Treason and Plot. [Traditional]

15 There was a young lady of Riga, / Who rode with a smile on a tiger; / They returned from the ride / With the lady inside, / And the smile on the face of the tiger. [Limerick]

16 There was an old man of Boulogne, / Who sang a most topical song, / It wasn't the words / Which frightened the birds, / But the horrible double-entendre. [Limerick]

17 Thirty days hath September, / April, June, and November; / All the rest have thirty-one, / Excepting February alone, / And that has twenty-eight days clear / And twenty-nine in each leap-year. [*Stevens MS* (c. 1555)]

Sayings

18 A beast, but a just beast. [Of Dr Temple, Headmaster of Rugby]

19 Earned a precarious living by taking in one another's washing. [Quoted in *The Commonweal*, 6 Aug. 1887. Attr. by William Morris to Mark Twain]

20 The eternal triangle. [Book review, *Daily Chronicle*, 5 Dec. 1907]

21 From ghoulies and ghosties and long-leggety beasties / And things that go bump in the night, / Good Lord, deliver us! [Scottish prayer]

22 How different, how very different from the home life of our own dear Queen! [Quoted in Irvin S. Cobb, *A Laugh a Day*. The alleged remark of a British matron during a performance of *Antony and Cleopatra*]

23 An intelligent Russian once remarked to us, 'Every country has its own constitution; ours is absolutism moderated by assassination'. [Count Münster, *Political Sketches of the State of Europe* (1868)]

24 The King over the water. [Jacobite toast]

1 Muscular Christianity. [Description of Kingsley's doctrine. *Edinburgh Review*, Jan. 1858]

2 A place within the meaning of the Act. [*The Betting Act*]

Songs

3 Absence makes the heart grow fonder. [From *Davison's Poetical Rhapsody* (1602)]

4 The animals went in one by one, / There's one more river to cross. [*One More River*]

5 As I sat on a sunny bank, / On Christmas Day in the morning, / I spied three ships come sailing by. [Carol: *As I sat on a Sunny Bank*]

6 Begone, dull care! I prithee begone from me! / Begone, dull care, you and I shall never agree. [*Begone Dull Care*]

7 The bells of hell go ting-a-ling-a-ling / For you but not for me. [Song of the 1914–18 War]

8 Bring us in no browne bred, for that is made of brane, / Nor bring us in no white bred, for therein is no gane, / But bring us in good ale! [*Bring us in Good Ale*]

9 But such a woe, believe me, as wins more hearts, / Than Mirth can do with her enticing parts. [*I saw my Lady weep*, set by John Dowland]

10 The Campbells are comin', oho, oho. [*The Campbells are Comin'* (c. 1715)]

11 Casey Jones, he mounted to the cabin, / Casey Jones, with his orders in his hand! / Casey Jones, he mounted to the cabin, / Took his farewell trip into the promised land. [*Casey Jones*]

12 Come lasses and lads, get leave of your dads, / And away to the Maypole hie, / For every he has got him a she, / And the fiddler's standing by. [*Come Lasses and Lads*]

13 Early one morning, just as the sun was rising, / I heard a maid singing in the valley below: / 'Oh, don't deceive me; Oh, never leave me! / How could you use a poor maiden so?' [*Early One Morning*]

14 Farewell and adieu to you, / Fair Spanish Ladies, / Farewell and adieu to you, Ladies of Spain. [*Spanish Ladies*]

15 For there was a man, sold lily-vite sand, / In Cupid's net had caught her; / And right over head and ears in love / Vent the putty little ratcatcher's daughter. [*The Ratcatcher's Daughter*]

16 For they're hangin' men and women there for the wearin' o' the Green. [*The Wearin' o' the Green*. Irish street ballad]

17 Frankie and Johnny were lovers, my gawd, how they could love, / Swore to be true to each other, true as the stars above; / He was her man, but he done her wrong. [*Frankie and Johnny*]

18 God rest you merry, gentlemen, / Let nothing you dismay; / Remember Christ our Saviour, / Was born on Christmas Day. [Carol: *God Rest You*]

19 Greensleeves was all my joy. / Greensleeves was my delight, / Greensleeves was my heart of gold, / And who but Lady Greensleeves? [*Greensleeves*]

20 Alas my love! ye do me wrong / To cast me off discourteously.

21 Ha-ha-ha, you and me, / Little brown jug, don't I love thee! [*The Little Brown Jug*]

22 He was a wight of high renown, / And thou art but of low degree; / 'Tis pride that pulls the country down; / Then take thine auld cloak about thee! [*The Old Cloak*, sung in *Othello*, II. iii]

23 Here we come a-wassailing. [Carol]

24 Hierusalem, my happie home / When shall I come to thee? [*Song*, 'made by F.D.P.']

25 The holly and the ivy, / When they are both full grown / Of all the trees that are in the wood, / The holly bears the crown: / The rising of the sun / And the running of the deer, / The playing of the merry organ, / Sweet singing in the choir. [Carol: *The Holly and the Ivy*]

26 I feel no pain, dear mother, now / But oh! I am so dry! / Oh, take me to a brewery / And leave me there to die. [Shanty]

27 In Dublin's fair city, where girls are so pretty, / I first set my eyes on sweet Molly Malone, / As she wheeled her wheelbarrow through streets broad and narrow, / Crying, Cockles and mussels! alive, alive, oh! [*Cockles and Mussels*]

28 In good King Charles's golden days, / When loyalty no harm meant; / A furious High-Churchman I was, / And so I gained preferment. [*The Vicar of Bray*]

29 And damned are those who dare resist, / Or touch the Lord's Anointed. / And this is law, I will maintain, / Unto my dying day, Sir, / That whatsoever King shall reign, / I will be the Vicar of Bray, Sir!

Anonymous

1 When George in pudding time came o'er, / And moderate men looked big, Sir.

2 Is that Mr Reilly, can anyone tell? / Is that Mr Reilly who owns the hotel? / Well, if that's Mr Reilly they speak of so highly, / Upon me soul, Reilly, you're doin' quite well. [*Is that Mr Reilly*, Chorus (1882)]

3 It is good to be merry and wise, / It is good to be honest and true, / It is best to be off with the old love, / Before you are on with the new. [*Songs of England and Scotland* (1835)]

4 It's love that makes the world go round. [Translation of French song]

5 King Stephen was a worthy peer; / His breeches cost him but a crown; / He held them sixpence all too dear, / Therefore he called the tailor lown. / Like a fine old English gentleman, / All of the olden time. [*The Fine Old English Gentleman*]

6 O, No, John! No, John! No, John! No! [*O No, John*]

7 Oh, Shenandoah, I long to hear you. / Away, you rolling river. [Shanty: *Oh, Shenandoah*]

8 Oh, 'tis my delight on a shining night, in the season of the year. [*The Lincolnshire Poacher*]

9 Oh! where is my wandering boy to-night? / The boy who was bravest of all. [*Oh! Where is my Boy To-night?*]

10 O ye'll tak' the high road, and I'll tak' the low road, / And I'll be in Scotland afore ye, / But me and my true love will never meet again, / On the bonnie, bonnie banks o' Loch Lomon'. [*The Bonnie Banks o' Loch Lomon'*]

11 An old Soldier of the Queen's, / And the Queen's old Soldier. [*An Old Soldier of the Queen's*]

12 Old soldiers never die; / They only fade away! [Song of the 1914–18 War]

13 She was poor but she was honest, / Victim of the squire's whim: / First he loved her, then he left her, / And she lost her honest name. [Song of the 1914–18 War, of which there are many versions]

14 See the little old-world village / Where her aged parents live, / Drinking the champagne she sends them; / But they never can forgive.

15 Standing on the bridge at midnight, / She says: 'Farewell, blighted Love.' / There's a scream, a splash – Good Heavens! / What is she a-doing of?

16 It's the same the whole world over, / It's the poor what gets the blame, / It's the rich what gets the pleasure, / Isn't it a blooming shame?

17 Some talk of Alexander, and some of Hercules; / Of Hector and Lysander, and such great names as these; / But of all the world's brave heroes, there's none that can compare / With the tow, row, row, row, row, row, for the British Grenadier. [*The British Grenadier*]

18 Swing low sweet chariot, / Comin' for to carry me home; / I looked over Jordan, an' what did I see? / A band of Angels coming after me, / Comin' for to carry me home. [Negro spiritual]

19 There is a tavern in the town, / And there my true love sits him down. [*There is a Tavern in the Town*]

20 Fare thee well, for I must leave thee, / Do not let this parting grieve thee, / And remember that the best of friends must part.

21 Adieu, adieu, kind friends, adieu, adieu, adieu, / I can no longer stay with you, stay with you. / I'll hang my harp on a weeping willow-tree. / And may the world go well with thee.

22 Tom Pearse, Tom Pearse, lend me your grey mare, / All along, down along, out along lee. / For I want for to go to Widdicombe Fair, / Wi' Bill Brewer, Jan Stewer, Peter Gurney, Peter Davey, Dan'l Whiddon, Harry Hawk, / Old Uncle Tom Cobbleigh and all. [*Widdicombe Fair*]

23 Until he came to a mer-ma-id / At the bottom of the deep blue sea, / Singing, Rule Britannia, Britannia, rule the waves! / Britons never, never never shall be marr-i-ed to a mer-ma-id / At the bottom of the deep blue sea. [*Oh! 'Twas in the Broad Atlantic*]

24 Wash me in the water / Where you wash your dirty daughter / And I shall be whiter / Than the whitewash on the wall. [*The Top of the Dixie Lid*. Song of the 1914–18 War]

25 We're here because we're here because we're here because we're here. [American song of the 1914–18 War]

26 Weep you no more, sad fountains; / What need you flow so fast? / Look how the snowy

mountains / Heaven's sun doth gently waste. [*Weep you no more*, set by John Dowland]

1 What is our life? a play of passion, / Our mirth the music of derision, / Our mothers' wombs the tiring houses be, / Where we are dressed for this short comedy. [*On the Life of Man*, from Orlando Gibbons, *First Set of Madrigals and Motets*]

2 Only we die in earnest, that's no jest.

3 What shall we do with the drunken sailor? / Early in the morning? [Shanty]

Greek

4 Know thyself. [Written up in the temple at Delphi]

5 Nothing to excess. [Written up in the temple at Delphi, according to Plato's *Protagoras*]

Latin

6 *Adeste fideles, / Laete triumphantes; / Venite, venite in Bethlehem.* [Hymn, 18 Cent. See F. Oakely for trans.]

7 *Ave Caesar, morituri te salutant.* – Hail Caesar, those about to die salute you. [Gladiators' salute on entering the arena]

8 *Cras amet qui nunquam amavit quique amavit cras amet.* – Tomorrow may he love who never loved before, and may he who has loved love too. [*Pervigilium Veneris*]

9 *Et in Arcadia ego.* – I too am in Arcadia. [Inscription on a tomb, the subject of paintings by Nicolas Poussin and others]

10 *Gaudeamus igitur, / Iuvenes dum sumus.* – Let us live then and be glad / While young life's before us. [Medieval students' song]

11 *Quidquid agas, prudenter agas, et respice finem.* – Whatever you do, do cautiously, and look to the end. [*Gesta Romanorum*, cap. 103]

12 *Tempora mutantur, et nos mutamur in illis.* – Times change, and we change with them. [Quoted in Harrison, *Description of Britain* (1577), Pt III. Ch. iii]

French

13 *Ah! ça ira, ça ira, ça ira, ça ira, / Les aristocrates à la lanterne.* – Oh, it'll be, it'll be, it'll be, it'll be, / The aristocrats will hang. [Refrain of the French Revolution. The phrase 'ça ira' is pre-revolutionary]

14 *Cet animal est très méchant. Quand on l'attaque il se défend.* – This creature is very wicked. He defends himself when attacked. [*La Ménagerie*, by Théodore P.K., identity unknown (1868)]

15 *Il ne faut pas être plus royaliste que le roi.* – You must not be more royalist than the king. [A phrase current in the reign of Louis XVI; see Chateaubriand, *La Monarchie selon la Charte*]

16 *Ils ne passeront pas.* – They shall not pass. [Watchword during defence of Verdun, 1916 (see 308:5). The phrase was used again during the defence of Madrid by the Government 1936–8 in the Spanish form of ¡*no pasarán!* (see 214:2)]

17 *Liberté! Égalité! Fraternité!* – Liberty! Equality! Fraternity! [Phrase used in the French Revolution, but actually earlier in origin]

18 *Revenons à ces moutons.* – Let us return to those sheep: i.e. to the subject. [*La Farce de Maître Pathelin*, III. iv]

19 *Le roi est mort, vive le roi.* – The king is dead, long live the king. [Phrase used by the heralds to proclaim the death of one French king and the accession of his successor. First used in 1461]

Italian

20 *Se non è vero, è molto ben trovato.* – If it is not true, it is a very happy invention. [Common saying, quoted by Giordano Bruno, 1585]

APPIUS CAECUS 4 Cent. BC

21 *Fabrum esse suae quemque fortunae.* – Each man the architect of his own fate. [Quoted by Sallust, *De Civitate*, I. 2]

THOMAS APPLETON 1812–1884

22 Good Americans, when they die, go to Paris. [Quoted in O. W. Holmes, *Autocrat of the Breakfast Table*, Ch. 6]

ARABIAN NIGHTS

23 Who will change old lamps for new? ... new lamps for old? [*The History of Aladdin*]

24 Open Sesame! [*The History of Ali Baba*]

ARCHIMEDES 287–212 BC

25 *Eureka!* – I have found it! [On making a discovery]

26 Give me a firm spot on which to stand, and I will move the earth. [On the lever]

HANNAH ARENDT 1906–1975

27 The banality of evil. [Referring to the

revelations of the Eichmann trial in Jerusalem in her book *Eichmann in Jerusalem*]

COMTE D'ARGENSON 1652–1721

1 ABBÉ GUYOT DESFONTAINES (excusing himself for having written a libellous pamphlet): *Il faut que je vive.* – But I must live.
D'ARGENSON: *Je n'en vois pas la nécessité.* – I do not see the necessity. [Quoted in Voltaire, *Alzire*, 'Discours préliminaire']

LUDOVICO ARIOSTO 1474–1533

2 *Natura il fece, e poi ruppe la stampa.* – Nature made him, and then broke the mould. [*Orlando Furioso*, X. 84]

ARISTOTLE 384–322 BC

3 A tragedy is the imitation of an action that is serious, and also, as having magnitude, complete in itself . . . with incidents arousing pity and terror, with which to accomplish its purgation of these emotions. [*Poetics*, 6]

4 Tragedy is an imitation of a whole and complete action of some amplitude. . . . Now a whole is that which has a beginning, a middle, and an end. [7]

5 Poetry is more philosophical and of higher value than history. [9]

6 A plausible impossibility is always preferable to an unconvincing possibility. [24]

7 Man is by nature a political animal. [*Politics*, I. 2]

8 Either a beast or a god. [14]

9 Plato is dear to me, but dearer still is truth. [Attr.]

JOHN ARMSTRONG 1709–1779

10 Th' athletic fool, to whom what Heaven denied / Of soul, is well compensated in limbs. [*Art of Preserving Health*, III. 206]

11 Distrust yourself, and sleep before you fight. / 'Tis not too late tomorrow to be brave. [IV. 457]

NEIL ARMSTRONG 1930–

12 That's one small step for [a] man. One giant leap for mankind. [On landing on the moon, 21 July 1969. In the transcript the word 'a' is inaudible]

SIR ROBERT [later LORD] ARMSTRONG 1927–

13 (Of his evidence at the Peter Wright–MI5 trial in Melbourne.) It contains a misleading impression, not a lie. It was being economical with the truth. [Quoted in the *Observer*, 'Sayings of the Year', 28 Dec. 1986. The phrase dates back at least to R. S. Surtees in the nineteenth century]

PETER ARNO 1904–1968

14 I consider your conduct unethical and lousy. [Cartoon caption]

15 Well, back to the old drawing board. [Cartoon caption, as designer walks away from crashed plane]

SIR EDWIN ARNOLD 1832–1904

16 Veil after veil will lift – but there must be / Veil upon veil behind. [*The Light of Asia*, VIII]

17 Nor ever be ashamed / So we be named / Press-men; Slaves of the Lamp; Servants of Light. [*The Tenth Muse*]

GEORGE ARNOLD 1834–1865

18 The living need charity more than the dead. [*The Jolly Old Pedagogue*]

MATTHEW ARNOLD 1822–1888

19 And we forget because we must / And not because we will. [*Absence*]

20 And then he thinks he knows / The hills where his life rose, / And the sea where it goes. [*The Buried Life*]

21 The Sea of Faith / Was once, too, at the full and round earth's shore / Lay like the folds of a bright girdle furled. / But now I only hear / Its melancholy, long, withdrawing roar, / Retreating, to the breath / Of the night-wind, down the vast edges drear / And naked shingles of the world. [*Dover Beach*]

22 And we are here as on a darkling plain / Swept with confused alarms of struggle and flight, / Where ignorant armies clash by night.

23 Is it so small a thing / To have enjoyed the sun, / To have lived light in the spring, / To have loved, to have thought, to have done? [*Empedocles on Etna*, I. ii. 397]

24 Not here, O Apollo! / Are haunts meet for

thee. / But, where Helicon breaks down / In cliff to the sea. [II. 421]

1 'Tis Apollo comes leading / His choir, the Nine. / The leader is fairest, / But all are divine. [445]

2 Eyes too expressive to be blue, / Too lovely to be grey. [*Faded Leaves*, 4]

3 Come, dear children, let us away; / Down and away below. [*The Forsaken Merman*, 1]

4 Now the great winds shoreward blow, / Now the salt tides seaward flow; / Now the wild white horses play, / Champ and chafe and toss in the spray. [4]

5 ˙Where the great whales come sailing by, / Sail and sail, with unshut eye. [43]

6 Children dear, was it yesterday / (Call yet once) that she went away? [48]

7 A wanderer is man from his birth. / He was born in a ship / On the breast of the river of Time. [*The Future*]

8 Wandering between two worlds, one dead, / The other powerless to be born. [*The Grande Chartreuse*, 85]

9 Years hence, perhaps, may dawn an age, / More fortunate, alas! than we, / Which without hardness will be sage, / And gay without frivolity. [157]

10 Creep into thy narrow bed, / Creep, and let no more be said! [*The Last Word*]

11 Let the long contention cease! / Geese are swans, and swans are geese.

12 Let the victors, when they come, / When the forts of folly fall, / Find thy body by the wall.

13 He bears the seed of ruin in himself. [*Merope*, 856]

14 We cannot kindle when we will / The fire which in the heart resides, / The spirit bloweth and is still, / In mystery our soul abides. [*Morality*]

15 Now he is dead! Far hence he lies / In the lorn Syrian town; / And on his grave, with shining eyes, / The Syrian stars look down. [*Obermann Once More*, 173]

16 Strew on her roses, roses, / And never a spray of yew. / In quiet she reposes: / Ah! would that I did too! [*Requiescat*]

17 To-night it doth inherit / The vasty hall of death.

18 Not deep the poet sees, but wide. [*Resignation*, 214]

19 Friends who set forth at our side, / Falter, are lost in the storm. / We, we only, are left! [*Rugby Chapel*, 102]

20 Go, for they call you, shepherd, from the hill. [*The Scholar-Gypsy*, 1]

21 All the live murmur of a summer's day. [20]

22 Tired of knocking at Preferment's door. [35]

23 Crossing the stripling Thames at Bablock-hithe, / Trailing in the cool stream thy fingers wet, / As the slow punt swings round. [74]

24 Waiting for the spark from heaven to fall. [120]

25 Sad Patience, too near neighbour to despair. [195]

26 This strange disease of modern life. [203]

27 Still nursing the unconquerable hope, / Still clutching the inviolable shade. [211]

28 The young light-hearted masters of the waves. [241]

29 Shy traffickers, the dark Iberians come: / And on the beach undid his corded bales. [249]

30 Others abide our question. Thou art free. / We ask and ask: Thou smilest and art still, / Out-topping knowledge. [*Shakespeare*]

31 And thou, who didst the stars and sunbeams know, / Self-schooled, self-scanned, self-honoured, self-secure / Didst tread on earth unguessed at. Better so!

32 Truth sits upon the lips of dying men. [*Sohrab and Rustum*, 656]

33 But the majestic river floated on, / Out of the mist and hum of that low land, / Into the frosty starlight, and there moved, / Rejoicing, through the hushed Chorasmian waste, / Under the solitary moon. [875]

34 The shorn and parcelled Oxus strains along / Through beds of sand and matted rushy isles – / Oxus, forgetting the bright speed he had / In his high mountain cradle in Pamere, / A foiled circuitous wanderer – till at last / The longed-for dash of waves is heard. [884]

35 From whose floor the new-bathed stars / Emerge, and shine upon the Aral Sea. [891]

36 And see all sights from pole to pole, / And glance, and nod, and bustle by; / And never

once possess our soul / Before we die. [*A Southern Night*, 69]

1 The signal-elm, that looks on Ilsley downs. [*Thyrsis*, 14]

2 That sweet city with her dreaming spires. [(Oxford) 19]

3 He went; his piping took a troubled sound / Of storms that rage outside our happy ground. [48]

4 The bloom is gone, and with the bloom go I. [60]

5 Too quick despairer, wherefore wilt thou go? / Soon will the high midsummer pomps come on. [61]

6 The heart less bounding at emotion new, / The hope, once crushed, less quick to spring again. [139]

7 Roam on! The light we sought is shining still. / Dost thou ask proof? Our tree yet crowns the hill, / Our Scholar travels yet the loved hillside. [238]

8 Who saw life steadily, and saw it whole: / The mellow glory of the Attic stage. [(Sophocles) *To a Friend*]

9 Dotting the shoreless watery wild, / We mortal millions live *alone*. [*To Marguerite, Isolation*]

10 The unplumbed, salt, estranging sea.

11 France, famed in all great arts, in none supreme. [*To a Republican Friend*]

12 Culture being a pursuit of our total perfection by means of getting to know, on all the matters which most concern us, the best which has been thought and said in the world. [*Culture and Anarchy*, Preface]

13 Our society distributes itself into Barbarians, Philistines, and Populace.

14 The pursuit of perfection, then, is the pursuit of sweetness and light. [Ch. 1]

15 *Philistine* gives the notion of something particularly stiff-necked and perverse in the resistance to light and its children; and therein it specially suits our middle-class. [3]

16 The governing idea of Hellenism is spontaneity of consciousness; that of Hebraism, strictness of conscience. [4]

17 No man, who knows nothing else, knows even his Bible. [5]

18 The magnificent roaring of the young lions of the *Daily Telegraph*. [*Essays in Criticism*, First Series, Preface]

19 [Oxford] whispering from her towers the last enchantments of the Middle Age . . . Home of lost causes, and forsaken beliefs, and unpopular names, and impossible loyalties!

20 I am bound by my own definition of criticism: a disinterested endeavour to learn and propagate the best that is known and thought in the world. ['The Function of Criticism at the Present Time']

21 Philistine must have originally meant, in the mind of those who invented the nickname, a strong, dogged, unenlightened opponent of the chosen people, of the children of light. ['Heinrich Heine']

22 Philistinism! – We have not the expression in English. Perhaps we have not the word because we have so much of the thing.

23 [Shelley] a beautiful and ineffectual angel beating in the void his luminous wings in vain. [*Essays in Criticism*, Second Series, 'Byron']

24 He never spoke out. [(Quoting letter from Gray's friend, James Brown) 'Gray']

25 Gray, a born poet, fell upon an age of reason.

26 The difference between genuine poetry and the poetry of Dryden, Pope, and all their school, is briefly this: their poetry is conceived in their wits, genuine poetry is conceived and composed in the soul.

27 [Poetry] a criticism of life under the conditions fixed for such a criticism by the laws of poetic truth and poetic beauty. ['The Study of Poetry']

28 He [Chaucer] lacks the high seriousness of the great classics, and therewith an important part of their virtue.

29 His expression may often be called bald . . . but it is bald as the bare mountain tops are bald, with a baldness full of grandeur. ['Wordsworth']

30 Culture, the acquainting ourselves with the best that has been known and said in the world, and thus with the history of the human spirit. [*Literature and Dogma*, Preface to edn. of 1873]

31 Miracles do not happen. [Preface to edn. of 1883]

32 The true meaning of religion is thus not simply morality, but morality touched by emotion. [Ch. 1. §2]

1 Conduct is three-fourths of our life and its largest concern. [§3]

2 The eternal *not ourselves* that makes for righteousness. [8. §1]

3 But there remains the question: what righteousness really is. The method and secret and sweet reasonableness of Jesus. [12. §2]

4 He will find one English book and one only, where, as in the *Iliad* itself, perfect plainness of speech is allied with perfect nobleness; and that book is the Bible. [*On Translating Homer*, 3]

5 I think it will be found that the grand style arises in poetry, when a noble nature, poetically gifted, treats with simplicity or with severity a serious subject. [Final words]

SAMUEL J. ARNOLD 1774–1852

6 For England, home, and beauty. [*The Death of Nelson* (see also 337:16)]

THOMAS ARNOLD 1795–1842

7 What we must look for here is, first, religious and moral principles; secondly, gentlemanly conduct; thirdly, intellectual ability. [Address to his scholars at Rugby School]

GEORGE ASAF [GEORGE H. POWELL] 1880–1951

8 What's the use of worrying? / It never was worth while, / So, pack up your troubles in your old kit-bag, / And smile, smile, smile. [*Pack up Your Troubles in Your Old Kit-bag*]

LORD ASHBURTON 1731–1783

9 The power of the Crown has increased, is increasing, and ought to be diminished. [Motion in the House of Commons, 1780]

'DAISY ASHFORD' 1881–1972

10 Mr Salteena was an elderly man of 42 and was fond of asking peaple to stay with him. [*The Young Visiters*, Ch. 1]

11 I am parshial to ladies if they are nice I suppose it is my nature. I am not quite a gentleman but you would hardly notice it but cant be helped anyhow.

12 I am very pale owing to the drains in this house. [2]

13 What I say is what dose it matter we cant all be of the Blood royal can we. [5]

14 My own idear is that these things are as piffle before the wind.

15 I am very fond of fresh air and royalties.

16 Here I am tied down to this life he said ... being royal has many painfull drawbacks. [6]

17 My life will be sour grapes and ashes without you. [8]

18 Oh Bernard muttered Ethel this is so sudden. No no cried Bernard and taking the bull by both horns he kissed her violently on her dainty face. My bride to be he murmered several times. [9]

19 She had very nice feet and plenty of money. [12]

H. H. ASQUITH, EARL OF OXFORD 1852–1928

20 We must wait and see. [Speech in House of Commons, 4 Apr. 1910, referring to the Budget. Later interpreted as referring to the war]

MARGOT ASQUITH 1865–1945

21 He [Lloyd George] could not see a belt without hitting below it. [*Autobiography*, quoted in the *Listener*, 11 June 1953]

22 Lord Birkenhead is very clever, but sometimes his brains go to his head.

23 Jean Harlow [Hollywood's sexy actress] kept calling Margot Asquith by her first name, or kept trying to: she pronounced it Mar*got*. Finally Margot set her right. 'No, no, Jean. The *t* is silent as in Harlow.' [Quoted in T. S. Matthews, *Great Tom*, Ch. 7]

E. L. ATKINSON 1882–1929 and APSLEY CHERRY GARRARD 1886–1959

24 A very gallant gentleman. [Inscription on the burial-place of Captain Oates in the Antarctic, 1912]

JOHN AUBREY 1626–1697

25 He was so fair that they called him *the lady* of Christ's College. [*Brief Lives*, 'John Milton']

ALEXANDER BOSWELL, LORD AUCHINLECK 1706–1782

26 He [Cromwell] gart kings ken they had a lith [joint] in their neck. [Quoted in Boswell, *Tour of the Hebrides*, note, 6 Nov. 1773]

W. H. AUDEN 1907–1973

1 August for the people and their favourite islands. / Daily the steamers sidle up to meet / The effusive welcome of the pier. [*August for the people*]

2 Hinting at the forbidden like a wicked uncle, / Night after night to the farmer's children you beckon. [*The Capital*]

3 Speechless Evil / Borrowed the language of Good / And reduced it to noise. [*The Cave of Making*, Postscript]

4 Within these breakwaters English is spoken; without / Is the immense, improbable atlas. [*Dover*]

5 Let us honour if we can / The vertical man / Though we value none / But the horizontal one. [*Epigraph*]

6 He knew human folly like the back of his hand, / And was greatly interested in armies and fleets; / When he laughed, respectable senators burst with laughter, / And when he cried the little children died in the streets. [*Epitaph on a Tyrant* (see also 289:11)]

7 One tapped my shoulder and asked me 'How did you fall, sir?' / Whereat I awakened. [*1st January 1931*]

8 Alone, alone, about the dreadful wood / Of conscious evil runs a lost mankind, / Dreading to find its Father. [*For the Time Being*, 'Chorus']

9 When the Sex War ended with the slaughter of the Grandmothers, / They found a bachelor's baby suffocating under them; / Somebody called him George and that was the end of it: / They hitched him up to the Army. ['Soldiers']

10 To us he is no more a person / Now but a climate of opinion / Under whom we conduct our differing lives. [*In Memory of Sigmund Freud*]

11 In the nightmare of the dark / All the dogs of Europe bark, / And the living nations wait, / Each sequestered in its hate. [*In Memory of W. B. Yeats*]

12 Intellectual disgrace / Stares from every human face, / And the seas of pity lie / Locked and frozen in each eye.

13 When I try to imagine a faultless love / Or the life to come, what I hear is the murmur / Of underground streams, what I see is a limestone landscape. [*In Praise of Limestone*]

14 And on the issue of their charm depended / A land laid waste, with all its young men slain, / The women weeping, and its towns in terror. [*In Time of War*, xix]

15 It is time for the destruction of error. / The chairs are being brought in from the garden, / The summer talk stopped on that savage coast / Before the storms. [*It is time*]

16 To throw away the key and walk away, / Not abrupt exile, the neighbours asking why / But following a line with left and right, / An altered gradient at another rate. [*The Journey*]

17 Lay your sleeping head, my love, / Human on my faithless arm. [*Lay your sleeping head*]

18 Look, stranger, at this island now / The leaping light for your delight discovers. [*Look Stranger*]

19 Private faces in public places / Are wiser and nicer / Than public faces in private places. [*Marginalia*]

20 Five minutes on even the nicest mountain / Is awfully long. [*Mountains*]

21 About suffering they were never wrong, / The Old Masters. [*Musée des Beaux Arts*]

22 Even the dreadful martyrdom must run its course / Anyhow in a corner, some untidy spot / Where the dogs go on with their doggy life.

23 O Unicorn among the cedars, / To whom no magic charm can lead us, / White childhood moving like a sigh / Through the green woods. [*New Year Letter*, Pt III]

24 God bless the USA, so large, / So friendly, and so rich. [*On the Circuit*]

25 The glacier knocks in the cupboard, / The desert sighs in the bed, / And the crack in the tea-cup opens / A lane to the land of the dead. [*One Evening*]

26 To the man-in-the-street, who, I'm sorry to say, / Is a keen observer of life, / The word 'Intellectual' suggests straight away / A man who's untrue to his wife. [*The Orators*, Epigraph]

27 Attractions for their coming week / Are Masters Wet, Dim, Drip and Bleak. [Ode, 'Roar Gloucestershire']

28 The Oxford Don: 'I don't feel quite happy about pleasure.' ['Journal of an Airman']

29 Only those in the last stage of disease could believe that children are true judges of character.

1 To ask the hard question is simple. [*The Question*]

2 Verse was a special illness of the ear; / Integrity was not enough. [*Rimbaud*]

3 His truth acceptable to lying men.

4 Over the heather the west wind blows, / I've lice in my tunic and a cold in my nose. / The rain comes pattering out of the sky, / I'm a Wall soldier and I don't know why. [*Roman Wall Blues*]

5 Embrace me, belly, like a bride. [*The Sea and the Mirror*, II, 'Stephano's Song']

6 At Dirty Dick's and Sloppy Joe's / We drank our liquor straight, / Some went upstairs with Margery, / And some, alas, with Kate. ['Song of the Master and the Boatswain']

7 The nightingales are sobbing in / The orchards of our mothers, / And hearts that we broke long ago / Have long been breaking others.

8 My Dear One is mine as mirrors are lonely.

9 There is no such thing as the State / And no one exists alone; / Hunger allows no choice / To the citizen or the police; / We must love one another or die. [*September 1, 1939*]

10 Out of the air a voice without a face / Proved by statistics that some cause was just. [*The Shield of Achilles*]

11 No hero is mortal till he dies. [*A Short Ode to a Philologist*]

12 Their fate must always be the same as yours, / To suffer the loss they were afraid of, yes, / Holders of one position, wrong for years. [*Since you are going to begin today*]

13 Harrow the house of the dead; look shining at / New styles of architecture, a change of heart. [Sonnet: *Sir, no man's enemy*]

14 O for doors to be open and an invite with gilded edges / To dine with Lord Lobcock and Count Asthma. [*Song*]

15 So take your proper share, man, of / Dope and drink: / Aren't you the Chairman of / Ego, Inc? [*Song of the Devil*]

16 The stars are dead; the animals will not look: / We are left alone with our day, and the time is short and / History to the defeated / May say Alas but cannot help or pardon. [*Spain 1937*]

17 Noises at dawn will bring / Freedom for some, but not this peace / No bird can contradict. [*Taller Today*]

18 A shilling life will give you all the facts. [*Who's Who*]

19 This great society is going smash; / They cannot fool us with how fast they go, / How much they cost each other and the gods! / A culture is no better than its woods. [*Winds*]

20 Be clean, be tidy, oil the lock, / Weed the garden, wind the clock; / Remember the Two. [*The Witnesses*]

21 Some books are undeservedly forgotten; none are undeservedly remembered. [*The Dyer's Hand*, Pt. I, 'Reading']

22 No poet or novelist wishes he were the only one who ever lived, but most of them wish they were the only one alive, and quite a number fondly believe their wish has been granted. ['Writing']

23 When I find myself in the company of scientists, I feel like a shabby curate who has strayed by mistake into a drawing room full of dukes. [2, 'The Poet and the City']

24 Man is a history-making creature who can neither repeat his past nor leave it behind. [5, 'D. H. Lawrence']

25 A verbal art like poetry is reflective; it stops to think. Music is immediate; it goes on to become. [8, 'Notes on Music']

26 Geniuses are the luckiest of mortals because what they must do is the same as what they most want to do. [Foreword to Dag Hammarskjöld, *Markings*]

27 Music is the best means we have of digesting time. [Quoted in Robert Craft, *Stravinsky: The Chronicle of a Friendship*]

28 A professor is one who talks in someone else's sleep. [Quoted in Charles Osborne, *Auden: The Life of a Poet*, Ch. 13]

ÉMILE AUGIER 1820–1889

29 *La nostalgie de la boue.* – A yearning for the gutter. [*Le Mariage d'Olympe*, I. i]

ST AUGUSTINE 354–430

30 Thou hast created us for Thyself, and our heart is not quiet until it rests in Thee. [*Confessions*, I. 1]

31 To Carthage I came, where there sang all around my ears a cauldron of unholy loves. [III. 1]

1 It is impossible that the son of these tears should perish. [III. 12]

2 Give me chastity and continency, but not yet. [VIII. 7]

3 The verdict of the world is final. [*Contra Epistolam Parmeniani*, III. 24]

4 There is no salvation outside the Church. [*De Bapt.* IV. 17]

5 Hear the other side. [*De Duabus Animabus*, XIV. 2]

6 Love, and do what you will. [*In Epist. Ioann. Tract.* VIII. 7]

7 Rome has spoken; the case is concluded. [*Sermons*, Bk i]

MARCUS AURELIUS ANTONINUS
121–180

8 Whatever this is that I am, it is a little flesh and breath, and the ruling part. [*Meditations*, II. 2]

9 And thou wilt give thyself relief, if thou doest every act of thy life as if it were the last. [5]

10 Remember that no man loses any other life than this which he now lives, nor lives any other than this which he now loses. [14]

11 All things from eternity are of like forms and come round in a circle.

12 The universe is transformation; our life is what our thoughts make it. [IV. 3]

13 Everything that happens happens as it should, and if you observe carefully, you will find this to be so. [10]

14 Remember this, that there is a proper value and proportion to be observed in the performance of every act. [32]

15 Everything is only for a day, both that which remembers and that which is remembered. [35]

16 Time is like a river made up of the events which happen, and its current is strong; no sooner does anything appear than it is swept away, and another comes in its place, and will be swept away too. [43]

17 Nothing happens to any man that he is not formed by nature to bear. [V. 18]

18 Live with the gods. And he does so who constantly shows them that his soul is satisfied with what is assigned to him. [27]

19 Remember that to change your mind and follow him who sets you right is to be none the less free than you were before. [VIII. 16]

20 Whatever may happen to you was prepared for you from all eternity; and the implication of causes was from eternity spinning the thread of your being. [X. 5]

JANE AUSTEN 1775–1817

21 An egg boiled very soft is not unwholesome. [(Mr Woodhouse) *Emma*, Ch. 3]

22 One half of the world cannot understand the pleasures of the other. [(Emma) 9]

23 A basin of nice smooth gruel, thin, but not too thin. [12]

24 Drinking too much of Mr Weston's good wine. [15]

25 Human nature is so well disposed towards those who are in interesting situations, that a young person, who either marries or dies, is sure to be kindly spoken of. [22]

26 The sooner every party breaks up the better. [(Mr Woodhouse) 25]

27 But, surely, Mr Churchill, nobody would think of opening the windows at Randalls. Nobody could be so imprudent. [(Mr Woodhouse) 29]

28 Business, you know, may bring money, but friendship hardly ever does. [(John Knightley) 34]

29 One has no great hopes from Birmingham. I always say there is something direful in the sound. [(Mrs Elton) 36]

30 'And what are you reading, Miss ——?' 'Oh! it is only a novel!' . . . or, in short, only some work in which the most thorough knowledge of human nature, the happiest delineation of its varieties, the liveliest effusions of wit and humour are conveyed to the world in the best chosen language. [*Northanger Abbey*, Ch. 5]

31 I have heard that something very shocking indeed will soon come out in London. [(Catherine) 14]

32 My sore throats are always worse than anyone's. [(Mary Musgrove) *Persuasion*, Ch. 18]

33 All the privilege I claim for my own sex . . . is that of loving longest, when existence or when hope is gone. [(Anne) 23]

1 It is a truth universally acknowledged, that a single man in possession of a good fortune, must be in want of a wife. [*Pride and Prejudice*, Ch. 1]

2 She was a woman of mean understanding, little information, and uncertain temper. [(Mrs Bennet)]

3 A lady's imagination is very rapid; it jumps from admiration to love, from love to matrimony in a moment. [(Darcy) 6]

4 How can you contrive to write so even? [(Miss Bingley) 10]

5 It is happy for you that you possess the talent of flattering with delicacy. May I ask whether these pleasing attentions proceed from the impulse of the moment, or are the result of previous study? [(Mr Bennet) 14]

6 You have delighted us long enough. [(Mr Bennet) 18]

7 It does not appear to me that my hand is unworthy your acceptance, or that the establishment I can offer would be any other than highly desirable. [(Mr Collins) 19]

8 From this day you must be a stranger to one of your parents. – Your mother will never see you again if you do *not* marry Mr Collins, and I will never see you again if you *do.* [(Mr Bennet) 20]

9 Nobody is on my side, nobody takes part with me: I am cruelly used, nobody feels for my poor nerves. [(Mrs Bennet)]

10 'If it was not for the entail I should not mind it.'
   'What should not you mind?'
   'I should not mind anything at all.'
   'Let us be thankful that you are preserved from a state of such insensibility.' [(Mrs and Mr Bennet) 23]

11 Next to being married, a girl likes to be crossed in love a little now and then. [(Mr Bennet) 24]

12 One cannot be always laughing at a man without now and then stumbling on something witty. [(Elizabeth) 40]

13 You ought certainly to forgive them, as a Christian, but never to admit them in your sight, or allow their names to be mentioned in your hearing. [(Mr Collins) 57]

14 An annuity is a very serious business. [(Mrs Dashwood) *Sense and Sensibility*, Ch. 2]

15 The pleasantness of an employment does not always evince its propriety. [(Elinor) 13]

16 What dreadful hot weather we have! It keeps me in a continual state of inelegance. [*Letters*, 18 Sept. 1796]

17 Mrs Hall of Sherbourne was brought to bed yesterday of a dead child, some weeks before she expected, owing to a fright. I suppose she happened unawares to look at her husband. [27 Oct. 1798]

18 I do not want people to be very agreeable, as it saves me the trouble of liking them a great deal. [24 Dec. 1798]

19 The little bit (two inches wide) of ivory on which I work with so fine a brush, as produces little effect after much labour. [16 Dec. 1816]

ALFRED AUSTIN 1835–1913

20 Across the wires the electric message came: / 'He is no better, he is much the same.' [*On the Illness of the Prince of Wales*, attr. to Austin, but probably not his]

W. E. AYTOUN 1813–1865

21 Take away the star and garter – / Hide them from my aching sight! / Neither king nor prince shall tempt me / From my lonely room this night. [*Charles Edward at Versailles on the Anniversary of Culloden*]

22 Fhairshon swore a feud / Against the clan M'Tavish; / Marched into their land / To murder and to rafish; / For he did resolve / To extirpate the vipers, / With four-and-twenty men / And five-and-thirty pipers. [*The Massacre of the Macpherson*]

B

LAUREN BACALL 1924–

1 You know how to whistle, don't you, Steve? You just put your lips together and blow. [To Humphrey Bogart in film *To Have and Have Not*. Script by Jules Furthman and William Faulkner]

FRANCIS BACON 1561–1626

2 If a man will begin with certainties, he shall end in doubts; but if he will be content to begin with doubts, he shall end in certainties. [*The Advancement of Learning*, I. v. 8]

3 [Knowledge is] a rich storehouse for the glory of the Creator, and the relief of man's estate. [11]

4 They are ill discoverers that think there is no land, when they can see nothing but sea. [vii. 5]

5 But men must know, that in this theatre of man's life it is reserved only for God and angels to be lookers-on. [II. xx. 8]

6 We are much beholden to Machiavel and others, that write what men do, and not what they ought to do. [xxi. 9]

7 All good moral philosophy is but the handmaid to religion. [xxii. 14]

8 Fortunes ... come tumbling into some men's laps. [xxiii. 43]

9 That other principle of Lysander, 'That children are to be deceived with comfits, and men with oaths'. [45]

10 Anger makes dull men witty, but it keeps them poor. [*Apothegms*, 5. Attr. by Bacon to Queen Elizabeth I]

11 Hope is a good breakfast, but it is a bad supper. [36]

12 Like strawberry wives, that laid two or three great strawberries at the mouth of their pot, and all the rest were little ones. [54. Attr. to Queen Elizabeth I]

13 One of the Seven was wont to say: 'That laws were like cobwebs; where the small flies were caught, and the great brake through.' [181]

14 Riches are a good handmaiden, but the worst mistress. [*De dignitate et augmentis scientiarium*, Pt I. vi. 3. 6]

15 I have often thought upon death, and I find it the least of all evils. [*An Essay on Death*]

16 My essays ... come home, to men's business, and bosoms. [*Essays*, Dedication (1625)]

17 What is truth? said jesting Pilate; and would not stay for an answer. [1, 'Of Truth']

18 A mixture of a lie doth ever add pleasure.

19 It is not the lie that passeth through the mind, but the lie that sinketh in and settleth in it, that doth the hurt.

20 Certainly it is a heaven upon earth, to have a man's mind to move in charity, rest in providence, and turn upon the poles of truth.

21 Men fear death, as children fear to go in the dark; and as that natural fear in children is increased with tales, so is the other. [2, 'Of Death']

22 Revenge triumphs over death; love slights it; honour aspireth to it; grief flieth to it.

23 It is as natural to die as to be born; and to a little infant, perhaps, the one is as painful as the other.

24 All colours will agree in the dark. [3, 'Of Unity in Religion']

1 Revenge is a kind of wild justice. [4, 'Of Revenge']

2 A man that studieth revenge keeps his own wounds green.

3 Prosperity is the blessing of the Old Testament, adversity is the blessing of the New. [5, 'Of Adversity']

4 Prosperity is not without many fears and distastes; and adversity is not without comforts and hopes.

5 Prosperity doth best discover vice, but adversity doth best discover virtue.

6 Nakedness is uncomely as well in mind, as body. [6, 'Of Simulation and Dissimulation']

7 The joys of parents are secret, and so are their griefs and fears. [7, 'Of Parents and Children']

8 Children sweeten labours; but they make misfortunes more bitter.

9 The noblest works and foundations have proceeded from childless men.

10 He that hath wife and children, hath given hostages to fortune; for they are impediments to great enterprises, either of virtue, or mischief. [8, 'Of Marriage and Single Life']

11 There are some other that account wife and children but as bills of charges.

12 Wives are young men's mistresses; companions for middle age; and old men's nurses.

13 He was reputed one of the wise men that made answer to the question, when a man should marry? 'A young man not yet, an elder man not at all.'

14 The speaking in a perpetual hyperbole is comely in nothing but in love. [10, 'Of Love']

15 The arch-flatterer, with whom all the petty flatterers have intelligence, is a man's self.

16 Nuptial love maketh mankind; friendly love perfecteth it; but wanton love corrupteth and embaseth it.

17 Men in great place are thrice servants: servants of the sovereign or state; servants of fame; and servants of business. [11, 'Of Great Place']

18 It is a strange desire to seek power and to lose liberty.

19 Set it down to thyself, as well to create good precedents as to follow them.

20 Severity breedeth fear, but roughness breedeth hate. Even reproofs from authority ought to be grave and not taunting.

21 As in nature things move violently to their place and calmly in their place, so virtue in ambition is violent, in authority settled and calm.

22 He said it, that knew it best. [12, 'Of Boldness']

23 There is in human nature generally more of the fool than of the wise.

24 In civil business; what first? Boldness; what second, and third? Boldness. And yet boldness is a child of ignorance and baseness.

25 Boldness is an ill-keeper of promise.

26 If the hill will not come to Mahomet, Mahomet will go to the hill.

27 In charity there is no excess. [13, 'Of Goodness and Goodness of Nature']

28 If a man be gracious and courteous to strangers, it shows he is a citizen of the world.

29 New nobility is but the act of power, but ancient nobility is the act of time. [14, 'Of Nobility']

30 Nobility of birth commonly abateth industry.

31 The four pillars of government . . . (which are religion, justice, counsel, and treasure). [15, 'Of Seditions and Troubles']

32 The surest way to prevent seditions (if the times do bear it) is to take away the matter of them.

33 Money is like muck, not good except it be spread.

34 The remedy is worse than the disease.

35 God never wrought miracle to convince atheism, because his ordinary works convince it. [16, 'Of Atheism']

36 A little philosophy inclineth man's mind to atheism; but depth in philosophy bringeth men's minds about to religion.

37 For none deny there is a God, but those for whom it maketh that there were no God.

38 It were better to have no opinion of God at all, than such an opinion as is unworthy of him. [17, 'Of Superstition']

39 There is a superstition in avoiding superstition.

40 Travel, in the younger sort, is a part of education; in the elder, a part of experience. [18, 'Of Travel']

41 Let diaries, therefore, be brought in use.

1 Books will speak plain when counsellors blanch. [20, 'Of Counsel']

2 There be that can pack the cards, and yet cannot play well. [22, 'Of Cunning']

3 When he wrote a letter, he would put that which was most material in the postscript, as if it had been a by-matter.

4 Nothing doth more hurt in a state than that cunning men pass for wise.

5 Be so true to thyself, as thou be not false to others. [23, 'Of Wisdom for a Man's Self']

6 Certainly it is the nature of extreme self-lovers, as they will set an house on fire, and it were but to roast their eggs.

7 It is the wisdom of the crocodiles, that shed tears when they would devour.

8 He that will not apply new remedies must expect new evils; for time is the greatest innovator. [24, 'Of Innovations']

9 A wise man that had it for a by-word, when he saw men hasten to a conclusion, 'Stay a little, that we may make an end the sooner'. [25, 'Of Dispatch']

10 To choose time is to save time.

11 The French are wiser than they seem, and the Spaniards seem wiser than they are. [26, 'Of Seeming Wise']

12 It had been hard for him that spake it to have put more truth and untruth together, in few words, than in that speech: 'Whosoever is delighted in solitude is either a wild beast, or a god'. [27, 'Of Friendship']

13 A crowd is not company, and faces are but a gallery of pictures.

14 Cure the disease and kill the patient.

15 Riches are for spending. [28, 'Of Expense']

16 Neither is money the sinews of war (as it is trivially said). [29, 'Of The True Greatness of Kingdoms']

17 He that commands the sea is at great liberty, and may take as much and as little of the war as he will.

18 Age will not be defied. [30, 'Of Regimen of Health']

19 Suspicions amongst thoughts are like bats amongst birds, they ever fly by twilight. [31, 'Of Suspicion']

20 There is nothing makes a man suspect much, more than to know little.

21 Intermingle . . . jest with earnest. [32, 'Of Discourse']

22 [Dreams and predictions] ought to serve but for winter talk by the fireside. [35, 'Of Prophecies']

23 Nature is often hidden; sometimes overcome; seldom extinguished. [38, 'Of Nature in Men']

24 A man's nature runs either to herbs, or to weeds; therefore let him seasonably water the one, and destroy the other.

25 Virtue is like a rich stone, best plain set. [43, 'Of Beauty']

26 Houses are built to live in and not to look on. [45, 'Of Building']

27 God Almighty first planted a garden; and, indeed, it is the purest of human pleasures. [46, 'Of Gardens']

28 There is little friendship in the world, and least of all between equals. [48, 'Of Followers']

29 Studies serve for delight, for ornament, and for ability. [50, 'Of Studies']

30 To spend too much time in studies is sloth.

31 Read not to contradict and confute, nor to believe and take for granted, nor to find talk and discourse, but to weigh and consider.

32 Some books are to be tasted, others to be swallowed, and some few to be chewed and digested.

33 Reading maketh a full man; conference a ready man; and writing an exact man.

34 Histories make men wise; poets, witty; the mathematics, subtle; natural philosophy, deep; moral, grave; logic and rhetoric, able to contend.

35 A wise man will make more opportunities than he finds. [52, 'Of Ceremonies and Respects']

36 Fame is like a river, that beareth up things light and swollen, and drowns things weighty and solid. [53, 'Of Praise']

37 It was prettily devised of Aesop, 'The fly sat upon the axle-tree of the chariot-wheel and said, What a dust do I raise'. [54, 'Of Vain-glory']

38 The place of justice is a hallowed place. [56, 'Of Judicature']

39 Lucid intervals and happy pauses. [*The History of King Henry VII*, §3]

1 I would live to study and not study to live. [*Memorial of Access*]

2 For knowledge itself is power. [*Religious Meditations, 'Of Heresies'*]

3 The world's a bubble; and the life of man, / Less than a span. [*The World*]

4 Who then to frail mortality shall trust, / But limns the water, or but writes in dust.

5 What is it then to have or have no wife, / But single thraldom, or a double strife?

6 What then remains, but that we still should cry, / Not to be born, or being born, to die?

7 I have taken all knowledge to be my province. [Letter to Lord Burleigh, 1592]

WALTER BAGEHOT 1826–1877

8 The best reason why Monarchy is a strong government is that it is an intelligible government. The mass of mankind understand it, and they hardly anywhere in the world understand any other. [*The English Constitution*, Ch. 2]

9 Of all nations in the world the English are perhaps the least a nation of pure philosophers.

P. J. BAILEY 1816–1902

10 We live in deeds, not years; in thoughts, not breaths; / In feelings, not in figures on a dial. / We should count time by heart-throbs. He most lives / Who thinks most – feels the noblest – acts the best. [*Festus*, 5]

BRUCE BAIRNSFATHER 1888–1959

11 Well, if you knows of a better 'ole, go to it. [*Fragments from France*, 1]

SIR H. W. BAKER 1821–1877

12 The King of love my Shepherd is, / Whose goodness faileth never; / I nothing lack if I am His, / And He is mine for ever. [Hymn]

GEORGES BALANDIER 1920–

13 *Le Tiers Monde.* – the Third World. [Based on *Le Tiers État*. Attr. also to Alfred Sauvy]

STANLEY, EARL BALDWIN 1867–1947

14 A lot of hard-faced men who look as if they had done well out of the war. [Of the House of Commons returned in the 1918 election.

Quoted by J. M. Keynes, *Economic Consequences of the Peace*, Ch. 5]

15 What the proprietorship of these papers [referring to Beaverbrook and Rothermere] is aiming at is power, and power without responsibility – the prerogative of the harlot through the ages. [By-election speech, 18 Mar. 1931. Lord Birkenhead claims in *Rudyard Kipling*, Ch. 20, that the phrase originated with Kipling and was borrowed by his cousin, Stanley Baldwin. See also 135:16, 241:35, 408:10]

16 When you think about the defence of England, you no longer think of the chalk cliffs of Dover. You think of the Rhine. That is where our frontier lies today. [Speech in House of Commons, 30 July 1934]

17 My lips are not yet unsealed. Were these troubles over I would make a case, and I guarantee that not a man would go into the Lobby against us. [Speech on the Abyssinia crisis, 10 Dec. 1935]

18 Then comes Winston with his hundred-horse-power mind and what can I do? [Quoted in G. M. Young, *Stanley Baldwin*, Ch. 11]

19 There are three groups that no British Prime Minister should provoke: the Vatican, the Treasury and the miners. [Attr. There are variants from other politicians. R. A. Butler's version of Baldwin's 'Do not run up your nose dead against the Pope and the NUM [National Union of Mineworkers]' in his *The Art of Memory*, p. 110]

A. J. BALFOUR 1848–1930

20 Defence of philosophic doubt. [Article in *Mind*, 1878]

21 The energies of our system will decay, the glory of the sun will be dimmed, and the earth, tideless and inert, will no longer tolerate the race which has for a moment disturbed its solitude. Man will go down into the pit, and all his thoughts will perish. [*The Foundations of Belief*, Pt I. Ch. 1]

22 It is unfortunate, considering that enthusiasm moves the world, that so few enthusiasts can be trusted to speak the truth. [Letter to Mrs Drew, 1918]

23 Christianity naturally, but why journalism? [Said to Frank Harris, who claimed that the two greatest curses of civilization were Christianity and journalism. Quoted in Margot Asquith, *Autobiography*, Ch. 10]

1 Nothing matters very much, and very few things matter at all. [Attr.]

JOHN BALL ?–1381

2 When Adam delved and Eve span, / Who was then the gentleman? [Text for sermon at outbreak of Peasants' Revolt. Adapted from poem by Richard Rolle of Hampole]

BALLADS

3 'O prithee, sweetheart, canst thou tell me / Whether thou dost know / The bailiff's daughter of Islington?' / 'She's dead, sir, long ago.' [The Bailiff's Daughter of Islington]

4 But I hae dreamed a dreary dream, / Beyond the Isle of Skye; / I saw a dead man win a fight, / And I think that man was I. [The Battle of Otterbourne]

5 It fell about the Lammas tide / /When husbands win their hay, / The doughty Douglas bound him to ride, / In England to take a prey. [The Battle of Otterburn]

6 There were twa sisters sat in a bour; / Binnorie, O Binnorie! / There came a knight to be their wooer, / By the bonnie milldams o' Binnorie. [Binnorie]

7 Ye Highlands and ye Lawlands, / Oh where have you been? / They have slain the Earl of Murray, / And they laid him on the green. [The Bonny Earl of Murray]

8 He was a braw gallant, / And he played at the glove; / And the bonny Earl of Murray, / Oh he was the Queen's love!

9 O then bespoke our Saviour, / All in his mother's womb; / 'Bow down, good cherry-tree, / To my mother's hand.' [The Cherry-Tree Carol]

10 The Percy out of Northumberland, / An avow to God made he / That he would hunt in the mountains / Of Cheviot within days three, / In the maugre of doughty Douglas, / And all that e'er with him be. [Chevy Chase]

11 Clerk Saunders and May Margaret / Walked o'er yon gravelled green, / And sad and heavy was the love, / I wot, it fell these twa between. [Clerk Saunders]

12 She had not sailed a league, a league, / A league but barely three, / When dismal grew his countenance, / And drumlie grew his ee. [The Daemon Lover]

13 'O what hills are yon, yon pleasant hills, / That the sun shines sweetly on?' / 'O yon are the hills of heaven,' he said, / 'Where you will never won.'

14 He strack the top-mast wi' his hand, / The fore-mast wi' his knee, / And he brake the gallant ship in twain, / And sank her in the sea.

15 'And what will ye leave to you ain mither dear, Edward, Edward? / And what will ye leave to your ain mither dear, / Me dear son, now tell me, O?' / 'The curse of hell frae me sall ye bear, Mither, Mither: / The curse of hell frae me sall ye bear: / Sic counsels ye gave to me, O.' [Edward]

16 'O where are ye gaun?' / Quo' the false knight upon the road: / 'I'm gaun to the school,' / Quo' the wee boy and still he stood. [The False Knight Upon the Road]

17 But ne'er a word wad ane o' them speak, / For barring of the door. [Get up and Bar the Door]

18 Goodman, you've spoken the foremost word, / Get up and bar the door.

19 A ship I have got in the North Country / And she goes by the name of the Golden Vanity. / O I fear she'll be taken by a Spanish Ga-la-lee, / As she sails by the Low-lands low. [The Golden Vanity]

20 He bored with his auger, he bored once and twice, / And some were playing cards and some were playing dice.

21 I wish I were where Helen lies, / Night and day on me she cries; / O that I were where Helen lies, / On fair Kirkconnell lea! [Helen of Kirkconnell]

22 Cursed be the heart that thought the thought, / And cursed be the hand that fired the shot, / When in my arms burd Helen dropped, / And died to succour me!

23 Gae hame, gae hame, my mither dear, / Prepare my winding sheet, / And at the back o' merry Lincoln / The morn I will you meet. [Hugh of Lincoln]

24 O he's gart build a bonny ship, / To sail on the salt sea; / The mast was o' the beaten gold, / The sails o' cramoisie. [The Lass of Lochroyan]

25 'O where ha you been, Lord Randal, my son? / And where ha you been, my handsome young man?' / 'I ha been at the greenwood; mother, make my bed soon, / For I'm wearied

wi' hunting, and fain would lie down.' [*Lord Randal*]

1 This ae nighte, this ae nighte, / *Every nighte and alle*, / Fire and fleet and candle-lighte, / *And Christ receive thy saule.* [*A Lyke-Wake Dirge*]

2 When captains courageous, whom death could not daunt, / Did march to the siege of the city of Gaunt. [*Mary Ambree*]

3 For, in my mind, of all mankind / I love but you alone. [*The Nut Brown Maid*]

4 For I must to the green-wood go / Alone, a banished man.

5 Yestreen the Queen had four Maries, / The night she'll hae but three; / There was Marie Seaton, and Marie Beaton, / And Marie Carmichael, and me. [*The Queen's Maries*]

6 But the merriest month in all the year / Is the merry month of May. [*Robin Hood and the Three Squires*]

7 Let me have length and breadth enough, / With a green sod under my head; / That they may say when I am dead, / Here lies bold Robin Hood. [*Robin Hood's Death*]

8 The king sits in Dunfermline town / Drinking the blude-red wine. [*Sir Patrick Spens*]

9 The king has written a braid letter, / And signed it wi' his hand, / And sent it to Sir Patrick Spens / Was walking on the strand.

10 To Noroway, to Noroway, / To Noroway o'er the faem; / The king's daughter o' Noroway, / 'Tis thou must bring her hame.

11 Late, late yestreen I saw the new moon, / Wi' the auld moon in her arm.

12 O lang, lang may the ladies stand, / Wi' their gold kems in their hair, / Waiting for their ain dear lords, / For they'll see them na mair.

13 Half owre, half owre to Aberdour, / 'Tis fifty fathom deep, / And there lies guid Sir Patrick Spens / Wi' the Scots lords at his feet.

14 Janet has kilted her green kirtle / A little aboon her knee, / And she has braided her yellow hair / A little aboon her bree. [*Tam Lin*]

15 She turned about her milk-white steed, / And took true Thomas up behind. [*Thomas Rhymer*]

16 It was mirk, mirk night, there was nae starlight. / They waded thro' red blude to the knee; / For all the blude that's shed on the earth / Runs through the springs o' that country.

17 And see not ye that braid, braid road, / That lies across yon lilly leven? / That is the path of wickedness, / Tho' some call it the road to heaven.

18 There were three ravens sat on a tree, / They were as black as black might be. / Then one of them said to his mate, / 'Where shall we our breakfast take?' [*The Three Ravens*]

19 As I was walking all alane, / I heard twa corbies making a mane; / The tane unto the tither did say, / 'Where sall we gang and dine to-day?'

'In behint yon auld fail dyke, / I wot there lies a new-slain knight; / And naebody kens that he lies there, / But his hawk, his hound, and lady fair.

'His hound is to the hunting gane, / His hawk to fetch the wild-fowl hame, / His lady's ta'en anither mate, / So we may mak our dinner sweet.' [*The Twa Corbies*]

20 O'er his white banes, when they are bare, / The wind sall blaw for evermair.

21 The wind doth blow today, my love, / And a few small drops of rain; / I never had but one true-love, / In cold grave she was lain. [*The Unquiet Grave*]

22 'Tis I, my love, sits on your grave, / And will not let you sleep; / For I crave one kiss of your clay-cold lips, / And that is all I seek.

23 O waly, waly, up the bank, / And waly, waly, down the brae, / And waly, waly, yon burn-side, / Where I and my love wont to gae. [*Waly, Waly*]

24 But had I wist, before I kissed, / That love had been sae ill to win, / I had locked my heart in a case o' gowd, / And pinned it wi' a siller pin.

HONORÉ DE BALZAC 1799–1850

25 *Elles doivent avoir les défauts de leurs qualités.* – They must have the defects of their qualities. [*Le Lys dans la vallée*]

J. C. BAMPFYLDE 1754–1796

26 Rugged the breast that beauty cannot tame. [*Sonnet in Praise of Delia*]

EDWARD BANGS *fl.* 1775

27 Yankee Doodle came to town, / Riding on a

pony; / Stuck a feather in his cap / And called it Macaroni. [*Yankee Doodle*]

TALLULAH BANKHEAD 1903–1968

1 Cocaine isn't habit-forming. I should know – I've been using it for years. [Quoted in Lillian Hellman, *Pentimento*, 'Theatre']

2 There is less of this than meets the eye. [Said of the revival of a Maeterlinck play. Quoted in Alexander Woollcott, *Shouts and Murmurs*, 'Capsule Criticism']

THÉODORE DE BANVILLE 1823–1891

3 *Nous n'irons plus aux bois, les lauriers sont coupés.* – We will go to the woods no more, the laurels are cut down. [*Les Cariatides*]

ANNA LETITIA BARBAULD 1743–1825

4 Life! we've been long together, / Through pleasant and through cloudy weather; / 'Tis hard to part when friends are dear, / Perhaps 'twill cost a sigh, a tear; / Then steal away, give little warning; / Choose thine own time; / Say not 'Good-night'; but in some brighter clime / Bid me 'Good-morning'. [*Ode to Life*]

JOHN BARBOUR 1316?–1395

5 A! fredome is a noble thing! / Fredome mayse man to haiff liking. / Fredome al solace to man giffis; / He levys at eas that frely levys. [*The Bruce*, 225]

REV. R. H. BARHAM 1788–1845

6 'Pooh!' says his pal, 'you great dunce! / You've pouched the good gentleman's money, / So out with your whinger at once, / And scrag Jane, while I spiflicate Johnny!' [*The Babes in the Wood*]

7 Why, Captain! – my Lord! – Here's the devil to pay! / The fellow's been cut down and taken away! / What's to be done? / We've missed all the fun! – / Why, they'll laugh at and quiz us all over the town, / We are all of us done so uncommonly brown! [*Hon. Mr Sucklethumbkin's Story*]

8 The Jackdaw sat in the Cardinal's chair! / Bishop and abbot and prior were there; / Many a monk, and many a friar, / Many a knight, and many a squire, / With a great many more

of lesser degree. / In sooth a goodly company; / And they served the Lord Primate on bended knee. / Never, I ween, / Was a prouder seen, / Read of in books, or dreamt of in dreams, / Than the Cardinal Lord Archbishop of Rheims. [*The Jackdaw of Rheims*]

9 And six little singing-boys, – dear little souls! / In nice clean faces, and nice white stoles.

10 And a nice little boy had a nice cake of soap, / Worthy of washing the hands of the Pope.

11 In holy anger, and pious grief, / He solemnly cursed that rascally thief! / He cursed him at board, he cursed him in bed; / From the sole of his foot to the crown of his head; / He cursed him in sleeping, that every night / He should dream of the devil, and wake in a fright.

12 Never was heard such a terrible curse!! / But what gave rise / To no little surprise, / Nobody seemed one penny the worse!

13 His head was as bald as the palm of your hand; / His eye so dim, / So wasted each limb, / That, heedless of grammar, they all cried, 'THAT'S HIM!'

14 The Lady Jane was tall and slim, / The Lady Jane was fair. [*The Knight and the Lady*]

15 He would pore by the hour, o'er a weed or a flower, / Or the slugs that come crawling out after a shower.

16 Ah, ha! my good friend! – Don't you wish you may get it? [*The Lay of St Aloys*]

17 A Franklyn's Dogge leped over a style, / And hys name was littel Byngo. [*A Lay of St Gengulphus*]

18 He had no little handkerchief to wipe his little nose. [*Misadventures at Margate*]

19 And now I'm here, from this here pier it is my fixed intent / To jump, as Mr Levi did from off the Monu-ment.

20 But when the Crier cried, 'O Yes!' the people cried, 'O No!'

21 And then he hitched his trousers up, as is, I'm told, their use, / – It's very odd that Sailormen should wear those things so loose.

22 He smiled and said, 'Sir, does your mother know that you are out?'

23 They were a little less than 'kin', and rather more than 'kind'. [*Nell Cook*]

1 She drank prussic acid without any water, / And died like a Duke-and-a-Duchess's daughter! [*The Tragedy*]

MAURICE BARING 1874–1945

2 If you would know what the Lord God thinks of money, you have only to look at those to whom He gives it. [Quoted by Dorothy Parker in Malcolm Cowley (ed.), *Writers at Work*, First Series]

S. BARING-GOULD 1834–1924

3 Now the day is over, / Night is drawing nigh, / Shadows of the evening / Steal across the sky. [Hymn]

4 Onward, Christian soldiers, / Marching as to war, / With the Cross of Jesus / Going on before. [Hymn]

5 Through the night of doubt and sorrow / Onward goes the pilgrim band, / Singing songs of expectation, / Marching to the Promised Land. [Hymn]

LADY ANNE BARNARD 1750–1825

6 My father argued sair – my mother didna speak, / But she lookèd in my face till my heart was like to break; / They gied him my hand but my heart was in the sea; / And so auld Robin Gray, he was gudeman to me. [*Auld Robin Gray*]

WILLIAM BARNES 1801–1886

7 My love is the maid ov all maïdens, / Though all mid be comely. [*In the Spring*]

8 Since I noo mwore do zee your feäce / Up steäirs or down below. [*The Wife A-Lost*]

9 When sycamore leaves wer a spreadèn, / Green-ruddy, in hedges, / Bezide the red doust o' the ridges, / A-dried at Woak Hill. [*Woak Hill*]

RICHARD BARNFIELD 1574–1627

10 As it fell upon a day, / In the merry month of May. [*Ode*]

11 King Pandion, he is dead, / All thy friends are lapped in lead.

12 My flocks feed not, / My ewes breed not, / My rams speed not, / All is amiss. / Love is dying, / Faith's defying, / Heart's denying, / Causer of this. [*A Shepherd's Complaint*]

13 Nothing more certain than incertainties; / Fortune is full of fresh variety: / Constant in nothing but inconstancy. [*The Shepherd's Content*, xi]

PHINEAS T. BARNUM 1810–1891

14 The Greatest Show on Earth. [Slogan for his circus, 1881]

15 There's a sucker born every minute. [Attr., but in fact coined by 'Paper-collar Joe', according to A. H. Saxon, *P. T. Barnum: The Legend and the Man*]

SIR JAMES BARRIE 1860–1937

16 His lordship may compel us to be equal upstairs, but there will never be equality in the servants' hall. [*The Admirable Crichton*, I]

17 Fame is rot; daughters are the thing. [*Dear Brutus*, II]

18 The same kind, beaming smile that children could warm their hands at. [III]

19 If it's heaven for climate, it's hell for company. [*The Little Minister*, Ch. 3]

20 It's grand, and ye canna expect to be baith grand and comfortable. [10]

21 I do loathe explanations. [*My Lady Nicotine*, Ch. 14]

22 When the first baby laughed for the first time, the laugh broke into a thousand pieces and they all went skipping about, and that was the beginning of fairies. [*Peter Pan*, I]

23 Everytime a child says, 'I don't believe in fairies,' there's a little fairy somewhere that falls down dead.

24 To die will be an awfully big adventure. [III]

25 But the gladness of her gladness / And the sadness of her sadness / Are as nothing, Charles, / To the badness of her badness when she's bad. [*Rosalind*]

26 It might be said of these two boys that Shovel knew everything but Tommy knew other things. [*Sentimental Tommy*, Ch. 3]

27 One's religion is whatever he is most interested in, and yours is Success. [*The Twelve-Pound Look*, I]

28 It's a sort of bloom on a woman. If you have it [charm], you don't need to have anything else; and if you don't have it, it doesn't

much matter what else you have. [*What Every Woman Knows*, I]

1 A young Scotsman of your ability let loose upon the world with £300, what could he not do? It's almost appalling to think of; especially if he went among the English.

2 You've forgotten the greatest moral attribute of a Scotsman, Maggie, that he'll do nothing which might damage his career. [II]

3 There are few more impressive sights in the world than a Scotsman on the make.

4 He had the most atrocious bow-wow public park manner. [III]

5 I have always found that the man whose second thoughts are good is worth watching.

6 Never ascribe to an opponent motives meaner than your own. ['Courage', rectorial address, St Andrews University, 3 May 1922]

GEORGE BARRINGTON 1755–*c.* 1835

7 True patriots we; for be it understood, / We left our country for our country's good. [*Prologue for the opening of the Playhouse, Sydney, N.S.W.*, 1796 (the company being composed of convicts). Also attr. to Henry Carter]

BERNARD M. BARUCH 1870–1965

8 The cold war. [Said on 16 Apr. 1947, Columbia, South Carolina. Quoted in the *Boston Globe*, 1 Apr. 1949. In fact, Baruch gave credit for the phrase to his speech-writer, H. B. Swope]

WILLIAM BASSE ?–1653?

9 Renownèd Spenser, lie a thought more nigh / To learned Chaucer, and rare Beaumont lie / A little nearer Spenser, to make room / For Shakespeare, in your threefold, fourfold tomb. [*On Shakespeare*]

EDGAR BATEMAN 19 Cent.

10 Wiv a ladder and some glasses, / You could see to 'Ackney Marshes, / If it wasn't for the 'ouses in between. [*If it wasn't for the 'ouses in between*]

CHARLES BAUDELAIRE 1821–1867

11 *Le Poète est semblable au prince des nuées / Qui hante la tempête et se rit de l'archer; / Exilé sur le sol, au milieu des huées, / Ses ailes de géant l'empêchent de marcher.* – The poet is like the prince of the clouds, who rides the tempest and scorns the archer. Exiled on the ground, amidst boos and insults, his giant's wings prevent his walking. [*L'Albatros*]

12 *Hypocrite lecteur! mon semblable, mon frère!* – Hypocritical reader, my double, my brother! [*Au Lecteur*]

13 *La nature est un temple où de vivants piliers / Laissent parfois sortir de confuses paroles; / L'homme y passe à travers des forêts de symboles / Qui l'observent avec des regards familiers.* – Nature is a temple in which living columns sometimes emit confused words. Man approaches it through forests of symbols, which observe him with familiar glances. [*Correspondances*]

14 *Voici le soir charmant, ami du criminel; / Il vient comme un complice, à pas de loup.* – Here is the charming evening, the criminal's friend. It comes like an accomplice, with stealthy tread. [*Le Crépuscule du soir*]

15 *Entends, ma chère, entends la douce Nuit qui marche.* – Listen, my darling, listen to soft night approaching. [*Recueillement*]

16 *Fourmillante cité, cité pleine de rêves, / Où le spectre en plein jour raccroche le passant! / Les mystères partout coulent comme des sèves / Dans les canaux étroits du colosse puissant.* – Swarming city, city full of dreams, where a ghost in daylight clutches a passer-by! Mysteries everywhere flow like sap in the narrow channels of the great giant. [*Les Sept Vieillards*]

17 *J'ai plus de souvenirs que si j'avais mille ans.* – I have more memories than if I were a thousand years old. [*Spleen*]

18 *Ô Mort, vieux capitaine, il est temps! levons l'ancre!* – Death, old captain, it is time, let us raise anchor! [*Le Voyage*]

19 *Quelle est cette île triste et noir? – C'est Cythère, / Nous dit-on, un pays fameux dans les chansons, /Eldorado banal de tous les vieux garçons. / Regardez! après tout, c'est une pauvre terre.* – What is that sad, dark island? It is Cythera, they tell us, a country famous in song, banal Eldorado of every elderly bachelor. Look, after all, it is a poor land! [*Un Voyage à Cythère*]

L. FRANK BAUM 1856–1919

20 The road to the City of Emeralds is paved

with yellow brick. [*The Wonderful Wizard of Oz*, Ch. 2. This became 'Follow the yellow brick road' in the musical version]

RICHARD BAXTER 1615–1691

1 I preached as never sure to preach again, / And as a dying man to dying men! [*Love Breathing Thanks and Praise*, 2]

SEIGNEUR DE BAYARD 1476–1524

2 *Le chevalier sans peur et sans reproche.* – Knight without fear and without reproach. [Description of him]

T. H. BAYLY 1797–1839

3 I'd be a butterfly; living a rover, / Dying when fair things are fading away. [*I'd be a Butterfly*]

4 Absence makes the heart grow fonder, / Isle of Beauty, fare thee well! [*Isle of Beauty*]

5 It was a dream of perfect bliss, / Too beautiful to last. [*It was a Dream*]

6 The mistletoe hung in the castle hall, / The holly branch shone on the old oak wall. [*The Mistletoe Bough*]

7 Oh, pilot! 'tis a fearful night, / There's danger on the deep. [*The Pilot*]

8 She wore a wreath of roses, / The night that first we met. [*She Wore a Wreath of Roses*]

9 We met, 'twas in a crowd, and I thought he would shun me. [*We Met, 'twas in a Crowd*]

10 Gaily the Troubadour / Touched his guitar. [*Welcome Me Home*]

11 Why don't the men propose, mamma, / Why don't the men propose? [*Why Don't the Men Propose?*]

VICE-ADMIRAL EARL BEATTY 1871–1936

12 Chatfield, there seems to be something wrong with our bloody ships today. [Attr. On sinking of battle-cruisers at Battle of Jutland, 30 May 1916, according to Winston Churchill, *The World Crisis*, Ch. 41]

PIERRE-AUGUSTIN DE BEAUMARCHAIS 1732–1799

13 *Aujourd'hui, ce qui ne vaut pas la peine d'être dit, on le chante.* – Today when something is not worth saying, they sing it. [*Le Barbier de Séville*, I. ii]

14 *Je me presse de rire de tout, de peur d'être obligé d'en pleurer.* – I force myself to laugh at everything, for fear of being compelled to weep.

15 *Boire sans soif et faire l'amour en tout temps, Madame; il n'y a que ça qui nous distingue des autres bêtes.* – Drinking when we are not thirsty and making love at all seasons, madam: that is all there is to distinguish us from the other animals. [*Le Mariage de Figaro*, II. xxi]

16 *Parce que vous êtes un grand seigneur, vous vous croyez un grand génie! ... Vous vous êtes donné la peine de naître, et rien de plus.* – Because you are a great lord, you think you are a great genius! ... You took the trouble to be born, and that is all. [V. iii]

FRANCIS BEAUMONT 1584–1616

17 What things have we seen, / Done at the Mermaid! heard words that have been / So nimble, and so full of subtle flame, / As if that every one from whence they came / Had meant to put his whole wit in a jest, / And had resolved to live a fool, the rest / Of his dull life. [*Letter to Ben Jonson*]

18 Mortality, behold and fear! / What a change of flesh is here! [*On the Tombs in Westminster Abbey*]

FRANCIS BEAUMONT
and JOHN FLETCHER 1579–1625

19 Bad's the best of us. [*The Bloody Brother*, IV. ii]

20 You are no better than you should be. [*The Coxcomb*, IV. iii]

21 But what is past my help is past my care. [*The Double Marriage*, I. i]

22 Nose, nose, jolly red nose, / And who gave thee this jolly red nose? ... / Nutmegs and ginger, cinnamon and cloves, / And they gave me this jolly red nose. [*The Knight of the Burning Pestle*, I. iii]

23 This is a pretty flim-flam. [II. iii]

24 Thou wilt scarce be a man before thy mother. [*Love's Cure*, II. ii]

25 Upon my buried body lie / Lightly, gentle earth. [*The Maid's Tragedy*, II. i]

26 Nothing's so dainty sweet as lovely melancholy. [*The Nice Valour*, III. iii, Song]

1 As men / Do walk a mile, women should talk an hour, / After supper. 'Tis their exercise. [*Philaster*, II. iv]

2 All your better deeds / Shall be in water writ, but this in marble. [V. iii]

3 Oh, love will make a dog howl in rhyme. [*The Queen of Corinth*, IV. i]

4 Kiss till the cow come home. [*The Scornful Lady*, II. ii]

5 There is no other purgatory but a woman. [III. i]

6 Daisies smell-less, yet most quaint, / And sweet thyme true, / Primrose, first born child of Ver, / Merry Spring-time's harbinger. [*Two Noble Kinsmen*, I. i]

7 Care-charming Sleep, thou easer of all woes, / Brother to Death. [*Valentinian*, V. ii]

8 Come sing now, sing; for I know ye sing well, / I see ye have a singing face. [*The Wild Goose Chase*, II. ii]

SAMUEL BECKETT 1906–1989

9 We could have saved sixpence. We have saved fivepence. (*Pause*) But at what cost? [*All That Fall*]

10 CLOV: Do you believe in the life to come? HAMM: Mine was always that. [*Endgame*]

11 Personally I have no bone to pick with graveyards. [*First Love*]

12 For why be discouraged, one of thieves was saved, that is a generous percentage. [*Malone Dies*]

13 There is no return game between a man and his stars. [*Murphy*]

14 VLADIMIR: That passed the time. ESTRAGON: It would have passed in any case. VLADIMIR: Yes, but not so rapidly. [*Waiting for Godot*, I]

15 ESTRAGON: . . . Let's go. VLADIMIR: We can't. ESTRAGON: Why not? VLADIMIR: We're waiting for Godot.

16 We are all born mad. Some remain so.

WILLIAM BECKFORD 1759–1844

17 He did not think . . . that it was necessary to make a hell of this world to enjoy paradise in the next. [*Vathek*]

18 I am not over-fond of resisting temptation.

THOMAS BECON 1512–1567

19 For when the wine is in, the wit is out. [*Catechism*, 375]

T. L. BEDDOES 1798–1851

20 If thou wilt ease thine heart / Of love and all its smart, / Then sleep, dear, sleep. [*Death's Jest Book*, II. ii]

21 Old Adam, the carrion crow. [V. iv]

22 If there were dreams to sell, / What would you buy? / Some cost a passing bell; / Some a light sigh, / That shakes from Life's fresh crown / Only a roseleaf down. [*Dream-Pedlary*]

THE VENERABLE BEDE 673–735

23 When we compare the present life of man with that time of which we have no knowledge, it seems to me like the swift flight of a lone sparrow through the banqueting-hall where you sit in the winter months . . . This sparrow flies swiftly in through one door of the hall, and out through another . . . Similarly, man appears on earth for a little while, but we know nothing of what went on before this life, and what follows. [*History of the English Church and People*, 2. Ch. 13, trans. L. Sherley-Price]

BERNARD BEE 1823–1861

24 There is Jackson standing like a stone wall. [At first battle of Bull Run, 1861]

SIR THOMAS BEECHAM 1879–1961

25 A musicologist is a man who can read music but can't hear it. [Quoted in H. Proctor-Gregg, *Beecham Remembered*, 'Beecham's Obiter Dicta']

MAX BEERBOHM 1872–1956

26 He cannot see beyond his own nose. Even the fingers he outstretches from it to the world are (as I shall suggest) often invisible to him. [*Around Theatres*, 'A Conspectus of G.B.S.']

27 I believe the twenty-four hour day has come to stay. [*A Christmas Garland*, 'Perkins and Mankind']

28 It is doubtful whether the people of southern England have even yet realized how much introspection there is going on all the time in the Five Towns. ['Scruts']

1 Most women are not so young as they are painted. [*A Defence of Cosmetics*]

2 There is always something rather absurd about the past. [*1880*]

3 To give an accurate and exhaustive account of that period would need a far less brilliant pen than mine.

4 A swear-word in a rustic slum / A simple swear-word is to some, / To Masefield something more. [*Fifty Caricatures*, caption; parody of W. Wordsworth]

5 Undergraduates owe their happiness chiefly to the consciousness that they are no longer at school. The nonsense which was knocked out of them at school is all put gently back at Oxford or Cambridge. [*Going Back to School*]

6 None, it is said, of all who revelled with the Regent, was half so wicked as Lord George Hell. [*The Happy Hypocrite*, Ch. 1]

7 No Roman ever was able to say, 'I dined last night with the Borgias'. [*Hosts and Guests*]

8 Fate wrote her [Queen Caroline] a most tremendous tragedy, and she played it in tights. [*King George the Fourth*]

9 'After all,' as a pretty girl once said to me, 'women are a sex by themselves, so to speak.' [*The Pervasion of Rouge*]

10 O the disgrace of it! – / The scandal, the incredible come-down! [*Savonarola Brown*]

11 I looked out for what the metropolitan reviewers would have to say. They seemed to fall into two classes: those who had little to say and those who had nothing. [*Seven Men*, 'Enoch Soames']

12 A hundred eyes were fixed on her, and half as many hearts lost to her. [*Zuleika Dobson*, Ch. 1]

13 Zuleika, on a desert island, would have spent most of her time in looking for a man's footprint. [2]

14 The dullard's envy of brilliant men is always assuaged by the suspicion that they will come to a bad end. [4]

15 You will find that the woman who is really kind to dogs is always one who has failed to inspire sympathy in men. [6]

16 You will think me lamentably crude: my experience of life has been drawn from life itself. [7]

17 The Socratic manner is not a game at which two can play. [15]

18 'Ah, say that again,' she murmured. 'Your voice is music.'

He repeated his question.

'Music,' she said dreamily; and such is the force of habit that 'I don't,' she added, 'know anything about music, really. But I know what I like.' [16]

19 And love levels all, doesn't it? Love and the Board school. [17]

20 What were they going to do with the Grail when they found it, Mr Rossetti? [Caption to a cartoon]

21 Of course we all know that [William] Morris was a wonderful all-round man, but the act of walking round him has always tired me. [Quoted in S. N. Behrman, *Conversations with Max*, Ch. 2]

BRENDAN BEHAN 1923–1964

22 Other people have a nationality. The Irish and the Jews have a psychosis. [*Richard's Cork Leg*, I]

APHRA BEHN 1640–1689

23 Love ceases to be a pleasure, when it ceases to be a secret. [*The Lover's Watch*, 'Four o'Clock']

24 Faith, sir, we are here today, and gone tomorrow. [*The Lucky Chance*, IV]

25 Variety is the soul of pleasure. [*The Rover*, Pt II. I]

26 Come away; poverty's catching.

27 Money speaks sense in a language all nations understand. [III. i]

CLIVE BELL 1881–1964

28 It would follow that 'significant form' was form behind which we catch a sense of ultimate reality. [*Art*, Pt I. Ch. 3]

29 Comfort came in with the middle classes. [*Civilization*, Ch. 4]

JAMES WARNER BELLAH 1899–1976
and WILLIS GOLDBECK 1899–1979

30 When the legend becomes fact, print the legend. [From the film *Who Shot Liberty Valance?*]

W. H. BELLAMY 19 Cent.

1 Old Simon the Cellarer keeps a rare store / Of malmsey and malvoisie. [*Simon the Cellarer*]

JOACHIM DU BELLAY *see* DU BELLAY, JOACHIM

HILAIRE BELLOC 1870–1953

2 When people call this beast to mind, / They marvel more and more / At such a little tail behind, / So large a trunk before. [*The Bad Child's Book of Beasts*, 'The Elephant']

3 I shoot the Hippopotamus / With bullets made of platinum, / Because if I use leaden ones / His hide is sure to flatten 'em. ['The Hippopotamus']

4 The nicest child I ever knew / Was Charles Augustus Fortescue. [*Cautionary Tales*, 'Charles Augustus Fortescue']

5 Alas! That such affected tricks / Should flourish in a child of six! ['Godolphin Horne']

6 The chief defect of Henry King / Was chewing little bits of string. ['Henry King']

7 They answered, as they took their fees, / 'There is no cure for this disease'.

8 There was a boy whose name was Jim; / His friends were very good to him. ['Jim']

9 'Ponto!' he cried, with angry frown, / 'Let go, Sir! Down, Sir! Put it down!'

10 And always keep a hold of Nurse / For fear of finding something worse.

11 Lord Lundy from his earliest years / Was far too freely moved to tears. ['Lord Lundy']

12 In my opinion butlers ought / To know their place, and not to play / The Old Retainer night and day.

13 We had intended you to be / The next Prime Minister but three.

14 My language fails! / Go out and govern New South Wales!

15 Matilda told such dreadful lies, / It made one gasp and stretch one's eyes; / Her aunt, who, from her earliest youth, / Had kept a strict regard for truth, / Attempted to believe Matilda: / The effort very nearly killed her. ['Matilda']

16 And summoned the immediate aid / Of London's noble Fire Brigade.

17 Her aunt was off to the theatre / To see that interesting play / *The Second Mrs Tanqueray*.

18 For every time she shouted 'Fire!' / They only answered 'Little liar!'

19 A trick that everyone abhors / In little girls is slamming doors. ['Rebecca']

20 Child! do not throw this book about! / Refrain from the unholy pleasure / Of cutting all the pictures out! [*Dedication on the Gift of a Book to a Child*]

21 From quiet homes and first beginning, / Out to the undiscovered ends, / There's nothing worth the wear of winning, / But laughter and the love of friends. [*Dedicatory Ode*]

22 They died to save their country and they only saved the world. [*The English Graves*]

23 I said to Heart, 'How goes it?' Heart replied: / 'Right as a Ribstone Pippin!' But it lied. [*Epigrams*, 'The False Heart']

24 I'm tired of Love: I'm still more tired of Rhyme. / But Money gives me pleasure all the time. ['Fatigue']

25 Of this bad world the loveliest and best / Has smiled and said 'Good Night', and gone to rest. ['On a Dead Hostess']

26 The accursed power which stands on Privilege / (And goes with Women, and Champagne, and Bridge) / Broke – and Democracy resumed her reign: / (Which goes with Bridge, and Women, and Champagne). ['On a General Election']

27 When I am dead, I hope it may be said: / 'His sins were scarlet, but his books were read'. ['On His Books']

28 The Devil, having nothing else to do, / Went off to tempt my Lady Poltagrue. / My Lady, tempted by a private whim, / To his extreme annoyance, tempted him. ['On Lady Poltagrue']

29 Pale Ebenezer thought it wrong to fight, / But Roaring Bill (who killed him) thought it right. ['The Pacifist']

30 Sally is gone that was so kindly, / Sally is gone from Ha'nacker Hill. [*Ha'nacker Mill*]

31 Remote and ineffectual Don / That dared attack my Chesterton. [*Lines to a Don*]

32 Dons admirable! Dons of might! / Uprising on my inward sight / Compact of ancient tales, and port, / And sleep – and learning of a sort.

33 Oh! let us never, never doubt / What nobody is sure about! [*More Beasts for Worse Children*, 'The Microbe']

1 I had an aunt in Yucatan / Who bought a python from a man / And kept it for a pet. / She died, because she never knew / These simple little rules and few: – / The snake is living yet. ['The Python']

2 The Moral is (I think, at least) / That Man is an UNGRATEFUL BEAST. [*New Cautionary Tales*, 'A Reproof of Gluttony']

3 When I am living in the Midlands / That are sodden and unkind. [*The South Country*]

4 I will hold my house in the high wood / Within a walk of the sea, / And the men that were boys when I was a boy / Shall sit and drink with me.

5 Do you remember an inn, / Miranda? [*Tarantella*]

6 The fleas that tease in the high Pyrenees.

7 It is the best of all trades, to make songs, and the second best to sing them. [*On Everything*, 'On Song']

8 The Servile State. [Title of a book]

9 When you have lost your inns drown your empty selves, for you will have lost the last of England. [*This and That*, 'On Inns']

10 The poor darlings [the Jews], I'm awfully fond of them and I'm awfully sorry for them, but it's their own silly fault – they ought to have let God alone. [Letter to the author, quoted in Robert Speight, *Life of Hilaire Belloc*, Ch. 19]

SAUL BELLOW 1915–

11 Conquered people tend to be witty. [*Mr Sammler's Planet*, Ch. 2]

P.-L. DE BELLOY 1727–1775

12 *Plus je vis d'étrangers, plus j'aimai ma patrie.* – The more foreigners I saw, the more I loved my native land. [*Le Siège de Calais*, II. iii]

ROBERT BENCHLEY 1889–1945

13 STREETS FULL OF WATER. PLEASE ADVISE. [Telegram on arriving in Venice]

JULIEN BENDA 1867–1956

14 *La Trahison des clercs.* – The treason of the intellectuals. [Title of book (1927)]

STEPHEN VINCENT BENÉT 1898–1943

15 Bury my heart at Wounded Knee. [*American Names*]

ARNOLD BENNETT 1867–1931

16 'Ye can call it influenza if ye like,' said Mrs Machin. 'There was no influenza in my young days. We called a cold a cold.' [*The Card*, Ch. 8]

17 'What great cause is he identified with?'
'He's identified ... with the great cause of cheering us all up.' [Last words of the book]

18 Pessimism, when you get used to it, is just as agreeable as optimism. [*Things that have Interested Me*, 'The Slump in Pessimism']

19 Being a husband is a whole-time job. That is why so many husbands fail. They cannot give their entire attention to it. [*The Title*, I]

20 Journalists say a thing that they know isn't true, in the hope that if they keep on saying it long enough it *will* be true. [II]

A. C. BENSON 1862–1925

21 Land of Hope and Glory, Mother of the Free, / How shall we extol thee, who are born of thee? / Wider still and wider shall thy bounds be set; / God who made thee mighty, make thee mightier yet. [Song from *Pomp and Circumstance*, to music by Sir Edward Elgar]

JEREMY BENTHAM 1748–1832

22 The greatest happiness of the greatest number is the foundation of morals and legislation. [*The Commonplace Book*]

23 All punishment is mischief: all punishment in itself is evil. [*Principles of Morals and Legislation*, Ch. 13]

E. C. BENTLEY 1875–1956

24 I cannot think of any repartee, / I simply wag my great, long, furry ears. [*Ballade of Plain Common Sense*]

25 Geography is about maps, / But Biography is about chaps. [*Biography for Beginners*]

26 What I like about Clive / Is that he is no longer alive. / There is a great deal to be said / For being dead. ['Clive']

27 George the Third / Ought never to have occurred. / One can only wonder / At so grotesque a blunder. ['George III']

28 Sir Christopher Wren / Said, 'I am going to dine with some men, / If anybody calls / Say I am designing St Paul's.' ['Sir Christopher Wren']

RICHARD BENTLEY 1662–1742

1 It is a pretty poem, Mr Pope, but you must not call it Homer. [Of Pope's *Iliad*. Quoted in Samuel Johnson, *Life of Pope*]

2 It is a maxim with me that no man was ever written out of reputation but by himself. [Quoted in Monk, *Life of Bentley*]

PIERRE-JEAN DE BÉRANGER 1780–1857

3 *Nos amis, les ennemis.* – Our friends, the enemy. [*L'Opinion de ces demoiselles*]

BERNARD BERENSON 1865–1959

4 In figure painting, the type of all painting, I have endeavoured to set forth that the principal if not sole source of life enchantments are Tactile Values, Movement and Space Composition. [*The Decline of Art*]

INGRID BERGMAN 1915–1982

5 Play it, Sam. Play 'As Time Goes By'. [In the film *Casablanca*. Script by Julius J. Epstein, Philip G. Epstein and Howard Koch. Usually misquoted as 'Play it again, Sam' and falsely attr. to Humphrey Bogart in that film]

BISHOP GEORGE BERKELEY 1685–1753

6 Westward the course of empire takes its way; / The four first acts already past, / A fifth shall close the drama with the day: / Time's noblest offspring is the last. [*On the Prospects of Planting Arts and Learning in America*]

IRVING BERLIN 1888–1989

7 Come on and hear, come on and hear, Alexander's Ragtime Band. [Song: *Alexander's Ragtime Band*]

8 There's No Business Like Show Business. [Title of song in musical *Annie Get Your Gun*]

9 The Hostess with the Mostes' on the Ball. [Title of song in musical *Call Me Madam*, I]

10 I'm dreaming of a white Christmas, / Just like the ones I used to know. [Song: *White Christmas*, in musical *Holiday Inn*]

11 The song is ended / But the melody lingers on. [Song: *The Song is Ended*, in musical *Ziegfeld Follies*]

W. B. BERNARD 1807–1875

12 A Storm in a Teacup. [Title of a farce]

THEOBALD VON BETHMANN HOLLWEG 1856–1921

13 Just for a word – 'neutrality', a word which in wartime has so often been disregarded, just for a scrap of paper – Great Britain is going to make war. [To Sir Edward Goschen, 4 Aug. 1914]

JOHN BETJEMAN 1906–1984

14 And is it true? And is it true, / This most tremendous tale of all, / Seen in a stained-glass window's hue, / A Baby in an ox's stall? [*Christmas*]

15 Spirits of well-shot woodcock, partridge, snipe / Flutter and bear him up the Norfolk sky. [*Death of King George V*]

16 As beefy ATS / Without their hats / Come shooting through the bridge, / And 'cheerioh' and 'cheeri-bye' / Across the waste of waters die. [*Henley-on-Thames*]

17 Phone for the fish-knives, Norman, / As Cook is a little unnerved; / You kiddies have crumpled the serviettes / And I must have things daintily served. [*How to Get on in Society*]

18 The Church's Restoration / In eighteen-eighty-three / Has left for contemplation / Not what there used to be. [*Hymn*]

19 In the licorice fields at Pontefract / My love and I did meet ... / Her sturdy legs were flannel-slack'd, / The strongest legs in Pontefract. [*The Licorice Fields at Pontefract*]

20 Pam, I adore you, Pam, you great big mountainous sports girl / Whizzing them over the net, full of the strength of five. [*Pot Pourri from a Surrey Garden*]

21 Rumbling under blackened girders, Midland, bound for Cricklewood, / Puffed its sulphur to the sunset where that Land of Laundries stood. [*Parliament Hill Fields*]

22 The gas was on in the Institute, / The flare was up in the gym. [*A Shropshire Lad*]

23 Come, friendly bombs, and fall on Slough. / It isn't fit for humans now. [*Slough*]

24 Miss J. Hunter Dunn, Miss J. Hunter Dunn, / Furnish'd and burnish'd by Aldershot sun. [*A Subaltern's Love-song*]

1 Childhood is measured out by sounds and smells / And sights, before the dark of reason grows. [*Summoned by Bells*, IV]

2 But I'm dying now and done for, / What on earth was all the fun for? / For I'm old and ill and terrified and tight. [*Sun and Fun*]

3 Broad of Church and broad of mind, / Broad before and broad behind, / A keen ecclesiologist, / A rather dirty Wykehamist. [*The Wykehamist*]

JACOB BEULER 19 Cent.

4 If I had a donkey wot wouldn't go / D'ye think I'd wollop him? no, no, no. [Song (*c.* 1822)]

ANEURIN BEVAN 1897–1960

5 This island is almost made of coal and surrounded by fish. Only an organizing genius could produce a shortage of coal and fish in Great Britain at the same time. [Speech at Blackpool, 18 May 1945]

6 No attempt at ethical or social seduction can eradicate from my heart a deep burning hatred for the Tory Party ... So far as I am concerned they are lower than vermin. [Speech at Manchester, 4 July 1948]

7 I know that the right kind of political leader for the Labour Party is a desiccated calculating machine. [Always assumed (though Bevan denied it) to refer to Hugh Gaitskell. At Labour Party Conference, 29 Sept. 1954]

8 If you carry this resolution and follow out all its implications and do not run away from it, you will send a Foreign Secretary, whoever he was, naked into the conference chamber. [On unilateral disarmament, at Labour Party Conference, 3 Oct. 1957]

BHAGAVAD-GITA

9 It is not that I have never existed before, nor thou, nor all these kings. Nor is it that all shall cease to exist hereafter.

As in this body the embodied soul passes through childhood, youth and old age, in the same manner it goes from one body to another; therefore the wise are never deluded regarding it. [Ch. 2. 12]

10 He who considers this [Self] as a slayer or he who thinks that this [Self] is slain, neither of these knows the Truth. For it does not slay, nor is it slain. [19]

11 For that which is born death is certain, and for the dead birth is certain. Therefore grieve not over that which is unavoidable. [27]

12 If the radiance of a thousand suns / were to burst into the sky / that would be like / the splendour of the Mighty One. [(Epigraph to Robert Jungk, *Brighter than A Thousand Suns*, used to describe the first atomic explosions) 11.12]

THE BIBLE

OLD TESTAMENT

Genesis

13 In the beginning God created the heaven and the earth.

And the earth was without form, and void; and darkness was upon the face of the deep. [1:1]

14 And God said, Let there be light: and there was light. [1:3]

15 *Fiat lux.* [*Vulgate* version]

16 So God created man in his own image, in the image of God created he him; male and female created he them. [1:27]

17 Be fruitful, and multiply, and replenish the earth. [1:28]

18 And God saw everything that he had made, and, behold, it was very good. [1:31]

19 And the Lord God formed man of the dust of the ground, and breathed into his nostrils the breath of life; and man became a living soul. [2:7]

20 And the Lord God said, It is not good that the man should be alone. [2:18]

21 This is now bone of my bones, and flesh of my flesh. [2:23]

22 Therefore shall a man leave his father and his mother, and shall cleave unto his wife: and they shall be one flesh. [2:24]

23 Now the serpent was more subtil than any beast of the field. [3:1]

24 Ye shall be as gods, knowing good and evil. [3:5]

25 And they sewed fig-leaves together, and made themselves aprons. [('breeches' for 'aprons' in *Genevan Bible*, 1560) 3:7]

26 And they heard the voice of the Lord God walking in the garden in the cool of the day. [3:8]

1 I was afraid, because I was naked; and I hid myself. [3:10]

2 Upon thy belly shalt thou go, and dust shalt thou eat all the days of thy life. [3:14]

3 In sorrow thou shalt bring forth children. [3:16]

4 In the sweat of thy face shalt thou eat bread. [3:19]

5 For dust thou art, and unto dust shalt thou return.

6 The mother of all living. [3:20]

7 Am I my brother's keeper? [4:9]

8 The voice of thy brother's blood crieth unto me from the ground. [4:10]

9 My punishment is greater than I can bear. [4:13]

10 And the Lord set a mark upon Cain. [4:15]

11 Dwelt in the land of Nod, on the east of Eden. [4:16]

12 The sons of God saw the daughters of men, that they were fair. [6:2]

13 There were giants in the earth in those days. [6:4]

14 Mighty men which were of old, men of renown.

15 The same day were all the fountains of the great deep broken up, and the windows of heaven were opened. [7:11]

16 But the dove found no rest for the sole of her foot. [8:9]

17 In her mouth was an olive-leaf pluckt off. [8:11]

18 Whoso sheddeth man's blood, by man shall his blood be shed. [9:6]

19 I do set my bow in the cloud, and it shall be for a token of a covenant between me and the earth. [9:13]

20 Nimrod the mighty hunter before the Lord. [10:9]

21 Thou shalt be buried in a good old age. [15:15]

22 His hand will be against every man, and every man's hand against him. [16:12]

23 Shall not the Judge of all the earth do right? [18:25]

24 Behold behind him a ram caught in the thicket by his horns. [22:13]

25 Esau selleth his birthright for a mess of pottage. [25. Chapter heading in *Genevan Bible*]

26 The voice is Jacob's voice, but the hands are the hands of Esau. [27:22]

27 And Mizpah; for he said, The Lord watch between thee and me, when we are absent one from another. [31:49]

28 I will not let thee go, except thou bless me. [32:26]

29 He made him a coat of many colours. [37:3]

30 Behold, this dreamer cometh. [37:19]

31 And the lean and the ill favoured kine did eat up the first seven fat kine. [41:20]

32 Jacob saw that there was corn in Egypt. [42:1]

33 Ye are spies; to see the nakedness of the land ye are come. [42:9]

34 Then shall ye bring down my grey hairs with sorrow to the grave. [42:38]

35 Ye shall eat the fat of the land. [45:18]

36 See that ye fall not out by the way. [45:24]

37 Few and evil have the days of the years of my life been. [47:9]

38 Unstable as water, thou shalt not excel. [49:4]

Exodus

39 Now there arose up a new king over Egypt, which knew not Joseph. [1:8]

40 I have been a stranger in a strange land. [2:22]

41 Behold, the bush burned with fire, and the bush was not consumed. [3:2]

42 A land flowing with milk and honey. [3:8]

43 And God said unto Moses, I AM THAT I AM. [3:14]

44 But I am slow of speech, and of a slow tongue. [4:10]

45 Ye shall no more give the people straw to make brick. [5:7]

46 Multiply my signs and my wonders in the land of Egypt. [7:3]

47 Even darkness which may be felt. [10:21]

48 With your loins girded, your shoes on your feet, and your staff in your hand. [12:11]

49 They spoiled the Egyptians. [12:36]

50 In the land of Egypt, when we sat by the flesh pots, and when we did eat bread to the full. [16:3]

1 Eye for eye, tooth for tooth, hand for hand, foot for foot. [21:24; also *Deuteronomy*, 19:21]

2 Thou shalt not seethe a kid in his mother's milk. [23:19]

3 Thou art a stiff-necked people. [33:3]

4 There shall no man see me, and live. [33:20]

Leviticus

5 Let him go for a scapegoat into the wilderness. [16:10]

6 Thou shalt love thy neighbour as thyself. [19:18; also *St Matthew*, 19:19]

Numbers

7 The Lord bless thee, and keep thee.
   The Lord make his face shine upon thee, and be gracious unto thee. [6:24]

8 Sent to spy out the land. [13:16]

9 Smote him with the edge of the sword. [21:24]

10 Let me die the death of the righteous, and let my last end be like his! [23:10]

11 Be sure your sin will find you out. [32:23]

Deuteronomy

12 Man doth not live by bread only, but by every word that proceedeth out of the mouth of the Lord doth man live. [8:3; also *St Matthew*, 4:4 and *St Luke*, 4:4 (with 'alone' for 'only')]

13 If there arise among you a prophet, or a dreamer of dreams. [13:1]

14 The wife of thy bosom. [13:6]

15 Thou shalt not muzzle the ox when he treadeth out the corn. [25:4]

16 In the morning thou shalt say, Would God it were even! and at even thou shalt say, Would God it were morning! [28:67]

17 He kept him as the apple of his eye. [32:10]

18 Jeshurun waxed fat, and kicked. [32:15]

19 As thy days, so shall thy strength be. [33:25]

20 The eternal God is thy refuge, and underneath are the everlasting arms. [33:27]

Joshua

21 This line of scarlet thread. [2:18]

22 Hewers of wood and drawers of water. [9:21]

23 I am going the way of all the earth. [23:14]

Judges

24 I arose a mother in Israel. [5:7]

25 The stars in their courses fought against Sisera. [5:20]

26 She brought forth butter in a lordly dish. [5:25]

27 At her feet he bowed, he fell, he lay down. [5:27]

28 Why tarry the wheels of his chariots? [5:28]

29 Have they not divided the prey; to every man a damsel or two? [5:30]

30 Faint, yet pursuing. [8:4]

31 Out of the eater came forth meat, and out of the strong came forth sweetness. [14:14]

32 If ye had not plowed with my heifer, ye had not found out my riddle. [14:18]

33 He smote them hip and thigh. [15:8]

34 The Philistines be upon thee. [16:9]

35 He wist not that the Lord was departed from him. [16:20]

36 From Dan even to Beer-sheba. [20:1]

37 The people arose as one man. [20:8]

Ruth

38 Whither thou goest, I will go; and where thou lodgest, I will lodge: thy people shall be my people, and thy God my God. [1:16]

39 The Lord do so to me, and more also, if ought but death part thee and me. [1:17]

1 Samuel

40 Speak, Lord; for thy servant heareth. [3:9]

41 Be strong, and quit yourselves like men. [4:9]

42 I-chabod, saying, The glory is departed from Israel. [4:21]

43 Is Saul also among the prophets? [10:11]

44 The Lord hath sought him a man after his own heart. [13:14]

45 Agag came unto him delicately. And Agag said, Surely the bitterness of death is past. [15:32]

46 Saul hath slain his thousands, and David his ten thousands. [18:7]

2 Samuel

47 Tell it not in Gath, publish it not in the streets of Askelon; lest the daughters of the

Philistines rejoice, lest the daughters of the un-circumcised triumph. [1:20]

1 Saul and Jonathan were lovely and pleasant in their lives, and in their death they were not divided. [1:23]

2 How are the mighty fallen in the midst of the battle! [1:25]

3 Thy love to me was wonderful, passing the love of women. [1:26]

4 Abner with the hinder end of the spear smote him under the fifth rib. [2:23]

5 Tarry at Jericho until your beards be grown. [10:5]

6 The poor man had nothing, save one little ewe lamb. [12:3]

7 And Nathan said to David, Thou art the man. [12:7]

8 Come out, come out, thou bloody man, and thou man of Belial. [16:7]

9 Would God I had died for thee, O Absalom, my son, my son! [18:33]

1 Kings

10 A proverb and a byword among all people. [9:7]

11 Behold, the half was not told me. [10:7]

12 My father hath chastised you with whips, but I will chastise you with scorpions. [12:11]

13 To your tents, O Israel. [12:16]

14 He slept with his fathers. [14:20]

15 How long halt ye between two opinions? [18:21]

16 He is talking, or he is pursuing, or he is in a journey, or peradventure he sleepeth, and must be awaked. [18:27]

17 There ariseth a little cloud out of the sea, like a man's hand. [18:44]

18 And after the fire a still small voice. [19:12]

19 Elijah passed by him, and cast his mantle upon him. [19:19]

20 Hast thou found me, O mine enemy? [21:20]

21 I saw all Israel scattered upon the hills, as sheep that have not a shepherd. [22:17]

22 And a certain man drew a bow at a venture, and smote the king of Israel between the joints of the harness. [22:34]

2 Kings

23 Go up, thou bald head. [2:23]

24 Is it well with the child? And she answered, It is well. [4:26]

25 There is death in the pot. [4:40]

26 He shall know that there is a prophet in Israel. [5:8]

27 Is thy servant a dog, that he should do this great thing? [8:13]

28 The driving is like the driving of Jehu, the son of Nimshi; for he driveth furiously. [9:20]

29 Had Zimri peace, who slew his master? [9:31]

Esther

30 Let it be written among the laws of the Persians and the Medes, that it be not altered. [1:19]

31 Thus shall it be done to the man whom the king delighteth to honour. [6:9]

Job

32 One that feared God, and eschewed evil. [1:1]

33 And the Lord said unto Satan, Whence comest thou? Then Satan answered the Lord, and said, From going to and fro in the earth, and from walking up and down in it. [1:7]

34 Naked came I out of my mother's womb, and naked shall I return thither: the Lord gave, and the Lord hath taken away; blessed be the name of the Lord. [1:21]

35 Skin for skin, yea, all that a man hath will he give for his life. [2:4]

36 Curse God, and die. [2:9]

37 There the wicked cease from troubling; and there the weary be at rest. [3:17]

38 The hair of my flesh stood up. [4:15]

39 Shall mortal man be more just than God? Shall a man be more pure than his maker? [4:17]

40 Man is born unto trouble, as the sparks fly upward. [5:7]

41 My days are swifter than a weaver's shuttle, and are spent without hope. [7:6]

42 He shall return no more to his house, neither shall his place know him any more. [7:10]

43 Canst thou by searching find out God? [11:7]

44 No doubt but ye are the people, and wisdom shall die with you. [12:2]

1 Man that is born of a woman is of few days, and full of trouble. [14:1]

2 Miserable comforters are ye all. [16:2]

3 I am escaped with the skin of my teeth. [19:20]

4 I know that my redeemer liveth, and that he shall stand at the latter day upon the earth. [19:25]

5 Seeing the root of the matter is found in me. [19:28]

6 The price of wisdom is above rubies. [28:18]

7 I was eyes to the blind, and feet was I to the lame.

I was a father to the poor: and the cause which I knew not I searched out. [29:15]

8 That mine adversary had written a book. [31:35]

9 Who is this that darkeneth counsel by words without knowledge? [38:2]

10 Gird up now thy loins like a man. [38:3]

11 When the morning stars sang together, and all the sons of God shouted for joy. [38:7]

12 Canst thou bind the sweet influences of the Pleiades, or loose the bands of Orion? [38:31]

13 He saith among the trumpets, Ha, ha; and he smelleth the battle afar off, the thunder of the captains, and the shouting. [39:25]

14 Canst thou draw out leviathan with an hook? [41:1]

15 He maketh the deep to boil like a pot. [41:31]

16 I have heard of thee by the hearing of the ear: but now mine eye seeth thee. [42:5]

17 So the Lord blessed the latter end of Job more than his beginning. [42:12]

Psalms

18 Nor sitteth in the seat of the scornful. [1:1]

19 Why do the heathen rage, and the people imagine a vain thing? [2:1]

20 Thou shalt break them with a rod of iron; thou shalt dash them in pieces like a potter's vessel. [2:9]

21 Stand in awe, and sin not: commune with your heart upon your bed, and be still. [4:4]

22 Lord, lift thou up the light of thy countenance upon us. [4:6]

23 Let them perish through their own imaginations. [5:11, *Book of Common Prayer* version]

24 God is a righteous Judge, strong and patient: and God is provoked every day. [7:12, *Book of Common Prayer* version]

25 Out of the mouth of babes and sucklings hast thou ordained strength. [8:2]

26 Thou hast made him a little lower than the angels. [8:5]

27 The fowl of the air, and the fish of the sea, and whatsoever passeth through the paths of the seas. [8:8]

28 Their memorial is perished with them. [9:6]

29 Up, Lord, and let not man have the upper hand. [9:19, *Book of Common Prayer* version]

30 They do but flatter with their lips, and dissemble in their double heart. [12:2, *Book of Common Prayer* version]

31 The fool hath said in his heart, There is no God. [14:1 and 53:1]

32 He that sweareth to his own hurt, and changeth not. [15:4]

33 The lines are fallen unto me in pleasant places; yea, I have a goodly heritage. [16:6]

34 Keep me as the apple of the eye; hide me under the shadow of thy wings. [17:8]

35 Yea, he did fly upon the wings of the wind. [18:10]

36 The heavens declare the glory of God; and the firmament sheweth his handiwork.

Day unto day uttereth speech, and night unto night sheweth knowledge. [19:1]

37 More to be desired are they than gold, yea, than much fine gold: sweeter also than honey and the honeycomb. [19:10]

38 Let the words of my mouth, and the meditation of my heart, be acceptable in thy sight, O Lord. [19:14]

39 Some trust in chariots, and some in horses: but we will remember the name of the Lord our God. [20:7]

40 My God, my God, why hast thou forsaken me? [22:1; also *St Matthew*, 27:46 and *St Mark*, 15:34]

41 O my God, I cry in the daytime, but thou hearest not; and in the night season, and am not silent. [22:2]

42 But I am a worm, and no man; a reproach of men, and despised of the people. [22:6]

43 Strong bulls of Bashan have beset me round. [22:12]

1 They pierced my hands and my feet.

I may tell all my bones: they look and stare upon me.

They part my garments among them, and cast lots upon my vesture. [22:16]

2 The Lord is my shepherd; I shall not want.

He maketh me to lie down in green pastures: He leadeth me beside the still waters. [23:1]

3 Yea, though I walk through the valley of the shadow of death, I will fear no evil: for thou art with me; thy rod and thy staff they comfort me. [23:4]

4 The earth is the Lord's, and the fulness thereof; the world, and they that dwell therein. [24:1]

5 Lift up your heads, O ye gates; and be ye lift up, ye everlasting doors; and the King of glory shall come in.

Who is this King of glory? The Lord strong and mighty, the Lord mighty in battle. [24:7]

6 Remember not the sins of my youth, nor my transgressions. [25:7]

7 I should utterly have fainted: but that I believe verily to see the goodness of the Lord in the land of the living. [27:15, *Book of Common Prayer* version]

8 Weeping may endure for a night, but joy cometh in the morning. [30:5]

9 Into thy hands I commend my spirit. [31:6, *Book of Common Prayer* version]

10 I am clean forgotten, as a dead man out of mind. [31:14, *Book of Common Prayer* version]

11 Thou shalt keep them secretly in a pavilion from the strife of tongues. [31:20]

12 Sing unto him a new song; play skilfully with a loud noise. [33:3]

13 The Lord bringeth the counsel of the heathen to nought. [33:10]

14 Eschew evil, and do good: seek peace, and ensue it. [34:14, *Book of Common Prayer* version]

15 I have been young, and now am old; yet have I not seen the righteous forsaken, nor his seed begging bread. [37:25]

16 I myself have seen the ungodly in great power: and flourishing like a green bay-tree. [37:36, *Book of Common Prayer* version]

17 He heapeth up riches, and knoweth not who shall gather them. [39:6]

18 Thou makest his beauty to consume away, like as it were a moth fretting a garment: every man therefore is but vanity. [39:12, *Book of Common Prayer* version]

19 Blessed is he that considereth the poor: the Lord will deliver him in time of trouble. [41:1]

20 Yea, mine own familiar friend, in whom I trusted, which did eat of my bread, hath lifted up his heel against me. [41:9]

21 As the hart panteth after the water brooks, so panteth my soul after thee, O God. [42:1]

22 Deep calleth unto deep. [42:7]

23 My heart is inditing a great matter: I speak of the things which I have made touching the king: my tongue is the pen of a ready writer. [45:1]

24 God is our refuge and strength, a very present help in trouble. [46:1]

25 He maketh wars to cease unto the end of the earth; he breaketh the bow, and cutteth the spear in sunder; he burneth the chariot in the fire.

Be still, and know that I am God. [46:9]

26 He shall subdue the people under us, and the nations under our feet. [47:3]

27 God is gone up with a merry noise: and the Lord with the sound of the trump. [47:5, *Book of Common Prayer* version]

28 Their inward thought is, that their houses shall continue for ever, and their dwelling-places to all generations; they call their lands after their own names.

Nevertheless, man being in honour abideth not: he is like the beasts that perish. [49:11]

29 For every beast of the forest is mine, and the cattle upon a thousand hills. [50:10]

30 Purge me with hyssop, and I shall be clean: wash me, and I shall be whiter than snow. [51:7]

31 The sacrifices of God are a broken spirit; a broken and a contrite heart, O God, thou wilt not despise. [51:17]

32 O that I had wings like a dove! for then would I fly away, and be at rest. [55:6]

33 We took sweet counsel together, and walked unto the house of God in company. [55:14]

34 The words of his mouth were smoother than butter, but war was in his heart: his

words were softer than oil, yet were they drawn swords. [55:21]

1 They have digged a pit before me, into the midst whereof they are fallen themselves. [57:6]

2 They are like the deaf adder that stoppeth her ear;
Which will not hearken to the voice of charmers, charm he never so wisely. [58:4]

3 They grin like a dog, and run about through the city. [59:6, *Book of Common Prayer* version]

4 Moab is my wash-pot; over Edom will I cast out my shoe. [60:8]

5 Give us help from trouble: for vain is the help of man. [60:11 and 108:12]

6 He only is my rock and my salvation: he is my defence; I shall not be moved. [62:6]

7 If riches increase, set not your heart upon them.
God hath spoken once; twice have I heard this; that power belongeth unto God. [62:10]

8 When I remember thee upon my bed, and meditate on thee in the night watches. [63:6]

9 They shall fall by the sword: they shall be a portion for foxes. [63:10]

10 O thou that hearest prayer, unto thee shall all flesh come. [65:2]

11 Thou crownest the year with thy goodness; and thy paths drop fatness.
They drop upon the pastures of the wilderness: and the little hills rejoice on every side. [65:11]

12 God be merciful unto us, and bless us: and shew us the light of his countenance, and be merciful unto us. [67:1, *Book of Common Prayer* version]

13 Let God arise, let his enemies be scattered: let them also that hate him flee before him.
As smoke is driven away, so drive them away: as wax melteth before the fire, so let the wicked perish at the presence of God. [68:1]

14 A father of the fatherless, and a judge of the widows, is God in his holy habitation. [68:5]

15 Why leap ye, ye high hills? [68:16]

16 Thou hast ascended on high, thou hast led captivity captive. [68:18]

17 The singers went before, the players on instruments followed after; amongst them were the damsels playing with timbrels. [68:25]

18 They gave me also gall for my meat; and in my thirst they gave me vinegar to drink. [69:21]

19 His enemies shall lick the dust. [72:9]

20 God is the judge: he putteth down one, and setteth up another. [75:7]

21 In the hand of the Lord, there is a cup, and the wine is red. [75:8]

22 A stubborn and rebellious generation. [78:8]

23 Man did eat angels' food. [78:25]

24 Then the Lord awaked as one out of sleep, and like a mighty man that shouteth by reason of wine.
And he smote his enemies in the hinder parts. [78:65]

25 Thou feedest them with the bread of tears. [80:5]

26 They go from strength to strength. [84:7]

27 For a day in thy courts is better than a thousand. I had rather be a doorkeeper in the house of my God, than to dwell in the tents of wickedness. [84:10]

28 Mercy and truth are met together; righteousness and peace have kissed each other. [85:10]

29 Before the mountains were brought forth, or ever thou hadst formed the earth and the world, even from everlasting to everlasting, thou art God. [90:2]

30 Thou art God from everlasting, and world without end. [*Book of Common Prayer* version]

31 For a thousand years in thy sight are but as yesterday when it is past, and as a watch in the night. [90:4]

32 In the morning they are like grass which groweth up.
In the morning it flourisheth, and groweth up; in the evening it is cut down, and withereth. [90:5]

33 We spend our years as a tale that is told.
The days of our years are threescore years and ten; and if by reason of strength they be fourscore years, yet is their strength labour and sorrow; for it is soon cut off, and we fly away. [90:9]

34 So teach us to number our days, that we may apply our hearts unto wisdom. [90:12]

35 Surely he shall deliver thee from the snare of the fowler, and from the noisome pestilence. [91:3]

1 Thou shalt not be afraid for the terror by night; nor for the arrow that flieth by day.

Nor for the pestilence that walketh in darkness; nor for the destruction that wasteth at noonday.

A thousand shall fall at thy side, and ten thousand at thy right hand; but it shall not come nigh thee. [91:5]

2 For he shall give his angels charge over thee, to keep thee in all thy ways.

They shall bear thee up in their hands, lest thou dash thy foot against a stone. [91:11]

3 But my horn shalt thou exalt like the horn of an unicorn: I shall be anointed with fresh oil. [92:10]

4 The righteous shall flourish like the palm-tree: he shall grow like a cedar in Lebanon. [92:12]

5 They shall bring forth fruit in old age; they shall be fat and flourishing. [92:14]

6 He that planted the ear, shall he not hear? he that formed the eye, shall he not see? [94:9]

7 O sing unto the Lord a new song. [96:1 and 98:1]

8 Let the floods clap their hands: let the hills be joyful together. [98:8]

9 I am like a pelican of the wilderness: I am like an owl of the desert.

I watch, and am as a sparrow alone upon the house-top. [102:6]

10 As for man, his days are as grass: as a flower of the field, so he flourisheth.

For the wind passeth over it, and it is gone; and the place thereof shall know it no more. [103:15]

11 And wine that maketh glad the heart of man, and oil to make his face to shine, and bread which strengtheneth man's heart. [104:15]

12 The young lions roar after their prey, and seek their meat from God. [104:21]

13 Man goeth forth to his work, and to his labour until the evening. [104:23]

14 Thus were they defiled with their own works, and went a whoring with their own inventions. [106:39]

15 He brought them out of darkness and the shadow of death, and brake their bands in sunder. [107:14]

16 They were even hard at death's door. [107:18, *Book of Common Prayer* version]

17 They that go down to the sea in ships, that do business in great waters.

These see the works of the Lord, and his wonders in the deep. [107:23]

18 They reel to and fro, and stagger like a drunken man, and are at their wit's end. [107:27]

19 Sit thou at my right hand, until I make thine enemies thy footstool. [110:1]

20 The fear of the Lord is the beginning of wisdom. [111:10]

21 He raiseth up the poor out of the dust, and lifteth the needy out of the dunghill. [113:7]

22 The mountains skipped like rams, and the little hills like lambs. [114:4]

23 They have mouths, but they speak not: eyes have they, but they see not.

They have ears, but they hear not; noses have they, but they smell not. [115:5]

24 I said in my haste, All men are liars. [116:11]

25 Precious in the sight of the Lord is the death of his saints. [116:15]

26 The stone which the builders refused is become the head stone of the corner. [118:22]

27 Thy word is a lamp unto my feet, and a light unto my path. [119:105]

28 Woe is me, that I sojourn in Mesech, that I dwell in the tents of Kedar. [120:5]

29 I am for peace: but when I speak, they are for war. [120:7]

30 I will lift up mine eyes unto the hills from whence cometh my help. [121:1]

31 He will not suffer thy foot to be moved: he that keepeth thee will not slumber. [121:3]

32 The Lord is thy keeper: the Lord is the shade upon thy right hand.

The sun shall not smite thee by day, nor the moon by night. [121.5]

33 The Lord shall preserve thy going out, and thy coming in, from this time forth, and even for evermore. [121:8]

34 Peace be within thy walls, and prosperity within thy palaces. [122:7]

35 The Lord hath done great things for us; whereof we are glad.

Turn again our captivity, O Lord, as the streams in the south.

They that sow in tears, shall reap in joy. [126:3]

1 Except the Lord build the house, they labour in vain that build it. [127:1]

2 It is vain for you to rise up early, to sit up late, to eat the bread of sorrows: for so he giveth his beloved sleep. [127:2]

3 Happy is the man that hath his quiver full of them [children]. [127:5]

4 Thy children like the olive-branches round about thy table. [128:3, *Book of Common Prayer* version]

5 Out of the depths have I cried unto thee, O Lord. [130:1]

6 If thou, Lord, shouldest mark iniquities, O Lord, who shall stand? [130:3]

7 Behold, how good and how pleasant it is for brethren to dwell together in unity!

It is like the precious ointment upon the head that ran down upon the beard, even Aaron's beard, that went down to the skirts of his garments. [133:1]

8 His mercy endureth for ever. [136:1]

9 By the rivers of Babylon, there we sat down, yea, we wept when we remembered Zion.

We hanged our harps upon the willows in the midst thereof. [137: 1]

10 Sing us one of the songs of Zion.

How shall we sing the Lord's song in a strange land?

If I forget thee, O Jerusalem, let my right hand forget her cunning. [137:3]

11 If I take the wings of the morning, and dwell in the uttermost parts of the sea;

Even there shall thy hand lead me, and thy right hand shall hold me. [139:9]

12 I am fearfully and wonderfully made. [139:14]

13 Set a watch, O Lord, before my mouth, keep the door of my lips. [141:3]

14 Let the wicked fall into their own nets, whilst that I withal escape. [141:10]

15 Put not your trust in princes, nor in the son of man, in whom there is no help. [146:3]

16 He gathereth together the outcasts of Israel.

He healeth the broken in heart, and bindeth up their wounds. [147:2]

17 He delighteth not in the strength of the horse: he taketh not pleasure in the legs of a man. [147:10]

18 Let the saints be joyful in glory: let them sing aloud upon their beds.

Let the high praises of God be in their mouth, and a two-edged sword in their hand;

To execute vengeance upon the heathen and punishments upon the people;

To bind their kings with chains, and their nobles with fetters of iron. [149:5]

19 Praise him upon the loud cymbals; praise him upon the high-sounding cymbals. [150:5]

Proverbs

20 The fear of the Lord is the beginning of knowledge. [1:7]

21 Surely in vain the net is spread in the sight of the bird. [1:17]

22 Wisdom crieth without; she uttereth her voice in the streets. [1:20]

23 Her ways are ways of pleasantness, and all her paths are peace. [3:17]

24 Wisdom is the principal thing; therefore get wisdom: and with all thy getting get understanding. [4:7]

25 The path of the just is as the shining light, that shineth more and more unto the perfect day. [4:18]

26 Go to the ant, thou sluggard, consider her ways, and be wise. [6:6]

27 Yet a little sleep, a little slumber, a little folding of the hands to sleep. [6:10]

28 Can a man take fire in his bosom, and his clothes not be burned? [6:27]

29 He goeth after her, straightway, as an ox goeth to the slaughter, or as a fool to the correction of the stocks. [7:22]

30 Wisdom is better than rubies. [8:11]

31 Stolen waters are sweet, and bread eaten in secret is pleasant. [9:17]

32 A wise son maketh a glad father: but a foolish son is the heaviness of his mother. [10:1]

33 The rich man's wealth is his strong city: the destruction of the poor is their poverty. [10:15]

34 Where no counsel is, the people fall: but in the multitude of counsellors there is safety. [11:14]

35 He that is surety for a stranger shall smart for it. [11:15]

1 As a jewel of gold in a swine's snout, so is a fair woman which is without discretion. [11:22]

2 A virtuous woman is a crown to her husband: but she that maketh ashamed is as rottenness in his bones. [12:4]

3 A righteous man regardeth the life of his beast. [12:10]

4 Hope deferred maketh the heart sick. [13:12]

5 The way of transgressors is hard. [13:15]

6 The desire accomplished is sweet to the soul. [13:19]

7 He that spareth his rod hateth his son. [13:24]

8 Fools make a mock at sin. [14:9]

9 In all labour there is profit: but the talk of the lips tendeth only to penury. [14:23]

10 Righteousness exalteth a nation. [14:34]

11 A soft answer turneth away wrath: but grievous words stir up anger. [15:1]

12 A merry heart maketh a cheerful countenance. [15:13]

13 Better is a dinner of herbs where love is, than a stalled ox and hatred therewith. [15:17]

14 A word spoken in due season, how good is it! [15:23]

15 Pride goeth before destruction, and an haughty spirit before a fall. [16:18]

16 The hoary head is a crown of glory, if it be found in the way of righteousness. [16:31]

17 He that repeateth a matter separateth very friends. [17:9]

18 Let a bear robbed of her whelps meet a man, rather than a fool in his folly. [17:12]

19 He that begetteth a fool doeth it to his sorrow. [17:21]

20 He that hath knowledge spareth his words. [17:27]

21 A wounded spirit who can bear? [18:14]

22 There is a friend that sticketh closer than a brother. [18:24]

23 Wine is a mocker, strong drink is raging. [20:1]

24 Every fool will be meddling. [20:3]

25 Even a child is known by his doings. [20:11]

26 It is naught, it is naught, saith the buyer: but when he is gone his way, then he boasteth. [20:14]

27 It is better to dwell in a corner of the house-top, than with a brawling woman in a wide house. [21:9]

28 A good name is rather to be chosen than great riches. [22:1]

29 The rich and poor meet together: the Lord is the maker of them all. [22:2]

30 Train up a child in the way he should go: and when he is old, he will not depart from it. [22:6]

31 Remove not the ancient landmark, which thy fathers have set. [22:28]

32 Riches certainly make themselves wings. [23:5]

33 Look not upon the wine when it is red. [23:31]

34 The heart of kings is unsearchable. [25:3]

35 Heap coals of fire upon his head. [25:22]

36 As cold waters to a thirsty soul, so is good news from a far country. [25:25]

37 A whip for the horse, a bridle for the ass, and a rod for the fool's back. [26:3]

38 Answer not a fool according to his folly, lest thou also be like unto him. [26:4]

39 Answer a fool according to his folly, lest he be wise in his own conceit. [26:5]

40 As a dog returneth to his vomit, so a fool returneth to his folly. [26:11]

41 Seest thou a man wise in his own conceit? there is more hope of a fool than of him. [26:12]

42 The slothful man saith, There is a lion in the way; a lion is in the streets. [26:13]

43 The sluggard is wiser in his own conceit than seven men that can render a reason. [26:16]

44 Whoso diggeth a pit shall fall therein: and he that rolleth a stone, it will return upon him. [26:27]

45 Boast not thyself of to-morrow; for thou knowest not what a day may bring forth. [27:1]

46 Faithful are the wounds of a friend. [27:6]

47 A continual dropping in a very rainy day and a contentious woman are alike. [27:15]

48 Iron sharpeneth iron; so a man sharpeneth the countenance of his friend. [27:17]

1 Though thou shouldst bray a fool in a mortar among wheat with a pestle, yet will not his foolishness depart from him. [27:22]

2 The wicked flee when no man pursueth: but the righteous are bold as a lion. [28:1]

3 He that maketh haste to be rich shall not be innocent. [28:20]

4 A fool uttereth all his mind. [29:11]

5 Where there is no vision, the people perish. [29:18]

6 Give me neither poverty nor riches; feed me with food convenient for me. [30:8]

7 The horseleach hath two daughters, crying, Give, give. [30:15]

8 The way of an eagle in the air; the way of a serpent upon a rock; the way of a ship in the midst of the sea; and the way of a man with a maid. [30:19]

9 The spider taketh hold with her hands, and is in kings' palaces. [30:28]

10 Who can find a virtuous woman? for her price is far above rubies. [31:10]

11 Her children arise up, and call her blessed. [31:28]

Ecclesiastes

12 Vanity of vanities, saith the Preacher, vanity of vanities; all is vanity.

What profit hath a man of all his labour which he taketh under the sun?

One generation passeth away, and another generation cometh. [1:2]

13 All the rivers run into the sea; yet the sea is not full. [1:7]

14 All things are full of labour; man cannot utter it: the eye is not satisfied with seeing, nor the ear filled with hearing.

The thing that hath been, it is that which shall be; and that which is done is that which shall be done: and there is no new thing under the sun. [1:8]

15 All is vanity and vexation of spirit. [1:14]

16 In much wisdom is much grief: and he that increaseth knowledge increaseth sorrow. [1:18]

17 Wisdom excelleth folly, as far as light excelleth darkness. [2:13]

18 One event happeneth to them all. [2:14]

19 To every thing there is a season, and a time to every purpose under the heaven.

A time to be born, and a time to die; a time to plant, and a time to pluck up that which is planted. [3:1]

20 I praised the dead which are already dead more than the living which are yet alive. [4:2]

21 Woe to him that is alone when he falleth, for he hath not another to help him up. [4:10]

22 A threefold cord is not quickly broken. [4:12]

23 God is in heaven, and thou upon earth: therefore let thy words be few. [5:2]

24 Better is it that thou shouldst not vow, than that thou shouldst vow and not pay. [5:5]

25 The sleep of a labouring man is sweet. [5:12]

26 A good name is better than precious ointment; and the day of death than the day of one's birth.

It is better to go to the house of mourning, than to go to the house of feasting. [7:1]

27 As the crackling of thorns under a pot, so is the laughter of the fool. [7:6]

28 Better is the end of a thing than the beginning thereof. [7:8]

29 Say not thou, What is the cause that the former days were better than these? for thou dost not enquire wisely concerning this. [7:10]

30 In the day of prosperity be joyful, but in the day of adversity consider. [7:14]

31 Be not righteous over much; neither make thyself over wise. [7:16]

32 One man among a thousand have I found; but a woman among all those have I not found. [7:28]

33 God hath made man upright; but they have sought out many inventions. [7:29]

34 There is no discharge in that war. [8:8]

35 A man hath no better thing under the sun than to eat, and to drink and to be merry. [8:15]

36 A living dog is better than a dead lion. [9:4]

37 Whatsoever thy hand findeth to do, do it with thy might; for there is no work, nor device, nor knowledge, nor wisdom, in the grave whither thou goest. [9:10]

38 The race is not to the swift, nor the battle to the strong. [9:11]

39 Dead flies cause the ointment of the apothecary to send forth a stinking savour. [10:1]

1 He that diggeth a pit shall fall into it. [10:8]

2 Wine maketh merry: but money answereth all things. [10:19]

3 Curse not the king, no not in thy thought; and curse not the rich in thy bedchamber: for a bird of the air shall carry the voice, and that which hath wings shall tell the matter. [10:20]

4 Cast thy bread upon the waters: for thou shalt find it after many days. [11:1]

5 In the place where the tree falleth, there it shall be. [11:3]

6 He that observeth the wind shall not sow; and he that regardeth the clouds shall not reap. [11:4]

7 Truly the light is sweet, and a pleasant thing it is for the eyes to behold the sun. [11:7]

8 Rejoice, O young man, in thy youth. [11:9]

9 Remember now thy Creator in the days of thy youth, while the evil days come not, nor the years draw nigh, when thou shalt say, I have no pleasure in them. [12:1]

10 The strong men shall bow themselves, and the grinders cease because they are few. [12:3]

11 The almond-tree shall flourish, and the grasshopper shall be a burden, and desire shall fail: because man goeth to his long home. [12:5]

12 Or ever the silver cord be loosed, or the golden bowl be broken, or the pitcher be broken at the fountain, or the wheel broken at the cistern.

Then shall the dust return to the earth as it was: and the spirit shall return unto God who gave it. [12:6]

13 The words of the wise are as goads. [12:11]

14 Of making many books there is no end; and much study is a weariness of the flesh. [12:12]

15 Fear God, and keep his commandments: for this is the whole duty of man. [12:13]

Song of Solomon

16 Let him kiss me with the kisses of his mouth: for thy love is better than wine. [1:2]

17 I am black, but comely, O ye daughters of Jerusalem. [1:5]

18 As the lily among thorns, so is my love among the daughters. [2:2]

19 Stay me with flagons, comfort me with apples: for I am sick of love. [2:5]

20 Rise up, my love, my fair one, and come away.

For, lo, the winter is past, the rain is over and gone;

The flowers appear on the earth; the time of the singing birds is come, and the voice of the turtle is heard in our land. [2:10]

21 Take us the foxes, the little foxes, that spoil the vines. [2:15]

22 Until the day break, and the shadows flee away. [2:17]

23 A fountain of gardens, a well of living waters, and streams from Lebanon. [4:15]

24 I sleep, but my heart waketh. [5:2]

25 Fair as the moon, clear as the sun, and terrible as an army with banners. [6:10]

26 Thy belly is like an heap of wheat set about with lilies.

Thy two breasts are like two young roes that are twins. [7:2]

27 Set me as a seal upon thine heart, as a seal upon thine arm; for love is strong as death; jealousy is cruel as the grave. [8:6]

28 Many waters cannot quench love, neither can the floods drown it. [8:7]

29 We have a little sister, and she hath no breasts. [8:8]

Isaiah

30 The ox knoweth his owner, and the ass his master's crib. [1:3]

31 Bring no more vain oblations; incense is an abomination unto me; the new moons and sabbaths, the calling of assemblies, I cannot away with. [1:13]

32 Though your sins be as scarlet, they shall be as white as snow. [1:18]

33 They shall beat their swords into plow-shares, and their spears into pruning-hooks: nation shall not lift up sword against nation, neither shall they learn war any more. [2:4; also *Micah*, 4:3 ('a sword' for 'sword')]

34 What mean ye that ye beat my people to pieces, and grind the faces of the poor? [3:15]

35 Woe unto them that join house to house, that lay field to field, till there be no place, that they may be placed alone in the midst of the earth! [5:8]

36 Woe unto them that call evil good, and good evil. [5:20]

1 Woe unto them that are wise in their own eyes, and prudent in their own sight! [5:21]

2 Above it stood the seraphims: each one had six wings; with twain he covered his face, and with twain he covered his feet, and with twain he did fly. [6:2]

3 Then said I, Lord, how long? [6:11]

4 Behold, a virgin shall conceive, and bear a son, and shall call his name Immanuel. [7:14]

5 For a stone of stumbling and for a rock of offence. [8:14]

6 Wizards that peep, and that mutter. [8:19]

7 The people that walked in darkness have seen a great light: they that dwell in the land of the shadow of death, upon them hath the light shined. [9:2]

8 For unto us a child is born, unto us a son is given: and the government shall be upon his shoulder: and his name shall be called Wonderful, Counsellor, The mighty God, The everlasting Father, The Prince of Peace. [9:6]

9 And there shall come forth a rod out of the stem of Jesse, and a Branch shall grow out of his roots. [11:1]

10 The wolf also shall dwell with the lamb, and the leopard shall lie down with the kid; and the calf and the young lion and the fatling together; and a little child shall lead them. [11:6]

11 Hell from beneath is moved for thee to meet thee at thy coming. [14:9]

12 How art thou fallen from heaven, O Lucifer, son of the morning! [14:12]

13 Watchman, what of the night?
The watchman said, The morning cometh, and also the night. [21:11]

14 Tyre, the crowning city, whose merchants are princes. [23:8]

15 For precept must be upon precept, precept upon precept; line upon line, line upon line; here a little, and there a little. [28:10]

16 They are drunken, but not with wine. [29:9, cf. 51:21]

17 Their strength is to sit still. [30:7]

18 Speak unto us smooth things, prophesy deceits. [30:10]

19 In quietness and in confidence shall be your strength. [30:15]

20 One thousand shall flee at the rebuke of one. [30:17]

21 Though the Lord give you the bread of adversity. [30:20]

22 This is the way, walk ye in it. [30:21]

23 An habitation of dragons, and a court for owls. [34:13]

24 The desert shall rejoice, and blossom as the rose. [35:1]

25 Sorrow and sighing shall flee away. [35:10]

26 Lo, thou trustest in the staff of this broken reed, on Egypt; whereon, if a man lean, it will go into his hand and pierce it. [36:6, cf. 2 Kings, 18:21]

27 Set thine house in order: for thou shalt die. [38:1]

28 I shall go softly all my years in the bitterness of my soul. [38:15]

29 Comfort ye, comfort ye my people, saith your God. [40:1]

30 The voice of him that crieth in the wilderness, Prepare ye the way of the Lord. [40:3]

31 Every valley shall be exalted, and every mountain and hill shall be made low: and the crooked shall be made straight, and the rough places plain. [40:4]

32 All flesh is grass, and all the goodliness thereof is as the flower of the field. [40:6, cf. 1 Peter, 1:24]

33 The grass withereth, the flower fadeth: because the spirit of the Lord bloweth upon it: surely the people is grass. [40:7]

34 He shall feed his flock like a shepherd: he shall gather the lambs with his arm, and carry them in his bosom, and shall gently lead those that are with young. [40:11]

35 Behold, the nations are as a drop of a bucket, and are counted as the small dust of the balance. [40:15]

36 Have ye not known? have ye not heard? hath it not been told you from the beginning? [40:21]

37 They that wait upon the Lord shall renew their strength; they shall mount up with wings as eagles. [40:31]

38 A bruised reed shall he not break, and the smoking flax shall he not quench. [42:3]

39 Seeing many things, but thou observest not. [42:20]

40 He warmeth himself, and saith, Aha, I am warm, I have seen the fire. [44:16]

1 Shall the clay say to him that fashioneth it, What makest thou? [45:9]

2 I have chosen thee in the furnace of affliction. [48:10]

3 There is no peace, saith the Lord, unto the wicked. [48:22]

4 How beautiful upon the mountains are the feet of him that bringeth good tidings, that publisheth peace. [52:7]

5 They shall see eye to eye, when the Lord shall bring again Zion. [52:8]

6 The Lord hath comforted his people, he hath redeemed Jerusalem. [52:9]

7 He is despised and rejected of men; a man of sorrows, and acquainted with grief. [53:3]

8 All we like sheep have gone astray. [53:6]

9 He was oppressed, and he was afflicted, yet he opened not his mouth: he is brought as a lamb to the slaughter, and as a sheep before her shearers is dumb, so he openeth not his mouth. [53:7]

10 He was cut off out of the land of the living. [53:8]

11 He was numbered with the transgressors; and he bare the sin of many. [53·:12]

12 Seek ye the Lord while he may be found, call ye upon him while he is near. [55:6]

13 For my thoughts are not your thoughts, neither are your ways my ways, saith the Lord. [55:8]

14 I will give them an everlasting name, that shall not be cut off. [56:5]

15 They are all dumb dogs, they cannot bark. [56:10]

16 Their feet run to evil, and they make haste to shed innocent blood. [59:7]

17 Arise, shine, for thy light is come. [60:1]

18 He hath sent me to bind up the broken-hearted, to proclaim liberty to the captives, and the opening of the prison to them that are bound;

To proclaim the acceptable year of the Lord, and the day of vengeance of our God; to comfort all that mourn. [61:1]

19 To give unto them beauty for ashes. [61:3]

20 I have trodden the winepress alone. [63:3]

21 All our righteousnesses are as filthy rags; and we all do fade as a leaf. [64:6]

22 For, behold, I create new heavens and a new earth. [65:17]

23 As one whom his mother comforteth, so will I comfort you. [66:13]

Jeremiah

24 They were as fed horses in the morning: every one neighed after his neighbour's wife. [5:8]

25 Saying, Peace, peace; when there is no peace. [6:14]

26 The harvest is past, the summer is ended, and we are not saved. [8:20]

27 Is there no balm in Gilead; is there no physician there? [8:22]

28 I was like a lamb or an ox that is brought to the slaughter. [11:19]

29 Can the Ethiopian change his skin, or the leopard his spots? [13:23]

30 The heart is deceitful above all things, and desperately wicked. [17:9]

Lamentations

31 Is it nothing to you, all ye that pass by? behold, and see if there be any sorrow like unto my sorrow. [1:12]

Ezekiel

32 They four had one likeness, as if a wheel had been in the midst of a wheel. [10:10]

33 The fathers have eaten sour grapes, and the children's teeth are set on edge. [18:2]

34 The king of Babylon stood at the parting of the way. [21:21]

35 She doted upon the Assyrians her neighbours, captains and rulers clothed most gorgeously, horsemen riding upon horses, all of them desirable young men. [23:12]

36 Set me down in the midst of the valley which was full of bones. [37:1]

37 And he said unto me, Son of man, can these bones live? [37:3]

38 Prophesy unto the wind. [37:9]

39 Son of man, set thy face against Gog, the land of Magog. [38:2]

Daniel

40 This image's head was of fine gold, his breast and his arms of silver, his belly and his thighs of brass,

His legs of iron, his feet part of iron and part of clay. [2:32]

1 The sound of the cornet, flute, harp, sackbut, psaltery, dulcimer, and all kinds of music. [3:5]

2 Cast into the midst of a burning fiery furnace. [3:11]

3 MENE, MENE, TEKEL, UPHARSIN. [5:25]

4 Thou art weighed in the balances, and art found wanting. [5:27]

5 Thy kingdom is divided, and given to the Medes and Persians. [5:28]

6 The Ancient of days did sit, whose garment was white as snow. [7:9]

Hosea

7 They have sown the wind, and they shall reap the whirlwind. [8:7]

8 Ye have plowed wickedness, ye have reaped iniquity. [10:13]

9 I drew them with cords of a man, with bands of love. [11:4]

10 I have multiplied visions, and used similitudes. [12:10]

Joel

11 That which the palmerworm hath left hath the locust eaten. [1:4]

12 Your sons and your daughters shall prophesy, your old men shall dream dreams, your young men shall see visions. [2:28]

13 Multitudes in the valley of decision. [3:14]

Amos

14 Can two walk together, except they be agreed? [3:3]

15 As a firebrand plucked out of the burning. [4:11]

Jonah

16 So they cast lots, and the lot fell upon Jonah. [1:7]

17 And also much cattle. [4:11]

Micah

18 They shall sit every man under his vine and under his fig-tree. [4:4]

19 What doth the Lord require of thee, but to do justly, and to love mercy, and to walk humbly with thy God? [6:8]

Habakkuk

20 Write the vision, and make it plain upon tables, that he may run that readeth it. [2:2]

Zechariah

21 For who hath despised the day of small things? [4:10]

22 Turn you to the stronghold, ye prisoners of hope. [9:12]

23 Woe to the idle shepherd that leaveth the flock! [11:17]

24 I was wounded in the house of my friends. [13:6]

Malachi

25 Have we not all one father? hath not one God created us? [2:10]

26 Those that oppress the hireling in his wages. [3:5]

27 Unto you that fear my name shall the Sun of righteousness arise with healing in his wings. [4:2]

APOCRYPHA

1 Esdras

28 Women are strongest: but above all things Truth beareth away the victory. [13:12]

29 Great is truth, and mighty above all things. [4:41]

30 *Magna est veritas et praevalet.* [*Vulgate* version]

2 Esdras

31 If he went not through the narrow, how could he come into the broad? [7:5]

32 I shall light a candle of understanding in thine heart, which shall not be put out. [14:25 (see also 248:25)]

Tobit

33 So they went forth both, and the young man's dog with them. [5:16]

Wisdom of Solomon

34 Love righteousness, ye that be judges of the earth. [1:1]

35 The ear of jealousy heareth all things. [1:10]

36 Let us crown ourselves with rosebuds, before they be withered. [2:8]

37 Through envy of the devil came death into the world. [2:24]

38 The souls of the righteous are in the hand of God, and there shall no torment touch them. [3:1]

39 Having been a little chastised, they shall be greatly rewarded. [3:5]

Ecclesiasticus

1 My son, if thou come to serve the Lord, prepare thy soul for temptation. [2:1]

2 Be not curious in unnecessary matters: for more things are shewed unto thee than men understand. [3:23]

3 There is a shame that bringeth sin, and there is a shame which is glory and grace. [4:21]

4 A faithful friend is the medicine of life. [6:16]

5 Miss not the discourse of the elders. [8:9]

6 Open not thine heart to every man, lest he requite thee with a shrewd turn. [8:19]

7 Forsake not an old friend; for the new is not comparable to him; a new friend is as new wine; when it is old, thou shalt drink it with pleasure. [9:10]

8 Many kings have sat upon the ground; and one that was never thought of hath worn the crown. [11:5]

9 Judge none blessed before his death. [11:28]

10 He that toucheth pitch shall be defiled therewith. [13:1]

11 How agree the kettle and the earthen pot together? for if the one be smitten against the other, it shall be broken. [13:2]

12 Be not made a beggar by banqueting upon borrowing. [18:33]

13 He that contemneth small things shall fall by little and little. [19:1]

14 Make little weeping for the dead, for he is at rest: but the life of the fool is worse than death. [22:11]

15 All wickedness is but little to the wickedness of a woman. [25:19]

16 The stroke of the whip maketh marks in the flesh; but the stroke of the tongue breaketh bones. [28:17]

17 Envy and wrath shorten the life. [30:24]

18 Leave off first for manners' sake. [31:17]

19 Let thy speech be short, comprehending much in few words. [32:8]

20 Leave not a stain in thine honour. [33:22]

21 There is a friend, which is only a friend in name. [37:1]

22 Honour a physician with the honour due unto him for the uses which you may have of him: for the Lord hath created him. [38:1]

23 Take no heaviness to heart: drive it away, and remember the last end. [38:20]

24 How can he get wisdom . . . whose talk is of bullocks? [38:25]

25 They will maintain the state of the world, and all their desire is in the work of their craft. [38:34]

26 Better it is to die than to beg. [40:28]

27 Let us now praise famous men, and our fathers that begat us. [44:1]

28 All these were honoured in their generations. [44:7]

29 There be of them that have left a name behind them. [44:8]

30 Their bodies are buried in peace; but their name liveth for evermore. [44:14]

2 Maccabees

31 It is a foolish thing to make a long prologue, and to be short in the story itself. [2:32]

32 When he was at the last gasp. [7:9]

33 Nicanor lay dead in his harness. [15:28]

NEW TESTAMENT

St Matthew

34 Rachel weeping for her children, and would not be comforted, because they are not. [2:18]

35 The voice of one crying in the wilderness. [3:3]

36 His meat was locusts and wild honey. [3:4]

37 O generation of vipers, who hath warned you to flee from the wrath to come? [3:7]

38 And now also the axe is laid unto the root of the trees. [3:10]

39 Man shall not live by bread alone. [4:4]

40 I will make you fishers of men. [4:19]

41 Blessed are the poor in spirit: for theirs is the kingdom of heaven. [5:3]

42 Blessed are the pure in heart: for they shall see God.
Blessed are the peacemakers: for they shall be called the children of God. [5:8]

43 Ye are the salt of the earth: but if the salt hath lost his savour, wherewith shall it be salted? [5:13]

44 Neither do men light a candle, and put it under a bushel. [5:15]

1 Whoever shall say, Thou fool, shall be in danger of hell fire. [5:22]

2 Agree with thine adversary quickly, whilst thou art in the way with him. [5:25]

3 Till thou hast paid the uttermost farthing. [5:26]

4 Resist not evil: but whosoever shall smite thee on thy right cheek, turn to him the other also. [5:39]

5 Love your enemies. [5:44]

6 He maketh his sun rise on the evil and on the good, and sendeth rain on the just and on the unjust. [5:45]

7 Let not thy left hand know what thy right hand doeth. [6:3]

8 Give us this day our daily bread. [6:11]

9 Forgive us our debts, as we forgive our debtors. [6:12]

10 Lead us not into temptation, but deliver us from evil. [6:13]

11 Where moth and rust doth corrupt, and where thieves break through and steal. [6:19]

12 Where your treasure is, there will your heart be also. [6:21]

13 No man can serve two masters. [6:24]

14 Ye cannot serve God and mammon.

15 Which of you by taking thought can add one cubit unto his stature? [6:27]

16 Consider the lilies of the field, how they grow; they toil not, neither do they spin:
  And yet I say unto you, that even Solomon in all his glory was not arrayed like one of these. [6:28]

17 Seek ye first the kingdom of God, and his righteousness; and all these things shall be added unto you. [6:33]

18 Take therefore no thought for the morrow: for the morrow shall take thought for the things of itself. Sufficient unto the day is the evil thereof. [6:34]

19 Judge not, that ye be not judged. [7:1]

20 Why beholdest thou the mote that is in thy brother's eye, but considerest not the beam that is in thine own eye? [7:3]

21 Neither cast ye your pearls before swine. [7:6]

22 Ask, and it shall be given you; seek, and ye shall find; knock, and it shall be opened unto you. [7:7]

23 What man is there of you, whom if his son ask bread, will he give him a stone? [7:9]

24 Therefore all things whatsoever ye would that men should do to you, do ye even so to them: for this is the law and the prophets. [7:12]

25 Wide is the gate, and broad is the way, that leadeth to destruction. [7:13]

26 Strait is the gate, and narrow is the way, which leadeth unto life, and few there be that find it. [7:14]

27 Beware of false prophets, which come to you in sheep's clothing, but inwardly they are ravening wolves. [7:15]

28 By their fruits ye shall know them. [7:20]

29 I have not found so great faith, no, not in Israel. [8:10]

30 But the children of the kingdom shall be cast out into outer darkness: there shall be weeping and gnashing of teeth. [8:12]

31 The foxes have holes, and the birds of the air have nests; but the Son of man hath not where to lay his head. [8:20]

32 Let the dead bury their dead. [8:22]

33 They that be whole need not a physician, but they that are sick. [9:12]

34 Neither do men put new wine into old bottles. [9:17]

35 The maid is not dead, but sleepeth. [9:24]

36 The harvest truly is plenteous, but the labourers are few. [9:37]

37 Freely ye have received, freely give. [10:8]

38 When ye depart out of that house or city, shake off the dust of your feet. [10:14]

39 Be ye therefore wise as serpents, and harmless as doves. [10:16]

40 He that endureth to the end shall be saved. [10:22]

41 Are not two sparrows sold for a farthing? and one of them shall not fall on the ground without your Father. [10:29]

42 The very hairs of your head are all numbered. [10:30]

43 I came not to send peace, but a sword. [10:34]

44 He that findeth his life shall lose it: and he that loseth his life for my sake shall find it. [10:39]

1 What went ye out into the wilderness to see? A reed shaken with the wind? [11:7]

2 The kingdom of heaven suffereth violence, and the violent take it by force. [11:12]

3 Wisdom is justified of her children. [11:19]

4 Come unto me, all ye that labour and are heavy laden, and I will give you rest. [11:28]

5 He that is not with me is against me. [12:30]

6 The blasphemy against the Holy Ghost shall not be forgiven unto men. [12:31]

7 Every idle word that men shall speak, they shall give account thereof in the day of judgement. [12:36]

8 An evil and adulterous generation seeketh after a sign. [12:39]

9 He findeth it empty, swept, and garnished. [12:44]

10 The last state of that man is worse than the first. [12:45]

11 Some seeds fell by the way side. [13:4]

12 An enemy hath done this. [13:28]

13 Found one pearl of great price. [13:46]

14 A prophet is not without honour, save in his own country. [13:57]

15 Be of good cheer; it is I; be not afraid. [14:27]

16 O thou of little faith, wherefore didst thou doubt? [14:31]

17 Besought him that they might only touch the hem of his garment. [14:36]

18 Not that which goeth into the mouth defileth a man; but that which cometh out of the mouth, this defileth a man. [15:11]

19 If the blind lead the blind, both shall fall into the ditch. [15:14]

20 It is not meet to take the children's bread, and to cast it to dogs. [15:26]

21 The dogs eat of the crumbs which fall from their masters' table. [15:27]

22 Can ye not discern the signs of the times? [16:3]

23 Thou art Peter, and upon this rock I will build my church; and the gates of hell shall not prevail against it. [16:18]

24 Get thee behind me, Satan. [16:23]

25 Let him deny himself, and take up his cross, and follow me. [16:24]

26 What is a man profited, if he shall gain the whole world, and lose his own soul? [16:26]

27 If ye have faith as a grain of mustard seed, ye shall say unto this mountain, Remove hence to yonder place; and it shall remove. [17:20]

28 Except ye be converted, and become as little children, ye shall not enter into the kingdom of heaven. [18:3]

29 Whoso shall offend one of these little ones which believe in me, it were better that a millstone were hanged about his neck, and that he were drowned in the depth of the sea. [18:6]

30 It must needs be that offences come; but woe to that man by whom the offence cometh! [18:7]

31 If thine eye offend thee, pluck it out. [18:9]

32 Until seventy times seven. [18:22]

33 For this cause shall a man leave father and mother, and shall cleave to his wife: and they twain shall be one flesh. [19:5]

34 What therefore God hath joined together, let not man put asunder. [19:6]

35 Thou shalt love thy neighbour as thyself. [19:19; also *Leviticus*, 19:18]

36 Thou shalt have treasure in heaven. [19:21]

37 He went away sorrowful: for he had great possessions. [19:22]

38 It is easier for a camel to go through the eye of a needle, than for a rich man to enter into the kingdom of God. [19:24]

39 With God all things are possible. [19:26]

40 But many that are first shall be last; and the last shall be first. [19:30]

41 Borne the burden and heat of the day. [20:12]

42 Is it not lawful for me to do what I will with mine own? Is thine eye evil, because I am good? [20:15]

43 Whosoever will be chief among you, let him be your servant. [20:27]

44 My house shall be called the house of prayer; but ye have made it a den of thieves. [21:13]

45 Out of the mouths of babes and sucklings thou hast perfected praise. [21:16]

46 The stone which the builders rejected, the same is become the head of the corner. [21:42 (see also 40:26)]

47 A man which had not on a wedding garment. [22:11]

1 Cast him into outer darkness; there shall be weeping and gnashing of teeth. [22:13]

2 Many are called, but few are chosen. [22:14]

3 Render therefore unto Caesar the things which are Caesar's; and unto God the things that are God's. [22:21]

4 For in the resurrection they neither marry, nor are given in marriage. [22:30]

5 All their works they do for to be seen of men. [23:5]

6 Whosoever shall exalt himself shall be abased; and he that shall humble himself shall be exalted. [23:12]

7 Ye blind guides, which strain at a gnat, and swallow a camel. [23:24]

8 Ye are like unto whited sepulchres, which indeed appear beautiful outward, but are within full of dead men's bones, and of all uncleanness. [23:27]

9 Ye shall hear of wars and rumours of wars. [24:6]

10 The end is not yet.

11 The abomination of desolation. [24:15]

12 Wheresoever the carcase is, there will the eagles be gathered together. [24:28]

13 Eating and drinking, marrying and giving in marriage. [24:38]

14 Well done, good and faithful servant. [25:23]

15 Unto every one that hath shall be given, and he shall have abundance: but from him that hath not shall be taken away even that which he hath. [25:29]

16 He shall separate them one from another, as a shepherd divideth his sheep from the goats. [25:32]

17 I was an hungered, and ye gave me meat: I was thirsty, and ye gave me drink: I was a stranger, and ye took me in. [25:35]

18 They covenanted with him for thirty pieces of silver. [26:15]

19 It had been good for that man if he had not been born. [26:24]

20 Before the cock crow, thou shalt deny me thrice. [26:34]

21 Let this cup pass from me. [26:39]

22 Watch and pray, that ye enter not into temptation: the spirit indeed is willing, but the flesh is weak. [26:41]

23 All they that take the sword shall perish with the sword. [26:52]

24 He took water, and washed his hands before the multitude, saying, I am innocent of the blood of this just person. [27:24]

25 His blood be on us, and on our children. [27:25]

26 He saved others, himself he cannot save. [27:42]

27 My God, my God, why hast thou forsaken me? [27:46]

St Mark

28 The sabbath was made for man, and not man for the sabbath. [2:27]

29 And if a house be divided against itself, that house cannot stand. [3:25]

30 He that hath ears to hear, let him hear. [4:9]

31 With what measure ye mete, it shall be measured to you. [4:24]

32 My name is Legion: for we are many. [5:9]

33 Sitting, and clothed, and in his right mind. [5:15]

34 Knowing in himself that virtue had gone out of him. [5:30]

35 I see men as trees, walking. [8:24]

36 What shall it profit a man, if he shall gain the whole world, and lose his own soul? [8:36]

37 Lord, I believe; help thou mine unbelief. [9:24]

38 Where their worm dieth not, and the fire is not quenched. [9:44]

39 Suffer the little children to come unto me, and forbid them not: for of such is the kingdom of heaven. [10:14]

40 Which devour widows' houses, and for a pretence make long prayers. [12:40]

41 And there came a certain poor widow, and she threw in two mites. [12:42]

St Luke

42 My soul doth magnify the Lord,
    And my spirit hath rejoiced in God my Saviour. [1:46]

43 To give light to them that sit in darkness and in the shadow of death, to guide our feet into the way of peace. [1:79]

44 Because there was no room for them in the inn. [2:7]

1 And lo, the angel of the Lord came upon them, and the glory of the Lord shone round about them: and they were sore afraid. [2:9]

2 Glory to God in the highest, and on earth peace, good will toward men. [2:14]

3 Lord, now lettest thou thy servant depart in peace, according to thy word. [2:29]

4 Wist ye not that I must be about my Father's business? [2:49]

5 Shewed unto him all the kingdoms of the world in a moment of time. [4:5]

6 Physician, heal thyself. [4:23]

7 Woe unto you, when all men shall speak well of you! [6:26]

8 The only son of his mother, and she was a widow. [7:12]

9 The labourer is worthy of his hire. [10:7]

10 Fell among thieves. [10:30]

11 He passed by on the other side. [10:31]

12 Go, and do thou likewise. [10:37]

13 Mary hath chosen that good part, which shall not be taken away from her. [10:42]

14 When a strong man armed keepeth his palace, his goods are in peace. [11:21]

15 His armour wherein he trusted. [11:22]

16 He that is not with me is against me. [11:23]

17 Thou fool, this night thy soul shall be required of thee. [12:20]

18 Let your loins be girded about, and your lights burning. [12:35]

19 Go and sit down in the lowest room; that when he that bade thee cometh, he may say to thee, Friend, go up higher. [14:10]

20 I have married a wife, and therefore I cannot come. [14:20]

21 The poor, and the maimed, and the halt, and the blind. [14:21]

22 Go out into the highways and hedges, and compel them to come in. [14:23]

23 Rejoice with me; for I have found my sheep which was lost. [15:6]

24 Joy shall be in heaven over one sinner that repenteth, more than over ninety and nine just persons, which need no repentance. [15:7]

25 Took his journey into a far country, and there wasted his substance with riotous living. [15:13]

26 He would fain have filled his belly with the husks that the swine did eat. [15:16]

27 Bring hither the fatted calf, and kill it. [15:23]

28 I cannot dig; to beg I am ashamed. [16:3]

29 The children of this world are in their generation wiser than the children of light. [16:8]

30 Make to yourselves friends of the mammon of unrighteousness. [16:9]

31 Clothed in purple and fine linen. [16:19]

32 The crumbs which fell from the rich man's table. [16:21]

33 Between us and you there is a great gulf fixed. [16:26]

34 We are unprofitable servants: we have done that which was our duty to do. [17:10]

35 The kingdom of God is within you. [17:21]

36 Remember Lot's wife. [17:32]

37 God, I thank thee, that I am not as other men are. [18:11]

38 God, be merciful to me a sinner. [18:13]

39 Out of thine own mouth will I judge thee. [19:22]

40 If these should hold their peace, the stones would immediately cry out. [19:40]

41 And when they heard it, they said, God forbid. [20:16]

42 In your patience possess ye your souls. [21:19]

43 Nevertheless, not my will, but thine, be done. [22:42]

44 If they do these things in a green tree, what shall be done in the dry? [23:31]

45 Father, forgive them; for they know not what they do. [23:34]

46 Why seek ye the living among the dead? [24:5]

47 And their words seemed to them as idle tales. [24:11]

St John

48 In the beginning was the Word, and the Word was with God, and the Word was God. [1:1]

49 The light shineth in darkness; and the darkness comprehended it not. [1:5]

50 There was a man sent from God, whose name was John. [1:6]

51 He was not that Light, but was sent to bear witness of that Light. [1:8]

1 He came unto his own, and his own received him not. [1:11]

2 And the Word was made flesh, and dwelt among us. [1:14]

3 Whose shoe's latchet I am not worthy to unloose. [1:27]

4 Can there any good thing come out of Nazareth? [1:46]

5 Woman, what have I to do with thee? mine hour is not yet come. [2:4]

6 The wind bloweth where it listeth, and thou hearest the sound thereof, but canst not tell whence it cometh, and whither it goeth. [3:8]

7 How can these things be? [3:9]

8 God so loved the world, that he gave his only begotten Son, that whosoever believeth in him should not perish, but have everlasting life. [3:16]

9 Men loved darkness rather than light, because their deeds were evil. [3:19]

10 God is a Spirit; and they that worship him must worship him in spirit and in truth. [4:24]

11 They are white already to harvest. [4:35]

12 Rise, take up thy bed, and walk. [5:8]

13 He was a burning and a shining light. [5:35]

14 Search the scriptures. [5:39]

15 It is the spirit that quickeneth. [6:63]

16 Judge not according to the appearance. [7:24]

17 He that is without sin among you, let him first cast a stone at her. [8:7]

18 The truth shall make you free. [8:32]

19 He was a murderer from the beginning, and abode not in the truth, because there is no truth in him. [8:44]

20 He is a liar, and the father of it.

21 The night cometh, when no man can work. [9:4]

22 The good shepherd giveth his life for the sheep. [10:11]

23 I am the resurrection, and the life. [11:25]

24 Jesus wept. [11:35]

25 For the poor always ye have with you. [12:8]

26 A new commandment I give unto you, That ye love one another. [13:34]

27 In my Father's house are many mansions. [14:2]

28 I am the way, the truth, and the life: no man cometh unto the Father, but by me. [14:6]

29 Greater love hath no man than this, that a man lay down his life for his friends. [15:13]

30 Whither goest thou? [16:5]

31 Quo vadis? [Vulgate version]

32 Pilate saith unto him, What is truth? [18:38]

33 Now Barabbas was a robber. [18:40]

34 Behold the man! [19:5]

35 Ecce homo! [Vulgate version]

36 What I have written, I have written. [19:22]

37 It is finished. [19:30]

38 Consummatum est. [Vulgate version]

39 Touch me not. [20:17]

40 Noli me tangere. [Vulgate version]

41 Feed my sheep. [21:16]

Acts of the Apostles

42 Cloven tongues like as of fire. [2:3]

43 Silver and gold have I none; but such as I have give I thee. [3:6]

44 Thy money perish with thee. [8:20]

45 Breathing out threatenings and slaughter. [9:1]

46 It is hard for thee to kick against the pricks. [9:5]

47 The street which is called Straight. [9:11]

48 This woman was full of good works. [9:36]

49 God is no respecter of persons. [10:34]

50 We also are men of like passions with you. [14:15]

51 Come over into Macedonia, and help us. [16:9]

52 Certain lewd fellows of the baser sort. [17:5]

53 For all the Athenians and strangers which were there spent their time in nothing else, but either to tell, or to hear some new thing. [17:21]

54 An altar with its inscription, TO THE UNKNOWN GOD. [17:23]

55 For in him we live, and move, and have our being. [17:28]

1 As certain also of our own poets have said.

2 Gallio cared for none of these things. [18:17]

3 Great is Diana of the Ephesians. [19:34]

4 It is more blessed to give than to receive. [20:35]

5 A citizen of no mean city. [21:39]

6 Brought up in this city at the feet of Gamaliel. [22:3]

7 A conscience void of offence toward God, and toward men. [24:16]

8 I appeal unto Caesar. [25:11]

9 Hast thou appealed unto Caesar? unto Caesar shalt thou go. [25:12]

10 Paul, thou art beside thyself; much learning doth make thee mad. [26:24]

11 For this thing was not done in a corner. [26:26]

12 Almost thou persuadest me to be a Christian. [26:28]

Romans

13 Without ceasing I make mention of you always in my prayers. [1:9]

14 The just shall live by faith. [1:17]

15 Served the creature more than the Creator. [1:25]

16 These, having not the law, are a law unto themselves. [2:14]

17 Let God be true, but every man a liar. [3:4]

18 (Some affirm that we say,) Let us do evil, that good may come. [3:8]

19 Where no law is, there is no transgression. [4:15]

20 Who against hope believed in hope. [4:18]

21 Hope maketh not ashamed. [5:5]

22 Where sin abounded, grace did much more abound. [5:20]

23 Death hath no more dominion over him. [6:9]

24 The wages of sin is death. [6:23]

25 For the good that I would I do not: but the evil which I would not, that I do. [7:19]

26 Who shall deliver me from the body of this death? [7:24]

27 To be carnally minded is death. [8:6]

28 We know that the whole creation groaneth, and travaileth in pain together until now. [8:22]

29 All things work together for good to them that love God. [8:28]

30 If God be for us, who can be against us? [8:31]

31 Neither death, nor life, nor angels, nor principalities, nor powers, nor things present, nor things to come,

Nor height, nor depth, nor any other creature, shall be able to separate us from the love of God. [8:38]

32 My kinsmen according to the flesh. [9:3]

33 Hath not the potter power over the clay, of the same lump to make one vessel unto honour, and another unto dishonour? [9:21]

34 A zeal of God, but not according to knowledge. [10:2]

35 Let love be without dissimulation. [12:9]

36 Rejoice with them that do rejoice, and weep with them that weep. [12:15]

37 Be not wise in your own conceits. [12:16]

38 Vengeance is mine; I will repay, saith the Lord. [12:19]

39 Be not overcome of evil, but overcome evil with good. [12:21]

40 Let every soul be subject unto the higher powers. [13:1]

41 The powers that be are ordained of God.

42 Render therefore to all their dues: tribute to whom tribute is due; custom to whom custom; fear to whom fear; honour to whom honour. [13:7]

43 Love is the fulfilling of the law. [13:10]

44 The night is far spent, the day is at hand. [13:12]

45 Him that is weak in the faith receive ye, but not to doubtful disputations. [14:1]

46 Let every man be fully persuaded in his own mind. [14:5]

47 None of us liveth to himself. [14:7]

48 That no man put a stumbling-block or an occasion to fall in his brother's way. [14:13]

49 We then that are strong ought to bear the infirmities of the weak. [15:1]

1 Corinthians

50 God hath chosen the foolish things of the world to confound the wise. [1:27]

51 I have planted, Apollos watered; but God gave the increase. [3:6]

1 Every man's work shall be made manifest. [3:13]

2 The wisdom of this world is foolishness with God. [3:19]

3 A spectacle unto the world, and to angels, and to men. [4:9]

4 Absent in body, but present in spirit. [5:3]

5 Know ye not that a little leaven leaveneth the whole lump? [5:6]

6 Your body is the temple of the Holy Ghost. [6:19]

7 It is better to marry than to burn. [7:9]

8 The fashion of this world passeth away. [7:31]

9 Knowledge puffeth up, but charity edifieth. [8:1]

10 I am made all things to all men. [9:22]

11 They do it to obtain a corruptible crown; but we an incorruptible. [9:25]

12 So fight I, not as one that beateth the air. [9:26]

13 But I keep under my body, and bring it into subjection. [9:27]

14 Let him that thinketh he standeth take heed lest he fall. [10:12]

15 God is faithful, who will not suffer you to be tempted above that ye are able. [10:13]

16 All things are lawful for me, but all things are not expedient. [10:23]

17 For the earth is the Lord's, and the fulness thereof. [10:26]

18 Whether therefore ye eat, or drink, or whatsoever ye do, do all to the glory of God. (10:31]

19 If a woman have long hair, it is a glory to her. [11:15]

20 Now there are diversities of gifts, but the same Spirit. [12:4]

21 Though I speak with the tongues of men and of angels, and have not charity, I am become as sounding brass, or a tinkling cymbal. [13:1]

22 Charity suffereth long, and is kind. [13:4]

23 Charity never faileth: but whether there be prophecies, they shall fail. [13:8]

24 For we know in part, and we prophesy in part. [13:9]

25 When I was a child, I spake as a child, I understood as a child, I thought as a child: but when I became a man, I put away childish things.

For now we see through a glass, darkly; but then face to face. [13:11]

26 And now abideth faith, hope, charity, these three; but the greatest of these is charity. [13:13]

27 Let your women keep silence in the churches. [14:34]

28 Let all things be done decently and in order. [14:40]

29 One born out of due time. [15:8]

30 I laboured more abundantly than they all: yet not I, but the grace of God which was with me. [15:10]

31 We are of all men most miserable. [15:19]

32 As in Adam all die, even so in Christ shall all be made alive. [15:22]

33 The last enemy that shall be destroyed is death. [15:26]

34 Let us eat and drink; for to morrow we die. [15:32, cf. *Isaiah*, 22:13]

35 Evil communications corrupt good manners. [15:33]

36 One star differeth from another star in glory. [15:41]

37 It is sown in corruption; it is raised in incorruption. [15:42]

38 The first man is of the earth, earthy. [15:47]

39 In a moment, in the twinkling of an eye, at the last trump. [15:52]

40 O death, where is thy sting? O grave, where is thy victory? [15:55]

41 Quit you like men, be strong. [16:13]

42 Let him be Anathema, Maran-atha. [16:22]

2 Corinthians

43 Not in tables of stone, but in fleshy tables of the heart. [3:3]

44 The letter killeth, but the spirit giveth life. [3:6]

45 An house not made with hands. [5:1]

46 We walk by faith, not by sight. [5:7]

47 We are ambassadors for Christ. [5:20]

48 Behold, now is the accepted time; behold, now is the day of salvation. [6:2]

1 As having nothing, and yet possessing all things. [6:10]

2 God loveth a cheerful giver. [9:7]

3 For ye suffer fools gladly, seeing ye yourselves are wise. [11:19]

4 Whether in the body, I cannot tell; or whether out of the body, I cannot tell: God knoweth. [12:2]

5 There was given to me a thorn in the flesh. [12:7]

6 My strength is made perfect in weakness. [12:9]

Galatians

7 The right hands of fellowship. [2:9]

8 Weak and beggarly elements. [4:9]

9 I have bestowed upon you labour in vain. [4:11]

10 Which things are an allegory. [4:24]

11 Ye are fallen from grace. [5:4]

12 Be not deceived; God is not mocked: for whatsoever a man soweth, that shall he also reap. [6:7]

13 Let us not be weary in well doing. [6:9]

Ephesians

14 The unsearchable riches of Christ. [3:8]

15 To be strengthened with might by his Spirit in the inner man. [3:16]

16 Carried about with every wind of doctrine. [4:14]

17 We are members one of another. [4:25]

18 Be ye angry and sin not: let not the sun go down upon your wrath. [4:26]

19 Let no man deceive you with vain words: for because of these things cometh the wrath of God upon the children of disobedience. [5:6]

20 Redeeming the time, because the days are evil. [5:16]

21 Put on the whole armour of God. [6:11]

22 For we wrestle not against flesh and blood, but against principalities, against powers, against the rulers of the darkness of this world, against spiritual wickedness in high places. [6:12]

Philippians

23 For to me to live is Christ, and to die is gain. [1:21]

24 Work out your own salvation with fear and trembling. [2:12]

25 But what things were gain for me, those I counted loss for Christ. [3:7]

26 Whose God is their belly, and whose glory is in their shame. [3:19]

27 Rejoice in the Lord alway: and again I say, Rejoice. [4:4]

28 The peace of God, which passeth all understanding. [4:7]

29 Whatsoever things are true, whatsoever things are honest, whatsoever things are just, whatsoever things are pure, whatsoever things are lovely, whatsoever things are of good report; if there be any virtue, and if there be any praise, think on these things. [4:8]

30 I have learned, in whatsoever state I am, therewith to be content. [4:11]

Colossians

31 Touch not; taste not; handle not. [2:21]

32 Husbands, love your wives, and be not bitter against them. [3:19]

33 Let your speech be alway with grace, seasoned with salt. [4:6]

1 Thessalonians

34 Remembering without ceasing your work of faith, and labour of love. [1:3]

35 Study to be quiet, and to do your own business. [4:11]

36 Pray without ceasing. [5:17]

37 Prove all things; hold fast that which is good. [5:21]

2 Thessalonians

38 If any would not work, neither should he eat. [3:10]

1 Timothy

39 Neither give heed to fables and endless genealogies. [1:4]

40 I did it ignorantly in unbelief. [1:13]

41 Not greedy of filthy lucre. [3:3]

42 Every creature of God is good. [4:4]

43 But refuse profane and old wives' fables. [4:7]

44 Worse than an infidel. [5:8]

45 Drink no longer water, but use a little wine for thy stomach's sake and thine often infirmities. [5:23]

1 For we brought nothing into this world, and it is certain we can carry nothing out. [6:7]

2 The love of money is the root of all evil. [6:10]

3 Fight the good fight of faith. [6:12]

4 Rich in good works. [6:18]

5 Oppositions of science falsely so called. [6:20]

2 Timothy

6 Be instant in season, out of season. [4:2]

7 I have fought a good fight, I have finished my course, I have kept the faith. [4:7]

8 The Lord reward him according to his works. [4:14]

Titus

9 Unto the pure all things are pure. [1:15]

Hebrews

10 For the word of God is quick, and powerful, and sharper than any two-edged sword, piercing even to the dividing asunder of soul and spirit. [4:12]

11 It is a fearful thing to fall into the hands of the living God. [10:31]

12 Faith is the substance of things hoped for, the evidence of things not seen. [11:1]

13 Confessed that they were strangers and pilgrims on the earth. [11:13]

14 Seeing we also are compassed about with so great a cloud of witnesses. [12:1]

15 Whom the Lord loveth he chasteneth. [12:6]

16 The spirits of just men made perfect. [12:23]

17 Let brotherly love continue.

Be not forgetful to entertain strangers: for thereby some have entertained angels unawares. [13:1]

18 Jesus Christ the same yesterday, and to day, and for ever. [13:8]

19 For here we have no continuing city, but we seek one to come. [13:14]

James

20 Every good gift and every perfect gift is from above, and cometh down from the Father of lights, with whom is no variableness, neither shadow of turning. [1:17]

21 Let every man be swift to hear, slow to speak, slow to wrath. [1:19]

22 Pure religion and undefiled before God and the Father is this, To visit the fatherless and widows in their affliction, and to keep himself unspotted from the world. [1:27]

23 Faith without works is dead. [2:20]

24 How great a matter a little fire kindleth! [3:5]

25 The tongue can no man tame; it is an unruly evil. [(Commonly misquoted as 'The tongue is an unruly member') 3:8]

26 Resist the devil, and he will flee from you. [4:7]

27 Ye have heard of the patience of Job. [5:11]

28 Let your yea be yea; and your nay, nay. [5:12]

1 Peter

29 Be sober, and hope to the end. [1:13]

30 As newborn babes, desire the sincere milk of the word. [2:2]

31 But ye are a chosen generation, a royal priesthood, an holy nation, a peculiar people. [2:9]

32 Honour all men. Love the brotherhood. Fear God. Honour the king. [2:17]

33 Even the ornament of a meek and quiet spirit. [3:4]

34 Giving honour unto the wife, as unto the weaker vessel. [3:7]

35 Charity shall cover the multitude of sins. [4:8]

36 Be sober, be vigilant; because your adversary the devil, as a roaring lion, walketh about, seeking whom he may devour. [5:8]

2 Peter

37 The dog is turned to his own vomit again; and the sow that was washed to her wallowing in the mire. [2:22]

1 John

38 If we say that we have no sin, we deceive ourselves, and the truth is not in us. [1:8]

39 Shutteth up his bowels of compassion. [3:17]

40 He that loveth not knoweth not God; for God is love. [4:8]

41 There is no fear in love; but perfect love casteth out fear. [4:18]

1 He that loveth not his brother whom he hath seen, how can he love God whom he hath not seen? [4:20]

Jude

2 Wandering stars, to whom is reserved the blackness of darkness for ever. [13]

Revelation of St John

3 His head and his hairs were white like wool, as white as snow; and his eyes were as a flame of fire. [1:14]

4 His voice as the sound of many waters. [1:15]

5 I am he that liveth, and was dead. [1:18]

6 I have somewhat against thee, because thou hast left thy first love. [2:4]

7 Be thou faithful unto death, and I will give thee a crown of life. [2:10]

8 He shall rule them with a rod of iron. [2:27]

9 I will not blot out his name out of the book of life. [3:5]

10 Because thou art lukewarm, and neither cold nor hot, I will spue thee out of my mouth. [3:16]

11 Behold, I stand at the door, and knock. [3:20]

12 Four beasts full of eyes before and behind. [4:6]

13 He went forth conquering, and to conquer. [6:2]

14 Behold, a pale horse: and his name that sat on him was Death. [6:8]

15 A great multitude, which no man could number, of all nations, and kindreds, and people, and tongues. [7:9]

16 These are they which came out of great tribulation, and have washed their robes, and made them white in the blood of the Lamb. [7:14]

17 When he had opened the seventh seal, there was silence in heaven about the space of half an hour. [8:1]

18 Those men which have not the seal of God in their foreheads. [9:4]

19 And there were stings in their tails. [9:10]

20 A woman clothed with the sun, and the moon under her feet, and upon her head a crown of twelve stars. [12:1]

21 The devil is come down unto you, having great wrath, because he knoweth that he hath but a short time. [12:12]

22 Let him that hath understanding count the number of the beast: for it is the number of a man; and his number is Six hundred threescore and six. [13:18]

23 Babylon is fallen, is fallen, that great city. [14:8]

24 Blessed are the dead which die in the Lord from henceforth: Yea, saith the Spirit, that they may rest from their labours; and their works do follow them. [14:13]

25 Behold, I come as a thief. [16:15]

26 A place called in the Hebrew tongue Armageddon. [16:16]

27 I will shew unto thee the judgement of the great whore that sitteth upon many waters. [17:1]

28 The woman was arrayed in purple and scarlet colour. [17:4]

29 And he laid hold on the dragon, that old serpent, which is the Devil, and Satan, and bound him a thousand years. [20:2]

30 The sea gave up the dead which were in it. [20:13]

31 And I saw a new heaven and a new earth: for the first heaven and the first earth were passed away; and there was no more sea. [21:1]

32 The holy city, new Jerusalem, coming down from God out of heaven, prepared as a bride adorned for her husband. [21:2]

33 And God shall wipe away all tears from their eyes; and there shall be no more death, neither sorrow, nor crying, neither shall there be any more pain: for the former things are passed away. [21:4]

34 Behold, I make all things new. [21:5]

35 I will give unto him that is athirst of the fountain of the water of life freely. [21:6]

36 The street of the city was pure gold. [21:21]

37 And the leaves of the tree were for the healing of the nations. [22:2]

38 I am Alpha and Omega, the beginning and the end, the first and the last. [22:13]

39 Whosoever loveth and maketh a lie. [22:15]

ISAAC BICKERSTAFFE 1735?–1812?

1 There was a jolly miller once, / Lived on the river Dee; / He worked and sang from morn till night; / No lark more blithe than he. [*Love in a Village*, I. v]

2 And this the burden of his song / For ever used to be, / I care for nobody, not I, / If no one cares for me.

3 We all love a pretty girl – under the rose. [II. ii]

AMBROSE BIERCE 1842–1914

4 When Eve saw her reflection in a pool, she sought Adam and accused him of infidelity. [*The Devil's Dictionary*]

5 *Applause*, n. The echo of a platitude.

6 *Bore*, n. A person who talks when you wish him to listen.

7 *Brain*, n. An apparatus with which we think that we think.

8 Calamities are of two kinds: misfortune to ourselves, and good fortune to others.

9 *Debauchee*, n. One who has so earnestly pursued pleasure that he has had the misfortune to overtake it.

10 While your friend holds you affectionately by both your hands you are safe, because you can watch both his. [Entry under *Epigram*]

11 *Faith*, n. Belief without evidence in what is told by one who speaks without knowledge, of things without parallel.

12 *Future*, n. That period of time in which our affairs prosper, our friends are true and our happiness is assured.

13 *Marriage*, n. The state or condition of a community consisting of a master, a mistress and two slaves, making in all two.

14 *Patience*, n. A minor form of despair, disguised as a virtue.

15 *Peace*, n. In international affairs, a period of cheating between two periods of fighting.

JOSH BILLINGS *see* SHAW, HENRY WHEELER

LAURENCE BINYON 1869–1943

16 Now is the time for the burning of the leaves. [*The Burning of the Leaves*]

17 With proud thanksgiving, a mother for her children, / England mourns for her dead across the sea. [*For the Fallen*]

18 They shall grow not old, as we that are left grow old: / Age shall not weary them, nor the years condemn. / At the going down of the sun and in the morning / We will remember them.

F. E. SMITH, EARL OF BIRKENHEAD 1872–1930

19 JUDGE: You are offensive, sir.
F. E. S.: We both are; the difference is that I'm trying to be and you can't help it. [C. E. Bechofer Roberts ('Ephesian'), *Lord Birkenhead*, Ch. 3]

AUGUSTINE BIRRELL 1850–1933

20 That great dust-heap called 'history'. [*Obiter Dicta*, 'Carlyle']

OTTO VON BISMARCK 1815–1898

21 Politics is no exact science. [Speech in Prussian Chamber, 18 Dec. 1863]

22 Politics is the art of the possible. [In conversation with Meyer von Waldeck, 11 Aug. 1867 (see also 271:11)]

23 We shall not go to Canossa [i.e. 'give way']. [Speech in the Reichstag, 14 May 1872]

24 An honest broker. [Speech in the Reichstag, 19 Feb. 1878]

25 Blood and iron. [Speech in Prussian Chamber, 28 Jan. 1886. 'Iron and blood' used by him, 29 Sept. 1862]

VALENTINE BLACKER 1778–1823

26 Put your trust in God, my boys, and keep your powder dry. [*Oliver Cromwell's Advice*]

SIR WILLIAM BLACKSTONE 1723–1780

27 Man was formed for society. [*Commentary on the Laws of England*, Introduction]

28 The king never dies. [Bk i. 7]

29 Time whereof the memory of man runneth not to the contrary. [18]

30 That the king can do no wrong is a necessary and fundamental principle of the English constitution. [iii. 17]

31 It is better that ten guilty persons escape than one innocent suffer. [iv. 27]

HELEN BLACKWOOD, LADY DUFFERIN 1807–1867

1 I'm sitting on the stile, Mary, / Where we sat, side by side. [*Lament of the Irish Emigrant*]

2 And the red was on your lip, Mary, / The love-light in your eye.

3 They say there's bread and work for all, / And the sun shines always there: / But I'll not forget old Ireland, / Were it fifty times as fair.

ROBERT BLAIR 1699–1746

4 The schoolboy, with his satchel in his hand, / Whistling aloud to bear his courage up. [*The Grave*, 58]

5 Its visits, / Like those of angels, short, and far between. [588]

CHARLES DUPEE BLAKE 1846–1903

6 Rock-a-bye baby on the tree top, / When the wind blows the cradle will rock, / When the bough bends the cradle will fall, / Down comes the baby, cradle and all. [Attr.]

WILLIAM BLAKE 1757–1827

7 For everything that lives is holy, life delights in life. [*America*, 71]

8 To see a World in a grain of sand, / And a Heaven in a wild flower, / Hold Infinity in the palm of your hand, / And Eternity in an hour. [*Auguries of Innocence*]

9 A robin redbreast in a cage / Puts all Heaven in a rage.

10 A dog starved at his master's gate / Predicts the ruin of the State.

11 A skylark wounded in the wing, / A cherubim does cease to sing.

12 Every wolf's and lion's howl / Raises from Hell a human soul.

13 He who shall hurt the little wren / Shall never be beloved by men.

14 The caterpillar on the leaf / Repeats to thee thy mother's grief.

15 A truth that's told with bad intent / Beats all the lies you can invent.

16 Every tear from every eye / Becomes a babe in Eternity.

17 He who shall teach the child to doubt / The rotting grave shall ne'er get out.

18 The strongest poison ever known / Came from Caesar's laurel crown.

19 If the Sun and Moon should doubt, / They'd immediately go out.

20 The harlot's cry from street to street / Shall weave old England's winding-sheet.

21 Does the Eagle know what is in the pit / Or wilt thou go ask the Mole? / Can Wisdom be put in a silver rod, / Or Love in a golden bowl? [*The Book of Thel*, Thel's motto]

22 The Vision of Christ that thou dost see / Is my vision's greatest enemy. [*The Everlasting Gospel*, α]

23 Both read the Bible day and night, / But thou read'st black where I read white.

24 Humility is only doubt, / And does the sun and moon blot out. [γ]

25 This life's five windows of the soul / Distorts the Heavens from pole to pole, / And leads you to believe a lie / When you see with, not thro', the eye.

26 I am sure this Jesus will not do, / Either for Englishman or Jew. ['Epilogue']

27 Mutual Forgiveness of each vice, / Such are the Gates of Paradise. [*The Gates of Paradise*, Prologue]

28 Truly, my Satan, thou art but a dunce, / And dost not know the garment from the man; / Every harlot was a virgin once, / Nor canst thou ever change Kate into Nan.

Tho' thou art worshipped by the names divine / Of Jesus and Jehovah, thou art still / The Son of Morn in weary Night's decline, / The lost traveller's dream under the hill. [Epilogue]

29 Great things are done when men and mountains meet; / This is not done by jostling in the street. [*Gnomic Verses*]

30 The Angel that presided o'er my birth / Said 'Little creature, formed of joy and mirth, / Go, love without the help of anything on earth.' ['Riches']

31 He who bends to himself a Joy / Doth the wingèd life destroy; / But he who kisses the Joy as it flies / Lives in Eternity's sunrise. ['Several Questions Answered']

32 I must Create a System, or be enslaved by another Man's; / I will not Reason and Compare; my business is to Create. [*Jerusalem*, f. 10. 20]

1 I see the Fourfold Man; the Humanity in deadly sleep, / And its fallen Emanation, the Spectre and its cruel Shadow. / I see the Past, Present, and Future existing all at once / Before me. [f. 15. 6]

2 The fields from Islington to Marybone, / To Primrose Hill and Saint John's Wood, / Were builded over with pillars of gold; / And there Jerusalem's pillars stood. [f. 27]

3 For a tear is an intellectual thing; / And a sigh is the sword of an angel king; / And the bitter groan of a martyr's woe / Is an arrow from the Almighty's bow. [f. 52]

4 I give you the end of a golden string; / Only wind it into a ball, / It will lead you in at Heaven's gate, / Built in Jerusalem's wall. [f. 77]

5 England! awake! awake! awake! / Jerusalem thy sister calls! / Why wilt thou sleep the sleep of death, / And close her from thy ancient walls?

6 And now the time returns again: / Our souls exult, and London's towers / Receive the Lamb of God to dwell / In England's green and pleasant bowers.

7 I care not whether a man is good or evil; all that I care / Is whether he is a wise man or a fool. Go! put off holiness, / And put on intellect. [f. 91:54]

8 'Father, O father! what do we here / In this land of unbelief and fear? / The Land of Dreams is better far, / Above the light of the morning star.' [The Land of Dreams]

9 And did those feet in ancient time / Walk upon England's mountains green? / And was the holy Lamb of God / On England's pleasant pastures seen?

And did the Countenance Divine / Shine forth upon our clouded hills? / And was Jerusalem builded here / Among these dark Satanic mills?

Bring me my bow of burning gold! / Bring me my arrows of desire! / Bring me my spear! O clouds, unfold! / Bring me my chariot of fire!

I will not cease from mental fight, / Nor shall my sword sleep in my hand, / Till we have built Jerusalem / In England's green and pleasant land. [Milton, Preface]

10 When a man has married a wife, he finds out whether / Her knees and elbows are only glued together. [Miscellaneous Epigrams]

11 Mock on, mock on, Voltaire, Rousseau; / Mock on, mock on; 'tis all in vain! / You throw the sand against the wind, / And the wind blows it back again. [Mock on, mock on, Voltaire, Rousseau]

12 My Spectre around me night and day / Like a wild beast guards my way; / My Emanation far within / Weeps incessantly for my sin. [My Spectre around me night and day]

13 Never seek to tell thy love, / Love that never told can be; / For the gentle wind does move / Silently, invisibly. [Never seek to tell thy Love]

14 Soon as she was gone from me, / A traveller came by, / Silently, invisibly: / He took her with a sigh.

15 When Sir Joshua Reynolds died / All Nature was degraded; / The King dropped a tear in the Queen's ear, / And all his pictures faded. [On Art and Artists]

16 A petty sneaking thief I knew – / O! Mr Cr—, how do you do? [On Cromek]

17 Hear the voice of the Bard! / Who present, past, and future sees; / Whose ears have heard / The Holy Word / That walked among the ancient trees. [Songs of Experience, Introduction]

18 Ah, Sun-flower! weary of time, / Who countest the steps of the sun; / Seeking after that sweet golden clime, / Where the traveller's journey is done;

Where the Youth pined away with desire, / And the pale Virgin shrouded in snow, / Arise from their graves, and aspire / Where my Sun-flower wishes to go. ['Ah! Sun-Flower']

19 Love seeketh not itself to please, / Nor for itself hath any care, / But for another gives its ease, / And builds a Heaven in Hell's despair. ['The Clod and the Pebble']

20 And the gates of this Chapel were shut, / And 'Thou shalt not' writ over the door. ['The Garden of Love']

21 And priests in black gowns were walking their rounds, / And binding with briars my joys and desires.

22 Pity would be no more / If we did not make somebody poor; / And Mercy no more could be / If all were as happy as we. ['The Human Abstract']

23 My mother groaned, my father wept, / Into

William Blake

the dangerous world I leapt; / Helpless, naked, piping loud, / Like a fiend hid in a cloud. ['Infant Sorrow']

1 But if at the Church they would give us some ale, / And a pleasant fire our souls to regale, / We'd sing and we'd pray all the live-long day, / Nor ever once wish from the Church to stray. ['The Little Vagabond']

2 I was angry with my friend: / I told my wrath, my wrath did end. / I was angry with my foe: / I told it not, my wrath did grow. ['A Poison Tree']

3 O Rose, thou art sick! / The invisible worm, / That flies in the night, / In the howling storm,

Has found out thy bed / Of crimson joy; / And his dark secret love / Does thy life destroy. ['The Sick Rose']

4 Tiger! Tiger! burning bright / In the forests of the night, / What immortal hand or eye / Could frame thy fearful symmetry? ['The Tiger']

5 When the stars threw down their spears, / And watered heaven with their tears, / Did he smile his work to see? / Did he who made the Lamb make thee?

6 Piping down the valleys wild, / Piping songs of pleasant glee, / On a cloud I saw a child. [*Songs of Innocence*, Introduction]

7 'Pipe a song about a Lamb!' / So I piped with merry cheer.

8 And I made a rural pen, / And I stained the water clear, / And I wrote my happy songs / Every child may joy to hear.

9 When my mother died, I was very young, / And my father sold me while yet my tongue / Could scarcely cry "'weep! 'weep! 'weep! 'weep!' / So your chimneys I sweep, and in soot I sleep. ['The Chimney Sweeper']

10 To Mercy, Pity, Peace, and Love / All pray in their distress. ['The Divine Image']

11 For Mercy has a human heart, / Pity a human face, / And Love, the human form divine, / And Peace, the human dress. [See 62:23]

12 'Twas on a Holy Thursday, their innocent faces clean, / The children walking two and two, in red and blue and green. ['Holy Thursday']

13 Then cherish pity, lest you drive an angel from your door.

14 'I have no name: / I am but two days old.' /

What shall I call thee? / 'I happy am, / Joy is my name.' / Sweet joy befall thee! ['Infant Joy']

15 Little Lamb, who made thee? / Dost thou know who made thee? / Gave thee life, and bid thee feed, / By the stream and o'er the mead; / Gave thee clothing of delight, / Softest clothing, woolly, bright; / Gave thee such a tender voice, Making all the vales rejoice? ['The Lamb']

16 He is meek, and He is mild; / He became a little child. / I a child, and thou a lamb, / We are callèd by His name. / Little Lamb, God bless thee!

17 When the green woods laugh with the voice of joy. ['Laughing Song']

18 My mother bore me in the southern wild, / And I am black, but O! my soul is white. ['The Little Black Boy']

19 Father! father! where are you going? / O do not walk so fast. / Speak, father, speak to your little boy, / Or else I shall be lost. ['The Little Boy Lost']

20 Farewell, green fields and happy groves, / Where flocks have took delight, / Where lambs have nibbled, silent moves / The feet of angels bright; / Unseen they pour blessing, / And joy without ceasing, / On each bud and blossom, / And each sleeping bosom. ['Night']

21 When the voices of children are heard on the green, / And laughing is heard on the hill, / My heart is at rest within my breast, / And everything else is still. ['Nurse's Song']

22 Can I see another's woe, / And not be in sorrow too? ['On Another's Sorrow']

23 Cruelty has a human heart, / And Jealousy a human face; / Terror the human form divine, / And Secrecy the human dress. [*Appendix to the Songs of Innocence and of Experience*, 'A Divine Image'; see 62:11]

24 I mock thee not, though I by thee am mocked; / Thou call'st me madman, but I call thee blockhead. [*To Flaxman*]

25 Thy friendship oft has made my heart to ache: / Do be my enemy – for friendship's sake. [*To Hayley*]

26 Whether on Ida's shady brow, / Or in the chambers of the East, / The chambers of the sun, that now / From ancient melody have ceased;

Whether in Heaven ye wander fair, / Or the green corners of the earth, / Or the blue regions of the air / Where the melodious winds have birth. [*To the Muses*]

1 Wandering in many a coral grove, / Fair Nine, forsaking Poetry!

2 The sound is forced, the notes are few!

3 O! why was I born with a different face? / Why was I not born like the rest of my race? [*To Thomas Butts*]

4 Without contraries is no progression. [*The Marriage of Heaven and Hell*, 'The Argument']

5 Man has no Body distinct from his Soul; for that called Body is a portion of Soul discerned by the five Senses, the chief inlets of Soul in this age. ['The Voice of the Devil']

6 Energy is eternal delight!

7 Those who restrain Desire, do so because theirs is weak enough to be restrained. ['Those who restrain Desire . . .']

8 The reason Milton wrote in fetters when he wrote of Angels and God, and at liberty when of Devils and Hell, is because he was a true poet, and of the Devil's party without knowing it. ['note']

9 In seed time learn, in harvest teach, in winter enjoy. ['Proverbs of Hell']

10 The road of excess leads to the palace of wisdom.

11 He who desires but acts not breeds pestilence.

12 The cut worm forgives the plough.

13 A fool sees not the same tree that a wise man sees.

14 Eternity is in love with the productions of time.

15 If the fool would persist in his folly he would become wise.

16 Prisons are built with stones of Law, brothels with bricks of Religion.

17 The pride of the peacock is the glory of God. / The lust of the goat is the bounty of God. / The wrath of the lion is the wisdom of God. / The nakedness of woman is the work of God.

18 What is now proved was once only imagined.

19 The tigers of wrath are wiser than the horses of instruction.

20 Damn braces. Bless relaxes.

21 Truth can never be told so as to be understood, and not be believed.

22 Then I asked: 'Does a firm persuasion that a thing is so, make it so?'

He replied: 'All Poets believe that it does, and in ages of imagination this firm persuasion removed mountains; but many are not capable of a firm persuasion of anything.' ['A Memorable Fancy: "The Prophets Isaiah and Ezekiel . . ." ']

23 If the doors of perception were cleansed, everything would appear to man as it is, infinite. ['The ancient tradition . . .']

24 I was in a Printing-house in Hell, and saw the method in which knowledge is transmitted from generation to generation. ['A Memorable Fancy: "I was in a Printing-house . . ." ']

25 Man's Desires are limited by his Perceptions; none can desire what he has not perceived. [*There is no Natural Religion*]

26 The Desire of Man being Infinite, the possession is Infinite, and himself Infinite.

27 To generalize is to be an idiot. [Quoted in Alexander Gilchrist, *Life of Blake*]

PHILIP BLISS 1838–1876

28 Hold the fort, for I am coming. [*Ho, my Comrades, see the Signal*]

KAREN BLIXEN *see* **DINESEN, 'ISAK'**

ALEXANDER BLOK 1880–1921

29 The right words in the right order. [Of poetry. Quoted in D. Burg and G. Feifer, *Solzhenitsyn*. See also 118:31]

ROBERT BLOOMFIELD 1766–1823

30 Strange to the world, he wore a bashful look, / The fields his study, Nature was his book. [*Farmer's Boy*, 'Spring', 31]

MARSHAL BLÜCHER 1742–1814

31 What a place to plunder! [Alleged remark on seeing London in 1814]

EDMUND BLUNDEN 1896–1974

32 I am for the woods against the world, / But are the woods for me? [*The Kiss*]

33 I have been young, and now am not too old; / And I have seen the righteous forsaken, / His health, his honour and his quality taken, / This is not what we were formerly told. [*Report on Experience*]

W. SCAWEN BLUNT 1840–1922

1 I like the hunting of the hare / Better than that of the fox. [*The Old Squire*]

BOETHIUS 480?–524

2 For in all adversity of fortune the worst sort of misery is to have been happy. [*Consolation of Philosophy*, Bk ii. Prose 4]

HUMPHREY BOGART 1899–1957

3 Here's looking at you, kid. [In film *Casablanca*, script by Julius J. Epstein, Philip G. Epstein and Howard Koch. See also 32:5 for the line usually attr. – falsely – to him]

JAKOB BÖHME 1575–1624

4 THE SCHOLAR: Whither goes the soul when the body dies?
THE MASTER: There is no necessity for it to go anywhere. [*Of Heaven and Hell, A Dialogue*]

NIELS BOHR 1885–1962

5 Two sorts of truth: trivialities, where opposites are obviously absurd, and profound truths, recognized by the fact that the opposite is also a profound truth. [Quoted in S. Rozental, *Niels Bohr: His Life and Work*]

6 An expert is a man who has made all the mistakes, which can be made, in a very narrow field. [Quoted in A. L. Mackay, ed., *A Dictionary of Scientific Quotations*]

NICOLAS BOILEAU 1636–1711

7 *Quelque sujet qu'on traite, ou plaisant, ou sublime, / Que toujours le bon sens s'accorde avec la rime.* – Whether one is treating a light or an exalted subject, let the sense and the rhyme always agree. [*L'Art poétique*, I. 27]

8 *Qui ne sait se borner ne sut jamais écrire.* – No one who cannot limit himself has ever been able to write. [63]

9 *Souvent la peur d'un mal nous conduit dans un pire.* – Often the fear of one evil leads us into a worse. [64]

10 *Enfin Malherbe vint, et, le premier en France, / Fit sentir dans les vers une juste cadence.* – At last came Malherbe, and made verse run smoothly – the first in France to do so. [131]

11 *Vingt fois sur le métier remettez votre ouvrage; / Polissez-le sans cesse et le repolissez.* – Bring your work back to the workshop twenty times. Polish it continuously, and polish it again. [172]

12 *Un sot trouve toujours un plus sot qui l'admire.* – A fool always finds a greater fool to admire him. [232]

13 *Qu'en un lieu, qu'en un jour, un seul fait accompli, / Tienne jusqu'à la fin le théâtre rempli.* – Let a single complete action, in one place and one day, keep the theatre packed to the last. [III. 45]

14 *Soyez plutôt maçon, si c'est votre talent.* – Be a mason instead, if you have a talent for that. [IV. 26]

15 *Ma pensée au grand jour partout s'offre et s'expose, /Et mon vers, bien ou mal, dit toujours quelque chose.* – Everywhere my thought offers and exposes itself to the light of day, and my verse, whether good or bad, always says something. [*Épîtres*, IX. 59]

16 *Le pénible fardeau de n'avoir rien à faire.* – The dreadful burden of having nothing to do. [XI. 86]

17 *Reprenez vos esprits et souvenez-vous bien / Qu'un dîner réchauffé ne valut jamais rien.* – Take fresh heart and never forget that a warmed-up dinner is worth nothing at all. [*Le Lutrin*, 103]

18 *Grand roi, cesse de vaincre, ou je cesse d'écrire.* – Great king, cease winning victories, or I shall give up writing. [*Satires*, VIII. 1]

HENRY ST JOHN, VISCOUNT BOLINGBROKE 1678–1751

19 They make truth serve as a stalking-horse to error. [*On the Study of History*, Letter 1]

20 Nations, like men, have their infancy. [4]

21 They [Thucydides and Xenophon] maintained the dignity of history. [5]

22 Truth lies within a little and certain compass, but error is immense. [*Reflections upon Exile*]

SIR DAVID BONE 1874–1959

23 It's 'Damn you, Jack – I'm all right!' with you chaps. [*The Brassbounder*, Ch. 3]

JAMES BONE 1872–1962

24 He made righteousness readable. [Of C. P. Scott of the *Manchester Guardian*]

DIETRICH BONHOEFFER 1906–1945

1 A God who let us prove his existence would be an idol. [*No Rusty Swords*]

DANIEL BOORSTIN 1914–

2 A best-seller was a book which somehow sold well simply because it was selling well. [*The Image*, Ch. 4]

BARTON BOOTH 1681–1733

3 True as the needle to the pole, / Or as the dial to the sun. [*Song*]

GENERAL WILLIAM BOOTH 1829–1912

4 This Submerged Tenth – is it, then, beyond the reach of the nine-tenths in the midst of whom they live? [*In Darkest England*, I. ii. 23]

JORGE LUIS BORGES 1899–1986

5 Writing is nothing more than a guided dream. [*Doctor Brodie's Report*, Preface]

LUDWIG BÖRNE 1786–1837

6 Let us have no care, but be glad of the approaching springtime of the peoples. Let us have no fear of the movement into the open. [*Gesammelte Schriften* (1829), III. 135]

GEORGE BORROW 1803–1881

7 The author of 'Amelia' [Fielding], the most singular genius which their island ever produced, whose works it has long been the fashion to abuse in public and to read in secret. [*The Bible in Spain*, Ch. 1]

8 The genuine spirit of localism. [31]

9 There are no countries in the world less known by the British than those selfsame British Islands. [*Lavengro*, Preface]

10 Translation is at best an echo. [25]

11 There's night and day, brother, both sweet things; sun, moon, and stars, brother, all sweet things; there's likewise a wind on the heath. Life is very sweet, brother; who would wish to die?

12 A losing trade, I assure you, sir: literature is a drug. [30]

13 Youth will be served, every dog has his day, and mine has been a fine one. [92]

14 Sherry . . . a sickly compound, the use of which will transform a nation, however bold and warlike by nature, into a race of sketchers, scribblers and punsters, in fact into what Englishmen are at the present day. [*Wild Wales*, Ch. 28]

MARÉCHAL BOSQUET 1810–1861

15 *C'est magnifique, mais ce n'est pas la guerre.* – It is magnificent, but it is not war. [Comment on the Charge of the Light Brigade, 1854]

J. C. BOSSIDY 1860–1928

16 And this is good old Boston, / The home of the bean and the cod, / Where the Lowells talk to the Cabots, / And the Cabots talk only to God. [Toast proposed at Harvard dinner, 1910]

JACQUES BÉNIGNE BOSSUET 1627–1704

17 *L'Angleterre, ah! la perfide Angleterre.* – England, oh, perfidious England! [*Sermon sur la Circoncision*. (By the time of the French Revolution this had become *Albion perfide*)]

HORATIO BOTTOMLEY 1860–1933

18 VISITOR: Ah Bottomley, sewing?
BOTTOMLEY: No, reaping. [When discovered sewing mail bags by a prison visitor. Quoted in Julian Symons, *Horatio Bottomley*, Ch. 19]

BOULAY DE LA MEURTHE 1761–1840

19 *C'est pire qu'un crime, c'est une faute.* – It is worse than a crime, it is a blunder. [Comment on the execution of the Duc d'Enghien, 21 Mar. 1804, also attr. to Talleyrand]

SIR H. E. BOULTON 1859–1935

20 Speed, bonny boat, like a bird on the wing; / 'Onward', the sailors cry; / Carry the lad that's born to be king / Over the sea to Skye. [*Skye Boat Song*]

F. W. BOURDILLON 1852–1921

21 The night has a thousand eyes, / And the day but one; / Yet the light of the bright world dies / With the dying sun. [*Light*]

LORD BOWEN 1835–1894

22 The rain it raineth on the just / And also

on the unjust fella: / But chiefly on the just, because / The unjust steals the just's umbrella. [Quoted in Walter Sichel, *Sands of Time*]

1 *On a metaphysician:* A blind man in a dark room, looking for a black hat which is not there. [Attr. in *Notes & Queries*, 182. 123]

E. E. BOWEN 1836–1901

2 Forty years on, when afar and asunder / Parted are those who are singing today. [*Forty Years On*, Harrow School Song]

ELIZABETH BOWEN 1899–1973

3 Experience isn't interesting till it begins to repeat itself – in fact, till it does that, it hardly *is* experience. [*The Death of the Heart*, Pt I. Ch. 1]

4 The heart may think it knows better: the senses know that absence blots people out. We have really no absent friends. [II.2]

W. L. BOWLES 1762–1850

5 The Cause of Freedom is the cause of God! [*Edmund Burke*, 78]

E. BOYD-JONES 19 Cent.
and PAUL A. RICHARDS 19 Cent.

6 Tell Me Pretty Maiden, Are There Any More At Home Like You? [Title of song in musical *Floradora*, II]

MALCOLM BRADBURY 1932–

7 I like the English. They have the most rigid code of immorality in the world. [*Eating People is Wrong*, Ch. 5]

RAY BRADBURY 1920–

8 The Day It Rained Forever. [Title of book]

JOHN BRADFORD 1510?–1555

9 But for the grace of God, there goes John Bradford. [On seeing some criminals led to execution]

F. H. BRADLEY 1846–1924

10 Metaphysics is the finding of bad reasons for what we believe upon instinct; but to find these reasons is no less an instinct. [*Appearance and Reality*, Preface]

11 A ballet dance of bloodless categories. [*Logic*]

12 His mind is open; yes, it is so open that nothing is retained; ideas simply pass through him. [Quoted in Evan Esar (ed.), *Treasury of Humorous Quotations*]

GENERAL OMAR BRADLEY 1893–1981

13 The wrong war, at the wrong place, at the wrong time, and with the wrong enemy. [At the Senate inquiry over General MacArthur's proposal to carry the Korean conflict into China, 15 May 1951]

JOHN BRAHAM 1774?–1856

14 England, home and beauty. [*The Americans*, Song]

JOHN BRAINE 1922–1986

15 Room At the Top. [Title of book]

HARRY BRAISTED 19 Cent.

16 If you want to win her hand, / Let the maiden understand / That she's not the only pebble on the beach. [*You're not the only Pebble on the Beach*]

ERNEST BRAMAH [E. B. SMITH] 1868–1942

17 An expression of no-encouragement. [*The Wallet of Kai Lung*, 'Confession of Kai Lung']

18 The whole narrative is permeated with the odour of joss-sticks and honourable high-mindedness. ['Kin Yen']

G. W. BRANDT 20 Cent.

19 Surrounded on all sides, I won the war single-handed. [Quoted in *Cassell's Encyclopaedia of Literature*, 'Plot']

SEBASTIAN BRANT 1458–1521

20 *Die Welt die will betrogen sein.* – The world, which wishes to be deceived. [*Das Narrenschiff*]

RICHARD BRATHWAITE 1588?–1673

21 I saw a Puritan-one / Hanging of his cat on Monday, / For killing of a mouse on Sunday. [*Barnabee's Journal*, Pt I]

BERTOLT BRECHT 1898–1956

1 You want justice, but do you want to pay for it, hm? When you go to a butcher you know you have to pay, but you people go to a judge as if you were off to a funeral supper. [*The Caucasian Chalk Circle*, V, trans. Eric Bentley]

2 Take note of what men of old concluded: / That what there is shall go to those who are good for it, / Children to the motherly, that they prosper, / Carts to good drivers, that they be driven well, / The valley to the waterers, that it yield fruit.

3 It was never decreed that a god mustn't pay hotel bills. [*The Good Woman of Setzuan*, Prologue, trans. Eric Bentley]

4 Unhappy the land that has no heroes ... No. Unhappy the land that is in need of heroes. [*The Life of Galileo*, 13, trans. Desmond I. Vesey]

5 What they could do with round here is a good war. What else can you expect with peace running wild all over the place? You know what the trouble with peace is? No organization. [*Mother Courage*, I, trans. Eric Bentley]

6 When a soldier sees a clean face, there's one more whore in the world. [III]

7 THE CHAPLAIN: We're in God's hands now! MOTHER C.: I hope we're not as desperate as that, but it *is* hard to sleep at night.

8 What happens to the hole when the cheese is gone? [VI]

9 War is like love, it always finds a way.

10 She's not so pretty anyone would want to ruin her.

11 Don't tell me peace has broken out. [VIII]

12 THE COOK [*to the Chaplain*]: As a grown man, you should know better than to go round advising people.

13 As the old Czech proverb has it, 'Sweaty feet seldom come singly.' [*Schweyk in the Second World War*, II, trans. William Rowlinson]

14 A man who sees another man on the street corner with only a stump for an arm will be so shocked the first time he'll give him sixpence. But the second time it'll only be a threepenny bit. And if he sees him a third time, he'll have him cold-bloodedly handed over to the police. [*The Threepenny Opera*, I. i, trans. Desmond I. Vesey and Eric Bentley]

15 The wickedness of the world is so great you have to run your legs off to avoid having them stolen from under you. [I. iii]

16 Grub first, then ethics. [II. i]

17 What is robbing a bank compared to founding one? [III. i]

18 Oh the shark has pretty teeth, dear, / And he shows them pearly white. / Just a jack-knife has Macheath / And he keeps it out of sight.

GERALD BRENAN 1894–1987

19 In a happy marriage it is the wife who provides the climate, the husband the landscape. [*Thoughts in a Dry Season*, 'Marriage']

NICHOLAS BRETON 1545?–1626?

20 I wish my deadly foe no worse / Than want of friends, and empty purse. [*A Farewell to Town*]

21 A Mad World, My Masters. [Title of dialogue]

22 Much ado there was, God wot, / He would love, and she would not. [*Phillida and Corydon*]

ROBERT BRIDGES 1844–1930

23 Awake, my heart, to be loved, awake, awake! / The darkness silvers away, the morn doth break. [*Awake, my heart, to be loved*]

24 Wherefore to-night so full of care, / My soul, revolving hopeless strife? [*Dejection*]

25 For beauty being the best of all we know / Sums up the unsearchable and secret aims / Of nature. [*The Growth of Love*, 8]

26 Beauty sat with me all the summer day, / Awaiting the sure triumph of her eye; / Nor mark'd I till we parted, how, hard by, / Love in her train stood ready for his prey. [56]

27 The hill pines were sighing, / O'ercast and chill was the day: / A mist in the valley lying / Blotted the pleasant May. [*The Hill Pines were Sighing*]

28 I heard a linnet courting / His lady in the spring. [*I heard a linnet*]

29 I will not let thee go. / Had not the great sun seen, I might; / Or were he reckoned slow / To bring the false to light, / Then might I let thee go. [*I will not let thee go*]

30 When men were all asleep the snow came flying, / In large white flakes falling on the city

brown, / Stealthily and perpetually settling and loosely lying, / Hushing the latest traffic of the drowsy town. [*London Snow*]

1 'O look at the trees!' they cried, 'O look at the trees!'

2 The south-wind strengthens to a gale, / Across the moon the clouds fly fast, / The house is smitten as with a flail, / The chimney shudders to the blast. [*Low Barometer*]

3 And Reason kens he herits in / A haunted house. Tenants unknown / Assert their squalid lease of sin / With earlier title than his own.

4 My delight and thy delight / Walking, like two angels white, / In the gardens of the night. [*My Delight and thy Delight*]

5 Beautiful must be the mountains whence ye come, / And bright in the fruitful valleys the streams, wherefrom / Ye learn your song. [*Nightingales*]

6 Perfect little body, without fault or stain on thee. [*On a dead Child*]

7 Whither, O splendid ship, thy white sails crowding, / Leaning across the bosom of the urgent West. [*A Passer-by*]

8 Spring goeth all in white, / Crowned with milk-white may: / In fleecy flocks of light / O'er heaven the white clouds stray. [*Spring goeth all in White*]

9 When death to either shall come, – / I pray it be first to me. [*When Death to either shall come*]

10 The day begins to droop, – / Its course is done: / But nothing tells the place / Of the setting sun. [*Winter Nightfall*]

JOHN BRIGHT 1811–1889

11 My opinion is that the Northern States will manage somehow to muddle through. [Said during the American Civil War]

12 The angel of death has been abroad throughout the land; you may almost hear the beating of his wings. [Speech in House of Commons, 23 Feb. 1855]

13 I am for 'Peace, retrenchment and reform', the watchword of the great Liberal party thirty years ago. [Speech at Birmingham, 28 Apr. 1859]

14 England is the mother of Parliaments. [18 Jan. 1865]

15 The right honourable gentleman ... has retired into what may be called his political Cave of Adullam – and he has called about him everyone that was in distress and everyone that was discontented. [Speech in House of Commons, 13 Mar. 1866]

16 A free breakfast table. [Address to Edinburgh Chamber of Commerce in favour of repeal of food duties, 1868]

17 Force is not a remedy. [Speech at Birmingham, 16 Nov. 1880]

18 The knowledge of the ancient languages is mainly a luxury. [Letter in *Pall Mall Gazette*, 30 Nov. 1886]

19 And he adores his maker. [Attr., when told that he should give Disraeli credit for being a self-made man]

ANTHELME BRILLAT-SAVARIN 1755–1826

20 *Dis-moi ce que tu manges, je te dirai ce que tu es.* – Tell me what you eat, and I will tell you what you are. [*Physiologie du goût*, 'Méditation', IV]

RICHARD BROME ?–1652?

21 I am a gentleman, though spoiled i' the breeding. The Buzzards are all gentlemen. We came in with the Conqueror. [*The English Moor*, III, ii]

J. BRONOWSKI 1908–1974

22 And he was a genius, in the sense that a genius is a man who has *two* great ideas. [(Of John von Neumann) *The Ascent of Man*, Ch. 3]

CHARLOTTE BRONTË 1816–1855

23 Reader, I married him. [*Jane Eyre*, Ch. 38]

EMILY BRONTË 1818–1848

24 No coward soul is mine, / No trembler in the world's storm-troubled sphere: / I see Heaven's glories shine, / And faith shines equal, arming me from fear. [*Last Lines*]

25 Vain are the thousand creeds / That move men's hearts: unutterably vain.

26 Though earth and man were gone, / And suns and universes ceased to be, / And Thou were left alone, / Every existence would exist in Thee.

1 There is not room for Death, / Nor atom that his might could render void: / Thou – Thou art Being and Breath, / And what Thou art may never be destroyed.

2 Oh! dreadful is the check – intense the agony – / When the ear begins to hear, and the eye begins to see; / When the pulse begins to throb, the brain to think again; / The soul to feel the flesh, and the flesh to feel the chain. [*The Prisoner*]

3 Cold in the earth – and the deep snow piled above thee, / Far, far, removed, cold in the dreary grave! [*Remembrance*]

4 Once drinking deep of that divinest anguish, / How could I seek the empty world again?

5 I lingered round them, under that benign sky: watched the moths fluttering among the heath and harebells; listened to the soft wind breathing through the grass; and wondered how anyone could ever imagine unquiet slumbers for the sleepers in that quiet earth. [*Wuthering Heights*, conclusion]

RUPERT BROOKE 1887–1915

6 Blow out, you bugles, over the rich Dead! / There's none of these so lonely and poor of old, / But, dying, has made us rarer gifts than gold. / These laid the world away; poured out the red / Sweet wine of youth; gave up the years to be / Of work and joy, and that unhoped serene, / That men call age; and those who would have been, / Their sons, they gave, their immortality. [*The Dead*]

7 Honour has come back, as a king, to earth, / And paid his subjects with a royal wage; / And Nobleness walks in our ways again; / And we have come into our heritage.

8 Unfading moths, immortal flies, / And the worm that never dies. / And in that Heaven of all their wish, / There shall be no more land, say fish. [*Heaven*]

9 Breathless, we flung us on the windy hill, / Laughed in the sun, and kissed the lovely grass. [*The Hill*]

10 And then you suddenly cried and turned away.

11 Here tulips bloom as they are told; / Unkempt about those hedges blows / An English unofficial rose; / And there the unregulated sun / Slopes down to rest when day is done, / And

wakes a vague unpunctual star, / A slippered Hesper. [*The Old Vicarage, Grantchester*]

12 And spectral dance, before the dawn, / A hundred Vicars down the lawn; / Curates, long dust, will come and go / On lissom, clerical, printless toe; / And oft between the boughs is seen / The sly shade of a Rural Dean.

13 For England's the one land, I know, / Where men with Splendid Hearts may go; / And Cambridgeshire, of all England, / The shire for Men who Understand.

14 For Cambridge people rarely smile, / Being urban, squat, and packed with guile.

15 They love the Good; they worship Truth; / They laugh uproariously in youth; / (And when they get to feeling old, / They up and shoot themselves, I'm told).

16 Stands the Church clock at ten to three? / And is there honey still for tea?

17 Now, God be thanked who has matched us with His hour, / And caught our youth, and wakened us from sleeping. [*Peace*]

18 And the worst friend and enemy is but Death.

19 War knows no power. Safe shall be my going, / Secretly armed against all death's endeavour; / Safe though all safety's lost; safe where men fall; / And if these poor limbs die, safest of all. [*Safety*]

20 If I should die, think only this of me: / That there's some corner of a foreign field / That is for ever England. There shall be / In that rich earth a richer dust concealed. [*The Soldier*]

21 And think, this heart, all evil shed away, / A pulse in the eternal mind, no less / Gives somewhere back the thoughts by England given.

22 In hearts at peace, under an English heaven.

23 Spend in pure converse our eternal day; / Think each in each, immediately wise; / Learn all we lacked before; hear, know, and say / What this tumultuous body now denies; / And feel, who have laid our groping hands away; / And see, no longer blinded by our eyes. [Sonnet: *Not with vain Tears*]

24 Oh! Death will find me long before I tire / Of watching you; and swing me suddenly / Into the shade and loneliness and mire / Of the last land! [Sonnet: *Oh! Death will find me*]

LOUISE BROOKS 1908–1985

1 I never gave away anything without wishing I had kept it; nor kept it without wishing I had given it away. [Her own epitaph, quoted in Kenneth Tynan, *Show People*]

PHILLIPS BROOKS 1835–1893

2 O little town of Bethlehem, / How still we see thee lie; / Above thy deep and dreamless sleep / The silent stars go by. [Hymn]

SHIRLEY BROOKS 1816–1874

3 I takes and paints, / Hears no complaints, / And sells before I'm dry; / Till savage Ruskin / He sticks his tusk in, / Then nobody will buy. [*Poem by a Perfectly Furious Academician*]

4 Says Hyam to Moses, / 'Let's cut off our noses.' / Says Moses to Hyam, / 'Ma tear, who vould buy 'em?' [*A Practical Answer*]

R. B. BROUGH 1828–1860

5 My Lord Tomnoddy is thirty-four; / The Earl can last but a few years more. / My Lord in the Peers will take his place: / Her Majesty's councils his words will grace. / Office he'll hold and patronage sway; / Fortunes and lives he will vote away; / And what are his qualifications? ONE / He's the Earl of Fitzdotterel's eldest son. [*My Lord Tomnoddy*]

LORD BROUGHAM 1778–1868

6 The schoolmaster is abroad, and I trust more to him, armed with his primer, than I do to the soldier in full military array, for upholding and extending the liberties of his country. [Speech in House of Commons, 29 Jan. 1828]

7 Education makes a people easy to lead, but difficult to drive; easy to govern but impossible to enslave. [Attr.]

8 The great Unwashed. [Attr.]

LEW BROWN 1899–1958

9 Climb upon my knee, Sonny Boy; / Though you're only three, Sonny Boy. [Song: *Sonny Boy*, sung by Al Jolson]

10 Life is Just a Bowl of Cherries. [Title of song in musical *Scandals*, music by Ray Henderson, sung by Ethel Merman]

T. E. BROWN 1830–1897

11 O blackbird, what a boy you are! / How you do go it! [*The Blackbird*]

12 A rich man's joke is always funny. [*The Doctor*]

13 A garden is a lovesome thing, God wot! [*My Garden*]

THOMAS BROWN 1663–1704

14 I do not love thee, Doctor Fell, / The reason why I cannot tell; / But this alone I know full well, / I do not love thee, Doctor Fell. [Trans. of Martial, i. 32]

SIR THOMAS BROWNE 1605–1682

15 They do most by Books, who could do much without them, and he that chiefly owes himself unto himself, is the substantial Man. [*Christian Morals*, II. 11]

16 Life is itself but the shadow of death, and souls departed but the shadows of the living. All things fall under this name. The sun itself is but the dark *simulacrum*, and light but the shadow of God. [*The Garden of Cyrus*, Ch. 4]

17 But the quincunx of heaven runs low, and 'tis time to close the five ports of knowledge. [5]

18 And though in the bed of Cleopatra, can hardly with any delight raise up the ghost of a rose.

19 The huntsmen are up in America, and they are already past their first sleep in Persia.

20 Dreams out of the ivory gate, and visions before midnight. [*On Dreams*]

21 I dare, without usurpation, assume the honourable style of a Christian. [*Religio Medici*, Pt I. 1]

22 Yet at my devotion I love to use the civility of my knee, my hat, and hand. [3]

23 Methinks there be not impossibilities enough in Religion for an active faith. [9]

24 I love to lose myself in a mystery; to pursue my reason to an O altitudo!

25 We carry with us the wonders we seek without us: there is all Africa and her prodigies in us. [15]

26 All things are artificial; for nature is the art of God. [16]

27 Thus the devil played at chess with me, and yielding a pawn, thought to gain a queen of

me, taking advantage of my honest endeavours. [18]

1 For my part, I have ever believed, and do now know, that there are witches. [30]

2 Thus we are men and we know not how: there is something in us that can be without us, and will be after us. [35]

3 Certainly there is no happiness within this circle of flesh, nor is it in the optics of these eyes to behold felicity. The first day of our jubilee is death. [43]

4 To believe only possibilities is not faith, but mere philosophy. [48]

5 There is no road or ready way to virtue. [55]

6 The multitude: that numerous piece of monstrosity, which, taken asunder, seem men, and the reasonable creatures of God; but, confused together, make but one great beast, and a monstrosity more hideous than Hydra. [II. 1]

7 It is the common wonder of all men, how among so many millions of faces, there should be none alike. [2]

8 No man can justly censure or condemn another, because indeed no man truly knows another. [4]

9 *Charity begins at home*, is the voice of the world.

10 The whole world was made for man; but the twelfth part of man for woman: man is the whole world, and the breath of God; woman the rib and crooked piece of man. I could be content that we might procreate like trees, without conjunction, or that there were any way to perpetuate the world without this trivial and vulgar way of union. [9]

11 Sure there is music even in the beauty, and the silent note which Cupid strikes, far sweeter than the sound of an instrument. For there is music where ever there is a harmony, order, or proportion: and thus far we may maintain the music of the spheres.

12 We all labour against our own cure; for death is the cure of all diseases.

13 For the world, I count it not an inn, but an hospital; and a place not to live but to die in. [11]

14 There is surely a piece of divinity in us, something that was before the elements, and owes no homage unto the sun.

15 Sleep is a death; O make me try, / By sleeping, what it is to die; / And as gently lay my head / On my grave, as now my bed. [12]

16 Old mortality, the ruins of forgotten times. [*Urn Burial*, Preface]

17 What song the Syrens sang, or what name Achilles assumed when he hid himself among women, though puzzling questions, are not beyond all conjecture. [Ch. 5]

18 But the iniquity of oblivion blindly scattereth her poppy, and deals with the memory of men without distinction to merit of perpetuity.

19 The night of time far surpasseth the day, and who knows when was the equinox?

20 Man is a noble animal, splendid in ashes, and pompous in the grave.

WILLIAM BROWNE 1590?–1645?

21 Underneath this sable hearse / Lies the subject of all verse: / Sidney's sister, Pembroke's mother: / Death, ere thou hast slain another, / Fair, and learned, and good as she, / Time shall throw a dart at thee. [*Epitaph on the Dowager Countess of Pembroke*]

22 Steer hither, steer, your winged pines, / All beaten mariners, / Here lie love's undiscovered mines, / A prey to passengers. ['Song of the Sirens', from the *Inner Temple Masque*]

SIR WILLIAM BROWNE 1692–1774

23 The King to Oxford sent a troop of horse, / For Tories own no argument but force: / With equal skill to Cambridge books he sent, / For Whigs admit no force but argument. [Reply to epigram by Joseph Trapp (see 431:19)]

ELIZABETH BARRETT BROWNING 1806–1861

24 Since when was genius found respectable? [*Aurora Leigh*, Bk vi]

25 And kings crept out again to feel the sun. [*Crowned and Buried*]

26 Do you hear the children weeping, O my brothers, / Ere the sorrow comes with years? [*The Cry of the Children*]

27 In the pleasant orchard closes, / 'God bless all our gains', say we; / But 'May God bless all our losses' / Better suits with our degree. [*The Lost Bower*]

Robert Browning

1 What was he doing, the great god Pan, / Down in the reeds by the river? / Spreading ruin and scattering ban, / Splashing and paddling with hoofs of a goat, / And breaking the golden lilies afloat / With the dragon-fly on the river. [*A Musical Instrument*]

2 O earth, so full of dreary noises! / O men, with wailing in your voices! / O delvèd gold, the wailers heap! / O strife, O curse, that o'er it fall! / God strikes a silence through you all, / And giveth his beloved, sleep. [*The Sleep*]

3 I tell you, hopeless grief is passionless. [Sonnet: *Grief*]

4 'Guess now who holds thee?' – 'Death', I said, but there / The silver answer rang, . . . 'Not Death, but Love.' [*Sonnets from the Portuguese*, 7]

5 If thou must love me, let it be for naught / Except for love's sake only. [14]

6 God's gifts put man's best gifts to shame. [26]

7 How do I love thee? Let me count the ways. / I love thee to the depth and breadth and height / My soul can reach, when feeling out of sight / For the ends of Being and ideal Grace. [43]

8 I love thee with a love I seemed to lose / With my lost saints – I love thee with the breath, / Smiles, tears, of all my life! – and, if God choose, / I shall but love thee better after death.

9 Thou large-brained woman and large-hearted man. [*To George Sand, A Desire*]

10 Life treads on life, and heart on heart: / We press too close in church and mart / To keep a dream or grave apart. [*A Vision of Poets*, conclusion]

11 Our Euripides, the human, / With his droppings of warm tears, / And his touches of things common / Till they rose to touch the spheres. [*Wine of Cyprus*, xii]

ROBERT BROWNING 1812–1889

12 The high that proved too high, the heroic for earth too hard, / The passion that left the ground to lose itself in the sky, / Are music sent up to God by the lover and the bard; / Enough that he heard it once; we shall hear it by-and-by. [*Abt Vogler*, 10]

13 The rest may reason and welcome; 'tis we musicians know. [11]

14 Well, it is earth with me; silence resumes her reign: / I will be patient and proud, and soberly acquiesce. [12]

15 I have dared and done, for my resting-place is found, / The C major of this life: so, now I will try to sleep.

16 How he lies in his rights of a man! / Death has done all death can. [*After*]

17 Love, we are in God's hand. / How strange now, looks the life he makes us lead. / So free we seem, so fettered fast we are! [*Andrea del Sarto*, 49]

18 Ah, but a man's reach should exceed his grasp, / Or what's a heaven for? [96]

19 Four great walls in the New Jerusalem, / Meted on each side by the angel's reed, / For Leonard, Rafael, Agnolo and me / To cover. [261]

20 Again the Cousin's whistle! Go, my Love. [267]

21 Why need the other women know so much? [*Any Wife to Any Husband*]

22 It's wiser being good than bad; / It's safer being meek than fierce; / It's fitter being sane than mad. / My own hope is, a sun will pierce / The thickest cloud earth ever stretched; / That, after Last returns the First, / Though a wide compass round be fetched; / That what began best can't end worst, / Nor what God blessed once, prove accurst. [*Apparent Failure*]

23 Hatred and cark and care, what place have they / In yon blue liberality of heaven? [*Aristophanes' Apology*, 52]

24 My sun sets to rise again. [*At the 'Mermaid'*]

25 Lo, life again knocked laughing at the door! / The world goes on, goes ever, in and through, / And out again o' the cloud. [*Balaustion's Adventure*, John Murray's edn., Vol. i. p. 650. 1. 2]

26 So, you despise me, Mr Gigadibs. [*Bishop Blougram's Apology*, John Murray's edn., Vol. i. p. 528. 1. 13]

27 Truth that peeps / Over the glasses' edge when dinner's done, / And body gets its sop and holds its noise / And leaves soul free a little. [16]

28 Best be yourself, imperial, plain and true! [529. 55]

29 We mortals cross the ocean of this world / Each in his average cabin of a life. [530. 8]

1 Just when we are safest, there's a sunset-touch, / A fancy from a flower-bell, someone's death, / A chorus-ending from Euripides, – / And that's enough for fifty hopes and fears / As old and new at once as nature's self, / To rap and knock and enter in our soul. [531. 17]

2 The grand Perhaps! [25]

3 All we have gained then by our unbelief / Is a life of doubt diversified by faith, / For one of faith diversified by doubt: / We called the chess-board white, – we call it black. [45]

4 You, for example, clever to a fault, / The rough and ready man that write apace, / Read somewhat seldomer, think perhaps even less. [534. 25]

5 And that's what all the blessed evil's for. [537. 26]

6 No, when the fight begins within himself, / A man's worth something. [65]

7 Gigadibs the literary man, / Who played with spoons, explored his plate's design, / And ranged the olive stones about its edge. [541. 40]

8 He said true things, but called them by wrong names. [61]

9 By this time he has tested his first plough, / And studied his last chapter of St John. [542. 5]

10 Saint Praxed's ever was the church for peace. [*The Bishop orders his Tomb*]

11 Horses for ye, and brown Greek manuscripts, / And mistresses with great smooth marbly limbs.

12 I shall lie through centuries, / And hear the blessed mutter of the mass, / And see God made and eaten all day long.

13 There's a woman like a dew-drop, she's so purer than the purest. [*A Blot in the 'Scutcheon*, I. iii]

14 How well I know what I mean to do / When the long, dark autumn-evenings come. [*By the Fire Side*, 1]

15 Not verse now, only prose! [2]

16 That great brow / And the spirit-small hand propping it. [23]

17 When earth breaks up and heaven expands, / How will the change strike me and you / In the house not made with hands? [27]

18 We two stood there with never a third. [38]

19 Oh, the little more, and how much it is! / And the little less, and what worlds away! [39]

20 If two lives join, there is oft a scar, / They are one and one, with a shadowy third; / One near one is too far. [46]

21 Setebos, Setebos, and Setebos! / 'Thinketh, He dwelleth i' the cold o' the moon. / 'Thinketh He made it, with the sun to match, / But not the stars; the stars came otherwise. [*Caliban upon Setebos*, 24]

22 'Let twenty pass, and stone the twenty-first, / Loving not, hating not, just choosing so. [103]

23 This Quiet, all it hath a mind to do, doth. [138]

24 'Tis the Last Judgement's fire must cure this place, / Calcine its clods and set my prisoners free. [*'Childe Roland to the Dark Tower Came'*, 11]

25 As for the grass, it grew as scant as hair / In leprosy. [13]

26 One stiff blind horse, his every bone a-stare, / Stood stupefied, however he came there: / Thrust out past service from the devil's stud!

27 I never saw a brute I hated so; / He must be wicked to deserve such pain. [14]

28 The hills, like giants at a hunting, lay, / Chin upon hand, to see the game at bay. [32]

29 Dauntless the slug-horn to my lips I set, / And blew. [34]

30 Though Rome's gross yoke / Drops off, no more to be endured, / Her teaching is not so obscured / By errors and perversities, / That no truth shines athwart the lies. [*Christmas Eve*, 11]

31 I watched my foolish heart expand / In the lazy glow of benevolence, / O'er the various modes of man's belief. [20]

32 I have written three books on the soul, / Proving absurd all written hitherto, / And putting us to ignorance again. [*Cleon*, 57]

33 Certain slaves / Who touched on this same isle, preached him and Christ; / And (as I gather from a bystander) / Their doctrine could be held by no sane man. [250]

34 What is he buzzing in my ears? / 'Now that I come to die, / Do I view the world as a vale of tears?' / Ah, reverend sir, not I! [*Confessions*]

35 How sad and bad and mad it was – / But then, how it was sweet!

1 Ages past the soul existed, / Here an age 'tis resting merely. [*Cristina*]

2 Your ghost will walk, you lover of trees / (If our loves remain) / In an English lane, / By a cornfield-side a-flutter with poppies. [*'De Gustibus –'*]

3 And let them pass, as they will too soon, / With the bean-flowers' boon, / And the black-bird's tune, / And May, and June!

4 Open my heart and you will see / Graved inside of it, 'Italy'.

5 Such ever was love's way; to rise, it stoops. [*A Death in the Desert*, 134]

6 For life, with all its yields of joy and woe, / And hope and fear, – believe the aged friend – / Is just a chance o' the prize of learning love. [245]

7 For I say, this is death, and the sole death, / When a man's loss comes to him from his gain, / Darkness from light, from knowledge ignorance, / And lack of love from love made manifest. [482]

8 Man partly is and wholly hopes to be. [588]

9 Reads verse and thinks she understands. [*Dis aliter visum*, 4]

10 Schumann's our music-maker now; / Has his march-movement youth and mouth? / Ingres's the modern man that paints; / Which will lean on me, of his saints? / Heine for songs; for kisses, how? [8]

11 How very hard it is / To be a Christian! [*Easter-Day*, 1]

12 At last awake / From life, that insane dream we take / For waking now. [14]

13 A fierce vindictive scribble of red. [15]

14 At the midnight in the silence of the sleep-time, / When you set your fancies free. [*Epilogue to Asolando*]

15 Oh to love so, be so loved, yet so mistaken!

16 One who never turned his back but marched breast forward, / Never doubted clouds would break, / Never dreamed, though right were worsted, wrong would triumph, / Held we fall to rise, are baffled to fight better, / Sleep to wake.

17 Karshish, the picker-up of learning's crumbs, / The not-incurious in God's handiwork. [*An Epistle . . . of Karshish, the Arab Physician*, 1]

18 – That he was dead and then restored to life / By a Nazarene physician of his tribe. [98]

19 'But love I gave thee, with myself to love. / And thou must love me who have died for thee!' / The madman saith He said so: it is strange. [Final lines]

20 There, that is our secret: go to sleep! / You will wake, and remember, and understand. [*Evelyn Hope*]

21 I am poor brother Lippo, by your leave! [*Fra Lippo Lippi*, 1]

22 Where sportive ladies leave their doors ajar. [6]

23 He's Judas to a tittle, that man is! / Just such a face! [25]

24 Flower o' the broom, / Take away love, and our earth is a tomb! [53]

25 If you get simple beauty and nought else, / You get about the best thing God invents. [217]

26 You should not take a fellow eight years old / And make him swear to never kiss the girls. [224]

27 This is our master, famous, calm, and dead, / Borne on our shoulders. [*A Grammarian's Funeral*, 27]

28 He said, 'What's time? Leave Now for dogs and apes! / Man has Forever.' [83]

29 *Calculus* racked him: / Leaden before, his eyes grew dross of lead: / *Tussis* attacked him. [86]

30 He settled *Hoti's* business – let it be! – / Properly based *Oun* – / Gave us the doctrine of the enclitic *De*, / Dead from the waist down. [129]

31 Give both the infinitudes their due – / Infinite mercy, but, I wis, / As infinite a justice too. [*The Heretic's Tragedy*]

32 I liken his Grace to an acorned hog. [*Holy-Cross Day*]

33 The Lord will have mercy on Jacob yet, / And again in his border see Israel set.

34 Oh, to be in England, / Now that April's there. [*Home-Thoughts from Abroad*]

35 While the chaffinch sings on the orchard bough / In England – now!

36 And after April, when May follows, / And the whitethroat builds, and all the swallows!

37 That's the wise thrush; he sings each song

twice over, / Lest you should think he never could recapture / The first fine careless rapture!

1 Nobly, nobly Cape Saint Vincent to the North-west died away; / Sunset ran, one glorious blood-red, reeking into Cadiz bay. [*Home-Thoughts from the Sea*]

2 'Here and here did England help me: how can I help England?' – say, / Whoso turns as I, this evening, turn to God to praise and pray, / While Jove's planet rises yonder, silent over Africa.

3 'With this same key / Shakespeare unlocked his heart', once more! / Did Shakespeare? If so, the less Shakespeare he! [*House*]

4 I sprang to the stirrup, and Joris, and he; / I galloped, Dirck galloped, we galloped all three. ['*How they brought the Good News from Ghent to Aix*']

5 I count life just a stuff / To try the soul's strength on. [*In a Balcony*, 651]

6 The moth's kiss, first! / Kiss me as if you made believe / You were not sure, this eve, / How my face, your flower, had pursed / Its petals up. [*In a Gondola*]

7 The bee's kiss, now! / Kiss me as if you entered gay / My heart at some noonday.

8 Still ailing, Wind? Wilt be appeased or no? [*James Lee's Wife*, VI]

9 Oh, good gigantic smile o' the brown old earth. [VII]

10 There's heaven above, and night by night / I look right through its gorgeous roof. [*Johannes Agricola in Meditation*]

11 So, one day more I am deified. / Who knows but the world may end tonight? [*The Last Ride Together*, 2]

12 Where had I been now if the worst befell? / And here we are riding, she and I. [4]

13 What if we still ride on, we two / With life forever old yet new, / Changed not in kind but in degree, / The instant made eternity – / And heaven just prove that I and she / Ride, ride together, for ever ride? [10]

14 Escape me? / Never – / Beloved! / While I am I, and you are you, / So long as the world contains us both, / Me the loving and you the loth, / While the one eludes, must the other pursue. [*Life in a Love*]

15 To dry one's eyes and laugh at a fall, / And, baffled, get up and begin again.

16 And, Robert Browning, you writer of plays, / Here's a subject made to your hand! [*A Light Woman*, 14]

17 Just for a handful of silver he left us, / Just for a riband to stick in his coat. [*The Lost Leader* (Wordsworth)]

18 Shakespeare was with us, Milton was for us / Burns, Shelley, were with us, – they watch from their graves.

19 Blot out his name, then, record one lost soul more, / One task more declined, one more footpath untrod, / One more devil's-triumph and sorrow for angels, / One wrong more to man, one more insult to God!

20 All's over, then; does truth sound bitter / As one at first believes? / Hark, 'tis the sparrows' good-night twitter / About your cottage eaves! [*The Lost Mistress*]

21 I will hold your hand but as long as all may, / Or so very little longer!

22 Where the quiet-coloured end of evening smiles, / Miles and miles. [*Love among the Ruins*, 1]

23 Love is best. [7]

24 The only fault's with time; / All men become good creatures: but so slow! [*Luria*, V]

25 Backward and forward each throwing his shuttle, / Death ending all with a knife. [*Master Hugues of Saxe-Gotha*, 22]

26 What, you want, do you, to come unawares, / Sweeping the church up for first morning-prayers, / And find a poor devil has ended his cares / At the foot of your rotten-runged rat-riddled stairs? / Do I carry the moon in my pocket? [29]

27 A tap at the pane, the quick sharp scratch / And blue spurt of a lighted match, / And a voice less loud, thro' its joys and fears, / Than the two hearts beating each to each. [*Meeting at Night*]

28 Ah, did you once see Shelley plain, / And did he stop and speak to you / And did he speak to you again? / How strange it seems and new! [*Memorabilia*]

29 A moulted feather, an eagle-feather! / Well, I forget the rest.

30 This is a spray the Bird clung to. [*Misconceptions*]

31 This is a heart the Queen leant on.

Robert Browning

1 If such as came for wool, sir, went home shorn, / Where is the wrong I did them? [*Mr Sludge, 'The Medium'*, 630]

2 There's a real love of a lie, / Liars find ready-made for lies they make, / As hand for glove, or tongue for sugar-plum. [689]

3 There's a more hateful form of foolery – / The social sage's, Solomon of saloons / And philosophic diner-out, the fribble / Who wants a doctrine for a chopping-block / To try the edge of his faculty upon. [772]

4 Why should I set so fine a gloss on things? [1354]

5 Boston's a hole, the herring-pond is wide. [Two lines from end]

6 She had / A heart – how shall I say? – too soon made glad, / Too easily impressed. [*My Last Duchess*]

7 Give me of Nelson only a touch. [*Nationality in Drinks*]

8 Never the time and the place / And the loved one all together! [*Never the Time and the Place*]

9 What's come to perfection perishes. / Things learned on earth, we shall practise in heaven. / Works done least rapidly, Art most cherishes. [*Old Pictures in Florence*, 17]

10 Suddenly, as rare things will, it vanished. [*One Word More*, 4]

11 Dante, who loved well because he hated, / Hated wickedness that hinders loving. [5]

12 God be thanked, the meanest of his creatures / Boasts two soul-sides, one to face the world with, / One to show a woman when he loves her. [17]

13 Oh, their Rafael of the dead Madonnas, / Oh, their Dante of the dread Inferno, / Wrote one song – and in my brain I sing it, / Drew one angel – borne, see, on my bosom! [19]

14 Unless God send his hail / Or blinding fire balls, sleet or stifling snow, / In some time, his good time, I shall arrive. [*Paracelsus*, Pt I]

15 PARACELSUS: I am he that aspired to *know*: and thou?
APRILE: I would *love* infinitely, and be loved! [II]

16 God is the perfect poet, / Who in his person acts his own creations.

17 Heap cassia, sandal-buds and stripes / Of labdanum, and aloe-balls, / Smeared with dull nard an Indian wipes / From out her hair. [IV]

18 Progress is / The law of life, man is not man as yet. [V]

19 Round the cape of a sudden came the sea, / And the sun looked over the mountain's rim: / And straight was a path of gold for him, / And the need of a world of men for me. [*Parting at Morning*]

20 It was roses, roses, all the way, / With myrtle mixed in my path like mad. [*The Patriot*]

21 Sun-treader, I believe in God and truth / And love. [(Shelley) *Pauline*]

22 Hamelin Town's in Brunswick, / By famous Hanover city; / The river Weser, deep and wide, / Washes its wall on the southern side; / A pleasanter spot you never spied. [*The Pied Piper of Hamelin*, 1]

23 Rats! / They fought the dogs and killed the cats, / And bit the babies in the cradles, / And ate the cheeses out of the vats. [2]

24 With shrieking and squeaking / In fifty different sharps and flats.

25 Save when at noon his paunch grew mutinous / For a plate of turtle green and glutinous. [4]

26 And the muttering grew to a grumbling; / And the grumbling grew to a mighty rumbling; / And out of the houses the rats came tumbling. [7]

27 I heard a sound as of scraping tripe, / And putting apples wondrous ripe, / Into a cider-press's gripe.

28 So munch on, crunch on, take your nuncheon, / Breakfast, supper, dinner, luncheon!

29 The year's at the spring / And day's at the morn; / Morning's at seven; / The hillside's dew-pearled; / The lark's on the wing; / The snail's on the thorn; / God's in his heaven – / All's right with the world! [*Pippa Passes*, Pt 1. 222]

30 God must be glad one loves His world so much. [III. 73]

31 A king lived long ago, / In the morning of the world, / When earth was nigher heaven than now. [164]

32 Such grace had kings when the world begun! [1222]

1 All service ranks the same with God – / With God, whose puppets, best and worst, / Are we: there is no last or first. [IV. 113]

2 Stand still, true poet that you are! / I know you; let me try and draw you. / Some night you'll fail us: when afar / You rise, remember one man saw you, / Knew you and named a star! [*Popularity*]

3 Who fished the murex up? / What porridge had John Keats?

4 The rain set early in to-night, / The sullen wind was soon awake. / It tore the elm-tops down for spite. / And did its worst to vex the lake. [*Porphyria's Lover*]

5 No pain felt she; / I am quite sure she felt no pain.

6 Fear death? – to feel the fog in my throat, / The mist in my face. [*Prospice*]

7 Where he stands, the Arch Fear in a visible form, / Yet the strong man must go.

8 I was ever a fighter, so – one fight more, / The best and the last!

9 No! let me taste the whole of it, fare like my peers / The heroes of old, / Bear the brunt, in a minute pay glad life's arrears / Of pain, darkness and cold.

10 O thou soul of my soul! I shall clasp thee again, / And with God be the rest!

11 Grow old along with me! / The best is yet to be, / The last of life, for which the first was made: / Our times are in His hand / Who saith, 'A whole I planned, / Youth shows but half; trust God: see all nor be afraid!' [*Rabbi ben Ezra*, 1]

12 Irks care the crop-full bird? Frets doubt the maw-crammed beast? [4]

13 Then, welcome each rebuff / That turns earth's smoothness rough, / Each sting that bids nor sit nor stand but go! [6]

14 For thence – a paradox / Which comforts while it mocks, – / Shall life succeed in that it seems to fail: / What I aspired to be, / And was not, comforts me: / A brute I might have been, but would not sink i' the scale. [7]

15 I see the whole design, / I, who saw power, see now love perfect too. [10]

16 Let us not always say / 'Spite of this flesh today / I strove, made head, gained ground upon the whole!' / As the bird wings and sings, / Let us cry 'All good things / Are ours, nor soul helps flesh more, now, than flesh helps soul.' [12]

17 Therefore I summon age / To grant youth's heritage. [13]

18 For note, when evening shuts, / A certain moment cuts / The deed off, calls the glory from the grey. [16]

19 Now, who shall arbitrate? / Ten men love what I hate, / Shun what I follow, slight what I receive; / Ten who in ears and eyes / Match me: we all surmise, / They this thing, and I that: whom shall my soul believe? [22]

20 But all, the world's coarse thumb / And finger failed to plumb, / So passed in making up the main account. [24]

21 Thoughts hardly to be packed / Into a narrow act, / Fancies that broke through language and escaped. [25]

22 Let age approve of youth, and death complete the same. [32]

23 Do you see this square old yellow Book, I toss / I' the air, and catch again? [*The Ring and the Book*, I. 33]

24 The Life, Death, Miracles of Saint Somebody, / Saint Somebody Else, his Miracles, Death and Life, – / With this, one glance at the lettered back of which, / And 'Stall!' cried I: a *lira* made it mine. [80]

25 Well, British Public, ye who like me not, / (God love you!) and will have your proper laugh / At the dark question, laugh it! I laugh first. [410]

26 Whom but a dusk misfeatured messenger, / No other than the angel of this life, / Whose care is lest men see too much at once. [593]

27 Our murder has been done three days ago, / The frost is over and done, the south wind laughs, / And, to the very tiles of each red roof / A-smoke i' the sunshine, Rome lies gold and glad. [904]

28 Vows can't change nature, priests are only men, / And love likes stratagem and subterfuge. [1057]

29 O lyric Love, half angel and half bird / And all a wonder and a wild desire. [1391]

30 Never may I commence my song, my due / To God who best taught song by gift of thee, / Except with bent head and beseeching hand – / That still, despite the distance and the dark, / What was, again may be. [1403]

Robert Browning

1 Everyone soon or late comes round by Rome. [V. 296]

2 Creation purged o' the miscreate, man redeemed, / A spittle wiped off from the face of God! [VI. 1478]

3 But I, not privileged to see a saint / Of old when such walked earth with crown and palm, / If I call 'saint' what saints call something else – / The saints must bear with me. [VII. 1512]

4 O lover of my life, O soldier-saint. [1786]

5 Through such souls alone / God stooping shows sufficient of His light / For us i' the dark to rise by. And I rise. [1843]

6 On our Pompilia, faultless to a fault. [IX. 1175]

7 Just the one prize vouchsafed unworthy me, / Seven years a gardener of the untoward ground. [X. 1030]

8 Thou at first prompting of what I call God, / And fools call Nature, didst hear, comprehend, / Accept the obligation laid on thee. [1073]

9 Why comes temptation but for man to meet / And master and make crouch beneath his foot, / And so be pedestaled in triumph? [1184]

10 White shall not neutralize the black, nor good / Compensate bad in man, absolve him so: / Life's business being just the terrible choice. [1235]

11 There's a new tribunal now, / Higher than God's – the educated man's! [1975]

12 Abate, – Cardinal, – Christ, – Maria, – God ... /Pompilia, will you let them murder me? [XI. 2424]

13 It is the glory and the good of Art, / That Art remains the one way possible / Of speaking truth, to minds like mine at least. [XII. 842]

14 Oh, the wild joys of living! the leaping from rock up to rock, / The strong rending of boughs from the fir-tree, the cool silver shock / Of the plunge in a pool's living water. [Saul, 9]

15 Leave the flesh to the fate it was fit for! the spirit be thine! [13]

16 I have gone the whole round of creation: I saw and I spoke: / I, a work of God's hand for that purpose, received in my brain / And pronounced on the rest of his handwork – returned him again / His creation's approval or censure: I spoke as I saw: / I report, as a man may of God's work – all's love, yet all's law. [17]

17 In the first is the last, in thy will is my power to believe. [18]

18 He who did most, shall bear most; the strongest shall stand the most weak.

19 The iron gate / Ground its teeth to let me pass! [A Serenade at the Villa]

20 Because a man has shop to mind / In time and place, since flesh must live, / Needs spirit lack all life behind, / All stray thoughts, fancies fugitive, / All loves except what trade can give?

I want to know a butcher paints, / A baker rhymes for his pursuit, / Candlestick-maker much acquaints / His soul with song, or, haply mute, / Blows out his brains upon the flute! [Shop, 20]

21 Gr-r-r – there go, my heart's abhorrence! / Water your damned flower-pots, do! / If hate killed men, Brother Lawrence, / God's blood, would not mine kill you! [Soliloquy of the Spanish Cloister]

22 What's the Greek name for Swine's Snout?

23 There's a great text in Galatians, / Once you trip on it, entails / Twenty-nine distinct damnations, / One sure if another fails.

24 Or, my scrofulous French novel / On grey paper with blunt type! / Simply glance at it, you grovel / Hand and foot in Belial's gripe.

25 'St, there's Vespers! *Plena gratiâ / Ave, Virgo!* Gr-r-r – you swine!

26 Nay but you, who do not love her, / Is she not pure gold, my mistress? [Song]

27 Who will, may hear Sordello's story told. [Sordello, 1]

28 Sidney's self, the starry paladin.

29 Still more labyrinthine buds the rose.

30 A touch divine – / And the scaled eyeball owns the mystic rod; / Visibly through his garden walketh God.

31 Who would has heard Sordello's story told. [6]

32 I have known *Four-and-twenty* leaders of revolts. [A Soul's Tragedy, last words]

33 She looked at him, as one who awakes: / The past was a sleep, and her life began. [The Statue and the Bust, 10]

34 The world and its way have a certain worth. [46]

35 The glory dropped from their youth and love, / And both perceived they had dreamed a dream. [51]

1 And the sin I impute to each frustrate ghost / Is – the unlit lamp and the ungirt loin. [82]

2 There may be heaven; there must be hell; / Meantime, there is our earth here – well! [*Time's Revenges*]

3 What of soul was left, I wonder, when the kissing had to stop? [*A Toccata of Galuppi's*, 14]

4 Dear dead women, with such hair, too – what's become of all the gold / Used to hang and brush their bosoms? I feel chilly and grow old. [15]

5 Another Boehme with a tougher book / And subtler meanings of what roses say. ['*Transcendentalism*']

6 Where is the thread now? Off again! / The old trick! only I discern – / Infinite passion, and the pain / Of finite hearts that yearn. [*Two in the Campagna*, 12]

7 Had I but plenty of money, money enough and to spare, / The house for me, no doubt, were a house in the city-square. [*Up at a Villa – Down in the City*, 1]

8 *Bang-whang-whang* goes the drum, *tootle-te-tootle* the fife; / No keeping one's haunches still: it's the greatest pleasure in life.

9 What's become of Waring / Since he gave us all the slip? [*Waring*, I. 1]

10 Oh, never star / Was lost here, but it rose afar! / Look East, where whole new thousands are! / In Vishnu-land what Avatar? [II. 3]

11 Let's contend no more, Love, / Strive nor weep: / All be as before, Love, / – Only sleep! [*A Woman's Last Word*]

12 Where the apple reddens / Never pry – / Lest we lose our Edens, / Eve and I.

13 I knew you once: but in Paradise, / If we meet, I will pass nor turn my face. [*The Worst of It*, 19]

14 For spring bade the sparrows pair, / And the boys and girls gave guesses, / And stalls in our street looked rare / With bulrush and water-cresses. [*Youth and Art*, 9]

15 And nobody calls you a dunce, / And people suppose me clever: / This could but have happened once, / And we missed it, lost it for ever. [17]

LENNY BRUCE 1923–1966

16 A lot of people say to me, 'Why did you kill Christ?' I dunno, it was one of those parties, got out of hand, you know. [Quoted in J. Cohen (ed.), *The Essential Lenny Bruce*]

MICHAEL BRUCE 1746–1767

17 Thou hast no sorrow in thy song, / No winter in thy year! [*To the Cuckoo*. Also attr. to John Logan]

'BEAU' BRUMMELL 1778–1840

18 Who's your fat friend? [Of George, Prince of Wales. Quoted in Gronow, *Reminiscences*]

W. J. BRYAN 1860–1925

19 You shall not press down upon the brow of labour this crown of thorns, you shall not crucify mankind upon a cross of gold. [Speech at the Democratic National Convention, Chicago, 8 July 1896]

JOHN BUCHAN [LORD TWEEDSMUIR] 1875–1940

20 An atheist is a man who has no invisible means of support. [Quoted in H. E. Fosdick, *On Being a Real Person*. Ch. 10. See 167:24]

R. W. BUCHANAN 1841–1901

21 The Fleshly School of Poetry. [Title of article in the *Contemporary Review*, Oct. 1871]

22 She just wore / Enough for modesty – no more. [*White Rose and Red*, I. v. 60]

GEORGE VILLIERS, SECOND DUKE OF BUCKINGHAM 1628–1687

23 The world is made up for the most part of fools and knaves. [*To Mr Clifford, on his 'Humane Reason'*]

24 What the devil does the plot signify, except to bring in fine things? [*The Rehearsal*, III. i]

25 Ay, now the plot thickens very much upon us. [ii]

JOHN SHEFFIELD, FIRST DUKE OF BUCKINGHAM AND NORMANBY 1648–1721

26 Read Homer once, and you can read no more, / For all books else appear so mean, so poor, / Verse will seem prose; but still persist to

read, / And Homer will be all the books you need. [*An Essay on Poetry*]

1 A faultless monster which the world ne'er saw.

H. J. BUCKOLL 1803–1871

2 Lord, dismiss us with Thy blessing, / Thanks for mercies past received. [Hymn]

J. B. BUCKSTONE 1802–1879

3 On such an occasion as this, / All time and nonsense scorning, / Nothing shall come amiss, / And we won't go home till morning. [*Billy Taylor*, I. ii]

BUDDHA [SIDDHĀRTHA GAUTAMA]
c. 563–c. 483 BC

4 This Ariyan Eightfold Path, that is to say: Right view, right aim, right speech, right action, right living, right effort, right mindfulness, right contemplation. [F. L. Woodward, *Some Sayings of the Buddha*, p. 8]

5 Ye must leave righteous ways behind, not to speak of unrighteous ways. [317]

6 All things, oh priests, are on fire ... The eye is on fire; forms are on fire; eye-consciousness is on fire; impressions received by the eye are on fire. [*The Fire Sermon*]

GEORGE-LOUIS DE BUFFON 1707–1788

7 *Le style est l'homme même.* – Style is the man himself. [*Discours sur le style*]

8 *Le génie n'est qu'une grande aptitude à la patience.* – Genius is nothing but a great aptitude for patience. [Attr. in Hérault de Séchelles, *Voyage à Montbar*]

ARTHUR BULLER 1874–1944

9 There was a young lady named Bright, / Whose speed was far faster than light; / She set out one day / In a relative way, / And returned home the previous night. [Limerick in *Punch*, 19 Dec. 1923]

ALFRED BUNN 1796?–1860

10 Alice, where art thou? [Title of song]

11 I dreamt that I dwelt in marble halls, / With vassals and serfs at my side. [*The Bohemian Girl*, II]

'BUGS BUNNY'

12 What's up Doc? [Catch phrase from film cartoon, 1937 by 'Tex' (Fred) Avery]

JOHN BUNYAN 1628–1688

13 Some said, 'John, print it'; others said, 'Not so.' / Some said, 'It might do good'; others said, 'No'. [*The Pilgrim's Progress*, Apology for his Book]

14 As I walked through the wilderness of this world. [Pt I]

15 Do you see yonder wicket-gate?

16 The name of the slough was Despond.

17 The gentleman's name was Mr Worldly-Wise-Man.

18 I come from the city of Destruction.

19 Set down my name, Sir.

20 A very stately palace before him, the name of which was Beautiful.

21 The valley of Humiliation.

22 Then Apollyon straddled quite over the whole breadth of the way.

23 It beareth the name of Vanity Fair, because the town where 'tis kept, is lighter than vanity.

24 So soon as the man overtook me, he was but a word and a blow.

25 Hanging is too good for him.

26 My great grandfather was but a waterman, looking one way, and rowing another. [Mr By-Ends. See also 86:7]

27 They are for religion when in rags and contempt, but I am for him when he walks in his golden slippers in the sunshine and with applause. [Mr By-Ends]

28 A castle, called Doubting Castle, the owner whereof was Giant Despair.

29 They came to the Delectable Mountains.

30 Then I saw that there was a way to Hell, even from the gates of heaven.

31 So I awoke, and behold it was a dream.

32 One Great-heart. [II]

33 He that is down needs fear no fall, / He that is low no pride. [Shepherd Boy's Song]

34 Come wind, come weather.

35 He who would valiant be / 'Gainst all disaster / Let him in constancy / Follow the Master. / There's no discouragement / Shall make him once relent, / His first avowed intent / To be a pilgrim. [*English Hymnal* version]

1 Who so beset him round / With dismal stories, / Do but themselves confound; / His strength the more is.

2 Then fancies flee away! / I'll fear not what men say. / I'll labour night and day / To be a pilgrim.

3 Mr Standfast.

4 So he passed over, and all the trumpets sounded for him on the other side. [Mr Valiant-for-Truth]

GOTTFRIED AUGUST BURGER 1708–1775

5 *O Mutter, Mutter! Hin ist hin! / Verloren ist verloren!* – Oh mother, mother! Gone is gone! Lost is lost! [*Lenore*]

ANTHONY BURGESS 1917–

6 Who ever heard of a clockwork orange? ... The attempt to impose upon man, a creature of growth and capable of sweetness, to ooze juicily at the last round the bearded lips of God, to attempt to impose, I say, laws and conditions appropriate to a mechanical creation, against this I raise my sword-pen. [*The Clockwork Orange*, Ch. 2]

GELETT BURGESS 1866–1951

7 I never saw a Purple Cow, / I never hope to see one; / But I can tell you, anyhow, / I'd rather see than be one! [*Burgess Nonsense Book*, 'The Purple Cow']

8 Ah, yes! I wrote the 'Purple Cow' – / I'm sorry, now, I wrote it! / But I can tell you anyhow, / I'll kill you if you quote it! ['*Cinq Ans après*']

J. W. BURGON 1813–1888

9 Match me such marvel save in Eastern clime, / A rose-red city – 'half as old as time'! [*Petra*, l. 132]

JOHN BURGOYNE 1722–1792

10 You have only, when before your glass, to keep pronouncing to yourself nimini-pimini – the lips cannot fail of taking their plie. [*The Heiress*, III. ii]

EDMUND BURKE 1729–1797

11 The greater the power, the more dangerous the abuse. [Speech on the Middlesex Election, 1771]

12 Your representative owes you, not his industry only, but his judgement; and he betrays instead of serving you if he sacrifices it to your opinion. [Speech to the electors of Bristol, 3 Nov. 1774]

13 I have in general no very exalted opinion of the virtue of paper government. [Speech on conciliation with America, 22 Mar. 1775]

14 The concessions of the weak are the concessions of fear.

15 Through a wise and salutary neglect, a generous nature has been suffered to take her own way to perfection.

16 The use of force alone is but *temporary*. It may subdue for a moment; but it does not remove the necessity of subduing again; and a nation is not governed, which is perpetually to be conquered.

17 Abstract liberty, like other mere abstractions, is not to be found.

18 The mysterious virtue of wax and parchment.

19 I do not know the method of drawing up an indictment against a whole people.

20 The march of the human mind is slow.

21 All government, indeed every human benefit and enjoyment, every virtue, and every prudent act, is founded on compromise and barter.

22 Slavery they can have anywhere. It is a weed that grows in every soil.

23 Magnanimity in politics is not seldom the truest wisdom; and a great empire and little minds go ill together.

24 Not merely a chip off the old 'block', but the old block itself. [On William Pitt the Younger's maiden speech in House of Commons, Jan. 1781]

25 A rapacious and licentious soldiery. [Speech on Fox's East India Bill, 1 Dec. 1783]

26 What the greatest inquest of the nation has begun, its highest Tribunal [the House of Commons] will accomplish. [Impeachment of Warren Hastings, 15 Feb. 1788]

27 Religious persecution may shield itself under the guise of a mistaken and over-zealous piety. [17 Feb.]

28 A thing may look specious in theory, and

yet be ruinous in practice; a thing may look evil in theory, and yet be in practice excellent. [19 Feb.]

1 An event has happened, upon which it is difficult to speak, and impossible to be silent. [5 May 1789]

2 Dangers by being despised grow great. [Speech on the Petition of the Unitarians, 1792]

3 There is but one law for all, namely, that law which governs all law, the law of our Creator, the law of humanity, justice, equity – the law of nature, and of nations. [28 May 1794]

4 There is, however, a limit at which forbearance ceases to be a virtue. [*Observations on 'The Present State of the Nation'*]

5 It is a general popular error to imagine the loudest complainers for the public to be the most anxious for its welfare.

6 I am convinced that we have a degree of delight, and that no small one, in the real misfortunes and pains of others. [*On the Sublime and Beautiful*, I. xiv]

7 No passion so effectually robs the mind of all its powers of acting and reasoning as fear. [II. ii]

8 Beauty in distress is much the most affecting beauty. [III. ix]

9 Custom reconciles us to everything. [IV. xviii]

10 Whenever our neighbour's house is on fire, it cannot be amiss for the engines to play a little on our own. [*Reflections on the Revolution in France*]

11 A state without the means of some change is without the means of its conservation.

12 Government is a contrivance of human wisdom to provide for human *wants*. Men have a right that these wants should be provided for by this wisdom.

13 But the age of chivalry is gone. That of sophisters, economists, and calculators, has succeeded; and the glory of Europe is extinguished for ever.

14 That chastity of honour, that felt a stain like a wound.

15 Vice itself lost half its evil, by losing all its grossness.

16 Kings will be tyrants from policy, when subjects are rebels from principle.

17 Because half a dozen grasshoppers under a fern make the field ring with their importunate chink . . . do not imagine that those who make the noise are the only inhabitants of the field.

18 The little, meagre, shrivelled, hopping, though loud and troublesome *insects* of the hour.

19 Man is by his constitution a religious animal.

20 A perfect democracy is therefore the most shameless thing in the world.

21 The men of England, the men, I mean, of light and leading in England.

22 Superstition is the religion of feeble minds.

23 He that wrestles with us strengthens our nerves, and sharpens our skill. Our antagonist is our helper.

24 Our patience will achieve more than our force.

25 Good order is the foundation of all things.

26 Having first looked to government for bread, on the very first scarcity they will turn and bite the hand that fed them. [*Thoughts and Details on Scarcity*]

27 The wisdom of our ancestors. [*Thoughts on the Cause of the Present Discontents*]

28 When bad men combine, the good must associate; else they will fall, one by one, an unpitied sacrifice in a contemptible struggle.

29 'Not men but measures'; a sort of charm by which many people get loose from every honourable engagement.

30 So to be patriots as not to forget that we are gentlemen.

31 The only infallible criterion of wisdom to vulgar minds – success. [*Letter to a Member of the National Assembly*]

32 You can never plan the future by the past.

33 To innovate is not to reform. [*A Letter to a Noble Lord*, 1796]

34 These gentle historians, on the contrary, dip their pens in nothing but the milk of human kindness.

35 I know that many have been taught to think that moderation, in a case like this, is a sort of treason. [*Letter to the Sheriffs of Bristol*]

36 If any ask me what a free government is, I

answer, that for any practical purpose, it is what the people think so.

1 Liberty, too, must be limited in order to be possessed.

2 Nothing is so fatal to religion as indifference, which is, at least, half infidelity. [Letter to William Smith, 29 Jan. 1795]

3 Somebody has said, that a king may make a nobleman, but he cannot make a gentleman.

4 If we command our wealth, we shall be rich and free; if our wealth commands us, we are poor indeed. [Letters on a Regicide Peace, 1]

5 Example is the school of mankind, and they will learn at no other.

JOHNNY BURKE 1908–1964

6 Don't you know each cloud contains / Pennies from Heaven? [Song: Pennies from Heaven, music by A. Johnston]

WILLIAM CECIL, LORD BURLEIGH 1520–1598

7 What! all this for a song? [To Queen Elizabeth when ordered to pay Spenser £100. Quoted in Birch, Life of Spenser]

BISHOP GILBERT BURNET 1643–1715

8 There was a sure way never to see it lost, and that was to die in the last ditch. [History of My Own Times, I, speech attr. to William III]

9 He [Halifax] had said that he had known many kicked downstairs, but he never knew any kicked upstairs before. [Original Memoirs]

FANNY BURNEY [MME D'ARBLAY] 1752–1840

10 In the bosom of her respectable family resided Camilla. [Camilla, I. Ch. 1]

11 Travelling is the ruin of all happiness! There's no looking at a building here after seeing Italy. [Cecilia, IV, 2]

12 'True, very true, ma'am,' said he, yawning, 'one really lives nowhere; one does but vegetate, and wish it all at an end.' [VII. 5]

13 Indeed, the freedom with which Dr Johnson condemns whatever he disapproves is astonishing. [Diary, 23 Aug. 1778]

14 'Why, what the D—l,' cried the Captain, 'do you come to the play, without knowing what it is?'

'O yes, Sir, yes, very frequently; I have no time to read play-bills; one merely comes to meet one's friends, and show that one's alive.' [Evelina, Letter 20]

15 Now I am ashamed of confessing that I have nothing to confess. [59]

J. D. BURNS 1823–1864

16 Hushed was the evening hymn, – The temple courts were dark; / The lamp was burning dim / Before the sacred Ark, / When suddenly a voice divine / Rang through the silence of the shrine. [Hymn: The Child Samuel]

JOHN BURNS 1858–1943

17 Every drop of the Thames is liquid 'istory. [Said to Transatlantic visitors, attr. by Sir Frederick Whyte, quoted in Daily Mail 25 Jan. 1943]

ROBERT BURNS 1759–1796

18 O thou! whatever title suit thee, / Auld Hornie, Satan, Nick, or Clootie. [Address to the Deil, 1]

19 But faith! he'll turn a corner jinkin' / An' cheat you yet. [119]

20 But fare you weel, auld Nickie-ben! / O wad ye tak a thought an' men'! / Ye aiblins might – I dinna ken – / Still hae a stake: / I'm wae to think upo' yon den, / Ev'n for your sake! [121]

21 Then gently scan your brother man, / Still gentler sister woman; / Tho' they may gang a kennin wrang, / To step aside is human. [Address to the Unco Guid, 49]

22 What's done we partly may compute, / But know not what's resisted. [63]

23 Ae fond kiss, and then we sever! [Ae Fond Kiss]

24 But to see her was to love her, / Love but her, and love for ever.

25 Had we never lov'd sae kindly, / Had we never lov'd sae blindly, / Never met – or never parted, / We had ne'er been broken-hearted.

26 Should auld acquaintance be forgot, / And never brought to min'? [Auld Lang Syne]

27 We'll tak a cup o' kindness yet, / For auld lang syne.

28 And there's a hand, my trusty fiere, / And gie's a hand o' thine.

29 Freedom and Whisky gang thegither! [The Author's Earnest Cry and Prayer, 185]

Robert Burns

1 O saw ye bonnie Lesley / As she gaed o'er the border? / She's gane, like Alexander, / To spread her conquests farther.

To see her is to love her, / And love but her for ever: / For Nature made her what she is, / And never made anither! [*Bonnie Lesley*]

2 Gin a body meet a body / Coming through the rye; / Gin a body kiss a body, / Need a body cry? [*Coming through the Rye*]

3 Contented wi' little, and cantie wi' mair. [*Contented wi' Little*]

4 The mother, wi' her needle and her shears, / Gars auld claes look amaist as weel's the new. [*The Cotter's Saturday Night*, 43]

5 The halesome parritch, chief of Scotia's food. [92]

6 He wales a portion with judicious care, / And 'Let us worship God!' he says with solemn air. [107]

7 From scenes like these old Scotia's grandeur springs, / That makes her loved at home, revered abroad: / Princes and lords are but the breath of kings, / 'An honest man's the noblest work of God.' [163 (the last line quotes Pope: see 88:15, 215:11, 314:9)]

8 I wasna fou, but just had plenty. [*Death and Dr Hornbook*, 14]

9 On ev'ry hand it will allow'd be, / He's just – nae better than he should be. [*A Dedication to Gavin Hamilton*, 25]

10 There's threesome reels, and foursome reels, / There's hornpipes and strathspeys, man; / But the ae best dance e'er cam to our lan', / Was – the De'il's awa' wi' the Exciseman. [*The De'il's awa' wi' the Exciseman*]

11 But Facts are chiels that winna ding, / An' downa be disputed. [*A Dream*, 30]

12 If honest nature made you fools, / What sairs your grammars? [*Epistle to John Lapraik*, 63]

13 Gie me ae spark o' Nature's fire, / That's a' the learning I desire. [73]

14 The social, friendly, honest man, / Whate'er he be, / 'Tis he fulfils great Nature's plan, / And none but he! [*Epistle to Lapraik*, No. 2, 87]

15 Perhaps it may turn out a sang, / Perhaps turn out a sermon. [*Epistle to a Young Friend*, 7]

16 But still keep something to yoursel / Ye scarcely tell to ony. [35]

17 I waive the quantum o' the sin, / The hazard of concealing; / But oh! it hardens a' within, / And petrifies the feeling! [45]

18 Here lie Willie Michie's banes; / O Satan, when ye tak him, / Gie him the schoolin' of your weans, / For clever deils he'll mak them! [*Epitaph on a Schoolmaster*]

19 A man's a man for a' that! [*For a' that and a' that*]

20 Go fetch to me a pint o' wine, / An' fill it in a silver tassie. [*Go Fetch to me a Pint o' Wine*]

21 Green grow the rashes O; / The sweetest hours that e'er I spend, / Are spent among the lasses O! [*Green grow the Rashes*]

22 What signifies the life o' man, / An' 'twere na for the lasses O.

23 Auld nature swears, the lovely dears / Her noblest work she classes O; / Her prentice han' she tried on man, / An' then she made the lasses O.

24 O, gie me the lass that has acres o' charms, / O, gie me the lass wi' the weel-stockit farms. [*Hey for a Lass wi' a Tocher*]

25 The golden hours on angel wings / Flew o'er me and my dearie; / For dear to me as light and life / Was my sweet Highland Mary. [*Highland Mary*]

26 Here some are thinkin' on their sins, / An' some upo' their claes. [*The Holy Fair*, 82]

27 There's some are fou o' love divine, / There's some are fou o' brandy. [239]

28 There's death in the cup – sae beware! [*Inscription on a Goblet*]

29 It was a' for our rightfu' King, / We left fair Scotland's strand. [*It was a' for our Rightfu' King*]

30 He turn'd him right and round about / Upon the Irish shore; / And gae his bridle-reins a shake, / With adieu for evermore, / My dear, / Adieu for evermore.

31 John Anderson my jo, John, / When we were first acquent, / Your locks were like the raven, / Your bonnie brow was brent. [*John Anderson My Jo*]

32 There was three Kings into the east, / Three kings both great and high, / And they hae sworn a solemn oath / John Barleycorn should die. [*John Barleycorn*]

33 Let them cant about decorum / Who have characters to lose. [*The Jolly Beggars*, 310]

1 Nature's law, / That man was made to mourn. [*Man was made to Mourn*, 31]

2 Man's inhumanity to man / Makes countless thousands mourn! [55]

3 My heart's in the Highlands, my heart is not here; / My heart's in the Highlands a-chasing the deer. [*My Heart's in the Highlands*]

4 O, my Luve's like a red red rose / That's newly sprung in June: / O, my Luve's like the melodie / That's sweetly play'd in tune. [*My Love is like a Red Red Rose*]

5 Of a' the airts the wind can blaw, / I dearly like the west. [*Of a' the Airts*]

6 Hear, Land o' Cakes, and brither Scots. [*On the Late Capt. Grose's Peregrinations*]

7 O, wert thou in the cauld blast, / On yonder lea, on yonder lea, / My plaidie to the angry airt, / I'd shelter thee, I'd shelter thee. [*O, Wert Thou in the Cauld Blast*]

8 The desert were a paradise, / If thou wert there, if thou wert there.

9 The mair they talk I'm kent the better, / E'en let them clash. [*The Poet's Welcome to his Love-begotten Daughter*]

10 Scots, wha hae wi' Wallace bled, / Scots, wham Bruce has aften led, / Welcome to your gory bed, / Or to victorie. [*Scots, Wha hae*]

11 Liberty's in every blow! / Let us do or die!

12 Some hae meat, and canna eat, / And some wad eat that want it, / But we hae meat and we can eat, / And sae the Lord be thankit. [*The Selkirk Grace*]

13 Where sits our sulky sullen dame, / Gathering her brows like gathering storm, / Nursing her wrath to keep it warm. [*Tam o' Shanter*, 10]

14 Auld Ayr, wham ne'er a town surpasses / For honest men and bonnie lasses. [15]

15 Ah, gentle dames! It gars me greet / To think how mony counsels sweet, / How mony lengthen'd sage advices, / The husband frae the wife despises! [33]

16 His ancient, trusty, drouthy crony; / Tam lo'ed him like a vera brither; / They had been fou for weeks thegither. [42]

17 Kings may be blest, but Tam was glorious, / O'er a' the ills o' life victorious! [57]

18 But pleasures are like poppies spread – / You seize the flow'r, its bloom is shed; / Or like the snow falls in the river – A moment white, then melts for ever. [59]

19 That hour, o' night's black arch the key-stane. [69]

20 Inspiring bold John Barleycorn! / What dangers thou canst make us scorn! / Wi' tippenny, we fear nae evil; / Wi' usquebae, we'll face the devil! [105]

21 As Tammie glowr'd, amaz'd, and curious, / The mirth and fun grew fast and furious. [143]

22 Ah, Tam! ah, Tam! thou'll get thy fairin'! / In hell they'll roast thee like a herrin' ! [201]

23 He'll hae misfortunes great and sma', / But aye a heart aboon them a'. [*There was a Lad*]

24 Fair fa' your honest sonsie face, / Great chieftain o' the puddin'-race! / Aboon them a' ye tak your place, / Painch, tripe, or thairm: / Weel are ye worthy o' a grace / As lang's my arm. [*To a Haggis*]

25 O wad some Pow'r the giftie gie us / To see oursels as others see us! / It wad frae mony a blunder free us, / And foolish notion. [*To a Louse*]

26 Wee modest crimson-tippèd flow'r. [*To a Mountain Daisy*]

27 Wee, sleekit, cow'rin', tim'rous beastie, / O what a panic's in thy breastie! / Thou need na start awa sae hasty, / Wi' bickering brattle! [*To a Mouse*]

28 The best laid schemes o' mice an' men / Gang aft a-gley.

29 To make a happy fire-side clime / To weans and wife, / That's the true pathos and sublime / Of human life. [*To Dr Blacklock*]

30 We labour soon, we labour late, / To feed the titled knave, man; / And a' the comfort we're to get / Is that ayont the grave, man. [*The Tree of Liberty*, attr. to Burns]

31 His lockèd, letter'd, braw brass collar, / Shew'd him the gentleman and scholar. [*The Twa dogs*, 13]

32 But human bodies are sic fools, / For a' their colleges and schools, / That when nae real ills perplex them, / They make enow themselves to vex them. [195]

33 But yet the light that led astray / Was light from Heaven. [*The Vision*, 239]

34 O Whistle, and I'll come to you, my lad. [*Whistle, and I'll come to you, my Lad*]

35 Ye banks and braes o' bonnie Doon, / How can ye bloom sae fresh and fair? / How can ye

chant, ye little birds, / And I sae weary fu' o' care? [*Ye Banks and Braes*]

1 And my fause lover stole my rose, / But ah! he left the thorn wi' me.

2 Don't let the awkward squad fire over me. [Quoted in A. Cunningham's *Life*, Vol. i. p. 344]

B. H. BURT ?–1950

3 When you're all dressed up and no place to go. [Title of song]

ROBERT BURTON 1577–1640

4 All my joys to this are folly, / Naught so sweet as melancholy. [*Anatomy of Melancholy*, 'The Author's Abstract']

5 They lard their lean books with the fat of others' works. ['Democritus to the Reader']

6 We can say nothing but what hath been said . . . Our poets steal from Homer . . . he that comes last is commonly best.

7 Like watermen, that row one way and look another. [See also 80:26]

8 All poets are mad.

9 Were it not that they are loath to lay out money on a rope, they would be hanged forthwith, and sometimes die to save charges. [Pt I. §2. Memb. 3. 12]

10 One was never married, and that's his hell; another is, and that's his plague. [Memb. 4. 7]

11 If there is a hell upon earth, it is to be found in a melancholy man's heart. [§4. Memb. 1. 3]

12 [Fabricius] finds certain spots and clouds in the sun. [II. §2. Memb. 3]

13 Who cannot give good counsel? 'Tis cheap, it costs them nothing. [§3. Memb. 3]

14 What is a ship but a prison? [Memb. 4]

15 All places are distant from heaven alike.

16 Tobacco, divine, rare, superexcellent tobacco, which goes far beyond all their panaceas, potable gold, and philosopher's stones, a sovereign remedy to all diseases . . . But, as it is commonly abused by most men, which take it as tinkers do ale, 'tis a plague, a mischief, a violent purger of goods, lands, health, hellish, devilish, and damned tobacco, the ruin and overthrow of body and soul. [§4. Memb. 2. 1]

17 'Let me not live,' said Aretine's Antonia, 'if I had not rather hear thy discourse than see a play.' [III. §1. Memb. 1. 1]

18 To enlarge and illustrate this – is to set a candle in the sun. [§2. Memb. 1. 2]

19 Cornelia kept her in talk till her children came from school, and these, said she, are my jewels. [Memb. 2. 3]

20 England is a paradise for women, and hell for horses: Italy a paradise for horses, hell for women, as the diverb goes. [§3. Memb. 1. 2]

21 The miller sees not all the water that goes by his mill. [Memb. 4. 1]

22 The fear of some divine and supreme powers keeps men in obedience. [§4. Memb. 1. 2]

23 One religion is as true as another. [Memb. 2. 1]

WILHELM BUSCH 1832–1908

24 *Max und Moritz ihrerseits / Fanden darin keinen Reiz.* – Max and Moritz for their part found no attraction in it. [*Max und Moritz*]

COMTE DE BUSSY-RABUTIN 1618–1693

25 *Comme vous savez, Dieu est d'ordinaire pour les gros escadrons contre les petits.* – As you know, God is usually on the side of the big battalions against the small. [Letter to the Comte de Limoges, 18 Oct. 1677. Also ascr. to Marshal Turenne; see 433:8, 443:1]

BISHOP JOSEPH BUTLER 1692–1752

26 That which is the foundation of all our hopes and of all our fears; all our hopes and fears which are of any consideration: I mean a Future Life. [*The Analogy of Religion*, Introduction]

27 But to *us*, probability is the very guide of life.

28 Things and actions are what they are, and the consequences of them will be what they will be: why then should we desire to be deceived? [*Fifteen Sermons*, 7. 16]

29 Sir, the pretending to extraordinary revelations and gifts of the Holy Ghost is a horrid thing, a very horrid thing. [To John Wesley. Quoted in Wesley, *Works*, xiii. 449]

NICHOLAS MURRAY BUTLER 1862–1947

30 An expert is one who knows more and more about less and less. [Commencement Address, Columbia University]

R. A. BUTLER [later LORD BUTLER]
1902–1982

1 QUESTION: Mr Butler, would you say that this is the best Prime Minister we have?
ANSWER: Yes. [In interview about Sir Anthony Eden's premiership, London Airport, Dec. 1955]

SAMUEL BUTLER 1612–1680

2 When civil dudgeon first grew high, / And men fell out they knew not why. [*Hudibras*, I. i. 1]

3 Besides 'tis known he could speak Greek, / As naturally as pigs squeak. [51]

4 He could distinguish, and divide / A hair 'twixt south and south-west side. / On either which he would dispute, / Confute, change hands, and still confute. [63]

5 For he by geometric scale / Could take the size of pots of ale. [121]

6 For every why he had a wherefore. [132]

7 He knew what's what, and that's as high / As metaphysic wit can fly. [149]

8 'Twas Presbyterian true blue. [189]

9 Such as do build their faith upon / The holy text of pike and gun. [193]

10 And prove their doctrine orthodox / By apostolic blows and knocks. [197]

11 Compound for sins, they are inclined to / By damning those they have no mind to. [213]

12 He ne'er considered it, as loath / To look a gift-horse in the mouth. [483]

13 Quoth Hudibras, I smell a rat; / Ralpho, thou dost prevaricate. [815]

14 Through perils both of wind and limb, / Through thick and thin she followed him. [ii. 369]

15 Ay me! what perils do environ / The man that meddles with cold iron! [iii. 1]

16 I'll make the fur / Fly round the ears of the old cur. [277]

17 Cleric before, and Lay behind; / A lawless linsy-woolsy brother, / Half of one order, half another. [1226]

18 Quoth Hudibras, Friend Ralph, thou hast / Outrun the constable at last. [1367]

19 Love is a boy, by poets styled, / Then spare the rod, and spoil the child. [II. i. 844]

20 And like a lobster boiled, the morn / From black to red began to turn. [ii. 31]

21 Have always been at daggers-drawing, / And one another clapper-clawing. [79]

22 Oaths are but words, and words but wind. [107]

23 He made an instrument to know / If the moon shine at full or no. [iii. 261]

24 To swallow gudgeons ere they're catched, And count their chickens ere they're hatched. [923]

25 Still amorous, and fond, and billing, / Like Philip and Mary on a shilling. [III. i. 687]

26 Neither have the hearts to stay, / Nor wit enough to run away. [ii. 569]

27 For, those that fly, may fight again, / Which he can never do that's slain. [iii. 243]

28 He that complies against his will, / Is of his own opinion still. [547]

29 The souls of women are so small, / That some believe they've none at all. [*Miscellaneous Thoughts*]

SAMUEL BUTLER 1835–1902

30 Some who had received a liberal education at the Colleges of Unreason, and taken the highest degrees in hypothetics, which are their principal study. [*Erewhon*, Ch. 9]

31 Straighteners, managers and cashiers of the Musical Banks.

32 While to deny the existence of an unseen kingdom is bad, to pretend that we know more about it than its bare existence is no better. [15]

33 The wish to spread those opinions that we hold conducive to our own welfare is so deeply rooted in the English character that few of us can escape its influence. [20]

34 It has been said that the love of money is the root of all evil. The want of money is so quite as truly.

35 Spontaneity is only a term for man's ignorance of the gods. [25]

36 It has, I believe, been often remarked that a hen is only an egg's way of making another egg. [*Life and Habit*, Ch. 8]

37 Life is one long process of getting tired. [*Notebooks*, Ch. 1, 'Life', 7]

38 Life is the art of drawing sufficient conclusions from insufficient premises. [9]

1 All progress is based upon a universal innate desire on the part of every organism to live beyond its income. [16]

2 The healthy stomach is nothing if not conservative. Few radicals have good digestions. [Ch. 6, 'Indigestion']

3 Though analogy is often misleading, it is the least misleading thing we have. [Ch. 7, 'Thought and Word', 2]

4 When a man is in doubt about this or that in his writing, it will often guide him if he asks himself how it will tell a hundred years hence. [Final note]

5 If Bach wriggles, Wagner writhes. [Ch. 8, 'Musical Criticism']

6 The history of art is the history of revivals. ['Anachronism']

7 The phrase 'unconscious humour' is the one contribution I have made to the current literature of the day. ['*Homo Unius Libri*: Myself and "Unconscious Humour"']

8 I am the *enfant terrible* of literature and science. [Ch. 12, 'Myself']

9 Virgil was no good because Tennyson ran him, and as for Tennyson – well, Tennyson goes without saying. ['Blake, Dante, etc.']

10 An apology for the Devil – it must be remembered that we have only heard one side of the case. God has written all the books. [Ch. 14, 'An Apology for the Devil']

11 God is Love – I dare say. But what a mischievous devil Love is! ['God is Love']

12 To live is like to love – all reason is against it, and all healthy instinct for it. ['Life and Love']

13 The public buys its opinions as it buys its meat, or takes in its milk, on the principle that it is cheaper to do this than to keep a cow. So it is, but the milk is more likely to be watered. [Ch. 17, 'Public Opinion']

14 To be at all is to be religious more or less. [Ch. 22, 'Religion']

15 An honest God's the noblest work of man. [*Further Extracts*, Vol. i, 'An Honest God' (reversing Pope, 314:9). See also 84:7, 215:11]

16 Brigands demand money or your life, whereas women require both. [Vol. iv, 'Women and Brigands']

17 Taking numbers into account, I should think more mental suffering had been undergone in the streets leading from St George's, Hanover Square, than in the condemned cells of Newgate. [*The Way of all Flesh*, Ch. 13]

18 Every man's work, whether it be literature or music or pictures or architecture or anything else, is always a portrait of himself. [14]

19 That vice pays homage to virtue is notorious; we call it hypocrisy. [19]

20 Pleasure after all is a safer guide than either right or duty.

21 The advantage of doing one's praising for oneself is that one can lay it on so thick and exactly in the right places. [34]

22 There's many a good tune played on an old fiddle. [61]

23 'Tis better to have loved and lost than never to have lost at all. [77]

24 Stowed away in a Montreal lumber room / The Discobolus standeth and turneth his face to the wall; / Dusty, cobweb-covered, maimed and set at naught, / Beauty crieth in an attic and no man regardeth: / O God! O Montreal! [*Psalm of Montreal*]

WILLIAM BUTLER 1535–1618

25 Doubtless God could have made a better berry [than the strawberry], but doubtless God never did. [Quoted in I. Walton, *The Compleat Angler*, Pt I. Ch. 5]

JOHN BYROM 1692 1763

26 Some say, that Signor Bononcini, / Compared to Handel's a mere ninny; / Others aver, to him, that Handel / Is scarcely fit to hold a candle. / Strange! that such high dispute should be / 'Twixt Tweedledum and Tweedledee. [*Epigram on the Feuds between Handel and Bononcini*]

27 Bone and Skin, two millers thin, / Would starve us all, or near it; / But be it known to Skin and Bone / That Flesh and Blood can't bear it. [*Epigram on Two Monopolists*]

28 I shall prove it – as clear as a whistle. [*Epistle to Lloyd*, I. xii]

29 Christians awake, salute the happy morn, / Whereon the Saviour of the world was born. [*Hymn for Christmas Day*]

30 God bless the King, I mean the Faith's Defender; / God bless – no harm in blessing – the

Pretender; / But who Pretender is, or who is King, / God bless us all – that's quite another thing. [*To an Officer in the Army*]

GEORGE GORDON, LORD BYRON
1788–1824

1 The 'good old times' – all times when old are good – / Are gone. [*The Age of Bronze,* 1]

2 For what were all these country patriots born? / To hunt, and vote, and raise the price of corn? [14]

3 The land of self-interest groans from shore to shore, / For fear that plenty should attain the poor.

4 In short, he was a perfect cavaliero, / And to his very valet seemed a hero. [*Beppo,* 33]

5 His heart was one of those which most enamour us, / Wax to receive, and marble to retain. [34]

6 The nursery still lisps out in all they utter – / Besides, they always smell of bread and butter. [39]

7 Know ye the land where the cypress and myrtle / Are emblems of deeds that are done in their clime? / Where the rage of the vulture, the love of the turtle, / Now melt into sorrow, now madden to crime! [*The Bride of Abydos,* I. 1]

8 Where the virgins are soft as the roses they twine, / And all, save the spirit of man, is divine.

9 Mark! where his carnage and his conquests cease! / He makes a solitude, and calls it – peace! [20]

10 Hark! to the hurried question of Despair: / 'Where is my child?' – an Echo answers – 'Where?' [27]

11 Maidens, like moths, are ever caught by glare, / And Mammon wins his way where Seraphs might despair. [*Childe Harold's Pilgrimage,* 9]

12 Adieu, adieu! my native shore / Fades o'er the waters blue. [13]

13 My native Land – Good Night!

14 War, war is still the cry, 'War even to the knife!' [86]

15 Well didst thou speak, Athena's wisest son! / 'All that we know is, nothing can be known,' [II. 7]

16 Ah! happy years! once more who would not be a boy? [23]

17 Foul Superstition! howsoe'er disguised, / Idol, saint, virgin, prophet, crescent, cross, / For whatsoever symbol thou art prized, / Thou sacerdotal gain, but general loss! / Who from true worship's gold can separate thy dross? [44]

18 Hereditary bondsmen! know ye not / Who would be free themselves must strike the blow? [76]

19 Where'er we tread 'tis haunted, holy ground. [88]

20 What is the worst of woes that wait on age? / What stamps the wrinkle deeper on the brow? / To view each loved one blotted from life's page. / And be alone on earth, as I am now. [98]

21 There was a sound of revelry by night; / And Belgium's capital had gathered then / Her Beauty and her Chivalry, and bright / The lamps shone o'er fair women and brave men; / A thousand hearts beat happily; and when / Music arose with its voluptuous swell, / Soft eyes looked love to eyes that spake again, / And all went merry as a marriage bell; / But hush! hark! a deep sound strikes like a rising knell! [III. 21]

22 Did ye not hear it? – No; 'twas but the wind, / Or the car rattling o'er the stony street; / On with the dance! let joy be unconfined; / No sleep till morn, when Youth and Pleasure meet / To chase the glowing Hours with flying feet. [22]

23 Arm! Arm! it is – it is – the cannon's opening roar!

24 Or whispering, with white lips – 'The foe! they come! they come!' [25]

25 Rider and horse, – friend, foe, – in one red burial blent! [28]

26 But Life will suit / Itself to Sorrow's most detested fruit, / Like to the apples on the Dead Sea's shore, / All ashes to the taste. [34]

27 The castle crag of Drachenfels / Frowns o'er the wide and winding Rhine. [55]

28 To fly from, need not be to hate, mankind: / All are not fit with them to stir and toil, / Nor is it discontent to keep the mind / Deep in its fountain. [69]

29 I live not in myself, but I become / Portion

of that around me; and to me / High mountains are a feeling, but the hum / Of human cities torture. [72]

1 Ye stars! which are the poetry of heaven! [88]

2 Then stirs the feeling infinite, so felt / In solitude, where we are *least* alone. [90]

3 I have not loved the world, nor the world me; / I have not flattered its rank breath, nor bowed / To its idolatries a patient knee, / Nor coined my cheek to smiles, nor cried aloud / In worship of an echo. [113]

4 I stood / Among them, but not of them; in a shroud / Of thoughts which were not their thoughts.

5 I stood in Venice, on the Bridge of Sighs; / A palace and a prison on each hand. [IV. 1]

6 Where Venice sat in state, throned on her hundred isles!

7 The Ariosto of the North. [(Walter Scott) 40]

8 Let these describe the indescribable. [53]

9 Then farewell, Horace; whom I hated so, / Not for thy faults, but mine. [77]

10 Yet, Freedom! yet thy banner, torn, but flying, / Streams like the thunder-storm *against* the wind. [98]

11 Alas! our young affections run to waste, / Or water but the desert. [120]

12 Of its own beauty is the mind diseased, / And fevers into false creation. [122]

13 Time, the avenger! unto thee I lift / My hands, and eyes, and heart, and crave of thee a gift. [130]

14 I see before me the Gladiator lie: / He leans upon his hand – his manly brow / Consents to death, but conquers agony. [140]

15 The arena swims around him – he is gone, / Ere ceased the inhuman shout which hailed the wretch who won.

16 He heard it, but he heeded not – his eyes / Were with his heart, and that was far away; / He recked not of the life he lost nor prize, / But where his rude hut by the Danube lay, / *There* were his young barbarians all at play, / *There* was their Dacian mother – he, their sire, / Butchered to make a Roman holiday. [141]

17 While stands the Coliseum, Rome shall stand; / When falls the Coliseum, Rome shall fall; / And when Rome falls – the World. [145]

18 Oh! that the Desert were my dwelling-place, / With one fair Spirit for my minister, / That I might all forget the human race, / And, hating no one, love but only her! [177]

19 There is a pleasure in the pathless woods, / There is a rapture on the lonely shore, / There is society, where none intrudes, / By the deep sea, and music in its roar: / I love not man the less, but Nature more. [178]

20 Roll on, thou deep and dark blue Ocean – roll! / Ten thousand fleets sweep over thee in vain; / Man marks the earth with ruin – his control / Stops with the shore. [179]

21 He sinks into thy depths with bubbling groan, / Without a grave, unknelled, uncoffined, and unknown.

22 Time writes no wrinkle on thine azure brow: / Such as creation's dawn beheld, thou rollest now. [182]

23 Dark-heaving – boundless, endless, and sublime, / The image of eternity, the throne / Of the Invisible. [183]

24 And I have loved thee, Ocean! and my joy / Of youthful sports was on thy breast to be / Borne, like thy bubbles, onward: from a boy / I wantoned with thy breakers. [184]

25 The fatal facility of the octosyllabic verse. [*The Corsair*, Dedication]

26 Such hath it been – shall be – beneath the sun / The many still must labour for the one! [I. 8]

27 The spirit burning but unbent, / May writhe, rebel – the weak alone repent! [II. 10]

28 She for him had given / Her all on earth, and more than all in heaven! [III. 17]

29 He left a Corsair's name to other times, / Linked with one virtue, and a thousand crimes. [24]

30 I tell thee, be not rash; a golden bridge / Is for a flying enemy. [*The Deformed Transformed*, II. 2]

31 Explaining metaphysics to the nation – / I wish he would explain his explanation. [(Of Coleridge) *Don Juan*, Dedication, 2]

32 In virtues nothing earthly could surpass her, / Save thine 'incomparable oil', Macassar! [I. 17]

33 But – Oh! ye lords of ladies intellectual, / Inform us truly, have they not hen-pecked you all? [22]

1 She / Was married, charming, chaste, 'and twenty-three. [49]

2 What men call gallantry, and gods adultery, / Is much more common where the climate's sultry. [63]

3 Christians have burnt each other, quite persuaded / That all the Apostles would have done as they did. [83]

4 A little still she strove, and much repented, / And whispering 'I will ne'er consent' – consented. [117]

5 Sweet is revenge – especially to women. [124]

6 Pleasure's a sin, and sometimes sin's a pleasure. [133]

7 Man's love is of man's life a thing apart, / 'Tis woman's whole existence. [194]

8 So for a good old-gentlemanly vice, / I think I must take up with avarice. [216]

9 There's nought, no doubt, so much the spirit calms / As rum and true religion. [II. 34]

10 If this be true, indeed, / Some Christians have a comfortable creed. [86]

11 He could, perhaps, have passed the Hellespont, / As once (a feat on which ourselves we prided) / Leander, Mr Ekenhead, and I did. [105]

12 Let us have wine and women, mirth and laughter, / Sermons and soda-water the day after. [178]

13 Man, being reasonable, must get drunk; / The best of life is but intoxication. [179]

14 Alas! the love of women! it is known / To be a lovely and a fearful thing. [199]

15 In her first passion woman loves her lover, / In all the others all she loves is love. [III. 3]

16 For no one cares for matrimonial cooings, / There's nothing wrong in a connubial kiss: / Think you, if Laura had been Petrarch's wife, / He would have written sonnets all his life? [8]

17 All tragedies are finished by a death, / All comedies are ended by a marriage. [9]

18 Dreading that climax of all human ills, / The inflammation of his weekly bills. [34]

19 He was the mildest mannered man / That ever scuttled ship or cut a throat. [41]

20 Though sages may pour out their wisdom's treasure, / There is no sterner moralist than Pleasure. [64]

21 But Shakespeare also says, 'tis very silly / 'To gild refinèd gold, or paint the lily'. [76]

22 Agree to a short armistice with truth. [83]

23 The isles of Greece, the isles of Greece! / Where burning Sappho loved and sung, / Where grew the arts of war and peace, / Where Delos rose, and Phoebus sprung! / Eternal summer gilds them yet, / But all, except their sun, is set. [86. 1]

24 The mountains look on Marathon – / And Marathon looks on the sea; / And musing there an hour alone, / I dreamed that Greece might yet be free. [86. 3]

25 He counted them at break of day – / And when the sun set where were they? [86. 4]

26 Of the three hundred grant but three, / To make a new Thermopylae! [86. 7]

27 Fill high the cup with Samian wine! [86. 9]

28 Milton's the prince of poets – so we say; / A little heavy, but no less divine. [91]

29 Nothing so difficult as a beginning / In poesy, unless perhaps the end. [IV. 1]

30 Imagination droops her pinion. [3]

31 And if I laugh at any mortal thing, / 'Tis that I may not weep. [4]

32 'Whom the gods love die young' was said of yore. [12]

33 'Arcades ambo', *id est* – blackguards both. [93]

34 I've stood upon Achilles' tomb, / And heard Troy doubted, time will doubt of Rome. [101]

35 Oh! 'darkly, deeply, beautifully blue', / As someone somewhere sings about the sky. [110]

36 The negroes more philosophy displayed, – / Used to it, no doubt, as eels are to be flayed. [V. 7]

37 I thought it would appear / That there had been a lady in the case. [19]

38 And put himself upon his good behaviour. [47]

39 That all-softening, overpowering knell, / The tocsin of the soul – the dinner-bell. [49]

40 A moral (like all morals) melancholy. [63]

41 Not to admire is all the art I know. [101]

42 Why don't they knead two virtuous souls for life / Into that moral centaur, man and wife? [158]

43 There is a tide in the affairs of women, /

Which, taken at the flood, leads – God knows where. [VI. 12]

1 A lady of a 'certain age', which means / Certainly aged. [69]

2 A 'strange coincidence', to use a phrase / By which such things are settled nowadays. [78]

3 He said / Little, but to the purpose. [IX. 83]

4 When Bishop Berkeley said 'there was no matter', / And proved it – 'twas no matter what he said. [XI. 1]

5 But Tom's no more – and so no more of Tom. [20]

6 And, after all, what is a lie? 'Tis but / The truth in masquerade. [37]

7 'Tis strange the mind, that very fiery particle, / Should let itself be snuffed out by an article. [(John Keats) 60]

8 And hold up to the sun my little taper. [XII. 21]

9 A finished gentleman from top to toe. [84]

10 Now hatred is by far the longest pleasure; / Men love in haste, but they detest at leisure. [XIII. 6]

11 Cool, and quite English, imperturbable. [14]

12 The English winter – ending in July, / To recommence in August. [42]

13 Society is now one polished horde, / Formed of two mighty tribes, the *Bores* and *Bored*. [95]

14 I for one venerate a petticoat. [XIV. 26]

15 Of all the horrid, hideous notes of woe, / Sadder than owl-songs or the midnight blast, / Is that portentous phrase, 'I told you so'. [50]

16 She had consented to create again / That Adam, called 'the happiest of men'. [55]

17 'Tis strange – but true; for truth is always strange; / Stranger than fiction. [101]

18 Not so her gracious, graceful, graceless Grace. [XVI. 49]

19 The loudest wit I e'er was deafened with. [81]

20 And both were young, and one was beautiful. [*The Dream*, 2]

21 Still must I hear? – shall hoarse Fitzgerald bawl / His creaking couplets in a tavern hall, / And I not sing? [*English Bards and Scotch Reviewers*, 1]

22 I'll publish, right or wrong: / Fools are my theme, let satire be my song. [5]

23 'Tis pleasant, sure, to see one's name in print; / A book's a book, although there's nothing in't. [51]

24 A man must serve his time to every trade / Save censure – critics all are ready made. / Take hackneyed jokes from Miller, got by rote, / With just enough of learning to misquote. [63]

25 As soon / Seek roses in December – ice in June; / Hope constancy in wind, or corn in chaff; / Believe a woman or an epitaph, / Or any other thing that's false, before / You trust in critics. [75]

26 Better to err with Pope, than shine with Pye. [102]

27 The simple Wordsworth . . . / Who, both by precept and example, shows / That prose is verse, and verse is merely prose. [237]

28 Be warm, but pure; be amorous, but be chaste. [306]

29 Comus all allows; / Champagne, dice, music or your neighbour's spouse. [650]

30 But who forgives the senior's ceaseless verse, / Whose hairs grow hoary as his rhymes grow worse? [729]

31 Let simple Wordsworth chime his childish verse, / And brother Coleridge lull the babe at nurse. [917]

32 Nay more, though all my rival rhymesters frown, / I too can hunt a poetaster down. [1063]

33 The world is a bundle of hay, / Mankind are the asses who pull; / Each tugs it a different way, / And the greatest of all is John Bull. [*Epigram*]

34 Dear Doctor, I have read your play, / Which is a good one in its way, – / Purges the eyes and moves the bowels, / And drenches handkerchiefs like towels. [*Epistle from Mr Murray to Dr Polidori*]

35 With death doomed to grapple, / Beneath this cold slab, he / Who lied in the chapel / Now lies in the Abbey. [*Epitaph for William Pitt*]

36 And know, whatever thou hast been, / 'Tis something better not to be. [*Euthanasia*]

37 Fare thee well! and if for ever, / Still for ever, fare thee well. [*Fare thee well*]

1 Clime of the unforgotten brave! / Whose land from plain to mountain-cave / Was Freedom's home or Glory's grave! [*The Giaour*, 103]

2 For Freedom's battle once begun, / Bequeathed by bleeding Sire to Son, / Though baffled oft is ever won. [123]

3 I die, – but first I have possessed, / And come what may, I *have been* blessed. [1127]

4 The Assyrian came down like the wolf on the fold, / And his cohorts were gleaming in purple and gold; / And the sheen of their spears was like stars on the sea, / When the blue wave rolls nightly on deep Galilee. [*Hebrew Melodies*, 'The Destruction of Sennacherib']

5 For the Angel of Death spread his wings on the blast.

6 And the might of the Gentile, unsmote by the sword, / Hath melted like snow in the glance of the Lord!

7 Oh! snatched away in beauty's bloom, / On thee shall press no ponderous tomb. ['Oh! Snatched away']

8 She walks in beauty, like the night / Of cloudless climes and starry skies; / And all that's best of dark and bright / Meet in her aspect and her eyes. ['She walks in Beauty']

9 A mind at peace with all below, / A heart whose love is innocent!

10 Friendship is Love without his wings! [*Hours of Idleness*, 'L'Amitié']

11 Though women are angels, yet wedlock's the devil. ['To Eliza']

12 Who killed John Keats? / 'I,' says the Quarterly, / So savage and Tartarly; / ''Twas one of my feats.' [*John Keats*]

13 Maid of Athens, ere we part, / Give, oh give me back my heart! [*Maid of Athens*]

14 When the moon is on the wave, / And the glow-worm in the grass, / And the meteor on the grave, / And the wisp on the morass; / When the falling stars are shooting, / And the answered owls are hooting, / And the silent leaves are still / In the shadow of the hill. [*Manfred*, I. 1]

15 In truth, he was a noble steed. [*Mazeppa*, 9]

16 The Cincinnatus of the West, / Whom envy dared not hate, / Bequeathed the name of Washington, / To make man blush there was but one! [*Ode to Napoleon Buonaparte*, 19]

17 My hair is grey, but not with years, / Nor grew it white / In a single night, / As men's have grown from sudden fears. [*The Prisoner of Chillon*, 1]

18 A light broke in upon my brain, – / It was the carol of a bird; / It ceased, and then it came again, / The sweetest song ear ever heard. [10]

19 Even I / Regained my freedom with a sigh. [14]

20 I am the very slave of circumstance / And impulse – borne away with every breath! [*Sardanapalus*, IV. 1]

21 So, we'll go no more a roving / So late into the night, / Though the heart be still as loving, / And the moon be still as bright.

For the sword outwears its sheath, / And the soul wears out the breast, / And the heart must pause to breathe, / And love itself have rest.

Though the night was made for loving, / And the day returns too soon, / Yet we'll go no more a roving / By the light of the moon. [*So, we'll go no more a roving*]

22 Eternal Spirit of the chainless Mind! / Brightest in dungeons, Liberty! thou art. [*Sonnet on Chillon*]

23 Chillon! thy prison is a holy place, / And thy sad floor an altar.

24 May none these marks efface! / For they appeal from tyranny to God.

25 There be none of Beauty's daughters / With a magic like thee. [*Stanzas for Music*, 'There be none of Beauty's daughters']

26 There's not a joy the world can give like that it takes away. ['There's not a joy']

27 Nor be, what man should ever be, / The friend of Beauty in distress? [*To Florence*]

28 Saint Peter sat by the celestial gate: / His keys were rusty, and the lock was dull. [*The Vision of Judgement*, 1]

29 The angels all were singing out of tune, / And hoarse with having little else to do, / Excepting to wind up the sun and moon, / Or curb a runaway young star or two. [2]

30 A better farmer ne'er brushed dew from lawn, / A worse king never left a realm undone! [(George III) 8]

31 That household virtue, most uncommon, / Of constancy to a bad, ugly woman. [12]

32 But he, with first a start and then a wink, /

Said, 'There's another star gone out, I think!' [16]

1 An old man / With an old soul, and both extremely blind. [23]

2 He pattered with his keys at a great rate, / And sweated through his apostolic skin: / Of course his perspiration was but ichor, / Or some such other spiritual liquor. [25]

3 By many stories, / And true, we learn the angels are all Tories. [26]

4 Though they did not kiss, / Yet still between his Darkness and his Brightness / There passed a mutual glance of great politeness. [35]

5 Satan met his ancient friend / With more hauteur, as might an old Castilian / Poor noble meet a mushroom rich civilian. [36]

6 He had written much blank verse, and blanker prose. [(Southey) 98]

7 All I saw farther, in the last confusion, / Was, that King George slipped into heaven for one; / And when the tumult dwindled to a calm, / I left him practising the hundredth psalm. [106]

8 When we two parted / In silence and tears, / Half broken-hearted / To sever for years, / Pale grew thy cheek and cold, / Colder thy kiss; / Truly that hour foretold / Sorrow to this. [*When We Two Parted*]

9 If I should meet thee / After long years, / How should I greet thee? / With silence and tears.

10 By headless Charles see heartless Henry lies. [*Windsor Poetics*]

11 My Princess of Parallelograms. [Description of Annabella Milbanke in letter to Lady Melbourne, 18 Oct. 1812]

12 I awoke one morning and found myself famous. [On instantaneous success of *Childe Harold*. Quoted in T. Moore, *Life of Byron*, 1. 347]

13 Friendship may, and often does, grow into love, but love never subsides into friendship. [Attr.]

HENRY J. BYRON 1834–1884

14 I'm going to 'go it' a bit before *I* settle down. [*Our Boys*, a comedy, I]

15 Life's too short for chess.

C

JAMES BRANCH CABELL 1879–1958

1 I am willing to taste any drink once. [*Jurgen*, Ch. 1]

2 Why is the King of Hearts the only one that hasn't a moustache? [*The Rivet in Grandfather's Neck*]

3 The optimist proclaims that we live in the best of all possible worlds; and the pessimist fears this is so. [*The Silver Stallion*, Bk iv. Ch. 2]

AUGUSTUS CAESAR 63 BC–AD 14

4 *Quintili Vari, legiones redde.* – Quintilius Varus, give me back my legions. [Suetonius, *Divus Augustus*, 23]

5 *Ad kalendas Graecas soluturos.* – To be paid at the Greek Kalends. [87]

JULIUS CAESAR 102?–44 BC

6 *Gallia est omnis divisa in partes tres.* – The whole of Gaul is divided into three parts. [*De Bello Gallico*, I. i]

7 *Iacta alea est.* – The die is cast. [(At the crossing of the Rubicon) Suetonius, *Divus Julius*, 32]

8 *Veni, vidi, vici.* – I came, I saw, I conquered. [37. 2]

9 Caesar's wife must be above suspicion. [Traditional, based on Plutarch's *Life of Julius Caesar*, x. 6]

10 *Et tu, Brute?* – You also, Brutus? [Alleged dying words, for which there is no authority]

PEDRO CALDERÓN DE LA BARCA 1600–1681

11 *Pues el delito mayor / del hombre es haber nacido.* – For man's greatest crime is to have been born. [*La Vida es Sueño*, I]

12 *Pues veo estando dormido / que sueñe estando despierto.* – For I see now that I am asleep that I dream when I am awake. [II]

13 *Que aún en sueños / no se pierde el hacer bien.* – For even in dreams a good deed is not lost.

CALIGULA 12–41

14 *Utinam populus Romanus unam cervicem haberet!* – I wish the Roman people had only one neck! [Suetonius, *Caligula*, 30]

C. S. CALVERLEY 1831–1884

15 The auld wife sat at her ivied door, / (*Butter and eggs and a pound of cheese*) / A thing she had frequently done before; / And her spectacles lay on her aproned knees. [*Ballad*]

16 And this song is considered a perfect gem, / And as to the meaning, it's what you please.

17 O Beer! O Hodgson, Guinness, Allsop, Bass! / Names that should be on every infant's tongue! [*Beer*]

18 I cannot sing the old songs now! / It is not that I deem them low; / 'Tis that I can't remember how / They go. [*Changed*]

19 You see this pebble-stone? It's a thing I bought / Of a bit of a chit of a boy i' the mid o' the day – / I like to dock the smaller parts-o'-speech, / As we curtail the already cur-tail'd cur. [*The Cock and the Bull*]

20 Complete with hat and gloves, / One on and one a-dangle i' my hand, / And ombrifuge (Lord love you!), case o' rain. / I flopp'd forth, 'sbuddikins! on my own ten toes.

1 The boy, a bare-legged beggarly son of a gun.

2 Get out, you blazing ass! / Gabble o' the goose. Don't bugaboo-baby *me*!

3 Life is with such all beer and skittles; / They are not difficult to please / About their victuals. [*Contentment*]

4 Grinder, who serenely grindest / At my door the Hundredth Psalm. [*Lines on hearing the Organ*]

5 Meaning, however, is no great matter. [*Lovers, and a Reflection*]

6 I must mention again it was gorgeous weather, / Rhymes are so scarce in this world of ours.

7 Thou who, when fears attack, / Bidst them avaunt, and Black / Care, at the horseman's back / Perching, unseatest; / Sweet, when the morn is gray; / Sweet when they've cleared away / Lunch; and at close of day / Possibly sweetest. [*Ode to Tobacco*]

8 Manifold / Stories, I know, are told, / Not to thy credit.

9 How they who use fusees / All grow by slow degrees / Brainless as chimpanzees, / Meagre as lizards; / Go mad, and beat their wives; / Plunge (after shocking lives) / Razors and carving knives / Into their gizzards.

10 Cats may have had their goose / Cooked by tobacco-juice; / Still why deny its use / Thoughtfully taken?

11 Yet it is better to drop thy friends, O my daughter, than to drop thy 'H.s'. [*Proverbial Philosophy*, 'Of Friendship']

12 Study first Propriety: for she is indeed the Pole-star. ['Of Propriety']

13 Read not Milton, for he is dry; nor Shakespeare, for he wrote of common life. ['Of Reading']

14 Eugene Aram, though a thief, a liar, and a murderer, / Yet, being intellectual, was amongst the noblest of mankind.

BARON DE CAMBRONNE 1770–1842

15 *La Garde meurt, mais ne se rend pas.* – The Guards die, but do not surrender. [When called on to surrender at Waterloo. Attr. to Cambronne but always disclaimed by him. He insisted that he just said '*Merde*' ('Shit'). Elsewhere attr. to Col. Michel]

WILLIAM CAMDEN 1551–1623

16 Betwixt the stirrup and the ground / Mercy I asked, mercy I found. [*Epitaph for a Man killed by falling from his Horse*]

SIMON CAMERON 1799–1889

17 An honest politician is one who, when he is bought, will stay bought. [In conversation, *c.* 1860]

JANE MONTGOMERY CAMPBELL 1817–1878

18 We plough the fields, and scatter / The good seed on the land, / But it is fed and watered / By God's Almighty Hand.

He sends the snow in winter, / The warmth to swell the grain, / The breezes and the sunshine, / And soft refreshing rain. [Hymn]

19 He paints the wayside flower, / He lights the evening star.

MRS PATRICK CAMPBELL 1865–1940

20 It doesn't matter what you do in the bedroom as long as you don't do it in the street and frighten the horses. [Quoted in Daphne Fielding, *The Duchess of Jermyn Street*, Ch. 2]

21 Marriage is the result of the longing for the deep, deep peace of the double-bed after the hurly-burly of the chaise-longue. [Quoted in A. Woollcott, *While Rome Burns*, 'the First Mrs Tanqueray']

ROY CAMPBELL 1902–1957

22 Or like a poet woo the moon, / Riding an arm-chair for my steed, / And with a flashing pen harpoon / Terrific metaphors of speed. [*The Festivals of Flight*]

23 You praise the firm restraint with which they write – / I'm with you there, of course: / They use the snaffle and the bit all right, / But where's the bloody horse? [*On Some South African Novelists*]

THOMAS CAMPBELL 1777–1844

24 Of Nelson and the North / Sing the glorious

day's renown, / When to battle fierce came forth / All the might of Denmark's crown, / And her arms along the deep proudly shone. [*Battle of the Baltic*]

1 There was silence deep as death, / And the boldest held his breath / For a time.

2 Ye are brothers, ye are men, / And we conquer but to save.

3 Spare, woodman, spare the beechen tree. [*The Beech-Tree's Petition*]

4 Tomorrow let us do or die! [*Gertrude of Wyoming*, Pt III. 37]

5 And wherever I went was my poor dog Tray. [*The Harper*]

6 On Linden, when the sun was low, / All bloodless lay the untrodden snow, / And dark as winter was the flow / Of Iser, rolling rapidly. [*Hohenlinden*]

7 The combat deepens. On, ye brave, / Who rush to glory, or the grave! / Wave, Munich! all thy banners wave, / And charge with all thy chivalry!

8 Lochiel, Lochiel! beware of the day / When the Lowlands shall meet thee in battle array! [*Lochiel's Warning*]

9 A chieftain to the Highlands bound / Cries, 'Boatman, do not tarry! / And I'll give thee a silver pound / To row us o'er the ferry.' [*Lord Ullin's Daughter*]

10 O, I'm the chief of Ulva's isle, / And this Lord Ullin's daughter.

11 I'll meet the raging of the skies, / But not an angry father.

12 The waters wild went o'er his child, / And he was left lamenting.

13 'Tis distance lends enchantment to the view, / And robes the mountain in its azure hue. [*Pleasures of Hope*, 1. 7]

14 The proud, the cold untroubled heart of stone, / That never mused on sorrow but its own. [185]

15 Hope, for a season, bade the world farewell, / And Freedom shrieked – as Kosciusko fell! [381]

16 And muse on Nature with a poet's eye. [II. 98]

17 What though my wingèd hours of bliss have been, / Like angel-visits, few and far between? [377]

18 Our bugles sang truce – for the night-cloud had lowered, / And the sentinel stars set their watch in the sky. [*The Soldier's Dream*]

19 Star that bringest home the bee, / And settest the weary labourer free! [*Song to the Evening Star*]

20 Ye Mariners of England / That guard our native seas, / Whose flag has braved, a thousand years, / The battle and the breeze. [*Ye Mariners of England*]

21 While the battle rages loud and long, / And the stormy winds do blow.

22 Britannia needs no bulwarks, / No towers along the steep; / Her march is o'er the mountain waves, / Her home is on the deep.

23 Now Barabbas was a publisher. [Often also attr. to Byron]

THOMAS CAMPION 1567–1620

24 Follow thy fair sun, unhappy shadow. [*Follow Thy Fair Sun*]

25 Follow your saint, follow with accents sweet; / Haste you, sad notes, fall at her flying feet. [*Follow Your Saint*]

26 Rose-cheeked Laura, come; / Sing thou smoothly with thy beauty's / Silent music, either other/ Sweetly gracing. [*Laura*]

27 Good thoughts his only friends, / His wealth a well-spent age, / The earth his sober inn / And quiet pilgrimage. [*The Man of Life Upright*]

28 Never weather-beaten sail more willing bent to shore, / Never tired pilgrim's limbs affected slumber more. [*Never Weather-beaten Sail*]

29 The Summer hath his joys, / And Winter his delights. / Though Love and all his pleasures are but toys, / They shorten tedious nights. [*Now Winter Nights Enlarge*]

30 There is a garden in her face, / Where roses and white lilies grow; / A heavenly paradise is that place, / Wherein all pleasant fruits do flow. / There cherries grow which none may buy, / Till 'Cherry-ripe' themselves do cry. [*There is a Garden in her Face*]

31 When thou must home to shades of under-ground, / And there arrived, a new admirèd guest, / The beauteous spirits do engirt thee round, / White Iope, blithe Helen, and the rest. [*When Thou Must Home*]

ALBERT CAMUS 1913–1960

1 I am well aware that an addiction to silk underwear does not necessarily imply that one's feet are dirty. None the less, style, like sheer silk, too often hides eczema. [*The Fall*]

2 A single sentence will suffice for modern man: he fornicated and read the papers.

3 How many crimes committed merely because their authors could not endure being wrong!

4 You know what charm is: a way of getting the answer yes without having asked any clear question.

5 Don't wait for the Last Judgement. It takes place every day.

6 Too many people have decided to do without generosity in order to practise charity.

7 The absurd is sin without God. [*The Myth of Sisyphus*, 'Absurd Walls', trans. J. O'Brien]

8 The struggle itself towards the heights is enough to fill a man's heart. One must imagine Sisyphus happy. [Title essay]

9 An intellectual is someone whose mind watches itself. [*Notebooks, 1935–42*]

10 What is a rebel? A man who says no. [*The Rebel*, Ch. 1]

GEORGE CANNING 1770–1827

11 Needy Knife-grinder! whither are you going? / Rough is the road, your wheel is out of order – / Bleak blows the blast; – your hat has got a hole in't. / So have your breeches. [*The Friend of Humanity and the Knife-Grinder*]

12 Story! God bless you! I have none to tell, Sir.

13 *I* give thee sixpence! I will see thee damned first – / Wretch! whom no sense of wrongs can rouse to vengeance; / Sordid, unfeeling, reprobate, degraded, / Spiritless outcast!

14 A steady patriot of the world alone, / The friend of every country but his own. [*New Morality*, 113]

15 And finds, with keen discriminating sight, / Black's not so black; – nor white so very white. [199]

16 But of all plagues, good Heaven, thy wrath can send, / Save me, oh, save me, from the candid friend! [209]

17 Pitt is to Addington / As London is to Paddington. [*The Oracle*]

18 Here's to the Pilot that weathered the storm. [(Of William Pitt) *The Pilot*]

19 Whene'er with haggard eyes I view / This Dungeon, that I'm rotting in, / I think of those Companions true / Who studied with me in the U– / –NIVERSITY OF GOTTINGEN, – / –NIVERSITY OF GOTTINGEN. [*Song*]

20 In matters of commerce the fault of the Dutch / Is offering too little and asking too much. / The French are with equal advantage content, / So we clap on Dutch bottoms just twenty per cent. [Dispatch to British Ambassador at The Hague, 31 Jan. 1826]

21 I called the New World into existence, to redress the balance of the Old. [Speech, 12 Dec.]

HUGHIE CANNON 1877–1912

22 Won't you come home, Bill Bailey, won't you come home? [Song: *Won't You Come Home, Bill Bailey?*]

JOHN CAPLES 1900–

23 They laughed when I sat down at the piano. But when I started to play! [Advertisement for US school of music]

PRINCE FRANCESCO CARACCIOLO 1752–1799

24 There are in England sixty different religious sects, but only one sauce. [Attr.]

THOMAS CAREW 1595?–1639

25 He that loves a rosy cheek, / Or a coral lip admires, / Or, from star-like eyes, doth seek / Fuel to maintain his fires; / As old Time makes these decay, / So his flames must waste away. [*Disdain Returned*]

26 Here lies a King that ruled, as he thought fit, / The universal monarchy of wit. [*Elegy on the Death of Dr Donne*]

27 Good to the poor, to kindred dear, / To servants kind, to friendship clear, / To nothing but herself severe. [*Inscription on the Tomb of Lady Mary Wentworth*]

28 Give me more love or more disdain; / The torrid or the frozen zone. [*Mediocrity in Love Rejected*]

29 Ask me no more where Jove bestows, /

When June is past, the fading rose; / For in your beauty's orient deep / These flowers, as in their causes, sleep. [Song: *Ask me no more*]

1 Then fly betimes, for only they / Conquer Love that run away. [Song: *Conquest by Flight*]

HENRY CAREY 1693?–1743

2 Go call a coach, and let a coach be call'd; / And let the man who calls it be the caller; / And in his calling let him nothing call / But Coach, Coach, Coach! O for a Coach, Ye Gods! [*Chrononhotonthologos*, II. 4]

3 Ha! Dead! Impossible! It cannot be! / I'd not believe it though himself should swear it.

4 God save our gracious king! / Long live our noble king! / God save the king! [*God save the King*]

5 Confound their politics, / Frustrate their knavish tricks.

6 Of all the girls that are so smart / There's none like pretty Sally, / She is the darling of my heart, / And she lives in our alley. [*Sally in our Alley*]

7 Of all the days that's in the week / I dearly love but one day – / And that's the day that comes betwixt / A Saturday and Monday.

JANE WELSH CARLYLE 1801–1866

8 When one has been threatened with a great injustice, one accepts a smaller as a favour. [*Journal*, 21 Nov. 1855]

THOMAS CARLYLE 1795–1881

9 A poet without love were a physical and metaphysical impossibility. [*Critical and Miscellaneous Essays*, 'Burns']

10 A witty statesman said, you might prove anything by figures. ['Chartism', Ch. 2]

11 In epochs when cash payment has become the sole nexus of man to man. [6]

12 All reform except a moral one will prove unavailing. ['Corn Law Rhymes']

13 The foul sluggard's comfort: 'It will last my time'. ['Count Cagliostro. Flight Last']

14 Thou wretched fraction, wilt thou be the ninth part even of a tailor? ['Doctor Francia']

15 This Mirabeau's work, then, is done. He sleeps with the primeval giants. He has gone over to the majority: *Abiit ad plures*. [(This last phrase quotes 308:8) 'Mirabeau']

16 History is the essence of innumerable biographies. ['On History']

17 A well-written Life is almost as rare as a well-spent one. ['Richter']

18 Poetry and Religion (and it is really worth knowing) are 'a product of the smaller intestines'. ['Signs of the Times']

19 Silence is deep as Eternity; speech is shallow as Time. ['Sir Walter Scott']

20 To the very last, he [Napoleon] had a kind of idea; that, namely, of *La carrière ouverte aux talents*, The tools to him that can handle them.

21 The three great elements of modern civilization, Gunpowder, Printing, and the Protestant Religion. ['The State of German Literature']

22 Literary men are . . . a perpetual priesthood.

23 Genius (which means transcendent capacity of taking trouble, first of all). [*Frederick the Great*, Bk iv. Ch. 3]

24 Happy the people whose annals are blank in history books! [xvi. 1]

25 France was long a despotism tempered by epigrams. [*French Revolution*, Pt I. Bk i. Ch. 1]

26 To a shower of gold most things are penetrable. [I. iii. 7]

27 A whiff of grapeshot. [I. v. 3]

28 The gospel according to Jean Jacques. [(Rousseau) II. i. 6]

29 The seagreen Incorruptible. [(Robespierre) iv. 4]

30 Worship is transcendent wonder. [*Heroes and Hero-Worship*, i, 'The Hero as Divinity']

31 No great man lives in vain. The history of the world is but the biography of great men.

32 The true University of these days is a collection of books. [v. 'The Hero as Man of Letters']

33 Burke said that there were Three Estates in Parliament; but, in the Reporters' Gallery yonder, there sat a *Fourth Estate*, more important far than they all. [See also 262:6]

34 For one man that can stand prosperity, there are a hundred that will stand adversity.

35 Respectable Professors of the Dismal Science. [(Political Economy) *Latter Day Pamphlets*, 1, 'The Present Time']

36 A Parliament speaking through reporters to Buncombe and the twenty-seven millions mostly fools. [6, 'Parliaments']

1 A healthy hatred of scoundrels. [12]

2 Transcendental moonshine. [*Life of John Sterling*, Pt I. Ch. 15]

3 Blessed is he who has found his work; let him ask no other blessedness. [*Past and Present*, Bk i. 11]

4 Captains of Industry. [iv. 4, title]

5 Work is the grand cure of all the maladies and miseries that ever beset mankind. [Rectorial Address at Edinburgh University, 2 Apr. 1886]

6 I never heard tell of any clever man that came of entirely stupid people.

7 No man who has once heartily and wholly laughed can be altogether irreclaimably bad. [*Sartor Resartus*, Bk i. Ch. 4]

8 Man is a tool-using animal ... Without tools he is nothing, with tools he is all. [5]

9 Be not the slave of Words. [8]

10 Sarcasm I now see to be, in general, the language of the devil. [ii. 4]

11 The everlasting No. [7, title]

12 Man's unhappiness, as I construe, comes of his greatness; it is because there is an Infinite in him, which with all his cunning he cannot quite bury under the Finite. [9]

13 Close thy Byron; open thy Goethe.

14 'Do the duty that lies nearest thee', which thou knowest to be a duty! Thy second duty will already have become clearer.

15 Produce! Produce! Were it but the pitifullest infinitesimal fraction of a product, produce it in God's name! 'Tis the utmost thou hast in thee: out with it, then.

16 The Public is an old woman. Let her maunder and mumble. [*Journal*, 1835]

17 It were better to perish than to continue schoolmastering. [Remark, quoted in D. A. Wilson, *Carlyle till Marriage*]

18 If Jesus Christ were to come to-day, people wouldn't even crucify him. They would ask him to dinner, and hear what he had to say, and make fun of it. [Remark, quoted in D. A. Wilson, *Carlyle at his Zenith*]

19 I don't pretend to understand the Universe – it's a great deal bigger than I am ... People ought to be modester. [Remark to William Allingham, quoted in D. A. Wilson and D. Wilson McArthur, *Carlyle in Old Age*]

20 Macaulay is well for a while, but one wouldn't *live* under Niagara. [Remark, quoted in R. M. Milnes, *Notebook*]

21 There is only one post fit for you, and that is the office of perpetual president of the Heaven and Hell Amalgamation Society. [Remark to Lord Houghton, quoted in T. E. Wemyss Reid, *Life of Lord Houghton*]

22 MARGARET FULLER: I accept the universe. CARLYLE: Gad! she'd better! [Attr.]

DALE CARNEGIE 1888–1955

23 How to Win Friends and Influence People. [Title of book]

JULIA CARNEY 1823–1908

24 Little drops of water, little grains of sand, / Make the mighty ocean, and the pleasant land. / So the little minutes, humble though they be, / Make the mighty ages of eternity. [*Little Things*. Wrongly attr. to various other writers]

25 Little deeds of kindness, little words of love, / Help to make earth happy, like the heaven above. / [Later reading of second line: 'Make this earth an Eden']

J. E. CARPENTER 1813–1885

26 What are the wild waves saying / Sister, the whole day long. / That ever amid our playing, / I hear but their low lone song? [*What are the Wild Waves Saying?*]

LEWIS CARROLL [CHARLES DODGSON] 1832–1898

27 'What is the use of a book,' thought Alice, 'without pictures or conversations?' [*Alice in Wonderland*, Ch. 1]

28 Do cats eat bats? – Do bats eat cats?

29 Curiouser and curiouser! [2]

30 How doth the little crocodile / Improve his shining tail, / And pour the waters of the Nile, / On every golden scale! [See 447:12]

31 'I'll be judge, I'll be jury,' said cunning old Fury: / 'I'll try the whole cause, and condemn you to death.' [3]

32 The Duchess! The Duchess! Oh my dear paws! Oh my fur and whiskers! [4]

33 'You are old, Father William,' the young man said, / 'And your hair has become very white; / And yet you incessantly stand on your head – / Do you think at your age, it is right?'

'In my youth,' Father William replied to his son, / 'I feared it might injure the brain; / But now that I'm perfectly sure I have none, / Why, I do it again and again.' [5 (See 401:22)]

1 Do you think I can listen all day to such stuff? / Be off, or I'll kick you downstairs!

2 'If everybody minded their own business,' the Duchess said in a hoarse growl, 'the world would go round a deal faster than it does.' [6]

3 Speak roughly to your little boy, / And beat him when he sneezes: / He only does it to annoy, / Because he knows it teases.

4 It [the Cheshire Cat] vanished quite slowly, beginning with the end of the tail, and ending with the grin, which remained some time after the rest of it had gone.

5 'Then you should say what you mean,' the March Hare went on.

'I do,' Alice hastily replied; 'at least – at least I mean what I say – that's the same thing, you know.' [7]

6 It was the *best* butter.

7 Twinkle, twinkle, little bat! / How I wonder what you're at! / Up above the world you fly, / Like a tea-tray in the sky. [See 415:6]

8 They lived at the bottom of a well – ... They lived on treacle.

9 Off with her head! [8]

10 Everything's got a moral, if only you can find it. [9]

11 Take care of the sense, and the sounds will take care of themselves.

12 That's nothing to what I could say if I chose.

13 We called him Tortoise because he taught us.

14 'Reeling and Writhing, of course, to begin with,' the Mock Turtle replied; 'and then the different branches of Arithmetic – Ambition, Distraction, Uglification, and Derision.'

15 *He* taught us Drawling, Stretching and Fainting in Coils.

16 'That's the reason they're called lessons,' the Gryphon remarked: 'because they lessen from day to day.'

17 'Will you walk a little faster?' said a whiting to a snail, / 'There's a porpoise close behind us, and he's treading on my tail.' [10]

18 Will you, won't you, will you, won't you, will you join the dance?

19 The further off from England, the nearer is to France – / Then turn not pale, beloved snail, but come and join the dance.

20 Soup of the evening, beautiful Soup!

21 'Begin at the beginning,' the King said, gravely, 'and go on till you come to the end; then stop.' [12]

22 They told me you had been to her, / And mentioned me to him: / She gave me a good character, / But said I could not swim.

23 Sentence first – verdict afterwards.

24 'Twas brillig, and the slithy toves / Did gyre and gimble in the wabe; / All mimsy were the borogoves, / And the mome raths outgrabe. [*Through the Looking Glass*, Ch. 1]

25 Beware the Jabberwock, my son! / The jaws that bite, the claws that catch! / Beware the Jubjub bird, and shun / The frumious Bandersnatch!

26 One, two! One, two! and through and through / The vorpal blade went snicker-snack! / He left it dead, and with its head / He went galumphing back.

27 'And hast thou slain the Jabberwock? / Come to my arms, my beamish boy! / O frabjous day: Callooh! Callay!' / He chortled in his joy.

28 Curtsey while you're thinking what to say. It saves time. [2]

29 Now, *here*, you see, it takes all the running *you* can do, to stay in the same place. If you want to get somewhere else, you must run at least twice as fast as that!

30 'If you think we're wax-works,' he said, 'you ought to pay, you know. Wax-works weren't made to be looked at for nothing. Nohow!' [4]

31 Tweedledum and Tweedledee / Agreed to have a battle; / For Tweedledum said Tweedledee / Had spoiled his nice new rattle.

32 'Contrariwise,' continued Tweedledee, 'if it was so, it might be; and if it were so, it would be: but as it isn't, it ain't. That's logic.'

33 The sun was shining on the sea, / Shining with all his might: / He did his very best to make / The billows smooth and bright – / And this was odd because it was / The middle of the night. [4]

1 'It's very rude of him,' she said, / 'To come and spoil the fun!'

2 You could not see a cloud, because / No cloud was in the sky: / No birds were flying overhead – / There were no birds to fly.

3 The Walrus and the Carpenter / Were walking close at hand; / They wept like anything to see / Such quantities of sand: / 'If this were only cleared away,' / They said, 'it *would* be grand!'

'If seven maids with seven mops / Swept it for half a year, / Do you suppose,' the Walrus said, / 'That they could get it clear?' / 'I doubt it,' said the Carpenter, / And shed a bitter tear.

4 And thick and fast they came at last, / And more, and more, and more.

5 'The time has come,' the Walrus said, / 'To talk of many things: / Of shoes – and ships – and sealing-wax – / Of cabbages – and kings – / Of why the sea is boiling hot – / And whether pigs have wings.'

6 'The night is fine,' the Walrus said. / 'Do you admire the view?'

7 The Carpenter said nothing but, / 'The butter's spread too thick!'

8 'I weep for you,' the Walrus said: / 'I deeply sympathize.' / With sobs and tears he sorted out / Those of the largest size, / Holding his pocket-handkerchief / Before his streaming eyes.

9 But answer came there none – / And this was scarcely odd because / They'd eaten every one.

10 The rule is, jam to-morrow and jam yesterday – but never jam to-day. [5]

11 They gave it me . . . for an un-birthday present. [6]

12 The little fishes of the sea, / They sent an answer back to me. / The little fishes' answer was / 'We cannot do it, Sir, because –'

13 I said it very loud and clear; / I went and shouted in his ear.

14 He's an Anglo-Saxon Messenger – and those are Anglo-Saxon attitudes. [7]

15 The other Messenger's called Hatta. I must have *two*, you know – to come and go. One to come, and one to go.

16 It's as large as life, and twice as natural!

17 It's my own invention. [8]

18 But I was thinking of a plan / To dye one's whiskers green.

19 Or madly squeeze a right-hand foot / Into a left-hand shoe.

20 No admittance till the week after next. [9]

21 What I tell you three times is true. [*The Hunting of the Snark*, Fit 1]

22 He would answer to 'Hi!' or to any loud cry, / Such as 'Fry me!' or 'Fritter my wig!' / To 'What-you-may-call-um!' or 'What-was-his-name!' / But especially 'Thing-um-a-jig!'

23 His intimate friends called him 'Candle-ends', / And his enemies 'Toasted-cheese'.

24 Then the bowsprit got mixed with the rudder sometimes. [2]

25 You may seek it with thimbles – and seek it with care; / You may hunt it with forks and hope; / You may threaten its life with a railway-share; / You may charm it with smiles and soap. [3]

26 I said it in Hebrew – I said it in Dutch – / I said it in German and Greek; / But I wholly forgot (and it vexes me much) / That English is what you speak! [4]

27 In the midst of the word he was trying to say / In the midst of his laughter and glee, / He had softly and suddenly vanished away – / For the Snark *was* a Boojum, you see. [8]

28 He thought he saw an Elephant, / That practised on a fife: / He looked again, and found it was / A letter from his wife. / 'At length I realize,' he said, / 'The bitterness of life!' [*Sylvie and Bruno*, Ch. 5]

29 He thought he saw a Banker's Clerk / Descending from the bus: / He looked again, and found it was / A Hippopotamus. / 'If this should stay to dine,' he said, / 'There won't be much for us!' [7]

WILLIAM LORENZO CARTER 1813–1860

30 'O daughter, dear,' her mother said, 'this blanket round you fold, / 'Tis such a dreadful night abroad, you will catch your death of cold.' [*Young* (or *Fair*) *Charlotte*]

31 Young ladies, think of this fair girl and always dress aright, / And never venture thinly clad on such a wintry night.

JOYCE CARY 1888–1957

32 The only good government . . . is a bad one in a hell of a fright. [*The Horse's Mouth*, Ch. 32]

PHOEBE CARY 1824–1871

1 And though hard be the task, / 'Keep a stiff upper lip'. [*Keep a Stiff Upper Lip*]

PHILA HENRIETTA CASE *fl.* 1864

2 Oh! why does the wind blow upon me so wild? – Is it because I'm nobody's child? [*Nobody's Child*]

HARRY CASTLING 19 Cent.

3 Let's all go down the Strand. [Title of song]

EDWARD CASWALL 1814–1878

4 Days and moments quickly flying, / Blend the living with the dead; / Soon will you and I be lying / Each within our narrow bed. [Hymn]

5 My God, I love Thee; not because / I hope for heaven thereby. [Hymn]

6 Sleep, Holy Babe, / Upon thy mother's breast! [Hymn]

ST CATHERINE OF SIENA 1347–1380

7 All the way to heaven is *heaven.* [Quoted in the Weekend *Guardian,* 1–2 July 1989]

CATO THE ELDER 234–149 BC

8 *Delenda est Carthago.* – Carthage must be destroyed. [Plutarch, *Life of Cato*]

CATULLUS 87–54? BC

9 *Lugete, o Veneres Cupidinesque, / Et quantum est hominum venustiorum. / Passer mortuus est meae puellae, / Passer deliciae meae puellae, /Quem plus illa oculis suis amabat.* – Mourn, O Graces and Loves, and all men whom the Graces love. My mistress's sparrow is dead, my mistress's pet, which she loved more than her very eyes. [*Carmina*, 3]

10 *Qui nunc it per iter tenebricosum / Illuc, unde negant redire quemquam.* – Now he is treading that dark road to the place from which they say no one has ever returned.

11 *Vivamus, mea Lesbia, atque amemus, / Rumoresque senum severiorum /Omnes unius aestimemus assis. / Soles occidere et redire possunt: / Nobis cum semel occidit brevis lux, / Nox est perpetua una dormienda.* – Let us live, my Lesbia, and love, and not give a farthing for the talk of censorious old men. Suns may set and rise again. As for us, when the brief light has once set, we must sleep one endless night. [5]

12 *Da mi basia mille, deinde centum, / Dein mille altera.* – Give me a thousand kisses, then a hundred, then a thousand more.

13 *Miser Catulle, desinas ineptire, / Et quod vides perisse perditum ducas.* – Poor Catullus, cease your folly and give up for lost what you see is lost. [8]

14 *Nam castum esse decet pium poetam / Ipsum, versiculos nihil necesse est.* – For the godly poet must be chaste himself, but there is no need for his verses to be so. [16]

15 *Paene insularum, Sirmio, insularumque / Ocelle.* – Sirmio, little eye of peninsulas and islands. [31]

16 *O quid solutis est beatius curis? / Cum mens onus reponit, ac peregrino / Labore fessi venimus larem ad nostrum, / Desideratoque acquiescimus lecto. / Hoc est, quod unum est pro laboribus tantis.* – O what is more blessed than to throw cares aside, as the mind puts down its burden and, weary with the labour of far journeys, we return home and rest on the couch that we longed for? This alone is worth all that labour.

17 *Nam risu inepto res ineptior nulla est.* – There is nothing sillier than a silly laugh. [39]

18 *Iam ver egelidos refert tepores, / Iam caeli furor aequinoctialis / Iucundis Zephyri silescit auris.* – Now Spring restores the balmy heat, now Zephyr's sweet breezes calm the rage of the equinoctial sky. [46]

19 *Gratias tibi maximas Catullus / Agit pessimus omnium poeta /Tanto pessimus omnium poeta / Quanto tu optimus omnium's patronus.* – Catullus, the worst of all poets, gives you his warmest thanks; he being as much the worst of all poets as you are the best of all patrons. [49]

20 *Vesper adest, iuvenes, consurgite: Vesper Olympo / Exspectata diu vix tandem lumina tollit.* – Rise up, lads, the evening is coming. The evening star is just raising his long-awaited light in heaven. [62]

21 *Ut flos in saeptis secretus nascitur hortis, / Ignotus pecori, nullo contusus aratro, / Quem mulcent aurae, firmat sol, educat imber; / Multi illum pueri, multae optavere puellae.* – As a flower springs up secretly in a fenced garden, known to no cattle, bruised by no plough, caressed by the winds, strengthened by the sun, and drawn

up by the shower, so many a boy and many a girl desire it.

1 *Sed mulier cupido quod dicit amanti / In vento et rapida scribere oportet aqua.* – But what a woman says to her desirous lover should be written in wind and swift-flowing water. [70]

2 *Siqua recordanti benefacta priora voluptas / Est homini.* – If a man can take pleasure in recalling the kindnesses he has done. [76]

3 *Difficile est longum subito deponere amorem. / Difficile est, verum hoc qua lubet efficias.* – It is difficult suddenly to put aside a long-standing love; it is difficult, but somehow you must do it. [85]

4 *O di, reddite mi hoc pro pietate mea.* – O gods, grant me this in return for my piety.

5 *Odi et amo: quare id faciam, fortasse requiris. / Nescio, sed fieri sentio et excrucior.* – I hate and love. You may ask why I do so. I do not know, but I feel it and am in torment. [85]

6 *Nunc tamen interea haec prisco quae more parentum / Tradita sunt tristi munere ad inferias, / Accipe fraterno multum manantia fletu. / Atque in perpetuum, frater, ave atque vale.* – But now meanwhile take these offerings, according to the old custom of our fathers, the tribute of sorrow, for a funeral sacrifice. Take them, wet with many a tear of your brother's. And for ever, Brother, hail and farewell. [101]

CHARLES CAUSLEY 1917–

7 Ears like bombs and teeth like splinters: / A blitz of a boy is Timothy Winters. [*Timothy Winters*]

CONSTANTINE CAVAFY 1863–1933

8 And now, what will become of us without barbarians? Those people were a kind of solution. [*Waiting for the Barbarians*]

EDITH CAVELL 1865–1915

9 I realize that patriotism is not enough. I must have no hatred or bitterness towards anyone. [Last words, 12 Oct. 1915]

MADISON JULIUS CAWEIN 1865–1914

10 An old Spanish saying is that 'a kiss without a moustache is like an egg without salt'. [*Nature-Notes*]

THOMAS OF CELANO *c.* 1190–1260

11 *Dies irae, dies illa / Solvet saeclum in favilla, / Teste David cum Sibylla.* – Day of wrath and doom impending, / David's word with Sibyl's blending, / Heaven and earth in ashes ending. [*Analecta Hymnica*, trans. Dr W. J. Irons in *The English Hymnal*]

SUSANNAH CENTLIVRE 1667?–1723

12 The real Simon Pure. [*A Bold Stroke for a Wife*, V. i]

MIGUEL CERVANTES 1547–1616

13 I swear by all the orders of chivalry in the world to pay you every single *real*, and perfumed into the bargain. [*Don Quixote*, Pt I. Ch. 4]

14 I know who I am, and I know too that I am capable of being not only the characters I have named, but all the Twelve Peers of France, and all the Nine Worthies as well. [5]

15 Wouldn't it be better to stay peacefully at home, and not roam about the world seeking better bread than is made of wheat, never considering that many go for wool and come back shorn? [7]

16 Take care, your worship, those things over there are not giants but windmills. [8]

17 I hate to keep things long in case they go mouldy from over-keeping. [17]

18 Didn't I tell you, Don Quixote, sir, to turn back, for they were not armies you were going to attack, but flocks of sheep? [18]

19 Wasn't it my father's son who got tossed in the blanket yesterday? [18]

20 The Knight of the Sad Countenance. [19]

21 Fear has many eyes and can see things underground. [20]

22 A leap over the hedge is better than good men's prayers. [21]

23 I have always heard, Sancho, that doing good to base fellows is like throwing water into the sea. [23]

24 Let them eat the lie and swallow it with their bread. Whether the two were lovers or no, they'll have accounted to God for it by now. I have my own fish to fry. I know nothing. I'm not one to pry into other people's lives. It's no good lying about the price; your purse always

knows better. What's more, I was born naked and naked I am now: I neither lose nor win. Suppose they were lovers, what's that to me? Plenty of people expect to find bacon where there's not so much as a hook to hang it on. Who can hedge in the cuckoo? [25]

1 A knight errant who turns mad for a reason deserves neither merit nor thanks. The thing is to do it without cause.

2 One shouldn't talk of halters in the hanged man's house.

3 She isn't a bad bit of goods, the Queen! I wish all the fleas in my bed were as good. [30]

4 In me the need to talk is a primary impulse, and I can't help saying right off what comes to my tongue.

5 If you don't believe me, you'll see it when the eggs are fried. [37]

6 Oh, sir, sir, there are more tricks done in the village than make a noise – saving her ladyship's presence. [46]

7 Every man's the son of his own deeds; and since I am a man I can become pope. [47]

8 Have you no mind to do what nobody can do for you? [48]

9 I've as large a soul as the next man, and as stout a body as the best of them, and I'd be as good a king of my estate as any other King. [50]

10 The sage left nothing in his ink-horn. [II. 3]

11 Without a governorship you came out of your mother's womb, without a governorship you've lived to this day, and without a governorship you'll go – or they'll take you – to the grave. [5]

12 Hunger is the best sauce in the world.

13 An honest woman and a broken leg are best at home, and for an honest girl a job of work's her holiday.

14 We cannot all be friars, and many are the ways by which God bears his chosen to heaven. [8]

15 Well, now, there's a remedy for everything except death. [10]

16 Never meddle with play-actors, for they're a favoured race. [11]

17 All the physicians and authors in the world could not give a clear account of his madness. He is mad in patches, full of lucid intervals. [18]

18 There are only two families in the world, my old grandmother used to say, the *Haves* and the *Have-nots*. [20]

19 If that should not be, cousin, I say: patience and shuffle the cards. [23]

20 'If I had a water thirst,' replied Sancho, 'there are wells on the road where I could have quenched it.' [24]

21 God bless the inventor of sleep, the cloak that covers all men's thoughts, the food that cures all hunger . . . the balancing weight that levels the shepherd with the king and the simple with the wise. [68]

JOSEPH CHAMBERLAIN 1836–1914

22 Provided that the City of London remains as it is at present, the clearing-house of the world. [Speech in London, 19 Jan. 1904]

23 Learn to think Imperially.

24 The day of small nations has long passed away. The day of Empires has come. [Speech at Birmingham, 12 May]

NEVILLE CHAMBERLAIN 1869–1940

25 In war, whichever side may call itself the victor, there are no winners, but all are losers. [Speech at Kettering, 3 July 1938]

26 How horrible, fantastic, incredible it is that we should be digging trenches and trying on gas-masks here because of a quarrel in a far-away country between people of whom we know nothing! [Radio broadcast of 27 Sept.]

27 I believe it is peace for our time . . . peace with honour. [Speech after Munich Agreement, 30 Sept. See also 143:10]

28 Whatever may be the reason – whether it was that Hitler thought he might get away with what he had got without fighting for it, or whether it was that after all the preparations were not sufficiently complete – however, one thing is certain: he missed the bus. [Speech to Conservative and Unionist Associations, 4 Apr. 1940]

CHARLES HADDON CHAMBERS
1860–1921

29 The long arm of coincidence. [*Captain Swift*, II]

NICOLAS CHAMFORT 1741–1794

1 *Quelqu'un disait d'un homme très personnel: il brûlerait votre maison pour se faire cuire deux œufs.* – Someone said of a very great egotist: 'He would burn your house down to cook himself a couple of eggs.' [*Caractères et anecdotes*]

2 *La plus perdue de toutes les journées est celle où l'on n'a pas ri.* – The most wasted of all days is that on which one has not laughed. [*Maximes et pensées*]

3 *L'amour, tel qu'il existe dans la société, n'est que l'échange de deux fantaisies et le contact de deux épidermes.* – Love, in present-day society, is just the exchange of two imaginary pictures, and the contact of one epidermis with another.

JOHN CHANDLER 1806–1876

4 Conquering kings their titles take / From the foes they captive make: / Jesu, by a nobler deed, / From the thousands He hath freed. [Hymn]

RAYMOND CHANDLER 1888–1959

5 She gave me a smile I could feel in my hip pocket. [*Farewell My Lovely*, Ch. 18]

6 Down these mean streets a man must go who is not himself mean. [*Pearls Are a Nuisance*, 'The Simple Art of Murder']

7 A city with no more personality than a paper cup. [(Of Los Angeles) *The Little Sister*, Ch. 26]

8 Any man who can write a page of living prose adds something to our life, and the man who can, as I can, is surely the last to resent someone who can do it even better. An artist cannot deny art, nor would he want to. If you believe in an ideal, you don't own it, it owns you. [Quoted in F. MacShane, *The Life of Raymond Chandler*]

9 If my books had been any worse, I should not have been invited to Hollywood, and if they had been any better, I should not have come. [Letter to Charles Morton, assoc. ed. of the *Atlantic Monthly*, 12 Dec. 1945]

10 Would you convey my compliments to the purist who reads your proofs and tell him or her that I write in a sort of broken-down patois which is something like the way a Swiss waiter talks, and that when I split an infinitive, God damn it, I split it so it will stay split. [Letter to Edward Weeks, ed. of the *Atlantic Monthly*, 18 Jan. 1947]

SIR CHARLES CHAPLIN 1889–1977

11 Life is a tragedy when seen in close-up, but a comedy in long-shot. [Quoted in obituary, *Guardian*, 28 Dec. 1977]

GEORGE CHAPMAN 1559?–1634

12 An Englishman, / Being flattered, is a lamb; threatened, a lion. [*Alphonsus*, I. ii]

13 Give me a spirit that on this life's rough sea / Loves t'have his sails filled with a lusty wind, / Even till his sail-yards tremble, his masts crack, / And his rapt ship run on her side so low / That she drinks water, and her keel ploughs air. [*Byron's Conspiracy*, III. i]

14 We have watered our horses in Helicon. [*May-Day*, III. iii]

15 His naked Ulysses clad in eternal fiction. [*Odyssey of Homer*, Epistle Dedicatory]

16 And let a scholar all Earth's volumes carry, / He will be but a walking dictionary. [*Tears of Peace*, 266]

CHARLES I 1600–1649

17 Never make a defence of apology before you be accused. [Letter to Lord Wentworth, 3 Sept. 1636]

18 I see all the birds are flown. [In House of Commons, 4 Jan. 1642, when he arrived to arrest five members]

19 And therefore I tell you (and I pray God it be not laid to your charge) that I am the Martyr of the People. [Speech on the scaffold, 30 Jan. 1649]

CHARLES II 1630–1685

20 Better than a play! [On the Lords' debate on Lord Ross's Divorce Bill, 1670]

21 This is very true: for my words are my own, and my actions are my ministers'. [Reply to Lord Rochester's premature epitaph on him – see 328:7]

22 Not a religion for gentlemen. [(Presbyterianism) Burnet, *History of My Own Time*, Vol. i. Bk ii. Ch. 2]

23 Let not poor Nelly starve. [(Of Nell Gwynn, on his deathbed, 5 Feb. 1685, to his brother James) 17]

24 Brother, I am too old to go again to my travels. [Hume, *History of Great Britain*, Vol. ii. Ch. 7]

1 He had been, he said, an unconscionable time dying; but he hoped that they would excuse it. [T. B. Macaulay, *History of England*, Vol. i. Ch. 4]

EMPEROR CHARLES V 1500–1558

2 I speak Spanish to God, Italian to women, French to men, and German to my horse. [Attr.]

SALMON PORTLAND CHASE 1808–1873

3 The only way to resumption is to resume. [Letter to Horace Greely, 17 May 1866]

FRANÇOIS-RENÉ DE CHATEAUBRIAND 1768–1848

4 An original writer is not one who imitates nobody, but one whom nobody can imitate. [*Génie du Christianisme*]

EARL OF CHATHAM *see* PITT, WILLIAM

THOMAS CHATTERTON 1752–1770

5 O! synge untoe mie roundelaie, / O! droppe the brynie teare wythe mee, / Daunce ne moe atte hallie daie, / Lycke a reynynge ryver bee; / Mie love ys dedde, / Gon to hys death-bedde, / Al under the wyllowe-tree. [*Mynstrelles Songe*]

GEOFFREY CHAUCER 1340?–1400

6 Flee fro the press, and dwelle with sothfast-nesse ... / Forth, pilgrim, forth! Forth, beste, out of thy stal! / Know thy contree, look up, thank God of al! / Hold the hye wey, and lat thy gost thee lede; / And trouthe shall delivere, hit is no drede. [*Balade de Bon Conseyl*]

7 Whan that Aprille with his shoures soote / The droghte of March hath perced to the roote. [*Canterbury Tales*, 'Prologue', 1]

8 And smale fowles maken melodye, / That slepen al the night with open yë / (So priketh hem nature in hir corages): / Than longen folk to goon on pilgrimages. [9]

9 And of his port as meke as is a mayde. [69]

10 He was a verray, parfit gentil knight. [72]

11 He was as fresh as is the month of May. [92]

12 Ful wel she song the service divyne, / En-tuned in hir nose ful semely; / And Frensh she spak ful faire and fetisly, / After the scole of Stratford atte Bowe, / For Frensh of Paris was to hir unknowe. [122]

13 Ther was first write a crowned A, / And after, '*Amor vincit omnia*'. [161 (see also 441:21)]

14 He yaf not of that text a pulled hen, / That seith that hunters been nat holy men. [177]

15 His palfrey was as broun as is a berye. [207]

16 He knew the tavernes wel in every toun. [240]

17 A Clerk ther was of Oxenford also. [285]

18 As lene was his hors as is a rake. [287]

19 For him was lever have at his beddes heed / Twenty bokes, clad in blak or reed, / Of Aristotle and his philosophye, / Than robes riche, or fithele, or gay sautrye. / But al be that he was a philosophre, / Yet hadde he put litel gold in cofre. [293]

20 And gladly wolde he lerne and gladly teche. [308]

21 No-wher so bisy a man as he ther nas, / And yet he semed bisier than he was. [321]

22 It snewed in his hous of mete and drinke. [345]

23 His studie was but litel on the Bible. [438]

24 She was a worthy womman al hir lyve: / Housbondes at chirche-dore she hadde fyve, / Withouten other companye in youthe. [459]

25 This noble ensample to his sheep he yaf, / That first he wroghte, and afterward he taughte. [496]

26 If gold ruste, what shal iren do? [500]

27 But Cristes lore and his apostles twelve, / He taughte, first he folwed it himselve. [527]

28 That hadde a fyr-reed cherubinnes face. [624]

29 His walet lay biforn him in his lappe, / Bretful of pardoun comen from Rome al hoot. [686]

30 Love wol nat ben constreyned by maistrye; / Whan maistrie comth, the God of Love anon / Beteth his winges, and farewel! he is gon! ['The Franklin's Tale', 36]

31 Trouthe is the hyeste thing that man may kepe. [751]

32 The carl spak oo thing, but he thoghte another. ['The Friar's Tale', 270]

1 And thefore, at the kinges court, my brother, / Ech man for him-self, ther is non other. ['The Knight's Tale', 323]

2 The bisy larke, messager of day. [633]

3 The smyler with the knyf under the cloke. [1141]

4 Up roos the sonne, and up roos Emelye. [1415]

5 What is this world? what asketh men to have? / Now with his love, now in his colde grave / Allone, withouten any companye. [1919]

6 This world nis but a thurghfare ful of wo, / And we been pilgrimes, passinge to and fro; / Deeth is an ende of every worldly sore. [1989]

7 'Tehee!' quod she, and clapte the window to. ['The Miller's Tale', 554]

8 Tragedie is to seyn a certeyn storie, / As olde bokes maken us memorie, / Of him that stood in greet prosperitee / And is y-fallen out of heigh degree / Into miserie, and endeth wrecchedly. ['The Monk's Prologue', 85]

9 Mordre wol out, that see we day by day. ['The Nun's Priest's Tale', 232]

10 She was as digne as water in a dich. ['The Reeve's Tale', 44]

11 The gretteste clerkes been noght the wysest men. [134]

12 So was hir joly whistle wel y-wet. [235]

13 Thou lokest as thou woldest finde an hare, / For ever upon the ground I see thee stare. ['Prologue to Sir Thopas', 6]

14 That in his owene grece I made him frye. ['The Wife of Bath's Prologue', 487]

15 And for to see, and eke for to be seye. [552]

16 A womman cast hir shame away, / Whan she cast of her smok. [782]

17 Wommen desyren to have sovereyntee / As wel over hir housbond as hir love. ['The Tale of the Wife of Bath', 182]

18 Whan that the month of May / Is comen, and that I here the foules singe, / And that the floures ginnen for to springe, / Farwel my book and my devocioun! [The Legend of Good Women, Prologue, 36 (second version)]

19 Of alle the floures in the mede, / Than love I most these floures whyte and rede, / Swiche as men callen daysies in our toun. [41]

20 And she was fair as is the rose in May. ['Legend of Cleopatra', 34]

21 The lyf so short, the craft so long to lerne, / Th' assay so hard, so sharp the conquering. [The Parliament of Fowls, 1]

22 Unknowe, unkist, and lost that is unsought. [Troilus and Criseyde, i. 809]

23 For I have seyne, of a ful misty morwe / Folwen ful ofte a mery someres day. [iii. 1060]

24 Right as an aspes leef she gan to quake. [1200]

25 For of fortunes sharp adversitee / The worst kinde of infortune is this, / A man to have ben in prosperitee, / And it remembren, whan it passed is. [1625]

26 Oon ere it herde, at the other out it wente. [iv. 434]

27 Paradys stood formed in hir yën. [v. 817]

28 Ye, farewel al the snow of ferne yere! [1176]

29 Th' entente is al, and nought the lettres space. [1630]

30 Go, litel book, go litel myn tragedie. [1786]

31 O moral Gower, this book I directe / To thee. [1856]

ANTON CHEKHOV 1860–1904

32 LIUBOV ANDREEVNA: Are you still a student?
TROFIMOV: I expect I shall be a student to the end of my days. [The Cherry Orchard, I]

33 I cannon off the cushion! I pot into the middle pocket. [II et passim]

34 MEDVIENKO: Why do you always wear black?
MASHA: I am in mourning for my life. I am unhappy. [The Seagull, I]

35 The time's come: there's a terrific thundercloud advancing upon us, a mighty storm is coming to freshen us up . . . It's going to blow away all this idleness and indifference, and prejudice against work . . . I'm going to work, and in twenty-five or thirty years' time every man and woman will be working. [Three Sisters, I]

36 If only we could go back to Moscow! Sell the house, finish with our life here, and go back to Moscow.

37 It seemed that the next minute they would discover a solution. Yet it was clear to both of them that the end was still far, far off, and that

the hardest and most complicated part was only just beginning. [*The Lady with the Dog*]

1 If you are afraid of loneliness, don't marry. [Quoted in Roger Hall, *Conjugal Rites*]

ANDREW CHERRY 1762–1812

2 The next day, / There she lay, / In the Bay of Biscay, O: [*The Bay of Biscay*]

CHARLIE CHESTER 1914–

3 Down in the jungle / Living in a tent, / Better than a prefab – / No rent! [From BBC Radio comedy series *Stand Easy*]

EARL OF CHESTERFIELD 1694–1773

4 Be wiser than other people if you can, but do not tell them so. [Letter to his son, 19 Nov. 1745]

5 An injury is much sooner forgotten than an insult. [9 Oct. 1746]

6 Courts and camps are the only places to learn the world in. [2 Oct. 1747]

7 Take the tone of the company you are in. [9 Oct.]

8 I knew once a very covetous, sordid fellow [perhaps William Lowndes], who used to say, 'Take care of the pence, for the pounds will take care of themselves.' [6 Nov.]

9 Advice is seldom welcome; and those who want it the most always want it the least. [29 Jan. 1748]

10 Sacrifice to the Graces. [9 Mar.]

11 I am sure that since I have had the full use of my reason, nobody has ever heard me laugh.

12 A man of sense only trifles with them [women], plays with them, humours and flatters them, as he does with a sprightly and forward child; but he neither consults them about, nor trusts them with, serious matters. [5 Sept.]

13 Due attention to the inside of books, and due contempt for the outside, is the proper relation between a man of sense and his books. [10 Jan. 1749]

14 Idleness is only the refuge of weak minds. [20 July]

15 Women are much more like each other than men: they have, in truth, but two passions, vanity and love; these are their universal characteristics. [19 Dec.]

16 Is it possible to love such a man? No. The utmost I can do for him is to consider him as a respectable Hottentot. [(Dr Johnson, or Lord Lyttelton) 28 Feb. 1751]

17 Every woman is infallibly to be gained by every sort of flattery, and every man by one sort or other. [16 Mar. 1752]

18 A chapter of accidents. [16 Feb. 1753]

19 Religion is by no means a proper subject of conversation in a mixed company. [Letter to his godson No. 112 (undated)]

20 Tyrawley and I have been dead these two years; but we don't choose to have it known. [Quoted in Boswell, *Life of Johnson*, 3 Apr. 1773]

21 He once exclaimed to Anstis, Garter King at Arms, 'You foolish man, you do not even know your own foolish business'. [Quoted in Jesse, *Memoirs of the Court of England*, Vol. ii]

22 Unlike my subject will I frame my song, / It shall be witty and it shan't be long. [*Epigram on 'Long' Sir Thomas Robinson*]

23 Give Dayrolles a chair. [Last words]

G. K. CHESTERTON 1874–1936

24 Are they clinging to their crosses, / F. E. Smith? [*Antichrist*]

25 But the souls of Christian peoples ... / Chuck it, Smith!

26 Before the gods that made the gods / Had seen their sunrise pass, / The White Horse of the White Horse Vale / Was cut out of the grass. [*The Ballad of the White Horse*, I]

27 I tell you naught for your comfort, / Yea, naught for your desire, / Save that the sky grows darker yet / And the sea rises higher.

28 For the great Gaels of Ireland / Are the men that God made mad, / For all their wars are merry, / And all their songs are sad. [II]

29 I rose politely in the club / And said, 'I feel a little bored; / Will someone take me to a pub?' [*A Ballade of an Anti-Puritan*]

30 The gallows in my garden, people say, / Is new and neat and adequately tall. [*A Ballade of Suicide*]

31 After all / I think I will not hang myself today.

32 The wine they drink in Paradise / They make in Haute Lorraine. [*A Cider Song*]

1 The road from heaven to Hereford / Where the apple wood of Hereford / Goes all the way to Wales.

2 The men that worked for England / They have their graves at home. [*Elegy in a Country Churchyard*]

3 And they that rule in England, / In stately conclave met, / Alas, alas for England / They have no graves as yet.

4 With monstrous head and sickening cry / And ears like errant wings, / The devil's walking parody / On all four-footed things. [*The Donkey*]

5 Fools! for I also had my hour; / One far fierce hour and sweet: / There was a shout about my ears, / And palms before my feet.

6 St George he was for England, / And before he killed the dragon / He drank a pint of English ale / Out of an English flagon. [*The Englishman*]

7 Merrily taking twopenny ale and cheese with a pocket knife; / But these were luxuries not for him who went for the Simple Life. [*The Good Rich Man*]

8 White founts falling in the courts of the sun, / And the Soldan of Byzantium is smiling as they run. [*Lepanto*]

9 Strong gongs groaning as the guns boom far, / Don John of Austria is going to the war.

10 The folk that live in Liverpool, their heart is in their boots; / They go to hell like lambs, they do, because the hooter hoots. [*Me Heart*]

11 You have weighed the stars in the balance, and grasped the skies in a span: / Take, if you must have answer, the word of a common man. [*The Pessimist*]

12 Before the Roman came to Rye or out to Severn strode, / The rolling English drunkard made the rolling English road. [*The Rolling English Road*]

13 That night we went to Birmingham by way of Beachy Head.

14 For there is good news yet to hear and fine things to be seen, / Before we go to Paradise by way of Kensal Green.

15 Smile at us, pay us, pass us; but do not quite forget. / For we are the people of England, that never have spoken yet. [*The Secret People*]

16 God made the wicked Grocer / For a mystery and a sign, / That men might shun the awful shop / And go to inns to dine. [*The Song against Grocers*]

17 He crams with cans of poisoned meat / The subjects of the King, / And when they die by thousands / Why, he laughs like anything.

18 Earth will grow worse till men redeem it, / And wars more evil, ere all wars cease. [*A Song of Defeat*]

19 And we were angry and poor and happy, / And proud of seeing our names in print.

20 The Nothing scrawled on a five-foot page.

21 They haven't got no noses, / The fallen sons of Eve. [*The Song of Quoodle*]

22 And goodness only knowses / The Noselessness of Man.

23 If an angel out of heaven / Brings you other things to drink, / Thank him for his kind attentions, / Go and pour them down the sink. [*The Song of Right and Wrong*]

24 Tea, although an Oriental, / Is a gentleman at least; / Cocoa is a cad and coward, / Cocoa is a vulgar beast.

25 And Noah he often said to his wife when he sat down to dine, / 'I don't care where the water goes if it doesn't get into the wine'. [*Wine and Water*]

26 A great deal of contemporary criticism reads to me like a man saying: 'Of course I do not like green cheese: I am very fond of brown sherry.' [*All I Survey*, 'On Jonathan Swift']

27 'My country, right or wrong,' is a thing no patriot would think of saying except in a desperate case. It is like saying, 'My mother, drunk or sober.' [*The Defendant* (See 133:10)]

28 A good novel tells us the truth about its hero; but a bad novel tells us the truth about its author. [*Heretics*, 15]

29 The artistic temperament is a disease that afflicts amateurs. [17]

30 An artist will betray himself by some sort of sincerity. [*The Incredulity of Father Brown*, 'The Dagger with Wings']

31 To be clever enough to get all that money, one must be stupid enough to want it. [*The Innocence of Father Brown*, 'The Paradise of Thieves']

32 Where does a wise man kick a pebble? On the beach. Where does a wise man hide a leaf? In the forest. ['The Broken Sword']

33 The human race, to which so many of my readers belong. [*The Napoleon of Notting Hill*, Ch. 1]

1 Mr Shaw is (I suspect) the only man on earth who has never written any poetry. [*Orthodoxy*, Ch. 3]

2 Every politician is emphatically a promising politician. [*The Red Moon of Meru*]

3 Lying in bed would be an altogether perfect and supreme experience if only one had a coloured pencil long enough to draw on the ceiling. [*Tremendous Trifles*]

4 Hardy went down to botanize in the swamp, while Meredith climbed towards the sun. Meredith became, at his best, a sort of daintily dressed Walt Whitman: Hardy became a sort of village atheist brooding and blaspheming over the village idiot. [*The Victorian Age in Literature*, Ch. 2]

5 If a thing is worth doing it is worth doing badly. [*What's Wrong with the World*, 'Folly and Female Education']

6 'The Christian ideal,' it is said, 'has not been tried and found wanting; it has been found difficult and left untried.' ['The Unfinished Temple']

7 Journalism largely consists in saying 'Lord Jones Dead' to people who never knew Lord Jones was alive. [*The Wisdom of Father Brown*, 'The Purple Wig']

8 Blasphemy itself could not survive religion; if anyone doubts that, let him try to blaspheme Odin. [In the *Daily News*, 24 June 1904]

9 When you break the big laws, you do not get liberty; you do not even get anarchy. You get the small laws. [29 July 1905]

10 A dying monarchy is always one that has too much power, not too little; a dying religion always interferes more than it ought, not less. [11 Mar. 1911]

11 Democracy means government by the uneducated, while aristocracy means government by the badly educated. [In *The New York Times*, 1 Feb. 1931]

HENRY CHETTLE *c.* 1560–1607

12 Diaphenia, like the daffadowndilly, / White as the sun, fair as the lily, / Heigh ho, how I do love thee! [*Diaphenia*, also attr. to Henry Constable]

ALBERT CHEVALIER 1861–1923

13 Wot's the good of Hanyfink? – Why – Nuffink! [Music-hall refrain]

14 There ain't a lady livin' in the land / As I'd swop for my dear old Dutch! [*My Old Dutch*]

15 Laugh! I thought I should 'ave died, / Knocked 'em in the Old Kent Road. [*Wot Cher*, or *Knocked 'em in the Old Kent Road*]

MAURICE CHEVALIER 1888–1972

16 Old age isn't so bad when you consider the alternative. [Quoted in M. Freedland, *Maurice Chevalier*, Ch. 20]

NOAM CHOMSKY 1928–

17 Colourless green ideas sleep furiously. [(Sentence to illustrate grammatical structure as independent of meaning) *Syntactic Structures*, 2. 3]

H. F. CHORLEY 1808–1872

18 God the All-terrible! King, who ordainest / Great winds Thy clarions, the lightnings Thy sword. [Hymn]

CHUANG TSU 369–286 Cent. BC

19 I do not know whether I was then a man dreaming I was a butterfly, or whether I am now a butterfly dreaming I am a man. [*On Levelling All Things*, 2]

CHARLES CHURCHILL 1731–1764

20 Though by whim, envy, or resentment led, / They damn those authors whom they never read. [*The Candidate*, 57]

21 Be England what she will, / With all her faults, she is my country still. [*The Farewell*, 27]

22 Just to the windward of the law. [*The Ghost*, III. 56]

23 Who often, but without success, have prayed / For apt Alliteration's artful aid. [*The Prophecy of Famine*, 85]

24 Genius is of no country; her pure ray / Spreads all abroad, as general as the day. [*The Rosciad*, 207]

25 Statesman all over, in plots famous grown, / He mouths a sentence, as curs mouth a bone. [321]

26 So loud each tongue, so empty was each head, / So much they talked, so very little said. [549]

27 With various readings stored his empty

skull, / Learn'd without sense, and venerably dull. [591]

1 Those who would make us feel, must feel themselves. [962]

2 Where he falls short, 'tis Nature's fault alone; / Where he succeeds, the merit's all his own. [1025]

3 The best things carried to excess are wrong. [1039]

LORD RANDOLPH CHURCHILL
1849–1894

4 The old gang. [(Members of the Conservative Government) Speech in House of Commons, 7 Mar. 1878]

5 Ulster will fight; Ulster will be right. [Letter, 7 May 1886]

6 I never could make out what those damn dots meant. [(Of the decimal point) Quoted by Winston Churchill, *Lord Randolph Churchill*, Vol. ii. p. 184]

WINSTON CHURCHILL 1874–1965

7 The wars of the peoples will be more terrible than those of kings. [Speech in House of Commons on Army Estimates, 1901. Quoted in *Maxims and Reflections*, Sect. V]

8 It cannot in the opinion of His Majesty's Government be classified as slavery in the extreme acceptance of the word without some risk of terminological inexactitude. [Speech in House of Commons, 22 Feb. 1906]

9 He [Lord Charles Beresford] is one of those orators of whom it was well said, 'Before they get up they do not know what they are going to say; when they are speaking, they do not know what they are saying; and when they sit down they do not know what they have said.' [Speech in House of Commons, 20 Dec. 1912]

10 The maxim of the British people is 'Business as usual'. [Speech at Guildhall, 9 Nov. 1914]

11 The grass grows green on the battlefield, but never on the scaffold. [Attr. remark on Irish Rebellion, 1916]

12 A hopeful disposition is not the sole qualification to be a prophet. [Speech in House of Commons, 30 Apr. 1927]

13 I have waited fifty years to see the Boneless Wonder [Ramsay MacDonald] sitting on the Treasury Bench. [28 Jan. 1931]

14 We know that he [Ramsay MacDonald] has, more than any other man, the gift of compressing the largest amount of words into the smallest amount of thought. [23 Mar. 1933]

15 So they [the Government] go on in strange paradox, decided only to be undecided, resolved to be irresolute, adamant for drift, solid for fluidity, all-powerful for impotence. [12 Nov. 1936]

16 We have sustained a defeat without a war. [(Describing Munich) Speech in House of Commons, 5 Oct. 1938]

17 I cannot forecast to you the action of Russia. It is a riddle wrapped in a mystery inside an enigma; but perhaps there is a key. That key is Russian national interest. [BBC Radio broadcast in London, 1 Oct. 1939]

18 I would say to the House, as I said to those who have joined this Government, 'I have nothing to offer but blood, toil, tears and sweat.' [First speech in House of Commons as Prime Minister, 13 May 1940]

19 You ask: 'What is our aim?' I can answer in one word: 'Victory!' Victory at all costs, victory in spite of all terror, victory however long and hard the road may be: for without victory there is no survival.

20 We shall defend our island, whatever the cost may be, we shall fight on the beaches, we shall fight on the landing grounds, we shall fight in the fields and in the streets, we shall fight in the hills; we shall never surrender. [4 June]

21 Learn to get used to it [bombing]. Eels get used to skinning. [Notes for speech, 20 June]

22 What General Weygand called the 'Battle of France' is over. I expect the Battle of Britain is about to begin . . . [Speech in House of Commons, 18 June]

23 Let us therefore brace ourselves to our duties, and so bear ourselves that, if the British Empire and its Commonwealth last for a thousand years, men will still say: 'This was their finest hour.' [18 June]

24 Never in the field of human conflict was so much owed by so many to so few. [(The Battle of Britain) 20 Aug.]

25 We are waiting for the long-promised invasion. So are the fishes. [Broadcast to the French people, 21 Oct.]

1 Give us the tools, and we will finish the job. [Broadcast, addressed to President Roosevelt, 9 Feb. 1941]

2 You [Hitler] do your worst, and we will do our best. [Speech at Civil Defence Services' Luncheon, 14 July]

3 It becomes still more difficult to reconcile Japanese action with prudence or even sanity. What kind of people do they think we are? [Speech to US Congress, 24 Dec.]

4 'In three weeks England will have her neck wrung like a chicken.' Some chicken; some neck! [Speech to Canadian Senate, 30 Dec. See 451:22]

5 This is not the end. It is not even the beginning of the end. But it is, perhaps, the end of the beginning. [(Of the victory in Egypt) Speech at the Mansion House, 10 Nov. 1942]

6 I have not become the King's First Minister in order to preside over the liquidation of the British Empire.

7 There is no finer investment for any community than putting milk into babies. [BBC Radio broadcast, 21 Mar. 1943]

8 The empires of the future are the empires of the mind. [Speech at Harvard University, 16 Sept.]

9 There are few virtues which the Poles do not possess and there are few errors they have ever avoided. [Speech in House of Commons after Potsdam Conference, 16 Aug. 1945]

10 An iron curtain has descended across the Continent. [Address at Westminster College, Fulton, USA, 5 Mar. 1946. See also 179:11, 400:17]

11 No one pretends that democracy is perfect or all-wise. Indeed, it has been said that democracy is the worst form of government except all those other forms that have been tried from time to time. [Speech in House of Commons, 11 Nov. 1947]

12 Perhaps it is better to be irresponsible and right than to be responsible and wrong. [Party Political Broadcast, London, 26 Aug. 1950]

13 Talking jaw-jaw is always better than war-war. [Speech in White House, Washington, 26 June 1954. See also 264:7]

14 It was a nation and race dwelling all around the globe that had the lion heart. I had the luck to be called upon to give the roar. [Speech at

Palace of Westminster on his 80th birthday, 30 Nov.]

15 Headmasters have powers at their disposal with which Prime Ministers have never yet been invested. [*My Early Life*, Ch. 2]

16 It is a good thing for an uneducated man to read books of quotations. [(Of himself) 9]

17 One voyage to India is enough; the others are merely repletion. [10]

18 Moral of the Work. In war: resolution. In defeat: defiance. In victory: magnanimity. In peace: goodwill. [Epigraph to *The Second World War*, but originally used to describe the 1914–18 War]

19 'Winston is back.' [Signal of Board of Admiralty to the Fleet on his return as First Lord, 1939. *The Second World War*, Vol. i, *The Gathering Storm*, Ch. 22]

20 I felt as if I were walking with destiny, and that all my past life had been but a preparation for this hour and this trial ... My warnings over the last six years had been so numerous, so detailed, and were now so terribly vindicated, that no one could gainsay me ... I was sure I should not fail. Therefore, although impatient for the morning, I slept soundly and had no need for cheering dreams. Facts are better than dreams. [(Closing words) 38]

21 No one can guarantee success in war, but only deserve it. [*The Second World War*, Vol. ii, *Their Finest Hour*]

22 Before Alamein we never had a victory. After Alamein we never had a defeat. [Vol. iv, *The Hinge of Fate*, Ch. 33]

23 Tell them from me they are unloading history. [(Telegram to the Port Commandant at Tripoli) 40]

24 Well, the principle seems the same. The water still keeps falling over. [When asked whether the Niagara Falls looked the same as when he first saw them. [v, *Closing the Ring*, Ch. 5]

25 Dictators ride to and fro upon tigers which they dare not dismount. And the tigers are getting hungry. [*While England Slept*]

26 He's a modest little man with much to be modest about. [Remark on Clement Attlee's becoming Prime Minister. Attr. in Michael Foot, *Aneurin Bevan*]

27 There, but for the grace of God, goes God.

[Of Sir Stafford Cripps. Quoted in L. Kronenberger, *The Cutting Edge*, but also ascr. to H. J. Mankiewicz on Orson Welles]

1 In defeat unbeatable; in victory unbearable. [(On Viscount Montgomery) Quoted in Edward Marsh, *Ambrosia and Small Beer*, Ch. 5. Sect. ii]

2 The difference between him [Mr Asquith] and Arthur [Balfour] is that Arthur is wicked and moral, Asquith is good and immoral. [Quoted in E. T. Raymond, *Mr Balfour*, Ch. 13]

3 You and I must take care not to lose the next war. [To Lord Ismay, apropos the Nuremberg trials. Quoted by A. J. P. Taylor in BBC TV programme *The Warlords*, 6 Sept. 1976]

4 We should have the art [of making atomic bombs] rather than the article [the bombs themselves] [Secret memo to Lord Cherwell, Nov. 1951]

5 This is the sort of English up with which I will not put. [Marginal comment on state document, quoted in Sir Ernest Gowers, *Plain Words*]

COLLEY CIBBER 1671–1757

6 Whilst thus I sing, I am a King, / Altho' a poor blind boy. [*The Blind Boy*]

7 Dumb's a sly dog. [*Love makes the Man*, IV. i]

8 One had as good be out of the world, as out of the fashion. [*Love's Last Shift*, II]

9 Off with his head – so much for Buckingham. [*Richard III* (altered), IV. iii]

10 Conscience avaunt, Richard's himself again. [V. iii]

11 Perish the thought! [V. v]

MARCUS TULLIUS CICERO 106–43 BC

12 *Nihil tam absurde dici potest, quod non dicatur ab aliquo philosophorum.* Nothing so absurd can be said, that some philosopher has not said it. [*De Divinatione*, ii. 58]

13 *Salus populi suprema est lex.* – The good of the people is the chief law. [*De Legibus*, III. iii]

14 *'Ipse dixit.' 'Ipse' autem erat Pythagoras.* – 'He himself said it,' and this *self* was Pythagoras. [*De Natura Deorum*, I. v. 10]

15 *Summum bonum.* – The highest good. [*De Officiis*, I. ii]

16 *Cedant arma togae, concedant laurea laudi.* – Let arms give place to civic robes, laurels to paeans. [I. xxii]

17 *O tempora, O mores!* – What times! What habits! [*In Catilinam*, I. i]

18 *Abiit, excessit, evasit, erupit.* – He departed, withdrew, rushed off, broke away. [II. i]

19 *Civis Romanus sum.* – I am a Roman citizen. [*In Verrem*, V. lvii]

20 *Quod di omen avertant.* – May the gods avert the omen. [*Philippic*, III. xiv]

21 *Silent enim leges inter arma.* – Laws are dumb in time of war. [*Pro Milone*, IV. xi]

22 *Cui bono?* – To whose profit? [XII. xxxii]

23 *Errare, mehercule, malo cum Platone . . . quam cum istis vera sentire.* – I swear I would rather be wrong with Plato than see the truth with men like these. [(The Pythagoreans) *Tusculanae Disp.* I. 17]

24 *O fortunatam natam me consule Romam!* – O happy Rome, born when I was consul! [Quoted in *Juvenal*, X. 122]

JOHN CLARE 1793–1864

25 He could not die when trees were green, / For he loved the time too well. [*The Dying Child*]

26 I am: yet what I am none cares, or knows. [*I am*]

27 I long for scenes where man has never trod; / A place where woman never smiled or wept; / There to abide with my Creator, God, / And sleep as I in childhood sweetly slept: / Untroubling and untroubled where I lie; – The grass below – above the vaulted sky.

28 Love lies beyond / The tomb, the earth, which fades like dew! / I love the fond, / The faithful, and the true. ['*Love lies beyond the Tomb*']

29 If life had a second edition, how I would correct the proofs. [Letter to a friend]

EDWARD HYDE, EARL OF CLARENDON 1609–1674

30 So much enamoured on peace that he [Falkland] would have been glad the King should have bought it at any price. [*Selections from the History of the Rebellion*, 9]

31 He [Hampden] had a head to contrive, a tongue to persuade, and a hand to execute any mischief. [(Quoting a description of Cinna) 21]

KARL VON CLAUSEWITZ 1780–1831

32 War is nothing more than the continuation of politics by other means. [*On War*, I. i]

HENRY CLAY 1777–1852

1 I had rather be right than be President. [Speech, 1850]

GEORGES CLEMENCEAU 1841–1929

2 War is much too important a thing to be left to the generals. [(1886) Quoted in G. Suarez, *Clemenceau*, but also attr. to Talleyrand, 414:13, among others]

SAMUEL LANGHORNE CLEMENS *see* **TWAIN, MARK**

JOHN CLEVELAND 1613–1658

3 Strafford who was hurried hence / 'Twixt treason and convenience. [*Epitaph on the Earl of Strafford*]

4 Had Cain been Scot, God would have changed his doom / Not forced him wander, but confined him home. [*The Rebel Scot*]

ROBERT, LORD CLIVE 1725–1774

5 By God, Mr Chairman, at this moment I stand astonished at my own moderation! [Reply during Parliamentary inquiry, 1773]

THE CLOUD OF UNKNOWING 14 Cent.

6 And smite upon that thick cloud of unknowing with a sharp dart of longing love; and go not thence for thing that befalleth. [Ch. 6]

ARTHUR HUGH CLOUGH 1819–1861

7 Well, I know, after all, it is only juxtaposition, – / Juxtaposition, in short; and what is juxtaposition? [*Amours de voyage*, I. 11]

8 I am in love, you say; I do not think so, exactly. [II. 10]

9 *Action will furnish belief,* – but will that belief be the true one? / This is the point, you know. [V. 2]

10 Whither depart the souls of the brave that die in the battle, / Die in the lost, lost fight, for the cause that perishes with them? [V. 6]

11 Still more plain the Tutor, the grave man, nicknamed Adam, / White-tied, clerical, silent, with antique square-cut waistcoat / Formal, unchanged, of black cloth, but with sense and

feeling beneath it. [*The Bothie of Tober-na-Vuolich*, I. 20]

12 *Shady* in Latin, said Lindsay, but *topping* in Plays and Aldrich. [I. 25]

13 Good are the Ethics, I wis; good absolute, not for me, though; / Good, too, Logic, of course; in itself, but not in fine weather. [II. 225]

14 Gay in the mazy, / Moving, imbibing the rosy, and pointing a gun at the horny! [III. 97]

15 Grace is given of God, but knowledge is born in the market. [IV. 81]

16 A world where nothing is had for nothing. [VIII. 5]

17 How pleasant it is to have money, heigh-ho! / How pleasant it is to have money. [*Dipsychus*, I. ii]

18 And almost every one when age, / Disease, or sorrows strike him, / Inclines to think there is a God, / Or something very like Him. [I. v]

19 This world is very odd we see, / We do not comprehend it; / But in one fact we all agree, / God won't, and we can't mend it. [II. ii]

20 Trust me, I've read your German sage / To far more purpose than e'er you did; / You find it in his wisest page, / Whom God deludes is well deluded.

21 Thou shalt have one God only; who / Would be at the expense of two? [*The Latest Decalogue*]

22 Thou shalt not kill; but needst not strive / Officiously to keep alive.

23 Thou shalt not covet, but tradition / Approves all forms of competition.

24 'Tis better to have fought and lost, / Than never to have fought at all. [*Peschiera*]

25 Say not the struggle naught availeth, / The labour and the wounds are vain, / The enemy faints not, nor faileth, / And as things have been, things remain. [*Say not the Struggle Naught Availeth*]

26 And not by eastern windows only, / When daylight comes, comes in the light, / In front the sun climbs slow, how slowly, / But westward, look, the land is bright.

WILLIAM COBBETT 1762–1835

27 The slavery of the tea and coffee and other slop-kettle. [*Advice to Young Men*, Letter 1]

28 The great wen of all. [(London) *Rural Rides* (1821)]

CHARLES COBORN 1852–1945

1 Two lovely black eyes, / Oh, what a surprise! / Only for telling a man he was wrong. / Two lovely black eyes! [*Two Lovely Black Eyes*]

ALISON COCKBURN 1713–1794

2 For the flowers of the forest are withered away. [*The Flowers of the Forest* (See also 158:4)]

JEAN COCTEAU 1889–1963

3 The essential tact in daring is to know how far one can go too far. [*Le Coq et l'Arlequin*]

4 Hugo was a madman who believed he was Hugo. [*Opium*, p. 77]

CODE NAPOLÉON 1804

5 *La recherche de la paternité est interdite.* – Investigations into paternity are forbidden. [Article 340]

GEORGE M. COHAN 1878–1942

6 We'll be over, we're coming over, / And we won't come back till it's over over there. [*Over There*, US song of the 1914–18 War]

SIR EDWARD COKE 1552–1634

7 How long soever it hath continued, if it be against reason, it is of no force in law. [*Institutes*, 'Commentary upon Littleton', I. 80]

8 The gladsome light of Jurisprudence. [I. Epilogue]

9 For a man's house is his castle. [III. 73]

10 Magna Charta is such a fellow, that he will have no sovereign. [On the Lords' Amendment to the Petition of Right, 17 May 1628]

11 They [corporations] cannot commit treason, nor be outlawed, nor excommunicate, for they have no souls. [*Sutton's Hospital Case*]

12 Six hours in sleep, in law's grave study six, / Four spend in prayer, the rest on Nature fix. [Epigram (See also 224:19)]

FRANK COLBY 1865–1925

13 Men will confess to treason, murder, arson, false teeth, or a wig. How many of them will own up to a lack of humour? [*Essays*, I]

14 I have found some of the best reasons I ever had for remaining at the bottom simply by looking at the men at the top. [II]

HARTLEY COLERIDGE 1796–1849

15 She is not fair to outward view / As many maidens be; / Her loveliness I never knew / Until she smiled on me. [Song: *She is not Fair*]

16 Her very frowns are fairer far, / Than smiles of other maidens are.

MARY COLERIDGE 1861–1907

17 We were young, we were merry, we were very, very wise, / And the door stood open at our feast, / When there passed us a woman with the West in her eyes, / And a man with his back to the East. [*Unwelcome*]

S. T. COLERIDGE 1772–1834

18 It is an ancient mariner, / And he stoppeth one of three. [*The Ancient Mariner*, Pt I]

19 The guests are met, the feast is set. / May'st hear the merry din.

20 He holds him with his glittering eye.

21 The ship was cheered, the harbour cleared, / Merrily did we drop.

22 The sun came up upon the left, / Out of the sea came he! / And he shone bright, and on the right / Went down into the sea.

23 The bride hath paced into the hall, / Red as a rose is she.

24 And ice, mast-high, came floating by, / As green as emerald.

25 The ice was here, the ice was there, / The ice was all around; / It cracked and growled, and roared and howled, / Like noises in a swound!

26 The fair breeze blew, the white foam flew, / The furrow followed free; / We were the first that ever burst / Into that silent sea. [II]

27 As idle as a painted ship / Upon a painted ocean.

28 Water, water, everywhere, / Nor any drop to drink.

29 Yea, slimy things did crawl with legs / Upon the slimy sea.

30 The Nightmare Life-in-Death was she, / Who thicks man's blood with cold. [III]

31 'The game is done! I've won, I've won!' / Quoth she, and whistles thrice.

1 The sun's rim dips; the stars rush out: / At one stride comes the dark.

2 Till clomb above the eastern bar / The hornèd moon, with one bright star / Within the nether tip.

3 I fear thee, ancient Mariner! / I fear thy skinny hand! [IV]

4 Alone, alone, all, all alone, / Alone on a wide, wide sea!

5 The moving moon went up the sky, / And nowhere did abide: / Softly she was going up, / And a star or two beside.

6 A spring of love gushed from my heart, / And I blessed them unaware.

7 Oh sleep! it is a gentle thing, / Beloved from pole to pole! [V]

8 We were a ghastly crew.

9 A noise like of a hidden brook. / In the leafy month of June, / That to the sleeping woods all night / Singeth a quiet tune.

10 Like one that on a lonesome road / Doth walk in fear and dread. / And having once turned round walks on, / And turns no more his head; / Because he knows, a frightful fiend / Doth close behind him tread. [VI]

11 No voice; but oh! the silence sank / Like music on my heart.

12 When the ivy-tod is heavy with snow, / And the owlet whoops to the wolf below. [VII]

13 I pass, like night, from land to land; / I have strange power of speech.

14 O Wedding-Guest! this soul hath been / Alone on a wide wide sea; / So lonely 'twas that God himself / Scarce seemèd there to be.

15 He prayeth well, who loveth well / Both man and bird and beast.

16 He prayeth best, who loveth best / All things both great and small; / For the dear God who loveth us,/ He made and loveth all.

17 A sadder and a wiser man, / He rose the morrow morn.

18 And the Spring comes slowly up this way. [Christabel, Pt I. 22]

19 The one red leaf, the last of its clan, / That dances as often as dance it can, / Hanging so light, and hanging so high, / On the topmost twig that looks up at the sky. [49]

20 And what can ail the mastiff bitch? [149]

21 A sight to dream of, not to tell! [253]

22 Saints will aid if men will call: / For the blue sky bends over all! [330]

23 Life is thorny; and youth is vain; / And to be wroth with one we love / Doth work like madness in the brain. [II. 413]

24 I counted two and seventy stenches, / All well defined, and several stinks! [Cologne]

25 Well! If the Bard was weather-wise, who made / The grand old ballad of Sir Patrick Spence. [Dejection: an Ode, 1]

26 I see them all so excellently fair, / I see, not feel, how beautiful they are! [37]

27 I may not hope from outward forms to win / The passion and the life, whose fountains are within. [45]

28 O Lady! we receive but what we give, / And in our life alone does Nature live. [47]

29 Swans sing before they die – 'twere no bad thing / Did certain persons die before they sing. [Epigram on a Volunteer Singer]

30 The Frost performs its secret ministry, / Unhelped by any wind. [Frost at Midnight, 1]

31 Therefore all seasons shall be sweet to thee, / Whether the summer clothe the general earth / With greenness, or the redbreast sit and sing / Betwixt the tufts of snow on the bare branch / Of mossy apple tree. [65]

32 Whether the eave-drops fall / Heard only in the trances of the blast, / Or if the secret ministry of frost / Shall hang them up in silent icicles, / Quietly shining to the quiet moon. [70]

33 The Knight's bones are dust, / And his good sword rust; – / His soul is with the saints, I trust. [The Knight's Tomb]

34 At this moment he was unfortunately called out by a person on business from Porlock. [Kubla Khan, 'Introductory Note', frequently quoted as 'the person from Porlock']

35 In Xanadu did Kubla Khan / A stately pleasure-dome decree; / Where Alph, the sacred river, ran / Through caverns measureless to man / Down to a sunless sea.

So twice five miles of fertile ground / With walls and towers was girdled round: / And there were gardens bright with sinuous rills, / Where blossomed many an incense-bearing tree; / And here were forests ancient as the hills, / Enfolding sunny spots of greenery.

36 A savage place! as holy and enchanted / As

e'er beneath a waning moon was haunted / By woman wailing for her demon lover!

1 As if this earth in fast thick pants were breathing.

2 Five miles meandering with a mazy motion.

3 Ancestral voices prophesying war!

4 It was a miracle of rare device, / A sunny pleasure-dome with caves of ice!

5 A damsel with a dulcimer / In a vision once I saw: / It was an Abyssinian maid, / And on her dulcimer she played, / Singing of Mount Abora.

6 And all should cry, Beware! Beware! / His flashing eyes, his floating hair! / Weave a circle round him thrice, / And close your eyes with holy dread, / For he on honey-dew hath fed, / And drunk the milk of Paradise.

7 All thoughts, all passions, all delights, / Whatever stirs this mortal frame, / All are but ministers of Love, / And feed his sacred flame. [*Love*]

8 With Donne whose muse on dromedary trots, / Wreathe iron pokers into true-love knots. [*On Donne's Poetry*]

9 In the hexameter rises the fountain's silvery column; / In the pentameter aye falling in melody back. [*Ovidian Elegiac Metre*]

10 Something Childish, but very Natural. [Title of poem]

11 So for the mother's sake the child was dear, / And dearer was the mother for the child. [*Sonnet to a Friend . . .*]

12 And this reft house is that the which he built, / Lamented Jack! [*Sonnets Attempted in the Manner of Contemporary Writers*, 3]

13 This lime-tree bower my prison! [*This Lime-tree Bower my Prison*]

14 Life went a-maying / With Nature, Hope, and Poesy, / When I was young! [*Youth and Age*]

15 He who begins by loving Christianity better than Truth will proceed by loving his own sect or church better than Christianity, and end by loving himself better than all. [*Aids to Reflection, Moral and Religious Aphorisms*, 25]

16 If a man could pass through Paradise in a dream, and have a flower presented to him as a pledge that his soul had really been there, and if he found that flower in his hand when he

awoke – Aye, and what then? [*Anima Poetae* (1816)]

17 The primary imagination I hold to be the living power and prime agent of all human perception, and as a repetition in the finite mind of the eternal act of creation in the infinite I AM. [*Biographia Literaria*, Ch. 13]

18 The Fancy is indeed no other than a mode of memory emancipated from the order of time and space.

19 That willing suspension of disbelief for the moment, which constitutes poetic faith. [14]

20 Nothing can permanently please, which does not contain in itself the reason why it is so, and not otherwise.

21 Our *myriad-minded* Shakespeare. [15]

22 No man was ever yet a great poet, without being at the same time a profound philosopher.

23 The dwarf sees farther than the giant, when he has the giant's shoulder to mount on. [*The Friend*, I. 8 (See 294:7)]

24 Poetry is not the proper antithesis to prose, but to science. Poetry is opposed to science, and prose to metre. [*Lectures and notes of 1818*, Sect. I]

25 To read Dryden, Pope, etc., you need only count syllables; but to read Donne you must measure *time*, and discover the time of each word by the sense of passion.

26 Reviewers are usually people who would have been poets, historians, biographers, etc., if they could; they have tried their talents at one or at the other, and have failed; therefore they turn critics. [*Lectures on Shakespeare and Milton*, I]

27 The faults of great authors are generally excellences carried to an excess. [*Miscellanies*, 149]

28 Summer has set in with its usual severity. [Remark quoted in Charles Lamb's letter to V. Novello, 9 May 1826]

29 Schiller has the material sublime. [*Table Talk*, 29 Dec. 1822]

30 You abuse snuff! Perhaps it is the final cause of the human nose. [4 Jan. 1823]

31 Prose = words in their best order; poetry = the *best* words in the best order. [12 July 1827 (see 63:29)]

32 The man's desire is for the woman; but the woman's desire is rarely other than for the desire of the man. [23 July]

1 My mind is in a state of philosophical doubt. [30 Apr. 1830]

2 Poetry is certainly something more than good sense, but it must be good sense at all events; just as a palace is more than a house, but it must be a house, at least. [9 May]

3 I believe the souls of five hundred Sir Isaac Newtons would go to the making up of a Shakespeare or a Milton. [Letter to Thomas Poole, 23 Mar. 1801]

JESSE COLLINGS 1831–1920

4 Three acres and a cow. [Slogan for Land Reform, 1885]

MICHAEL COLLINS 1890–1922

5 Early this morning, I signed my death warrant. [(On signing the Irish Treaty. He was assassinated a few months afterwards) Letter, 6 Dec. 1921]

MORTIMER COLLINS 1827–1876

6 A man is as old as he's feeling, / A woman as old as she looks. [The Unknown Quantity]

WILKIE COLLINS 1824–1889

7 I am not against hasty marriages, where a mutual flame is fanned by an adequate income. [No Name, Sc. iv. Ch. 8]

WILLIAM COLLINS 1721–1759

8 To fair Fidele's grassy tomb / Soft maids and village hinds shall bring / Each opening sweet, of earliest bloom, / And rifle all the breathing Spring. [Dirge in Cymbeline]

9 Beloved, till life can charm no more; / And mourned, till Pity's self be dead.

10 If aught of oaten stop, or pastoral song, / May hope, chaste Eve, to soothe thy modest ear. [Ode to Evening]

11 While now the bright-haired sun / Sits in yon western tent, whose cloudy skirts, / With brede ethereal wove, / O'erhang his wavy bed: / Now air is hushed, save where the weak-eyed bat, / With short shrill shriek flits by on leathern wing, / Or where the beetle winds / His small but sullen horn.

12 Hamlets brown, and dim-discovered spires.

13 Bathe thy breathing tresses, meekest Eve!

14 Faints the cold work till thou inspire the whole. [Ode to Simplicity]

15 How sleep the brave, who sink to rest, / By all their country's wishes blest! [Ode written in the Year 1746]

16 By fairy hands their knell is rung; / By forms unseen their dirge is sung.

17 When Music, heav'nly maid, was young. [The Passions, An Ode for Music, 1]

18 With eyes upraised, as one inspired, / Pale Melancholy sat retired; / And from her wild sequestered seat, / In notes by distance made more sweet, / Poured through the mellow horn her pensive soul. [57]

19 In hollow murmurs died away. [68]

20 O Music! sphere-descended maid, / Friend of Pleasure, Wisdom's aid! [95]

GEORGE COLMAN THE ELDER
  1732–1794

21 Love and a cottage! Eh, Fanny! Ah, give me indifference and a coach and six! [The Clandestine Marriage, I. ii]

GEORGE COLMAN THE YOUNGER
  1762–1836

22 Mum's the word. [The Battle of Hexham, II. i]

23 Lord help you! Tell 'em Queen Anne's dead. [The Heir-at-Law, I. i]

24 Not to be sneezed at. [II.i]

25 His heart runs away with his head. [Who Wants a Guinea? I. i]

26 Like two single gentlemen rolled into one. [Lodgings for Single Gentlemen]

27 When taken, / To be well shaken. [The Newcastle Apothecary]

28 Says he, 'I am a handsome man, but I'm a gay deceiver.' [Unfortunate Miss Bailey]

29 Crying, 'Bless you, Wicked Captain Smith, remember poor Miss Bailey.'

CHARLES COLTON 1780?–1832

30 Men will wrangle for religion; write for it; fight for it; anything but – live for it. [Lacon, I. 25]

31 When you have nothing to say, say nothing. [183]

32 Examinations are formidable even to the

best prepared, for the greatest fool may ask more than the wisest man can answer. [322]

1 The debt which cancels all others. [II. 66]

IVY COMPTON-BURNETT 1892–1969

2 There is more difference within the sexes than between them. [*Mother and Son*, 10]

WILLIAM CONGREVE 1670–1729

3 There is nothing more unbecoming a man of quality than to laugh; 'tis such a vulgar expression of the passion! [*The Double Dealer*, I. iv]

4 See how love and murder will out. [IV. vi]

5 Thou liar of the first magnitude. [*Love for Love*, II. v]

6 I came upstairs into the world; for I was born in a cellar. [vii]

7 O fie miss, you must not kiss and tell. [x]

8 I know that's a secret, for it's whispered everywhere. [III. iii]

9 If I marry, Sir Sampson, I'm for a good estate with any man, and for any man with a good estate. [v]

10 He that first cries out stop thief, is often he that has stolen the treasure. [xiv]

11 A branch of one of your antediluvian families, fellows that the flood could not wash away. [V. ii]

12 'Tis well enough for a servant to be bred at an university: but the education is a little too pedantic for a gentleman. [iii]

13 Music hath charms to soothe a savage breast, / To soften rocks, or bend a knotted oak. [*The Mourning Bride*, I. i]

14 Heaven has no rage like love to hatred turned, / Nor hell a fury, like a woman scorned. [III. viii]

15 Is he then dead? / What, dead at last, quite, quite for ever dead! [V. xi]

16 In my conscience I believe the baggage loves me: for she never speaks well of me herself, nor suffers anybody else to rail at me. [*The Old Bachelor*, I. iii]

17 One of love's April-fools. [iv]

18 Well, Sir Joseph, you have such a winning way with you. [V. vii]

19 I could find it in my heart to marry thee, purely to be rid of thee. [x]

20 Courtship to marriage, as a very witty prologue to a very dull play.

21 They come together like the coroner's inquest, to sit upon the murdered reputations of the week. [*The Way of the World*, I. i]

22 She once used me with that insolence, that in revenge I took her to pieces; sifted her, and separated her failings; I studied 'em, and got 'em by rote. The catalogue was so large, that I was not without hopes, one day or other to hate her heartily. [iii]

23 O the pious friendships of the female sex! [II. iii]

24 Here she comes i' faith full sail, with her fan spread and streamers out, and a shoal of fools for tenders. [iv]

25 O ay, letters – I had letters – I am persecuted with letters – I hate letters – nobody knows how to write letters; and yet one has 'em, one does not know why – they serve one to pin up one's hair.

26 Only with those in verse, Mr Witwoud. I never pin up my hair with prose.

27 If I have not fretted myself till I am pale again, there's no veracity in me. [III. i]

28 Yes, but tenderness becomes me best – a sort of dyingness – you see that picture has a sort of a – ha, Foible? A swimmingness in the eyes. [v]

29 Love's but the frailty of the mind, – When 'tis not with ambition joined. [xii]

30 No, I'm no enemy to learning; it hurts not me. [xiii]

31 Rise to meet him in a pretty disorder – yes – O, nothing is more alluring than a levee from a couch in some confusion. [IV. i]

32 I nauseate walking; 'tis a country diversion, I loathe the country. [iv]

33 Wife, spouse, my dear, joy, jewel, love, sweet-heart and the rest of that nauseous cant, in which men and their wives are so fulsomely familiar. [v]

34 Let us be very strange and well-bred: Let us be as strange as if we had been married a great while; and as well-bred as if we were not married at all.

35 These articles subscribed, if I continue to endure you a little longer, I may by degrees dwindle into a wife.

1 I hope you do not think me prone to an iteration of nuptials. [xii]

2 You are all camphire and frankincense, all chastity and odour.

3 O, she is the antidote to desire. [xiv]

4 I chiefly made it my own care to initiate her very infancy in the rudiments of virtue, and to impress upon her tender years a young odium and aversion to the very sight of men. [V. v]

5 Careless she is with artful care, / Affecting to seem unaffected. [*Amoret*]

6 The good received, the giver is forgot. [*Epistle to Lord Halifax*, 40]

7 Whom she refuses, she treats still / With so much sweet behaviour, / That her refusal, through her skill, / Looks almost like a favour. [Song: *Doris*]

8 Would she could make of me a saint, / Or I of her a sinner. [Song: *Pious Selinda goes to Prayers*]

JAMES CONNELL 1852–1929

9 Then raise the scarlet standard high! / Beneath its shade we'll live and die! / Though cowards flinch, and traitors jeer, / We'll keep the Red Flag flying here! [*The Red Flag*]

CYRIL CONNOLLY 1903–1974

10 It is closing time in the gardens of the West and from now on an artist will be judged only by the resonance of his solitude or the quality of his despair. [*The Condemned Playground*]

11 I shall christen this style the Mandarin, since it is beloved by literary pundits. It is the style of all those writers whose tendency is to make their language convey more than they mean or more than they feel, it is the style of most artists and all humbugs. [*Enemies of Promise*, Ch. 2]

12 The ape-like virtues without which no one can enjoy a public school.

13 Literature is the art of writing something that will be read twice; journalism what will be grasped at once. [3]

14 Whom the gods wish to destroy they first call promising. [13]

15 There is no more sombre enemy of good art than the pram in the hall. [14]

16 I have always disliked myself at any given moment; the total of such moments is my life. [18]

17 No city should be too large for a man to walk out of in a morning. [*The Unquiet Grave*, 1]

18 Everything is a dangerous drug to me except reality, which is unendurable.

19 Imprisoned in every fat man a thin one is wildly signalling to be let out. [2 (See also 300:17, 448:8, 453:10)]

20 The true index of a man's character is the health of his wife.

T. W. CONNOR 19 Cent.

21 She was one of the early birds, / And I was one of the worms. [*She was a Dear Little Dickie-Bird*]

JOSEPH CONRAD 1857–1924

22 Mistah Kurtz – he dead. [*The Heart of Darkness*, Ch. 3]

23 A work that aspires, however humbly, to the condition of art should carry its justification in every line. [*The Nigger of the Narcissus*, Preface]

24 This could have occurred nowhere but in England, where men and sea interpenetrate, so to speak. [*Youth*]

CONSERVATIVE PARTY PRESS RELEASE

25 This would, at a stroke, reduce the rise in prices, increase productivity and reduce unemployment. [Distributed at press conference, 16 June 1960. Wrongly attr. to Edward Heath at the conference, according to D. Butler and A. Sloman, *British Political Facts 1900–1975*]

BENJAMIN CONSTANT 1767–1830

26 *Je ne suis pas la rose, mais j'ai vécu avec elle.* – I am not the rose, but I have lived with her. [Attr.]

EMPEROR CONSTANTINE 288?–337

27 *In hoc signo vinces.* – Beneath this sign thou shalt conquer. [Words heard in a vision]

J. GORDON COOGLER 1869–?

28 Alas! for the South, her books have grown

fewer – / She was never much given to literature. [*Purely Original Verse*]

A. J. COOK 1885–1931

1 Not a penny off the pay; not a second on the day. [Slogan of Coal Strike, 1926]

DAN COOK 1926–

2 The opera ain't over till the fat lady sings. [In baseball commentary on US TV, Apr. 1978, quoted in the *Washington Post*, 11 June 1978. Often wrongly ascr. to Dick Motta, coach of Washington Bullets, who adopted it]

ELIZA COOK 1818–1889

3 I love it, I love it; and who shall dare / To chide me for loving that old arm-chair? [*The Old Arm-Chair*]

PETER COOK 1937–

4 I am very interested in the Universe – I am specializing in the Universe and all that surrounds it. [In *Beyond the Fringe*]

PRESIDENT CALVIN COOLIDGE 1872–1933

5 The chief business of the American people is business. [Speech in Washington, DC, 17 Jan. 1925, commonly misquoted as 'The business of America is business']

6 He said he was against it. [On being asked what a clergyman had said in a sermon on sin, attr. J. H. McKee, *Coolidge: Wit and Wisdom*]

7 They hired the money, didn't they? [Of the Allies' war-debt, 1925) Attr. but not authenticated by his biographer, Claude M. Fuess]

JAMES FENIMORE COOPER 1789–1851

8 The Last of the Mohicans. [Title of novel]

RICHARD CORBET 1582–1635

9 Farewell rewards and fairies, / Good housewives now may say, / But now foul sluts in dairies / Do fare as well as they, / And though they sweep their hearths no less / Than maids were wont to do, / Yet who of late for cleanliness, / Finds sixpence in her shoe? [*The Fairies' Farewell*]

10 By which we note the fairies / Were of the

old profession; / Their songs were Ave Maries, / Their dances were procession.

TRISTAN CORBIÈRE 1845–1875

11 *Mélange adultère de tout.* – Adulterous mixture of everything. [*Épitaphe*]

PIERRE CORNEILLE 1606–1684

12 *Cette obscure clarté qui tombe des étoiles.* – This dark brightness that falls from the stars. [*Le Cid*, IV. iii]

13 *Et le combat cessa, faute de combattants.* – And the battle ended through lack of combatants.

14 *Je suis maître de moi comme de l'univers / Je le suis, je veux l'être.* – I am master of myself, as of the Universe; I am, and I wish to be so. [*Cinna*, V. iii]

15 *Faites votre devoir, et laissez faire aux dieux.* – Do your duty, and leave the rest to the gods. [*Horace*, II. viii]

16 *Hélas! je sors d'un mal pour tomber dans un pire.* – Alas, I emerge from one disaster to fall into a worse. [*Le Menteur*, III. ii]

17 *À raconter ses maux, souvent on les soulage.* – One often calms one's grief by recounting it. [*Polyeucte*, I. iii]

FRANCES CORNFORD 1886–1960

18 Magnificently unprepared / For the long littleness of life. [*Rupert Brooke*]

19 O why do you walk through the fields in gloves, / Missing so much and so much? / O fat white woman whom nobody loves. [*To a Fat Lady seen from the Train*]

ANNE BIGOT DE CORNUEL 1605–1694

20 *Il n'y a pas de héros pour son valet de chambre.* – No man is a hero to his valet. [*Lettres de Mlle Aïssé*, 13 Aug. 1728 (see also 285:20)]

ANTONIO CORREGGIO 1489?–1534

21 *Anch-io sono pittore!* – I am a painter too! [Attr. on seeing Raphael's *St Cecilia* at Bologna *c.* 1525]

W. J. CORY 1823–1892

22 Jolly boating weather, / And a hay harvest

breeze, / Blade on the feather, / Shade off the trees. [*Eton Boating Song*]

1 They told me, Heraclitus, they told me you were dead, / They brought me bitter news to hear, and bitter tears to shed. [*Heraclitus*]

2 How often you and I / Had tired the sun with talking and sent him down the sky.

3 A handful of grey ashes, long, long ago at rest.

4 Still are thy pleasant voices, thy nightingales, awake; / For Death, he taketh all away, but them he cannot take.

NATHANIEL COTTON 1705–1788

5 Yet still we hug the dear deceit. [*Visions*, 'Content']

ÉMILE COUÉ 1857–1926

6 *Tous les jours, à tous points de vue, je vais de mieux en mieux.* – Every day, in every way, I'm getting better and better. [Formula of his faith-cures]

VICTOR COUSIN 1792–1867

7 *Il faut de la religion pour la religion, de la morale pour la morale, de l'art pour l'art.* – We need religion for religion's sake, morality for morality's sake and art for art's sake. [*Cours de philosophie*]

THOMAS, BARON COVENTRY 1578–1640

8 The wooden walls are the best walls of this kingdom. [Speech to the Judges, 17 June 1635]

NOËL COWARD 1899–1973

9 I believe that since my life began / The most I've had is just / A talent to amuse. [*Bitter Sweet*, II. i, 'If Love were All']

10 We have no reliable guarantee that the afterlife will be any less exasperating than this one, have we? [*Blithe Spirit*, I]

11 Never mind, dear, we're all made the same, though some more than others. [*Collected Sketches and Lyrics*, 'The Café de la Paix']

12 We're Regency Rakes / And each of us makes / A personal issue / Of adipose tissue. [*Conversation Piece*, I. iv]

13 There's always something fishy about the French! [vi]

14 Don't let's be beastly to the Germans. [Lyric: *Don't Let's be Beastly to the Germans*]

15 Don't put your daughter on the stage, Mrs Worthington. [Lyric: *Don't Put your Daughter on the Stage*]

16 When it's raspberry time in Runcorn, / In Runcorn, in Runcorn, / The air is like a draught of wine. / The undertaker cleans his sign, / The Hull express goes off line, / When it's raspberry time in Runcorn. [*On With the Dance*, 'Poor Little Rich Girl']

17 And though the Van Dycks have to go / And we pawn the Bechstein grand, / We'll stand by the Stately Homes of England. [*Operette*, I. vii]

18 Very flat, Norfolk. [*Private Lives*, I]

19 Extraordinary how potent cheap music is. [Some versions give 'strange' as the first word]

20 Certain women should be struck regularly, like gongs. [III]

21 But why, oh why, do the wrong people travel, / When the right people stay at home? [*Sail Away*, 'Why Do . . . ?']

22 There are bad times just around the corner, / We can all look forward to despair, / It's as clear as crystal / From Bridlington to Bristol / That we can't save democracy / And we don't much care. [Lyric: *There Are Bad Times*]

23 A room with a view / And you. [*This Year of Grace*, 'A Room with A View']

24 There's sand in the porridge and sand in the bed, / And if this is pleasure we'd rather be dead. ['Mother's Complaint']

25 Dance, dance, dance little lady, / Leave tomorrow behind. ['Dance Little Lady']

26 Whatever crimes the Proletariat commits / It can't be beastly to the Children of the Ritz. [*Words and Music*, 'The Children of the Rich']

27 Mad dogs and Englishmen go out in the midday sun.

28 The sun never sets on Government House. ['Planters' Wives']

29 Mad about the boy.

30 Learn the lines and don't bump into the furniture. [Advice to a young actor. Attr.]

ABRAHAM COWLEY 1618–1667

31 The thirsty earth soaks up the rain, / And drinks, and gapes for drink again. / The plants

suck in the earth and are / With constant drinking fresh and fair. [*Anacreontic: Drinking*]

1 For why / Should every creature drink but I, / Why, man of morals, tell me why?

2 Love in her sunny eyes does basking play; / Love walks the pleasant mazes of her hair; / Love does on both her lips for ever stray; / And sows and reaps a thousand kisses there. / In all her outward parts Love's always seen; / But, oh, he never went within. [*The Change*]

3 God the first garden made, and the first city Cain. [*The Garden*]

4 The world's a scene of changes, and to be / Constant, in Nature were inconstancy. [*Inconstancy*]

5 This only grant me, that my means may lie / Too low for envy, for contempt too high. [*Of Myself*]

6 But boldly say each night, / To-morrow let my sun his beams display, / Or in clouds hide them; I have lived to-day.

7 Hail, old patrician trees, so great and good! [*Of Solitude*]

8 Thou needst not make new songs, but say the old. [*On the Death of Mr Crashaw*]

9 His faith perhaps in some nice tenets might / Be wrong; his life, I'm sure, was always in the right.

10 And I myself a Catholic will be, / So far at least, great saint, to pray to thee. / Hail, Bard triumphant! and some care bestow / On us, the Poets militant below.

11 Though you be absent here, I needs must say / The trees as beauteous are, and flowers as gay, / As ever they were wont to be. [*The Spring*]

12 Life is an incurable disease. [*To Dr Scarborough*]

13 Well then; I now do plainly see, / This busy world and I shall ne'er agree. [*The Wish*]

14 Ah, yet, e'er I descend to th' grave / May I a small house, and large garden have! / And a few friends, and many books, both true, / Both wise, and both delightful too! / And since Love ne'er will from me flee, / A mistress moderately fair, / And good as guardian-angels are, / Only beloved, and loving me!

HANNAH COWLEY 1743–1809

15 I have been five minutes too late all my life-time! [*The Belle's Stratagem*, I. i]

16 But what is woman? – only one of Nature's agreeable blunders. [*Who's the Dupe?* II. ii]

WILLIAM COWPER 1731–1800

17 When the British warrior queen, / Bleeding from the Roman rods, / Sought, with an indignant mien, / Counsel of her country's gods. [*Boadicea*]

18 Rome shall perish – write that word / In the blood that she has spilt.

19 Hark! The Gaul is at her gates!

20 Regions Caesar never knew / Thy posterity shall sway.

21 But misery still delights to trace / Its semblance in another's case. [*The Castaway*]

22 We perished, each alone: / But I beneath a rougher sea, / And whelmed in deeper gulfs than he.

23 Grief is itself a med'cine. [*Charity*, 159]

24 He found it inconvenient to be poor. [189]

25 Heaven held his hand, the likeness must be true. [434]

26 With outstretched hoe I slew him at the door, / And taught him NEVER TO COME THERE NO MORE. [(A viper that attacked three kittens) *The Colubriad*]

27 A fool must now and then be right, by chance. [*Conversation*, 96]

28 Contradiction for its own dear sake. [106]

29 A noisy man is always in the right. [114]

30 Pernicious weed! whose scent the fair annoys, / Unfriendly to society's chief joys, / Thy worst effect is banishing for hours / The sex whose presence civilizes ours. [251]

31 A fool with judges, amongst fools a judge: / He says but little, and that little said / Owes all its weight, like loaded dice, to lead. / His wit invites you by his looks to come, / But when you knock, it never is at home. [300]

32 Some farrier should prescribe his proper course, / Whose only fit companion is his horse. [411]

33 An honest man, close-buttoned to the chin, / Broadcloth without, and a warm heart within. [*Epistle to Joseph Hill*]

34 The busy trifler dreams himself alone, / Frames many a purpose, and God works his own. [*Expostulation*, 322]

1 Thousands, careless of the damning sin, / Kiss the book's outside who ne'er look within. [388]

2 'Twas April, as the bumpkins say, / The legislature called it May. [*A Fable*]

3 The man that hails you Tom or Jack, / And proves by thumps upon your back / How he esteems your merit, / Is such a friend, that one had need / Be very much his friend indeed / To pardon or to bear it. [*Friendship*, 163]

4 And diff'ring judgements serve but to declare, / That truth lies somewhere, if we knew but where. [*Hope*, 423]

5 Absence from whom we love is worse than death. ['*Hope, like the Short-lived Ray*']

6 John Gilpin was a citizen / Of credit and renown, / A train-band captain eke was he / Of famous London town. [*John Gilpin*, 1]

7 To-morrow is our wedding-day, / And we will then repair / Unto the Bell at Edmonton, / All in a chaise and pair. [3]

8 So you must ride / On horseback after we. [4]

9 O'erjoyed was he to find / That, though on pleasure she was bent, / She had a frugal mind. [8]

10 And up he got, in haste to ride, / But soon came down again. [12]

11 For loss of time, / Although it grieved him sore, / Yet loss of pence, full well he knew, / Would trouble him much more. [14]

12 Away went Gilpin, neck or naught, / Away went hat and wig! [25]

13 The dogs did bark, the children screamed, / Up flew the windows all; / And every soul bawled out, Well done! / As loud as he could bawl. [28]

14 Away went Gilpin – Who but he? / His fame soon spread around – He carries weight! he rides a race! / 'Tis for a thousand pound! [29]

15 The dinner waits, and we are tired: / Said Gilpin – So am I! [37]

16 My hat and wig will soon be here, / They are upon the road. [44]

17 Right glad to find / His friend in merry pin. [45]

18 Says John, It is my wedding-day, / And all the world would stare, / If wife should dine at Edmonton, / And I should dine at Ware. [49]

19 So turning to his horse, he said, / I am in haste to dine; / 'Twas for your pleasure you came here, / You shall go back for mine. [50]

20 Now let us sing, Long live the king, / And Gilpin, long live he; / And when he next doth ride abroad, / May I be there to see! [63]

21 No dancing bear was so genteel, / Or half so *dégagé*. [*Of Himself*]

22 Oh for a closer walk with God, / A calm and heavenly frame; / A light to shine upon the road / That leads me to the Lamb! [*Olney Hymns*, 1]

23 What peaceful hours I once enjoyed! / How sweet their memory still! / But they have left an aching void / The world can never fill.

24 Nor sword nor spear the stripling took, / But chose a pebble from the brook. [4]

25 My God, till I received thy stroke, / How like a beast was I! / So unaccustomed to the yoke, / So backward to comply. [12]

26 There is a fountain filled with blood / Drawn from Emmanuel's veins; / And sinners, plunged beneath that flood, / Lose all their guilty stains. [15]

27 When this poor, lisping, stammering tongue / Lies silent in the grave.

28 Can a woman's tender care / Cease towards the child she bare? / Yes, she may forgetful be, / Yet will I remember thee. [18]

29 I seem forsaken and alone, / I hear the lion roar; / And every door is shut but one, / And that is Mercy's door. [33]

30 God moves in a mysterious way, / His wonders to perform; / He plants his footsteps in the sea, / And rides upon the storm. [35]

31 Behind a frowning providence / He hides a smiling face.

32 The bud may have a bitter taste, / But sweet will be the flower.

33 Toll for the brave – / The brave! that are no more; / All sunk beneath the wave, / Fast by their native shore. [*On the Loss of the Royal George*]

34 A land-breeze shook the shrouds, / And she was overset; / Down went the Royal George, / With all her crew complete.

35 It was not in the battle, / No tempest gave the shock, / She sprang no fatal leak, / She ran upon no rock; / His sword was in the sheath, /

His fingers held the pen, / When Kempenfelt went down / With twice four hundred men.

1 There goes the parson, oh! illustrious spark, / And there, scarce less illustrious, goes the clerk! [*On Observing Some Names of Little Note recorded in the 'Biographica Britannica'*]

2 Oh that those lips had language! Life has passed / With me but roughly since I heard thee last. [*On the Receipt of My Mother's Picture*, 1]

3 Blest be the art that can immortalize. [8]

4 Wretch even then, life's journey just begun. [24]

5 May I but meet thee on that peaceful shore, / The parting word shall pass my lips no more! [34]

6 Dupe of to-morrow even from a child. [41]

7 Thy morning bounties ere I left my home, / The biscuit or confectionary plum. [60]

8 Not scorned in Heaven, though little noticed here. [73]

9 Me howling blasts drive devious, tempest-tossed, / Sails ripped, seams opening wide, and compass lost. [102]

10 I shall not ask Jean Jacques Rousseau / If birds confabulate or no. [*Pairing Time Anticipated*]

11 The poplars are felled, farewell to the shade, / And the whispering sound of the cool colonnade! [*The Poplar Field*]

12 Unmissed but by his dogs and by his groom. [*The Progress of Error*, 95]

13 Oh, laugh or mourn with me the rueful jest, / A cassocked huntsman and a fiddling priest! [110]

14 Himself a wanderer from the narrow way, / His silly sheep, what wonder if they stray? [118]

15 Remorse, the fatal egg by Pleasure laid / In every bosom where her nest is made. [239]

16 Mortals, whose pleasures are their only care, / First wish to be imposed on, and then are. [289]

17 Thou god of our idolatry, the Press. [461]

18 Then, shifting his side (as a lawyer knows how). [*The Report of an Adjudged Case*]

19 For 'tis a truth well known to most, / That whatsoever thing is lost – / We seek it, ere it come to light, / In every cranny but the right. [*The Retired Cat*, 95]

20 Always, ere he mounted, kissed his horse. [*Retirement*, 578]

21 Absence of occupation is not rest, / A mind quite vacant is a mind distressed. [623]

22 Built God a church, and laughed his Word to scorn. [(Voltaire) 688]

23 Philologists who chase / A panting syllable through time and space, / Start it at home, and hunt it in the dark, / To Gaul, to Greece, and into Noah's ark. [691]

24 Beggars invention and makes fancy lame. [710]

25 Mary! I want a lyre with other strings. [*Sonnet to Mrs Unwin*]

26 And, of all lies (be that one poet's boast) / The lie that flatters I abhor the most. [*Table Talk*, 87]

27 As if the world and they were hand and glove. [173]

28 Stop, while ye may; suspend your mad career! [435]

29 Made poetry a mere mechanic art; / And every warbler has his tune by heart. [(Pope) 656]

30 I sing the Sofa. [*The Task*, Bk i, 'The Sofa', 1]

31 The nurse sleeps sweetly, hired to watch the sick, / Whom, snoring, she disturbs. [89]

32 He, not unlike the great ones of mankind, / Disfigures earth; and, plotting in the dark, / Toils much to earn a monumental pile, / That may record the mischiefs he has done. [(Of the mole) 274]

33 God made the country, and man made the town. [749]

34 Oh for a lodge in some vast wilderness, / Some boundless contiguity of shade, / Where rumour of oppression and deceit, / Of unsuccessful or successful war, / Might never reach me more! [ii, 'The Timepiece', 1]

35 Mountains interposed / Make enemies of nations, who had else, / Like kindred drops, been mingled into one. [17]

36 Slaves cannot breathe in England; if their lungs / Receive our air, that moment they are free; / They touch our country, and their shackles fall. [40]

37 England, with all thy faults, I love thee still – / My country! [206]

1 There is a pleasure in poetic pains / Which only poets know. [285]

2 Variety's the very spice of life, / That gives it all its flavour. [606]

3 Let her pass, and charioted along / In guilty splendour, shake the public ways! [iii, 'The Garden'. 69]

4 I was a stricken deer, that left the herd / Long since. [108]

5 Charge / His mind with meanings that he never had. [148]

6 Great contest follows, and much learned dust / Involves the combatants. [161]

7 From reveries so airy, from the toil / Of dropping buckets into empty wells, / And growing old in drawing nothing up. [188]

8 Riches have wings, and grandeur is a dream. [263]

9 Detested sport, / That owes its pleasures to another's pain. [326]

10 How various his employments, whom the world / Calls idle; and who justly, in return, / Esteems that busy world an idler too! [352]

11 Who loves a garden loves a greenhouse too. [566]

12 Now stir the fire, and close the shutters fast, / Let fall the curtains, wheel the sofa round, / And, while the bubbling and loud-hissing urn / Throws up a steamy column, and the cups, / That cheer but not inebriate, wait on each, / So let us welcome peaceful evening in. [iv, 'The Winter Evening', 36]

13 'Tis pleasant, through the loopholes of retreat, / To peep at such a world; to see the stir / Of the great Babel, and not feel the crowd. [88]

14 O Winter, ruler of th' inverted year. [120]

15 Spare feast! a radish and an egg. [173]

16 With spots quadrangular of diamond form, / Ensanguined hearts, clubs typical of strife, / And spades, the emblem of untimely graves. [217]

17 In indolent vacuity of thought. [297]

18 It seems the part of wisdom. [336]

19 'Tis your country bids! / Gloriously drunk, obey th' important call! [509]

20 Shaggy, and lean, and shrewd, with pointed ears, / And tail cropped short, half lurcher and half cur. [v, 'The Winter Morning Walk', 45]

21 Great princes have great playthings. [177]

22 But war's a game, which, were their subjects wise, / Kings would not play at. [187]

23 And the first smith was the first murderer's son. [219]

24 All constraint, / Except what wisdom lays on evil men, / Is evil. [448]

25 Meditation here / May think down hours to moments. Here the heart / May give a useful lesson to the head, / And Learning wiser grow without his books. [vi, 'The Winter Walk at Noon', 84]

26 Nature is but a name for an effect, / Whose cause is God. [223]

27 A cheap but wholesome salad from the brook. [304]

28 I would not enter on my list of friends / (Though graced with polished manners and fine sense, / Yet wanting sensibility) the man / Who needlessly sets foot upon a worm. [560]

29 Shine by the side of every path we tread / With such a lustre, he who runs may read. [*Tirocinium*, 79]

30 The parson knows enough who knows a duke. [403]

31 As a priest, / A piece of mere church furniture at best. [425]

32 Thy lot thy brethren of the slimy fin / Would envy, could they know that thou wast doomed / To feed a bard, and to be praised in verse. [*To the Immortal Memory of the Halibut on which I Dined*]

33 Greece, sound thy Homer's, Rome thy Virgil's name, / But England's Milton equals both in fame. [*To John Milton*]

34 The twentieth year is well-nigh past, / Since first our sky was overcast; / Ah would that this might be the last! / My Mary! [*To Mary*]

35 All thy threads with magic art / Have wound themselves about this heart.

36 Just knows, and knows no more, her Bible true – / A truth the brilliant Frenchman never knew. [*Truth*, 327]

37 I am monarch of all I survey, / My right there is none to dispute; / From the centre all round to the sea / I am lord of the fowl and the brute. / Oh, solitude, where are the charms / That sages have seen in thy face? / Better dwell in the midst of alarms, / Than reign in this horrible place. [*Verses supposed to be written by Alexander Selkirk*]

1 Society, friendship, and love, / Divinely bestowed upon man, / Oh, had I the wings of a dove, / How soon would I taste you again!

2 But the sea-fowl has gone to her nest, / The beast is laid down in his lair.

3 He kissed likewise the maid in the kitchen, and seemed upon the whole a most loving, kissing, kind-hearted gentleman. [Letter to the Rev. J. Newton, 29 Mar. 1784]

GEORGE CRABBE 1754–1832

4 What is a church? – Our honest sexton tells, / 'Tis a tall building, with a tower and bells. [*The Borough*, Letter 2, 'The Church', 11]

5 Habit with him was all the test of truth, / 'It must be right: I've done it from my youth.' [3, 'The Vicar', 138]

6 Books cannot always please, however good; / Minds are not ever craving for their food. [24, 'Schools', 402]

7 The ring so worn, as you behold, / So thin, so pale, is yet of gold. [*His Mother's Wedding Ring*]

8 A master-passion is the love of news. [*The Newspaper*, 279]

9 Oh! rather give me commentators plain, / Who with no deep researches vex the brain; / Who from the dark and doubtful love to run, / And hold their glimmering tapers to the sun. [*The Parish Register*, 'Baptisms', 89]

10 When the coarse cloth she saw, with many a stain, / Soiled by rude hands, who cut and came again. [*Tales*, vii, 'The Widow's Tale', 25]

11 But 'twas a maxim he had often tried, / That right was right, and there he would abide. [xv, 'The Squire and the Priest', 365]

12 He tried the luxury of doing good. [*Tales of the Hall*, iii. 'Boys at School', 139]

13 'The game,' said he, 'is never lost till won.' [xv, 'Gretna Green', 334]

DINAH MARIA CRAIK [*née* MULOCK] 1826–1887

14 Douglas, Douglas, tender and true. [*Songs of our Youth*, 'Douglas, Douglas']

HART CRANE 1899–1932

15 Our Meistersinger, thou set breath in steel; / And it was thou who on the boldest heel / Stood up and flung the span on even wing / Of that great Bridge, our Myth, whereof I sing. [(Of Walt Whitman and Brooklyn Bridge) *The Bridge*]

THOMAS CRANMER 1489–1556

16 This hand hath offended. [Said at his burning, of the hand that had signed a recantation, 21 Mar. 1556]

RICHARD CRASHAW 1613?–1649

17 O thou undaunted daughter of desires! / By all thy dower of lights and fires; / By all the eagle in thee, all the dove; / By all thy lives and deaths of love; / By thy large draughts of intellectual day. [*The Flaming Heart upon the Book of Saint Teresa*, 93]

18 By the full kingdom of that final kiss / That seized thy parting soul, and sealed thee His; / By all the Heavens thou hast in Him – / Fair sister of the Seraphim! [101]

19 It was Thy day, sweet! and did rise / Not from the East, but from Thine eyes. [*Hymn of the Nativity*, 21]

20 Love, thou art absolute sole Lord / Of life and death. [*Hymn to Saint Teresa*, 1]

21 Farewell house, and farewell home! / She's for the Moors, and martyrdom. [63]

22 I would be married, but I'd have no wife, / I would be married to a single life. [*On Marriage*]

23 *Nympha pudica Deum vidit, et erubuit.* – The conscious water saw its God, and blushed. [*Sacred Epigram*, in Latin and English]

24 Two walking baths; two weeping motions; / Portable, and compendious oceans. [*Saint Mary Magdalene, or The Weeper*, 19]

25 Does the day-star rise? / Still thy stars do fall and fall. / Does day close his eyes? / Still the fountain weeps for all. / Let night or day do what they will, / Thou hast thy task; thou weepest still. [23]

26 Whoe'er she be, / That not impossible she / That shall command my heart and me;

Where e'er she lie, / Lockt up from mortal eye, / In shady leaves of destiny. [*Wishes to his Supposed Mistress*, 1]

27 Life, that dares send / A challenge to his end, / And when it comes say, 'Welcome, friend!' [85]

MRS EDMUND CRASTER ?–1874

1 The Centipede was happy quite, / Until the Toad in fun / Said, 'Pray which leg goes after which?' / And worked her mind to such a pitch, / She lay distracted in the ditch / Considering how to run. [Attr.]

JULIA CRAWFORD *fl.* 1835

2 Kathleen Mavourneen! the grey dawn is breaking, / The horn of the hunter is heard on the hill. [*Kathleen Mavourneen*]

3 It may be for years, and it may be for ever, / Oh! why art thou silent, thou voice of my heart?

JAMES CREELMAN 1901–1941
and RUTH ROSE 20 Cent.

4 Oh no, it wasn't the aeroplanes. It was Beauty killed the Beast. [Final words of film *King Kong* (1933 version)]

QUENTIN CRISP 1908–

5 There was no need to do any housework at all. After the first four years the dirt doesn't get any worse. [*The Naked Civil Servant*, 15]

JOHN WILSON CROKER 1780–1857

6 We now are, as we always have been, decidedly and conscientiously attached to what is called the Tory, and which might with more propriety be called the Conservative, party. [*Quarterly Review*, Jan. 1830]

7 A game which a sharper once played with a dupe, entitled, 'Heads I win, tails you lose.' [*Croker Papers*]

RICHMAL CROMPTON 1890–1969

8 Violet Elizabeth [Bott] dried her tears. She saw that they were useless and she did not believe in wasting her effects. 'All right,' she said calmly, 'I'll thcream then. I'll thcream, an' thcream, an' thcream till I'm thick.' [*Just William*]

OLIVER CROMWELL 1599–1658

9 A few honest men are better than numbers. [Letter to Sir W. Spring, Sept. 1643]

10 Such men as had the fear of God before them ... the plain russet-coated captain that knows what he fights for and loves what he knows. [Letter, Sept. 1643]

11 The State, in choosing men to serve it, takes no notice of their opinions. If they be willing faithfully to serve it, that satisfies. [Before Marston Moor, 2 July 1644]

12 I beseech you, in the bowels of Christ, think it possible you may be mistaken. [Letter to the Church of Scotland, 3 Aug. 1650]

13 It [the Battle of Worcester] is for aught I know a crowning mercy. [Letter to William Lenthall, 4 Sept. 1651]

14 Remark all these roughnesses, pimples, warts, and everything as you see me, otherwise I will never pay a farthing for it. [Instructions to Lely, on the painting of his portrait]

15 What shall we do with this bauble? There, take it away. [(The mace) When dismissing Parliament, 20 Apr. 1653]

16 You have sat too long here for any good you have been doing. Depart, I say, and let us have done with you. In the name of God, go! [Speech to the Rump Parliament, 22 Jan. 1654. See also 4:23]

17 Necessity hath no law. Feigned necessities, imaginary necessities ... are the greatest cozenage that men can put upon the Providence of God, and make pretences to break known rules by. [Speech to Parliament, 12 Sept.]

18 It is not my design to drink or to sleep, but my design is to make what haste I can to be gone. [Dying words, quoted in J. Morley, *Life*, v. Ch. 10]

T. W. H. CROSLAND 1868–1924

19 The Unspeakable Scot. [Title of an essay]

BISHOP RICHARD CUMBERLAND
1631–1718

20 It is better to wear out than to rust out. [Quoted in G. Horne, *The Duty of Contending for the Faith*]

E. E. CUMMINGS 1894–1962

21 who knows if the moon's / a balloon, coming out of a keen city / in the sky – filled with pretty people? [*& [AND]*]

22 he sang his didn't he danced his did [*50 Poems*, 29]

1 for whatever we lose (like a you or a me) / it's always ourselves we find in the sea ['maggie and milly and molly and may']

2 next to of course god america i / love you land of the pilgrims and so forth oh [*next to of course god*]

3 in every language even deafanddumb / thy sons acclaim your glorious name by gorry / by jingo by gee by gosh by gum

4 (and down went / my Uncle / Sol / and started a worm farm) [*nobody loses all the time*]

5 a politician is an arse upon which everyone has sat except a man [*A politician*]

6 Olaf (upon what were once knees) / does almost ceaselessly repeat / 'there is some shit I will not eat' [204]

ALLAN CUNNINGHAM 1784–1842

7 It's hame and it's hame, hame fain wad I be, / O, hame, hame, hame to my ain countree! [*It's Hame and It's Hame*]

8 Wha the deil hae we got for a king, / But a wee, wee German lairdie! [*The Wee, Wee German Lairdie*]

9 A wet sheet and a flowing sea, / A wind that follows fast / And fills the white and rustling sail / And bends the gallant mast. [*A Wet Sheet and a Flowing Sea*]

ROBERT CUNNINGHAME-GRAHAM 1735–1797

10 If doughty deeds my lady please, / Right soon I'll mount my steed. [*If Doughty Deeds My Lady Please*]

WILL CUPPY 1884–1949

11 The Dodo never had a chance. He seems to have been invented for the sole purpose of becoming extinct and that was all he was good for. [*How to Become Extinct*, p. 163)

JOHN PHILPOT CURRAN 1750–1817

12 The condition upon which God hath given liberty to man is eternal vigilance. [Speech on the right of election of Lord Mayor of Dublin, 10 July 1790]

'COLIN CURZON' 20 Cent.

13 I'll tell you in a phrase, my sweet, exactly what I mean: / . . . Not tonight, Josephine. [*Not tonight, Josephine*]

CYRANO DE BERGERAC 1620–1655

14 *Périsse l'Univers, pourvu que je me venge.* – Perish the Universe, provided I have my revenge. [*Agrippine*, IV. iii]

D

HARRY DACRE End of 19 Cent.

1 Daisy, Daisy, give me your answer, do! / I'm half crazy, all for the love of you! / It won't be a stylish marriage, / I can't afford a carriage, / But you'll look sweet upon the seat / Of a bicycle made for two! [*Daisy Bell*]

DAILY MIRROR

2 Whose finger on the trigger? [Front-page headline, on eve of election, 25 Oct. 1951]

EDOUARD DALADIER 1884–1970

3 *C'est un drôle de guerre.* [(This became 'It is a phoney war.' in trans.) Speech in Chamber of Deputies, Paris, 22 Dec. 1939]

SERGEANT DAN DALY [US Marines]
    20 Cent.

4 Come on, you sons of bitches! Do you want to live for ever? [Attr. at the battle of Belleau Wood, 6 June 1918. See also 169:3]

CHARLES A. DANA 1819–1897

5 When a dog bites a man that is not news, but when a man bites a dog that is news. ['What is News?', *New York Sun*, 1882]

SAMUEL DANIEL 1562–1619

6 Princes in this case / Do hate the traitor, though they love the treason. [*Tragedy of Cleopatra*, IV. i]

7 Love is a sickness full of woes, / All remedies refusing; / A plant that with most cutting grows, / Most barren with best using. / Why so? / More we enjoy it, more it dies; / If not enjoyed, it sighing cries, / Hey ho. [*Hymen's Triumph*, I. v]

8 How dost thou wear and weary out thy days, / Restless Ambition, never at an end! [*Philotas*, chorus]

9 Fair is my love, and cruel as she's fair, / Her brow shades frowns, although her eyes are sunny. [*Sonnets to Delia*, 6]

10 Care-charmer Sleep, son of the sable Night, / Brother to Death, in silent darkness born, / Relieve my languish, and restore the light, / With dark forgetting of my cares return. / And let the day be time enough to mourn / The shipwreck of my ill-adventured youth. [44]

11 Unless above himself he can / Erect himself, how poor a thing is man. [*To the Lady Margaret, Countess of Cumberland*, 12]

12 Come, worthy Greek! Ulysses, come; / Possess these shores with me! / The winds and seas are troublesome / And here we may be free. [*Ulysses and the Siren*, 1]

13 Custom, that is before all law; Nature, that is above all art. [*A Defence of Rhyme*]

DANTE ALIGHIERI 1265–1321

14 *Nel mezzo del cammin di nostra vita.* – In the mid-course of our life. [*Divina Commedia*, 'Inferno', i. 1]

15 *Lasciate ogni speranza voi ch'entrate.* – All hope abandon, ye who enter here. [iii. 9]

16 *Il gran rifiuto.* – The great refusal. [60]

17 *Nessun maggior dolore / Che ricordarsi del*

131

tempo felice /Nella miseria. – There is no greater grief than to recall a time of happiness when in misery. [v. 121]

1 *E'n la sua volontade è nostra pace.* – In His will is our peace. ['Paradiso', iii. 85]

2 *L'amor che move il sole e l'altre stelle.* – Love that moves the sun and the other stars. [xxxiii. 145]

GEORGES JACQUES DANTON 1759–1794

3 *De l'audace, encore de l'audace, et toujours de l'audace!* – Boldness, more boldness, and perpetual boldness! [Speech in the Legislative Assembly, 2 Sept. 1792]

MR JUSTICE DARLING 1849–1936

4 The law-courts of England are open to all men like the doors of the Ritz Hotel. [Also attr. to Lord Justice Sir James Mathew and Judge Sturgess]

RICHARD DARRÉ 1895–1953

5 *Blut and Boden.* – Blood and soil. [*Law for the Establishment of Hereditary Farms*, 29 Sept. 1933]

CHARLES DARWIN 1809–1882

6 The highest possible stage in moral culture is when we recognize that we ought to control our thoughts. [*The Descent of Man*, Ch. 4]

7 Man with all his noble qualities, with sympathy that feels for the most debased, with benevolence which extends not only to other men but to the humblest living creature, with his godlike intellect which has penetrated into the movements and constitution of the solar system – with all these exalted powers – still bears in his bodily frame the indelible stamp of his lowly origin. [Conclusion]

8 I have called this principle, by which each slight variation, if useful, is preserved, by the term of Natural Selection. [*The Origin of Species*, Ch. 3]

9 We will now discuss in a little more detail the struggle for existence.

10 The expression often used by Mr Herbert Spencer of the Survival of the Fittest is more accurate, and is sometimes equally convenient.

ERASMUS DARWIN 1731–1802

11 Soon shall thy arm, unconquered steam! afar / Drag the slow barge, or drive the rapid car; / Or on wide-waving wings expanded bear / The flying chariot through the field of air. [*The Botanic Garden*, I. i. 289]

CHARLES DAVENANT 1656–1714

12 Custom, that unwritten law, / By which the people keep even kings in awe. [*Circe*, II. iii]

SIR WILLIAM DAVENANT 1606–1668

13 The lark now leaves his watery nest / And climbing, shakes his dewy wings; / He takes this window for the east; / And to implore your light, he sings, / Awake, awake, the morn will never rise, / Till she can dress her beauty at your eyes. [*Song*]

JOHN DAVIDSON 1857–1909

14 When the pods went pop on the broom, green broom. [*A Runnable Stag*]

15 As I went down to Dymchurch Wall, / I heard the South sing o'er the land. [*In Romney Marsh*]

16 With thirty bob a week to keep a bride / He fell in love and married in his teens: / At thirty bob he stuck; but he knows it isn't luck: / He knows the seas are deeper than tureens. [50]

SIR JOHN DAVIES 1569–1626

17 Wedlock, indeed, hath oft comparèd been / To public feasts, where meet a public rout; / Where they that are without would fain go in. / And they that are within would fain go out. [*A Contention betwixt a Wife, A Widow and a Maid*, 196]

18 Judge not the play before the play be done. [*Respice Finem*]

W. H. DAVIES 1870–1940

19 And hear the pleasant cuckoo, loud and long – / The simple bird that thinks two notes a song. [*April's Charms*]

20 A rainbow and a cuckoo's song / May never come together again; / May never come / This side the tomb. [*A Great Time*]

21 It was the Rainbow gave thee birth, / And left thee all her lovely hues. [*The Kingfisher*]

1 What is this life if, full of care, / We have no time to stand and stare? [*Leisure*]

2 Sweet Stay-at-Home, sweet Well-content. [*Sweet Stay-at-Home*]

JEFFERSON DAVIS 1808–1889

3 All we ask is to be let alone. [Inaugural address as President of the Confederate States of America, 18 Feb. 1861. Attr.]

T. O. DAVIS 1814–1845

4 Come in the evening, or come in the morning, / Come when you're looked for, or come without warning. [*The Welcome*]

C. DAY LEWIS 1904–1972

5 I sang as one / Who on a tilting deck sings / To keep men's courage up, though the wave hangs / That shall cut off their sun. [*The Conflict*]

6 Now the peak of summer's past, the sky is overcast / And the love we swore would last for an age seems deceit. [*Hornpipe*]

7 Suppose that we, to-morrow or the next day, / Came to an end – in storm the shafting broken, / Or a mistaken signal, the flange lifting – / Would that be premature, a text for sorrow? [*Suppose that we*]

EUGENE V. DEBS 1855–1926

8 While there is a lower class, I am in it; while there is a criminal element, I am of it; while there is a soul in prison, I am not free. [Speech in Cleveland, Ohio, 9 Sept. 1917]

CLAUDE DEBUSSY 1862–1918

9 A beautiful sunset that was mistaken for a dawn. [Of Wagner's music, attr.]

STEPHEN DECATUR 1779–1820

10 Our country! In her intercourse with foreign nations, may she always be in the right; but our country, right or wrong. [Toast given at Norfolk, Virginia, Apr. 1816. See 110:27]

CHARLES DEDERICH 20 Cent.

11 Today is the first day of the rest of your life. [Hippie slogan of late 1960s]

MARQUISE DU DEFFAND 1697–1780

12 *La distance n'y fait rien; il n'y a que le premier pas qui coûte.* – Distance doesn't matter; it is only the first step that is difficult. [(On the legend that St Denis walked six miles, carrying his head in his hand) Letter to d'Alembert, 7 July 1763]

DANIEL DEFOE 1661?–1731

13 He bade me observe it, and I should always find, that the calamities of life were shared among the upper and lower part of mankind; but that the middle station had the fewest disasters. [*Robinson Crusoe*, Pt I]

14 One day, about noon, going towards my boat, I was exceedingly surprised with the print of a man's naked foot on the shore, which was very plain to be seen in the sand.

15 I takes my man Friday with me.

16 The best of men cannot suspend their fate: / The good die early, and the bad die late. [*Character of the late Dr S. Annesley*]

17 All men would be tyrants if they could. [*The Kentish Petition*, addenda, 11]

18 Wherever God erects a house of prayer, / The Devil always builds a chapel there; / And 'twill be found, upon examination, / The latter has the largest congregation. [*The True-Born Englishman*, (Pt I. 1]

EDGAR DEGAS 1834–1917

19 Monet's pictures are always too draughty for me. [In conversation. Quoted in *Memoirs of Julie Manet* (Mme Renoir)]

CHARLES DE GAULLE *see* GAULLE, GENERAL DE

THOMAS DEKKER 1572?–1632

20 The best of men / That e'er wore earth about him, was a sufferer, / A soft, meek, patient, humble, tranquil spirit, / The first true gentleman that ever breathed. [*The Honest Whore*, Pt I. I. ii]

21 Art thou poor, yet hast thou golden slumbers? / O sweet content! / Art thou rich, yet is thy mind perplexed? / O punishment! [*Patient Grissill*, I]

1 To add to golden numbers, golden numbers.

2 Honest labour bears a lovely face.

3 Golden slumbers kiss your eyes, / Smiles awake you when you rise. / Sleep, pretty wantons, do not cry, / And I will sing a lullaby. [IV. ii]

4 Brave shoemakers, all gentlemen of the gentle craft. [*The Shoemaker's Holiday*, III. i]

WALTER DE LA MARE 1873–1956

5 Ann, Ann! / Come! quick as you can! / There's a fish that *talks* / In the frying pan. [*Alas, Alack*]

6 Oh, no man knows / Through what wild centuries / Roves back the rose. [*All That's Past*]

7 Very old are we men; / Our dreams are tales / Told in dim Eden / By Eve's nightingales.

8 Silence and sleep like fields / Of amaranth lie.

9 Far are the shades of Arabia, / Where the Princes ride at noon. [*Arabia*]

10 He is crazed with the spell of far Arabia, / They have stolen his wits away.

11 Has anybody seen my Mopser? – / A comely dog is he, / With hair the colour of a Charles the Fifth, / And teeth like ships at sea. [*The Bandog*]

12 When I lie where shades of darkness / Shall no more assail mine eyes. [*Fare Well*]

13 Look thy last on all things lovely, / Every hour.

14 Since that all things thou wouldst praise / Beauty took from those who loved them / In other days.

15 Nought but vast sorrow was there – / The sweet cheat gone. *The Ghost*]

16 He is the Ancient Tapster of this Hostel, / To him at length even we all keys must resign. [*Hospital*]

17 Three jolly gentlemen, / In coats of red, / Rode their horses / Up to bed. [*The Huntsmen*]

18 I can't abear a Butcher, / I can't abide his meat. [*I Can't Abear*]

19 Do diddle di do, / Poor Jim Jay / Got stuck fast / In Yesterday. [*Jim Jay*]

20 'Is there anybody there?' said the Traveller, / Knocking on the moonlit door. [*The Listeners*]

21 'Tell them I came, and no-one answered, / That I kept my word,' he said.

22 And how the silence surged softly backward, / When the plunging hoofs were gone.

23 It's a very odd thing – / As odd as can be – / That whatever Miss T. Eats / Turns into Miss T. [*Miss T.*]

24 Softly along the road of evening, / In a twilight dim with rose, / Wrinkled with age, and drenched with dew, / Old Nod, the shepherd, goes. [*Nod*]

25 Three jolly Farmers / Once bet a pound / Each dance the other would / Off the ground. [*Off the Ground*]

26 Slowly, silently, now the moon / Walks the night in her silver shoon. [*Silver*]

27 Who said, 'Peacock Pie'? / The old king to the sparrow: / Who said, 'Crops are ripe'? / Rust to the harrow. [*The Song of the Mad Prince*]

28 Who said, 'Where sleeps she now? / Where rests she now her head, / Bathed in eve's loveliness'? / That's what I said.

29 Who said, 'Ay, mum's the word'? / Sexton to willow.

30 Life's troubled bubble broken.

31 Too tired to yawn, too tired to sleep: / Poor tired Tim! It's sad for him. [*Tired Tim*]

ABBÉ JACQUES DELILLE 1738–1813

32 *Le sort fait les parents, la choix fait les amis.* – Fate chooses your relations, you choose your friends. [*Malheur et pitié*, I]

SIR JOHN DENHAM 1615–1669

33 O could I flow like thee, and make my stream / My great example, as it is my theme! / Though deep, yet clear, though gentle, yet not dull, / Strong without rage, without o'erflowing full. [*Cooper's Hill*, 189]

THOMAS, LORD DENMAN 1779–1854

34 Trial by jury itself . . . will be a delusion, a mockery, and a snare. [Judgement in O'Connell *v.* the Queen, 4 Sept. 1844]

C. J. DENNIS 1876–1938

35 Me name is Mud. [*The Sentimental Bloke*]

JOHN DENNIS 1657–1734

36 A man who could make so vile a pun

would not scruple to pick a pocket. [In the *Gentleman's Magazine*, 1781]

1 Damn them! they will not let my play run, but they steal my thunder! [Attr., on hearing his stage effects used by another dramatist]

SENATOR CHAUNCEY DEPEW 1834–1928

2 If you will refrain from telling lies about the Republican Party, I'll promise not to tell the truth about the Democrats. [Attr. in J. F. Parker, *If Elected, I Promise . . .* Reused in reversed form by Adlai Stevenson, in speech in Fresno, 10 Sept. 1952, as quoted in Suzy Platt (ed.), *Respectfully Quoted*]

THOMAS DE QUINCEY 1785–1859

3 So then, Oxford Street, stony-hearted stepmother, thou that listenest to the sighs of orphans, and drinkest the tears of children, at length I was dismissed from thee. [*Confessions of an English Opium Eater*, Pt I]

4 Everlasting farewells! and again, and yet again reverberated – everlasting farewells! [II]

5 Murder Considered as One of the Fine Arts. [Title of essay]

6 If once a man indulges himself in murder, very soon he comes to think little of robbing; and from robbing he comes next to drinking and sabbath-breaking, and from that to incivility and procrastination. [*On Murder*]

EDWARD, EARL OF DERBY 1799–1869

7 A great Whig authority used always to say that the duty of an Opposition was very simple – it was, to oppose everything, and propose nothing. [Speech in House of Commons, 4 June 1841]

8 Don't you see that we have dished the Whigs? [In reference to the Reform Bill of 1867]

LORD DESART 1845–1898

9 Mother Hubbard, you see, was old: there being no mention of others, we may presume she was alone; a widow – a friendless, old, solitary widow. Yet did she despair? Did she sit down and weep, or read a novel, or wring her hands? No! She went to the cupboard. [*Mock Sermon: Old Mother Hubbard*]

RENÉ DESCARTES 1596–1650

10 *Le bon sens est la chose du monde la mieux partagée: car chacun pense en être si bien pourvu, que ceux même qui sont les plus difficiles à contenter en toute autre chose n'ont point coutume d'en désirer plus qu'ils en ont.* – Common sense is the most widely distributed commodity in the world, for everyone thinks himself so well endowed with it that those who are hardest to please in every other respect generally have no desire to possess more of it than they have. [*Le Discours de la méthode*, I]

11 *La lecture de tous les bons livres est comme une conversation avec les plus honnêtes gens des siècles passés.* – The reading of all good books is like a conversation with the finest persons of past centuries.

12 *C'est quasi le même de converser avec ceux des autres siècles que de voyager.* – Travelling is almost like talking with those of other centuries.

13 *Cogito, ergo sum.* – I think, therefore I am. [IV]

EUSTACHE DESCHAMPS 1345–1406

14 *Qui pendra la sonnette au chat?* – Who will bell the cat? [*Ballade: Le Chat et les souris* (see also 147:2)]

PHILIPPE DESTOUCHES 1680–1754

15 *Les absents ont toujours tort.* – The absent are always in the wrong. [*L'Obstacle imprévu*, 1. vi]

EDWARD DE VERE *see* OXFORD, EARL OF

DUKE OF DEVONSHIRE 1895–1950

16 Good God, that's done it. He's lost us the tarts' vote. [(On hearing Baldwin's attack on the press barons; see 21:15, 241:35, 408:10) N. Rees, *Quote . . . Unquote*, cites Harold Macmillan, the duke's son-in-law, as witness to the two remarks being made in 1931 at a by-election meeting]

PETER DE VRIES 1910–

17 Gluttony is an emotional escape, a sign something is eating us. [*Comfort Me with Apples*, 15]

1 We must love one another, yes, yes, that's all true enough, but nothing says we have to like each other. [*The Glory of the Hummingbird*, Ch. 1]

2 I was thinking that we all learn by experience, but some of us have to go to summer school. [*Tunnel of Love*, 14]

SERGE DIAGHILEV 1872–1929

3 *Étonne-moi!* – Astonish me! [(Said to Jean Cocteau, in 1912, when dispirited through lack of encouragement) Quoted in *The Journals of Jean Cocteau*, 1]

PORFIRIO DIAZ 1830–1915

4 Poor Mexico, so far from God and so near to the United States! [Also attr. to Ambrose Bierce]

CHARLES DIBDIN 1745–1814

5 Did you ever hear of Captain Wattle? / He was all for love and a little for the bottle. [*Captain Wattle and Miss Roe*]

6 What argufies pride and ambition? / Soon or late death will take us in tow: / Each bullet has got its commission, / And when our time's come we must go. [*Each Bullet has its Commission*]

7 In every mess I find a friend, / In every port a wife. [*Jack in his Element*]

8 Then trust me, there's nothing like drinking / So pleasant on this side the grave; / It keeps the unhappy from thinking, / And makes e'en the valiant more brave. [*Nothing like Grog*]

9 For they say there's a Providence sits up aloft, / To keep watch for the life of poor Jack! [*Poor Jack*]

10 The lass that loves a sailor. [*The Round Robin*]

11 Here, a sheer hulk, lies poor Tom Bowling, / The darling of our crew. [*Tom Bowling*]

12 Faithful, below, he did his duty; / But now he's gone aloft.

THOMAS DIBDIN 1771–1841

13 Oh! it's a snug little island, / A right little, tight little island! [*The Snug Little Island*]

CHARLES DICKENS 1812–1870

14 Rather a tough customer in argeyment, Joe, if anybody was to try and tackle him. [(Parkes) *Barnaby Rudge*, Ch. 1]

15 Something will come of this. I hope it mayn't be human gore. [(Simon Tappertit) 4]

16 'There are strings,' said Mr Tappertit, '... in the human heart that had better not be wibrated.' [22]

17 Oh gracious, why wasn't I born old and ugly? [(Miss Miggs) 70]

18 This is a London particular ... A fog, miss. [*Bleak House*, Ch. 3]

19 I expect a judgment. Shortly. [Miss Flite]

20 Educating the natives of Borrioboola-Gha, on the left bank of the Niger. [(Mrs Jellyby) 4]

21 I am always conscious of an uncomfortable sensation now and then when the wind is blowing in the east. [(Mr Jarndyce) 6]

22 I only ask to be free. The butterflies are free. [Harold Skimpole]

23 Think! I've got enough to do, and little enough to get for it, without thinking. [Coavinses]

24 Not to put too fine a point upon it. [(Mr Snagsby) 11]

25 He wos very good to me, he wos! [Jo]

26 He [Mr Turveydrop] is celebrated almost everywhere, for his Deportment. [(Caddy) 14]

27 What is peace? Is it war? No. Is it strife? No. Is it lovely, and gentle, and beautiful, and pleasant, and serene, and joyful? O yes! [(Mr Chadband) 19]

28 Jobling, there *are* chords in the human mind. [(Guppy) 20]

29 Mrs Jellyby was looking far away into Africa. [23]

30 'It is,' says Chadband, 'the ray of rays, the sun of suns, the moon of moons, the star of stars. It is the light of Terewth.' [25]

31 It's my old girl that advises. She has the head. But I never own to it before her. Discipline must be maintained. [(Mr Bagnet) 27]

32 'Old girl,' said Mr Bagnet, 'give him my opinion. You know it.'

33 It is a melancholy truth that even great men have their poor relations. [28]

34 She's Colour-Serjeant of the Nonpareil battalion. [(Mr Bagnet) 52]

35 Far better hang wrong fler than no fler. [(The debilitated cousin) 53]

36 Oh let us love our occupations, / Bless the

squire and his relations, / Live upon our daily rations, / And always know our proper stations. [*The Chimes*, Second Quarter]

1 In came a fiddler – and tuned like fifty stomach-aches. / In came Mrs Fezziwig, one vast substantial smile. [*A Christmas Carol*, Stave 2]

2 'God bless us every one!' said Tiny Tim, the last of all. [3]

3 'Somebody's sharp.' 'Who is?' asked the gentleman, laughing . . . 'Only Brooks of Sheffield,' said Mr Murdstone. [*David Copperfield*, Ch. 2]

4 'I am a lone lorn creetur',' were Mrs Gummidge's words . . . 'and everythink goes contrairy with me.' [3]

5 'I feel it more than other people,' said Mrs Gummidge.

6 She's been thinking of the old 'un! [Mr Peggotty of Mrs Gummidge]

7 Barkis is willin'. [5]

8 I live on broken wittles – and I sleep on the coals. [The Waiter]

9 Experientia does it – as papa used to say. [(Mrs Micawber) 11]

10 'In case anything turned up,' which was his favourite expression. [Mr Micawber]

11 I never will desert Mr Micawber. [(Mrs Micawber) 12]

12 Annual income twenty pounds, annual expenditure nineteen nineteen six, result happiness. Annual income twenty pounds, annual expenditure twenty pounds ought and six, result misery. [Mr Micawber]

13 The mistake was made of putting some of the trouble out of King Charles's head into my head. [(Mr Dick) 17]

14 We are so very 'umble. [Uriah Heep]

15 Uriah, with his long hands slowly twining over one another, made a ghastly writhe from the waist upwards.

16 'Orses and dorgs is some men's fancy. They're wittles and drink to me. [(The Gentleman on the Coach) 19]

17 I only ask for information. [(Rosa Dartle) 20]

18 'It was as true,' said Mr Barkis, '. . . as taxes is. And nothing's truer than them.' [21]

19 What a world of gammon and spinnage it is, though, ain't it! [(Miss Mowcher) 22]

20 Ain't I volatile? [Miss Mowcher]

21 I should be happy, myself, to propose two months . . . but I have a partner, Mr Jorkins. [(Mr Spenlow) 23]

22 I assure you she's the dearest girl. [(Traddles) 27]

23 Accidents will occur in the best-regulated families. [(Mr Micawber) 28]

24 He's a going out with the tide. [(Mr Peggotty) 30]

25 You know, Trotwood, I don't want to swing a cat. I never do swing a cat. [(Mr Dick) 35]

26 Only my child-wife. [(Dora) 44]

27 Circumstances beyond my individual control. [(Mr Micawber) 49]

28 I'm Gormed – and I can't say no fairer than that! [(Mr Peggotty) 63]

29 He's tough, ma'am, tough, is J. B. Tough and devilish sly! [(Major Bagstock) *Dombey and Son*, Ch. 7]

30 I want to know what it says . . . The sea, Floy, what it is that it keeps on saying. [(Paul Dombey) 8]

31 'Wal'r, my boy,' replied the Captain, 'in the Proverbs of Solomon you will find the following words, "May we never want a friend in need, nor a bottle to give him!" When found, make a note of.' [(Captain Cuttle) 15]

32 Train up a fig-tree in the way it should go, and when you are old sit under the shade of it. [(Captain Cuttle) 19]

33 Cows are my passion. What I have ever sighed for has been to retreat to a Swiss farm, and live entirely surrounded by cows – and china. [(Mrs Skewton) 21]

34 The bearings of this observation lays in the application on it. [(Bunsby) 23]

35 Say, like those wicked Turks, there is no What's-his-name but Thingummy, and What-you-may-call-it is his prophet! [(Mrs Skewton) 27]

36 I positively adore Miss Dombey; – I–I am perfectly sore with loving her. [(Mr Toots) 30]

37 If you could see my legs when I take my boots off, you'd form some idea of what unrequited affection is. [(Mr Toots) 48]

38 Stranger, pause and ask thyself the question, Canst thou do likewise? If not, with a blush retire. [(Mrs Sapsea's epitaph) *Edwin Drood*, Ch. 4]

1 'Dear me,' said Mr Grewgious, peeping in, 'it's like looking down the throat of Old Time.' [9]

2 There's a young man hid with me, in comparison with which young man I am a Angel. That young man hears the words I speak. That young man has a secret way pecooliar to himself, of getting at a boy and at his heart, and at his liver. [(Magwitch) *Great Expectations*, Ch. 1]

3 He calls the knaves, Jacks, this boy! . . . And what coarse hands he has! And what thick boots! [(Estella) 8]

4 I've a pretty large experience of boys, and you're a bad set of fellows. Now mind . . . you behave yourself! [(Mr Jaggers) 11]

5 On the Rampage, Pip, and off the Rampage, Pip; such is Life! [(Joe Gargery) 15]

6 You don't object to an aged parent, I hope? [(Wemmick) 25]

7 We didn't find that it [London] come up to its likeness in the red bills – it is there drawd too architectooralooral. [(Joe Gargery) 27]

8 Halloa! Here's a church! . . . Let's go in! . . . Here's Miss Skiffins! Let's have a wedding. [(Wemmick) 55]

9 Now, what I want is Facts . . . Facts alone are wanted in life. [(Mr Gradgrind) *Hard Times*, Bk i. Ch. 1]

10 It couldn't exist without allonging and marshonging to something or other. [(Mr Meagles) *Little Dorrit*, Bk i. Ch. 2]

11 Whatever was required to be done, the Circumlocution Office was beforehand with all the public departments in the art of perceiving – HOW NOT TO DO IT. [10]

12 Look here. Upon my soul you mustn't come into the place saying you want to know, you know. [Barnacle Junior]

13 I hate a fool! [(Mr F.'s Aunt) 13]

14 Take a little time – count five-and-twenty, Tattycoram. [(Mr Meagles) 16]

15 In company with several other old ladies of both sexes. [17]

16 It was not a bosom to repose upon, but it was a capital bosom to hang jewels upon. [(Mrs Merdle's) 21]

17 There's milestones on the Dover Road! [(Mr F.'s Aunt) 23]

18 It came like magic in a pint bottle; it was not ecstasy but it was comfort. [(Flora Finching) 24]

19 Papa, potatoes, poultry, prunes and prism, are all very good words for the lips; especially prunes and prism. [(Mrs General) ii. 5]

20 Once a gentleman, and always a gentleman. [(Rigaud) 28]

21 The Lord No Zoo. [(Toby Chuzzlewit) *Martin Chuzzlewit*, Ch. 1]

22 Any man may be in good spirits and good temper when he's well dressed. There an't much credit in that. [(Mark Tapley) 5]

23 There might be some credit in being jolly. [Mark Tapley]

24 A highly geological home-made cake.

25 With affection beaming in one eye, and calculation out of the other. [(Mrs Todgers) 8]

26 'Do not repine, my friends,' said Mr Pecksniff, tenderly. 'Do not weep for me. It is chronic.' [9]

27 Let us be moral. Let us contemplate existence. [Mr Pecksniff]

28 Here's the rule for bargains: 'Do other men, for they would do you.' That's the true business precept. [(Jonas Chuzzlewit) 11]

29 Buy an annuity cheap, and make your life interesting to yourself and everybody else that watches the speculation. [18]

30 'Mrs Harris,' I says, 'leave the bottle on the chimley-piece, and don't ask me to take none, but let me put my lips to it when I am so dispoged.' [(Mrs Gamp) 19]

31 Some people . . . may be Rooshans, and others may be Prooshans; they are born so, and will please themselves. Them which is of other naturs thinks different. [Mrs Gamp]

32 Therefore I *do* require it, which I makes confession, to be brought reg'lar and draw'd mild. [(Mrs Gamp) 25]

33 'She's the sort of woman now,' said Mould . . . 'one would almost feel disposed to bury for nothing: and do it neatly too!'

34 He'd make a lovely corpse. [Mrs Gamp]

35 'Sairey,' said Mrs Harris, 'sech is life. Vich likeways is the hend of all things!' [(Mrs Gamp) 29]

36 Our backs is easy ris. We must be cracked-up, or they rises, and we snarls. We shows our teeth, I tell you, fierce. You'd better crack us up, you had! [(Chollop) 33]

1 Oh Sairey, Sairey, little do we know wot lays afore us! [(Mrs Gamp) 40]

2 'Bother Mrs Harris!' said Betsey Prig . . . 'I don't believe there's no sich a person!' [49]

3 But the words she spoke of Mrs Harris, lambs could not forgive . . . nor worms forget. [Mrs Gamp]

4 Which fiddle-strings is weakness to expredge my nerves this night! [(Mrs Gamp) 51]

5 United Metropolitan Improved Hot Muffin and Crumpet and Punctual Delivery Company. [*Nicholas Nickleby*, Ch. 2]

6 At Mr Wackford Squeers's Academy, Dotheboys Hall . . . Youth are boarded, clothed, booked, furnished with pocket-money, provided with all necessaries, instructed in all languages living and dead. [3]

7 He had but one eye and the popular prejudice runs in favour of two. [(Mr Squeers) 4]

8 Subdue your appetites, my dears, and you've conquered human natur. [(Mr Squeers) 5]

9 Here's richness! [Mr Squeers]

10 C-l-e-a-n, clean, verb active, to make bright, to scour. W-i-n, win, d-e-r, der, winder, a casement. When the boy knows this out of the book, he goes and does it. [(Mr Squeers) 8]

11 When he has learnt that bottinney means a knowledge of plants, he goes and knows 'em. That's our system, Nickleby; what do you think of it? [Mr Squeers]

12 As she frequently remarked when she made any such mistake, it would be all the same a hundred years hence. [(Mrs Squeers) 9]

13 There are two styles of portrait painting; the serious and the smirk. [(Miss La Creevy) 10]

14 One mask of brooses both blue and green. [(Fanny Squeers) 15]

15 I pity his ignorance and despise him. [Fanny Squeers]

16 We've got a private master comes to teach us at home, but we ain't proud, because ma says it's sinful. [(Mrs Kenwigs) 16]

17 'What's the water in French, sir?' 'L'eau,' replied Nicholas. 'Ah!' said Mr Lillywick, shaking his head mournfully. 'I thought as much. Lo, eh? I don't think anything of that language – nothing at all.'

18 Language was not powerful enough to describe the infant phenomenon. [23]

19 She's the only sylph I ever saw, who could stand upon one leg, and play the tambourine on her other knee, *like* a sylph. [(Mr Crummles) 25]

20 I am a demd villain! . . . I will fill my pockets with change for a sovereign in half-pence and drown myself in the Thames . . . who for her sake will become a demd, damp, moist, unpleasant body! [(Mr Mantalini) 34]

21 In the absence of the planet Venus, who has gone on business to the Horse Guards. [(The Gentleman in the Small-clothes) 41]

22 She is come at last – at last – and all is gas and gaiters! [(The Gentleman in the Small-clothes) 49]

23 My life is one demd horrid grind! [(Mr Mantalini) 64]

24 He has gone to the demnition bow-wows. [Mr Mantalini]

25 Is the old min agreeable? [(Dick Swiveller) *Old Curiosity Shop*, Ch. 2]

26 What is the odds so long as the fire of soul is kindled at the taper of conwiviality, and the wing of friendship never moults a feather! [Dick Swiveller]

27 Pass the rosy wine. [(Dick Swiveller) 7]

28 Codlin's the friend, not Short. [(Codlin) 19]

29 It's calm and – what's that word again – critical! – no – classical, that's it – it is calm and classical. [(Mrs Jarley) 27]

30 We cannot have single gentlemen to come into this establishment and sleep like double gentlemen without paying extra for it . . . an equal quantity of slumber was never got out of one bed and bedstead, and if you want to sleep in that way, you must pay for a double-bedded room. [(Dick Swiveller) 35]

31 It was a maxim with Foxey – our revered father, gentlemen – 'Always suspect everybody'. [(Sampson Brass) 66]

32 Oliver Twist has asked for more! [(Bumble) *Oliver Twist*, Ch. 2]

33 Known by the *sobriquet* of 'The artful Dodger'. [8]

34 'Hard,' replied the Dodger. 'As nails,' added Charley Bates. [9]

35 There is a passion for hunting something deeply implanted in the human breast. [10]

1 I only know two sorts of boys, Mealy boys, and beef-faced boys. [(Mr Grimwig) 14]

2 A beadle! A parish beadle, or I'll eat my head! [(Mr Grimwig) 17]

3 There's light enough for what I've got to do. [(Bill Sikes) 47]

4 'If the law supposes that,' said Mr Bumble, . . . 'the law is a ass – a idiot.' [*Oliver Twist*, 51]

5 A literary man – *with* a wooden leg. [(Mr Boffin on Silas Wegg) *Our Mutual Friend*, Bk i. Ch. 5]

6 Professionally he declines and falls, and as a friend he drops into poetry. [Mr Boffin on Silas Wegg]

7 Decline-and-Fall-Off-the-Rooshan-Empire. [Mr Boffin]

8 'Mrs Boffin, Wegg,' said Boffin, 'is a high-flyer at Fashion.'

9 Meaty jelly, too, especially when a little salt, which is the case when there's ham, is mellering to the organ. [Silas Wegg]

10 Mr Podsnap settled that whatever he put behind him he put out of existence . . . Mr Podsnap had even acquired a peculiar flourish of his right arm in often clearing the world of its most difficult problems, by sweeping them behind him. [11]

11 The question [with Mr Podsnap] was, would it bring a blush into the cheek of the young person?

12 Oh! *I* know their tricks and their manners. [(Fanny Cleaver) ii. 1]

13 I think . . . that it is the best club in London. [(Mr Twemlow, on the House of Commons) 3]

14 Queer Street is full of lodgers just at present. [(Fledgeby) iii. 1]

15 O Mrs Higden, Mrs Higden, you was a woman and a mother, and a mangler in a million million. [(Sloppy) 9]

16 T'other governor. [(Mr Riderhood) iv. 1]

17 The dodgerest of the dodgers. [(Mr Fledgeby) 8]

18 The Golden Dustman. [(Mr Boffin) 11]

19 He had used the word in its Pickwickian sense. [(Mr Blotton) *Pickwick Papers*, Ch. 1]

20 'An observer of human nature, sir,' said Mr Pickwick. [2]

21 Half a crown in the bill, if you look at the waiter. [Jingle]

22 Not presume to dictate, but broiled fowl and mushrooms – capital thing! [Jingle]

23 Kent, sir – everybody knows Kent – apples, cherries, hops and women. [(Jingle) 2]

24 I wants to make your flesh creep. [(The Fat Boy) 8]

25 'It's always best on these occasions to do what the mob do.' 'But suppose there are two mobs?' suggested Mr Snodgrass. 'Shout with the largest,' replied Mr Pickwick. [13]

26 Can I unmoved see thee dying / On a log, / Expiring frog! [(Mrs Leo Hunter) 15]

27 Tongue; well, that's a wery good thing when it ain't a woman's. [(Mr Weller) 19]

28 Battledore and shuttlecock's a wery good game, vhen you an't the shuttlecock and two lawyers the battledores, in which case it gets too excitin' to be pleasant. [(Mr Weller) 20]

29 Mr Weller's knowledge of London was extensive and peculiar.

30 Take example by your father, my boy, and be wery careful o' vidders all your life, specially if they've kept a public house, Sammy. [Mr Weller]

31 The wictim o' connubiality, as Blue Beard's domestic chaplain said, with a tear of pity, ven he buried him. [Mr Weller]

32 Poverty and oysters always seem to go together. [(Sam Weller) 22]

33 Wery good power o' suction, Sammy . . . You'd ha' made an uncommon fine oyster, Sammy, if you'd been born in that station o' life. [(Mr Weller) 23]

34 It's over, and can't be helped, and that's one consolation, as they always say in Turkey, ven they cuts the wrong man's head off. [Sam Weller]

35 Dumb as a drum vith a hole in it, sir. [(Sam Weller) 25]

36 Wery glad to see you, indeed, and hope our acquaintance may be a long 'un, as the gen'l'm'n said to the fi' pun' note. [Sam Weller]

37 Subscribe to our noble society for providing the infant negroes in the West Indies with flannel waistcoats and moral pocket handkerchiefs. [(Mr Stiggins) 27]

38 Vether it's worth goin' through so much, to learn so little, as the charity-boy said ven he got to the end of the alphabet, is a matter o' taste. [(Mr Weller) 27]

1 Eccentricities of genius. [30]

2 A double glass o' the inwariable. [(Mr Weller) 33]

3 Poetry's unnat'ral; no man ever talked poetry 'cept a beadle on boxin' day. [Mr Weller]

4 I am afeerd that werges on the poetical, Sammy. [Mr Weller]

5 'That's rather a sudden pull up, ain't it, Sammy?' inquired Mr Weller.

'Not a bit on it,' said Sam; 'she'll vish there wos more, and that's the great art o' letter writin'.'

6 Never sign a walentine with your own name. [Sam Weller]

7 If your governor don't prove a alleybi, he'll be what the Italians call reg'larly flummoxed. [Mr Weller]

8 She's a swellin' wisibly before my wery eyes. [Mr Weller]

9 It's my opinion, sir, that this meeting is drunk. [Mr Stiggins]

10 A Being, erect upon two legs, and bearing all the outward semblance of a man, and not of a monster. [Sergeant Buzfuz) 34]

11 'Do you spell it with a "V" or a "W"?' inquired the judge.

'That depends upon the taste and fancy of the speller, my Lord,' replied Sam.

12 'Oh, quite enough to get, sir, as the soldier said ven they ordered him three hundred and fifty lashes, ' replied Sam.

'You must not tell us what the soldier, or any other man, said, sir,' interposed the judge; 'it's not evidence.'

13 'Yes I have a pair of eyes,' replied Sam, 'and that's just it. If they wos a pair o' patent double million magnifyin' gas microscopes of hextra power, p'raps I might be able to see through a flight o' stairs and a deal door; but bein' only eyes, you see, my wision's limited.'

14 Oh Sammy, Sammy, vy worn't there a alleybi! [Mr Weller]

15 A friendly swarry, consisting of a boiled leg of mutton with the usual trimmings. [37]

16 'You disliked the killibeate taste, perhaps?'

'I don't know much about that 'ere,' said Sam. 'I thought they'd a wery strong flavour o' warm flat-irons.'

'That is the killibeate, Mr Weller,' observed Mr John Smauker, contemptuously.

17 'That 'ere young lady,' replied Sam. 'She knows wot's wot, she does.'

18 We know, Mr Weller – we, who are men of the world – that a good uniform must work its way with the women, sooner or later. [The Gentleman in Blue]

19 Anythin' for a quiet life, as the man said wen he took the sitivation at the lighthouse. [(Sam Weller) 43]

20 Wich is your partickler wanity? Wich wanity do you like the flavour on best, sir? [(Sam Weller) 45]

21 I'm wery much mistaken if that 'ere Jingle worn't a doin' somethin' in the water-cart way. [Sam Weller]

22 'Never ... see a dead postboy, did you?' inquired Sam ... 'No,' rejoined Bob, 'I never did.' 'No,' rejoined Sam triumphantly. 'Nor never vill; and there's another thing that no man never see, and that's a dead donkey.' [51]

23 'There's a Providence in it all,' said Sam.

'O' course there is,' replied his father with a nod of grave approval. 'Wot 'ud become o' the undertakers vithout it, Sammy?' [52]

24 Grief never mended no broken bones, and as good people's wery scarce, what I says is, make the most on 'em. [Sketches by Boz, 'Scenes', Ch. 22, 'Gin-Shops']

25 A smattering of everything, and a knowledge of nothing. [(Minerva House) 'Tales', Ch. 3, 'Sentiment']

26 It was the best of times, it was the worst of times. [A Tale of Two Cities, opening words]

27 I pass my whole life, miss, in turning an immense pecuniary Mangle. [(Mr Lorry) i. 4]

28 Although it's a long time on the road, it is on the road and coming. I tell thee it never retreats, and never stops. [(Mme Defarge) ii. 16]

29 'It is possible that it may not come, during our lives. We shall not see the triumph.' [Defarge]

'We shall have helped it,' returned madame.

30 'It is a far, far better thing that I do, than I have ever done; it is a far, far better rest, that I go to, than I have ever known.' [(Sidney Carton) iii. 15]

EMILY DICKINSON 1830–1886

31 Ample make this bed. / Make this bed with awe; / In it wait till judgement break / Excellent and fair. [Ample make this Bed]

1 Because I could not stop for Death, / He kindly stopped for me; / The carriage held but just ourselves / And Immortality. [*The Chariot*]

2 It was not death, for I stood up, / And all the dead lie down; / It was not night, for all the bells / Put out their tongues, for noon. [*It was not Death, for I stood up*]

3 How dreary to be somebody! / How public, like a frog / To tell your name the livelong day / To an admiring bog! [*Life*]

4 Our journey has advanced; / Our feet were almost come / To that odd fork in Being's road, / Eternity by term. [*Our Journey had Advanced*]

5 My life closed twice before its close; / It yet remains to see / If Immortality unveil / A third event to me. [*Parting*]

6 Parting is all we know of heaven, / And all we need of hell.

7 There came a wind like a bugle; / It quivered through the grass. [*There came a Wind*]

8 How much can come / And much can go, / And yet abide the world!

9 There's a certain slant of light, / On winter afternoons, / That oppresses, like the weight / Of cathedral tunes. [*There's a certain Slant of Light*]

10 I never saw a moor, / I never saw the sea; / Yet know I how the heather looks, / And what a wave must be. [*Time and Eternity*]

DENIS DIDEROT 1713–1784

11 *Faire son devoir tellement quellement, toujours dire du bien de M. le prieur et laisser aller le monde à sa fantaisie.* – To do his duty somehow, always to speak well of the Prior, and let the world go its own way. [*Le Neveu de Rameau*]

12 *L'esprit de l'escalier.* – Staircase wit (i.e. the good retort thought of after the conversation is finished). [*Paradoxe sur le comédien*]

13 *On a dit que l'amour qui ôtait l'esprit à ceux qui en avaient en donnait à ceux qui n'en avaient pas.* – It has been said that love robs those who have it of their wit, and gives it to those who have none.

'ISAK' DINESEN [KAREN BLIXEN] 1885–1962

14 What is man, when you come to think upon him, but a minutely set, ingenious machine for turning, with infinite artfulness, the red wine of Shiraz into urine? [*Seven Gothic Tales*, 'The Dreamers']

DIODORUS SICULUS Second half of 1 Cent. BC

15 Medicine for the soul. [Inscription quoted, I. 49. 3]

DIOGENES *fl. c.* 380 BC

16 Stand a little less between me and the sun. [(When asked by Alexander if he lacked anything) Plutarch's *Life of Alexander*, 14]

DIONYSIUS OF HALICARNASSUS *c.* 40–8 BC

17 History is philosophy drawn from examples. [*Ars rhetorica*, 11. 2]

WALT DISNEY 1901–1966

18 Supercalifragilisticexpialidocious. [Song from film musical *Mary Poppins*, words by Richard M. and Robert R. Sherman]

19 Who's Afraid of the Big Bad Wolf? [Title of song in cartoon film *Silly Symphony*, lyric and music by Frank E. Churchill and Ann Ronell]

20 Whistle While You Work. [Title of song in cartoon film *Snow White*, lyric by Larry Morey]

21 Heigh ho, heigh ho! / It's off to work we go. [Song]

BENJAMIN DISRAELI 1804–1881

22 Though I sit down now, the time will come when you will hear me. [Maiden speech in House of Commons, 7 Dec. 1837]

23 The Continent will not suffer England to be the workshop of the world. [Speech in House of Commons, 15 Mar. 1838]

24 The noble Lord [Lord Stanley] is the Rupert of parliamentary discussion. [24 Apr. 1844]

25 The right honourable gentleman [Sir Robert Peel] caught the Whigs bathing and walked away with their clothes. [28 Feb. 1845]

26 A Conservative government is an organized hypocrisy. [17 Mar.]

27 A precedent embalms a principle. [22 Feb. 1848]

28 England does not love coalitions. [16 Dec. 1852]

1 Finality is not the language of politics. [28 Feb. 1859]

2 I am myself a gentleman of the Press, and I bear no other scutcheon. [18 Feb. 1863]

3 The characteristic of the present age is a craving credulity. [Speech at Oxford Diocesan Conference, 25 Nov. 1864]

4 Man . . . is a being born to believe.

5 Is man an ape or an angel? Now I am on the side of the angels.

6 I had to prepare the mind of the country [for Reform], and . . . to educate our party. [Speech at Edinburgh, 29 Oct. 1867]

7 You behold a range of exhausted volcanoes. [(Referring to ministers on the Government Bench) Speech at Manchester, 3 Apr. 1872]

8 A University should be a place of light, of liberty, and of learning. [Speech in House of Commons, 11 Mar. 1873]

9 An author who speaks about his own books is almost as bad as a mother who talks about her own children. [Speech at banquet in Glasgow, 19 Nov. 1873]

10 Lord Salisbury and myself have brought you back peace – but a peace I hope with honour. [Speech in House of Commons, 16 July 1878. See 105:27]

11 A sophistical rhetorician inebriated with the exuberance of his own verbosity. [(Gladstone) Speech at banquet, 27 July]

12 No Government can be long secure without a formidable Opposition. [*Coningsby*, Bk ii. Ch. 1]

13 The Arch-Mediocrity who presided, rather than ruled, over this Cabinet of Mediocrities.

14 A sound Conservative government . . . Tory men and Whig measures. [6]

15 Youth is a blunder; Manhood a struggle; Old Age a regret. [iii. 1]

16 Read no history: nothing but biography, for that is life without theory. [*Contarini Fleming*, Pt I. Ch. 23]

17 'Sensible men are all of the same religion.' 'And pray, what is that?' inquired the prince. 'Sensible men never tell.' [*Endymion*, Bk i. Ch. 81]

18 Time is the great physician. [vi. 9]

19 They [the Furies] mean well; their feelings are strong, but their hearts are in the right place. [*The Infernal Marriage*, Pt I. 1]

20 The blue ribbon of the turf. [(The Derby) *Life of Lord George Bentinck*, Ch. 26]

21 The gondola of London. [(A hansom cab) *Lothair*, Ch. 27]

22 When a man fell into his anecdotage it was a sign for him to retire from the world. [28]

23 Every woman should marry – and no man. [30]

24 Little things affect little minds. [*Sybil*, Bk iii. Ch. 2]

25 Mr Kremlin himself was distinguished for ignorance, for he had only one idea, – and that was wrong. [iv. 5]

26 I was told that the Privileged and the People formed Two Nations. [8]

27 London is a modern Babylon. [*Tancred*, Bk v. Ch. 5]

28 I repeat . . . that all power is a trust – that we are accountable for its exercise – that, from the people, and for the people, all springs, and all must exist. [*Vivian Grey*, Bk vi. Ch. 7]

29 All Paradise opens! Let me die eating ortolans to the sound of soft music! [*The Young Duke*, Bk i. Ch. 10]

30 A *dark* horse, which had never been thought of . . . rushed past the grand stand to sweeping triumph. [ii. 5]

31 A man may speak very well in the House of Commons, and fail very completely in the House of Lords. There are two distinct styles requisite: I intend, in the course of my career, if I have time, to give a specimen of both. [v. 6]

32 Everyone likes flattery; and when you come to Royalty you should lay it on with a trowel. [Attr. remark to Matthew Arnold, quoted in G. W. E. Russell, *Collections and Recollections*, Ch. 23]

33 I am dead: dead, but in the Elysian fields. [(When translated to the House of Lords) In 1876, quoted in R. Blake, *Disraeli*, Ch. 24]

34 If a traveller were informed that such a man [Lord John Russell] was leader of the House of Commons, he may well begin to comprehend how the Egyptians worshipped an insect. [Attr.]

35 Pray remember, Mr Dean, no dogma, no Dean. [Quoted in F. Monypenny and G. E. Buckle, *Life*, Vol. iv. p. 368]

36 We authors, Ma'am. [(Attr. remark to Queen Victoria) v. 49]

1 When I want to read a novel I write one. [vi. 636]

2 There are three kinds of lies – lies, damned lies and statistics. [Quoted in Mark Twain, *Autobiography*, Pt V. Ch. 1, but also ascr. to others]

3 Your dexterity seems a happy compound of the smartness of an attorney's clerk and the intrigue of a Greek of the lower empire. [Attr. remark to Lord Palmerston]

SYDNEY DOBELL 1824–1874

4 The murmur of the mourning ghost / That keeps the shadowy kine, / 'O Keith of Ravelston, / The sorrows of thy line!' [*A Nuptial Eve*]

AUSTIN DOBSON 1840–1921

5 And I wove the thing to a random rhyme, / For the Rose is Beauty, the Gardener, Time. [*A Fancy from Fontenelle*]

6 The ladies of St James's! / They're painted to the eyes, / Their white it stays for ever, / Their red it never dies: / But Phyllida, my Phyllida! / Her colour comes and goes; / It trembles to a lily, – / It wavers to a rose. [*The Ladies of St James's*]

7 I intended an Ode, / And it turned to a Sonnet. [*Rose Leaves*]

8 For I respectfully decline / To dignify the Serpentine, / And make *hors-d'œuvres* for fishes. [*To 'Lydia Languish'*]

PHILIP DODDRIDGE 1702–1751

9 Behold the bleeding Lamb of God, / Our spotless sacrifice! [Hymn]

10 O God of Bethel, by whose hand / Thy people still are fed. [(Later altered to 'O God of Jacob') Hymn]

11 Return, my roving heart, return. [Hymn]

CHARLES FLETCHER DOLE 1845–1927

12 Democracy is on trial in the world, on a more colossal scale than ever before. [*The Spirit of Democracy*]

AELIUS DONATUS 4 Cent.

13 *Pereant qui ante nos nostra dixerunt.* – Confound the men who have made our remarks before us. [Quoted in St Jerome, *Commentary on Ecclesiastes*, Ch. 1]

JOHN DONNE 1571?–1631

14 Twice or thrice had I loved thee / Before I knew thy face or name, / So in a voice, so in a shapeless flame, / Angels affect us oft, and worshipped be. [*Air and Angels*]

15 Only our love hath no decay; / This, no tomorrow hath, nor yesterday, / Running it never runs from us away, / But truly keeps his first, last, everlasting day. [*The Anniversary*]

16 Come live with me, and be my love, / And we will some new pleasures prove / Of golden sands and crystal brooks / With silken lines, and silver hooks. [*The Bait*]

17 The day breaks not, it is my heart. [(Also attributed to John Dowland) *Break of Day*]

18 For God's sake hold your tongue, and let me love. [*The Canonization*]

19 Dear love, for nothing less than thee / Would I have broke this happy dream, / It was a theme / For reason, much too strong for fantasy, / Therefore thou waked'st me wisely; yet / My dream thou brok'st not, but continued'st it. [*The Dream*]

20 She, and comparisons are odious. [*Elegies*, 8, 'The Comparison', 54]

21 No spring, nor summer beauty hath such grace, / As I have seen in one autumnal face. [9, 'The Autumnal', 1]

22 So, if I dream I have you, I have you, / For all our joys are but fantastical. [10, 'The Dream', 13]

23 By our first strange and fatal interview. [16, 'On His Mistress', 1]

24 Nurse, O my love is slain, I saw him go / O'er the white Alps alone. [52]

25 Whoever loves, if he do not propose / The right true end of love, he's one that goes / To sea for nothing but to make him sick. [18, 'Love's Progress', 1]

26 O my America! my new-found-land. [19, 'To His Mistress Going to Bed', 27]

27 The household bird, with the red stomacher. [*Epithalamions*, 'On the Lady Elizabeth and Count Palatine', 8]

28 So, so, break off this last lamenting kiss, / Which sucks two souls, and vapours both away, / Turn thou ghost that way, and let me turn this, / And let our selves benight our happiest day. [*The Expiration*]

1 Where, like a pillow on a bed, / A pregnant bank swelled up, to rest / The violet's reclining head, / Sat we two, one another's best. [*The Extasie*, 1]

2 Pictures in our eyes to get / Was all our propagation. [11]

3 All day, the same our postures were, / And we said nothing all the day. [19]

4 But O alas, so long, so far / Our bodies why do we forbear? / They're ours, though they're not we, we are / The intelligences, they the sphere. [49]

5 So must pure lovers' souls descend / T'affections, and to faculties, / Which sense may reach and apprehend, / Else a great Prince in prison lies. [65]

6 Who ever comes to shroud me, do not harm / Nor question much / That subtle wreath of hair, which crowns my arm. [*The Funeral*]

7 Since you would save none of me, I bury some of you.

8 I wonder by my troth, what thou, and I / Did, till we loved? were we not weaned till then, / But sucked on country pleasures, childishly / Or snorted we in the seven sleepers' den? [*The Good-Morrow*]

9 And now good morrow to our waking souls, / Which watch not one another out of fear.

10 For love, all love of other sights controls, / And makes one little room, an everywhere.

11 Where can we find two better hemispheres / Without sharp North, without declining West?

12 Thou hast made me, and shall thy work decay? [*Holy Sonnets*, 1]

13 I am a little world made cunningly / Of elements, and an angelic spright. [5]

14 This is my play's last scene, here heavens appoint / My pilgrimage's last mile. [6]

15 At the round earth's imagined corners, blow / Your trumpets, Angels, and arise, arise / From death, you numberless infinities / Of souls. [7]

16 All whom the flood did, and the fire shall o'erthrow, / All whom war, dearth, age, agues, tyrannies, / Despair, law, chance, hath slain.

17 But let them sleep, Lord, and me mourn a space.

18 Death be not proud, though some have called thee / Mighty and dreadful, for, thou art not so, / For, those whom thou think'st, thou dost overthrow / Die not, poor death. [10]

19 One short sleep past, we wake eternally, / And death shall be no more; death, thou shalt die.

20 Spit in my face you Jews, and pierce my side. [11]

21 What if this present were the world's last night? [13]

22 Batter my heart, three personed God; for you / As yet but knock, breathe, shine and seek to mend. [14]

23 I, like an usurpt town, to another due, / Labour to admit you, but Oh, to no end.

24 For I / Except you enthrall me, never shall be free, / Nor ever chaste, except you ravish me.

25 Show me, dear Christ, thy spouse, so bright and clear. [18]

26 Wilt thou forgive that sin, where I begun, / Which is my sin, though it were done before? / Wilt thou forgive those sins through which I run / And do them still, though still I do deplore? / When thou hast done, thou hast not done, / For I have more. [*Hymn to God the Father*]

27 Since I am coming to that holy room, / Where, with thy quire of Saints for evermore, / I shall be made thy Music; As I come / I tune the instrument here at the door, / And what I must do then, think here before. [*Hymn to God in My Sickness*]

28 When I died last, and, Dear, I die / As often as from thee I go, / Though it be but an hour ago, / And lovers' hours be full eternity. [*The Legacy*]

29 If yet I have not all thy love, / Dear, I shall never have it all. [*Lovers' Infiniteness*]

30 I long to talk with some old lover's ghost, / Who died before the god of love was born. [*Love's Deity*]

31 Rebel and Atheist too, why murmur I, / As though I felt the worst that love could do?

32 Send home my long strayed eyes to me, / Which, Oh, too long have dwelt on thee. [*The Message*]

33 'Tis the year's midnight, and it is the day's. [*Nocturnal upon St Lucy's Day*]

1 The world's whole sap is sunk: / The general balm th' hydroptic earth hath drunk.

2 Nature's great masterpiece, an elephant / The only harmless great thing. [*The Progress of the Soul*, 381]

3 When my grave is broke up again / Some second guest to entertain. [*The Relique*]

4 A bracelet of bright hair about the bone.

5 Her pure and eloquent blood / Spoke in her cheeks, and so distinctly wrought, / That one might almost say, her body thought. [*The Second Anniversary*, 244]

6 Sweetest love, I do not go, / For weariness of thee, / Nor in hope the world can show / A fitter Love for me; / But since that I / Must die at last, 'tis best / To use myself in jest, / Thus by feigned deaths to die. [Song: '*Sweetest love . . .*']

7 Go, and catch a falling star, / Get with child a mandrake root, / Tell me, where all past years are, / Or who cleft the Devil's foot. [Song: '*Go and Catch . . .*']

8 Ride ten thousand days and nights, / Till age snow white hairs on thee.

9 Though she were true, when you met her, / And last, till you write your letter, / Yet she / Will be / False, ere I come, to two, or three.

10 Busy old fool, unruly Sun, / Why dost thou thus, / Through windows, and through curtains call on us? / Must to thy motions lovers' seasons run? [*The Sun Rising*]

11 Love all alike, no season knows, nor clime, / Nor hours, days, months, which are the rags of time.

12 She is all States, and all Princes, I, / Nothing else is. / Princes do but play us.

13 Shine here to us, and thou art everywhere, / This bed thy centre is, these walls, thy sphere.

14 I am two fools, I know, / For loving, and for saying so, / In whining Poetry. [*The Triple Fool*]

15 I have done one braver thing / Than all the Worthies did, / And yet a braver thence doth spring, / Which is to keep that hid. [*The Undertaking*]

16 As virtuous men pass mildly away, / And whisper to their souls to go, / Whilst some of their sad friends do say, / The breath goes now, and some say no. [*Valediction: Forbidding Mourning*]

17 If they be two, they are two so / As stiff twin compasses are two, / Thy soul the fixt foot makes no show / To move, but doth, if the other do.

And though it in the centre sit, / Yet when the other far doth roam, / It leans, and hearkens after it, / And grows erect, as that comes home.

18 On a round ball / A workman that hath copies by, can lay / An Europe, Afrique and an Asia, / And quickly make that, which was nothing, All. [*Valediction: Of Weeping*]

19 But I do nothing upon myself, and yet I am mine own Executioner. [*Devotions*, 12]

20 No man is an Island, entire of itself; every man is a piece of the Continent, a part of the main. [17]

21 Any man's death diminishes me, because I am involved in Mankind; And therefore never send to know for whom the bell tolls; it tolls for thee.

22 I neglect God and his Angels, for the noise of a fly, for the rattling of a coach, for the whining of a door. [*Sermons*, I. 80]

THOMAS SACKVILLE, EARL OF DORSET 1536–1608

23 His drink, the running stream; his cup, the bare / Of his palm closed; his bed, the hard, cold ground. [*Mirour for Magistrates*, Induction, 264]

24 His withered fist still knocking at Death's door. [334]

25 So, in this way of writing without thinking, / Thou hast a strange alacrity in sinking. [*Satire on Edward Howard*]

FYODOR DOSTOEVSKY 1821–1881

26 If you were to destroy in mankind the belief in immortality, not only love but every living force maintaining the life of the world would at once be dried up. Moreover, nothing then would be immortal, everything would be permissible, even cannibalism. [*Brothers Karamazov*, Pt I. Bk i. Ch. 6]

27 I think if the devil doesn't exist, but man has created him, he has created him in his own image and likeness. [II. v. 4]

28 It's not God that I don't accept, Alyosha, only I most respectfully return Him the ticket.

SARAH DOUDNEY 1843–1926

29 But the waiting time, my brothers, / Is the hardest time of all. [*Psalm of Life*, 'The Hardest Time of All']

LORD ALFRED DOUGLAS 1870–1945

1 I am the Love that dare not speak its name. [*Two Loves*]

ARCHIBALD DOUGLAS, FIFTH EARL OF ANGUS 1449–1514

2 I'll bell the cat. [Said at a meeting of Scottish nobles, 1482]

JAMES DOUGLAS 20 Cent.

3 I would rather put a phial of prussic acid in the hands of a healthy boy or girl than the book in question. [Reviewing Radclyffe Hall's *The Well of Loneliness* in the *Sunday Express*]

KEITH DOUGLAS 1920–1944

4 Remember me when I am dead / And simplify me when I'm dead. [*Simplify me when I'm dead*]

NORMAN DOUGLAS 1868–1952

5 Many a man who thinks to found a home discovers that he has merely opened a tavern for his friends. [*South Wind*, Ch. 24]

WILLIAM DOUGLAS 1672–1748

6 And for bonnie Annie Laurie / I'll lay me doun and dee. [*Annie Laurie*]

SIR ALEC DOUGLAS-HOME [EARL OF HOME] 1903–

7 As far as the 14th Earl is concerned, I suppose Mr Wilson, when you come to think of it, is the 14th Mr Wilson. [In TV interview, 21 Oct. 1963]

LORENZO DOW 1777–1834

8 You will be damned if you do – And you will be damned if you don't. [Definition of Calvinism from *Reflections on the Love of God*, 6]

ERNEST DOWSON 1867–1900

9 And I was desolate and sick of an old passion. [*Non Sum Qualis Eram*]

10 I have been faithful to thee, Cynara! in my fashion.

11 They are not long, the weeping and the laughter, / Love and desire and hate: / I think they have no portion in us after / We pass the gate. [*Vita Summa Brevis*]

12 They are not long, the days of wine and roses: / Out of a misty dream / Our path emerges for a while, then closes / Within a dream.

SIR ARTHUR CONAN DOYLE 1859–1930

13 Singularity is almost invariably a clue. The more featureless and commonplace a crime is, the more difficult is it to bring it home. [*The Adventures of Sherlock Holmes*, 'The Boscombe Valley Mystery']

14 You know my method. It is founded upon the observance of trifles.

15 A little monograph on the ashes of one hundred and forty different varieties of pipe, cigar, and cigarette tobacco.

16 It has long been an axiom of mine that the little things are infinitely the most important. ['A Case of Identity']

17 It is my belief, Watson, founded upon my experience, that the lowest and vilest alleys of London do not present a more dreadful record of sin than does the smiling and beautiful countryside. ['The Copper Beeches']

18 It is quite a three-pipe problem. ['The Red-Headed League']

19 I have nothing to do today. My practice is never very absorbing.

20 All other men are specialists, but his specialism is omniscience. [*His Last Bow*, 'The Bruce-Partington Plans']

21 But here, unless I am mistaken, is our client. ['Wisteria Lodge']

22 The giant rat of Sumatra, a story for which the world is not yet prepared. [*The Sussex Vampire*]

23 You know my methods, Watson. [*The Memoirs of Sherlock Holmes*, 'The Crooked Man']

24 'Excellent!' I cried. 'Elementary,' said he.

25 He [Professor Moriarty] is the Napoleon of crime. ['The Final Problem']

26 You mentioned your name as if I should recognize it, but beyond the obvious facts that you are a bachelor, a solicitor, a Freemason, and an asthmatic, I know nothing whatever about you. ['The Norwood Builder']

27 A long shot, Watson; a very long shot! ['Silver Blaze']

1 'Is there any point to which you would wish to draw my attention?'
'To the curious incident of the dog in the night-time.'
'The dog did nothing in the night-time.'
'That was the curious incident,' remarked Sherlock Holmes.

2 Now, Watson, the fair sex is your department. [*The Return of Sherlock Holmes*, 'The Second Stain']

3 In an experience of women that extends over many nations and three separate continents, I have never looked upon a face which gave a clearer promise of a refined and sensitive nature. [(Dr Watson) *The Sign of Four*, Ch. 2]

4 How often have I said to you that when you have eliminated the impossible, whatever remains, however improbable, must be the truth. [Ch. 6]

5 The Baker Street irregulars. [Ch. 8]

6 'I am inclined to think –' said I. 'I should do so,' Sherlock Holmes remarked impatiently. [*The Valley of Fear*, Ch. 1]

7 The vocabulary of 'Bradshaw' is nervous and terse, but limited.

SIR FRANCIS DOYLE 1810–1888

8 Last night among his fellow roughs, / He jested, quaffed, and swore; / A drunken private of the Buffs, / Who never looked before. [*The Private of the Buffs*]

SIR FRANCIS DRAKE 1540?–1596

9 There is plenty of time to win this game, and to thrash the Spaniards too. [Attr. saying, when the Armada was sighted, 20 July 1588]

10 I remember Drake . . . would call the Enterprise [of Cadiz, 1587] the singeing of the King of Spain's beard. [Quoted in Bacon, *Considerations touching a War with Spain*]

RUTH DRAPER 1889–1956

11 As a matter of fact, you know I am rather sorry you should see the garden now, because, alas! it is not looking at its best. Oh, it doesn't *compare* to what it was last year. [*Showing the Garden*]

12 And as for my poor *Glubjullas*, they never came up at all! . . . I can't think why, because I generally have great luck with my *Glubjullas*.

MICHAEL DRAYTON 1563–1631

13 Fair stood the wind for France, / When we our sails advance, / Nor now to prove our chance, / Longer will tarry. [*Ballad of Agincourt*]

14 Upon Saint Crispin's Day / Fought was this noble fray, / Which fame did not delay, / To England to carry. / O when shall English men / With such acts fill a pen, / Or England breed again / Such a King Harry?

15 Had in him those brave translunary things / That the first poets had. [(Christopher Marlowe) *To Henry Reynolds, of Poets and Poesy*, 106]

16 For that fine madness still he did retain / Which rightly should possess a poet's brain. [109]

17 Next these, learn'd Jonson, in this list I bring, / Who had drunk deep of the Pierian spring. [129]

18 I pray thee leave, love me no more, / Call home the heart you gave me, / I but in vain the saint adore, / That can, but will not, save me. [*To His Coy Love*]

19 And Queens hereafter shall be glad to live / Upon the alms of thy superfluous praise. [*Sonnets*, 'Idea', 6]

20 Since there's no help, come let us kiss and part. [61]

21 Shake hands for ever, cancel all our vows, / And when we meet at any time again, / Be it not seen in either of our brows, / That we one jot of former love retain.

22 When faith is kneeling by his bed of death, / And innocence is closing up his eyes, / Now if thou would'st, when all have given him over, / From death to life, thou might'st him yet recover.

WILLIAM DRENNAN 1754–1820

23 The men of the Emerald Isle. [*Erin*]

JOHN DRINKWATER 1882–1937

24 Moon-washed apples of wonder. [*Moonlit Apples*]

THOMAS DRUMMOND 1797–1840

25 Property has its duties as well as its rights. [Letter to Earl of Donoughmore, 22 May 1838]

WILLIAM DRUMMOND 1585–1649

1 The last and greatest herald of Heaven's King, / Girt with rough skins, hies to the deserts wild. [*For the Baptist*]

2 Phoebus arise, / And paint the sable skies / With azure, white, and red. [Song: *Phoebus Arise*]

3 Of this fair volume which we world do name / If we the sheets and leaves could turn with care. [*The World*]

JOHN DRYDEN 1631–1700

4 In pious times, ere priestcraft did begin, / Before polygamy was made a sin. [*Absalom and Achitophel*, Pt I. 1]

5 And, wide as his command, / Scattered his Maker's image through the land. [9]

6 Whate'er he did was done with so much ease, / In him alone 'twas natural to please. [27]

7 God's pampered people whom, debauched with ease, / No king could govern, nor no God could please. [47]

8 Plots, true or false, are necessary things, / To raise up commonwealths, and ruin kings. [83]

9 Of these the false Achitophel was first: / A name to all succeeding ages curst. [150]

10 A fiery soul, which working out its way, / Fretted the pigmy-body to decay: / And o'erinformed the tenement of clay. / A daring pilot in extremity; / Pleased with the danger, when the waves went high, / He sought the storms; but for a calm unfit, / Would steer too nigh the sands to boast his wit. / Great wits are sure to madness near allied, / And thin partitions do their bounds divide. [156]

11 Bankrupt of life, yet prodigal of ease. [168]

12 And all to leave, what with this toil he won, / To that unfeathered, two-legged thing, a son. [169]

13 Born a shapeless lump, like Anarchy. [172]

14 Resolved to ruin or to rule the state. [174]

15 For politicians neither love nor hate. [223]

16 The people's prayer, the glad diviner's theme, / The young men's vision, and the old men's dream! [238]

17 Than a successive title, long, and dark, / Drawn from the mouldy rolls of Noah's ark. [301]

18 All empire is no more than power in trust. [411]

19 But far more numerous was the herd of such, / Who think too little, and who talk too much. [533]

20 A man so various that he seemed to be / Not one, but all mankind's epitome. / Stiff in opinions, always in the wrong; / Was everything by starts and nothing long: / But, in the course of one revolving moon, / Was chemist, fiddler, statesman, and buffoon. [545]

21 So over-violent, or over-civil, / That every man, with him, was God or Devil. [557]

22 In squandering wealth was his peculiar art: / Nothing went unrewarded but desert. / Beggared by fools, whom still he found too late: / He had his jest, and they had his estate. [559]

23 Did wisely from expensive sins refrain, / And never broke the Sabbath, but for gain. [587]

24 During his office, treason was no crime. / The sons of Belial had a glorious time. [597]

25 His tribe were God Almighty's gentlemen. [645]

26 Youth, beauty, graceful action, seldom fail: / But common interest always will prevail. [723]

27 Nor is the people's judgement always true; / The most may err as grossly as the few. [781]

28 Beware the fury of a patient man. [1005]

29 Doeg, though without knowing how or why, / Made still a blundering kind of melody; / Spurred boldly on, and dashed through thick and thin, / Through sense and nonsense, never out nor in; / Free from all meaning, whether good or bad, / And in one word, heroically mad. [II. 412]

30 For every inch that is not fool is rogue. [463]

31 To die for faction is a common evil, / But to be hanged for nonsense is the Devil. [498]

32 The lovely Thais by his side, / Sat like a blooming Eastern bride. [*Alexander's Feast*, 9]

33 None but the brave deserves the fair. [15]

34 With ravished ears / The monarch hears, / Assumes the god, / Affects to nod, / And seems to shake the spheres. [37]

35 Bacchus ever fair, and ever young. [44]

36 Drinking is the soldier's pleasure. [57]

John Dryden

1 Rich the treasure, / Sweet the pleasure; / Sweet is pleasure after pain. [58]

2 Fought all his battles o'er again; / And thrice he routed all his foes; and thrice he slew the slain. [67]

3 Fallen from his high estate / And welt'ring in his blood. [78]

4 War, he sung, is toil and trouble; / Honour but an empty bubble; / Never ending, still beginning, / Fighting still, and still destroying. / If all the world be worth thy winning, / Think, oh think, it worth enjoying. [99]

5 Sighed and looked, and sighed again. [120]

6 Revenge, revenge, Timotheus cries, / See the Furies arise! [131]

7 And, like another Helen, fired another Troy. [154]

8 Could swell the soul to rage, or kindle soft desire. [160]

9 He raised a mortal to the skies; / She drew an angel down. [179]

10 So sicken waning moons too near the sun, / And blunt their crescents on the edge of day. [*Annus Mirabilis*, 125]

11 By viewing Nature, Nature's handmaid, art, / Makes mighty things from small beginnings grow. [155]

12 An horrid stillness first invades the ear, / And in that stillness we the tempest fear. [*Astraea Redux*, 7]

13 Of seeming arms to make a short essay, / Then hasten to be drunk, the business of the day. [*Cymon and Iphigenia*, 407]

14 Better to hunt in fields, for health unbought, / Than fee the doctor for a nauseous draught. / The wise, for cure, on exercise depend; / God never made his work for man to mend. [*Epistle to John Driden of Chesterton*, 92]

15 Theirs was the giant race, before the flood. [*Epistle to Mr Congreve*, 5]

16 Here lies my wife: here let her lie! / Now she's at rest, and so am I. [*Epitaph intended for his Wife*]

17 She feared no danger for she knew no sin. [*The Hind and the Panther*, I. 4]

18 For truth has such a face and such a mien / As to be loved needs only to be seen. [33]

19 My thoughtless youth was winged with vain desires, / My manhood, long misled by wandering fires, / Followed false lights; and when their glimpse was gone, / My pride struck out new sparkles of her own. / Such was I, such by nature still I am. / Be thine the glory, and be mine the shame. [72]

20 Reason to rule but mercy to forgive: / The first is law, the last prerogative. [261]

21 Too black for heav'n, and yet too white for hell. [343]

22 Much malice mingles with a little wit. [III. 1]

23 They found the new Messiah by the star. [176]

24 By education most have been misled; / So they believe, because they so were bred. / The priest continues what the nurse began, / And thus the child imposes on the man. [389]

25 T' abhor the makers, and their laws approve, / Is to hate traitors, and the treason love. [706]

26 Three poets, in three distant ages born, / Greece, Italy, and England, did adorn. / The first in loftiness of thought surpassed; / The next in majesty, in both the last. / The force of nature could no further go; / To make a third she joined the former two. [*Lines Printed under the Engraved Portrait of Milton*]

27 All human things are subject to decay, / And when fate summons, monarchs must obey. [*Mac Flecknoe*, 1]

28 The rest to some faint meaning make pretence, / But Shadwell never deviates into sense. / Some beams of wit on other souls may fall, / Strike through and make a lucid interval. / But Shadwell's genuine night admits no ray, / His rising fogs prevail upon the day. [19]

29 And torture one poor word ten thousand ways. [208]

30 To live at ease, and not be bound to think. [*The Medal*, 236]

31 So poetry, which is in Oxford made / An art, in London only is a trade. [*Prologue to the University of Oxford*]

32 And this unpolished rugged verse I chose / As fittest for discourse and nearest prose. [*Religio Laici*, 453]

33 From harmony, from heavenly harmony / This universal frame began: / From harmony to harmony / Through all the compass of the notes it ran, / The diapason closing full in Man. [*Song for St Cecilia's Day*, 1]

1 What passion cannot music raise and quell! [2]

2 The trumpet's loud clangour / Excites us to arms. [3]

3 The soft complaining flute. [4]

4 The trumpet shall be heard on high, / The dead shall live, the living die, / And music shall untune the sky. [8]

5 Farewell, too little and too lately known, / Whom I began to think and call my own. [*To the Memory of Mr Oldham*]

6 Wit will shine / Through the harsh cadence of a rugged line.

7 While yet a young probationer, / And candidate of heaven. [*To the Memory of Mrs Killigrew*, 21]

8 When rattling bones together fly, / From the four corners of the sky. [184]

9 Happy the man, and happy he alone, / He, who can call to-day his own: / He who, secure within, can say, / To-morrow do thy worst, for I have lived to-day. [Trans. of Horace, Bk iii. xxix]

10 Look round the habitable world! how few / Know their own good; or knowing it, pursue. [Trans. of Juvenal, x]

11 To see and to be seen, in heaps they run; / Some to undo, and some to be undone. [Trans. of Ovid, *Ars amatoria*, i. 109]

12 Who, for false quantities, was whipped at school. [Trans. of Persius, *Satires*, i. 135]

13 She knows her man, and when you rant or swear, / Can draw you to her with a single hair. [v. 246]

14 Errors, like straws, upon the surface flow; / He who would search for pearls must dive below. [*All for Love*, Prologue, 25]

15 She deserves / More worlds than I can lose. [I. i]

16 Fool that I was, upon my eagle's wings / I bore this wren till I was tired with soaring, / And now he mounts above me. [II. i]

17 Witness ye days and nights, and all ye hours, / That danced away with down upon your feet.

18 Men are but children of a larger growth. [IV. i]

19 Your Cleopatra; Dolabella's Cleopatra; every man's Cleopatra.

20 Whistling to keep myself from being afraid. [*Amphitryon*, III. i]

21 I am as free as nature first made man, / Ere the base laws of servitude began, / When wild in woods the noble savage ran. [*The Conquest of Granada*, Pt I. I. i]

22 Forgiveness to the injured does belong; / For they ne'er pardon, who have done the wrong. [II. I. ii]

23 This is the porcelain clay of humankind. [*Don Sebastian*, I. i]

24 And love's the noblest frailty of the mind. [*The Indian Emperor*, II. ii]

25 All heiresses are beautiful. [*King Arthur*, I. i]

26 I am to be married within these three days; married past redemption. [*Marriage à la Mode*, I. i]

27 For, Heaven be thanked, we live in such an age, / When no man dies for love, but on the stage. [*Mithridates*, Epilogue]

28 All, all of a piece throughout; / Thy chase had a beast in view; / Thy wars brought nothing about; / Thy lovers were all untrue. / 'Tis well an old age is out, / And time to begin a new. [*The Secular Masque*]

29 There is a pleasure sure / In being mad, which none but madmen know! [*The Spanish Friar*, II. i]

30 Dying bless the hand that gave the blow.

31 Looks as he were Lord of humankind. [ii]

32 A thing well said will be wit in all languages. [*Essay of Dramatic Poesy*]

33 He [Shakespeare] was the man who of all modern, and perhaps ancient poets, had the largest and most comprehensive soul ... He was naturally learned; he needed not the spectacles of books to read nature; he looked inwards, and found her there.

34 'Tis sufficient to say [of Chaucer], according to the proverb, that here is God's plenty. [Preface to *Fables*]

35 He [Chaucer] is a perpetual fountain of good sense.

36 A man is to be cheated into passion, but to be reasoned into truth. [Preface to *Religio Laici*]

37 Cousin Swift, you will never be a poet. [Quoted in Johnson's *Lives of the Poets*, 'Swift']

ALEXANDER DUBČEK 1921–

38 Socialism with a Human Face. [Motto of

the Prague Spring of 1968. Coined by Radovan Richta, according to R. Stewart (comp.), *Penguin Dictionary of Political Quotations*]

JOACHIM DU BELLAY 1515–1560

1 *France, mère des arts, des armes et des lois.* – France, mother of the arts, of arms and of law. [*Les Regrets*, 9]

2 *Heureux qui, comme Ulysse, a fait un beau voyage.* – Happy is he who, like Ulysses, has made a fine voyage. [31]

AL DUBIN 1891–1945

3 Tiptoe through the tulips with me. [Song: *Tiptoe Through the Tulips* from the musical *Gold Diggers of Broadway*]

4 You may not be an angel / 'Cause angels are so few, / But until the day that one comes along / I'll string along with you. [*Twenty Million Sweethearts*]

GEORGE DUFFIELD 1818–1888

5 Stand up! stand up for Jesus! [Hymn]

JOHN FOSTER DULLES 1888–1959

6 If EDC [European Defence Community] should fail, the United States might be compelled to make an 'agonizing reappraisal' of its basic policy. [Speech at North Atlantic Council in Paris, 14 Dec. 1953]

7 If you are scared to go to the brink, you are lost. [Interview in *Life* magazine, 16 Jan. 1956]

ALEXANDRE DUMAS 1803–1870

8 *Il y a une femme dans toutes les affaires; aussitôt qu'on me fait un rapport, je dis: 'Cherchez la femme'.* – There is a woman in every case; as soon as they bring me a report, I say, 'Look for the woman'. [*Les Mohicans de Paris*, II. iii]

9 *Tous pour un, un pour tous.* – All for one, one for all. [Motto, *Les Trois Mousquetaires*]

ALEXANDRE DUMAS *fils* 1824–1895

10 All generalizations are dangerous, even this one. [Quoted in Evan Esar (ed.), *Treasury of Humorous Quotations*]

DAPHNE DU MAURIER 1907–1989

11 Last night I dreamt I went to Manderlay again. [*Rebecca*, Ch. 1]

MARÉCHAL DUMOURIEZ 1739–1823

12 *Les courtisans qui l'entourent* [Louis XVIII] *n'ont rien oublié et n'ont rien appris.* – The courtiers who surround him have forgotten nothing and learnt nothing. [*Examen* (See also 414:8)]

WILLIAM DUNBAR 1460?–1520?

13 Our plesance heir is all vain glory, / This fals warld is bot transitory, / The flesche is brukle, the Fend is sle; / Timor mortis conturbat me. [*Lament for the Makaris*]

14 London, thou art the flour of cities all! [*London*]

15 Done is a battell on the dragon blak, / Our campioun Christ confountet hes his force; / The yettis of hell ar brokin with a crak, / The signe triumphall rasit is of the croce. [*On the Resurrection of Christ*]

FINLEY PETER DUNNE 1867–1936

16 Th' dead ar-re always pop'lar. I knowed a society wanst to vote a monyment to a man an' refuse to help his fam'ly, all in wan night. [*Mr Dooley in Peace and War*, 'On Charity']

17 'Th' American nation in th' Sixth Ward is a fine people,' he says. 'They love th' eagle,' he says, 'on th' back iv a dollar.' ['Oratory on Politics']

THOMAS D'URFEY 1653–1723

18 Neighbours o'er the Herring Pond. [*Pills to Purge Melancholy*, Vol. ii, 'Fable of the Lady, the Lurcher and the Marrow-Puddings']

LEO DUROCHER [Manager of Brooklyn Dodgers baseball team, 1951–4] 1906–

19 Nice guys finish last. [(Of 1948 New York Giants) According to P. F. Boller, jun., and J. George, *They Never Said It*, he really said 'Nice guys. Finish last.']

LAWRENCE DURRELL 1912–1990

20 The Good Lord Nelson had a swollen gland, / Little of the scripture did he understand / Till a woman led him to the promised land / Aboard the Victory, Victory O. [*A Ballad of the Good Lord Nelson*]

SIR EDWARD DYER 1540?–1607

1 My mind to me a kingdom is, / Such present joys therein I find, / That it excels all other bliss / That earth affords or grows by kind. [*My Mind to me a Kingdom is*]

JOHN DYER Early 18 Cent.

2 And he that will this health deny, / Down among the dead men let him lie. [Toast: *Here's a Health to the King*]

JOHN DYER 1700?–1758

3 Ever charming, ever new, / When will the landscape tire the view? [*Grongar Hill*, 5]

4 A little rule, a little sway, / A sunbeam in a winter's day, / Is all the proud and mighty have / Between the cradle and the grave. [89]

BOB DYLAN 1941–

5 How many roads must a man walk down / Before you call him a man? [Song: *Blowin' in the Wind*]

6 Yes, 'n' how many years can some people exist / Before they're allowed to be free? / Yes, 'n' how many times can a man turn his head, / Pretending he just doesn't see? / The answer, my friend, is blowin' in the wind.

7 A Hard Rain's A-Gonna Fall. [Title of song]

8 Keep a clean nose / Watch the plain clothes / You don't need a weather man / To know which way the wind blows. [Song: *Subterranean Homesick Blues*]

9 Twenty years of schoolin' / And they put you on the day shift.

10 Come mothers and fathers / Throughout the land / And don't criticize / What you can't understand. [Song: *The Times They Are A-Changin'*]

E

ANTHONY EDEN, EARL OF AVON 1895–1977

1 We are not at war with Egypt. We are in an armed conflict. [Speech in House of Commons, 4 Nov. 1956]

LADY CLARISSA EDEN 1920–1985

2 During the last few weeks I have felt sometimes that the Suez Canal was flowing through my drawing room. [Of the Suez crisis, when opening Gateshead Conservative Association HQ, 20 Nov. 1956]

MARIA EDGEWORTH 1767–1849

3 Well, some people talk of morality, and some of religion, but give me a little snug property. [*The Absentee*, Ch. 2]

4 And all the young ladies said that a love-match was the only thing for happiness, where the parties could anyway afford it. [*Castle Rackrent*, 'Continuation of Memoirs']

5 I've a great fancy to see my own funeral afore I die.

6 Come when you're called, / And do as you're bid; / Shut the door after you, / And you'll never be chid. [*The Contrast*, Ch. 1]

7 Business was his pleasure; pleasure was his business. [2]

THOMAS ALVA EDISON 1847–1931

8 Genius is one per cent inspiration and ninety-nine per cent perspiration. [Newspaper interview in 1903, quoted in *Life*, Ch. 24]

EDWARD III OF ENGLAND 1312–1377

9 Let the boy win his spurs. [Of the Black Prince at Crécy]

EDWARD VII 1841–1910

10 We are all Socialists nowadays. [Speech at Mansion House, 5 Nov. 1895]

EDWARD VIII 1894–1972

11 Something must be done. [Speech during tour of unemployment areas in South Wales, 18 Nov. 1936]

12 But you must believe me when I tell you that I have found it impossible to carry the heavy burden of responsibility and to discharge my duties as King as I would wish to do, without the help and support of the woman I love. [Abdication speech, 11 Dec. 1936]

RICHARD EDWARDES 1523?–1566

13 The falling out of faithful friends, renewing is of love. [*Amantium Irae*]

OLIVER EDWARDS 1711–1791

14 You are a philosopher, Dr Johnson. I have tried too in my time to be a philosopher; but I don't know how, cheerfulness was always breaking in. [Quoted in Boswell's *Life of Johnson*, 17 Apr. 1778]

ALBERT EINSTEIN 1879–1955

15 $E = mc^2$

Energy equals mass times the speed of light

squared. [Statement of the mass–energy equivalence relationship]

1 Science without religion is lame, religion without science is blind. [Paper for conference on science, New York, 9/11 Sept. 1940]

2 The Lord God is subtle but he is not malicious. [Quip carved in German above the fireplace of Fine Hall, the Mathematical Institute of Princeton University]

3 If only I had known, I should have become a watchmaker. [Of his making the atom bomb possible, 1945]

4 I cannot believe that God plays dice with the cosmos. [*Observer*, 'Sayings of the Week', 5 Apr. 1953, but used earlier in letter to Max Born, 4 Dec. 1926]

PRESIDENT DWIGHT D. EISENHOWER
1890–1969

5 You have a row of dominoes set up. You knock over the first one, and what will happen to the last one is a certainty that it will go over very quickly. [Press Conference, 7 Apr. 1954, on the strategic importance of Indochina]

6 The military-industrial complex. [Farewell radio and TV address as President, 17 Jan. 1961]

GEORGE ELIOT [MARY ANN CROSS]
1819–1880

7 It's but little good you'll do a-watering the last year's crop. [*Adam Bede*, Ch. 18]

8 It was a pity he couldna be hatched o'er again, an' hatched different.

9 It's them that take advantage that get advantage i' this world. [32]

10 He was like a cock who thought the sun had risen to hear him crow. [33]

11 We hand folks over to God's mercy, and show none ourselves. [42]

12 I'm not denyin' the women are foolish: God Almighty made 'em to match the men. [53]

13 Men's men: gentle or simple, they're much of a muchness. [*Daniel Deronda*, Bk iv. Ch. 21]

14 The law's made to take care o' raskills. [*The Mill on the Floss*, Bk iii. Ch. 4]

15 I've never any pity for conceited people, because I think they carry their comfort about with them. [v. 4]

16 The happiest women, like the happiest nations, have no history. [vi. 3]

17 'Character,' says Novalis, in one of his questionable aphorisms – 'character is destiny.' [6]

18 In every parting there is an image of death. [*Scenes of Clerical Life*, 'Amos Barton', Ch. 10]

19 Animals are such agreeable friends – they ask no questions, they pass no criticisms. ['Mr Gilfil's Love-Story', Ch. 7]

20 Debasing the moral currency. [*Theophrastus Such*, title of essay]

21 Oh may I join the choir invisible / Of those immortal dead who live again / In minds made better by their presence. [*Poems*, 'Oh May I Join the Choir Invisible']

T. S. ELIOT 1888–1965

22 Pray for us now and at the hour of our birth. [*Animula*]

23 Because I do not hope to turn again / Because I do not hope / Because I do not hope to turn. [*Ash Wednesday*, I]

24 Teach us to care and not to care / Teach us to sit still.

25 Lady, three white leopards sat under a juniper tree / In the cool of the day. [II]

26 At the first turning of the second stair / I turned and saw below / The same shape twisted on the banister. [III]

27 Redeem / The time. Redeem / The unread vision in the higher dream. [IV]

28 Will the veiled sister pray / For children at the gate / Who will not go away and cannot pray. [V]

29 Time present and time past / Are both perhaps present in time future, / And time future contained in time past. [*Four Quartets*, 'Burnt Norton', I]

30 Footfalls echo in the memory / Down the passage which we did not take / Towards the door we never opened / Into the rose-garden.

31 Human kind / Cannot bear very much reality.

32 At the still point of the turning world. [II]

33 In my beginning is my end. ['East Coker', I]

34 The intolerable wrestle / With words and meanings. [II]

35 The houses are all gone under the sea. / The dancers are all gone under the hill.

36 The wounded surgeon plies the steel / That questions the distempered part. [IV]

1 So here I am, in the middle way, having had twenty years – / Twenty years largely wasted, the years of *l'entre deux guerres*. [V]

2 Undisciplined squads of emotion.

3 In my end is my beginning.

4 I do not know much about gods; but I think that the river / Is a strong brown god. ['Dry Salvages', I]

5 The river is within us, the sea is all about us.

6 You are not the same people who left that station / Or who will arrive at any terminus, / While the narrowing rails slide together behind you. [III]

7 Not fare well, / But fare forward, voyagers.

8 Ash on an old man's sleeve / Is all the ash the burnt roses leave, / Dust in the air suspended / Marks the place where a story ended. ['Little Gidding', II]

9 The dove descending breaks the air / With flame of incandescent terror. [IV]

10 Here I am, an old man in a dry month, / Being read to by a boy. [*Gerontion*]

11 In the juvescence of the year / Came Christ the tiger.

12 After such knowledge, what forgiveness? Think now / History has many cunning passages, contrived corridors / And issues.

13 Tenants of the house, / Thoughts of a dry brain in a dry season.

14 We are the hollow men / We are the stuffed men / Leaning together. [*The Hollow Men*, I]

15 Here we go round the prickly pear / At five o'clock in the morning. [V]

16 Between the idea / And the reality / Between the motion / And the act / Falls the Shadow.

17 This is the way the world ends / Not with a bang but a whimper.

18 A cold coming we had of it, / Just the worst time of the year / For a journey. [*Journey of the Magi*]

19 When the evening is spread out against the sky / Like a patient etherised upon a table. [*Love Song of J. Alfred Prufrock*]

20 In the room the women come and go / Talking of Michelangelo.

21 The yellow fog that rubs its back upon the windowpanes.

22 I have measured out my life with coffee spoons.

23 I should have been a pair of ragged claws / Scuttling across the floors of silent seas.

24 And I have seen the eternal Footman hold my coat, and snicker, / And in short, I was afraid.

25 No! I am not Prince Hamlet, nor was meant to be; / Am an attendant lord.

26 I grow old . . . I grow old . . . / I shall wear the bottoms of my trousers rolled.

27 He always has an alibi, and one or two to spare: / At whatever time the deed took place – Macavity wasn't there! [*Macavity: The Mystery Cat*]

28 I am aware of the damp souls of housemaids /Sprouting despondently at area gates. [*Morning at the Window*]

29 To hear the latest Pole / transmit the Preludes, through his hair and fingertips. [*Portrait of a Lady*]

30 The winter evening settles down / With smell of steaks in passage ways. [*Preludes*, I]

31 The worlds revolve like ancient women / Gathering fuel in vacant lots. [IV]

32 Birth, and copulation, and death. / That's all the facts when you come to brass tacks. [*Sweeney Agonistes*, 'Fragment of an Agon')

33 April is the cruellest month, breeding / Lilacs out of the dead land. [*The Waste Land*, 1]

34 I read, much of the night, and go south in the winter. [18]

35 And I will show you something different from either / Your shadow at morning striding behind you / Or your shadow at evening rising to meet you; / I will show you fear in a handful of dust [27]

36 Madame Sosostris, famous clairvoyante, / Had a bad cold, nevertheless / Is known to be the wisest woman in Europe, / With a wicked pack of cards. [43]

37 Here, said she, / Is your card, the drowned Phoenician Sailor. [46]

38 Unreal City, / Under the brown fog of a winter dawn, / A crowd flowed over London Bridge, so many, / I had not thought death had undone so many. [60]

39 That corpse you planted last year in your garden, / Has it begun to sprout? Will it bloom this year? [71]

40 The Chair she sat in, like a burnished throne, / Glowed on the marble. [77]

1 The change of Philomel, by the barbarous king / So rudely forced. [99]

2 'Jug jug' to dirty ears. [103]

3 My nerves are bad to-night. Yes, bad. [111]

4 When Lil's husband got demobbed, I said – / I didn't mince my words, I said to her myself, / Hurry up please, it's time. [139]

5 Musing upon the king my brother's wreck / And on the king my father's death before him. [191]

6 O the moon shone bright on Mrs Porter / And on her daughter / They wash their feet in soda water. [199]

7 One of the low on whom assurance sits / As a silk hat on a Bradford millionaire. [233]

8 When lovely woman stoops to folly and / Paces about her room again, alone, / She smoothes her hair with automatic hand, / And puts a record on the gramophone. [253]

9 A woman drew her long black hair out tight / And fiddled whisper music on those strings / And bats with baby faces in the violet light / Whistled. [377]

10 Webster was much possessed by death / And saw the skull beneath the skin. [*Whispers of Immortality*]

11 Uncorseted, her friendly bust / Gives promise of pneumatic bliss.

12 Donne, I suppose, was such another / Who found no substitute for sense. / To seize and clutch and penetrate; / Expert beyond experience.

13 The clock has stopped in the dark. [*The Family Reunion*, II. iii]

14 Since golden October declined into sombre November / And the apples were gathered and stored, and the land became brown sharp points of death in a waste of water and mud. [*Murder in the Cathedral*, I]

15 Yet we have gone on living, / Living and partly living.

16 The last temptation is the greatest treason: / To do the right deed for the wrong reason.

17 Clear the air! clean the sky! wash the wind! take stone from stone and wash them. [II]

18 The only way of expressing emotion in the form of art is by finding an 'objective correlative'; in other words, a set of objects, a situation, a chain of events which shall be the formula of that particular emotion. [*Selected Essays*, 'Tradition and the Individual Talent']

19 After the erection of the Chinese Wall of Milton, blank verse has suffered not only arrest but retrogression. ['Christopher Marlowe']

20 The majority of poems one outgrows and outlives, as one outgrows and outlives the majority of human passions. Dante's is one of those that one can only just hope to grow up to at the end of life. ['Dante']

21 Tennyson and Browning are poets, and they think; but they do not feel their thought as immediately as the odour of a rose. A thought to Donne was an experience; it modified his sensibility. ['Metaphysical Poets']

22 In the seventeenth century a dissociation of sensibility set in.

ELIZABETH I 1533–1603

23 I will make you shorter by a head. [Quoted in Chamberlin, *Sayings of Queen Elizabeth*]

24 Madam, I may not call you; mistress I am ashamed to call you; and so I know not what to call you; but howsoever, I thank you. [(To the wife of the Archbishop of Canterbury) Quoted in Harington, *Brief View of the State of the Church*]

25 God forgive you, but I never can. [(To the Countess of Nottingham) Hume, *History of England under the House of Tudor*, Vol. ii. Ch. 7]

26 I know I have the body of a weak and feeble woman, but I have the heart and stomach of a king, and of a king of England too. [Speech at Tilbury, on the approach of the Spanish Armada, 1588]

27 All my possessions for a moment of time. [Last words]

QUEEN ELIZABETH II 1926–

28 I think everybody really will concede that on this, of all days, I should begin my speech with the words 'My husband and I'. [Speech at Silver Wedding Banquet, Guildhall, London, 20 Nov. 1972, but phrase was used as far back as her Christmas Broadcast, 1953]

ALF ELLERTON 20 Cent.

29 Belgium Put the Kibosh on the Kaiser. [Title of song of 1914–18 War. Music by Mark Sheridan]

JOHN ELLERTON 1826–1893

1 Now the labourer's task is o'er; / Now the battle-day is past; / Now upon the further shore / Lands the voyager at last. [Hymn]

CHARLOTTE ELLIOTT 1789–1871

2 Christian, seek not yet repose, / Hear thy guardian angel say, / 'Thou art in the midst of foes; / Watch and pray'. [Hymn]

EBENEZER ELLIOTT 1781–1849

3 What is a communist? One who hath yearnings / For equal division of unequal earnings. [Epigram]

JANE ELLIOTT 1727–1805

4 I've heard them lilting, at our ewe milking, / Lasses a' lilting, before dawn of day: / But now they are moaning on ilka green loaning; / The flowers o' the forest are a' wede away. [The Flowers of the Forest (See also 116:2)]

GEORGE ELLIS [SIR GEORGE GANDER] 1753–1815

5 Snowy, Flowy, Blowy, / Showery, Flowery, Bowery, / Hoppy, Croppy, Droppy, / Breezy, Sneezy, Freezy. [The Twelve Months]

HENRY HAVELOCK ELLIS 1859–1939

6 Every artist writes his own autobiography. [The New Spirit, 'Tolstoi', II]

ELSTOW Early 16 Cent.

7 We know the way to heaven to be as ready by water as by land. [(When threatened with drowning by Henry VIII) Quoted in Stow, Annals]

PAUL ÉLUARD 1895–1952

8 Adieu tristesse / Bonjour tristesse / Tu es inscrite dans les lignes du plafond. – Farewell sadness, / Good day sadness. / You are written in the lines on the ceiling. [La Vie immédiate]

RALPH WALDO EMERSON 1803–1882

9 If the red slayer thinks he slays, / Or if the slain think he is slain, / They know not well the subtle ways / I keep, and pass, and turn again. [Brahma]

10 I am the doubter and the doubt, / And I the hymn the Brahmin sings.

11 Heartily know, / When half-gods go, / The gods arrive. [Give All to Love]

12 Here once the embattled farmers stood, / And fired the shot heard round the world. [Hymn sung at the Completion of the Concord Monument]

13 Things are in the saddle, / And ride mankind. [Ode, inscribed to W. H. Channing]

14 He builded better than he knew; – / The conscious stone to beauty grew. [The Problem]

15 Some of your hurts you have cured, / And the sharpest you still have survived, / But what torments of grief you endured / From evils which never arrived! [Quatrains, 'Borrowing' (from the French)]

16 So nigh is grandeur to our dust, / So near is God to man, / When Duty whispers low, Thou must, / The youth replies, I can. [Voluntaries, 3]

17 Art is a jealous mistress. [Conduct of Life, 'Wealth']

18 The louder he talked of his honour, the faster we counted our spoons. ['Worship']

19 Though we travel the world over to find the beautiful, we must carry it with us or we find it not. [Essays, 'Art']

20 Beware when the great God lets loose a thinker on this planet. ['Circles']

21 Nothing great was ever achieved without enthusiasm.

22 The wise through excess of wisdom is made a fool. ['Experience']

23 Thou art to me a delicious torment. ['Friendship']

24 A friend is a person with whom I may be sincere. Before him I may think aloud.

25 The only reward of virtue is virtue; the only way to have a friend is to be one.

26 There is properly no history; only biography. ['History']

27 All mankind love a lover. ['Love']

28 Men are conservatives when they are least vigorous, or when they are most luxurious. They are conservatives after dinner. ['New England Reformers']

29 We are wiser than we know. [Essays, 'The Over-Soul']

30 The faith that stands on authority is not faith.

1 Language is fossil poetry. ['The Poet']

2 Whoso would be a man must be a noncon-formist. ['Self-Reliance']

3 A foolish consistency is the hobgoblin of little minds, adored by little statesmen and philosophers and divines.

4 To be great is to be misunderstood.

5 I like the silent church before the service begins better than any preaching.

6 An institution is the lengthened shadow of one man.

7 What is a weed? A plant whose virtues have not yet been discovered. [*Fortune of the Republic*]

8 Talent alone cannot make a writer. There must be a man behind the book. [*Representative Men*, 'Goethe']

9 Every hero becomes a bore at last. ['Uses of Great Men']

10 I have heard with admiring submission the experience of the lady who declared that the sense of being well-dressed gives a feeling of inward tranquillity which religion is powerless to bestow. [*Social Aims*]

11 Never read any book that is not a year old. [*Society and Solitude*, 'Books']

12 Hitch your wagon to a star. ['Civilization']

13 We boil at different degrees. ['Eloquence']

14 America is a country of young men. ['Old Age']

15 Every man is a borrower and a mimic, life is theatrical and literature a quotation. ['Success']

16 If a man can write a better book, preach a better sermon, or make a better mouse-trap than his neighbour, though he build his house in the woods, the world will make a beaten path to his door. [Lecture noted down by Sarah Yule, quoted in her *Borrowings*. Also ascr. to Elbert Hubbard]

17 We are always getting ready to live, but never living. [*Journals*, 13 Apr. 1834]

18 I hate quotations. Tell me what you know. [May 1849]

EMPEDOCLES 5 Cent. BC

19 God is a circle whose centre is everywhere and whose circumference is nowhere.

SIR WILLIAM EMPSON 1906–1984

20 It seemed the best thing to be up and go. [*Aubade*]

21 The heart of standing is you cannot fly.

22 Waiting for the end, boys, waiting for the end. [*Just a Smack at Auden*)

23 Slowly the poison the whole blood stream fills . . . / The waste remains, the waste remains and kills. [*Missing Dates*]

24 Seven Types of Ambiguity. [Title of book]

PÈRE PROSPER ENFANTIN 1796–1864

25 Exploitation without work of man by man. [*Œuvres de Saint Simon et Enfantin*]

FRIEDRICH ENGELS 1820–1895

26 The state is not 'abolished', it withers away. [*Anti-Dühring*]

27 Look at the Paris Commune. That was the Dictatorship of the Proletariat. [Preface to Karl Marx, *The Civil War in France*, (1891 edn.)]

HENRY ERSKINE 1746–1817

28 The rule of the road is a paradox quite, / Both in riding and driving along; / If you keep to the left, you are sure to be right, / If you keep to the right you are wrong. [*The Rule of the Road*]

LORD ERSKINE 1750–1823

29 The uncontrolled licentiousness of a brutal and insolent soldiery. [*In defence of William Stone*]

HENRI ESTIENNE 1531–1598

30 *Si jeunesse savait; si vieillesse pouvait.* – If youth knew, if age could. [*Les Prémices*, 191]

SIR GEORGE ETHEREDGE 1635–1691

31 Whate'er you say, I know all beyond High-Park's a desert to you. [*The Man of Mode*, V. ii]

RENÉ ETIEMBLE 1909–

32 *Parlez-vous Franglais?* [Title of book]

EUCLID *fl. c.* 300 BC

33 *Quod erat demonstrandum.* – Which was to be proved. [Trans. from Greek]

EURIPIDES 480–406 BC

1 Whom God wishes to destroy, he first makes mad. [*Fragments* (Exists in many forms; the Latin version *'Quos deus vult perdere, prius dementat'* is quoted in Boswell, *Life of Johnson*)]

ANTHONY EUWER 1877–1955

2 As a beauty I'm not a great star. / Others are handsomer far; / But my face – I don't mind it / Because I'm behind it; / It's the folk out in front that I jar. [Limerick]

ABEL EVANS 1679–1737

3 When Tadlow walks the streets, the paviours cry, / 'God bless you, Sir!' and lay their rammers by. [Epigram: *On Dr Tadlow*]

4 Under this stone, reader, survey / Dead Sir John Vanbrugh's house of clay. / Lie heavy on him, Earth! For he / Laid many heavy loads on thee! [*Epitaph*]

JOHN EVELYN 1620–1706

5 A studious decliner of honours and titles. [*Diary*, Introduction]

6 I saw Hamlet Prince of Denmark played; but now the old plays begin to disgust this refined age. [26 Nov. 1661]

DAVID EVERETT 1770–1813

7 Large streams from little fountains flow, / Tall oaks from little acorns grow. [*Lines written for a School Declamation*]

GAVIN EWART 1916–

8 Miss Twye was soaping her breasts in her bath / When she heard behind her a meaning laugh / And to her amazement she discovered / A wicked man in the bathroom cupboard. [*Miss Twye*]

W. N. EWER 1885–1976

9 How odd / Of God / To choose / The Jews. [*How Odd*]

F

F. W. FABER 1814–1863

1 Have mercy on us worms of earth. [Hymn]

2 My God, how wonderful Thou art, / Thy majesty how bright, / How beautiful Thy mercy-seat / In depths of burning light! [Hymn]

3 The music of the Gospel leads us home. [Hymn: *The Pilgrims of the Night*]

ROBERT FABYAN ?–1513

4 Finally he paid the debt of nature. [*Chronicles*, Pt II. 41]

5 Ranulphe says he [King Henry I] took a surfeit by eating of a lamprey, and thereof died. [(Ranulphe did not, in fact, specify) 229]

6 The Duke of Clarence . . . a prisoner in the Tower, was secretly put to death and drowned in a barrel of Malmesey wine. [1477 (early edns. give 'malvesye')]

HANS FALLADA 1893–1947

7 *Kleiner Mann, was nun?* – Little Man, What Now? [Title of novel]

FRANTZ FANON 1925–1961

8 However painful it may be for me to accept this conclusion, I am obliged to state it: for the black man there is only one destiny. And it is white. [*Black Skin, White Masks*, Introduction]

9 Violence is man re-creating himself. [*The Wretched of the Earth*, Ch. 1]

CATHERINE MARIA FANSHAWE
   1765–1834

10 'Twas whispered in heaven, 'twas muttered in hell, / And echo caught faintly the sound as it fell; / On the confines of earth 'twas permitted to rest, / And the depths of the ocean its presence confessed. [*Enigma, The Letter H*]

HERBERT FARJEON 1887–1945

11 I've danced with a man, who's danced with a girl, who's danced with the Prince of Wales. [*Picnic*]

EDWARD FARMER 1809?–1876

12 I have no pain, dear mother, now; but oh! I am so dry: / Just moisten poor Jim's lips once more; and, mother, do not cry! [*The Collier's Dying Child*]

GEORGE FARQUHAR 1678–1707

13 Sir, you shall taste my *Anno Domini*. [*The Beaux' Stratagem*, I. i]

14 I have fed purely upon ale; I have eat my ale, drank my ale, and I always sleep upon ale.

15 My Lady Bountiful.

16 Says little, thinks less, and does – nothing at all, faith.

17 There's no scandal like rags, nor any crime so shameful as poverty.

18 'Twas for the good of my country that I should be abroad. Anything for the good of one's country – I'm a Roman for that. [III. ii]

19 Captain is a good travelling name and so I take it.

20 How a little love and good company improves a woman! [IV. i]

21 Spare all I have, and take my life. [V. ii]

1 Charming women can true converts make, / We love the precepts for the teacher's sake. [*The Constant Couple*, V. iii. See also 203:28]

2 Poetry's a mere drug, Sir. [*Love and a Bottle*, III. ii]

3 Hanging and marriage, you know, go by Destiny. [*The Recruiting Officer*, III. ii]

DEAN FARRAR 1831–1903

4 Russell, let me always call you Edwin, and call me Eric. [*Eric, or Little by Little*, Ch. 4]

5 'What a surly devil that is,' said Eric . . .
'A surly – ? Oh, Eric, that's the first time I ever heard you swear.' [8]

WILLIAM FAULKNER 1897–1962

6 If a writer has to rob his mother, he will not hesitate; the 'Ode to a Grecian Urn' is worth any number of old ladies. [In M. Cowley (ed.), *Writers at Work*, first series]

GUY FAWKES 1570–1606

7 A desperate disease requires a dangerous remedy. [(Of Gunpowder Plot 5 Nov. 1605) Echoing Hippocrates; see 201:16]

FRANÇOIS DE FÉNELON 1651–1715

8 Nothing is more despicable than a professional talker who uses his words as a quack uses his remedies. [Letter to M. Dacier]

9 A good historian is timeless; although he is a patriot, he will never flatter his country in any respect.

EMPEROR FERDINAND I 1506–1564

10 *Fiat justitia et pereat mundus.* – Let justice be done, though the world perish. [Motto]

JOHN FERRIAR 1761–1815

11 Now cheaply bought for thrice their weight in gold. [*Illustrations of Sterne*, 'Bibliomania']

LUDWIG FEUERBACH 1804–1872

12 *Der Mensch ist, was er isst.* – A man is what he eats. [*Blätter für Literarische Unterhaltung*, 12 Nov. 1850]

EUGENE FIELD 1850–1895

13 Listen to my tale of woe. [*The Little Peach*]

14 Wynken, Blynken and Nod one night / Sailed off in a wooden shoe – / Sailed on a river of crystal light, / Into a sea of dew. [*Wynken, Blynken and Nod*]

HENRY FIELDING 1707–1754

15 'Tace, madam,' answered Murphy, 'is Latin for a candle.' [*Amelia*, Bk i. Ch. 10]

16 When widows exclaim loudly against second marriage, I would always lay a wager that the man, if not the wedding-day, is absolutely fixed on. [vi. 8]

17 One of my illustrious predecessors. [*Covent Garden Journal*, No. 3, 11 Jan. 1752]

18 I am as sober as a judge. [*Don Quixote in England*, III. xiv]

19 Oh! The roast beef of England, / And old England's roast beef. [*Grub Street Opera*, III. iii]

20 Never trust the man who hath reason to suspect that you know he hath injured you. [*Jonathan Wild*, Bk. iii. Ch. 4]

21 He in a few minutes ravished this fair creature, or at least would have ravished her, if she had not, by a timely compliance, prevented him. [7]

22 But pray, Mr Wild, why bitch? [8]

23 For clergy are men as well as other folks. [*Joseph Andrews*, Bk ii. Ch. 6]

24 To whom nothing is given, of him can nothing be required. [8]

25 I describe not men, but manners; not an individual, but a species. [iii. 1]

26 Public schools are the nurseries of all vice and immorality. [5]

27 Some folks rail against other folks, because other folks have what some folks would be glad of. [iv. 6]

28 Love and scandal are the best sweeteners of tea. [*Love in Several Masques*, IV. xi]

29 Every physician almost hath his favourite disease. [*Tom Jones*, Bk ii. Ch. 9]

30 Thwackum was for doing justice, and leaving mercy to heaven. [iii. 10]

31 O! more than Gothic ignorance. [vii. 3]

32 An amiable weakness. [x. 8]

33 His designs were strictly honourable, as the

saying is; that is, to rob a lady of her fortune by way of marriage. [xi. 4]

1 Composed that monstrous animal a husband and wife. [xv. 9]

2 All Nature wears one universal grin. [*Tom Thumb the Great*, I. i]

3 To sun myself in Huncamunca's eyes. [iii]

4 When I'm not thanked at all, I'm thanked enough, / I've done my duty, and I've done no more.

5 The hounds all join in glorious cry, / The huntsman winds his horn: / And a-hunting we will go. [*A-Hunting We Will Go*]

GRACIE FIELDS 1898–1979

6 We're going to string old Hitler / From the very highest bough / Of the biggest aspidistra in the world. [Song: *The Biggest Aspidistra*, written by J. Harper, W. Haines and T. Connor]

J. T. FIELDS 1816–1881

7 'I'm an owl; you're another. Sir Critic, good day!' / And the barber kept on shaving. [*The Owl-Critic*]

W. C. FIELDS 1879–1946

8 A woman is like an elephant – I like to look at 'em, but I wouldn't want to own one. [In film *Mississippi*]

9 It's a funny old world – a man's lucky if he gets out of it alive. [In film *You're Telling Me*]

10 Fish fuck in it. [When asked why he never drank water. Quoted in L. Halliwell, *The Filmgoer's Book of Quotes*]

11 Never Give a Sucker an Even Break. [Film title; the line originated with E. F. Albee]

12 On the whole I would rather be in Philadelphia. [Supposed epitaph, but apocryphal]

13 Anyone who hates children and dogs can't be all bad. [Falsely attr. to W. C. Fields. In fact said at a banquet in his honour, 1939, by Leo C. Rosten, and of 'babies' not 'children'. See 332:7]

RONALD FIRBANK 1886–1926

14 She made a ravishing corpse. [*The Eccentricities of Cardinal Pirelli*, Ch. 8]

15 'O, help me heaven,' she prayed, 'to be decorative and to do right.' [*Flower Beneath the Foot*, Ch. 2]

16 It is said, I believe, that to behold the Englishman at his *best* one should watch him play tip-and-run. [Ch. 14]

17 All millionaires love a baked apple. [*Vainglory*, Ch. 13]

JOHN ARBUTHNOT, LORD FISHER
1841–1920

18 You will always be fools! We shall never be gentlemen. [Quoted as the saying of a German Naval officer to his British confrère]

19 Sack the lot! [Letter to *The Times*, 2 Sept. 1919]

CLYDE FITCH 20 Cent.

20 The Woman in the Case. [Title of play]

ALBERT H. FITZ 20 Cent.

21 You are my honey, honeysuckle, I am the bee. [Song: *The Honeysuckle and the Bee*. Music by W. H. Penn]

EDWARD FITZGERALD 1809–1883

22 Awake! for Morning in the Bowl of Night / Has flung the Stone that puts the Stars to Flight: / And Lo! the Hunter of the East has caught / The Sultan's Turret in a Noose of Light. [*The Rubá'iyát of Omar Khayyám*, Edn. 1. 1]

23 Dreaming when Dawn's Left Hand was in the sky / I heard a Voice within the Tavern cry: / 'Awake, my Little ones, and fill the Cup / Before Life's Liquor in its Cup be dry.' [2]

24 Now the New Year reviving old Desires, / The thoughtful Soul to Solitude retires, / Where the White Hand of Moses on the Bough / Puts out, and Jesus from the Ground suspires. [4]

25 But still the Vine her ancient Ruby yields, / And still a Garden by the Water blows. [5]

26 Come, fill the Cup, and in the Fire of Spring / The Winter Garment of Repentance fling: / The Bird of Time has but a little way / To fly – and Lo! the Bird is on the Wing. [7]

27 The Wine of Life keeps oozing drop by drop, / The Leaves of Life keep falling one by one. [8]

28 Each Morn a thousand Roses brings, you

say: / Yes, but where leaves the Rose of Yesterday? [9]

1 Here with a Loaf of Bread beneath the Bough, / A Flask of Wine, a Book of Verse – and Thou / Beside me singing in the Wilderness – / And Wilderness is Paradise enow. [11]

2 A Book of Verses underneath the Bough / A Jug of Wine, a Loaf of Bread – and Thou. [12]

3 Ah, take the Cash, and let the Credit go, / Nor heed the rumble of a distant Drum! [13]

4 The Worldly Hope men set their Hearts upon / Turns Ashes – or it prospers; and anon, / Like Snow upon the Desert's dusty face, / Lighting a little Hour or two – is gone. [14]

5 This battered Caravanserai / Whose Portals are alternate Night and Day. [Edn. 4. 17]

6 They say the Lion and the Lizard keep / The Courts where Jamshýd gloried and drank deep: / And Bahrám, that great Hunter – the Wild Ass / Stamps o'er his Head, and he lies fast asleep. [Edn. 1. 17]

7 I sometimes think that never blows so red / The Rose as where some buried Caesar bled; / That every Hyacinth the Garden wears / Dropt in her Lap from some once lovely Head. [18]

8 To-morrow? – Why, To-morrow I may be / Myself with Yesterday's Sev'n Thousand Years. [20]

9 One by one crept silently to Rest. [21]

10 One thing is certain, that Life flies; / One thing is certain, and the Rest is Lies; / The Flower that once has blown for ever dies. [26]

11 Myself when young did eagerly frequent / Doctor and Saint, and heard great Argument / About it and about: but evermore / Came out by the same Door as in I went. [27]

12 I came like Water, and like Wind I go. [28]

13 Into this Universe, and Why not knowing / Nor Whence, like Water willy-nilly flowing: / And out of it, as Wind along the Waste, / I know not Whither, willy-nilly blowing. [29]

14 There was a Door to which I found no Key: / There was a Veil past which I could not see. [32]

15 Ah, fill the Cup: what boots it to repeat / How Time is slipping underneath our Feet. [37]

16 One Moment in Annihilation's Waste, / One Moment, of the Well of Life to taste – / The Stars are setting and the Caravan / Starts for the Dawn of Nothing – Oh, make haste! [38]

17 The Grape that can with Logic absolute / The Two-and-Seventy jarring Sects confute. [43]

18 'Tis all a Chequer-board of Nights and Days / Where Destiny with Men for Pieces plays / Hither and thither moves, and mates, and slays, / And one by one back in the Closet lays. [49]

19 The Ball no question makes of Ayes and Noes, / But Here or There as strikes the Player goes. [Edn. 4. 70]

20 The Moving Finger writes; and, having writ, / Moves on: nor all thy Piety nor Wit / Shall lure it back to cancel half a Line, / Nor all thy Tears wash out a Word of it. [Edn. 1. 51]

21 And that inverted Bowl we call The Sky, / Whereunder crawling coop't we live and die, / Lift not thy hands to It for help – for It / Rolls impotently on as Thou or I. [52]

22 One Flash of It within the Tavern caught / Better than in the Temple lost outright. [Edn. 4. 77]

23 O Thou who didst with Pitfall and with Gin / Beset the Road I was to wander in, / Thou wilt not with Predestination round / Enmesh me, and impute my Fall to Sin? [Edn. 1. 57]

24 Oh, Thou, who Man of baser Earth didst make, / And who with Eden didst devise the Snake; / For all the Sin wherewith the Face of Man / Is blackened. Man's Forgiveness give – and take! [58]

25 Who is the Potter, pray, and who the Pot? [60]

26 Said one: 'Folks of a surly Tapster tell, / And daub his Visage with the Smoke of Hell; / They talk of some strict Testing of us – Pish! / He's a Good Fellow, and 'twill all be well.' [64]

27 Indeed the Idols I have loved so long / Have done my credit in this World much wrong: / Have drowned my Honour in a Shallow Cup / And sold my Reputation for a Song. [69]

28 I often wonder what the Vintners buy / One half so precious as the Goods they sell. [71]

29 Alas, that Spring should vanish with the Rose! / That Youth's sweet-scented Manuscript should close! [72]

30 Ah Love! Could thou and I with Fate conspire / To grasp this sorry Scheme of Things entire, / Would not we shatter it to bits – and then / Re-mould it nearer to the Heart's Desire! [73]

1 Ah, Moon of my Delight who know'st no wane, / The Moon of Heav'n is rising once again: / How oft hereafter rising shall she look; / Through this same Garden after me – in vain! [74]

2 And when Thyself with shining Foot shall pass / Among the Guests Star-scattered on the Grass, / And in thy joyous Errand reach the Spot / Where I made one – turn down an empty Glass! [75]

3 And when like her, O Saki, you shall pass. [Edn. 4. 101]

4 A Mr Wilkinson, a clergyman. [Parody of Wordsworth, quoted in Hallam Tennyson, *Tennyson*, ii. 276]

F. SCOTT FITZGERALD 1896–1940

5 In a real dark night of the soul it is always three o'clock in the morning, day after day. [*The Crack-Up*]

6 Though the Jazz Age continued, it became less and less of an affair of youth. The sequel was like a children's party taken over by the elders. ['Echoes of the Jazz Age']

7 If you want to kiss me any time during the evening, Nick, just let me know and I'll be glad to arrange it for you. Just mention my name. [*The Great Gatsby*, Ch. 6]

8 Her voice is full of money. [7]

9 Gatsby believed in the green light, the orgastic future that year by year recedes before us. It eluded us then, but that's no matter – tomorrow we will run faster, stretch out our arms further . . . And one fine morning – So we beat on, boats against the current, borne back ceaselessly into the past. [9]

10 There are no second acts in American lives. [*The Last Tycoon*, 'Notes']

11 Show me a hero and I will write you a tragedy. [*Notebooks*, E]

12 All good writing is *swimming under water* and holding your breath. [Undated letter to Frances Scott Fitzgerald]

13 First you take a drink, then the drink takes a drink, then the drink takes you. [Quoted in Jules Feiffer, *Ackroyd*, '1964 May 7']

14 Let me tell you about the very rich. They are different from you and me. [*The Rich Boy*. In *Notebooks*, E, Fitzgerald records Hemingway's rejoinder: 'Yes, they have more money'; but elsewhere Hemingway spoke thus of the rich and Mary Colum gave the put-down]

15 An author ought to write for the youth of his own generation, the critics of the next, and the schoolmasters of ever afterwards. [Quoted in the *Guardian*, 13 Nov. 1964]

BOB FITZSIMMONS 1862–1917

16 The bigger they come, the harder they fall. [Before fight with J. Jeffries, San Francisco, 9 June 1899]

BUD FLANAGAN 1896–1968

17 Underneath the arches / We dream our dreams away. [Song: *Underneath the Arches*]

18 Run, Rabbit. [Title of song; words by Noël Gay and Ralph Butler]

MICHAEL FLANDERS 1922–1975

19 Eating people is wrong. [Song: *The Reluctant Cannibal*]

GUSTAVE FLAUBERT 1821–1880

20 I maintain that ideas are events. It is more difficult to make them interesting, I know, but if you fail the style is at fault. [Letter to Louise Colet, 15 Jan. 1853]

21 All one's inventions are true, you can be sure of that. Poetry is as exact a science as geometry. [14 Aug.]

22 Do not read, as children do, to amuse yourself, or like the ambitious, for the purpose of instruction. No, read in order to live. [Letter to Mlle de Chantepie, June 1857]

23 Language is a cracked kettle on which we beat out tunes for bears to dance to, while all the time we long to move the stars to pity. [Quoted in Julian Barnes, *Flaubert's Parrot*, 4]

24 The author in his book must be like God in his universe, everywhere present and nowhere visible.

JAMES ELROY FLECKER 1884–1915

25 For pines are gossip pines the wide world through. [*Brumana*]

26 West of these out to seas colder than the Hebrides I must go, / Where the fleet of stars is anchored and the young star-captains glow. [*The Dying Patriot*]

1 The dragon-green, the luminous, the dark, the serpent-haunted sea. [*The Gates of Damascus*, 'West Gate']

2 We who with songs beguile your pilgrimage / And swear that Beauty lives though lilies die, / We poets of the proud old lineage / Who sing to find your hearts, we know not why, – / What shall we tell you? Tales, marvellous tales / Of ships and stars and isles where good men rest. [*The Golden Journey to Samarkand*, Prologue]

3 When the great markets by the sea shut fast / All that calm Sunday that goes on and on: / When even lovers find their peace at last, / And Earth is but a star, that once had shone.

4 And some to Mecca turn to pray, and I toward thy bed, Yasmin. [*Hassan*, I. ii]

5 For one night or the other night / Will come the Gardener in white, and gathered flowers are dead, Yasmin.

6 For lust of knowing what should not be known, / We take the Golden Road to Samarkand. [V. ii]

7 What would ye, ladies? It was ever thus. / Men are unwise and curiously planned.

8 I have seen old ships sail like swans asleep / Beyond the village which men still call Tyre. [*The Old Ships*]

9 And with great lies about his wooden horse / Set the crew laughing and forgot his course.

10 It was so old a ship – who knows, who knows? / And yet so beautiful, I watched in vain / To see the mast burst open with a rose / And the whole deck put on its leaves again.

11 A ship, an isle, a sickle moon – / With few but with how splendid stars / The mirrors of the sea are strewn / Between their silver bars. [*A Ship, an Isle, a Sickle Moon*]

12 And old Maeonides the blind / Said it three thousand years ago. [*To a Poet a Thousand Years Hence*]

MARJORIE FLEMING 1803–1811

13 A direful death indeed they had / That would put any parent mad / But she was more than usual calm / She did not give a singel dam. [*Journal*, 1]

14 Today I pronounced a word which should never come out of a lady's lips it was that I called John a Impudent Bitch. [2]

15 Sentiment is what I am not acquainted with. [3]

ANDREW FLETCHER OF SALTOUN 1655–1716

16 I knew a very wise man so much of Sir Christopher's sentiment, that he believed if a man were permitted to make all the ballads, he need not care who should make the laws of a nation. [*Letter to the Marquis of Montrose and others*]

JOHN FLETCHER see under BEAUMONT, FRANCIS

PHINEAS FLETCHER 1582–1650

17 Drop, drop, slow tears, / And bathe those beauteous feet, / Which brought from Heaven / The news and Prince of Peace. [*An Hymn*]

18 Love is like linen often changed, the sweeter. [*Sicelides*, III. v]

19 The coward's weapon, poison. [V. iii]

20 Love's tongue is in his eyes. [*Piscatory Eclogues*, V. xiii]

JOHN FLORIO 1553?–1625

21 England is the paradise of women, the purgatory of men, and the hell of horses. [*Second Fruits*]

MARSHAL FOCH 1851–1929

22 My centre is giving way, my right is in retreat; situation excellent. I am attacking. [Message to Joffre, 8 Sept. 1914, on eve of Battle of the Marne]

SAMUEL FOOTE 1720–1777

23 Born in a cellar . . . and living in a garret. [*The Author*, III]

24 So she went into the garden to cut a cabbage-leaf, to make an apple-pie; and at the same time a great she-bear, coming up the street, pops its head into the shop. 'What! no soap?' So he died, and she very imprudently married the barber. [Nonsense, quoted by Maria Edgeworth in *Harry and Lucy Concluded*]

25 The great Panjandrum himself.

26 They all fell to playing the game of catch as

catch can, till the gun powder ran out at the heels of their boots.

1 When house and land are gone and spent, / Then learning is most excellent. [*Taste*, I. i]

2 He is not only dull in himself, but the cause of dullness in others. [Remark quoted in Boswell, *Life of Johnson*]

GERALD FORD 1913–

3 I am a Ford, not a Lincoln. [On becoming Vice-President, 6 Dec. 1973]

HENRY FORD 1863–1947

4 History is more or less bunk. [Interview in the *Chicago Tribune*, 25 May 1916]

5 Any colour, so long as it's black. [Advertisement for Model-T Ford car. Attr., in Allan Nevins, *Ford*, vol. 2, Ch. 15]

JOHN FORD 1586–1639?

6 I am ... a mushroom / On whom the dew of heaven drops now and then. [*The Broken Heart*, I. iii]

7 Revenge proves its own executioner. [IV. i]

8 He hath shook hands with time. [V. ii]

9 They are the silent griefs which cut the heart-strings. [iii]

10 We can drink till all look blue. [*The Lady's Trial*, IV. ii]

11 Why, I hold fate / Clasped in my fist, and could command the course / Of time's eternal motion, hadst thou been / One thought more steady than an ebbing sea. [*'Tis Pity She's a Whore*. V. v]

LENA FORD 1870–1916

12 Keep the home fires burning while your hearts are yearning, / Though your lads are far away, they dream of home. / There's a silver lining through the dark cloud shining: / Turn the dark cloud inside out, till the boys come home. [*Keep the Home Fires Burning*, music by Ivor Novello, also sometimes credited with first line]

THOMAS FORD 1580?–1648

13 There is a lady sweet and kind, / Was never face so pleased my mind; / I did but see her passing by, / And yet I love her till I die. [*There is a Lady*]

LIEUTENANT-COMMANDER FORGY [US Naval Chaplain] 1908–1983

14 Praise the Lord and pass the ammunition. [Said at Pearl Harbor, 7 Dec. 1941]

E. M. FORSTER 1879–1970

15 It is not that the Englishman can't feel – it is that he is afraid to feel. He has been taught at his public school that feeling is bad form. He must not express great joy or sorrow, or even open his mouth too wide when he talks – his pipe might fall out if he did. [*Abinger Harvest*, 'Notes on the English Character']

16 Yes – oh dear, yes – the novel tells a story. [*Aspects of the Novel*, Ch. 2]

17 *Ulysses* ... is a dogged attempt to cover the universe with mud. [6]

18 Only connect! [*Howards End*, Epigraph]

19 Beethoven's Fifth Symphony is the most sublime noise that has ever penetrated into the ear of man. [Ch. 5]

20 She felt increasingly ... that, though the people are important, the relations between them are not. [*A Passage to India*, 13]

21 'Can you always tell whether a stranger is your friend?' 'Yes.' 'Then you are an Oriental.' [36]

22 If I had to choose between betraying my *country* and betraying my *friend*, I hope I should have the guts to betray my *country*. [*Two Cheers for Democracy*, 'What I Believe']

23 So Two cheers for Democracy: one because it admits variety and two because it permits criticism. Two cheers are quite enough; there is no occasion to give three. Only Love the Beloved Republic deserves that.

H. E. FOSDICK 1878–1969

24 An atheist is a man who has no invisible means of support. [Attr. also to John Buchan. See 79:20]

CHARLES FOSTER 1828–1904

25 Isn't this a billion dollar country? [Retorting to a gibe about 'a million dollar Congress']

SIR GEORGE FOSTER 1847–1931

1 In these somewhat troublesome days when the great Mother Empire stands splendidly isolated in Europe. [Speech in Canadian House of Commons, 16 Jan. 1896]

S. C. FOSTER 1826–1864

2 Beautiful dreamer, wake unto me. [*Beautiful Dreamer*]

3 Oh! doodah day! / Gwine to run all night! / Gwine to run all day! / I bet my money on the bobtail nag. / Somebody bet on the bay. [*Camptown Races*]

4 I dream of Jeanie with the light brown hair. [*Jeanie with the Light Brown Hair*]

5 Weep no more, my lady, / Oh! weep no more today! / We will sing one song for the old Kentucky Home, / For the old Kentucky Home far away. [*My Old Kentucky Home*]

6 The sun shines bright in the old Kentucky home.

7 O, Susanna! O, don't you cry for me, / I've come from Alabama, wid my banjo on my knee. [*O, Susanna*]

8 Way down upon de Swanee Ribber, / Far, far away, / Dere's where my heart is turning ebber: / Dere's where de old folks stay. / All up and down de whole creation / Sadly I roam, / Still longing for de old plantation, / And for de old folks at home. [*Old Folks at Home*]

9 He had no wool on de top of his head / In de place where de wool ought to grow. [*Uncle Ned*]

10 Dere's no more work for poor old Ned, / He's gone whar de good niggers go.

CHARLES JAMES FOX 1749–1806

11 How much the greatest event it is that ever happened in the world! and how much the best! [Letter to Richard Fitzpatrick, 30 July 1789, on the fall of the Bastille]

GEORGE FOX 1624–1690

12 I heard a voice which said, 'There is one, even Christ Jesus, that can speak to thy condition', and when I heard it, my heart did leap for joy. [*Journal*]

13 When the Lord sent me forth into the world, He forbade me to put off my hat to any, high or low.

W. T. B. FOX 20 Cent.

14 The Super Powers. [Title of book (1944), coining the phrase; subtitled *Their Responsibility for Peace*]

ANATOLE FRANCE 1844–1924

15 *Le bon critique est celui qui raconte les aventures de son âme au milieu des chefs-d'œuvre.* – A good critic is one who narrates the adventures of his mind among masterpieces. [*La Vie littéraire*, I, Preface]

FRANCIS I, KING OF FRANCE 1494–1547

16 *Tout est perdu fors l'honneur.* – All is lost save honour. [On the loss of the battle of Pavia (in slightly different form in letter to his mother), 23 Feb. 1525]

BENJAMIN FRANKLIN 1706–1790

17 Remember that time is money. [*Advice to Young Tradesmen*]

18 Here Skugg lies snug / As a bug in a rug. [Letter to Miss G. Shipley, 26 Sept. 1772]

19 There never was a good war or a bad peace. [Letter to Josiah Quincy, 11 Sept. 1783]

20 In this world nothing can be said to be certain, except death and taxes. [Letter to Jean-Baptiste Le Roy, 13 Nov. 1789]

21 A little neglect may breed mischief . . . for want of a nail the shoe was lost; for want of a shoe the horse was lost; and for want of a horse the rider was lost. [*Maxims* . . . prefixed to *Poor Richard's Almanac*]

22 Some are weather-wise, some are otherwise. [*Poor Richard's Almanac*, Feb. 1735]

23 He that lives upon hope will die fasting. [Preface, 1758]

24 Poor man, said I, you pay too much for your whistle. [*The Whistle*, 10 Nov. 1779]

25 Yes, we must, indeed, all hang together or, most assuredly, we shall all hang separately. [Remark at signing of Declaration of Independence, 4 July 1776]

26 Man is a tool-making animal. [Quoted in Boswell, *Life of Johnson*, 7 Apr. 1778]

KARL EMIL FRANZOS 1848–1904

1 *Jedes Land hat die Juden, die es verdient.*
– Every country has the Jews that it deserves.
[*Schlüssel zur neueren Geschichte der Juden*]

FREDERICK THE GREAT OF PRUSSIA 1712–1786

2 *Lorsque Auguste buvait, la Pologne était ivre.*
– When Augustus drank, Poland became
drunk. [*Les Trois Sultanes*, iii. 3]

3 You rogues, do you want to live for ever?
[When the Guards hesitated at Kolin, 18 June
1757. See also 131:4]

4 A German singer! I should as soon expect
to get pleasure from the neighing of my horse.
[Quoted in Evan Esar (ed.), *Treasury of Humorous Quotations*]

ARTHUR FREED 1894–1973

5 I'm singing in the rain, just singing in the
rain; What a wonderful feeling, I'm happy
again. [Song: *Singing in the Rain*, from musical
Hollywood Review of 1929. Music by Nacio Herb
Brown]

JOHN FREEMAN 1880–1929

6 Than these November skies / Is no sky
lovelier. The clouds are deep; / Into their grey
the subtle spies / Of colour creep, / Changing
their high austerity to delight, / Till ev'n the
leaden interfolds are bright. [*November Skies*]

7 Last night a sword-light in the sky / Flashed
a swift terror on the dark. / In that sharp light
the fields did lie / Naked and stone-like; each
tree stood / Like a tranced woman, bound and
stark, / Far off the wood / With darkness ridged
the riven dark. [*Stone Trees*]

PERCY FRENCH ?–1920

8 Where the mountains of Mourne sweep
down to the sea. [Song: *The Mountains of Mourne*]

JOHN HOOKHAM FRERE 1769–1846

9 The feathered race with pinions skim the
air – / Not so the mackerel, and still less the
bear. [*Progress of Man*, 34]

10 A Conservative is only a Tory who is
ashamed of himself. [Attr.]

SIGMUND FREUD 1856–1939

11 We are so made that we can derive intense
enjoyment from a contrast and very little from
a state of things. [*Civilization and Its Discontents*,
Ch. 2]

12 The myth of King Oedipus, who killed his
father and took his mother to wife, reveals,
with little modification, the infantile wish,
which is later opposed and repudiated by the
barrier against incest. Shakespeare's *Hamlet* is
equally rooted in the soil of the incest-complex,
but under a better disguise. [*Five Lectures on
Psycho-Analysis*, IV]

13 At bottom God is nothing more than an
exalted father. [*Totem & Taboo*]

14 The great question ... which I have not
been able to answer, despite my thirty years of
research into the feminine soul, is 'What does a
woman want?' [Quoted in Charles Rolo, *Psychiatry in American Life*]

MAX FRISCH 1911–1991

15 Technology . . . the knack of so arranging the
world that we don't have to experience it.
[*Homo Faber*, Pt 2]

CHARLES FROHMAN 1860–1915

16 Why fear death? It is the most beautiful
adventure in life. [Last words before going down
in the *Lusitania*, 7 May 1915]

ERICH FROMM 1900–1980

17 Modern man lives under the illusion that
he knows what he wants, while he actually
wants what he is supposed to want. [*Escape
from Freedom*, Pt X, Ch. 7]

18 Man always dies before he is fully born.
[*Man for Himself*, Ch. 3]

19 In the nineteenth century the problem was
that God is dead; in the twentieth century the
problem is that man is dead. [*The Sane Society*,
Ch. 9]

ROBERT FROST 1874–1963

20 Earth's the right place for love; / I don't
know where it's likely to go better. [*Birches*]

21 One could do worse than be a swinger of
birches.

1 Forgive, O Lord, my little jokes on Thee / And I'll forgive Thy great big one on me. [*Cluster of Faith*]

2 'Home is the place where, when you have to go there, / They have to take you in.' / 'I should have called it / Something you somehow haven't to deserve.' [*The Death of the Hired Man*]

3 I would have written of me on my stone: / I had a lover's quarrel with the world. [*Epitaph*]

4 Some say the world will end in fire, / Some say in ice. / From what I've tasted of desire / I hold with those who favour fire, / But if I had to perish twice, / I think I know enough of hate / To say that for destruction ice / Is also great / And would suffice. [*Fire and Ice*]

5 The land was ours before we were the land's. / She was our land more than a hundred years / Before we were her people. / Such as we were we gave ourselves outright / (The deed of gift was many deeds of war) / To the land vaguely realizing westward, / But still unstoried, artless, unenhanced, / Such as she was, such as she has become. [*The Gift Outright*]

6 Keep cold, young orchard. Goodbye and keep cold. / Dread fifty above more than fifty below. [*Goodbye and Keep Cold*]

7 This as it will be seen is other far / Than with brooks taken otherwhere in song. / We love the things we love for what they are. [*Hyla Brook*]

8 Something there is that doesn't love a wall. [*Mending a Wall*]

9 My apple trees will never get across / And eat the cones under his pines, I tell him. / He only says, 'Good fences make good neighbours'.

10 I never dared be radical when young / For fear it would make me conservative when old. [*Precaution*]

11 I shall be telling this with a sigh / Somewhere ages and ages hence: / Two roads diverged in a wood, and I – / I took the one less travelled by, / And that has made all the difference. [*The Road not Taken*]

12 Pressed into service means pressed out of shape. [*The Self-Seeker*]

13 The best way out is always through. [*A Servant to Servants*]

14 The woods are lovely, dark and deep. / But I have promises to keep, / And miles to go before I sleep. [*Stopping by Woods on a Snowy Evening*]

15 Writing free verse is like playing tennis with the net down. [Address at Milton Academy, Mass., 17 May 1935]

16 Poetry is a way of taking life by the throat. [*Comment*]

17 A diplomat is a man who always remembers a woman's birthday but never remembers her age. [Quoted in Evan Esar (ed.), *Treasury of Humorous Quotations*]

JAMES ANTHONY FROUDE 1818–1894

18 Wild animals never kill for sport. Man is the only one to whom the torture and death of his fellow-creatures is amusing in itself. [*Oceana*, Ch. 5]

CHRISTOPHER FRY 1907–

19 I know your cause is lost, but in the heart / Of all right causes is a cause that cannot lose. [*The Dark is Light Enough*, III]

20 The Lady's not for Burning. [Title of play]

21 I travel light; as light, / That is, as a man can travel who will / Still carry his body around because / Of its sentimental value. [I]

22 What after all / Is a halo? It's only one more thing to keep clean.

23 Always fornicate / Between clean sheets and spit on a well-scrubbed floor. [II]

24 The moon is nothing / But a circumambulatory aphrodisiac / Divinely subsidized to provoke the world / Into a rising birth-rate. [III]

ROGER FRY 1866–1934

25 Manet and the Post-Impressionists. [(Name of exhibition 'struck out in talk with a journalist') Virginia Woolf, *Roger Fry*, Ch. 7]

R. BUCKMINSTER FULLER 1895–1983

26 One outstandingly important fact regarding Spaceship Earth, and that is that no instruction book came with it. [*Operating Manual for Spaceship Earth*, Ch. 4]

THOMAS FULLER 1608–1661

27 There is a great difference between painting a face and not washing it. [*Church History*, Bk vii. Sect. i. 32]

28 He knows little, who tells his wife all he knows. [*Holy State*, Bk i. Ch. 3]

1 A little skill in antiquity inclines a man to Popery; but depth in that study brings him about again to our religion. [ii. 6]

2 Light (God's eldest daughter!) is a principal beauty in a building. [7]

3 Anger is one of the sinews of the soul; he that wants it hath a maimed mind. [iii. 8]

4 The pyramids themselves, doting with age, have forgotten the names of their founders. [14]

5 Learning hath gained most by those books by which the printers have lost. [18]

6 Men have a touchstone whereby to try gold, but gold is the touchstone whereby to try men. [iv. 7]

7 Security is the mother of danger and the grandmother of destruction. [v. 18. 1]

8 Often the cockloft is empty in those which nature hath built many stories high. [9]

9 Much matter decocted into a few words. [(Definition of a proverb) *The Worthies of England*, Ch. 2]

ALFRED FUNKE 1869–?

10 *Gott strafe England!* – God punish England! [*Schwert und Myrte*]

DOUGLAS FURBER ?–1961

11 Any time you're Lambeth way, / Any evening, any day, / You'll find us all doin' the Lambeth walk. [Song: *Doin' the Lambeth Walk*]

HENRY FUSELI 1741–1825

12 Blake is damned good to steal from. [Quoted in Alexander Gilchrist, *Life of Blake*, Ch. 7]

13 Nature puts me out. [39]

ROSE FYLEMAN 1877–1957

14 There are fairies at the bottom of our garden. [*Fairies*]

G

HUGH GAITSKELL 1906–1963

1 There are some of us, Mr Chairman, who will fight and fight again to save the party we love. [Speech at Labour Party Conference, Scarborough, 3 Oct. 1960]

GAIUS 2 Cent.

2 *Damnosa hereditas.* – Ruinous inheritance. [*Institutes*, ii. 163]

J. K. GALBRAITH 1908–

3 The Affluent Society. [Title of book]

4 It is a far, far better thing to have a firm anchor in nonsense than to put out on the troubled seas of thought. [11. iv]

5 Meetings are indispensable when you don't want to do anything. [*Ambassador's Journal*]

GALILEO GALILEI 1564–1642

6 *E pur si muove.* – Yet it does move. [Attr. saying in 1632, after being forced to recant his doctrine that the earth moves round the sun]

ADOLF GALLAND 20 Cent.

7 It felt as if angels were pushing. [(On his first flight in a jet aircraft, the Messerschmitt 262, May 1943) *The First and the Last*]

JOHN GALSWORTHY 1867–1933

8 Nobody tells me anything. [*The Man of Property*, Pt I. Ch. 1]

9 'Very haughty!' he said, 'the wild Buccaneer.'

10 He would be setting up as a man of property next, with a place in the country.

11 Oh, your precious 'lame ducks'! [II. 12]

12 The French cook; we open tins. [Quoted in Evan Esar (ed.), *Treasury of Humorous Quotations*]

LÉON GAMBETTA 1838–1882

13 *Il n'y pas de question sociale.* – There is no social question. [Favourite saying]

14 *Les temps héroïques sont passés.* – The heroic times have passed away. [Saying]

MAHATMA GANDHI 1869–1948

15 I think it would be a good idea. [Attr., when asked by an interviewer what he thought of Western civilization]

GRETA GARBO 1905–1990

16 I want to be alone. [Attr., but she always insisted she had only said: 'I want to be left alone.' Subsequently used in her film *Grand Hotel*, script by William A. Drake]

FREDERICO GARCÍA LORCA 1899–1936

17 *A las cinco de la tarde. / Eran las cinco en punto de la tarde. / Un niño trajo la blanca sábana / a las cinco de la tarde.* – At five in the afternoon. It was exactly five in the afternoon. A boy brought the white sheet at five in the afternon. [*Llanto por Ignacio Sánchez Mejías*]

18 *Cuando sale la luna / de cien rostros iguales, / la moneda de plata / solloza en el bolsillo.* – When the moon of a hundred identical faces comes out, the silver coins sob in the pocket. [*La luna asoma*]

1 *Ni un solo momento, viejo hermoso Walt Whitman, / he dejado de ver tu barba llena de mariposas.* – Not for a moment, beautiful aged Walt Whitman, have I failed to see your beard full of butterflies. [*Oda a Walt Whitman*]

2 *Con el alma de charol / vienen por la carrera.* – With their patent-leather souls, they [the Civil Guards] come along the road. [*Romance de la Guardia civil española*]

3 *El jinete se acercaba/ tocando el tambor del llano. /Dentro de la fragua el niño / tiene los ojos cerrados.* – Drumming the plain, the horseman is coming. Inside the smithy the child has closed his eyes. [*Romance de la luna, luna*]

4 *Verde que te quiero verde. / Verde viento. Verde ramas. / El barco sobre el mar / y el caballo en la montaña.* – Green how I love you green. Green wind. Green boughs. The ship on the sea and the horse on the mountain. [*Romance sonambulo*]

DAVID GARRICK 1717–1779

5 Come cheer up, my lads! 'tis to glory we steer, / To add something more to this wonderful year; / To honour we call you, not press you like slaves, / For who are so free as the sons of the waves? / Heart of oak are our ships, / Heart of oak are our men: / We always are ready; / Steady, boys, steady; / We'll fight and we'll conquer again again. [*Heart of Oak*]

6 Here lies Nolly Goldsmith, for shortness called Noll, / Who wrote like an angel, but talked like poor Poll. [*Impromptu Epitaph*]

7 A fellow-feeling makes one wondrous kind. [*Occasional Prologue on Quitting the Theatre*]

WILLIAM LLOYD GARRISON 1805–1879

8 I am in earnest – I will not equivocate – I will not excuse – I will not retreat a single inch – and I will be heard! [*Salutatory Address of the Liberator*, 1 Jan. 1831]

SIR SAMUEL GARTH 1661–1719

9 Hard was their lodging, homely was their food, / For all their luxury was doing good. [*Claremont*, 148]

10 A barren superfluity of words. [*The Dispensary*, II. 95]

11 Some fell by laudanum, and some by steel, / And death in ambush lay in every pill. [IV. 62]

ELIZABETH GASKELL 1810–1865

12 A man ... is *so* in the way in the house! [*Cranford*, Ch. 1]

13 We were none of us musical, though Miss Jenkyns beat time, out of time, by way of appearing to be so.

14 Bombazine would have shown a deeper sense of her loss. [7]

GENERAL DE GAULLE 1890–1970

15 *Toute ma vie je me suis fait une certaine idée de la France.* – All my life I have thought of France in a certain way. [*War Memoirs*, Vol. I: *The Call to Honour*, Ch. 1]

16 France has lost the battle but she has not lost the war. [Broadcast from London after the fall of France, 18 June 1940]

17 As for me, I have never, in any one of my speeches, spoken of *l'Europe des patries* although it is always claimed that I have. [At a press conference, 15 May 1962]

THÉOPHILE GAUTIER 1811–1872

18 *Ce que j'écris n'est pas pour les petites filles.* – What I write is not for little girls. [*Albertus*, 98]

19 *Oui, l'œuvre sort plus belle / D'une forme au travail / Rebelle, / Vers, marbre, onyx, émail.* – Yes, the work comes out more beautiful from a material that resists the process, verse, marble, onyx, or enamel. [*L'Art*]

20 *Je suis un homme pour qui le monde extérieur existe.* – I am a man for whom the outside world exists. [Quoted in *Journal des Goncourt*, 1 May 1857]

GAVARNI [S. G. CHEVALIER] 1804–1866

21 *Les enfants terribles.* – The embarrassing young. [Title of a series of prints]

JOHN GAY 1685–1732

22 I rage, I melt, I burn, / The feeble God has stabbed me to the heart. [*Acis and Galatea*, II]

23 Bring me a hundred reeds of decent growth, / To make a pipe for my capacious mouth.

24 O ruddier than the cherry, / O sweeter than the berry, / O nymph more bright / Than

moonshine night, / Like kidlings blithe and merry.

1 'Tis woman that seduces all mankind, / By her we first were taught the wheedling arts. [*The Beggar's Opera*, I. ii]

2 How, like a moth, the simple maid / Still plays about the flame! [iv]

3 Our Polly is a sad slut! nor heeds what we have taught her. / I wonder any man alive will ever rear a daughter! [viii]

4 O Polly, you might have toyed and kissed. / By keeping men off, you keep them on. [ix]

5 A fox may steal your hens, sir, / ... If lawyer's hand is fee'd sir, / He steals your whole estate. [x]

6 For on the rope that hangs my dear / Depends poor Polly's life. [xii]

7 I sipped each flower, / I changed ev'ry hour, / But here ev'ry flower is united. [xiii]

8 If with me you'll fondly stray, / Over the hills and far away.

9 Fill ev'ry glass, for wine inspires us, / And fires us / With courage, love and joy. / Women and wine should life employ. / Is there aught else on earth desirous? [II. i]

10 If the heart of a man is depressed with cares. / The mist is dispelled when a woman appears. [iii]

11 Youth's the season made for joys, / Love is then our duty. [iv]

12 Man may escape from rope and gun; / Nay, some have out-lived the doctor's pill; / Who takes a woman must be undone, / That basilisk is sure to kill. [viii]

13 The fly that sips treacle is lost in the sweets.

14 Do like other widows – buy yourself weeds, and be cheerful. [xi]

15 How happy could I be with either, / Were t'other dear charmer away! / But while ye thus tease me together, / To neither a word will I say. [xiii]

16 One wife is too much for most husbands to hear, / But two at a time there's no mortal can bear. [III. xi]

17 The charge is prepared; the lawyers are met, / The judges all ranged (a terrible show!).

18 She who has never loved has never lived. [*Captives*, II. i]

19 Where yet was ever found a mother, / Who'd give her booby for another? [*Fables*, Pt I. iii. 33]

20 In every age and clime we see, / Two of a trade can ne'er agree. [xxi. 43]

21 'While there is life, there's hope,' he cried; / 'Then why such haste?' so groaned and died. [xxvii. 49]

22 And when a lady's in the case, / You know, all other things give place. [l. 41]

23 'Tis a gross error, held in schools, / That Fortune always favours fools. [II. xii. 119]

24 Life is a jest; and all things show it. / I thought so at once; but now I know it. [*My own Epitaph*]

25 All in the Downs the fleet was moored, / The streamers waving in the wind, / When black-eyed Susan came aboard. [*Sweet William's Farewell*]

26 We only part to meet again. / Change, as ye list, ye winds; my heart shall be / The faithful compass that still points to thee.

27 Adieu! she cries; and waved her lily hand.

28 'Twas when the seas were roaring / With hollow blasts of wind; / A damsel lay deploring, / All on a rock reclined. [*The What D'Ye Call It*, II. viii]

SIR ERIC GEDDES 1875–1937

29 We will get everything out of her [Germany] that you can squeeze out of a lemon, and a bit more ... I will squeeze her until you can hear the pips squeak. [Speech at Cambridge, 9 Dec. 1918]

GEORGE I 1660–1727

30 I hate all Boets and Bainters. [Quotation in Campbell, *Lives of the Chief Justices*, Ch. 30]

GEORGE II 1683–1760

31 KING [replying to Queen Caroline's death-bed injunctions to marry again]: *Non, j'aurai des maîtresses.* – No, I will take mistresses.
QUEEN CAROLINE: *Ah! mon Dieu! Cela n'empêche pas.* – But, goodness me, that won't prevent you! [Hervey, *Memoirs of George II*]

32 Oh! he [General Wolfe] is mad, is he? Then I wish he would *bite* some other of my generals. [F. Thackeray, *History of William Pitt*]

GEORGE III 1738–1820

33 Born and educated in this country, I glory

in the name of Briton. [First speech from the throne, 18 Nov. 1760]

1 'Was there ever,' cried he, 'such stuff as great part of Shakespeare? Only one mustn't say so!' [Fanny Burney's *Diary*, 19 Dec. 1785]

GEORGE V 1865–1936

2 Wake up, England. [Title of reprinted speech at Guildhall, London, 5 Dec. 1901]

3 How is the Empire? [Official last words, as quoted in *The Times*, 21 Jun. 1936]

4 Bugger Bognor! [Attr. dying words when told by his physician he would soon be convalescing in Bognor.]

IRA GERSHWIN 1896–1983

5 Oh, I got plenty o' nuthin', / An' nuthin's plenty fo' me. [Song: *I Got Plenty o' Nuthin'*, from musical *Porgy and Bess*. Music by George Gershwin]

6 It ain't necessarily so, / It ain't necessarily so – / De t'ings dat yo' li'ble / To read in de Bible – / It ain't necessarily so. [Song: *It Ain't Necessarily So*, from *Porgy and Bess*]

EDWARD GIBBON 1737–1794

7 The romance of *Tom Jones*, that exquisite picture of human manners, will outlive the palace of the Escurial and the imperial eagle of the house of Austria. [*Autobiography*]

8 To the University of Oxford I acknowledge no obligation; and she will as willingly renounce me for a son, as I am willing to disclaim her for a mother. I spent fourteen months at Magdalen College; they proved the fourteen months the most idle and unprofitable of my whole life.

9 Decent easy men, who supinely enjoyed the gifts of the founder.

10 I sighed as a lover, I obeyed as a son.

11 Crowds without company, and dissipation without pleasure. [Of London]

12 My English text is chaste, and all licentious passages are left in the decent obscurity of a learned language.

13 The various modes of worship, which prevailed in the Roman world, were all considered by the people as equally true; by the philosopher, as equally false; and by the magistrate, as equally useful. [*The Decline and Fall of the Roman Empire*, Ch. 2]

14 The principles of a free constitution are irrevocably lost when the legislative power is nominated by the executive. [3]

15 His reign is marked by the rare advantage of furnishing very few materials for history; which is, indeed, little more than the register of the crimes, follies and misfortunes of mankind.

16 It has been calculated by the ablest politicians that no State, without becoming soon exhausted, can maintain above the hundredth part of its members in arms and idleness. [5]

17 Twenty-two acknowledged concubines, and a library of sixty-two thousand volumes, attested the variety of his inclinations; and from the productions which he left behind him, it appears that the former as well as the latter were designed for use rather than ostentation. [7]

18 All taxes must, at last, fall upon agriculture. [8]

19 Corruption, the most infallible symptom of constitutional liberty. [21]

20 The ecclesiastical writers, who, in the heat of religious faction, are apt to despise the profane virtues of sincerity and moderation. [26]

21 In every deed of mischief he [Comenus] had a heart to resolve, a head to contrive, and a hand to execute. [48]

22 Our sympathy is cold to the relation of distant misery. [49]

23 All that is human must be retrograde if it does not advance. [71]

STELLA GIBBONS 1902–1989

24 Something nasty in the woodshed. [*Cold Comfort Farm, passim*]

25 Graceless, Pointless, Feckless and Aimless waited their turn to be milked. [Ch. 3]

KAHLIL GIBRAN 1883–1931

26 You were born together, and together you shall be for evermore . . . but let there be spaces in your togetherness. And let the winds of the heavens dance between you. [*The Prophet*, 'Of Marriage']

27 I have never agreed with my other self wholly. The truth of the matter seems to lie between us. [*Sand and Foam*]

W. W. GIBSON 1878–1962

1 But we, how shall we turn to little things / And listen to the birds and winds and streams / Made holy by their dreams, / Nor feel the heart-break in the heart of things? [*A Lament*]

ANDRÉ GIDE 1869–1951

2 *L'acte gratuite.* – The unmotivated action. [*Les Caves du Vatican, passim*]

3 Hugo – alas! [In a letter to Paul Valéry, when asked to name the greatest French poet, quoted in Claude Martin, *La Maturité de André Gide*, p. 502]

RICHARD GIFFORD 1725–1807

4 Revolves the sad vicissitude of things. [*Contemplation*]

WILLIAM GIFFORD 1756–1826

5 The insatiate itch of scribbling. [Trans. of Juvenal, *Satires*, vii. 79. See 228:2]

6 His namby-pamby madrigals of love. [*The Baviad*, 176]

FRED GILBERT 1850–1903

7 As I walk along the Bois Bou-long, / With an independent air, / You can hear the girls declare, / 'He must be a millionaire'; / You can hear them sigh and wish to die, / You can see them wink the other eye / At the man who broke the Bank at Monte Carlo. [*The Man who Broke the Bank at Monte Carlo*]

SIR HUMPHREY GILBERT 1539?–1583

8 We are as near to heaven by sea as by land. [Hakluyt, *Voyages*, III. p. 159]

SIR W. S. GILBERT 1836–1911

9 But they couldn't chat together – they had not been introduced. [*Bab Ballads*, 'Etiquette']

10 There were captains by the hundred, there were baronets by dozens. ['Ferdinando and Elvira']

11 The padre said, 'Whatever have you been and gone and done?' ['Gentle Alice Brown']

12 The mildest curate going. ['The Rival Curates']

13 Then they began to sing / That extremely lovely thing, / 'Scherzando! ma non troppo, ppp.' ['The Story of Prince Agib']

14 Oh, I am a cook and captain bold, / And the mate of the *Nancy* brig, / And a bo'sun tight, and a midshipmite, / And the crew of the captain's gig. ['The Yarn of the Nancy Bell']

15 He led his regiment from behind – / He found it less exciting. [*The Gondoliers*, I]

16 That celebrated, / Cultivated, / Underrated / Nobleman, / The Duke of Plaza-Toro!

17 Of that there is no manner of doubt – / No probable, possible shadow of doubt – / No possible doubt whatever.

18 A taste for drink, combined with gout, / Had doubled him up for ever.

19 Try we life-long, we can never / Straighten out life's tangled skein.

20 Life's a pudding full of plums.

21 Oh, 'tis a glorious thing, I ween, / To be a regular Royal Queen! / No half-and-half-affair, I mean, / But a right-down regular Royal Queen!

22 Take a pair of sparkling eyes. [II]

23 Take my counsel, happy man; / Act upon it, if you can!

24 Dukes were three a penny.

25 When everyone is somebodee, / Then no one's anybody.

26 I'm called Little Buttercup – dear Little Buttercup, / Though I could never tell why. [*H.M.S. Pinafore*, I]

27 Though 'Bother it' I may / Occasionally say, / I never use a big, big D. –
ALL: What never?
CAPT: No, never!
ALL: What, *never*?
CAPT: Hardly ever!

28 And so do his sisters, and his cousins, and his aunts!

29 When I was a lad I served a term / As office-boy to an Attorney's firm; / I cleaned the windows and I swept the floor, / And I polished up the handle of the big front door. / I polished up that handle so successfullee, / That now I am the Ruler of the Queen's Navee!

30 And I copied all the letters in a big round hand.

31 And I always voted at my party's call, / And I never thought of thinking for myself at all.

1 Things are seldom what they seem, / Skim milk masquerades as cream. [II]

2 Never mind the why and wherefore.

3 He is an Englishman! / For he himself has said it, / And it's greatly to his credit, / That he is an Englishman!

4 For he might have been a Roosian, / A French, or Turk, or Proosian, / O perhaps Italian! / But in spite of all temptations / To belong to other nations, / He remains an Englishman!

5 Bow, bow, ye lower middle classes! / Bow, bow, ye tradesmen, bow, ye masses. [*Iolanthe*, I]

6 The Law is the true embodiment / Of everything that's excellent. / It has no kind of fault or flaw, / And I, my lords, embody the Law.

7 The constitutional guardian I, / Of pretty young Wards in Chancery.

8 A pleasant occupation for / A rather susceptible Chancellor!

9 Hearts just as pure and fair / May beat in Belgrave Square / As in the lowly air / Of Seven Dials.

10 When I went to the Bar as a very young man, / (Said I to myself, said I).

11 I often think it's comical / How Nature always does contrive / That every boy and every gal, / That's born into the world alive, / Is either a little Liberal, / Or else a little Conservative! [II]

12 The House of Peers, throughout the war, / Did nothing in particular, / And did it very well.

13 When you're lying awake with a dismal headache, and repose is tabooed by anxiety, / I conceive you may use any language you choose to indulge in without impropriety.

14 For you dream you are crossing the Channel, and tossing about in a steamer from Harwich, / Which is something between a large bathing-machine and a very small second-class carriage.

15 Pooh-Bah (Lord High Everything Else). [*The Mikado*, Dramatis Personae]

16 A wandering minstrel I – / A thing of shreds and patches. [I]

17 And I am right, / And you are right, / And all is right as right can be!

18 I can trace my ancestry back to a protoplasmal primordial atomic globule. Consequently, my family pride is something inconceivable. I can't help it. I was born sneering.

19 It revolts me, but I do it!

20 As some day it may happen that a victim must be found, / I've got a little list – I've got a little list / Of society offenders who might well be underground, / And who never would be missed / who never would be missed!

21 Three little maids from school are we, / Pert as a schoolgirl well can be / Filled to the brim with girlish glee!

22 Life is a joke that's just begun.

23 Three little maids who, all unwary, / Come from a ladies' seminary.

24 Modified rapture!

25 We are not shy; / We're very wide awake, / The moon and I!

26 Here's a how-de-doo! [II]

27 My object all sublime / I shall achieve in time – / To let the punishment fit the crime.

28 A source of innocent merriment.

29 On a cloth untrue / With a twisted cue, / And elliptical billiard balls.

30 I drew my snickersnee!

31 Something lingering with boiling oil in it, I fancy.

32 Merely corroborative detail, intended to give artistic verisimilitude to an otherwise bald and unconvincing narrative.

33 The flowers that bloom in the spring, / Tra la, / Have nothing to do with the case.

34 I've got to take under my wing, / Tra la, / A most unattractive old thing, / Tra la, / With a caricature of a face.

35 On a tree by a river a little tomtit / Sang 'Willow, titwillow, titwillow.'

36 Twenty love-sick maidens we, / Love-sick all against our will. [*Patience*, I]

37 When I first put this uniform on.

38 If you're anxious for to shine in the high aesthetic line, as a man of culture rare.

39 The meaning doesn't matter if it's only idle chatter of a transcendental kind.

40 Why, what a very singularly deep young man, this deep young man must be!

41 An attachment à la Plato for a bashful young potato, or a not-too-French French bean.

42 By no endeavour, / Can magnet ever / Attract a silver churn! [II]

43 Sing 'Hey to you – good day to you' – / Sing 'Bah to you – ha! ha! to you.'

1 Francesca di Rimini, miminy, piminy, / 'Je-ne-sais-quoi' young man!

2 I'm a greenery-yallery, Grosvenor Gallery, / Foot-in-the-grave young man!

3 I am the very model of a modern Major-General. [*Pirates of Penzance*, I]

4 When the foeman bares his steel, / Tarantara, tarantara! / We uncomfortable feel. [II]

5 When constabulary duty's to be done, / The policeman's lot is not a happy one.

6 When the enterprising burglar's not a-burgling.

7 Politics we bar, / They are not our bent: / On the whole we are / Not intelligent. [*Princess Ida*, I]

8 We will hang you, never fear, / Most politely, most politely!

9 Man's a ribald – Man's a rake, / Man is Nature's sole mistake. [II]

10 All baronets are bad. [*Ruddigore*, I]

11 He uses language that would make your hair curl.

12 Such a bright little, tight little, / Slight little, light little, / Trim little, prim little craft! [II]

13 Some word that teems with hidden meaning – like 'Basingstoke'.

14 Time was when Love and I were well acquainted. [*The Sorcerer*, I]

15 I was a pale young curate then.

16 So I fell in love with a rich attorney's / Elderly ugly daughter. [*Trial by Jury*]

17 She may very well pass for forty-three / In the dusk with a light behind her!

18 And many a burglar I've restored / To his friends and his relations.

19 For now I am a Judge, / And a good Judge too.

20 Is life a boon? / If so, it must befall / That death, whene'er he call, / Must call too soon. [*The Yeomen of the Guard*, I]

21 It's the song of a merryman, moping mum, / Whose soul was sad, and whose glance was glum, / Who supped no sup, and who craved no crumb, / As he sighed for the love of a ladye.

22 Sir, I view the proposal to hold an inter-national exhibition at San Francisco with an equanimity bordering on indifference. [Quoted in Hesketh Pearson, *Gilbert, His Life and Strife*, Ch.19]

23 Sir, Sunday morning, although recurring at regular and well foreseen intervals, always seems to take this railway by surprise. [In a letter of complaint to the Stationmaster at Baker Street on the Metropolitan line, quoted in John Julius Norwich, *A Christmas Cracker*]

24 Funny without being vulgar. [Attr. remark on Irving's *Hamlet*]

S. W. GILLINAN 19 Cent.

25 Adam/ Had 'em. [*On the Antiquity of Microbes*]

JAMES GILLRAY 1757–1815

26 Political Ravishment, or The Old Lady of Threadneedle Street in Danger. [Caption of a caricature, 1797]

ALLEN GINSBERG 1926–

27 I saw the best minds of my generation destroyed by madness, starving hysterical naked. [*Howl*]

MME DE GIRARDIN 1804–1855

28 Business is other people's money. [*Marguerites*, Vol. ii. p. 104]

JEAN GIRAUDOUX 1882–1944

29 It's odd how people waiting for you stand out far less clearly than people you are waiting for. [*Tiger at the Gates*, I]

GEORGE GISSING 1857–1903

30 It is because nations tend towards stupidity and baseness that mankind moves so slowly; it is because individuals have a capacity for better things that it moves at all. [*The Private Papers of Henry Ryecroft*, 'Spring', XVI]

W. E. GLADSTONE 1809–1898

31 You cannot fight against the future. Time is on our side. [Speech on the Reform Bill, 1866]

32 [The Turks] one and all, bag and baggage, shall, I hope, clear out from the province they

have desolated and profaned. [Speech in House of Commons, 7 May 1877]

1 Out of the range of practical politics. [Speech at Dalkeith, 26 Nov. 1879]

2 The resources of civilization are not yet exhausted. [Speech at Leeds, 7 Oct. 1881]

3 I would tell them of my own intention to keep my own counsel ... and I will venture to recommend them, as an old Parliamentary hand, to do the same. [Speech in House of Commons, 21 Jan. 1886]

4 All the world over, I will back the masses against the classes. [Speech at Liverpool, 28 June]

5 This is the negation of God erected into a system of government. [Letter to the Earl of Aberdeen on the state of Naples, 1851]

WILLIAM HENRY, DUKE OF GLOUCESTER 1743–1805

6 Another damned, thick, square book! Always scribble, scribble, scribble! Eh! Mr Gibbon? [Quoted in note to Boswell, *Life of Johnson*]

JOHN A. GLOVER-KIND ?–1918

7 I do Like to be Beside the Seaside. [Title of song]

JEAN-LUC GODARD 1930–

8 Photography is truth. And cinema is truth twenty-four times a second. [Film, *Le Petit Soldat*]

CHARLES GODFREY ?–1935

9 When we go to meet the foe, / It's the English-speaking race against the world. [Song: *We're Brothers of the Selfsame Race*]

A. D. GODLEY 1856–1925

10 What is this that roareth thus? / Can it be a Motor Bus? / Yes, the smell and hideous hum / Indicat Motorem Bum. [*The Motor Bus*]

JOSEF GOEBBELS 1897–1945

11 An iron curtain would at once descend on this territory. [*Das Reich*, 25 Feb. 1945. See also 113:10, 400:17]

HERMANN GOERING 1893–1946

12 Guns will make us powerful; butter will only make us fat. [Broadcast Summer 1936 – the juxtaposition used also that year by Josef Goebbels]

13 I herewith commission you to carry out all preparations with regard to ... a *total solution* of the Jewish question in those territories of Europe which are under German influence. [Instructions to Heydrich, 31 July 1941, quoted in W. L. Shirer, *The Rise and Fall of the Third Reich*, Bk v. Ch. 27]

14 When I hear the word Culture, I reach for my revolver. [Attr. but actually from Hanns Johst, *Schlageter*, 224:16]

JOHANN WOLFGANG VON GOETHE 1749–1832

15 *Es irrt der Mensch, so lang er strebt.* – Man errs so long as he strives. [*Faust*, Pt I, 'Prolog im Himmel']

16 *Da steh' ich nun, ich armer Tor! / Und bin so klug als wie zuvor.* – There I am, a poor fool, and am no wiser than I was before. ['Nacht']

17 *Der Geist, der stets verneint!* – The spirit that always denies. ['Studierzimmer']

18 *Entbehren sollst du, sollst entbehren! / Das ist der ewige Gesang.* – You shall abstain, shall abstain. That is the eternal song.

19 *Werd ich zum Augenblicke sagen: / Verweile doch! Du bist so schön! –* / If I say to the moment: 'Stay now! You are so beautiful!'

20 *Denn eben, wo Begriffe fehlen, / Da stellt ein Wort zur rechten Zeit sich ein.* – For just when ideas fail, a word comes in to save the situation.

21 *Meine Ruh' ist hin, / Mein Herz ist schwer.* – My peace is gone, my heart is heavy. ['Gretchens Stube']

22 *Wer immer strebend sich bemüht, / Den können wir erlösen.* – If a man makes continuous efforts, we can save him. [II, 'Bergschluchten, Wald, Fels und Einöde']

23 *Alles Vergängliche / Ist nur ein Gleichnis.* – All that is transitory is only an image.

24 *Das Ewig-Weibliche, / Zieht uns hinan.* – The eternal in woman draws us on.

25 *Du musst herrschen und gewinnen, / Oder dienen und verlieren, / Leiden oder triumphieren, / Amboss oder Hammer sein.* – You must either

William Henry, Duke of Gloucester · Johann Wolfgang Von Goethe

179

conquer and rule or serve and lose, suffer or triumph, be the anvil or the hammer. [*Der Gross-Cophta*, II]

1 *Ein unnütz Leben ist ein früher Tod.* – A useless life is an early death. [*Iphigenie*, I. ii]

2 *Es bildet ein Talent sich in der Stille, / Sich ein Charakter in dem Strom der Welt.* – Genius is formed in quiet, character in the stream of human life. [*Tasso*, I. ii]

3 *Und so lang du das nicht hast, / Dieses: Stirb und werde! / Bist du nur ein trüber Gast /Auf der dunklen Erde.* – And until you have grasped this: 'Die and be transformed!' you will be nothing but a sombre guest on the sorry earth. [*Selige Sehnsucht*]

4 *In der Beschränkung zeigt sich erst der Meister.* – It is in self-limitation that a master first shows himself. [*Sonett: Natur und Kunst*]

5 *Über allen Gipfeln / Ist Ruh'.* – On all the peaks lies peace. [*Wanderers Nachtlied*]

6 *In der Kunst ist das Beste gut genug.* – In art the best is good enough. [*Italienische Reise*]

7 *Wer nie sein Brot mit Tränen ass, / Wer nie die kummervollen Nächte / Auf seinem Bette weinend sass, /Der kennt euch nicht, ihr himmlischen Mächte.* – Who never ate his bread with tears, who never sat through the sorrowful night, weeping upon his bed, does not know you, O heavenly powers. [*Wilhelm Meister*, ii. 13]

8 *Denn alle Schuld rächt sich auf Erden.* – For all guilt is punished on earth.

9 *Kennst du das Land wo die Zitronen blühn?* – Do you know the land where the lemon-trees flower? ['*Mignonslied*']

10 *Was hat man dir, du armes Kind, getan?* What have they done to you, my poor child?

11 *Lord Byron is nur gross, wenn er dichtet; so bald er reflektiert ist er ein Kind.* – Lord Byron is only great as a poet; as soon as he reflects he is a child. [*Gespräche mit Eckermann*, 18 Jan. 1825]

12 *Nationalliteratur will jetzt nicht viel sagen, die Epoche der Weltliteratur ist an der Zeit.* – National literature no longer means very much, the age of world literature is due. [31 Jan. 1827]

13 *Ich habe unter meinen Papieren ein Blatt gefunden ... wo ich die Baukunst eine erstarrte Musik nenne.* – I have found among my papers a sheet ... in which I call architecture frozen music. [23 Mar. 1829, but also ascr. to Friedrich von Schelling, *Die Philosophie der Kunst*, 1807. See 338:6]

14 *Mehr Licht!* – More light! [Reported dying words. Actually he asked for the second shutter of his window to be opened so that more light could come in]

VINCENT VAN GOGH 1853–1890

15 How to achieve such anomalies, such alterations and re-fashionings of reality so what comes out of it are lies, if you like, but lies that are more than literal truth. [Quoted by Francis Bacon, in the *Observer*, 25 Sept. 1988]

OLIVER GOLDSMITH 1728–1774

16 Sweet Auburn! loveliest village of the plain. [*The Deserted Village*, 1]

17 The bashful virgin's side-long looks of love, / The matron's glance that would those looks reprove. [29]

18 Ill fares the land, so hastening ills a prey, / Where wealth accumulates, and men decay; / Princes and lords may flourish, or may fade; / A breath can make them, as a breath has made; / But a bold peasantry, their country's pride, / When once destroyed, can never be supplied. [51]

19 For him light labour spread her wholesome store, / Just gave what life required, but gave no more; / His best companions, innocence and health; / And his best riches, ignorance of wealth. [59]

20 How happy he who crowns in shades like these, / A youth of labour with an age of ease. [99]

21 And, all his prospects brightening to the last, / His heaven commences ere the world be past! [111]

22 The watch-dog's voice that bayed the whispering wind, / And the loud laugh that spoke the vacant mind. [121]

23 A man he was, to all the country dear, / And passing rich with forty pounds a year; / Remote from towns he ran his godly race, / Nor e'er had changed, nor wished to change his place. [141]

24 Far other aims his heart had learned to prize, / More skilled to raise the wretched than to rise. / His house was known to all the

vagrant train, / He chid their wanderings, but relieved their pain. [147]

1 And e'en his failings leaned to Virtue's side. [164]

2 He tried each art, reproved each dull delay. / Allured to brighter worlds, and led the way. [169]

3 And fools, who came to scoff, remained to pray. [180]

4 Even children followed with endearing wile, / And plucked his gown, to share the good man's smile. [183]

5 Beside yon straggling fence that skirts the way, / With blossomed furze unprofitably gay. [193]

6 A man severe he was, and stern to view, / I knew him well, and every truant knew; / Well had the boding tremblers learned to trace / The day's disasters in his morning face; / Full well they laughed with counterfeited glee, / At all his jokes, for many a joke had he; / Full well the busy whisper, circling round, / Conveyed the dismal tidings when he frowned; / Yet he was kind, or if severe in aught, / The love he bore to learning was in fault. [197]

7 In arguing too, the parson owned his skill, / For e'en though vanquished, he could argue still; / While words of learned length, and thundering sound, / Amazed the gazing rustics ranged around; / And still they gazed, and still the wonder grew, / That one small head could carry all he knew. [211]

8 Where village statesmen talked with looks profound, / And news much older than their ale went round. [223]

9 The white-washed wall, the nicely sanded floor, / The varnished clock that clicked behind the door; / The chest contrived a double debt to pay, / A bed by night, a chest of drawers by day. [227]

10 The twelve good rules, the royal game of goose. [232]

11 And, e'en while fashion's brightest arts decoy, / The heart distrusting asks, if this be joy. [263]

12 How wide the limits stand / Between a splendid and an happy land. [267]

13 Sweet as the primrose peeps beneath the thorn. [330]

14 In all the silent manliness of grief. [384]

15 Thou source of all my bliss, and all my woe, / That foundst me poor at first, and keepst me so. [413]

16 The king himself has followed her, – / When she has walked before. [*Elegy on Mrs Mary Blaize*]

17 Too nice for a statesman, too proud for a wit. [(Edmund Burke) *Retaliation*, 38]

18 Too fond of the *right* to pursue the *expedient*. [(Edmund Burke) 40]

19 An abridgement of all that was pleasant in man. [(David Garrick) 94]

20 As a wit, if not first, in the very first line. [(Garrick) 96]

21 On the stage he was natural, simple, affecting, / 'Twas only that, when he was off, he was acting. [(Garrick) 101]

22 When they talked of their Raphaels, Correggios and stuff, / He shifted his trumpet, and only took snuff. [(Reynolds) 145]

23 Thou best-humoured man with the worst-humoured muse. [(Whitefoord) 174]

24 O Memory! thou fond deceiver, / Still importunate and vain, / To former joys recurring ever, / And turning all the past to pain! [Song: *O Memory*]

25 Where'er I roam, whatever realms to see, / My heart untravelled fondly turns to thee. [*The Traveller*, 7]

26 And learn the luxury of doing good. [22]

27 These little things are great to little man. [42]

28 Such is the patriot's boast, where'er we roam, / His first, best country ever is at home. [73]

29 The land of scholars, and the nurse of arms. [356]

30 Laws grind the poor, and rich men rule the law. [386]

31 How small, of all that human hearts endure, / That part which laws or kings can cause or cure. [429]

32 Still to ourselves in every place consigned, / Our own felicity we make or find. [431]

33 You may all go to pot. [*Verses in Reply to an Invitation to Dinner at Dr Baker's*]

34 As writers become more numerous, it is natural for readers to become more indolent. [*The Bee*, No. 175, 'Upon Unfortunate Merit']

35 'The Republic of Letters' is a very common

expression among the Europeans. [*The Citizen of the World*, 20]

1 A night-cap decked his brows instead of bay, / A cap by night – a stocking all the day! [30]

2 'Did I say so?' replied he coolly; 'to be sure, if I said so, it was so.' [54]

3 I hate the French because they are all slaves, and wear wooden shoes. [*Essays*, 24, 'Distresses of a Common Soldier']

4 Hope, like the gleaming taper's light, / Adorns and cheers our way; / And still, as darker grows the night, / Emits a brighter ray. [*The Captivity*, II]

5 This same philosophy is a good horse in the stable, but an arrant jade on a journey. [*The Good-Natured Man*, I]

6 I'm now no more than a mere lodger in my own house.

7 Friendship is a disinterested commerce between equals; love, an abject intercourse between tyrants and slaves.

8 Don't let's make imaginary evils, when you know we have so many real ones to encounter.

9 LEONTINE: An only son, sir, might expect more indulgence.

CROAKER: An only father, sir, might expect more obedience.

10 I am told he makes a very handsome corpse, and becomes his coffin prodigiously.

11 Silence is become his mother tongue. [II]

12 In my time, the follies of the town crept slowly among us, but now they travel faster than a stage-coach. [*She Stoops to Conquer*, I]

13 I love everything that's old: old friends, old times, old manners, old books, old wines.

14 As for disappointing them, I should not so much mind; but I can't abide to disappoint myself.

15 The very pink of perfection.

16 Let schoolmasters puzzle their brain, / With grammar, and nonsense, and learning, / Good liquor, I stoutly maintain, / Gives genius a better discerning. [Song]

17 It's a damned long, dark, boggy, dirty, dangerous way.

18 This is Liberty-Hall, gentlemen. [II]

19 The first blow is half the battle.

20 We are the boys / That fear no noise / Where the thundering cannons roar.

21 Was there ever such a cross-grained brute? [III]

22 As for murmurs, mother, we grumble a little now and then, to be sure. But there's no love lost between us. [IV]

23 A book may be amusing with numerous errors, or it may be very dull without a single absurdity. [*The Vicar of Wakefield*, Preface)

24 I was ever of the opinion, that the honest man who married and brought up a large family, did more service than he who continued single, and only talked of population. [Ch. 1]

25 I . . . chose my wife, as she did her wedding gown, not for a fine glossy surface, but such qualities as would wear well.

26 I was never much displeased with those harmless delusions that tend to make us more happy. [3]

27 I find you want me to furnish you with argument and intellects too. [7]

28 That's a good girl. I find you are perfectly qualified for making converts, and so go help your mother to make the gooseberry-pie.

29 Man wants but little here below, / Nor wants that little long. [8, *A Ballad*, 30. See also 203:29, 472:25]

30 By the living jingo, she was all of a muck of sweat. [9]

31 With other fashionable topics, such as pictures, taste, Shakespeare, and the musical glasses.

32 It seemed to me pretty plain, that they had more of love than matrimony in them. [16]

33 Good people all, of every sort, / Give ear unto my song; / And if you do find it wondrous short, / It cannot hold you long. [17, *An Elegy on the Death of a Mad Dog*]

34 That still a godly race he ran, / Whene'er he went to pray.

35 The naked every day he clad, / When he put on his clothes.

36 The dog, to gain some private ends, / Went mad and bit the man.

37 The man recovered of the bite, / The dog it was that died.

38 When lovely woman stoops to folly, / And finds too late that men betray, / What charm can soothe her melancholy, / What art can wash her guilt away? [29]

39 There is no arguing with Johnson; for when

his pistol misses fire, he knocks you down with the butt end of it. [Quoted in Boswell, *Life of Johnson*, 26 Oct. 1769]

1 As I take my shoes from the shoemaker, and my coat from the tailor, so I take my religion from the priest. [9 Apr. 1773]

2 If you were to make little fishes talk, they would talk like whales. [(Said to Johnson) 27 Apr. 1773]

3 Is he like Burke, who winds into a subject like a serpent? [(To Boswell, of Johnson) 10 May 1773]

4 A pampered menial. [Alteration of a phrase in T. Moss, *Beggar's Petition*]

SENATOR BARRY GOLDWATER 1909–

5 I would remind you that extremism in the defence of liberty is no vice. And let me remind you also that moderation in the pursuit of justice is no virtue! [Speech on accepting Republican nomination, San Francisco, 16 July 1964]

SAMUEL GOLDWYN 1882–1974

6 For years I have been known for saying 'include me out'; but today I am giving it up for ever. [Address at Balliol, Oxford, 1 Mar. 1945. He always denied it was actually first said at Association of Motion Picture Producers, 1933]

7 Let's have some new clichés. [*Observer*, 'Sayings of the Week', 24 Oct. 1948]

8 Why should people go out and pay money to see bad films when they can stay at home and see bad television for nothing? [*Observer*, 'Sayings of the Week', 9 Sept. 1956]

9 A wide screen just makes a bad film twice as bad. [Said on 9 Sept. 1956]

10 Anybody who goes to see a psychiatrist ought to have his head examined. [Attr., but probably invented by one of his staff]

11 I'll give you a definite maybe. [Attr.]

12 In two words: im-possible. [Attr. (by Charles Chaplin?), but apocryphal, Quoted in Alva Johnston, *The Great Goldwyn*]

13 His [Joseph M. Schenk's] verbal contract is worth more than the paper it's written on. [Became Goldwynized to:] A verbal contract isn't worth the paper it's written on. [Carol Easton, *Search for Goldwyn*]

14 I read part of it all the way through. [Attr., quoted in Philip French, *The Movie Moguls*, Ch. 4, but probably apocryphal]

EDMOND and JULES DE GONCOURT
1822–1896 and 1830–1870

15 *Les historiens sont des raconteurs du passé, les romanciers des raconteurs du présent.* – Historians tell the story of the past, novelists the story of the present. [*Idées et Sensations*]

JOE GOODWIN 1889–1943
and LARRY SHAY 1897–1988

16 When you're smiling the whole world smiles with you. [Song: *When You're Smiling*, music by Mark Fisher]

ADAM LINDSAY GORDON 1833–1870

17 Life is mostly froth and bubble, / Two things stand like stone, / Kindness in another's trouble, / Courage in your own. [*Ye Wearie Wayfarer*, Fytte 8]

LORD GOSCHEN 1831–1907

18 I have not the temerity to give a political blank cheque to Lord Salisbury. [Speech in House of Commons, 19 Feb. 1884]

19 We have stood alone in that which is called isolation – our splendid isolation, as one of our colonial friends was good enough to call it. [(See under Sir George Foster, 168:1) Speech at Lewes, 26 Feb. 1896]

VINCENT DE GOURNAY 1712–1759

20 *Laissez faire, laissez passer.* – Liberty of action, liberty of movement. [Speech, Sept. 1758. Also attr. to Marquis d'Argenson and François Quesnay]

GRAFFITI

21 Fighting for peace is like fucking for chastity. [Quoted in *Knave* magazine, Mar. 1977]

22 God is not Dead but Alive and Well and working on a Much Less Ambitious Project. [Noted in a Greenwich pub. Quoted in the *Guardian*, 'London Letter', 27 Nov. 1975]

23 Hey, hey, L.B.J., how many kids did you kill today? [At period of Vietnam War. Quoted in Robert Reisner, *Graffiti*]

1 Is there intelligent life on earth? Yes, but I'm only visiting. [Noted in Cambridge. Quoted by Norman Shrapnel in the *Guardian*, 17 Oct. 1970]

2 Is there life before death? [Noted at Notting Hill Gate; quoted in *London Graffiti*]

3 *Je suis Marxiste, tendance Groucho*. [Noted in Paris, 1968]

4 When God created man, she was only experimenting. I always thought men were a phallusy. [Noted in a ladies' lavatory]

5 A woman without a man is like a fish without a bicycle. [Noted on the campus at Birmingham University and elsewhere. Quoted in N. Rees, *Quote . . . Unquote*]

RICHARD GRAFTON ?–1572?

6 Thirty days hath November, / April, June and September, / February hath twenty-eight alone, / And all the rest have thirty-one. [*Abridgement of the Chronicles of England*, Introduction (1570)]

HARRY GRAHAM 1874–1936

7 'There's been an accident!' they said, / 'Your servant's cut in half; he's dead!' / 'Indeed!' said Mr Jones, 'and please / Send me the half that's got my keys.' [*Ruthless Rhymes*, 'Mr Jones']

8 Billy, in one of his nice new sashes, / Fell in the fire and was burnt to ashes; / Now, although the room grows chilly, / I haven't the heart to poke poor Billy. ['Tender Heartedness']

JAMES GRAHAME 1765–1811

9 Hail, Sabbath, thee I hail, the poor man's day. [*The Sabbath*, 29]

KENNETH GRAHAME 1859–1932

10 'O Mr Hodgitts!' I heard her cry, 'you are brave! for my sake do not be rash!' He was not rash. [*The Golden Age*, 'The Burglars']

11 Monkeys, who very sensibly refrain from speech, lest they should be set to earn their livings. ['The Magic Ring']

12 There is nothing – absolutely nothing – half so much worth doing as simply messing about in boats. [*The Wind in the Willows*, Ch. 1]

13 The clever men at Oxford / Know all that there is to be knowed. / But they none of them know one half as much / As intelligent Mr Toad. [10, Song]

JAMES GRAINGER 1721?–1766

14 What is fame? an empty bubble; / Gold? a transient, shining trouble. [*Solitude*, 96]

ANTONIO GRAMSCI 1891–1937

15 Pessimism of the spirit; optimism of the will. [Attr., description of intelligence]

SIR ROBERT GRANT 1779–1838

16 O worship the King, all glorious above! / O gratefully sing his power and his love! / Our Shield and Defender – the Ancient of Days, / Pavilioned in splendour, and girded with praise. [Hymn]

17 The earth with its store of wonders untold, / Almighty! thy power hath founded of old; / Hath 'stablished it fast by a changeless decree, / And round it hath cast like a mantle the sea.

18 Thy mercies how tender, how firm to the end, / Our Maker, Defender, Redeemer and Friend!

GENERAL ULYSSES S. GRANT 1822–1885

19 I purpose to fight it out on this line, if it takes all summer. [Dispatch to Washington, 11 May 1864]

20 No terms except unconditional and immediate surrender can be accepted. [To General Buckner at Fort Donelson, 16 Feb. 1862]

GEORGE GRANVILLE, BARON LANSDOWNE 1667–1735

21 Of all the plagues with which the world is cursed, / Of every ill, a woman is the worst. [*The British Enchanters*, II. i]

LORD GRANVILLE 1815–1891

22 Spheres of action. [Letter to Count Münster, 29 Apr. 1885]

GÜNTER GRASS 1927–

23 Even bad books are books and therefore sacred. [*The Tin Drum*, 'Rasputin and the Alphabet']

A. P. GRAVES 1846–1931

24 Och! Father O'Flynn, you've the wonderful way wid you. [*Father O'Flynn*]

1 Checkin' the crazy ones, coaxin' onaisy ones, / Liftin' the lazy ones on wid the stick.

J. W. GRAVES 1795–1886

2 D'ye ken John Peel with his coat so gray? / D'ye ken John Peel at the break of the day? / D'ye ken John Peel when he's far far away / With his hounds and his horn in the morning?

'Twas the sound of his horn called me from my bed, / And the cry of his hounds has me oft-times led; / For Peel's view-hallo would waken the dead, / Or a fox from his lair in the morning. [John Peel]

ROBERT GRAVES 1895–1985

3 No escape, / No such thing; to dream of new dimensions, / Cheating checkmate by painting the king's robe / So that he slides like a queen. [The Castle]

4 Christ of his gentleness, / Thirsting and hungering / Walked in the wilderness; / Soft words of grace he spoke / Unto lost desert-folk / That listened wondering. [In the Wilderness]

5 Across two counties he can hear / And catch your words before you speak. / The woodlouse or the maggot's weak / Clamour rings in his sad ear, / And noise so slight it would surpass / Credence. [Lost Love]

6 Those famous men of old, the Ogres – / They had long beards and stinking armpits, / They were wide-mouthed, long-yarded and great-bellied / Yet of no taller stature, Sirs, than you. [Ogres and Pygmies]

7 The thundering text, the snivelling commentary.

8 Any honest housewife would sort them out, / Having a nose for fish, an eye for apples. [The Poets]

9 You reading over my shoulder, peering beneath / My writing arm. [The Reader Over my Shoulder (also title of a book of criticism)]

10 Take your delight in momentariness, / Walk between dark and dark – a shining space / With the grave's narrowness, though not its peace. [Sick Love]

11 Why have such scores of lovely, gifted girls / Married impossible men? [A Slice of Wedding Cake]

12 'How is your trade, Aquarius, / This frosty night?' / 'Complaints is many and various / And my feet are cold,' says Aquarius. [Star-talk]

13 Love is a universal migraine / A bright stain on the vision / Blotting out reason. [Symptoms of Love]

14 They carry / Time looped so river-wise about their house / There's no way in by history's road / To name or number them. [Through Nightmare]

15 To bring the dead to life / Is no great magic. / Few are wholly dead: / Blow on a dead man's embers / And a live flame will start. [To Bring the Dead to Life]

16 It's an old story – f's for s's – / But good enough for them, the suckers. [Wm. Brazier]

17 Goodbye to All That. [Title of book]

HAROLD GRAY 1894–1968

18 Little Orphan Annie. [Title of American comic-strip serial, 1925. Derived from song by J. W. Riley]

THOMAS GRAY 1716–1771

19 Ruin seize thee, ruthless King! / Confusion on thy banners wait; / Though fanned by Conquest's crimson wing, / They mock the air with idle state. [The Bard, I. 1]

20 Vocal no more, since Cambria's fatal day, / To high-born Hoel's harp, or soft Llewellyn's lay. [2]

21 Dear as the light that visits these sad eyes; / Dear as the ruddy drops that warm my heart. [3]

22 Weave the warp, and weave the woof, / The winding-sheet of Edward's race. / Give ample room, and verge enough / The characters of hell to trace. [II. 1]

23 The swarm that in thy noontide beam were born, / Gone to salute the rising morn. [2]

24 In gallant trim the gilded vessel goes, / Youth on the prow, and Pleasure at the helm; / Regardless of the sweeping whirlwind's sway, / That, hushed in grim repose, expects his evening prey.

25 Ye towers of Julius, London's lasting shame, / With many a foul and midnight murther fed. [3]

26 Visions of glory, spare my aching sight, / Ye unborn ages, crowd not on my soul! [III. 1]

27 The curfew tolls the knell of parting day, / The lowing herd winds slowly o'er the lea, /

Thomas Gray

The ploughman homeward plods his weary way, / And leaves the world to darkness and to me. [*Elegy Written in a Country Churchyard,* 1]

1 Now fades the glimmering landscape on the sight, / And all the air a solemn stillness holds, / Save where the beetle wheels his droning flight, / And drowsy tinklings lull the distant fold. [2]

2 Save that from yonder ivy-mantled tower, / The moping owl does to the moon complain. [3]

3 Each in his narrow cell for ever laid, / The rude forefathers of the hamlet sleep. [4]

4 The breezy call of incense-breathing Morn, / The swallow twittering from the straw-built shed, / The cock's shrill clarion, or the echoing horn, / No more shall rouse them from their lowly bed. [5]

5 Let not ambition mock their useful toil, / Their homely joys and destiny obscure; / Nor grandeur hear, with a disdainful smile, / The short and simple annals of the poor. [8]

6 The boast of heraldry, the pomp of power, / And all that beauty, all that wealth e'er gave, / Awaits alike th' inevitable hour, / The paths of glory lead but to the grave. [9]

7 Where through the long-drawn aisle and fretted vault / The pealing anthem swells the note of praise. [10]

8 Can storied urn or animated bust / Back to its mansion call the fleeting breath? / Can honour's voice provoke the silent dust, / Or flattery soothe the dull cold ear of death? [11]

9 Hands, that the rod of empire might have swayed, / Or waked to ecstasy the living lyre. [12]

10 Full many a gem of purest ray serene / The dark unfathomed caves of ocean bear: / Full many a flower is born to blush unseen, / And waste its sweetness on the desert air. [14]

11 Some village Hampden, that with dauntless breast / The little tyrant of his fields withstood; / Some mute inglorious Milton here may rest, / Some Cromwell guiltless of his country's blood. [15]

12 Th' applause of listening senates to command, / The threats of pain and ruin to despise, / To scatter plenty o'er a smiling land, / And read their history in a nation's eyes. [16]

13 Forbade to wade through slaughter to a throne, / And shut the gates of mercy on mankind. [17]

14 Far from the madding crowd's ignoble strife, / Their sober wishes never learned to stray; / Along the cool sequestered vale of life / They kept the noiseless tenor of their way. [19]

15 For who to dumb Forgetfulness a prey, / This pleasing anxious being e'er resigned, / Left the warm precincts of the cheerful day / Nor cast one longing ling'ring look behind? [22]

16 On some fond breast the parting soul relies, / Some pious drops the closing eye requires; / E'en from the tomb the voice of Nature cries, / E'en in our ashes live their wonted fires. [23]

17 Brushing with hasty steps the dews away / To meet the sun upon the upland lawn. [25]

18 Here rests the head upon the lap of Earth / A youth to fortune and to fame unknown. / Fair Science frowned not on his humble birth, / And Melancholy marked him for her own.

Large was his bounty, and his soul sincere, / Heav'n did a recompense as largely send: / He gave to Mis'ry all he had, a tear, / He gained from Heav'n ('twas all he wished) a friend.

No farther seek his merits to disclose, / Or draw his frailties from their dread abode, / (There they alike in trembling hope repose), / The bosom of his Father and his God. [30]

19 Daughter of Jove, relentless power, / Thou tamer of the human breast, / Whose iron scourge and tort'ring hour / The bad affright, afflict the best. [*Hymn to Adversity*]

20 And leave us leisure to be good.

21 Owls would have hooted in St Peter's choir, / And foxes stunk and littered in St Paul's. [*Impromptu on Lord Holland's Seat*]

22 Hence, avaunt! ('tis holy ground). [*Ode for Music*]

23 Servitude that hugs her chain.

24 There sit the sainted sage, the bard divine, / The few, whom genius gave to shine / Through every unborn age, and undiscovered clime.

25 Their tears, their little triumphs o'er, / Their human passions now no more.

26 Demurest of the tabby kind, / The pensive Selima, reclined. [*Ode on the Death of a Favourite Cat*]

27 What female heart can gold despise? / What cat's averse to fish?

28 A fav'rite has no friend.

29 Not all that tempts your wand'ring eyes /

And heedless hearts, is lawful prize; / Nor all that glisters, gold.

1 Ye distant spires! ye antique towers. [*Ode on a Distant Prospect of Eton College*, 1]

2 Where once my careless childhood strayed, / A stranger yet to pain. [2]

3 Who foremost now delight to cleave / With pliant arm thy glassy wave? [3]

4 Urge the flying ball.

5 They hear a voice in every wind, / And snatch a fearful joy. [4]

6 To each his suff'rings: all are men, / Condemned alike to groan; / The tender for another's pain, / Th' unfeeling for his own. / Yet ah! why should they know their fate? / Since sorrow never comes too late, / And happiness too swiftly flies. / Thought would destroy their paradise. / No more; where ignorance is bliss, / 'Tis folly to be wise. [10]

7 The meanest flowret of the vale, / The simplest note that swells the gale, / The common sun, the air, and skies, / To him are opening paradise. [*Ode on the Pleasure arising from Vicissitude*]

8 The Attic warbler pours her throat, / Responsive to the cuckoo's note. [*Ode on the Spring*]

9 To Contemplation's sober eye. / Such is the race of Man.

10 The sun is set, the spring is gone – / We frolic while 'tis May.

11 Woods that wave o'er Delphi's steep, / Isles that crown th' Aegean deep. [*The Progress of Poesy*, II. 3]

12 Far from the sun and summer-gale, / In thy green lap was Nature's darling laid. [(Shakespeare) III. 1]

13 Or ope the sacred source of sympathetic tears.

14 He passed the flaming bounds of space and time: / The living throne, the sapphire-blaze, / Where angels tremble while they gaze, / He saw; but blasted with excess of light, / Closed his eyes in endless night. [(Milton) 2]

15 Beyond the limits of a vulgar fate, / Beneath the good how far – but far above the great. [(Dryden) 3]

16 Too poor for a bribe, and too proud to importune, / He had not the method of making a fortune. [*Sketch of His own Character*]

17 And weep the more, because I weep in vain. [*Sonnet on the Death of Richard West*]

18 The language of the age is never the language of poetry, except among the French, whose verse, where the thought or image does not support it, differs in nothing from prose. [Letter to Richard West, Apr. 1742]

19 I shall be but a shrimp of an author. [Letter to Horace Walpole, 25 Feb. 1768 (long after the publication of his *Elegy*)]

HORACE GREELEY 1811–1872

20 Go West, young man, and grow up with the country. [*Hints towards Reform*, but originally said by J. B. L. Soule (see 401:6)]

MATTHEW GREEN 1696–1737

21 They politics like ours profess, / The greater prey upon the less. [*The Grotto*, 69]

22 To cure the mind's wrong bias, Spleen, / Some recommend the bowling-green; / Some, hilly walks; all, exercise; / Fling but a stone, the giant dies. / Laugh and be well. [*The Spleen*, 89]

GRAHAM GREENE 1904–1991

23 Catholics and Communists have committed great crimes, but at least they have not stood aside, like an established society, and been indifferent. I would rather have blood on my hands than water like Pilate. [*The Comedians*, III. 4. iv]

24 So many of his prayers had remained unanswered that he had hopes that this one prayer of his had lodged all the time like wax in the Eternal ear. [*Monsignor Quixote*, Pt I. Ch. 1.]

25 A solitary laugh is often a laugh of superiority. [9]

26 That whisky priest, I wish we had never had him in the house. [*The Power and the Glory*, Pt I. ii and *passim*]

27 Of course, before we *know* he is a saint, there will have to be miracles. [IV]

28 Sentimentality – that's what we call the sentiment we don't share. [Quoted in A. Andrews, *Quotations for Speakers and Writers*]

ROBERT GREENE 1560?–1592

29 Weep not, my wanton, smile upon my knee; / When thou art old there's grief enough for thee. / Mother's wag, pretty boy, / Father's sorrow, father's joy. [*Sephestia's Song*]

1 The wanton smiled, father wept; / Mother cried, baby lept.

2 If country loves such sweet desires gain, / What lady would not love a shepherd swain? [*The Shepherd's Wife's Song*]

3 For there is an upstart crow, beautified with our feathers, that with his tiger's heart wrapped in a player's hide, supposes he is as well able to bumbast out a blank verse as the best of you; and being an absolute *Iohannes fac totum*, is in his own conceit the only Shakescene in a country. [*Groatsworth of Wit*]

GERMAINE GREER 1939–

4 Man is jealous because of his *amour propre*; woman is jealous because of her lack of it. [*The Female Eunuch*, 'Egotism']

GREGORY I 540–604

5 *Responsum est, quod Angli vocarentur. At ille: 'Bene,' inquit; 'nam et angelicam habent faciem, et tales angelorum in caelis decet esse coherides.'* –The reply was that they were Angles. 'It is well,' said he, 'for they have the faces of angels, and such should be the co-heirs of the angels in heaven.' [(Traditionally quoted as '*Non Angli sed Angeli*' – 'Not Angles but angels') The Venerable Bede, *Ecclesiastical History*, II. i]

GREGORY VII 1020–1085

6 I have loved justice and hated iniquity; therefore I die in exile. [Attr.]

ÉTIENNE DE GRELLET [STEPHEN GRELLET] 1773–1855

7 I shall pass through this world but once. If, therefore, there be any kindness I can show, or any good thing I can do, let me do it now; let me not defer it or neglect it, for I shall not pass this way again. [Attr. to Grellet, and to others]

JULIAN GRENFELL 1888–1915

8 And he is dead who will not fight; / And who dies fighting has increase. [*Into Battle*]

FULKE GREVILLE, LORD BROOKE 1554–1628

9 If in my heart all saints else be defaced, / Honour the shrine where you alone are placed. [*Caelica*, Sonnet 3]

10 Silence augmenteth grief, writing increaseth rage, / Staled are my thoughts, which loved and lost the wonder of our age; / Yet quickened now with fire, though dead with frost ere now, / Enraged I write I know not what; dead, quick, I know not how. [*Epitaph on Sir Philip Sidney*]

11 Vast Superstition! Glorious style of weakness! / Sprung from the deep disquiet of Man's passion, / To desolation, and despair of Nature. [*Mustapha*, Chorus 5]

12 Oh wearisome condition of humanity! / Born under one law, to another bound: / Vainly begot, and yet forbidden vanity; / Created sick, commanded to be sound. [V. iv]

VISCOUNT GREY OF FALLODEN 1862–1933

13 The lamps are going out all over Europe; we shall not see them lit again in our lifetime. [On the eve of war, 3 Aug. 1914]

MERVYN GRIFFITH-JONES 1909–1978

14 Would you allow your wife or your servant to read this book? [Presenting the case for the prosecution of *Lady Chatterley's Lover*, 20 Oct. 1960]

GEORG GRODDECK 20 Cent.

15 Whatever you blame, that you have done yourself. [Quoted in 'Palinurus' (Cyril Connolly), *The Unquiet Grave*, Pt III]

GEORGE and WEEDON GROSSMITH 1847–1912 and 1854–1919

16 What's the good of a home if you are never in it? [*The Diary of a Nobody*, Ch. 1]

17 I left the room with silent dignity, but caught my foot in the mat. [12]

18 I am a poor man, but I would gladly give ten shillings to find out who sent me the insulting Christmas card I received this morning. [13]

GEORGE GROSSMITH THE YOUNGER 1874–1935
and FRED THOMPSON 1884–1949

19 Another little drink wouldn't do us any harm. [*The Bing Boys*, 'Another Little Drink']

20 If you were the only girl in the world, / And I were the only boy. ['If you were the Only Girl']

PHILIP GUEDALLA 1889–1944

1 The work of Henry James has always seemed divisible by a simple dynastic arrangement into three reigns: James I, James II, and the Old Pretender. [*Collected Essays*, 'Mr Henry James']

2 Any stigma, as the old saying is, will serve to beat a dogma. [Quoted in Evan Esar (ed.), *Treasury of Humorous Quotations*]

'TEXAS' GUINAN 1884–1933

3 Hello, sucker! [Welcome to night-club customers]

4 Fifty million Frenchmen can be wrong. [Attr. in *New York World-Telegram*, 21 Mar. 1931, when denied entry into France]

ARTHUR GUITERMAN 1871–1943

5 The Prophet's Cam-u-el, that primal Desert Ship. [*The Legend of the First Cam-u-el*]

6 Lightly we follow our cue, / 'Exit, pursued by a bear'. [*The Shakespearean Bear*]

FRANÇOIS GUIZOT 1787–1874

7 *Enrichissez-vous!* – Enrich yourselves! [Speech, 1 Mar. 1843]

DOROTHY GURNEY 1858–1932

8 The kiss of the sun for pardon, / The song of the birds for mirth, / One is nearer God's Heart in a garden / Than anywhere else on earth. [*God's Garden*]

WOODY GUTHRIE 1912–1967

9 So Long, It's Been Good to Know Yuh. [Title of song]

10 This Land is Your Land, this Land is My Land. [Song: *This Land is Your Land*]

JOHN HABBERTON 1842–1921

1 Want to shee the wheels go wound. [*Helen's Babies*, 1]

EMPEROR HADRIAN 76–138

2 *Animula vagula blandula, / Hospes comesque corporis, / Quae nunc abibis in loca / Pallidula rigida nudula, / Nec ut soles dabis iocos!* – Little soul, wandering and pleasant guest and companion of the body, into what places will you now depart, pale, stiff, and naked; and you will sport no longer as you did! [Poem]

H. RIDER HAGGARD 1856–1925

3 She-who-must-be-obeyed. [*She, passim*]

EARL HAIG 1861–1928

4 Every position must be held to the last man: there must be no retirement. With our backs to the wall, and believing in the justice of our cause, each one of us must fight on to the end. [Order to the British troops, 12 Apr. 1918]

J. B. S. HALDANE 1892–1964

5 An angel whose muscles developed no more power weight for weight than those of an eagle or a pigeon would require a breast projecting for about four feet to house the muscles engaged in working its wings, while to economize in weight, its legs would have to be reduced to mere stilts. [*Possible Worlds*, 'On Being the Right Size']

6 My own suspicion is that the universe is not only queerer than we suppose, but queerer than we *can* suppose. [Title essay]

SARAH HALE 1788–1879

7 Mary had a little lamb, / Its fleece was white as snow, / And everywhere that Mary went / The lamb was sure to go. [*Mary's Little Lamb*]

THOMAS CHANDLER HALIBURTON 1796–1865

8 I want you to see Peel, Stanley, Graham, Shiel, Russell, Macaulay, Old Joe, and so on. These men are all upper crust here. [*Sam Slick in England*, Ch. 24]

MARQUIS OF HALIFAX 1633–1695

9 The innocent word 'Trimmer' signifies no more than this, that if men are together in a boat, and one part of the company would weigh it down on one side, another would make it lean as much to the contrary. [*Character of a Trimmer*, Preface]

10 Popularity is a crime from the moment it is sought; it is only a virtue where men have it whether they will or no. [*Moral Thoughts and Reflections*]

11 Men are not hanged for stealing horses, but that horses may not be stolen. [*Political Thoughts and Reflections*, 'Of Punishment']

CHARLES SPRAGUE HALL *fl.* 1860

12 John Brown's body lies a-mouldering in the grave, / His soul is marching on! [*John Brown's Body*]

JOSEPH HALL 1574–1656

13 Death borders upon our birth, and our cradle stands in the grave. [*Epistles*, 2]

1 I first adventure, follow me who list / And be the second English satirist. [*Virgidemiae*, Prologue]

OWEN HALL [JAMES DAVIS] 1854–1907

2 Tell me, pretty maiden, are there any more at home like you? [*Florodora*, II]

ROBERT HALL 1764–1831

3 Glass of brandy and water! That is the current but not the appropriate name: ask for a glass of liquid fire and distilled damnation. [Gregory, *Life*]

GAIL HAMILTON [MARY ABIGAIL DODGE] 1838–1896

4 The total depravity of inanimate things. [*Epigram*]

WILLIAM HAMILTON 1704–1754

5 Busk ye, busk ye, my bonny bonny bride, / Busk ye, busk ye, my winsome marrow. [*The Braes of Yarrow*]

SIR WILLIAM HAMILTON 1788–1856

6 On earth there is nothing great but man; in man there is nothing great but mind. [*Lectures on Metaphysics*]

WILLIAM GERARD HAMILTON 1729–1796

7 Johnson is dead. – Let us go to the next best: – There is nobody; no man can be said to put you in mind of Johnson. [Boswell, *Life of Johnson*, 1784]

DAG HAMMARSKJÖLD 1905–1961

8 In the last analysis, it is our conception of death which decides our answers to all the questions that life puts to us. [*Diaries* (1958)]

OSCAR HAMMERSTEIN 1895–1960

9 The last time I saw Paris, her heart was warm and gay, / I heard the laughter of her heart in every street café. [Song: *The Last Time I Saw Paris*]

10 Oh, what a beautiful mornin'! / Oh, what a beautiful day! [Song: *Oh, What a Beautiful Mornin'*, from musical *Oklahoma!* Music by Richard Rodgers]

11 The corn is as high as an elephant's eye.

12 Ol' man river, dat ol' man river, / He must know sumpin', but don't say nothin', / He just keeps rollin', he keeps on rollin' along. [Song: *Ol' Man River*, from musical *Show Boat*, I. Music by Jerome Kern]

13 The hills are alive with the sound of music / With the songs they have sung / For a thousand years. [Title song from the musical *The Sound of Music*. Music by Richard Rodgers]

14 Some enchanted evening, / you may see a stranger / 'Cross a crowded room. [Song: *Some Enchanted Evening*, from musical *South Pacific*, I. Music by Richard Rodgers]

15 I'm Gonna Wash That Man Right Out of My Hair. [Title of song in *South Pacific*]

CHRISTOPHER HAMPTON 1946–

16 If I had to give a definition of capitalism, I would say: the process whereby American girls turn into American women. [*Savages*, Sc. 16]

17 Asking a working writer what he thinks about critics is like asking a lamp-post how it feels about dogs. [Quoted in the *Sunday Times Magazine*, 16 Oct. 1977]

MINNY MAUD HANFF 1880–1942

18 Since then they called him Sunny Jim. [Advertisement for Force, a breakfast food]

KATHERINE HANKEY 1834–1911

19 Tell me the old, old story. [Hymn]

ERNST AUGUST, ELECTOR OF HANOVER 1629–1698

20 *Les chevaux du roi de France sont mieux logés que moi.* – The king of France's horses are better housed than I. [On seeing Louis XIV's stables at Versailles]

BRIAN HANRAHAN 1949–

21 I'm not allowed to say how many planes joined the raid but I counted them all out and I counted them all back. [(On British attack in the Falklands War) BBC Broadcast, 1 May 1982]

EDMOND HARAUCOURT 1856–1941

1 *Partir c'est mourir un peu, / C'est mourir à ce qu'on aime.* – To part is to die a little, to die to what one loves. [*Seul, 'Rondel de l'Adieu'*]

OTTO HARBACH 1873–1963

2 Smoke Gets in Your Eyes. [Title of song from musical *Roberta*]

OTTO HARBACH 1873–1963
  and **FRANK MANDEL** 20 Cent.

3 Tea for Two, and Two for Tea. [Title of song from musical *No, No, Nanette*, II. Music by Vincent Youmans]

E. Y. HARBURG 1898–1981

4 Brother, Can You Spare a Dime? [Title of song from musical *New Americana*. Music by Jay Gorney]

5 Say, it's only a paper moon, / Sailing over a cardboard sea. [Song: *Paper Moon*, from musical *Take A Chance*]

6 Somewhere over the rainbow, / Way up high: / There's a land that I heard of / Once in a lullaby. [Song: *Over the Rainbow*, from film *The Wizard of Oz*. Music by Harold Arlen]

EARL OF HARDWICKE 1690–1764

7 His doubts are better than most people's certainties. [Reference to Dirleton's *Doubts*, quoted in Boswell, *Life of Johnson*]

REV. E. J. HARDY 20 Cent.

8 How To Be Happy Though Married. [Title of book (1910)]

THOMAS HARDY 1840–1928

9 When the Present has latched its postern behind my tremulous stay, / And the May month flaps its glad green leaves like wings, / Delicate-filmed as new-spun silk, will the neighbours say, / 'He was a man who used to notice such things'? [*Afterwards*]

10 Where once we danced, where once we sang, Gentlemen, / The floors are shrunken, cobwebs hang. [*An Ancient to Ancients*]

11 The bower we shrined to Tennyson, / Gentlemen, / Is roof-wrecked; damps there drip upon / Sagged seats, the creeper-nails are rust, / The spider is sole denizen.

12 Any little old song / Will do for me. [*Any little old song*]

13 So zestfully canst thou sing? / And all this indignity, / With God's consent, on thee! / Blinded ere yet a-wing. [*The Blinded Bird*]

14 The Immanent Will that stirs and urges everything. [*The Convergence of the Twain*]

15 So little cause for carolings / Of such ecstatic sound / Was written on terrestrial things / Afar or nigh around, / That I could think there trembled through / His happy good-night air / Some blessed Hope, whereof he knew / And I was unaware. [*The Darkling Thrush*]

16 His landmark is a kopje-crest / That breaks the veldt around; / And foreign constellations west / Each night above his mound. [*Drummer Hodge*]

17 Smile out; but still suffer: / The paths of love are rougher / Than thoroughfares of stones. [*The End of the Episode*]

18 We two kept house, the Past and I. [*The Ghost of the Past*]

19 O man-projected Figure, of late / Imaged as we, thy knell who shall survive? / Whence came it we were tempted to create / One whom we can no longer keep alive? [*God's Funeral*]

20 Crass Casualty obstructs the sun and rain, / And dicing Time for gladness casts a moan . . . / These purblind Doomsters had as readily strown / Blisses about my pilgrimage as pain. [*Hap*]

21 Well, World, you have kept faith with me, / Kept faith with me; / Upon the whole you have proved to be / Much as you said you were. [*He never expected much*]

22 I am the family face; / Flesh perishes, I live on, / Projecting trait and trace / Through time to times anon, / And leaping from place to place / Over oblivion. [*Heredity*]

23 I need not go / Through sleet and snow / To where I know / She waits for me: / She will tarry there / Till I find it fair, / And have time to spare / From company. [*I need not go*]

24 Who holds that if way to the Better there be, it exacts a full look at the Worst. [*In Tenebris, II*]

25 Only a man harrowing clods / In a slow silent walk / With an old horse that stumbles

and nods / Half asleep as they stalk. [*In the Time of 'The Breaking of Nations'*]

1 Yonder a maid and her wight / Come whispering by: / War's annals will cloud into night / Ere their story die.

2 Let me enjoy the earth no less / Because the all-enacting Might / That fashioned forth its loveliness / Had other aims than my delight. [*Let me enjoy*]

3 There's not a modest maiden elf / But dreads the final Trumpet, / Lest half of her should rise herself, / And half some sturdy strumpet! [*The Levelled Churchyard*]

4 What of the faith and fire within us / Men who march away / Ere the barncocks say / Night is growing gray, / Leaving all that here can win us? [*Men who march away*]

5 In the third-class seat sat the journeying boy, / And the roof-lamp's oily flame / Played down on his listless form and face, / Bewrapt past knowing to what he was going, / Or whence he came. [*Midnight on the Great Western*]

6 And both of us, scorning parochial ways, / Had lived like the wives in the patriarchs' days. [*Over the Coffin*]

7 Christmas Eve, and twelve of the clock. / 'Now they are all on their knees.' [*Oxen*]

8 If someone said on Christmas Eve, / 'Come see the oxen kneel . . .' / I should go with him in the gloom, / Hoping it might be so.

9 A pinch of unseen, unguarded dust. [*Shelley's Skylark*]

10 'What do you think of it, Moon, / As you go? / Is life much or no?' / 'O, I think of it, often think of it / As a show / God ought surely to shut up soon, / As I go.' [*To the Moon*]

11 A star looks down at me, / And says: 'Here I and you / Stand, each in our degree: / What do you mean to do?' [*Waiting Both*]

12 This is the weather the cuckoo likes / And so do I. [*Weathers*]

13 When I set out for Lyonnesse, / A hundred miles away, / The rime was on the spray. [*When I set out for Lyonnesse*]

14 Who's in the next room? – who? / I seemed to see / Somebody in the dawning passing through, / Unknown to me. [*Who's in the next room?*]

15 A local cult, called Christianity. [*The Dynasts*, I. vi]

16 To persons standing alone on a hill during a clear midnight such as this, the roll of the world eastward is almost a palpable movement. [*Far From the Madding Crowd*, Ch. 2]

17 A nice unparticular man. [8]

18 Ethelberta breathed a sort of exclamation, not right out, but stealthily, like a parson's damn. [*The Hand of Ethelberta*]

19 Done because we are too menny. [*Jude the Obscure*, Pt VI. Ch. 2]

20 Life's Little Ironies. [Title of volume of stories]

21 All her shining keys will be took from her, and her cupboards opened, and things a' didn't wish seen, anybody will see; and her little wishes and ways will all be as nothing. [*The Mayor of Casterbridge*, Ch. 18]

22 The long, laborious road, dry, empty, and white. It was quite open to the heath on each side, and bisected that vast dark surface like the parting-line on a head of black hair, diminishing and bending away on the furthest horizon. [*The Return of the Native*, Ch. 2]

23 A little one-eyed, blinking sort o' place. [*Tess of the D'Urbervilles*, Ch. 1]

24 'Justice' was done, and the President of the Immortals, in Aeschylean phrase, had ended his sport with Tess. [59]

25 Good, but not religious-good. [*Under the Greenwood Tree*, I. Ch. 2]

26 I like a story with a bad moral . . . all good stories have a coarse touch or a bad moral, depend on't. If the story-tellers could ha' got decency and good morals from true stories, who'd have troubled to invent parables? [8]

27 Silent? ah, he is silent! He can keep silence well. That man's silence is wonderful to listen to. [II.5]

28 You was a good man, and did good things. [*The Woodlanders*, Ch. 48]

JULIUS and AUGUSTUS HARE
1795–1855 and 1792–1834

29 Half the failures in life arise from pulling in one's horse as he is leaping. [*Guesses at Truth*, I]

30 Purity is the feminine, Truth the masculine, of Honour.

MAURICE E. HARE 1886–1967

31 There once was a man who said, 'Damn! /

It is borne in upon me I am / An engine that moves / In predestinate grooves, / I'm not even a bus, I'm a tram.' [Limerick]

W. F. HARGREAVES 1846–1919

1 I'm Burlington Bertie: I rise at ten thirty. [*Burlington Bertie*]

2 I walk down the Strand / With my gloves on my hand, / And I walk down again / With them off.

3 P. C. 49. [Title of music-hall song]

SIR JOHN HARINGTON 1561–1612

4 Treason doth never prosper: what's the reason? / For if it prosper, none dare call it treason. [*Epigrams*, 'Of Treason']

J. P. HARRINGTON 19 Cent.

5 Now your country calls you far across the sea, / To do a soldier's duty / For England, home and beauty. [Song: *The Girls You Leave Behind You*]

J. P. HARRINGTON
and GEORGE LE BRUN ?–1905

6 Everything in the Garden's Lovely! [Title of music-hall song, sung by Marie Lloyd]

CHARLES K. HARRIS 1865–1930

7 Many a heart is aching, if you could read them all, / Many the hopes that have vanished, after the ball. [*After the Ball*]

CLIFFORD HARRIS 20 Cent.

8 You called me Baby Doll a year ago, [*A Broken Doll*]

JOEL CHANDLER HARRIS 1848–1908

9 'Law, Brer Tarrypin!' sez Brer Fox, sezee, 'you ain't see no trouble yit. Ef you wanter see sho' nuff trouble, you des oughter go 'longer me; I'm de man w'at kin show you trouble', sezee. [*Nights with Uncle Remus*, Ch. 17]

10 Hit look lak sparrer-grass, hit feel lak sparrer-grass, hit tas'e lak sparrer-grass, en I bless ef 'taint sparrer-grass. [(Asparagus), 27]

11 A contrapshun what he call a Tar-Baby. [*Uncle Remus*, Ch. 2]

12 Tar-Baby ain't sayin' nuthin', en Brer Fox, he lay low.

13 Ez shoshubble ez a baskit er kittens. [3]

14 Bred en bawn in a brier-patch, Brer Fox. [4]

15 Lounjun' 'round' en suffer'n. [12]

16 I'm de'f in one year, en I can't hear out'n de udder. [19]

17 Ole man Know-All died las' year. [34]

18 Lazy fokes' stummucks don't git tired.

19 Licker talks mighty loud w'en it git loose from de jug.

20 Oh, war shill we go w'en de great day comes, / Wid be blowin' er de trumpits en de bangin' er de drums? / How many po' sinners'll be kotched out late / En find no latch ter de golden gate? [*Uncle Remus: His Songs*, I]

LORENZ HART 1895–1943

21 Bewitched, Bothered and Bewildered. [Title of song in musical, *Pal Joey*]

FRANCIS BRETT [BRET] HARTE
1836–1902

22 Thar ain't no sense / In gittin' riled! [*Jim*]

23 Which I wish to remark, / And my language is plain, / That for ways that are dark / and for tricks that are vain, / The heathen Chinee is peculiar, / Which the same I would rise to explain. [*Plain Language from Truthful James*]

24 But he smiled as he sat by the table, / With the smile that was childlike and bland.

25 And the same with intent to deceive.

26 We are ruined by Chinese cheap labour.

27 I reside at Table Mountain, and my name is Truthful James. [*The Society upon the Stanislaus*]

28 And he smiled a kind of sickly smile, and curled up on the floor, / And the subsequent proceedings interested him no more.

L. P. HARTLEY 1895–1972

29 The past is a foreign country: they do things differently there. [*The Go-Between*, opening words]

MINNIE HASKINS 1875–1957

30 And I said to the man who stood at the gate of the year: 'Give me a light that I may tread safely into the unknown.' And he replied:

'Go out into the darkness and put your hand into the hand of God. That shall be to you better than light and safer than a known way.' [*The Desert*, Introduction. Quoted by King George VI in his Christmas Broadcast, 1939]

H. DE CRONIN HASTINGS 1902–

1 Worm's eye view. [Caption to photograph in the *Architectural Review, c.* 1932 and *passim*]

STEPHEN HAWES *c.* 1475–before 1530

2 For though the day be never so longe, / At last the belles ringeth to evensonge. [*Passetyme of Pleasure*, 42]

R. S. HAWKER 1803–1875

3 And have they fixed the where and when? / And shall Trelawny die? / Here's twenty thousand Cornish men / Will know the reason why! [*Song of the Western Men* (The last three lines are traditional)]

NATHANIEL HAWTHORNE 1804–1864

4 Life is made up of marble and mud. [*The House of the Seven Gables*, Ch. 2]

5 What other dungeon is so dark as one's own heart! What jailer so inexorable as one's self! [11]

6 She named the infant 'Pearl', as being of great price – purchased with all she had. [*The Scarlet Letter*, Ch. 6]

7 Dr Johnson's morality was as English an article as a beefsteak. [*Our Old Home*, 'Lichfield and Uttoxeter']

LORD CHARLES HAY ?–1760

8 Gentlemen of the French Guard, fire first! [At Battle of Fontenoy, 1745]

IAN HAY [JOHN HAY BEITH] 1876–1952

9 Funny peculiar, or funny ha-ha? [*The House-master*, III]

J. MILTON HAYES 1884–1940

10 There's a one-eyed yellow idol to the north of Khatmandu; / There's a little marble cross below the town; / And a broken-hearted woman tends the grave of 'Mad Carew', / While the yellow god forever gazes down. [*The Green Eye of the Little Yellow God*, written (1911), with Cuthbert Clarke]

11 The Whitest Man I Know. [Title of song, music by R. Fenton Gower. See also 226:28, 247:21]

WILLIAM HAZLITT 1778–1830

12 The least pain in our little finger gives us more concern and uneasiness than the destruction of millions of our fellow-beings. [*American Literature*, 'Dr Channing']

13 If the world were good for nothing else, it is a fine subject for speculation. [*Characteristics*, 302]

14 His sayings are generally like women's letters; all the pith is in the postcript. [(Charles Lamb) *Conversations of Northcote*, 'Boswell Redivivus']

15 His worst is better than any other person's best. [(Scott) *English Literature*, Ch. 14]

16 His works (taken together) are almost like a new edition of human nature.

17 When a person dies who does any one thing better than anyone else in the world, which so many others are trying to do well, it leaves a gap in society. [(On the death of John Cavanagh, the fives-player) *The Indian Jugglers*]

18 He [Coleridge] talked on for ever; and you wished him to talk on for ever. [*Lectures on the English Poets*, 8]

19 So have I loitered my life away, reading books, looking at pictures, going to plays, hearing, thinking, writing on what pleased me best. I have wanted only one thing to make me happy, but wanting that have wanted everything. [*My First Acquaintance with Poets*]

20 There is nothing good to be had in the country, or, if there is, they will not let you have it. [*Observations on Mr Wordsworth's* Excursion]

21 Those who make their dress a principal part of themselves, will, in general, become of no more value than their dress. [*On the Clerical Character*]

22 I do not think there is anything deserving the name of society to be found out of London. [*On Coffee-House Politicians*]

23 The English (it must be owned) are rather a foul-mouthed nation. [*On Criticism*]

1 There is an unseemly exposure of the mind, as well as of the body. [*On Disagreeable People*]

2 No young man believes he shall ever die. [*On the Feeling of Immortality in Youth*]

3 One of the pleasantest things in the world is going a journey; but I like to go by myself. [*On Going a Journey*]

4 When I am in the country I wish to vegetate like the country.

5 Give me the clear blue sky above my head, and the green turf beneath my feet, a winding road before me, and a three hours' march to dinner – and then to thinking! It is hard if I cannot start some game on these lone heaths.

6 The *incognito* of an inn is one of its striking privileges.

7 It is great to shake off the trammels of the world and of public opinion . . . and become the creature of the moment . . . known by no other title than *The Gentleman in the Parlour*!

8 It is better to be able neither to read nor write than to be able to do nothing else. [*On the Ignorance of the Learned*]

9 You will hear more good things on the outside of a stagecoach from London to Oxford than if you were to pass a twelve-month with the undergraduates, or heads of colleges, of that famous university.

10 There is not a more mean, stupid, dastardly, pitiful, selfish, spiteful, envious, ungrateful animal than the Public. It is the greatest of cowards, for it is afraid of itself. [*On Living to One's Self*]

11 The art of pleasing consists in being pleased. [*On Manner*]

12 A nickname is the heaviest stone that the devil can throw at a man. [*On Nicknames*]

13 Venerate art as art. [*On Patronage*]

14 We never do anything well till we cease to think about the manner of doing it. [*On Prejudice*]

15 Violent antipathies are always suspicious, and betray a secret affinity. [*On Vulgarity and Affectation*]

16 Ignorance alone makes monsters or bugbears; our actual acquaintances are all very common-place people. [*Why Distant Objects Please*]

17 We can scarcely hate anyone that we know.

18 Well, I've had a happy life. [Last words, quoted in W. C. Hazlitt, *Memoirs of William Hazlitt*]

DENIS HEALEY 1917–

19 That part of his speech was rather like being savaged by a dead sheep. [On being attacked in a parliamentary debate by Geoffrey Howe over his Budget proposals, House of Commons, 14 June, 1978]

SEAMUS HEANEY 1939–

20 When they spoke of the mammon of iniquity / The coins in my pockets reddened like stove-lids. [*Terminus*]

EDWARD HEATH 1916–

21 It is the unpleasant and unacceptable face of capitalism. [(Of the Lonrho Affair) In House of Commons, 15 May 1973]

BISHOP HEBER 1782–1826

22 Brightest and best of the sons of the morning. / Dawn on our darkness, and lend us Thine aid! [Hymn]

23 By cool Siloam's shady rill / How sweet the lily grows! / How sweet the breath beneath the hill / Of Sharon's dewy rose! [Hymn]

24 From Greenland's icy mountains, / From India's coral strand, / Where Afric's sunny fountains / Roll down their golden sand. [Hymn]

25 What though the spicy breezes / Blow soft o'er Ceylon's isle, / Though every prospect pleases, / And only man is vile.

In vain with lavish kindness / The gifts of God are strown, / The heathen in his blindness / Bows down to wood and stone.

26 Holy, holy, holy, Lord God Almighty! / Early in the morning our song shall rise to thee. [Hymn]

27 Holy, holy, holy! all the saints adore Thee, / Casting down their golden crowns around the glassy sea; / Cherubim and seraphim falling down before thee, / Which wert, and art, and evermore shalt be.

GEORG WILHELM HEGEL 1770–1831

28 What experience and history teach is this –

that people and governments never have learnt anything from history, or acted on principles deduced from it. [*Philosophy of History*, Introduction]

HEINRICH HEINE 1797–1856

1 *Auf Flügeln des Gesanges.* – On wings of song. [Title of song]

2 *Ich weiss nicht, was soll es bedeuten, / Dass ich so traurig bin; / Ein Märchen aus alten Zeiten, / Das kommt mir nicht aus dem Sinn.* – I do not know why it should be, but I am so sad; there is an old-time story which I cannot get out of my head. [*Die Lorelei*]

3 *Du bist wie eine Blume.* – You are like a flower. [*Du Bist wie eine Blume*]

4 *Ich grolle nicht, und wenn das Herz auch bricht.* – I do not complain, even if my heart breaks. [Title of song]

5 *Gut ist der Schlaf, der Tod ist besser – freilich / Das beste wäre, nie geboren sein.* – Sleep is good, death is better; but of course, the best thing would be never to have been born at all. [*Morphine*]

6 *Dort, wo man Bücher verbrennt, verbrennt man am Ende auch Menschen.* – Wherever they burn books they will also end up burning people. [(Used as inscription on memorial at Dachau concentration camp) *Almansor*]

7 *Dieu me pardonnera, c'est son métier.* – God will pardon me, it is His trade. [Last words]

8 It is extremely difficult for a Jew to be converted, for how can he bring himself to believe in the divinity of – another Jew? [Attr.]

JOSEPH HELLER 1923–

9 There was only one catch and that was Catch-22, which specified that a concern for one's own safety in the face of dangers that were real and immediate was the process of a rational mind. [*Catch-22*, Ch. 5]

LILLIAN HELLMAN 1905–1984

10 I cannot and will not cut my conscience to fit this year's fashions. [Letter to the House Committee on un-American Activities, 19 May 1952]

SIR ARTHUR HELPS 1813–1875

11 Reading is sometimes an ingenious device for avoiding thought. [*Friends in Council*, Bk ii. Ch. 1]

FELICIA HEMANS 1793–1835

12 Not there, not there, my child! [*The Better Land*]

13 The boy stood on the burning deck – / Whence all but he had fled. [*Casabianca*]

14 They grew in beauty, side by side, / They filled one home with glee; – / Their graves are severed, far and wide, / By mount, and stream, and sea. [*The Graves of a Household*]

15 He Never Smiled Again. [(Henry I) Title of poem]

16 The stately homes of England, / How beautiful they stand! [*The Homes of England*]

17 The cottage homes of England! / By thousands on her plains.

ERNEST HEMINGWAY 1899–1961

18 But did thee feel the earth move? [*For Whom the Bell Tolls*, Ch. 13]

19 If you are lucky enough to have lived in Paris as a young man, then wherever you go for the rest of your life, it stays with you, for Paris is a moveable feast. [*A Moveable Feast* (epigraph), to a friend]

20 A man can be destroyed but not defeated. [*The Old Man and the Sea*]

21 Grace under pressure. [Definition of courage. Quoted in J. F. Kennedy, *Profiles in Courage*, Ch. 1]

22 I started out very quiet and I beat Mr Turgenev. Then I trained hard and I beat Mr de Maupassant. I've fought two draws with Mr Stendhal, and I think I had an edge in the last one. But nobody's going to get me in any ring with Mr Tolstoy unless I'm crazy or I keep getting better. [In *New Yorker*, 13 May 1950. Quoted in Lillian Ross, *Portrait of Hemingway*]

W. E. HENLEY 1849–1903

23 What have I done for you, / England, my England? / What is there I would not do, / England, my own? [*For England's Sake*, 3]

24 Out of the night that covers me, / Black as the pit from pole to pole, / I thank whatever gods may be / For my unconquerable soul. [*Invictus*]

25 Under the bludgeonings of chance / My head is bloody, but unbowed.

26 It matters not how strait the gate, / How

charged with punishments the scroll, / I am the master of my fate: / I am the captain of my soul.

1 Night with her train of stars / And her great gift of sleep. [*Margaritae Sororis*]

2 Or ever the knightly years were gone / With the old world to the grave, / I was a King in Babylon / And you were a Christian slave. [*To W.A.*]

HENRI IV, OF FRANCE 1553–1610

3 I want there to be no peasant in my kingdom so poor that he cannot have a chicken in his pot every Sunday. [Attr.]

4 Paris is well worth a mass. [Attr. also to his minister Sully]

5 The wisest fool in Christendom. [(James I) Attr. also to Sully]

HENRY II 1133–1189

6 Who will rid me of this turbulent priest? [(Archbishop Thomas Becket) Attr.]

HENRY VIII 1491–1547

7 This man [Thomas Cranmer] hath the sow by the right ear. [Letter to Edward Foxe and Stephen Gardiner, 3 Aug. 1529]

MATTHEW HENRY 1662–1714

8 Many a dangerous temptation comes to us in gay, fine colours, that are but skin-deep. [*Commentaries, Genesis*, 3:1]

9 To their own second and sober thoughts. [*Job*, 6:29]

10 He rolls it under his tongue as a sweet morsel. [*Psalms*, 36:2]

11 Men of polite learning and a liberal education. [*Acts*, 10:1]

12 All this and heaven too. [*Life of Philip Henry*]

O. HENRY [W. S. PORTER] 1862–1910

13 Busy as a one-armed man with the nettle-rash pasting on wall-paper. [*The Ethics of Pig*]

14 It couldn't have happened anywhere but in little old New York. [*A Little Local Colour*]

15 Baghdad-on-the-Subway. [Said of New York in *A Madison Square Arabian Night*, also in other stories]

16 If men knew how women pass the time when they are alone, they'd never marry. [*Memoirs of a Yellow Dog*]

17 He had the artistic metempsychosis which is half drunk when sober and looks down on airships when stimulated. [*A Midsummer Masquerade*]

18 It was beautiful and simple as all truly great swindles are. [*The Octopus Marooned*]

19 Whenever he saw a dollar in another man's hands he took it as a personal grudge, if he couldn't take it any other way.

20 A straw vote only shows which way the hot air blows. [*A Ruler of Men*]

21 Take it from me – he's got the goods. [*The Unprofitable Servant*]

22 Turn up the lights, I don't want to go home in the dark. [Last words, 5 June 1910, quoting popular song. See 457:11]

PATRICK HENRY 1736–1799

23 I know not what course others may take; but as for me, give me liberty or give me death. [Speech to Virginia Convention, 23 Mar. 1775, but not recorded by William Wirt until 40 years later, so wording in some doubt]

HERACLITUS *c.* 544–483 BC

24 All is flux, nothing stays still. [Diels, *Fragments of the Pre-Socratics*]

25 The way up is the way down.

26 You cannot step twice into the same river.

SIR A. P. HERBERT 1890–1971

27 Don't let's go to the dogs tonight, / For mother will be there. [*Don't let's go*]

28 Not huffy or stuffy, nor tiny or tall, / But fluffy, just fluffy, with no brains at all. [*I Like them Fluffy*]

29 It may be life, but ain't it slow? [*It May Be Life*]

30 Other people's babies – / That's my life! / Mother to dozens, / And nobody's wife. [*Other People's Babies*]

31 Nothing is wasted, nothing is in vain: / The seas roll over but the rocks remain. [*Tough at the Top*]

32 Holy Deadlock. [Title of novel]

33 People must not do things for fun. We are

not here for fun. There is no reference to fun in any Act of Parliament. [*Uncommon Law*, p. 33]

1 The critical period in matrimony is break-fast time. [p. 98]

GEORGE HERBERT 1593–1633

2 Let all the world in every corner sing / My God and King. [*Temple*, 'Antiphon']

3 A verse may find him who a sermon flies. / And turn delight into a sacrifice. ['Church Porch', 1]

4 Drink not the third glass which thou canst not tame / When once it is within thee. [5]

5 Dare to be true: nothing can need a lie; / A fault, which needs it most, grows two thereby. [13]

6 Do all things like a man, not sneakingly: / Think the King sees thee still; for his King does. [21]

7 I struck the board, and cried, 'No more; / I will abroad.' / What, shall I ever sigh and pine? / My lines and life are free; free as the road, / Loose as the wind, as large as store. ['The Collar']

8 But as I raved and grew more fierce and wild / At every word, / Methought I heard one calling, 'Child'; / And I replied, 'My Lord'.

9 Throw away thy rod, / Throw away they wrath: / O my God. / Take the gentle path. ['Discipline']

10 Love is swift of foot; / Love's a man of war, / And can shoot, / And can hit from far.

11 I got Thee flowers to strew Thy way, / I got me boughs off many a tree; / But Thou wast up by break of day, / And brought'st Thy sweets along with Thee. ['Easter']

12 Teach me, my god and King, / In all things Thee to see, / And what I do in anything / To do it as for Thee. ['The Elixir']

13 Who sweeps a room, as for Thy laws, / Makes that and th' action fine.

14 He that is weary, let him sit. / My soul would stir / And trade in courtesies and wit. ['Employment']

15 Death is still working like a mole, / And digs my grave at each remove. ['Grace']

16 Who says that fictions only and false hair / Become a verse? Is there in truth no beauty? / Is all good structure in a winding stair? ['Jordan']

17 I envy no man's nightingale or spring; / Nor let them punish me with loss of rhyme, / Who plainly say, 'My God my King'.

18 Love bade me welcome; yet my soul drew back / Guilty of dust and sin. ['Love']

19 'You must sit down,' says Love, 'and taste my meat.' / So I did sit and eat.

20 When God at first made man, / Having a glass of blessings standing by, / Let us (said he) pour on him all we can: / Let the world's riches, which dispersèd lie, / Contract into a span. ['The Pulley']

21 Let him be rich and weary, that at least, / If goodness lead him not, yet weariness / May toss him to my breast.

22 At length I heard a ragged noise and mirth / Of thieves and murderers: there I him espied, / Who straight, 'Your suit is granted,' said, and died. ['Redemption']

23 But who does hawk at eagles with a dove? ['The Sacrifice', 23]

24 Bibles laid open, millions of surprises. ['Sin']

25 Sweet day, so cool, so calm, so bright, / The bridal of the earth and sky, / The dew shall weep thy fall to-night; / For thou must die. ['Virtue']

26 Sweet spring, full of sweet days and roses, / A box where sweets compacted lie.

27 Only a sweet and virtuous soul, / Like seasoned timber, never gives; / But though the whole world turn to coal, / Then chiefly lives.

28 Lord, how can man preach thy eternal word? / He is a brittle crazy glass: / Yet in thy Temple thou dost him afford / This glorious and transcendent place, / To be a window, through thy grace. ['Windows']

29 Do well and right, and let the world sink. [*Priest to the Temple*, Ch. 29]

J. M. DE HERÉDIA 1842–1905

30 *Et sur elle courbé, l'ardent Imperator, / Vit dans ses larges yeux étoilés de points d'or / Toute une mer immense où fuyaient des galères.* – And bending over her, the ardent Emperor saw in her great eyes, flecked with golden points, a whole great sea, with galleys fleeing across it. [*Antoine et Cléopatre*]

31 *Où penchés à l'avant des blanches caravelles, / Ils regardaient monter en un ciel ignoré / Du fond*

de l'Océan des étoiles nouvelles. – Where leaning over the prow of white four-masters, they saw new stars climb from the depths of the ocean into an unknown sky. [Les Conquérants]

OLIVER HERFORD 1863–1935

1 King Barumph has a whim of iron. [Excuse It Please, 'Impossible Pudding']

ROBERT HERRICK 1591–1674

2 I sing of brooks, of blossoms, birds, and bowers: / Of April, May, of June, and July-flowers. / I sing of maypoles, hock-carts, wassails, wakes, / Of bridegrooms, brides, and of their bridal cakes. [Hesperides, 'The Argument']

3 Fair pledges of a fruitful tree, / Why do ye fall so fast? ['Blossoms']

4 Cherry ripe, ripe, ripe, I cry / Full and fair ones; come and buy; / If so be, you ask me where / They do grow? I answer there, / Where my Julia's lips do smile; / There's the land, or cherry-isle. ['Cherry Ripe']

5 A sweet disorder in the dress / Kindles in clothes a wantonness. ['Delight in Disorder']

6 A winning wave (deserving note) / In the tempestuous petticoat: / A careless shoe-string, in whose tie / I see a wild civility: / Do more bewitch me than when art / Is too precise in every part.

7 Only a little more / I have to write, / Then I'll give o'er, / And bid the world good-night. ['His Poetry his Pillar']

8 You say, to me-wards your affection's strong; / Pray love me little, so you love me long. ['Love me Little, Love me Long']

9 Her eyes the glow-worm lend thee, / The shooting-stars attend thee; / And the elves also, / Whose little eyes glow, / Like the sparks of fire, befriend thee. ['The Night-Piece, to Julia']

10 Night makes no difference 'twixt the priest and clerk; / Joan as my lady is as good i' th' dark. ['No Difference i' th' Dark']

11 Fain would I kiss my Julia's dainty leg, / Which is as white and hairless as an egg. ['On Julia's Legs']

12 A little saint best fits a little shrine, / A little prop best fits a little vine, / As my small cruse best fits my little wine. ['A Ternary of Littles']

13 Bid me to live, and I will live / Thy Prot-estant to be: / Or bid me love, and I will give / A loving heart to thee. ['To Anthea, Who May Command Him Anything']

14 Bid me to weep, and I will weep, / While I have eyes to see.

15 Fair daffodils, we weep to see / You haste away so soon: / As yet the early-rising sun / Has not attained his noon. ['To Daffodils']

16 I dare not ask a kiss; / I dare not beg a smile; / Lest having that, or this, / I might grow proud the while. ['To Electra']

17 Only to kiss that air, / That lately kissèd thee.

18 Welcome maids of honour, / You do bring / In the Spring; / And wait upon her. ['To Violets']

19 Gather ye rosebuds while ye may, / Old Time is still a-flying: / And this same flower that smiles to-day, / To-morrow will be dying. ['To Virgins, to Make Much of Time']

20 Her pretty feet / Like snails did creep / A little out, and then, / As if they started at bo-peep, / Did soon draw in agen. ['Upon her Feet']

21 Whenas in silks my Julia goes, / Then, then (methinks) how sweetly flows / That liquefaction of her clothes. ['Upon Julia's Clothes']

22 Here a little child I stand, / Heaving up my either hand; / Cold as paddocks though they be, / Here I lift them up to Thee, / For a benison to fall / On our meat, and on us all. Amen. [Noble Numbers, 'Another Grace for a Child']

JAMES HERVEY 1714–1758

23 E'en crosses from his sov'reign hand / Are blessings in disguise. [Reflections on a Flower-Garden]

HERMANN HESSE 1877–1962

24 If you hate a person, you hate something in him that is part of yourself. What isn't part of ourselves doesn't disturb us. [Demian, Ch. 6]

25 As a body everyone is single, as a soul never. [Steppenwolf, 'Treatise on the Steppen-wolf']

LORD JUSTICE HEWART 1870–1943

26 A long line of cases shows that it is not

merely of some importance, but it is of fundamental importance, that justice should not only
be done, but should manifestly and undoubtedly
be seen to be done. [Rex v. Sussex Justices,
9 Nov. 1923]

JOHN HEYWOOD 1497?–1580?

1 Let the world slide, let the world go: / A fig
for care, and a fig for woe! / If I can't pay, why
I can owe, / And death makes equal the high
and the low. [*Be Merry, Friends*]

2 All a green willow is my garland. [*The Green
Willow*]

THOMAS HEYWOOD 1572?–1641

3 Seven cities warred for Homer, being dead,
/ Who, living, had no roof to shroud his head.
[*Hierachy of the Blessed Angels*]

4 A Woman Killed with Kindness. [Title of
play]

SEYMOUR HICKS 1871–1949

5 You will recognize, my boy, the first sign
of age: it is when you go out into the streets of
London and realize for the first time how
young the policemen look. [*Between Ourselves*]

WILLIAM EDWARD HICKSON 1803–1870

6 'Tis a lesson you should heed, / Try, try
again. / If at first you don't succeed, / Try, try
again. [*Try and Try Again*]

'DR BREWSTER HIGLEY' 19 Cent.

7 Oh give me a home where the buffalo roam,
/ Where the deer and the antelope play, / Where
seldom is heard a discouraging word / And the
skies are not cloudy all day. [*Home on the Range*]

AARON HILL 1685–1750

8 Tender-handed stroke a nettle, / And it
stings you for your pains; / Grasp it like a man
of mettle, / And it soft as silk remains. [*Verses
Written on a Window*]

JOE HILL 1879–1915

9 Work and pray, live on hay. / You'll get pie
in the sky when you die. [Song: *The Preacher
and the Slave*]

10 Don't waste any time mourning – organize!
[Letter to W. D. Haywood, the day before being
shot by firing squad, Utah State Penitentiary,
19 Nov. 1915]

PATTY SMITH HILL 1868–1946
and E. MILDRED HILL ?–1916

11 Happy birthday to you, happy birthday to
you. [Song: *Happy Birthday*]

ROWLAND HILL 1744–1833

12 He did not see any reason why the devil
should have all the good tunes. [E. W. Broome,
Rev. Rowland Hill, Ch. 7]

FRANK HILLEBRAND 1893–1963

13 Home, James And Don't Spare the Horses.
[Title of song, ascr. by Dennis Norden in the
Guardian, 'Notes and Queries', 18 June 1990]

JAMES HILTON 1900–1954

14 Anno domini – that's the most fatal complaint of all in the end. [*Good-bye, Mr Chips*,
Ch. 1]

HIPPOCRATES c. 460–357 BC

15 The life so short, the craft so long to learn.
[*Aphorisms*, I. i (trans. Chaucer). Often quoted
in Latin: *Ars longa, vita brevis*]

16 Extreme remedies are most appropriate for
extreme diseases. [vi]

ADOLF HITLER 1889–1945

17 The great masses of the people ... will
more easily fall victims to a great lie than to a
small one. [*Mein Kampf*, Ch. 10]

18 I go the way that Providence dictates with
the assurance of a sleepwalker. [Speech at
Munich, 15 Mar. 1936, after successful re-
occupation of the Rhineland]

19 It [the Sudetenland] is the last territorial
claim that I have to make in Europe. [Speech,
26 Sept. 1938]

20 Well, he [Chamberlain] seemed such a nice
old gentleman, I thought I would give him
my autograph as a souvenir. [After Munich.
Attr.]

21 Is Paris burning? [On the liberation of Paris,
25 Aug. 1944]

PRINCE HOARE 1755–1834

1 The saucy Arethusa. [Song: *The Arethusa*]

RUSSELL HOBAN 1925–

2 There were times when it seemed to him that the different parts of him were not all under the same management. [*The Lion of Boaz-Jachin and Jachin-Boaz*, Ch. 15]

3 After all, when you come right down to it, how many people speak the same language even when they speak the same language?[27]

THOMAS HOBBES 1588–1679

4 The condition of man ... is a condition of war of everyone against everyone. [*Leviathan*, Pt I. Ch. 4]

5 Words are wise men's counters, they do but reckon with them, but they are the money of fools.

6 Sudden glory is the passion which maketh those grimaces called laughter. [6]

7 No arts; no letters; no society; and which is worst of all, continual fear and danger of violent death; and the life of man, solitary, poor, nasty, brutish, and short. [13]

8 The Papacy is not other than the Ghost of the deceased Roman Empire, sitting crowned upon the grave thereof. [iv. 47]

9 I am about to take my last voyage, a great leap in the dark. [Last words]

JOHN CAM HOBHOUSE, BARON BROUGHTON 1786–1869

10 When I invented the phrase 'His Majesty's Opposition' [Canning] paid me a compliment on the fortunate hit. [*Recollections of a Long Life*, ii. Ch. 12. See also 328:15]

EDWARD WALLIS HOCH 1849–1925

11 There is so much good in the worst of us, / And so much bad in the best of us, / That it hardly becomes any of us / To talk about the rest of us. [*Good and Bad* (Authorship not absolutely certain)]

RALPH HODGSON 1871–1962

12 'Twould ring the bells of Heaven / The wildest peal for years, / If Parson lost his senses / And people came to theirs. [*The Bells of Heaven*]

13 See an old unhappy bull, / Sick in soul and body both. [*The Bull*]

14 Reason has moons, but moons not hers / Lie mirror'd on her sea, / Confounding her astronomers, / But, O! delighting me. [*Reason Has Moons*]

15 I climbed a hill as light fell short, / And rooks came home in scramble sort, / And filled the trees and flapped and fought / And sang themselves to sleep. [*The Song of Honour*]

16 When stately ships are twirled and spun / Like whipping tops and help there's none / And mighty ships ten thousand ton / Go down like lumps of lead.

17 Without a wish, without a will, / I stood upon that silent hill / And stared into the sky until / My eyes were blind with stars and still / I stared into the sky.

18 Time, you old gipsy man, / Will you not stay, / Put up your caravan / Just for one day? [*Time, You Old Gipsy Man*]

SAMUEL HOFFENSTEIN 1890–1947

19 Babies haven't any hair; / Old men's heads are just as bare; – / Between the cradle and the grave / Lies a haircut and a shave. [*Songs of Faith in the Year after Next*, 8]

ELISHA B. HOFFMAN 1839–?

20 Have you been to Jesus for the cleansing power? / Are you washed in the blood of the Lamb? [Hymn]

E. T. A. HOFFMAN 1776–1822

21 He's a wicked man that comes after children when they won't go to bed and throws handfuls of sand in their eyes. [*The Sandman*]

HEINRICH HOFFMAN 1809–1874

22 Augustus was a chubby lad; / Fat ruddy cheeks Augustus had; / And everybody saw with joy / The plump and hearty healthy boy. [*Struwwelpeter*, 'Augustus']

23 Take the soup away! / O take the nasty soup away! / I won't have any soup today.

24 Here is cruel Frederick, see! / A horrid wicked boy was he. ['Cruel Frederick']

25 The trough was full and faithful Tray / Came out to drink one sultry day.

26 At this good Tray grew very red, / And growled and bit him till he bled.

1 But Fidgety Phil / He won't sit still; / He wriggles / And giggles, / and then, I declare, / Swings backwards and forwards, / And tilts up his chair. ['Fidgety Phil']

2 'Me-ow,' they said, 'me-ow, me-o, / You'll burn to death, if you do so.' ['Harriet and the Matches']

3 Now tall Agrippa lived close by, – / So tall he almost touched the sky; / He had a mighty inkstand too, / In which a great goose-feather grew. ['The Inky Boys']

4 Look at little Johnny there, / Little Johnny Head-In-Air. ['Johnny Head-In-Air' (See also 322:1)]

5 The door flew open, in he ran, / The great, long, red-legged scissor-man. ['The Little-Suck-a-Thumb']

6 Snip! Snap! Snip! They go so fast. / That both his thumbs are off at last.

7 The hare sits snug in leaves and grass, / And laughs to see the green man pass. ['The Man that went out Shooting']

8 Anything to me is sweeter / Than to see Shock-headed Peter. ['Shock-headed Peter']

COLONEL MAX HOFFMAN 1869–1927

9 LUDENDORFF: The English soldiers fight like lions.
HOFFMAN: True. But don't we know that they are lions led by donkeys. [Of 1915 battles. Quoted in A. Clark, The Donkeys]

HEINRICH HOFFMANN VON FALLERSLEBEN 1798–1876

10 Deutschland, Deutschland über alles. – Germany, Germany before all else. [Poem]

JAMES HOGG 1770–1835

11 Come weel, come wo, we'll gather and go, / And live or die wi' Charlie. [Jacobite Relics of Scotland, 76, 'O'er the Water to Charlie']

12 There grows a bonny brier bush in our kail yard. [78, 'An You Be He']

13 Will you no come back again? / Better lo'ed you'll never be, / And will ye no come back again? [195, 'Will Ye No Come Back Again?']

14 Where the pools are bright and deep, / Where the grey trout lies asleep, / Up the river and o'er the lea, / That's the way for Billy and me. [A Boy's Song]

15 Late, late in the gloamin' Kilmeny came hame! [Kilmeny]

16 My love she's but a lassie yet. [Title of song]

SIR RICHARD HOGGART 1918–

17 The Uses of Literacy. [Title of book]

SIR RICHARD HOLLAND Mid 15 Cent.

18 O Dowglas, O Dowglas, tendir and trewe! [Buke of the Howlat, 31]

REV. J. H. HOLMES 1879–1964

19 The universe is not hostile, nor yet is it friendly. It is simply indifferent. [The Sensible Man's View of Religion]

OLIVER WENDELL HOLMES 1809–1894

20 It was a tall young oysterman lived by the riverside. [The Ballad of the Oysterman]

21 And now they keep an oyster shop for mermaids down below.

22 Have you heard of the wonderful one-hoss shay, / That was built in such a logical way / It ran a hundred years to a day? [The Deacon's Masterpiece]

23 Day has put on his jacket, and around / His burning bosom buttoned it with stars. [Evening]

24 And since, I never dare to write / As funny as I can. [The Height of the Ridiculous]

25 When the last reader reads no more. [The Last Reader]

26 And silence, like a poultice, comes / To heal the blows of sound. [The Music Grinders]

27 For him in vain the envious seasons roll / Who bears eternal summer in his soul. [The Old Player]

28 We love the precepts for the teacher's sake. [A Rhymed Lesson (See also 162:1)]

29 Man wants but little drink below, / But wants that little strong. [A Song of Other Days (Parody of Goldsmith 182:29)]

30 Man has his will – but woman has her way. [The Autocrat of the Breakfast Table, Ch. 1]

31 Build thee more stately mansions, O my soul, / As the swift seasons roll! [4, 'The Chambered Nautilus']

32 The axis of the earth sticks out visibly through the centre of each and every town or city. [6]

1 The world's great men have not commonly been scholars, nor its great scholars great men.

2 Depart, – be off, – excede, – evade, – erump! [11]

3 A moment's insight is sometimes worth a life's experience. [*The Professor at the Breakfast Table*, Ch. 10]

4 To be seventy years young is sometimes far more hopeful than to be forty years old. [*On the Seventieth Birthday of Julia Ward Howe*]

JOHN HOME 1722–1808

5 My name is Norval; on the Grampian hills / My father feeds his flocks; a frugal swain, / Whose constant cares were to increase his store. [*Douglas*, II. i]

6 He seldom errs / Who thinks the worst he can of womankind. [III. iii]

7 Like Douglas conquer, or like Douglas die. [v]

HOMER *c.* 900 BC

8 He went off without a word along the shore of the sounding sea. [*Iliad*, I. 34, trans. E. V. Rieu]

9 Winged words. [201]

10 Over the wine-dark sea. [350]

11 Men in their generations are like the leaves of the trees. The wind blows and one year's leaves are scattered on the ground; but the trees burst into bud and put on fresh ones when the spring comes round. [VI. 146]

12 She [Andromache] was smiling through her tears. [484]

13 He saw the cities of many peoples and learnt their ways. He suffered many hardships on the high seas in his struggles to preserve his life and bring his comrades home. [*Odyssey*, I. 4, trans. E. V. Rieu]

14 As soon as Dawn with her rose-tinted hands had lit the East. [II. 1]

15 Put me on earth again, and I would rather be a serf in the house of some landless man . . . than king of all these dead men that have done with life. [XI. 489]

16 Bear, O my heart; thou hast borne a yet harder thing. [XX. 18]

WILLIAM HONE 1780–1842

17 John Jones may be descibed as 'one of the has beens'. [*Every-Day Book*, II. 820]

THOMAS HOOD 1799–1845

18 It was not in the winter / Our loving lot was cast! / It was the time of roses, / We plucked them as we passed! [Ballad: *It was not in the Winter*]

19 One more Unfortunate, / Weary of breath, / Rashly importunate, / Gone to her death. Take her up tenderly, / Lift her with care; / Fashioned so slenderly, / Young, and so fair! [*The Bridge of Sighs*]

20 Our very hopes belied our fears, / Our fears our hopes belied – / We thought her dying when she slept, / And sleeping when she died! [*The Death Bed*]

21 Ben Battle was a soldier bold, / And used to war's alarms: / But a cannon-ball took off his legs, / So he laid down his arms. [*Faithless Nelly Gray*]

22 For here I leave my second leg, / And the Forty-second Foot.

23 The love that loves a scarlet coat / Should be more uniform.

24 His death which happened in his berth, / At forty-odd befell: / They went and told the sexton, and / The sexton toll'd the bell. [*Faithless Sally Brown*]

25 A hollow voice is all I have / But this I tell you plain, / Marry come up! – you marry, Ma'am, / And I'll come up again. [*The Ghost*]

26 I remember, I remember, / The house where I was born, / The little window where the sun / Came peeping in at morn. [*I Remember*]

27 Alas! my everlasting peace / Is broken into pieces. [*Mary's Ghost*]

28 And then, in the fullness of joy and hope, / Seem'd washing his hands with invisible soap, / In imperceptible water. [*Miss Kilmansegg*, 'Her Christening']

29 There's Bardus, a six-foot column of fop, / A lighthouse without any light atop. ['Her First Step']

30 For one of the pleasures of having a rout, / Is the pleasure of having it over. ['Her Dream']

31 No sun – no moon! / No morn – no noon – / No dawn – no dusk – no proper time of day – [*No!*]

32 No shade, no shine, no butterflies, no bees, / No fruits, no flowers, no leaves, no birds, – November!

1 I saw old Autumn in the misty morn / Stand shadowless like Silence, listening / To silence. [Ode: *Autumn*]

2 She stood breast high amid the corn. [*Ruth*]

3 With fingers weary and worn, / With eyelids heavy and red, / A woman sat in unwomanly rags, / Plying her needle and thread – / Stitch! stitch! stitch! [*The Song of the Shirt*]

4 'Extremes meet', as the whiting said with its tail in its mouth. [*The Doves and the Crows*]

TOM HOOD THE YOUNGER 1834–1874

5 If you were queen of bloaters / And I were king of soles, / The sea we'd wag our fins in. / Nor heed the crooked pins in / The water, dropped by boaters / To catch our heedless joles. [*A Catch*]

6 I never nursed a dear gazelle, / To glad me with its dappled hide, / But when it came to know me well / It fell upon the buttered side. [*Muddled Metaphors*]

RICHARD HOOKER 1554?–1600

7 He that goeth about to persuade a multitude that they are not so well governed as they ought to be, shall never want attentive and favourable hearers. [*Ecclesiastical Polity*, Bk i. §i]

8 Change is not made without inconvenience, even from worse to better. [Quoted by Samuel Johnson in the Preface to his *English Dictionary*]

ELLEN STURGIS HOOPER 1816–1841

9 I slept, and dreamed that life was Beauty; / I woke, and found that life was Duty. [*Life a Duty*]

PRESIDENT HERBERT HOOVER 1874–1964

10 The American system of rugged individualism. [Campaign speech in New York, 22 Oct. 1928]

ANTHONY HOPE [SIR ANTHONY HOPE HAWKINS] 1863–1933

11 Economy is going without something you do want in case you should, some day, want something you probably won't want. [*The Dolly Dialogues*, 12]

12 Unless one is a genius, it is best to aim at being intelligible. [15]

13 'Boys will be boys –'
'And even that wouldn't matter if we could only prevent girls from being girls.'[16]

14 '*Bourgeois*', I observed, 'is an epithet which the riff-raff apply to what is respectable, and the aristocracy to what is decent.' [17]

15 He is very fond of making things which he does not want, and then giving them to people who have no use for them.

16 Good families are generally worse than any others. [*The Prisoner of Zenda*, Ch. 1]

17 His foe was folly and his weapon wit. [Inscription on tablet to Sir W. S. Gilbert.]

LAURENCE HOPE [ADELA FLORENCE NICOLSON] 1865–1904

18 Less than the dust beneath thy chariot wheel, / Less than the weed that grows beside they door. [*Indian Love Lyrics*, 'Less than the Dust']

19 Pale hands I loved beside the Shalimar, / Where are you now? Who lies beneath your spell? ['Pale Hands I Loved']

GERARD MANLEY HOPKINS 1844–1889

20 As kingfishers catch fire, dragonflies draw flame; / As tumbled over rim in roundy wells / Stones ring. [*As Kingfishers catch Fire*]

21 Just for lack / Of answer the eagerer a-wanting Jessy or Jack / There God to aggrándise, God to glorify. [*The Candle Indoors*]

22 Not, I'll not, carrion comfort, Despair, not feast on thee; / Not untwist – slack they may be – these last strands of man / In me ór, most weary, cry *I can no more.* I can; / Can something, hope, wish day come, not choose not to be. [*Carrion Comfort*]

23 That night, that year / Of now done darkness I wretch lay wrestling with (my God!) my God.

24 Felix Randal the farrier, O he is dead then? [*Felix Randal*]

25 Didst fettle for the great grey drayhorse his bright and battering sandal!

26 The world is charged with the grandeur of God. [*God's Grandeur*]

27 Elected Silence, sing to me / And beat upon my whorlèd ear. [*Habit of Perfection*]

28 Hard as hurdle arms, with a broth of goldish flue / Breathed round. [*Harry Ploughman*]

1 I have desired to go / Where springs not fail, / To fields where flies no sharp and sided hail / And a few lilies blow. [*Heaven-Haven*]

2 Where no storms come, / Where the green swell is in the havens dumb, / And out of the swing of the sea.

3 I wake and feel the fell of dark, not day. / What hours, O what black hoürs we have spent / This night! [*I wake and feel the fell*]

4 And my lament / Is cries countless, cries like dead letters sent / To dearest him that lives alas! away.

5 I am gall, I am heartburn.

6 I see / The lost are like this, and their scourge to be / As I am mine, their sweating selves; but worse.

7 What would the world be, once bereft / Of wet and of wildness? Let them be left, / O let them be left, wildness and wet; / Long live the weeds and the wilderness yet. [*Inversnaid*]

8 No worst, there is none. Pitched past pitch of grief, / More pangs will, schooled at fore-pangs, wilder wring. / Comforter, where, where is your comforting? [*No worst, there is none*]

9 O the mind, mind has mountains; cliffs of fall / Frightful, sheer, no-man-fathomed. Hold them cheap / May who ne'er hung there.

10 Áll / Life death does end and each day dies with sleep.

11 Glory be to God for dappled things – / For skies of couple-colour as a brindled cow; / For rose-moles all in stipple upon trout that swim. [*Pied Beauty*]

12 All trádes, their gear and tackle and trim.

13 All things counter, original, spare, strange; / Whatever is fickle, freckled (who knows how?) / With swift, slow; sweet, sour; adazzle, dim; / he fathers-forth whose beauty is past change. / Praise him.

14 Honour is flashed off exploit, so we say. [*St Alphonsus Rodriguez*]

15 Look at the stars! look, look up at the skies! / O look at all the fire-folk sitting in the air! / The bright boroughs, the circle-citadels there! [*The Starlight Night*]

16 This piece-bright paling shuts the spouse / Christ home, Christ and his mother and all his hallows.

17 Thou art indeed just, Lord, if I contend / With thee; but, sir, so what I plead is just. / Why do sinners' ways prosper? and why must / Disappointment all I endeavour end? [*Thou art indeed just, Lord*]

18 Birds build – but not I build; no, but strain, / Time's eunuch, and not breed one work that wakes. / Mine, O thou lord of life, send my roots rain.

19 The fine delight that fathers thought; the strong / Spur, live and lancing like the blowpipe flame, / Breathes once and, quenchèd faster than it came, / Leaves yet the mind a mother of immortal song. [*To R. B.*]

20 O then if in my lagging lines you miss / The roll, the rise, the carol, the creation.

21 I caught this morning morning's minion, kingdom of daylight's dauphin, dapple-dawn-drawn Falcon. [*The Windhover*]

22 The achieve of, the mastery of the thing!

23 A few other little things; some in sprung rhythm, with various other experiments. [Letter to R. W. Dixon, 5 Oct. 1878]

24 Now it is the virtue of design, pattern, or inscape to be distinctive and it is the vice of distinctiveness to become queer. [Letter to Robert Bridges, 15 Feb. 1879]

25 The poetical language of an age should be the current language heightened. [14 Aug.]

JOSEPH HOPKINSON 1770–1842

26 Hail, Columbia! happy land! / Hail, ye heroes! heaven-born band! [*Hail, Columbia* (1798)]

HORACE 65–8 BC

27 'Pictoribus atque poetis / Quidlibet audendi semper fuit aequa potestas.' / Scimus, et hanc veniam petimusque damusque vicissim. – 'Painters and poets', you say, 'have always had an equal licence for bold invention.' We know this; we claim the liberty for ourselves and we give it to others. [*Ars Poetica*, 9]

28 Inceptis gravibus plerumque et magna professis / Purpureus, late qui splendeat, unus et alter / Adsuitur pannus. – Often a purple patch or two is tacked on to a serious work of high promise, to give an effect of colour. [14]

29 Brevis esse laboro, / Obscurus fio. – It is when I struggle to be brief that I become obscure. [25]

1 *Grammatici certant et adhuc sub iudice lis est.* – Grammarians dispute, and the case is still before the courts. [78]

2 *Proicit ampullas et sesquipedalia verba.* – He tosses aside his paint-pots and his words a foot and a half long. [97]

3 *Parturient montes, nascetur ridiculus mus.* – Mountains will be in labour, and the birth will be an absurd little mouse. [139 (See also 244:14)]

4 *Semper ad eventum festinat et in medias res / Non secus ac notas auditorem rapit.* – He always hurries to the issue, rushing his readers into the middle of the story as if they knew it already. [148]

5 *Difficilis, querulus, laudator temporis acti / Se puero.* – Testy, querulous and given to praising the way things were when he was a boy. [173]

6 *Vos exemplaria Graeca / Nocturna versate manu, versate diurna.* – As for you, turn over the pages of the Greeks, as exemplars, by night and by day. [268]

7 *Grais ingenium, Grais dedit ore rotundo / Musa loqui.* – The Muse gave the Greeks genius and the art of the well-turned phrase. [323]

8 *Omne tulit punctum qui miscuit utile dulci, / Lectorem delectando pariterque monendo.* – He has won every vote who mingles profit with pleasure, by delighting and instructing the reader at the same time. [343]

9 *Indignor quandoque bonus dormitat Homerus.* – But if Homer, who is good, nods for a moment, I think it a shame. [359]

10 *Ut pictura poesis.* – As in painting, so in poetry. [361]

11 *Mediocribus esse poetis / Non homines, non di, non concessere columnae.* – Neither men nor gods nor bookstalls have ever allowed poets to be mediocre. [372]

12 *Nonumque prematur in annum.* – Let it not be published until the ninth year. [368]

13 *Virtus est vitium fugere, et sapientia prima / Stultitia caruisse.* – To flee vice is a virtue, and the beginning of wisdom is to be done with folly. [*Epistles,* I. i. 41]

14 *Si possis recte, si non, quocumque modo rem.* – By right means, if you can, but by any means make money. [66]

15 *Quidquid delirant reges, plectuntur Achivi.* – For every folly of their princes, the Greeks feel the lash. [ii. 14]

16 *Dimidium facti qui coepit habet: sapere aude.* – He who has begun has half done. Have the courage to be wise. [40]

17 *Ira furor brevis est.* – Anger is a brief madness. [62]

18 *Omnem crede diem tibi diluxisse supremum. / Grata superveniet quae non sperabitur hora. / Me pinguem et nitidum bene curata cute vises / Cum ridere voles Epicuri de grege porcum.* – Think to yourself that every day is your last; the hour to which you do not look forward will come as a welcome surprise. As for me, when you want a good laugh, you will find me, in a fine state, fat and sleek, a true hog of Epicurus' sty. [iv. 13]

19 *Naturam expellas furca, tamen usque recurret.* – Though you drive Nature out with a pitchfork, she will still find her way back. [x. 24]

20 *Caelum non animum mutant qui trans mare currunt.* – They change their skies but not their souls who run across the sea. [xi. 27]

21 *Quod petis hic est, / Est Ulubris, animus si te non deficit aequus.* – What you seek is here, at Ulubrae, if you have but equanimity. [29]

22 *Concordia discors.* – Harmony in discord. [xii. 19]

23 *Principibus placuisse viris non ultima laus est. / Non cuivis homini contingit adire Corinthum.* – It is no mean glory to have found favour with the leaders of men. It is not everyone that can get to Corinth. [xvii. 35]

24 *Et semel emissum volat irrevocabile verbum.* – Once a word has been allowed to escape, it cannot be recalled. [xviii. 71]

25 *Nam tua res agitur, paries cum proximus ardet.* – When your neighbour's wall is on fire, it becomes your business. [84]

26 *Nulla placere diu nec vivere carmina possunt / Quae scribuntur aquae potoribus.* – No poems can please for long or live that are written by water-drinkers. [xix. 2]

27 *Atque inter silvas Academi quaerere verum.* – And seek the truth in the groves of Academus. [II. ii. 45]

28 *Singula de nobis anni praedantur euntes.* – The years as they pass plunder one thing after another. [55]

29 *Multa fero, ut placem genus irritabile vatum.* – I put up with a great deal to pacify the touchy tribe of poets. [102]

30 *Lusisti satis, edisti satis atque bibisti: / Tempus*

abire tibi est. – You have played enough; you have eaten and drunk enough. Now it is time for you to depart. [214]

1 *Beatus ille, qui procul negotiis, / Ut prisca gens mortalium, / Paterna rura bubus exercet suis, / Solutus omni faenore.* – Happy the man who, far from business schemes, like the early race of mortals, ploughs and reploughs his ancestral land, with oxen of his own breeding, and no slavish yoke round his neck. [*Epodes*, II. 1]

2 *Quodsi me lyricis vatibus inseres, / Sublimi feriam sidera vertice.* – But if you place me among the lyric bards, I shall touch the stars with my exalted head. [*Odes*, I. i. 35]

3 *Illi robur et aes triplex / Circa pectus erat, qui fragilem truci / Commisit pelago ratem / Primus.* – His heart was mailed with oak and triple brass who first committed a frail ship to the wild seas. [iii. 9]

4 *Pallida Mors aequo pulsat pede pauperum tabernas / Regumque turris.* – Pale Death knocks with impartial foot at poor men's hovels and kings' palaces. [iv. 13]

5 *Vitae summa brevis spem nos vetat incohare longam.* – Life's short span forbids our embarking on far-reaching hopes. [15]

6 *Nil desperandum Teucro duce et auspice Teucro.* – With Teucer as leader and under Teucer's star, never despair. [vii. 27]

7 *Cras ingens iterabimus aequor.* – Tomorrow we take our course once more over the mighty seas. [32]

8 *Permitte divis cetera.* – Leave the rest to the gods. [ix. 9]

9 *Tu ne quaesieris, scire nefas.* – Do not ask. Such knowledge is not for us. [xi. 1]

10 *Carpe diem, quam minimum credula postero.* – Seize today, and put as little trust as you can in the morrow. [8]

11 *O matre pulchra filia pulchrior.* – O fairer daughter of a fair mother. [xvi. 1]

12 *Integer vitae scelerisque purus.* – The man of upright life, unstained by guilt. [xxii. 1]

13 *Dulce ridentem Lalagen amabo, / Dulce loquentem.* – I will love the sweetly laughing, sweetly chattering Lalage. [23]

14 *Nunc est bibendum, nunc pede libero / Pulsanda tellus.* – Now is the time for drinking, now the time to beat the earth with unfettered foot. [xxxvii. 1]

15 *Persicos odi, puer, apparatus.* – Boy, I loathe Persian luxury. [xxxviii. 1]

16 *Aequam memento rebus in arduis / Servare mentem.* – Remember, when life's path is steep, to keep an even mind. [II. iii. 1]

17 *Omnes eodem cogimur.* – We are all driven into the same fold. [25]

18 *Auream quisquis mediocritatem / Diligit.* – Whoever prizes the golden mean. [x. 5]

19 *Neque semper arcum / Tendit Apollo.* – Apollo does not always keep his bow strung. [19]

20 *Eheu fugaces, Postume, Postume, / Labuntur anni.* – Alas, Postumus, Postumus, the fleeting years are slipping by. [xiv. 1]

21 *Nihil est ab omni / Parte beatum.* – No lot is in all respects happy. [xvi. 27]

22 *Odi profanum vulgus et arceo; / Favete linguis; carmina non prius / Audita Musarum sacerdos / Virginibus puerisque canto.* – I hate the uninitiated crowd and keep them away. Observe silence! I, the Muses' priest, sing for girls and boys songs never heard before. [III. i. 1]

23 *Post equitem sedet atra Cura.* – Black Care takes her seat behind the horseman. [40]

24 *Dulce et decorum est pro patria mori.* – It is a sweet and seemly thing to die for one's country. [ii. 13 (See also 302:10)]

25 *Iustum et tenacem propositi virum / Non civium ardor prava iubentium, / Non vultus instantis tyranni / Mente quatit solida.* – The man who is tenacious of purpose in a rightful cause is not shaken from his firm resolve by the frenzy of his fellow citizens clamouring for what is wrong, or by the tyrant's threatening face. [iii. 1]

26 *Si fractus illabitur orbis / Impavidum ferient ruinae.* – If the vault of heaven crack, the ruins will strike him fearless still. [7]

27 *Auditis an me ludit amabilis / Insania?* – Do you hear, or does some fond illusion mock me? [iv. 5]

28 *Fratesque tendentes opaco / Pelion imposuisse Olympo.* – The brothers who strove to pile Pelion on shady Olympus. [51]

29 *Vis consili expers mole ruit sua.* – Brute force without wisdom falls by its own weight. [65]

30 *Delicta maiorum immeritus lues.* – Though guiltless, you must expiate your fathers' sins. [vi. 1]

1 *Splendide mendax et in omne virgo / Nobilis aevum.* – Gloriously false, a maid famous for all time. [xi. 35]

2 *O fons Bandusiae splendidior vitro.* – O spring of Bandusia, brighter than glass. [xiii. 1]

3 *Magnas inter opes inops.* – A pauper in the midst of wealth. [xvi. 28]

4 *Vixi puellis nuper idoneus / Et militavi non sine gloria; / Nunc arma defunctumque bello / Barbiton hic paries habebit.* – Till lately I was still fit for the maidens, and served in battle not without renown. Now my armour and my lute, whose campaigns are over, will hang on yonder wall. [xxvi. 1]

5 *Exegi monumentum aere perennius.* – I have completed a monument more lasting than brass. [xxx. 1]

6 *Non omnis moriar.* – I shall not altogether die. [6]

7 *Non sum qualis eram bonae / Sub regno Cinarae. Desine, dulcium / Mater saeva Cupidinum.* – I am not what I was when kindly Cinara was queen. Strive no more, cruel mother of sweet loves. [IV. i. 3 (last line repeats *Odes*, I. xix. 1)]

8 *Merses profundo: pulchrior evenit.* – Plunge it in the depths; it comes up fairer. [iv. 65]

9 *Diffugere nives, redeunt iam gramina campis / Arboribusque comae.* – The snows have fled; already the grass is returning to the fields and the leaves to the trees. [vii. 1]

10 *Misce stultitiam consiliis brevem: / Dulce est desipere in loco.* – Mingle some brief folly with your wisdom. To forget it in due place is sweet. [xii. 27]

11 *Mutato nomine de te / Fabula narratur.* – Change the name, and the tale is about you. [*Satires*, I. i. 69]

12 *Hoc genus omne.* – All that tribe. [ii. 2]

13 *Tempora certa modosque, et quod prius ordine verbum est / Posterius facias, praeponens ultima primis . . . / Invenias etiam disiecti membra poetae.* – Take away the rhythm and the metre, and put the first word last and the last first; still the dispersed limbs are those of a poet. [iv. 58-9 and 62]

14 *Ad unguem / Factus homo.* – An accomplished man to his fingertips. [v. 32]

15 *Credat Iudaeus Apella, / Non ego.* – Let Apella the Jew believe that, not I. [v. 100]

16 *Par nobile fratrum.* – A noble pair of brothers. [iii. 243]

17 *Hoc erat in votis: modus agri non ita magnus, / Hortus ubi et tecto vicinus iugis aquae fons / Et paulum silvae super his foret.* – This was what I prayed for: a plot of land not too large, containing a garden, and near the house a fresh spring of water, and a bit of forest to complete it. [vi. 1]

18 *O noctes cenaeque deum!* – O nights and feasts of the gods! [65]

RICHARD HENRY [HENGIST] HORNE
1803–1884

19 'Tis always morning somewhere in the world. [*Orion*, Bk iii. Canto 2]

ZILPHIA HORTON 1907–1957

20 We Shall Overcome. [Title of Song, original version. Later additions by Pete Seeger, Frank Hamilton, Guy Carawan]

A. E. HOUSMAN 1859–1936

21 The Grizzly Bear is huge and wild; / He has devoured the infant child. / The infant child is not aware / He has been eaten by the bear. [*Infant Innocence*]

22 Pass me the can, lad; there's an end of May. [*Last Poems*, 9]

23 May will be fine next year as like as not: / Oh ay, but then we shall be twenty-four.

24 We for a certainty are not the first / Have sat in taverns while the tempest hurled / Their hopeful plans to emptiness, and cursed / Whatever brute and blackguard made the world.

25 The troubles of our proud and angry dust / Are from eternity, and shall not fail. / Bear them we can, and if we can we must. / Shoulder the sky, my lad, and drink your ale.

26 But men at whiles are sober / And think by fits and starts, / And if they think, they fasten / Their hands upon their hearts. [10]

27 I, a stranger and afraid / In a world I never made. [12]

28 And then the clock collected in the tower / Its strength and struck. [15, 'Eight O'Clock']

29 Made of earth and sea / His overcoat for ever, / And wears the turning globe. [20]

30 The fairies break their dances / And leave the printed lawn. [21]

1 The young man feels his pockets / And wonders what's to pay.

2 These, in the day when heaven was falling. / The hour when earth's foundations fled, / Followed their mercenary calling / And took their wages and are dead.

Their shoulders held the skies suspended; / They stood, and earth's foundations stay; / What God abandoned, these defended, / And saved the sum of things for pay. [37, 'Epitaph on an Army of Mercenaries']

3 To air the ditty / and to earth I. / Tomorrow, more's the pity, / Away we both must hie. [41, 'Fancy's Knell']

4 The rainy Pleiads wester, / Orion plunges prone, / The stroke of midnight ceases, / And I lie down alone. [*More Poems*, 11]

5 Loveliest of trees, the cherry now / Is hung with bloom along the bough. [*A Shropshire Lad*, 2]

6 Now, of my threescore years and ten, / Twenty will not come again.

7 About the woodlands I will go / To see the cherry hung with snow.

8 Clay lies still, but blood's a rover; / Breath's a ware that will not keep. / Up, lad; when the journey's over / There'll be time enough for sleep. [4, 'Reveille']

9 A neck God made for other use / Than strangling in a string. [9]

10 Lovers lying two by two / Ask not whom they sleep beside, / And the bridegroom all night through / Never turns him to the bride. [12]

11 When I was one-and-twenty / I heard a wise man say, / 'Give crowns and pounds and guineas / But not your heart away.' [13]

12 Oh, when I was in love with you, / Then I was clean and brave. [18]

13 And silence sounds no worse than cheers / After death has stopped the ears. [19, 'To an Athlete Dying Young']

14 In summertime on Bredon / The bells they sound so clear; / Round both the shires they ring them / In steeples far and near, / A happy noise to hear.

15 Here of a Sunday morning / My love and I would lie, / And see the coloured counties, / And hear the larks so high / About us in the sky. [21, 'Bredon Hill']

16 'Come all to church, good people,' – / Oh, noisy bells, be dumb; / I hear you, I will come.

17 They carry back bright to the coiner the mintage of man, / The lads that will die in their glory and never be old. [23]

18 Is my team ploughing, / That I was used to drive? [27]

19 No change, though you lie under / The land you used to plough.

20 The goal stands up, the keeper / Stands up to keep the goal.

21 The flag of morn in conqueror's state / Enters at the English gate: / the vanquished eve, as night prevails, / Bleeds upon the road to Wales. [28, 'The Welsh Marches']

22 Today the Roman and his trouble / Are ashes under Uricon. [31]

23 From far, from eve and morning / And yon twelve-winded sky, / The stuff of life to knit me / Blew hither: here am I. [32]

24 White in the moon the long road lies. [36]

25 Into my heart an air that kills / From yon far country blows: / What are those blue remembered hills, / What spires, what farms are those? [40]

26 That is the land of lost content, / I see it shining plain, / The happy highways where I went / And cannot come again.

27 And the feather pate of folly / Bears the falling of the sky. [49]

28 Think no more; 'tis only thinking / Lays lads underground.

29 With rue my heart is laden / For golden friends I had, / For many a rose-lipt maiden / And many a lightfoot lad. [54]

30 Malt does more than Milton can / To justify God's ways to man. [62]

31 Ale, man, ale's the stuff to drink / For fellows whom it hurts to think.

32 Mithridates, he died old.

33 Good religious poetry ... is likely to be most justly appreciated and most discriminately relished by the undevout. [*The Name and Nature of Poetry*]

34 Even when poetry has a meaning, as it usually has, it may be inadvisable to draw it out ... Perfect understanding will sometimes almost extinguish pleasure.

35 If a line of poetry strays into my memory, my skin bristles so that the razor ceases to act.

1 Cambridge has seen many strange sights. It has seen Wordsworth drunk, it has seen Porson sober. I am a greater scholar than Wordsworth and I am a greater poet than Porson. So I fall betwixt and between. [Speech, on leaving University College, London, to take up the Chair of Latin at Cambridge, 1911. Quoted in R. P. Graves, *A. E. Housman, the Scholar-poet*, Ch. 5]

BISHOP W. W. HOW 1823–1897

2 For all the Saints who from their labours rest, / Who Thee by faith before the world confessed, / Thy name, O Jesu, be for ever blest. / Alleluia! [Hymn]

SAMUEL HOWARD 1710–1782

3 Gentle Shepherd, tell me where. [*Song*]

JULIA WARD HOWE 1819–1910

4 Mine eyes have seen the glory of the coming of the Lord: / He is trampling out the vintage where the grapes of wrath are stored. [*Battle Hymn of the American Republic*]

5 Oh! be swift, my soul, to answer Him! be jubilant, my feet!/ Our God is marching on.

6 In the beauty of the lilies Christ was born across the sea, / With a glory in his bosom that transfigures you and me: / As he died to make men holy, let us die to make men free, / While God is marching on.

JAMES HOWELL 1594?–1666

7 Some hold translations not unlike to be / The wrong side of a Turkish tapestry. [*Familiar Letters*, Bk i. 6]

8 This life at best is but an inn, / And we the passengers. [73]

WILLIAM DEAN HOWELLS 1837–1920

9 Some people can stay longer in an hour than others can in a week. [Attr. in Evan Esar (ed.), *Treasury of Humorous Quotations*]

MARY HOWITT 1799–1888

10 Buttercups and daisies, / Oh, the pretty flowers; / Coming ere the Springtime, / To tell of sunny hours. [*Buttercups and Daisies*]

11 'Will you walk into my parlour?' said a spider to a fly: / 'Tis the prettiest little parlour that ever you did spy.' [*The Spider and the Fly*]

EDMOND HOYLE 1672–1769

12 When in doubt, win the trick. [*Hoyle's Games*, 'Whist: 'Twenty-four Short Rules for Learners']

ELBERT HUBBARD 1856–1915

13 Life is just one damned thing after another. [*One Thousand and One Epigrams*. Elsewhere attr. to F. W. O'Malley. See also 273:20]

'KIN' HUBBARD 1868–1930

14 Nobody ever forgets where he buried a hatchet. [*Abe Martin's Broadcast*, (1930)]

THOMAS HUGHES 1822–1896

15 He never wants anything but what's right and fair; only when you come to settle what's right and fair, it's everything that he wants and nothing that you want. [*Tom Brown's Schooldays*, Pt II. Ch. 2]

16 It's more than a game. It's an institution. [(Cricket) 7]

VICTOR HUGO 1802–1885

17 *Car le mot, c'est le Verbe, et le Verbe, c'est Dieu.* – For words are the Word, and the Word is God. [*Les Contemplations*, I. i. 8]

18 *Waterloo! Waterloo! Waterloo! Morne plaine! / Comme une onde qui bout dans une urne trop pleine, / Dans ton cirque de bois, de coteaux, de vallons, / La pâle mort mêlait les sombres bataillons.* – Waterloo! Waterloo! Waterloo! Sad plain! Like a wave breaking into an overfilled cup, pale death mingled the dark batallions in your arena of woods, hills, and valleys. [*L'Expiation*, ii. 1]

19 *Lorsque l'enfant parait, le cercle de famille / Applaudit à grands cris.* – When the child appears, the family greet it with loud cries. [*Les Feuilles d'automne*, xix. 1]

20 *Oh! combien de marins, combien de capitaines / Qui sont partis joyeux pour des courses lointaines, / Dans ce morne horizon se sont évanouis.* – Oh! how many sailors, how many captains who have gaily set out for long voyages have vanished behind that sad horizon! [*Oceano Nox*]

21 *Les champs n'étaient point noirs, les cieux n'étaient pas mornes.* – The fields were not dark, the skies were not dull. [*Tristesse d'Olympio*]

1 *La popularité? c'est la gloire en gros sous.* – Popularity? It's glory's small change. [*Ruy Blas*, iii. 4]

2 *Vous créez un frisson nouveau.* – You create a new shiver of horror. [Letter to Charles Baudelaire, 6 Oct. 1859]

T. E. HULME 1883–1917

3 I walked abroad, / And saw the ruddy moon lean over a hedge / Like a red-faced farmer. / I did not stop to speak, but nodded, / And round about were the wistful stars / With white faces like town children. [*Autumn*]

DAVID HUME 1711–1776

4 Avarice, the spur of industry. [*Essays*, 'Of Civil Liberty']

5 Beauty in things exists in the mind which contemplates them. ['Of Tragedy']

6 Custom, then, is the great guide of human life. [*An Enquiry Concerning Human Understanding*, Sect. V. Pt I]

7 Never literary attempt was more unfortunate than my Treatise of Human Nature. It fell *dead-born from the press*. [*My Own Life*, Ch. 1]

MARGARET HUNGERFORD 1855–1897

8 Beauty is in the eye of the beholder. [Quoted in *Molly Bawn*]

G. W. HUNT *c.* 1825–1904

9 We don't want to fight; but, by Jingo, if we do, / We've got the ships, we've got the men, we've got the money too. [Music-hall song, 1878]

J. H. LEIGH HUNT 1784–1859

10 Abou Ben Adhem (may his tribe increase!) / Awoke one night from a deep dream of peace. [*Abou Ben Adhem and the Angel*]

11 Write me as one that loves his fellow-men.

12 And lo! Ben Adhem's name led all the rest.

13 A Venus grown fat! [*Blue-stocking Revels*]

14 The laughing queen that caught the world's great hands. [*The Nile*]

15 If you become a nun, dear, / A friar I will be. [*The Nun*]

16 Jenny kissed me when we met, / Jumping from the chair she sat in; / Time, you thief, who love to get / Sweets into your list, put that in. [*Rondeau*]

17 This Adonis in loveliness was a corpulent man of fifty. [(The Prince Regent) *The Examiner*, 22 Mar. 1812]

18 The Earl of Liverpool, whom Madame de Staël is said to have described as having 'a talent for silence'. [*Autobiography*, Ch. 11]

ANNIE HUNTER 1742–1821

19 My mother bids me bind my hair / With bands of rosy hue. [*My Mother Bids Me Bind My Hair*]

JOHN HUSS 1373–1415

20 *O sancta simplicitas!* – O holy simplicity! [At the stake, on seeing a peasant bringing a faggot to throw on the pile]

FRANCIS HUTCHESON 1694–1746

21 Wisdom denotes the pursuing of the best ends by the best means. [*Inquiry into the Original of Our Ideas of Beauty and Virtue*, I. v]

22 That action is best which procures the greatest happiness for the greatest numbers. [II. iii]

ALDOUS HUXLEY 1894–1963

23 There are few who would not rather be taken in adultery than in provincialism. [*Antic Hay*, 10]

24 Lady Capricorn, he understood, was still keeping open bed. [21]

25 'Going to the Feelies this evening, Henry?' enquired the Assistant Predestinator. 'I hear the new one at the Alhambra is first-rate. There's a love scene on a bearskin rug; they say it's marvellous. Every hair of the bear reproduced.' [*Brave New World*, Ch. 3]

26 Our Ford . . . had been the first to reveal the appalling dangers of family life.

27 Oh, she's a splendid girl. Wonderfully pneumatic.

28 The sexophones wailed like melodious cats under the moon. [5]

29 I can sympathize with people's pains, but not with their pleasures. There is something curiously boring about somebody else's happiness. [*Limbo*, 'Cynthia']

1 Forgetting that several excuses are always less convincing than one. [*Point Counter Point*, Ch. 1]

2 Parodies and caricatures are the most penetrating of criticisms. [28]

3 Happiness is like coke – something you get as a by-product in the process of making something else. [30]

4 Burlap walked home. He was feeling pleased with himself and the world at large. 'I accept the Universe', was how, only an hour before, he had concluded his next week's leader. [37]

5 At thirty-three ... Lilian Aldwinkle appealed to all the instinctive bigamist in one. She was eighteen in the attics and widow Dido on the floors below. [*Those Barren Leaves*, I. 2]

6 How appallingly thorough these Germans always managed to be, how emphatic! In sex no less than in war – in scholarship, in science. Diving deeper than anyone else and coming up muddier. [*Time Must Have a Stop*, 6]

7 There isn't any formula or method. You learn to love by loving – by paying attention and doing what one thereby discovers has to be done. [30]

8 But when the wearied Band / Swoons to a waltz, I take her hand, / And there we sit in peaceful calm, / Quietly sweating palm to palm. [*Frascati's*]

9 A million million spermatozoa, / All of them alive: / Out of their cataclysm but one poor Noah / Dare hope to survive. / And among that billion minus one / Might have chanced to be / Shakespeare, another Newton, a new Donne – / But the One was Me. [*The Fifth Philosopher's Song*]

10 Beauty for some provides escape, / Who gain a happiness in eyeing / The gorgeous buttocks of the ape / Or Autumn sunsets exquisitely dying. [*The Ninth Philosopher's Song*]

T. H. HUXLEY 1825–1895

11 Science is nothing but trained and organized common sense. [*Collected Essays*, iv, 'The Method of Zadig']

12 Irrationally held truths may be more harmful than reasoned errors. [xii, 'The Coming of Age of the Origin of Species']

13 It is the customary fate of new truths to begin as heresies and to end as superstitions.

14 I took thought, and invented what I conceived to be the appropriate title of 'agnostic'. [*Science and Christian Tradition*. Ch. 7]

I

DOLORES IBÁRRURI ['LA PASIONARIA'] 1895–1989

1 It is better to die on your feet than to live on your knees! [Republican slogan broadcast in the Spanish Civil War, but coined by Emiliano Zapata in Mexico in 1910. Quoted in Hugh Thomas, *The Spanish Civil War*, Ch. 16]

2 ¡no pasarán! – They shall not pass. [Rallying cry to Spanish Republicans in Civil War, 1936. The call echoes the French *Ils ne passeront pas* of 1916 at Verdun. See 9:16, 308:5]

HENRIK IBSEN 1828–1906

3 When did the squirrel get home? [*A Doll's House*, I, trans. Michael Meyer]

4 Home life ceases to be free and beautiful as soon as it is founded on borrowing and debt.

5 I don't wish you anything but just what you are – my own sweet little song-bird.

6 In that moment it burst upon me that I had been living here these eight years with a strange man, and had borne him three children. [III]

7 The minority is always right. [*An Enemy of the People*, IV]

8 One should never put on one's best trousers to go out to battle for freedom and truth. [v]

9 The strongest man upon earth is the man who stands most alone.

10 Mother, give me the sun. [*Ghosts*, III]

11 I can see him. With vine leaves in his hair. [*Hedda Gabler*, II]

12 But, merciful God! People don't do such things! [IV]

13 Some day, youth will come here and thunder on my door, and force its way in to me. [*The Master Builder*, I]

14 Go round, Peer! [*Peer Gynt*, II. vii]

15 What should a man be? Himself. That's all. [IV. i]

16 Emperor? You old fake! / You're no Emperor. You're just an onion. / Now then, little Peer, I'm going to peel you. [V. v]

17 As you can see, I'm a button-moulder. / You must go into my casting ladle. [vii]

18 Sleep, O sleep, my dearest boy. / I will cradle you, I will guard you. [x, Solveig's song]

19 They may soon expect the white horse at Rosmersholm now. [*Rosmersholm*, II]

20 It was love for me – *her* kind of love – that drove her into the mill-race. [III]

21 Always do that, wild duck. Stick at the bottom. Deep as they can get. . . . And so they never come up again. [*The Wild Duck*, II]

22 Deprive the average human being of his life-lie, and you rob him of his happiness. [V]

23 Oh, life would be all right if we didn't have to put up with these damned creditors who keep pestering us with the demands of their ideals.

24 BELLING: And what, if I may ask, is your destiny?
GREGERS: To be the thirteenth at table.

HAROLD L. ICKES 1874–1952

25 I am against government by crony. [On resigning as US Secretary of the Interior, Feb. 1946]

REV. CHARLES INGE 1868–1957

1 This very remarkable man / Commends a most practical plan: / You can do what you want / If you don't think you can't, / So don't think you can't if you can. [*On M. Coué*]

W. R. INGE, DEAN OF ST PAUL'S 1860–1954

2 The vulgar mind always mistakes the exceptional for the important. [*Lay Thoughts of a Dean*, Pt. III., Ch. 1, 'Private Notebooks']

3 Many people believe that they are attracted by God or by nature, when they are only repelled by man.

4 To become a popular religion, it is only necessary for a superstition to enslave a philosophy. [*Outspoken Essays*, Second Series, 'The Idea of Progress']

5 Christianity promises to make men free; it never promises to make them independent. [*The Philosophy of Plotinus*]

6 Literature flourishes best when it is half a trade and half an art. [*The Victorian Age*, p. 49]

7 A man may build himself a throne of bayonets, but he cannot sit on it. [Marchant, *Wit and Wisdom of Dean Inge*, 108]

JEAN INGELOW 1820–1897

8 Play uppe 'The Brides of Enderby'. [*The High Tide on the Coast of Lincolnshire*]

9 'Cusha! Cusha! Cusha!' calling / Ere the early dews were falling.

10 A sweeter woman ne'er drew breath / Than my sonne's wife Elizabeth.

R. G. INGERSOLL 1833–1899

11 An honest God is the noblest work of man. [*Gods*, Pt I (See also 84:7, 88:15, 314:9)]

12 In nature there are neither rewards nor punishments – there are consequences. [*Lectures and Essays*, Third Series, 'Some Reasons Why']

13 Few rich men own their own property. The property owns them. [Address to the McKinley League, New York, 29 Oct. 1896]

EUGENE IONESCO 1912–

14 Describe a circle, stroke its back and it turns vicious. [*The Bold Prima-Donna*, II]

15 We haven't the time to take our time. [*Exit the King*]

16 There are more dead people than living. And their numbers are increasing. The living are getting rarer. [*Rhinoceros*, II]

WASHINGTON IRVING 1783–1859

17 A woman's whole life is a history of the affections. [*The Sketch Book*, 'The Broken Heart']

18 A sharp tongue is the only edged tool that grows keener with constant use. ['Rip Van Winkle']

19 The almighty dollar, that great object of universal devotion throughout our land, seems to have no genuine devotees in these peculiar villages. [*Wolfert's Roost*, 'The Creole Village']

CHRISTOPHER ISHERWOOD 1904–1986

20 I am a camera with its shutter open, quite passive, recording, not thinking. [*Goodbye to Berlin*, 'A Berlin Diary']

21 The common cormorant or shag / Lays eggs inside a paper bag / The reason you will see no doubt / It is to keep the lightning out / But what these unobservant birds / Have never noticed is that herds / Of wandering bears may come with buns / And steal the bags to hold the crumbs. [W. H. Auden and John Garrett (eds.), *The Poet's Tongue*]

J

PRESIDENT ANDREW JACKSON
1767–1845

1 Our Union: It must be preserved. [Toast at Jefferson Day Dinner, Apr. 13 1830]

2 One man with courage makes a majority. [Ascr. by Robert Kennedy in his foreword to his brother's *Profiles in Courage*]

'JOE' JACOBS [US boxing manager]
1896–1940

3 I should of stood [have stayed] in bed. [At World Baseball Series, Oct. 1935. Quoted in J. Lardner, *Strong Cigars and Lovely Women*]

4 We was robbed! [After Max Schmeling (whose manager he was) was declared loser in heavyweight-boxing title fight with Jack Sharkey, 21 June 1932]

W. W. JACOBS 1863–1943

5 'Sailor men 'ave their faults,' said the night-watchman, frankly. 'I'm not denying it. I used to 'ave myself when I was at sea.' [*The Lady of the Barge*, 'Bill's Paper Chase']

JAMES I OF ENGLAND AND VI OF SCOTLAND 1566–1625

6 A branch of the sin of drunkenness, which is the root of all sins. [*A Counterblast to Tobacco*]

7 Herein is not only a great vanity, but a great contempt of God's good gifts, that the sweetness of man's breath, being a good gift of God, should be wilfully corrupted by this stinking smoke.

8 He was a bold man who first swallowed an oyster. [Quoted in Dean Swift, *Polite Conversation*, Dialogue II]

9 Dr Donne's verses are like the peace of God; they pass all understanding. [Attr. by Archdeacon Plume]

10 No bishop, no king. [Attr.]

HENRY JAMES 1843–1916

11 The deep well of unconscious cerebration. [*The American*, Preface]

12 The historian, essentially, wants more documents than he can really use; the dramatist only wants more liberties than he can really take. [*The Aspern Papers*]

13 London doesn't love the latent or the lurking, has neither time, nor taste, nor sense for anything less discernible than the red flag in front of the steam-roller. It wants cash over the counter and letters ten feet high. [*The Awkward Age*, I. 2]

14 What could the thing that was to happen to him be, after all, but just this thing that had begun to happen? Her dying, her death, his consequent solitude – *that* was what he had figured as the beast in the jungle. [*The Beast in the Jungle*]

15 Vereker's secret, my dear man – the general intention of his books: the string the pearls were strung on, the buried treasure, the figure in the carpet. [*The Figure in the Carpet*, Ch. 11]

16 Cats and monkeys, monkeys and cats – all human life is there. [*The Madonna of the Future*]

17 We work in the dark – we do what we can – we give what we have. Our doubt is our passion, and our passion is our task. The rest is the madness of art. [*The Middle Years*]

1 The Real Right Thing. [Title of story]

2 We must grant the artist his subject, his idea, his *donné*: our criticism is applied only to what he makes of it. [*The Art of Fiction*, 'Partial Portraits']

3 The time-honoured bread-sauce of the happy ending. [*Theatricals, Second Series*]

4 Summer afternoon – summer afternoon; to me those have always been the two most beautiful words in the English language. [Quoted in Edith Wharton, *A Backward Glance*, Ch. 10]

5 So here it is at last, the distinguished thing! [(Said by a 'voice' heard as he suffered his first stroke, often wrongly described as his last words) 14]

6 Kidd, turn off the light to spare my blushes. [Said to the maid after Edmund Gosse had told him he had been awarded the Order of Merit. Quoted in James S. Bain, *A Bookseller Looks Back*]

7 It is art that *makes* life, makes interest, makes importance, for our consideration and application of these things, and I know of no substitute whatever for the force and beauty of its process. [Letter to H. G. Wells, 10 July 1915]

8 Tell the boys to follow, to be faithful, to take me seriously. [Last recorded words, said to Alice James. Quoted in H. Montgomery Hyde, *Henry James at Home*, Ch. 7. iv]

WILLIAM JAMES 1842–1910

9 I think you will practically recognise the two types of mental make-up that I mean if I head the columns by the titles 'tender-minded' and 'tough-minded' respectively. [*Pragmatism*]

10 There is no more miserable human being than one in whom nothing is habitual but indecision. [*Psychology*, Ch. 10]

11 The whole drift of my education goes to persuade me that the world of our present consciousness is only one out of many worlds of consciousness that exist. [*The Varieties of Religious Experience*, Lecture XX]

12 The moral flabbiness born of the bitch-goddess Success. [Letter to H. G. Wells, 11 Sept. 1906]

13 A great many people think they are thinking when they are merely rearranging their prejudices. [Attr. in Clifton Fadiman, *American Treasury*]

14 [Environment is] a big, booming, buzzing confusion. [Quoted in Peter F. Smith, *The Dynamics of Urbanism*, Ch. 2]

15 Whenever two people meet there are really six people present. There is each man as he sees himself, each man as the other person sees him, and each man as he really is. [Quoted in Laurence J. Peter, *Peter's Quotations*]

RANDALL JARRELL 1914–1965

16 It is better to entertain an idea than to take it home to live with you for the rest of your life. [*Pictures from an Institution*, iv. 9]

17 I decided that Europeans and Americans are like men and women: they understand each other worse, and it matters less, than either of them suppose. [10]

18 In the United States, there one feels free . . . Except from the Americans – but every pearl has its oyster.

SIR JAMES JEANS 1887–1946

19 The universe begins to look more like a great thought than a great machine. [*The Mysterious Universe*, Ch. 5]

THOMAS JEFFERSON 1743–1826

20 We hold these truths to be sacred and undeniable; that all men are created equal and independent, that from that equal creation they derive rights inherent and inalienable, among which are the preservation of life, and liberty, and the pursuit of happiness. [Original draft for the American Declaration of Independence]

21 Error of opinion may be tolerated where reason is left free to combat it. [First inaugural address, 4 Mar. 1801]

22 Peace, commerce, and honest friendship with all nations – entangling alliances with none.

23 A little rebellion now and then is a good thing. [Letter to James Madison, 30 Jan. 1787]

24 The tree of liberty must be refreshed from time to time with the blood of patriots and tyrants. It is its natural manure. [Letter to W. S. Smith, 13 Nov. 1787]

25 Indeed I tremble for my country when I reflect that God is just. [*Notes on Virginia*, Query 18, 'Manners']

FRANCIS, LORD JEFFERY 1773–1850

1 This will never do. [(On Wordsworth's *Excursion*) *Edinburgh Review*, Nov. 1814]

PAUL JENNINGS 1918–1989

2 Resistentialism is concerned with what Things think about men. [*Even Oddlier*, 'Developments in Resistentialism']

3 When numbered pieces of toast and marmalade were dropped on various samples of carpet arranged in quality, from coir matting to the finest Kirman rugs, the marmalade-downwards-incidence ($\mu\delta\iota$) varied indirectly with the quality of the carpet (Qc) – the Principle of the Graduated Hostility of Things.

4 Ventre's stark dictum that *les choses sont contre nous*.

JEROME K. JEROME 1859–1927

5 It is impossible to enjoy idling thoroughly unless one has plenty of work to do. [*Idle thoughts of an Idle Fellow*, 'On Being Idle']

6 Love is like the measles; we all have to go through it. ['On Being in Love']

7 The only malady I could conclude I had not got was housemaid's knee. [*Three Men in a Boat*, Ch. 1]

8 I like work: it fascinates me. I can sit and look at it for hours. I love to keep it by me: the idea of getting rid of it nearly breaks my heart. [15]

9 The Passing of the Third Floor Back. [Title of play]

DOUGLAS JERROLD 1803–1857

10 Mrs Caudle's Curtain Lectures. [Title of book]

11 That fellow would vulgarize the day of judgement. [*Wit and Opinions*, 'A Comic Author']

12 Earth is here so kind [Australia], that just tickle her with a hoe and she laughs with a harvest. ['A Land of Plenty']

13 We love peace, as we abhor pusillanimity; / But not peace at any price. ['Peace']

14 Love's like the measles – all the worse when it comes late in life. ['A Philanthropist']

15 The only athletic sport I ever mastered was backgammon. [Quoted in W. Jerrold, *Douglas Jerrold*, Vol. i. Ch. 1]

SENATOR HIRAM JOHNSON 1866–1945

16 The first casualty when war comes is truth. [Speech in US Senate, 1918]

LIONEL JOHNSON 1867–1902

17 The saddest of all Kings / Crowned, and again discrowned. [*By the Statue of King Charles I at Charing Cross*]

18 Speak after sentence? Yea: / And to the end of time.

19 Some players upon plaintive strings / Publish their wistfulness abroad; / I have not spoken of these things, / Save to one man, and unto God. [*The Precept of Silence*]

PRESIDENT LYNDON B. JOHNSON 1908–1973

20 This administration today, here and now, declares unconditional war on poverty in America. [State of the Union address to Congress, 8 Jan. 1964]

21 I am going to build the kind of nation that President Roosevelt hoped for, President Truman worked for and President Kennedy died for. [Quoted in the *Sunday Times*, 27 Dec. 1964]

22 I'd much rather have that fellow inside my tent pissing out, than outside my tent pissing in. [On being asked why he kept J. Edgar Hoover at the FBI. Quoted by J. K. Galbraith in the *Guardian Weekly* 18 Dec. 1971]

23 Jerry Ford is so dumb that he can't fart and chew gum at the same time. [Quoted in R. Reeves, *A Ford, Not a Lincoln*, Ch. 1]

PHILANDER JOHNSON 1866–1939

24 Cheer up, the worst is yet to come. [*Shooting Stars*]

DR SAMUEL JOHNSON 1709–1784

25 Here falling houses thunder on your head, / And here a female atheist talks you dead. [*London*, 17]

26 Of all the griefs that harass the distressed, / Sure the most bitter is a scornful jest. [166]

27 This mournful truth is ev'rywhere confessed, / Slow rises worth by poverty depressed. [176]

1 Long-expected one and twenty, / Lingering year at length is flown. [*One and Twenty*]

2 I put my hat upon my head, / I walked into the Strand, / And there I met another man / Whose hat was in his hand. [*Parodies of the Hermit of Warkworth*]

3 When learning's triumph o'er her barb'rous foes / First reared the stage, immortal Shakespeare rose; / Each change of many-coloured life he drew, / Exhausted worlds, and then imagined new: / Existence saw him spurn her bounded reign, / And panting Time toiled after him in vain. [*Prologue at the Opening of Theatre in Drury Lane*]

4 The drama's laws, the drama's patrons give, / For we that live to please, must please to live.

5 Let observation, with extensive view, / Survey mankind from China to Peru. [*The Vanity of Human Wishes*, 1]

6 Deign on the passing world to turn thine eyes, / And pause awhile from letters, to be wise; / There mark what ills the scholar's life assail, / Toil, envy, want, the patron, and the jail. [157]

7 Around his tomb let Art and Genius weep / But hear his death, ye blockheads! hear and sleep. [173]

8 His fall was destined to a barren strand, / A petty fortress, and a dubious hand; / He left the name, at which the world grew pale, / To point a moral, or adorn a tale. [219]

9 Hides from himself his state, and shuns to know / That life protracted is protracted woe. [257]

10 In life's last scene what prodigies surprise, / Fears of the brave, and follies of the wise! / From Marlborough's eyes the streams of dotage flow, / And Swift expires a driv'ller and a show. [315]

11 Must helpless man, in ignorance sedate, / Roll darkling down the torrent of his fate? [345]

12 Still raise for good the supplicating voice, / But leave to Heaven the measure and the choice. [351]

13 With these celestial Wisdom calms the mind, / And makes the happiness she does not find. [367]

14 *Lexicographer*. A writer of dictionaries, a harmless drudge. [*Dictionary of the English Language*]

15 *Oats*. A grain, which in England is generally given to horses, but in Scotland supports the people.

16 *Patron*. Commonly a wretch who supports with insolence, and is paid with flattery.

17 When two Englishmen meet, their first talk is of the weather. [*The Idler*, 11]

18 Whatever withdraws us from the power of our senses; whatever makes the past, the distant, or the future, predominate over the present, advances us in the dignity of thinking beings. [*Journey to the Western Islands*, 'Inch Kenneth']

19 About things on which the public thinks long it commonly attains to think right. [*The Lives of the English Poets*, 'Addison']

20 The true genius is a mind of large general powers, accidentally determined to some particular direction. ['Cowley']

21 About the beginning of the seventeenth century appeared a race of writers that may be termed the *metaphysical poets*.

22 Their thoughts are often new, but seldom natural.

23 The most heterogeneous ideas are yoked by violence together.

24 The father of English criticism. ['Dryden']

25 The *Churchyard* abounds with images which find a mirror in every mind, and with sentiments to which every bosom returns an echo. ['Gray']

26 New things are made familiar, and familiar things are made new. ['Pope']

27 If Pope be not a poet, where is poetry to be found?

28 Preserve me from unseasonable and immoderate sleep. [*Prayers and Meditations* (1767)]

29 This world, where much is to be done and little to be known. ['Against Inquisitive and Perplexing Thoughts']

30 Nothing can please many, and please long, but just representations of general nature. Particular manners can be known to few, and, therefore, few only can judge how nearly they are copied. [*Preface to Shakespeare*]

31 In his tragic scenes there is always something wanting.

32 I have always suspected that the reading is right which requires many words to prove it

wrong, and the emendation wrong which cannot without so much labour appear to be right.

1 Notes are often necessary, but they are necessary evils.

2 Particulars are not to be examined till the whole has been surveyed.

3 I shall long to see the miseries of the world, since the sight of them is necessary to happiness. [*Rasselas*, Ch. 3]

4 To a poet nothing can be useless. [10]

5 The business of a poet, said Imlac, is to examine, not the individual but the species; to remark general properties and large appearances. He does not number the streaks of the tulip.

6 Human life is everywhere a state in which much is to be endured and little to be enjoyed. [11]

7 Marriage has many pains, but celibacy has no pleasures. [26]

8 Example is always more efficacious than precept. [29]

9 The endearing elegance of female friendship. [45]

10 The rod produces an effect which terminates in itself. A child is afraid of being whipped, and gets his task, and there's an end on't; whereas by exciting emulation and comparisons of superiority, you lay the foundation of lasting mischief; you make brothers and sisters hate each other. [(On Mr Hunter, his headmaster) Boswell, *Life of Johnson*, Introductory]

11 BOSWELL: That, Sir, was great fortitude of mind.
JOHNSON: No, Sir, stark insensibility. [1728]

12 Sir, we are a nest of singing birds. [(Of Pembroke College, Oxford) 1730]

13 If you call a dog *Hervey*, I shall love him. [1737]

14 Tom Birch is as brisk as a bee in conversation; but no sooner does he take a pen in his hand, than it becomes a torpedo to him, and benumbs all his faculties. [1743]

15 When asked how he felt upon the ill-success of his tragedy, he replied, 'Like the Monument'; meaning that he continued firm and unmoved as that column. [1749]

16 I'll come no more behind your scenes, David; for the silk stockings and white bosoms of your actresses excite my amorous propensities. [1750]

17 A man may write at any time, if he will set himself doggedly to it. [Mar. 1750]

18 Sir, he lived in London, and hung loose upon society. [(F. Lewis) 1750]

19 Wretched *un-idea'd* girls. [1753]

20 No man is well pleased to have his all neglected, be it ever so little. [Letter to Lord Chesterfield, 7 Feb. 1754]

21 Is not a patron, my lord, one who looks with unconcern on a man struggling for life in the water, and when he has reached ground, encumbers him with help?

22 The notice which you have been pleased to take of my labours, had it been early, had been kind; but it has been delayed till I am indifferent, and cannot enjoy it; till I am solitary, and cannot impart it; till I am known, and do not want it.

23 A fly, Sir, may sting a stately horse, and make him wince; but one is but an insect, and the other is a horse still. [Footnote on Warburton.]

24 This man, I thought, had been a Lord among wits; but, I find, he is only a wit among Lords. [Lord Chesterfield]

25 They teach the morals of a whore, and the manners of a dancing-master. [Lord Chesterfield's Letters]

26 Sir, he [Lord Bolingbroke] was a scoundrel and a coward: a scoundrel for charging a blunderbuss against religion and morality; a coward, because he had not resolution to fire it off himself, but left half a crown to a beggarly Scotchman [David Mallet], to draw the trigger after his death! [6 Mar.]

27 When the messenger who carried the last sheet [of Johnson's *Dictionary*] to Millar returned, Johnson asked him, 'Well, what did he say?' – 'Sir (answered the messenger), he said, thank God I have done with him.' – 'I am glad (replied Johnson with a smile,) that he thanks God for anything.' [Apr. 1755]

28 I respect Millar: he has raised the price of literature.

29 Ignorance, Madam, pure ignorance. [(On being asked how, in his *Dictionary*, he came to define *Pastern* as the knee of a horse) 1755]

1 If a man does not make new acquaintance as he advances through life, he will soon find himself alone. A man, Sir, should keep his friendship *in constant repair*.

2 No man will be a sailor who has contrivance enough to get himself into a jail; for being in a ship is being in a jail, with the chance of being drowned. . . . A man in a jail has more room, better food and commonly better company. [Mar. 1759]

3 BOSWELL: I do indeed come from Scotland, but I cannot help it . . .
JOHNSON: That, Sir, I find, is what a very great many of your countrymen cannot help. [16 May 1763]

4 When a butcher tells you his heart bleeds for his country, he has, in fact, no uneasy feeling.

5 Dr Blair . . . asked . . . whether he thought any man of a modern age could have written such poems [*Ossian*] . . . 'Yes, Sir, many men, many women, and many children.' [24 May]

6 He insisted on people praying with him; and I'd as lief pray with Kit Smart as anyone else.

7 Another charge was, that he [Smart] did not love clean linen; and I have no passion for it.

8 You may scold a carpenter who has made you a bad table, though you cannot make a table. It is not your trade to make tables. [25 June]

9 Campbell is a good man, a pious man. I am afraid he has not been in the inside of a church for many years; but he never passes a church without pulling off his hat. This shows that he has good principles. [1 July]

10 A man ought to read just as inclination leads him; for what he reads as a task will do him little good. [9 July]

11 If he does really think there is no distinction between virtue and vice, why, Sir, when he leaves our houses let us count our spoons.

12 Subordination tends greatly to human happiness. Were we all upon an equality, we should have no other enjoyment than mere animal pleasure. [20 July]

13 Truth, Sir, is a cow, which will yield such people [sceptics] no more milk, and so they are gone to milk the bull. [21 July]

14 Your levellers wish to level *down* as far as themselves; but they cannot bear levelling *up* to themselves.

15 Why, Sir, Sherry [Thomas Sheridan] is dull, naturally dull; but it must have taken a great deal of pains to become what we now see him. Such an excess of stupidity, Sir, is not in Nature. [28 July]

16 Sir, it is burning a farthing candle at Dover, to shew a light at Calais. [On Sheridan's influence upon the English language]

17 Sir, a woman's preaching is like a dog's walking on his hind legs. It is not done well; but you are surprised to find it done at all. [31 July]

18 I look upon it, that he who does not mind his belly, will hardly mind anything else. [5 Aug.]

19 This was a good dinner enough, to be sure; but it was not a dinner to *ask* a man to.

20 BOSWELL: It is impossible to refute it . . .
Johnson, striking his foot with mighty force against a large stone, till he rebounded from it, answered, 'I refute it *thus*.' [(On Bishop Berkeley's proof of the non-existence of matter) 6 Aug.]

21 A very unclubbable man. [(Sir John Hawkins) 1764]

22 I would consent to have a limb amputated to recover my spirits.

23 It was not for me to bandy civilities with my Sovereign. [Feb. 1767]

24 Well, (said he), we had a good talk.
BOSWELL: Yes, Sir, you tossed and gored several persons. [1768]

25 We *know* our will is free, and *there's* an end on't. [10 Oct. 1769]

26 In the description of night in *Macbeth*, the beetle and the bat detract from the general idea of darkness – inspissated gloom. [16 Oct.]

27 Shakespeare never has six lines together without a fault. [19 Oct.]

28 Most schemes of political improvement are very laughable things. [26 Oct.]

29 It matters not how a man dies, but how he lives. The act of dying is not of importance, it lasts so short a time.

30 His [a player's] conversation usually threatened and announced more than it performed; that he fed you with a continual renovation of

hope, to end in a constant succession of disappointment. [1770]

1 That man [Lord Lyttelton] sat down to write a book, to tell the world what the world had all his life been telling him.

2 That fellow seems to me to possess but one idea, and that is a wrong one. [Of a dull fellow]

3 A gentleman who had been very unhappy in marriage, married immediately after his wife died: Johnson said, it was the triumph of hope over experience.

4 He said that few people had intellectual resources sufficient to forgo the pleasures of wine. They could not otherwise contrive how to fill the interval between dinner and supper. [1772]

5 Sir, it is so far from being natural for a man and a woman to live in a state of marriage, that we find all the motives that they have for remaining in that connection, and the restraints which civilised society imposes to prevent separation, are hardly sufficient to keep them together. [31 Mar. 1772]

6 There is more knowledge of the heart in one letter of Richardson's, than in all *Tom Jones*. [6 Apr.]

7 Much ... may be made of a Scotchman, if he be *caught* young. [(On Lord Mansfield) 1772]

8 'What (said Elphinston), have you read it through?' ... 'No, Sir, do *you* read books *through?*' [19 Apr. 1773]

9 Read over your compositions, and where ever you meet with a passage which you think is particularly fine, strike it out. [(Quoting a college tutor) 30 Apr.]

10 The woman's a whore, and there's an end on't. (Lady Diana Beauclerk) 7 May]

11 I hope I shall never be deterred from detecting what I think a cheat, by the menaces of a ruffian. [Letter to James Macpherson, Feb. 1775]

12 There are few ways in which a man can be more innocently employed than in getting money. [(To William Strahan) 27 Mar.]

13 A man will turn over half a library to make one book. [6 Apr.]

14 Patriotism is the last refuge of a scoundrel. [7 Apr.]

15 Knowledge is of two kinds. We know a subject ourselves, or we know where we can find information upon it. [18 Apr.]

16 In lapidary inscriptions a man is not upon oath. [1775]

17 Nothing odd will do long. *Tristram Shandy* did not last. [20 Mar. 1776]

18 There is nothing which has yet been contrived by man, by which so much happiness is produced as by a good tavern or inn. [21 Mar.]

19 BOSWELL: Sir, you observed one day ... that a man is never happy for the present, but when he is drunk. Will you not add, – or when driving rapidly in a post-chaise?
JOHNSON: No, Sir, you are driving rapidly *from* something, or *to* something. [29 Mar.]

20 If a madman were to come into this room with a stick in his hand, no doubt we should pity the state of his mind; but our primary consideration would be to take care of ourselves. We should knock him down first, and pity him afterwards. [3 Apr.]

21 No man but a blockhead ever wrote, except for money. [5 Apr.]

22 A man who has not been in Italy, is always conscious of an inferiority. [11 Apr.]

23 BOSWELL: Then, Sir, what is poetry?
JOHNSON: Why, Sir, it is much easier to say what it is not. We all *know* what light is; but it is not easy to *tell* what it is.

24 *Olivarii Goldsmith, Poetae, Physici, Historici, qui nullum fere scribendi genus non tetigit, nullum quod tetigit non ornavit.* – To Oliver Goldsmith, poet, naturalist, and historian, who left hardly any style of writing untouched, and touched nothing that he did not adorn. [(Goldsmith's epitaph) 22 June]

25 If ... I had no duties, and no reference to futurity, I would spend my life in driving briskly in a post-chaise with a pretty woman. [19 Sept. 1777]

26 Depend upon it, Sir, when a man knows he is to be hanged in a fortnight, it concentrates his mind wonderfully.

27 When a man is tired of London he is tired of life; for there is in London all that life can afford. [20 Sept.]

28 It is wonderful that five thousand years have now elapsed since the creation of the world, and still it is undecided whether or not there has ever been an instance of the spirit of any person

appearing after death. All argument is against it; but all belief is for it. [31 Mar. 1778]

1 Every man thinks meanly of himself for not having been a soldier, or not having been at sea. [10 Apr.]

2 I am willing to love all mankind, *except an American.* [15 Apr.]

3 All censure of a man's self is oblique praise. It is in order to show how much he can spare. [25 Apr.]

4 I have always said, the first Whig was the Devil. [28 Apr.]

5 If it rained knowledge, I'd hold out my hand; but I would not give myself the trouble to go in quest of it. [12 May]

6 Claret is the liquor for boys; port for men; but he who aspires to be a hero . . . must drink brandy. [7 Apr. 1779]

7 BOSWELL: Is not the Giant's Causeway worth seeing?

JOHNSON: Worth seeing? yes; but not worth going to see. [12 Oct.]

8 If you are idle, be not solitary; if you are solitary, be not idle. [(Letter to Boswell) 27 Oct.]

9 Greek, Sir, . . . is like lace; every man gets as much of it as he can. [1780]

10 Sir, your wife, *under pretence of keeping a bawdy-house,* is a receiver of stolen goods.

11 There are people whom one should like very well to drop, but would not wish to be dropped by. [Mar. 1781]

12 He fills a chair. [(Lord North) 1 Apr.]

13 Sir, I have two cogent reasons for not printing any list of subscribers; – one, that I have lost all the names, – the other, that I have spent all the money. [May]

14 My dear friend, clear your *mind* of cant. [15 May 1783]

15 As I know more of mankind I expect less of them, and am ready now to call a man *a good man,* upon easier terms than I was formerly. [Sept.]

16 I should as soon think of contradicting a bishop. [(Of George Psalmanazar) 15 May 1784]

17 Milton . . . was a genius that could cut a Colossus from a rock, but could not carve heads upon cherry-stones. [13 June].

18 Who drives fat oxen should himself be fat. [(Line composed in parody of a line in a tragedy) June].

19 Sir, I have found you an argument; but I am not obliged to find you an understanding.

20 Sir, . . . there is not a sapling upon Parnassus more severely blown about by every wind of criticism. [Of a vain author]

21 A lawyer has no business with the justice or injustice of the cause which he undertakes, unless his client asks his opinion, and then he is bound to give it honestly. The justice or injustice of the cause is to be decided by the judge. [Boswell, *Tour of the Hebrides*, 15 Aug. 1773]

22 True, Sir; but sensation is sensation. [(On the 'kindness' of a tedious visit) 23 Aug.]

23 I have, all my life long, been lying till noon; yet I tell all young men, and tell them with great sincerity, that nobody who does not rise early will ever do any good. [14 Sept.]

24 I inherited a vile melancholy from my father, which has made me mad all my life, at least not sober. [16 Sept.]

25 Wickedness is always easier than virtue; for it takes the short cut to everything. [17 Sept.]

26 I am always sorry when any language is lost, because languages are the pedigree of nations. [18 Sept.]

27 I do not like much to see a Whig in any dress; but I hate to see a Whig in a parson's gown. [24 Sept.]

28 A fellow who makes no figure in company, and has a mind as narrow as the neck of a vinegar cruet. [30 Sept.]

29 A cucumber should be well sliced, and dressed with pepper and vinegar, and then thrown out, as good for nothing. [5 Oct.]

30 By seeing London, I have seen as much of life as the world can show. [11 Oct.]

31 It is ridiculous for a Whig to pretend to be honest. He cannot hold it out. [21 Oct.]

32 A man may be very sincere in good principles, without having good practice. [25 Oct.]

33 Sir, the noblest prospect that a Scotchman ever sees, is the high road that leads him to London. [10 Nov.]

34 I am sorry I have not learnt to play at cards. It is very useful in life: it generates kindness, and consolidates society. [11 Nov.]

1 Wheresoe'er I turn my view, / All is strange, yet nothing new; / Endless labour all along, / Endless labour to be wrong. [*Anecdotes of Johnson* by Mrs Piozzi]

2 Hermit hoar, in solemn cell, / Wearing out life's evening gray; / Strike thy bosom, sage! and tell / What is bliss, and which the way? / Thus I spoke, and speaking sighed, / Scarce repressed the starting tear, / When the hoary sage replied, / 'Come, my lad, and drink some beer.'

3 If a man who turnips cries, / Cry not when his father dies, / 'Tis a proof that he had rather / Have a turnip than a father. ['Burlesque of lines by Lope de Vega']

4 Dear Bathurst ... was a man to my very heart's content: he hated a fool, and he hated a rogue, and he hated a Whig; he was a very good hater.

5 Life is a pill which none of us can bear to swallow without gilding.

6 He will not, whither he is now gone, find much difference, I believe, either in the climate or the company. [Of a gentleman from Jamaica, recently dead]

7 I would advise no man to marry, Sir, ... who is not likely to propagate understanding.

8 You could not stand five minutes with that man [Edmund Burke] beneath a shed while it rained, but you must be convinced you had been standing with the greatest man you had ever yet seen. [Also quoted by Boswell]

9 Was there ever yet anything written by mere man that was wished longer by its readers, excepting *Don Quixote, Robinson Crusoe,* and the *Pilgrim's Progress?*

10 It is all cant; the dog knows he is miserable all the time. [On being told that anyone was happy]

11 I have heard him assert, that a tavern chair was the throne of human felicity. [Hawkins, *Life of Johnson*]

12 Difficult do you call it, Sir? I wish it were impossible. [(Of a violinist's playing) *Anecdotes by William Seward*]

13 Love is the wisdom of the fool and the folly of the wise. [William Cooke, *Life of Samuel Foote*]

14 No two men can be half an hour together, but one shall acquire an evident superiority over the other. [Attr.]

JOHN BENN JOHNSTONE 1803–1891

15 I want you to assist me in forcing her on board the lugger; once there, I'll frighten her into marriage. [(Commonly quoted as: 'Once aboard the lugger and the girl is mine') *The Gipsy Farmer*]

HANNS JOHST 1890–1978

16 When I hear anyone talk of culture, I reach for my revolver. [*Schlageter,* usually attr. wrongly to H. Goering. See 179:14]

AL JOLSON 1886–1950

17 You ain't heard nothin' yet, folks. [Remark in the first talking film, *The Jazz Singer,* July 1927]

JOHN PAUL JONES 1747–1792

18 I have not yet begun to fight. [Attr. as his ship, the *Bonhomme Richard,* appeared to be sinking after engaging with HMS *Serapis,* off Flamborough Head, Yorkshire, 23 Sept. 1779]

SIR WILLIAM JONES 1746–1794

19 Seven hours to law, to soothing slumber seven, / Ten to the world allot, and all to heaven. [*Lines in Substitution for those of Sir Edward Coke* (See 116:12)]

BEN JONSON 1573–1637

20 Fortune, that favours fools. [*The Alchemist,* Prologue]

21 I have a humour, / I would not willingly be gulled. [II. i]

22 Bells are profane, a tune may be religious. [III. ii]

23 I will eat exceedingly, and prophesy. [*Bartholomew Fair,* I. vi]

24 This is the very womb and bed of enormity. [II. i]

25 Neither do thou lust after that tawny weed tobacco. [vi]

26 Slow, slow, fresh fount, keep time with my salt tears; / Yet slower yet, O faintly, gentle springs. [*Cynthia's Revels,* I. i]

27 Queen and huntress, chaste and fair, / Now the sun is laid to sleep, / Seated in thy silver chair, / State in wonted manner keep: / Hesperus entreats thy light, / Goddess, excellently bright. [V. iii]

1 If he were / To be made honest by an act of parliament, / I should not alter in my faith of him. [*The Devil is an Ass*, IV. i]

2 Still to be neat, still to be drest, / As you were going to a feast. [*Epicœne*, I. i]

3 Lady, it is to be presumed, / Though art's hid causes are not found, / All is not sweet, all is not sound.

4 Such sweet neglect more taketh me, / Than all the adulteries of art; / They strike mine eyes, but not my heart.

5 Have you a stool there to be melancholy upon? [*Every Man in His Humour*, III. i]

6 I do hold it, and will affirm it before any prince in Europe, to be the most sovereign and precious weed that ever the earth rendered to the use of man. |ii]

7 I do honour the very flea of his dog. [IV. ii].

8 Apes are apes, though clothed in scarlet. [*The Poetasters*, V]

9 'Twas only fear first in the world made gods. [*Sejanus*, II. ii]

10 Good morning to the day: and next, my gold! – / Open the shrine that I may see my saint. [*Volpone*, I. i]

11 Come, my Celia, let us prove, / While we can, the sports of love. [III. vi]

12 Suns that set may rise again, / But if once we lose this light, / 'Tis with us perpetual night.

13 Have you seen but a bright lily grow, / Before rude hands have touched it? / Have you marked but the fall o' the snow / Before the soil hath smutched it? . . . O so white! O so soft! O so sweet is she! [*Celebration of Charis*, IV, 'Her Triumph']

14 She is Venus when she smiles; / But she's Juno when she walks, / And Minerva when she talks. [V]

15 Underneath this stone doth lie / As much beauty as could die. [*Epitaph on Elizabeth L. H.*]

16 It is not growing like a tree / In bulk, doth make men better be. [*Ode on the Death of Sir H. Morison*]

17 Wherein the graver had a strife / With Nature to out-do the life. [*On the Portrait of Shakespeare*]

18 Reader, look / Not on his picture, but his book.

19 Follow a shadow, it still flies you, / Seem to fly it, it will pursue. / So court a mistress, she denies you; / Let her alone, she will court you. / Say, are not women truly, then / Styled but the shadows of us men? [Song: *That Women are but Men's Shadows*]

20 Drink to me only with thine eyes, / And I will pledge with mine; / Or leave a kiss but in the cup, / And I'll not look for wine. [*To Celia*]

21 Soul of the Age! / The applause! delight! the wonder of our stage! / My Shakespeare, rise; I will not lodge thee by / Chaucer, or Spenser, or bid Beaumont lie / A little further, to make thee a room; / Thou art a monument without a tomb. [*To the Memory of Shakespeare*]

22 Sporting Kyd, or Marlowe's mighty line.

23 And though thou hadst small Latin, and less Greek.

24 He was not of an age, but for all time!

25 For a good poet's made as well as born.

26 Sweet swan of Avon!

27 I remember the players have often mentioned it as an honour to Shakespeare that in his writing (whatsoever he penned) he never blotted out a line. My answer hath been, 'Would he had blotted a thousand.' [*Timber, or Discoveries*, 64]

28 For I loved the man, and do honour his memory, on this side idolatry, as much as any. [Shakespeare]

29 There was ever more in him to be praised than to be pardoned. [Shakespeare]

30 The fear of every man that heard him was, lest he should make an end. [(Bacon) 78]

31 In his adversity I ever prayed, that God would give him strength; for greatness he could not want. [(Bacon) 80]

32 O rare Ben Jonson. [Epitaph on his tombstone]

DOROTHEA JORDAN 1762–1816

33 'Oh where, and Oh where is your Highland laddie gone?' / 'He's gone to fight the French, for King George upon the throne, / And it's Oh! in my heart, how I wish him safe at home!' [*The Blue Bells of Scotland*]

BENJAMIN JOWETT 1817–1893

34 The lie in the Soul is a true lie. [From the Introduction to his trans. of Plato's *Republic*]

JAMES JOYCE 1882–1941

1 riverrun, past Eve and Adam's, from swerve of shore to bend of bay, brings us by a commodius vicus of recirculation back to Howth Castle and Environs. [*Finnegans Wake* (1939), Pt I. p. 1]

2 the redaction known as the Sayings Attributive to H. C. Earwicker, prize on schillings, postlots free. [p. 36]

3 Have you heard of one Humpty Dumpty / How he fell with a roll and a rumble / And curled up like Lord Olofa Crumble / By the butt of the Magazine Wall, / (Chorus) Of the Magazine Wall, / Hump helmet and all? ['The Ballad of Persse O'Reilly'. 45]

4 He was fafafather of all schemes to bother us / Slow coaches and immaculate contraceptives for the populace.

5 Like the bumping bull of the Cassidys / All your butter is in your horns.

6 Mind my duvetyne dress above all! It's golded silvy, the newest sextones with princess effect. For Rutland blue's got out of passion. [148]

7 The Mookse and the Gripes, Gentes and laitymen, fullstopppers and semi-colonials, hybreds and lubberds! Eins within a space and a wearywide space it wast ere wohned a Mookse. [152]

8 Shem is as short for Shemus as Jem is joky for Jacob. [169]

9 O / tell me all about / Anna Livia! I want to hear all / about Anna Livia. Well, you know Anna Livia? Yes, of course, we all know Anna Livia. Tell me all. Tell me now. [196]

10 Can't hear with the waters of. The chittering waters of. Flittering bats, fieldmice bawk talk. Ho! Are you not gone ahome? [215]

11 Dark hawks near us. Night! Night! My ho head halls. I feel as heavy as yonder stone.

12 Beside the rivering waters of, hitherand-thithering waters of Night! [216]

13 Voyaging after maidens, belly jonah hunting the polly joans. [II. 323]

14 Three quarks for Muster Mark!

15 The Gracehoper was always jigging a jog, hoppy on akkant of his joyicity. [III. 414]

16 *The thing pleased him andt, and andt, / He larved ond he larved on he merd such a nauses / The Gracehoper feared he would mixplace his fauces.* [418]

17 A Portrait of the Artist as a Young Man. [Title of book]

18 Ireland is the old sow that eats her farrow. [Ch. 5]

19 I go to encounter for the millionth time the reality of experience, and to forge in the smithy of my soul the uncreated conscience of my race. Old father, old artificer, stand me now and ever in good stead. [Final words of Stephen Daedalus]

20 The snotgreen sea. The scrotumtightening sea. [*Ulysses* (Bodley Head, 1937), p. 3]

21 When I makes tea I makes tea, as old mother Grogan said. And when I makes water I makes water. [10]

22 History, Stephen said, is a nightmare from which I am trying to awake. [31]

23 As we read in the first chapter of Guinness'es. [122]

24 I caught a cold in the park. The gate was open. [126]

25 Gold by bronze heard iron steel. [256]

26 There's a bloody sight more pox than pax about that boyo. [(Of Edward VII) 315]

27 I dream of wellfilled hose. [351]

28 I regard him as the whitest man I know. He is down on his luck at present owing to the mortgaging of his extensive property at Agendath Netaim in faraway Asia Minor, slides of which will now be shown. [442 (See also 195:11, 247:21)]

29 I belong to the *faubourg Saint-Patrice* called Ireland for short [606]

30 Your battles inspired me – not the obvious material battles but those that were fought and won behind your forehead. [Letter to Henrik Ibsen, March 1901]

EMPEROR JULIAN, THE APOSTATE
  c. 331–363

31 *Vicisti, Galilaee.* – Thou hast conquered, O Galilean. [Latin translation of alleged dying words]

JULIANA OF NORWICH 14 Cent.

32 Sin is behovely, but all shall be well and all shall be well and all manner of thing shall be well. [*Revelations of Divine Love*, Ch. 27]

C. G. JUNG 1875–1961

1 A more or less superficial layer of the unconscious is undoubtedly personal. I call it the personal unconscious. But this personal unconscious rests upon a deeper layer, which does not derive from personal experience and is not a personal acquisition but is inborn. The deeper layer I call the collective unconscious . . . it has contents and modes of behaviour that are more or less the same everywhere and in all individuals. [*Archetypes and the Collective Unconscious*]

2 As far as we can discern, the sole purpose of human existence is to kindle a light in the darkness of mere being. [*Memories, Dreams, Reflections*, Ch. 11]

3 Religion, it might be said, is the term that designates the attitude peculiar to a consciousness which has been altered by the experience of the *numinosum*. [*Psychology and Religion*, Ch. 1]

4 Show me a sane man and I will cure him for you. [Quoted by Vincent Brome in the *Observer*, 19 July 1975]

5 The true leader is always led. [Quoted in the *Guardian Weekly*, 30 Oct. 1976]

6 I do not believe . . . I know. [(When asked if he believed in God.) Quoted in Laurens van der Post, *Jung and the Story of Our Time*]

7 We need more understanding of human nature, because the only real danger that exists is man himself . . . We know nothing of man, far too little. His psyche should be studied because we are the origin of all coming evil. [In BBC TV 'Face to Face' interview with John Freeman]

JUNIUS [identity unknown] 18 Cent.

8 The liberty of the Press is the *Palladium* of all the civil, political, and religious rights of an Englishman. [*Letters*, Dedication]

9 In all the mazes of metaphorical confusion. [7]

10 It is not that you do wrong by design, but that you should never do right by mistake. [12]

11 There is a holy mistaken zeal in politics as well as in religion. By persuading others, we convince ourselves. [35]

12 Whether it be the heart to conceive, the understanding to direct, or the hand to execute. [37]

13 The injustice done to an individual is sometimes of service to the public. [41]

GENERAL JUNOT 1771–1813

14 I am my own ancestor. [On being created duke]

JUVENAL 60–c. 130

15 *Probitas laudatur et alget.* – Honesty is praised and starves. [*Satires*, I. 74]

16 *Quidquid agunt homines, votum timor ira voluptas / Gaudia discursus nostri farrago libelli est.* – All men's activities – their wishes, fears, anger, pleasures, joys, and miscellaneous pursuits – is the hodge-podge of my book. [85]

17 *Dat veniam corvis, vexat censura columbas.* – Censure acquits the raven, but pursues the dove. [II. 63]

18 *Nemo repente fuit turpissimus.* – No one ever reached the depths of wickedness all at once. [83]

19 *Grammaticus rhetor geometres pictor aliptes / Augur schoenobates medicus magus, omnia novit / Graeculus esuriens; in caelum miseris, ibit.* – Grammarian, rhetorician, geometer, painter, ringmaster, soothsayer, rope-dancer, physician, magician – he knows everything. Tell the hungry little Greek to go to heaven, and he will go. [III. 76]

20 *Nil habet infelix paupertas durius in se / Quam quod ridiculos homines facit.* – Poverty is bitter, but it has no harder pang than that it makes men ridiculous. [152]

21 *Haud facile emergunt quorum virtutibus obstat / Res angusta domi.* – It is not easy for men to emerge from obscurity if their qualities are thwarted by narrow means at home. [164]

22 *Hic vivimus ambitiosa / Paupertate omnes.* – Here we all live in a state of ambitious poverty. [182]

23 *Omnia Romae / Cum pretio.* – At Rome, all things can be had at a price. [183]

24 *Rara avis in terris nigroque simillima cycno.* – A rare bird on earth, and very like a black swan. [VI. 165]

25 *Hoc volo, sic iubeo, sit pro ratione voluntas.* – I wish it, I command it. Let my will take the place of a reason. [223]

26 *Nulla fere causa est, in qua non femina litem*

moverit. – There is hardly a case in which the dispute was not caused by a woman. [242]

1 *Quis custodiet ipsos / Custodes?* – Who is to guard the guards themselves? [347]

2 *Tenet insanabile multos / Scribendi cacoethes et aegro in corde senescit.* – An inveterate and incurable itch for writing besets many and grows old with their sick hearts. [VII. 51. See 176:5]

3 *Occidit miseros crambe repetita magistros.* – Warmed up cabbage wears out the poor master's life. [154]

4 *Nobilitas sola est atque unica virtus.* – Virtue is the one and only nobility. [VIII. 20]

5 *Cantabit vacuus coram latrone viator.* – The traveller with empty pockets will sing in the thief's face. [X. 22]

6 *Duas tantum res anxius optat, / Panem et circenses.* – Limits the Romans' anxieties to two things – bread and games. [80]

7 *Orandum est ut sit mens sana in corpore sano.* – Your prayer must be for a sound mind in a sound body. [356]

8 *Prima est haec ultio quod se / Iudice nemo nocens absolvitur.* This is the first punishment, that by the verdict of his own heart no guilty man is acquitted. [XIII. 2]

K

FRANZ KAFKA 1883–1924

1 You may object that it is not a trial at all; you are quite right, for it is only a trial if I recognize it as such. [*The Trial*, 2, 'First Interrogation']

2 It's often safer to be in chains than to be free. [8]

3 Let me remind you of the old maxim: people under suspicion are better moving than at rest, since at rest they may be sitting in the balance without knowing it, being weighed together with their sins.

4 'But I am not guilty,' said K.; 'it's a misunderstanding. And if it comes to that, how can any man be called guilty?' [9, 'In the Cathedral']

5 If the French were German in their essence, then how the Germans would admire them! [*The Diaries of Franz Kafka*, 17 Dec. 1910]

GUS KAHN 1886–1941

6 Yes sir, That's my Baby; / No sir, Don't mean maybe; / Yes sir, That's my Baby now. [Song: *Yes Sir, That's My Baby*, music by Walter Donaldson]

GUS KAHN and RAYMOND B. EGAN 1890–1952

7 There's nothing surer, / The rich get rich and the poor get poorer, / In the meantime, in between time, / Ain't we got fun. [Song: *Ain't We got Fun*]

IMMANUEL KANT 1724–1804

8 Two things fill my mind with ever-increasing wonder and awe, the more often and the more intensely the reflection dwells on them: the starry heavens above me and the moral law within me. [*Critique of Pure Reason*, conclusion]

9 A categorical imperative would be one which represented an action as objectively necessary in itself, without reference to any other purpose. [*Fundamental Principles of Morals*, 2]

ALPHONSE KARR 1808–1890

10 *Si l'on veut abolir la peine de mort en ce cas, que MM. les assassins commencent.* – If we are to abolish the death penalty, let our friends the murderers make the first move. [*Les Guêpes*, 1840]

11 *Plus ça change, plus c'est la même chose.* – The more things change, the more they are the same. [Jan. 1849]

GEORGE S. KAUFMAN 1889–1961

12 Satire is something that closes on Saturday night. [Quoted in R. E. Drennan, *Wit's End*]

TED KAVANAGH 1892–1958

13 'After you, Claude.' / 'No, after you, Cecil.' [*Itma*, BBC Radio comedy series, catchphrase]

14 Can I do you now, sir? [Mrs Mop]

15 Don't forget the diver.

16 Foonf speaking.

17 I don't mind if I do. [Colonel Chinstrap]

1 It's being so cheerful as keeps me going. [Mona Lott.]

2 Wot, me? In my state of health! [Charles Atlas]

DENIS KEARNEY 1847–1907

3 Horny-handed sons of toil. [Speech in San Francisco, c. 1878]

JOHN KEATS 1795–1821

4 Bards of Passion and of Mirth, / Ye have left your souls on earth! Have ye souls in heaven too? [*Bards of Passion and of Mirth*]

5 The imagination of a boy is healthy, and the mature imagination of a man is healthy; but there is a space of life between, in which the soul is in a ferment, the character undecided, the way of life uncertain, the ambition thick-sighted: thence proceeds mawkishness. [*Endymion*, Preface]

6 A thing of beauty is a joy for ever: / Its loveliness increases; it will never / Pass into nothingness. [Bk i. 1]

7 Solitary thinkings; such as dodge / Conception to the very bourne of heaven, / Then leave the naked brain. [294]

8 Pleasure is oft a visitant; but pain / Clings cruelly to us. [906]

9 O Sorrow, / Why dost borrow / Heart's lightness from the merriment of May? [iv. 164]

10 To Sorrow / I bade good-morrow, / And thought to leave her far away behind; / But cheerly, cheerly, / She loves me dearly; / She is so constant to me, and so kind. [173]

11 Their smiles, / Wan as primroses gathered at midnight / By chilly-fingered Spring. [969]

12 It is a flaw / In happiness to see beyond our bourn, – / It forces us in summer skies to mourn, / It spoils the singing of the nightingale. [*Epistle to J. H. Reynolds*, 82]

13 St Agnes' Eve – Ah, bitter chill it was! / The owl, for all his feathers, was a-cold; / The hare limped trembling through the frozen grass, / And silent was the flock in woolly fold. [*The Eve of St Agnes*, 1]

14 Soon, up aloft, / The silver, snarling trumpets 'gan to chide. [4]

15 Upon the honeyed middle of the night. [6]

16 Out went the taper as she hurried in; / Its little smoke, in pallid moonshine, died. [23]

17 Full on this casement shone the wintry moon, / And threw warm gules on Madeline's fair breast. [25]

18 A heap / Of candied apple, quince, and plum, and gourd; / With jellies soother than the creamy curd, / And lucent syrops tinct with cinnamon. [30]

19 He played an ancient ditty, long since mute, / In Provence called 'La belle dame sans merci'. [33]

20 The arras, rich with horseman, hawk, and hound, / Fluttered in the besieging wind's uproar; / And the long carpets rose along the dusty floor. [40]

21 Fanatics have their dreams, wherewith they weave / A paradise for a sect. [*The Fall of Hyperion*, Bk i. 1]

22 Ever let the fancy roam, / Pleasure never is at home. [*Fancy*, 1]

23 Where's the cheek that doth not fade, / Too much gazed at? [69]

24 Where's the face / One would meet in every place? / Where's the voice, however soft, / One would hear so very oft? [73]

25 God of the golden bow, / And of the golden lyre, / And of the golden hair, / And of the golden fire, / Charioteer / Of the patient year, / Where – where slept thine ire? [*Hymn to Apollo*]

26 Deep in the shady sadness of a vale / Far sunken from the healthy breath of morn, / Far from the fiery noon, and eve's one star, / Sat gray-haired Saturn, quiet as a stone. [*Hyperion*, Bk i. 1]

27 No stir of air was there, / Not so much life as on a summer's day / Robs not one light seed from the feathered grass, / But where the dead leaf fell, there did it rest. [7]

28 O how frail / To that large utterance of the early Gods! [50]

29 As when, upon a trancèd summer-night, / Those green-robed senators of mighty woods, / Tall oaks, branch-charmèd by the earnest stars, / Dream, and so dream all night without a stir. [72]

30 A solitary sorrow best befits / Thy lips, and antheming a lonely grief. [iii. 5]

31 Point me out the way / To any one particular beauteous star. [99]

32 I stood tip-toe upon a little hill. ['*I stood tip-toe*', 1]

1 Here are sweet-peas, on tip-toe for a flight: / With wings of gentle flush o'er delicate white, / And taper fingers catching at all things, / To bind them all about with tiny rings. [57]

2 Lorenzo, a young palmer in Love's eye. [*Isabella*, 1]

3 Parting they seemed to tread upon the air, / Twin roses by the zephyr blown apart / Only to meet again more close. [10]

4 Why were they proud? again we ask aloud, / Why in the name of Glory were they proud? [16]

5 So the two brothers and their murdered man / Rode past fair Florence. [27]

6 O cruelty, / To steal my Basil-pot away from me! [63]

7 Oh what can ail thee, wretched wight, / Alone and palely loitering; / The sedge is withered from the lake, / And no birds sing. [*La Belle Dame sans Merci*, 1]

8 I see a lilly on thy brow, / With anguish moist and fever dew; / And on thy cheek a fading rose / Fast withereth too.

I met a lady in the meads / Full beautiful, a faery's child; / Her hair was long, her foot was light, / And her eyes were wild. [3]

9 She looked at me as she did love, / And made sweet moan. [6]

10 And sure in language strange she said, / I love thee true. [7]

11 And there I shut her wild, wild eyes / With kisses four. [(Lord Houghton's version) 8]

12 The latest dream I ever dreamed / On the cold hill side. [9]

13 I saw pale kings and princes too, / Pale warriors, death-pale were they all. / Who cry'd – 'La belle Dame sans merci / Hath thee in thrall!'

I saw their starved lips in the gloam / With horrid warning gapèd wide, / And I awoke, and found me here / On the cold hill side. [11]

14 Real are the dreams of Gods, and smoothly pass / Their pleasures in a long immortal dream. [*Lamia*, I. 127]

15 Love in a hut, with water and a crust, / Is – Love forgive us! – cinders, ashes, dust. [II. 1]

16 Philosophy will clip an angel's wings. [234]

17 Souls of poets dead and gone, / What Elysium have ye known, / Happy field or mossy cavern, / Choicer than the Mermaid Tavern? /

Have ye tippled drink more fine / Than mine host's Canary wine? [*Lines on the Mermaid Tavern*]

18 Thou still unravished bride of quietness, / Thou foster-child of silence and slow time. [*Ode on a Grecian Urn*, 1]

19 Heard melodies are sweet, but those unheard / Are sweeter; therefore, ye soft pipes, play on; / Not to the sensual ear, but, more endeared, / Pipe to the spirit ditties of no tone. [2]

20 She cannot fade, though thou hast not thy bliss, / For ever wilt thou love and she be fair.

21 For ever piping songs for ever new. [3]

22 All breathing human passion far above, / That leaves a heart high-sorrowful and cloyed, / A burning forehead and a parching tongue.

23 To what green altar, O mysterious priest, / Lead'st thou that heifer lowing at the skies, / And all her silken flanks with garlands drest? / What little town by river or sea shore, / Or mountain-built with peaceful citadel, / Is emptied of this folk, this pious morn? [4]

24 Thou, silent form, dost tease us out of thought / As doth eternity: Cold Pastoral! [5]

25 'Beauty is truth, truth beauty,' – That is all / Ye know on earth, and all ye need to know.

26 Leaving great verse unto a little clan. [*Ode to Maia*]

27 No, no, go not to Lethe, neither twist / Wolf's-bane, tight-rooted, for its poisonous wine. [*Ode on Melancholy*, 1]

28 But when the melancholy fit shall fall / Sudden from heaven like a weeping cloud, / That fosters the droop-headed flowers all, / And hides the green hill in an April shroud; / Then glut thy sorrow on a morning rose. [2]

29 She dwells with Beauty – Beauty that must die; / And Joy, whose hand is ever at his lips / Bidding adieu; and aching pleasure nigh, / Turning to Poison while the bee-mouth sips: / Ay, in the very temple of delight / Veiled Melancholy has her sovran shrine, / Though seen of none save him whose strenuous tongue / Can burst Joy's grape against his palate fine; / His soul shall taste the sadness of her might, / And be among her cloudy trophies hung. [3]

30 My heart aches, and a drowsy numbness pains / My sense, as though of hemlock I had drunk. [*Ode to a Nightingale*, 1]

John Keats

1 Thou, light-winged Dryad of the trees, / In some melodious plot / of beechen green, and shadows numberless, / Singest of summer in full-throated ease.

2 O for a draught of vintage! that hath been / Cooled a long age in the deep delvèd earth, / Tasting of flora and the country green, / Dance, and Provençal song, and sunburnt mirth! / O for a beaker full of the warm South, / Full of the true, the blushful Hippocrene, / With beaded bubbles winking at the brim, / And purple-stainèd mouth; / That I might drink, and leave the world unseen, / And with thee fade away into the forest dim.

Fade far away, dissolve, and quite forget / What thou among the leaves hast never known, / The weariness, the fever, and the fret / Here, where men sit and hear each other groan. [2]

3 Where youth grows pale and spectre-thin, and dies; / Where but to think is to be full of sorrow / And leaden-eyed despairs [3]

4 Away! away! for I will fly to thee, / Not charioted by Bacchus and his pards, / But on the viewless wings of Poesy. [4]

5 I cannot see what flowers are at my feet, / Nor what soft incense hangs upon the boughs. [5]

6 Mid-May's eldest child, / The coming musk-rose, full of dewy wine, / The murmurous haunt of flies on summer eves.

7 Darkling I listen; and, for many a time / I have been half in love with easeful death, / Called him soft names in many a musèd rhyme, / To take into the air my quiet breath; / Now more than ever it seems rich to die, / To cease upon the midnight with no pain, / While thou art pouring forth thy soul abroad / In such an ecstasy! / Still wouldst thou sing, and I have ears in vain – / To thy high requiem become a sod.

Thou wast not born for death, immortal Bird! / No hungry generations tread thee down; / The voice I hear this passing night was heard / In ancient days by emperor and clown: / Perhaps the self-same song that found a path / Through the sad heart of Ruth, when, sick for home, / She stood in tears amid the alien corn; / The same that oft-times hath / Charmed magic casements, opening on the foam / Of perilous seas, in faery lands forlorn.

Forlorn! the very word is like a bell / To toll me back from thee to my sole self! [6]

8 Thy plaintive anthem fades / Past the near meadows, over the still stream, / Up the hill-side; and now 'tis buried deep / In the next valley-glades: / Was it a vision or a waking dream? / Fled is that music: – Do I wake or sleep? [8]

9 O latest born and loveliest vision far / Of all Olympus' faded hierarchy. [*Ode to Psyche* 24]

10 Virgin-choir to make delicious moan / Upon the midnight hours. [30]

11 All the gardener Fancy e'er could feign, / Who breeding flowers, will never breed the same. [62]

12 A bright torch, and a casement ope at night, / To let the warm Love in. [66]

13 Stop and consider! life is but a day; / A fragile dew-drop on its perilous way / From a tree's summit; a poor Indian's sleep / While his boat hastens to the monstrous steep / Of Montmorenci. [*Sleep and Poetry*, 85]

14 O for ten years, that I may overwhelm / Myself in poesy; so I may do the deed / That my own soul has to itself decreed. [96]

15 A drainless shower / Of light is poesy; 'tis the supreme power; / 'Tis might half slumbering on his own right arm. [235]

16 They shall be accounted poet kings / Who simply tell the most heart-easing things. [267]

17 There was a naughty Boy, / And a naughty boy was he, / He ran away to Scotland / The people for to see – / Then he found / That the ground / Was as hard, / That a yard / Was as long, / That a song / Was as merry, / That a cherry / Was as red – / That lead / Was as weighty, / That fourscore / Was as eighty, / That a door / Was as wooden / As in England – / So he stood in his shoes / And he wondered. [*A Song about Myself*]

18 Bright star, would I were steadfast as thou art – / Not in lone splendour hung aloft the night / And watching, with eternal lids apart, / Like Nature's patient, sleepless Eremite, / The moving waters at their priestlike task / Of pure ablution round earth's human shores. [Sonnet: *Bright Star*]

19 Still, still to hear her tender-taken breath, / And so live ever – or else swoon to death.

20 Happy is England, sweet her artless daughters; / Enough their simple loveliness for me. [Sonnet: *Happy is England*]

1 Four seasons fill the measure of the year; / There are four seasons in the mind of man. [Sonnet: *The Human Seasons*]

2 Much have I travelled in the realms of gold, / And many goodly states and kingdoms seen; / Round many western islands have I been / Which bards in fealty to Apollo hold. [Sonnet: *On First Looking into Chapman's Homer*]

3 Then felt I like some watcher of the skies / When a new planet swims into his ken; / Or like stout Cortez, when with eagle eyes / He stared at the Pacific – and all his men / Looked at each other with a wild surmise – / Silent, upon a peak in Darien.

4 It keeps eternal whispering around / Desolate shores. [Sonnet: *On the Sea*]

5 Mortality / Weighs heavily on me like unwilling sleep. [Sonnet: *On seeing the Elgin Marbles*]

6 There is a budding morrow in midnight, / There is a triple sight in blindness keen. [Sonnet: *To Homer*]

7 To one who has been long in city pent, / 'Tis very sweet to look into the fair / And open face of heaven. [Sonnet: *To one who has been long in city pent*]

8 O soft embalmer of the still midnight, / Shutting, with careful fingers and benign / Our gloom-pleased eyes. [Sonnet: *To Sleep*]

9 Turn the key deftly in the oilèd wards, / And seal the hushèd Casket of my Soul.

10 When I have fears that I may cease to be / Before my pen has gleaned my teeming brain. [Sonnet: *When I have fears*]

11 When I behold, upon the night's starred face, / Huge cloudy symbols of a high romance.

12 Then on the shore / Of the wide world I stand alone, and think / Till love and fame to nothingness do sink.

13 Verse, Fame and Beauty are intense indeed, / But Death intenser – Death is Life's high meed. [Sonnet: *Why did I laugh to-night?*]

14 In a drear-nighted December, / Too happy, happy tree, / Thy branches ne'er remember / Their green felicity. [*Stanzas In a Drear-nighted December*]

15 But were there ever any / Writhed not at passed joy?

16 Season of mists and mellow fruitfulness, / Close bosom-friend of the maturing sun; / Conspiring with him how to load and bless / With fruit the vines that round the thatch-eaves run. [*To Autumn*, 1]

17 To set budding more, / And still more, later flowers for the bees, / Until they think warm days will never cease, / For summer has o'er-brimmed their clammy cells.

18 On a half-reapèd furrow sound asleep, / Drowsed with the fume of poppies, while thy hook / Spares the next swath and all its twinèd flowers. [2]

19 Where are the songs of Spring? Ay, where are they? / Think not of them, thou hast thy music too, [3]

20 Then in a wailful choir the small gnats mourn.

21 The red-breast whistles from a garden-croft; / And gathering swallows twitter in the skies.

22 A man should have the fine point of his soul taken off to become fit for this world. [Letter to J. H. Reynolds, 22 Nov. 1817]

23 I am certain of nothing but the holiness of the heart's affections and the truth of the imagination. – What the imagination seizes as beauty must be truth. [Letter to Benjamin Bailey, 22 Nov.]

24 I have never yet been able to perceive how anything can be known for truth by consecutive reasoning – and yet it must be.

25 O for a life of sensations rather than of thoughts!

26 Negative Capability, that is, when a man is capable of being in uncertainties, mysteries, doubts, without any irritable reaching after fact and reason. [Letter to G. and T. Keats, 21 Dec.]

27 There is nothing stable in the world; uproar's your only music. [Letter to G. and T. Keats, 13 Jan. 1818]

28 We hate poetry that has a palpable design upon us – and if we do not agree, seems to put its hand in its breeches pocket. Poetry should be great and unobtrusive, a thing which enters into one's soul, and does not startle or amaze it with itself, but with its subject. [Letter to J. H. Reynolds, 3 Feb.]

29 Poetry should surprise by a fine excess, and not by singularity; it should strike the reader as a wording of his own highest thoughts, and appear almost a remembrance. [Letter to John Taylor, 27 Feb.]

30 If poetry comes not as naturally as the leaves to a tree it had better not come at all.

1 Scenery is fine – but human nature is finer. [Letter to Benjamin Bailey, 13 Mar.]

2 We read fine things but never feel them to the full until we have gone the same steps as the author. [Letter to J. H. Reynolds, 3 May]

3 I compare human life to a large mansion of many apartments, two of which I can only describe, the doors of the rest being as yet shut upon me.

4 Were it in my choice I would reject a petrarchal coronation – on account of my dying day, and because women have cancers. [Letter to Benjamin Bailey, 10 June]

5 I wish I could say Tom was any better. His identity presses upon me so all day that I am obliged to go out. [Letter to C. W. Dilke, 21 Sept.]

6 I would sooner fail than not be among the greatest. [Letter to J. A. Hessey, 9 Oct.]

7 I think I shall be among the English poets after my death. [Letter to G. and G. Keats, 14 Oct.]

8 The roaring of the wind is my wife and the stars through the window pane are my children.

9 A poet is the most unpoetical of anything in existence, because he has no identity – he is continually informing and filling some other body. [Letter to R. Woodhouse, 27 Oct.]

10 It is true that in the height of enthusiasm I have been cheated into some fine passages; but that is not the thing. [Letter to B. R. Haydon, 8 Mar. 1819]

11 A man's life of any worth is a continual allegory – and very few eyes can see the mystery of his life – a life like the scriptures – figurative. [Letter to G. and G. Keats, 14 Feb. – 3 May]

12 Shakespeare led a life of allegory; his works are the comments on it.

13 Call the world if you please 'The Vale of Soul-making'.

14 I have two luxuries to brood over in my walks, your loveliness and the hour of my death. O that I could have possession of them both in the same minute. [Letter to Fanny Brawne, 25 July]

15 The only means of strengthening one's intellect is to make up one's mind about nothing – to let the mind be a thoroughfare for all thoughts. [Letter to G. and G. Keats, 17-27 Sept.]

16 'If I should die', said I to myself, 'I have left no immortal work behind me – nothing to make my friends proud of my memory – but I have loved the principle of beauty in all things, and if I had had time I would have made myself remembered.' [Letter to Fanny Brawne, Feb. 1820(?)]

17 You might curb your magnanimity, and be more of an artist, and load every rift of your subject with ore. [Letter to P. B. Shelley, Aug. 1820]

18 Here lies one whose name was writ in water. [Epitaph, written by himself]

JOHN KEBLE 1792–1866

19 New every morning is the love / Our wakening and uprising prove. [The Christian Year, 'Morning']

20 We need not bid, for cloistered cell, / Our neighbour and our work farewell. / Nor strive to wind ourselves too high / For sinful man beneath the sky.

21 The trivial round, the common task, / Would furnish all we ought to ask; / Room to deny ourselves, a road / To bring us, daily, nearer God.

22 And help us, this and every day, / To live more nearly as we pray.

23 Sun of my soul! Thou Saviour dear, / It is not night if thou be near. ['Evening']

24 Abide with me from morn to eve, / For without Thee I cannot live: / Abide with me when night is nigh. / For without Thee I dare not die.

25 Be every mourner's sleep tonight / Like infant's slumbers, pure and light.

26 The voice that breathed o'er Eden, / That earliest wedding day. [Poems, 'Holy Matrimony']

THOMAS KELLY 1769–1854

27 The Head that once was crowned with thorns / Is crowned with glory now. [Hymn]

WALT KELLY 1913–1973

28 We have met the enemy, and he is us. [In cartoon strip Pogo, parodying Captain Oliver Hazard Perry (1785–1819), 'We have met the

enemy and he is ours', at Battle of Lake Erie, 10 Sept. 1813]

J. P. KEMBLE 1757–1823

1 When late I attempted your pity to move, / Why seemed you so deaf to my prayers? / Perhaps it was right to dissemble your love, / But – why did you kick me downstairs? [*The Panel*, I. i (an adaptation of Isaac Bickerstaffe's comedy *'Tis Well 'tis no Worse*)]

THOMAS À KEMPIS *c.* 1380–1471

2 *O quam cito transit gloria mundi.* – Oh, how swiftly the glory of the world passes away! [*Imitation of Christ*, 3 (*Sic transit gloria mundi* – Thus passes the glory of the world – is used at the enthronement of a new Pope and is proverbial)]

3 It is much safer to obey than to rule. [9]

4 If you cannot mould yourself as you would wish, how can you expect other people to be entirely to your liking? [16]

5 Man proposes but God disposes. [19]

6 Would to God that we might spend a single day really well! [23]

JOHN KEMPTHORNE 1775–1838

7 Praise the Lord! ye heavens adore Him, / Praise Him, Angels in the height! [Hymn]

BISHOP THOMAS KEN 1637–1711

8 Awake, my soul, and with the sun / Thy daily stage of duty run; / Shake off dull sloth, and joyful rise, / To pay thy morning sacrifice. [*A Morning Hymn*]

9 Redeem thy mis-spent time that's past; / Live this day, as if 'twere thy last.

10 Teach me to live, that I may dread / The grave as little as my bed. [*An Evening Hymm*]

11 Praise God from whom all blessings flow, / Praise him all creatures here below. [*A Midnight Hymn*]

WILLIAM KENDRICK ?–1777

12 In durance vile. [*Falstaff's Wedding*, I. ii]

JIMMY KENNEDY 1902–1984

13 If you go down to the woods today / You're sure of a big surprise . . . / For every bear that ever there was / Will gather there for certain because / Today's the day the teddy bears have their picnic. [Song: *The Teddy Bears' Picnic* (music by John W. Bratton)]

PRESIDENT JOHN F. KENNEDY 1917–1963

14 We stand today on the edge of a new frontier. [Speech on his adoption as Democratic presidential candidate, 15 July 1960]

15 Let the word go forth from this time and place, to friend and foe alike, that the torch has been passed to a new generation of Americans – born in this century, tempered by war, disciplined by a hard and bitter peace. [Inaugural address as President, 20 Jan. 1961]

16 In the past, those who foolishly sought power by riding on the back of the tiger ended up inside.

17 Let us never negotiate out of fear. But let us never fear to negotiate.

18 Ask not what your country can do for you; ask what you can do for your country.

19 There's an old saying that victory has a hundred fathers, defeat is an orphan. [(Of Bay of Pigs) press conference, 21 Apr. 1961]

20 I think it's the most extraordinary collection of talent, of human knowledge, that has ever been gathered together at the White House – with the possible exception of when Thomas Jefferson dined alone. [At a dinner for Nobel prizewinners, 29 Apr. 1962]

21 The war against hunger is truly mankind's war of liberation. [Speech at opening of World Food Congress, 4 June 1963]

22 If we cannot now end our differences, at least we can help make the world safe for diversity. [Address, American University, Washington, DC, 10 June 1963]

23 All free men, wherever they may live, are citizens of Berlin. And therefore, as a free man, I take pride in the words: '*Ich bin ein Berliner*'. [Speech at West Berlin City Hall, 26 June 1963]

24 When power narrows the areas of man's concern, poetry reminds him of the richness and diversity of his existence. When power corrupts, poetry cleanses. [Address at Dedication of the Robert Frost Library, Amherst College, Mass., 26 Oct. 1963]

1 In free society art is not a weapon ... Artists are not engineers of the soul.

2 It was involuntary. They sank my boat. [(Remark when asked how he became a war hero) Arthur M. Schlesinger, jun., *A Thousand Days*, Ch. 4]

LADY CAROLINE KEPPEL 1735–?

3 O! they're all fled with thee, / Robin Adair. [*Robin Adair*]

JOSEPH KESSELRING 1902–

4 Arsenic and Old Lace. [Title of play]

WILLIAM KETHE ?–1608

5 All people that on earth do dwell, / Sing to the Lord with cheerful voice. [Hymn]

FRANCIS SCOTT KEY 1779–1843

6 'Tis the star-spangled banner, O! long may it wave / O'er the land of the free and the home of the brave! [*The Star-Spangled Banner*]

SIDNEY KEYES 1922–1943

7 He never loved the frenzy of the sun / Nor the clear seas. / He came with hero's arms and bullock's eyes / Afraid of nothing but his nagging gods. [*Dido's Lament for Aeneas*]

8 There is no virtue now in blind reliance / On place or person or the forms of love. / The storm bears down the pivotal tree, the cloud / Turns to the net of an inhuman fowler / And drags us from the air. [*The Kestrels*]

JOHN MAYNARD KEYNES 1883–1946

9 He [Clemenceau] had one illusion – France; and one disillusion – mankind. [*Economic Consequences of the Peace*, Ch. 4]

10 There is no harm in being sometimes wrong – especially if one is promptly found out. [*Essays in Biography*]

11 Regarded as a means, the businessman is tolerable; regarded as an end he is not so satisfactory. [*Essays in Persuasion*]

12 If the Treasury were to fill old bottles with banknotes, bury them at suitable depths in disused coalmines which are then filled up to the surface with town rubbish, and leave it to private enterprise on well-tried principles of *laissez-faire* to dig the notes up again ... there need be no more unemployment and, with the help of the repercussions, the real income of the community ... would probably become a good deal larger than it actually is. [*The General Theory of Employment*, Bk iii. Ch. 10]

13 It is better that a man should tyrannize over his bank balance than over his fellow citizens. [vi. 24]

14 The ideas of economists and political philosophers, both when they are right and when they are wrong, are more powerful than is commonly understood. Indeed the world is ruled by little else. Practical men, who believe themselves to be quite exempt from any intellectual influences, are usually the slaves of some defunct economist.

15 But this *long run* is a misleading guide to current affairs. *In the long run* we are all dead. [*A Tract on Monetary Reform*, Ch. 3]

16 Whenever you save 5s. you put a man out of work for a day. [(In 1931) *Observer*, 'Sayings of Our Times', 31 May 1953]

NIKITA S. KHRUSHCHEV 1894–1971

17 Comrades! We must abolish the cult of the individual decisively, once and for all. [(Often becomes 'the cult of personality') Speech to secret session of 20th Congress of Communist Party, 25 Feb. 1956]

18 Whether you like it or not, history is on our side. We will bury you. [Remark at Moscow reception, 18 Nov. 1956]

19 They talk about who won and who lost. Human reason won. Mankind won. [On the Cuban crisis. Quoted in the *Observer*, 11 Nov. 1962]

20 Politicians are the same all over. They promise to build a bridge even where there is no river. [Impromptu remark on visit to Yugoslavia, 21 Aug, 1963]

21 If you start throwing hedgehogs under me, I shall throw two porcupines under you. [Quoted in *Observer*, 'Sayings of the Week', 10 Nov. 1963]

SØREN KIERKEGAARD 1813–1855

22 *The Two Ways:* One is to suffer; the other is to become a professor of the fact that another

suffered. [W. H. Auden, *Kierkegaard Anthology*, p. 20]

1 That is the road we all have to take – over the Bridge of Sighs into eternity. [23]

2 Dread is a sympathetic antipathy and an antipathetic sympathy. [134]

JOYCE KILMER 1888–1918

3 I think that I shall never see / A poem lovely as a tree. [*Trees*. See also 292:16]

4 Poems are made by fools like me, / But only God can make a tree.

BENJAMIN KING 1857–1894

5 Nothing to do but work, / Nothing to eat but food, / Nothing to wear but clothes / To keep one from going nude. [*The Pessimist*]

6 Nowhere to fall but off, / Nowhere to stand but on!

BISHOP HENRY KING 1592–1669

7 Stay for me there; I will not fail / To meet thee in that hollow vale. / And think not much of my delay; / I am already on the way. [*The Exequy*, 79]

8 But hark! My pulse like a soft drum / Beats my approach, tells thee I come. [101]

MARTIN LUTHER KING, JUN. 1929–1968

9 I have a dream that my four little children will one day live in a nation where they will not be judged by the colour of their skin but by the content of their character. [Speech in Washington on completion of civil rights march, 28 Aug. 1963.]

10 A riot is at bottom the language of the unheard. [*Chaos or Community*, Ch. 4]

STODDARD KING 1889–1933

11 There's a long, long trail a-winding / Into the land of my dreams. [*The Long, Long Trail*]

CHARLES KINGSLEY 1819–1875

12 Airly Beacon, Airly Beacon; / Oh the pleasant sight to see / Shires and towns from Airly Beacon, / While my love climbed up to me! [*Airly Beacon*]

13 Be good, sweet maid, and let who will be clever; / Do noble things, not dream them, all day long; / And so make Life, and Death, and that For Ever, / One grand sweet song. [*A Farewell. To C.E.G.*]

14 Do the work that's nearest, / Though it's dull at whiles, / Helping, when we meet them, / Lame dogs over stiles. [*Letter to Thomas Hughes*]

15 O Mary, go and call the cattle home / And call the cattle home, / And call the cattle home, / Across the sands of Dee. [*The Sands of Dee*]

16 I once had a sweet little doll, dears, / The prettiest doll in the world. [*Songs from The Water Babies*, 'My Little Doll']

17 When all the world is young, lad, / And all the trees are green; / And every goose a swan, lad / And every lass a queen; / Then hey for boot and horse, lad, / And round the world away; / Young blood must have its course, lad, / And every dog his day. ['Young and Old']

18 Three fishers went sailing away to the west, / Away to the west as the sun went down. [*The Three Fishers*]

19 For men must work and women must weep. / And the sooner it's over, the sooner to sleep.

20 To be discontented with the divine discontent, and to be ashamed with the noble shame, is the very germ of the first upgrowth of all virtue. [*Health and Education*, 'The Science of Health']

21 Truth, for its own sake, had never been a virtue with the Romish clergy. Father Newman informs us that it need not, and on the whole ought not to be; that cunning is the weapon which Heaven has given to the saints wherewith to withstand the brute male force of the wicked world which marries and is given in marriage. Whether his notion be doctrinally correct or not, it is at least historically so. [Review of J. A. Froude's *History of England*]

22 He did not know that a keeper is only a poacher turned outside in, and a poacher a keeper turned inside out. [*The Water Babies*, Ch. 1]

23 As thorough an Englishman as ever coveted his neighbour's goods. [4]

24 Mrs Bedonebyasyoudid is coming. [5]

25 The loveliest fairy in the world; and her name is Mrs Doasyouwouldbedoneby.

26 All the butterflies and cockyolybirds would fly past me. [8]

1 More ways of killing a cat than choking her with cream. [*Westward Ho!*, Ch. 20]

2 Some say that the age of chivalry is past, that the spirit of romance is dead. The age of chivalry is never past, so long as there is a wrong left unredressed on earth. [Quoted in Mrs C. Kingsley, *Life*, ii. Ch. 28]

HUGH KINGSMILL 1889–1949

3 What still alive at twenty-two. / A clean, upstanding chap like you! / Sure, if your throat is hard to slit, / Slit your girl's and swing for it. [Parody of Housman. Quoted in H. Pearson and M. Muggeridge, *About Kingsmill*]

4 But bacon's not the only thing / That's cured by hanging from a string. [Parody of Housman. Quoted in *About Kingsmill*]

5 Friends are God's apology for relations. [Michael Holroyd (ed.), *The Best of Hugh Kingsmill*, Introduction]

RUDYARD KIPLING 1865–1936

6 When you've shouted 'Rule Britannia', when you've sung 'God save the Queen', / When you've finished killing Kruger with your mouth. [*The Absent-Minded Beggar*]

7 He's an absent-minded beggar, and his weaknesses are great – / But we and Paul must take him as we find him. / He's out on active service, wiping something off a slate – / And he's left a lot of little things behind him!

8 Duke's son – cook's son – son of a hundred kings – / (Fifty thousand horse and foot going to Table Bay!).

9 Pass the hat for your credit's sake, and pay – pay – pay!

10 Back to the army again, sergeant, / Back to the army again, / Out o' the cold an' the rain. [*Back to the Army Again*]

11 Oh, East is East, and West is West, and never the twain shall meet, / Till Earth and Sky stand presently at God's great Judgment Seat; / But there is neither East nor West, Border, nor Breed, nor Birth, / When two strong men stand face to face, though they come from the ends of the earth! [*The Ballad of East and West*]

12 Four things greater than all things are, – / Women and Horses and Power and War. [*The Ballad of the King's Jest*]

13 It was not preached to the crowd, / It was not taught by the State. / No man spoke it aloud, / When the English began to hate. [*The Beginnings*]

14 And a woman is only a woman, but a good cigar is a smoke. [*The Betrothed*]

15 Oh, where are you going to, all you Big Steamers, / With England's own coal, up and down the salt seas? [*Big Steamers*]

16 There's a little red-faced man, / Which is Bobs. / Rides the tallest 'orse 'e can – / Our Bobs. [*Bobs* – Lord Roberts]

17 (Boots – boots – boots – boots – movin' up and down again!) / There's no discharge in the war! [*Boots*]

18 I've a head like a concertina, I've a tongue like a button-stick, / I've a mouth like an old potato, and I'm more than a little sick. [*Cells*]

19 Teach us delight in simple things, / And mirth that has no bitter springs. [*The Children's Song*]

20 The coastwise lights of England watch the ships of England go! [*The Coastwise Lights*]

21 They know the worthy General as 'that most immoral man'. [*A Code of Morals*]

22 We know that the tail must wag the dog, for the horse is drawn by the cart; / But the Devil whoops, as he whooped of old: 'It's clever, but is it Art?' [*The Conundrum of the Workshops*]

23 Till the Devil whispered behind the leaves, / 'It's pretty, but is it Art?'

24 If once you have paid him the Dane-geld / You never get rid of the Dane. [*Dane-geld*]

25 O they're hangin' Danny Deever in the mornin'! [*Danny Deever*]

26 The 'eathen in 'is blindness bows down to wood and stone; / 'E don't obey no orders unless they is 'is own. [*The 'Eathen*]

27 The 'eathen in 'is blindness must end where 'e began, / But the backbone of the Army is the Non-commissioned Man!

28 Who are neither children nor gods, but men in a world of men! [*England's Answer*]

29 Winds of the World, give answer! They are whimpering to and fro – / And what should they know of England who only England know? [*The English Flag*]

30 Something lost behind the Ranges. Lost and waiting for you. Go! [*The Explorer*]

31 For the female of the species is more deadly than the male. [*The Female of the Species*]

1 The Hun is at the gate! [*For All We Have and Are*]

2 What stands if Freedom fall? / Who dies if England live?

3 So 'ere's to you, Fuzzy-Wuzzy, at your 'ome in the Soudan; / You're a pore benighted 'eathen but a first-class fightin' man. [*'Fuzzy-Wuzzy'*]

4 'E's all 'ot sand an' ginger when alive, / An' 'e's generally shammin' when 'e's dead.

5 To the legion of the lost ones, to the cohort of the damned. [*Gentlemen-Rankers*]

6 Gentlemen-Rankers out on the spree, / Damned from here to Eternity.

7 Oh, Adam was a gardener, and God who made him sees / That half a proper gardener's work is done upon his knees. [*The Glory of the Garden*, 8]

8 The uniform 'e wore / Was nothin' much before, / An' rather less than 'arf o' that be'ind. [*Gunga Din*]

9 An' for all 'is dirty 'ide / 'E was white, clear white inside / When 'e went to tend the wounded under fire.

10 You're a better man than I am, Gunga Din!

11 If you can keep your head when all about you / Are losing theirs and blaming it on you. [*If –*]

12 If you can meet with Triumph and Disaster / And treat those two impostors just the same.

13 If you can talk with crowds and keep your virtue, / Or walk with kings – nor lose the common touch.

14 If you can fill the unforgiving minute / With sixty seconds' worth of distance run, / Yours is the Earth and everything that's in it, / And – which is more – you'll be a Man, my son!

15 There are nine and sixty ways of constructing tribal lays, / And – every – single – one – of – them –'is – right! [*In the Neolithic Age*]

16 *No doubt but ye are the People – your throne is above the King's. / Whoso speaks in your presence must say acceptable things.* [*The Islanders*]

17 Then ye returned to your trinkets; then ye contented your souls / With the flannelled fools at the wicket or the muddied oafs at the goals.

18 And I'd like to roll to Rio / Some day before I'm old! [*Just-So Stories*, 'The Beginning of the Armadilloes']

19 I keep six honest serving-men / (They taught me all I knew); / Their names are What and Why and When / And How and Where and Who. [Follows 'The Elephant's Child']

20 We get the Hump – / Cameelious Hump – / The Hump that is black and blue! ['How the Camel Got His Hump']

21 'Confound Romance!' . . . And all unseen / Romance brought up the nine-fifteen. [*The King*]

22 For Allah created the English mad – the maddest of all mankind! [*Kitchener's School*]

23 There's times when you'll think that you mightn't, / There's times when you know that you might; / *But the things you will learn from the Yellow and Brown, / They'll 'elp you a lot with the White!* [*The Ladies*]

24 An' I learned about women from 'er!

25 I've taken my fun where I've found it / An' now I must pay for my fun.

26 For the Colonel's Lady an' Judy O'Grady / Are sisters under their skins!

27 Have it *jest* as you've a mind to, but I've proved it time on time, / If you want to change her nature you have *got* to give her lime. [*The Land*]

28 And Ye take mine honour from me if Ye take away the sea! [*The Last Chantey*]

29 Now this is the Law of the Jungle – as old and as true as the sky. [*The Law of the Jungle*]

30 We have had an Imperial lesson; it may make us an Empire yet! [*The Lesson*]

31 There's a whisper down the field where the year has shot her yield, / And the ricks stand grey to the sun, / Singing: – 'Over then, come over, for the bee has quit the clover, / And your English summer's done'. [*The Long Trail*]

32 You have heard the beat of the off-shore wind, / And the thresh of the deep-sea rain; / You have heard the song – how long? how long? / Pull out on the trail again!

33 Pull out, pull out on the Long Trail – the trail that is always new!

34 There be triple ways to take, of the eagle or the snake, / Or the way of a man with a maid.

35 Predestination in the stride o' yon connectin'-rod. [*McAndrew's Hymn*]

36 Though Thy Power brings / All skill to naught, Ye'll understand a man must think o' things.

Rudyard Kipling

1 Ye thought? Ye are not paid to think.

2 On the road to Mandalay, / Where the flyin'-fishes play, / An' the dawn comes up like thunder outer China 'crost the Bay! [*Mandalay*]

3 A-wastin' Christian kisses on an 'eathen idol's foot.

4 An' there ain' no buses runnin' from the Bank to Mandalay.

5 Tho' I walks with fifty 'ousemaids outer Chelsea to the Strand, / An' they talks a lot o' lovin', but wot do they understand?

6 Ship me somewhere east of Suez, where the best is like the worst, / Where there aren't no Ten Commandments, an' a man can raise a thirst: / For the temple-bells are callin', an' it's there that I would be – / By the old Moulmein Pagoda, looking lazy at the sea.

7 And your rooms at college was beastly – more like a whore's than a man's. [*The 'Mary Gloster'*]

8 Stiff-necked Glasgow beggar! I've heard he's prayed for my soul, / But he couldn't lie if you paid him, and he'd starve before he stole.

9 King Solomon drew merchantmen, / Because of his desire / For peacocks, apes and ivory, / From Tarshish unto Tyre. [*The Merchantmen*]

10 My new-cut ashlar takes the light / Where crimson-blank the windows flare. ['*My New-cut Ashlar*']

11 And the end of the fight is a tombstone white with the name of the late deceased, / And the epitaph drear: 'A fool lies here who tried to hustle the East'. [*Naulahka*, heading to Ch. 5]

12 Daughter am I in my mother's house, / But mistress in my own. [*Our Lady of the Snows*]

13 The toad beneath the harrow knows / Exactly where each tooth-point goes; / The butterfly upon the road / Preaches contentment to that toad. [*Pagett M.P.*]

14 Brothers and Sisters, I bid you beware / Of giving your heart to a dog to tear. [*The Power of the Dog*]

15 Little Tin Gods on Wheels. [*Public Waste*]

16 God of our fathers, known of old, / Lord of our far-flung battle-line. [*Recessional*]

17 The tumult and the shouting dies; / The Captains and the Kings depart: / Still stands thine ancient sacrifice, / An humble and a contrite heart. / Lord God of Hosts, be with us yet, / Lest we forget – lest we forget!

18 Such boastings as the Gentiles use, / Or lesser breeds without the Law.

19 *Brother, thy tail hangs down behind!* [*Road-Song of the 'Bandar-Log'*]

20 Shillin' a day, / Bloomin' good pay – / Lucky to touch it, a shillin' a day. [*Shillin' a Day*]

21 Brandy for the Parson, / 'Baccy for the Clerk; / Laces for a lady, letters for a spy, / Watch the wall, my darling, while the Gentlemen go by! [*A Smuggler's Song*]

22 'E's a kind of a giddy harumfrodite – soldier an' sailor too! [*Soldier an' Sailor too!*]

23 If blood be the price of admiralty, / Lord God, we ha' paid in full! [*The Song o' the Dead*]

24 Keep ye the Law – be swift in all obedience – / Clear the land of evil, drive the road and bridge the ford. [*A Song of the English*]

25 Through the Jungle very softly flits a shadow and a sigh – / He is Fear, O Little Hunter, he is Fear! [*The Song of the Little Hunter*]

26 'Let us now praise famous men' – / Men of little showing – / For their work continueth, / And their work continueth, / Broad and deep continueth, / Greater than their knowing! [*Stalky and Co.*, 'School Song']

27 You may carve it on his tombstone, you may cut it on his card, / That a young man married is a young man marred. [*The Story of the Gadsbys*]

28 God gives all men all earth to love, / But, since man's heart is small, / Ordains for each one spot shall prove / Belovèd over all. / Each to his choice, and I rejoice / The lot has fallen to me / In a fair ground – in a fair ground – / Yea, Sussex by the sea! [*Sussex*]

29 For the sin ye do by two and two ye must pay for one by one! [*Tomlinson*]

30 Oh, it's Tommy this, an' Tommy that, an' 'Tommy, go away'; / But it's 'Thank you, Mr Atkins', when the band begins to play. [*Tommy*]

31 We aren't no thin red 'eroes, nor we aren't no blackguards too. / But single men in barracks, most remarkable like you; / And if sometimes our conduck isn't all your fancy paints, / Why, single men in barracks don't grow into plaster saints.

1 Of all the trees that grow so fair, / Old England to adorn, / Greater are none beneath the Sun, / Than Oak and Ash and Thorn. [*A Tree Song*]

2 How very little, since things were made, / Things have altered in the building trade. [*A Truthful Song*]

3 But a fool must follow his natural bent / (Even as you and I!). [*The Vampire*]

4 They shut the road through the woods / Seventy years ago. [*The Way through the Woods*]

5 All the people like us are We, / And every one else is They. [*We and They*]

6 When the Earth's last picture is painted and the tubes are twisted and dried. [*When Earth's Last Picture*]

7 And, each in his separate star, / Shall draw the Thing as he sees it for the God of things as they are!

8 When 'Omer smote 'is bloomin' lyre, / He'd 'eard men sing by land an' sea; / An' what he thought 'e might require, / 'E went an' took – the same as me! [*When 'Omer Smote*]

9 Your new-caught, sullen peoples / Half devil and half child. [*The White Man's Burden*]

10 Take up the White Man's burden – / And reap his old reward: / The blame of those ye better, / The hate of those ye guard.

11 'Ave you 'eard o' the Widow at Windsor / With a hairy gold crown on 'er 'ead? [*The Widow at Windsor*]

12 But you won't get away from the tune that they play / To the bloomin' old rag over 'ead.

13 He travels the fastest who travels alone. [*The Winners*]

14 Politics are not my concern . . . They impressed me as a dog's life without a dog's decencies. [*A Diversity of Creatures*, 'The Village that Voted the Earth was Flat']

15 Good hunting! [*The Jungle Book*, 'Kaa's Hunting']

16 'We be of one blood, thou and I,' Mowgli answered, '. . . my kill shall be thy kill if ever thou art hungry.'

17 The Cat. He walked by himself, and all places were alike to him. [*Just So Stories*, 'The Cat That Walked by Himself']

18 An Elephant's Child – who was full of 'satiable curtiosity. ['The Elephant's Child']

19 The great grey-green, greasy Limpopo River, all set about with fever trees.

20 There lived a Parsee from whose hat the rays of the sun were reflected in more-than-oriental splendour. ['How the Rhinoceros Got His Skin']

21 You haf too much Ego in your Cosmos. [*Life's Handicap*, 'Bertran and Bimi']

22 What's the good of argifying? ['On Greenhow Hill']

23 The Light that Failed. [Title of a novel]

24 Never praise a sister to a sister, in the hope of your compliments reaching the proper ears. [*Plain Tales from the Hills*, 'False Dawn']

25 The silliest woman can manage a clever man; but it needs a very clever woman to manage a fool. ['Three and – an Extra']

26 But that is another story.

27 She was as immutable as the hills. But not quite so green. ['Venus Annodomini']

28 Being kissed by a man who didn't wax his moustache was – like eating an egg without salt. [*Soldiers Three*, 'The Gadsbys, Poor Dear Mamma']

29 Steady the Buffs.

30 A member of the most ancient profession in the world. ['On the City Wall']

31 I gloat! Hear me gloat! [*Stalky and Co*, Ch. 1]

32 'This man', said M'Turk, with conviction, 'is the Gadarene Swine,' ['The Flag of Their Country']

33 'Tisn't beauty, so to speak, nor good talk necessarily. It's just IT. [*Traffics and Discoveries*, 'Mrs Bathurst']

34 Words are, of course, the most powerful drug used by mankind. [Speech, 14 Feb. 1923]

35 Power without responsibility – the prerogative of the harlot throughout the ages. [See 21:15, 135:16, 408:10]

HENRY KISSINGER 1923–

36 The conventional army loses if it does not win. The guerrilla wins if he does not lose. [*Foreign Affairs*, XIII, 'The Vietnam Negotiations', Jan. 1969]

37 We are all the President's men. [Said in 1970 of the invasion of Cambodia]

1 Power is the ultimate aphrodisiac. [In *The New York Times*, 19 Jan, 1971]

2 Even a paranoid can have enemies. [Quoted in *Time* magazine, 24 Jan, 1977]

PAUL KLEE 1879–1940

3 An *active* line on a walk, moving freely, without goal. A walk for a walk's sake. [*Pedagogical Sketchbook*, I. 1]

FRIEDRICH VON KLINGER 1752–1831

4 *Sturm und Drang.* – Storm and stress. [Title of a play]

FRIEDRICH KLOPSTOCK 1724–1803

5 God and I both knew what it [a passage in one of his poems] meant once; now God alone knows. [Attr. by Cesare Lombroso, *The Man of Genius*, Pt I, Ch. 2. Also ascr. to Browning]

CHARLES KNIGHT 20 Cent.

6 Here we are! here we are!! here we are again!!! / There's Pat and Mac and Tommy and Jack and Joe. / When there's trouble brewing, / When there's something doing, / Are we downhearted? / No! Let 'em all come! [*Here we are! Here we are again!!*]

MARY KNOWLES 1733–1807

7 He [Dr Johnson] gets at the substance of a book directly; he tears the heart out of it. [Boswell, *Life of Johnson*, 15 Apr. 1778]

JOHN KNOX 1505–1572

8 The First Blast of the Trumpet Against the Monstrous Regiment of Women. [Title of pamphlet, 1558]

MGR. RONALD KNOX 1888–1957

9 There once was a man who said, 'God / Must find it exceedingly odd / If he finds that this tree / Continues to be / When there's no one about in the quad'. [Limerick]

ARTHUR KOESTLER 1905–1983

10 One may not regard the world as a sort of metaphysical brothel for emotions. [*Darkness at Noon*, 'The Second Hearing', Ch. 7]

11 Two half-truths do not make a truth, and two half-cultures do not make a culture. [(On the 'Two Cultures') *The Ghost in the Machine*, Preface]

12 A writer's ambition should be to trade a hundred contemporary readers for ten readers in ten years' time and for one reader in a hundred years' time. [Interview with Harvey Breit in the *New York Times Book Review*, 1 Apr. 1951]

ERNIE KOVACS 1919–1962

13 A medium, so called because it is neither rare nor well done. [Of television. Quoted in Leslie Halliwell, *The Filmgoer's Book of Quotes*]

KARL KRAUS 1874–1936

14 An aphorism never coincides with the truth: it is either a half-truth or one-and-a-half truths. [*Half-Truths and One-and-a-Half Truths*, 'Riddles']

15 Journalists write because they have nothing to say, and have something to say because they write. ['In Hollow Heads']

16 Psychoanalysis is that mental illness for which it regards itself as therapy.

17 A woman who cannot be ugly is not beautiful. ['Not for women']

J. KRISHNAMURTI 1895–1986

18 Religion is the frozen thought of men out of which they build temples. [Quoted in the *Observer*, 'Sayings of the Week', 22 Apr. 1928]

THOMAS KYD 1557–1595?

19 In time the savage bull sustains the yoke, / In time all haggard hawks will stoop to lure. / In time small wedges cleave the hardest oak, / In time the flint is pierced with softest shower. [*The Spanish Tragedy*, I. vi. See also 372:26]

20 Oh eyes, no eyes, but fountains fraught with tears; / O life, no life, but lively form of death; / Oh world, no world, but mass of public wrongs. [III. ii]

21 Why then, I'll fit you. [IV. i. 69. Quoted in T. S. Eliot's *Waste Land*, 431; followed by 'Hieronymo's mad againe']

22 My son – and what's a son? A thing begot / Within a pair of minutes, thereabouts, / A lump bred up in darkness. [III. xi. Anonymous additions]

L

HENRY LABOUCHERE 1831–1912

1 He [Labouchere] did not object, he once said, to Gladstone's always having the ace of trumps up his sleeve, but only to his pretence that God put it there. [Quoted in *Dictionary of National Biography*]

JEAN DE LA BRUYÈRE 1645–1696

2 Liberality lies less in giving liberally than in the timeliness of the gift. [*Les Caractères*, 'Du cœur', 47]

3 One must laugh before one is happy, or one may die without ever laughing at all. [63]

4 Women run to extremes; they are either better or worse than men. ['*Des femmes*', 53]

5 There are only three events in a man's life; birth, life, and death; he is not conscious of being born, he dies in pain, and he forgets to live. ['*De l'homme*', 48]

6 The majority of men devote the greater part of their lives to making their remaining years unhappy. [102]

7 A strict observer is one who would be an atheist under an atheistic king. ['*De la mode*', 21]

8 Everything has been said, and we come too late after more than seven thousand years in which man has existed and thought. ['*Des ouvrages de l'esprit*', 1]

9 Making books is a skilled trade, like making clocks. [3]

10 The pleasure of criticizing robs us of the pleasure of being moved by some very fine things. [20]

11 The former [Corneille] paints men as they should be, the latter [Racine] paints them as they are. [54]

12 The punishment of a criminal is an example to the rabble; but every decent man is concerned if an innocent person is condemned. ['*De quelques usages*', 52]

13 There are some who speak one moment before they think. ['*De la société et la conversation*', 15]

ALAN LADD 1913–1964

14 A man's gotta do what a man's gotta do. [In film *Shane*. Screenplay by A. B. Guthrie, jun., from Jack Schaefer novel]

JEAN DE LA FONTAINE 1621–1695

15 *Elle alla crier famine / Chez la fourmi sa voisine.* – She went to cry famine at her neighbour's, the ant's. [*Fables*, I. 1, '*La Cigale et la Fourmi*']

16 *La fourmi n'est pas prêteuse: / C'est là son moindre défaut.* – The ant is no lender; that is the least of her faults.

17 *Vous chantiez? j'en suis fort aise: / Eh bien, dansez maintenant.* – You sang? I am delighted. Well, dance now.

18 *Apprenez que tout flatteur / Vit aux dépens de celui qui l'écoute.* – Be advised that all flatterers live at the expense of those who listen to them. [2, '*Le Corbeau et le Renard*']

19 *Cette leçon vaut bien un fromage sans doute.* – That lesson is undoubtedly well worth a cheese.

20 *Mais quelqu'un troubla la fête.* – But someone

disturbed the feast. [9, *'Le Rat de Ville et le Rat des Champs'*]

1 *La raison du plus fort est toujours la meilleure.* – The stronger man's argument is always the best. [10, *'Le Loup et l'Agneau'*]

2 *Plutôt souffrir que mourir, / C'est la devise des hommes.* – Rather suffer than die is man's motto. [16, *'La Mort et le Bûcheron'*]

3 *Hé! mon ami, tire-moi de danger: / Tu feras après ta harangue.* – Well, my friend, get me out of danger. You can make your speech afterwards. [19, *'L'Enfant et le Maître d'École'*]

4 *Je plie et ne romps pas.* – I bend but do not break. [22, *'Le Chêne et le Roseau'*]

5 *Il faut, autant qu'on peut, obliger tout le monde: / On a souvent besoin d'un plus petit que soi.* – One should oblige everyone to the extent of one's ability. One often needs someone smaller than oneself. [II. 11, *'Le Lion et le Rat'*]

6 *Patience et longueur de temps / Font plus que force ni que rage.* – Patience and passage of time do more than strength and fury.

7 *C'est double plaisir de tromper le trompeur.* – It's a double pleasure to trick the trickster. [15, *'Le Coq et le Renard'*]

8 *Le plus âne des trois n'est pas celui qu'on pense.* – The greatest ass of the three is not the one you would think. [III. 1, *'Le Meunier, son Fils et l'Âne'*]

9 *Celui-ci ne voyait pas plus loin que son nez.* – This fellow did not see further than his own nose. [5, *'Le Renard et le Bouc'*]

10 *En toute chose il faut considérer la fin.* – In all matters one must consider the end.

11 *Ils sont trop verts, dit-il, et bon pour des goujats.* – They are too green, he said, and only good for boobies. [11, *'Le Renard et les Raisins'*]

12 *Chacun se dit ami: mais fou qui s'y repose; / Rien n'est plus commun que le nom, / Rien n'est plus rare que la chose.* – Everyone calls himself a friend, but only a fool relies on it; nothing is commoner than the name, nothing rarer than the thing. [IV. 17, *'Parole de Socrate'*]

13 *Ne t'attends qu'à toi seul; c'est un commun proverbe.* – Rely only on yourself; it is a common proverb. [22, *'L'Alouette et ses Petits avec le Maître d'un Champ'*]

14 *Une montagne en mal d'enfant / Jetait une clameur si haute / Que chacun, au bruit accourant, / Crut qu'elle accoucherait sans faute / D'une cité plus grosse que Paris: / Elle accoucha d'une souris.* – A mountain in labour shouted so loud that everyone, summoned by the noise, ran up expecting that she would be delivered of a city bigger than Paris; she brought forth a mouse. [V. 10, *'La Montagne qui accouche'* (See 207:3)]

15 *Il m'a dit qu'il ne faut jamais / Vendre la peau de l'ours qu'on ne l'ait mis par terre.* – He told me never to sell the bear's skin before one has killed the beast. [20. *'L'Ours et les deux Compagnons'*]

16 *Aide-toi, le ciel t'aidera.* – Help yourself, and heaven will help you. [VI. 18, *'Le Chartier embourbé'*]

17 *Ne soyons pas si difficiles: / Les plus accommodants, ce sont les plus habiles.* – Let us not be so difficult; the most accommodating are the cleverest. [VII. 4, *'Le Héron'*]

18 *Le lait tombe: adieu veau, vache, cochon, couvée.* – The milk falls, farewell calf, cow, pig, and clutch of eggs. [9, *'La Laitière et le Pot au Lait'*]

19 *Il faut s'entr'aider: c'est la loi de nature.* – People must help one another; it is nature's law. [VIII. 17, *'L'Âne et le Chien'*]

20 *Mais un fripon d'enfant (cet âge est sans pitié).* – But a rascally child – that is a pitiless age. [IX. 2, *'Les Deux Pigeons'*]

21 *Ventre affamé n'a point d'oreilles.* – A hungry stomach has no ears. [18, *'Le Milan et le Rossignol'*]

22 *Mais les ouvrages les plus courts / Sont toujours les meilleurs.* – But the shortest works are always the best. [X. 14, *'Les Lapins'*]

ALPHONSE DE LAMARTINE 1790–1869

23 *O temps! suspends ton vol; et vous, heures propices! / Suspendez votre cours: / Laissez-nous savourer les rapides délices / Des plus beaux de nos jours!* – O time, suspend your flight, and you, happy hours, stay your feet! Let us savour the swift delights of our life's loveliest days! [*Le Lac*, 21]

24 *J'aimais les voix du soir dans les airs répandues, / Le bruit lointain des chars gémissant sous leur poids, / Et le sourd tintement des cloches suspendues / Au cou des chevreaux dans les bois.* – I loved voices drifting down the breeze at evening, the distant sound of carts creaking beneath their loads, and the dull jangling of bells hung on the kid-goats' necks in the woods. [*Les Préludes*, 328]

A. J. LAMB 1870–1928

1 She's a Bird in Gilded Cage. [Title of song]

LADY CAROLINE LAMB 1785–1828

2 Mad, bad, and dangerous to know. [(Byron, at their first meeting, Mar. 1812) *Journal*]

CHARLES LAMB 1775–1834

3 For thy sake, Tobacco, I / Would do anything but die. [*A Farewell to Tobacco*, 122]

4 Gone before / To that unknown and silent shore. [*Hester*]

5 Angel-duck, angel-duck, winged and silly, / Pouring a watering-pot over a lily. [*Nonsense Verses*]

6 I have had playmates, I have had companions, / In my days of childhood, in my joyful school-days, – All, all are gone, the old familiar faces. [*The Old Familiar Faces*]

7 Riddle of destiny, who can show / What thy short visit meant, or know / What thy errand here below? [*On an Infant Dying as soon as Born*]

8 Who first invented work and bound the free / And holiday-rejoicing spirit down? [*Work*]

9 Truths, which transcend the searching School-men's vein, / And half had staggered that stout Stagirite. [*Written at Cambridge*]

10 Good Master Raymund Lully, you look wise. Pray correct that error. [*Essays of Elia*, 'All Fools' Day']

11 Nothing is to me more distasteful than that entire complacency and satisfaction which beam in the countenances of a new-married couple. ['A Bachelor's Complaint of Married People']

12 I have no ear. ['A Chapter on Ears']

13 I even think that sentimentally I am disposed to harmony. But organically I am incapable of a tune.

14 'Presents', I often say, 'endear absents.' ['A Dissertation upon Roast Pig']

15 We are nothing; less than nothing, and dreams. We are only what might have been, and must wait upon the tedious shores of Lethe millions of ages before we have existence, and a name. ['Dream Children']

16 I hate a man who swallows it [his food], affecting not to know what he is eating. I suspect his taste in higher matters. ['Grace before Meat']

17 C – [Coleridge] holds that a man cannot have a pure mind who refuses apple-dumplings.

18 I am, in plainer words, a bundle of prejudices – made up of likings and dislikings. ['Imperfect Sympathies']

19 I have been trying all my life to like Scotchmen, and am obliged to desist from the experiment in despair.

20 You must beware of indirect expressions before a Caledonian. Clap an extinguisher on your irony, if you are unhappily blessed with a vein of it.

21 'A clear fire, a clean hearth, and the rigour of the game.' This was the celebrated wish of old Sarah Battle (now with God), who, next to her devotions, loved a good game at whist. ['Mrs Battle's Opinions on Whist']

22 They do not play at cards, but only play at playing at them.

23 All people have their blind side – their superstitions; and I have heard her declare, under the rose, that hearts were her favourite suit.

24 She unbent her mind afterwards – over a book.

25 Man is a gaming animal. He must always be trying to get the better in something or other.

26 Boys are capital fellows in their own way, among their mates; but they are unwholesome companions for grown people. ['The Old and the New Schoolmaster']

27 The human species, according to the best theory I can form of it, is composed of two distinct races, *the men who borrow* and *the men who lend*. ['The Two Races of Men']

28 What a liberal confounding of those pedantic distinctions of *meum* and *tuum*! or rather what a noble simplification of language!

29 Your *borrowers of books* – those mutilators of collections – spoilers of the symmetry of shelves, and creators of odd volumes.

30 Not many sounds in life, and I include all urban and rural sounds, exceed in interest a knock at the door. ['Valentine's Day']

31 Credulity is the man's weakness, but the child's strength. ['Witches and other Night Fears']

1 How sickness enlarges the dimensions of a man's self to himself. [*Last Essays of Elia*, 'The Convalescent']

2 I love to lose myself in other men's minds. When I am not walking, I am reading; I cannot sit and think. Books think for me. ['Detached Thoughts on Books and Reading']

3 Newspapers always excite curiosity. No one ever lays one down without a feeling of disappointment.

4 A poor relation – is the most irrelevant thing in nature. ['Poor Relations']

5 It [a pun] is a pistol let off at the ear; not a feather to tickle the intellect. ['Popular Fallacies', 9]

6 I would not call that man my friend who should be offended with 'the divine chit-chat of Cowper'. [Letter to Coleridge, 5 Dec. 1796]

7 I came home . . . hungry as a hunter. [Letter to Coleridge, Apr. 1800]

8 Separate from the pleasure of your company, I don't much care if I never see another mountain in my life. [Letter to Wordsworth, 30 Jan. 1801]

9 The man must have a rare recipe for melancholy, who can be dull in Fleet Street. [Letter to T. Manning, 15 Feb. 1802]

10 A little thin, flowery border round, neat, not gaudy. [Letter to Wordsworth, June 1806]

11 Nothing puzzles me more than time and space; and yet nothing troubles me less, as I never think about them. [Letter to T. Manning, 2 Jan. 1810]

12 Anything awful makes me laugh. I misbehaved once at a funeral. [Letter to Southey, 9 Aug. 1815]

13 His face when he repeats his verses hath its ancient glory, an Archangel a little damaged. [(Coleridge) Letter to Wordsworth, 26 Apr. 1816]

14 How I like to be liked, and what I do to be liked! [Letter to Dorothy Wordsworth, 8 Jan. 1821]

15 When my sonnet was rejected, I exclaimed, 'Damn the age; I will write for Antiquity!' [Letter to B. W. Procter, 22 Jan. 1829]

16 What a lass that were to go a-gipsying through the world with. ['The Jovial Crew', *The Examiner*, July 1819]

17 The greatest pleasure I know is to do a good action by stealth, and to have it found out by accident. ['Table Talk by the late Elia', *The Athenaeum*, 4 Jan. 1834]

MARY LAMB 1764–1847

18 A child's a plaything for an hour. [*Parental Recollections*]

JOHN LAMBTON, EARL OF DURHAM 1792–1840

19 He said he considered £40,000 a year a moderate income – such a one as a man *might jog on with*. [Quoted in *The Creevey Papers* 13 Sept. 1821]

WILLIAM JAMES LAMPTON 1859–1917

20 Same old slippers, / Same old rice, / Same old glimpse of / Paradise. [*June Weddings*]

LETITIA LANDON 1802–1838

21 As beautiful as woman's blush, – / As evanescent too. [*Apple Blossoms*]

WALTER SAVAGE LANDOR 1775–1864

22 Child of a day, thou knowest not / The tears that overflow thy urn. [*Child of a Day*]

23 Stand close around, ye Stygian set, / With Dirce in one boat conveyed! / Or Charon, seeing, may forget / That he is old and she a shade. [*Dirce*]

24 George the First was always reckoned / Vile, but viler George the Second; / And what mortal ever heard / Any good of George the Third? / When from earth the Fourth descended / God be praised, the Georges ended! [*Epigram*]

25 I strove with none; for none was worth my strife; / Nature I loved, and, next to Nature, Art; / I warmed both hands before the fire of life; / It sinks, and I am ready to depart. [*I Strove with None*]

26 I loved him not; and yet now he is gone / I feel I am alone. [*Maid's Lament*]

27 Proud word you never spoke, but you will speak / Four not exempt from pride some future day. / Resting on one white hand a warm wet cheek / Over my open volume you will say, / 'This man loved *me*!' then rise and trip away. [*Proud Word You Never Spoke*]

28 Ah, what avails the sceptred race! / Ah, what the form divine! [*Rose Aylmer*]

1 There is delight in singing, tho' none hear / Beside the singer. [*To Robert Browning*]

2 Browning! Since Chaucer was alive and hale, / No man hath walked along our roads with step / So active, so inquiring eye, or tongue / So varied in discourse.

3 The Siren waits thee, singing song for song.

4 Laodameia died; Helen died; Leda, the beloved of Jupiter, went before. [*Imaginary Conversations*, 'Aesop and Rhodope']

5 There are no fields of amaranth on this side of the grave: there are no voices, O Rhodope! that are not soon mute, however tuneful: there is no name, with whatever emphasis of passionate love repeated, of which the echo is not faint at last.

GEORGE MARTIN LANE 1823–1897

6 The waiter roars it through the hall: / 'We don't give bread with one fish-ball!' [*The Lay of the Lone Fish-Ball*]

ANDREW LANG 1844–1912

7 *I* am the batsman and the bat, / *I* am the bowler and the ball, / The umpire, the pavilion cat, / The roller, pitch, and stumps, and all. [*Brahma* (imitation of Emerson)]

8 He uses statistics as a drunken man uses lamp-posts – for support rather than illumination. [Quoted in A. L. Mackay, ed., *A Dictionary of Scientific Quotations*]

JULIA LANG 1921–

9 Are you sitting comfortably? Then I'll begin. [BBC radio programme, *Listen with Mother*, passim]

FREDERICK LANGBRIDGE 1849–1923

10 Two men look out through the same bars: / One sees the mud, and one the stars. [*Cluster of Quiet Thoughts*]

WILLIAM LANGLAND 1330?–1400?

11 In a somer seson whan soft was the sonne. [*Piers Plowman*, B Text, Prologue, 1]

12 A faire felde ful of folke fonde I there bitwene, / Of alle manner of men, the mene and the riche, / Worching and wandring as the worlde asketh. [17]

13 Dowel, Dobet and Dobest. [Passus 8]

14 Ac on a May morwenyng on Maluerne hulles / Me befel for to slepe for weyrynesse of wandryng. [C Text, Passus 1.6]

15 'After sharpest shoures,' quath Pees, 'most sheene is the sonne; / Is no weder warmer than after watery cloudes.' [21.456]

ARCHBISHOP STEPHEN LANGTON ?–1228

16 *Veni, Sancte Spiritus, / Et emitte coelitus / Lucis tuae radium.* – Come, thou holy Paraclete, / And from thy celestial seat / Send thy light and brilliancy. [Trans. J. M. Neale]

LAO TZU *c.* 604–531BC

17 The Way is empty yet use will not drain it. [*Tao te Ching*, 4, trans. D. C. Lau. Attr. to Lao Tzu but published 4 Cent. BC]

18 Heaven and earth are ruthless and treat the myriad creatures as straw dogs. [5]

PHILIP LARKIN 1922–1985

19 Sexual intercourse began in nineteen sixty-three / – (which was rather late for me) – / Between the end of the *Chatterley* ban / And the Beatles' first LP. [*Annus Mirabilis*]

20 Perhaps being old is having lighted rooms / Inside your head, and people in them, acting. / People you know, yet can't quite name. [*The Old Fools*]

21 Here's to the whitest man I know, / Though white is not my favourite colour. [*Sympathy in White Major*. See also 195:11, 226:28]

22 They fuck you up, your mum and dad. / They may not mean to, but they do. / They fill you with the faults they had / And add some extra, just for you. [*This be the Verse*]

23 Why should I let the toad *work* / Squat on my life? [*Toads*]

DUC DE LA ROCHEFOUCAULD 1613–1680

24 We have all enough strength to bear other people's troubles. [*Les Maximes*, 19]

25 We need greater virtues to bear good fortune than bad. [25]

26 If we had no faults we should not take so much pleasure in noticing them in others. [31]

1 One is never as fortunate or as unfortunate as one imagines. [49]

2 To establish oneself in the world one has to do all one can to appear established. [56]

3 If one judges love by the majority of its effects, it is more like hatred than like friendship. [72]

4 Love of justice in most men is no more than the fear of suffering injustice. [78]

5 It is more shameful to distrust one's friends than to be deceived by them. [84]

6 Everyone complains of his memory, but no one complains of his judgement. [89]

7 The intellect is always fooled by the heart. [102]

8 One gives nothing so freely as advice. [110]

9 One had rather malign oneself than not speak of oneself at all. [138]

10 To refuse praise reveals a desire to be praised twice over. [149]

11 Flattery is false coin that is only current thanks to our vanity. [158]

12 Hypocrisy is the homage paid by vice to virtue. [218]

13 One's over-great haste to repay an obligation is a kind of ingratitude. [226]

14 It takes great cleverness to be able to conceal one's cleverness. [245]

15 We only confess our little faults to persuade people that we have no large ones. [327]

16 We seldom attribute common sense except to those who agree with us. [347]

17 We may give advice, but we can never prompt behaviour. [378]

18 Nothing prevents us from being natural so much as the desire to appear so. [431]

19 Quarrels would not last so long if the fault were on only one side. [496]

20 In the misfortunes of our best friends, we find something that is not unpleasing. [*Maximes supprimés*, 583]

21 Most usually our virtues are only vices in disguise. [Added to the fourth edn. of *Les Maximes*]

22 Anything may happen in France. [Attr. remark to Mazarin, quoted by Sainte-Beuve, *Portraits de femmes*]

DUC DE LA ROCHEFOUCAULD-LIANCOURT 1747–1827

23 LOUIS XVI: *C'est une révolte?* – Is it a revolt? THE DUKE: *Non, Sire, c'est une révolution.* – No, Sire, it's a revolution. [On hearing of the Fall of the Bastille, 15 July 1789]

HAROLD LASSWELL 1902–1978

24 Politics: Who Gets What, When, How. [Title of book]

BISHOP HUGH LATIMER 1485?–1555

25 Be of good comfort, Master Ridley, and play the man. We shall this day light such a candle by God's grace in England, as (I trust) shall never be put out. [Said when he and Ridley were about to be burned, 16 Oct. 1555 (see also 47:32)]

SIR HARRY LAUDER 1870–1950

26 I love a lassie. [Song]

27 Just a wee deoch-an-duoris / Before we gang awa' . . . / If y' can say / It's a braw brecht moonlecht necht, / Yer a' recht, that's a'. [Song]

28 Keep right on to the end of the road. [Song]

29 O! it's nice to get up in the mornin', / But it's nicer to stay in bed. [Song]

30 Roamin' in the gloamin', / By the bonny banks of Clyde. [Song]

WILLIAM L. LAURENCE 1888–1977

31 At first it [the first atomic explosion] was a giant column that soon took the shape of a supramundane mushroom. [*New York Times*, 26 Sept. 1945]

D. H. LAWRENCE 1885–1930

32 Is it the secret of the long-nosed Etruscans? / The long-nosed, sensitive footed, subtly-smiling Etruscans, / Who made so little noise outside the cypress groves? [*Cypresses*]

33 Evil, what is evil? / There is only one evil, to deny life / As Rome denied Etruria / And mechanical America Montezuma still.

34 Along the avenue of cypresses, / All in their scarlet cloaks and surplices / Of linen, go the chanting choristers, / The priests in gold and black, the villagers. [*Giorno dei Morti*]

1 How beastly the bourgeois is especially the male of the species. [*How Beastly the Bourgeois Is*]

2 Too much of the humble Willy wet-leg / And the holy can't-help-it touch. [*Now It's Happened*]

3 A snake came to my water-trough / On a hot, hot day, and I in pyjamas for the heat, / To drink there. [*Snake*]

4 Not I, not I, but the wind that blows through me! / A fine wind is blowing the new direction of Time. [*Song of a Man Who Has Come Through*]

5 The English people on the whole are surely the *nicest* people in the world, and everyone makes everything so easy for everybody else, that there is almost nothing to resist at all. [*Dull London*]

6 To the Puritan all things are impure. [*Etruscan Places*]

7 Morality which is based on ideas, or on an ideal, is an unmitigated evil. [*Fantasia of the Unconscious* 7]

8 Every race which has become self-conscious and idea-bound in the past has perished.

9 Death is the only pure, beautiful conclusion of a great passion. [15]

10 You may be the most liberal Liberal Englishman, and yet you cannot fail to see the categorical difference between the responsible and the irresponsible classes. [*Kangaroo*, Ch. 1]

11 Man's ultimate love for man? Yes, yes, but only in the separate darkness of man's love for the present, unknowable God. [17]

12 It's all this cold-hearted fucking that is death and idiocy. [*Lady Chatterley's Lover*, Ch. 14]

13 This is John Thomas marryin' Lady Jane. [15]

14 But tha mun dress thysen, an' go back to thy stately homes of England, how beautiful they stand. Time's up! Time's up for Sir John, an' for little Lady Jane! Put thy shimmy on, Lady Chatterley!

15 No absolute is going to make the lion lie down with the lamb unless the lamb is inside. [*The Later D. H. Lawrence*]

16 It is as if the life had retreated eastwards. As if the Germanic life were slowly ebbing away from contact with western Europe, ebbing to the deserts of the east. [*A Letter from Germany* (1924)]

17 Sentimentalism is the working off on yourself of feelings you haven't really got. [*Phoenix* 'John Galsworthy']

18 Pornography is the attempt to insult sex, to do dirt on it. ['Pornography and Obscenity']

19 It is no good casting out devils. They belong to us, we must accept them and be at peace with them. ['The Reality of Peace']

20 'It [Mexico] is a country where men despise sex, and live for it,' said Ramón. 'Which is suicide.' [*The Plumed Serpent*]

21 Be a good animal, true to your animal instincts. [*The White Peacock*, Pt II, Ch. 2]

22 I think more of a bird with broad wings flying and lapsing through the air, than anything, when I think of metre. [Letter to Edward Marsh, Nov. 1913]

23 I like to write when I feel spiteful: it's like having a good sneeze. [Letter to Lady Cynthia Asquith, Nov. 1913]

24 The ordinary novel would trace the history of the diamond – but I say, 'Diamond, what! This is carbon.' And my diamond may be coal or soot and my theme is carbon. [Letter to Edward Garnett, 5 June 1914]

25 I cannot get any sense of an enemy – only of a disaster. [Letter to Edward Marsh, Autumn 1914]

26 The autumn always gets me badly, as it breaks into colours. I want to go south, where there is no autumn, where the cold doesn't crouch over one like a snow-leopard waiting to pounce. The heart of the North is dead, and the fingers are corpse fingers. [Letter to J. M. Murry, 3 Oct. 1924]

JEROME LAWRENCE 1916–

27 A neurotic is the man who builds a castle in the air. A psychotic is the man who lives in it. A psychiatrist is the man who collects the rent. [Quoted in Laurence J. Peter, *Peter's Quotations*]

T. E. LAWRENCE 1888–1935

28 I loved you, so I drew these tides of men into my hands and wrote my will across the sky in stars. [*Seven Pillars of Wisdom*, Dedication]

29 All men dream: but not equally. Those who dream by night in the dusty recesses of their

minds wake in the day to find that it was vanity: but the dreamers of the day are dangerous men, for they may act their dream with open eyes, to make it possible. [Ch. 1]

SIR AUSTEN HENRY LAYARD 1817–1894

1 ... If we sent the right man to fill the right place. [Speech in House of Commons, 15 Jan. 1855]

EMMA LAZARUS 1849–1887

2 Give me your tired, your poor, / Your huddled masses yearning to breathe free. [Inscription on the Statue of Liberty, New York harbour]

STEPHEN LEACOCK 1869–1944

3 'A', whispered C, 'I think I'm going fast.' 'How fast do you think you'll go, old man?' murmured A. 'I don't know,' said C, 'but I'm going at any rate.' [Literary Lapses, 'A, B and C']

4 The landlady of a boarding-house is a parallelogram – that is, an oblong angular figure, which cannot be described, but which is equal to anything. ['Boarding-House Geometry']

5 On the same bill and on the same side of it there should not be two charges for the same thing.

6 I detest life-insurance agents; they always argue that I shall some day die, which is not so. ['Insurance Up to Date']

7 Astronomy teaches the correct use of the sun and the planets. ['A Manual of Education']

8 Electricity is of two kinds, positive and negative. The difference is, I presume, that one comes a little more expensive, but is more durable; the other is a cheaper thing, but the moths get into it.

9 He flung himself from the room, flung himself upon his horse and rode madly off in all directions. [Nonesense Novels, 'Gertrude the Governess']

10 Advertising may be described as the science of arresting the human intelligence long enough to get money from it. [The Penguin Stephen Leacock]

11 The general idea, of course, in any first-class laundry is to see that no shirt or collar

ever comes back twice. [Winnowed Wisdom, Ch. 6]

EDWARD LEAR 1812–1888

12 There was an old Man who said, 'Hush! / I perceive a young bird in this bush!' / When they said, 'Is it small?' / He replied, 'Not at all!/ It is four times as big as the bush!' [Book of Nonsense]

13 There was an Old Man with a beard, / Who said, 'It is just as I feared!– / Two owls and a hen, / Four larks and a wren, / Have all built their nest in my beard!'

14 'How pleasant to know Mr Lear!' / Who has written such volumes of stuff! / Some think him ill-tempered and queer, / But a few think him pleasant enough. [Nonsense Songs, Preface]

15 Who or why, or which or what, / Is the Akond of Swat? ['The Akond of Swat']

16 On the coast of Coromandel / Where the early pumpkins blow, / In the middle of the woods / Lived the Yonghy-Bonghy-Bò. / Two old chairs, and half a candle,– / One old jug without a handle,– / These were all his wordly goods. ['The Courtship of the Yonghy-Bonghy-Bò']

17 When awful darkness and silence reign / Over the great Gromboolian plain. ['The Dong with a Luminous Nose']

18 When Storm-clouds brood on the towering heights / Of the Hills of the Chankly Bore.

19 The Dong!– the Dong! / The wandering Dong through the forest goes! / The Dong!– the Dong! / The Dong with a luminous Nose!

20 And who so happy,– O who, / As the Duck and the Kangaroo? ['The Duck and the Kangaroo']

21 In spite of all their friends could say, / On a winter's morn, on a stormy day, / In a sieve they went to sea! ['The Jumblies']

22 Far and few, far and few, / Are the lands where the Jumblies live; / Their heads are green, and their hands are blue, / And they went to sea in a sieve.

23 And they bought an Owl, and a useful Cart, / And a pound of Rice, and a Cranberry Tart.

24 The Owl and the Pussy-Cat went to sea/ In a beautiful pea-green boat, / They took some honey, and plenty of money, / Wrapped up in a

five-pound note / The Owl looked up to the stars above, / And sang to a small guitar, / 'O lovely Pussy! O Pussy, my love, / What a beautiful Pussy you are!' ['The Owl and the Pussy-Cat']

1 Pussy said to the Owl, 'You elegant fowl! / How charmingly sweet you sing! / O let us be married! too long we have tarried: / But what shall we do for a ring?' / They sailed away for a year and a day, / To the land where the Bong-Tree grows, / And there in a wood a Piggy-wig stood, / With a ring at the end of his nose.

2 'Dear Pig, are you willing to sell for one shilling / Your ring?' Said the Piggy, 'I will.'

3 They dined on mince, and slices of quince, / Which they ate with a runcible spoon; / And hand in hand, on the edge of the sand, / They danced by the light of the moon.

4 Ploffskin, Pluffskin, Pelican jee! / We think no Birds so happy as we! / Plumpskin, Ploshkin, Pelican jill! / We think so then and we thought so still. ['The Pelican Chorus']

5 The Pobble who has no toes / Had once as many as we; / When they said, 'Some day you may lose them all'; / He replied – 'Fish fiddle de-dee!' ['The Pobble who has no Toes']

6 He has gone to fish for his Aunt Jobiska's / Runcible Cat with crimson whiskers!

7 It's a fact the whole world knows, / That Pobbles are happier without their toes.

8 Two old Bachelors were living in one house; / One caught a Muffin, the other caught a Mouse. ['The Two Old Bachelors']

9 There was an old man of Thermopylae, / Who never did anything properly; / But they said, 'If you choose / To boil eggs in your shoes, / You shall never remain in Thermopylae.' [*One Hundred Nonsense Pictures*]

10 Serve up in a clean dish, and throw the whole out of the window as fast as possible. [*To make an Amblongus Pie*]

TIMOTHY LEARY 1920–

11 If you take the game of life seriously, if you take your nervous system seriously, if you take your sense organs seriously, if you take the energy process seriously, you must turn on, tune in, and drop out. [*The Politics of Ecstasy*, Ch. 21]

MARY LEASE 1853–1933

12 Kansas had better stop raising corn and begin raising hell. [Attr.]

FRAN LEBOWITZ 1946–

13 Original thought is like original sin: both happened before you were born to people you could not possibly have met. [*Social Studies*, 'People']

14 Remember that as a teenager you are at the last stage in your life when you will be happy to hear that the phone is for you. ['Tips for Teens']

15 If you're going to America, bring your own food. ['Fran Lebowitz's Travel Hints']

STANISLAW LEC 1909–1966

16 Is it progress if a cannibal uses knife and fork? [*Unkempt Thoughts*]

17 When smashing monuments, save the pedestals – they always come in handy.

JOHN LE CARRÉ 1931–

18 The Spy Who Came in from the Cold. [Title of novel]

19 A committee is an animal with four back legs. [*Tinker, Tailor, Soldier, Spy*, Pt III. Ch. 34]

LE CORBUSIER 1887–1965

20 *Une maison est une machine-à-habiter.* – A house is a machine for living in. [*Vers une architecture*]

GYPSY ROSE LEE 1914–1970

21 God is love but get it in writing: [Catch-phrase]

HENRY LEE 1756–1818

22 First in war, first in peace, first in the hearts of his fellow countrymen. [(George Washington) Speech in House of Representatives, 19 Dec. 1799]

NATHANIEL LEE 1655–1692

23 Then he will talk, – good gods, how he will talk! [*The Rival Queens*, I. iii]

24 When Greeks joined Greeks, then was the tug of war! [IV. ii]

25 Man, false man, smiling, destructive man. [*Theodosius*, III. ii]

RICHARD LE GALLIENNE 1866–1947

26 The cry of the Little Peoples goes up to God

in vain, / For the world is given over to the cruel sons of Cain. [*The Cry of the Little Peoples*]

1 She's somewhere in the sunlight strong, / Her tears are in the falling rain, / She calls me in the wind's soft song, / And with the flowers she comes again. [*Song*]

2 What of the Darkness? Is it very fair? [*What of the Darkness?*]

TOM LEHRER 1928–

3 Life is like a sewer. What you get out of it depends on what you put in. [Preamble to song: *We Will All Go Together When We Go*]

4 It is sobering to consider that when Mozart was my age he had already been dead for a year. [Quoted in N. Shapiro, *An Encyclopedia of Quotations about Music*]

FRED W. LEIGH ?–1924

5 There was I, waiting at the church, / Waiting at the church, waiting at the church, / When I found he'd left me in the lurch, / Lor', how it did upset me!. . . / Can't get away to marry you today – / My wife won't let me! [Song: *Waiting at the Church*. Music by Henry E. Peter. Sung by Vesta Victoria]

FRED W. LEIGH and CHARLES COLLINS ?–1923

6 My old man said, 'Follow the van, / Don't dilly dally on the way!' [Music-hall song: *Don't Dilly Dally*]

7 Why am I always a bridesmaid, never a blushing bride? [Music-hall song: *Why Am I Always a Bridesmaid?*, sung by Lily Morris]

H. S. LEIGH 1837–1883

8 That loathsome centipede, Remorse, / Invaded with a stealthy tread / My nasal organ. [*An Allegory, written in Deep Dejection*]

9 I wondered hugely what she meant, / And said, 'I'm bad at riddles; / But I know where little girls are sent / For telling taradiddles.' [*Only Seven*]

10 In form and feature, face and limb, / I grew so like my brother / That folks got taking me for him / And each for one another. [*The Twins*]

11 For one of us was born a twin / And not a soul knew which.

C. G. LELAND 1824–1903

12 I tont dink mooch of beoplesh / Dat goes mit demselfs alone. [*Breitmann Ballads*, 'Ballad']

13 She drawed him oonder der wasser, / De maiden mit nodings on.

14 Hans Breitmann gife a barty; / Dey had biano-blayin', / I felled in lofe mit a Merican frau, / Her name vas Madilda Yane. ['Hans Breitmann's Barty']

15 Und efery dime she gife a shoomp / She make de vindows sound.

16 Dey rolled in more ash sefen kecks / Of foost-rate lager beer.

17 Hans Breitmann gife a barty – / Vhere ish dat barty now? / Vhere ish de lofely golden cloud / Dat float on de moundain's prow?

18 All goned afay mit de lager beer – / Afay in de ewigkeit!

GENERAL CURTIS LEMAY 1906–1990

19 My solution to the problem [of North Vietnam] would be to tell them frankly that they've got to draw in their horns and stop their aggression, or we're going to bomb them back into the Stone Age. [*Mission with LeMay*, p. 565]

NINON DE LENCLOS 1620–1705

20 *La vieillesse est l'enfer des femmes.* – Old age is woman's hell. [Attr.]

VLADIMIR ILYICH [ULYANOV] LENIN 1870–1924

21 If it were necessary to give the briefest possible definition of imperialism, we should have to say that imperialism is the monopoly stage of capitalism. [*Imperialism, the Highest Stage of Capitalism*, Ch. 7]

22 So long as the state exists there is no freedom. When there is freedom there will be no state. [*The State and Revolution*, 5. iv]

23 Under socialism *all* will govern in turn and will soon become accustomed to no one governing. [6. iii]

24 Every cook has to learn how to govern the state. [*Will the Bolsheviks Retain Government Power?*]

25 Communism is Soviet power plus the electrification of the whole country. [Slogan promoting the electrification programme, at Congress of Soviets, 22 Dec. 1920]

1 Who, whom? We or they? [Quoted in Fitzroy Maclean, *Disputed Barricade*]

2 It is true that liberty is precious – so precious that it must be rationed. [Quoted in Sidney and Beatrice Webb, *Soviet Communism*, Ch. 12]

JOHN LENNON 1940–1980

3 Will people in the cheaper seats clap your hands? All the rest of you just rattle your jewellery. [At Royal Variety Performance, 15 Nov. 1963]

4 We're more popular than Jesus Christ now. I don't know which will go first. Rock and roll or Christianity. [*The Beatles' Illustrated Lyrics*]

JOHN LENNON and PAUL McCARTNEY 1942–

5 How does it feel to be one of the beautiful people, now that that you know who you are? [Song: *Baby You're a Rich Man*]

6 For I don't care too much for money, / For money can't buy me love. [Song: *Can't Buy Me Love*]

7 All the lonely people, where do they all come from? / All the lonely people, where do they all belong? [Song: *Eleanor Rigby*]

8 If there's anything that you want, / If there's anything I can do, / Just call on me, / And I'll send it along with love from me to you. [Song: *From Me to You*]

9 I've got to admit it's getting better. / It's a little better all the time. [Song: *Getting Better*]

10 It's been a hard day's night. [Song: *A Hard Day's Night* (and film title)]

11 He's a real Nowhere Man, / Sitting in his Nowhere Land, / Making all his nowhere plans for nobody. / Doesn't have a point of view, / Knows not where he's going to, / Isn't he a bit like you and me? [Song: *Nowhere Man*]

12 Sergeant Pepper's Lonely Hearts Club Band. [Title of song]

13 She's leaving home after living alone for so many years. [Song: *She's Leaving Home*]

14 She loves you, yeh, yeh, yeh, / And with a love like that you know you should be glad. [Song: *She Loves You*]

15 She's got a ticket to ride, but she don't care. [Song: *Ticket to Ride*]

16 Will you still need me, will you still feed me, / When I'm sixty-four? [Song: *When I'm Sixty-four*]

17 I get by with a little help from my friends. [Song: *With a Little Help from My Friends*]

LUIS DE LEÓN 1528?–1591

18 As I was saying the other day. [Resuming a lecture at Salamanca University, 1577, interrupted by five years' imprisonment]

HUGH LEONARD 1926–

19 The problem with Ireland is that it's a country full of genius, but with absolutely no talent. [Interview in *The Times*, Aug. 1977]

ALAN JAY LERNER 1918–1986

20 I'm getting married in the morning! / Ding dong! the bells are gonna chime. / Pull out the stopper! Let's have a whopper! / But get me to the church on time! [*My Fair Lady*, II. iii]

21 Why can't a woman be more like a man? / Men are so honest, so thoroughly square; / Eternally noble, historically fair. [iv]

22 I've grown accustomed to the trace / Of something in the air, / Accustomed to her face. [vi]

ALAIN RENÉ LESAGE 1668–1747

23 Justice is such a fine thing that we cannot pay too dearly for it. [*Crispin rival de son maître*, IX]

24 They made peace between us; we embraced, and we have been mortal enemies ever since. [*Le Diable boiteux*, Ch. 3]

GOTTHOLD EPHRAIM LESSING 1729–1781

25 A man who does not lose his reason over certain things has none to lose. [*Emilia Galotti*, IV. vii]

26 Mocking laughter from Hell. [V. ii]

27 A single grateful thought raised to heaven is the most perfect prayer. [*Minna von Barnhelm*, II. vii]

28 Absolute truth belongs to Thee alone. [*Wolfenbüttler Fragmente*]

ALFRED LESTER 1874–1925

29 Call out the Boys of the Old Brigade, / Who made Old England free – / Send out my Mother, my Sister and my Brother, / But for God's sake don't send me! [*Conscientious Objector's Lament*]

SIR ROGER L'ESTRANGE 1616–1704

1 It is with our passions as it is with fire and water, they are good servants, but bad masters. [*Aesop's Fables*, 38]

2 Though this may be play to you, 'tis death to us. [398]

EUGEN LEVINÉ 20 Cent.

3 We Communists are dead men on leave. [At his trial. Quoted in R. Leviné-Meyer, *Leviné: the Life of a Revolutionary*, Ch. 3]

DUC DE LÉVIS 1764–1830

4 *Noblesse oblige.* – Nobility carries its obligations [*Maximes et réflexions*, 73]

G. H. LEWES 1817–1878

5 Murder, like talent, seems occasionally to run in families. [*The Physiology of Common Life*, Ch. 12]

C. S. LEWIS 1898–1963

6 There must be several young women who would render the Christian life intensely difficult to him if only you could persuade him to marry one of them. [*Screwtape Letters*, XIX]

SIR GEORGE CORNEWALL LEWIS 1806–1863

7 Life would be tolerable, were it not for its amusements. [Quoted in Sagittarius and George, *The Perpetual Pessimist*. Also attr. to Edward Bulwer-Lytton]

JOHN LEWIS [PARTNERSHIP]

8 We are never knowingly undersold. [Shop slogan]

SINCLAIR LEWIS 1885–1951

9 Our American professors like their literature clear and cold and pure and very dead. [Address in Stockholm on receiving the Nobel Prize, 12 Dec. 1930]

ROBERT LEY 1890–1945

10 *Kraft durch Freude.* – Strength through joy. [German Labour Front slogan, first used 2 Dec. 1933]

GEORGE LEYBOURNE ?–1884

11 O, he flies through the air with the greatest of ease, / This daring young man on the flying trapeze. [*The Man on the Flying Trapeze*]

[WLADZIU VALENTINO] LIBERACE 1919–1987

12 I cried all the way to the bank. [Reaction to hostile criticism in 1954. Quoted in Bob Thomas, *Liberace: The True Story*]

PRINCE DE LIGNE 1735–1814

13 *Le congrès ne marche pas, il danse.* – The Congress makes no progress, but it dances. [Remark on the Congress of Vienna, 1814]

ABRAHAM LINCOLN 1809–1865

14 The ballot is stronger than the bullet. [Speech, 19 May 1856]

15 What is conservatism? Is it not adherence to the old and tried, against the new and untried? [27 Feb. 1860]

16 In giving freedom to the slave, we assure freedom to the free, – honourable alike in what we give and what we preserve. [1 Dec. 1862]

17 That this nation, under God, shall have a new birth of freedom; and that government of the people, by the people, and for the people, shall not perish from the earth. [The Gettysburg Address, 19 Nov. 1863]

18 An old Dutch farmer, who remarked to a companion once that it was not best to swap horses when crossing a stream. [9 June 1864]

19 With malice toward none; with charity for all; with firmness in the right, as God gives us to see the right, let us strive on to finish the work we are in. [Second inaugural address, 4 Mar. 1865]

20 You can fool all the people some of the time, and some of the people all the time, but you cannot fool all the people all the time. [Attr. words in speech at Clinton, Illinois, 8 Sept. 1858. Also attr. to P. T. Barnum]

21 I intend no modification of my oft-expressed personal wish that all men everywhere could be free. [Letter, 22 Aug. 1862]

22 I claim not to have controlled events, but confess plainly that events have controlled me. [Letter, 4 Apr. 1864]

1 People who like this sort of thing will find this the sort of thing they like. [Of a book]

2 The Lord prefers common-looking people. That is the reason he makes so many of them. [(23 Dec. 1863) Attr. by J. Hay, *Letters*, Vol. i. p. 142]

N. VACHEL LINDSAY 1879–1931

3 Then I saw the Congo, creeping through the black, / Cutting through the jungle with a golden track. [*The Congo*, 1]

4 Mumbo-Jumbo is dead in the jungle. [3]

GEORGE LINLEY 1798–1865

5 Oh, let the prayer re-echo: / 'God bless the Prince of Wales!' [*God Bless the Prince of Wales*]

6 Tho' lost to sight, to mem'ry dear/ Thou ever wilt remain. [Attr. song]

W. J. LINTON 1812–1898

7 For he's one of Nature's Gentlemen, the best of every time. [*Nature's Gentleman*]

MAXIM LITVINOV 1876–1951

8 Peace is indivisible. [Speech at League of Nations, Geneva, 1 July 1936]

LIVY 59 BC–AD 17

9 *Vae victis.* – Woe to the vanquished. [*History*, V. 48]

MARIE LLOYD 1870–1922

10 A little of what you fancy does you good. [Song]

11 I'm one of the ruins that Cromwell knocked about a bit. [Song]

12 Oh, mister porter, what shall I do? / I wanted to go to Birmingham, but they've carried me on to Crewe. [Song, words by George Le Brun]

ROBERT LLOYD 1733–1764

13 Slow and steady wins the race. [*The Hare and the Tortoise*]

DAVID, EARL LLOYD GEORGE 1863–1945

14 Mr Balfour's Poodle. [Description of House of Lords, in reply to a claim that the Lords were 'the watchdog of the nation', House of Commons, 26 June 1907]

15 A fully equipped Duke costs as much to keep up as two Dreadnoughts, and Dukes are just as great a terror, and they last longer. [Speech on the Budget, 9 Oct. 1909]

16 What is our task? To make Britain a fit country for heroes to live in. [Speech, 24 Nov. 1918]

17 May I ask of Protestants and Catholics alike that in these days of rejoicing [Christmas] we shall not forget the pitiful Madonna of the Slums with her pallid children. [Speech in London, 18 Dec. 1925]

18 He [Neville Chamberlain] saw foreign policy through the wrong end of a municipal drainpipe. [Quoted in Harris, *The Fine Art of Political Wit*, Ch. 6]

19 The Right Hon. gentleman [Sir John Simon] has sat so long on the fence that the iron has entered his soul. [Attr. in speech in House of Commons]

20 He was brilliant to the top of his army boots. [Of Field-Marshal, Lord Haig. Attr. in J. Wintle, *The Dictionary of War Quotations*]

JOHN LOCKE 1632–1704

21 New opinions are always suspected, and usually opposed, without any other reason but because they are not already common. [*Essay on the Human Understanding*, Dedication]

22 All men are liable to error; and most men are, in many points, by passion or interest, under temptation to it. [Ch. 20. 17]

FREDERICK LOCKER-LAMPSON 1821–1895

23 The world's as ugly, ay, as sin, / And almost as delightful. [*The Jester's Plea*]

24 And many are afraid of God – / And more of Mrs Grundy.

J. G. LOCKHART 1794–1854

25 Here lies that peerless peer Lord Peter, / Who broke the laws of God and man and metre. [*Epitaph for Lord Robertson*. Also attr. in slightly different form to Sir Walter Scott and Francis, Lord Jeffery]

DAVID LODGE 1935–

26 Literature is mostly about having sex and

not much about having children; life is the other way round. [*The British Museum is Falling Down*, Ch. 4]

THOMAS LODGE 1558?–1625

1 Love, in my bosom, like a bee, / Doth suck his sweet. [*Love, in my Bosom* Also attr. to Robert Greene]

2 Devils are not so black as they are painted. [*Margarite of America*]

3 Heigh ho, would she were mine! [*Rosalind's Description*]

FRANK LOESSER 1910–1969

4 I'd like to get you / On a slow boat to China. [Song: *Slow Boat to China*]

5 See what the boys in the back room will have, / And tell them I'll have the same. [Song in film *Destry Rides Again*, sung by Marlene Dietrich]

JOHN LOGAN 1748–1788

6 Thou hast no sorrow in thy song, / No winter in thy year. [*To the Cuckoo*, attr.]

CESARE LOMBROSO 1836–1909

7 The ignorant man always adores what he cannot understand. [*The Man of Genius*, Pt III, Ch. 3]

H. W. LONGFELLOW 1807–1882

8 I shot an arrow in the air, / It fell to earth, I know not where. [*The Arrow and the Song*]

9 And the song, from beginning to end, / I found again in the heart of a friend.

10 I know a maiden fair to see, / Take care! / She can both false and friendly be, / Beware! Beware! [*Beware!*]

11 I stood on the bridge at midnight, / As the clocks were striking the hour. [*The Bridge*]

12 Build me straight, O worthy Master! / Staunch and strong, a goodly vessel, / That shall laugh at all disaster, / And with wave and whirlwind wrestle! [*The Building of the Ship*]

13 Thou, too, sail on, O Ship of State! / Sail on, O Union, strong and great! / Humanity with all its fears, / With all the hopes of future years, / Is hanging breathless on thy fate!

14 Between the dark and the daylight, / When the night is beginning to lower, / Comes a pause in the day's occupations, / That is known as the Children's Hour. [*The Children's Hour*]

15 I hear in the chamber above me / The patter of little feet.

16 Singing the Hundredth Psalm, the grand old Puritan anthem. [*The Courtship of Miles Standish*, 3]

17 Archly the maiden smiled, with eyes over-running with laughter, / Said, in a tremulous voice, 'Why don't you speak for yourself, John?'

18 The bards sublime, / Whose distant foot-steps echo / Through the corridors of Time. [*The Day is Done*]

19 The cares that infest the day / Shall fold their tents, like the Arabs, / And as silently steal away. [*The Day is Done*]

20 This is the forest primeval. [*Evangeline*, 'Prelude']

21 Silently one by one, in the infinite meadows of heaven / Blossomed the lovely stars, the forget-me-nots of the angels. [I. 3]

22 Sorrow and silence are strong, and patient endurance is godlike. [II. 1]

23 The shades of night were falling fast, / As through an Alpine village passed / A youth, who bore, 'mid snow and ice, / A banner with the strange device, / Excelsior! [*Excelsior*]

24 'Try not the pass!' the old man said; / 'Dark lowers the tempest overhead.'

25 Beware the pine-tree's withered branch! / Beware the awful avalanche!

26 A traveller, by the faithful hound, / Half-buried in the snow was found.

27 Giotto's tower, / The lily of Florence blossom-ing in stone. [*Giotto's Tower*]

28 Saint Augustine! well hast thou said, / That of our vices we can frame / A ladder, if we will but tread / Beneath our feet each deed of shame! [*The Ladder of St Augustine*]

29 The heights by great men reached and kept / Were not attained by sudden flight, / But they, while their companions slept, / Were toil-ing upward in the night.

30 You would attain to the divine perfection, / And yet not turn your back upon the world. [*Michael Angelo*, I. 5]

31 A boy's will is the wind's will, / And the

thoughts of youth are long, long thoughts. [*My Lost Youth*]

1 Not in the clamour of the crowded street, / Not in the shouts and plaudits of the throng, / But in ourselves, are triumph and defeat. [*The Poets*]

2 Tell me not in mournful numbers, / Life is but an empty dream! / For the soul is dead that slumbers, / And things are not what they seem.

Life is real! Life is earnest! / And the grave is not its goal. / Dust thou art, to dust returnest, / Was not spoken of the soul. [*A Psalm of Life*]

3 Art is long, and Time is fleeting.

4 Trust no Future, howe'er pleasant / Let the dead Past bury its dead! / Act – act in the living Present! / Heart within, and God o'erhead!

5 Lives of great men all remind us / We can make our lives sublime, / And, departing, leave behind us / Footprints on the sands of time.

6 Let us, then, be up and doing. / With a heart for any fate; / Still achieving, still pursuing, / Learn to labour and to wait.

7 There is a Reaper whose name is Death, / And, with his sickle keen, / He reaps the bearded grain at a breath, / And the flowers that grow between. [*The Reaper and the Flowers*]

8 Though the mills of God grind slowly, yet they grind exceeding small; / Though with patience He stands waiting, with exactness grinds He all. [*Retribution*, (trans. of Friedrich von Logau)]

9 A Lady with a Lamp shall stand / In the great history of the land. / A noble type of good, / Heroic womanhood. [*Santa Filomena*]

10 'Wouldst thou' – so the helmsman answered. – / 'Learn the secret of the sea? / Only those who brave its dangers / Comprehend its mystery!' [*The Secret of the Sea*]

11 Beside the ungathered rice he lay. / His sickle in his hand. [*The Slave's Dream*]

12 By the shining Big-Sea-Water. [*The Song of Hiawatha*, 3]

13 From the waterfall he named her, / Minnehaha, Laughing Water. [4]

14 As unto the bow the cord is, / So unto the man is woman; / Though she bends him, she obeys him, / Though she draws him, yet she follows; / Useless each without the other! [10]

15 He seemed the incarnate 'Well, I told you so!' [*Tales of A Wayside Inn*, Pt I, 'The Poet's Tale']

16 Our ingress into the world / Was naked and bare; / Our progress through the world / Is trouble and care. [II, 'The Student's Tale']

17 Ships that pass in the night, and speak each other in passing; / Only a signal shown and a distant voice in the darkness; / So on the ocean of life we pass and speak one another, / Only a look and a voice; then darkness again and a silence. [III, 'The Theologian's Tale']

18 There was a little girl / Who had a little curl / Right in the middle of her forehead; / And when she was good / She was very, very good, / But when she was bad she was horrid. [*There was a Little Girl*]

19 Under the spreading chestnut tree / The village smithy stands; / The smith, a mighty man is he, / With large and sinewy hands; / And the muscles of his brawny arms / Are strong as iron bands. [*The Village Blacksmith*]

20 Looks the whole world in the face, / For he owes not any man.

21 Something attempted, something done, / Has earned a night's repose.

22 It was the schooner Hesperus, / That sailed the wintry sea; / And the skipper had taken his little daughter, / To bear him company. [*The Wreck of the Hesperus*]

23 But the father answered never a word. / A frozen corpse was he.

ALICE ROOSEVELT LONGWORTH
1884–1980

24 If you can't say anything good about someone, sit right here by me. [Embroidered on a cushion in her sitting room]

ANITA LOOS 1893–1981

25 So this gentleman said a girl with brains ought to do something else with them besides think. [*Gentlemen Prefer Blondes*, Ch. 1]

26 Kissing your hand may make you feel very, very good but a diamond and safire bracelet lasts for ever. [4]

27 So then Dr Froyd said all I needed was to cultivate a few inhibitions and get some sleep. [5]

LORCA *see* GARCÍA LORCA

LORD LOTHIAN 1882–1940

1 A limitation of armaments by political appeasement. [Letter to *The Times*, May 1934]

LOUIS XIV 1638–1715

2 *Ah! si je n'étais pas roi, je me mettrais en colère.* – Ah, if I were not king, I should lose my temper. [Attr.]

3 *Dieu, a-t-il donc oublié ce que j'ai fait pour lui?* – Has God then forgotten what I have done for him? [Attr., after the battle of Malplaquet]

4 *L'Etat c'est moi.* – I am the state. [Attr. to speech, 13 Apr. 1655]

5 *Il n'y a plus de Pyrénées.* – The Pyrenees are no more. [Attr. by Voltaire, *The Century of Louis XIV*, Ch. 28]

6 *J'ai failli attendre!* – I very nearly had to wait! [Attr.]

7 *Les premiers sentiments sont toujours les plus naturels.* – First feelings are always the most natural. [Reported by Mme de Sévigné]

LOUIS XVIII 1755–1824

8 *L'exactitude est la politesse des rois.* – Punctuality is the politeness of kings. [Attr.]

LOUIS-PHILIPPE 1773–1850

9 *La cordiale entente qui existe entre mon gouvernement et le sien* [Great Britain]. – The cordial understanding that exists between our two governments. [Speech, 27 Dec. 1843]

RICHARD LOVELACE 1618–1658

10 And when she ceased, we sighing saw / The floor lay paved with broken hearts. [*Gratiana Dancing and Singing*]

11 Lady, it is already morn, / And 'twas last night I swore to thee / That fond impossibility. [*The Scrutiny*]

12 Fishes, that tipple in the deep, / Know no such liberty. [*To Althea, From Prison*]

13 Stone walls do not a prison make / Nor iron bars a cage; / Minds innocent and quiet take / That for an hermitage.

14 Tell me not, Sweet, I am unkind, / That

from the nunnery / Of thy chaste breast, and quiet mind, / To war and arms I fly. [*To Lucasta, Going to the Wars*]

15 Yet this inconstancy is such, / As you too shall adore; / I could not love thee, Dear, so much / Loved I not honour more.

MARIE LOVELL 1803–1877

16 Two souls with but a single thought, / Two hearts that beat as one. [*Ingomar the Barbarian*, II (trans. of Friedrich Halm)]

ROBERT LOVEMAN 1864–1923

17 It is not raining rain to me, / It's raining violets. [*April Rain*]

SAMUEL LOVER 1797–1868

18 'There's luck in odd numbers,' says Rory O'More. [*Rory O'More*]

19 'Now women are mostly troublesome cattle to deal with mostly,' said Goggins. [*Handy Andy*, Ch. 36]

JAMES RUSSELL LOWELL 1819–1891

20 An' you've gut to git up airly / Ef you want to take in God. [*The Biglow Papers*, First Series, 1]

21 He's been true to *one* party – an' thet is himself. [2]

22 A marciful Providunce fashioned us holler, / O' purpose thet we might our principles swaller. [4]

23 But libbaty's a kind o'thing / That don't agree with niggers. [6]

24 An' in convartin' public trusts / To very privit uses.

25 I *don't* believe in princerple, / But oh, I *du* in interest.

26 I scent wich pays the best, an' then / Go into it baldheaded.

27 God makes sech nights, all white and still, / Fur'z you can look or listen. [Second Series, 'The Courtin']

28 All kin' o' smily round the lips, / An' teary round the lashes.

29 My gran'ther's rule was safer 'n 't is to crow: / Don't never prophesy – onless ye know. [2]

1 Of all the sarse that I can call to mind, /
England does make the most onpleasant kind: /
It's you're the sinner 'ollers, she's the saint; /
Wut's good's all English, all thet isn't ain't.

2 There comes Emerson first, whose rich words,
every one, / Are like gold nails in temples to hang
trophies on; / Whose prose is grand verse, while
his verse, the Lord knows, / Is some of it pr – No,
'tis not even prose. [*A Fable for Critics*]

3 There comes Poe, with his raven, like
Barnaby Rudge, / Three fifths of him genius
and two fifths sheer fudge.

4 A wise scepticism is the first attribute of a
good critic. [*Among My Books*, 'Shakespeare
Once More']

5 There is no good in arguing with the inevitable. The only argument available with an east
wind is to put on your overcoat. [*Democracy
and Addresses*, 'Democracy']

6 The misfortunes hardest to bear are those
which never come.

ROBERT LOWELL 1917–1977

7 If we see light at the end of the tunnel, / It's
the light of the oncoming train. [*Day by Day*]

8 The monument sticks like a fishbone / in
the city's throat. [*For the Union Dead*]

9 This is death / To die and know it. This is the
Black Widow, death. [*Mr Edwards and the Spider*]

10 The Lord survives the rainbow of His will.
[*The Quaker Graveyard in Nantucket*]

SAINT IGNATIUS LOYOLA 1491–1556

11 To give and not to count the cost; / To fight
and not to heed the wounds; / To toil and not
to seek for rest; / To labour and not ask for any
reward / Save that of knowing that we do Thy
will. [*Prayer for Generosity*]

LUCAN 39–65

12 *Victrix causa deis placuit, sed victa Catoni.*
– The victorious cause pleased the Gods, but the
conquered one pleased Cato. [*Pharsalia*, I. 128]

13 *Stat magni nominis umbra.* – There stands
the shadow of a glorious name. [135]

14 *Vivit post proelia Magnus, sed fortuna perit.*
– Pompey lives after his battles, but his fortune
has perished. [VIII. 84]

15 *Clarum et venerabile nomen / Gentibus.* – An
illustrious name, revered by the nations. [IX.
203]

16 *Estne Dei sedes nisi terra, et pontus, et aer, /
Et coelum, et virtus? Superos quid quaerimus ultra?
/ Iupiter est quodcumque vides, quocumque mov-
eris.* – Is the abode of God anywhere but in the
earth, and sea, and sky, and air, and virtue?
Why do we seek the heavenly ones beyond?
Whatever you see, and whatever you touch,
that is Jupiter. [578]

LUCRETIUS 99–55 BC

17 *Ergo vivida vis animi pervicit, et extra / Proces-
sit longe flammantia moenia mundi / Atque omne
immensum peragravit, mente animoque.* – So the
lively force of his mind has broken down all
barriers, and he has passed far beyond the fiery
walls of the world, and in mind and spirit has
traversed the boundless universe. [*De Rerum
Natura*, I. 72]

18 *Tantum religio potuit suadere malorum.*
– Such are the heights of wickedness to which
men are driven by religion. [101]

19 *Nil posse creari / De nilo.* – Nothing can be
created out of nothing. [155]

20 *Stilicidi casus lapidem cavat.* – Constant dripping hollows out a stone. [313]

21 *Suave, mari magno turbantibus aequora ventis,
/ E terra magnum alterius spectare laborem.*
– Sweet it is, when on the high seas the winds
are lashing the waters, to gaze from the land
on another's struggles. [II. 1]

22 *Inque brevi spatio mutantur saecla animantum
/ Et quasi cursores vitai lampada tradunt.* – The
generations of living things pass in a short
time, and like runners hand on the torch of life.
[78]

23 *Ut quod ali cibus est aliis fuat acre venenum.*
– What is food to one man is bitter poison to
others. [IV. 637]

24 *Medio de fonte leporum / Surgit amari aliquid
quod in ipsis floribus angat.* – From the heart of
the fountain of delight rises a jet of bitterness
that tortures us among the very flowers. [1133]

DOCTOR KARL LUEGER [Mayor of
Vienna] 1844–1910

25 I decide who is a Jew. [Quoted in Alan
Bullock, *Hitler*, Ch. 1. Sect. I. Sometimes
wrongly attr. to Goering]

MARTIN LUTHER 1483-1546

1 *Esto peccator et pecca fortiter, sed fortius fide et gaude in Christo.* – Be a sinner and strong in your sins, but be stronger in your faith and rejoice in Christ. [Letter to Melanchthon]

2 *Hier stehe ich, ich kann nicht anders.* – Here I stand, I cannot do otherwise. [Speech at the Diet of Worms, 18 Apr. 1521]

3 *Ein' feste Burg ist unser Gott, / Ein' gute Wehr und Waffen.* – A safe stronghold our God is still, / A trusty shield and weapon. [*Ein' feste Burg,* trans. T. Carlyle]

4 *Gedanken sind zollfrei.* – Thoughts pay no duty. [Motto of *Von weltlicher Obrigkeit*]

5 *Wer nicht liebt Wein, Weib und Gesang, / Der bleibt ein Narr sein Lebe lang.* – Who loves not wine, woman and song, / Remains a fool his whole life long. [Inscription at Wartburg, attr.]

ROSA LUXEMBURG 1871-1919

6 Freedom is always and exclusively freedom for the one who thinks differently. [*Social Reform or Revolution*]

JOHN LYDGATE 1370?-1451?

7 Sithe of our language he was the lodesterre. [(Chaucer) *The Falls of Princes,* Prologue, 252]

JOHN LYLY 1554?-1606

8 Cupid and my Campaspe played / At cards for kisses, Cupid paid. [*Campaspe,* III. v]

9 What bird so sings, yet so does wail? / O 'tis the ravished nightingale. / Jug, jug, jug, jug, tereu, she cries. [V. i]

10 None but the lark so shrill and clear; / How at heaven's gates she claps her wings, / The morn not waking till she sings.

11 It seems to me (said she) that you are in some brown study. [*Euphues* (Arber Edn., p. 80]

H. F. LYTE 1793-1847

12 Abide with me! Fast falls the eventide; / The darkness deepens: Lord, with me abide! / When other helpers fail, and comforts flee, / Help of the helpless, O abide with me! [Hymn]

13 Change and decay in all around I see; / O Thou, who changest not, abide with me!

GEORGE LYTTELTON 1709-1773

14 What is your sex's earliest, latest care, / Your heart's supreme ambition? – To be fair. [*Advice to a Lady*]

15 Where none admire, 'tis useless to excel; / Where none are beaux, 'tis vain to be a belle. [*Soliloquy of a Beauty*]

EDWARD BULWER-LYTTON 1803-1873

16 Revolutions are not made with rosewater. [*The Parisians,* Bk. v. Ch. 7]

17 Beneath the rule of men entirely great, / The pen is mightier than the sword. [*Richelieu,* II. ii]

18 In the lexicon of youth, which fate reserves / For a bright manhood, there is no such word / As – *fail.*

EARL OF LYTTON *see* MEREDITH, OWEN

M

THE MABINOGION

1 He could see a tall tree on the river bank, and the one half of it was burning from its root to its tip, and the other half with green leaves on it. [*Peredur Son of Efrawg*]

GENERAL MacARTHUR 1880–1964

2 I shall return. [On leaving the Philippines, 12 Mar. 1942]

ROSE MACAULAY 1889–1958

3 'Take my camel, dear', said my aunt Dot, as she climbed down from this animal on her return from High Mass. [*The Towers of Trebizond*, Ch. 1]

4 It was a book to kill time for those who like it better dead. [Quoted in Evan Esar (ed.), *Treasury of Humorous Quotations*]

THOMAS BABINGTON MACAULAY 1800–1859

5 Attend, all ye who list to hear our noble England's praise; / I tell of the thrice-noble deeds she wrought in ancient days. [*The Armada*]

6 The sentinel on Whitehall gate looked forth into the night.

7 Obadiah Bind-their-kings-in-chains-and-their-nobles-with-links-of-iron. [*The Battle of Naseby*]

8 Oh, wherefore come ye forth in triumph from the north, / With your hands, and your feet, and your raiment all red? / And wherefore doth your rout send forth a joyous shout? / And whence be the grapes of the wine-press which ye tread?

9 By those white cliffs I never more must see, / By that dear language which I spake like thee, / Forget all feuds, and shed one English tear / O'er English dust. A broken heart lies here. [*A Jacobite's Epitaph*]

10 One of us two, Herminius, / Shall never more go home. / I will lay on for Tusculum, / And lay thou on for Rome! [*Lays of Ancient Rome*, 'The Battle of Lake Regillus', 27]

11 These be the great Twin Brethren / To whom the Dorians pray. [40]

12 Lars Porsena of Clusium / By the nine gods he swore / That the great house of Tarquin / Should suffer wrong no more. / By the Nine Gods he swore it, / And named a trysting day, / And bade his messengers ride forth, / East and west and south and north, / To summon his array. ['Horatius', 1]

13 Then out spake brave Horatius, / The Captain of the Gate: / 'To every man upon this earth / Death cometh soon or late. / And how can man die better / Than facing fearful odds, / For the ashes of his fathers, / And the temples of his Gods?' [27]

14 Now who will stand on either hand / And keep the bridge with me? [29]

15 Then none was for a party; / Then all were for the state; / Then the great man helped the poor. / And the poor man loved the great. [32]

16 The Romans were like brothers / In the brave days of old.

17 Oh Tiber! father Tiber! / To whom the Romans pray, / A Roman's life, a Roman's arms, / Take thou in charge this day! [59]

1 And even the ranks of Tuscany / Could scarce forbear to cheer. [60]

2 Ye diners-out from whom we guard our spoons. [*Political Georgics* (letter to Hannah Macaulay, 29 June 1831]

3 The object of oratory alone is not truth but persuasion. [*Essay on Athenian Orators*]

4 In order that he might rob a neighbour whom he had promised to defend, black men fought on the coast of Coromandel, and red men scalped each other by the Great Lakes of North America. [*Historical Essays*, 'Frederic the Great']

5 The business of everybody is the business of nobody. ['Hallam's Constitutional History']

6 The gallery in which the reporters sit has become a fourth estate of the realm. [See 99:33]

7 Every schoolboy knows who imprisoned Montezuma, and who strangled Atahualpa. ['Lord Clive']

8 They [the Nabobs] raised the price of everything in their neighbourhood, from fresh eggs to rotten boroughs.

9 The reluctant obedience of distant provinces generally costs more than it is worth. ['Lord Mahon's War of the Succession']

10 The history of England is emphatically the history of progress. ['Sir J. Mackintosh's History of the Revolution']

11 When some traveller from New Zealand shall, in the midst of a vast solitude, take his stand on a broken arch of London Bridge to sketch the ruins of St Paul's. ['Von Ranke']

12 She [the Roman Church] thoroughly understands what no other Church has ever understood, how to deal with enthusiasts.

13 The Chief Justice was rich, quiet, and infamous. ['Warren Hastings']

14 The great Proconsul.

15 Thus our democracy was, from an early period, the most aristocratic, and our aristocracy the most democratic in the world. [*History of England*, I. Ch. 1]

16 He ... felt towards those whom he had deserted that peculiar malignity which has, in all ages, been characteristic of apostates.

17 The Puritan hated bear-baiting, not because it gave pain to the bear, but because it gave pleasure to the spectators. [2]

18 There were gentlemen and there were seamen in the navy of Charles the Second. But the seamen were not gentlemen: and the gentlemen were not seamen. [3]

19 He [Rumbold] never would believe that Providence had sent a few men into the world ready booted and spurred to ride, and millions ready saddled and bridled to be ridden. [5]

20 In every age the vilest specimens of human nature are to be found among demagogues.

21 Boswell is the first of biographers. [*Literary Essays*, 'Boswell's Life of Johnson']

22 The conformation of his mind was such that whatever was little seemed to him great, and whatever was great seemed to him little. ['Horace Walpole']

23 An acre in Middlesex is better than a principality in Utopia. ['Lord Bacon']

24 A sort of broken Johnsonese. ['Madame d'Arblay']

25 The dust and silence of the upper shelf. ['Milton']

26 As civilisation advances, poetry almost necessarily declines.

27 Perhaps no person can be a poet, or can even enjoy poetry, without a certain unsoundness of mind.

28 Nobles by the right of an earlier creation, and priests by the imposition of a mightier hand.

29 A propensity which, for want of a better name, we will venture to christen Boswellism.

30 We know no spectacle so ridiculous as the British public in one of its periodical fits of morality. ['Moore's Life of Byron']

31 From the poetry of Lord Byron they drew a system of ethics, compounded of misanthropy and voluptuousness, in which the two great commandments were, to hate your neighbour, and to love your neighbour's wife.

32 We have heard it said that five per cent is the natural interest of money. ['Southey's Colloquies']

33 The English Bible, a book which, if everything else in our language should perish, would alone suffice to show the whole extent of its beauty and power. [*On John Dryden*]

34 I shall not be satisfied unless I produce something that shall for a few days supersede

the last fasionable novel on the tables of young ladies. [Letter to Macvey Napier, 5 Nov. 1841]

1 There is only one cure for the evils which newly acquired freedom produces; and that is freedom. [Quoted in the *Sunday Times*, June 1990]

GENERAL A. C. McAULIFFE 1898–1975

2 Nuts! [Reply to German demand to surrender Bastogne, 22 Dec. 1944]

JOSEPH McCARTHY 20 Cent.

3 You made me love you, / I didn't want to do it. [Song]

SENATOR JOSEPH R. McCARTHY 1908–1957

4 McCarthyism is Americanism with its sleeves rolled. [In a speech in Wisconsin in 1952. Quoted in R. Rovere, *Senator Joe McCarthy*, Ch. 1]

MARY McCARTHY 1912–1989

5 Every word she [Lillian Hellman] writes is a lie, including 'and' and 'the'. [Discussing the 1930s in TV interview on Dick Cavett Show, 25/6 Jan. 1980]

GEORGE McCLELLAN 1826–1885

6 All quiet along the Potomac. [Attr., in the American Civil War]

HUGH MacDIARMID 1892–1978

7 I'll ha'e nae hauf-way hoose, but aye be whaur / Extremes meet – it's the only way I ken / To dodge the curst conceit o'bein' richt / That damns the vast majority o' men. [*A Drunk Man Looks at the Thistle*]

8 Hauf his soul a Scot maun use / Indulgin' in illusions, / And hauf in gettin' rid o' them / And comin' to conclusions.

9 There are plenty of ruined buildings in the world but no ruined stones. [*On a Raised Beach*]

GEORGE MACDONALD 1824–1905

10 Where did you come from, baby dear? / Out of the everywhere into here. [*At the Back of the North Wind*, Ch. 33, Song]

11 Where did you get your eyes so blue? / Out of the sky as I came through.

12 Here lie I, Martin Elginbrodde: / Hae mercy o' my soul, Lord God; / As I wod do, were I Lord God, / And ye were Martin Elginbrodde. [*David Elginbrod*, Bk i. Ch. 13]

FELIX McGLENNON ?–1943

13 They may build their ships, my lads, and think they know the game, / But they can't build boys of the bulldog breed / Who made old England's name. [*Sons of the Sea*]

WILLIAM McGONAGALL 1825–1902

14 Beautiful Railway Bridge of the Silv'ry Tay! / Alas, I am very sorry to say / That ninety lives have been taken away / On the last Sabbath day of 1879, / Which will be remember'd for a very long time. [*The Tay Bridge Disaster*]

CHARLES MACKAY 1814–1889

15 There's a good time coming, boys. [*The Good Time Coming*]

16 Cheer! Boys, cheer! [Title of song]

HENRY MACKENZIE 1745–1831

17 The Man of Feeling. [Title of novel]

SIR JAMES MACKINTOSH 1765–1831

18 Disciplined inaction. [*The Causes of the Revolution*, Ch. 7]

19 The Commons, faithful to their system, remained in a wise and masterly inactivity. [*Vindiciae Gallicae*, 1]

ARCHIBALD MACLEISH 1892–1982

20 A poem should be palpable and mute / As a globed fruit, / Dumb / As old medallions to the thumb . . . / A poem should be equal to / Not true . . . / A poem should not mean / But be. [*Ars Poetica*]

FIONA MACLEOD [WILLIAM SHARP] 1856–1905

21 How beautiful they are, / The lordly ones, / Who dwell in the hills, / In the hollow hills. [*The Immortal Hour*, ii]

22 My heart is a lonely hunter that hunts on a lonely hill. [*The Lonely Hunter*, vi]

NORMAN MACLEOD 1812–1872

1 Courage, brother! do not stumble, / Though thy path be dark as night; / There's a star to guide the humble: / 'Trust in God, and do the Right'. [Hymn: *Trust in God*]

MARSHALL McLUHAN 1911–1981

2 The new electronic interdependence re-creates the world in the image of a global village. [*The Gutenberg Galaxy*]

3 The medium is the message. This is merely to say that the personal and social consequences of any medium ... result from the new scale that is introduced into our affairs by each extension of ourselves or by any new technology. [*Understanding Media*, Ch. 1]

MARSHAL McMAHON 1808–1893

4 *J'y suis, j'y reste.* – Here I am and here I stay. [Attr., at taking of Malakoff, 8 Sept. 1855]

HAROLD MACMILLAN, LORD STOCKTON 1894–1986

5 You've never had it so good. [Speech on financial situation at Bedford, 20 July 1957 (originally US presidential election slogan, 1952)]

6 I thought the best thing to do was to settle up these little local difficulties, and then turn to the wider vision of the Commonwealth. [Said at London Airport, 7 Jan. 1958, referring to resignation of Treasury Ministers]

7 Jaw-jaw is better than war-war. [Said at Canberra, 30 Jan. 1958. See 113:13]

8 The wind of change is blowing through this Continent, and whether we like it or not, this growth of national consciousness is a political fact. [Speech, Cape Town, 3 Feb. 1960]

9 Fifteen fingers on the safety catch. [Speech in House of Commons, 30 May 1960, on breakdown of summit conference on nuclear disarmament]

LEONARD McNALLY 1752–1820

10 On Richmond Hill there lives a lass, / More sweet than May day morn, / Whose charms all other maids surpass, / A rose without a thorn. [*The Lass of Richmond Hill*]

LOUIS MACNEICE 1907–1963

11 It's no go the merrygoround, it's no go the rickshaw, / All we want is a limousine and a ticket for the peepshow. / Their knickers are made of crêpe-de-chine, their shoes are made of python, / Their halls are lined with tiger rugs and their walls with heads of bison. [*Bagpipe Music*]

12 It's no go, my honey love, it's no go, my poppet; / Work your hands from day to day, the winds will blow the profit. / The glass is falling hour by hour, the glass will fall for ever, / But if you break the bloody glass you won't hold up the weather.

13 Between the enormous fluted Ionic columns / There seeps from heavily jowled or hawk-like foreign faces / The guttural sorrow of the refugees. [*The British Museum Reading Room*]

14 When our brother Fire was having his dog's day / Jumping the London streets with millions of tin cans / Clanking at his tail, we heard some shadow say / 'Give the dog a bone'. [*Brother Fire*]

15 Crumbling between the fingers, under the feet, / Crumbling behind the eyes, / Their world gives way and dies / And something twangs and breaks at the end of the street. [*Débâcle*]

16 Time was away and somewhere else, / There were two glasses and two chairs / And two people with one pulse. [*Meeting Point*]

JAMES MACPHERSON 1736–1796

17 They came forth to war, but they always fell. [*Ossian*, 'Cath-Loda', 2]

JOHN MACRAE 1872–1918

18 In Flanders fields the poppies blow / Between the crosses, row on row. [*In Flanders Fields*]

MAURICE DE MAETERLINCK 1862–1949

19 *Il n'y a par de morts.* – There are no dead. [*L'Oiseau bleu*, IV, ii]

MAGNA CARTA 1215

20 *Nisi per legale iudicium parium suorum vel per legem terrae.* – Except by the legal judgement of his equals or the law of the land. [Clause 39]

GUSTAV MAHLER 1860–1911

1 At last, fortissimo! [On visiting Niagara. Quoted in K. Blaukopf, *Mahler*, Ch. 8]

F. S. MAHONY *see* PROUT, FATHER

JOSEPH DE MAISTRE 1754–1821

2 Every nation has the government that it deserves. [Letter on the subject of Russia, 15 Aug. 1811]

3 Scratch the Russian and·you will find the Tartar. [Attr. also to Napoleon and Prince de Ligne]

FRANÇOIS DE MALHERBE 1555–1628

4 *Mais elle etait du monde où les plus belles choses / Ont le pire destin; / Et rose, elle a vécu ce que vivent les roses, / L'espace d'un matin.* – But she was of the world where the fairest things have the worst fate. Like a rose, she has lived as long as roses live, the space of one morning. [*Consolation à M. du Périer*]

STÉPHANE MALLARMÉ 1842–1898

5 *La chair est triste, hélas ! et j'ai lu tous les livres.* – The flesh, alas, is sad, and I have read all the books. [*Brise marine*]

6 *Mais, ô mon cœur, entends le chant des matelots.* – But, O my soul, hear the song of the sailors.

7 *Donner un sens plus pur aux mots de la tribu.* – To give a purer sense to the language of the tribe. [*Le Tombeau d'Edgar Poe*]

G. H. L. MALLORY 1886–1924

8 Because it's there. [When asked why he wanted to climb Everest. Quoted in John Hunt, *The Ascent of Everest*, Ch. 1]

SIR THOMAS MALORY ?–1471

9 Whoso pulleth out this sword of this stone and anvil is rightwise king born of all England. [*Morte d'Arthur*, Bk. i. Ch 4]

10 This beast went to the well and drank, and the noise was in the beast's belly like unto the questing of thirty couple hounds, but all the while the beast drank there was no noise in the beast's belly. [19]

11 King Pellinore that time followed the questing beast.

12 So they rode till they came to a lake that was a fair water and broad. And in the midst Arthur was ware of an arm clothed in white samite, that held a fair sword in that hand. [25]

13 What, nephew, said the king, is the wind in that door? [vii. 34]

14 And anon there came in a dove at a window, and in her mouth there seemed a little censer of gold, and therewithal there was such a savour as all the spicery of the world had been there. [xi. 2]

15 For, as I suppose, no man in this world hath lived better than I have done, to achieve that I have done. [xvii. 16]

16 The month of May was come, when every lusty heart beginneth to blossom, and to bring forth fruit. [xviii. 25]

17 For love that time was not as love is nowadays. [xx. 3]

18 And much more am I sorrier for my good knights' loss than for the loss of my fair queen; for queens I might have enough, but such a fellowship of good knights shall never be together in no company. [9]

19 I saw nothing but waters wap [lap] and waves wanne [come]. [xxi. 5]

20 Through this same man and me hath all this war been wrought, and the death of the most noblest knights of the world; for through our love that we have loved together is my most noble lord slain. [9]

21 For as well as I have loved thee heretofore, mine heart will not serve now to see thee; for through thee and me is the flower of kings and knights destroyed.

22 Then Sir Launcelot saw her visage, but he wept not greatly, but sighed! [11]

23 Thou wert never matched of earthly knight's hand ... And thou wert the truest friend to thy lover that ever bestrad horse, and thou wert the truest lover of a sinful man that ever loved woman; and thou wert the kindest man that ever struck with sword. And thou wert the goodliest person that ever came among press of knights; and thou wert the meekest man and the gentlest that ever ate in hall among ladies, and thou wert the sternest knight

to thy mortal foe that ever put spear in the rest. [xxi. 13]

T. R. MALTHUS 1766–1834

1 The perpetual struggle for room and food. [*On Population*, Ch. 31]

W. R. MANDALE 19 Cent.

2 Up and down the City Road, / In and out the Eagle, / That's the way the money goes – / Pop goes the weasel! [*Pop Goes the Weasel*]

OSIP MANDELSTAM 1891–1938

3 But whenever there's a snatch of talk / it turns to the Kremlin mountaineer, / the ten thick worms his fingers, / his words like measures of weight, / the huge laughing cockroaches on his top lip, / The glitter of his boot-rims. [*Poems*, No. 286, 'Stalin Epigram']

J.C. MANGAN 1803–1849

4 My Dark Rosaleen! [Title of poem]

HERMAN J. MANKIEWICZ 1897–1953 and ORSON WELLES 1915–1985 [*see also under* WELLES]

5 It [death] is the only disease you don't look forward to being cured of. [In film *Citizen Kane*].

6 I guess Rosebud is just a piece in a jigsaw puzzle – a missing piece.

LORD JOHN MANNERS 1818–1906

7 Let wealth and commerce, laws and learning die, / But leave us still our old nobility. [*England's Trust*, Pt III. 227]

MAO ZEDONG 1893–1976

8 The enemy advances, we retreat; the enemy camps, we harass; the enemy tires, we attack; the enemy retreats, we pursue. [Letter, 5 Jan. 1930, but in fact quoting a letter from the Front Committee to the Central Committee of the Chinese Communist Party]

9 Every Communist must grasp the truth, 'Political power grows out of the barrel of a gun.' [Speech to Central Committee, Communist Party, 6 Nov. 1938]

10 We are advocates of the abolition of war, we do not want war; but war can only be abolished through war, and in order to get rid of the gun it is necessary to take up the gun.

11 Letting a hundred flowers blossom and a hundred schools of thought contend is the policy for promoting the progress of the arts and the sciences. [*On the Correct Handling of Contradictions*, 27 Feb. 1957]

12 All reactionaries are paper tigers. [Speech to International Congress, Moscow, 18 Nov. 1957]

WALTER MAP c. 1140–c. 1209

13 If die I must, let me die drinking in an inn. [*De Nugis Curialium*]

MARCUS AURELIUS ANTONINUS see AURELIUS

SENATOR WILLIAM MARCY 1786–1857

14 They see nothing wrong in the rule that to the victors belong the spoils of the enemy. [Speech in US Senate, 25 Jan. 1832]

QUEEN MARIE-ANTOINETTE 1755–1793

15 *Qu'ils mangent de la brioche.* – Let them eat cake. [Attr., on being told that the people could not afford bread. In fact pre-dated by reference in Rousseau, *Confessions*, Bk. vi]

SARAH, FIRST DUCHESS OF MARLBOROUGH 1660–1744

16 The Duke returned from the wars today and did pleasure me in his top-boots. [Attr., and various versions]

CHRISTOPHER MARLOWE 1564–1593

17 Live and die in Aristotle's works. [*Doctor Faustus*, 33]

18 I'll have them fly to India for gold, / Ransack the ocean for orient pearl. [110]

19 Unhappy spirits that fell with Lucifer, / Conspired against our God with Lucifer, / And are for ever damned with Lucifer. [310]

20 Hell hath no limits, nor is circumscribed / In one self place; for where we are is hell, / And where hell is, must we ever be. [560]

21 When all the world dissolves, / And every creature shall be purified, / All place shall be hell that is not heaven. [563]

22 Was this the face that launched a thousand

ships, / And burnt the topless towers of Ilium? / Sweet Helen, make me immortal with a kiss! / Her lips suck forth my soul: see, where it flies! – / Come, Helen, come give me my soul again. / Here will I dwell, for heaven be in these lips, / And all is dross that is not Helena. [1354]

1 Oh, thou art fairer than the evening air / Clad in the beauty of a thousand stars. [1367]

2 Now hast thou but one bare hour to live / And then thou must be damned perpetually! / Stand still, you ever-moving spheres of heaven, / That time may cease and midnight never come. [1450]

3 *O lente, lente currite noctis equi!* / The stars move still, time runs, the clock will strike, / The devil will come, and Faustus must be damned. / Oh, I'll leap up to my God! Who pulls me down? / See, see, where Christ's blood streams in the firmament! / One drop would save my soul, half a drop: ah, my Christ! [1458]

4 You stars that reigned at my nativity, / Whose influence hath allotted death and hell, / Now draw up Faustus, like a foggy mist, / Into the entrails of yon labouring cloud. [1473]

5 O soul, be changed into little waterdrops, / And fall into the ocean, ne'er be found! [1502]

6 Ugly hell, gape not! come not, Lucifer! / I'll burn my books! [1506]

7 Cut is the branch that might have grown full straight, / And burnèd is Apollo's laurel-bough, / That sometime grew within this learnèd man. [1508]

8 My men like satyrs grazing on the lawns, / Shall with their goat-feet dance an antic hay. [*Edward II*, I. i. 59]

9 I count religion but a childish toy, / And hold there is no sin but ignorance. [*The Jew of Malta*, Prologue, 14]

10 As their wealth increaseth, so enclose / Infinite riches in a little room. [I. i. 36]

11 BARNARDINE: Thou hast committed – BARABAS: Fornication? But that was in an other country: and besides, the wench is dead. [IV. i. 40]

12 I'm arm'd with more than complete steel – / The justice of my quarrel. [*Lust's Dominion*, IV. iii (authorship of play doubtful)]

13 Jigging veins of rhyming mother wits. [*Tamburlaine the Great*, Prologue]

14 Our swords shall play the orators for us. [Pt I. I. ii. 132]

15 Accursed be he that first invented war. [II. iv. 1]

16 Is it not passing brave to be a king, / And ride in triumph through Persepolis? [II. v. 53]

17 Ah, fair Zenocrate!– divine Zenocrate! / Fair is too foul an epithet for thee. [V. i. 135]

18 Now walk the angels on the walls of heaven, / As sentinels to warn th' immortal souls / To entertain divine Zenocrate. [Pt 2. II. iv. 15]

19 Yet let me kiss my lord before I die, / And let me die with kissing of my lord. [69]

20 Holla, ye pampered jades of Asia! / What, can ye draw but twenty miles a day? [IV. iii. 1]

21 For Tamburlaine, the scourge of God, must die. [V. iii. 249]

22 Who ever loved, that loved not at first sight? [*Hero and Leander*, I. 176]

23 Come live with me and be my love, / And we will all the pleasures prove / That hills and valleys, dales and fields, / Woods, or steepy mountain yields. [*The Passionate Shepherd to his Love*]

24 By shallow rivers to whose falls / Melodious birds sing madrigals.

25 And I will make thee beds of roses / And a thousand fragrant posies.

CLÉMENT MAROT 1495–1544

26 *Pipeur, larron, jureur, blasphémateur, / Sentant la hart de cent pas à la ronde, / Au demeurant le meilleur fils du monde.* – A cheat, a thief, a swearer and blasphemer, who smelt of the rope from a hundred yards away, but for the rest the best lad in the world. [*Epîtres*, XXIX]

DON MARQUIS 1878–1937

27 toujours gai archy toujours gai. [*archys life of mehitabel*, III, 'mehitabels first mistake']

28 procrastination is the / art of keeping / up with yesterday [XII, 'certain maxims of archy']

29 its cheerio / my deario that / pulls a lady through [XXIV, 'cheerio my deario']

30 now and then / there is a person born / who is so unlucky / that he runs into accidents / which started out to happen / to somebody else [XLI, 'archy the cockroach says']

31 jamais triste archy jamais triste / that is my motto [XLVI, 'mehitabel sees paris']

32 The art of newspaper paragraphing is / to stroke a platitude until it purrs like an epigram. [*New York Sun*: 'The Sun Dial']

1 An idea isn't responsible for the people who believe in it.

2 Ours is a world where people don't know what they want and are willing to go through hell to get it. [Quoted in Evan Esar (ed.), *Treasury of Humorous Quotations*]

CAPTAIN FREDERICK MARRYAT
1792–1848

3 As savage as a bear with a sore head. [*The King's Own*, Ch. 26]

4 If you please, ma'am, it was a very little one. [(Excusing an illegitimate baby) *Midshipman Easy*, Ch. 31]

5 All zeal, Mr Easy. [9]

6 It's just six of one and half-a-dozen of the other. [*The Pirate*, Ch. 4]

7 Every man paddle his own canoe. [*Settlers in Canada*, Ch. 8]

VICE PRESIDENT T. R. MARSHALL
1854–1925

8 What this country needs is a really good five-cent cigar. [Said to Henry M. Rose. Quoted in *New York Tribune*, 4 Jan. 1920]

MARTIAL *c.* 40–*c.* 104

9 *Laudant illa sed ista legunt.* – Those they praise, but they read the others. [*Epigrammata*, IV. 49]

10 *Non est vivere, sed valere vita est.* – Life is not living, but being in health. [VI. 70]

11 *Rus in urbe.* – The country in town. [XII. 57]

ANDREW MARVELL 1621–1678

12 Where the remote Bermudas ride, / In the ocean's bosom unespied. [*Bermudas*, I]

13 He hangs in shades the orange bright, / Like golden lamps in a green night. [17]

14 Echo beyond the Mexique Bay. [36]

15 My love is of a birth as rare / As 'tis, for object, strange and high; / It was begotten by despair, / Upon impossibility. [*The Definition of Love*]

16 As lines, so loves oblique, may well / Themselves in every angle greet: / But ours so truly parallel, / Though infinite, can never meet.

Therefore the love which us doth bind, / But Fate so enviously debars, / Is the conjunction of the mind, / And opposition of the stars.

17 Earth cannot show so brave a sight, / As when a single soul does fence / The batteries of alluring sense / And Heaven views it with delight. [*A Dialogue between the Resolved Soul and Created Pleasure*, 45]

18 How vainly men themselves amaze, / To win the palm, the oak, or bays; / And their incessant labours see / Crowned from some single herb or tree. [*The Garden*, 1]

19 Fair quiet, have I found thee here / And innocence thy sister dear? [9]

20 The nectarine, and curious peach, / Into my hands themselves do reach; / Stumbling on melons, as I pass, / Ensnared with flowers, I fall on grass. [37]

21 The mind, that ocean where each kind / Does straight its own resemblance find; / Yet it creates, transcending these, / Far other worlds, and other seas, / Annihilating all that's made / To a green thought in a green shade. [41]

22 Here at the fountain's sliding foot, / Or at some fruit tree's mossy root, / Casting the body's vest aside, / My soul into the boughs does glide. [49]

23 But 'twas beyond a mortal's share / To wander solitary there: / Two paradises 'twere in one, / To live in paradise alone. [61]

24 The inglorious arts of peace. [*An Horatian Ode upon Cromwell's Return from Ireland*, 10]

25 He nothing common did, or mean, / Upon that memorable scene, / But with his keener eye / The axe's edge did try. [57]

26 So much one man can do / That does both act and know. [75]

27 Ye country comets, that portend / No war nor prince's funeral, / Shining unto no higher end / Than to presage the grass's fall. [*The Mower to the Glow Worms*]

28 Had it lived long, it would have been / Lilies without, roses within. [*The Nymph Complaining for the Death of her Fawn*, 91]

29 Who can foretell for what high cause / This darling of the Gods was born? [*The Picture of Little T.C. in a Prospect of Flowers*]

30 Gather the flowers, but spare the buds.

31 Had we but world enough, and time, / This coyness, lady, were no crime. [*To His Coy Mistress*]

1 I would / Love you ten years before the flood, / And you should if you please refuse / Till the conversion of the Jews; / My vegetable love should grow / Vaster than empires and more slow.

2 But at my back I always hear / Time's wingèd chariot hurrying near, / And yonder all before us lie / Deserts of vast eternity. / Thy beauty shall no more be found, / Nor, in thy marble vaults, shall sound / My echoing song; then worms shall try / That long-preserved virginity, / And your quaint honour turn to dust, / And into ashes all my lust: / The grave's a fine and private place, / But none, I think, do there embrace.

3 Thus, though we cannot make our sun / Stand still, yet we will make him run.

4 The tawny mowers enter next, / Who seem like Israelites to be / Walking on foot through a green sea. [*Upon Appleton House*, 388]

5 And now the salmon-fishers moist / Their leathern boats begin to hoist; / And like Antipodes in shoes, / Have shod their heads in their canoes. [769]

GROUCHO MARX 1895–1977

6 Send two dozen roses to Room 424 and put 'Emily, I love you' on the back of the bill. [In film *A Day at the Races*, screenplay by Robert Pirosh, George Seaton and George Oppenheimer]

7 Do you suppose I could buy back my introduction to you? [In film *Monkey Business*, script by S. J. Perelman, Will B. Johnstone and Arthur Sheekman]

8 I've worked myself up from nothing to a state of extreme poverty.

9 I didn't like the play, but then I saw it under adverse conditions – the curtain was up. [Quoted in Laurence J. Peter, *Peter's Quotations*]

10 Military intelligence is a contradiction in terms. [Quoted in A. Spiegelman and B. Schneider, *Whole Grains*]

11 I never forget a face, but I'll make an exception in your case. [Quoted in the *Guardian*, 18 June 1965]

12 Please accept my resignation. I don't want to belong to any club that will accept me as a member. [*Groucho and Me*, Ch. 26]

KARL MARX 1818–1883

13 A spectre is haunting Europe – the spectre of Communism. [*The Communist Manifesto*, opening words]

14 The workers have nothing to lose but their chains. They have a world to gain. Workers of the world, unite. [Closing words]

15 From each according to his abilities, to each according to his needs. [*Criticism of the Gotha Programme*]

16 Religion . . . is the opium of the people. [*Criticism of Hegel's Philosophy of Right*, Introduction]

17 Hegel says somewhere that all great events and personalities in world history reappear in one way or another. He forgot to add: the first time as tragedy, the second as farce. [*The Eighteenth Brumaire of Louis Napoleon*, Pt I]

18 The dictatorship of the proletariat. [Letter to Weydemeyer, 5 Mar. 1852]

MARY TUDOR 1516–1558

19 When I am dead and opened, you shall find 'Calais' lying in my heart. [Holinshed, *Chronicles*, III]

ERIC MASCHWITZ 1901–1969

20 A Nightingale Sang in Berkeley Square. [Title of song]

21 These foolish things / Remind me of you. [Song: *These Foolish Things*]

JOHN MASEFIELD 1878–1967

22 Coming in solemn beauty like slow old tunes of Spain. [*Beauty*]

23 Oh some are fond of Spanish wine, and some are fond of French. [*Captain Stratton's Fancy*]

24 Quinquireme of Nineveh from distant Ophir / Rowing home to haven in sunny Palestine, / With a cargo of ivory, / And apes and peacocks, /Sandalwood, cedarwood and sweet white wine. [*Cargoes*]

25 Dirty British coaster with a salt-caked smoke stack, / Butting through the Channel in the mad March days, / With a cargo of Tyne coal, / Road-rail, pig-lead, / Firewood, iron-ware, and cheap tin-trays.

26 Laugh and be merry, remember, better the

world with a song. / Better the world with a blow in the teeth of a wrong. [*Laugh and Be Merry*]

1 One road leads to London, / One road runs to Wales, / My road leads me seawards / To the white dipping sails. [*Roadways*]

2 I must down to the seas again, to the lonely sea and the sky, / And all I ask is a tall ship and a star to steer her by, / And the wheel's kick and the wind's song and the white sail's shaking. / And a grey mist on the sea's face and a grey dawn breaking [*Sea Fever*]

3 I must down to the sea again, for the call of the running tide / Is a wild call and a clear call that may not be denied.

4 I must down to the seas again, to the vagrant gypsy life, / To the gull's way and the whale's way where the wind's like a whetted knife; / And all I ask is a merry yarn from a laughing fellow-rover, / And quiet sleep and a sweet dream when the long trick's over.

5 It's a warm wind, the west wind, full of birds' cries. [*The West Wind*]

WALT MASON 1862–1939

6 He's the Man Who Delivers the Goods. [*The Man Who Delivers the Goods*]

WILLIAM MASON 1724–1797

7 The fattest hog in Epicurus' sty. [*An Heroic Epistle*, 24]

PHILIP MASSINGER 1583–1640

8 He that would govern others, first should be / The master of himself. [*The Bondman*, I. iii]

9 Now speak, / Or be for ever silent. [*The Duke of Milan*, IV. iii]

10 I am driven / Into a desperate strait and cannot steer / A middle course. [*The Great Duke of Florence*, III. i]

11 The devil turned precisian! [*A New Way to Pay Old Debts*, I. i]

12 Death hath a thousand doors to let out life: / I shall find one. [*A Very Woman*, V. iv]

HENRI MATISSE 1869–1954

13 I don't know whether I believe in God or not. I think, really, I'm some sort of Buddhist. But the essential thing is to put oneself in a frame of mind which is close to that of prayer. [Quoted in Françoise Gilot and Carlton Lake, *Life with Picasso*, Part VI]

14 Exactitude is not truth. [Essay title quoted in J. D. Flam (ed.), *Matisse on Art*]

REGINALD MAUDLING 1917–1977

15 There comes a time in every man's life when he must make way for an older man. [Remark made in Smoking Room of House of Commons on being dropped from Mrs Thatcher's Shadow Cabinet and replaced by a man older than himself. Quoted in the *Guardian*, 20 Nov. 1976]

W. SOMERSET MAUGHAM 1874–1965

16 You know, of course, that the Tasmanians, who never committed adultery, are now extinct. [*The Bread-Winner*, iii]

17 A woman will always sacrifice herself if you give her the opportunity. It is her favourite form of self-indulgence. [*The Circle*, III]

18 When married people don't get on they can separate, but if they're not married it's impossible. It's a tie that only death can sever.

19 It's only if a man's a gentleman that he won't hesitate to do an ungentlemanly thing. Mortimer is on the boundary line and it makes him careful. [*The Constant Wife*, II]

20 The degree of a nation's civilization is marked by its disregard for the necessities of existence. [*Our Betters*, I]

21 'But I can do nothing unless I am in complete possession of the facts.' 'Obviously you can't cook them unless you have them.' [*Cakes and Ale*, Ch. 9]

22 Impropriety is the soul of wit. [*The Moon and Sixpence*, Ch. 4]

23 People ask you for criticism, but they only want praise. [*Of Human Bondage*, Ch. 50]

24 Money is like a sixth sense, without which you cannot make a complete use of the other five. [51]

25 For to write good prose is an affair of good manners. It is, unlike verse, a civic art ... Poetry is baroque. [*The Summing Up*, Ch. 12]

26 I would sooner read a time-table or a catalogue than nothing at all ... They are much more entertaining than half the novels that are written. [25]

1 Music-hall songs provide the dull with wit, just as proverbs provide them with wisdom. [*A Writer's Notebook*, 1892]

2 Men have an extraordinarily erroneous opinion of their position in nature; and the error is ineradicable. [1896]

3 There are times when I look over the various parts of my character with perplexity. I recognize that I am made up of several persons and that the person that at the moment has the upper hand will inevitably give place to another. But which is the real one? All of them or none?

4 The highest activities of consciousness have their origins in physical occurrences of the brain just as the loveliest melodies are not too sublime to be expressed by notes. [1902]

5 I can't think of a single Russian novel in which one of the characters goes to a picture gallery. [1917]

6 Sentimentality is only sentiment that rubs you up the wrong way. [1941]

SIR WILLIAM MAULE 1788–1858

7 My lords, we are vertebrate animals, we are mammalia! My learned friend's manner would be intolerable in Almighty God to a black beetle. [In court]

JAMES MAXTON 1885–1946

8 Sit down, man. You're a bloody tragedy. [To Ramsay MacDonald on the occasion of the last speech he made in House of Commons. Attr.]

VLADIMIR MAYAKOVSKY 1893–1930

9 Our planet / is poorly equipped / for delight. / One must snatch / gladness / from the days that are. / In this life / it's not difficult to die. / To make life / is more difficult by far. [*Sergei Yessenin*, trans. Herbert Marshall]

HUGHES MEARNS 1875–1965

10 As I was going up the stair / I met a man who wasn't there. / He wasn't there again today. / I wish, I wish he'd go away. [*The Psychoed*]

SIR PETER MEDAWAR 1915–1987

11 If politics is the art of the possible, research

is surely the art of the soluble. [*The Art of the Soluble*, (See 59:22)]

WILLIAM MEE 1788–1862

12 She's all my fancy painted her; / She's lovely, she's divine. [*Alice Gray*]

VISCOUNT MELBOURNE 1779–1848

13 I wish that I was as cocksure of anything as Tom Macaulay is of everything. [Attr. by Earl Cowper, preface to *Lord Melbourne's Papers*]

14 Things have come to a pretty pass when religion is allowed to invade the sphere of private life. [Attr. by G. W. E. Russell]

THOMAS MELLOR 1880–1926

15 I Wouldn't Leave My Little Wooden Hut for You. [Title of song]

HERMAN MELVILLE 1819–1891

16 Call me Ishmael. [*Moby Dick*, opening words]

17 Better sleep with a sober cannibal than a drunken Christian. [Ch. 3]

18 This, shipmates, this is that other lesson; and woe to that pilot of the living God who slights it. [9]

19 A whale ship was my Yale College and my Harvard. [24]

H. L. MENCKEN 1880–1956

20 No man is genuinely happy, married, who has to drink worse gin than he used to drink when he was single. [*Prejudices*, Fourth Series, 14]

21 I've made it a rule never to drink by daylight and never to refuse a drink after dark. [*New York Post*, 18 Sept. 1945]

JOHNNY MERCER 1906–1976

22 Days of wine and roses laugh and run away, / Like a child at play. [Song: *Days of Wine and Roses*]

23 That old black magic has me in its spell. [Song: *That Old Black Magic*]

24 You must have been a beautiful baby, / 'Cos baby just look at you now. [Song: *You Must Have Been a Beautiful Baby*]

LOUIS-SÉBASTIEN MERCIER 1740–1814

1 *Les extrèmes se touchent.* – Extremes meet.
[*Tableau de Paris*, Vol. iv. Ch. 348, heading]

GEORGE MEREDITH 1828–1909

2 Under yonder beech-tree single on the green-sward, / Couched with her arms behind her golden head, / Knees and tresses folded to slip and ripple idly, / Lies my young love sleeping in the shade. [*Love in the Valley*, 1]

3 She whom I love is hard to catch and conquer, / Hard, but O the glory of the winning were she won! [2]

4 Lovely are the curves of the white owl sweeping / Wavy in the dusk lit by one large star. / Lone on the fir-branch, his rattle-note unvaried. / Brooding o'er the gloom, spins the brown eve-jar. / Darker grows the valley, more and more forgetting: / So were it with me if forgetting could be willed. [5]

5 Love that so desires would fain keep her changeless; / Fain would fling the net, and fain have her free. [6]

6 On a starred night Prince Lucifer uprose. / Tired of his dark dominion swung the fiend. [*Lucifer in Starlight*]

7 Around the ancient track marched, rank on rank, / The army of unalterable law.

8 Not till the fire is dying in the grate, / Look we for any kinship with the stars. [*Modern Love*, 4]

9 And if I drink oblivion of a day, / So shorten I the stature of my soul. [12]

10 That rarest gift / To Beauty, Common Sense. [32]

11 In tragic life, God wot, / No villain need be! Passions spin the plot: / We are betrayed by what is false within. [43]

12 Ah, what a dusty answer gets the soul / When hot for certainties in this our life. [50]

13 Bring the army of the faithful through. [*To J[ohn] M[orley]*]

14 Sweet as Eden is the air, / And Eden-sweet the ray. [*Woodland Peace*]

15 Enter these enchanted woods, / You who dare. [*The Woods of Westermain*]

16 'Tis Ireland gives England her soldiers, her generals too. [*Diana of the Crossways*, Ch. 2]

17 'Hog's my feed,' said Andrew Hedger . . .'Ah could eat hog a solid hower.' [8]

18 'But how divine is utterance,' she said. 'As we to the brutes, poets are to us.' [16]

19 Cynicism is intellectual dandyism. [*The Egoist*, Ch. 7]

20 An aged and a great wine. [20]

21 None of your dam punctilio. [*One of Our Conquerors*, Ch. 1]

22 I expect that Woman will be the last thing civilized by Man. [*The Ordeal of Richard Feverel*, Ch. 1]

23 Who rises from prayer a better man, his prayer is answered. [12]

24 Kissing don't last: cookery do! [28]

25 Speech is the small change of silence. [34]

OWEN MEREDITH [EARL OF LYTTON] 1831–1891

26 Genius does what it must, and Talent does what it can. [*Last Words of a Sensitive Second-Rate Poet*]

DIXON MERRITT 1879–1954

27 A wonderful bird is the pelican, / His bill will hold more than his belican. / He can take in his beak / Enough food for a week, / But I'm darned if I know how the helican. [*The Pelican*]

PRINCE METTERNICH 1773–1859

28 Italy is a geographical expression. [Letter to Lord Palmerston, 6 Aug. 1847]

ALICE MEYNELL 1847–1922

29 Flocks of the memories of the day draw near / The dovecot doors of sleep. [*At Night*]

30 I must not think of thee; and, tired yet strong, / I shun the thought that lurks in all delight – / The thought of thee – and in the blue heaven's height, / And in the sweetest passage of a song. [*Renouncement*]

31 She walks – the lady of my delight – / A shepherdess of sheep. [*The Shepherdess*]

JULES MICHELET 1798–1874

32 You are one of the forces of nature. [Letter to Alexandre Dumas, quoted in Dumas' *Memoirs*, Vol. vi. Ch. 138]

WILLIAM MICKLE 1735–1788

33 The dews of summer night did fall, / The moon, sweet regent of the sky, / Silvered the

walls of Cumnor Hall, / And many an oak that grew thereby. [*Cumnor Hall*]

THOMAS MIDDLETON 1570?–1627

1 A wondrous necessary man. [*The Changeling*, V. i]

2 Beneath the stars, upon yon meteor / Ever hung my fate, 'mongst things corruptible. [V. iii]

3 By many a happy accident. [*No Wit, No Help, Like a Woman's*, IV. i]

4 Though I be poor, I'm honest. [*The Witch*, III. ii]

5 There's no hate lost between us. [IV. ii]

6 Black spirits and white, red spirits and gray, / Mingle, mingle, mingle, you that mingle may! [V. ii]

A. MIDLANE 1825–1909

7 There's a Friend for little children / Above the bright blue sky, / A Friend who never changes, / Whose love will never die. [Hymn]

LUDWIG MIES VAN DER ROHE 1886–1969

8 Less is more. [Quoted in his obituary, *The Times*, 19 Aug. 1969]

GEORGE MIKES 1912–1987

9 Continental people have sex life; the English have hot-water bottles. [*How to be an Alien*]

JOHN STUART MILL 1806–1873

10 Ask yourself whether you are happy, and you cease to be so. [*Autobiography*, Ch. 5]

11 Unearned increment. [*Dissertations and Discussions*, IV]

12 He who knows only his own side of the case knows little of that. [*On Liberty*, Ch. 2]

13 The liberty of the individual must be thus far limited; he must not make himself a nuisance to other people. [3]

14 All good things which exist are the fruits of originality.

15 Liberty consists in doing what one desires. [5]

16 The worth of a State, in the long run, is the worth of the individuals composing it.

EDNA ST VINCENT MILLAY 1892–1950

17 Euclid alone / Has looked on Beauty bare, Fortunate they / Who, though once only and then but far away, / Have heard her massive sandal set on stone. [*Euclid alone has looked on Beauty bare*]

18 My candle burns at both ends; / It will not last the night; / But, ah, my foes, and oh, my friends – / It gives a lovely light. [*A Few Figs from Thistles*, 'First Fig']

19 And if I loved you Wednesday, / Well what is that to you? / I do not love you Thursday – / So much is true. [*Thursday*]

20 It is not true that life is one damn thing after another – it is one damn thing over and over. [(Capping Elbert Hubbard; see 211:13) *Letters of Edna St Vincent Millay*]

ARTHUR MILLER 1915–

21 Oh, Elizabeth, your justice would freeze beer! [*The Crucible*, II]

22 He's liked, but he's not well liked. [*Death of a Salesman*, I]

23 Never fight fair with a stranger, boy. You'll never get out of the jungle that way.

24 Willy Loman never made a lot of money. His name was never in the paper. He's not the finest character that ever lived. But he's a human being, and a terrible thing is happening to him. So attention must be paid.

25 He's a man way out there in the blue, riding on a smile and a shoeshine. And when they start not smiling back – that's an earthquake ... A salesman is got to dream, boy. It comes with the territory. [II, 'Death Requiem']

26 A good newspaper, I suppose, is a nation talking to itself. [*Observer*, 'Sayings of the Week', 26 Nov. 1961]

MRS E. MILLER 1833–1913

27 I love to hear the story / Which angel voices tell. [Hymn]

HARRY MILLER ?–1983

28 A Boy's Best Friend is His Mother [Title of song]

JONATHAN MILLER 1934–

29 I'm not really a Jew; just Jew-ish, not the whole hog. [*Beyond the Fringe*]

WILLIAM MILLER 1810–1872

1 Wee Willie Winkie runs through the town, / Upstairs and downstairs in his nicht-gown. [*Willie Winkie*]

SPIKE MILLIGAN 1918–

2 'Do you come here often?'
'Only in the mating season.' [BBC radio comedy series *The Goon Show* (running gag)]

3 You silly twisted boy!

4 I'm walking backwards for Christmas.

5 The dreaded lergy.

6 It's all in the mind, you know.

7 I'm a hero wid coward's legs, I'm a hero from the waist up. [*Puckoon*, Ch. 2]

8 When she saw the sign 'Members only' she thought of him. [3]

9 Money can't buy friends, but you can get a better class of enemy. [6]

A. J. MILLS 1872–?

10 All the Nice Girls Love a Sailor. [Title of song]

11 Just like the Ivy I'll cling to you. [Title of song]

HENRY MILMAN 1791–1868

12 Ride on! ride on in majesty! / In lowly pomp ride on to die. [*Ride On*]

A. A. MILNE 1882–1956

13 They're changing guard at Buckingham Palace – / Christopher Robin went down with Alice. [*When We Were Very Young*, 'Buckingham Palace']

14 James James / Morrison Morrison / Weatherby George Dupree / Took great / Care of his Mother / Though he was only three. ['Disobedience']

15 You must never go down to the end of the town if you don't go down with me.

16 The King asked / The Queen, and / The Queen asked / The Dairymaid: / 'Could we have some butter for / The Royal slice of bread?' ['The King's Breakfast']

17 Nobody, my darling, could call me / A fussy man – / BUT / I do like a little bit of butter to my bread!

18 Hush! Hush! Whisper who dares! / Christopher Robin is saying his prayers. ['Vespers']

19 And nobody knows / (Tiddely pom), / How cold my toes / (Tiddely pom), / How cold my toes / (Tiddely pom), / Are growing. [*House at Pooh Corner*, Ch. 1]

20 Tiggers don't like honey. [2]

21 'Well, I sort of made it up,' said Pooh . . .'it comes to me sometimes.' 'Ah!' said Rabbit, who never let things come to him, but always went and fetched them. [Ch. 5]

22 He respects Owl, because you can't help respecting anybody who can spell TUESDAY, even if he doesn't spell it right.

23 When you are a Bear of Very Little Brain, and you Think of Things, you find sometimes that a Thing which seemed very Thingish inside you is quite different when it gets out into the open and has other people looking at it. [6]

24 Isn't it funny / How a bear likes honey? / Buzz! Buzz! Buzz! / I wonder why he does? [*Winnie-the-Pooh*, Ch. 1]

25 How sweet to be a Cloud / Floating in the Blue!

26 When Rabbit said, 'Honey or condensed milk with your bread?' he was so excited that he said, 'Both,' and then, so as not to seem greedy, he added, 'But don't bother about the bread, please.' [2]

27 I am a Bear of Very Little Brain and long words Bother Me. [4]

28 I have decided to catch a Heffalump. [5]

29 I'm giving him a Useful Pot to Keep Things In. [6]

30 'Pathetic,' he said. 'That's what it is. Pathetic.' [6]

31 Time for a little something.

32 Kanga and Baby Roo. [7]

33 On Monday, when the sun is hot, / I wonder to myself a lot: / 'Now is it true, or is it not, / That what is which and which is what?'

34 An Expotition to the North Pole. [8, heading]

LORD MILNER 1854–1925

35 If we believe a thing to be bad, and if we have a right to prevent it, it is our duty to try to prevent it and to damn the consequences. [Speech in Glasgow, 26 Nov. 1909]

JOHN MILTON 1608–1674

1 Such sweet compulsion doth in music lie. [*Arcades*, 68]

2 Blest pair of Sirens, pledges of Heav'n's joy, / Sphere-born harmonious sisters, voice and verse. [*At a Solemn Music*, 1]

3 Before the starry threshold of Jove's Court / My mansion is. [*Comus*, 1]

4 Above the smoke and stir of this dim spot, / Which men call earth. [5]

5 An old, and haughty nation proud in arms. [33]

6 Bacchus, that first from out the purple grape, / Crushed the sweet poison of misusèd wine. [46]

7 What hath night to do with sleep? [122]

8 Ere the blabbing Eastern scout, / The nice Morn on th' Indian steep / From her cabined loop-hole peep. [138]

9 Come, knit hands, and beat the ground, / in a light fantastic round. [143]

10 When the grey-hooded Ev'n / Like a sad votarist in palmer's weed, / Rose from the hindmost wheels of Phoebus' wain. [188]

11 The stars, / That nature hung in heaven, and filled their lamps / With everlasting oil, to give due light / To the misled and lonely traveller. [197]

12 O welcome pure-eyed Faith, white-handed Hope, / Thou hovering angel girt with golden wings. [213]

13 Was I deceived, or did a sable cloud / Turn forth her silver lining on the night? [221]

14 By slow Meander's margent green, / And in the violet-embroidered vale. [232]

15 Dingle, or bushy dell of this wild wood, / And every bosky bourn from side to side. [313]

16 With thy long levelled rule of streaming light. [340]

17 Virtue could see to do what Virtue would / By her own radiant light, though sun and moon / Were in the flat sea sunk. [373]

18 He that has light within his own clear breast / May sit i' th' centre, and enjoy bright day, / But he that hides a dark soul, and foul thoughts / Benighted walks under the midday sun. [381]

19 The unsunned heaps / Of miser's treasure. [398]

20 'Tis Chastity, my brother, Chastity: / She that has that is clad in complete steel. [420]

21 How charming is divine philosophy! / Not harsh, and crabbèd as dull fools suppose, / But musical as is Apollo's lute, / And a perpetual feast of nectared sweets, / Where no crude surfeit reigns. [476]

22 Storied of old in high immortal verse / Of dire chimeras and enchanted isles, / And rifted rocks whose entrance leads to Hell. [516]

23 Wrapt in a pleasing fit of melancholy. [546]

24 And filled the air with barbarous dissonance. [550]

25 I was all ear / And took in strains that might create a soul / Under the ribs of Death. [560]

26 That power / Which erring men call Chance. [587]

27 Virtue may be assailed, but never hurt, / Surprised by unjust force, but not enthralled. [589]

28 If this fail, / The pillared firmament is rottenness, / And earth's base built on stubble. [597]

29 Those budge doctors of the Stoic fur. [707]

30 Praising the lean and sallow abstinence. [709]

31 Beauty is Nature's coin, must not be hoarded, / But must be current. [739]

32 Beauty is Nature's brag, and must be shown / In courts, at feasts, and high solemnities. [745]

33 It is for homely features to keep home, / They had their name thence; coarse complexions / And cheeks of sorry grain will serve to ply / The sampler, and to tease the housewife's wool. / What need a vermeil-tinctured lip for that, / Love-darting eyes, or tresses like the morn? [748]

34 Sabrina fair, / Listen where thou art sitting / Under the glassy, cool, translucent wave, / In twisted braids of lilies knitting / The loose train of thy amber-dropping hair. [859]

35 Mortals, that would follow me, / Love virtue, she alone is free, / She can teach ye how to climb / Higher than the sphery chime; / Or if virtue feeble were, / Heav'n itself would stoop to her. [1018]

36 Hence, vain deluding joys, / The brood of Folly without father bred. [*Il Penseroso*, 1]

John Milton

1 The gay motes that people the sunbeams. [8]

2 Hail divinest melancholy. [12]

3 Sober, steadfast, and demure. [32]

4 And looks commercing with the skies, / Thy rapt soul sitting in thine eyes. [39]

5 Him that yon soars on golden wing, / Guiding the fiery-wheelèd throne, / The Cherub Contemplation. [52]

6 Sweet bird, that shunn'st the noise of folly, / Most musical, most melancholy! [61]

7 To behold the wandering moon, / Riding near her highest noon, / Like one that had been led astray / Through the heav'n's wide pathless way; / And oft, as if her head she bowed, / Stooping through a fleecy cloud. [67]

8 I hear the far-off curfew sound, / Over some wide-watered shore, / Swinging slow with sullen roar. [74]

9 Far from all resort of mirth, / Save the cricket on the hearth! [81]

10 Sometime let gorgeous Tragedy / In sceptred pall come sweeping by, / Presenting Thebes, or Pelops' line, / Or the tale of Troy divine. [97]

11 Or bid the soul of Orpheus sing / Such notes as, warbled to the string, / Drew iron tears down Pluto's cheek. [105]

12 Or call up him that left half told / The story of Cambuscan bold. [109]

13 Where more is meant than meets the ear. [120]

14 Hide me from day's garish eye / While the bee with honied thigh / That at her flowery work doth sing. [141]

15 With antique pillars massy proof, / And storied windows richly dight, / Casting a dim religious light. / There let the pealing organ blow, / To the full-voiced quire below. [158]

16 Till old experience do attain / To something like prophetic strain. [173]

17 Hence loathèd Melancholy, / Of Cerberus and blackest Midnight born. [*L'Allegro*, 1]

18 So buxom, blithe, and debonair. [24]

19 Haste thee, nymph, and bring with thee / Jest and youthful jollity, / Quips and cranks, and wanton wiles, / Nods, and becks, and wreathèd smiles. [25]

20 Sport that wrinkled Care derides, / And Laughter holding both his sides. / Come and trip it as ye go / On the light fantastic toe. [31]

21 The mountain nymph, sweet Liberty. [36]

22 To hear the lark begin his flight, / And singing startle the dull night, / From his watchtower in the skies, / Till the dappled dawn doth rise. [41]

23 While the cock with lively din, / Scatters the rear of darkness thin, / And to the stack, or the barn door, / Stoutly struts his dames before. [49]

24 Right against the eastern gate, / Where the great sun begins his state. [59]

25 And every shepherd tells his tale / Under the hawthorn in the dale. [67]

26 Meadows trim with daisies pied, / Shallow brooks and rivers wide, / Towers, and battlements it sees / Bosomed high in tufted trees, / Where perhaps some beauty lies, / The cynosure of neighbouring eyes. [75]

27 Of herbs and other country messes, / Which the neat-handed Phyllis dresses. [85]

28 To many a youth and many a maid, / Dancing in the chequered shade. [95]

29 Then to the spicy nut-brown ale. [100]

30 Towered cities please us then / And the busy hum of men. [117]

31 Store of ladies, whose bright eyes / Rain influence, and judge the prize. [121]

32 Then to the well-trod stage anon, / If Jonson's learnèd sock be on, / Or sweetest Shakespeare, Fancy's child, / Warble his native wood-notes wild. [131]

33 And ever, against eating cares, / Lap me in soft Lydian airs, / Married to immortal verse / Such as the meeting soul may pierce / In notes, with many a winding bout / Of linkèd sweetness long drawn out. [135]

34 The melting voice through mazes running; / Untwisting all the chains that tie / The hidden soul of harmony. [142]

35 Such strains as would have won the ear / Of Pluto, to have quite set free / His half-regained Eurydice. [148]

36 Yet once more, O ye laurels, and once more / Ye myrtles brown, with ivy never sere, / I come to pluck your berries harsh and crude, / And with forced fingers rude, / Shatter your leaves before the mellowing year. [*Lycidas*, 1]

1 He knew / Himself to sing, and build the lofty rhyme. [10]

2 Without the meed of some melodious tear. [14]

3 Under the opening eye-lids of the morn. [26]

4 But O the heavy change, now thou art gone, / Now thou art gone, and never must return! [37]

5 Gadding vine. [40]

6 As killing as the canker to the rose. [45]

7 And strictly meditate the thankless Muse. [66]

8 To sport with Amaryllis in the shade, / Or with tangles of Neaera's hair. [68]

9 Fame is the spur that the clear spirit doth raise / (That last infirmity of noble mind) / To scorn delights, and live laborious days; / But the fair guerdon when we hope to find, / And think to burst out into sudden blaze, / Comes the blind Fury with th' abhorred shears, / And slits the thin-spun life. [70]

10 Fame is no plant that grows on mortal soil. [78]

11 It was that fatal and perfidious bark / Built in th' eclipse, and rigged with curses dark. [100]

12 Last came, and last did go, / The Pilot of the Galilean lake, / Two massy keys he bore, of metals twain, / (The golden opes, the iron shuts amain). [108]

13 Blind mouths! that scarce themselves know how to hold / A sheep-hook. [119]

14 And when they list, their lean and flashy songs / Grate on their scrannel pipes of wretched straw, / The hungry sheep look up, and are not fed, / But swoln with wind, and the rank mist they draw, / Rot inwardly, and foul contagion spread. [123]

15 But that two-handed engine at the door, / Stands ready to smite once, and smite no more. [130]

16 Throw hither all your quaint enamelled eyes / That on the green turf suck the honied showers, / And purple all the ground with vernal flowers. / Bring the rathe primrose that forsaken dies, / The tufted crow-toe and pale jessamine, / The white pink, and the pansy freaked with jet, / The glowing violet, / The muskrose and the well-attired woodbine, / With cowslips wan that hang the pensive head, / And every flower that sad embroidery wears: / Bid amaranthus all his beauty shed, / And daffadillies fill their cups with tears, / To strew the laureate hearse where Lycid lies. [139]

17 So sinks the day-star in the ocean bed, / And yet anon repairs his drooping head, / And tricks his beams, and with new-spangled ore, / Flames in the forehead of the morning sky. [168]

18 At last he rose, and twitched his mantle blue; / Tomorrow to fresh woods, and pastures new. [192]

19 O fairest flower, no sooner blown but blasted, / Soft silken primrose fading timelessly. [On the Death of a Fair Infant, 1]

20 This is the month and this the happy morn. [On the Morning of Christ's Nativity, 1]

21 Forsook the courts of everlasting day. [13]

22 It was the winter wild, / While the Heaven-born child, / All meanly wrapt in the rude manger lies. [29]

23 Nor war, or battle's sound / Was heard the world around. [53]

24 Time will run back, and fetch the age of gold. [135]

25 The oracles are dumb. [173]

26 No nightly trance or breathèd spell, / Inspires the pale-eyed priest from the prophetic cell. [179]

27 So when the sun in bed, / Curtained with cloudy red, / Pillows his chin upon an orient wave. [229]

28 What needs my Shakespeare, for his honoured bones, / The labour of an age in pilèd stones? [On Shakespeare]

29 Dear son of memory, great heir of fame, / What need'st thou such weak witness of thy name?

30 Rhyme being no necessary adjunct or true ornament of poem or good verse, in longer works especially, but the invention of a barbarous age, to set off wretched matter with lame metre. [Paradise Lost, Preface: The Verse]

31 The troublesome and modern bondage of rhyming.

32 Of Man's first disobedience, and the fruit / Of that forbidden tree, whose mortal taste / Brought death into the world, and all our woe, / With loss of Eden. [Bk i. 1]

John Milton

1 Things unattempted yet in prose or rhyme. [16]

2 What in me is dark / Illumine, what is low raise and support; / That to the height of this great argument / I may assert eternal Providence, / And justify the ways of God to men. [22]

3 To bottomless perdition, there to dwell / In adamantine chains and penal fire. [47]

4 As far as angels' ken. [59]

5 Yet from those flames / No light, but rather darkness visible / Served only to discover sights of woe, / Regions of sorrow, doleful shades where peace / And rest can never dwell, hope never comes / That comes to all. [62]

6 Sense of injured merit. [98]

7 What though the field be lost? / All is not lost; th' unconquerable will, / And study of revenge, immortal hate, / And courage never to submit or yield: / And what is else not to be overcome? [105]

8 To be weak is miserable / Doing or suffering. [157]

9 And out of good still to find means of evil. [165]

10 Farewell happy fields / Where joy for ever dwells: Hail horrors, hail! [249]

11 A mind not to be changed by place or time. / The mind is its own place, and in itself / Can make a heav'n of hell, a hell of heav'n. [253]

12 Better to reign in hell than serve in heav'n. [263]

13 Thick as autumnal leaves that strow the brooks / In Vallombrosa, where th' Etrurian shades / High overarched imbower. [302]

14 Awake, arise, or be for ever fall'n! [330]

15 Execute their aery purposes. [430]

16 When night / Darkens the streets, then wander forth the sons / Of Belial, flown with insolence and wine. [500]

17 The imperial ensign, which, full high advanced, / Shone like a meteor, streaming to the wind. [536]

18 A shout that tore hell's concave, and beyond / Frightened the reign of Chaos and old Night. [542]

19 In perfect phalanx to the Dorian mood / Of flutes and soft recorders. [550]

20 His form had yet not lost / All her original brightness, nor appeared / Less than archangel ruined, and th' excess / Of glory obscured. [591]

21 In dim eclipse disastrous twilight sheds / On half the nations, and with fear of change / Perplexes monarchs. [597]

22 Care / Sat on his faded cheek. [601]

23 Tears such as angels weep, burst forth. [620]

24 Who overcomes / By force, hath overcome but half his foe. [648]

25 Let none admire / That riches grow in hell; that soil may best / Deserve the precious bane. [690]

26 Anon out of the earth a fabric huge / Rose like an exhalation. [710]

27 From morn / To noon he fell, from noon to dewy eve, / A summer's day; and with the setting sun / Dropt from the zenith like a falling star. [742]

28 Pandemonium, the high capital / Of Satan and his peers. [756]

29 Fairy elves, / Whose midnight revels, by a forest side / Or fountain, some belated peasant sees, / Or dreams he sees, while overhead the moon / Sits arbitress. [781]

30 Satan exalted sat, by merit raised / To that bad eminence. [ii. 5]

31 Rather than be less / Cared not to be at all. [47]

32 My sentence is for open war; of wiles, / More unexpert, I boast not. [51]

33 Though his tongue / Dropt manna, and could make the worse appear / The better reason. [112]

34 For who would lose, / Though full of pain, this intellectual being, / Those thoughts that wander through eternity, / To perish rather, swallowed up and lost / In the wide womb of uncreated night, / Devoid of sense and motion? [146]

35 His red right hand. [174]

36 Unrespited, unpitied, unreprieved, / Ages of hopeless end. [185]

37 Thus Belial, with words clothed in reason's garb, / Counselled ignoble ease, and peaceful sloth, / Not peace. [226]

38 With grave / Aspect he rose, and in his rising seemed / A pillar of state; deep on his

front engraven / Deliberation sat and public care; / And princely counsel in his face yet shone, / Majestic though in ruin. [300]

1 Through the palpable obscure find out / His uncouth way. [406]

2 Long is the way / and hard, that out of hell leads up to light. [432]

3 Vain wisdom all, and false philosophy. [565]

4 O'er many a frozen, many a fiery Alp, / Rocks, caves, lakes, fens, bogs, dens, and shades of death. [620]

5 The other shape, / If shape it might be called that shape had none. [666]

6 Black it stood as night, / Fierce as ten furies, terrible as hell, / And shook a dreadful dart. [670]

7 Whence and what art thou, execrable shape? [681]

8 Sable-vested Night, eldest of things. [962]

9 With ruin upon ruin, rout on rout, / Confusion worse confounded. [995]

10 Hail holy light, offspring of heav'n firstborn, / Or of th' Eternal co-eternal beam. [iii. 1]

11 The rising world of waters dark and deep. [11]

12 Then feed on thoughts, that voluntary move / Harmonious numbers. [37]

13 Thus with the year / Seasons return, but not to me returns / Day, or the sweet approach of ev'n or morn, / Or sight of vernal bloom, or summer's rose, / Or flocks, or herds, or human face divine. [40]

14 From the cheerful ways of men / Cut off, and for the book of knowledge fair / Presented with a universal blank / Of nature's works to me expunged and razed, / And wisdom at one entrance quite shut out. [46]

15 Dark with excessive bright. [380]

16 Embryos and idiots, eremites and friars / White, black, and grey, with all their trumpery. [474]

17 Into a Limbo large and broad, since called / The paradise of fools, to few unknown. [495]

18 At whose sight all the stars / Hide their diminished heads. [iv. 34]

19 Me miserable! which way shall I fly / Infinite wrath, and infinite despair? / Which way I fly is hell; myself am hell; / And in th' lowest deep a lower deep / Still threatening to devour me opens wide, / To which the hell I suffer seems a heav'n. [73]

20 So farewell hope, and with hope farewell fear, / Farewell remorse: all good to me is lost; / Evil be thou my Good. [108]

21 Sabean odours from the spicy shore / Of Araby the blest. [162]

22 Thence up he flew, and on the Tree of Life, / The middle tree and highest there that grew, / Sat like a cormorant. [194]

23 A heav'n on earth. [208]

24 Flowers of all hue, and without thorn the rose. [256]

25 The mantling vine. [258]

26 For contemplation he and valour formed; / For softness she and sweet attractive grace, / He for God only, she for God in him: / His fair large front and eye sublime declared / Absolute rule. [297]

27 Implied / Subjection, but required with gentle sway / And by her yielded, by him best received; / Yielded with coy submission, modest pride, / And sweet reluctant amorous delay. [307]

28 Adam the goodliest man of men since born / His sons, the fairest of her daughters Eve. [323]

29 With necessity, / The tyrant's plea, excused his devilish deeds. [393]

30 Imparadised in one another's arms. [506]

31 All but the wakeful nightingale; / She all night long her amorous descant sung. [602]

32 God is thy law, thou mine: to know no more / Is woman's happiest knowledge, and her praise. [637]

33 With thee conversing I forget all time. [639]

34 Sweet the coming on / Of grateful evening mild; then silent night / With this her solemn bird and this fair moon, / And these the gems of heaven, her starry train. [646]

35 Hail wedded love, mysterious law, true source / Of human offspring, sole propriety / In Paradise of all things common else. [750]

36 Blest pair; and O yet happiest if ye seek / no happier state, and know to know no more. [774]

37 Squat like a toad, close at the ear of Eve. [800]

1 Not to know me argues yourselves un-known. [830]

2 Abashed the devil stood, / And felt how awful goodness is. [846]

3 Wherefore with thee / Came not all hell broke loose? [917]

4 The starry cope of heaven. [992]

5 Fled / Murmuring, and with him fled the shades of night. [1014]

6 Now morn her rosy steps in th' eastern clime / Advancing, sowed the earth with orient pearl. [v. 1]

7 My fairest, my espoused, my latest found, / Heaven's last best gift, my ever new delight. [18]

8 Best image of myself and dearer half. [95]

9 These are thy glorious works, Parent of good! [153]

10 Him first, him last, him midst, and without end. [165]

11 A wilderness of sweets. [294]

12 Freely we serve / Because we freely love, as in our will / To love or not; in this we stand or fall. [538]

13 Thrones, dominations, princedoms, virtues, powers. [601]

14 All seemed well pleased, all seemed but were not all. [617]

15 The seraph Abdiel, faithful found, / Among the faithless, faithful only he. [893]

16 Servant of God, well done, well hast thou fought / The better fight, who singly hast main-tained / Against revolted multitudes the cause / Of truth, in word mightier than they in arms. [vi. 29]

17 He onward came, far off his coming shone. [768]

18 More safe I sing with mortal voice, un-changed / To hoarse or mute though fall'n on evil days, / On evil days though fall'n, and evil tongues; / In darkness, and with dangers com-passed round, / And solitude. [vii. 24]

19 Still govern thou my song, / Urania, and fit audience find, though few. [30]

20 Endued / With sanctity of reason. [507]

21 Liquid lapse of murmuring streams. [viii. 263]

22 And feel that I am happier than I know. [282]

23 Grace was in all her steps, heaven in her eye, / In every gesture dignity and love. [488]

24 Her virtue and the conscience of her worth, / That would be wooed, and not unsought be won. [502]

25 The sum of earthly bliss. [522]

26 So absolute she seems / And in herself complete, so well to know / Her own, that what she wills to do or say, / Seems wisest, virtuousest, discreetest, best. [547]

27 Accuse not Nature, she hath done her part; / Do thou but thine. [561]

28 A smile that glowed / Celestial rosy red, love's proper hue. [618]

29 My unpremeditated verse. [ix. 24]

30 Since first this subject for heroic song / Pleased me long choosing, and beginning late. [25]

31 The serpent subtlest beast of all the field. [86]

32 For solitude sometimes is best society, / And short retirement urges sweet return. [249]

33 She fair, divinely fair, fit love for Gods. [489]

34 God so commanded, and left that command / Sole daughter of his voice; the rest we live / Law to ourselves, our reason is our law. [652]

35 Earth felt the wound, and Nature from her seat / Sighing through all her works gave signs of woe, / That all was lost. [782]

36 O fairest of creation! last and best / Of all God's works! Creature in whom excelled / What-ever can to sight or thought be formed, / Holy, divine, good, amiable, or sweet! [896]

37 A pillared shade / High overarched, and echoing walks between. [1106]

38 Yet shall I temper so / Justice with mercy. [x. 77]

39 Demoniac frenzy, moping melancholy, / And moon-struck madness. [xi. 485]

40 Nor love thy life, nor hate; but what thou liv'st, / Live well, how long or short permit to heav'n. [553]

41 The evening star, / Love's harbinger. [588]

42 The brazen throat of war had ceased to roar; / All now was turned to jollity and game, / To luxury and riot, feast and dance. [713]

43 Now I see / Peace to corrupt no less than war to waste. [783]

1 Some natural tears they dropped, but wiped them soon; / The world was all before them, where to choose / Their place of rest, and Providence their guide: / They hand in hand with wandering steps and slow / Through Eden took their solitary way. [xii. 645]

2 Most men admire / Virtue, who follow not her lore. [*Paradise Regained*, Bk i. 482]

3 Beauty stands / In the admiration only of weak minds / Led captive. [ii. 220]

4 Fairy damsels met in forest wide / By knights of Logres, or of Lyones, / Lancelot or Pelleas, or Pellenore. [359]

5 Of whom to be dispraised were no small praise. [iii. 56]

6 The childhood shows the man, / As morning shows the day. Be famous then / By wisdom; as thy empire must extend, / So let extend thy mind o'er all the world. [iv. 220]

7 Athens, the eye of Greece, mother of arts / And eloquence. [240]

8 The olive-grove of Academe, / Plato's retirement, where the Attic bird / Trills her thick-warbled notes the summer long. [244]

9 The first and wisest of them all professed / To know this only, that he nothing knew. [293]

10 Deep versed in books and shallow in himself. [327]

11 Till morning fair / Came forth with pilgrim steps in amice grey. [426]

12 He unobserved / Home to his mother's house private returned. [638]

13 Let us with a gladsome mind / Praise the Lord, for he is kind, / For his mercies ay endure, / Ever faithful, ever sure. [*Psalm* 136]

14 A little onward lend thy guiding hand / To these dark steps, a little further on. [*Samson Agonistes*, 1]

15 Eyeless in Gaza at the mill with slaves. [41]

16 O dark, dark, dark, amid the blaze of noon, / Irrecoverably dark, total eclipse / Without all hope of day! [80]

17 The sun to me is dark / And silent as the moon, / When she deserts the night / Hid in her vacant, interlunar cave. [86]

18 To live a life half-dead, a living death. [100]

19 Ran on embattled armies clad in iron, / And weaponless himself, / Made arms ridiculous. [129]

20 Wisest men / Have erred, and by bad women been deceived; / And shall again, pretend they ne'er so wise. [210]

21 Just are the ways of God, / And justifiable to men; Unless there be who think not God at all. [293]

22 What boots it at one gate to make defence, / And at another to let in the foe? [560]

23 My race of glory run, and race of shame, / And I shall shortly be with them that rest. [597]

24 But who is this, what thing of sea or land? / Female of sex it seems, / That so bedecked, ornate, and gay, / Comes this way sailing / Like a stately ship / Of Tarsus, bound for th' isles / Of Javan or Gadier / With all her bravery on, and tackle trim, / Sails filled, and streamers waving, / Courted by all the winds that hold them play, / An amber scent of odorous perfume / Her harbinger. [710]

25 Yet beauty, though injurious, hath strange power, / After offence returning, to regain / Love once possessed. [1003]

26 He's gone and who knows how he may report / Thy words by adding fuel to the flame? [1350]

27 For evil news rides post, while good news baits. [1538]

28 Like that self-begotten bird / In the Arabian woods embost, / That no second knows nor third, / And lay ere while a holocaust. [1699]

29 Nothing is here for tears, nothing to wail / Or knock the breast, no weakness, no contempt, / Dispraise, or blame; nothing but well and fair, / And what may quiet us in a death so noble. [1721]

30 All is best, though we oft doubt, / What the unsearchable dispose. [1745]

31 Oft he seems to hide his face, / But unexpectedly returns / And to his faithful champion hath in place / Bore witness gloriously. [1749]

32 He with new acquist / Of true experience from this great event / With peace and consolation hath dismissed, / And calm of mind, all passion spent. [1755]

33 The bright morning star, day's harbinger. [Song: *On May Morning*]

34 How soon hath Time, the subtle thief of youth, / Stoln on his wing my three and twentieth year! [Sonnet: *On being arrived at the age of twenty-three*]

1 All is, if I have grace to use it so, / As ever in my great Task-Master's eye.

2 Licence they mean when they cry liberty. [Sonnet: *On the detraction . . .*]

3 When I consider how my light is spent / Ere half my days in this dark world and wide, / And that one talent which is death to hide, / Lodged with me useless. [Sonnet: *On his blindness*]

4 Doth God exact day-labour, light denied? / I fondly ask; but patience, to prevent / That murmur, soon replies, God doth not need/ Either man's work or his own gifts; who best / Bear his mild yoke, they serve him best; his state / Is kingly; thousands at his bidding speed, / And post o'er land and ocean without rest, / They also serve who only stand and wait.

5 Methought I saw my late espousèd saint / Brought to me like Alcestis, from the grave. [Sonnet: *On his deceased wife*]

6 But O as to embrace me she inclined, / I waked, she fled, and day brought back my night.

7 Avenge, O Lord, thy slaughtered saints, whose bones / Lie scattered on the Alpine mountains cold; / Even them who kept thy truth so pure of old / When all our fathers worshipped stocks and stones. [Sonnet: *On the late massacre in Piedmont*]

8 The bloody Piedmontese that rolled / Mother with infant down the rocks.

9 New Presbyter is but old Priest writ large. [Sonnet: *On the new forcers of conscience*]

10 Peace hath her victories / No less renowned than war. [Sonnet: *To Cromwell*]

11 For what can war, but endless war still breed? [Sonnet: *To Fairfax*]

12 O nightingale, that on yon bloomy spray / Warblest at eve, when all the woods are still. [Sonnet: *To the nightingale*]

13 Captain, or colonel, or knight in arms. [Sonnet: *When the assault was intended to the city*]

14 He who would not be frustrate of his hope to write well hereafter in laudable things ought himself to be a true poem. [*Apology for Smectymnuus*]

15 Books are not absolutely dead things, but do contain a potency of life in them to be as active as that soul was whose progeny they are; nay they do preserve as in a vial the purest efficacy and extraction of that living intellect that bred them. [*Areopagitica*]

16 As good almost kill a man as kill a good book; who kills a man kills a reasonable creature, God's image; but he who destroys a good book, kills reason itself, kills the image of God, as it were in the eye.

17 A good book is the precious life-blood of a master spirit, embalmed and treasured up on purpose to a life beyond life.

18 I cannot praise a fugitive and cloistered virtue, unexercised and unbreathed, that never sallies out and sees her adversary, but slinks out of the race, where that immortal garland is to be run for, not without dust and heat.

19 Our sage and serious poet Spenser.

20 God is decreeing to begin some new and great period in His Church, even to the reforming of the Reformation itself. What does he then but reveal Himself to His servants, and as His manner is, first to His Englishmen?

21 Methinks I see in my mind a noble and puissant nation rousing herself like a strong man after sleep, and shaking her invincible locks. Methinks I see her as an eagle mewing her mighty youth, and kindling her undazzled eyes at the full midday beam.

22 To chronicle the wars of kites and crows, fighting in the air. [*The History of Britain*, Bk iv]

23 Rhetoric ... To which poetry would be made subsequent, or indeed rather precedent, as being less subtle and fine, but more simple, sensuous and passionate. [*Of Education*]

24 A poet soaring in the high region of his fancies with his garland and singing robes about him. [*The Reason of Church Government*, Bk ii, Introduction]

25 None can love freedom heartily, but good men; the rest love not freedom, but licence. [*The Tenure of Kings and Magistrates*]

26 One tongue is sufficient for a woman. [Attr., when asked whether he would instruct his daughters in foreign languages]

COMTE DE MIRABEAU 1749–1791

27 War is Prussia's national industry. [Attr. to Mirabeau by Albert Sorel, but probably a misquotation of a longer passage in his *Monarchie prussienne*]

MISSAL

1 *O felix culpa, quae talem ac tantum meruit habere Redemptorem.* – O happy fault, which has earned the possession of such, and so great a Redeemer. [*Exsultet* on Holy Saturday]

MARY RUSSELL MITFORD 1787–1855

2 She [Jane Austen] was then the prettiest, silliest, most affected, husband-hunting butter-fly she ever remembers. [Letter, 3 Apr. 1815]

3 Perpendicular, precise and taciturn. [(Jane Austen) Quoted in *Life and Letters of Mary R. Mitford*, I. p. 306]

NANCY MITFORD 1904–1973

4 All the heat there was seemed to concentrate in the Hons' cupboard, which was always stifling. Here we would sit, huddled up on the slatted shelves, and talk for hours about life and death. [*The Pursuit of Love*, Ch. 2]

WILSON MIZNER 1876–1933

5 Be nice to people on your way up because you'll meet 'em on your way down. [Quoted in A. Johnston, *The Legendary Mizners*, Ch. 4. Also attr. to Jimmy Durante]

6 If you steal from one author it's plagiarism. If you steal from many its research.

7 A trip through a sewer in a glass-bottomed boat. [(Of Hollywood) Quoted in A. Johnston, *Legend of a Sport; the New Yorker*. See also 444:5]

GENERAL EMILIO MOLA 1887–1937

8 We have four columns advancing on Madrid. The fifth column will arise at the proper time. [Radio speech, Oct. 1936]

J. B. POQUELIN, called MOLIÈRE
1622–1673

9 M. JOURDAIN: *Quoi? quand je dis: 'Nicole, apportez moi mes pantoufles, et me donnez mon bonnet de nuit', c'est de la prose?* – What? When I say, 'Nicole, bring me my slippers and give me my nightcap'; that's prose?
LE MAÎTRE DE PHILOSOPHIE: *Oui, monsieur.* – Yes, sir.
M. JOURDAIN: *Par ma foi! il y a plus de quarante ans que je dis de la prose sans que j'en susse rien.* – Gracious me! I've been talking prose for the last forty years and have never known it. [*Le Bourgeois Gentilhomme*, II. iv]

10 *Ah, la belle chose que de savoir quelquechose.* – Oh, how fine it is to know a thing or two. [vi]

11 *On ne meurt qu'une fois, et c'est pour si longtemps!* – One only dies once – but one is dead so long! [*Le Dépit amoureux*, V. iii]

12 *Il n'est rien d'égal au tabac; c'est la passion des honnêtes gens, et qui vit sans tabac n'est pas digne de vivre.* – There's nothing like tobacco; it is the passion of all decent people; someone who lives without tobacco does not deserve to live. [*Don Juan*, I. i]

13 *Je consens qu'une femme ait des clartés de tout, / Mais je ne lui veux point la passion choquante / De se rendre savante afin d'être savante / Et j'aime que souvent, aux questions qu'on fait, / Elle sache ignorer les choses qu'elle sait.* – I am quite agreeable that a woman shall be informed about everything, but I cannot allow her the shocking passion for acquiring learning in order to be learned. When she is asked questions, I like her often to know how not to know the things she does know. [*Les Femmes savantes*, I. iii]

14 *La grammaire qui sait régenter jusqu'aux rois.* – Grammar, which can govern even kings. [II. vi]

15 *Je vis de bonne soupe, et non de beau langage.* – I live on good soup, not on fine words. [vii]

16 *Guenille, si l'on veut: ma guenille m'est chère.* – Rags they may be, but I love my rags.

17 *Et je vous suis garant / Qu'un sot savant est sot plus qu'un sot ignorant.* – I assure you that a learned fool is more foolish than an ignorant fool. [IV. iii]

18 *Que diable allait-il faire dans cette galère?* – What the devil was he up to in that galley? [*Les Fourberies de Scapin*, II. vii]

19 *Vous l'avez voulu, George Dandin, vous l'avez voulu.* – You asked for it, George Dandin, you asked for it. [*George Dandin*, I. ix]

20 *Il faut qu'il ait tué bien des gens pour s'être fait si riche.* – He must have killed a lot of men to have made so much money. [*Le Malade imaginaire*, I. v]

21 *Je veux qu'il me batte, moi . . . Il me plait d'être battue.* – I want him to beat me . . . I like being beaten. [*Le Médecin malgré lui*, I. ii]

22 GÉRONTE: *Il me semble que vous les placez*

autrement qu'ils ne sont; que le cœur est du côté gauche, et le foie du côté droit. – I think you are locating them in the wrong places. The heart is on the left and the liver on the right.

SGANARELLE: *Oui, cela était autrefois ainsi, mais nous avons changé tout cela,–* Yes, that was so in the old days. But we have changed all that. [II. iv]

1 *Je veux qu'on me distingue; et pour le trancher net, / L'ami du genre humain n'est pas du tout mon trait.* – I want to be understood; to be quite frank, the friend of the human race is not in the least my role. [*Le Misanthrope*, I. i]

2 *Ces haines vigoureuses / Que doit donner le vice aux âmes vertueuses.* – Those strong dislikes that vice should inspire in virtuous souls.

3 *Il faut, parmi le monde, une vertu traitable.* – Virtue in this world should be malleable.

4 *La parfaite raison fuit tout extrémité / Et veut que l'on soit sage avec sobriété.* – Pure reason avoids extremes, and requires one to be wise in moderation.

5 *C'est une folie à nulle autre seconde, / De vouloir se mêler à corriger le monde.* – It is a stupidity second to none, to busy oneself with the correction of the world.

6 *Si le roi m'avait donné / Paris, sa grand'ville, / Et qu'il me fallût quitter / L'amour de ma mie, / Je dirais au roi Henri: / Reprenez votre Paris.* – If the king gave me Paris, his great city, and I had to give up my darling's love, I should say to King Henry, Take your Paris back. [(Old song) I. ii]

7 *Et les deux bras croisés, du haut de son esprit, / Il regarde en pitié tout ce que chacun dit.* – And with his arms crossed he looks pityingly down from his spiritual height on everything that anyone says. [II. ii]

8 *On doit se regarder soi-même un fort long temps, / Avant que de songer à condamner les gens.* – One should examine oneself for a very long time before thinking of condemning others. [III. iv]

9 *L'âge amènera tout, et ce n'est pas le temps, / Madame, comme on sait, d'être prude à vingt ans.* – Age will bring all things, and everyone knows, Madame, that twenty is no age to be a prude.

10 *Oui, je vous l'ai déjà dit, ils commencent ici* [Paris] *par faire pendre un homme et puis ils lui font son procès.* – Yes, as I have already told you, here they hang a man first and try him afterwards. [*Monsieur de Pourceaugnac*, III. i]

11 *Les gens de qualité savent tout sans avoir rien appris.* – People of quality know everything without learning anything. [*Les Précieuses ridicules*, ix]

12 *Le pauvre homme!* – Poor man! [*Tartuffe*, I. iv, *passim*]

13 *Couvrez ce sein que je ne saurais voir: / Par de pareils objets les âmes sont blessées / Et cela fait venir de coupables pensées.* – Cover that bosom. I must not see it. Souls are wounded by such things, and they arouse wicked thoughts. [III. ii]

14 *Ah! pour être dévot, je n'en suis pas moins homme!* – Oh, I may be devout, but I am human all the same. [iii]

15 *Le ciel défend, de vrai, certains contentements: / Mais on trouve avec lui des accommodements.* – Of course heaven forbids certain pleasures, but one finds means of compromise. [IV. v]

16 *La scandale du monde est ce qui fait l'offense, / Et ce n'est pas pécher que pécher en silence.* – It is a public scandal that offends; to sin in secret is no sin at all.

17 *L'homme est, je vous l'avoue, un méchant animal.* – Man is, I confess, a wicked creature. [V. vi]

COSMO MONKHOUSE 1840–1901

18 There was an old party of Lyme, / Who married three wives at one time, / When asked, 'Why the third?' / He replied, 'One's absurd, / And bigamy, sir, is a crime!' [Limerick]

DUKE OF MONMOUTH 1649–1685

19 Do not hack me as you did my Lord Russell. [Words to his executioner. Quoted in T. B. Macaulay, *The History of England*, Vol. i. Ch. 5]

HAROLD MONRO 1879–1932

20 When the tea is brought at five o'clock, / And all the neat curtains are drawn with care, / The little black cat with bright green eyes / Is suddenly purring there. [*Milk for the Cat*]

21 The white saucer like some full moon descends / At last from the clouds of the table above.

JOHN MONSELL 1811–1875

22 Fight the good fight with all thy might, /

Christ is thy strength and Christ thy right. / Lay hold on life, and it shall be / Thy joy and crown eternally. [Hymn]

LADY MARY WORTLEY MONTAGU
1689–1762

1 Be plain in dress, and sober in your diet; / In short, my deary! kiss me, and be quiet. [*Summary of Lord Lyttelton's Advice*]

2 Satire should, like a polished razor keen, / Wound with a touch that's scarcely felt or seen. [*To the Imitator of the First Satire of Horace*, Bk ii]

3 This world consists of men, women, and Herveys. [*Letters and Works*, 'Introductory Anecdotes']

C. E. MONTAGUE 1867–1928

4 I was born below par to th' extent of two whiskies. [*Fiery Particles*]

MICHEL DE MONTAIGNE 1533–1592

5 Unless a man feels he has a good enough memory, he should never venture to lie. [*Essays*, I. 9]

6 The continuous labour of your life is to build the house of death. [20]

7 One must always have one's boots on and be ready to go.

8 The value of life lies, not in the length of days, but in the use we make of them; a man may live long, yet live very little. Satisfaction in life depends not on the number of your years, but on your will.

9 The daughter-in-law of Pythagoras said that a woman who goes to bed with a man ought to lay aside her modesty with her skirt, and put it on again with her petticoat. [21]

10 A little of everything and nothing thoroughly, after the French fashion. [26]

11 If I were pressed to say why I loved him, I feel that my only reply could be: 'Because it was he, because it was I'. [28]

12 The greatest thing in the world is to know how to be self-sufficient. [39]

13 There's as much difference between us and ourselves as between us and others. [II. 1]

14 To know how to live is my trade and my art. [6]

15 Virtue will have nothing to do with ease . . . It demands a steep and thorny road. [11]

16 When I play with my cat, who knows whether she is not amusing herself with me more than I with her. [12]

17 Life is a dream; when we sleep we are awake, and when awake we sleep.

18 *Que sais-je?* – What do I know? [Also inscribed on Montaigne's medal]

19 There is, in public affairs, no state so bad, provided it has age and stability on its side, that it is not preferable to change and disturbance. [17]

20 Many a man has been a wonder to the world, whose wife and valet have seen nothing in him that was even remarkable. Few men have been admired by their servants. [III. 2. See also 122:20]

21 It [marriage] is like a cage; one sees the birds outside desperate to get in, and those inside equally desperate to get out. [5]

22 The world is but a school of inquiry. [8]

23 Poverty of goods is easily cured; poverty of soul, impossible. [10]

24 It might well be said of me that here I have merely made up a bunch of other men's flowers, and provided nothing of my own but the string to bind them. [12]

25 A man who fears suffering is already suffering from what he fears. [13]

LEON MONTENAEKEN 1859–?

26 *La vie est vaine: / Un peu d'amour, / Un peu de haine . . . / Et puis – bonjour!*

La vie est brève: / Un peu d'espoir, / Un peu de rêve / Et puis – bon soir!

Life is fruitless: a little love, a little hate . . . and then – good morning.

Life is brief: a little hope, a little dream and then – good night! [*Peu de chose*]

CHARLES, BARON DE MONTESQUIEU
1689–1755

27 An empire founded by war has to maintain itself by war. [*Considérations sur les causes de la grandeur des Romains et de leur décadence*, Ch. 8]

28 Liberty is the right to do everything which the laws allow. [*L'Esprit des lois*, XI. 3]

1 There is a very good saying that if triangles invented a god, they would make him three-sided. [*Lettres persanes*, 59]

2 I suffer from the disease of writing books and being ashamed of them when they are finished. [*Pensées diverses*, 'Portrait de Montesquieu par lui-même']

JAMES MONTGOMERY 1771-1854

3 Here in the body pent, / Absent from Him I roam, / Yet nightly pitch my moving tent / A day's march nearer home. [Hymn: *For Ever with the Lord*]

ROBERT MONTGOMERY 1807-1855

4 The solitary monk who shook the world. [*Luther, Man's Need and God's Supply*, 68]

MARQUIS OF MONTROSE 1612-1650

5 My dear and only love, I pray / This noble world of thee, / Be governed by no other sway / But purest monarchy. [*My dear and only Love*]

6 He either fears his fate too much, / Or his deserts are small, / That puts it not unto the touch / To win or lose it all.

7 But if thou wilt be constant then, / And faithful of thy word, / I'll make thee glorious by my pen, / And famous by my sword.

PERCY MONTROSE 19 Cent.

8 In a cavern, in a canyon, / Excavating for a mine / Dwelt a miner, Forty-niner, / And his daughter, Clementine. / Oh, my darling, Oh, my darling, Oh, my darling Clementine! / Thou art lost and gone for ever, dreadful sorry, Clementine. [*Clementine*]

9 Light she was and like a fairy. / And her shoes were number nine; / Herring boxes without topses, / Sandals were for Clementine.

10 But I kissed her little sister, / And forgot my Clementine.

MONTY PYTHON'S FLYING CIRCUS 1969-1974

11 I'm a lumberjack / And I'm OK / I sleep all night / And I work all day. [*Monty Python's Big Red Book*]

12 It's not pining, it's passed on. This parrot is no more. It's ceased to be. It's expired. It's gone to meet its maker. This is a late parrot. It's a stiff. Bereft of life it rests in peace. It would be pushing up the daisies if you hadn't nailed it to the perch. It's rung down the curtain and joined the choir invisible. It's an ex-parrot. [BBC TV comedy series, programme of 14 Dec. 1969]

13 Nudge, nudge, wink, wink. Know what I mean? [*Passim* in series, with variants]

14 And now for something completely different.

EDWARD MOORE 1712-1757

15 This is adding insult to injuries. [*The Foundling*, V. ii]

16 I am rich beyond the dreams of avarice. [*The Gamester*, II. ii]

GEORGE MOORE 1852-1933

17 All reformers are bachelors. [*The Bending of the Bough*, I]

18 A man travels the world over in search of what he needs and returns home to find it. [*The Brook Kerith*, Ch. 11]

19 Acting is therefore the lowest of the arts, if it is an art at all. [*Mummer-Worship*]

MARIANNE MOORE 1887-1972

20 My father used to say, / 'Superior people never make long visits.' [*Silence*]

THOMAS MOORE 1779-1852

21 Row, brothers, row, the stream runs fast, / The Rapids are near and the daylight's past. [*A Canadian Boat Song*]

22 Believe me, if all those endearing young charms, / Which I gaze on so fondly to-day. [*Irish Melodies*, 'Believe me, if all . . .']

23 As the sun-flower turns on her god, when he sets, / The same look which she turned, when he rose.

24 Eyes of most unholy blue! ['By that Lake']

25 You may break, you may shatter the vase, if you will, / But the scent of the roses will hang round it still. ['Farewell! But Whenever']

26 The harp that once through Tara's halls / The soul of music shed, / Now hangs as mute as Tara's walls / As if that soul were fled. ['The Harp that Once']

1 No, there's nothing half so sweet in life / As love's young dream. ['Love's Young Dream']

2 The Minstrel Boy to the war is gone, / In the ranks of death you'll find him; / His father's sword he has girded on, / And his wild harp slung behind him. ['The Minstrel Boy']

3 Oh! blame not the bard. ['Oh! Blame Not']

4 Oh! breathe not his name, let it sleep in the shade, / Where cold and unhonoured his relics are laid. ['Oh! Breathe Not']

5 Rich and rare were the gems she wore, / And a bright gold ring on her hand she bore. ['Rich and Rare']

6 She is far from the land where her young hero sleeps, / And lovers are round her, sighing: / But coldly she turns from their gaze, and weeps, / For her heart in his grave is lying. ['She is Far']

7 The light, that lies / In woman's eyes, / Has been my heart's undoing. ['The Time I've Lost']

8 'Tis the last rose of summer / Left blooming alone; / All her lovely companions / Are faded and gone. [''Tis the Last Rose']

9 Then awake! the heavens look bright, my dear; / 'Tis never too late for delight, my dear; / And the best of all ways / To lengthen our days / Is to steal a few hours from the night, my dear! ['The Young May Moon']

10 'Come, come,' said Tom's father, 'at your time of life, / There's no longer excuse for thus playing the rake – / It is time you should think, boy, of taking a wife' – 'Why, so it is, father – whose wife shall I take?' [A Joke Versified]

11 I never nursed a dear gazelle, / To glad me with its soft black eye, / But when it came to know me well, / And love me, it was sure to die! [Lalla-Rookh, 'Fire-Worshippers', i. 279]

12 Like Dead Sea fruits, that tempt the eye, / But turn to ashes on the lips! [484]

13 Some flow'rets of Eden ye still inherit, / But the trail of the serpent is over them all! ['Paradise and the Peri', 206]

14 Oft in the stilly night, / Ere Slumber's chain has bound me, / Fond Memory brings the light / Of other days around me; / The smiles, the tears, / Of boyhood's years, / The words of love then spoken; / The eyes that shone, / Now dimmed and gone, / The cheerful hearts now broken! [National Airs, 'Oft in the Stilly Night']

15 I feel like one / Who treads alone / Some banquet-hall deserted, / Whose lights are fled, / Whose garlands dead / And all but he departed!

16 Disguise our bondage as we will, / 'Tis woman, woman, rules us still. [Sovereign Woman]

POP MORAND 20 Cent.

17 Keeping Up With the Joneses. [Title of cartoon strip which first appeared in 1914 and ran till 1958]

THOMAS MORDAUNT 1730–1809

18 Sound, sound the clarion, fill the fife, / Throughout the sensual world proclaim, / One crowded hour of glorious life / Is worth an age without a name. [Verses written during the War 1756–63]

SIR THOMAS MORE 1478–1535

19 Your sheep, that were wont to be so meek and tame and so small eaters, now, as I hear say, be become so great devourers, and so wild, that they eat up and swallow down the very men themselves. [Utopia, Bk i]

20 This hath not offended the king. [(As he pushed his beard aside at his execution) Bacon, Apophthegms, 22]

21 Yea, marry, now it is somewhat, for now it is rhyme; before, it was neither rhyme nor reason. [(To a friend who had versified an indifferent book) 287]

22 Is not this house [the Tower of London] as nigh heaven as my own? [Roper, Life of Sir T. More]

23 I pray you, Master Lieutenant, see me safe up, and for my coming down let me shift for myself. [On mounting the scaffold, 7 July 1535]

ERIC MORECAMBE 1926–1984 and ERNIE WISE 1925–

24 Q: What do you think of the show so far? A: Rubbish. [Running gag in TV show The Morecambe and Wise Show, scripts by Eddie Braben]

25 Short, fat, hairy legs.

J. M. MOREHEAD 1796–1866

26 It's a long time between drinks. [Said to the

Governor of South Carolina, when Morehead was Governor of North Carolina. Quoted in R. L. Stevenson, *The Wrong Box*, Ch. 8]

THOMAS MORELL 1703–1784

1 See, the conquering hero comes! / Sound the trumpets, beat the drums! [*Joshua*, Pt III]

AUGUSTUS DE MORGAN 1806–1871

2 Great fleas have little fleas upon their backs to bite 'em, / And little fleas have lesser fleas, and so *ad infinitum*. [*A Budget of Paradoxes*, p. 377. See also 410:16]

CHRISTIAN MORGENSTERN 1871–1914

3 *Es gibt ein Gespenst / das frisst Taschentücher; / es begleitet dich / auf deiner Reise.* – There is a ghost / That eats handkerchiefs; / It keeps you company / On all your travels. [*Galgenlieder*, 'Gespenst' ('The Ghost'), trans. R. F. C. Hull]

CHRISTOPHER MORLEY 1890–1957

4 A human being: an ingenious assembly of portable plumbing. [*Human Being*, Ch. 11]

5 Life is a foreign language: all men mispronounce it. [*Thunder on the Left*, 14]

6 My theology, briefly, is that the universe was dictated but not signed. [Quoted in A. Andrews, *Quotations for Speakers and Writers*]

CHARLES MORRIS 1745–1838

7 If one must have a villa in summer to dwell, / Oh give me the sweet shady side of Pall Mall! [*The Contrast*, last lines]

DESMOND MORRIS 1928–

8 There are one hundred and ninety-three living species of monkeys and apes. One hundred and ninety-two of them are covered with hair. The exception is a naked ape self-named *Homo sapiens*. [*The Naked Ape*, Introduction]

G. P. MORRIS 1802–1864

9 Woodman, spare that tree! / Touch not a single bough! / In youth it sheltered me, / And I'll protect it now. [*Woodman, spare that Tree*]

WILLIAM MORRIS 1834–1896

10 The idle singer of an empty day. [*The Earthly Paradise*, 'An Apology']

11 Dreamer of dreams, born out of my due time, / Why should I strive to set the crooked straight? / Let it suffice me that my murmuring rhyme / Beats with light wing against the ivory gate, / Telling a tale not too importunate.

12 Forget six counties overhung with smoke, / Forget the snorting steam and piston stroke, / Forget the spreading of the hideous town; / Think rather of the pack-horse on the down, / And dream of London, small and white and clean, / The clear Thames bordered by its gardens green. [Prologue, 'The Wanderers']

13 Had she come all the way for this, / To part at last without a kiss? [*The Haystack in the Floods*]

14 Swerve to the left, son Roger, he said, / When you catch his eyes through the helmet-slit, / Swerve to the left, then out at his head, / And the Lord God give you the joy of it! [*The Judgement of God*]

15 I know a little garden close / Set thick with lily and red rose, / Where I would wander if I might / From dewy dawn to dewy night. / And have one with me wandering. [*The Life and Death of Jason*, IV. 577]

16 Love is enough: though the world be a-waning, / And the woods have no voice but the voice of complaining. [*Love is Enough*]

17 There were four of us about that bed; / The mass-priest knelt at the side, / I and his mother stood at the head, / Over his feet lay the bride. [*Shameful Death*]

18 He did not die in the night, / He did not die in the day, / But in the morning twilight / His spirit passed away.

19 Pray but one prayer for me 'twixt thy closed lips. [*Summer Dawn*]

20 Speak but one word to me over the corn, / Over the tender, bowed locks of the corn.

21 There was a knight came riding by / In early spring, when the roads were dry; / And he heard that lady sing at the noon, / *Two red roses across the moon*. [*Two Red Roses across the Moon*]

22 Wind, wind! thou art sad, art thou kind? / Wind, wind, unhappy! thou art blind, / Yet still thou wanderest the lily-seed to find. [*The Wind*]

23 Fellowship is heaven, and lack of fellowship is hell; fellowship is life, and lack of fellowship is death; and the deeds that ye do upon the

earth, it is for fellowship's sake that ye do them. [*The Dream of John Ball*, Ch. 4]

1 Have nothing in your houses that you do not know to be useful, or believe to be beautiful. [*The Beauty of Life*]

JIM MORRISON 1943–1971

2 The old get old, the young get younger, / They got the guns but we got the numbers. [Song: *Five to One*]

J. B. MORTON ['BEACHCOMBER'] 1893–1979

3 To fairy flutes, / As the light advances, / In square black boots / The cabman dances. [*The Best of Beachcomber* 12, 'The Saga of the Saucy Mrs Flobster: The Dancing Cabman']

4 SIXTY HORSES WEDGED IN A CHIMNEY The story to fit this sensational headline has not turned up yet. [13, 'Mr Justice Cocklecarrot: Home Life']

5 Dr Strabismus (Whom God Preserve) of Utrecht is carrying out research work with a view to crossing salmon with mosquitoes. He says it will mean a bite every time for fishermen. [*By the Way*, January Tail-piece]

THOMAS MORTON 1764–1838

6 Push on – keep moving. [*A Cure for the Heartache*, II. i]

7 Approbation from Sir Hubert Stanley is praise indeed. [V. ii]

8 Always ding, dinging Dame Grundy into my ears – What will Mrs Grundy say? What will Mrs Grundy think? [*Speed the Plough*, I. i]

SIR OSWALD MOSLEY 1896–1980

9 I am not, and never have been, a man of the right. My position was on the left and is now in the centre of politics. [Letter to *The Times*, 26 Apr. 1968]

WILLIAM MOTHERWELL 1797–1835

10 I've wandered east, I've wandered west, / Through many a weary way; / But never, never can forget / The love o' life's young day. [*Jeannie Morrison*]

J. L. MOTLEY 1814–1877

11 As long as he lived, he was the guiding-star of a whole brave nation, and when he died the little children cried in the streets. [(William the Silent) *The Rise of the Dutch Republic*, Pt VI. Ch. 7. See also 14:6]

12 Give us the luxuries of life, and we will dispense with its necessities. [Quoted in O. W. Holmes, *Autocrat of the Breakfast Table*, Ch. 6]

PETER MOTTEUX 1660–1718

13 The devil was sick, the devil a monk wou'd be: / The devil was well, and the devil a monk he'd be. [Trans. of Rabelais, *Gargantua and Pantagruel*, Bk iv. Ch. 24]

MALCOLM MUGGERIDGE 1903–1990

14 The orgasm has replaced the Cross as the focus of longing and the image of fulfilment. [*The Most of Malcolm Muggeridge*, 'Down with Sex']

15 He [Sir Anthony Eden] is not only a bore but he bores for England. ['Boring for England', reprinted in Edward Hyams, *Newstatesmanship*]

EDWIN MUIR 1887–1959

16 We have seen / Good men made evil wrangling with the evil, / Straight minds grown crooked fighting crooked minds. / Our peace betrayed us; we betrayed our peace. / Look at it well. This was the good town once. [*The Good Town*]

17 Oh these deceits are strong almost as life, / Last night I dreamt I was in the labyrinth, / And woke far on. I did not know the place. [*The Labyrinth*]

18 There is a road that turning always / Cuts off the country of Again. / Archers stand there on every side / And as it runs Time's deer is slain, / And lies where it has lain. [*The Road*]

19 See him, the gentle Bible beast, / With lacquered hoofs and curling mane, / His wondering journey from the East / Half done, between the rock and plain. [*The Toy Horse*]

DINAH MULOCK *see* CRAIK, DINAH

ANTHONY MUNDAY 1553–1633

20 Beauty sat bathing by a spring. [*To Colin Clout*]

H. H. MUNRO *see* **SAKI**

ERNST MÜNSTER 1766–1839

1 Absolutism tempered by assassination. [(Quoting description of the Russian Constitution) *Political Sketches* (See 326:15)]

IRIS MURDOCH 1918–

2 Writing is like getting married. One should never commit oneself until one is amazed at one's luck. [*The Black Prince*, 'Bradley Pearson's Foreword']

3 'We aren't getting anywhere. You know that as well as I do.' 'One doesn't have to get anywhere in a marriage. It's not a public conveyance.' [*A Severed Head*, Ch. 3]

ARTHUR MURPHY 1727–1805

4 Above the vulgar flight of common souls. [*Zenobia*, V. i]

C. W. MURPHY 19 Cent.

5 Has anybody here seen Kelly? / Kelly from the Isle of Man? [Song: *Has Anybody Here seen Kelly?* Sung by Florrie Forde]

EDWARD A. MURPHY 1918–

6 If there is a wrong way to do something, then someone will do it. [*Murphy's Law*]

FRED MURRAY ?–1922
    and **GEORGE EVERARD** 20 Cent.

7 And it's all right in the summer time, / In the summer time it's lovely! / While my old man's painting hard, / I'm posing in the old back yard. / But oh, oh! In the winter-time / It's another thing you know, / With a little red nose, / And very little clothes, / And the stormy winds do blow. [Song: *It's All Right in the Summer Time*]

FRED MURRAY and R. P. WESTON ?–1936

8 I'm Henery the Eighth, I am ... I got married to the widder next door. / She's been married seven times before, / Hevery one was a Henery, / She wouldn't have a Willy or a Sam. [Song: *I'm Henery the Eighth*, sung by Harry Champion]

ROBERT MUSIL 1880–1942

9 Progress would be wonderful – if only it would stop. [Attr.]

ALFRED DE MUSSET 1810–1857

10 *Je ne puis: – malgré moi l'infini me tourmente.* – I cannot help it;– in spite of myself, infinity torments me. [*L'Espoir en Dieu*, 9]

11 *Les plus désespérés sont les chants les plus beaux / Et j'en sais d'immortels qui sont de purs sanglots.* – The most despairing songs are the most beautiful, and I know some immortal ones that are pure tears. [*La Nuit de mai*]

12 *Les grands artistes n'ont pas de patrie.* – Great artists have no country. [*Lorenzaccio*, I. v]

13 *Il faut qu'une porte soit ouverte ou fermée.* – A Door must be either Open or Shut. [Title of comedy]

14 *On ne badine pas avec l'amour.* – One Must not Trifle with Love. [Title of comedy]

BENITO MUSSOLINI 1883–1945

15 CURZON: What is your foreign programme?
MUSSOLINI: My foreign policy is 'Nothing for Nothing'. [Quoted in George Seldes, *Sawdust Caesar*, Ch. 12]

16 Fascism is not an article for export. [(German press report, 1932) Ch. 24]

N

VLADIMIR NABOKOV 1899–1977

1 Lolita, light of my life, fire of my loins. My sin, my soul. Lo-lee-ta: the tip of the tongue taking a trip of three steps down the palate to tap, at three, on the teeth. Lo. Lee. Ta. [Opening sentences of *Lolita*]

2 I think like a genius, I write like a distinguished author, and I speak like a child. [*Strong Opinions*, Foreword]

3 Satire is a lesson, parody is a game. [6]

IAN NAIRN 1930–1983

4 Subtopia. [Title of article in *Architectural Review*, June 1955]

LADY NAIRNE 1766–1845

5 Better lo'ed ye canna be, / Will ye no come back again? [*Bonnie Charlie's now awa!*]

6 Wha'll buy my caller herrin'? / They're bonnie fish and halesome farin'. [*Caller Herring*]

7 Charlie is my darling, my darling, my darling, / Charlie is my darling, the young Chevalier. [*Charlie is my Darling*]

8 Wi' a hundred pipers an' a', an' a'. [*The Hundred Pipers*]

9 I was daft to refuse the Laird o' Cockpen. [*The Laird o' Cockpen*]

10 I'm wearin' awa'. / To the land o' the leal. [*The Land o' the Leal*]

FRIDTJOF NANSEN 1861–1930

11 The difficult is what takes a little time; the impossible is what takes a little longer. [Also attr. to others. Variant form was motto placarded at South-East Asia HQ in 1939–45 War]

SIR CHARLES NAPIER 1782–1853

12 *Peccavi*. [(I have Sind) Dispatch after victory of Hyderabad in Sind, Feb. 1843]

NAPOLEON BONAPARTE 1769–1821

13 Soldiers, consider that from the summit of these pyramids, forty centuries look down upon you. [Speech before the Battle of the Pyramids, 21 July 1798]

14 In war, moral considerations account for three-quarters, the balance of actual forces only for the other quarter. [Letter, 27 Aug. 1808]

15 There rises the sun of Austerlitz. [Before Moscow, 1812]

16 From the sublime to the ridiculous there is only one step. [After the retreat from Moscow, 1812]

17 The bullet that is to kill me has not yet been moulded. [Said in 1814, when the Spanish king asked whether he had ever been hit by a cannon-ball]

18 A revolution is an opinion backed by bayonets. [*Maxims*]

19 Every French soldier carries in his cartridge-pouch the baton of a marshal of France. [Quoted in E. Blaze, *La Vie militaire sous l'empire*]

20 *Le courage de l'improvisite.* – Spontaneous courage. [Quoted in Las Cases, *Mémorial de Ste Hélène*]

21 England is a nation of shopkeepers. [(Quoting Adam Smith – see 398:17) B. E. O'Meara, *Napoleon at St Helena*]

1 *La carrière ouverte aux talents.* – The career open to talents. [Quoted in B. E. O'Meara, *Napoleon in Exile*]

2 An army marches on its stomach. [Attr.]

3 *Tête d'Armée.* – Chief of the Army. [Last words]

4 Love then, and even later, was the whole concern of everyone's life. That is always the fate of leisured societies. [Quoted by F. L. Lucas in *Tragedy*]

OGDEN NASH 1902–1971

5 A bit of talcum / Is always walcum. [*The Baby*]

6 The camel has a single hump; / The dromedary, two; / Or else the other way around. / I'm never sure. Are you? [*The Camel*]

7 The song of canaries / Never varies, / And when they're moulting / They're pretty revolting. [*The Canary*]

8 The cow is of the bovine ilk; / One end is moo, the other, milk. [*The Cow*]

9 Beneath this slab / John Brown is stowed. / He watched the ads, / And not the road. [*Lather as You Go*]

10 Tell me, O Octopus, I begs, / Is those things arms, or is they legs? / I marvel at thee, Octopus; If I were thou, I'd call me Us. [*The Octopus*]

11 Children aren't happy with nothing to ignore, / And that's what parents were created for. [*The Parent*]

12 Middle-aged life is merry, and I love to lead it. [*Peekaboo, I almost See You*]

13 Candy is dandy, / But liquor is quicker. [*Reflection on Ice-Breaking*]

14 When Ah itchez, Ah scratchez. [*Requiem*]

15 What chills the finger not a bit / Is so frigid upon the fundament. [*Samson Agonistes*]

16 I think that I shall never see / A billboard lovely as a tree. / Perhaps unless the billboards fall, / I'll never see a tree at all. [*Song of the Open Road*, see also 237:3]

17 The turtle lives 'twixt plated decks / Which practically conceal its sex. / I think it clever of the turtle / In such a fix to be so fertile. [*The Turtle*]

18 Life is not having been told that the man has just waxed the floor. [*You and Me and P. B. Shelley*]

THOMAS NASHE 1567–1601

19 Adieu, farewell earth's bliss, / This world uncertain is. [*In Plague Time*]

20 Beauty is but a flower / Which wrinkles will devour; / Brightness falls from the air, / Queens have died young and fair, / Dust hath closed Helen's eye, / I am sick, I must die. / Lord, have mercy on us!

21 Spring, the sweet spring, is the year's pleasant king; / Then blooms each thing, then maids dance in a ring, / Cold doth not sting, the pretty birds do sing: / Cuckoo, jug-jug, pu-we, to-witta-woo! [*Spring*]

JAMES NAYLOR 1860–1945

22 King David and King Solomon / Led merry, merry lives. [*Ancient Authors*]

JOHN MASON NEALE 1818–1866

23 Around the throne of God, a band / Of glorious angels ever stand. [Hymn]

24 Art thou weary, art thou languid, / Art thou sore distressed? [Hymn]

25 Christian! dost thou see them / On the holy ground, / How the troops of Midian / Prowl and prowl around? / Christian! up and smite them. / Counting gain but loss; / Smite them by the merit / Of the Holy Cross! [Hymn]

26 Ever Three and ever One; / Consubstantial, co-eternal, / While unending ages run. [Hymn: *Come ye Faithful*]

27 Good King Wenceslas looked out, / On the Feast of Stephen; / When the snow lay round about, / Deep and crisp and even. [Carol]

28 Hither, page, and stand by me, / If thou know'st it, telling, / Yonder peasant, who is he? / Where and what his dwelling?

29 In his master's steps he trod, / Where the snow lay dinted.

30 Jerusalem the golden, / With milk and honey blest, / Beneath thy contemplation / Sink heart and voice opprest. [Hymn]

HORATIO, VISCOUNT NELSON 1758–1805

31 The Nelson touch. [Private diary, 9 Oct. 1805]

32 You must hate a Frenchman as you hate the devil. [Quoted in R. Southey, *Life of Nelson*, Ch. 3]

1 Westminster Abbey or victory! [(At Battle of Cape St Vincent) 4]

2 Before this time tomorrow I shall have gained a peerage, or Westminster Abbey. [(Battle of Nile) 5]

3 It is warm work; and this day may be the last to any of us at a moment. But mark you! I would not be elsewhere for thousands. [(Battle of Copenhagen) 7]

4 I have a right to be blind sometimes ... I really do not see the signal! [Putting the telescope to his blind eye at the Battle of Copenhagen]

5 England expects every man will do his duty. [(Battle of Trafalgar) 9]

6 Thank God, I have done my duty.

7 Kiss me, Hardy.

EMPEROR NERO 37–68

8 *Qualis artifex pereo!* – What an artist dies in me! [Dying words, quoted by Suetonius, *Life of Nero*, 49]

GÉRARD DE NERVAL 1808–1855

9 *Je suis le ténébreux, – le veuf, – l'inconsolé, / Le prince d'Aquitaine à la tour abolie.* – I am the shadowy one – the widower – the unconsoled – the prince of Aquitaine whose tower has been destroyed. [*El Desdichado*]

E. NESBIT 1858–1924

10 Oh! little brown brother, / Are you awake in the dark? [*Baby Seed Song*]

ALLAN NEVINS 1890–1971

11 Offering Germany too little, and offering even that too late. [*Current History*, May 1935]

SIR HENRY NEWBOLT 1862–1938

12 Here's to the bold and free! [*Admirals All*]

13 Admirals all, for England's sake.

14 To set the cause above renown, / To love the game beyond the prize, / To honour, while you strike him down, / The foe that comes with fearless eyes. [*Clifton Chapel*]

15 'Qui procul hinc', the legend's writ, – / The frontier-grave is far away – / 'Qui ante diem periit: / Sed miles, sed pro patria.' [Who died far from here, before his time, but as a soldier, and for his country]

16 Take my drum to England, hang et by the shore. / Strike et when your powder's runnin' low; / If the Dons sight Devon, I'll quit the port o' Heaven, / An' drum them up the Channel as we drummed them long ago. [*Drake's Drum*]

17 Drake he's in his hammock till the great Armadas come. (Capten, art tha sleepin' there below?)

18 Where the old trade's plyin', an' the old flag flyin'.

19 She's the Fighting Téméraire. [*The Fighting Téméraire*]

20 'Ye have robbed,' said he, 'ye have slaughtered and made an end, / Take your ill-got plunder, and bury the dead.' [*He Fell Among Thieves*]

21 There'a a breathless hush in the Close tonight – / Ten to make and the match to win – / A bumping pitch and a blinding light, / An hour to play and the last man in. / And it's not for the sake of a ribboned coat, / Or the selfish hope of a season's fame, / But his Captain's hand on his shoulder smote – / 'Play up! play up! and play the game!' [*Vitae Lampada*]

22 The sand of the desert is sodden red, – Red with the wreck of a square that broke; – / The gatling's jammed and the colonel dead, / And the regiment blind with the dust and smoke. / The river of death has brimmed its banks / And England's far and honour a name, / But the voice of a schoolboy rallies the ranks: / 'Play up! play up! and play the game!'

MARGARET, DUCHESS OF NEWCASTLE 1624?–1673

23 For all the Brothers were valiant, and all the Sisters virtuous. [Her epitaph in Westminster Abbey]

ANTHONY NEWLEY 1931– and LESLIE BRICUSSE 1931–

24 Stop the World, I Want to Get Off. [Title of Musical]

CARDINAL NEWMAN 1801–1890

25 He has attempted (as I may call it) to *poison the wells*. [*Apologia Pro Vita Sua*, 'Mr Kingsley's Method of Disputation']

1 I recollect an acquaintance saying to me that 'the Oriel Common Room stank of Logic.' [*History of My Religious Opinions*]

2 It is almost a definition of a gentleman to say that he is one who never inflicts pain. [*The Idea of a University*, 'Knowledge and Religious Duty']

3 Lead, Kindly Light, amid the encircling gloom, / Lead Thou me on! / The night is dark, and I am far from home – / Lead Thou me on! [Hymn]

4 I loved the garish day, and, spite of fears, / Pride ruled my will: remember not past years.

5 And with the morn those angel faces smile / Which I have loved long since, and lost awhile.

NEWS OF THE WORLD

6 All human life is there. [Newspaper's slogan]

SIR ISAAC NEWTON 1642–1727

7 If I have seen further, it is by standing on the shoulders of giants. [Letter to Robert Hooke, 5 Feb. 1675/76 (variants of the phrase in Lucan, Robert Burton, see also 118:23)]

8 I do not know what I may appear to the world, but to myself I seem to have been only like a boy playing on the sea-shore, and diverting myself in now and then finding a smoother pebble or a prettier shell than ordinary, whilst the great ocean of truth lay all undiscovered before me. [D. Brewster, *Memoirs of Newton*, II. Ch. 27]

9 O Diamond! Diamond! thou little knowest the mischief done! [Attr. remark to a dog that 'destroyed the almost finished labours of some years']

JOHN NEWTON 1725–1807

10 Glorious things of thee are spoken, / Zion, city of our God. [*Olney Hymns*, 'Glorious Things']

11 How sweet the name of Jesus sounds / In a believer's ear! ['The Name of Jesus']

NICHOLAS I OF RUSSIA 1796–1855

12 We have a sick man – a seriously sick man on our hands. [(Turkey) Quoted in a letter by Sir G. H. Seymour, 11 Jan. 1853]

13 Russia has two generals in whom she can trust – Generals Janvier and Février. [*Punch*, 10 Mar. 1853]

VIVIAN NICHOLSON 1936–

14 Spend, spend, spend. [When asked in Sept. 1961 what she was going to do with record football pools win. Also used as title of her autobiography]

ADELA NICOLSON *see* HOPE, LAURENCE

REINHOLD NIEBUHR 1892–1971

15 God grant me the serenity to accept things I cannot change, courage to change things I can, and wisdom to know the difference. [Attr., but never claimed by him, probably 18 Cent. German, if not earlier]

16 Man's capacity for evil makes democracy necessary and man's capacity for good makes democracy possible. [*The Children of Light and the Children of Darkness*, Foreword]

MARTIN NIEMÖLLER 1892–1984

17 In Germany, the Nazis came for the Communists and I didn't speak up because I was not a Communist. Then they came for the Jews and I didn't speak up because I was not a Jew. Then they came for the trade unionists and I didn't speak up because I was not a trade unionist. Then they came for the Catholics and I was a Protestant so I didn't speak up. Then they came for me . . . By that time there was no one to speak up for anyone. [Attr. in *Congressional Record*, 14 Oct. 1968]

FRIEDRICH NIETZSCHE 1844–1900

18 I teach you the superman. Man is something that is to be surpassed. [*Also sprach Zarathustra*, Prologue, Ch. 3]

19 As an artist, a man has no home in Europe save in Paris. [*Ecce Homo*]

20 My time has not yet come either; some are born posthumously.

21 The masters have been abolished; the morality of the common man has triumphed. [*Genealogie der Moral*, Aphorism 9]

22 Morality in Europe today is herd-morality. [*Jenseits von Gut und Böse*]

1 Is not life a hundred times too short for us to bore ourselves?

FLORENCE NIGHTINGALE 1820–1910

2 Too kind – too kind. [When handed the insignia of the Order of Merit on her deathbed. Quoted in Lytton Strachey, *Eminent Victorians*]

NIMROD [CHARLES APPERLEY] 1779–1843

3 'But he'll be drowned,' exclaims Lord Kinnaird.
'I shouldn't wonder,' observes Mr William Coke. 'But the pace is too good to inquire.' [*The Chase*]

4 Quite the cream of the thing.

PRESIDENT RICHARD NIXON 1913–

5 You won't have Nixon to kick around any more, gentlemen. This is my last Press Conference. [Press conference for governorship of California, 7 Nov. 1962]

6 This is the greatest week in the history of the world since the creation. [Of man's first moon-landing, said on board the *Hornet*, 24 July 1969]

7 The great silent majority of my fellow Americans – I ask for your support. [TV address on Vietnam War, 3 Nov. 1969]

8 There can be no whitewash at the White House. [TV address on the Watergate crisis, 30 Apr. 1973. Quoted in C. Bernstein and B. Woodward, *All the President's Men*]

9 If some of my judgements were wrong, and some were wrong, they were made in what I believed at the time to be the best interest of the nation. [In his resignation speech, 8 Aug. 1974]

10 When the President does it, that means it is not illegal. [In TV interview with David Frost, 20 May 1977]

MILTON NOBLES 1847–1924

11 The villain still pursued her. [*Phoenix*, I. iii]

A. J. NOCK 1873–1945

12 It is an economic axiom as old as the hills that goods and services can be paid for only with goods and services. [*Memoirs of a Superfluous Man*, III. Ch. 3]

THOMAS NOEL 1799–1861

13 Rattle his bones over the stones; / He's only a pauper, whom nobody owns! [*The Pauper's Drive*]

DENIS NORDEN 1922–

14 It's a funny kind of month, October. For the really keen cricket fan it's when you discover that your wife left you in May. [In *She* magazine, Oct. 1977]

REV. JOHN NORRIS 1657–1711

15 Like Angels' visits, short and bright; / Mortality's too weak to bear them long. [*The Parting*]

CHRISTOPHER NORTH [JOHN WILSON] 1785–1854

16 His Majesty's dominions, on which the sun never sets. [*Noctes Ambrosianae*, 20 (See 338:12)]

17 Laws were made to be broken. [24]

LORD NORTHCLIFFE 1865–1922

18 They are only ten. [Said to have been written up in his offices to remind the staff of their public's mental age]

19 When I want a peerage, I will pay for it like an honest man. [Quoted in Reginald Pound and Geoffrey Harmsworth, *Northcliffe*, Ch. 11]

SIR STAFFORD NORTHCOTE 1818–1887

20 That grand old man, the Prime Minister. [(Gladstone) Speech, 12 Apr. 1882]

CAROLINE NORTON 1808–1877

21 The Arab's Farewell to his Steed. [Title of poem]

22 I do not love thee! – no! I do not love thee! / And yet when thou art absent I am sad. [*I Do Not Love Thee*]

23 All our calm is in that balm – / Not lost but gone before. [*Not Lost But Gone Before*]

JACK NORWORTH 1878–1959

24 Oh! shine on, shine on, harvest moon / Up in the sky. / I ain't had no lovin' / Since April, January, June or July. [Song: *Shine On, Harvest Moon*, music by Nora Bayes-Norworth]

NOVALIS [FRIEDRICH VON HARDENBERG] 1772–1801

1 *Ein Gott-betrunkener Mensch.* – A God-intoxicated man. [Description of Spinoza]

IVOR NOVELLO 1893–1951

2 And Her Mother Came Too. [Title of song]

ALFRED NOYES 1880–1958

3 Go down to Kew in lilac-time, in lilac-time, in lilac-time. [*The Barrel Organ*]

NURSERY RHYMES

For sources, see Oxford Dictionary of Nursery Rhymes

4 A was an apple-pie; / B bit it; / C cut it.

5 As I was going to St Ives, / I met a man with seven wives.

6 Baa, baa, black sheep, / Have you any wool? / Yes sir, yes, sir, / Three bags full.

7 Bobby Shaftoe's gone to sea, / Silver buckles at his knee; / He'll come back and marry me, / Bonny Bobby Shaftoe.

8 Boys and girls come out to play, / The moon doth shine as bright as day.

9 Bye, baby bunting. / Daddy's gone a-hunting, / Gone to get a rabbit skin / To wrap the baby bunting in.

10 Cock a doodle doo! / My dame has lost her shoe, / My master's lost his fiddling stick, / And knows not what to do.

11 Come, let's to bed, / Says Sleepy-head; / Tarry a while, says Slow; / Put on the pan, says Greedy Nan, / We'll sup before we go.

12 Daffy-down-dilly is new come to town, / With a yellow petticoat, and a green gown.

13 Ding, dong, bell, / Pussy's in the well. / Who put her in? / Little Johnny Green.

14 Fee, fi, fo, fum, / I smell the blood of an Englishman; / Be he alive or be he dead, / I'll grind his bones to make my bread.

15 A frog he would a wooing go. / 'Heigh ho!' says Rowley.

16 Georgie Porgie, pudding and pie, / Kissed the girls and made them cry; / When the boys came out to play, / Georgie Porgie ran away.

17 Goosey goosey gander, / Whither shall I wander? / Upstairs and downstairs / And in my lady's chamber. / There I met an old man / Who would not say his prayers; / I took him by the left leg, / And threw him down the stairs.

18 Here is the church, and here is the steeple; / Open the door and here are the people.

19 Hey diddle, diddle, / The cat and the fiddle, / The cow jumped over the moon; / The little dog laughed / To see such sport, / And the dish ran away with the spoon.

20 Hickory, dickory, dock, / The mouse ran up the clock. / The clock struck one, / The mouse ran down, / Hickory, dickory, dock.

21 Hot cross buns! Hot cross buns! / One a penny, two a penny, / Hot cross buns!

22 How many miles to Babylon? / Three-score and ten. / Can I get there by candle-light? / Yes, and back again.

23 Humpty Dumpty sat on a wall, / Humpty Dumpty had a great fall; / All the King's horses, and all the King's men, / Couldn't put Humpty together again.

24 Hush-a-bye, baby, on the tree top, / When the wind blows the cradle will rock; / When the bough breaks the cradle will fall, / Down will come baby, cradle, and all.

25 I had a little nut tree, / Nothing would it bear / But a silver nutmeg / And a golden pear; / The King of Spain's daughter / Came to visit me, / And all for the sake / Of my little nut tree.

26 I love little pussy, / Her coat is so warm, / And if I don't hurt her, / She'll do me no harm.

27 I love sixpence, jolly little sixpence, / I love sixpence better than my life.

28 I'm the king of the castle, / Get down you dirty rascal.

29 Jack and Jill / Went up the hill, / To fetch a pail of water; / Jack fell down, / And broke his crown, / And Jill came tumbling after.

30 Jack Sprat could eat no fat, / His wife could eat no lean; / And so between them both, you see, / They licked the platter clean.

31 Ladybird, ladybird, / Fly away home, / Your house is on fire, / And your children all gone.

32 The lion and the unicorn / Were fighting for the crown; / The lion beat the unicorn / All around the town.

Some gave them white bread, / And some gave them brown; / Some gave them plum cake / And drummed them out of town.

1 Little Bo-Peep has lost her sheep, / And doesn't know where to find them; / Leave them alone, and they'll come home, / Bringing their tails behind them.

2 Little boy blue, / Come blow up your horn, / The sheep's in the meadow, / The cow's in the corn. / Where is the boy / Who looks after the sheep? / He's under a haycock / Fast asleep.

3 Little Jack Horner / Sat in the corner, / Eating a Christmas pie; / He put in his thumb, and pulled out a plum, / And said, 'What a good boy am I!'

4 Little Miss Muffet / Sat on a tuffet, / Eating her curds and whey; / There came a big spider, / Who sat down beside her / And frightened Miss Muffet away.

5 Little Polly Flinders / Sat among the cinders.

6 Little Tommy Tucker, / Sings for his supper. / What shall we give him? / White bread and butter.

7 London bridge is broken down, / My fair lady.

8 Mary had a little lamb, / His fleece was white as snow; / And everywhere that Mary went / The lamb was sure to go.

9 Mary, Mary, quite contrary, / How does your garden grow? / With silver bells, and cockle shells, / And pretty maids all in a row.

10 Monday's child is fair of face, / Tuesday's child is full of grace.

11 The north wind doth blow, / And we shall have snow, / And what will poor Robin do then? / Poor thing.

He'll sit in a barn, / And keep himself warm, / And hide his head under his wing, / Poor thing.

12 O dear, what can the matter be? / Johnny's so long at the fair. [Continued in next entry]

13 He promised he'd bring me a bunch of blue ribbons / To tie up my bonny brown hair.

14 Old King Cole / Was a merry old soul, / And a merry old soul was he; / He called for his pipe, / And he called for his bowl, / And he called for his fiddlers three.

15 Old Mother Hubbard / Went to the cupboard, / To get her poor dog a bone; / But when she got there, / The cupboard was bare, / And so the poor dog had none.

16 One, two, / Buckle my shoe; / Three, four,/ Knock at the door.

17 Oranges and lemons, / Say the bells of St Clement's. [Continued in next entry]

18 You owe me five farthings, / Say the bells of St Martin's. / When will you pay me? / Say the bells at Old Bailey. When I grow rich, / Say the bells at Shoreditch. [Continued in next entry]

19 Here comes a candle to light you to bed, / Here comes a chopper to chop off your head.

20 Pat-a-cake, pat-a-cake, baker's man, / Bake me a cake as fast as you can.

21 Pease porridge hot / Pease porridge cold, / Pease porridge in the pot / Nine days old.

22 Peter Piper picked a peck of pickled pepper.

23 Pussy cat, pussy cat, / Where have you been? / I've been up to London / To look at the Queen, / Pussy cat, pussy cat, What did you there? / I frightened a little mouse / Under her chair.

24 The Queen of Hearts / She made some tarts, / All on a summer's day; / The Knave of Hearts / He stole the tarts, / And took them clean away.

25 Rain, rain, go away, / Come again another day.

26 Ride a cock-horse to Banbury Cross, / To see a fine lady upon a white horse; / Rings on her fingers and bells on her toes, / And she shall have music wherever she goes.

27 Ring-a-ring o' roses, / A pocket full of posies, / A-tishoo! A-tishoo! / We all fall down.

28 Round and round the rugged rock / The ragged rascal ran.

29 See-saw, Margery Daw, / Johnny shall have a new master; / He shall have but a penny a day, / Because he can't work any faster.

30 Simple Simon met a pieman / Going to the fair.

31 Sing a song of sixpence, / A pocket full of rye; / Four and twenty blackbirds, / Baked in a pie.

When the pie was opened, / The birds began to sing; / Was not that a dainty dish, / To set before the king?

The king was in his counting-house, / Counting out his money; / The queen was in the parlour, / Eating bread and honey.

The maid was in the garden, / Hanging out the clothes, / When down came a blackbird / And pecked off her nose.

1 Solomon Grundy, / Born on a Monday.

2 Taffy was a Welshman, / Taffy was a thief; / Taffy came to my house, / And stole a piece of beef.

3 Tell tale, tit! / Your tongue shall be split, / And all the dogs in the town / Shall have a little bit.

4 There was a crooked man, / And he walked a crooked mile, / He found a crooked sixpence / Against a crooked stile.

5 There was an old woman who lived in a shoe, / She had so many children she didn't know what to do.

6 This is the farmer sowing his corn, / That kept the cock that crowed in the morn, / That waked the priest all shaven and shorn, / That married the man all tattered and torn, / That kissed the maiden all forlorn, / That milked the cow with the crumpled horn, / That tossed the dog, / That worried the cat, / That killed the rat, / That ate the malt, / That lay in the house that Jack built.

7 This little pig went to market; / This little pig stayed at home.

8 Three blind mice, see how they run! / They all ran after the farmer's wife, / Who cut off their tails with a carving knife, / Did ever you see such a thing in your life, / As three blind mice?

9 Three wise men of Gotham / Went to sea in a bowl; / And if the bowl had been stronger, / My song would have been longer.

10 Tom, he was a piper's son, / He learned to play when he was young, / But all the tune that he could play / Was, 'Over the hills and far away.' [Continued in next entry]

11 Tom, Tom, the piper's son, / Stole a pig and away he run; / The pig was eat, and Tom was beat, / And Tom went howling down the street.

12 We are all in the dumps, / For diamonds are trumps; / The kittens are gone to St Paul's. / The babies are bit, / The Moon's in a fit, / And the houses are built without walls.

13 Wee Willie Winkie runs through the town, / Upstairs and downstairs in his nightgown.

14 What are little boys made of? / What are little boys made of? / Frogs and snails / And puppy-dogs' tails, / That's what little boys are made of.

What are little girls made of? / What are little girls made of? / Sugar and spice / And all things nice, / That's what little girls are made of.

15 Where are you going to, my pretty maid? / I'm going a-milking, sir, she said. [Continued in next entry]

16 My face is my fortune, sir, she said. [Continued in next entry]

17 Then I can't marry you, my pretty maid. / Nobody asked you, sir she said.

18 Who killed Cock Robin? / I, said the Sparrow, / With my bow and arrow, / I killed Cock Robin. [Continued in next entry]

19 Who saw him die? / I, said the Fly, / With my little eye, / I saw him die.

O

FREDERICK OAKELEY 1802–1880

1 O come all ye faithful, / Joyful and triumphant, / O come ye, O come ye to Bethlehem. [Hymn, trans. from Latin, *Adeste Fideles*]

JOHN OATES 1880–1912

2 I am just going outside, and may be some time. [Last words, 16 Mar. 1912. Quoted in R. F. Scott's diary, *Scott's Last Expedition*, Ch. 20]

FLANN O'BRIEN [MYLES NA GOPALEEN] 1910–1966

3 The conclusion of your syllogism, I said lightly, is fallacious, being based upon licensed premises. [*At Swim-Two-Birds*, Ch. 1]

4 A thing of duty is a boy for ever. [On the perennial youthfulness of policemen. Quoted in the *Listener*, 24 Feb. 1977]

SEAN O'CASEY 1880–1964

5 I killin' meself workin', an' he sthruttin' about from mornin' till night like a paycock! [*Juno and the Paycock*, I]

6 He's an oul' butty o' mine – oh, he's a darlin' man, a daarlin' man.

7 The whole worl's in a state o' chassis.

8 It's only a little cold I have; there's nothing derogatory wrong with me. [*The Plough and the Stars*, I]

9 There's no reason to bring religion into it. I think we ought to have as great a regard for religion as we can, so as to keep it out of as many things as possible.

10 A man should always be drunk, Minnie, when he talks politics – it's the only way in which to make them important. [*The Shadow of a Gunman*, I]

11 English literature's performing flea. [Of P. G. Wodehouse. Quoted in P. G. Wodehouse, *Performing Flea*, 'Postscript']

ADOLPH OCHS 1858–1935

12 All the news that's fit to print. [Motto of the *New York Times*]

JOHN O'KEEFE 1747–1833

13 Amo, amas, I love a lass, / As a cedar tall and slender; / Sweet cowslip's grace / Is her nominative case, / And she's of the feminine gender. [*The Agreeable Surprise*, II. ii]

14 Fat, fair and forty. [*Irish Minnie*, ii]

15 You shall always except the present company. [*The London Hermit*, I. ii]

PATRICK O'KEEFE 1872–1934

16 Say it with flowers. [Slogan for Society of American Florists]

DENNIS O'KELLY 1720?–1787

17 It will be Eclipse first, the rest nowhere. [At Epsom, 3 May 1769]

JOHN OLDHAM 1653–1683

18 Racks, gibbets, halters, were their arguments. [*Satires upon the Jesuits*, 'Garnet's Ghost', 176]

WILLIAM OLDYS 1696–1761

19 Busy, curious, thirsty fly / Drink with me, and drink as I. [*Busy, Curious, Thirsty Fly*]

EUGENE O'NEILL 1888–1953

1 For de little stealin' dey gits you in jail soon or late. For de big stealin' dey makes you emperor and puts you in de Hall o' Fame when you croaks. [*The Emperor Jones*]

JOHN OPIE 1761–1806

2 I mix them with brains, sir. [When asked how he mixed his colours. Quoted in Samuel Smiles, *Self-Help*, Ch. 4]

J. ROBERT OPPENHEIMER 1904–1967

3 We knew the world would not be the same. [(After first atomic test) *The Decision to Drop the Bomb*]

4 The physicists have known sin; and this is a knowledge which they cannot lose. [Lecture at Massachusetts Institute of Technology, 25 Nov. 1947]

BARONESS ORCZY 1865–1947

5 We seek him here, we seek him there, / Those Frenchies seek him everywhere. / Is he in heaven? – Is he in hell? / That demmed, elusive Pimpernel? [*The Scarlet Pimpernel*, Ch. 12]

J. B. O'REILLY 1844–1890

6 The organized charity, scrimped and iced, / In the name of a cautious, statistical Christ. [*In Bohemia*]

META ORRED 19 Cent.

7 In the gloaming, O, my darling! / When the lights are dim and low, / And the quiet shadows falling / Softly come and softly go. [*In the Gloaming*]

JOSE ORTEGA Y GASSET 1883–1955

8 The world is the sum-total of our vital possibilities. [*The Revolt of the Masses*, Ch. 4]

JOE ORTON 1933–1967

9 I'd the upbringing a nun would envy and that's the truth. Until I was fifteen I was more familiar with Africa than my own body. [*Entertaining Mr Sloane*, I]

10 It's all any reasonable child can expect if the dad is present at the conception. [3]

GEORGE ORWELL 1903–1950

11 Man is the only creature that consumes without producing. [*Animal Farm*, Ch. 1]

12 Four legs good, two legs bad. [3]

13 Napoleon had commanded that once a week there should be held something called a Spontaneous Demonstration. [9]

14 He intended, he said, to devote the rest of his life to learning the remaining twenty-two letters of the alphabet.

15 All animals are equal, but some animals are more equal than others. [10]

16 The creatures outside looked from pig to man, and from man to pig, and from pig to man again; but already it was impossible to say which was which.

17 I'm fat, but I'm thin inside. Has it ever struck you that there's a thin man inside every fat man, just as they say there's a statue inside every block of stone? [*Coming up for Air*, I. 3 (See also 121:19, 448:8, 453:10)]

18 Probably the Battle of Waterloo *was* won on the playing-fields of Eton, but the opening battles of all subsequent wars have been lost there. [*The Lion and the Unicorn*, 'England, Your England']

19 A family with the wrong members in control – that, perhaps, is as near as one can come to describing England in a phrase. ['The Ruling Class']

20 Big Brother is watching you. [*1984*, Pt I. Ch. 1]

21 Only the Thought Police mattered.

22 War is Peace / Freedom is Slavery / Ignorance is Strength.

23 Who controls the past controls the future . . . Who controls the present controls the past. [Ch. 3]

24 Newspeak was the official language of Oceania. [Footnote]

25 His mind . . . fetched up with a bump against the Newspeak word *doublethink*.

26 The Two Minutes Hate.

27 The proles are not human beings. [5]

28 Hate Week.

29 There can hardly be a town in the South of England where you could throw a brick without hitting the niece of a bishop. [*The Road to Wigan Pier*, Ch. 7]

1 We of the sinking middle class ... may sink without further struggles into the working class where we belong, and probably when we get there it will not be so dreadful as we feared, for, after all, we have nothing to lose but our aitches. [13]

2 The aim of a joke is not to degrade the human being but to remind him that he is already degraded. [*Selected Essays*, 'Funny But Not Vulgar']

3 The inflated style is itself a kind of euphemism. A mass of Latin words falls upon the facts like soft snow, blurring the outlines and covering up all the details. The great enemy of clear language is insincerity. ['Politics and the English Language']

4 In prose, the worst thing one can do with words is surrender to them.

5 The Catholic and the Communist are alike in assuming that an opponent cannot be both honest and intelligent. ['The Prevention of Literature']

6 The quickest way of ending a war is to lose it. [*Shooting an Elephant*, 'Second Thoughts on James Burnham']

7 Serious sport has nothing to do with fair play. It is bound up with hatred, jealousy, boastfulness, disregard of all rules and sadistic pleasure in witnessing violence. In other words, it is war minus the shooting. ['The Sporting Spirit']

8 One cannot really be a Catholic and grown-up. [(Of Evelyn Waugh, in his notebook) *Collected Essays* (Penguin edn.), p.576]

JOHN OSBORNE 1929–

9 Don't clap too hard – It's a very old building. [*The Entertainer*, vii]

10 He really deserves some sort of decoration ... a medal inscribed 'For Vaguery in the Field'. [*Look Back in Anger*, I]

11 I'm not mentioned at all because my name is a dirty word.

12 I don't think one 'comes down' from Jimmy's university. According to him, it's not even red brick, but white tile. [II. i]

13 They spend their time mostly looking forward to the past.

14 Poor old Daddy – just one of those sturdy old plants left over from the Edwardian Wilderness, that can't understand why the sun isn't shining any more. [ii]

ARTHUR O'SHAUGHNESSY 1844–1881

15 We are the music-makers / And we are the dreamers of dreams, / Wandering by lone sea-breakers, / And sitting by desolate streams; / World-losers and world-forsakers, / On whom the pale moon gleams: / Yet we are the movers and shakers / Of the world forever, it seems. [*Ode*]

16 One man with a dream, at pleasure, / Shall go forth and conquer a crown; / And three with a new song's measure / Can trample a kingdom down.

17 For each age is a dream that is dying, / Or one that is coming to birth.

JAMES OTIS 1725–1783

18 Taxation without representation is tyranny. [Watchword of the American Revolution. Attr., but probably apocryphal]

THOMAS OTWAY 1652–1685

19 Destructive, damnable, deceitful woman! [*The Orphan*, III. i]

20 O woman! lovely woman! Nature made thee / To temper man: we had been brutes without you; / Angels are painted fair, to look like you. [*Venice Preserved*, I. i]

SIR THOMAS OVERBURY 1581–1613

21 In part to blame is she, / Which hath without consent been only tried: / He comes too near that comes to be denied. [*A Wife*, 26]

OVID 43 BC–AD 17

22 *Procul hinc, procul este, severae!* – Stay far hence, far hence, forbidding women! [*Amores*, II. i. 3]

23 *Forsitan et nostrum nomen miscebitur istis.* – Perhaps too our name will be joined with these. [*Ars Amatoria*, iii. 339]

24 *Gutta cavat lapidem, consumitur anulus usu.* – The dropping of rain hollows out a stone, a ring is worn by use. [*Epistulae Ex Ponto*, IV, x. 5]

25 *Iam seges est ubi Troia fuit.* – Now there are fields where Troy once was. [*Heroides*, I. i. 53]

26 *Medio tutissimus ibis.* – You will go most safely in the middle. [*Metamorphoses*, II. 137]

1 *Inopem me copia fecit.* – Plenty makes me poor. [III. 466]

2 *Video meliora, proboque; / Deteriora sequor.* – I see better things and approve; I follow the worse. [VII. 20]

3 *Tempus edax rerum.* – Time the devourer of things. [XXV. 234]

4 *Tu quoque.* – Thou also. [*Tristia*, ii. 39]

ROBERT OWEN 1771–1858

5 All the world is queer save thee and me, and even thou art a little queer. [Attr., when ending his partnership with William Allen, 1828]

WILFRED OWEN 1893–1918

6 My subject is war, and the pity of War. The Poetry is in the pity. [Preface to *Poems*]

7 What passing-bells for these who die as cattle? / Only the monstrous anger of the guns./ Only the stuttering rifles' rapid rattle / Can patter out their hasty orisons. [*Anthem for doomed Youth*]

8 And bugles calling for them from sad shires.

9 And each slow dusk a drawing-down of blinds.

10 The old Lie: *Dulce et decorum est / Pro patria mori.* [*Dulce et decorum est* (see 208:24)]

11 Move him into the sun – / Gently its touch awoke him once / At home. [*Futility*]

12 Red lips are not so red / As the stained stones kissed by the English dead. / Kindness of wooed and wooer / Seems shame to their love pure. [*Greater Love*]

13 Whatever mourns when many leave these shores; / Whatever shares / The eternal reciprocity of tears. [*Insensibility*]

14 My soul looked down from a vague height with Death, / As unremembering how I rose or why, / And saw a sad land, weak with sweats of dearth. [*The Show*]

15 It seemed that out of battle I escaped / Down some profound dull tunnel, long since scooped / Through granites which titanic wars had groined. [*Strange Meeting*]

16 One sprang up, and stared / With piteous recognition in fixed eyes, / Lifting distressful hands, as if to bless.

17 'Strange friend,' I said, 'here is no cause to mourn.' / 'None,' said the other, 'save the undone years, / The hopelessness. Whatever hope is yours / Was my life also; I went hunting wild / After the wildest beauty in the world.'

18 Courage was mine, and I had mystery, / Wisdom was mine, and I had mastery; / To miss the march of the retreating world / Into vain citadels that are not walled.

EDWARD OXENFORD 1847–1929

19 I fear no foe in shining armour. [Song]

AXEL COUNT OXENSTIERNA 1583–1654

20 Do you not know, my son, with how little wisdom the world is governed? [Letter to his son, 1648]

EDWARD DE VERE, EARL OF OXFORD 1550–1604

21 If women could be fair and yet not fond. [*Women's Changeableness*]

P

THOMAS PAINE 1737–1809

1 The sublime and the ridiculous are often so nearly related that it is difficult to class them separately. One step above the sublime makes the ridiculous; and one step above the ridiculous makes the sublime again. [*The Age of Reason*, ii, note]

2 These are times that try men's souls. The summer soldier and the sunshine patriot will, in this crisis, shrink from the service of his country; but he that stands it *now* deserves the love and thanks of man and woman. ['The American Crisis', in the *Pennsylvania Journal*, 23 Dec. 1776]

3 Government, even in its best state, is but a necessary evil; in its worst state, an intolerable one. [*Common Sense*, Ch. 1]

4 The final event to himself [Mr Burke] has been, that as he rose like a rocket, he fell like the stick. [*Letter to the Addressers on the late Proclamation*]

5 [Burke] is not affected by the reality of distress touching his heart, but by the showy resemblance of it striking his imagination. He pities the plumage, but forgets the dying bird. [(On Burke, *Reflections on the Revolution in France*) *The Rights of Man*, Pt I]

6 My country is the world, and my religion is to do good. [Pt I. Ch. 5]

7 The religion of humanity. [Attr. by Edmund Gosse]

JOSÉ DE PALAFOX 1776–1847

8 War to the knife. [When summoned to surrender Saragossa, 4 Aug. 1808. Perhaps in fact: 'War *and* the knife']

REV. WILLIAM PALEY 1743–1805

9 Who can refute a sneer? [*Moral Philosophy*, V. Ch. 9]

SAMUEL PALMER 1805–1881

10 A picture has been said to be something between a thing and a thought. [Quoted in Arthur Symons, *Life of Blake*]

VISCOUNT PALMERSTON 1784–1865

11 You may call it a coalition, you may call it the accidental and fortuitous concurrence of atoms. [Speech in House of Commons, 5 Mar. 1857]

12 Die, my dear Doctor, that's the last thing I shall do! [Attr. last words]

EDWARD PARAMORE 1895–1956

13 Hard-boiled as a picnic egg. [*The Ballad of Yukon Jake*]

DOROTHY PARKER 1893–1967

14 Some men break your heart in two, / Some men fawn and flatter, / Some men never look at you; / And that cleans up the matter. [*Experience*]

15 Four be the things I'd been better without: / Love, curiosity, freckles, and doubt. [*Inventory*]

16 Men seldom make passes / At girls who wear glasses. [*News Item*]

17 Why is it no one ever sent me yet / One perfect limousine, do you suppose? / Ah no, it's always just my luck to get / One perfect rose. [*One Perfect Rose*]

1 Guns aren't lawful; / Nooses give; / Gas smells awful; / You might as well live. [*Résumé*]

2 Where's the man could ease a heart, / Like a satin gown? [*The Satin Dress*]

3 By the time you swear you're his, / Shivering and sighing, / And he vows his passion is / Infinite, undying – / Lady, make a note of this: / One of you is lying. [*Unfortunate Coincidence*]

4 Three highballs, and I think I'm St Francis of Assisi. [*Just A Little One*]

5 Wit's End. [Nickname for Alexander Woollcott's New York apartment. Quoted in James Thurber, *The Years with Ross*, Ch. 15]

6 Enjoyed it! One more drink and I'd have been under the host. [When asked whether she had enjoyed a cocktail party. Quoted in R. E. Drennan, *Wit's End*]

7 You can't teach an old dogma new tricks.

8 How could they tell? [On being told that ex-President Coolidge had died. Similar joke ascr. to Wilson Mizner in A. Johnston, *Legend of a Sport; the New Yorker*]

9 This is not a novel to be tossed aside lightly. It should be thrown with great force. [Book review]

10 She ran the whole gamut of her emotions from A to B. [Of Katharine Hepburn in play *The Lake*, 1933, quoted in A. Woollcott, *While Rome Burns*, 'Our Mrs Parker']

11 Good work Mary . . . We all knew you had it in you [Telegram to friend on her new baby]

12 Hollywood money isn't money. It's congealed snow, melts in your hand, and there you are. [In Malcolm Cowley (ed.), *Writers at Work*, First Series]

13 Seventy-two suburbs in search of a city. [Of Los Angeles, but others are attr. with the description. Quoted in Leslie Halliwell, *The Filmgoer's Book of Quotes*]

14 You can lead a whore to culture but you can't make her think. [Speech to American Horticultural Society]

15 This is on me. [Suggested epitaph for her own tombstone. Quoted in J. Keats, *You Might As Well Live*, Pt 1. Ch 5]

16 Oh, don't worry about Alan . . . Alan will always land on somebody's feet. [(Of her husband on the day their divorce became final) IV. 1]

17 Excuse my dust. [Alternative epitaph, quoted in A. Woollcott, *While Rome Burns*, 'Our Mrs Parker']

MARTIN PARKER ?–1656

18 You gentlemen of England / Who live at home at ease, / How little do you think / On the dangers of the seas. [*The Valiant Sailors*]

19 The Man in the Moon may wear out his shoon, By running after Charles-his-Wain, / But all's to no end; for the times will not mend / Till the King enjoys his own again. [*When the King enjoys his Own again*]

ROSS PARKER 1914–1974
and HUGHIE CHARLES 1907–

20 There'll always be an England / While there's a country lane, / Wherever there's a cottage small / Beside a field of grain. [*There'll Always Be an England*]

C. NORTHCOTE PARKINSON 1909–

21 Work expands so as to fill the time available for its completion. General recognition of this fact is shown in the proverbial phrase 'It is the busiest man who has time to spare.' [*Parkinson's Law*, Ch. 1]

22 The rise in the total of those employed is governed by Parkinson's Law and would be much the same whether the volume of work were to increase, diminish or even disappear.

CHARLES STEWART PARNELL 1846–1891

23 No man has a right to fix the boundary of the march of a nation; no man has a right to say to his country – thus far shalt thou go and no further. [Speech at Cork, 21 Jan. 1885]

THOMAS PARNELL 1679–1717

24 We call it only pretty Fanny's way. [*An Elegy to an old Beauty*]

25 Remote from man, with God he passed the days, / Prayer all his business, all his pleasure praise. [*The Hermit*, 5]

26 Still an angel appear to each lover beside, / But still be a woman to you. [Song: *When thy Beauty Appears*]

SAMUEL PARR 1747–1825

1 Now that the old lion is dead, every ass thinks he may kick at him. [(Dr Johnson) Quoted in Boswell, *Life of Johnson*, 1784]

BLAISE PASCAL 1623–1662

2 Not to care for philosophy is to be a true philosopher. [*Pensées*, I. 4]

3 The more intelligence one has the more people one finds original. Commonplace people see no difference between men. [I. 7]

4 The last thing one discovers in writing a book is what to put first. [19]

5 When one finds a natural style, one is amazed and delighted, for where one expected to see an author, one discovers a man. [29]

6 If you want people to think well of you, do not speak well of yourself. [44]

7 Man of wit, bad character. [46]

8 I cannot forgive Descartes; in all his philosophy he did his best to dispense with God. But he could not avoid making Him set the world in motion with a flip of His thumb; after that he had no more use for God. [II. 77]

9 If Cleopatra's nose had been shorter, the whole face of the earth would have changed. [162]

10 The heart has its reasons, which are quite unknown to the head. [IV. 277]

11 Man is no more than a reed, the weakest in nature. But he is a thinking reed. [VI. 347]

12 The I is hateful. [VII. 434]

13 Be comforted. You would not be seeking Me if you had not found Me. [552]

BORIS PASTERNAK 1890–1960

14 No bad man can be a good poet. [Quoted in Ilya Ehrenburg, *Truce*]

WALTER PATER 1839–1894

15 All art constantly aspires towards the condition of music. [*The Renaissance*, 'Giorgione']

16 She is older than the rocks among which she sits; like the vampire, she has been dead many times, and learned the secrets of the grave; and has been a diver in deep seas, and keeps their fallen day about her; and trafficked for strange webs with Eastern merchants: and,

as Leda, was the mother of Helen of Troy, and, as Saint Anne, the mother of Mary; and all this has been to her but as the sound of lyres and flutes, and lives only in the delicacy with which it has moulded the changing lineaments, and tinged the eyelids and the hands. [(Mona Lisa) 'Leonardo da Vinci']

17 Art comes to you proposing frankly to give nothing but the highest quality to your moments as they pass, and simply for those moments' sake. [Conclusion]

18 To burn always with this hard, gem-like flame, to maintain this ecstasy, is success in life.

ANDREW PATERSON 1864–1941

19 Once a jolly swagman camped by a billabong, / Under the shade of a coolibah tree, / And he sang as he sat and waited till his billy boiled, / 'You'll come a-waltzing, Matilda, with me.' [*Waltzing Matilda*]

COVENTRY PATMORE 1823–1896

20 Ah, wasteful woman, she who may / On her sweet self set her own price, / Knowing man cannot choose but pay, / How has she cheapened paradise; / How given for nought her priceless gift, / How spoiled the bread and spilled the wine, / Which, spent with due respective thrift, / Had made brutes men and men divine. [*The Angel in the House*, Bk i. 3, Prelude 3]

21 Love's perfect blossom only blows / Where noble manners veil defect. / Angels may be familiar; those / Who err each other must respect. [i. 11, Prelude 2]

22 'I saw you take his kiss!' ' 'Tis true.' / 'Oh, modesty!' 'Twas strictly kept: / He thought me asleep; at least, I knew / He thought I thought he thought I slept.' [ii. 8, Prelude 3]

23 A woman is a foreign land, / Of which, though there he settle young, / A man will ne'er quite understand / The customs, politics, and tongue. [9, Prelude 2]

24 Why, having won her, do I woo? / Because her spirit's vestal grace / Provokes me always to pursue, / But, spirit-like, eludes embrace. [12, Prelude 1]

25 I, singularly moved / To love the lovely that are not beloved, / Of all the seasons, most / Love winter. [*The Unknown Eros*, Bk i. 3, 'Winter']

1 And the only loveless look the look with which you passed. [8, 'Departure']

2 My little son, who looked from thoughtful eyes / And moved and spoke in quiet grown-up wise, / Having my law the seventh time disobeyed, / I struck him, and dismissed / With hard words and unkissed, / His mother, who was patient, being dead. [10, 'The Toys']

3 Here, in this little bay, / Full of tumultuous life and great repose, / Where, twice a day, / The purposeless, glad ocean comes and goes. [12, 'Magna est Veritas']

4 For want of me the world's course will not fail; / When all its work is done, the lie shall rot; / The truth is great, and shall prevail, / When none cares whether it prevail or not.

5 With all my will, but much against my heart, / We two now part, / My Very Dear, / Our solace is, the sad road lies so clear. [16, 'A Farewell']

JEAN PAUL [J. P. RICHTER] 1763–1825

6 *Diesen Weltschmerz kann er, so zu sagen, nur aushalten durch den Anblick der Seligkeit.* – He can, so to speak, only bear the sorrow of this world by gazing on blessedness. [*Selina*]

7 Providence has given to the French the empire of the land, to the English that of the sea, and to the Germans that of the air. [Quoted by Carlyle]

LESLIE PAUL 1905–

8 Angry Young Man. [Title of book (1951)]

JAMES PAYN 1830–1898

9 I never had a piece of toast / Particularly long and wide / But fell upon the sandy floor / And always on the buttered side. ['Parody', *Chambers' Journal*, 1884]

J. H. PAYNE 1792–1852

10 'Mid pleasures and palaces though we may roam, / Be it ever so humble, there's no place like home. [*Clari, the Maid of Milan*, 'Home, Sweet Home']

SIR EUSTACE PEACHTREE 17 Cent.

11 When men heard thunder on the left the gods had somewhat of special advertisement to impart. [*The Dangers of this Mortal Life*]

T. L. PEACOCK 1785–1866

12 A book that furnishes no quotation is, *me judice*, no book – it is a plaything. [*Crotchet Castle*, Ch. 9]

13 My house has been broken open on the most scientific principles. [17]

14 Not drunk is he who from the floor / Can rise alone and still drink more; / But drunk is he, who prostrate lies, / Without the power to drink or rise. [*The Misfortunes of Elphin*, Ch. 3, heading]

15 The mountain sheep are sweeter, / But the valley sheep are fatter; / We therefore deemed it meeter / To carry off the latter. [11]

16 He was sent, as usual, to a public school, where a little learning was painfully beaten into him, and from thence to the university, where it was carefully taken out of him. [*Nightmare Abbey*, Ch. 1]

17 Laughter is pleasant, but the exertion is too much for me. [(Hon. Mr Listless) 5]

18 Seamen three! what men be ye? / Gotham's three Wise Men we be. / Whither in your bowl so free? / To rake the moon from out the sea. / The bowl goes trim. The moon doth shine, / And our ballast is old wine. [11, 'Three Men of Gotham']

NORMAN VINCENT PEALE 1898–

19 The Power of Positive Thinking. [Title of book]

COMMANDER R. PEARY 1856–1920

20 The Eskimo had his own explanation. Said he: 'The devil is asleep or having trouble with his wife, or we should never have come back so easily.' [*The North Pole*]

GEORGE PEELE 1558?–1597?

21 God in the whizzing of a pleasant wind / Shall march upon the tops of mulberry trees. [*David and Bethsabe*, XII]

22 Whenas the rye reach to the chin, / And chopcherry, chopcherry ripe within, / Strawberries swimming in the cream, / And schoolboys playing in the stream; / Then O, then O, / then O, my true love said, / Till that time come again / She could not live a maid. [*The Old Wife's Tale*]

23 His golden locks time hath to silver turned;

/ O time too swift, O swiftness never ceasing!
[*Polyhymnia*, 'The Old Knight']

1 His helmet now shall make a hive for bees;
/ And lovers' sonnets turned to holy psalms, /
A man-at-alms must now serve on his knees, /
And feed on prayers, which are age's aims.

2 Goddess, allow this aged man his right, /
To be your beadsman now, that was your
knight.

CHARLES PÉGUY 1873–1914

3 The Social Revolution will be moral, or it
will not be. [*Basic Verities*]

4 What will God say to us, if some of us go to
him without the others? [Quoted in W. Neil,
Concise Dictionary of Religious Quotations]

EARL OF PEMBROKE 1734–1794

5 Dr Johnson's sayings would not appear so
extraordinary were it not for his *bow-wow way*.
[Boswell, *Life of Johnson*, 27 Mar. 1775, note]

WILLIAM PENN 1644–1718

6 No pain, no palm; no thorns, no throne; no
gall, no glory; no cross, no crown. [*No Cross,
No Crown*]

7 Men are more careful of the breed of their
horses and dogs than of their children. [*Reflexions and Maxims*, i. 85]

SAMUEL PEPYS 1633–1703

8 And so to bed. [*Diary*, 20 Apr. 1660 and
passim]

9 A silk suit, which cost me much money,
and I pray God to make me able to pay for it. [1
July 1660]

10 A good honest and painful sermon. [17
Mar. 1661]

11 But Lord! to see the absurd nature of Englishmen that cannot forbear laughing and jeering at
everything that looks strange. [27 Nov. 1662]

12 My wife, who, poor wretch, is troubled with
her lonely life. [19 Dec.]

13 No high-flyer. [27 May 1663]

14 Most of their discourse was about hunting,
in a dialect I understand very little. [22 Nov.]

15 Several poor creatures carried by, by constables, for being at a conventicle . . . I would to

God they would either conform, or be more
wise, and not be catched! [7 Aug. 1664]

16 Pretty witty Nell. [(Gwynne) 3 Apr. 1665]

17 But Lord! what a sad time it is to see no
boats upon the River, and grass grows all up
and down White Hall Court. [20 Sept.]

18 Strange to say what delight we married
people have to see these poor fools decoyed into
our condition. [25 Dec.]

19 Music and women I cannot but give way
to, whatever my business is. [9 Mar. 1666]

20 Home, and, being washing-day, dined upon
cold meat. [4 Apr.]

21 And mighty proud I am (and ought to be
thankful to God Almighty) that I am able to
have a spare bed for my friends. [8 Aug.]

22 But it is pretty to see what money will do.
[21 Mar. 1667]

23 To church; and with my mourning, very
handsome, and new periwig, make a great
show. [31 Mar.]

24 My wife hath something in her gizzard,
that only waits an opportunity of being provoked to bring up. [17 June 1668]

25 A good dinner, and company that pleased
me mightily, being all eminent men in their
way. [19 July]

26 And so I betake myself that course, which
is almost as much as to see myself go into my
grave; for which, and all the discomforts that
will accompany my being blind, the good God
prepare me. [Final entry]

JOHN PERCY 19 Cent.

27 Your Molly has never been false, she declares, / Since last time we parted at Wapping
Old Stairs. [Song: *Wapping Old Stairs*]

S. J. PERELMAN 1904–1979

28 There had been a heavy fall of talcum several
hours before and as far as the ground could see the
eye was white. [*Crazy like A Fox*, 'The Love Decoy']

29 You've a sharp tongue in your head, Mr
Essick. Look out it doesn't cut your throat. [*The
Rising Gorge*, 'All Out. . .']

30 Love is not the dying moan of a distant
violin – it's the triumphant twang of a bedspring. [Quoted in A. Andrews, *Quotations for
Speakers and Writers*]

CHARLES PERRAULT 1628–1703

1 'Sister Anne, Sister Anne, can you see nothing coming?' And her sister Anne answered her, 'I see nothing but the sun which raises a dust, and the grass growing green.' [*Fairy Tales*, 'Bluebeard']

EDWARD PERRONET 1726–1792

2 All hail, the power of Jesus' name! / Let angels prostrate fall. [Hymn]

PERSIUS 34–62

3 *Virtutem videant, intabescantque relicta.* – Let them look upon virtue and pine because they have lost her. [*Satires*, III. 38]

4 *Venienti occurrite morbo.* – Meet the disease on its first appearance. [III. 64]

MARSHAL PÉTAIN 1856–1951

5 They shall not pass. [Attr. at Battle of Verdun, 26 Feb. 1916. Also used in General Nivelle's Order of the Day, 23 Jun. 1916, as 'You will not let them pass!' and adopted in the Spanish Civil War. See 9:16, 214:2]

LAURENCE J. PETER 1919–

6 A pessimist is a man who looks both ways before crossing a one-way street, [*Peter's Quotations*]

LAURENCE J. PETER and
RAYMOND HULL

7 *The Peter Principle*: In a Hierarchy Every Employee Tends to Rise to his Level of Incompetence. [*The Peter Principle*, Ch. 1]

PETRONIUS ?–c. 66

8 *Abiit ad plures.* – He has joined the great majority. [*Cena Trimalchionis*, 42.5]

9 *Horatii curiosa felicitas.* – The studied felicity of Horace. [*Satyricon*, 118]

E. J. PHELPS 1822–1900

10 The man who makes no mistakes does not usually make anything. [Speech at Mansion House, 24 Jan. 1899]

ADMIRAL J. W. PHILIP 1840–1900

11 Don't cheer, boys; those poor devils are dying. [On passing a burning Spanish ship at Battle of Santiago, 3 July 1898]

AMBROSE PHILIPS c. 1674–1749

12 The flowers anew, returning seasons bring! / But beauty faded has no second spring. [*The First Pastoral*, 55]

JOHN PHILIPS 1676–1709

13 Happy the man, who, void of cares and strife, / In silken or in leathern purse retains / A Splendid Shilling. [*The Splendid Shilling*, 1]

STEPHEN PHILLIPS 1864–1915

14 A man not old, but mellow, like good wine, [*Ulysses*, III. ii]

WENDELL PHILLIPS 1811–1884

15 We live under a government of men and morning newspapers. [*Address*, 'The Press']

16 Eternal vigilance is the price of liberty – power is ever stealing from the many to the few. [Speech in Boston, Mass., 28 Jan. 1852. This sometimes has been considered a quotation by Phillips from Jefferson, but without justification. Also attr. to Patrick Henry]

17 One, on God's side, is a majority. [Speech at Brooklyn, 1 Nov. 1859]

18 Every man meets his Waterloo at last.

EDEN PHILLPOTTS 1862–1961

19 His father's sister had bats in the belfry and was put away. [*Peacock House*, 'My First Murder']

PABLO PICASSO 1881–1973

20 God is really only another artist. He invented the giraffe, the elephant, and the cat. He has no real style. He just goes on trying other things. [Quoted in Françoise Gilot and Carlton Lake, *Life with Picasso*, Pt I]

21 Painting is a blind man's profession. He paints not what he sees, but what he feels, what he tells himself about what he has seen. [Quoted in Jean Cocteau, *Journals*, 'Childhood']

22 You do something, and then somebody else

comes along and does it pretty. [To Gertrude Stein, quoted by F. Scott Fitzgerald in letter to Frances Scott Fitzgerald, 7 May 1940]

WILFRED PICKLES 1904–1978

1 Are you courting? [*Passim*, in BBC Radio series *Have a Go*]

2 Give him the money, Barney. [Addressed to Barney Colehan]

PINDAR 518–*c*. 437 BC

3 Water is best. [(Inscription over the Pump Room, Bath) *Olympian Odes*, I]

PETER PINDAR [JOHN WOLCOT] 1738–1819

4 Care to our coffin adds a nail no doubt; / And ev'ry grin, so merry, draws one out. [*Expostulatory Odes*, 15]

5 A fellow in a market town, / Most musical, cried razors up and down. [*Some More Lyric Odes*, 3]

6 What rage for fame attends, both great and small! / Better be damned than mentioned not at all! [*To the Royal Academicians*, 8]

SIR ARTHUR PINERO 1855–1934

7 From forty to fifty a man is at heart either a stoic or a satyr. [*Second Mrs Tanqueray*, I]

8 I love fruit, when it is expensive.

HAROLD PINTER 1930–

9 If only I could get down to Sidcup! I've been waiting for the weather to break. He's got my papers, this man I left them with, it's got it all down there, I could prove everything. [*The Caretaker*, Act I]

10 I mean, don't forget the earth's about five thousand million years old, at least. Who can afford to live in the past? [*The Homecoming*, II]

11 In other words, apart from the known and the unknown, what else is there?

ROBERT M. PIRSIG 1928–

12 One thing about pioneers that you don't hear mentioned is that they are invariably, by their nature, messmakers. [*Zen and the Art of Motorcycle Maintenance*, Pt. III., Ch. 21]

13 Traditional scientific method has always been at the very *best*, 20-20 hindsight. It's good for seeing where you've been. [24]

14 We keep passing unseen through little moments of other people's lives.

WILLIAM PITT, EARL OF CHATHAM 1708–1778

15 The atrocious crime of being a young man ... I shall attempt neither to palliate nor to deny. [Speech in reply to Robert Walpole, 27 Jan. 1741]

16 Where laws end, tyranny begins. [Speech on the Wilkes case, 9 Jan. 1770]

17 We have a Calvinistic creed, a Popish liturgy, and an Arminian clergy. [Speech in House of Lords, 19 May 1772]

18 If I were an American, as I am an Englishman, while a foreign troop was landed in my country, I never would lay down my arms – never – never – never! [18 Nov. 1777]

19 It was a saying of Lord Chatham, that the parks were the lungs of London. [W. Windham in speech in House of Commons, 30 June 1808]

WILLIAM PITT 1759–1806

20 Necessity is the plea for every infringement of human freedom. It is the argument of tyrants; it is the creed of slaves. [Speech in House of Commons 18 Nov. 1783]

21 England has saved herself by her exertions; and will, as I trust, save Europe by her example. [Speech in Guildhall, London, 9 Nov. 1805]

22 Roll up that map [of Europe]; it will not be wanted these ten years. [Said in Dec. 1805, after Napoleon's victory at Austerlitz]

23 O my country! how I leave my country. [(Or 'love' for 'leave') Attr. last words in Lord Stanhope, *Life*, 1879 edn.]

24 I think I could eat one of Bellamy's veal pies. [Attr. last words 23 Jan. 1806]

J. R. PLANCHE 1796–1880

25 It would have made a cat laugh. [*The Queen of the Frogs*, I. iv]

SYLVIA PLATH 1932–1963

26 Dying / Is an art, like everything else. / I do it exceptionally well. [*Lady Lazarus*]

1 Love set you going like a fat gold watch. [*Morning Song*]

PLATO *c.* 428–347 BC

2 Socrates is guilty of corrupting the minds of the young, and of believing in deities of his own invention instead of the gods recognized by the State. [*Apology*, 24B]

3 I wonder if we could contrive ... some magnificent myth* that would in itself carry conviction to our whole community. [(*Also trans. as 'the noble lie') *Republic*, Bk. iii. 414]

4 There will be no end to the troubles of states, or indeed, my dear Glaucon, of humanity itself, till philosophers become kings in this world, or till those we now call kings and rulers really and truly become philosophers. [v. 473]

5 Democracy passes into despotism. [viii. 562]

PLAUTUS 254–184 BC

6 *Quem di diligunt / Adulescens moritur* – He whom the gods favour dies young. [*Bacchides*, IV. 816]

7 *Miles Gloriosus.* – Vainglorious Soldier. [Title of play]

PLINY THE ELDER 23–79

8 *Brutum fulmen.* – A harmless thunderbolt. [*Natural History*, Bk. ii. Ch. 43]

9 *Ut non sit satis aestimare, parens melior homini an tristior noveca fuerit.* – It is far from easy to determine whether she [Nature] has proved a kind parent to man or a merciless step-mother. [vii. 1]

10 *Ex Africa semper aliquid novi.* – There is always something new out of Africa. [Proverbial adaptation of *Natural History*, viii. 17].

11 *In vino veritas.* – Truth comes out in wine. [Proverbial adaptation of *Natural History*, xiv. 28]

12 *Sal Atticum.* – Attic salt. [xxxi. 41]

13 *Nulla dies sine linea.* – Not a day without a line. [Proverbial adaptation of *Natural History* xxxv, 36, 84]

PLOTINUS 205–270

14 And here we have, incidentally, lighted upon the cause of the Circuit of the All; it is a movement which seeks perpetuity by way of futurity. [*Enneads*, III. 7]

JOSEPH PLUNKETT 1887–1916

15 I see His blood upon the rose / And in the stars the glory of His eyes. [*I See His Blood*]

EDGAR ALLAN POE 1809–1849

16 I was a child and she was a child, / In this kingdom by the sea; / But we loved with a love that was more than love – / I and my Annabel Lee. [*Annabel Lee*]

17 Keeping time, time, time, / In a sort of Runic rhyme, / To the tintinnabulation that so musically wells / From the bells, bells, bells, bells. [*The Bells*, 9]

18 The viol, the violet, and the vine. [*The City in the Sea*]

19 That the play is the tragedy 'Man', / And its hero the Conqueror Worm. [*The Conqueror Worm*, 39]

20 All that we see or seem / Is but a dream within a dream. [*A Dream within a Dream*]

21 The fever called 'Living' / Is conquered at last. [*For Annie*]

22 This – all this – was in the olden Time long ago. [*The Haunted Palace*]

23 A dirge for her, the doubly dead, / In that she died so young. [*Lenore*]

24 Once upon a midnight dreary, while I pondered, weak and weary, / Over many a quaint and curious volume of forgotten lore, / While I nodded nearly napping, suddenly there came a tapping, / As of someone gently rapping. [*The Raven*, 1]

25 Deep into the darkness peering, long I stood there, wondering, fearing, / Doubting, dreaming dreams no mortal ever dared to dream before. [5]

26 'Prophet!' said I, 'thing of evil – prophet still, if bird or devil! / By that heaven that bends above us – by that God we both adore.' [16]

27 Take thy beak from out my heart and take thy form from off my door! / Quoth the Raven, 'Nevermore'. [17]

28 Helen, thy beauty is to me / Like those Nicean barks of yore. [*To Helen*]

29 Thy Naiad airs have brought me home / To the glory that was Greece. / And the grandeur that was Rome.

30 The skies they were ashen and sober; / The

leaves they were crispèd and sere – / The leaves they were withering and sere; / It was night in the lonesome October / Of my most immemorial year. [*Ulalume*]

HENRI POINCARÉ 1854–1912

1 Thought is only a flash between two long nights, but this flash is everything. [Quoted in H. L. Mencken, *A New Dictionary of Quotations*]

JACKSON POLLOCK 1912–1956

2 Painting is self-discovery. Every good artist paints what he is. [Quoted in F. V. O'Connor, *Jackson Pollock*]

MME DE POMPADOUR 1721–1764

3 *Après nous le déluge.* – After us the deluge. [After Battle of Rossbach, 1757]

JOHN POOLE 1786?–1872

4 I hope I don't intrude. [*Paul Pry*, I. ii]

ALEXANDER POPE 1688–1744

5 Ye gods! annihilate but space and time, / And make two lovers happy. [*The Art of Sinking in Poetry*, 11]

6 And thou Dalhousy, the great God of War, / Lieutenant-Colonel to the Earl of Mar.

7 Whether you choose Cervantes' serious air, / Or laugh and shake in Rabelais' armchair. [*The Dunciad*, Bk i. 21]

8 Poetic Justice, with her lifted scale, / Where, in nice balance, truth with gold she weighs, / And solid pudding against empty praise. [52]

9 Now night descending, the proud scene was o'er, / But lived in Settle's numbers one day more. [89]

10 While pensive poets painful vigils keep / Sleepless themselves to give their readers sleep. [93]

11 How here he sipped, how there he plundered snug, / And sucked all o'er, like an industrious bug. [129]

12 Or where the pictures for the page atone, / And Quarles is saved for beauties not his own. [139]

13 Some daemon stole my pen (forgive th' offence) / And once betrayed me into common sense. / Else all my prose and verse were much the same. [187]

14 A vast, vamped future, old, revived new piece. [284]

15 Loud thunder to its bottom shook the bog, / And the hoarse nation croaked, 'God save King Log!' [329]

16 A brain of feathers and a heart of lead. [ii. 44]

17 Peeled, patched, and piebald, linsey-wolsey brothers, / Grave mummers! sleeveless some, and shirtless others. [iii. 115]

18 All crowd, who foremost shall be damned to fame. [158]

19 So sweetly mawkish and so smoothly dull. [171]

20 Right well mine eyes arede the myster wight, / On parchment scraps y-fed and Wormius hight. [187]

21 And Alma Mater all dissolved in port. [338]

22 A wit with dunces, and a dunce with wits. [iv. 90]

23 Let standard-authors, thus, like trophies borne, / Appear more glorious as more hacked and torn. [123]

24 The right divine of kings to govern wrong. [188]

25 When man's whole frame is obvious to a flea. [238]

26 We bring to one dead level ev'ry mind. [268]

27 To happy convents, bosomed deep in vines, / Where slumber abbots, purple as their wines. [301]

28 Stretched on the rack of a too easy chair. [342]

29 Religion blushing veils her sacred fires, / And unawares morality expires. / Nor public flame, nor private, dares to shine; / Nor human spark is left nor glimpse divine! / Lo! thy dread empire, Chaos! is restored; / Light dies before thy uncreating word; / Thy hand, great Anarch! lets the curtain fall / And universal darkness buries all. [649]

30 Vital spark of heav'nly flame! / Quit, oh quit this mortal frame: / Trembling, hoping, ling'ring, flying, / Oh the pain, the bliss of dying. [*The Dying Christian to his Soul*]

31 I mount! I fly! / O grave! where is thy victory? / O death! where is thy sting?

Alexander Pope

1 What beck'ning ghost, along the moonlight shade / Invites my steps, and points to yonder glade? [*Elegy to the Memory of an Unfortunate Lady*, 1]

2 Is it, in heav'n, a crime to love too well? [6]

3 Is there no bright reversion in the sky, / For those who greatly think, or bravely die? [9]

4 Ambition first sprung from your bless'd abodes; / The glorious fault of angels and of gods. [13]

5 By foreign hands thy dying eyes were closed, / By foreign hands thy decent limbs composed, / By foreign hands thy humble grave adorned. / By strangers honoured, and by strangers mourned! [51]

6 Yet shall thy grave with rising flow'rs be dressed, / And the green turf lie lightly on thy breast. [63]

7 A heap of dust alone remains of thee; / 'Tis all thou art, and all the proud shall be! [73]

8 Speed the soft intercourse from soul to soul, / And waft a sigh from Indus to the Pole. [*Eloisa to Abelard* [57]

9 And love th' offender, yet detest th' offence. [192]

10 How happy is the blameless vestal's lot! / The world forgetting, by the world forgot. [207]

11 One thought of thee puts all the pomp to flight, / Priests, tapers, temples, swim before my sight. [273]

12 See my lips tremble, and my eye-balls roll, / Suck my last breath, and catch my flying soul! [323]

13 You beat your pate, and fancy wit will come: / Knock as you please, there's nobody at home. [Epigram: *An Empty House*]

14 Shut, shut the door, good John! fatigued I said. / Tie up the knocker, say I'm sick, I'm dead. / The dog-star rages! [*Epistle to Dr Arbuthnot*, 1]

15 Is there a parson, much bemused in beer, / A maudlin poetess, a rhyming peer, / A clerk foredoomed his father's soul to cross / Who pens a stanza, when he should engross? [15]

16 Fired that the house reject him, "Sdeath I'll print it, / And shame the fools.' [61]

17 No creature smarts so little as a fool. [84]

18 Destroy his fib or sophistry, in vain, / The creature's at his dirty work again. [91]

19 As yet a child, not yet a fool to fame, / I lisped in numbers, for the numbers came. [127]

20 This long disease, my life. [132]

21 And he whose fustian's so sublimely bad / It is not poetry, but prose run mad. [187]

22 Were there one whose fires / True genius kindles, and fair fame inspires; / Blest with each talent and each art to please, / And born to write, converse, and live with ease; / Should such a man, too fond to rule alone, / Bear, like the Turk, no brother near the throne, / View him with scornful, yet with jealous eyes, / And hate for arts that caused himself to rise; / Damn with faint praise, assent with civil leer, / And, without sneering, teach the rest to sneer; / Willing to wound, and yet afraid to strike, / Just hint a fault, and hesitate dislike. [(Addison) 193]

23 Alike reserved to blame, or to commend, / A tim'rous foe, and a suspicious friend; / Dreading e'en fools, by flatterers besieged, / And so obliging that he ne'er obliged; / Like Cato, give his little senate laws, / And sit attentive to his own applause; / . . . Who but must laugh, if such a man there be? / Who would not weep, if Atticus were he? [(Addison) 207]

24 Curst be the verse, how well soe'er it flow, / That tends to make one worthy man my foe. [283]

25 Let Sporus tremble. – What? that thing of silk, / Sporus, that mere white curd of ass's milk? / Satire or sense, alas! can Sporus feel? / Who breaks a butterfly upon a wheel?

Yet let me flap this bug with gilded wings – / This painted child of dirt, that stinks and stings. [(Lord Hervey) 305]

26 Eternal smiles his emptiness betray, / As shallow streams run dimpling all the way. [315]

27 He himself one vile antithesis. [325]

28 Wit that can creep, and pride that licks the dust. [333]

29 Unlearn'd, he knew no schoolman's subtle art, / No language, but the language of the heart. [398]

30 Nature and Nature's laws lay hid in night: / God said 'Let Newton be!' and all was light. [*Epitaph intended for Sir Isaac Newton* (See also 403:26)]

31 In wit a man; simplicity a child. [*Epitaph on Gay*]

1 Heav'n, as its purest gold, by tortures tried; / The saint sustained it, but the woman died. [*Epitaph on Mrs Corbet*]

2 'Tis with our judgements as our watches, none / Go just alike, yet each believes his own. [*An Essay on Criticism*, 9]

3 Pride, the never failing vice of fools. [204]

4 A little learning is a dang'rous thing; / Drink deep, or taste not the Pierian spring: / There shallow draughts intoxicate the brain, / And drinking largely sobers us again. [215]

5 Hills peep o'er hills, and Alps on Alps arise! [232]

6 Whoever thinks a faultless piece to see, / Thinks what ne'er was, nor is, nor e'er shall be. [253]

7 True wit is nature to advantage dressed, / What oft was thought but ne'er so well expressed. [297]

8 Words are like leaves; and where they most abound, / Much fruit of sense beneath is rarely found. [309]

9 Such laboured nothings, in so strange a style, / Amaze th' unlearn'd, and make the learned smile. [326]

10 Be not the first by whom the new are tried, / Nor yet the last to lay the old aside. [335]

11 As some to church repair, / Not for the doctrine, but the music there. [342]

12 While expletives their feeble aid do join, / And ten low words oft creep in one dull line. [346]

13 Where'er you find 'the cooling western breeze', / In the next line, it 'whispers through the trees': / If crystal streams 'with pleasing murmurs creep', / The reader's threatened, not in vain, with 'sleep'. / Then, at the last and only couplet fraught / With some unmeaning thing they call a thought, / A needless Alexandrine ends the song, / That, like a wounded snake, drags its slow length along. [350]

14 True ease in writing comes from art, not chance, / As those move easiest who have learned to dance. / 'Tis not enough no harshness gives offence, / The sound must seem an echo to the sense. [362]

15 For fools admire, but men of sense approve. [391]

16 But let a lord once own the happy lines, / How the wit brightens! how the style refines! [420]

17 Some praise at morning what they blame at night; / But always think the last opinion right. [430]

18 Nor in the critic let the man be lost. [523]

19 To err is human, to forgive, divine. [525]

20 Then unbelieving priests reformed the nation, / And taught more pleasant methods of salvation. [546]

21 All seems infected that th'infected spy, / As all looks yellow to the jaundiced eye. [558]

22 Men must be taught as if you taught them not, / And things unknown proposed as things forgot. [574]

23 The bookful blockhead, ignorantly read, / With loads of learned lumber in his head. [612]

24 For fools rush in where angels fear to tread. [625]

25 Awake my St John! Leave all meaner things / To low ambition, and the pride of kings. / Let us, since life can little more supply / Than just to look about us and to die, / Expatiate free o'er all this scene of man; / A mighty maze! but not without a plan. [*An Essay on Man*, I. 1]

26 Eye Nature's walks, shoot folly as it flies, / And catch the manners living as they rise; / Laugh where we must, be candid where we can; / But vindicate the ways of God to man. [13]

27 Who sees with equal eye, as God of all, / A hero perish, or a sparrow fall, / Atoms or systems into ruin hurled, / And now a bubble burst and now a world. [87]

28 Hope springs eternal in the human breast; / Man never is, but always to be blessed. [95]

29 Lo, the poor Indian! whose untutored mind / Sees God in clouds, or hears him in the wind; / His soul proud science never taught to stray / Far as the solar walk or milky way. [99]

30 Why has not man a microscopic eye? / For this plain reason, man is not a fly. [193]

31 Die of a rose in aromatic pain? [200]

32 The spider's touch, how exquisitely fine! / Feels at each thread, and lives along the line. [217]

33 All are but parts of one stupendous whole, / Whose body nature is, and God the soul. [267]

34 All nature is but art, unknown to thee; / All chance, direction which thou canst not see;

/ All discord, harmony not understood; / All partial evil, universal good; / And, spite of pride, in erring reason's spite, / One truth is clear, Whatever is, is right. [289]

1 Know then thyself, presume not God to scan; / The proper study of mankind is man. [II.1]

2 Chaos of thought and passion, all confused; / Still by himself abused, or disabused; / Created half to rise, and half to fall; / Great Lord of all things, yet a prey to all; / Sole judge of truth, in endless error hurled: / The glory, jest, and riddle of the world! [13]

3 And hence one master-passion in the breast, / Like Aaron's serpent, swallows up the rest. [131]

4 Vice is a monster of so frightful mien, / As to be hated needs but to be seen; / Yet seen too oft, familiar with her face, / We first endure, then pity, then embrace. [217]

5 Behold the child, by nature's kindly law / Pleased with a rattle, tickled with a straw: / Some livelier plaything gives his youth delight, / A little louder, but as empty quite: / Scarfs, garters, gold, amuse his riper stage, / And beads and prayer-books are the toys of age: / Pleased with this bauble still, as that before; / Till tired he sleeps, and life's poor play is o'er. [275]

6 For forms of government let fools contest, / Whate'er is best administered is best: / For modes of faith let graceless zealots fight; / His can't be wrong whose life is in the right. / In faith and hope the world will disagree, / But all mankind's concern is charity. [III. 303]

7 O happiness! our being's end and aim! / Good, pleasure, ease, content! whate'er thy name: / That something still which prompts th' eternal sigh, / For which we bear to live, or dare to die. [IV. 1]

8 Order is heaven's first law. [49]

9 An honest man's the noblest work of God. [248 (See 84:7, 88:15, 215:11)]

10 If parts allure thee, think how Bacon shined, / The wisest, brightest, meanest of mankind: / Or, ravished with the whistling of a name, / See Cromwell damned to everlasting fame. [281]

11 Slave to no sect, who takes no private road, / But looks through nature up to nature's God. [331]

12 Formed by thy converse happily to steer / From grave to gay, from lively to severe. [379]

13 Thou wert my guide, philosopher, and friend. [390]

14 That true self-love and social are the same. [396]

15 To observations which ourselves we make, / We grow more partial for th' observer's sake. [Moral Essays, Epistle I. 11]

16 Grant but as many sorts of mind as moss. [18]

17 Like following life through creatures you dissect, / You lose it in the moment you detect. [29]

18 'Tis education forms the common mind, / Just as the twig is bent, the tree's inclined. [149]

19 'Odious! in woollen! 'twould a saint provoke' / (Were the last words that poor Narcissa spoke). [246]

20 One would not, sure, be frightful when one's dead – / And, Betty, give this cheek a little red. [250]

21 And you, brave Cobham! to the latest breath / Shall feel your ruling passion strong in death. [262]

22 Most women have no characters at all. [II. 2]

23 Fine by defect and delicately weak. [43]

24 With too much quickness ever to be taught; / With too much thinking to have common thought. [97]

25 'With every pleasing, every prudent part, / Say, what can Chloe want?' – She wants a heart. [159]

26 Men, some to business, some to pleasure take; / But every woman is at heart a rake. [215]

27 See how the world its veterans rewards! / A youth of frolics, an old age of cards. [243]

28 She who ne'er answers till a husband cools, / Or if she rules him, never shows she rules; / Charms by accepting, by submitting sways, / Yet has her humour most when she obeys. [261]

29 And mistress of herself though China fall. [268]

30 Woman's at best a contradiction still. [270]

31 Who shall decide when doctors disagree? [III. 1]

32 But thousands die, without or this or that, / Die, and endow a college, or a cat. [95]

1 The ruling passion, be it what it will, / The ruling passion conquers reason still. [153]

2 Rise, honest Muse! and sing the Man of Ross. [250]

3 In the worst inn's worst room, with mat half-hung, / The floors of plaster and the walls of dung, / On once a flock-bed, but repaired with straw, / With tape-tied curtains, never meant to draw, / The George and Garter dangling from that bed / Where tawdry yellow strove with dirty red, / Great Villiers lies. [299]

4 To rest, the cushion and soft dean invite, / Who never mentions hell to ears polite. [IV. 149]

5 Statesman, yet friend to truth! of soul sincere / In action faithful, and in honour clear, / Who broke no promise, served no private end, / Who gained no title, and who lost no friend. [V. 67]

6 Happy the man whose wish and care / A few paternal acres bound, / Content to breathe his native air, / In his own ground. [*Ode on Solitude*]

7 Has she no faults then (Envy says), Sir? / Yes she has one, I must aver; / When all the world conspires to praise her, / The woman's deaf and does not hear. [*On a Certain Lady at Court*]

8 I am his Highness' dog at Kew; / Pray tell me, sir, whose dog are you? [*On the Collar of a Dog which I gave to his Royal Highness*]

9 Where'er you walk, cool gales shall fan the glade, / Trees where you sit shall crowd into a shade: / Where'er you tread, the blushing flowers shall rise, / And all things flourish where you turn your eyes. [*Pastorals*, 'Summer', 73]

10 To make mankind in conscious virtue bold, / Live o'er each scene, and be what they behold. [*Prologue to Mr Addison's 'Cato'*, 3]

11 What dire offence from am'rous causes springs, / What mighty contests rise from trivial things. [*The Rape of the Lock*, I. 1]

12 Now lap-dogs give themselves the rousing shake, / And sleepless lovers, just at twelve, awake. [15]

13 They shift the moving toyshop of their heart. [100]

14 And all Arabia breathes from yonder box. [134]

15 Here files of pins extend their shining rows, / Puffs, powders, patches, bibles, billet-doux. [137]

16 On her white breast a sparkling cross she wore, / Which Jews might kiss, and infidels adore. [II. 7]

17 If to her share some female errors fall, / Look on her face, and you'll forget 'em all. [17]

18 Fair tresses man's imperial race ensnare, / And beauty draws us with a single hair. [27]

19 Here thou, great Anna! whom three realms obey, / Dost sometimes counsel take – and sometimes tea. [III.7]

20 At ev'ry word a reputation dies. [16]

21 The hungry judges soon the sentence sign, / And wretches hang that jurymen may dine. [21]

22 'Let Spades be trumps!' she said, and trumps they were. [46]

23 Coffee, which makes the politician wise, / And see through all things with his half-shut eyes. [117]

24 Not louder shrieks to pitying heav'n are cast, / When husbands, or when lap-dogs breathe their last. [157]

25 She sighs for ever on her pensive bed, / Pain at her side, and Megrim at her head. [IV. 23]

26 Sir Plume, of amber snuff-box justly vain, / And the nice conduct of a clouded cane. [123]

27 Charms strike the sight, but merit wins the soul. [V. 34]

28 There St John mingles with my friendly bowl / The feast of reason and the flow of soul. [*Satires and Epistles of Horace Imitated*, Bk ii. Satire I. 127]

29 Shakespeare ... / For gain not glory, winged his roving flight, / And grew immortal in his own despite. [Epistle I. 69]

30 The people's voice is odd, / It is, and it is not, the voice of God. [89]

31 In quibbles angel and archangel join, / And God the Father turns a school divine. [101, on *Paradise Lost*]

32 The mob of gentlemen who wrote with ease. [108]

33 One simile, that solitary shines / In a dry desert of a thousand lines. [111]

34 Waller was smooth; but Dryden taught to

join / The varying verse, the full-resounding line, / The long majestic march, and energy divine. [267]

1 Ev'n copious Dryden wanted, or forgot, / The last and greatest art, the art to blot. [280]

2 The many-headed monster of the pit. [305]

3 The vulgar boil, the learned roast an egg. [II. 85]

4 Do good by stealth, and blush to find it fame. [Epilogue to the Satires, Dialogue I. 136]

5 Ask you what provocation I have had? / The strong antipathy of good to bad. [II. 197]

6 Yes; I am proud, I must be proud to see/ Men not afraid of God, afraid of me. [208]

7 Nor fame I slight, nor for her favours call; / She comes unlooked for, if she comes at all. [The Temple of Fame, 513]

8 Teach me to feel another's woe, / To hide the fault I see; / That mercy I to others show, / That mercy show to me. [The Universal Prayer]

9 Not chaos-like, together crushed and bruised, / But, as the world harmoniously confused: / Where order in variety we see, / And where, though all things differ, all agree. [Windsor Forest, 13]

10 Achilles' wrath, to Greece the direful spring / Of woes unnumbered, heavenly goddess sing! [Homer's Iliad, I. 1]

11 She moves a goddess, and she looks a queen. [III. 1]

12 True friendship's laws are by this rule expressed, / Welcome the coming, speed the parting guest. [Homer's Odyssey, XV. 83]

13 Not to admire, is all the art I know / To make men happy, and to keep them so. [Trans. of Horace, Epistle I. vi]

14 I never knew any man in my life who could not bear another's misfortunes perfectly like a Christian. [Thoughts on Various Subjects]

15 When men grow virtuous in their old age, they only make a sacrifice to God of the devil's leavings.

16 'Blessed is the man who expects nothing, for he shall never be disappointed' was the ninth beatitude. [Letter to Fortescue. 23 Sept. 1725]

SIR KARL POPPER 1902–

17 Our knowledge can only be finite, while our ignorance must necessarily be infinite. [Conjectures and Refutations]

18 But I shall certainly admit a system as empirical or scientific only if it is capable of being *tested* by experience. These considerations suggest that not the *verifiability* but the *falsifiability* of a system is to be taken as a criterion of demarcation ... *It must be possible for an empirical scientific system to be refuted by experience.* [The Logic of Scientific Discovery, Ch. 1, Sect. vi]

19 We may become the makers of our fate when we have ceased to pose as its prophets. [Quoted in an editorial in the *Observer*, 28 Dec. 1975]

RICHARD PORSON 1759–1808

20 When Dido found Aeneas would not come, / She mourned in silence, and was Di-do-dum. [Epigram on Latin Gerunds]

21 I went to Frankfort, and got drunk / With that most learn'd professor, Brunck, / I went to Wortz, and got more drunken, / With that more learn'd professor, Ruhnken. [Facetiae Cantabrigienses]

22 The Germans in Greek / Are sadly to seek; / Not five in five score, / But ninety-five more; / All, save only Hermann, / And Hermann's a German. [Quoted in M. L. Clarke, *Richard Porson*]

COLE PORTER 1891–1964

23 But I'm always true to you, darlin', in my fashion, / Yes I'm always true to you, darlin', in my way. [Song: *Always True to You in My Fashion*, from musical *Kiss Me, Kate*]

24 Now: heaven knows, anything goes. [Song: *Anything Goes*, and title of musical]

25 And we suddenly know, what heaven we're in, / When they begin the beguine. [Song: *Begin the Beguine* from musical *Jubilee*]

26 I love Paris in the springtime. [Song: *I Love Paris*, from musical *Can-Can*]

27 It's delightful, / it's delicious, / It's delectable, / It's delirious. [Song: *It's Delovely*, from musical *Red Hot and Blue*]

28 I've Got You Under My Skin. [Title of song, from musical *Born to Dance*]

29 If you want to buy my wares, / Follow me and climb the stairs. / Love for sale. [Song: *Love for Sale*, from musical *The New Yorkers*]

1 It's not 'cause I wouldn't / It's not 'cause I shouldn't / And, Lord knows, it's not 'cause I couldn't, / It's simply because I'm the laziest gal in town. [Song: *The Laziest Gal in Town*, from musical *Stage Fright*. Sung by Marlene Dietrich]

2 Miss Otis regrets she's unable to lunch today. [Song: *Miss Otis Regrets*, from musical *Hi Diddle Diddle*]

3 My heart belongs to Daddy / 'Cause my Daddy, he treats me so well. [Song: *My Heart Belongs to Daddy*, from musical *Leave It to Me*]

FRANCIS POTT 1832–1909

4 The strife is o'er, the battle done; / Now is the Victor's triumph won; / O let the song of praise be sung. Alleluia! [Hymn]

BEATRIX POTTER 1866–1943

5 I shall tell you a tale of four little rabbits whose names were Flopsy, Mopsy, Cottontail and Peter. [*The Tale of Peter Rabbit*]

6 You may go into the field or down the lane, but don't go into Mr McGregor's garden.

7 I am worn to a ravelling. [*The Tailor of Gloucester*]

8 I am undone and worn to a thread-paper for I have NO MORE TWIST.

9 It is said that the effect of eating too much lettuce is 'soporific'. [*The Tale of the Flopsy Bunnies*]

STEPHEN POTTER 1900–1969

10 Gamesmanship or, The Art of Winning Games without actually Cheating. [Title of book]

11 *How to be one up* – how to make the other man feel that something has gone wrong, however slightly. [*Lifemanship*]

12 There was one ploy of Gattling's which I found particularly effective, and I believe it must have been about this time that I first murmured to myself the word 'Lifemanship'.

13 Just as there are O.K.-words in conversation-ship so there are O.K.-*people to mention* in Newstatesmanship.

EZRA POUND 1885–1972

14 Winter is icummen in, / Lhude sing God-damm. / Raineth drop and staineth slop, / And how the wind doth ramm! / Sing: Goddamm. [*Ancient Music*]

15 Hang it all, Robert Browning, / There can be but one 'Sordello'. [*Cantos*, II]

16 And even I can remember / A day when the historians left blanks in their writings, / I mean for things they didn't know. [XIII]

17 Pull down thy vanity / Thou art a beaten dog beneath the hail, / A swollen magpie in a fitful sun, / Half black half white / Nor knowst 'ou wing from tail / Pull down thy vanity. [LXXXI]

18 *With Usura* / With usura hath no man a house of good stone / each block cut smooth and well fitting. [XLV]

19 Bah! I have sung women in three cities, / But it is all the same; / And I will sing of the sun. [*Cino*]

20 For three years, out of key with his time, / He strove to resuscitate the dead art / Of poetry; to maintain 'the sublime' / In the old sense. Wrong from the start. [*Hugh Selwyn Mauberley*, 'E.P. Ode pour l'élection de son sépulcre', I]

21 Observed the elegance of Circe's hair / Rather than the mottoes on sundials.

22 Caliban casts out Ariel. [III]

23 Walked eye-deep in hell / believing in old men's lies, then unbelieving / came home, home to a lie. [IV]

24 There died a myriad, / And of the best, among them, / For an old bitch gone in the teeth, / For a botched civilization. [V]

25 The apparition of these faces in the crowd; / Petals on a wet black bough. [*In a Station of the Metro*]

26 Real education must ultimately be limited to men who insist on knowing: the rest is mere sheep-herding. [*ABC of Reading*]

27 The author's conviction . . . is that music begins to atrophy when it departs too far from the dance; that poetry begins to atrophy when it gets too far from music ['Warning']

28 Literature is news that *stays* news. [Ch. 2]

29 Great Literature is simply language charged with meaning to the utmost possible degree. [*How to Read*, Pt II]

ANTHONY POWELL 1905–

30 He fell in love with himself at first sight and it is a passion to which he has always remained

faithful. Self-love seems so often unrequited. [*The Acceptance World*, Ch. 1]

1 All men are brothers, but, thank God, they aren't all brothers-in-law. [At *Lady Molly's*, Ch. 4]

2 People think that because a novel's invented, it isn't true. Exactly the reverse is the case. Biography and memoirs can never be wholly true, since they cannot include every conceivable circumstance of what happened. The novel can do that. [*Hearing Secret Harmonies*, Ch. 3]

3 One of the worst things about life is not how nasty the nasty people are. You know that already. It is how nasty the nice people can be. [*The Kindly Ones*, Ch. 4]

4 Growing old is like being increasingly penalized for a crime you haven't committed. [*Temporary Kings*, Ch. 1]

ENOCH POWELL 1912–

5 As I look ahead, I am filled with foreboding. Like the Roman, I seem to see 'the River Tiber foaming with much blood'. [Speech in Birmingham, 20 Apr. 1968]

W. M. PRAED 1802–1839

6 I think that nought is worth a thought, / And I'm a fool for thinking. [*The Chant of the Brazen Head*]

7 The ice of her Ladyship's manners, / The ice of his Lordship's champagne. [*Goodnight to the Season*]

8 My own Araminta, say 'No!' [*A Letter of Advice*]

9 For all who understood admired, / And some who did not understand them. [*The Vicar*]

THE BOOK OF COMMON PRAYER

10 A Table of the Moveable Feasts. [Introductory pages]

11 Dearly beloved brethren, the Scripture moveth us in sundry places to acknowledge and confess our manifold sins and wickedness. [*Morning Prayer*, 'The Invitation to Confession']

12 We have erred and strayed from thy ways like lost sheep. ['General Confession']

13 We have left undone those things which we ought to have done; And we have done those things which we ought not to have done; And there is no health in us.

14 A godly, righteous, and sober life.

15 And forgive us our trespasses, As we forgive them that trespass against us. ['Lord's Prayer']

16 PRIEST: O Lord, open thou our lips.
ANSWER: And our mouth shall shew forth thy praise.
PRIEST: O God, make speed to save us.
ANSWER: O Lord, make haste to help us. ['Versicles and Responses']

17 As it was in the beginning, is now, and ever shall be: world without end. Amen. ['Gloria']

18 Lord God of Sabaoth. ['Te Deum']

19 The noble army of Martyrs.

20 Of an infinite Majesty.

21 O all ye Works of the Lord, bless ye the Lord: praise him and magnify him for ever. ['Benedicite']

22 O ye Whales, and all that move in the Waters.

23 Give peace in our time, O Lord. ['Versicles']

24 Jesus Christ his only Son our Lord. Who was conceived by the Holy Ghost, Born of the Virgin Mary, Suffered under Pontius Pilate, Was crucified, dead, and buried. ['Apostles' Creed']

25 The holy Catholic Church, the Communion of Saints; the Forgiveness of sins; the Resurrection of the body, And the life everlasting.

26 Lord have mercy upon us.
[Response] Christ have mercy upon us. ['Responses']

27 Whose service is perfect freedom. ['Second Collect, for Peace']

28 Neither run into any kind of danger. ['Third Collect, for Grace']

29 In choirs and places where they sing, here followeth the anthem. [Rubric]

30 The fountain of all goodness. ['Prayer for the Royal Family']

31 The continual dew of thy blessing. ['Prayer for the Clergy and People']

32 Lighten our darkness, we beseech thee, O Lord. [*Evening Prayer*, 'Third Collect']

33 Neither confounding the Persons: nor dividing the Substance. [*Athanasian Creed*]

34 Not three Gods: but one God.

1 Have mercy upon us miserable sinners. [*Litany*]

2 Envy, hatred, and malice, and all uncharitableness.

3 The world, the flesh, and the devil.

4 From battle and murder, and from sudden death.

5 In the hour of death, and in the day of judgement.

6 Unity, peace, and concord.

7 The kindly fruits of the earth.

8 PRIEST: O Lord, deal not with us after our sins. ANSWER: Neither reward us after our iniquities.

9 All sorts and conditions of men. [*Prayer for All Conditions of Men*]

10 Our creation, preservation, and all the blessings of this life. [*A General Thanksgiving*]

11 For the means of grace, and for the hope of glory.

12 Put upon us the armour of light, now in the time of this mortal life. [*Collect, First Sunday in Advent*]

13 Read, mark, learn, and inwardly digest. [*Collect, Second Sunday in Advent*]

14 That most excellent gift of charity. [*Collect, Quinquagesima Sunday*]

15 Jews, Turks, Infidels, and Heretics. [*Third Collect for Good Friday*]

16 The author and giver of all good things. [*Collect, Seventh Sunday after Trinity*]

17 Serve thee with a quiet mind. [*Collect, 21st Sunday after Trinity*]

18 Whom truly to know is everlasting life. [*Collect, St Philip and St James's Day*]

19 Unto whom all hearts be open, all desires known, and from whom no secrets are hid. [*Holy Communion, Collect*]

20 Ye that do truly and earnestly repent you of your sins, and are in love and charity with your neighbours. ['Invitation']

21 Very God of Very God, Begotten not made. ['The Nicene Creed']

22 Hear what comfortable words. ['Priest's Exhortation']

23 Be amongst you and remain with you always. ['Blessing']

24 All our works, begun, continued, and ended in thee. ['Collect after the Offertory']

25 The old Adam in this Child may be so buried, that the new man may be raised up in him. [*Public Baptism of Infants*, 'Blessing']

26 Renounce the devil and all his works. [*passim*]

27 Such as are of Riper Years. [*Public Baptism. . .*]

28 The pomps and vanity of this wicked world. [*Catechism*]

29 Governors, teachers, spiritual pastors and masters.

30 To keep my hands from picking and stealing.

31 To do my duty in that state of life unto which it shall please God to call me.

32 An outward and visible sign of an inward and spiritual grace.

33 In their Mother Tongue. [Rubric]

34 Laying on of Hands. [*Confirmation*, section heading]

35 Being now come to years of discretion. [Preface]

36 If any of you know cause, or just impediment. [*Solemnization of Matrimony*, 'Banns']

37 This is the first time of asking.

38 Brute beasts that have no understanding. ['Exhortation']

39 First, it was ordained for the procreation of children.

40 Let him now speak, or else hereafter for ever hold his peace.

41 Wilt thou have this woman to thy wedded wife? ['Betrothal']

42 To have and to hold from this day forward, for better for worse, for richer for poorer, in sickness and in health, to love and to cherish, till death us do part.

43 To love, cherish and to obey.

44 With this ring I thee wed, with my body I thee worship, and with all my worldly goods I thee endow.

45 Those whom God hath joined together let no man put asunder. [Prayer]

46 Holy wedlock. ['Priest's Address']

47 Peace be to this house. [*The Visitation of the Sick*]

48 The inner man. ['Prayer . . . when there appeareth small hope of recovery']

1 Against the hour of death.

2 Laid violent hands upon themselves. [*The Burial of the Dead*, opening rubric]

3 Man that is born of a woman hath but a short time to live, and is full of misery. [Anthem]

4 In the midst of life we are in death.

5 We therefore commit his body to the ground; earth to earth; ashes to ashes; dust to dust; in sure and certain hope of the Resurrection to eternal life. ['Committal']

6 We therefore commit his body to the deep, to be turned into corruption, looking for the resurrection of the body, (when the Sea shall give up her dead). [*At the Burial of their Dead at Sea*]

7 Of Works of Supererogation. [*Articles of Religion*, XIV, heading]

8 Fond thing vainly invented. [XXII 'Of Purgatory']

9 The Bishop of *Rome* hath no jurisdiction in this Realm of *England*. [XXXVII]

10 A Man may not marry his Grandmother. [*Table of Kindred*]

JACQUES PRÉVERT 1900–1977

11 *Notre Père qui êtes aux cieux / Restez-y / Et nous resterons sur la terre / Qui est quelquefois si jolie.* – Our Father that art in heaven, stay there and we will stay on earth which is sometimes so pretty. [*Pater Noster*]

J. B. PRIESTLEY 1894–1984

12 A number of anxious dwarfs trying to grill a whale. [(Of Politicians) *Outcries and Asides*]

13 Comedy, we may say, is society protecting itself – with a smile. [*George Meredith*]

14 Our great-grandchildren, when they learn how we began this war by snatching glory out of defeat ... may also learn how the little holiday steamers made an excursion to hell and came back glorious. [(On Dunkirk) BBC Radio broadcast, 5 June 1940]

MATTHEW PRIOR 1664–1721

15 Dear Cloe, how blubbered is that pretty face! [*A Better Answer*]

16 Odds life! must one swear to the truth of a song?

17 I court others in verse: but I love thee in prose; / And they have my whimsies, but thou hast my heart.

18 Be to her virtues very kind; / Be to her faults a little blind; / Let all her ways be unconfined; / And clap your padlock – on her mind. [*An English Padlock*]

19 To John I owed great obligation; / But John, unhappily, thought fit / To publish it to all the nation: / Sure John and I are more than quit. [*Epigram*]

20 Nobles and heralds, by your leave, / Here lies what once was Matthew Prior; / The son of Adam and of Eve, / Can Bourbon or Nassau go higher? [*Epitaph on Himself*]

21 He bought her sermons, psalms, and graces, / And doubled down the useful places. [*Hans Carvel*, 51]

22 Her religion so well with her learning did suit / That in practice sincere, and in controverse mute, / She shewed she knew better to live than dispute. [*Jinny the Just*]

23 The merchant, to secure his treasure, / Conveys it in a borrowed name: / Euphelia serves to grace my measure; / But Cloe is my real flame. [*An Ode, 'The Merchant to Secure his Treasure'*]

24 She chuckled when a bawd was carted: / And thought the nation ne'er would thrive, / Till all the whores were burnt alive. [*Paolo Purganti and his Wife*, 44]

25 The doctor understood the call; / But had not always wherewithal. [81]

26 Cured yesterday of my disease, / I died last night of my physician. [*The Remedy Worse than the Disease*]

27 Abra was ready ere I called her name; / And, though I called another, Abra came. [*Solomon*, II. 362]

28 For hope is but the dream of those that wake. [III. 102]

29 Now fitted the halter, now traversed the cart; / And often took leave, but was loath to depart. [*The Thief and the Cordelier*]

30 For, as our different ages move, / 'Tis so ordained (would fate but mend it!) / That I shall be past making love / When she begins to comprehend it. [*To a Child of Quality, Five Years Old*]

31 They never taste who always drink; / They always talk, who never think. [*Upon this Passage in Scaligerana*]

V. S. PRITCHETT 1900–

1 Human beings are simply archaic, ivy-covered ruins, preserved by the connoisseur, and they stand out oddly in the new world of the masses. [*New Writing and Daylight*, 'The Future of Fiction']

ADELAIDE PROCTER 1825–1864

2 Seated one day at the organ, / I was weary and ill at ease, / And my fingers wandered idly / Over the noisy keys. [*A Lost Chord*]

3 But I struck one chord of music, / Like the sound of a great Amen.

PROTAGORAS c.485–415 BC

4 Man is the measure of all things. [Quoted by Plato in *Theaetetus*, 160D]

PIERRE-JOSEPH PROUDHON 1809–1865

5 *La propriété c'est le vol.* – Property is theft. [*Qu'est-ce que la propriété?*]

MARCEL PROUST 1871–1922

6 The taste was that of the little crumb of madeleine which on Sunday mornings at Combray . . . when I used to say good-day to her in her bedroom, my aunt Léonie used to give me, dipping it first in her own cup of real or of lime-flower tea. [*Remembrance of Things Past: Swann's Way*, 'Overture' trans. C. K. Scott Moncrieff and Terence Kilmartin]

7 In theory one is aware that the earth revolves, but in practice one does not perceive it, the ground upon which one treads seems not to move, and one can live undisturbed. So it is with Time in one's life. [*Within a Budding Grove*, 'Madame Swann at Home']

8 A powerful idea communicates some of its power to the man who contradicts it.

9 There can be no peace of mind in love, since the advantage one has secured is never anything but a fresh starting-point for further desires.

10 It is our noticing them that puts things in a room, our growing used to them that takes them away again and clears a space for us. ['Place Names']

11 He strode rapidly across the whole width of the hotel, seeming to be in pursuit of his mon-ocle, which kept darting away in front of him like a butterfly.

12 The human face is indeed, like the face of the God of some oriental theogony, a whole cluster of faces, juxtaposed on different planes so that one does not see them all at once. ['Elstir']

13 She's the sort of woman who does a tremendous lot for her old governesses. [*The Guermantes Way*, Vol. i. Ch. 1]

14 Everything we think of as great has come to us from neurotics. It is they and they alone who found religions and create great works of art. The world will never realize how much it owes to them, and what they have suffered in order to bestow their gifts on it. ['Decline and Death of My Grandmother']

15 It has even been said that the highest praise of God consists in the denial of him by the atheist who finds creation so perfect that he can dispense with a creator. [Vol. ii. Ch. 2]

16 Good-bye, I've barely said a word to you, but it's always like that at parties – we never really see each other, we never say the things we should like to; in fact it's the same everywhere in this life. Let's hope that when we are dead things will be better arranged. [*Cities of the Plain*, Vol. i. Pt. II. Ch. 1]

17 Illness is the most heeded of doctors: to kindness and wisdom we make promises only; pain we obey.

18 If habit is a second nature it prevents us from knowing whose cruelties it lacks as well as it's enchantments.

19 I have a horror of sunsets, they're so romantic, so operatic. [ii. 2]

20 Happiness is beneficial for the body, but it is grief that develops the powers of the mind. [*Time Regained*, Ch. 2, trans. C. K. Scott Moncrieff, Terence Kilmartin and Andreas Mayor]

FATHER PROUT [F. S. MAHONY] 1804–1866

21 'Tis the bells of Shandon, / That sound so grand on / The pleasant waters / Of the River Lee. [*The Bells of Shandon*]

W. J. PROWSE 1836–1870

22 Though the latitude's rather uncertain, / And the longitude also is vague, / The persons I

pity who know not the city, / The beautiful city of Prague. [*The City of Prague*]

PUBLILIUS SYRUS *see* **SYRUS, PUBLILIUS**

JOHN PUDNEY 1909–1977

1 Do not despair / For Johnny Head-in-Air. / He sleeps as sound / As Johnny Underground. [Lines scribbled on an envelope during an air-raid in 1941. Later used for the film *The Way to the Stars*. See also 203:4]

WILLIAM PULTENEY, EARL OF BATH
   1684–1764

2 Since twelve honest men have decided the cause, / And were judges of fact, tho' not judges of laws. [*The Honest Jury*, 3]

PUNCH

3 Advice to persons about to marry. – Don't. [Vol. viii. p. 1 1845]

4 You pays your money and you takes your choice. [x. 17. 1846]

5 Never do to-day what you can put off till to-morrow. [xvii. 241. 1849]

6 Who's 'im, Bill?
   A stranger!
   'Eave 'arf a brick at 'im. [xxvi. 82. 1854]

7 It's the 'ammer, 'ammer, 'ammer along the 'ard 'igh road. [xxx. 218. 1856]

8 Mun, a had na' been the-erre abune twa hoours when – *bang* – went *saxpence*!! [lv. 235. 1868]

9 Nothink for nothink 'ere, and precious little for sixpence! [lvii. 152, 1869]

10 It appears the Americans have taken umbrage –
   The deuce they have! Whereabouts is that? [lxiii. 189. 1872]

11 Go directly, – see what she's doing and tell her she mustn't! [202]

12 There was *one* poor tiger that *hadn't got* a Christian! [lxviii. 143. 1875]

13 What did *you* take out of the bag, Mamma? *I* only got sixpence. [lxx. 139. 1876]

14 I never read books – I *write* them. [lxxiv. 210. 1878]

15 I used your soap two years ago; since then I have used no other. [lxxxvi. 197. 1884]

16 Don't look at me, Sir, with – ah – in that tone of voice, Sir! [lxxxvii. 38. 1884]

17 Nearly all our best men are dead! Carlyle, Tennyson, Browning, George Eliot! – I'm not feeling very well myself! [civ. 210. 1893]

18 I'm afraid you've got a bad egg, Mr Jones!
   Oh no, my Lord, I assure you! Parts of it are excellent! [cix. 222. 1895]

19 Look here, Steward, if this is coffee, I want tea; but if this is tea, then I wish for coffee. [cxxiii. 44, 1902]

ISRAEL PUTNAM 1715–1790

20 Don't one of you fire until you see the whites of their eyes. [At Bunker Hill, 17 June 1775. Also attr. to W. Prescott and others]

MARIO PUZO 1920–

21 I'll make him an offer he can't refuse. [*passim* in novel and film *The Godfather*, screenplay with Francis Ford Coppola]

Q

FRANCIS QUARLES 1592–1644

1 Be wisely worldly, be not worldly wise. [*Emblems*, Bk. ii. 2:46]

2 My soul, sit thou a patient looker-on; / Judge not the play before the play is done; / Her plot hath many changes; every day / Speaks a new scene; the last act crowns the play. [Epigram: *Respice Finem*]

3 We'll cry both arts and learning down, / And hey! then up go we! [*The Shepherd's Oracles*, 'Song of Anarchus', 4]

SIR ARTHUR QUILLER COUCH 1863–1944

4 Know you her secret none can utter? / – Hers of the Book, the tripled Crown? [*Alma Mater*]

JOSIAH QUINCY JUN. 1772–1864

5 As it will be the right of all, so it will be the duty of some, definitely to prepare for a separation, amicably if they can, violently if they must. [Speech in US House of Representatives, 14 Jan. 1811]

R

FRANÇOIS RABELAIS c.1492–1553

1 I drink for the thirst to come. [*Gargantua*, Ch. 5]

2 *L'appétit vient en mangeant.* – Appetite comes with eating.

3 Hope to catch larks if the heavens fell. [11]

4 The strength of a war waged without monetary reserves is as fleeting as a breath. Money is the sinews of battle. [46]

5 *A la venue des cocquecigrues.* – About the coming of the cocklicranes. [49]

6 *En leur reigle n'estoit que ceste clause: Fais ce que voudras.* – In their rules there was only one clause: Do what you will. [57]

7 I was born and brought up as a child in Touraine, which is the garden of France. [*Pantagruel*, Ch. 9]

8 So Anarch became a good crier of green sauce. [31]

9 Man never found the deities so kindly / As to assure him that he'd live tomorrow. [III. 2]

10 Not everyone is a debtor who wishes to be; not everyone who wishes makes creditors. [(Panurge) 3]

11 This is a great year for cuckolds. [9]

12 This flea that I have in my ear has been tickling me. [(Panurge) 31]

13 The dice of judgement ... the same dice as you gentlemen use in this supreme court of yours. [(Bridlegoose) 39]

14 Few and signally blest are those whom Jupiter has destined to be cabbage-planters. For they've always one foot on the ground, and the other not far from it. [(Panurge) IV. 18]

15 'Devil take me,' began Friar John.
'I'll go halves with him,' interrupted Panurge. [23]

16 *Vogue la galère.* – Let her go.

17 You can keep your litter and your hay and your oats. Long live the thistles of the field, for there you can play the stallion to your heart's content. [V.7]

18 On the other square, to the left, was elegantly engraved in capital letters this sentence. ALL THINGS MOVE TO THEIR END. [37]

19 Then this one word was heard: *Trink*. [45]

20 *Trink* is a panomphaean word. It speaks oracles, that is to say, in all languages. [46]

21 *Tirez le rideau, la farce est jouée.* – Ring down the curtain, the farce is over. [Attr. last words]

22 *Je m'en vais chercher un grand peut-être.* – I am going in search of a great perhaps. [Alternative attr. last words]

JEAN RACINE 1639–1699

23 *Ah! je l'ai trop aimé pour ne le point haïr!* – Oh, I have loved him too much to feel no hate for him. [*Andromaque*, II. i. 416]

24 *Mon innocence enfin commence à me peser.* – Now my innocence begins to weigh me down. [III. i. 772]

25 *Je t'aimais inconstant, qu'aurais-je fait fidèle?* – I loved you when you were inconstant. What should I have done if you had been faithful? [IV. v. 1365]

26 *C'était pendant l'horreur d'une profonde nuit.* – It was during the horror of an intensely dark night. [*Athalie*, II. v. 490]

27 *Elle flotte, elle hésite; en un mot, elle est*

femme. – She wavers, she hesitates; in one word, she is a woman. [III. iii. 876]

1 *Ce n'est plus une ardeur dans mes veines cachée: / C'est Vénus toute entière à sa proie attachée.* – It is no longer a heat concealed in my blood, it is Venus herself grasping her prey. [*Phèdre*, II. v. 304]

2 *Ainsi que la vertue le crime a ses degrés.* – Crime, like virtue, has its degrees. [IV. ii. 1096]

3 *Le jour n'est pas plus pur que le fond de mon cœur.* – Day is not purer than the depths of my heart. [IV. ii. 1112]

4 *On apprend à hurler, dit l'autre, avec les loups.* – One learns, said the other, to howl with the wolves. [*Les Plaideurs*, I. i. 6]

THOMAS RAINBOROWE ?–1648

5 The poorest he that is in England hath a life to live as the greatest he. [*Army Debates at Putney*, 29 Oct. 1647]

SIR WALTER RALEIGH c.1552–1618

6 As you came from the holy land / Of Walsinghame, / Met you not with my true love / By the way as you came?

How shall I know your true love, / That have met many one / As I went to the holy land, / That have come, that have gone? [*As you Came*]

7 Go, Soul, the body's guest, / Upon a thankless arrant: / Fear not to touch the best; / The truth shall be thy warrant: / Go, since I needs must die, / And give the world the lie. [*The Lie*]

8 Give me my scallop-shell of quiet, / My staff of faith to walk upon, / My scrip of joy, immortal diet, / My bottle of salvation, / My gown of glory, hope's true gage, / And thus I'll take my pilgrimage. [*The Passionate Man's Pilgrimage*]

9 O eloquent, just, and mighty Death! whom none could advise, thou hast persuaded; what none hath dared, thou hast done; and whom all the world hath flattered, thou only hast cast out of the world and despised; thou hast drawn together all the far-stretched greatness, all the pride, cruelty, and ambition of man, and covered it all over with these two narrow words. *Hic jacet.* [*A History of the World*, Bk v, Ch. 6]

10 Fain would I climb, yet fear I to fall. [Line written on a window-pane. Queen Elizabeth is said to have written under it, 'If the heart fails thee, climb not at all.']

11 The world itself is but a large prison, out of which some are daily led to execution. [When returning to prison from his trial]

12 'Tis a sharp remedy [the executioner's axe], but a sure one for all ills. [Attr. by David Hume, *History of Great Britain*, Vol. i. Ch. 4]

13 So the heart be right, it is no matter which way the head lieth. [When laying his head on the block]

SIR WALTER A. RALEIGH 1861–1922

14 I wish I loved the Human Race; / I wish I loved its silly face; / I wish I liked the way it walks; / I wish I liked the way it talks; / And when I'm introduced to one / I wish I thought *What Jolly Fun!* [*Laughter from a Cloud*, 'Wishes of an Elderly Man']

JULIAN RALPH 1853–1903

15 News value. [Lecture at Columbia University, 1892]

ALLAN RAMSAY 1686–1758

16 Farewell to Lochaber, and farewell my Jean. [*Lochaber No More*]

J. R. RANDALL 1839–1908

17 The despot's heel is on thy shore, Maryland! [*Maryland, My Maryland*]

J. E. RANKIN 1828–1904

18 God be with you till we meet again; / By His counsels guide, uphold you, / With His sheep securely fold you. [Hymn]

JOHN CROWE RANSOM 1888–1974

19 Here lies a lady of beauty and high degree. / Of chills and fevers she died, of fever and chills. [*Here lies a Lady*]

20 Two evils, monstrous either one apart, / Possessed me, and were long and loath at going; / A cry of Absence, Absence, in the heart, / And in the wood the furious winter blowing. [*Winter Remembered*]

ARTHUR RANSOME 1884–1967

21 BETTER DROWNED THAN DUFFERS IF NOT DUFFERS WONT DROWN [*Swallows and Amazons*, Ch. 1]

TERENCE RATTIGAN 1911–1977

1 She has ideas above her station ... How would you say that in French? ... you can't say au-dessus de sa gare. It isn't that sort of station. [*French without Tears*, I]

2 A nice, – respectable, – middle-class, middle-aged maiden lady, with time on her hands and the money to help her pass it ... Let us call her Aunt Edna ... Aunt Edna is universal, and to those who may feel that all the problems of the modern theatre might be solved by her liquidation, let me add that ... she is also immortal. [*Collected Plays*, Vol. ii, Preface]

THOMAS RAVENSCROFT 1592?–1635?

3 We be three poor mariners / Newly come from the seas. [*Deuteromelia*]

SIR HERBERT READ 1893–1968

4 I saw him stab / And stab again / A well-killed Boche. / This is the happy warrior. / This is he ... [*The Happy Warrior*]

CHARLES READE 1814–1884

5 *Courage, l'ami, le diable est mort.* – Courage, my friend, the devil is dead. [*The Cloister and the Hearth*, Ch. 24]

6 Make 'em laugh; make 'em cry; make 'em wait. [Recipe for novel-writing in serial form]

NANCY REAGAN 1921–

7 A woman is like a teabag. It's only when she's in hot water that you realize how strong she is. [Address to U S Women's Congress, quoted in the *Observer* Sayings of the Week, 29 Mar. 1981]

PRESIDENT RONALD REAGAN 1911–

8 You can tell a lot about a fellow's character from the way he eats jelly beans. [Quoted in the *Daily Mail*, 22 Jan. 1981]

9 My fellow Americans, I am pleased to tell you I have just signed legislation that will outlaw Russia for ever. We begin bombing in five minutes. [Rehearsal for TV programme, transmitted in error, 13 Aug. 1984]

HENRY REED 1914–1986

10 To-day we have naming of parts. Yesterday / We had daily cleaning. And tomorrow morning, / We shall have what to do after firing. But to-day, / To-day we have naming of parts. [*Naming of Parts*]

11 They call it easing the Spring; it is perfectly easy / If you have any strength in your thumb: like the bolt, / And the breech, and the cocking-piece, and the point of balance, / Which in our case we have not got.

12 And the various holds and rolls and throws and breakfalls / Somehow or other I always seemed to put / In the wrong place. And as for war, my wars / Were global from the start. [*Unarmed Combat*]

JOHN REED 1887–1920

13 Ten Days that Shook the World. [Title of book on Russian Revolution]

CHARLES A. REICH 1928–

14 The Greening of America. [Title of book]

LORD REITH 1889–1971

15 Despotism tempered by assassination. [On the best form of government. Quoted in the *Observer*, 12 Nov. 1972. See 290:1]

ERICH MARIA REMARQUE 1898–1970

16 *Im Westen nichts Neues.* – All Quiet on the Western Front. [Title of novel]

M. J. RENDALL 1862–1950

17 Nation shall speak peace unto nation. [Motto of BBC, 1927]

EBEN REXFORD 1848–1916

18 Darling, I am growing old, / Silver threads among the gold. [*Silver Threads among the Gold*]

FREDERIC REYNOLDS 1764–1841

19 How goes the enemy? [(Said by Mr Ennui, 'the time-killer') *The Dramatist*, I. i]

SIR JOSHUA REYNOLDS 1723–1792

20 If you have great talents, industry will improve them: if you have but moderate abilities,

industry will supply their deficiency. [*Discourses*, 2]

1 A mere copier of nature can never produce anything great. [3]

MALVINA REYNOLDS 1900–1978

2 They're all made out of ticky-tacky, and they all look just the same. [Song: *Little Boxes* about the tract houses in the hills south of San Francisco. Quoted in *The Times* obituary, 7 Apr. 1978. Sung by Pete Seeger]

CECIL RHODES 1853–1902

3 Remember that you are an Englishman, and have consequently won first prize in the lottery of life. [Quoted in Peter Ustinov, *Dear Me*, Ch. 4]

4 So little done, so much to do. [Last words]

GRANTLAND RICE 1880–1954

5 For when the One Great Scorer comes / To write against your name, / He marks – not that you won or lost – / But how you played the game. [*Alumnus Football*]

SIR STEPHEN RICE 1637–1715

6 'I will drive,' he used to say, 'a coach and six through the Act of Settlement.' [T. B. Macaulay, *History of England*, Ch. 12]

MANDY RICE-DAVIES 1944–

7 He would, wouldn't he? [When told Lord Astor had denied any involvement with her, at trial of Stephen Ward, 28 June 1963]

CARDINAL RICHELIEU 1585–1642

8 If you give me six lines written by the most honest man, I will find something in them to hang him. [Attr. in various forms and to other authors]

DAVID RIESMAN 1909–

9 The Lonely Crowd. [Title of book]

J. W. RILEY 1852–1916

10 An' the gobble-uns 'll git you / Ef you don't watch out! [*Little Orphan Annie*]

RAINER MARIA RILKE 1875–1926

11 It was the sinister, princely death which the chamberlain had carried with him and had himself nourished during his whole life. [*Notebooks of Malte Laurids Brigge*, Pt I]

12 It is good to say it aloud: 'Nothing has happened', Once again: 'Nothing has happened'. Does that help?

13 *Wunderlich nah ist der Held doch den jugendlich Toten.* – The hero is strangely akin to those who die young. [*Duineser Elegien* VI]

14 *Abgewendet schon, stand er am Ende der Lächeln, anders.* – But already withdrawn, he stood at the end of smiles, different.

15 *Unser / Leben geht hin mit Verwandlung.* – Our life passes in transformation. [VII]

16 *So leben wir und nehmen immer Abschied.* – Thus we live, for ever taking leave.

17 *Ist er ein Hiesiger? Nein, aus beiden / Reichen erwuchs seine weite Natur.* – Is he a man of this side? No, his broad nature grew from both realms. [*Die Sonette an Orpheus* I. vi]

18 *O dieses ist das Tier, das es nicht gibt.* – O this is the animal that does not exist. [II. iv]

19 *Alle die dich suchen, versuchen dich. / Und die, sie dich finden, binden dich, / an Bild und Gebärde.* – All who seek you tempt you, and as soon as they find you, bind you to an image and a posture. [*Das Stundenbuch, 'Alle welche dich suchen'*]

20 *Was wirst du tun, Gott, wenn ich sterbe? / Ich bin dein Krug (wenn ich zerscherbe?).* – What will you do, God, if I die? I am your pitcher (if I break?). [*Was wirst du tun, Gott'*]

ARTHUR RIMBAUD 1854–1891

21 *A noir, E blanc, I rouge, U vert, O bleu, voyelles.* – A black, E white, I red, U green, O blue, vowels. [*Voyelles*]

R. L. RIPLEY 1893–1949

22 Believe it or not. [Title of newspaper feature]

ANTOINE DE RIVAROL 1753–1801

23 *Ce qui n'est pas clair n'est pas français.* – What is not clear is not French. [*De l'universalité de la langue française*]

GEORGE ROBEY 1869–1954

24 The Prime Minister of Mirth. [Sobriquet of unknown origin]

1 I said 'Archibald, certainly not'. [Song refrain]

2 They knew her by the pimple, / The pimple on her nose. [Song: *The Simple Pimple*]

LEO ROBIN 1900–1984

3 Thanks For the Memory. [Title of song from musical *Big Broadcast*]

SIR BOYLE ROCHE 1743–1807

4 What has posterity done for us? [Speech in Irish Parliament, 1780]

5 Mr Speaker I smell a rat; I see him forming in the air and darkening the sky; but I'll nip him in the bud. [Attr.]

JOHN WILMOT, EARL OF ROCHESTER 1647–1680

6 The best good man, with the worst-natured muse. [(Lord Buckhurst) *An Allusion to Horace*]

7 Here lies our sovereign lord the king / Whose promise none relies on; / He never said a foolish thing, / Nor ever did a wise one. [*Epitaph on Charles II*. Various forms exist. For Charles's reply, see 106:21]

8 If I, by miracle, can be / This live-long minute true to thee, / 'Tis all that heaven allows. [*Love and Life, A Song*]

9 I'd be a dog, a monkey, or a bear, / Or anything but that vain animal, / Who is so proud of being rational. [*A Satire against Mankind*, 5]

10 Reason, an *ignis fatuus* of the mind. [12]

11 Then old age, and experience, hand in hand, / Lead him to death, and make him understand, / After a search so painful, and so long, / That all his life he has been in the wrong. [25]

12 Most men are cowards, all men should be knaves. [158]

13 A merry monarch, scandalous and poor. [*A Satire on King Charles II*]

14 Nothing, thou elder brother ev'n to shade, / Thou hadst a being ere the world was made. [*Upon Nothing*]

LUDWIG VON ROENNE 1804–1891

15 If anything can give us a claim to the title of his Majesty's loyal opposition, it is, I think, our present debate, and our present resolution. [Speech in Prussian House, 1863. See also 202:10]

THEODORE ROETHKE 1908–1963

16 Over this damp grave I speak the words of my love: / I, with no rights in this matter, / Neither father nor lover. [*Elegy for Jane*]

17 In a dark time the eye begins to see. [*In a Dark Time*]

18 I wake to sleep, and take my waking slow. / I learn by going where I have to go. [*The Waking*]

E. W. ROGERS 1864–1913

19 Ev'ry member of the force / Has a watch and chain, of course; / If you want to know the time, / Ask a P'liceman! [*Ask a P'liceman*]

20 Hi-tiddley-hi-ti. [Title of song]

J. E. T. ROGERS 1823–1900

21 While ladling butter from alternate tubs / Stubbs butters Freeman, Freeman butters Stubbs. [Attr. by W. H. Hutton, *Letters of Bishop Stubbs*]

R. C. ROGERS 1862–1912

22 The hours I spent with thee, dear heart, / Are as a string of pearls to me; / I count them over, every one apart, / My rosary. [*My Rosary*]

SAMUEL ROGERS 1763–1855

23 Ward has no heart, they say; but I deny it: / He has a heart, and gets his speeches by it. [*Epigram upon Lord Dudley*]

24 Think nothing done while aught remains to do. [*Human Life*, 49]

25 Never less alone than when alone, / Those whom he loved so long and sees no more, / Loved and still loves – not dead – but gone before, / He gathers round him. [755]

26 Oh! she was good as she was fair. / None – none on earth above her! / As pure in thought as angels are, / To know her was to love her. [*Jacqueline*, I. 68]

27 Sheridan was listened to with such attention that you might have heard a pin drop. [*Table Talk*]

1 It doesn't much signify whom one marries, for one is sure to find next morning that it was someone else.

2 When a new book is published, read an old one. [Attr.]

3 A man who attempts to read all the new productions must do as the fleas do – skip. [Attr.]

WILL ROGERS 1879–1935

4 A comedian can only last till he either takes himself serious or his audience takes him serious. [Newspaper article, 28 June 1931]

5 It's great to be great but it's greater to be human. [*Autobiography*, Ch. 15]

6 Everything is funny as long as it's happening to somebody else. [*The Illiterate Digest*]

7 My folks didn't come over on the *Mayflower*, but they were there to meet the boat. [Quoted in Evan Esar (ed.), *Treasury of Humorous Quotations*]

MME ROLAND 1754–1793

8 *O Liberté! O Liberté! que de crimes on commet en ton nom.* – O Liberty, Liberty, what crimes are committed in your name! [On passing the statue of Liberty, on her way to the scaffold. Quoted in A. de Lamartine, *Histoire des Girondins*]

JAMES ROLMAZ 19 Cent.

9 Where did you get that hat? / Where did you get that tile? [*Where Did You Get That Hat?*]

PIERRE DE RONSARD 1524/5–1585

10 *Mignonne, allons voir si la rose / Qui ce matin avait déclose / Sa robe de pourpre au soleil / A point perdu cette vesprée / Les plis de sa robe pourprée, / Et son teint au vôtre pareil.* – Darling, let us go to see if the rose, which this morning had spread her purple robe to the sun, has not this evening lost the folds of her purple robe and her colour, that is like yours. [*Odes, À Cassandre*, 17]

11 *Quand vous serez bien vieille, au soir à la chandelle, / Assise auprès du feu, dévidant et filant, / Direz, chantant mes vers, en vous émerveillant, / Ronsard me célébrait du temps que j'étais belle.* – When you are very old and sit at evening beside the fire, by candlelight, carding and spinning, you will say with wonder, as you recite my verses: 'Ronsard sang of me in the time when I was fair.' [*Sonnets à Hélène*, II. 43]

FRANKLIN D. ROOSEVELT 1882–1945

12 The forgotten man at the bottom of the economic pyramid. [Broadcast speech, 7 Apr. 1932]

13 I pledge you – I pledge myself – to a new deal for the American people. [Speech at convention, Chicago, 2 July]

14 Let me assert my firm belief that the only thing we have to fear is fear itself. [First inaugural address, 4 Mar. 1933]

15 In the field of world policy I would dedicate this nation to the policy of the good neighbour.

16 This generation of Americans has a rendezvous with destiny. [Speech accepting renomination, 27 June 1936]

17 We have always known that heedless self-interest was bad morals; we know now that it is bad economics. [Second inaugural address, 20 Jan. 1937]

18 I see one-third of a nation ill-housed, ill-clad, ill-nourished.

19 The change in the moral climate of America.

20 Quarantine the aggressors. [Speech at Chicago, 5 Oct.]

21 I have told you once and I will tell you again – your boys will not be sent into any foreign wars. [Election speech, 30 Oct. 1940]

22 We must be the great arsenal of democracy. [*Fireside Chat*, radio address 29 Dec.]

23 A world founded upon four essential freedoms. The first is freedom of speech and expression – everywhere in the world. The second is freedom of every person to worship God in his own way – everywhere in the world. The third is freedom from want . . . everywhere in the world. The fourth is freedom from fear . . . anywhere in the world. [Speech, 6 Jan. 1941]

24 Never before have we had so little time in which to do so much. [*Fireside Chat*, radio address, 23 Feb. 1942]

25 The only limit to our realization of tomorrow will be our doubts of today. [Address

written for Jefferson Day dinner to have been given 13 Apr. 1945. He died on the 12th]

1 A radical is a man with both feet firmly planted – in the air. [Radio address, 26 Oct. 1939]

THEODORE ROOSEVELT 1858–1919

2 I wish to preach, not the doctrine of ignoble ease, but the doctrine of the strenuous life. [Speech at Chicago, 10 Apr. 1899]

3 Speak softly and carry a big stick; you will go far. [Speech at Chicago, 2 Apr. 1901]

4 A man who is good enough to shed his blood for his country is good enough to be given a square deal afterwards. More than that no man is entitled to, and less than that no man shall have. [Speech at Springfield, Illinois, 4 July 1903]

5 The men with the muck-rakes are often indispensable to the well-being of society but only if they know when to stop raking the muck. [At laying of corner-stone, House of Representatives, 14 Apr. 1906]

6 Hyphenated Americanism. [Speech in New York, Oct. 1915]

7 One of our defects as a nation is a tendency to use what have been called 'weasel words'. When a weasel sucks eggs the meat is sucked out of the egg. If you use a 'weasel word' after another there is nothing left of the other. [Speech in St Louis, 31 May 1916]

8 There can be no fifty-fifty Americanism in this country. There is room here for only one hundred per cent Americanism. [Speech at Saratoga, N.Y. 19 July 1918]

9 The lunatic fringe in all reform movements. [*Autobiography*, Ch. 7]

10 No man is justified in doing evil on the ground of expediency. [*The Strenuous Life*, 'Latitude and Longitude among Reformers']

11 The most successful politician is he who says what everybody is thinking most often and in the loudest voice. [Quoted in Evan Esar (ed.), *Treasury of Humorous Quotations*]

EARL OF ROSCOMMON 1637–1685

12 Choose an author as you choose a friend. [*Essay on Translated Verse*, 96]

13 Immodest words admit of no defence, / For want of decency is want of sense. [113]

14 The multitude is always in the wrong. [183]

BILLY ROSE [WILLIAM ROSENBERG] 1899–1966

15 Does the Spearmint Lose Its Flavour on the Bedpost Overnight? [Title of song by Marty Bloom and Ernest Breller]

EARL OF ROSEBERY 1847–1929

16 The Empire is a Commonwealth of Nations. [Speech at Adelaide, S. Australia, 18 Jan. 1884]

17 It is beginning to be hinted that we are a nation of amateurs. [Rectorial Address, Glasgow University, 16 Nov. 1900]

18 I must plough my own furrow alone. [Speech at City of London Liberal Club, 19 July 1901]

19 You have to clean your plate. [(Advice to the Liberal Party) Speech at Chesterfield, 16 Dec.]

ISAAC ROSENBERG 1890–1918

20 Droll rat, they would shoot you if they knew / Your cosmopolitan sympathies (And God knows what antipathies). [*Break of Day in the Trenches*]

21 Death could drop from the dark / As easily as song. [*Returning, We hear the Larks*]

ALAN S. C. ROSS 1907–1978

22 U and Non-U, An Essay in Sociological Linguistics. [Title of essay, included in *Noblesse Oblige*]

ALEXANDER ROSS 1699–1784

23 Married, and wooed, and a'! / And was she nae very weel off / That was wooed, and married, and a'? [*Wooed, and Married, and A'*]

HAROLD W. ROSS 1892–1951

24 The *New Yorker* will not be edited for the old lady from Dubuque. [On founding the *New Yorker*, 1925. Later she became 'the little old lady']

25 On one of Mr Benchley's manuscripts he

wrote in the margin opposite 'Andromache', 'Who he?' Mr Benchley wrote back, 'You keep out of this.' [Quoted by Dorothy Parker in Malcolm Cowley (ed.), *Writers at Work*, First Series]

CHRISTINA ROSSETTI 1830–1894

1 My heart is like a singing bird / Whose nest is in a watered shoot; / My heart is like an apple-tree / Whose boughs are bent with thick-set fruit; / My heart is like a rainbow shell / That paddles in a halcyon sea; My heart is gladder than all these / Because my love is come to me. [*A Birthday*]

2 Because the birthday of my life / Is come, my love is come to me.

3 'Come cheer up my lads, 'tis to glory we steer' – As the soldier remarked whose post lay in the rear. [*Couplet*]

4 For there is no friend like a sister / In calm or stormy weather. [*Goblin Market*, toward the end]

5 Snow had fallen, snow on snow, / Snow on snow, / In the bleak mid-winter, / Long ago. [*Mid-Winter*]

6 Remember me when I am gone away, / Gone far away into the silent land. [*Remember*]

7 Better by far you should forget and smile / Than that you should remember and be sad.

8 Darkness more clear than noonday holdeth her, / Silence more musical than any song. [*Rest*]

9 Who has seen the wind? / Neither you nor I; / But when the trees bow down their heads / The wind is passing by. [*Sing-Song*]

10 But pluck an ivy branch for me / Grown old before my time. [Song: *Oh Roses for the Flush*]

11 When I am dead, my dearest, / Sing no sad songs for me; / Plant thou no roses at my head, / Nor shady cypress tree; / Be the green grass above me / With showers and dewdrops wet; / And if thou wilt, remember, / And if thou wilt, forget. [Song: *When I am Dead, my Dearest*]

12 'Does the road wind up-hill all the way?' / 'Yes, to the very end.' / 'Will the day's journey take the whole long day?' / 'From morn to night, my friend.' [*Up-Hill*]

13 'May not the darkness hide it from my face?' / 'You cannot miss that inn.'

14 'Will there be beds for me and all who seek?' / 'Yea, beds for all who come.'

DANTE GABRIEL ROSSETTI 1828–1882

15 The blessed damozel leaned out / From the gold bar of heaven; / Her eyes were deeper than the depth / Of waters stilled at even; / She had three lilies in her hand / And the stars in her hair were seven. [*The Blessed Damozel*, 1]

16 Her hair that lay along her back / Was yellow like ripe corn. [2]

17 As low as where this earth / Spins like a fretful midge. [6]

18 And the souls mounting up to God / Went by her like thin flames. [7]

19 'Was it a friend or foe that spread these lies?' / 'Nay, who but infants question in such wise? / 'Twas one of my most intimate enemies.' [*Fragment*]

20 A sonnet is a moment's monument, – / Memorial from the Soul's eternity / To one dead deathless hour. [*The House of Life*, 1, Introduction]

21 'Tis visible silence, still as the hour-glass, / Deep in the sun-searched growths the dragon-fly / Hangs like a blue thread loosened from the sky: – / So this winged hour is dropped to us from above. [19, 'Silent Noon']

22 And though thy soul sail leagues and leagues beyond, – Still, leagues beyond those leagues, there is more sea. [73, 'The Choice']

23 This is that Lady Beauty, in whose praise / Thy voice and hand shake still, – long known to thee / By flying hair and fluttering hem, – the beat / Following her daily of thy heart and feet, / How passionately and irretrievably, / In what fond flight, how many ways and days! [77, 'Soul's Beauty']

24 I do not see them here; but after death / God knows I know the faces I shall see, / Each one a murdered self, with low last breath. / 'I am thyself, – what hast thou done to me?' / 'And I – and I – thyself' (lo! each one saith,) / 'And thou thyself to all eternity!' [86 'Lost Days']

25 My name is Might-have-been; / I am also called No-more, Too-late, Farewell. [97, 'A Superscription']

26 O Mother, Mary Mother, / Three days today, between Hell and Heaven. [*Sister Helen*]

1 I have been here before, / But when or how I cannot tell: / I know the grass beyond the door, / The sweet keen smell, / The sighing sound, the lights around the shore. [*Sudden Light*]

2 Conception, my boy, *fundamental brain-work*, is what makes the difference in all art. [Letter to Hall Caine, quoted in his *Recollections of Rossetti*]

3 The Stealthy School of Criticism. [Title of a letter to the *Athenaeum*, 1871]

GIOACCHINO ROSSINI 1792–1868

4 Give me a laundry-list and I'll set it to music. [Quoted in Evan Esar (ed.), *Treasury of Humorous Quotations*]

EDMOND ROSTAND 1868–1918

5 *Énorme, mon nez! / – Vil camus, sot camard, tête plate, apprenez / Que je m'enorgueillis d'un pareil appendice, / Attendu qu'un grand nez est proprement l'indice / D'un homme affable, bon, courtois, spirituel, / Libéral, courageux, tel que je suis.* – My nose is huge! Vile snub-nose, flat-nosed ass, flat-head, let me inform you that I am proud of such an appendage, since a big nose is the proper sign of a friendly, good, courteous, witty, liberal, and brave man, such as I am. [*Cyrano de Bergerac*, I. i]

6 *À la fin de l'envoi, je touche.* – At the end of the envoy, I shall strike [iv]

LEO C. ROSTEN 1908–

7 Anybody who hates dogs and babies can't be all bad. [Often misquoted as 'children and dogs' and wrongly attr. to W. C. Fields. Said *of* Fields at Masquers' Club Dinner, Hollywood, 16 Feb. 1939. See 163:13]

PHILIP ROTH 1933–

8 A Jewish man with parents alive is a fifteen-year-old boy, and will remain a fifteen-year-old boy till they die. [*Portnoy's Complaint*]

ROUGET DE LISLE 1760–1836

9 *Allons, enfants de la patrie, / Le jour de gloire est arrivé.* – Come, children of our native land. / The day of glory has arrived. [*La Marseillaise*]

10 *Aux armes, citoyens!* – To arms, citizens!

M. E. ROURKE 1867–1933

11 And when I told them how beautiful you are / They didn't believe me! They didn't believe me! [Song: *They Didn't Believe Me*, Music by Jerome D. Kern]

JEAN-JACQUES ROUSSEAU 1712–1778

12 *L'homme est né libre, et partout il est dans les fers.* – Man was born free, and everywhere he is in chains. [*Du contrat social*, Ch. 1]

13 Everything is good when it leaves the Creator's hands; everything degenerates in the hands of man. [*Émile*, I. i]

14 Happiness: a good bank account, a good cook, and a good digestion. [Quoted in Nat Shapiro (ed.), *An Encyclopedia of Quotations about Music*]

MARTIN ROUTH 1755–1854

15 You will find it a very good practice always to verify your references, sir. [Attr. by Burgon in *Quarterly Review* July 1878]

NICHOLAS ROWE 1674–1718

16 At length the morn and cold indifference came. [*The Fair Penitent*, I. i]

17 Is this that haughty, gallant, gay Lothario? [V. i]

RICHARD ROWLAND ?1881–1947

18 The lunatics have taken over the asylum. [Comment when United Artists was taken over by Chaplin, Pickford, Fairbanks and Griffith. Quoted in Leslie Halliwell, *The Filmgoer's Book of Quotes*]

'RED ROWLEY' 20 Cent.

19 Mademoiselle from Armenteers, / Hasn't been kissed for forty years, / Hinky pinky, parley-voo. [*Mademoiselle from Armentières*]

JEAN DE ROYE 1425–?

20 *Chronique scandaleuse.* – Scandalous Chronicle. [Title given to his Journal in the edn. of 1611]

PAUL RUBENS 1875–1917

21 We Don't Want To Lose You But We Think You Ought To Go. [Song: *Your King and Country Want You*]

DAMON RUNYON 1884–1946

1 My boy ... always try to rub up against money, for if you rub up against money long enough, some of it may rub off on you. [*Furthermore*, 'A Very Honourable Guy']

2 'In fact,' Sam the Gonoph says, 'I long ago came to the conclusion that all life is six to five against.' ['A Nice Price']

3 She is a smart old broad. It is a pity she is so nefarious. [*Runyon à la carte*, 'Broadway Incident']

4 These citizens are always willing to bet that what Nicely-Nicely dies of will be over-feeding and never anything small like pneumonia, for Nicely-Nicely is known far and wide as a character who dearly loves to commit eating. [*Take It Easy*, 'Lonely Heart']

5 He is without strict doubt a Hoorah Henry, and he is generally figured as nothing but a lob as far as doing anything useful in this world is concerned. ['Tight Shoes']

DEAN RUSK 1909–

6 We're eyeball to eyeball, and the other fellow just blinked. [On the Cuban missile crisis, 24 Oct. 1962. Quoted in Eric de Mauny, *Russian Prospect*]

JOHN RUSKIN 1819–1900

7 You hear of me, among others, as a respectable architectural man-milliner; and you send for me that I may tell you the leading fashion. [*The Crown of Wild Olive*, 'Traffic', §3]

8 I have seen, and heard, much of cockney impudence before now; but never expected to hear a coxcomb ask two hundred guineas for flinging a pot of paint in the public's face. [(Of Whistler's *Nocturne in Black and Gold*) *Fors Clavigera*, Letter 79]

9 A falseness in all our impressions of external things, which I would generally characterize as the 'pathetic fallacy'. [*Modern Painters*, Vol. III. Pt iv; Ch. 12]

10 Mountains are the beginning and the end of all natural scenery. [IV. v. 20, beginning]

11 Be sure that you go to the author to get at *his* meaning, not to find yours. [*Sesame and Lilies*, 1. §13]

12 Which of us ... is to do the hard and dirty work for the rest – and for what pay? Who is to do the pleasant and clean work, and for what pay? [§30, note]

13 When we build, let us think that we build for ever. [*The Seven Lamps of Architecture*, Ch. 5. §10]

14 Remember that the most beautiful things in the world are the most useless; peacocks and lilies for instance. [*The Stones of Venice*, I. Ch. 2. §17]

15 The purest and most thoughtful minds are those which love colour the most. [5.§30]

16 Fine art is that in which the hand, the head, and the heart of man go together. [*The Two Paths*, Lecture II]

17 Not only is there but one way of *doing* things rightly, but there is only one way of *seeing* them, and that is seeing the whole of them.

18 There is no wealth but Life. [*Unto this Last*, IV. §77]

19 Trust thou thy Love: if she be proud, is she not sweet? / Trust thou thy Love: if she be mute, is she not pure? / Lay thou thy soul full in her hands, low at her feet; – / Fail, sun and breath! – Yet for thy peace, she shall endure. [*Trust Thou Thy Love*]

20 Tell me what you like, and I'll tell you what you are. [Quoted by Dennis Potter in *With Great Pleasure*, Vol. II]

BERTRAND, LORD RUSSELL 1872–1970

21 Brief and powerless is Man's life; on him and all his race the slow, sure doom falls pitiless and dark. [*Mysticism and Logic*, 'A Free Man's Worship']

22 Mathematics possesses not only truth, but supreme beauty – a beauty cold and austere, like that of sculpture. [Ch. 4]

23 Mathematics may be defined as the subject in which we never know what we are talking about, nor whether what we are saying is true.

24 Matter ... a convenient formula for describing what happens where it isn't. [*An Outline of Philosophy*]

25 What men really want is not knowledge but certainty. [Quoted by G. M. Carstairs in the *Listener*, 30 July 1964]

26 Many people would sooner die than think.

In fact they do. [Quoted as epigraph in A. Flew, *Thinking About Thinking*]

1 Patriots always talk of dying for their country, and never of killing for their country. [Attr.]

LORD JOHN RUSSELL 1792–1878

2 Among the defects of the Bill, which were numerous, one provision was conspicuous by its presence and another by its absence. [Speech to his constituents, Apr. 1859]

3 A proverb is one man's wit and all men's wisdom. [Attr.]

SIR WILLIAM RUSSELL 1820–1907

4 [The Russians] dash on towards the thin red line tipped with steel. [*The British Expedition to the Crimea*]

GILBERT RYLE 1900–1976

5 The dogma of the Ghost in the Machine. [*The Concept of Mind*, Ch. 1]

6 So too Plato was, in my view, a very unreliable Platonist. He was too much of a philosopher to think that anything he had said was the last word. [*Dilemmas*, Ch. 1]

S

WINIFRED SACKVILLE STONER JUN.

1 In fourteen hundred and ninety-two / Columbus sailed the ocean blue. [Quoted in the *Observer*, 10 Feb. 1991]

VICTORIA SACKVILLE-WEST 1892–1962

2 The greater cats with golden eyes / Stare out between the bars. [*King's Daughter*, II. 1]

MICHAEL SADLEIR 1888–1952

3 Fanny by Gaslight. [Title of book]

MORT SAHL 1926–

4 Would you buy a second-hand car from this man? [Of President Nixon, attr.]

CHARLES-AUGUSTIN SAINTE- BEUVE 1804–1869

5 Et Vigny, plus secret, / Comme en son tour d'ivoire, avant midi, rentrait. – And Vigny, more discreet, as if in his ivory tower, returned before noon. [*À M. Villemain*]

6 Every additional man who learns to read is another reader for Molière. [*Portraits littéraires*, Vol. ii]

ANTOINE DE SAINT-EXUPÉRY 1900–1944

7 Grown-ups never understand anything for themselves, and it is tiresome for children to be always and forever explaining things to them. [*The Little Prince*, Ch. 1]

JOHN L. ST JOHN 20 Cent.

8 Archibald – certainly not! [Title of song]

MARQUIS DE SAINT-LAMBERT 1716–1803

9 *Souvent j'écoute encor quand le chant a cessé.* – Often I am still listening when the song is over. [*Les Saisons*, 'Le Printemps']

W. ST LEGER 1850–c. 1915

10 There is a fine stuffed chavender, / A chavender, or chub, / That decks the rural pavender, / The pavender, or pub, / Wherein I eat my gravender, / My gravender or grub. [*A False Gallop of Analogies*]

SAKI [H. H. MUNRO] 1870–1916

11 You can't expect a boy to be depraved until he has been to a good school. [*A Baker's Dozen*]

12 'The man is a common murderer.'
'A common murderer, possibly, but a very uncommon cook.' [*The Blind Spot*]

13 Addresses are given to us to conceal our whereabouts. [*Cross Currents*]

14 'I believe I take precedence,' he said coldly; 'you are merely the club Bore: I am the club Liar.' [*A Defensive Diamond*]

15 Waldo is one of those people who would be enormously improved by death. [*The Feast of Nemesis*]

16 Children with Hyacinth's temperament don't know better as they grow older; they merely know more. [*Hyacinth*]

1 In baiting a mouse-trap with cheese, always leave room for the mouse. [*The Infernal Parliament*]

2 I might have been a gold-fish in a glass bowl for all the privacy I got. [*The Innocence of Reginald*]

3 The people of Crete unfortunately make more history than they can consume locally. [*The Jesting of Arlington Stringham*]

4 He's simply got the instinct for being unhappy highly developed. [*The Match-Maker*]

5 There's nothing in Christianity or Buddhism that quite matches the sympathetic unselfishness of an oyster.

6 The cook was a good cook, as cooks go; and as cooks go she went. [*Reginald on Besetting Sins*]

7 People may say what they like about the decay of Christianity; the religious system that produced green Chartreuse can never really die. [*Reginald on Christmas Presents*]

8 I always say beauty is only sin deep. [*Reginald's Choir Treat*]

9 His 'Noontide Peace', a study of two dun cows under a walnut tree, was followed by 'A Mid-day Sanctuary', a study of a walnut tree with two dun cows under it. [*The Stalled Ox*]

10 This story has no moral. If it points out an evil, at any rate it suggests no remedy. [*The Unbearable Bassington*, author's note]

11 A woman whose dresses are made in Paris and whose marriage has been made in Heaven might be equally biased for and against free imports. [Ch. 9]

12 Sherard Blaw, the dramatist who had discovered himself, and who had given so ungrudgingly of his discovery to the world. [13]

J. D. SALINGER 1919–

13 Sex is something I really don't understand too hot. You never know *where* the hell you are. I keep making up these sex rules for myself, and then I break them right away. [*The Catcher in the Rye*, Ch. 9]

14 They didn't act like people and they didn't act like actors. It's hard to explain. They acted more like they knew they were celebrities and all. I mean they were good, but they were *too* good. [17]

15 The trouble with girls is, if they like a boy, no matter how big a bastard he is, they'll say he has an inferiority complex, and if they *don't* like him, no matter how nice a guy he is, or how big an inferiority complex he has, they'll say he's conceited. Even smart girls do it. [18]

16 Sally said I was a sacrilegious atheist. I probably am. The thing Jesus *really* would've liked would be the guy that plays the kettle drums in the orchestra.

17 For Esmé, With Love and Squalor. [Title of story]

18 Poetry, surely, is a crisis, perhaps the only actionable one we can call our own. [*Seymour: An Introduction*]

19 A confessional passage has probably never been written that didn't stink a little bit of the writer's pride in having given up his pride.

20 One of the thousand reasons I quit going to the theatre when I was about twenty was that I resented like hell filing out of the theatre just because some playwright was forever slamming down his silly curtain.

LORD SALISBURY 1830–1903

21 We are part of the community of Europe and we must do our duty as such. [Speech at Caernarvon, 10 Apr. 1888]

22 By office boys for office boys. [Description of the *Daily Mail*]

SALLUST 86–34 BC

23 Coveting other men's property, and squandering his own. [*Catiline*, 5]

24 To like and dislike the same things, that is indeed true friendship. [20]

COMTE DE SALVANDY 1795–1856

25 We are dancing on a volcano. [Said just before the revolution of 1830]

LORD SAMUEL 1870–1963

26 A difficulty for every solution. [Of the Civil Service. Attr.]

CARL SANDBURG 1878–1967

27 When Abraham Lincoln was shovelled into the tombs, / he forgot the copperheads and the

assassin ... / in the dust, in the cool tombs. [*Cool Tombs*]

1 The fog comes / on little cat feet. [*Fog*]

2 Pile the bodies high at Austerlitz and Waterloo, / Shovel them under and let me work – / I am the grass; I cover all. [*Grass*]

3 Sometime they'll give a war and nobody will come. [*The People, Yes.*]

4 Hog Butcher for the World. [Of Chicago in *Chicago*]

5 Poetry is the achievement of the synthesis of hyacinths and biscuits. ['Poetry Considered', in the *Atlantic Monthly*, Mar. 1923]

6 Slang is a language that rolls up its sleeves, spits on its hands and goes to work. [In *The New York Times*, 13 Feb. 1959]

IRA D. SANKEY 1840–1908

7 Gather with the saints at the river, / That flows by the throne of God. [*Sacred Songs*, 'Shall We Gather']

8 In the sweet by-and-by, / We shall meet on that beautiful shore. ['Sweet By-and-by']

GEORGE SANTAYANA 1863–1952

9 The Bible is literature, not dogma. [*Introduction to the Ethics of Spinoza*]

10 Progress far from consisting in change, depends on retentiveness ... Those who do not remember the past are condemned to repeat it. [*The Life of Reason*, Vol. i. Ch. 12]

11 England is the paradise of individuality, eccentricity, heresy, anomalies, hobbies, and humours. [*Soliloquies in England*, 'The British Character']

12 Friendship is almost always the union of a part of one mind with a part of another; people are friends in spots. ['Friendships']

13 There is no cure for birth and death save to enjoy the interval. ['War Shrines']

14 It is a great advantage for a system of philosophy to be substantially true. [*The Unknowable*]

15 Life is not a spectacle or a feast; it is a predicament. [Quoted in Sagittarius and D. George, *The Perpetual Pessimist*]

EPES SARGENT 1813–1880

16 A life on the ocean wave, / A home on the rolling deep. [*A Life on the Ocean Wave*. These

lines were taken from a song by Samuel J. Arnold (see 13:6)]

JOHN SINGER SARGENT 1856–1925

17 A portrait is a picture in which there is just a tiny little something not quite right about the mouth. [Quoted in Donald Hall and Pat Corrington-Wykes (eds.), *Anecdotes of Modern Art*]

18 Every time I paint a portrait I lose a friend. [Quoted in Evan Esar (ed.), *Treasury of Humorous Quotations*]

JEAN-PAUL SARTRE 1905–1980

19 When one does nothing, one believes oneself responsible for everything. [*Altona*, I]

20 Man is a useless passion. [*Being and Nothingness* Pt IV, Ch. 2]

21 In reality, people read because they want to write. Anyway, reading is a sort of rewriting. [*Between Existentialism and Marxism*. 'The Purposes of Writing']

22 Man is condemned to be free. [*Existentialism is a Humanism*]

23 Hell is other people. [*Huis clos*, Sc. v (English title: *In Camera*)]

24 Three o'clock is always too late or too early for anything you want to do. [*Nausea*, trans. Robert Baldick]

25 At the time, a refined family had to include at least one delicate child. I was a perfect subject because I had some thought of dying at birth. [*Words*, trans. Irene Clephane]

26 Polite Society believed in God so that it need not talk of Him.

SIEGFRIED SASSOON 1886–1967

27 If I were fierce and bald and short of breath, / I'd live with scarlet Majors at the Base, / And speed glum heroes up the line to death. [*Base Details*]

28 I'd like to see a Tank come down the stalls, / Lurching to rag-time tunes, or 'Home, sweet Home', / And there'd be no more jokes in Music-halls / To mock the riddled corpses round Bapaume. ['*Blighters*']

29 Soldiers are citizens of death's grey land, / Drawing no dividend from time's tomorrows. [*Dreamers*]

30 Everyone suddenly burst out singing. [*Everyone Sang*]

1 The song was wordless; / The singing will never be done.

2 'He's a cheery old card,' grunted Harry to Jack / As they slogged up to Arras with rifle and pack ... / But he did for them both by his plan of attack. [*The General*]

3 I am making this statement as a wilful defiance of military authority because I believe that the War is being deliberately prolonged by those who have the power to end it. [Letter quoted in *Memoirs of an Infantry Officer*, X. 3]

RICHARD SAVAGE 1698–1743

4 No tenth transmitter of a foolish face. [*The Bastard*, 8]

HENRY SAYERS 1855–1932

5 Ta-ra-ra-boom-de-ay! [Title of song]

FRIEDRICH VON SCHELLING 1775–1854

6 It [architecture] is music in space, as it were a frozen music. [*Die Philosophie der Kunst*, p. 576. See also 180:13]

FRIEDRICH VON SCHILLER 1759–1805

7 *Freude, schöner Götterfunken, / Tochter aus Elysium.* – Joy, lovely radiance of the god, thou daughter of Elysium. [*An die Freude*]

8 *Alle Menschen werden Brüder.* – All men become brothers.

9 *Seid umschlungen, Millionen!* – Embrace one another, ye millions!

10 *Sieh da! sieh da, Timotheus, / Die Kraniche des Ibykus!* – See there, see there, Timotheus, the cranes of Ibykus! [*Die Kraniche des Ibykus*]

11 *Die Weltgeschichte ist das Weltgericht.* – World history is the world's court of judgement. [*Resignation*]

12 *Die Sonne geht in meinem Staat nicht unter.* – The sun does not set in my dominions. [(Philip II) *Don Carlos*, I. vi. See also 295:16]

13 *Mit der Dummheit kämpfen Götter selbst vergebens.* – Against stupidity the gods themselves struggle in vain. [*Die Jungfrau von Orleans*, III. vi]

14 *Ein ruheloser Marsch war unser Leben / Und wie des Windes Sausen, heimatlos, / Durchstürmten wir die kriegbewegte Erde.* – Our life was but a battle and a march / And like the wind's blast, never-resting, homeless, / We stormed across the war-convulsèd heath. [*Wallensteins Tod*, III. 15, trans. Coleridge]

FRIEDRICH VON SCHLEGEL 1772–1829

15 A historian is a prophet in reverse. [*Athenäum*, I, 'Fragmente']

16 Revolution from above. [*Concordia*, 38]

F. E. D. SCHLEIERMACHER 1768–1834

17 To be silent in seven languages. [Of the philologist, Immanuel Becker, attr.]

FIELD MARSHAL VON SCHLIEFFEN 1833–1913

18 When you march into France, let the last man on the right brush the Channel with his sleeve. [Of the Schlieffen plan. Quoted in B. Tuchman, *The Guns of August*, Ch. 2]

ARTUR SCHNABEL 1882–1951

19 Interpretation is a free walk on firm ground. [*My Life and Music*, II. 10]

20 The notes I handle no better than many pianists. But the pauses between the notes – ah, that is where the art resides. [Quoted in the *Chicago Daily News*, 11 June. 1958]

21 The sonatas of Mozart are unique; they are too easy for children, and too difficult for artists. [Quoted in Nat Shapiro (ed.), *An Encyclopedia of Quotations about Music*]

MAX SCHNECKENBURGER 1819–1849

22 *Die Wacht am Rhein.* – The Watch on the Rhine. [Title of song]

LOUIS SCHNEIDER 1805–1878

23 *O Tannenbaum, O Tannenbaum, / Wie grün sind deine Blätter.* – O pine-tree, O pine-tree, / How green are your leaves! [*Der Kurmärker und die Picarde*. Modernization of lines from a folksong, previously rendered by August Zarnack (1777–1827): 'Wie treu sind deine Blätter']

ARNOLD SCHOENBERG 1874–1951

24 Very well, I can wait. [Attr. remark when told his violin concerto needed a soloist with six fingers. Quoted in Nat Shapiro (ed.), *An Encyclo-*

pedia of Quotations about Music. Another version is: 'I want the little finger to become longer. I can wait.']

ARTHUR SCHOPENHAUER 1788–1860

1 To be alone is the fate of all great minds – a fate deplored at times, but still always chosen as the less grievous of two evils. [*Aphorismen zur Lebensweisheit, 'Von dem was Einer ist'*]

2 Intellect is invisible to the man who has none. ['*Von dem was Einer vorstellt*']

3 Every parting gives a foretaste of death; every coming together again a foretaste of the resurrection. [*Gedanken über vielerlei Gegenstände, XXVI, 'Psychologische Bemerkungen'*]

4 The fundamental fault of the female character is that it has no sense of justice. [XXVII, '*über die Weiber*']

CHARLES M. SCHULZ 1922–

5 Happiness is a Warm Puppy. [Title of book]

6 Good Grief, Charlie Brown. [Catch phrase in cartoon strip]

E. F. SCHUMACHER 1911–1977

7 Small is Beautiful. [Title of book subtitled *A Study of Economics as if People Mattered*]

SCIPIO AFRICANUS 236–184? BC

8 Never less idle than when unoccupied, nor less alone than when without company. [Quoted by Cicero, *De Officiis*, III. i]

C. P. SCOTT 1846–1932

9 Comment is free but facts are sacred. [*Manchester Guardian*, 5 May 1921]

CAPTAIN R. F. SCOTT 1868–1912

10 For God's sake look after our people. [*Journal*, 29 Mar. 1912]

SIR WALTER SCOTT 1771–1832

11 To the Lords of Convention 'twas Claver'se who spoke. ['Bonny Dundee', *The Doom of Devorgoil*, II. 2]

12 Come fill up my cup, come fill up my can, / Come saddle your horses, and call up your men; / Come open the West Port, and let me gang free, / And it's room for the bonnets of Bonny Dundee.

13 Look back, and smile at perils past. [*The Bridal of Triermain*, Introduction, ii]

14 But answer came there none. [III. 10]

15 The stag at eve had drunk his fill, / When danced the moon on Monan's rill. [*The Lady of the Lake*, I. 1]

16 In listening mood, she seemed to stand, / The guardian Naiad of the strand. [17]

17 Forward and frolic glee was there, / The will to do, the soul to dare. [21]

18 Yet seemed that tone, and gesture bland, / Less used to sue than to command.

19 Soldier, rest! thy warfare o'er, / Dream of fighting fields no more: / Sleep the sleep that knows not breaking. / Morn of toil, nor night of waking. [31]

20 Hail to the chief who in triumph advances! [II. 19]

21 Like the dew on the mountain, / Like the foam on the river, / Like the bubble on the fountain, / Thou art gone, and for ever. [III. 16]

22 And the stern joy which warriors feel / In foemen worthy of their steel. [V. 10]

23 The way was long, the wind was cold, / The Minstrel was infirm and old; / His withered cheek and tresses grey / Seemed to have known a better day. [*The Lay of the Last Minstrel*, Introduction]

24 The unpremeditated lay.

25 To her bidding she could bow / The viewless forms of air. [I. 12]

26 If thou wouldst view fair Melrose aright, / Go visit it by the pale moonlight. [II. 1]

27 Love rules the court, the camp, the grove, / And men below, and saints above; / For love is heaven, and heaven is love. [III. 2]

28 For ne'er / Was flattery lost on poet's ear: / A simple race! they waste their toil / For the vain tribute of a smile. [IV, Conclusion]

29 Call it not vain; they do not err, / Who say, that when the Poet dies, / Mute Nature mourns her worshipper, / And celebrates his obsequies. [V. 1]

30 True love's the gift which God has given / To man alone beneath the heaven. [13]

31 Breathes there the man, with soul so dead,

/ Who never to himself hath said, / This is my own, my native land! [VI. 1]

1 The wretch, concentred all in self, / Living, shall forfeit fair renown, / And, doubly dying, shall go down / To the vile dust from whence he sprung, / Unwept, unhonoured, and unsung.

2 O Caledonia! stern and wild, / Meet nurse for a poetic child! / Land of brown heath and shaggy wood, / Land of the mountain and the flood, / Land of my sires! [VI. 2]

3 That day of wrath, that dreadful day, / When heaven and earth shall pass away. [31]

4 His bright and brief career is o'er. [*The Lord of the Isles*, IV. 11]

5 O! many a shaft, at random sent / Finds mark the archer little meant! / And many a word, at random spoken, / May soothe or wound a heart that's broken! [V. 28]

6 To that dark inn, the grave! [VI. 26]

7 O hush thee, my babie, thy sire was a knight, / Thy mother a lady, both lovely and bright. [*Lullaby of an Infant Chief*]

8 November's sky is chill and drear, / November's leaf is red and sear. [*Marmion*, I, Introduction]

9 But search the land of living men, / Where wilt thou find their like agen! [I. 11]

10 And come he slow, or come he fast, / It is but Death who comes at last. [II. 30]

11 O, young Lochinvar is come out of the west, / Through all the wide Border his steed was the best. [V.12]

12 So faithful in love, and so dauntless in war, / There never was knight like the young Lochinvar.

13 With a smile on her lips, and a tear in her eye.

14 Heap on more wood! the wind is chill; / But let it whistle as it will. / We'll keep our Christmas merry still. [VI, Introduction]

15 England was merry England, when / Old Christmas brought his sports again.

16 And dar'st thou then / To beard the lion in his den, / The Douglas in his hall? [14]

17 What, warder, ho! / Let the portcullis fall.

18 O, what a tangled web we weave, / When first we practise to deceive! [17]

19 O Woman! In our hours of ease, / Uncer-

tain, coy, and hard to please, / And variable as the shade / By the light quivering aspen made; / When pain and anguish wring the brow, / A ministering angel thou! [30]

20 'Charge, Chester, charge! On, Stanley, on!' / Were the last words of Marmion. [32]

21 The stubborn spear-men still made good / Their dark impenetrable wood, / Each stepping where his comrade stood, / The instant that he fell. [34]

22 Come as the winds come, when / Forests are rended; / Come as the waves come, when / Navies are stranded! [*Pibroch of Donuil Dhu*]

23 Still are the thoughts to memory dear. [*Rokeby*, I. 33]

24 A weary lot is thine, fair maid, / A weary lot is thine. [III. 28]

25 Whirled them to the back o'beyont. [*The Antiquary*, Ch. 2]

26 Look not thou on beauty's charming, – / Sit thou still while kings are arming, – / Taste not when the wine-cup glistens, – / Speak not when the people listens, – / Stop thine ear against the singer, – / From the red gold keep thy finger; – / Vacant heart and hand, and eye, – / Easy live and quiet die. [*The Bride of Lammermoor*, Ch. 3]

27 It's ill taking the breeks aff a wild Highlandman. [*The Fair Maid of Perth*, Ch. 5]

28 For a con-si-de-ra-tion. [22]

29 Ever after designated as a 'stickit minister'. [*Guy Mannering*, Ch. 2]

30 MRS BERTRAM: That sounds like nonsense, my dear.

MR BERTRAM: May be so, my dear; but it may be very good law for all that. [9]

31 'Pro-di-gi-ous!' exclaimed Dominie Sampson. [14]

32 The ancient and now forgotten pastime of high jinks. [36]

33 The hour is come, but not the man. [*The Heart of Midlothian*, Ch. 4, heading]

34 Proud Maisie is in the wood, / Walking so early, / Sweet Robin sits in the bush, / Singing so rarely. [40]

35 There is a Southern proverb, – fine words butter no parsnips. [*The Legend of Montrose*, Ch. 3]

36 And it's ill speaking between a fou man

and a fasting. [*Redgauntlet*, Letter 11. 'Wandering Willie's Tale']

1 Come weal, come woe, we'll gather and go, / And live or die with Charlie. [Ch. 11]

2 Among the sea of upturned faces which bent their eyes on the pulpit as a common centre. [*Rob Roy*, Ch. 20]

3 If your honour disna ken when ye hae a gude servant, I ken when I hae a gude master. [24]

4 There's a gude time coming. [32]

5 My foot is on my native heath, and my name is MacGregor! [34]

6 The play-bill, which is said to have announced the tragedy of Hamlet, the character of the Prince of Denmark being left out. [*The Talisman*, Introduction]

7 My heart's in the Highlands, my heart is not here, / My heart's in the Highlands a-chasing the deer. [*Waverley*, Ch. 28]

8 But I must say to the Muse of fiction, as the Earl of Pembroke said to the ejected nun of Wilton, 'Go spin, you jade, go spin!' [*Journal*, 9 Feb. 1826]

9 The Big Bow-Wow strain I can do myself like anyone now going; but the exquisite touch, which renders ordinary commonplace things and characters interesting, from the truth of the description and the sentiment, is denied to me. [(Of Jane Austen) 14 Mar.]

10 I would like to be there, were it but to see how the cat jumps. [7 Oct.]

11 From the lone shieling of the misty island / Mountains divide us and the waste of seas – / Yet still the blood is strong, the heart is Highland, / And we in dreams behold the Hebrides! [*Canadian Boat Song* (authorship disputed)]

WILLIAM SCOTT, LORD STOWELL 1745–1836

12 The elegant simplicity of the three per cents. [Lord Campbell, *Lives of the Chancellors*, Vol. x Ch. 212]

13 A dinner lubricates business. [Boswell, *Life of Johnson*, 1781]

14 A precedent embalms a principle. [Attr. opinion, while Advocate-General]

RONALD SEARLE 1920–

15 The Terror of St Trinian's. [Title of book by D. B. Wyndham Lewis (Timothy Shy) and illustrated by Searle]

E. H. SEARS 1810–1876

16 It came upon the midnight clear, / That glorious song of old, / From Angels bending near the earth / To touch their harps of gold; / 'Peace on the earth; good will to man / From Heaven's all gracious King.' / The world in solemn stillness lay / To hear the angels sing. [*That Glorious Song of Old*]

GENERAL SEBASTIANI 1772–1851

17 At the moment of writing, calm [or 'order'] reigned in Warsaw. [After brutal suppression of the Polish rising, 1831]

SIR CHARLES SEDLEY 1639?–1701

18 Love still has something of the sea / From whence his mother rose. [*Love still has Something*]

19 Not, Celia, that I juster am / Or better than the rest. [*Not, Celia, that I juster am*]

20 When change itself can give no more, / 'Tis easy to be true.

21 Phyllis is my only joy, / Faithless as the winds or seas; / Sometimes coming, sometimes coy, / Yet she never fails to please. [*Phyllis is my only Joy*]

22 Phyllis, without frown or smile, / Sat and knotted all the while. [*Phyllis Knotting*]

ALAN SEEGER 1888–1916

23 I have a rendezvous with Death / At some disputed barricade. [*I Have a Rendezvous with Death*]

PETE SEEGER 1919–

24 Where have all the flowers gone? / Young girls picked them every one. [Song: *Where Have All the Flowers Gone?* Words by Derek Collyer 1936–85 and David Cummings 1934–]

SIR J. R. SEELEY 1834–1895

25 We seem, as it were, to have conquered and peopled half the world in a fit of absence of mind. [*The Expansion of England*, Lecture I]

ERICH SEGAL 1937–

26 Love means never having to say you're sorry. [Last line of film *Love Story*, screenplay by Erich Segal]

JOHN SELDEN 1584–1654

1 Old friends are best. King James used to call for his old shoes; they were easiest for his feet. [*Table Talk* 47]

2 'Tis not the eating, nor 'tis not the drinking, that is to be blamed, but the excess. [54]

3 Commonly we say a judgement falls on a man for something in him we cannot abide. [67]

4 A king is a thing men have made for their own sakes, for quietness' sake. Just as if in a family one man is appointed to buy the meat. [71]

5 Ignorance of the law excuses no man: not that all men know the law, but because 'tis an excuse every man will plead, and no man can tell how to refute him. [77]

6 Take a straw and throw it up into the air, you shall see by that which way the wind is. [81]

7 Marriage is nothing but a civil contract. [85]

8 There never was a merry world since the fairies left off dancing, and the parson left conjuring. [99]

9 Pleasure is nothing else but the intermission of pain. [104]

10 Pleasures are all alike simply considered in themselves ... He that takes pleasure to hear sermons enjoys himself as much as he that hears plays.

11 Preachers say, Do as I say, not as I do. [111]

GEORGE SELDES 1890–1970

12 Sawdust Caesar. [Title of biography of Benito Mussolini]

H. GORDON SELFRIDGE 1857–1947

13 The customer is always right. [Shop slogan]

W. C. SELLAR 1898–1951
and R. J. YEATMAN 1897–1968

14 1066 and All That. [Title of book]

15 The Roman Conquest was, however, a *Good Thing*. [Ch. 1]

16 The Venomous Bead (author of *The Rosary*). [3]

17 The Memorable Round Table made to have the Conferences at, so that it was impossible to say who was top knight. [6]

18 Whenever he returned to England he always set out again immediately for the Mediterranean and was therefore known as Richard Gare de Lyon. [17]

19 '*Honi soie qui mal y pense*' ('Honey, your silk stocking's hanging down'). [24]

20 Finding, however, that he was not memorable, he very patriotically abdicated in favour of Henry IV, part II. [26]

21 Lumbago and the Laxative Islands. [41]

22 Napoleon's armies always used to march on their stomachs, shouting: 'Vive l'Intérieur!' [48]

23 America became top nation and history came to a full stop. [62]

ROBERT W. SERVICE 1874–1958

24 Ah! the clock is always slow; / It is later than you think. [*It is Later than You Think*]

25 This is the Law of the Yukon, that only the Strong shall thrive; / That surely the Weak shall perish, and only the Fit survive. [*The Law of the Yukon*]

26 Back of the bar, in a solo game, sat Dangerous Dan McGrew, / And watching his luck was his light o' love, the lady that's known as Lou. [*The Shooting of Dan McGrew*]

MME DE SÉVIGNÉ 1626–1696

27 The more I see of men, the more I admire dogs. [Attr.]

W. H. SEWARD 1801–1872

28 But there is a higher law than the Constitution. [Speech in U S Senate, 11 Mar. 1850]

EDWARD SEXBY ?–1658

29 Killing no murder Briefly Discourst in Three Questions. [Title of pamphlet, 1657]

THOMAS SHADWELL 1642?–1692

30 Words may be false and full of art; / Sighs are the natural language of the heart. [*Psyche*, III]

31 And wit's the noblest frailty of the mind. [*A True Widow*, II. i]

1 Instantly, in the twinkling of a bed-staff. [*Virtuoso*, I. i]

ANTHONY ASHLEY COOPER, EARL OF SHAFTESBURY 1621–1683

2 Men of sense are really but of one religion ... 'Pray, my lord, what religion is that which men of sense agree in?' 'Madam,' says the earl immediately, 'men of sense never tell it.' [Onslow's note in Bishop Burnet, *History of My Own Time*, Vol. i. Bk ii. Ch. 1]

WILLIAM SHAKESPEARE 1564–1616

References are to the Oxford single-volume edn., ed. Craig.

Line references in scenes containing prose are in round brackets.

All's Well that Ends Well

3 It were all one / That I should love a bright particular star / And think to wed it, he is so above me. [I. i. (97)]

4 The hind that would be mated by the lion / Must die for love. [(103)]

5 Your old virginity is like one of our French withered pears; it looks ill, it eats drily. [(176)]

6 Our remedies oft in ourselves do lie, / Which we ascribe to heaven. [(235)]

7 My friends were poor but honest. [iii. (203)]

8 They say miracles are past. [II. iii. (1)]

9 A young man married is a man that's marred. [(315)]

10 The web of our life is of a mingled yarn, good and ill together. [IV. iii. (83)]

11 There's place and means for every man alive. [(379)]

12 Praising what is lost / Makes the remembrance dear. [V. iii. 19]

13 Mine eyes smell onions; I shall weep anon. [(325)]

Antony and Cleopatra

14 The triple pillar of the world transformed / Into a strumpet's fool. [I. i. 12]

15 There's beggary in the love that can be reckoned. [15]

16 Let Rome in Tiber melt, and the wide arch / Of the ranged empire fall! Here is my space. / Kingdoms are clay. [33]

17 In Nature's infinite book of secrecy / A little I can read. [ii. (11)]

18 I love long life better than figs. [(34)]

19 Mine, and most of our fortunes, to-night, shall be, – drunk to bed. [(47)]

20 Eternity was in our lips and eyes, / Bliss in our brows. [iii. 135]

21 Though age from folly could not give me freedom, / It does from childishness. [57]

22 Give me to drink mandragora. [v. 4]

23 That I might sleep out this great gap of time / My Antony is away. [5]

24 Where's my serpent of Old Nile? [25]

25 A morsel for a monarch. [31]

26 My salad days, / When I was green in judgement. [73]

27 No worse a husband than the best of men. [II. ii. 135]

28 The barge she sat in, like a burnished throne, / Burned on the water; the poop was beaten gold, / Purple the sails, and so perfumed, that / The winds were lovesick with them, the oars were silver / Which to the tune of flutes kept stroke, and made / The water which they beat to follow faster, / As amorous of their strokes. For her own person, / It beggared all description. [(199)]

29 The air; which, but for vacancy, / Had gone to gaze on Cleopatra too / And made a gap in nature. [(224)]

30 Age cannot wither her, nor custom stale / Her infinite variety; other women cloy / The appetites they feed. [(243)]

31 Music, moody food / Of us that trade in love. [v. 1]

32 Let's to billiards. [3]

33 Though it be honest, it is never good / To bring bad news. [85]

34 What manner o' thing is your crocodile? [vii. (47)]

35 Ambition, / The soldier's virtue. [III. i. 22]

36 Celerity is never more admired / Than by the negligent. [vii. 24]

37 We have kissed away / Kingdoms and provinces. [viii. 17]

38 I found you as a morsel, cold upon / Dead Caesar's trencher. [xi. 116]

39 Let's have one other gaudy night. [182]

1 Unarm, Eros; the long day's task is done / And we must sleep. [IV. xii. 35]

2 But I will be / A bridegroom in my death, and run into 't / As to a lover's bed. [99]

3 I am dying, Egypt, dying. [xiii. 18]

4 O! withered is the garland of the war, / The solider's pole is fallen; young boys and girls / Are level now with men; the odds is gone, / And there is nothing left remarkable / Beneath the visiting moon. [64]

5 Let's do it after the high Roman fashion, / And make death proud to take us. [87]

6 For his bounty, / There was no winter in't; an autumn 'twas / That grew the more by reaping . . . [V. ii. 86]

7 The bright day is done, / And we are for the dark. [192]

8 I shall see / Some squeaking Cleopatra boy my greatness. [218]

9 His biting is immortal; those that do die of it do seldom or never recover. [(246)]

10 I wish you joy o' the worm. [(281)]

11 Give me my robe, put on my crown; I have / Immortal longings in me. [(282)]

12 Dost thou not see my baby at my breast, / That sucks the nurse asleep? [(302)]

13 Now boast thee, death, in thy possession lies / A lass unparalleled. [(317)]

As You Like It

14 Fleet the time carelessly, as they did in the golden world. [I. i. (126)]

15 Let us sit and mock the good housewife Fortune from her wheel, that her gifts may henceforth be bestowed equally. [ii. (35)]

16 How now, wit! whither wander you? [(60)]

17 Well said: that was laid on with a trowel. [(113)]

18 Your heart's desires be with you! [(214)]

19 One out of suits with fortune. [(263)]

20 My pride fell with my fortunes. [(269)]

21 Hereafter in a better world than this, / I shall desire more love and knowledge of you. [ii. (301)]

22 O, how full of briers is this working-day world! [iii. (12)]

23 Beauty provoketh thieves sooner than gold. [(113)]

24 We'll have a swashing and a martial outside, / As many other mannish cowards have / That do outface it with their semblances. [(123)]

25 Sweet are the uses of adversity, / Which, like the toad, ugly and venomous, / Wears yet a precious jewel in his head; / And this our life, exempt from public haunt, / Finds tongues in trees, books in the running brooks, / Sermons in stones, and good in everything. [II. i. 12]

26 The big round tears / Coursed one another down his innocent nose, / In piteous chase. [38]

27 'Poor deer,' quoth he, 'thou makest a testament / As worldlings do, giving thy sum of more. / To that which had too much.' [47]

28 Sweep on, you fat and greasy citizens! [55]

29 For in my youth I never did apply / Hot and rebellious liquors to the blood. [iii. 48]

30 Therefore my age is as the lusty winter, / Frosty, but kindly. [52]

31 O good old man! how well in thee appears / The constant service of the antique world, / When service sweat for duty, not for meed! / Thou art not for the fashion of these times, / Where none will sweat but for promotion. [56]

32 Ay, now am I in Arden; the more fool I: when I was at home, I was in a better place: but travellers must be content. [iv. (16)]

33 If thou remember'st not the slightest folly / That ever love did make thee run into, / Thou has not loved. [(34)]

34 We that are true lovers run into strange capers. [(53)]

35 Thou speakest wiser than thou art ware of. [(57)]

36 I shall ne'er be ware of mine own wit till I break my shins against it. [(59)]

37 Under the greenwood tree / Who loves to lie with me, / And turn his merry note / Unto the sweet bird's throat, / Come hither, come hither, come hither: / Here shall he see / No enemy / But winter and rough weather. [v. 1]

38 I can suck melancholy out of a song, as a weasel sucks eggs. [(12)]

39 Who doth ambition shun, / And loves to live i' the sun, / Seeking the food he eats, / And pleased with what he gets. [(38)]

40 I'll rail against all the first-born of Egypt. [(60)]

1 A fool, a fool! I met a fool i' the forest, / A motley fool. [vii. 12]

2 And railed on Lady Fortune in good terms, / In good set terms. [16]

3 And then he drew a dial from his poke, / And looking on it with lack-lustre eye, / Says, very wisely, 'It is ten o'clock; / Thus may we see,' quoth he, 'how the world wags.' [20]

4 And so, from hour to hour we ripe and ripe, / And then from hour to hour we rot and rot, / And thereby hangs a tale. [26]

5 My lungs began to crow like chanticleer, / That fools should be so deep-contemplative, / And I did laugh sans intermission / An hour by his dial. [30]

6 Motley's the only wear. [34]

7 And says, if ladies be but young and fair, / They have the gift to know it; and in his brain, – / Which is as dry as the remainder biscuit / After a voyage, – he hath strange places crammed / With observation, the which he vents / In mangled forms. [37]

8 I must have liberty / Withal, as large a charter as the wind, / To blow on whom I please. [47]

9 The 'why' is plain as way to parish church. [52]

10 Whate'er you are / That in this desert inaccessible, / Under the shade of melancholy boughs, / Lose and neglect the creeping hours of time; / If ever you have looked on better days. [109]

11 All the world's a stage, / And all the men and women merely players: / They have their exits and their entrances; / And one man in his time plays many parts, / His acts being seven ages. At first the infant, / Mewling and puking in the nurse's arms. / And then the whining school-boy, with his satchel / And shining morning face, creeping like snail / Unwillingly to school. And then the lover / Sighing like furnace, with a woeful ballad / Made to his mistress' eyebrow. Then a soldier, / Full of strange oaths, and bearded like the pard, / Jealous in honour, sudden and quick in quarrel, / Seeking the bubble reputation / Even in the cannon's mouth. And then the justice, / In fair round belly with good capon lined, / With eyes severe, and beard of formal cut, / Full of wise saws and modern instances, / And so he plays his part. The sixth age shifts / Into the lean and slippered

pantaloon / With spectacles on nose and pouch on side, / His youthful hose well saved a world too wide / For his shrunk shank; and his big manly voice, / Turning again toward childish treble, pipes / And whistles in his sound. Last scene of all, / That ends this strange eventful history, / Is second childishness and mere oblivion, / Sans teeth, sans eyes, sans taste, sans everything. [139]

12 Blow, blow, thou winter wind, / Thou art not so unkind / As man's ingratitude: / Thy tooth is not so keen, / Because thou art not seen, / Although thy breath be rude. [174]

13 Most friendship is feigning, most loving mere folly. / Then heigh-ho! the holly! / This life is most jolly. [181]

14 The fair, the chaste and unexpressive she. [III. ii. 10]

15 Hast any philosophy in thee, shepherd? [(22)]

16 He that wants money, means, and content is without three good things. [(25)]

17 Truly, thou art damned like an ill-roasted egg, all on one side. [(39)]

18 Thou art in a parlous state. [(46)]

19 This is the very false gallop of verses. [(120)]

20 Let us make honourable retreat; though not with bag and baggage, yet with scrip and scrippage. [(170)]

21 O wonderful, wonderful, and most wonderful! and yet again wonderful, and after that, out of all whooping! [(202)]

22 Do you not know I am a woman? When I think, I must speak. [(265)]

23 I do desire we may be better strangers. [(276)]

24 Time travels in divers paces with divers persons. I'll tell you who Time ambles withal, who Time trots withal, who Time gallops withal and who he stands still withal. [(328)]

25 Every one fault seeming monstrous till his fellow-fault came to match it. [(377)]

26 Truly, I would the gods had made thee poetical. [iii. (16)]

27 I am not a slut, though I thank the gods I am foul. [(40)]

28 Down on your knees, / And thank heaven, fasting, for a good man's love. [v. 57]

1 It is a melancholy of mine own, compounded of many simples, extracted from many objects, and indeed the sundry contemplation of my travels, which by often rumination, wraps me in a most humorous sadness. [IV. i (16)]

2 I had rather have a fool to make me merry than experience to make me sad. [(28)]

3 Men have died from time to time, and worms have eaten them, but not for love. [(110)]

4 Men are April when they woo, December when they wed: maids are May when they are maids, but the sky changes when they are wives. [(153)]

5 The horn, the horn, the lusty horn / Is not a thing to laugh to scorn. [ii. (17)]

6 Chewing the food of sweet and bitter fancy. [iii. (103)]

7 It is meat and drink to me to see a clown. [V. i. (11)]

8 No sooner met but they looked; no sooner looked but they loved; no sooner loved but they sighed; no sooner sighed but they asked one another the reason; no sooner knew the reason but they sought the remedy. [ii. (37)]

9 Oh! how bitter a thing it is to look into happiness through another man's eyes. [(48)]

10 It is to be all made of sighs and tears; / And so am I for Phebe. [(91)]

11 It is to be all made of faith and service / . . . It is to be all made of fantasy, / All made of passion and all made of wishes, / All adoration, duty and observance, / All humbleness, all patience and impatience, / All purity, all trial, all obeisance. [ii. (96)]

12 It was a lover and his lass, / With a hey, and a ho, and a hey nonino, / That o'er the green cornfield did pass, / In the spring time, the only pretty ring time, / When birds do sing, hey ding a ding, ding; / Sweet lovers love the spring. [iii. (18)]

13 An ill-favoured thing, sir, but mine own. [iv. (60)]

14 The first, 'the retort courteous'; the second, 'the quip modest'; the third, 'the reply churlish'; the fourth, 'the reproof valiant'; the fifth, 'the countercheck quarrelsome'; the sixth, 'the lie with circumstance'; the seventh, 'the lie direct'. [(96)]

15 Your 'if' is the only peace-maker; much virtue in 'if'. [(108)]

16 He uses his folly like a stalking-horse, and under the presentation of that he shoots his wit. [(112)]

17 If it be true that 'good wine needs no bush', 'tis true that a good play needs no epilogue. [Epilogue, (3)]

The Comedy of Errors

18 The pleasing punishment that women bear. [I. i. 46]

19 They brought one Pinch, a hungry lean-faced villain, / A mere anatomy, a mountebank, / A threadbare juggler, and a fortune-teller, / A needy, hollow-eyed, sharp-looking wretch, / A living-dead man. [V. i. 238]

Coriolanus

20 Rubbing the poor itch of your opinion, / Make yourself scabs. [I. i. (171)]

21 They threw their caps / As they would hang them on the horns o' the moon, / Shouting their emulation. [(218)]

22 My gracious silence, hail! [II. i. (194)]

23 He himself stuck not to call us the many-headed multitude. [iii. 18]

24 Bid them wash their faces, / And keep their teeth clean. [(65)]

25 I thank you for your voices, thank you, / Your most sweet voices. [(179)]

26 The mutable, rank-scented many. [III. i. 65]

27 Hear you this Triton of the minnows? mark you / His absolute 'shall'? [88]

28 His nature is too noble for the world: / He would not flatter Neptune for his trident, / Or Jove for's power to thunder. [254]

29 You common cry of curs! whose breath I hate / As reek o' the rotten fens, whose loves I prize / As the dead carcasses of unburied men / That do corrupt my air, I banish you. [iii. 118]

30 The beast / With many heads butts me away. [IV. i. 1]

31 THIRD SERV: Where dwell'st thou? CORIOL: Under the canopy. [v. (40)]

32 O, a kiss / Long as my exile, sweet as my revenge! [V. iii. 44]

33 Chaste as the icicle / That's curdied by the frost from purest snow, / And hangs on Dian's temple. [65]

34 He wants nothing of a god but eternity and a heaven to throne in. [iv. (25)]

1 If you have writ your annals true, 'tis there, / That, like an eagle in a dovecote, I / Fluttered your Volscians in Corioli: / Alone I did it. [v. 114]

2 Thou hast done a deed whereat valour will weep. [134]

Cymbeline

3 She is alone the Arabian bird. [I. vi. 17]

4 Boldness be my friend! [18]

5 On her left breast / A mole cinque-spotted, like the crimson drops / I' the bottom of a cowslip. [II. ii. 37]

6 Hark! hark! the lark at heaven's gate sings, / And Phoebus 'gins arise, / His steeds to water at those springs / On chaliced flowers that lies; / And winking Mary-buds begin / To ope their golden eyes; / With everything that pretty is, / My lady sweet, arise. [iii. (22)]

7 Is there no way for men to be, but women / Must be half-workers? [v. 1]

8 There be many Caesars / Ere such another Julius. Britain is / A world by itself, and we will nothing pay / For wearing our own noses. [III. i. 11]

9 O! for a horse with wings! [ii. (49)]

10 Some jay of Italy. [iv. (51)]

11 I have not slept one wink. [(103)]

12 Weariness / Can snore upon the flint, when resty sloth / Finds the down pillow hard. [vi. 33]

13 Thou shalt not lack / The flower that's like thy face, pale primrose, nor / The azured hare-bell, like thy veins. [IV. ii. 220]

14 Thersites' body is as good as Ajax' / When neither are alive. [252]

15 Fear no more the heat o' the sun, / Nor the furious winter's rages; / Thou thy worldly task hast done, / Home art gone and ta'en thy wages: / Golden lads and girls all must: / As chimney-sweepers, come to dust.

Fear no more the frown o' the great, / Thou art past the tyrant's stroke. / Care no more to clothe and eat; / To thee the reed is as the oak: / The sceptre, learning, physic must, / All follow this, and come to dust. [258]

16 O! the charity of the penny cord. [V. iv. (169)]

17 He that sleeps feels not the toothache. [(176)]

18 Hang there like fruit, my soul, / Till the tree die! [v. 264]

Hamlet

19 For this relief much thanks, 'tis bitter cold, / And I am sick at heart. [I. i. 8]

20 Not a mouse stirring. [10]

21 But in the gross and scope of my opinion, / This bodes some strange eruption to our state. [68]

22 Whose sore task / Does not divide the Sunday from the week. [75]

23 This sweaty haste / Doth make the night joint-labourer with the day. [77]

24 In the most high and palmy state of Rome / A little ere the mightiest Julius fell, / The graves stood tenantless and the sheeted dead / Did squeak and gibber in the Roman streets. [113]

25 The moist star / Upon whose influence Neptune's empire stands / Was sick almost to doomsday with eclipse. [118]

26 Then it started like a guilty thing / Upon a fearful summons. [148]

27 But look, the morn, in russet mantle clad, / Walks o'er the dew of yon high eastern hill. [166]

28 The memory be green. [ii. 2]

29 With one auspicious and one dropping eye, / With mirth in funeral and with dirge in marriage, / In equal scale weighing delight and dole. [11]

30 The head is not more native to the heart. [47]

31 A little more than kin, and less than kind. [65]

32 Not so, my lord; I am too much i' the sun. [67]

33 All that live must die, / Passing through nature to eternity. [72]

34 Seems, madam! Nay, it is; I know not 'seems', / 'Tis not alone my inky cloak, good mother, / Nor customary suits of solemn black. [76]

35 But I have that within which passeth show; / These but the trappings and the suits of woe. [85]

36 O! that this too too solid flesh would melt, / Thaw, and resolve itself into a dew; / Or that the Everlasting had not fixed / His canon 'gainst

self-slaughter! O God! O God! / How weary, stale, flat, and unprofitable / Seem to me all the uses of this world. / Fie on't! O fie! 'tis an unweeded garden, / That grows to seed; things rank and gross in nature / Possess it merely. [129]

1 So excellent a king; that was, to this, / Hyperion to a satyr: so loving to my mother, / That he might not beteem the winds of heaven / Visit her face too roughly. [139]

2 Why, she would hang on him, / As if increase of appetite had grown / By what it fed on. [143]

3 Frailty, thy name is woman! [146]

4 Like Niobe, all tears. [149]

5 A beast that wants discourse of reason. [150]

6 It is not nor it cannot come to good. [158]

7 A truant disposition, good my lord. [169]

8 Thrift, thrift, Horatio! the funeral baked meats / Did coldly furnish forth the marriage tables. [180]

9 In my mind's eye, Horatio. [185]

10 He was a man, take him for all in all, / I shall not look upon his like again. [187]

11 Season your admiration for a while. [192]

12 In the dead vast and middle of the night. [198]

13 Armed at points exactly, cap-a-pe. [200]

14 A countenance more in sorrow than in anger. [231]

15 HAMLET: His beard was grizzled, no? HORATIO: It was, as I have seen it in his life, / A sable silvered. [239]

16 Give it an understanding but no tongue. [249]

17 All is not well; / I doubt some foul play. [254]

18 But you must fear, / His greatness weighed, his will is not his own. For he himself is subject to his birth. [iii. 16]

19 The chariest maid is prodigal enough / If she unmask her beauty to the moon. [36]

20 Do not, as some ungracious pastors do, / Show me the steep and thorny way to heaven, / Whiles, like a puffed and reckless libertine, / Himself the primrose path of dalliance treads, / And recks not his own rede. [47]

21 Give thy thoughts no tongue, / Nor any unproportioned thought his act. / Be thou familiar, but by no means vulgar. / Those friends thou hast, and their adoption tried, / Grapple them to thy soul with hoops of steel. [59]

22 Beware / Of entrance to a quarrel, but, being in, / Bear 't that the opposed may beware of thee, / Give every man thine ear, but few thy voice; / Take each man's censure, but reserve thy judgement. / Costly thy habit as thy purse can buy, / But not expressed in fancy; rich, not gaudy; / For the apparel oft proclaims the man. [65]

23 Neither a borrower, nor a lender be; / For loan oft loses both itself and friend, / And borrowing dulls the edge of husbandry. / This above all; to thine own self be true, / And it must follow, as the night the day, / Thou canst not then be false to any man. [75]

24 You speak like a green girl, / Unsifted in such perilous circumstance. [101]

25 Ay springes to catch woodcocks. [115]

26 Be somewhat scanter of your maiden presence. [121]

27 HAMLET: The air bites shrewdly; it is very cold.
HORATIO: It is a nipping and an eager air. [iv. 1]

28 But to my mind, – though I am native here, / And to the manner born, – it is a custom / More honoured in the breach than the observance. [14]

29 Angels and ministers of grace defend us! / Be thou a spirit of health or goblin damned, / Bring with thee airs from heaven or blasts from hell, / Be thy intents wicked or charitable, / Thou com'st in such a questionable shape / That I will speak to thee. [39]

30 Hath oped his ponderous and marble jaws. [50]

31 What may this mean, / That thou, dead corse, again in complete steel, / Revisit'st thus the glimpses of the moon, / Making night hideous? [51]

32 I do not set my life at a pin's fee; / And for my soul, what can it do to that, / Being a thing immortal as itself? [65]

33 Unhand me, gentlemen, / By heaven! I'll make a ghost of him that lets me. [84]

34 Something is rotten in the state of Denmark. [90]

1 But that I am forbid / To tell the secrets of my prison-house, / I could a tale unfold whose lightest word / Would harrow up thy soul, freeze thy young blood, / Make thy two eyes, like stars, start from their spheres, / Thy knotted and combinèd locks to part, / And each particular hair to stand on end, / Like quills upon the fretful porpentine: / But this eternal blazon must not be / To ears of flesh and blood. [v. 13]

2 Murder most foul, as in the best it is; / But this most foul, strange, and unnatural. [27]

3 With wings as swift / As meditation or the thoughts of love. [29]

4 And duller shouldst thou be than the fat weed / That rots itself in ease on Lethe wharf. [32]

5 O my prophetic soul! / My uncle! [40]

6 What a falling-off was there. [47]

7 But, soft! methinks I scent the morning air. [58]

8 In the porches of mine ears. [63]

9 Cut off even in the blossoms of my sin, / Unhouseled, disappointed, unaneled, / No reckoning made, but sent to my account / With all my imperfections on my head. [76]

10 Leave her to heaven, / And to those thorns that in her bosom lodge, / To prick and sting her. [86]

11 The glow-worm shows the matin to be near, / And 'gins to pale his uneffectual fire. [89]

12 While memory holds a seat / In this distracted globe. Remember thee! / Yea from the table of my memory / I'll wipe away all trivial fond records. [96]

13 O villain, villain, smiling, damned villain! / My tables, – meet it is I set it down, / That one may smile, and smile, and be a villain, / At least I'm sure it may be so in Denmark. [106]

14 There's ne'er a villain dwelling in all Denmark, / But he's an arrant knave. [123]

15 These are but wild and whirling words. [133]

16 There are more things in heaven and earth, Horatio, / Than are dreamt of in your philosophy. [166]

17 To put an antic disposition on. [172]

18 Rest, rest, perturbèd spirit! [182]

19 The time is out of joint; O cursèd spite, / That ever I was born to set it right! [188]

20 By indirections find directions out. [II. i. 66]

21 Brevity is the soul of wit. [ii. 90]

22 For, to define true madness, / What is't but to be nothing else but mad. [93]

23 More matter with less art. [95]

24 That he is mad, 'tis true; 'tis true 'tis pity; / And pity 'tis 'tis true. [97]

25 Doubt thou the stars are fire; / Doubt that the sun doth move; / Doubt truth to be a liar; / But never doubt I love. [(115)]

26 POLONIUS: Do you know me, my lord?
HAMLET: Excellent well; you are a fishmonger. [173]

27 To be honest, as this world goes, / Is to be one man picked out of ten thousand. [(179)]

28 Still harping on my daughter. [(190)]

29 POLONIUS: What do you read, my lord?
HAMLET: Words, words, words. [(195)]

30 Though this be madness, yet there is method in't. [(211)]

31 On Fortune's cap we are not the very button. [(237)]

32 Faith, her privates we. [(242)]

33 There is nothing either good or bad, but thinking makes it so. [(259)]

34 I could be bounded in a nutshell, and count myself a king of infinite space, were it not that I have bad dreams. [(264)]

35 Beggar that I am, I am even poor in thanks. [(286)]

36 It goes so heavily with my disposition that this goodly frame, the earth, seems to me a sterile promontory; this most excellent canopy, the air, look you, this brave o'erhanging firmament, this majestic roof fretted with golden fire, why, it appears no other thing to me but a foul and pestilent congregation of vapours! What a piece of work is a man! How noble in reason! how infinite in faculty! in form, in moving, how express and admirable! in action how like an angel! in apprehension how like a god! the beauty of the world! the paragon of animals! And yet, to me, what is this quintessence of dust? man delights not me; no, nor woman neither. [(316)]

37 What lenten entertainment the players shall receive from you. [(337)]

38 He that plays the king. [(341)]

1 I am but mad north-north-west; when the wind is southerly I know a hawk from a handsaw. [(405)]

2 The best actors in the world, either for tragedy, comedy, history, pastoral, pastoral-comical, historical-pastoral, tragical-historical, tragical-comical-historical-pastoral, scene individable or poem unlimited. [(424)]

3 Come, give us a taste of your quality. [(460)]

4 The play, I remember, pleased not the million; 'twas caviare to the general. [(465)]

5 The moblèd queen. [(533)]

6 They are the abstracts and brief chronicles of the time: after your death you were better have a bad epitaph than their ill report while you live. [(555)]

7 Use every man after his desert and who would 'scape whipping? [(561)]

8 O! what a rogue and peasant slave am I; / Is it not monstrous that this player here, / But in a fiction, in a dream of passion, / Could force his soul so to his own conceit. [(584)]

9 What's Hecuba to him or he to Hecuba / That he should weep for her? [(593)]

10 A dull and muddy-metalled rascal. [(602)]

11 I should have fatted all the region kites / With this slave's offal. Bloody, bawdy villain! / Remorseless, treacherous, lecherous, kindless villain! [(615)]

12 The play's the thing / Wherein I'll catch the conscience of the king. [(641)]

13 With devotion's visage / And pious action we do sugar o'er / The devil himself. [III. i. 47]

14 To be or not to be: that is the question: / Whether 'tis nobler in the mind to suffer / The slings and arrows of outrageous fortune, / Or to take arms against a sea of troubles, / And by opposing end them? To die: to sleep; / No more; and by a sleep to say we end / The heart-ache and the thousand natural shocks / That flesh is heir to, 'tis a consummation / Devoutly to be wished. To die, to sleep; / To sleep: perchance to dream: ay, there's the rub. / For in that sleep of death what dreams may come / When we have shuffled off this mortal coil, / Must give us pause. There's the respect / That makes calamity of so long life; / For who would bear the whips and scorns of time, / The oppressor's wrong, the proud man's contumely, / The pangs of disprized love, the law's delay, / The insolence of office, and the spurs / That patient merit of the unworthy takes, / When he himself might his quietus make / With a bare bodkin? who would fardels bear, / To grunt and sweat under a weary life, / But that the dread of something after death, / The undiscovered country from whose bourn / No traveller returns, puzzles the will, / And makes us rather bear those ills we have / Than fly to others that we know not of? / Thus conscience does make cowards of us all; / And thus the native hue of resolution / Is sicklied o'er with the pale cast of thought, / And enterprises of great pith and moment / With this regard their currents turn awry, / And lose the name of action. [56]

15 Nymph, in thy orisons / Be all my sins remembered. [89]

16 For to the noble mind / Rich gifts wax poor when givers prove unkind. [100]

17 Get thee to a nunnery. [(124)]

18 Be thou as chaste as ice, as pure as snow, thou shalt not escape calumny. [(142)]

19 I have heard of your paintings too, well enough. God hath given you one face, and you make yourselves another. [(150)]

20 I say, we will have no more marriages. [(156)]

21 O, what a noble mind is here o'erthrown: / The courtier's, soldier's, scholar's eye, tongue, sword; / The expectancy and rose of the fair state, / The glass of fashion, and the mould of form, / The observed of all observers, quite, quite down! [(159)]

22 That noble and most sovereign reason, / Like sweet bells jangled, out of tune and harsh; / That unmatched form and figure of blown youth / Blasted with ecstasy. [(166)]

23 Speak the speech, I pray you, as I pronounced it to you, trippingly on the tongue; but if you mouth it as many of your players do, I had as lief the town-crier spoke my lines. Nor do not saw the air too much with your hand, thus; but use all gently. [ii. 1]

24 Tear a passion to tatters, to very rags, to split the ears of the groundlings. [(11)]

25 It out-herods Herod. [(16)]

26 Suit the action to the word, the word to the action; with this special observance, that you o'erstep not the modesty of nature. [(20)]

1 The purpose of playing, whose end, both at the first and now, was and is, to hold, as 'twere, the mirror up to nature. [(24)]

2 I have thought some of nature's journey-men had made men, and not made them well, they imitated humanity so abominably. [(38)]

3 A man that fortune's buffets and rewards / Hast ta'en with equal thanks; and blessed are those / Whose blood and judgement are so well co-mingled / That they are not a pipe for fortune's finger / To sound what stop she please. [(72)]

4 Give me that man / That is not passion's slave, and I will wear him / In my heart's core, ay, in my heart of heart, / As I do thee. [(76)]

5 My imaginations are as foul / As Vulcan's stithy. [(88)]

6 The chameleon's dish: I eat the air promise-crammed. [(98)]

7 Here's metal more attractive. [(117)]

8 This is miching mallecho; it means mischief. [(148)]

9 OPHELIA: 'Tis brief, my lord.
HAMLET: As woman's love. [(165)]

10 The lady doth protest too much, methinks. [(242)]

11 Let the galled jade wince, our withers are unwrung. [(256)]

12 The story is extant, and writ in very choice Italian. [(277)]

13 What! frighted with false fire? [(282)]

14 Why, let the stricken deer go weep, / The hart ungallèd play; / For some must watch, while some must sleep: / So runs the world away. [(287)]

15 We shall obey, were she ten times our mother. [(352)]

16 The proverb is something musty. [(366)]

17 You would play upon me; you would seem to know my stops; you would pluck out the heart of my mystery; you would sound me from my lowest note to the top of my compass. [(387)]

18 Do you see yonder cloud that's almost in shape of a camel? [(400)]

19 They fool me to the top of my bent. [(408)]

20 'Tis now the very witching time of night, / When churchyards yawn and hell itself breathes out / Contagion to this world. [(413)]

21 Let me be cruel, not unnatural; / I will speak daggers to her but use none. [(420)]

22 O! my offence is rank, it smells to heaven. [iii. 36]

23 Now might I do it pat, now he is praying. [73]

24 My words fly up, my thoughts remain below: / Words without thoughts never to heaven go. [97]

25 How now! a rat? Dead for a ducat, dead! [iv. 23]

26 As false as dicers' oaths. [45]

27 Look here upon this picture, and on this; / The counterfeit presentment of two brothers. / See what a grace was seated on this brow; / Hyperion's curls; the front of Jove himself, / An eye like Mars, to threaten and command, / A station like the herald Mercury / New-lighted on a heaven-kissing hill, / A combination and a form indeed, / Where every god did seem to set his seal. To give the world assurance of a man. [53]

28 Could you on this fair mountain leave to feed, / And batten on this moor? [66]

29 You cannot call it love; for at your age / The hey-day in the blood is tame, it's humble / And waits upon the judgement. [68]

30 A cut-purse of the empire and the rule, / That from a shelf the precious diadem stole, / And put it in his pocket! [99]

31 A king of shreds and patches. [102]

32 This is the very coinage of your brain. [136]

33 Lay not that flattering unction to your soul. [145]

34 Assume a virtue, if you have it not. [160]

35 I must be cruel only to be kind. [178]

36 For 'tis the sport to have the engineer / Hoist with his own petar. [206]

37 I'll lug the guts into the neighbour room. [212]

38 Diseases desperate grown, / By desperate appliance are relieved, / Or not at all. [iv. iii. 9]

39 A certain convocation of politic worms are e'en at him. [(21)]

40 A man may fish with the worm that hath eat of a king, and eat of the fish that hath fed of that worm. [(29)]

41 How all occasions do inform against me, /

And spur my dull revenge! What is a man, / If his chief good and market of his time / Be but to sleep and feed? a beast, no more. / Sure he that made us with such large discourse, / Looking before and after, gave us not / That capability and god-like reason / To fust in us unused. [iv. 32]

1 Some craven scruple / Or thinking too precisely on the event. [40]

2 Rightly to be great / Is not to stir without great argument, / But greatly to find quarrel in a straw / When honour's at the stake. [53]

3 So full of artless jealousy is guilt, / It spills itself in fearing to be spilt. [v. 19]

4 How should I your true love know / From another one? / By his cockle hat and staff, / And his sandal shoon. [(23)]

5 He is dead and gone, lady, / He is dead and gone; / At his head a grass-green turf, / At his heels a stone. [(29)]

6 We know what we are, but know not what we may be. [(43)]

7 I a maid at your window / To be your Valentine. [(51)]

8 Come, my coach! Good-night, ladies; good-night, sweet ladies; good-night, good-night. [(72)]

9 When sorrows come, they come not single spies, / But in battalions. [(78)]

10 We have done but greenly, / In hugger-mugger to inter him. [(83)]

11 There's such divinity doth hedge a king, / That treason can but peep to what it would. [(123)]

12 To hell, allegiance! vows to the blackest devil! / Conscience and grace to the profoundest pit! / I dare damnation. [(130)]

13 They bore him barefaced on the bier; / Hey non nonny, nonny, hey nonny; / And in his grave rained many a tear. [(163)]

14 There's rosemary, that's for remembrance; pray, love, remember: and there is pansies, that's for thoughts. [(174)]

15 You must wear your rue with a difference. [(181)]

16 They say he made a good end. [(184)]

17 A very riband in the cap of youth. [vii. (77)]

18 One woe doth tread upon another's heel, / So fast they follow. [(164)]

19 There is a willow grows aslant a brook, / That shows his hoar leaves in the glassy stream. [(167)]

20 Her clothes spread wide, / And, mermaid-like, awhile they bore her up; / Which time she chanted snatches of old tunes, / As one incapable of her own distress, / Or like a creature native and indued / Unto that element; but long it could not be / Till that her garments, heavy with their drink, / Pulled the poor wretch from her melodious lay / To muddy death. [(176)]

21 Cudgel thy brains no more about it. [V. i. (61)]

22 Has this fellow no feeling of his business? [(71)]

23 The hand of little employment hath the daintier sense. [(75)]

24 How absolute the knave is! we must speak by the card, or equivocation will undo us. [(147)]

25 Alas! poor Yorick. I knew him, Horatio; a fellow of infinite jest, of most excellent fancy; he hath borne me on his back a thousand times; and now, how abhorred in my imagination it is! my gorge rises at it. [(201)]

26 Where be your gibes now? your gambols? your songs? your flashes of merriment, that were wont to set the table in a roar? [(207)]

27 Now get you to my lady's chamber, and tell her let her paint an inch thick, to this favour she must come. [(211)]

28 To what base uses we may return, Horatio! Why may not imagination trace the noble dust of Alexander, till he find it stopping a bung-hole? [(222)]

29 Imperious Caesar, dead and turned to clay, / Might stop a hole to keep the wind away. [(235)]

30 Lay her i' the earth; / And from her fair and unpolluted flesh / May violets spring! [(260)]

31 A ministering angel shall my sister be. [(263)]

32 Sweets to the sweet; farewell! [(265)]

33 I thought thy bride-bed to have decked, sweet maid, / And not have strewed thy grave. [(267)]

34 Forty thousand brothers / Could not, with all their quantity of love, / Make up my sum. [(291)]

1 Nay, an thou'lt mouth, / I'll rant as well as thou. [(305)]

2 Let Hercules himself do what he may, / The cat will mew and dog will have his day. [(313)]

3 There's a divinity that shapes our ends, / Rough-hew them how we will. [ii. 10]

4 It did me yeoman's service. [36]

5 Not shriving-time allowed. [47]

6 Into a towering passion. [80]

7 The phrase would be more german to the matter, if we could carry cannon by our sides. [(165)]

8 Not a whit, we defy augury; there's a special providence in the fall of a sparrow. If it be now, 'tis not to come; if it be not to come, it will be now; if it be not now, yet it will come: the readiness is all. [(232)]

9 A hit, a very palpable hit. [(295)]

10 This fell sergeant, death, / Is strict in his arrest. [(350)]

11 Report me and my cause aright. [(353)]

12 If thou didst ever hold me in thy heart, / Absent thee from felicity awhile, / And in this harsh world draw thy breath in pain, / To tell my story. [(360)]

13 The rest is silence. [(372)]

14 Now cracks a noble heart. Good-night, sweet prince, / And flights of angels sing thee to thy rest! [(373)]

Henry IV, Pt I

15 So shaken as we are, so wan with care. [I. i. 1]

16 In those holy fields / Over whose acres walked those blessed feet / Which fourteen hundred years ago were nailed / For our advantage on the bitter cross. [(24)]

17 Let us be Diana's foresters, gentlemen of the shade, minions of the moon. [ii. (28)]

18 FALSTAFF: And is not my hostess of the tavern a most sweet wench?
PRINCE: As the honey of Hybla, my old lad of the castle. [(44)]

19 What, in thy quips and thy quiddities? [(50)]

20 Old father antick the law. [(69)]

21 O! thou hast damnable iteration, and art indeed able to corrupt a saint. [(101)]

22 Now am I, if a man should speak truly, little better than one of the wicked. [(105)]

23 'Tis my vocation, Hal; 'tis no sin for a man to labour in his vocation. [(116)]

24 There's neither honesty, manhood, nor good fellowship in thee. [(154)]

25 Farewell, thou latter spring! Farewell, All-hallown summer! [(176)]

26 I know you all, and will awhile uphold / The unyoked humour of your idleness. [(217)]

27 If all the year were playing holidays, / To sport would be as tedious as to work. [(226)]

28 A certain lord, neat, and trimly dressed, / Fresh as a bridegroom; and his chin new-reaped, / Showed like a stubble-land at harvest-home. / He was perfumèd like a milliner, / And 'twixt his finger and his thumb he held / A pouncet-box, which ever and anon / He gave his nose and took't away again. [iii.33]

29 And as the soldiers bore dead bodies by, / He called them untaught knaves, unmannerly, / To bring a slovenly unhandsome corpse / Betwixt the wind and his nobility. [42]

30 He made me mad / To see him shine so brisk and smell so sweet / And talk so like a waiting-gentlewoman / Of guns, and drums, and wounds, – God save the mark! – / And telling me the sovereign'st thing on earth / Was parmaceti for an inward bruise; / And that it was great pity, so it was, / This villainous salt-petre should be digged / Out of the bowels of the harmless earth, / Which many a good tall fellow had destroyed / So cowardly; and but for these vile guns, / He would himself have been a soldier. [53]

31 O! the blood more stirs / To rouse a lion than to start a hare. [197]

32 By heaven methinks it were an easy leap / To pluck bright honour from the pale-faced moon, / Or dive into the bottom of the deep, / Where fathom-line could never touch the ground, / And pluck up drownèd honour by the locks. [201]

33 Why what a candy deal of courtesy / This fawning greyhound then did proffer me! [251]

34 I know a trick worth two of that. [II. i. (40)]

35 I am bewitched with the rogue's company: / If the rascal have not given me medicines to make me love him, I'll be hanged. [ii. (19)]

36 It would be argument for a week, laughter for a month, and a good jest for ever. [(104)]

1 Falstaff sweats to death, / And lards the lean earth as he walks along. [(119)]

2 Out of this nettle, danger, we pluck this flower, safety. [iii. (11)]

3 Constant you are, / But yet a woman. [(113)]

4 A Corinthian, a lad of mettle, a good boy. [iv. (13)]

5 He that kills me some six or seven dozen of Scots at a breakfast, washes his hands, and says to his wife, 'Fie upon this quiet life! I want work.' [(117)]

6 A plague of all cowards, I say. [(129)]

7 There live not three good men unhanged in England, and one of them is fat and grows old. [(146)]

8 Call you that backing of your friends? A plague upon such backing! Give me them that will face me. [(168)]

9 I am a Jew else; an Ebrew Jew. [(201)]

10 I have peppered two of them; two I am sure I have paid, two rogues in buckram suits. I tell thee what, Hal, if I tell thee a lie, spit in my face, call me horse. Thou knowest my old ward; here I lay, and thus I bore my point. Four rogues in buckram let drive at me. [(214)]

11 O monstrous! eleven buckram men grown out of two. [(247)]

12 Three misbegotten knaves in Kendal Green. [(249)]

13 Give you a reason on compulsion! If reasons were as plentiful as blackberries, I would give no man a reason upon compulsion, I. [(267)]

14 Mark now, how a plain tale shall put you down. [(285)]

15 Ah! No more of that, Hal, an thou lovest me. [(316)]

16 A plague of sighing and grief! It blows a man up like a bladder. [(370)]

17 I will do it in King Cambyses' vein. [(430)]

18 That reverend vice, that grey iniquity, that father ruffian, that vanity in years. [(505)]

19 Banish plump Jack and banish all the world. [(534)]

20 O monstrous! but one half-pennyworth of bread to this intolerable deal of sack! [(598)]

21 I am not in the roll of common men. [III. i. (43)]

22 GLENDOWER: I can call spirits from the vasty deep.

HOTSPUR: Why so can I, or so can any man; / But will they come when you do call for them? [(53)]

23 O! while you live, tell truth, and shame the devil! [(62)]

24 I had rather be a kitten and cry mew / Than one of these same metre ballad-mongers. [(128)]

25 Mincing poetry. [(133)]

26 And such a deal of skimble-skamble stuff. [(153)]

27 I understand thy kisses and thou mine, / And that's a feeling disputation. [(204)]

28 Swear me, Kate, like a lady as thou art, / A good mouth-filling oath. [(257)]

29 A fellow of no mark, nor likelihood. [ii. 45]

30 He was but as the cuckoo is in June, / Heard but not regarded. [75]

31 Do I not bate? do I not dwindle? Why, my skin hangs about me like an old lady's loose gown; I am withered like an old apple-john. [iii. (2)]

32 Company, villanous company, hath been the spoil of me. [(10)]

33 Shall I not take mine ease at mine inn? [(91)]

34 I have more flesh than another man, and therefore more frailty. [(187)]

35 That daffed the world aside, / And bid it pass. [IV. i. 96]

36 I saw young Harry with his beaver on, / His cushes on his thighs, gallantly armed, / Rise from the ground like feathered Mercury, / And vaulted with such ease into his seat / As if an angel dropped down from the clouds, / To turn the wind a fiery Pegasus / And witch the world with noble horsemanship. [104]

37 Doomsday is near; die all, die merrily. [134]

38 The cankers of a calm world and a long peace. [ii. (32)]

39 Food for powder; they'll fill a pit as well as better: tush, man, mortal men, mortal men. [(73)]

40 To the latter end of a fray and the beginning of a feast / Fits a dull fighter and a keen guest. [(86)]

41 Rebellion lay in his way, and he found it. [V. i. 28]

1 I would it were bed-time, Hal, and all well. [(125)]

2 Honour pricks me on. Yea, but how if honour prick me off when I come on? – how then? Can honour set-to a leg? No. Or an arm? No. Or take away the grief of a wound? No. Honour hath no skill in surgery, then? No. What is honour? A word. What is that word, honour? Air. A trim reckoning! Who hath it? He that died o' Wednesday. Doth he feel it? No. Doth he hear it? No. It is insensible then? Yea, to the dead. But will it not live with the living? No. Why? Detraction will not suffer it. Therefore I'll none of it: honour is a mere scutcheon: and so ends my catechism. [(131)]

3 The time of life is short; / To spend that shortness basely were too long. [ii. 81]

4 Two stars keep not their motion in one sphere. [iv. 65]

5 But thought's the slave of life, and life's time's fool; / And time, that takes survey of all the world, / Must have a stop. [(81)]

6 Ill-weaved ambition, how much art thou shrunk! / When that this body did contain a spirit, / A kingdom for it was too small a bound; / But now, two paces of the vilest earth / Is room enough: this earth, that bears thee dead, / Bears not alive so stout a gentleman. [(88)]

7 What! old acquaintance! could not all this flesh / Keep in a little life? Poor Jack, farewell / I could have better spared a better man. [(102)]

8 The better part of valour is discretion. [(120)]

9 Lord, Lord, how this world is given to lying! [(148)]

10 I'll purge, and leave sack, and live cleanly, as a nobleman should do. [(168)]

Henry IV, Pt II

11 Even such a man, so faint, so spiritless, / So dull, so dead in look, so woe-begone, / Drew Priam's curtain in the dead of night, / And would have told him half his Troy was burned. [I. i. 70]

12 Yet the first bringer of unwelcome news / Hath but a losing office, and his tongue / Sounds ever after as a sullen bell, / Remembered knolling a departed friend. [100]

13 I am not only witty in myself, but the cause that wit is in other men. I do here walk before thee like a sow that hath overwhelmed all her litter but one. [ii. (10)]

14 A rascally yea-forsooth knave. [(40)]

15 I am as poor as Job, my lord, but not so patient. [(145)]

16 We that are in the vaward of our youth. [(201)]

17 I was born about three of the clock in the afternoon, with a white head, and something a round belly. For my voice, I have lost it with hollaing, and singing of anthems. [(213)]

18 It was always yet the trick of our English nation, if they have a good thing, to make it too common. [(244)]

19 I can get no remedy against this consumption of the purse: borrowing only lingers and lingers it out, but the disease is incurable. [(268)]

20 Past and to come seems best; things present, worst. [iii. 108]

21 A poor lone woman. [II. i. (37)]

22 Away, you scullion! you rampallion! You fustilarian! I'll tickle your catastrophe. [(67)]

23 He hath eaten me out of house and home. [(82)]

24 Thou didst swear to me upon a parcel-gilt goblet, sitting in my Dolphin-chamber, at the round table, by a sea-coal fire, upon Wednesday in Wheeson week. [(97)]

25 Let the end try the man. [ii. (52)]

26 He was indeed the glass / Wherein the noble youth did dress themselves. [iii. 21]

27 I beseek you now, aggravate your choler. [iv. (174)]

28 Hollow pampered jades of Asia. [(177)]

29 Is it not strange that desire should so many years outlive performance? [(283)]

30 O sleep! O gentle sleep! / Nature's soft nurse, how have I frighted thee, / That thou no more wilt weigh mine eyelids down / And steep my senses in forgetfulness? [III. i. 5]

31 Wilt thou upon the high and giddy mast / Seal up the ship-boy's eyes, and rock his brains / In cradle of the rude imperious surge, / And in the visitation of the winds, / Who take the ruffian billows by the top, / Curling their monstrous heads, and hanging them / With deafening clamour in the slippery clouds, / That with the hurly death itself awakes? [18]

32 With all appliances and means to boot. [29]

1 Uneasy lies the head that wears a crown. [31]

2 There is a history in all men's lives. [80]

3 Death, as the Psalmist saith, is certain to all; all shall die. How a good yoke of bullocks at Stamford Fair? [ii. (41)]

4 We have heard the chimes at midnight. [(231)]

5 A man can die but once; we owe God a death. [(253)]

6 Lord, Lord, how subject we old men are to this vice of lying! [(329)]

7 Against ill chances men are ever merry, / But heaviness foreruns the good event. [IV. ii. 81]

8 A peace is of the nature of a conquest; / For then both parties nobly are subdued, / And neither party loser. [89]

9 I may justly say with the hook-nosed fellow of Rome, 'I came, saw and overcame'. [iii. (44)]

10 If I had a thousand sons, the first human principle I would teach them should be, to forswear thin potations and to addict themselves to sack. [(133)]

11 O polished perturbation! golden care! / That keep'st the ports of slumber open wide / To many a watchful night! [v. 22]

12 Thy wish was father, Harry, to that thought. [91]

13 Commit / The oldest sins the newest kind of ways. [124]

14 A joint of mutton, and any pretty little tiny kickshaws, tell William cook. [V. i. (28)]

15 Not Amurath an Amurath succeeds, / But Harry, Harry. [ii. 48]

16 A foutra for the world and worldlings base! / I speak of Africa and golden joys. [iii. (100)]

17 Under which king, Bezonian? speak or die. [(114)]

18 I know thee not, old man: fall to thy prayers; / How ill white hairs become a fool and jester! [v. 52]

Henry V

19 O! for a Muse of fire, that would ascend / The brightest heaven of invention. [Chorus, 1]

20 Can this cockpit hold / The vasty fields of France? or may we cram / Within this wooden O the very casques / That did affright the air at Agincourt? [11]

21 Consideration like an angel came, / And whipped the offending Adam out of him. [I. i. 28]

22 When he speaks, / The air, a chartered libertine, is still. [47]

23 And make your chronicle as rich with praise / As is the ooze and bottom of the sea / With sunken wreck and sumless treasuries. [ii. 163]

24 For so work the honey-bees, / Creatures that by a rule in nature teach / The act of order to a peopled kingdom. / They have a king and officers of sorts; / Where some, like magistrates, correct at home, / Others, like merchants, venture trade abroad, / Others, like soldiers, armèd in their stings, / Make boot upon the summer's velvet buds; / Which pillage they with merry march bring home / To the tent-royal of their emperor: / Who busied in his majesty, surveys/ The singing masons building roofs of gold, / The civil citizens kneading up the honey, / The poor mechanic porters crowding in / Their heavy burdens at his narrow gate, / The sad-eyed justice, with his surly hum, / Delivering o'er to executors pale / The lazy yawning drone. [187]

25 HENRY: What treasure, uncle?
EXETER: Tennis-balls, my liege. [258]

26 Now all the youth of England are on fire, / And silken dalliance in the wardrobe lies; / Now thrive the armourers, and honour's thought / Reigns solely in the breast of every man: / They sell the pasture now to buy the horse, / Following the mirror of all Christian kings, / With wingèd heels, as English Mercuries. / For now sits Expectation in the air. [II. Chorus, 1]

27 I dare not fight; but I will wink and hold out mine iron. [i. (7)]

28 Though patience be a tired mare, yet she will plod. [(25)]

29 Base is the slave that pays. [(100)]

30 He's in Arthur's bosom, if ever man went to Arthur's bosom. [iii. (9)]

31 Even at the turning o' the tide. [(13)]

32 His nose was as sharp as a pen, and a' babbled of green fields. [(17)]

33 Now I, to comfort him, bid him a' should not think of God, I hoped there was no need to trouble himself with any such thoughts yet. [(20)]

1 As cold as any stone. [(25)]

2 Trust none; / For oaths are straws, men's faiths are wafer-cakes, / And hold-fast is the only dog, my duck. [(53)]

3 Once more unto the breach, dear friends, once more; / Or close the wall up with our English dead. / In peace there's nothing so becomes a man / As modest stillness and humility: / But when the blast of war blows in our ears, / Then imitate the action of the tiger; / Stiffen the sinews, summon up the blood, / Disguise fair nature with hard-favoured rage. [III. i. 1]

4 On, on, you noblest English, / Whose blood is fet from fathers of war-proof! / Fathers that, like so many Alexanders, / Have in these parts from morn till even fought, / And sheathed their swords for lack of argument. [17]

5 And you, good yeomen, / Whose limbs were made in England, show us here / The mettle of your pasture. [25]

6 I see you stand like greyhounds in the slips, / Straining upon the start. The game's afoot: / Follow your spirit; and, upon this charge / Cry 'God for Harry! England and Saint George!' [31]

7 Men of few words are the best men. [ii. (40)]

8 I know the disciplines of wars. [(156)]

9 Now entertain conjecture of a time / When creeping murmur and the poring dark / Fills the wide vessel of the universe. / From camp to camp, through the foul womb of night, / The hum of either army stilly sounds. [IV. Chorus, 1]

10 How can they charitably dispose of anything when blood is their argument? [i. (150)]

11 Every subject's duty is the king's: but every subject's soul is his own. [(189)]

12 And what have kings that privates have not too, / Save ceremony, save general ceremony? [(258)]

13 Sleep so soundly as the wretched slave / Who with a body filled and vacant mind / Gets him to rest, crammed with distressful bread. [(288)]

14 O! that we now had here / But one ten thousand of those men in England / That do no work today. [iii. 16]

15 If we are marked to die, we are enow / To do our country loss; and if to live, / The fewer men, the greater share of honour. [20]

16 But if it be a sin to covet honour, / I am the most offending soul alive. [28]

17 This day is called the feast of Crispian. / He that outlives this day, and comes safe home, / Will stand a tip-toe when this day is named, / And rouse him at the name of Crispian. [40]

18 Old men forget: yet all shall be forgot, / But he'll remember with advantages / What feats he did that day. Then shall our names, / Familiar in his mouth as household words, / Harry the King, Bedford and Exeter, / Warwick and Talbot, Salisbury and Gloucester, / Be in their flowing cups freshly remembered. [49]

19 We few, we happy few, we band of brothers; / For he today that sheds his blood with me / Shall be my brother; be he ne'er so vile / This day shall gentle his condition: / And gentlemen in England now a-bed / Shall think themselves accursed they were not here, / And hold their manhoods cheap whiles any speaks / That fought with us upon Saint Crispin's day. [60]

20 Kill the poys and the luggage! [vii. 1]

21 But now behold, / In the quick forge and working-house of thought. [V. Chorus, 22]

22 There is occasions and causes why and wherefore in all things. [i. (3)]

23 By this leek, I will most horribly revenge. I eat and eat, I swear. [(49)]

24 For these fellows of infinite tongue, that can rhyme themselves into ladies' favours, they do always reason themselves out again. [ii. (162)]

25 Nice customs curtsey to great kings. [(291)]

Henry VI, Pt I

26 Hung be the heavens with black, yield day to night! [I. i. 1]

27 Unbidden guests / Are often welcomest when they are gone. [II. ii. 55]

28 Delays have dangerous ends. [III. ii. 33]

29 I owe him little duty and less love. [IV. iv. 34]

30 She's beautiful and therefore to be wooed; / She is a woman, therefore to be won. [V. iii. 78]

Henry VI, Pt II

31 Could I come near your beauty with my

nails / I'd set my ten commandments in your face. [I. iii. (144)]

1 Smooth runs the water where the brook is deep. [III. i. 53]

2 What stronger breastplate than a heart untainted! / Thrice is he armed that hath his quarrel just, / And he but naked, though locked up in steel, / Whose conscience with injustice is corrupted. [ii. 232]

3 I will make it felony to drink small beer. [IV. ii. (76)]

4 The first thing we do, let's kill all the lawyers. [(86)]

5 Away with him! away with him! he speaks Latin. [vii. (62)]

Henry VI, Pt III

6 O tiger's heart wrapped in a woman's hide! [I. iv. 137]

7 O God! methinks it were a happy life, / To be no better than a homely swain; / To sit upon a hill, as I do now, / To carve out dials, quaintly, point by point, / Thereby to see the minutes how they run, / How many make the hour full complete; / How many hours bring about the day; / How many days will finish up the year; / How many years a mortal man may live. [II.v. 21]

8 Gives not the hawthorn bush a sweeter shade / To shepherds looking on their silly sheep, / Than doth a rich embroidered canopy / To kings that fear their subjects' treachery? [42]

9 Warwick, peace; / Proud setter up and puller down of kings. [III. iii. 156]

10 A little fire is quickly trodden out, / Which being suffered, rivers cannot quench. [IV.viii. 7]

11 Down, down to hell; and say I sent thee thither. [V.vi. 67]

Henry VIII

12 Heat not a furnace for your foe so hot / That it do singe yourself. [I. i. 140]

13 If I chance to talk a little wild, forgive me; / I had it from my father. [iv. 26]

14 The mirror of all courtesy. [II. i. 53]

15 This bold bad man. [ii. (44)]

16 I swear 'tis better to be lowly born, / And range with humble livers in content, / Than to be perked up in a glistering grief, / And wear a golden sorrow. [iii. 19]

17 I would not be a queen / For all the world. [45]

18 Orpheus with his lute made trees, / And the mountain tops that freeze, / Bow themselves when he did sing. [III. i. 3]

19 In all you writ to Rome, or else / To foreign princes, 'Ego et Rex meus' / Was still inscribed. [314]

20 I have touched the highest point of all my greatness; / And from that full meridian of my glory, / I haste now to my setting: I shall fall / Like a bright exhalation in the evening, / And no man see me more. [ii. 224]

21 Farewell! a long farewell, to all my greatness! / This is the state of man: today he puts forth / The tender leaves of hope; tomorrow blossoms, / And bears his blushing honours thick upon him; / The third day comes a frost, a killing frost. / And when he thinks, good easy man, full surely / His greatness is a-ripening, nips his root, / And then he falls, as I do. I have ventured, / Like little wanton boys that swim on bladders, / This many summers in a sea of glory, / But far beyond my depth. [351]

22 Vain pomp and glory of this world, I hate ye: / I feel my heart new opened. O! how wretched / Is that poor man that hangs on princes' favours! / There is, betwixt that smile we would aspire to, / That sweet aspect of princes, and their ruin, / More pangs and fears than wars or women have; / And when he falls, he falls like Lucifer, / Never to hope again. [365]

23 A peace above all earthly dignities, / A still and quiet conscience. [380]

24 Cromwell, I charge thee, fling away ambition: / By that sin fell the angels. [441]

25 Love thyself last: cherish those hearts that hate thee; / Corruption wins not more than honesty. / Still in thy right hand carry gentle peace, / To silence envious tongues: be just, and fear not. / Let all the ends thou aim'st at be thy country's, / Thy God's, and truth's. [444]

26 Had I but served my God with half the zeal / I served my king, he would not in mine age / Have left me naked to mine enemies. [456]

27 An old man, broken with the storms of state, / Is come to lay his weary bones among ye; / Give him a little earth for charity. [IV. ii. 21]

28 He gave his honours to the world again, /

His blessed part to heaven, and slept in peace. [29]

1 So may he rest; his faults lie gently on him! [31]

2 He was a man / Of an unbounded stomach. [33]

3 Men's evil manners live in brass; their virtues / We write in water. [45]

4 He was a scholar, and a ripe and good one; / Exceeding wise, fair-spoken and persuading: / Lofty and sour to them that loved him not; / But to those men that sought him sweet as summer. [51]

5 Those twins of learning that he raised in you, / Ipswich, and Oxford! [58]

6 To dance attendance on their lordships' pleasures. [V. ii. 30]

7 Nor shall this peace sleep with her; but as when / The bird of wonder dies, the maiden phoenix, / Her ashes new-create another heir / As great in admiration as herself. [v. 40]

8 Some come to take their ease / And sleep an act or two. [Epilogue]

Julius Caesar

9 All that I live by is with the awl ... I am, indeed, sir, a surgeon to old shoes. [I. i. (23)]

10 As proper men as ever trod upon neat's-leather. [(27)]

11 You blocks, you stones, you worse than senseless things! [(39)]

12 Beware the ides of March. [ii. 18]

13 Well, honour is the subject of my story. / I cannot tell what you and other men / Think of this life: but, for my single self, / I had as lief not be as live to be / In awe of such a thing as I myself. [92]

14 And this man / Is now become a god. [115]

15 Ye gods, it doth amaze me, / A man of such a feeble temper should / So get the start of the majestic world, / And bear the palm alone. [128]

16 Why, man, he doth bestride the narrow world / Like a Colossus; and we petty men / Walk under his huge legs, and peep about / To find ourselves dishonourable graves. / Men at some time are masters of their fates; / The fault, dear Brutus, is not in our stars, / But in ourselves, that we are underlings. [134]

17 Upon what meat doth this our Caesar feed, / That he is grown so great? [148]

18 Let me have men about me that are fat; / Sleek-headed men and such as sleep o' nights; / Yond Cassius has a lean and hungry look; / He thinks too much: such men are dangerous. [191]

19 He reads much; / He is a great observer, and he looks / Quite through the deeds of men. [200]

20 Seldom he smiles, and smiles in such a sort / As if he mocked himself, and scorned his spirit, / That could be moved to smile at anything. [204]

21 'Tis very like: he hath the falling sickness. [255]

22 For my own part, it was Greek to me. [(288)]

23 Yesterday the bird of night did sit. / Even at noon-day, upon the market place, / Hooting and shrieking. [iii. 26]

24 So every bondman in his own hand bears / The power to cancel his captivity. [101]

25 It is the bright day that brings forth the adder: / And that craves wary walking. [II. i. 14]

26 That lowliness is young ambition's ladder, / Whereto the climber-upward turns his face; / But when he once attains the upmost round, / He then unto the ladder turns his back, / Looks in the clouds, scorning the base degrees / By which he did ascend. [22]

27 Between the acting of a dreadful thing / And the first motion, all the interim is / Like a phantasma or a hideous dream: / The genius and the mortal instruments / Are then in council; and the state of man, / Like to a little kingdom, suffers then / The nature of an insurrection. [63]

28 For he will never follow anything / That other men begin. [151]

29 Let us be sacrificers, but not butchers. [166]

30 Let's carve him as a dish fit for the gods. [173]

31 But when I tell him he hates flatterers, / He says he does, being then most flattered. [207]

32 Dwell I but in the suburbs / Of your good pleasure? If it be no more, / Portia is Brutus' harlot, not his wife. [285]

33 A lioness hath whelped in the streets; / And graves have yawned and yielded up their dead. [ii. 17]

1 When beggars die, there are no comets seen; / The heavens themselves blaze forth the death of princes. [30]

2 Cowards die many times before their deaths; / The valiant never taste of death but once. [32]

3 How hard it is for women to keep counsel. [iv. 9]

4 But I am constant as the northern star, / Of whose true fixed and resting quality / There is no fellow in the firmament. [III. i. 60]

5 Et tu, Brute! [77]

6 Why he that cuts off twenty years of life / Cuts off so many years of fearing death. [101]

7 How many ages hence / Shall this our lofty scene be acted o'er / In states unborn and accents yet unknown! [111]

8 O mighty Caesar! dost thou lie so low? / Are all thy conquests, glories, triumphs, spoils, / Shrunk to this little measure? [148]

9 The choice and master spirits of this age. [163]

10 Though last, not least in love. [189]

11 O! pardon me, thou bleeding piece of earth, / That I am meek and gentle with these butchers; / Thou art the ruins of the noblest man / That ever lived in the tide of times. [254]

12 Cry 'Havoc!' and let slip the dogs of war. [273]

13 As Caesar loved me, I weep for him; as he was fortunate, I rejoice at it; as he was valiant, I honour him; but as he was ambitious, I slew him . . . Who is there so base that would be a bondman? If any, speak; for him have I offended. [ii. (26)]

14 Friends, Romans, countrymen, lend me your ears; / I come to bury Caesar, not to praise him. / The evil that men do lives after them, / The good is oft interrèd with their bones. [(79)]

15 For Brutus is an honourable man; / So are they all, all honourable men. [(88)]

16 Ambition should be made of sterner stuff. [(98)]

17 O judgment! thou art fled to brutish beasts, / And men have lost their reason. [(110)]

18 But yesterday the word of Caesar might / Have stood against the world; now lies he there, / And none so poor to do him reverence. [(124)]

19 If you have tears, prepare to shed them now. [(174)]

20 See what a rent the envious Casca made. [(180)]

21 This was the most unkindest cut of all. [(188)]

22 O! what a fall was there, my countrymen; / Then I, and you, and all of us fell down, / Whilst bloody treason flourished over us. [(195)]

23 I come not, friends, to steal away your hearts. / I am no orator, as Brutus is; / But, as you know me all, a plain, blunt man, / That love my friend. [(220)]

24 Put a tongue / In every wound of Caesar, that should move / The stones of Rome to rise and mutiny. [(232)]

25 He shall not live; look, with a spot I damn him. [IV. i. 6]

26 When love begins to sicken and decay, / It useth an enforcèd ceremony! / There are no tricks in plain and simple faith. [ii. 20]

27 You yourself / Are much condemned to have an itching palm. [iii. 9]

28 I had rather be a dog and bay the moon, / Than such a Roman. [27]

29 Away, slight man! [37]

30 There is no terror, Cassius, in your threats; / For I am armed so strong in honesty / That they pass by me as the idle wind, / Which I respect not. [66]

31 A friend should bear his friend's infirmities, / But Brutus makes mine greater than they are. [85]

32 All his faults, observed, / Set in a notebook, learned, and conned by rote, / To cast into my teeth. [96]

33 There is a tide in the affairs of men, / Which, taken at the flood, leads on to fortune; / Omitted, all the voyage of their life / Is bound in shallows and in miseries. [217]

34 Never come such division 'tween our souls! [234]

35 For ever, and for ever, farewell, Cassius! / If we do meet again, why we shall smile! / If not, why then, this parting was well made. [V. i. 117]

36 O! that a man might know / The end of this day's business ere it come. [123]

1 O! Julius Caesar! thou art mighty yet! / Thy spirit walks abroad and turns our swords / In our own proper entrails. [iii. 94]

2 The last of all the Romans, fare thee well! [99]

3 Caesar, now be still; / I killed not thee with half so good a will. [v. 50]

4 This was the noblest Roman of them all. / All the conspirators save only he / Did that they did in envy of great Caesar. [68]

5 His life was gentle, and the elements / So mixed in him that Nature might stand up, / And say to all the world, 'This was a man!' [73]

King John

6 Lord of thy presence and no land beside. [I. i. 137]

7 For new-made honour doth forget men's names. [87]

8 For courage mounteth with occasion. [II. i. 82]

9 Saint George, that swinged the dragon, and e'er since / Sits on his horse back at mine hostess' door. [288]

10 Zounds! I was never so bethumped with words / Since I first called my brother's father dad. [466]

11 Mad world! mad kings! mad composition! [561]

12 That smooth-faced gentleman, tickling Commodity, / Commodity, the bias of the world. [573]

13 Well, whiles I am a beggar, I will rail, / And say there is no sin but to be rich; / And, being rich, my virtue then shall be / To say there is no vice but beggary. [593]

14 Here I and sorrows sit; / Here is my throne, bid kings come bow to it. [III. i. 73]

15 Thou wear a lion's hide! doff it for shame, / And hang a calf's-skin on those recreant limbs! [128]

16 Bell, book and candle shall not drive me back / When gold and silver becks me to come on. [iii. 12]

17 Grief fills the room up of my absent child, / Lies in his bed, walks up and down wih me, / Puts on his pretty looks, repeats his words, / Remembers me of all his gracious parts, / Stuffs out his vacant garments with his form. [iv. 93]

18 Life is as tedious as a twice-told tale, / Vexing the dull ear of a drowsy man. [108]

19 When Fortune means to men most good, / She looks upon them with a threatening eye. [119]

20 Heat me these irons hot. [IV. i. 1]

21 To gild refinèd gold, to paint the lily, / To throw a perfume on the violet, / To smooth the ice, or add another hue / Unto the rainbow, or with taper-light / To seek the beauteous eye of heaven to garnish, / Is wasteful and ridiculous excess. [ii. 11]

22 And oftentimes excusing of a fault / Doth make the fault the worse by the excuse. [30]

23 Another lean unwashed artificer. [201]

24 How oft the sight of means to do ill deeds / Makes ill deeds done! [219]

25 Heaven take my soul, and England keep my bones! [iii. 10]

26 Unthread the bold eye of rebellion, / And welcome home again discarded faith. [V. iv. 11]

27 I beg cold comfort. [vii. 42]

28 This England never did, nor never shall, / Lie at the proud foot of a conqueror, / But when it first did help to wound itself: / Now these her princes are come home again, / Come the three corners of the world in arms, / And we shall shock them, Nought shall make us rue / If England to itself do rest but true. [112]

King Lear

29 Nothing will come of nothing: speak again. [I. i. (92)]

30 LEAR: So young and so untender? CORDELIA: So young, my lord, and true. [(108)]

31 A still-soliciting eye. [(234)]

32 Why brand they us / With base? with baseness? bastardy? base, base? / . . . Edmund the base / Shall top the legitimate: – I grow, I prosper; / Now, gods stand up for bastards! [9 and 20]

33 These late eclipses in the sun and moon portend no good to us. [(115)]

34 This is the excellent foppery of the world . . . we make guilty of our disasters the sun, the moon and the stars, as if we were villains by necessity, fools by heavenly compulsion, knaves, thieves and treachers by spherical predominance, drunkards, liars and adulterers by an enforced obedience of planetary influence. [ii. (132)]

1 I should have been that I am had the maidenliest star in the firmament twinkled on my bastardizing. [(147)]

2 Pat he comes, like the catastrophe of the old comedy: my cue is villanous melancholy, with a sigh like Tom o' Bedlam. [(150)]

3 How sharper than a serpent's tooth it is / To have a thankless child! [iv. (312)]

4 Striving to better, oft we mar what's well. [(370)]

5 O! Let me not be mad, not mad, sweet heaven! / Keep me in temper; I would not be mad. [v. (51)]

6 The son and heir of a mongrel bitch. [II. ii. (23)]

7 Thou whoreson zed! thou unnecesssary letter! [(68)]

8 I am too old to learn. [(134)]

9 Fortune, good night, smile once more, turn thy wheel! [(180)]

10 Hysterica passio! down, thou climbing sorrow! / Thy element's below. [iv. (57)]

11 You are old; / Nature in you stands on the very verge / Of her confine. [(148)]

12 Necessity's sharp pinch. [(214)]

13 No, I'll not weep: / I have full cause of weeping, but this heart / Shall break into a hundred thousand flaws / Or ere I'll weep. O fool! I shall go mad. [(286)]

14 Blow, winds, and crack your cheeks! rage! blow! / You cataracts and hurricanoes spout / Till you have drenched our steeples, drowned the cocks! [III. ii. 1]

15 Rumble thy bellyful! Spit, fire! spout, rain! / Nor rain, wind, thunder, fire are my daughters / I tax you not, you elements, with unkindness. [(14)]

16 Here I stand, your slave, / A poor, infirm, weak, and despised old man. [(19)]

17 There was never yet fair woman but she made mouths in a glass. [(35)]

18 I will be the pattern of all patience. [(37)]

19 I am a man / More sinned against than sinning. [(59)]

20 Take physic, pomp; / Expose thyself to feel what wretches feel. [iv. 33]

21 Pillicock sat on Pillicock-hill: / Halloo, halloo, loo, loo! [(75)]

22 Defy the foul fiend. [(99)]

23 Unaccommodated man is no more but such a poor, bare, forked animal as thou art. [(109)]

24 'Tis a naughty night to swim in. [(113)]

25 Drinks the green mantle of the standing pool. [(136)]

26 The prince of darkness is a gentleman. [(148)]

27 Poor Tom's a-cold. [(151)]

28 Child Rowland to the dark tower came, / His word was still, Fie, foh, and fum, / I smell the blood of a British man. [(185)]

29 I am tied to the stake, and I must stand the course. [vii. (54)]

30 Out, vile jelly! / Where is thy lustre now? [(83)]

31 The lowest and most dejected thing of fortune. [IV. i. 3]

32 The worst is not; / So long as we can say, 'This is the worst.' [27]

33 As flies to wanton boys, are we to the gods; / They kill us for their sport. [36]

34 Wisdom and goodness to the vile seem vile; / Filths savour but themselves. [ii. 38]

35 It is the stars, / The stars above us, govern our conditions. [iii. 34]

36 How fearful / And dizzy 'tis to cast one's eyes so low! / The crows and choughs that wing the midway air / Show scarce so gross as beetles; half-way down / Hangs one that gathers samphire, dreadful trade! / Methinks he seems no bigger than his head. / The fishermen that walk upon the beach / Appear like mice, and yon tall anchoring bark / Diminished to her cock, her cock a buoy / Almost too small for sight. The murmuring surge / That on the unnumbered idle pebbles chafes, / Cannot be heard so high. [vi. 12]

37 Nature's above art in that respect. [(87)]

38 Ay, every inch a king. [(110)]

39 The wren goes to 't, and the small gilded fly / Does lecher in my sight. / Let copulation thrive. [(115)]

40 Give me an ounce of civet, good apothecary, to sweeten my imagination. [(133)]

41 GLOUC.: O! Let me kiss that hand!
LEAR: Let me wipe it first, it smells of mortality. [(136)]

42 See how yond justice rails upon yond simple thief. Hark in thine ear: change places; and handy-dandy, which is the justice, which is the thief? [(156)]

1 Through tattered clothes small vices do appear; / Robes and furred gowns hide all. [(169)]

2 Get thee glass eyes; / And, like a scurvy politician, seem / To see the things thou dost not. [(175)]

3 When we are born, we cry that we are come / To this great stage of fools. [(187)]

4 Mine enemy's dog, / Though he had bit me, should have stood that night / Against my fire. [vii. 36]

5 Thou art a soul in bliss; but I am bound / Upon a wheel of fire. [46]

6 I am a very foolish, fond old man, / Fourscore and upward, not an hour more or less; / And, to deal plainly, / I fear I am not in my perfect mind. [60]

7 Pray you now, forget and forgive. [(85)]

8 Men must endure / Their going hence, even as their coming hither: / Ripeness is all. [V. ii. 9]

9 Come, let's away to prison; / We two alone will sing like birds i' the cage: / When thou dost ask me blessing, I'll kneel down, / And ask of thee forgiveness: so we'll live, / And pray, and sing, and tell old tales, and laugh / At gilded butterflies, and hear poor rogues / Talk of court news; and we'll talk with them too, / Who loses and who wins; who's in, who's out; / And take upon 's the mystery of things. / As if we were God's spies; and we'll wear out, / In a walled prison, packs and sets of great ones / That ebb and flow by the moon. [iii. 8]

10 Upon such sacrifices, my Cordelia, / The gods themselves throw incense! [20]

11 The gods are just, and of our pleasant vices / Make instruments to plague us. [(172)]

12 The wheel is come full circle. [(176)]

13 Her voice was ever soft, / Gentle and low, an excellent thing in woman. [(274)]

14 Never, never, never, never, never! / Pray you, undo this button. [(310)]

15 Vex not his ghost: O! let him pass; he hates him / That would upon the rack of this tough world / Stretch him out longer. [(314)]

16 The oldest hath borne most: we that are young / Shall never see so much, nor live so long. [(327)]

Love's Labour's Lost

17 Spite of cormorant devouring Time. [I. i. 4]

18 Why, all delights are vain; but that most vain / Which, with pain purchased, doth inherit pain. [72]

19 Study is like the heaven's glorious sun, / That will not be deep-searched with saucy looks; / Small have continuous plodders ever won, / Save base authority from others' books. [84]

20 At Christmas I no more desire a rose / Than wish a snow in May's new-fangled mirth. [105]

21 A child of our grandmother Eve, a female; or, for thy more sweet understanding, a woman. [(263)]

22 Affliction may one day smile again; and till then, sit thee down, sorrow! [(312)]

23 Devise, wit; write, pen; for I am for whole volumes in folio. [ii. (194)]

24 Warble, child; make passionate my sense of hearing. [III. i. 1]

25 Remuneration! O! that's the Latin word for three farthings. [(143)]

26 A very beadle to a humorous sigh. [(185)]

27 This wimpled, whining, purblind, wayward boy, / This senior-junior, giant-dwarf, Dan Cupid; / Regent of love rhymes, lord of folded arms, / The anointed sovereign of sighs and groans, / Liege of all loiterers and malcontents. [(189)]

28 He hath not fed of the dainties that are bred in a book; he hath not eat paper, as it were; he hath not drunk ink. [IV. ii. (25)]

29 For where is any author in the world / Teaches such beauty as a woman's eye? / Learning is but an adjunct to ourself. [iii. (312)]

30 It adds a precious seeing to the eye; / A lover's eyes will gaze an eagle blind; / A lover's ear will hear the lowest sound. [(333)]

31 When Love speaks, the voice of all the gods / Makes heaven drowsy with the harmony. [(344)]

32 From women's eyes this doctrine I derive: / They sparkle still the right Promethean fire; / They are the books, the arts, the academes, / That show, contain, and nourish all the world. [(350)]

33 Priscian a little scratched; 'twill serve. [V. i. (31)]

1 They have been at a great feast of languages, and stolen the scraps. [(39)]

2 In the posteriors of this day; which the rude multitude call the afternoon. [(96)]

3 Taffeta phrases, silken terms precise, / Three-piled hyperboles, spruce affectation, / Figures pedantical. [ii. 407]

4 In russet yeas and honest kersey noes. [414]

5 A jest's prosperity lies in the ear / Of him that hears it, never in the tongue / Of him that makes it. [(869)]

6 When daisies pied and violets blue / And lady-smocks all silver-white / And cuckoo-buds of yellow hue / Do paint the meadows with delight, / The cuckoo then, on every tree, / Mocks married men; for thus sings he, / Cuckoo, / Cuckoo, cuckoo: O word of fear, / Unpleasing to a married ear. [(902)]

7 When icicles hang by the wall / And Dick the shepherd blows his nail, / And Tom bears logs into the hall / And milk comes frozen home in pail, / When blood is nipped, and ways be foul, / Then nightly sings the staring owl / Tu-who; / Tu-whit, tu-who – a merry note, / While greasy Joan doth keel the pot. [(920)]

8 When all aloud the wind doth blow, / And coughing drowns the parson's saw, / And birds sit brooding in the snow, / And Marian's nose looks red and raw, / When roasted crabs hiss in the bowl. [(929)]

9 The words of Mercury are harsh after the songs of Apollo. [(938)]

Macbeth

10 1ST WITCH: When shall we three meet again / In thunder, lightning, or in rain?
2ND WITCH: When the hurly-burly's done, / When the battle's lost and won. [I. i. 1]

11 Fair is foul, and foul is fair. [11]

12 What bloody man is that? [ii. 1]

13 He unseamed him from the nave to the chaps. [22]

14 Sleep shall neither night nor day / Hang upon his pent-house lid; / He shall live a man forbid: / Weary se'nnights nine times nine / Shall he dwindle, peak and pine. [iii. 19]

15 So foul and fair a day I have not seen. [38]

16 If you can look into the seeds of time, / And say which grain will grow and which will not. [58]

17 And to be king / Stands not within the prospect of belief. [73]

18 The earth hath bubbles, as the water has, / And these are of them. [79]

19 Or have we eaten of the insane root / That takes the reason prisoner? [84]

20 And oftentimes, to win us to our harm, / The instruments of darkness tell us truths, / Win us with honest trifles, to betray's / In deepest consequence. [123]

21 Two truths are told, / As happy prologues to the swelling act / Of the imperial theme. [127]

22 This supernatural soliciting / Cannot be ill, cannot be good. [130]

23 Why do I yield to that suggestion / Whose horrid image doth unfix my hair / And make my seated heart knock at my ribs, / Against the use of nature? Present fears / Are less than horrible imaginings. [134]

24 Come what come may, / Time and the hour runs through the roughest day. [146]

25 Nothing in his life / Became him like the leaving it; he died / As one that had been studied in his death / To throw away the dearest thing he owed, / As 'twere a careless trifle. [iv. 7]

26 There's no art / To find the mind's construction in the face; / He was a gentleman on whom I built / An absolute trust. [11]

27 Yet do I fear thy nature; / It is too full o' the milk of human kindness / To catch the nearest way. [v. (17)]

28 What thou wouldst highly, / That wouldst thou holily; wouldst not play false, / And yet wouldst wrongly win. [(21)]

29 The golden round, / Which fate and metaphysical aid doth seem / To have thee crowned withal. [(29)]

30 The raven himself is hoarse / That croaks the fatal entrance of Duncan / Under my battlements. [(39)]

31 Unsex me here, / And fill me from the crown to the toe top full / Of direst cruelty! [(42)]

32 That no compunctious visitings of nature / Shake my fell purpose. [(46)]

33 Come to my woman's breasts / And take my milk for gall, you murdering ministers, /

Wherever in your sightless substances, / You wait on nature's mischief. [(48)]

1 Your face, my thane, is as a book where men / May read strange matters. [(63)]

2 Look like the innocent flower, / But be the serpent under 't. [(66)]

3 This castle hath a pleasant seat; the air / Nimbly and sweetly recommends itself / Unto our gentle senses. [vi. 1]

4 This guest of summer, / The temple-haunting martlet, does approve / By his loved mansionry that the heaven's breath / Smells wooingly here; no jutty, frieze, / Buttress nor coign of vantage, but this bird / Hath made his pendent bed and procreant cradle: / Where they most breed and haunt, I have observed, / The air is delicate. [3]

5 If it were done when 'tis done, then 'twere well / It were done quickly: if the assassination / Could trammel up the consequence, and catch /With his surcease success; that but this blow / Might be the be-all and the end-all here, / But here, upon this bank and shoal of time, / We'd jump the life to come. [vii. 1]

6 This even-handed justice. [10]

7 Besides, this Duncan / Hath borne his faculties so meek, hath been / So clear in his great office, that his virtues / Will plead like angels trumpet-tongued against / The deep damnation of his taking-off; / And pity, like a naked new-born babe, / Striding the blast, or heaven's cherubim, horsed / Upon the sightless couriers of the air, / Shall blow the horrid deed in every eye. [16]

8 I have no spur / To prick the sides of my intent, but only / Vaulting ambition, which o'er-leaps itself / And falls on the other. [25]

9 I have bought / Golden opinions of all sorts of people. [32]

10 Letting 'I dare not' wait upon 'I would', / Like the poor cat i' the adage. [44]

11 I dare do all that may become a man; / Who dares do more is none. [46]

12 I have given suck and know / How tender 'tis to love the babe that milks me: / I would, while it was smiling in my face, / Have plucked my nipple from his boneless gums, / And dashed the brains out, had I so sworn as you / Have done to this. [54]

13 MACBETH: If we should fail –

LADY MACBETH: We fail! / But screw your courage to the sticking place, / And we'll not fail. [59]

14 That memory, the warder of the brain, / Shall be a fume. [65]

15 Bring forth men children only. [72]

16 There's husbandry in heaven; / Their candles are all out. [II. i. 4]

17 Merciful powers! / Restrain in me the cursed thoughts that nature / Gives way to in repose. [7]

18 Shut up / In measureless content. [16]

19 Is this a dagger which I see before me, / The handle toward my hand? Come, let me clutch thee: / I have thee not, and yet I see thee still, / Art thou not, fatal vision, sensible / To feeling as to sight? or art thou but / A dagger of the mind, a false creation, / Proceeding from the heat-oppressèd brain? [33]

20 The bell invites me. / Hear it not, Duncan; for it is a knell / That summons thee to heaven or to hell. [62]

21 It was the owl that shrieked, the fatal bellman, / Which gives the stern'st good-night. [ii. 4]

22 The attempt and not the deed / Confounds us. [12]

23 As they had seen me with these hangman's hands. [29]

24 I had most need of blessing, and 'Amen' / Stuck in my throat. [33]

25 These deeds must not be thought / After these ways; so, it will make us mad. [34]

26 Methought I heard a voice cry, 'Sleep no more! / Macbeth does murder sleep', the innocent sleep, /Sleep that knits up the ravelled sleave of care, / The death of each day's life, sore labour's bath, / Balm of hurt minds, great nature's second course, / Chief nourisher in life's feast. [36]

27 Infirm of purpose! / Give me the daggers. The sleeping and the dead / Are but as pictures; 'tis the eye of childhood / That fears a painted devil. [53]

28 Will all great Neptune's ocean wash this blood / Clean from my hand? No, this my hand will rather / The multitudinous seas incarnadine, / Making the green one red. [61]

29 A little water clears us of this deed. [68]

1 The primrose way to the everlasting bonfire. [iii. (22)]

2 The labour we delight in physics pain. [(56)]

3 Confusion now hath made his masterpiece! / Most sacrilegious murder hath broke ope / The Lord's anointed temple, and stole thence / The life o' the building! [(72)]

4 Shake off this downy sleep, death's counterfeit, / And look on death itself! [(83)]

5 There's nothing serious in mortality. / All is but toys; renown and grace is dead, / The wine of life is drawn, and the mere lees / Is left this vault to brag of. [(100)]

6 Who can be wise, amazed, temperate and furious, / Loyal and neutral, in a moment? No man. [(115)]

7 Look to the lady. [(126)]

8 A falcon, towering in her pride of place, / Was by a mousing owl hawked at and killed. [iv. 12]

9 I must become a borrower of the night / For a dark hour or twain. [III. i. 27]

10 To be thus is nothing; / But to be safely thus. [48]

11 1ST MURDERER: We are men, my liege.
MACBETH: Ay, in the catalogue ye go for men. [91]

12 I am one, my liege, / Whom the vile blows and buffets of the world / Have so incensed that I am reckless what / I do to spite the world. [108]

13 Things without all remedy / Should be without regard: what's done is done. [ii. 11]

14 We have scotched the snake, not killed it. [13]

15 Duncan is in his grave; / After life's fitful fever he sleeps well; / Treason has done his worst: not steel, nor poison, / Malice domestic, foreign levy, nothing / Can touch him further. [22]

16 But in them nature's copy's not eterne. [38]

17 The shard-borne beetle with his drowsy hums / Hath rung night's yawning peal. [42]

18 A deed of dreadful note. [44]

19 Come, seeling night, / Scarf up the tender eye of pitiful day. [46]

20 Light thickens; and the crow / Makes wing to the rooky wood; / Good things of day begin to droop and drowse, / Whiles night's black agents to their preys do rouse. [50]

21 Now spurs the lated traveller apace / To gain the timely inn. [iii. 6]

22 BANQUO: It will be rain tonight.
1ST MURDERER: Let it come down. [16]

23 But now I am cabined, cribbed, confined, bound in / To saucy doubts and fears. [iv. 24]

24 Now, good digestion wait on appetite, / And health on both! [38]

25 Thou canst not say I did it: never shake / Thy gory locks at me. [50]

26 The air-drawn dagger. [62]

27 The times have been, / That when the brains were out, the man would die, / And there an end; but now they rise again, / With twenty mortal murders on their crowns, / And push us from our stools. [78]

28 Thou hast no speculation in those eyes / Which thou dost glare with. [95]

29 What man dare, I dare. [99]

30 Hence, horrible shadow! / Unreal mockery, hence! [106]

31 Can such things be / And overcome us like a summer's cloud, / Without our special wonder? [110]

32 Stand not upon the order of your going, / But go at once. [119]

33 MACBETH: What is the night?
LADY MACBETH: Almost at odds with morning, which is which. [126]

34 I am in blood / Stepped in so far that, should I wade no more, / Returning were as tedious as go o'er. [136]

35 Double, double, toil and trouble; / Fire burn and cauldron bubble. [IV. i. 10]

36 Eye of newt and toe of frog, / Wool of bat and tongue of dog. [14]

37 By the pricking of my thumbs, / Something wicked this way comes. / Open locks, / Whoever knocks. [44]

38 How now, you secret, black, and midnight hags! [48]

39 A deed without a name. [49]

40 Be bloody, bold, and resolute. [79]

41 But yet I'll make assurance double sure, / And take a bond of fate. [83]

1 Macbeth shall never vanquished be until / Great Birnam wood to high Dunsinane hill / Shall come against him. [92]

2 What! will the line stretch out to the crack of doom? [117]

3 The weird sisters. [136]

4 His flight was madness: when our actions do not, / Our fears do make us traitors. [ii. 3]

5 He wants the natural touch. [9]

6 Angels are bright still, though the brightest fell. [iii. 22]

7 Stands Scotland where it did? [164]

8 Give sorrow words: the grief that does not speak / Whispers the o'er-fraught heart, and bids it break. [209]

9 What! all my pretty chickens and their dam, / At one fell swoop? [218]

10 MALCOLM: Dispute it like a man.
MACDUFF: I shall do so; / But I must also feel it like a man; / I cannot but remember such things were, / That were most precious to me. [219]

11 Out, damned spot! out, I say! One; two: why then, 'tis time to do't. Hell is murky! Fie, my lord, fie! a soldier, and afeard? [V. i. (38)]

12 Yet who would have thought the old man to have had so much blood in him? [(42)]

13 The Thane of Fife had a wife: where is she now? What! will these hands ne'er be clean? [(46)]

14 Here's the smell of the blood still: all the perfumes of Arabia will not sweeten this little hand. [(55)]

15 Now does he feel his title / Hang loose about him like a giant's robe / Upon a dwarfish thief. [ii. 20]

16 The devil damn thee black, thou cream-faced loon! / Where gott'st thou that goose look? [iii. 11]

17 Thou lily-livered boy. [15]

18 I have lived long enough: my way of life / Is fall'n into the sear, the yellow leaf; / And that which should accompany old age, / As honour, love, obedience, troops of friends, / I must not look to have; but, in their stead, / Curses, not loud but deep, mouth-honour, breath, / Which the poor heart would fain deny and dare not. [22]

19 Canst thou not minister to a mind diseased,

/ Pluck from the memory a rooted sorrow, / Raze out the written troubles of the brain, / And with some sweet oblivious antidote / Cleanse the stuffed bosom of that perilous stuff / Which weighs upon the heart? [40]

20 Throw physic to the dogs; I'll none of it. [47]

21 If thou couldst, doctor, cast / The water of my land, find her disease, / And purge it to a sound and pristine health, / I would applaud thee to the very echo, / That should applaud again. [50]

22 Hang out the banners on the outward walls: / The cry is still 'They come'; our castle's strength / Will laugh a siege to scorn. [v. 1]

23 The time has been my senses would have cooled / To hear a night-shriek, and my fell of hair / Would at a dismal treatise rouse and stir / As life were in't. I have supped full with horrors; / Direness, familiar to my slaughterous thoughts, / Cannot once start me. [10]

24 She should have died hereafter: / There would have been a time for such a word. / To-morrow, and to-morrow, and to-morrow, / Creeps in this petty pace from day to day, / To the last syllable of recorded time; / And all our yesterdays have lighted fools / The way to dusty death. Out, out, brief candle! / Life's but a walking shadow, a poor player / That struts and frets his hour upon the stage, / And then is heard no more: it is a tale / Told by an idiot, full of sound and fury, / Signifying nothing. [17]

25 I 'gin to grow aweary of the sun, / And wish the estate o' the world were now undone. [49]

26 Blow, wind! Come, wrack! / At least we'll die with harness on our back [51]

27 They have tied me to a stake; I cannot fly, / But bear-like I must fight the course. [vii. 1]

28 Why should I play the Roman fool, and die / On mine own sword? [30]

29 I bear a charmèd life. [41]

30 Despair thy charm; / And let the angel whom thou still hast served / Tell thee, Macduff was from his mother's womb / Untimely ripped. [42]

31 And be these juggling fiends no more believed, / That palter with us in a double sense; / That keep the word of promise to our ear, / And break it to our hope. [48]

1 Live to be the show and gaze o' the time. [53]

2 Lay on, Macduff; / And damned be him that first cries, 'Hold, enough!' [62]

Measure for Measure

3 Spirits are not finely touched / But to fine issues. [I. i. 35]

4 I hold you as a thing enskyed and sainted. [iv. 34]

5 A man whose blood / Is very snow-broth; one who never feels / The wanton stings and motions of the sense. [57]

6 Our doubts are traitors, / And make us lose the good we oft might win, / By fearing to attempt. [77]

7 'Tis one thing to be tempted, Escalus, / Another thing to fall. I do not deny, / The jury, passing on the prisoner's life, / May in the sworn twelve have a thief or two / Guiltier than him they try. [II. i. 17]

8 Some rise by sin, and some by virtue fall. [38]

9 This will last out a night in Russia, / When nights are longest there. [144]

10 Condemn the fault and not the actor of it? [ii. 37]

11 No ceremony that to great ones 'longs, / Not the king's crown, nor the deputed sword, / The marshal's truncheon, nor the judge's robe, / Become them with one half so good a grace / As mercy does. [59]

12 How would you be, / If He, which is the top of judgement, should / But judge you as you are? [75]

13 The law hath not been dead, though it hath slept. [90]

14 O! it is excellent / To have a giant's strength, but it is tyrannous / To use it like a giant. [107]

15 But man, proud man, / Drest in a little brief authority, / Most ignorant of what he's most assured, / His glassy essence, like an angry ape, / Plays such fantastic tricks before high heaven / As make the angels weep. [117]

16 That in the captain's but a choleric word, / Which in the soldier is flat blasphemy. [130]

17 The miserable hath no other medicine / But only hope. [III. i. 2]

18 Be absolute for death; either death or life / Shall thereby be the sweeter. Reason thus with life: / If I do lose thee, I do lose a thing / That none but fools would keep: a breath thou art, / Servile to all the skyey influences. [5]

19 Palsied eld. [36]

20 The sense of death is most in apprehension, / And the poor beetle, that we tread upon, / In corporal sufferance finds a pang as great / As when a giant dies. [75]

21 If I must die, / I will encounter darkness as a bride, / And hug it in my arms. [81]

22 Ay, but to die, and go we know not where; / To lie in cold obstruction and to rot; / This sensible warm motion to become / A kneaded clod; and the delighted spirit / To bathe in fiery floods, or to reside / In thrilling region of thick-ribbèd ice; / To be imprisoned in the viewless winds, / And blown with restless violence round about / The pendant world! [116]

23 The weariest and most loathèd worldly life / That age, ache, penury and imprisonment / Can lay on nature is a paradise / To what we fear of death. [127]

24 Virtue is bold, and goodness never fearful. [(214)]

25 There, at the moated grange, resides this dejected Mariana. [(279)]

26 Take, O take those lips away, / That so sweetly were forsworn / And those eyes, the break of day, / Lights that do mislead the morn: / But my kisses bring again, bring again; / Seals of love, but sealed in vain, sealed in vain. [IV. i. 1]

27 Every true man's apparel fits your thief. [ii. (46)]

28 I am a kind of burr; I shall stick. [iii. (193)]

29 A forted residence 'gainst the tooth of time, / And razure of oblivion. [V. i. 12]

30 Haste still pays haste, and leisure answers leisure; / Like doth quit like, and Measure still for Measure. [(411)]

31 They say best men are moulded out of faults, / And for the most, become much more the better / For being a little bad. [(440)]

32 What's mine is yours, and what is yours is mine. [(539)]

The Merchant of Venice

33 Nature hath framed strange fellows in her time: / Some that will evermore peep through their eyes / And laugh like parrots at a bag-

piper: / And other of such vinegar aspect / That they'll not show their teeth in way of smile, / Though Nestor swear the jest be laughable. [I. i. 51]

1 I hold the world but as the world, Gratiano; / A stage where every man must play a part, / And mine a sad one. [77]

2 Why should a man whose blood is warm within, / Sit like his grandsire cut in alabaster? [83]

3 There are a sort of men whose visages / Do cream and mantle like a standing pond. [88]

4 As who would say, 'I am Sir Oracle, / And when I ope my lips, let no dog bark!' [93]

5 Gratiano speaks an infinite deal of nothing, more than any man in Venice. His reasons are as two grains of wheat, hid in two bushels of chaff: you shall seek all the day ere you find them; and, when you have them, they are not worth the search. [114]

6 They are as sick that surfeit with too much, as they that starve with nothing. [ii. (5)]

7 Superfluity comes sooner by white hairs, but competency lives longer. [(9)]

8 If to do were as easy as to know what were good to do, chapels had been churches, and poor men's cottages princes' palaces. [(13)]

9 God made him, and therefore let him pass for a man. [(59)]

10 I will do anything, Nerissa, ere I will be married to a sponge. [(105)]

11 I dote on his very absence. [(118)]

12 Ships are but boards, sailors but men; there be land-rats and water-rats, land-thieves and water-thieves. [iii. (22)]

13 How like a fawning publican he looks! / I hate him for he is a Christian. / But more for that in low simplicity / He lends out money gratis, and brings down / The rate of usance here with us in Venice. / If I can catch him once upon the hip, / I will feed fat the ancient grudge I bear him. / He hates our sacred nation, and he rails, / Even there where merchants most do congregate. [(42)]

14 The devil can cite Scripture for his purpose. [(99)]

15 A goodly apple rotten at the heart. / O, what a goodly outside falsehood hath! [(102)]

16 Many a time and oft / In the Rialto you have rated me. [(107)]

17 For sufferance is the badge of all our tribe. [(111)]

18 You call me misbeliever, cut-throat dog, / And spet upon my Jewish gaberdine. [(112)]

19 Shall I bend low, and in a bondman's key, / With bated breath, and whispering humbleness? [(124)]

20 O father Abram! what these Christians are, / Whose own hard dealing teaches them suspect / The thoughts of others! [(161)]

21 I like not fair terms and a villain's mind. [(180)]

22 Mislike me not for my complexion, / The shadowed livery of the burnished sun. [II. i. 1]

23 O heavens! this is my true-begotten father. [ii. (36)]

24 It is a wise father that knows his own child. [(83)]

25 There is some ill a-brewing towards my rest, / For I did dream of money-bags to-night. [v. 17]

26 And the vile squealing of the wry-necked fife. [(30)]

27 But love is blind, and lovers cannot see / The pretty follies that themselves commit. [vi. 36]

28 What! must I hold a candle to my shames? [41]

29 My daughter! O my ducats! O my daughter! Fled with a Christian! O my Christian ducats! [viii. 15]

30 Hanging and wiving goes by destiny. [ix.83]

31 Let him look to his bond. [III. i. (51, 52, 54)]

32 Hath not a Jew eyes? hath not a Jew hands, organs, dimensions, senses, affections, passions? [(63)]

33 If you prick us, do we not bleed? If you tickle us, do we not laugh? If you poison us, do we not die? and if you wrong us, shall we not revenge? [(69)]

34 The villany you teach me I will execute, and it shall go hard but I will better the instruction. [(76)]

35 I would not have given it for a wilderness of monkeys. [(130)]

36 He makes a swan-like end, / Fading in music. [ii. 44]

1 Tell me where is fancy bred, / Or in the heart or in the head? How begot, how nourishèd? [63]

2 The world is still deceived with ornament. / In law, what plea so tainted and corrupt / But, being seasoned with a gracious voice, / Obscures the show of evil? [74]

3 Thus ornament is but the guilèd shore / To a most dangerous sea; the beauteous scarf / Veiling an Indian beauty; in a word, / The seeming truth which cunning times put on / To entrap the wisest. [97]

4 An unlessoned girl, unschooled, unpractised; / Happy in this, she is not yet so old / But she may learn. [160]

5 Here are a few of the unpleasant'st words / That ever blotted paper! [252]

6 I'll not answer that: / But say it is my humour. [IV. i. 42]

7 A harmless necessary cat. [55]

8 I am a tainted wether of the flock, / Meetest for death: the weakest kind of fruit / Drops earliest to the ground. [114]

9 The quality of mercy is not strained, / It droppeth as the gentle rain from heaven / Upon the place beneath: it is twice blessed; / It blesseth him that gives and him that takes: / 'Tis mightiest in the mightiest; it becomes / The thronèd monarch better than his crown; / His sceptre shows the force of temporal power, / The attribute to awe and majesty, / Wherein doth sit the dread and fear of kings; / But mercy is above the sceptred sway, / It is enthronèd in the hearts of kings, / It is an attribute of God himself, / And earthly power doth then show likest God's / When mercy seasons justice. Therefore, Jew, / Though justice be thy plea, consider this, / That in the course of justice none of us / Should see salvation: we do pray for mercy, / And that same prayer doth teach us all to render / The deeds of mercy. [(184)]

10 Wrest once the law to your authority: / To do a great right, do a little wrong. [(215)]

11 A Daniel come to judgement! yea! a Daniel! / O wise young judge, how I do honour thee! [(223)]

12 'Tis not in the bond. [(263)]

13 For, as thou urgest justice, be assured / Thou shalt have justice, more than thou desir'st. [(316)]

14 A second Daniel, a Daniel, Jew! / Now, infidel, I have thee on the hip. [(334)]

15 I thank thee, Jew, for teaching me that word. [(342)]

16 You take my house when you do take the prop / That doth sustain my house; you take my life / When you do take the means whereby I live. [(376)]

17 He is well paid that is well satisfied. [(416)]

18 LORENZO: In such a night / Troilus methinks mounted the Troyan walls, / And sighed his soul toward the Grecian tents, / Where Cressid lay that night.

JESSICA: In such a night / Did Thisbe fearfully o'ertrip the dew, / And saw the lion's shadow ere himself, / And ran dismayed away.

LORENZO: In such a night / Stood Dido with a willow in her hand / Upon the wild sea-banks, and waft her love / To come again to Carthage.

JESSICA: In such a night / Medea gathered the enchanted herbs / That did renew old Aeson. [V. i. 3]

19 How sweet the moonlight sleeps upon this bank! / Here will we sit, and let the sounds of music / Creep in our ears: soft stillness and the night / Become the touches of sweet harmony. [54]

20 Look how the floor of heaven / Is thick inlaid with patines of bright gold: / There's not the smallest orb which thou behold'st / But in his motion like an angel sings. / Still quiring to the young-eyed cherubins; / Such harmony is in immortal souls; / But, whilst this muddy vesture of decay / Doth grossly close it in, we cannot hear it. [58]

21 I am never merry when I hear sweet music. [69]

22 The man that hath not music in himself, / Nor is not moved with concord of sweet sounds, / Is fit for treasons, stratagems, and spoils; / The motions of his spirit are dull as night, / And his affections dark as Erebus: / Let no such man be trusted. [83]

23 How far that little candle throws his beams! / So shines a good deed in a naughty world. [90]

24 How many things by season seasoned are / To their right praise and true perfection! [107]

25 For a light wife doth make a heavy husband. [130]

The Merry Wives of Windsor

26 I will make a Star-chamber matter of it. [I. i. 1]

1 She has brown hair, and speaks small like a woman. [(48)]

2 Seven hundred pounds and possibilities is goot gifts. [(63)]

3 I had rather than forty shillings I had my Book of Songs and Sonnets here. [(205)]

4 'Convey' the wise it call. 'Steal!' foh! a fico for the phrase. [iii. (30)]

5 Here will be an old abusing of God's patience and the king's English. [iv. (5)]

6 We burn daylight. [II. i. (54)]

7 Faith, thou hast some crotchets in thy head. [(158)]

8 Why then the world's mine oyster, / Which I with sword will open. [ii. 2]

9 O sweet Anne Page! [III. i. (72)]

10 I cannot tell what the dickens his name is. [ii. 19]

11 O what a world of vile ill-favoured faults / Looks handsome in three hundred pounds a year! [iv. (32)]

12 I have a kind of alacrity in sinking. [v. (13)]

13 As good luck would have it. [(86)]

14 The rankest compound of villanous smell that ever offended nostril. [(95)]

15 A man of my kidney. [(119)]

16 There is a divinity in odd numbers, either in nativity, chance or death. [V. i. (3)]

A Midsummer Night's Dream

17 To live a barren sister all your life, / Chanting faint hymns to the cold fruitless moon. [I. i. 72]

18 But earthlier happy is the rose distilled, / Than that which withering on the virgin thorn, / Grows, lives, and dies, in single blessedness. [76]

19 And she, sweet lady, dotes, / Devoutly dotes, dotes in idolatry. [108]

20 For aught that ever I could read, / Could ever hear by tale or history, / The course of true love never did run smooth. [123]

21 Swift as a shadow, short as any dream, / Brief as the lightning in the collied night, / That, in a spleen, unfolds both heaven and earth, / And ere a man hath power to say, 'Behold!' / The jaws of darkness do devour it up: / So quick bright things come to confusion. [144]

22 Love looks not with the eyes, but with the mind, / And therefore is winged Cupid painted blind. [234]

23 The most lamentable comedy, and most cruel death of Pyramus and Thisby. [ii. (11)]

24 Masters, spread yourselves. [(16)]

25 A part to tear a cat in, to make all split. [(32)]

26 This is Ercles' vein. [(43)]

27 I'll speak in a monstrous little voice. [(55)]

28 I am slow of study. [(70)]

29 I will aggravate my voice so that I will roar you as gently as any sucking dove; I will roar you as 'twere any nightingale. [(84)]

30 A proper man, as one shall see in a summer's day. [(89)]

31 Over hill, over dale, / Thorough bush, thorough brier, / Over park, over pale, / Thorough flood, thorough fire. [II. i. 2]

32 I must go seek some dew-drops here, / And hang a pearl in every cowslip's ear. [14]

33 Ill met by moonlight, proud Titania. [60]

34 Thorough this distemperature we see / The seasons alter: hoary headed frosts / Fall in the fresh lap of the crimson rose. [106]

35 Since once I sat upon a promontory, / And heard a mermaid on a dolphin's back, / Uttering such dulcet and harmonious breath, / That the rude sea grew civil at her song, / And certain stars shot madly from their spheres, / To hear the sea-maid's music. [149]

36 And the imperial votaress passed on, / In maiden meditation, fancy-free. / Yet marked I where the bolt of Cupid fell; / It fell upon a little western flower, / Before milk-white, now purple with love's wound, / And maidens call it Love-in-idleness. [163]

37 I'll put a girdle round about the earth / In forty minutes. [175]

38 I know a bank whereon the wild thyme blows, / Where oxlips and the nodding violet grows / Quite over-canopied with luscious wood-bine, / With sweet musk-roses, and with eglan-tine. [249]

39 You spotted snakes with double tongue, / Thorny hedge-hogs, be not seen. [ii. 9]

40 God shield us! – a lion among ladies, is a most dreadful thing; for there is not a more fearful wild-fowl than your lion living. [III. i. (32)]

1 Look in the almanack, find out moonshine. [(55)]

2 What hempen homespuns have we swaggering here? [(82)]

3 Bless thee, Bottom! bless thee! thou art translated. [(124)]

4 Lord, what fools these mortals be! [ii. 115]

5 So we grew together, / Like to a double cherry, seeming parted, / But yet an union in partition; / Two lovely berries moulded on one stem. [208]

6 She was a vixen when she went to school: / And though she be but little, she is fierce. [324]

7 Jack shall have Jill; / Nought shall go ill; / The man shall have his mare again, / And all shall be well. [46]

8 I have a reasonable good ear in music: let us have the tongs and bones. [IV. i. (32)]

9 I have an exposition of sleep come upon me. [(44)]

10 My hounds are bred out of the Spartan kind, / So flewed, so sanded; and their heads are hung / With ears that sweep away the morning dew; / Crook-kneed, and dew-lapped like Thessalian bulls; / Slow in pursuit, but matched in mouth like bells. [(125)]

11 The eye of man hath not heard, the ear of man hath not seen, man's hand is not able to taste, his tongue to conceive, nor his heart to report, what my dream was. [(218)]

12 It shall be called Bottom's Dream, because it hath no bottom. [(222)]

13 The lunatic, the lover, and the poet, / Are of imagination all compact. [V. i. 7]

14 The lover, all as frantic, / Sees Helen's beauty in a brow of Egypt; / The poet's eye, in a fine frenzy rolling, / Doth glance from heaven to earth, from earth to heaven; / And, as imagination bodies forth / The forms of things unknown, the poet's pen / Turns them to shapes, and gives to airy nothing / A local habitation and a name. [10]

15 Or in the night, imagining some fear, / How easy is a bush supposed a bear! [21]

16 Very tragical mirth. [57]

17 That is the true beginning of our end. [111]

18 Whereat, with blade, with bloody blameful blade, / He bravely broached his boiling bloody breast. [(148)]

19 The best in this kind are but shadows, and the worst are no worse, if imagination amend them. [(215)]

20 The iron tongue of midnight hath told twelve; / Lovers to bed; 'tis almost fairy time. [(372)]

Much Ado About Nothing

21 He hath indeed better bettered expectation than you must expect of me to tell you how. [I. i. (15)]

22 He is a very valiant trencherman. [(52)]

23 I see, lady, the gentleman is not in your books. [(79)]

24 BEATRICE: I wonder that you will still be talking, Signior Benedick: nobody marks you.
BENEDICK: What! my dear Lady Disdain, are you yet living? [(121)]

25 Shall I never see a bachelor of three-score again? [(209)]

26 In time the savage bull doth bear the yoke. [(271) See also 242:19]

27 Benedick the married man. [(278)]

28 I could not endure a husband with a beard on his face: I had rather lie in the woollen. [II. i. (31)]

29 I have a good eye, uncle: I can see a church by daylight. [(86)]

30 Speak low, if you speak love. [(104)]

31 Friendship is constant in all other things / Save in the office and affairs of love. [(184)]

32 Silence is the perfectest herald of joy: I were but little happy if I could say how much. [(319)]

33 D. PEDRO: Will you have me, lady?
BEATRICE: No, my lord, unless I might have another for working days: your Grace is too costly to wear every day. [(341)]

34 There was a star danced, and under that was I born. [(351)]

35 Is it not strange that sheep's guts should hale souls out of men's bodies? [iii. (62)]

36 Sigh no more, ladies, sigh no more, / Men were deceivers ever; / One foot in sea, and one on shore, / To one thing constant never. [(65)]

37 Sits the wind in that corner? [(108)]

38 These paper bullets of the brain awe a man from the career of his humour. [(260)]

39 The world must be peopled. When I said I

would die a bachelor, I did not think I should live till I were married. [(262)]

1 He hath a heart as sound as a bell, and his tongue the clapper; for what his heart thinks his tongue speaks. [III. ii. (12)]

2 Well, every one can master a grief but he that has it. [(28)]

3 Are you good men and true? [iii. 1]

4 To be a well-favoured man is the gift of fortune; but to write and read comes by nature. [(14)]

5 You are thought here to be the most sense-less and fit man for the constable of the watch. [(22)]

6 2ND WATCH: How if a' will not stand? DOGBERRY: Why, then, take no note of him, but let him go; and presently call the rest of the watch together, and thank God you are rid of a knave. [(28)]

7 For the watch to babble and to talk is most tolerable and not to be endured. [(36)]

8 The most peaceable way for you, if you do take a thief, is to let him show himself what he is and steal out of your company. [(61)]

9 I am as honest as any man living that is an old man and no honester than I. [v. (15)]

10 Comparisons are odorous. [(18)]

11 If I were as tedious as a king, I could find in my heart to bestow it all of your worship. [(23)]

12 A good old man, sir; he will be talking; as they say, 'when the age is in, the wit is out'. [(36)]

13 Our watch, sir, hath indeed comprehended two aspicious persons. [(49)]

14 O! what men dare do! what men may do! what men daily do, not knowing what they do! [IV. i. (19)]

15 For it so falls out / That what we have we prize not to the worth / Whiles we enjoy it, but being lacked and lost, / Why then we rack the value. [(219)]

16 It is proved already that you are little better than false knaves, and it will go near to be thought so shortly. [ii. (23)]

17 Yea, marry, that's the eftest way. [(39)]

18 Flat burglary as ever was committed. [(54)]

19 Thou wilt be condemned into everlasting redemption for this. [(60)]

20 O that he were here to write me down an ass! [(80)]

21 A fellow that hath had losses; and one that hath two gowns, and everything handsome about him. [(90)]

22 Patch grief with proverbs. [V. i. 17]

23 For there was never yet philosopher / That could endure the toothache patiently. [35]

24 They have committed false report; more-over, they have spoken untruths; secondarily, they are slanders; sixth and lastly, they have belied a lady; thirdly, they have verified unjust things; and to conclude, they are lying knaves. [(224)]

25 No, I was not born under a rhyming planet. [ii. (40)]

26 Done to death by slanderous tongues. [iii. 3]

27 The wolves have preyed; and look, the gentle day, / Before the wheels of Phoebus, round about / Dapples the drowsy east with spots of grey. [25]

Othello

28 A fellow almost damned in a fair wife. [I. i. 21]

29 The bookish theoric. [24]

30 We cannot all be masters. [43]

31 In following him, I follow but myself. [58]

32 But I will wear my heart upon my sleeve / For daws to peck at. [64]

33 An old black ram / Is tupping your white ewe. [88]

34 You are one of those that will not serve God if the devil bid you. [108]

35 Your daughter and the Moor are now making the beast with two backs. [(117)]

36 Fathers, from hence trust not your daugh-ters' minds / By what you see them act. [(171)]

37 Keep up your bright swords, for the dew will rust them. [ii. 59]

38 The wealthy curlèd darlings of our nation. [68]

39 Most potent, grave, and reverend signiors, / My very noble and approved good masters. [iii. 76]

40 The very head and front of my offending / Hath this extent, no more. [80]

41 Rude am I in my speech, / And little blessed

with the soft phrase of peace, / For since these arms of mine had seven years' pith, / Till now some nine moons wasted, they have used / Their dearest action in the tented field. [81]

1 I will a round unvarnished tale deliver / Of my whole course of love. [90]

2 A maiden never bold; / Of spirit so still and quiet, that her motion / Blushed at herself. [94]

3 Wherein I spake of most disastrous chances, / Of moving accidents by flood and field, / Of hair-breadth 'scapes i' the imminent deadly breach. [134]

4 Antres vast and desarts idle, / Rough quarries, rocks, and hills whose heads touch heaven. [140]

5 The Cannibals that each other eat, / The Anthropophagi, and men whose heads/ Do grow beneath their shoulders. [143]

6 My story being done, / She gave me for my pains a world of sighs; / She swore, in faith, 'twas strange, 'twas passing strange; / 'Twas pitiful, 'twas wondrous pitiful: / She wished she had not heard it, yet she wished / That heaven had made her such a man; she thanked me, / And bade me, if I had a friend that loved her, / I should but teach him how to tell my story, / And that would woo her. Upon this hint I spake: / She loved me for the dangers I had passed, / And I loved her that she did pity them. / This only is the witchcraft I have used. [158]

7 To mourn a mischief that is past and gone, / Is the next way to draw new mischief on. [204]

8 The robbed that smiles steals something from the thief. [208]

9 Virtue! a fig! 'tis in ourselves that we are thus, or thus. [(323)]

10 Put money in thy purse. [(345)]

11 The food that to him now is as luscious as locusts shall be to him shortly as bitter as coloquintida. [(354)]

12 Framed to make women false. [(404)]

13 Do not put me to 't, / For I am nothing if not critical. [II. i. 118]

14 She never yet was foolish that was fair. [136]

15 To suckle fools and chronicle small beer. [160]

16 O most lame and impotent conclusion! [161]

17 Egregiously an ass. [(321)]

18 I have very poor and unhappy brains for drinking. [iii. (34)]

19 Potations pottle-deep. [(57)]

20 And let me the canakin clink: / A soldier's a man; / A life's but a span; / Why then let a soldier drink. [(73)]

21 Silence the dreadful bell! it frights the isle / From her propriety. [(177)]

22 But men are men; the best sometimes forget. [(243)]

23 Thy honesty and love doth mince this matter. [(249)]

24 Cassio, I love thee; / But never more be officer of mine. [(250)]

25 Reputation, reputation, reputation! O! I have lost my reputation, I have lost the immortal part of myself, and what remains is bestial. [(264)]

26 O God! that men should put an enemy in their mouths to steal away their brains. [(293)]

27 Good wine is a good familiar creature if it be well used. [(315)]

28 How poor are they that have not patience! / What wound did ever heal but by degrees? [III. ii. (379)]

29 Excellent wretch! Perdition catch my soul / But I do love thee! and when I love thee not, / Chaos is come again. [iii. 90]

30 Men should be what they seem. [126]

31 Good name in man and woman, dear my lord, / Is the immediate jewel of their souls; / Who steals my purse, steals trash; 'tis something, nothing; / 'Twas mine, 'tis his and has been slave to thousands; / But he that filches from me my good name / Robs me of that which not enriches him, / And makes me poor indeed. [153]

32 O! beware, my lord, of jealousy; / It is the green-eyed monster which doth mock / The meat it feeds on. [165]

33 If I do prove her haggard, / Though that her jesses were my dear heart-strings, / I'd whistle her off and let her down the wind, / To prey at fortune. [260]

34 For I am declined / Into the vale of years. [265]

1 O curse of marriage! / That we can call these delicate creatures ours, / And not their appetites. I had rather be a toad, / And live upon the vapour of a dungeon, / Than keep a corner in the thing I love / For others' uses. [268]

2 Trifles light as air / Are to the jealous confirmations strong / As proofs of holy writ. [323]

3 Not poppy, nor mandragora, / Nor all the drowsy syrups of the world, / Shall ever medicine thee to that sweet sleep / Which thou owedst yesterday. [331]

4 He that is robbed, not wanting what is stolen, / Let him not know't and he's not robbed at all. [343]

5 O! now for ever / Farewell the tranquil mind; farewell content! / Farewell the plumèd troop and the big wars / That make ambition virtue! O farewell! / Farewell the neighing steed and the shrill trump, / The spirit-stirring drum, the ear-piercing fife, / The royal banner, and all quality, / Pride, pomp, and circumstance of glorious war! [348]

6 Be sure of it; give me the ocular proof. [361]

7 On horror's head horrors accumulate. [371]

8 Take note, take note, O world! / To be direct and honest is not safe. [378]

9 But this denoted a foregone conclusion. [429]

10 Like to the Pontic sea, / Whose icy current and compulsive course / Ne'er feels retiring ebb, but keeps due on / To the Propontic and the Hellespont, / Even so my bloody thoughts, with violent pace, / Shall ne'er look back, ne'er ebb to humble love, / Till that a capable and wide revenge / Swallow them up. [454]

11 They are not ever jealous for the cause, / But jealous for they are jealous. [iv. (159)]

12 I would have him nine years a-killing. [(IV. i. (186)]

13 But yet the pity of it, Iago! [(205)]

14 Alas! to make me / The fixèd figure for the time of scorn / To point his slow and moving finger at. [ii. 52]

15 O thou weed! / Who art so lovely fair and smell'st so sweet / That the sense aches at thee, would thou hadst ne'er been born. [66]

16 O heaven! that such companions thou'dst unfold, / And put in every honest hand a whip / To lash the rascals naked through the world! [141]

17 The poor soul sat sighing by a sycamore tree, / Sing all a green willow; / Her hand on her bosom, her head on her knee, / Sing willow, willow, willow. [iii. (41)]

18 'Tis neither here nor there. [(59)]

19 He hath a daily beauty in his life / That makes me ugly. [V. i. 19]

20 This is the night / That either makes me or fordoes me quite. [128]

21 It is the cause, it is the cause, my soul; / Let me not name it to you, you chaste stars! / It is the cause. Yet I'll not shed her blood, / Nor scar that whiter skin of hers than snow, / And smooth as monumental alabaster. [ii. 1]

22 Put out the light and then put out the light. / If I quench thee, thou flaming minister, / I can again thy former light restore, / Should I repent me; but once put out thy light, / Thou cunning'st pattern of excelling nature, / I know not where is that Promethean heat / That can thy light relume. [7]

23 Curse his better angel from his side, / And fall to reprobation. [206]

24 Here is my journey's end, here is my butt, / And very sea-mark of my utmost sail. [266]

25 O ill-starred wench! / Pale as thy smock! when we shall meet at compt, / This look of thine will hurl my soul from heaven, / And fiends will snatch at it. [271]

26 Soft you; a word or two before you go. / I have done the state some service and they know't;/ No more of that: I pray you, in your letters, / When you shall these unlucky deeds relate, / Speak of me as I am; nothing extenuate, / Nor set down aught in malice: then must you speak / Of one that loved not wisely but too well; / Of one not easily jealous, but, being wrought, / Perplexed in the extreme; of one whose hand, / Like the base Indian, threw a pearl away / Richer than all his tribe; of one whose subdued eyes/ Albeit unusèd to the melting mood, / Drop tears as fast as the Arabian trees / Their med'cinable gum. Set you down this; / And say besides, that in Aleppo once, / Where a malignant and a turbaned Turk / Beat a Venetian and traduced the state, / I took by the throat the circumcisèd dog, / And smote him thus. [337]

1 I kissed thee ere I killed thee. [357]

Pericles

2 See, where she comes apparelled like the spring. [I. i. 12]

3 Few love to hear the sins they love to act. [92]

4 3RD FISHERMAN: I marvel how the fishes live in the sea.
1ST FISHERMAN: Why, as men do a-land; the great ones eat up the little ones. [II. i. (29)]

5 A man whom both the waters and the wind, / In that vast tennis-court, have made the ball / For them to play upon. [(64)]

6 This world to me is like a lasting storm, / Whirring me from my friends. [IV. i. 19]

Richard II

7 Old John of Gaunt, time-honoured Lancaster. [I. i. 1]

8 A jewel in a ten-times-barred-up chest / Is a bold spirit in a loyal breast. / Mine honour is my life; both grow in one; / Take honour from me, and my life is done. [180]

9 We were not born to sue, but to command. [196]

10 The daintiest last to make the end most sweet. [iii. 68]

11 This must my comfort be, / That sun that warms you here shall shine on me. [144]

12 How long a time lies in one little word! [213]

13 Things sweet to taste prove in digestion sour. [236]

14 All places that the eye of heaven visits / Are to a wise man ports and happy havens. / Teach thy necessity to reason thus; / There is no virtue like necessity. [275]

15 O! who can hold a fire in his hand / By thinking on the frosty Caucasus? / Or cloy the hungry edge of appetite / By bare imagination of a feast? / Or wallow naked in December snow / By thinking on fantastic summer's heat? / O, no! the apprehension of the good / Gives but the greater feeling to the worse. [294]

16 Methinks I am a prophet new inspired, / And thus expiring do foretell of him: / His rash fierce blaze of riot cannot last, / For violent fires soon burn out themselves; / Small showers last long, but sudden storms are short; / He tires betimes that spurs too fast betimes. [II. i. 31]

17 This royal throne of kings, this sceptered isle, / This earth of majesty, this seat of Mars, / This other Eden, demi-paradise, / This fortress built by Nature for herself / Against infection and the hand of war, / This happy breed of men, this little world, / This precious stone set in the silver sea, / Which serves it in the office of a wall, / Or as a moat defensive to a house, / Against the envy of less happier lands. / This blessed plot, this earth, this realm, this England, / This nurse, this teeming womb of royal kings, / Feared by their breed and famous by their birth, / Renownèd for their deeds as far from home – / For Christian service and true chivalry, – / As is the sepulchre in stubborn Jewry / Of the world's ransom, blessed Mary's Son: / This land of such dear souls, this dear, dear land. [40]

18 England, bound in with the triumphant sea, / Whose rocky shore beats back the envious siege / Of watery Neptune, is now bound in with shame, / With inky blots, and rotten parchment bonds: / That England, that was wont to conquer others, / Hath made a shameful conquest of itself. [61]

19 Can sick men play so nicely with their names? [84]

20 I am a stranger here in Gloucestershire: / These high wild hills and rough uneven ways / Draw out our miles and make them wearisome. [iii. 3]

21 I count myself in nothing else so happy / As in a soul remembering my good friends. [46]

22 Evermore thanks, the exchequer of the poor. [65]

23 Grace me no grace, nor uncle me no uncle. [87]

24 The caterpillars of the commonwealth. [166]

25 Things past redress are now with me past care. [171]

26 Eating the bitter bread of banishment. [III. i. 21]

27 Not all the water in the rough rude sea / Can wash the balm from an anointed king; / The breath of worldly men cannot depose / The deputy elected by the Lord. [ii. 54]

28 O! call back yesterday, bid time return. [69]

29 The worst is death, and death will have his day. [103]

1 Let's talk of graves, of worms and epitaphs; / Make dust our paper, and with rainy eyes / Write sorrow on the bosom of the earth; / Let's choose executors and talk of wills. [145]

2 For God's sake, let us sit upon the ground / And tell sad stories of the death of kings: / How some have been deposed, some slain in war, / Some haunted by the ghosts they have deposed; / Some poisoned by their wives, some sleeping killed; / All murdered: for within the hollow crown / That rounds the mortal temples of a king / Keeps Death his court, and there the antick sits, / Scoffing his state and grinning at his pomp; / Allowing him a breath, a little scene, / To monarchize, be feared, and killed with looks, / Infusing him with self and vain conceit / As if this flesh which walls about our life / Were brass impregnable; and humoured thus / Comes at the last, and with a little pin / Bores through his castle-wall, and farewell king! [155]

3 The purple testament of bleeding war. [iii. 940]

4 What must the king do now? Must he submit? / The king shall do it: must he be deposed? / The king shall be contented: must he lose / The name of king? o' God's name, let it go: / I'll give my jewels for a set of beads, / My gorgeous palace for a hermitage, / My gay apparel for an almsman's gown, / My figured goblets for a dish of wood, / My sceptre for a palmer's walking staff, / My subjects for a pair of carvèd saints, / And my large kingdom for a little grave, / A little little grave, an obscure grave. [143]

5 Some pretty match with shedding tears? / As thus; to drop them still upon one place / Till they have fretted us a pair of graves. [165]

6 Go, bind thou up yon dangling apricocks. [iv. 29]

7 If I dare eat, or drink, or breathe, or live, / I dare meet Surrey in a wilderness, / And spit upon him, whilst I say he lies, / And lies, and lies. [IV. i. 73]

8 Gave / His body to that pleasant country's earth, / And his pure soul unto his captain Christ. [97]

9 Peace shall go sleep with Turks and infidels. [139]

10 God save the king! Will no man say, amen? [172]

11 You may my glories and my state depose, / But not my griefs; still am I king of those. [192]

12 With mine own tears I wash away my balm, / With mine own hands I give away my crown. [207]

13 A mockery king of snow. [260]

14 Julius Caesar's ill-erected tower. [V. i. 2]

15 I am sworn brother, sweet, / To grim Necessity, and he and I / Will keep a league till death. [20]

16 As in a theatre, the eyes of men, / After a well-graced actor leaves the stage, / Are idly bent on him that enters next, / Thinking his prattle to be tedious. [ii. 23]

17 I have been studying how I may compare / The prison where I live unto the world. [V. v. 1]

18 How sour sweet music is / When time is broke and no proportion kept! / So is it in the music of men's lives. [42]

19 Mount, mount my soul! thy seat is up on high, / Whilst my gross flesh sinks downward, here to die. [112]

Richard III

20 Now is the winter of our discontent / Made glorious summer by this sun of York. [I. i. 1]

21 Our stern alarums changed to merry meetings; / Our dreadful marches to delightful measures. [7]

22 He capers nimbly to a lady's chamber / To the lascivious pleasing of a lute. [12]

23 Deformed, unfinished, sent before my time / Into this breathing world, scarce half made up, / And that so lamely and unfashionable / That dogs bark at me as I halt by them. [20]

24 In this weak piping time of peace. [24]

25 I am determinèd to prove a villain. [30]

26 No beast so fierce but knows some touch of pity. [ii. 71]

27 Was ever woman in this humour wooed? / Was ever woman in this humour won? [229]

28 Since every Jack became a gentleman / There's many a gentle person made a Jack. [iii. 72]

29 And thus I clothe my naked villany / With odd old ends stol'n forth of holy writ, / And seem a saint when most I play the devil. [336]

30 O, I have passed a miserable night, / So full

of ugly sights, of ghastly dreams, / That, as I am a Christian faithful man, / I would not spend another such a night, / Though 'twere to buy a world of happy days, / So full of dismal terror was the time! [iv. 2]

1 Lord, Lord! methought what pain it was to drown: / What dreadful noise of water in mine ears! / What sights of ugly death within mine eyes! Methought I saw a thousand fearful wracks; / A thousand men that fishes gnawed upon; / Wedges of gold, great anchors, heaps of pearl, / Inestimable stones, unvalued jewels, / All scattered in the bottom of the sea. / Some lay in dead men's skulls, and in those holes / Where eyes did once inhabit, there were crept, / As 'twere in scorn of eyes, reflecting gems, / That wooed the slimy bottom of the deep, / And mocked the dead bones that lay scattered by. [21]

2 I do not know that Englishman alive / With whom my soul is any jot at odds / More than the infant that is born tonight: / I thank my God for my humility. [II. i. 70]

3 So wise so young, they say, do never live long. [III. i. 79]

4 My Lord of Ely, when I was last in Holborn, / I saw good strawberries in your garden there. [iv. 31]

5 Thou art a traitor: / Off with his head! [74]

6 Cousin, thou wast not wont to be so dull: / Shall I be plain? I wish the bastards dead. [IV. ii. 17]

7 High-reaching Buckingham grows circumspect. [31]

8 I am not in the giving vein today. [115]

9 Their lips were four red roses on a stalk, / Which in their summer beauty kissed each other. [iii. 12]

10 The sons of Edward sleep in Abraham's bosom. [38]

11 Let not the heavens hear these tell-tale women / Rail on the Lord's anointed. [iv. 150]

12 An honest tale speeds best being plainly told. [359]

13 Harp not on that string. [365]

14 Is the chair empty? is the sword unswayed? / Is the king dead? the empire unpossessed? [470]

15 True hope is swift, and flies with swallow's wings; / Kings it makes gods, and meaner creatures kings. [V. ii. 23]

16 The king's name is a tower of strength. [iii. 12]

17 I have not that alacrity of spirit, / Nor cheer of mind, that I was wont to have. [73]

18 Give me another horse! bind up my wounds! / Have mercy, Jesu! Soft! I did but dream. / O coward conscience, how dost thou afflict me! [178]

19 My conscience hath a thousand several tongues, / And every tongue brings in a several tale, / And every tale condemns me for a villain. [194]

20 A horse! a horse! my kingdom for a horse! [iv. 7]

Romeo and Juliet

21 A pair of star-crossed lovers. [Prologue, 6]

22 The two hours' traffic of our stage. [12]

23 No, sir, I do not bite my thumb at you, sir; but I bite my thumb, sir. [I. i. (56)]

24 Remember thy swashing blow. [(68)]

25 Saint-seducing gold. [(220)]

26 When well-apparelled April on the heel / Of limping Winter treads. [ii. 27]

27 Pretty fool, it stinted and said 'Ay'. [iii. 48]

28 Thou wilt fall backward when thou comest to age. [56]

29 I am proverbed with a grandsire phrase. [iv. 37]

30 O! then, I see, Queen Mab hath been with you ... / She is the fairies' midwife, and she comes / In shape no bigger than an agate-stone / On the fore-finger of an alderman, / Drawn with a team of little atomies / Athwart men's noses as they lie asleep: / Her waggon-spokes made of long spinners' legs; / The cover, of the wings of grasshoppers; / The traces, of the smallest spider's web; / The collars, of the moonshine's watery beams; / Her whip, of cricket's bone; the lash, of film; / Her waggoner, a small grey-coated gnat, / Not half so big as a round little worm / Pricked from the lazy finger of a maid; / Her chariot is an empty hazel-nut, / Made by the joiner squirrel or old grub, / Time out o' mind the fairies' coachmakers. / And in this state she gallops night by night / Through lovers' brains, and then they dream of love; / O'er courtiers' knees, that dream on curtsies straight; / O'er lawyers' fingers, who straight dream on fees; / O'er ladies' lips, who straight on kisses dream. [53]

1 Sometimes she gallops o'er a courtier's nose, / And then dreams he of smelling out a suit; / And sometimes comes she with a tithe-pig's tail, / Tickling a parson's nose as a' lies asleep, / Then dreams he of another benefice; / Sometimes she driveth o'er a soldier's neck, / And then dreams he of cutting foreign throats. [78]

2 This is that very Mab / That plats the manes of horses in the night; / And bakes the elf-locks in foul sluttish hairs, / Which once untangled much misfortune bodes. [89]

3 For you and I are past our dancing days. [v. (35)]

4 O! she doth teach the torches to burn bright. / It seems she hangs upon the cheek of night / Like a rich jewel in an Ethiop's ear. [(48)]

5 We have a trifling foolish banquet towards. [(126)]

6 My only love sprung from my only hate! [(142)]

7 Young Adam Cupid, he that shot so trim / When King Cophetua loved the beggar-maid. [II. i. 13]

8 He jests at scars, that never felt a wound. / But, soft! what light through yonder window breaks? / It is the east, and Juliet is the sun. [ii. 1]

9 See! how she leans her cheek upon her hand: / O! that I were a glove upon that hand, / That I might touch that cheek. [23]

10 O Romeo, Romeo! wherefore art thou Romeo? [33]

11 What's in a name? that which we call a rose / By any other name would smell as sweet. [43]

12 For stony limits cannot hold love out. [67]

13 At lovers' perjuries, / They say, Jove laughs. [92]

14 I'll prove more true / Than those that have more cunning to be strange. [100]

15 O! swear not by the moon, the inconstant moon, / that monthly changes in her circled orb, / Lest that thy love prove likewise variable. [109]

16 The God of my idolatry. [114]

17 It is too rash, too unadvised, too sudden; / Too like the lightning, which doth cease to be / Ere one can say it lightens. [118]

18 Love goes toward love, as schoolboys from their books; / But love from love, toward school with heavy looks. [156]

19 How silver-sweet sound lovers' tongues by night, / Like softest music to attending ears! [165]

20 I would have thee gone; / And yet no further than a wanton's bird, / Who lets it hop a little from her hand, / Like a poor prisoner in his twisted gyves, / And with a silk thread plucks it back again, / So loving-jealous of his liberty. [176]

21 Good-night, good-night! parting is such sweet sorrow / That I shall say good-night till it be morrow. [184]

22 Virtue itself turns vice, being misapplied; / And vice sometime's by action dignified. [iii. 21]

23 Wisely and slow; they stumble that run fast. [94]

24 O flesh, flesh, how art thou fishified! [iv. (41)]

25 I am the very pink of courtesy. [(63)]

26 A gentleman, nurse, that loves to hear himself talk, and will speak more in a minute than he will stand to in a month. [(156)]

27 These violent delights have violent ends. [vi. 9]

28 Too swift arrives as tardy as too slow. [15]

29 O! so light of foot / Will ne'er wear out the everlasting flint. [16]

30 Thy head is as full of quarrels as an egg is full of meat. [III. i. (23)]

31 A word and a blow. [(43)]

32 No, 'tis not so deep as a well, nor so wide as a church door; but 'tis enough, 'twill serve. [(101)]

33 A plague o' both your houses! / They have made worms' meat of me. [(112)]

34 O! I am Fortune's fool. [(142)]

35 Gallop apace, you fiery-footed steeds, Towards Phoebus' lodging. [ii. 1]

36 Come, civil night, / Thou sober-suited matron, all in black. [10]

37 When he shall die, / Take him and cut him out in little stars, / And he will make the face of heaven so fine / That all the world will be in love with night, / And pay no worship to the garish sun. [21]

38 Thou art wedded to calamity. [iii. 3]

1 Adversity's sweet milk, philosophy. [54]

2 It was the nightingale, and not the lark, / That pierced the fearful hollow of thine ear; / Nightly she sings on yon pomegranate tree. [v. 2]

3 Night's candles are burnt out, and jocund day / Stands tiptoe on the misty mountain tops. [9]

4 Villain and he be many miles asunder. [82]

5 'Tis an ill cook that cannot lick his own fingers. [IV. ii. (6)]

6 My poverty, but not my will, consents. [V. i. 75]

7 The time and my intents are savage-wild, / More fierce and more inexorable far / Than empty tigers or the roaring sea. [iii. 37]

8 Tempt not a desperate man. [59]

9 How oft when men are at the point of death / Have they been merry! [88]

10 Beauty's ensign yet / Is crimson in thy lips and in thy cheeks, / And death's pale flag is not advancèd there. [94]

11 O! here / Will I set up my everlasting rest, / And shake the yoke of inauspicious stars / From this world-wearied flesh. Eyes look your last! / Arms, take your last embrace! [109]

The Taming of the Shrew

12 Look in the chronicles; we came in with Richard Conqueror. [Induction, i. (4)]

13 Twenty more such names and men as these, / Which never were, nor no man ever saw. [ii. (97)]

14 No profit grows where is no pleasure ta'en; / In brief, sir, study what you most affect. [I. i. 39]

15 There's small choice in rotten apples. [(137)]

16 Love in idleness. [(155)]

17 Nothing comes amiss, so money comes withal. [ii. (82)]

18 I must dance bare-foot on her wedding day, / And, for your love to her, lead apes in hell. [II. i. 33]

19 Kiss me, Kate. [318]

20 This is the way to kill a wife with kindness. [IV. i. (211)]

21 And as the sun breaks through the darkest clouds, / So honour peereth in the meanest habit. [iii. (175)]

22 O vile, / Intolerable, not to be endured! [V. ii. 93]

23 A woman moved is like a fountain troubled, / Muddy, ill-seeming, thick, bereft of beauty. [143]

24 Such duty as the subject owes the prince, / Even such a woman oweth to her husband. [156]

The Tempest

25 He hath no drowning mark upon him; his complexion is perfect gallows. [I. i. (33)]

26 What seest thou else / In the dark backward and abysm of time? [ii. 49]

27 Your tale, sir, would cure deafness. [106]

28 My library / Was dukedom large enough. [109]

29 A rotten carcass of a boat, not rigged, / Nor tackle, sail, nor mast; the very rats / Instinctively have quit it. [146]

30 Knowing I loved my books, he furnished me, / From mine own library with volumes that / I prize above my dukedom. [166]

31 From the still-vexed Bermoothes. [229]

32 I will be correspondent to command, / And do my spiriting gently. [297]

33 You taught me language; and my profit on't / Is, I know how to curse; the red plague rid you, / For learning me your language! [363]

34 Come unto these yellow sands, / And then take hands; / Curtsied when you have, and kissed, – / The wild waves whist. [375]

35 Full fathom five thy father lies; / Of his bones are coral made: / Those are pearls that were his eyes: / Nothing of him that doth fade, / But doth suffer a sea-change / Into something rich and strange. [394]

36 The fringèd curtains of thine eye advance, / And say what thou seest yond. [405]

37 He receives comfort like cold porridge. [II. i. (10)]

38 They'll take suggestion as a cat laps milk. [296]

39 Open-eyed conspiracy / His time doth take. [(309)]

40 A very ancient and fish-like smell. [ii. (27)]

41 Misery acquaints a man with strange bedfellows. [(42)]

42 Well, here's my comfort. (Drinks.) [(48)]

1 The master, the swabber, the boatswain and I, / The gunner and his mate, / Loved Mall, Meg and Marian and Margery, / But none of us cared for Kate; / For she had a tongue with a tang, / Would cry to a sailor 'Go hang!' [(49)]

2 'Ban, 'Ban, Ca-Caliban, / Has a new master – Get a new man. [(197)]

3 For several virtues / Have I liked several women. [III. i. 42]

4 FERDINAND: Here's my hand.
MIRANDA: And mine with my heart in't. [89]

5 Thou deboshed fish thou. [ii. (30)]

6 Flout 'em, and scout 'em; and scout 'em, and flout 'em; / Thought is free. [(133)]

7 He that dies pays all debts. [(143)]

8 Be not afeard: the isle is full of noises, / Sounds and sweet airs, that give delight and hurt not. [(147)]

9 You sun-burned sicklemen, of August weary. [IV. i. 134]

10 Our revels now are ended. These our actors, / As I foretold you, were all spirits and / Are melted into air, into thin air: / And, like the baseless fabric of this vision, / The cloud-capped towers, the gorgeous palaces, / The solemn temples, the great globe itself, / Yea, all which it inherit, shall dissolve / And, like this insubstantial pageant faded, / Leave not a rack behind. We are such stuff / As dreams are made on, and our little life / Is rounded with a sleep. [148]

11 I do begin to have bloody thoughts. [(221)]

12 With foreheads villanous low. [(252)]

13 Now does my object gather to a head. [V. i. 1]

14 The rarer action is / In virtue than in vengeance. [27]

15 Ye elves of hills, brooks, standing lakes and groves; / And ye, that on the sands with printless foot / Do chase the ebbing Neptune and do fly him / When he comes back. [33]

16 I'll break my staff, / Bury it certain fathoms in the earth, / And, deeper than did ever plummet sound, / I'll drown my book. [54]

17 Where the bee sucks, there suck I: / In a cowslip's bell I lie; / There I couch when owls do cry. / On the bat's back I do fly / After summer merrily: / Merrily, merrily shall I live now / Under the blossom that hangs on the bough. [88]

18 How beauteous mankind is! O brave new world, / That has such people in't! [183]

19 How camest thou in this pickle? [(281)]

20 Retire me to my Milan, where / Every third thought shall be my grave. [(310)]

Timon of Athens

21 Our poesy is as a gum, which oozes / From whence 'tis nourished. [I. i. 21]

22 'Tis not enough to help the feeble up, / But to support him after. [108]

23 I wonder men dare trust themselves with men. [ii. (45)]

24 Men shut their doors against a setting sun. [(152)]

25 We have seen better days. [IV. ii. 27]

26 Timon hath made his everlasting mansion / Upon the beachèd verge of the salt flood, / Who once a day with his embossèd froth / The turbulent surge shall cover. [V. i. (220)]

Titus Andronicus

27 He lives in fame that died in virtue's cause. [I. i. 390]

28 She is a woman, therefore may be wooed; / She is a woman, therefore may be won, / She is Lavinia, therefore must be loved. / What, man! more water glideth by the mill / Than wots the miller of; and easy it is / Of a cut loaf to steal a shive, we know. [II. i. 82]

29 Come, and take choice of all my library, / And so beguile thy sorrow. [IV. i. 34]

30 The eagle suffers little birds to sing, / And is not careful what they mean thereby. [iv. (82)]

31 If one good deed in all my life I did, / I do repent it from my very soul. [V. iii. 189]

Troilus and Cressida

32 I have had my labour for my travail. [I. i. (73)]

33 She's a merry Greek indeed. [ii. (116)]

34 Women are angels, wooing: / Things won are done; joy's soul lies in the doing: / That she beloved knows nought that knows not this: / Men prize the thing ungained more than it is. [(310)]

35 The heavens themselves, the planets, and this centre / Observe degree, priority, and place, / Insisture, course, proportion, season, form, / Office, and custom, in all line of order. [iii. 85]

1 Take but degree away, untune that string / And hark what discord follows; each thing meets / In mere oppugnancy. [109]

2 An envious fever / Of pale and bloodless emulation. [133]

3 To hear the wooden dialogue. [155]

4 The baby figure of the giant mass / Of things to come at large. [345]

5 'Tis mad idolatry / To make the service greater than the god. [II. ii. 56]

6 Thus to persist / In doing wrong extenuates not wrong, / But makes it much more heavy. [186]

7 That little little less than little wit. [iii. (14)]

8 I am giddy, expectation whirls me round. / The imaginary relish is so sweet / That it enchants my sense. [III. ii. (17)]

9 This is the monstruosity in love, lady, that the will is infinite and the execution confined. [(85)]

10 To be wise, and love, / Exceeds man's might. [(163)]

11 Let all pitiful goers-between be called to the world's end after my name; call them all Pandars. [(208)]

12 Time hath, my lord, a wallet at his back, / Wherein he puts alms for oblivion, / A great-sized monster of ingratitudes: / Those scraps are good deeds past: which are devoured / As fast as they are made, forgot as soon / As done. [iii. 145]

13 Perseverance, dear my lord, / Keeps honour bright: to have done, is to hang / Quite out of fashion, like a rusty mail / In monumental mockery. [150]

14 Time is like a fashionable host / That slightly shakes his parting guest by the hand, / And with his arms outstretched, as he would fly, / Grasps in the comer: welcome ever smiles, / And farewell goes out sighing. [165]

15 Envious and calumniating time. [174]

16 One touch of nature makes the whole world kin. [175]

17 And give to dust that is a little gilt / More laud than gilt o'er-dusted. [178]

18 My mind is troubled, like a fountain stirred; / And I myself see not the bottom of it. [(314)]

19 There's language in her eye, her cheek, her lip, / Nay, her foot speaks, her wanton spirits look out / At every joint and motive of her body. [IV. v. 55]

20 The end crowns all, / And that old common arbitrator, Time, / Will one day end it. [223]

21 Lechery, lechery; still, wars and lechery; nothing else holds fashion. [V. ii. (192)]

22 Words, words, mere words, no matter from the heart. [iii. (109)]

Twelfth Night

23 If music be the food of love, play on; / Give me excess of it, that, surfeiting, / The appetite may sicken, and so die. / That strain again! it had a dying fall: / O! it came o'er my ear like the sweet sound / That breathes upon a bank of violets, / Stealing and giving odour! [I. i. 1]

24 O spirit of love! how quick and fresh art thou, / That notwithstanding thy capacity / Receiveth as the sea, nought enters there, / Of what validity and pitch soe'er, / But falls into abatement and low price, / Even in a minute: so full of shapes is fancy, / That it alone is high fantastical. [9]

25 I am sure care's an enemy to life. [iii. (2)]

26 Speaks three or four languages word for word without book. [(28)]

27 Methinks sometimes I have no more wit than a Christian or an ordinary man has; but I am a great eater of beef, and I believe that does harm to my wit. [(90)]

28 Wherefore are these things hid? [(135)]

29 Is it a world to hide virtues in? [(142)]

30 Many a good hanging prevents a bad marriage. [v. (20)]

31 Good my mouse of virtue, answer me. [(68)]

32 A plague o' these pickle herring! [(127)]

33 One would think his mother's milk were scarce out of him. [(171)]

34 Lady, you are the cruell'st she alive. [(260)]

35 *Item*, Two lips, indifferent red; *Item*, Two grey eyes with lids to them; *Item*, One neck, one chin, and so forth. [(268)]

36 Make me a willow cabin at your gate, / And call upon my soul within the house; / Write loyal cantons of contemnèd love, / And sing them loud even in the dead of night; / Holla your name to the reverberate hills, / And make the babbling gossip of the air / Cry out, 'Olivia'. [(289)]

37 Farewell, fair cruelty. [(309)]

1 Not to be a-bed after midnight is to be up betimes. [II. iii. 1]

2 O mistress mine! where are you roaming? / O! stay and hear; your true love's coming, / That can sing both high and low. / Trip no further, pretty sweeting; / Journeys end in lovers meeting, / Every wise man's son doth know. [(42)]

3 In delay there lies no plenty; / Then come kiss me, sweet and twenty, / Youth's a stuff will not endure. [(53)]

4 He does it with a better grace, but I do it more natural. [(91)]

5 Is there no respect of place, persons, nor time in you? [(100)]

6 SIR TOBY: Dost thou think, because thou art virtuous, there shall be no more cakes and ale? CLOWN: Yes by Saint Anne; and ginger shall be hot i' the mouth too. [(124)]

7 My purpose is, indeed, a horse of that colour. [(184)]

8 I was adored once too. [(200)]

9 It gives a very echo to the seat / Where Love is throned. [iv. 21]

10 Let still the woman take / An elder than herself, so wears she to him, / So sways she level in her husband's heart: / For, boy, however we do praise ourselves, / Our fancies are more giddy and unfirm, / More longing, wavering, sooner lost and worn, / Than women's are. [29]

11 Then let thy love be younger than thyself, / Or thy affection cannot hold the bent. [36]

12 The spinsters and the knitters in the sun, / And the free maids that weave their thread with bones, / Do use to chant it: it is silly sooth, / And dallies with the innocence of love, / Like the old age. [44]

13 Come away, come away, death, / And in sad cypress let me be laid; / Fly away, fly away, breath: / I am slain by a fair cruel maid. / My shroud of white, stuck all with yew, / O! prepare it: / My part of death, no one so true / Did share it. [51]

14 DUKE: And what's her history? VIOLA: A blank, my lord. She never told her love, / But let concealment like a worm i' the bud, / Feed on her damask cheek: she pined in thought, / And with a green and yellow melancholy, / She sat like Patience on a monument, / Smiling at grief. [(111)]

15 I am all the daughters of my father's house, / And all the brothers too. [(122)]

16 Be not afraid of greatness: some men are born great, some achieve greatness, and some have greatness thrust upon them. [v. (158)]

17 Remember who commended thy yellow stockings, and wished to see thee ever cross-gartered. [(168)]

18 O world! how apt the poor are to be proud. [III. i. (141)]

19 O! what a deal of scorn looks beautiful / In the contempt and anger of his lip. [(159)]

20 Love sought is good, but giv'n unsought is better. [(170)]

21 You will hang like an icicle on a Dutchman's beard. [ii. (30)]

22 Let there be gall enough in thy ink, though thou write with a goose-pen, no matter. [(54)]

23 I think we do know the sweet Roman hand. [iv. (31)]

24 Why this is very midsummer madness. [(62)]

25 If this were played upon a stage now, / I could condemn it as an improbable fiction. [(142)]

26 More matter for a May morning. [(158)]

27 Still you keep o' the windy side of the law. [(183)]

28 Out of my lean and low ability I'll lend you something. [(380)]

29 I hate ingratitude more in a man / Than lying, vainness, babbling drunkenness, / Or any taint of vice whose strong corruption / Inhabits our frail blood. [(390)]

30 CLOWN: What is the opinion of Pythagoras concerning wild fowl? MALVOLIO: That the soul of our grandam might haply inhabit a bird. [IV. ii. (55)]

31 Leave thy vain bibble-babble. [(106)]

32 And thus the whirligig of time brings in his revenges. [V. i. (388)]

33 When that I was and a little tiny boy, / With hey, ho, the wind and the rain; / A foolish thing was but a toy, / For the rain it raineth every day. [(401)]

34 A great while ago the world begun, / With hey, ho, the wind and the rain; / But that's all one, our play is done, / And we'll strive to please you every day. [(417)]

The Two Gentlemen of Verona

1 Home-keeping youth have ever homely wits. [I. i. 2]

2 I have no other but a woman's reason: / I think him so, because I think him so. [ii. 23]

3 How wayward is this foolish love / That, like a testy babe, will scratch the nurse / And presently all humbled kiss the rod! [55]

4 O! how this spring of love resembleth / The uncertain glory of an April day. [iii. 84]

5 He makes sweet music with th' enamelled stones / Giving a gentle kiss to every sedge / He overtaketh in his pilgrimage. [II. vii. 28]

6 Except I be by Silvia in the night, / There is no music in the nightingale; / Unless I look on Silvia in the day, / There is no day for me to look upon. [III. i. 178]

7 Much is the force of heaven-bred poesy. [ii. 72]

8 Who is Silvia? What is she, / That all our swains commend her? [IV. ii. (40)]

9 How use doth breed a habit in a man! [V. iv. 1]

10 O heaven! were man / But constant, he were perfect. [110]

The Winter's Tale

11 Two lads that thought there was no more behind / But such a day tomorrow as today, / And to be boy eternal. [I. ii. 63]

12 We were as twinned lambs that did frisk i' the sun, / And bleat the one at the other: what we changed / Was innocence for innocence: we knew not / The doctrine of ill-doing, no, nor dreamed / That any did. [67]

13 Paddling palms and pinching fingers. [116]

14 A sad tale's best for winter. / I have one of sprites and goblins. [II. i. 24]

15 The silence often of pure innocence / Persuades when speaking fails. [ii. 41]

16 I am a feather for each wind that blows. [iii. 153]

17 What's gone and what's past help / Should be past grief. [III. ii. (223)]

18 *Exit, pursued by a bear.* [iii. 57, stage direction]

19 I would there were no age between sixteen and three-and-twenty, or that youth would sleep out the rest; for there is nothing in the between but getting wenches with child, wronging the ancientry, stealing, fighting. [58]

20 This is fairy gold. [(127)]

21 When daffodils begin to peer, / With heigh! the doxy, over the dale, / Why, then comes in the sweet o' the year; / For the red blood reigns in the winter's pale. [IV. ii. 1]

22 Set my pugging tooth on edge; / For a quart of ale is a dish for a king. [7]

23 Summer songs for me and my aunts, / While we lie tumbling in the hay. [11]

24 A snapper-up of unconsidered trifles. [(26)]

25 For the life to come, I sleep out the thought of it. [(30)]

26 Jog on, jog on, the foot-path way, / And merrily hent the stile-a: / A merry heart goes all the day, / Your sad tires in a mile-a. [(133)]

27 For you there's rosemary and rue, these keep / Seeming and savour all the winter long. [iii. 74]

28 Here's flowers for you; / Hot lavender, mints, savory, marjoram; / The marigold, that goes to bed wi' the sun, / And with him rises weeping. [103]

29 O Proserpina! / For the flowers now that frighted thou let'st fall / From Dis's waggon! daffodils, / That come before the swallow dares, and take / The winds of March with beauty; violets dim, / But sweeter than the lids of Juno's eyes / Or Cytherea's breath; pale primroses, / That die unmarried ere they can behold / Bright Phoebus in his strength – a malady / Most incident to maids; bold oxlips and / The crown imperial; lilies of all kinds, / The flower-de-luce being one. [116]

30 What you do / Still betters what is done. When you speak sweet, / I'd have you do it ever: when you sing, / I'd have you buy and sell so; so give alms; / Pray so; and, for the ordering your affairs, / To sing them too: when you do dance I wish you / A wave o' the sea; that you might ever do / Nothing but that; move still, still so, / And own no other function. [136]

31 Good sooth, she is / The queen of curds and cream. [160]

32 Lawn as white as driven snow. [(220)]

33 The self-same sun that shines upon his court / Hides not his visage from our cottage, but / Looks on alike. [(457)]

1 I'll queen it no inch further, / But milk my ewes and weep. [(462)]

2 Though I am not naturally honest, / I am so sometimes by chance. [(734)]

3 Let me have no lying: it becomes none but tradesmen. [(747)]

Poems

4 Crabbed age and youth cannot live together: / Youth is full of pleasance, age is full of care. [*The Passionate Pilgrim*, xii]

5 Age, I do abhor thee, youth, I do adore thee.

6 Beauty itself doth of itself persuade / The eyes of men without an orator. [*The Rape of Lucrece*, 29]

7 For greatest scandal waits on greatest state. [1006]

8 Cloud-kissing Ilion. [1370]

9 And now this pale swan in her watery nest / Begins the sad dirge of her certain ending. [1611]

10 To the only begetter of these insuing sonnets. [*Sonnets*, Dedication]

11 From fairest creatures we desire increase, / That thereby beauty's rose might never die. [1]

12 When forty winters shall besiege thy brow, / And dig deep trenches in thy beauty's field. [2]

13 Thou art thy mother's glass, and she in thee / Calls back the lovely April of her prime. [3]

14 When I do count the clock that tells the time, / I see the brave day sunk in hideous night; / When I behold the violet past prime, / And sable curls all silvered o'er with white; / When lofty trees I see barren of leaves, / Which erst from heat did canopy the herd, / And summer's green all girded up in sheaves, / Borne on the bier with white and bristly beard. [12]

15 If I could write the beauty of your eyes / And in fresh numbers number all your graces. [17]

16 And stretchèd metre of an antique song. [17]

17 Shall I compare thee to a summer's day? / Thou art more lovely and more temperate: / Rough winds do shake the darling buds of May, / And summer's lease hath all too short a date. / Sometimes too hot the eye of heaven shines, / And often is his gold complexion dimmed; / And every fair from fair sometime declines. [18]

18 But thy eternal summer shall not fade. [18]

19 O let my books be then the eloquence / And dumb presagers of my speaking breast. [23]

20 The painful warrior famousèd for fight, / After a thousand victories once foiled, / Is from the book of honour razèd quite, / And all the rest forgot for which he toiled. [25]

21 Weary with toil I haste me to my bed. [27]

22 When in disgrace with fortune and men's eyes / I all alone beweep my outcast state. [29]

23 Haply I think on thee – and then my state, / Like to the lark at break of day arising / From sullen earth, sings hymns at heaven's gate; / For the sweet love remembered such wealth brings / That then I scorn to change my state with kings.

24 When to the sessions of sweet silent thought / I summon up remembrance of things past, / I sigh the lack of many a thing I sought, / And with old woes new wail my dear times' waste: / Then can I drown an eye, unused to flow, / For precious friends hid in death's dateless night, / And weep afresh love's long since cancelled woe, / And moan the expense of many a vanished sight. [30]

25 But if the while I think on thee, dear friend, / All losses are restored and sorrows end.

26 But since he died, and poets better prove, / Theirs for their style I'll read, his for his love. [32]

27 Full many a glorious morning have I seen / Flatter the mountain tops with sovereign eye, / Kissing with golden face the meadows green, / Gilding pale streams with heavenly alchemy. [33]

28 Ah! but those tears are pearl which thy love sheds, / And they are rich and ransom all ill deeds. [34]

29 Roses have thorns, and silver fountains mud; / Clouds and eclipses stain both moon and sun. [35]

30 Not marble, nor the gilded monuments / Of princes shall outlive this powerful rhyme. [55]

31 Being your slave, what should I do but tend / Upon the hours and times of your desire? [57]

32 So true a fool is love that in your will, / Though you do anything, he thinks no ill.

33 Like as the waves make towards the pebbled

shore, / So do our minutes hasten to their end. [60]

1 Time doth transfix the flourish set on youth / And delves the parallels in beauty's brow.

2 When I have seen by Time's fell hand defaced / The rich-proud cost of outworn buried age. [64]

3 When I have seen the hungry ocean gain / Advantage on the kingdom of the shore.

4 Since brass, nor stone, nor earth, nor boundless sea, / But sad mortality o'ersways their power, / How with this rage shall beauty hold a plea, / Whose action is no stronger than a flower? [65]

5 Tired with all these, for restful death I cry. [66]

6 And art made tongue-tied by authority.

7 And simple truth miscalled simplicity, / And captive good attending captain ill.

8 No longer mourn for me when I am dead / Than you shall hear the surly sullen bell / Give warning to the world that I am fled / From this vile world, with vilest worms to dwell. [71]

9 O! if, – I say, you look upon this verse, / When I perhaps compounded am with clay, / Do not so much as my poor name rehearse, / But let your love even with my life decay.

10 That time of year thou mayst in me behold / When yellow leaves, or none, or few, do hang / Upon those boughs which shake against the cold, / Bare ruined choirs, where late the sweet birds sang. [73]

11 Your monument shall be my gentle verse, / Which eyes not yet created shall o'er-read; / And tongues to be, your being shall rehearse, / When all the breathers of this world are dead. [81]

12 Was it the proud full sail of this great verse, / Bound for the prize of all too precious you? [86]

13 That affable familiar ghost / Which nightly gulls him with intelligence.

14 Farewell! thou art too dear for my possessing, / And like enough thou know'st thy estimate. [87]

15 Thus have I had thee, as a dream doth flatter, / In sleep a king, but, waking, no such matter.

16 Ah! do not, when my heart hath 'scaped this sorrow, / Come in the rearward of a conquered woe; / Give not a windy night a rainy morrow, / To linger out a purposed overthrow. [90]

17 They that have power to hurt and will do none, / That do not do the thing they most do show, / Who, moving others, are themselves as stone, / Unmovèd, cold, and to temptation slow. [94]

18 The summer's flower is to the summer sweet, / Though to itself it only live and die.

19 For sweetest things turn sourest by their deeds; / Lilies that fester smell far worse than weeds.

20 From you have I been absent in the spring, / When proud-pied April, dressed in all his trim, / Hath put a spirit of youth in every thing. [98]

21 To me, fair friend, you never can be old, / For as you were when first your eye I eyed, / Such seems your beauty still. [104]

22 Ah! yet doth beauty, like a dial-hand, / Steal from his figure and no pace perceived.

23 Hear this, thou age unbred: / Ere you were born was beauty's summer dead.

24 When in the chronicle of wasted time / I see descriptions of the fairest wights, / And beauty making beautiful old rhyme, / In praise of ladies dead and lovely knights. [106]

25 For we, which now behold these present days, / Have eyes to wonder, but lack tongues to praise.

26 Not mine own fears, nor the prophetic soul / Of the wide world dreaming on things to come. [107]

27 And peace proclaims olives of endless age.

28 And thou in this shalt find thy monument, / When tyrants' crests and tombs of brass are spent.

29 O! never say that I was false of heart, / Though absence seemed my flame to qualify. [109]

30 Alas! 'tis true I have gone here and there, / And made myself a motley to the view. [110]

31 My nature is subdued / To what it works in, like the dyer's hand. [111]

32 Let me not to the marriage of true minds / Admit impediments. Love is not love / Which alters when it alteration finds, / Or tends with

the remover to remove: / O, no! it is an ever-fixèd mark. [116]

1 Love's not Time's fool, though rosy lips and cheeks / Within his bending sickle's compass come.

2 If this be error, and upon me proved, / I never writ, nor no man ever loved.

3 'Tis better to be vile than vile esteemed, / When not to be receives reproach of being. [121]

4 The expense of spirit in a waste of shame / Is lust in action; and till action, lust / Is perjured, murderous, bloody, full of blame, / Savage, extreme, rude, cruel, not to trust. [129]

5 Mad in pursuit and in possession so; / Had, having, and in quest to have, extreme; / A bliss in proof, – and proved, a very woe; / Before, a joy proposed; behind, a dream. / All this the world well knows; yet none knows well / To shun the heaven that leads men to this hell.

6 My mistress' eyes are nothing like the sun. [130]

7 Two loves I have of comfort and despair, / Which like two spirits do suggest me still: / The better angel is a man right fair, / The worser spirit a woman coloured ill. [144]

8 Poor soul, the centre of my sinful earth, / Fooled by these rebel powers that thee array, / Why dost thou pine within and suffer dearth, / Painting thy outward walls so costly gay? [146]

9 So shalt thou feed on Death, that feeds on men, / And Death once dead, there's no more dying then.

10 Hunting he loved, but love he laughed to scorn. [Venus and Adonis, 4]

11 Bid me discourse, I will enchant thine ear, / Or like a fairy, trip upon the green, / Or like a nymph, with long dishevelled hair, / Dance on the sands, and yet no footing seen: / Love is a spirit all compact of fire, / Not gross to sink, but light, and will aspire. [145]

12 Good friend, for Jesu's sake forbear / To dig the dust enclosèd here. / Blest be the man that spares these stones, / And curst be he that moves my bones. [His epitaph]

13 Item, I give unto my wife my second best bed. [Will]

G. BERNARD SHAW 1856–1950

14 All great truths begin as blasphemies. [Annajanska]

15 Whether you think Jesus was God or not, you must admit that he was a first-rate political economist. [Androcles and the Lion, Preface, 'Jesus as Economist']

16 Breakages, Limited, the biggest industrial corporation in the country. [The Apple Cart, I]

17 I never resist temptation, because I have found that things that are bad for me do not tempt me. [II]

18 What use are cartridges in battle? I always carry chocolate instead. [Arms and the Man, I]

19 You are a very poor soldier: a chocolate cream soldier!

20 I never apologize! [III]

21 You're not a man, you're a machine.

22 He is a barbarian, and thinks that the customs of his tribe and island Britain are the laws of nature. [Caesar and Cleopatra, II]

23 When a stupid man is doing something he is ashamed of, he always declares that it is his duty. [III]

24 We have no more right to consume happiness without producing it than to consume wealth without producing it. [Candida, I]

25 It is easy – terribly easy – to shake a man's faith in himself. To take advantage of that to break a man's spirit is devil's work.

26 I'm only a beer teetotaller, not a champagne teetotaller. [III]

27 The worst sin towards our fellow creatures is not to hate them, but to be indifferent to them; that's the essence of inhumanity. [The Devil's Disciple, II]

28 I never expect a soldier to think. [III]

29 The British soldier can stand up to anything except the British War Office.

30 Stimulate the phagocytes. Drugs are a delusion. [The Doctor's Dilemma, I]

31 All professions are conspiracies against the laity.

32 What God hath joined together no man shall ever put asunder: God will take care of that. [Getting Married, Preface]

33 Has he attained the seventh degree of concentration? [Heartbreak House, I]

G. Bernard Shaw

1 When our relatives are at home, we have to think of all their good points or it would be impossible to endure them. But when they are away, we console ourselves for their absence by dwelling on their vices.

2 She married a numskull.

3 Go anywhere in England where there are natural, wholesome, contented, and really nice English people: and what do you always find? That the stables are the real centre of the household. [III]

4 We must be thoroughly democratic, and patronize everybody without distinction of class. [*John Bull's Other Island*, II]

5 What really flatters a man is that you think him worth flattering.

6 There are only two qualities in the world: efficiency and inefficiency; and only two sorts of people: the efficient and the inefficient. [IV]

7 He is always breaking the law. He broke the law when he was born: his parents were not married. [*Major Barbara*, I]

8 I am a Millionaire. That is my religion. [II]

9 Wot prawce Selvytion nah?

10 He never does a proper thing without giving an improper reason for it. [III]

11 He knows nothing; and he thinks he knows everything. That points clearly to a political career.

12 Nothing is ever done in this world until men are prepared to kill one another if it is not done. [V]

13 CUSINS: Do you call poverty a crime?
UNDERSHAFT: The worst of all crimes. All the other crimes are virtues beside it. [IV]

14 Like all young men, you greatly exaggerate the difference between one young woman and another.

15 A lifetime of happiness! No man alive could bear it: it would be hell on earth. [*Man and Superman*, I]

16 The more things a man is ashamed of, the more respectable he is.

17 The true artist will let his wife starve, his children go barefoot, his mother drudge for his living at seventy, sooner than work at anything but his art.

18 It is a woman's business to get married as soon as possible, and a man's to keep unmarried as long as he can. [II]

19 Marry Ann; and at the end of a week you'll find no more inspiration in her than in a plate of muffins.

20 Hell is full of musical amateurs: music is the brandy of the damned. [III]

21 An Englishman thinks he is moral when he is only uncomfortable.

22 There are two tragedies in life. One is to lose your heart's desire. The other is to gain it. [IV (see also 455:31)]

23 Do not do unto others as you would they should do unto you. Their tastes may not be the same. ['Maxims for Revolutionists', 'The Golden Rule']

24 The golden rule is that there are no golden rules.

25 Do not love your neighbour as yourself. If you are on good terms with yourself it is an impertinence; if on bad, an injury.

26 Democracy substitutes election by the incompetent many for appointment by the corrupt few. ['Democracy']

27 He who can, does. He who cannot, teaches. ['Education']

28 Marriage is popular because it combines the maximum of temptation with the maximum of opportunity. ['Marriage']

29 If you strike a child, take care that you strike it in anger, even at the risk of maiming it for life. A blow in cold blood neither can nor should be forgiven. ['How to Beat Children']

30 The reasonable man adapts himself to the world; the unreasonable one persists in trying to adapt the world to himself. Therefore all progress depends on the unreasonable man. ['Reason']

31 Beware of the man whose god is in the skies. ['Religion']

32 Home is the girl's prison and the woman's workhouse. ['Women in the Home']

33 Every man over forty is a scoundrel. ['Stray Sayings']

34 There is nothing so bad or so good that you will not find an Englishman doing it; but you will never find an Englishman in the wrong. He does everything on principle. He fights you on patriotic principles; he robs you on business principles; he enslaves you on imperial principles. [*Man of Destiny*]

1 A great devotee of the Gospel of Getting On. [*Mrs Warren's Profession*, IV]

2 The fickleness of the women I love is only equalled by the infernal constancy of the women who love me. [*The Philanderer*, II]

3 There is only one religion though there are a hundred versions of it. [*Plays Pleasant*, Preface]

4 He's a gentleman: look at his boots. [*Pygmalion*, I]

5 PICKERING: Have you no morals, man?
DOOLITTLE: Can't afford them, Governor. Neither could you if you was as poor as me. [II]

6 My aunt died of influenza: so they said . . . But it's my belief they done the old woman in. [III]

7 Gin was mother's milk to her.

8 Not bloody likely.

9 West wind, wanton wind, wilful wind, womanish wind, false wind from over the water, will you never blow again? [*St Joan*, III]

10 How can what an Englishman believes be heresy? It is a contradiction in terms. [IV]

11 Assassination is the extreme form of censorship. [*The Shewing-Up of Blanco Posnet*, 'The Limits of Toleration']

12 Well, sir, you never can tell. That's a principle in life with me, sir, if you'll excuse my having such a thing, sir. [*You Never Can Tell*, II]

13 With the single exception of Homer, there is no eminent writer, not even Sir Walter Scott, whom I can despise so entirely as I despise Shakespeare when I measure my mind against his . . . It would positively be a relief to me to dig him up and throw stones at him. [*Dramatic Opinions and Essays*, Vol. ii. p. 52]

14 The trouble, Mr Goldwyn, is that you are only interested in art and I am only interested in money. [When declining to sell Goldwyn the screen rights of his plays. Quoted in Philip French, *The Movie Moguls*, Ch. 4]

15 England and America are two countries separated by the same language. [Attr. *Reader's Digest*, Nov. 1942]

HENRY WHEELER SHAW [JOSH BILLINGS] 1818–1885

16 Thrice is he armed that hath his quarrel just, / But four times he who gets his blow in fust. [*Josh Billings, his Sayings*]

17 It is better to know nothing than to know what ain't so. [*Proverb*]

SIR HARTLEY [later LORD] SHAWCROSS 1902–1989

18 We are the masters at the moment – and not only for the moment, but for a very long time to come. [Said in House of Commons in a debate on the trade unions, 2 Apr. 1946]

PATRICK SHAW-STEWART 1888–1917

19 I saw a man this morning / Who did not wish to die: / I ask, and cannot answer, / If otherwise would I. [Quoted in Evelyn Waugh, *Ronald Knox*, Pt 1. Ch. 4]

RICHARD SHEALE 16 Cent.

20 For when his legs were smitten off, / He fought upon his stumps. [*Ballad of Chevy Chase*, Pt II. 10]

A. F. SHELDON 1868–1935

21 He profits most who serves best. [*Motto for International Rotary*]

P. B. SHELLEY 1792–1822

22 The cemetery is an open space among the ruins, covered in winter with violets and daisies. It might make one in love with death, to think that one should be buried in so sweet a place. [*Adonais*, Preface]

23 I weep for Adonais – he is dead! / O, weep for Adonais! though our tears / Thaw not the frost that binds so dear a head! [1]

24 He went, unterrified, / Into the gulf of death; but his clear sprite / Yet reigns o'er earth; the third among the sons of light. [34]

25 To that high capital, where kingly Death / Keeps his pale court in beauty and decay, / He came. [55]

26 He will awake no more, oh, never more! [64]

27 She faded, like a cloud which had outwept its rain. [90]

28 Winter is come and gone, / But grief returns with the revolving year. [154]

29 Alas! that all we loved of him should be, / But for our grief, as if it had not been, / And grief itself be mortal! [181]

P. B. Shelley

1 The pilgrim of eternity, whose fame / Over his living head like Heaven is bent, / An early, but enduring monument. [264]

2 It is a dying lamp, a falling shower, / A breaking billow: – even whilst we speak / Is it not broken? [284]

3 Thou canst not soar where he is sitting now. – / Dust to the dust! but the pure spirit shall flow / Back to the burning fountain whence it came, / A portion of the eternal. [337]

4 He hath awakened from the dream of life – / 'Tis we, who lost in stormy visions, keep / With phantoms an unprofitable strife, / And in mad trance, strike with our spirit's knife / Invulnerable nothings. [344]

5 He has outsoared the shadow of our night; / Envy and calumny and hate and pain, / And that unrest which men miscall delight, / Can touch him not and torture not again; / From the contagion of the world's slow stain / He is secure. [352]

6 He is made one with Nature: there is heard / His voice in all her music. [370]

7 He is a portion of the loveliness / Which once he made more lovely. [379]

8 The one remains, the many change and pass; / Heaven's light forever shines, earth's shadows fly; / Life, like a dome of many-coloured glass, / Stains the white radiance of eternity. [460]

9 The soul of Adonais, like a star, / Beacons from the abode where the eternal are. [494]

10 At length upon the lone Chorasmian shore / He paused, a wide and melancholy waste / Of putrid marshes. [*Alastor*, 272]

11 Arethusa arose / From her couch of snows / In the Acroceraunian mountains. [*Arethusa*]

12 A widow bird sate mourning for her love / Upon a wintry bough; / The frozen wind crept on above, / The freezing stream below.
There was no leaf upon the forest bare, / No flower upon the ground, / And little motion in the air / Except the mill-wheel's sound. [*Charles I*, III. v]

13 I bring fresh showers for the thirsting flowers, / From the seas and the streams. [*The Cloud*, 1]

14 I wield the flail of the lashing hail, / And whiten the green plains under, / And then again I dissolve it in rain, / And laugh as I pass in thunder. [9]

15 Sublime on the towers of my skiey bowers, / Lightning my pilot sits; / In a cavern under is fettered the thunder, / It struggles and howls at fits. [17]

16 I am the daughter of Earth and Water, / And the nursling of the Sky; / I pass through the pores of the ocean and shores; / I change but I cannot die. [73]

17 Like a child from the womb, like a ghost from the tomb, / I arise and unbuild it again. [82]

18 How wonderful is Death, / Death and his brother Sleep! [*The Daemon of the World*, i. 1]

19 Yet both so passing strange and wonderful! [8]

20 Wail, for the world's wrong! [*A Dirge*]

21 Tell them that they are dull, / And bid them own that thou art beautiful. [*Epipsychidion*, Advertisement]

22 The spirit of the worm beneath the sod / In love and worship, blends itself with God. [128]

23 We – are we not formed, as notes of music are, / For one another, though dissimilar? [142]

24 I never was attached to that great sect, / Whose doctrine is, that each one should select / Out of the crowd a mistress or a friend, / And all the rest, though fair and wise, commend / To cold oblivion. [149]

25 Those poor slaves . . . / Who travel to their home among the dead / By the broad highway of the world, and so / With one chained friend, perhaps a jealous foe, / The dreariest and the longest journey go. [155]

26 A ship is floating in the harbour now, / A wind is hovering o'er the mountain's brow; / There is a path on the sea's azure floor, / No keel has ever ploughed that path before; / The halcyons brood around the foamless isles; / The treacherous ocean has forsworn its wiles; / The merry mariners are bold and free: / Say, my heart's sister, wilt thou sail with me? [408]

27 Earth and Ocean seem / To sleep in one another's arms, and dream / Of waves, flowers, clouds, woods, rocks, and all that we / Read in their smiles, and call reality. [509]

28 Chameleons feed on light and air: Poets' food is love and fame. [*An Exhortation*]

29 Time's printless torrent grew / A scroll of crystal, blazoning the name / Of Adonais! [*Fragment on Keats*]

1 A hater he came and sat by a ditch, / And he took an old cracked lute; / And he sang a song that was more of a screech / 'Gainst a woman that was a brute. [*A Hate-Song*]

2 The world's great age begins anew, / The golden years return, / The earth doth like a snake renew / Her winter weeds outworn: / Heaven smiles, and faiths and empires gleam, / Like wrecks of a dissolving dream. [*Hellas*, 1060]

3 A loftier Argo cleaves the main, / Fraught with a later prize; / Another Orpheus sings again, / And loves, and weeps, and dies. / A new Ulysses leaves once more / Calypso for his native shore. [1072]

4 Oh, write no more the tale of Troy. [1078]

5 Although a subtler sphinx renew / Riddles of death Thebes never knew. [1082]

6 Another Athens shall arise, / And to remoter time / Bequeath, like sunset to the skies, / The splendour of its prime. [1084]

7 Saturn and Love their long repose / Shall burst, more bright and good / Than all who fell, than One who rose, / Than many unsubdued. [1090]

8 Oh, cease! must hate and death return? / Cease! must men kill and die? / Cease! drain not to the dregs the urn / Of bitter prophecy. / The world is weary of the past, / Oh, might it die or rest at last! [1096]

9 Singing how down the vale of Maenalus / I pursued a maiden and clasped a reed. / Gods and men, we are all deluded thus! / It breaks in our bosom and then we bleed. [*Hymn of Pan*]

10 With fearful steps pursuing / Hopes of high talk with the departed dead. [*Hymn to Intellectual Beauty*, 51]

11 I arise from dreams of thee / In the first sweet sleep of night. / When the winds are breathing low, / And the stars are shining bright. [*The Indian Serenade*]

12 The nightingale's complaint, / It dies upon her heart.

13 Oh lift me from the grass! / I die! I faint! I fail! / Let thy love and kisses rain / On my lips and eyelids pale. / My cheek is cold and white, alas! / My heart beats loud and fast; – / Oh! press it to thine own again, / Where it will break at last.

14 Thou Paradise of exiles, Italy! [*Julian and Maddalo*, 57]

15 Most wretched men / Are cradled into poetry by wrong, / They learn in suffering what they teach in song. [544]

16 O world! O life! O time! / On whose last steps I climb, / Trembling at that where I had stood before; / When will return the glory of your prime? / No more – Oh, never more! [*A Lament*]

17 We watched the ocean and the sky together, / Under the roof of blue Italian weather. [*Letter to Maria Gisborne*, 146]

18 You will see Coleridge – he who sits obscure / In the exceeding lustre and the pure / Intense irradiation of a mind, / Which, with its own internal lightning blind, / Flags wearily through darkness and despair – / A cloud-encircled meteor of the air, / A hooded eagle among blinking owls. / You will see Hunt – one of those happy souls / Which are the salt of the earth, and without whom / This world would smell like what it is – a tomb. [202]

19 His [Peacock's] fine wit / Makes such a wound, the knife is lost in it. [240]

20 We'll have fires out of the Grand Duke's wood, / To thaw the six weeks' winter in our blood. / And then we'll talk. [308]

21 When the lamp is shattered / The light in the dust lies dead – / When the cloud is scattered / The rainbow's glory is shed. / When the lute is broken, / Sweet tones are remembered not: / When the lips have spoken, / Loved accents are soon forgot. [*Lines: When the Lamp is Shattered*]

22 O Love! who bewailest / The frailty of all things here, / Why choose you the frailest / For your cradle, your home, and your bier?

23 Many a green isle needs must be / In the deep wide sea of Misery. [*Lines written among the Euganean Hills*, 1]

24 Underneath Day's azure eyes / Ocean's nursling, Venice lies, / A peopled labyrinth of walls. [94]

25 Sun-girt City, thou hast been / Ocean's child, and then his queen; / Now is come a darker day, / And thou soon must be his prey. [115]

26 The mind which feeds this verse, / Peopling the lone universe. [318]

27 The fountains mingle with the river / And the rivers with the ocean, / The winds of heaven mix for ever / With a sweet emotion; / Nothing

in the world is single; / All things by a law divine / In one spirit meet and mingle. / Why not I with thine? [*Love's Philosophy*]

1 I met Murder on the way – / He had a mask like Castlereagh. [*The Mask of Anarchy*, 5]

2 Rise like lions after slumber / In unvanquishable number, / Shake your chains to earth like dew / Which in sleep had fallen on you – / Ye are many – they are few. [151]

3 Man's yesterday may ne'er be like his morrow; / Nought may endure but Mutability. [*Mutability*]

4 O wild West Wind, thou breath of Autumn's being, / Thou, from whose unseen presence the leaves dead / Are driven, like ghosts from an enchanter fleeing,

Yellow, and black, and pale, and hectic red, / Pestilence-stricken multitudes: O thou, / Who chariotest to their dark wintry bed

The wingèd seeds, where they lie cold and low, / Each like a corpse within its grave, until / Thine azure sister of the Spring shall blow

Her clarion o'er the dreaming earth. [*Ode to the West Wind*, 1]

5 Wild Spirit, which art moving everywhere; / Destroyer and preserver; hear, oh, hear! [13]

6 Thou dirge

Of the dying year, to which this closing night / Will be the dome of a vast sepulchre. [23]

7 Thou who didst waken from his summer dreams / The blue Mediterranean, where he lay, / Lulled by the coil of his crystálline streams,

Beside a pumice isle in Baiae's bay, / And saw in sleep old palaces and towers / Quivering within the wave's intenser day. [29]

8 If I were a dead leaf thou mightest bear; / If I were a swift cloud to fly with thee. [43]

9 If even / I were as in my boyhood, and could be The comrade of thy wanderings over heaven. [47]

10 Oh, lift me as a wave, a leaf, a cloud! / I fall upon the thorns of life! I bleed!

A heavy weight of hours has chained and bowed / One too like thee: tameless, and swift, and proud. [53]

11 Make me thy lyre, even as the forest is: / What if my leaves are falling like its own! [57]

12 Scatter, as from an unextinguished hearth / Ashes and sparks, my words among mankind! / Be through my lips to unawakened earth

The trumpet of a prophecy! O, Wind, / If Winter comes, can Spring be far behind? [66]

13 I met a traveller from an antique land / Who said: Two vast and trunkless legs of stone / Stand in the desert. [*Ozymandias*]

14 Whose frown / And wrinkled lip, and sneer of cold command, / Tell that its sculptor well those passions read / Which yet survive, stamped on these lifeless things.

15 My name is Ozymandias, king of kings: / Look on my works, ye mighty, and despair!

16 Sometimes / The Devil is a gentleman. [*Peter Bell the Third*, 81]

17 Hell is a city much like London – / A populous and a smoky city. [147]

18 Teas, / Where small talk dies in agonies. [204]

19 'Twas Peter's drift / To be a kind of moral eunuch. [313]

20 Whether he talked, wrote, or rehearsed – / Still with this dullness was he cursed – / Dull – beyond all conception – dull. [705]

21 Monarch of gods and daemons, and all spirits / But one, who throng those bright and rolling worlds. [*Prometheus Unbound*, I. 1]

22 The crawling glaciers pierce me with the spears / Of their moon-freezing crystals, the bright chains / Eat with their burning cold into my bones. [31]

23 The wingless, crawling hours, one among whom / – As some dark priest hales the reluctant victim, / Shall drag thee, cruel king, to kiss the blood / From these pale feet. [48]

24 Ere Babylon was dust, / The Magus Zoroaster, my dead child, / Met his own image, walking in the garden. [191]

25 Grief for a while is blind, and so was mine. / I wish no living thing to suffer pain. [304]

26 The good want power, but to weep barren tears. / The powerful goodness want: worse need for them. / The wise want love; and those who love want wisdom; / And all best things are thus confused with ill. [625]

27 Thy words are like a cloud of wingèd snakes; / And yet I pity those they torture not. [632]

1 Peace is in the grave. / The grave hides all things beautiful and good: / I am a God and cannot find it there. [638]

2 From the dust of creeds outworn. [697]

3 On a poet's lips I slept / Dreaming like a love-adept. [737]

4 Feeds on the aëreal kisses / Of shapes that haunt thought's wildernesses. [741]

5 Create he can / Forms more real than living man, / Nurslings of immortality! [747]

6 Leaves this peopled earth a solitude / When it returns no more. [II. iv. 17]

7 To know nor faith, nor love, nor law; to be / Omnipotent but friendless is to reign. [47]

8 He gave man speech, and speech created thought, / Which is the measure of the universe. [72]

9 All spirits are enslaved that serve things evil. [110]

10 All love is sweet, / Given or returned. Common as light is love, / And its familiar voice wearies not ever. [v. 39]

11 Life of Life! thy lips enkindle / With their love the breath between them; / And thy smiles before they dwindle / Make the cold air fire; then screen them / In those looks, where whoso gazes / Faints, entangled in their mazes. [48]

12 My soul is an enchanted boat, / Which, like a sleeping swan, doth float / Upon the silver waves of thy sweet singing. [72]

13 We have passed age's icy caves, / And manhood's dark and tossing waves, / And youth's smooth ocean, smiling to betray: / Beyond the glassy gulfs we flee / Of shadow-peopled infancy, / Through death and birth, to a diviner day. [98]

14 Death is the veil which those who live call life: / They sleep, and it is lifted. [III. iii. 113]

15 The loathsome mask has fallen, the man remains / Sceptreless, free, uncircumscribed, but man / Equal, unclassed, tribeless and nationless. [iv. 193]

16 Nor yet exempt, though ruling them like slaves, / From chance, and death, and mutability, / The clogs of that which else might oversoar / The loftiest star of unascended heaven, / Pinnacled dim in the intense inane. [200]

17 Familiar acts are beautiful through love. [IV. 403]

18 Man, who wert once a despot and a slave; / A dupe and a deceiver; a decay; / A traveller from the cradle to the grave / Through the dim light of this immortal day. [549]

19 To suffer woes which hope thinks infinite; / To forgive wrongs darker than death or night; / To defy power, which seems omnipotent; / To love, and bear; to hope till hope creates / From its own wreck the thing it contemplates; / Neither to change, nor falter, nor repent; / This, like thy glory, Titan, is to be / Good, great and joyous, beautiful and free; / This is alone life, joy, empire, and victory. [570]

20 I dreamed that, as I wandered by the way, / Bare winter suddenly was changed to spring. [The Question]

21 There grew pied wind-flowers and violets, / Daisies, those pearled Arcturi of the earth, / The constellated flower that never sets; / Faint oxslips; tender bluebells, at whose birth / The sod scarce heaved.

22 I hastened to the spot whence I had come, / That I might there present it! – Oh! to whom?

23 With hue like that when some great painter dips / His pencil in the gloom of earthquake and eclipse. [The Revolt of Islam, V. 1925]

24 A sensitive plant in a garden grew, / And the young winds fed it with silver dew. [The Sensitive Plant, I. 1]

25 It is a modest creed, and yet / Pleasant if one considers it, / To own that death itself must be, / Like all the rest, a mockery. [III. 126]

26 Rarely, rarely, comest thou, / Spirit of Delight! [Song: Rarely, Rarely, Comest Thou]

27 Let me set my mournful ditty / To a merry measure; / Thou wilt never come for pity, / Thou wilt come for pleasure.

28 Men of England, wherefore plough / For the lords who lay ye low? [Song to the Men of England]

29 The seed ye sow, another reaps; / The wealth ye find, another keeps.

30 An old, mad, blind, despised, and dying king. [Sonnet: England in 1819]

31 Lift not the painted veil which those who live / Call life. [Sonnet: Lift not the Painted Veil]

32 Through the unheeding many he did move, / A splendour among shadows, a bright blot / Upon this gloomy scene, a spirit that strove / For truth, and like the preacher found it not.

1 Away! the moor is dark beneath the moon, / Rapid clouds have drunk the last pale beam of even: / Away! the gathering winds will call the darkness soon, / And profoundest midnight shroud the serene lights of heaven. [*Stanzas – April 1814*]

2 Duty and dereliction guide thee back to solitude.

3 That content surpassing wealth / The sage in meditation found / And walked with inward glory crowned. [*Stanzas Written in Dejection*]

4 Yet now despair itself is mild, / Even as the winds and waters are; / I could lie down like a tired child, / And weep away the life of care / Which I have borne and yet must bear.

5 I fear thy kisses, gentle maiden, / Thou needest not fear mine. [*To —, I fear thy Kisses*]

6 Music, when soft voices die, / Vibrates in the memory – / Odours when sweet violets sicken, / Live within the sense they quicken.

Rose-leaves, when the rose is dead, / Are heaped for the belovèd's bed; / And so thy thoughts, when thou art gone, / Love itself shall slumber on. [*To —, Music, When Soft Voices Die*]

7 One word is too often profaned / For me to profane it, / One feeling too falsely disdained / For thee to disdain it. [*To —, One Word is Too Often Profaned*]

8 The worship the heart lifts above / And the Heavens reject not, – / The desire of the moth for the star, / Of the night for the morrow, / The devotion to something afar / From the sphere of our sorrow.

9 Best and brightest, come away! [*To Jane: The Invitation*]

10 I am gone into the fields / To take what this sweet hour yields; – / Reflection, you may come to-morrow, / Sit by the fireside with Sorrow.

11 Art thou pale for weariness / Of climbing heaven and gazing on the earth, / Wandering companionless / Among the stars that have a different birth, – / And ever changing, like a joyless eye / That finds no object worth its constancy? [*To the Moon*]

12 Swiftly walk o'er the western wave, / Spirit of Night! / Out of the misty eastern cave, / Where, all the long and lone daylight, / Thou wovest dreams of joy and fear. [*To Night*]

13 Kiss her until she be wearied out, / Then wander o'er city, and sea, and land, / Touching all with thine opiate wand – / Come, long-sought!

14 When I arose and saw the dawn, / I sighed for thee.

15 Thy brother Death came, and cried, / Wouldst thou me? / Thy sweet child Sleep, the filmy-eyed, / Murmured like a noontide bee, / Shall I nestle near thy side?

16 I ask of thee, belovèd Night – / Swift be thine approaching flight, / Come soon, soon!

17 Hail to thee, blithe spirit! / Bird thou never wert, / That from heaven, or near it, / Pourest thy full heart / In profuse strains of unpremeditated art. [*To a Skylark*, 1]

18 And singing still dost soar, and soaring ever singest. [10]

19 Like a star of Heaven, / In the broad daylight / Thou art unseen, but yet I hear thy shrill delight. [18]

20 Like a poet hidden / In the light of thought, / Singing hymns unbidden, / Till the world is wrought / To sympathy with hopes and fears it heeded not. [36]

21 We look before and after, / And pine for what is not: / Our sincerest laughter / With some pain is fraught; / Our sweetest songs are those that tell of saddest thought. [86]

22 Such harmonious madness / From my lips would flow / The world should listen then – as I am listening now. [103]

23 Then, what is life? I cried. [*The Triumph of Life*, 544]

24 And like a dying lady, lean and pale, / Who totters forth, wrapped in a gauzy veil, / Out of her chamber, led by the insane / And feeble wanderings of her fading brain, / The moon arose up in the murky east, / A white and shapeless mass – [*The Waning Moon*]

25 For she was beautiful – her beauty made / The bright world dim, and everything beside / Seemed like the fleeting image of a shade. [*The Witch of Atlas*, 137]

26 The rapid, blind / And fleeting generations of mankind. [615]

27 Ariel to Miranda: – Take / This slave of music, for the sake / Of him who is the slave of thee. [*With a Guitar, to Jane*]

28 The rich have become richer, and the poor have become poorer. [*A Defence of Poetry*]

1 Poetry is the record of the best and happiest moments of the happiest and best minds.

2 Poets are the unacknowledged legislators of the world.

WILLIAM SHENSTONE 1714–1763

3 Whoe'er has travelled life's dull round, / Where'er his stages may have been, / May sigh to think he still has found / The warmest welcome, at an inn. [*At an Inn at Henley*]

PHILIP H. SHERIDAN 1831–1888

4 The only good Indian is a dead Indian. [Attr., at Fort Cobb, Jan. 1869]

R. B. SHERIDAN 1751–1816

5 I was afterwards twice tapped for a dropsy, which declined into a very profitable consumption! [*The Critic*, I. ii]

6 Yes, sir, puffing is of various sorts: the principal are, the puff direct – the puff preliminary – the puff collateral – the puff collusive, and the puff oblique, or puff by implication.

7 No scandal about Queen Elizabeth, I hope? [II. i]

8 The Spanish fleet thou canst not see – because / – It is not yet in sight!

9 I must – I will – I can – I ought – I do.

10 All that can be said is, that two people happened to hit on the same thought – and Shakespeare made use of it first, that's all. [III. i]

11 I wish sir, you would practise this without me, I can't stay dying here all night.

12 *Enter Tilburina stark mad in white satin, and her confidant stark mad in white linen.* [Stage direction]

13 The wind whistles – the moon rises – see, / They have killed my squirrel in his cage! / Is this a grasshopper! Ha! no, it is my / Whiskerandos . . .

14 An oyster may be crossed in love.

15 I loved him for himself alone. [*The Duenna*, I. iii, song]

16 I was struck all on a heap. [II. ii]

17 I don't know any business you have to think at all. Thought does not become a young woman. [*The Rivals*, I. ii]

18 Illiterate him, I say, quite from your memory.

19 'Tis safest in matrimony to begin with a little aversion.

20 There's a little intricate hussy for you!

21 A circulating library in a town is as an ever-green tree of diabolical knowledge! It blossoms through the year!

22 A progeny of learning.

23 You gentlemen's gentlemen are so hasty. [II. ii]

24 He is the very pineapple of politeness! [III. iii]

25 It gives me the hydrostatics to such a degree.

26 The old weather-beaten she-dragon who guards you. [Of Mrs Malaprop]

27 An aspersion upon my parts of speech! was ever such a brute! Sure, if I reprehend anything in this world, it is the use of my oracular tongue, and a nice derangement of epitaphs!

28 She's as headstrong as an allegory on the banks of the Nile.

29 That's too civil by half. [III. iv]

30 No caparisons, miss, if you please. Caparisons don't become a young woman. [IV. ii]

31 You are not like Cerberus, three gentlemen at once, are you?

32 My valour is certainly going! – it is sneaking off! – I feel it oozing out as it were at the palms of my hands! [V. iii]

33 I own the soft impeachment.

34 You shall see them on a beautiful quarto page, where a neat rivulet of text shall meander through a meadow of margin. [*The School for Scandal*, I. i]

35 Here is the whole set! a character dead at every word. [II. ii]

36 I leave my character behind me.

37 Here's to the maiden of bashful fifteen; / Here's to the widow of fifty; / Here's to the flaunting extravagant quean. / And here's to the housewife that's thrifty. / Let the toast pass, – Drink to the lass, / I'll warrant she'll prove an excuse for the glass. [III. iii]

38 An unforgiving eye and a damned disinheriting countenance! [IV. i]

39 You write with ease, to show your breeding, / But easy writing's curst hard reading. [*Clio's Protest*]

1 A man may surely be allowed to take a glass of wine *by his own fireside*. [Refreshing himself at the Piazza Coffee House as his theatre in Drury Lane went up in flames, 24 Feb. 1809. Quoted in Thomas Moore, *Memoirs of the Life of Sheridan*, Vol. ii. Ch. 20]

2 The Right Honourable gentleman is indebted to his memory for his jests, and to his imagination for his facts. [(Speech in House of Commons in reply to Mr Dundas) Ch. 21]

GENERAL SHERMAN 1820–1891

3 I am tired and sick of war. Its glory is all moonshine ... War is hell. [Attr. words in address at Michigan Military Academy, 19 June 1879. Phrase repeated, Columbus, Ohio, 11 Aug. 1880]

JAMES SHIRLEY 1596–1666

4 The glories of our blood and state / Are shadows, not substantial things; / There is no armour against fate; / Death lays his icy hand on kings: / Sceptre and crown / Must tumble down, / And in the dust be equal made / With the poor crooked scythe and spade. [*The Contention of Ajax and Ulysses*, I. iii]

5 The garlands wither on your brow; / Then boast no more your mighty deeds! / Upon death's purple altar now, / See where the victor-victim bleeds. / Your heads must come / To the cold tomb: / Only the actions of the just / Smell sweet and blossom in their dust.

THE SHORTER CATECHISM

6 What is the chief end of man?
To glorify God and to enjoy him for ever.

J. H. SHORTHOUSE 1834–1903

7 'The Church of England', I said ... 'is no doubt a compromise.' [*John Inglesant*, Ch. 39]

DIMITRI SHOSTAKOVICH 1906–1975

8 A Soviet composer's reply to just criticism. [*Epigraph to his Fifth Symphony*]

ALGERNON SIDNEY 1622–1683

9 Liars ought to have good memories. [*Discourses Concerning Government*, Ch. 2, xv]

SIR PHILIP SIDNEY 1554–1586

10 My true love hath my heart and I have his, / By just exchange one for another given. [*Arcadia*, Bk iii]

11 'Fool,' said my Muse to me, 'look in thy heart and write.' [*Astrophel and Stella*, Sonnet 1]

12 With how sad steps, O Moon, thou climb'st the skies! / How silently, and with how wan a face! / What! may it be that even in heavenly place / That busy archer his sharp arrows tries? [31]

13 Do they above love to be loved, and yet / Those lovers scorn whom that love doth possess? / Do they call virtue there ungratefulness?

14 Come sleep! O sleep, the certain knot of peace, / The baiting place of wit, the balm of woe, / The poor man's wealth, the prisoner's release, / Th' indifferent judge between the high and low. [39]

15 That sweet enemy, France. [41]

16 Highway, since you my chief Parnassus be, / And that my Muse, to some ears not unsweet, / Tempers her words to trampling horses' feet / More oft than to a chamber-melody, / Now, blessed you, bear onward blessed me / To her, where I my heart, safe left, shall meet. [84]

17 Leave me, O Love, which reachest but to dust; / And thou, my mind, aspire to higher things; / Grow rich in that which never taketh rust; / Whatever fades, but fading pleasure brings. [110]

18 'Who is it that this dark night / Underneath my window plaineth?' / It is one who from thy sight, / Being, ah! exiled, disdaineth / Every other vulgar light. [Song 11]

19 There have been many most excellent poets that have never versified, and now swarm many versifiers that need never answer to the name of poets. [*The Defence of Poesy*]

20 With a tale, forsooth, he cometh unto you; with a tale which holdeth children from play, and old men from the chimney corner.

21 Certainly, I must confess mine own barbarousness, I never heard the old song of Percy and Douglas, that I found not my heart moved more than with a trumpet.

22 Our erected wit maketh us to know what perfection is.

1 To be rhymed to death as is said to be done in Ireland.

2 Thy necessity is yet greater than mine. [On giving his water-bottle to a dying soldier on the battlefield of Zutphen, 22 Sept. 1586. Often misquoted as 'Thy need']

ABBÉ SIEYÈS 1748–1836

3 *La mort, sans phrases.* – Death, and no phrases. [On voting for the death of Louis XVI, 19 Jan. 1793. (He himself denied having spoken the qualification)]

4 *J'ai vécu.* – I lived. [Reply when asked what he had done during the Terror]

EMPEROR SIGISMUND 1361–1437

5 I am the Roman Emperor, and am above grammar. [Reply to prelate who had criticized his Latin]

MAURICE SIGLER 1901–1961

6 Little Man, You've Had a Busy Day. [Title of song, written with Al Hoffman]

FRANK SILVER 1892–1960
  and IRVING CONN 1898–1961

7 Yes, we have no bananas, / We have no bananas today. [Song: *Yes, We Have No Bananas*]

PAUL SIMON 1942–

8 Like a bridge over troubled water, / I will ease your mind. [Song: *Bridge Over Troubled Water*]

9 Here's to you, Mrs Robinson, / Jesus loves you more than you will know. [Song: *Mrs Robinson*]

SIMONIDES *c.* 556–468 BC

10 Go, tell the Spartans, thou who passest by, / That here obedient to their laws we lie. [On the Spartan dead at the Battle of Thermopylae, 480 BC, trans. Mackail]

GEORGE R. SIMS 1847–1922

11 It is Christmas Day in the workhouse. [*Dragonet Ballads*, 'In the Workhouse: Christmas Day']

EDITH SITWELL 1887–1964

12 Jane, Jane, / Tall as a crane, / The morning light creaks down again. [*Aubade*]

13 Don Pasquito / Hid where the leaves drip with sweet . . . / But a word stung him like a mosquito . . . / For what they hear, they repeat! [*Façade*, 'I do like to be beside the Seaside']

14 'See me dance the polka' / Said Mr Wagg like a bear. ['Polka']

15 Lily O'Grady, / Silly and shady, / Longing to be / A lazy lady. ['Popular Song']

16 Do not take a bath in Jordan, / Gordon / On the holy Sabbath, on the peaceful day! ['Scotch Rhapsody']

17 Under great yellow flags and banners of the ancient Cold / Began the huge migrations / From some primeval disaster in the heart of Man. [*The Shadow of Cain*]

18 Who dreamed that Christ has died in vain? / He walks again on the Seas of Blood, He comes in the terrible Rain.

19 Still falls the Rain – / Dark as the world of man, black as our loss – / Blind as the nineteen hundred and forty nails / Upon the Cross. [*Still Falls the Rain*]

SIR OSBERT SITWELL 1892–1969

20 Do you remember Mr Goodbeare, the carpenter, / Godfearing and bearded Mr Goodbeare, / Who worked all day / At his carpenter's tray? [*Elegy for Mr Goodbeare*]

21 Now the nimble fingers are no more nimble, / And the silver thimble lies cold and tarnished black. [*Miss Mew's Window-Box*]

22 She did not recognise her enemy, / She thought him Dust: / But what is Dust, / Save Time's most lethal weapon, / Her faithful ally and our sneaking foe? [*Mrs Southern's Enemy*]

23 Education: in the holidays from Eton. [Entry in *Who's Who*]

JOHN SKELTON *c.* 1460–1529

24 With lullay, lullay, like a child, / Thou sleep'st too long, thou art beguiled. [*Lullay, Lullay like a Child*]

25 Vengeance I ask and cry, / By way of exclamation, / On the whole nation / Of cattes wild and tame: / God send them sorrow and shame! [*Philip Sparrow*]

1 O cat of churlish kind, / The fiend was in thy mind / When thou my bird untwined!

2 And robin readbreast, / He shall be the priest / The requiem mass to sing, / softly warbeling. [71]

3 Merry Margaret, / As midsummer flower, / Gentle as falcon / Or hawk of the tower. [*To Mistress Margaret Hussey*]

4 With solace and gladness, / Much mirth and no madness, / All good and no badness; / So joyously, / So maidenly, / So womanly, / Her demeaning.

PROFESSOR B. F. SKINNER 1904–1990

5 Education is what survives when what has been learnt has been forgotten. [*New Scientist*, 21 May 1964]

CHRISTOPHER SMART 1722–1771

6 I will consider my Cat Jeoffry. / For he is the servant of the Living God, duly and daily serving him. [*Jubilate Agno*, XIX. 51]

7 For adoration all the ranks / Of angels yield eternal thanks, / And David in the midst. [*Song to David*, 51]

8 Strong is the lion – like a coal / His eyeball – like a bastion's mole / His chest against the foes. [76]

9 Glorious the northern lights astream; / Glorious the song, when God's the theme; / Glorious the thunder's roar. [85]

10 And now the matchless deed's achieved, / Determined, dared, and done. [86]

F. E. SMEDLEY 1818–1864

11 You are looking as fresh as paint. [*Frank Fairleigh*, Ch. 41]

SAMUEL SMILES 1812–1904

12 We often discover what *will* do, by finding out what will not do; and probably he who never made a mistake never made a discovery. [*Self-Help*, Ch. 11]

13 A place for everything, and everything in its place. [*Thrift*, Ch. 5]

ADAM SMITH 1723–1790

14 People of the same trade seldom meet to-gether, even for merriment and diversion, but the conversation ends in a conspiracy against the public, or in some contrivance to raise prices. [*The Wealth of Nations*, Vol. ii. Bk i. Ch. 10. Pt ii]

15 With the greater part of rich people, the chief enjoyment of riches consists in the parade of riches. [Ch. 11]

16 Be assured, my young friend, that there is a great deal of *ruin* in a nation. [Letter to Sir John Sinclair, on the surrender at Saratoga, Oct. 1777]

17 To found a great empire for the sole purpose of raising up a people of customers, may at first sight appear a project fit only for a nation of shopkeepers. It is, however, a project altogether unfit for a nation of shopkeepers; but extremely fit for a nation that is governed by shopkeepers. [Vol. ii. Bk iv. Ch. 7. Pt iii (See also 291:21)]

ALEXANDER SMITH 1830–1867

18 In winter, when the dismal rain / Came down in slanting lines, / And Wind, that grand old harper, smote / His thunder-harp of pines. [*A Life Drama*, ii]

EDGAR SMITH 1857–1938

19 You may tempt the upper classes / With your villainous demi-tasses, / But Heaven will protect the Working Girl. [Song: *Heaven will Protect the Working Girl*]

JAMES and HORACE SMITH
1775–1839 and 1779–1849

20 What stately vision mocks my waking sense? / Hence, dear delusion, sweet enchantment, hence! [*Rejected Addresses*, 'An Address without a Phoenix']

21 I saw them go: one horse was blind, / The tails of both hung down behind, / Their shoes were on their feet. ['The Baby's Début']

22 Sated with home, of wife, of children tired. / The restless soul is driven abroad to roam; / Sated abroad, all seen and all admired, / The restless soul is driven to ramble home. ['*Cui Bono?*']

23 In the name of the Prophet – figs! ['Johnson's Ghost']

24 Hail, glorious edifice, stupendous work! / God bless the Regent and the Duke of York! ['Loyal Effusion']

1 Who makes the quartern loaf and Luddites rise? / Who fills the butchers' shops with large blue flies?

2 God bless the Army, bless their coats of scarlet, / God bless the Navy, bless the Princess Charlotte.

3 I am a blessed Glendoveer: / 'Tis mine to speak, and yours to hear. ['The Rebuilding']

4 'You, Clutterbuck, come, stir your stumps, / Why are you in such doleful dumps? / A fireman and afraid of bumps! – / What are they feared on? fools! 'od rot 'em!' / Were the last words of Higginbottom. ['A Tale of Drury Lane, The Burning']

5 John Richard William Alexander Dwyer / Was footman to Justinian Stubbs, Esquire. ['The Theatre', 76]

LOGAN PEARSALL SMITH 1865–1946

6 There are two things to aim at in life: first, to get what you want; and, after that, to enjoy it. Only the wisest of mankind achieve the second. [*Afterthoughts*, 1]

7 There are few sorrows, however poignant, in which a good income is of no avail.

8 What music is more enchanting than the voices of young people, when you can't hear what they say? [2]

9 It is the wretchedness of being rich that you have to live with rich people. [4]

10 People say that life is the thing, but I prefer reading. [6]

11 Thank heaven, the sun has gone in, and I don't have to go out and enjoy it.

REGINALD DORMAN SMITH 1899–1971

12 Let 'Dig for Victory' be the motto for everyone with a garden. [Radio broadcast to encourage vegetable growing, 4 Oct. 1939]

REV. SAMUEL F. SMITH 1808–1895

13 My country, 'tis of thee, / Sweet land of liberty, / Of thee I sing. [*America*]

STEVIE SMITH 1902–1971

14 A Good Time Was Had by All. [Title of book (1937), ascr. as source of phrase in Eric Partridge, *A Dictionary of Catch-Phrases*]

15 I was much too far out all my life. / And not waving but drowning. [*Not Waving But Drowning*]

16 Private Means is dead, / God rest his soul, / Officers and fellow-rankers said. [*Private Means is Dead*]

REV. SYDNEY SMITH 1771–1845

17 We cultivate literature on a little oatmeal. [(Proposed motto for the *Edinburgh Review*) *Works*, Vol. i, Preface]

18 I do not mean to be disrespectful, but the attempt of the Lords to stop the progress of Reform reminds me very forcibly of the great storm at Sidmouth, and of the conduct of the excellent Mrs Partington on that occasion. [Speech at Taunton, Oct. 1831]

19 Poverty is no disgrace to a man, but it is confoundedly inconvenient. [*His Wit and Wisdom*]

20 I look upon Switzerland as an inferior sort of Scotland. [Letter to Lord Holland, 1815]

21 I am convinced digestion is the great secret of life. [Letter to Arthur Kinglake, 30 Sept. 1837]

22 I have no relish for the country; it is a kind of healthy grave. [Letter to Miss G. Harcourt, 1838]

23 I am just going to pray for you at St Paul's, but with no very lively hope of success. [Letter to R. Monckton Milnes, 8 Nov. 1843]

24 It requires a surgical operation to get a joke well into a Scotch understanding. [Lady Holland, *Memoir*, Vol. i. Ch. 2]

25 I heard him [Jeffrey] speak disrespectfully of the Equator!

26 Looked as if she had walked straight out of the Ark. [7]

27 No furniture so charming as books. [9]

28 How can a bishop marry? How can he flirt? The most he can say is, 'I will see you in the vestry after service.'

29 I have, alas, only one illusion left, and that is the Archbishop of Canterbury.

30 Don't you know, as the French say, there are three sexes – men, women, and clergymen?

31 Heat, ma'am! It was so dreadful here that I found there was nothing left for it but to take off my flesh and sit in my bones.

32 Live always in the best company when you read. [10]

1 [Of marriage] A pair of shears, so joined that they cannot be separated; often moving in opposite directions, yet always punishing anyone who comes between them. [11]

2 He [Macaulay] has occasional flashes of silence that make his conversation perfectly delightful. [11]

3 Let onion atoms lurk within the bowl, / And, scarce-suspected, animate the whole. ['Recipe for Salad']

4 Serenely full, the epicure would say, / Fate cannot harm me, I have dined to-day.

5 Deserves to be preached to death by wild curates. [11]

6 What you don't know would make a great book.

7 I never read a book before reviewing it, it prejudices a man so. [H. Pearson, *The Smith of Smiths*, Ch. 3]

8 It is a place with only one post a day . . . In the country I always fear that creation will expire before tea-time. [5]

9 —'s idea of heaven is, eating *pâtées de foie gras* to the sound of trumpets. [10]

10 'Whewell's forte is science,' said someone. 'Yes, and his foible is omni-science,' added Sydney. [11]

11 What two ideas are more inseparable than Beer and Britannia?

TOBIAS SMOLLETT 1721–1771

12 Hark ye, Clinker, you are a most notorious offender. You stand convicted of sickness, hunger, wretchedness, and want. [*Humphrey Clinker*, Letter to Sir Watkin Phillips, 24 May]

13 He was formed for the ruin of our sex. [*Roderick Random*, Ch. 22]

14 That great Cham of literature, Samuel Johnson. [Letter to John Wilkes, 16 Mar. 1759, quoted in Boswell, *Life of Johnson*]

C. P. [later LORD] SNOW 1905–1980

15 The Two Cultures. [Title of article in the *New Statesman*, 6 Oct. 1956, on the gulf between the arts and the sciences]

16 The official world, the corridors of power. [*Homecomings*, Ch. 22 (later used as title for novel)]

VISCOUNTESS SNOWDEN 1881–1951

17 We were behind the 'iron curtain' at last! [*Through Bolshevik Russia* (1920). The phrase was later used by Goebbels (see 179:11) and taken up by Winston Churchill in his Fulton speech in 1946 (see 113:10). Derived from the safety curtain in a theatre]

SOCRATES 469–399 BC

18 The unexamined life is not worth living. [Quoted in Plato, *Apology*, 38]

19 Death is one of two things. Either it is annihilation, and the dead have no consciousness of anything; or, as we are told, it is really a change: a migration of the soul from this place to another. [41]

20 Nothing can harm a good man, either in life or after death. [42]

21 I am a citizen, not of Athens or Greece, but of the world. [Quoted in Plutarch, *De Exilio*, v]

22 Bad men live to eat and drink, whereas good men eat and drink in order to live. [Quoted in Plutarch, *Moralia*, 'How a Young Man Ought to Hear Poems', 4]

23 Crito, we ought to offer a cock to Asclepius. See to it, and don't forget. [Final words. Quoted in Plato, *Phaedo*, 118]

SOLON c. 640–c. 558 BC

24 Call no man happy till he dies, he is at best fortunate. [Quoted in Herodotus, *Histories*, I. 32]

25 But I grow old always learning many things. [Quoted in Plutarch, *Solon*, xxxi]

ALEXANDER SOLZHENITSYN 1918–

26 Nowadays we don't think much of a man's love for an animal; we laugh at people who are attached to cats. But if we stop loving animals, aren't we bound to stop loving humans too? [*Cancer Ward*, I. 20, trans. N. Bethell and D. Burg]

27 The camps had taught him that people who say nothing carry something within themselves. [II. 10]

28 No regime has ever loved great writers, only minor ones. [*The First Circle*, 57, trans. M. Guybon]

WILLIAM SOMERVILLE 1675–1742

1 The chase, the sport of kings; / Image of war, without its guilt. [*The Chase*, I. 13]

STEPHEN SONDHEIM 1930–

2 Everything's Coming Up Roses. [Song title from musical *Gypsy*]

SOPHOCLES 495–406 BC

3 Wonders are many, and none is more wonderful than man. [*Antigone*, 322]

4 I depict men as they ought to be, but Euripides portrays them as they are. [Quoted in Aristotle, *Poetics*, 25]

CHARLES SORLEY 1895–1915

5 Give them not praise. For, deaf, how should they know / It is not curses heaped on each gashed head? [*When You See Millions of the Mouthless Dead*]

J. B. L. SOULE 1815–1891

6 Go west, young man. [Article in the *Terre Haute* (Indiana) *Express*, 1851. See also 187:20]

ROBERT SOUTHEY 1774–1843

7 It was a summer evening, / Old Kaspar's work was done, / And he before his cottage door / Was sitting in the sun, / And by him sported on the green / His little grandchild Wilhelmine. [*The Battle of Blenheim*]

8 He came to ask what he had found, / That was so large, and smooth, and round.

9 But what they fought each other for, / I could not well make out.

10 'And everybody praised the Duke, / Who this great fight did win.' / 'But what good came of it at last?' / Quoth little Peterkin. / 'Why, that I cannot tell,' said he, / 'But 'twas a famous victory.'

11 How does the water / Come down at Lodore? [*The Cataract of Lodore*]

12 Curses are like young chickens, they always come home to roost. [*The Curse of Kehama*, Motto]

13 From his brimstone bed, at break of day / A walking the Devil is gone, / To look at his little snug farm of the World, / And see how his stock went on. [*The Devil's Walk* (a poem written in collaboration with Coleridge)]

14 How then was the Devil dressed? / O, he was in his Sunday best; / His coat was red, and his breeches were blue, / And there was a hole where his tail came through.

15 He passed a cottage with a double coach-house, / A cottage of gentility! / And he owned with a grin / That his favourite sin / Is pride that apes humility.

16 No stir in the air, no stir in the sea, / The ship was still as she could be. [*The Inchcape Rock*]

17 Till the vessel strikes with a shivering shock, – / 'O Christ, it is the Inchcape Rock!'

18 Sir Ralph the Rover tore his hair; / He curst himself in his despair.

19 And last of all an Admiral came, / A terrible man with a terrible name, – / A name which you all know by sight very well, / But which no one can speak, and no one can spell. [*The March to Moscow*, 8]

20 My days among the dead are past; / Around me I behold, / Where'er these casual eyes are cast, / The mighty minds of old. [*My Days among the Dead*]

21 Yet leaving here a name, I trust, / That will not perish in the dust.

22 You are old, Father William, the young man cried, / And pleasures with youth pass away, / And yet you lament not the days that are gone, / Now tell me the reason, I pray. [*The Old Man's Comforts*]

23 In the days of my youth I remembered my God! / And He hath not forgotten my age.

24 How beautiful is night! / A dewy freshness fills the silent air; / No mist obscures, nor cloud, nor speck, nor stain, / Breaks the serene of heaven. [*Thalaba the Destroyer*, I. 1]

25 The arts babblative and scribblative. [*Colloquies on the Progress and Prospects of Society*, X. Pt ii]

26 The march of intellect. [XIV]

27 The school that they have set up may properly be called the Satanic School. [*A Vision of Judgment*, Preface]

ROBERT SOUTHWELL 1561?–1595

28 As I in hoary winter's night stood shivering in the snow, / Surprised I was with sudden heat which made my heart to glow; / And lifting up a fearful eye to view what fire was

near, / A pretty Babe all burning bright did in the air appear. [*The Burning Babe*]

1 With this he vanished out of sight and swiftly shrunk away, / And straight I callèd unto mind that it was Christmas Day.

2 Behold, a silly tender Babe / In freezing winter night. [*New Prince, New Pomp*]

3 Times go by turns, and chances change by course, / From foul to fair, from better hap to worse. [*Times go by Turns*]

MURIEL SPARK 1918–

4 If you had been mine when you were seven you would have been the crème de la crème. [*The Prime of Miss Jean Brodie*, Ch. 2]

JOHNNY SPEIGHT 1920–

5 You silly moo. [Catch-phrase from BBC TV comedy series *Till Death Do Us Part*]

HERBERT SPENCER 1820–1903

6 Time: That which man is always trying to kill, but which ends in killing him. [*Definitions*]

7 Science is organized knowledge. [*Education*, Ch. 2]

8 This survival of the fittest. [*Principles of Biology*, III. Ch. 12, 'Indirect Equilibrium', 165]

9 Progress, therefore, is not an accident, but a necessity ... It is a part of nature. [*Social Statics* I. Ch. 2. 4]

10 Education has for its object the formation of character. [II. 4]

11 No one can be perfectly free till all are free; no one can be perfectly moral till all are moral; no one can be perfectly happy till all are happy. [IV. 30. 16]

12 It was remarked to me . . . that to play billiards was the sign of an ill-spent youth. [Quoted in Duncan, *Life and Letters of Spencer*, Ch. 20]

SIR STEPHEN SPENDER 1909–

13 After the first powerful manifesto / The black statement of pistons, without more fuss / But gliding like a queen, she leaves the station. [*The Express*]

14 I think continually of those who were truly great. / Who, from the womb, remembered the soul's history / Through corridors of light. [*I think continually of those*]

15 My parents kept me from children who were rough / And who threw words like stones and who wore torn clothes. [*My parents kept me from children who were rough*]

EDMUND SPENSER 1552?–1599

16 The merry cuckoo, messenger of spring, / His trumpet shrill hath thrice already sounded. [*Amoretti*, 19]

17 Fresh spring the herald of love's mighty king. [70]

18 One day I wrote her name upon the strand, / But came the waves and washèd it away: / Again, I wrote it with a second hand; / But came the tide, and made my pains his prey. / Vain man, said she, that dost in vain assay, / A mortal thing so to immortalize. [75]

19 Our love shall live, and later life renew.

20 Triton blowing loud his wreathèd horn. [*Colin Clout's Come Home Again*, 245]

21 The woods shall to me answer and my echo ring. [*Epithalamion*, 18]

22 Pour out the wine without restraint or stay, / Pour not by cups, but by the bellyful, / Pour out to all that wull. [250]

23 Ah! when will this long weary day have end, / And lend me leave to come unto my love? [278]

24 Now welcome, night, thou night so long expected, / That long day's labour dost at last defray. [315]

25 A gentle knight was pricking on the plain. [*The Faerie Queene*, Bk i. Canto 1. Stanza 1]

26 And on his breast a bloody cross he bore, / The dear remembrance of his dying Lord. [2]

27 A bold bad man! that dared to call by name / Great Gorgon, prince of darkness and dead night. [37]

28 Her angel's face, / As the great eye of heaven, shinèd bright, / And made a sunshine in the shady place. [3.6]

29 Still, as he fled, his eye was backward cast, / As if his fear still followed him behind. [9. 21]

30 Sleep after toil, port after stormy seas, / Ease after war, death after life, does greatly please. [40]

31 And all for love, and nothing for reward. [ii. 8. 2]

1 Gather therefore the rose, whilst yet is prime, / For soon comes age, that will her pride deflower. [12. 75]

2 Call me the Squire of Dames. [iii. 7. 51]

3 And as she looked about, she did behold, / How over that same door was likewise writ, / Be bold, be bold, and everywhere, Be bold. [11. 54]

4 Dan Chaucer, well of English undefiled, / On Fame's eternal beadroll worthy to be filed. [iv. 2. 32]

5 A monster, which the Blatant Beast men call, / A dreadful fiend, of gods and men ydrad. [v. 12. 37]

6 The gentle mind by gentle deeds is known: / For a man by nothing is so well bewrayed, / As by his manners. [vi. 3. 1]

7 It is the mind that maketh good or ill, / That maketh wretch or happy, rich or poor. [9. 30]

8 I was promised on a time, / To have reason for my rhyme; / From that time unto this season, / I received nor rhyme nor reason. [*Lines on his promised Pension* (traditional)]

9 Full little knowest thou that hast not tried, / What hell it is, in suing long to bide: / To lose good days, that might be better spent; / To waste long nights in pensive discontent; / To speed today, to be put back tomorrow; / To feed on hope, to pine with fear and sorrow. [*Mother Hubberd's Tale*, 895]

10 To eat thy heart through comfortless despairs: / To fawn, to crouch, to wait, to ride, to run, / To spend, to give, to want, to be undone. [904]

11 Calm was the day, and through the trembling air / Sweet-breathing Zephyrus did softly play. [*Prothalamion*, 1]

12 Against the bridal day, which is not long: / Sweet Thames! run softly, till I end my song. [17]

13 With that, I saw two swans of goodly hue / Come softly swimming down along the lee; / Two fairer birds I yet did never see. [37]

14 At length they all to merry London came, / To merry London, my most kindly nurse, / That to me gave this life's first native source: / Though from another place I take my name, / An house of ancient fame. [127]

BENEDICT SPINOZA 1632–1677

15 Nature abhors a vacuum. [*Ethics*, Pt I. 15, note]

16 Man is a social animal. [IV. 35, note]

17 We feel and know that we are eternal. [V. 23, note]

DR BENJAMIN SPOCK 1903–

18 You know more than you think you do. [Opening words of *Baby and Child Care*]

REV. W. A. SPOONER 1844–1930

19 Kinquering Congs their titles take. [Announcing the hymn in New College Chapel, 1879]

20 I remember your name perfectly, but I just can't think of your face. [Attr., but apocryphal]

21 Let us drink to the queer old Dean. [Attr.]

22 Sir, you have tasted two whole worms; you have hissed all my mystery lectures and been caught fighting a liar in the quad; you will leave Oxford by the next town drain. [Attr., but apocryphal]

SIR CECIL SPRING-RICE 1859–1918

23 I vow to thee, my country – all earthly things above – / Entire and whole and perfect, the service of my love. [*I vow to thee, my Country*]

24 And her ways are ways of gentleness, and all her paths are peace.

25 I am the Dean of Christ Church, Sir: / There's my wife; look well at her. / She's the Broad and I'm the High; / We are the University. [*The Masque of Balliol*]

SIR JOHN SQUIRE 1884–1958

26 It did not last: the Devil howling, 'Ho! / Let Einstein be!' restored the status quo. [*Answer to Pope's Epitaph on Sir Isaac Newton (see 312:30)*]

27 But I'm not so think as you drunk I am. [*Ballade of Soporific Absorption*]

28 At last incapable of further harm, / The lewd forefathers of the village sleep. [*If Gray had had to write his Elegy in the Cemetery of Spoon River*]

MME DE STAËL 1766–1817

29 *Tout comprendre c'est tout pardonner.* – To

understand all is to forgive all. [Common misquotation of *Corinne*, XVIII. Ch. 5]

JOSEPH STALIN 1879–1953

1 The Pope! How many divisions has he got? [To French Prime Minister Laval, who asked him to encourage Catholicism to please the Pope. Quoted in W. S. Churchill, *The Second World War*, Vol. i. Ch. 8, but also quoted by President Truman as said to Churchill at Potsdam conference]

SIR H. M. STANLEY 1841–1904

2 Dr Livingstone, I presume. [*How I found Livingstone*, Ch. 11]

COL. CHARLES E. STANTON 1859–1933

3 Lafayette, we are here! [At Lafayette's grave, Paris, 4 July 1917]

FRANK L. STANTON 1857–1927

4 Sweetes' li'l' feller, / Everybody knows; / Dunno what to call 'im, / But he's mighty lak' a rose! [*Sweetes' Li'l' Feller*]

JOHN STARK 1728–1822

5 We beat them to-day or Molly Stark's a widow. [Before the battle of Bennington, 16 Aug. 1777]

SIR RICHARD STEELE 1672–1729

6 There are so few who can grow old with a good grace. [*The Spectator*, 263]

7 Will Honeycomb calls these over-offended ladies the outrageously virtuous. [266]

8 It is to be noted that when any part of this paper appears dull, there is a design in it. [*The Tatler*, 38]

9 Though her mien carries much more invitation than command, to behold her is an immediate check to loose behaviour; to love her is a liberal education. [49]

10 The insupportable labour of doing nothing. [54]

11 Reading is to the mind what exercise is to the body. [147]

12 A little in drink, but at all times yr faithful husband. [Letter to his wife, 27 Sept. 1708]

LINCOLN STEFFENS 1866–1936

13 I have seen the future and it works. [Said to Bernard Baruch after a visit to the Soviet Union in 1919. Quoted in *Autobiography*, Ch. 18]

GERTRUDE STEIN 1874–1946

14 Rose is a rose is a rose is a rose. [*Sacred Emily*]

15 Pigeons on the grass alas. [*Four Saints in Three Acts*, III. iii]

16 In the United States there is more space where nobody is than where anybody is. That is what makes America what it is. [*The Geographical History of America*]

17 That's what you all are ... All of you young people who served in the war. You are a lost generation. [Quoted in Ernest Hemingway, *A Moveable Feast*, Ch. 3]

18 Just before she died she asked, 'What *is* the answer?' No answer came. She laughed and said, 'In that case what is the question?' Then she died. [Quoted by D. Sutherland in *Gertrude Stein: a Biography of her Work*, Ch. 6]

HENRI BEYLE called STENDHAL
1783–1842

19 Almost all our misfortunes in life come from the wrong notions we have about the things that happen to us. To know men thoroughly, to judge events sanely is, therefore, a great step towards happiness. [*Journal*, 10 Dec. 1801]

20 Romanticism is the art of presenting people with the literary works which are capable of affording them the greatest possible pleasure in the present state of their customs and beliefs.
Classicism, on the other hand, presents them with the literature that gave the greatest possible pleasure to their great-grandfathers. [*Racine et Shakespeare*, Ch. 3]

21 To the Happy Few [*Le Rouge et le noir*, epigraph]

22 *Politics* in the middle of things that concern the *imagination* are like a pistol shot in the middle of a concert. [Ch. 22]

23 A novel is a mirror walking along a main road. [49]

24 The only excuse for God is that he does not exist. [Quoted in J. Hick, *Evil and the God of Love*, 'Preface']

J. K. STEPHEN 1859–1892

1 Birthdays? yes, in a general way; / For the most if not for the best of men: / You were born (I suppose) on a certain day: / So was I: or perhaps in the night: what then? [*Sincere Flattery of R. B.*]

2 An old half-witted sheep / Which bleats articulate monotony, / And indicates that two and one are three. [*Sonnet* (in parody of Wordsworth)]

3 When the Rudyards cease from Kipling / And the Haggards ride no more. [*To R. K.*]

JAMES STEPHENS 1882–1950

4 I heard a bird at dawn / Singing sweetly on a tree, / That the dew was on the lawn, / And the wind was on the lea; / But I didn't listen to him, / For he didn't sing to me. [*The Rivals*]

5 I heard a sudden cry of pain! / There is a rabbit in a snare. [*The Snare*]

LAURENCE STERNE 1713–1768

6 They order, said I, this matter better in France. [*A Sentimental Journey*, opening]

7 I had had an affair with the moon, in which there was neither sin nor shame. ['The Monk, Calais']

8 As an Englishman does not travel to see Englishmen, I retired to my room. ['Preface, In the Desobligeant']

9 The learned Smelfungus. ['Calais, In the Street', 3]

10 I pity the man who can travel from Dan to Beersheba, and cry, 'Tis all barren.

11 There are worse occupations in this world than feeling a woman's pulse. ['The Pulse. Paris']

12 But in Paris, as none kiss each other but the men, I did what amounted to the same thing – I bid God bless her. ['The Fille de Chambre, Paris']

13 I am positive I have a soul: nor can all the books with which materialists have pestered the world ever convince me of the contrary. ['Maria, Moulines']

14 God tempers the wind, said Maria, to the shorn lamb. ['Maria']

15 So that when I stretched out my hand, I caught hold of the fille de chambre's – [Conclusion]

16 'Pray, my dear,' quoth my mother, 'have you not forgot to wind up the clock? –' 'Good G—!' cried my father, making an exclamation, but taking care to moderate his voice at the same time, – 'Did ever woman, since the creation of the world, interrupt a man with such a silly question?' [*Tristram Shandy*, Vol. i. Ch. 1]

17 So long as a man rides his hobby-horse peaceably and quietly along the king's highway, and neither compels you or me to get up behind him, – pray, Sir, what have either you or I to do with it? [7]

18 'Tis known by the name of perseverance in a good cause, – and of obstinacy in a bad one. [17]

19 My uncle Toby would never offer to answer this by any other kind of argument than that of whistling half a dozen bars of Lillabulero. [21]

20 Writing, when properly managed, (as you may be sure I think mine is) is but a different name for conversation. [ii. 11]

21 'I'll not hurt a hair of thy head: – Go,' says he, lifting up the sash and opening his hand as he spoke, to let it [a fly] escape; – 'go poor devil, get thee gone, why should I hurt thee? – This world surely is wide enough to hold both thee and me.' [12]

22 That's another story, replied my father. [17]

23 'I wish,' quoth my uncle Toby, 'you had seen what prodigious armies we had in Flanders.' [18]

24 'Our armies swore terribly in Flanders,' cried my uncle Toby, 'but nothing to this.' [iii. 11]

25 Of all the cants which are canted in this canting world, – though the cant of hypocrites may be the worst, – the cant of criticism is the most tormenting! [12]

26 The nonsense of the old women (of both sexes). [v. 16]

27 There is a North-west passage to the intellectual world. [42]

28 You forget the great Lipsius, quoth Yorick, who composed a work the day he was born; – they should have wiped it up, said my uncle Toby, and said no more about it. [vi. 2]

29 'He shall not die, by G—,' cried my uncle Toby. – The Accusing Spirit which flew up to heaven's chancery, blushed as he gave it in; – and the Recording Angel, as he wrote it down,

dropped a tear upon the word, and blotted it out for ever. [8]

1 A man should know something of his own country, too, before he goes abroad. [vii. 2]

2 'L—d!' said my mother, 'what is all this story about?' – 'A Cock and a Bull,' said Yorick. [ix. 33]

3 This sad vicissitude of things. [Sermon: *The Character of Shimei*]

WALLACE STEVENS 1879–1955

4 What counted was mythology of self, / Blotched out beyond unblotching. [*The Comedian as the Letter C*, I]

5 The only emperor is the emperor of ice-cream. [*The Emperor of Ice-Cream*]

6 Poetry is the supreme fiction, madame. / Take the moral law and make a nave of it / And from the nave build haunted heaven. [*A High-toned Old Christian Woman*]

7 If sex were all, then every trembling hand / Could make us squeak, like dolls, the wished-for words. [*Le Monocle de Mon Oncle*]

8 Beauty is momentary in the mind – / The fitful tracing of a portal; / But in the flesh it is immortal. [*Peter Quince at the Clavier*]

ADLAI STEVENSON 1900–1965

9 A lie is an abomination unto the Lord, and a very present help in trouble. [Speech, Springfield, Illinois, Jan. 1951]

10 Let's talk sense to the American people. Let's tell them the truth, that there are no gains without pains. [Speech in Chicago, 26 July 1952, accepting Democratic presidential nomination]

11 There is no evil in the atom; only in men's souls. [Speech in Hartford, Connecticut, 18 Sept.]

12 My definition of a free society is a society where it is safe to be unpopular. [Speech in Detroit, Oct.]

13 Flattery is all right – if you don't inhale. [Speech, 1 Feb. 1961]

14 She [Eleanor Roosevelt] would rather light candles than curse the darkness, and her glow has warmed the world. [Address to the United Nations General Assembly, 7 Nov. 1962, on her death]

15 Power corrupts, but lack of power corrupts absolutely. [Quoted in the *Observer*, Jan. 1963. Parody of Lord Acton (see 1:2)]

ROBERT LOUIS STEVENSON 1850–1894

16 Every one lives by selling something. [*Across the Plains*, 9, 'Beggars']

17 Politics is perhaps the only profession for which no preparation is thought necessary. [*Familiar Studies of Men and Books*, 'Yoshida-Torajiro']

18 Am I no a bonny fighter? [*Kidnapped*, Ch. 10]

19 I've a grand memory for forgetting, David. [18]

20 I have thus played the sedulous ape to Hazlitt, to Lamb, to Wordsworth, to Sir Thomas Browne, to Defoe, to Hawthorne, to Montaigne, to Baudelaire and to Obermann. [*Memories and Portraits*, Ch. 4]

21 I regard you with an indifference closely bordering on aversion. [*New Arabian Nights*, 'Story of the Bandbox']

22 For my part, I travel not to go anywhere, but to go. I travel for travel's sake. The great affair is to move. [*Travels with a Donkey*, 'Cheylard and Luc']

23 If landscapes were sold like the sheets of characters of my boyhood, one penny plain and twopence coloured, I should go the length of twopence every day of my life. ['Father Apollinaris']

24 Fifteen men on the dead man's chest – / Yo-ho-ho, and a bottle of rum! / Drink and the devil had done for the rest – [*Treasure Island*, Ch. 1]

25 Tip me the black spot. [3]

26 Pieces of eight! [10]

27 Many's the long night I've dreamed of cheese – toasted, mostly. [15]

28 In marriage, a man becomes slack and selfish, and undergoes a fatty degeneration of his moral being. [*Virginibus Puerisque*, I. 1]

29 Marriage is like life in this – that it is a field of battle, and not a bed of roses.

30 To marry is to domesticate the Recording Angel. Once you are married, there is nothing left for you, not even suicide, but to be good. [2]

1 The cruellest lies are often told in silence. [4, 'Truth of Intercourse']

2 Old and young, we are all on our last cruise. ['Crabbed Age and Youth']

3 Give me the young man who has brains enough to make a fool of himself!

4 Books are good enough in their own way, but they are a mighty bloodless substitute for life. ['An Apology for Idlers']

5 Extreme *busyness*, whether at school or college, kirk or market, is a symptom of deficient vitality.

6 There is no duty we so much underrate as the duty of being happy.

7 To travel hopefully is a better thing than to arrive, and the true success is to labour. ['El Dorado']

8 Though we are mighty fine fellows nowadays, we cannot write like Hazlitt. ['Walking Tours']

9 It's deadly commonplace, but, after all, the commonplaces are the great poetic truths. [*Weir of Hermiston*, Ch. 6]

10 Nothing like a little judicious levity. [*The Wrong Box*, Ch. 7]

11 I believe in an ultimate decency of things. [Letter, 23 Aug. 1893]

12 In winter I get up at night / And dress by yellow candle-light. / In summer quite the other way, / I have to go to bed by day. [*A Child's Garden of Verses*, 1, 'Bed in Summer']

13 A child should always say what's true / And speak when he is spoken to, / And behave mannerly at table: / At least as far as he is able. [5, 'Whole Duty of Children']

14 When I am grown to man's estate / I shall be very proud and great, / And tell the other girls and boys / Not to meddle with my toys. [11, 'Looking Forward']

15 The pleasant land of counterpane. [16, 'The Land of Counterpane']

16 I have a little shadow that goes in and out with me, / And what can be the use of him is more than I can see. [18, 'My Shadow']

17 The child that is not clean and neat, / With lots of toys and things to eat, / He is a naughty child, I'm sure – / Or else his dear papa is poor. [19, 'System']

18 The friendly cow, all red and white, / I love with all my heart: / She gives me cream with all her might, / To eat with apple-tart. [23, 'The Cow']

19 The world is so full of a number of things, / I'm sure we should all be as happy as kings. [24, 'Happy Thought']

20 Children, you are very little, / And your bones are very brittle. [27, 'Good and Bad Children']

21 Must we to bed indeed? Well then, / Let us arise and go like men, / And face with an undaunted tread / The long black passage up to bed. [41, 'North-West Passage, 1, Good-Night']

22 Give to me the life I love, / Let the lave go by me, / Give the jolly heaven above / And the byway nigh me. [*Songs of Travel*, 1, 'The Vagabond']

23 Wealth I ask not, hope nor love, / Nor a friend to know me; / All I seek, the heaven above / And the road below me.

24 I will make you brooches and toys for your delight / Of bird-song at morning and star-shine at night. [11]

25 In the highlands, in the country places, / Where the old plain men have rosy faces. [16]

26 Sing me a song of a lad that is gone, / Say, could that lad be I? / Merry of soul he sailed on a day / Over the sea to Skye. [42]

27 Blows the wind today, and the sun and the rain are flying, / Blows the wind on the moors today and now, / Where about the graves of the martyrs the whaups are crying, / My heart remembers how! [45, 'To S. R. Crockett']

28 Be it granted me to behold you again in dying, / Hills of home!

29 Go, little book, and wish to all / Flowers in the garden, meat in the hall, / A bin of wine, a spice of wit, / A house with lawns enclosing it, / A living river by the door, / A nightingale in the sycamore! [*Underwoods*, I. 1, 'Envoy']

30 There's nothing under Heaven so blue / That's fairly worth the travelling to. [2, 'A Song of the Road']

31 Under the wide and starry sky, / Dig the grave and let me lie. / Glad did I live and gladly die, / And I laid me down with a will. / This be the verse you grave for me: / 'Here he lies where he longed to be; / Home is the sailor, home from sea, / And the hunter home from the hill.' [21, 'Requiem']

1 I am a kind of farthing dip, / Unfriendly to the nose and eyes; / A blue-behinded ape, I skip / Upon the trees of Paradise. [30, 'A Portrait']

WILLIAM STEVENSON 1546?–1575

2 I can not eat but little meat, / My stomach is not good; / But sure I think, that I can drink / With him that wears a hood. / Though I go bare, take ye no care, / I am nothing a-cold; / I stuff my skin, so full within, / Of jolly good ale and old. [*Gammer Gurton's Needle*, II, song (authorship is disputed)]

SAMUEL J. STONE 1839–1901

3 The Church's one foundation / Is Jesus Christ her Lord; / She is His new creation / By water and the Word. [Hymn]

TOM STOPPARD 1937–

4 To attempt to sustain the attention of rival schools of academics by argument alone is tantamount to constructing a Gothic arch out of junket. [*Jumpers*, I]

5 We do on the stage the things that are supposed to happen off. Which is a kind of integrity, if you look on every exit being an entrance somewhere else. [*Rosencrantz and Guildenstern Are Dead*, I]

6 Eternity's a terrible thought. I mean, where's it going to end? [II]

7 The bad end unhappily, the good unluckily. That is what tragedy means.

8 What is an artist? For every thousand people there's nine hundred doing the work, ninety doing well, nine doing good, and one lucky bastard who's the artist. [*Travesties*, I. Also used with slightly different wording in *Artist Descending a Staircase*]

9 Do you think every *sole meunière* comes to you untouched by suffering? [II]

10 The House of Lords, an illusion to which I have never been able to subscribe – responsibility without power, the prerogative of the eunuch throughout the ages. [*Lord Malquist and Mr Moon*, VI. 1 (See also 21:15, 135:16, 241:35)]

11 I do not pretend to understand the universe. It is a great deal bigger than I am. [VI. 2]

HARRIET BEECHER STOWE 1811–1896

12 'Who was your mother?' 'Never had none,' said the child, with another grin. 'Never had any mother? What do you mean? Where were you born?' 'Never was born,' persisted Topsy: 'never had no father, nor mother, nor nothin'. I was raised by a speculator.' [*Uncle Tom's Cabin*, Ch. 20]

13 'Do you know who made you?' 'Nobody as I knows on,' said the child, with a short laugh . . . 'I 'spect I growed. Don't think nobody never made me.'

14 I's wicked – I is. I's mighty wicked, anyhow. I can't help it.

LYTTON STRACHEY 1880–1932

15 'Before she came', said a soldier, 'there was cussin' and swearin', but after that it was as 'oly as a church.' The most cherished privilege of the fighting man was abandoned for the sake of Miss Nightingale. [*Eminent Victorians*, 'Florence Nightingale']

16 Yet her conception of God was certainly not orthodox. She felt towards Him as she might have felt towards a glorified sanitary engineer; and in some of her speculations she seems hardly to distinguish between the Deity and the Drains.

17 It should not merely be useful and ornamental; it should preach a high moral lesson. [(On the Prince Consort's plans for the Great Exhibition) *Queen Victoria*, Ch. 4. vii]

18 Mr Gladstone was in his shirt-sleeves at Hawarden, cutting down a tree, when the royal message was brought to him. 'Very significant,' he remarked, when he had read the letter, and went on cutting down his tree. [8. i]

19 The Faery [Queen Victoria], he determined, should henceforth wave her wand for him [Disraeli] alone. [8. iii]

20 If this is dying, I don't think much of it. [Dying words. Quoted in Michael Holroyd, *Lytton Strachey*, Pt V. Ch. 17, Sect. viii]

EUGENE STRATTON 1861–1918

21 Little Dolly Daydream, pride of Idaho. [Song: *Little Dolly Daydream*, written by Leslie Stuart]

22 I know she likes me, / 'Cause she says so. [Song: *The Lily of Laguna*, written by Leslie Stuart]

IGOR STRAVINSKY 1882–1971

1 A good composer does not imitate; he steals. [Quoted in Peter Yates, *Twentieth Century Music*, Pt 1, Ch. 8]

2 My music is best understood by children and animals. [*Observer*, 'Sayings of the Week', 8 Oct. 1961]

BISHOP WILLIAM STUBBS 1825–1901

3 Froude believes Kingsley a divine. / And Kingsley goes to Froude for history. [Letter to J. R. Green, 17 Dec. 1871]

REV. G. A. STUDDERT KENNEDY 1883–1929

4 When Jesus came to Birmingham, they simply passed him by, / They never hurt a hair of him, they only let him die. [*The Unutterable Beauty* – 'Indifference']

SIR JOHN SUCKLING 1609–1642

5 Why so pale and wan, fond lover? / Prithee, why so pale? / Will, when looking well can't move her, / Looking ill prevail? / Prithee, why so pale? [*Aglaura*, IV. i, song]

6 If of herself she will not love, / Nothing can make her: / The devil take her!

7 Her feet beneath her petticoat, / Like little mice, stole in and out. / As if they feared the light. [*Ballad Upon a Wedding*]

8 Her lips were red, and one was thin, / Compared to that was next her chin / (Some bee had stung it newly).

9 Out upon it, I have loved / Three whole days together; / And am like to love three more, / If it prove fair weather.

Time shall moult away his wings, / Ere he shall discover / In the whole wide world again / Such a constant lover. [*A Poem with the Answer*]

SUETONIUS *c.* 70–*c.* 140

10 *Festina lente* – Hasten slowly. [*Augustus*, 25]

11 *Urbem . . . excoluit adeo, ut iure sit gloriatus marmoream se relinquere, quam latericiam accepisset.* – He so improved the city that he justly boasted he had found it brick and left it marble. [28]

12 *Ave, Imperator, morituri te salutant.* – Hail, Emperor, those about to die salute you. [*Claudius*, 21]

TERRY SULLIVAN ?–1950

13 She sells sea-shells on the sea-shore. / The shells she sells are sea-shells, I'm sure. [Song: *She Sells Sea-shells*, written in collaboration with Harry Gifford]

MAXIMILIEN, DUC DE SULLY 1559–1641

14 The English take their pleasures sadly after the fashion of their country. [*Memoirs*]

HENRY HOWARD, EARL OF SURREY 1517?–1547

15 Martial, the things for to attain / The happy life be these, I find: / The riches left, not got with pain; / The fruitful ground, the quiet mind. [*The Happy Life*]

16 The soote season, that bud and bloom forth brings, / With green hath clad the hill and eke the vale. [*Spring*]

R. S. SURTEES 1803–1864

17 The only infallible rule we know is, that the man who is always talking about being a gentleman never is one. [*Ask Mamma*, Ch. 1]

18 I'll fill hup the chinks wi' cheese. [*Handley Cross*, Ch. 1]

19 Full o' beans and benevolence. [27]

20 Hellish dark, and smells of cheese! [50]

21 Three things I never lends – my 'oss, my wife, and my name. [*Hillingdon Hall*, Ch. 33]

22 Champagne certainly gives one werry gentlemanly ideas, but for a continuance, I don't know but I should prefer mild hale. [*Jorrocks' Jaunts and Jollities*, No. 9]

23 Better be killed than frightened to death. [*Mr Facey Romford's Hounds*, Ch. 32]

24 The one thing that made her content to be a woman was that she would never have to marry one. [40]

25 The young ladies entered the drawing-room in the full fervour of sisterly animosity. [*Mr Sponge's Sporting Tour*, Ch. 17]

26 Women never look so well as when one comes in wet and dirty from hunting. [21]

1 He was a gentleman who was generally spoken of as having nothing a-year, paid quarterly. [24]

2 There is no secret so close as that between a rider and his horse. [31]

JONATHAN SWIFT 1667–1745

3 'Tis an old maxim in the schools, / That flattery's the food of fools; / Yet now and then your men of wit. / Will condescend to take a bit. [*Cadenus and Vanessa*. 758]

4 How haughtily he cocks his nose, / To tell what every schoolboy knows. [*The Country Life*, 81]

5 A coming shower your shooting corns presage. [*A Description of a City Shower*, 9]

6 I often wished that I had clear, / For life, six hundred pounds a-year, / A handsome house to lodge a friend; / A river at my garden's end, / A terrace walk, and half a rood / Of land set out to plant a wood. [*Imitation of Horace*, II. vi. 1]

7 Convey a libel in a frown, / And wink a reputation down. [*Journal of a Modern Lady*, 192]

8 Hail fellow, well met, / All dirty and wet: / Find out, if you can, / Who's master, who's man. [*My Lady's Lamentation*, 171]

9 Philosophy, the lumber of the schools. [*Ode to Sir W. Temple*, 2]

10 Some great misfortune to portend, / No enemy can match a friend. [*On the Death of Dr Swift*, 119]

11 The rest will give a shrug, and cry, / 'I'm sorry – but we all must die!' [211]

12 Yet malice never was his aim; / He lashed the vice, but spared the name; / No individual could resent, / Where thousands equally were meant. [512]

13 As learned commentators view / In Homer more than Homer knew. [*On Poetry*, 103]

14 Read all the prefaces of Dryden, / For these our critics much confide in; / (Tho' merely writ at first for filling, / To raise the volume's price a shilling). [251]

15 Hobbes clearly proves that every creature / Lives in a state of war by nature. [319]

16 So, naturalists observe, a flea / Hath smaller fleas that on him prey; / And these have smaller fleas to bite 'em, / And so proceed *ad infinitum*. [337 (See also 288:2)]

17 Hated by fools, and fools to hate / Be that my motto and my fate. [*To Dr Delaney, On the Libels*, 171]

18 A beggarly people! / A church and no steeple! [Of St Ann's Church, Dublin. Attr. by Edmund Malone]

19 Satire is a sort of glass, wherein beholders do generally discover everybody's face but their own. [*The Battle of the Books*, Preface]

20 Instead of dirt and poison we have rather chosen to fill our hives with honey and wax; thus furnishing mankind with the two noblest of things, which are sweetness and light.

21 I have heard of a man who had a mind to sell his house, and therefore carried a piece of brick in his pocket, which he showed as a pattern to encourage purchasers. [*The Drapier's Letters*, No. 2]

22 He [the emperor] is taller by almost the breadth of my nail than any of his court; which alone is enough to strike an awe into the beholders. [*Gulliver's Travels*, 'Voyage to Lilliput', Ch. 2]

23 Big-endians and small-endians. [4]

24 He could not forbear taking me up in his right hand, and stroking me gently with the other, after an hearty fit of laughing, asked me whether I were a Whig or a Tory. ['Voyage to Brobdingnag', 3]

25 I cannot but conclude the bulk of your natives to be the most pernicious race of little odious vermin that nature ever suffered to crawl upon the surface of the earth. [6]

26 He was amazed how so impotent and grovelling an insect as I (these were his expressions) could entertain such inhuman ideas. [7]

27 He gave it for his opinion, that whoever could make two ears of corn or two blades of grass to grow upon a spot of ground where only one grew before, would deserve better of mankind, and do more essential service to his country than the whole race of politicians put together.

28 He had been eight years upon a project for extracting sunbeams out of cucumbers, which were to be put into phials hermetically sealed, and let out to warm the air in raw inclement summers. ['Voyage to Laputa', 5]

1 I said the thing which was not. ['Voyage to the Houyhnhnms', 3]

2 I told him ... that we ate when we were not hungry, and drank without the provocation of thirst. [6]

3 My horses understand me tolerably well; I converse with them at least four hours every day. They are strangers to bridle or saddle; they live in great amity with me, and friendship to each other. [11]

4 With my own fair hands. [*Journal to Stella*, 4 Jan. 1711]

5 We are so fond of one another, because our ailments are the same. [1 Feb.]

6 I love good creditable acquaintance; I love to be the worst of the company. [17 May]

7 Monday is parson's holiday. [3 Mar. 1712]

8 I have been assured by a very knowing American of my acquaintance in London, that a young healthy child well nursed is at a year old a most delicious, nourishing, and wholesome food, whether stewed, roasted, baked, or boiled, and I make no doubt that it will equally serve in a fricassee, or a ragout. [*A Modest Proposal*]

9 Promises and pie-crust are made to be broken. [*Polite Conversation*, Dialogue 1]

10 Bachelor's fare; bread and cheese, and kisses.

11 Like an owl in an ivy-bush.

12 Why every one as they like; as the good woman said when she kissed her cow.

13 She wears her clothes, as if they were thrown on her with a pitchfork.

14 Faith, that's as well said as if I had said it myself. [2]

15 I always love to begin a journey on Sundays, because I shall have the prayers of the church, to preserve all that travel by land, or by water.

16 'Tis happy for him, that his father was before him. [3]

17 What though his head be empty, provided his commonplace book be full. [*A Tale of a Tub*, Sec. VII]

18 I never saw, heard, nor read, that the clergy were beloved in any nation where Christianity was the religion of the country. Nothing can render them popular but some degree of persecution. [*Thoughts on Religion*]

19 We have just enough religion to make us hate, but not enough to make us love one another. [*Thoughts on Various Subjects*]

20 The reason why so few marriages are happy is because young ladies spend their time in making nets, not in making cages.

21 A nice man is a man of nasty ideas.

22 Party is the madness of many, for the gain of a few.

23 Proper words in proper places, make the true definition of style. [*Letter to a Young Clergyman*, 9 Jan. 1720]

24 If Heaven had looked upon riches to be a valuable thing, it would not have given them to such a scoundrel. [Letter to Miss Vanhomrigh, 12 Aug.]

25 Principally I hate and detest that animal called man; although I heartily love John, Peter, Thomas, and so forth. [Letter to Pope, 29 Sept. 1725]

26 Not die here in a rage, like a poisoned rat in a hole. [Letter to Bolingbroke, 21 Mar. 1729]

27 I shall be like that tree, I shall die at the top. [Attr. in Sir Walter Scott, *Life of Swift*.]

28 Good God! What a genius I had when I wrote that book. [(Of *The Tale of A Tub*) Attr.]

29 Ah, a German and a genius! a prodigy, admit him! [Last words, when Handel was announced. Attr.]

30 *Ubi saeva indignatio ulterius cor lacerare nequit.* – Where fierce indignation can no longer tear his heart. [Swift's epitaph]

A. C. SWINBURNE 1837–1909

31 Maiden, and mistress of the months and stars / Now folded in the flowerless fields of heaven. [*Atalanta in Calydon*, opening]

32 When the hounds of spring are on winter's traces, / The mother of months in meadow or plain / Fills the shadows and windy places / With lisp of leaves and ripple of rain; / And the brown bright nightingale amorous / Is half assuaged for Itylus, / For the Thracian ships and the foreign faces, / The tongueless vigil and all the pain. [Chorus, 'When the Hounds of Spring, 1]

33 Bind on thy sandals, O thou most fleet, / Over the splendour and speed of thy feet; / For the faint east quickens, the wan west shivers, /

Round the feet of the day and the feet of the night. [2]

1 For winter's rains and ruins are over, / And all the season of snows and sins; / The days dividing lover and lover, / The light that loses, the night that wins. [4]

2 And in green underwood and cover / Blossom by blossom the spring begins.

3 Before the beginning of years / There came to the making of man / Time with a gift of tears, / Grief with a glass that ran. [Chorus, 'Before the Beginning of Years']

4 For a day and a night and a morrow, / That his strength might endure for a span / With travail and heavy sorrow, / The holy spirit of man.

5 And beauty and length of days. / And night, and sleep in the night.

6 He weaves, and is clothed with derision; / Sows, and he shall not reap; / His life is a watch or a vision / Between a sleep and a sleep.

7 Shall I strew on thee rose or rue or laurel, / Brother, on this that was the veil of thee? / Or quiet sea-flower moulded by the sea, / Or simplest growth of meadow-sweet or sorrel? [Ave atque Vale, 1]

8 For whom all winds are quiet as the sun, / All waters as the shore. [18]

9 Change in a trice! The lilies and languors of virtue / For the raptures and roses of vice. [Dolores, 9]

10 O sanguine and subtle Dolores, / Our Lady of Pain. [13]

11 Time turns the old days to derision, / Our loves into corpses or wives. [20]

12 Come down and redeem us from virtue, / Our Lady of Pain. [35]

13 I shall remember while the light lives yet / And in the night time I shall not forget. [Erotion]

14 In a coign of the cliff between lowland and highland, / At the sea-down's edge between windward and lee, / Walled round with rocks as an inland island, / The ghost of a garden fronts the sea. [A Forsaken Garden, 1]

15 The thorns he spares when the rose is taken; / The rocks are left when he wastes the plain. / The wind that wanders, the weeds wind-shaken, / These remain. [3]

16 As a god self-slain on his own strange altar, / Death lies dead. [10]

17 I am tired of tears and laughter, / And men that laugh and weep; / Of what may come hereafter / For men that sow and reap. [The Garden of Proserpine, 2]

18 Pale, beyond porch and portal, / Crowned with calm leaves, she stands, / Who gathers all things mortal / With cold immortal hands. [7]

19 We are not sure of sorrow, / And joy was never sure. [10]

20 We thank with brief thanksgiving / Whatever gods may be / That no man lives forever, / That dead men rise up never; / That even the weariest river / Winds somewhere safe to sea. [11]

21 I am that which began: / Out of me the years roll; / Out of me God and man; / I am equal and whole; / God changes, and man, and the form of them bodily; I am the soul. [Hertha, 1]

22 A creed is a rod, / And a crown is of night: / But this thing is God: / To be man with thy might, / To grow straight in the strength of thy spirit, and live out thy life as the light. [14]

23 Hope thou not much, and fear thou not at all. [Hope and Fear]

24 Glory to Man in the highest! for Man is the master of things. [Hymn of Man, last line]

25 I have lived long enough, having seen one thing, that love hath an end; / Goddess and maiden and queen, be near me now and befriend. [Hymn to Proserpine]

26 Yea, is not even Apollo, with hair and harpstring of gold, / A bitter God to follow, a beautiful God to behold?

27 Thou hast conquered, O pale Galilean; the world has grown grey from thy breath; / We have drunken of things Lethean, and fed on the fullness of death.

28 O ghastly glories of saints, dead limbs of gibbeted Gods!

29 A little soul for a little bears up this corpse which is man.

30 I remember the way we parted, / The day and the way we met: / You hoped we were both broken-hearted, / And knew we should both forget. [An Interlude]

31 And the best and the worst of this is / That neither is most to blame / If you have forgotten my kisses / And I have forgotten your name.

1 Swallow, my sister, O sister swallow, / How can thine heart be full of the spring? / A thousand summers are over and dead. / What hast thou found in the spring to follow? / What hast thou found in thine heart to sing? / What wilt thou do when the summer is shed? [*Itylus*, 1]

2 Till life forget and death remember, / Till thou remember and I forget. [5]

3 Let us go hence, my songs; she will not hear. [*A Leave-Taking*, 1]

4 While three men hold together, / The kingdoms are less by three. [*A Song in Time of Order*, 4]

5 I will go back to the great sweet mother, / Mother and lover of men, the sea. [*The Triumph of Time*, 33]

6 There lived a singer in France of old / By the tideless dolorous midland sea. / In a land of sand and ruin and gold / There shone one woman, and none but she. [41]

GEORGE 'BUDDY' DE SYLVA 1896–1950

7 California, Here I Come. [Title of song, written with Al Jolson]

ARTHUR SYMONS 1865–1945

8 As a perfume doth remain / In the folds where it hath lain, / So the thought of you, remaining / Deeply folded in my brain, / Will not leave me: all things leave me: / You remain. [*Memory*]

J. M. SYNGE 1871–1909

9 When I was writing 'The Shadow of the Glen' I got more aid than any learning would have given me from a chink in the floor of the old Wicklow house where I was staying, that let me hear what was being said by the servant girls in the kitchen. [*The Playboy of the Western World*, Preface]

10 I'd know his way of spitting, and he astride the moon. [III]

11 Oh, my grief, I've lost him surely. I've lost the only Playboy of the Western World. [Closing words]

PUBLILIUS SYRUS 1 Cent. BC

12 *Inopi beneficium bis dat qui dat celeriter.* – He gives the poor twice as much good who gives quickly. [*Maxims*, 6, becomes proverb: *Bis dat qui cito dat* – He gives twice who gives promptly]

13 *Necessitas dat legem, non ipsa accepit.* – Necessity gives the law, without acknowledging one itself. [399, becomes proverb: *Necessitas non habet legem* – Necessity has no law]

THOMAS SZASZ 1920–

14 Two wrongs don't make a right, but they make a good excuse. [*The Second Sin*, 'Social Relations']

15 If you talk to God, you are praying; if God talks to you, you have schizophrenia. If the dead talk to you, you are a spiritualist; if God talks to you, you are a schizophrenic. ['Schizophrenia']

ALBERT SZENT-GYÖRGYI 1893–1986

16 Discovery consists of seeing what everybody has seen and thinking what nobody has thought. [Quoted in I. J. Good, *The Scientist Speculates*]

T

JOSEPH TABRAR 1857–1931

1 Daddy wouldn't buy me a bow-wow, bow-wow, / I've got a little cat / And I'm very fond of that. [Song: *Daddy Wouldn't Buy Me a Bow-wow*]

2 In over a year and a half / I've only sung it once, / And I don't suppose I shall sing it again / For months and months and months. [*For Months and Months and Months*]

TACITUS *c*. 55–*c*. 117

3 Everything unknown is taken as marvellous; but now the limits of Britain are laid bare. [*Agricola*, 30]

4 Where they make a desert they call it peace.

5 It is a characteristic of the human mind to hate the man one has injured. [45]

6 *Elegantiae arbiter.* – Arbiter of taste. [(Of Petronius) *Annals*, xvi. 18]

HIPPOLYTE TAINE 1828–1893

7 Vice and virtues are products like sulphuric acid and sugar. [*Histoire de la littérature anglaise*, Introduction, iii]

CHARLES-MAURICE DE TALLEYRAND 1754–1838

8 *Ils n'ont rien appris, ni rien oublié.* – They have learnt nothing and forgotten nothing. [Of the exiled émigrés in 1796. Quoted by Chevalier de Panat in letter to Mallet du Pan. See also 152:12]

9 It is the beginning of the end. [Remark on Napoleon's Russian campaign, 1812]

10 *Défiez-vous des premiers mouvements; ils sont presque toujours bons.* – Mistrust first impulses; they are nearly always good. [Also attr. to Count Montrond]

11 *Pas trop de zèle.* – Not too much zeal. [Attr.]

12 Speech was given to man to disguise his thoughts. [Also attr. to many others]

13 War is much too serious a thing to be left to military men. [Attr. to him and others. Quoted by Aristide Briand to Lloyd George. See also 115:2]

BOOTH TARKINGTON 1869–1946

14 There are two things that will be believed of any man whatsoever, and one of them is that he has taken to drink. [*Penrod*, Ch. 10]

ALLEN TATE 1899–1979

15 Row upon row with strict impunity / The headstones yield their names to the element. [*Ode to the Confederate Dead*]

NAHUM TATE 1652–1715
and NICHOLAS BRADY 1659–1726

16 As pants the hart for cooling streams, / When heated in the chase. [Version of Psalm 42]

17 Through all the changing scenes of life. [Hymn]

18 While shepherds watched their flocks by night / All seated on the ground, / The angel of the Lord came down / And glory shone around.

'Fear not,' said he; for mighty dread/ Had seized their troubled mind; / 'Glad tidings of great joy

I bring / To you and all mankind.' [Christmas hymn]

A. J. P. TAYLOR 1906–1990

1 He [Lord Northcliffe] aspired to power instead of influence, and as a result forfeited both. [*English History, 1914–1945*, Ch. 1]

2 History gets thicker as it approaches recent time. [Bibliography]

3 A racing tipster who only reached Hitler's level of accuracy would not do well for his clients. [*The Origins of the Second World War*, 7]

ANN and JANE TAYLOR
1782–1866 and 1783–1827

4 I thank the goodness and the grace / Which on my birth have smiled, / And made me, in these Christian days, / A happy English child. [*A Child's Hymn of Praise*]

5 Thank you, pretty cow, that made / Pleasant milk to soak my bread. [*The Cow* (by Ann Taylor)]

6 Twinkle, twinkle, little star, / How I wonder what you are! / Up above the world so high, / Like a diamond in the sky! [*The Star* (by Jane Taylor)]

BAYARD TAYLOR 1825–1878

7 Till the sun grows cold, / And the stars are old, / And the leaves of the Judgement Book unfold. [*Bedouin Song*]

BISHOP JEREMY TAYLOR 1613–1667

8 Desperate by too quick a sense of constant infelicity. [*Holy Dying*, i. 5]

9 Every school-boy knows it. [*On the Real Presence*, V. §1]

10 The union of hands and hearts. [*Sermons*, 'The Marriage Ring', Pt I]

11 He that loves not his wife and children, feeds a lioness at home and broods a nest of sorrows. ['Married Love']

JOHN TAYLOR 1580–1653

12 'Tis a mad world, my masters. [*Western Voyage*, 1]

NORMAN TEBBIT 1931–

13 He didn't riot. He got on his bike and he looked for work. And he kept on looking until he found it. [Of his father, commonly misquoted as 'On your bike'. Speech at Conservative Party Conference, Blackpool, 15 Oct. 1981]

SIR WILLIAM TEMPLE 1628–1699

14 When all is done, human life is, at the greatest and the best, but like a froward child, that must be played with and humoured a little to keep it quiet till it falls asleep, and then the care is over. [*Essay on Poetry*]

ALFRED, LORD TENNYSON 1809–1892

15 Cleave ever to the sunnier side of doubt. [*The Ancient Sage*, 68]

16 A pasty costly made, / Where quail and pigeon, lark and leveret lay, / Like fossils of the rock, with golden yolks / Imbedded and injellied. [*Audley Court*, 22]

17 Dust are our frames; and gilded dust, our pride / Looks only for a moment whole and sound. [*Aylmer's Field*, 1]

18 Bare-footed came the beggar maid / Before the king Cophetua. [*The Beggar Maid*]

19 A happy bridesmaid makes a happy bride. [*The Bridesmaid*]

20 I come from haunts of coot and hern, / I make a sudden sally, / And sparkle out among the fern, / To bicker down a valley. [*The Brook*, song]

21 For men may come and men may go, / But I go on for ever.

22 I wind about, and in and out, / With here a blossom sailing, / And here and there a lusty trout, / And here and there a grayling.

23 Claspt hands and that petitionary grace / Of sweet seventeen subdued me ere she spoke. [112]

24 Half a league, half a league, / Half a league onward. / All in the valley of Death / Rode the six hundred. [*The Charge of the Light Brigade*]

25 'Forward the Light Brigade!'/ Was there a man dismayed?

26 Someone had blundered: / Theirs not to make reply, / Theirs not to reason why, / Theirs but to do and die.

27 Cannon to right of them, / Cannon to left of them, / Cannon in front of them / Volleyed and thundered.

Alfred, Lord Tennyson

1 Into the jaws of Death, / Into the mouth of Hell.

2 May there be no moaning of the bar, / When I put out to sea. [*Crossing the Bar*]

3 When that which drew from out the boundless deep / Turns again home.

4 Twilight and evening bell, / And after that the dark / And may there be no sadness of farewell, / When I embark;

For tho' from out our bourne of Time and Place / The flood may bear me far, / I hope to see my Pilot face to face / When I have crost the bar.

5 O love, what hours were thine and mine, / In lands of palm and southern pine. [*The Daisy*, 1]

6 I climbed the roofs at break of day; / Sun-smitten Alps before me lay. / I stood among the silent statues, / And statued pinnacles, mute as they. [61]

7 The bitter east, the misty summer / And gray metropolis of the North. [(Edinburgh) 103]

8 This proverb flashes thro' his head, / 'The many fail, the one succeeds'. [*The Day-Dream*, 'The Arrival', 15]

9 And is there any moral shut / Within the bosom of the rose? ['Moral', 7]

10 Dan Chaucer, the first warbler, whose sweet breath / Preluded those melodious bursts that fill / The spacious times of great Elizabeth. [*A Dream of Fair Women*, 5]

11 A daughter of the gods, divinely tall, / And most divinely fair. [87]

12 Ringed with the azure world, he stands. / The wrinkled sea beneath him crawls; / He watches from his mountain walls, / And like a thunderbolt he falls. [*The Eagle*]

13 Edward Bull / The curate; he was fatter than his cure. [*Edwin Morris*, 14]

14 God made the woman for the man, / And for the good and increase of the world. [43]

15 And when they buried him the little port / Had seldom seen a costlier funeral. [*Enoch Arden*, last lines]

16 Barbarous experiment, barbarous hexameters. [*Experiments in Quantity*, 'On Translations of Homer']

17 O mighty-mouthed inventor of harmonies, / O skilled to sing of Time or Eternity, / God-gifted organ voice of England, / Milton, a name to resound for ages. ['Milton, Alcaics']

18 O you chorus of indolent reviewers. ['Milton, Hendecasyllabics']

19 News from the humming city comes to it / In sound of funeral or of marriage bells. [*The Gardener's Daughter*, 35]

20 Half light, half shade, / She stood, a sight to make an old man young. [139]

21 Then she rode forth, clothed on with chastity. [*Godiva*, 53]

22 Light shall spread, and man be liker man / Thro' all the season of the golden year. [*The Golden Year*, 35]

23 Pray God our greatness may not fail / Thro' craven fears of being great. [*Hands all Round*]

24 Dreams are true while they last, and do we not live in dreams? [*The Higher Pantheism*]

25 Closer is He than breathing, and nearer than hands and feet.

26 Wearing the white flower of a blameless life. [*Idylls of the King*, Dedication, 24]

27 From the great deep to the great deep he goes. ['The Coming of Arthur', 410]

28 Live pure, speak true, right wrong, follow the King – / Else, wherefore born? ['Gareth and Lynette', 117]

29 Lead and I follow. [726]

30 No, no, too late! ye cannot enter now. ['Guinevere', 168]

31 To reverence the King, as if he were / Their conscience, and their conscience as their King, / To break the heathen and uphold the Christ, / To ride abroad redressing human wrongs, / To speak no slander, no, nor listen to it, / To honour his own word as if his God's. [465]

32 To love one maiden only, cleave to her, / And worship her by years of noble deeds, / Until they won her. [472]

33 Our fair father Christ. [559]

34 We needs must love the highest when we see it. [655]

35 For good ye are and bad, and like to coins, / Some true, some light, but every one of you / Stamped with the image of the King. ['The Holy Grail', 25]

36 God make thee good as thou art beautiful. [136]

37 His honour rooted in dishonour stood, /

And faith unfaithful kept him falsely true. ['Lancelot and Elaine', 871]

1 He makes no friend who never made a foe. [1082]

2 Our hoard is little, but our hearts are great. ['The Marriage of Geraint', 352]

3 For man is man and master of his fate. [355]

4 It is the little rift within the lute, / That by and by will make the music mute. ['Merlin and Vivien', 388]

5 Some black wether of St Satan's fold. [748]

6 For men at most differ as Heaven and Earth, / But women, worst and best, as Heaven and Hell. [812]

7 O great and sane and simple race of brutes / That own no lust because they have no law! ['Pelleas and Ettarre', 471]

8 I found Him in the shining of the stars, / I marked Him in the flowering of His fields, / But in His ways with men I find Him not. ['The Passing of Arthur', 9]

9 So all day long the noise of battle rolled / Among the mountains by the winter sea. [170]

10 On one side lay the Ocean, and on one / Lay a great water, and the moon was full. [179]

11 The sequel of to-day unsolders all / The goodliest fellowship of famous knights / Whereof this world holds record. [182]

12 An arm / Rose up from out the bosom of the lake, / Clothed in white samite, mystic, wonderful. [197]

13 This way and that dividing the swift mind. [227]

14 I heard the water lapping on the crag, / And the long ripple washing in the reeds. [284]

15 Authority forgets a dying king. [289]

16 For now I see the true old times are dead, / When every morning brought a noble chance, / And every chance brought out a noble knight. [397]

17 The days darken round me and the years, / Among new men, strange faces, other minds. [405]

18 The old order changeth, yielding place to new, / And God fulfils Himself in many ways, / Lest one good custom should corrupt the world. [408]

19 Pray for my soul. More things are wrought by prayer / Than this world dreams of. [415]

20 For what are men better than sheep or goats / That nourish a blind life within the brain, / If, knowing God, they lift not hands of prayer / Both for themselves and those who call them friend? / For so the whole round earth is every way / Bound by gold chains about the feet of God. [418]

21 Where falls not hail, or rain, or any snow, / Nor ever wind blows loudly. [428]

22 Shadows of three dead men and thou wast one of the three. [In the Garden at Swainston]

23 Believing where we cannot prove. [In Memoriam, Prologue]

24 Thou madest Death: and lo, thy foot / Is on the skull which thou hast made.

25 Thou madest man, he knows not why.

26 Our little systems have their day; / They have their day and cease to be; / They are but broken lights of thee, / And thou, O Lord, art more than they.

27 I held it truth with him who sings/ To one clear harp in divers tones, / That men may rise on stepping stones / Of their dead selves to higher things. [1 (Note: the stanza numbers used here refer to the later edn. of the poem which includes the additional stanza 39)]

28 Dark house, by which once more I stand / Here in the long unlovely street. [7]

29 On the bald street breaks the blank day.

30 Or where the kneeling hamlet drains / The chalice of the grapes of God. [10]

31 To-night the winds begin to rise / And roar from yonder dropping day: / The last red leaf is whirled away, / The rooks are blown about the skies. [15]

32 I do but sing because I must, / And pipe but as the linnets sing. [21]

33 The linnet born within the cage, / That never knew the summer woods. [27]

34 I hold it true, whate'er befall; / I feel it when I sorrow most; / 'Tis better to have loved and lost / Than never to have loved at all.

35 The time draws near the birth of Christ. [28]

36 Behold a man raised up by Christ. [31]

37 Her eyes are homes of silent prayer. [32]

38 'Twere best at once to sink to peace, / Like birds the charming serpent draws, / To drop

Alfred, Lord Tennyson

head-foremost in the jaws / Of vacant darkness and to cease. [34]

1 And so the Word had breath, and wrought / With human hands the creed of creeds / In loveliness of perfect deeds, / More strong than all poetic thought. [36]

2 How fares it with the happy dead? [44]

3 Be near me when my light is low, / When the blood creeps, and the nerves prick / And tingle; and the heart is sick, / And all the wheels of Being slow. [50]

4 Time, a maniac scattering dust, / And Life, a Fury slinging flame.

5 Do we indeed desire the dead / Should still be near us at our side? / Is there no baseness we would hide? / No inner vileness that we dread? [51]

6 Hold thou the good: define it well: / For fear divine philosophy / Should push beyond her mark and be / Procuress to the Lords of Hell. [53]

7 Oh yet we trust that somehow good / Will be the final goal of ill. [54]

8 But what am I? / An infant crying in the night: / An infant crying for the light: / And with no language but a cry.

9 So careful of the type she seems, / So careless of the single life. [55]

10 Nature, red in tooth and claw. [56]

11 What hope of answer or redress? / Behind the veil, behind the veil.

12 Peace; come away: we do him wrong / To sing so wildly: let us go. [57]

13 O Sorrow, wilt thou live with me / No casual mistress, but a wife. [59]

14 Sleep, Death's twin-brother, knows not Death, / Nor can I dream of thee as dead. [68]

15 I dreamed there would be Spring no more, / That Nature's ancient power was lost. [69]

16 So many worlds, so much to do, / So little done, such things to be. [73]

17 Round thee with the breeze of song / To stir a little praise of dust. [75]

18 God's finger touched him, and he slept. [85]

19 Fresh from brawling courts / And dusty purlieus of the law. [89]

20 There lives more faith in honest doubt, / Believe me, than in half the creeds. [96]

21 He seems so near and yet so far. [97]

22 Ring out, wild bells, to the wild sky. [106]

23 Ring out the old, ring in the new, / Ring, happy bells, across the snow: / The year is going, let him go;/ Ring out the false, ring in the true.

24 Ring out the feud of rich and poor, / Ring in redress to all mankind.

25 Ring out a slowly dying cause, / And ancient forms of party strife; / Ring in the nobler modes of life, / With sweeter manners, purer laws.

26 Ring out the want, the care, the sin, / The faithless coldness of the times.

27 Ring out false pride in blood and place, / The civic slander and the spite.

28 Ring out the thousand wars of old, / Ring in the thousand years of peace.

29 Not the schoolboy heat, / The blind hysterics of the Celt. [109]

30 The grand old name of gentleman. [111]

31 'Tis held that sorrow makes us wise. [113]

32 Now fades the long last streak of snow, / Now burgeons every maze of quick / About the flowering squares, and thick / By ashen roots the violets grow. [115]

33 The lark becomes a sightless song.

34 My regret / Becomes an April violet, / And buds and blossoms like the rest.

35 Trust that those we call the dead / Are breathers of an ampler day. [118]

36 But I was *born* to other things. [120]

37 There rolls the deep where grew the tree. [123]

38 Even tho' thrice again / The red fool-fury of the Seine / Should pile her barricades with dead. [127]

39 Thy voice is on the rolling air; / I hear thee where the waters run; / Thou standest in the rising sun, / And in the setting thou art fair. [130]

40 Wearing all that weight / Of learning lightly like a flower. [Conclusion]

41 That God, which ever lives and loves, / One God, one law, one element, / And one far-off divine event, / To which the whole creation moves.

42 All along the valley, stream that flashest white. [*In the Valley of the Cauteretz*]

1 The voice of the dead was a living voice to me.

2 Lady Clara Vere de Vere, / Of me you shall not win renown: / You thought to break a country heart / For pastime, ere you went to town. [*Lady Clara Vere de Vere*]

3 A simple maiden in her flower / Is worth a hundred coats-of-arms.

4 The lion on your old stone gates / Is not more cold to you than I.

5 The gardener Adam and his wife / Smile at the claims of long descent.

6 'Tis only noble to be good. / Kind hearts are more than coronets, / And simple faith than Norman blood.

7 On either side the river lie / Long fields of barley and of rye, / That clothe the wold and meet the sky; / And thro' the field the road runs by / To many-towered Camelot. [*The Lady of Shalott*, 1]

8 Willows whiten, aspens quiver, / Little breezes dusk and shiver / Thro' the wave that runs for ever / By the island in the river.

9 Only reapers, reaping early / In among the bearded barley.

10 She has heard a whisper say, / A curse is on her if she stay / To look down to Camelot. [2]

11 Or when the moon was overhead, / Came two young lovers lately wed; / 'I am half sick of shadows,' said / The Lady of Shalott.

12 A bow-shot from her bower-eaves, / He rode between the barley-sheaves, / The sun came dazzling thro' the leaves, / And flamed upon the brazen greaves / Of bold Sir Lancelot. [3]

13 'Tirra lirra,' by the river / Sang Sir Lancelot.

14 She left the web, she left the loom, / She made three paces thro' the room, / She saw the water-lily bloom, / She saw the helmet and the plume, / She looked down to Camelot. / Out flew the web and floated wide; / The mirror cracked from side to side; / 'The curse is come upon me,' cried The Lady of Shalott.

15 He said, 'She has a lovely face; / God in his mercy lend her grace, / The Lady of Shalott.' [4]

16 Ah God! the petty fools of rhyme / That shriek and sweat in pigmy wars. [*Literary Squabbles*]

17 The noblest answer unto such, / Is kindly silence when they brawl. [Altered in later version to 'perfect silence']

18 Nourishing a youth sublime / With the fairy tales of science, and the long result of Time. [*Locksley Hall*, 11]

19 In the spring a young man's fancy lightly turns to thoughts of love. [20]

20 As the husband is, the wife is: thou art mated with a clown. [47]

21 He will hold thee, when his passion shall have spent its novel force, / Something better than his dog, a little dearer than his horse. [49]

22 Cursed be the gold that gilds the straitened forehead of a fool! [62]

23 As the many-wintered crow that leads the clanging rookery home. [68]

24 Such a one do I remember, whom to look at was to love. [72]

25 Like a dog, he hunts in dreams, and thou art staring at the wall, / Where the dying night-lamp flickers, and the shadows rise and fall. [79]

26 Thou shalt hear the 'Never, never', whispered by the phantom years. [83]

27 With a little hoard of maxims preaching down a daughter's heart. [94]

28 But the jingling of the guinea helps the hurt that Honour feels. [105]

29 Men, my brothers, men the workers, ever reaping something new: / That which they have done but earnest of the things that they shall do. [117]

30 Heard the heavens fill with shouting, and there rained a ghastly dew / From the nations' airy navies grappling in the central blue. [123]

31 Till the war-drum throbbed no longer, and the battle-flags were furled / In the Parliament of man, the Federation of the world. [127]

32 The kindly earth shall slumber, lapt in universal law. [130]

33 So I triumphed ere my passion, sweeping thro' me, left me dry, / Left me with the palsied heart, and left me with the jaundiced eye. [131]

34 Yet I doubt not thro' the ages one increasing purpose runs, / And the thoughts of men are widened with the process of the suns. [137]

35 Knowledge comes, but wisdom lingers. [143]

Alfred, Lord Tennyson

1 I am shamed thro' all my nature to have loved so slight a thing. [148]

2 I will take some savage woman, she shall rear my savage race. [168]

3 Not with blinded eyesight poring over miserable books. [172]

4 I the heir of all the ages, in the foremost files of time. [178]

5 Let the great world spin for ever down the ringing grooves of change. [182]

6 Better fifty years of Europe than a cycle of Cathay. [184]

7 He is but a landscape-painter, / And a village maiden she. [*The Lord of Burleigh*, 7]

8 'Courage!' he said, and pointed toward the land, / 'This mounting wave will roll us shorewards soon.' / In the afternoon they came unto a land / In which it seemèd always afternoon. [*The Lotos-Eaters*, 1]

9 A land of streams! some, like a downward smoke, / Slow-dropping veils of thinnest lawn, did go. [10]

10 Our island home / Is far beyond the wave; we will no longer roam. [44]

11 Music that gentlier on the spirit lies, / Than tired eyelids upon tired eyes. ['Choric Song', 1]

12 All things have rest: why should we toil alone, / We only toil, who are the first of things. [2]

13 There is no joy but calm!

14 Ah, why / Should life all labour be? [4]

15 Time driveth onward fast, / And in a little while our lips are dumb. / Let us alone. What is it that will last? / All things are taken from us, and become / Portions and parcels of the dreadful Past.

16 Is there any peace / In ever climbing up the climbing wave?

17 Live and lie reclined / On the hills like Gods together, careless of mankind.

18 The clouds are lightly curled / Round their golden houses, girdled with the gleaming world.

19 Surely, surely, slumber is more sweet than toil, the shore / Than labour in the deep midocean, wind and wave and oar; / Oh rest ye, brother mariners, we will not wander more.

20 The rise / And long roll of the Hexameter. [*Lucretius*, 10]

21 I saw the flaring atom-streams / And torrents of her myriad universe, / Ruining along the illimitable inane. [38]

22 Weeded and worn the ancient thatch / Upon the lonely moated grange. [*Mariana*]

23 She only said, 'My life is dreary, / He cometh not,' she said: / She said, 'I am aweary, aweary, / I would that I were dead.'

24 Her tears fell with the dews at even; / Her tears fell ere the dews were dried.

25 Upon the middle of the night. / Waking she heard the night-fowl crow.

26 The blue fly sung in the pane; the mouse / Behind the mouldering wainscot shrieked.

27 Faultily faultless, icily regular, splendidly null, / Dead perfection, no more. [*Maud*, Pt I. ii]

28 One still strong man in a blatant land, / Whatever they call him, what care I, / Aristocrat, democrat, autocrat – one / Who can rule and dare not lie. [x. 5]

29 But ah for a man to arise in me, / That the man I am may cease to be! [6]

30 Birds in the high Hall-garden / When twilight was falling, / Maud, Maud, Maud, Maud, / They were crying and calling. [xii. 1]

31 Gorgonised me from head to foot / With a stony British stare. [xiii. 2]

32 Go not, happy day, / From the shining fields, / Go not, happy day, / Till the maiden yields. [xvii]

33 Come into the garden, Maud, / For the black bat, night, has flown, / Come into the garden, Maud, / I am here at the gate alone; / And the woodbine spices are wafted abroad, / And the musk of the rose is blown.

For a breeze of morning moves, / And the planet of Love is on high, Beginning to faint in the light that she loves / On a bed of daffodil sky. [xxii. 1]

34 All night have the roses heard / The flute, violin, bassoon; / All night has the casement jessamine stirred / To the dancers dancing in tune; / Till a silence fell with the waking bird, / And a hush with the setting moon. [3]

35 The rose was awake all night for your sake, / Knowing your promise to me; / The lilies and roses were all awake, / They sighed for the dawn and thee. [8]

36 Queen rose of the rosebud garden of girls. [9]

1 There has fallen a splendid tear / From the passion-flower at the gate. / She is coming, my dove, my dear; / She is coming, my life, my fate, / The red rose cries, 'She is near, she is near': / And the white rose weeps, 'She is late'. [10]

2 O that 'twere possible / After long grief and pain / To find the arms of my true love / Round me once again! [II. iv. 1]

3 I embrace the purpose of God and the doom assigned. [III. vi. 5]

4 You must wake and call me early, call me early, mother dear; / To-morrow 'ill be the happiest time of all the glad New-year; / Of all the glad New-year, mother, the maddest merriest day; / For I'm to be Queen o' the May, mother, I'm to be Queen o' the May. [*The May Queen*]

5 After it, follow it, / Follow The Gleam. [*Merlin and The Gleam*]

6 After-dinner talk / Across the walnuts and the wine. [*The Miller's Daughter*, 31]

7 What, it's you, / The padded man – that wears the stays. [*The New Timon and the Poets*]

8 Doesn't thou 'ear my 'erse's legs, as they canters awaäy? / Proputty, proputty, proputty – that's what I 'ears 'em saäy. [*Northern Farmer. New Style*, 1]

9 Doänt thou marry for munny, but goä wheer munny is! [5]

10 Maäybe she warn't a beauty:– I niver giv it a thowt. [6]

11 Taäke my word for it, Sammy, the poor in a loomp is bad. [12]

12 Bury the Great Duke / With an empire's lamentation. [*Ode on the Death of the Duke of Wellington*, 1]

13 The last great Englishman is low. [3]

14 O friends, our chief state-oracle is mute. [4]

15 Great in council and great in war, / Foremost captain of his time.

16 O fall'n at length that tower of strength / Which stood four-square to all the winds that blew!

17 This is England's greatest son, / He that gained a hundred fights, / Nor ever lost an English gun. [6]

18 In that world-earthquake, Waterloo!

19 Our loyal passion for our temperate kings. [7]

20 Who never sold the truth to serve the hour, / Nor paltered with eternal God for power.

21 Truth-teller was our England's Alfred named.

22 Not once or twice in our rough island-story, / The path of duty was the way to glory. [8]

23 The toppling crags of Duty scaled / Are close upon the shining table-lands / To which our God Himself is moon and sun.

24 There lies a vale in Ida, lovelier / Than all the valleys of Ionian hills. [*Oenone*, 1]

25 O mother Ida, many-fountained Ida, / Dear mother Ida, harken ere I die. [22]

26 I built my soul a lordly pleasure-house, / Wherein at ease for aye to dwell. [*The Palace of Art*, 1]

27 An English home – gray twilight poured / On dewy pastures, dewy trees, / Softer than sleep – all things in order stored, / A haunt of ancient Peace. [22]

28 Two godlike faces gazed below; / Plato the wise and large-browed Verulam, / The first of those who know. [41]

29 'Make me a cottage in the vale,' she said, / 'Where I may mourn and pray.' [73]

30 Our Playwright may show / In some fifth Act what this wild drama means. [*The Play*]

31 Dowered with the hate of hate, the scorn of scorn, / The love of love. [*The Poet*]

32 Then the maiden Aunt / Took this fair day for text, and from it preached / An universal culture for the crowd. [*The Princess*, Prologue, 107]

33 I seemed to move among a world of ghosts, / And feel myself the shadow of a dream. [I. 17]

34 As thro' the land at eve we went, / And plucked the ripened ears, / We fell out, my wife and I, / O we fell out I know not why, / And kissed again with tears. [II, Song]

35 O hard, when love and duty clash! [273]

36 Jewels five-words long / That on the stretched forefinger of all Time / Sparkle for ever. [355]

37 Sweet and low, sweet and low, / Wind of the western sea. [III, song]

38 Sleep, my little one, sleep, my pretty one, sleep.

39 The splendour falls on castle walls / And

snowy summits old in story: / The long light shakes across the lakes, / And the wild cataract leaps in glory. / Blow, bugle, blow, set the wild echoes flying, / Blow, bugle; answer, echoes, dying, dying, dying. [IV, Song]

1 O sweet and far from cliff and scar / The horns of Elfland faintly blowing!

2 Our echoes roll from soul to soul, / And grow for ever and for ever.

3 Tears, idle tears, I know not what they mean, / Tears from the depth of some divine despair. [Second song]

4 Looking on the happy Autumn-fields, / And thinking of the days that are no more.

5 Dear as remembered kisses after death.

6 O Swallow, Swallow, flying, flying South, / Fly to her, and fall upon her gilded eaves, / And tell her, tell her, what I tell to thee. [Third song]

7 Bright and fierce and fickle is the South, / And dark and true and tender is the North.

8 O tell her, brief is life but love is long.

9 Thy voice is heard thro' rolling drums, / That beat to battle where he stands. [Fourth song]

10 Man is the hunter; woman is his game: / The sleek and shining creatures of the chase, / We hunt them for the beauty of their skins. [V. 147]

11 Man for the field and woman for the hearth: / Man for the sword and for the needle she: / Man with the head and woman with the heart: / Man to command and woman to obey; / All else confusion. [427]

12 Home they brought her warrior dead: / She nor swooned, nor uttered cry: / All her maidens, watching, said, / 'She must weep or she will die.' [VI, Song]

13 The woman is so hard / Upon the woman. [205]

14 Ask me no more: thy fate and mine are sealed: / I strove against the stream and all in vain: / Let the great river take me to the main: / No more, dear love, for at a touch I yield; / Ask me no more. [VII, Song]

15 Now sleeps the crimson petal, now the white; / Nor waves the cypress in the palace walk; / Nor winks the gold fin in the porphyry font: / The fire-fly wakens: waken thou with me. [Second song]

16 Now lies the Earth all Danaë to the stars.

17 Now slides the silent meteor on, and leaves / A shining furrow, as thy thoughts in me.

18 Come down, O maid, from yonder mountain height: / What pleasure lives in height (the shepherd sang)? [Third song]

19 Love is of the valley, come thou down / And find him.

20 The moan of doves in immemorial elms / And murmuring of innumerable bees. [206]

21 The woman's cause is man's: they rise or sink / Together. [243]

22 Happy he / With such a mother! faith in womankind / Beats with his blood. [308]

23 Revolts, republics, revolutions, most / No graver than a schoolboys' barring out. [Conclusion, 65]

24 No little lily-handed Baronet he, / A great broad-shouldered genial Englishman, / A lord of fat prize-oxen and of sheep, / A raiser of huge melons and of pine, / A patron of some thirty charities. [84]

25 For it was in the golden prime / Of good Haroun Alraschid. [*Recollections of the Arabian Nights*, 11]

26 At Flores in the Azores Sir Richard Grenville lay. [*The Revenge*, 1]

27 I should count myself the coward if I left them, my Lord Howard, / To these Inquisition dogs and the devildoms of Spain. [2]

28 And they blest him in their pain, that they were not left to Spain, / To the thumbscrew and the stake, for the glory of the Lord. [3]

29 Shall we fight or shall we fly? / Good Sir Richard, tell us now, / For to fight is but to die! / There'll be little of us left by the time this sun is set. [4]

30 We be all good Englishmen. / Let us bang these dogs of Seville, the children of the devil, / For I never turned my back upon Don or devil yet.

31 And a dozen times we shook 'em off as a dog that shakes his ears / When he leaps from the water to the land. [8]

32 And the sun went down, and the stars came out far over the summer sea, / But never a moment ceased the fight of the one and the fifty-three. [9]

33 God of battles, was ever a battle like this in the world before?

1 A day less or more / At sea or ashore, / We die – does it matter when? [11]

2 Sink me the ship, Master Gunner – sink her, split her in twain! / Fall into the hands of God, not into the hands of Spain!

3 We have children, we have wives, / And the Lord hath spared our lives. / We will make the Spaniard promise, if we yield, to let us go: / We shall live to fight again and to strike another blow. [12]

4 They praised him to his face with their courtly foreign grace. [13]

5 I have fought for Queen and Faith like a valiant man and true; / I have only done my duty as a man is bound to do.

6 Riflemen, Riflemen, Riflemen form! [*Riflemen Form!*]

7 Deep on the convent-roof the snows / Are sparkling to the moon; / My breath to heaven like vapour goes: / May my soul follow soon! [*St Agnes' Eve*]

8 Make Thou my spirit pure and clear / As are the frosty skies.

9 The Sabbaths of Eternity, / One Sabbath deep and wide – / A light upon the shining sea – / The Bridegroom with his bride!

10 Battering the gates of heaven with storms of prayer. [*St Simeon Stylites*, 7]

11 A city clerk, but gently born and bred. [*Sea Dreams*, 1]

12 What does little birdie say / In her nest at peep of day? [Song]

13 Baby, sleep a little longer, / Till the little limbs are stronger.

14 My strength is as the strength of ten, / Because my heart is pure. [*Sir Galahad*, 1]

15 How sweet are looks that ladies bend / On whom their favours fall! [2]

16 A maiden knight – to me is given / Such hope, I know not fear. [6]

17 All armed I ride, whate'er betide, / Until I find the holy Grail. [7]

18 We were two daughters of one race. [*The Sisters*]

19 When cats run home and light is come, / And dew is cold upon the ground. [Song: *The Owl*]

20 Alone and warming his five wits, / The white owl in the belfry sits.

21 Oh teach me yet / Somewhat before the heavy clod / Weighs on me, and the busy fret / Of that sharp-headed worm begins / In the gross blackness underneath. [*Supposed Confessions of a Second-rate Sensitive Mind*, conclusion]

22 The woods decay, the woods decay and fall, / The vapours weep their burden to the ground, / Man comes and tills the field and lies beneath, / And after many a summer dies the swan. [*Tithonus*, 1]

23 Here at the quiet limit of the world, / A white-haired shadow roaming like a dream / The ever-silent spaces of the East. [7]

24 The Gods themselves cannot recall their gifts. [49]

25 The steam / Floats up from those dim fields about the homes / Of happy men that have the power to die, / And grassy barrows of the happier dead. [68]

26 A life that moves to gracious ends / Thro' troops of unrecording friends, / A deedful life, a silent voice. [*To —, after reading a Life and Letters*]

27 Betray the trust: / Keep nothing sacred: 'tis but just / The many-headed beast should know.

28 Wielder of the stateliest measure ever moulded by the lips of man. [*To Virgil*]

29 A still small voice spake unto me, / 'Thou art so full of misery, / Were it not better not to be?' [*The Two Voices*, 1]

30 This truth within thy mind rehearse, / That in a boundless universe / Is boundless better, boundless worse. [9]

31 I wept, 'Tho' I should die, I know / That all about the thorn will blow / In tufts of rosy-tinted snow.' [20]

32 Then comes the check, the change, the fall, / Pain rises up, old pleasures pall, / There is one remedy for all. [55]

33 'Consider well,' the voice replied, / 'His face, that two hours since hath died; / Wilt thou find passion, pain or pride?' [81]

34 Whatever crazy sorrow saith, / No life that breathes with human breath / Has ever truly longed for death. [132]

35 It little profits that an idle king, / By this still hearth, among these barren crags, / Matched with an aged wife, I mete and dole / Unequal laws unto a savage race. [*Ulysses*, 1]

1 I will drink / Life to the lees. [6]

2 Thro' scudding drifts the rainy Hyades / Vext the dim sea. [10]

3 Much have I seen and known; cities of men / And manners, climates, councils, governments, / Myself not least, but honoured of them all; / And drunk delight of battle with my peers, / Far on the ringing plains of windy Troy. [13]

4 All experience is an arch wherethro' / Gleams that untravelled world, whose margin fades / For ever and for ever when I move. [19]

5 To rust unburnished, not to shine in use. [23]

6 This gray spirit yearning in desire / To follow knowledge like a sinking star, / Beyond the utmost bound of human thought. [30]

7 This is my son, mine own Telemachus. [33]

8 Death closes all: but something ere the end, / Some work of noble note, may yet be done, / Not unbecoming men that strove with Gods. [51]

9 The long day wanes: the slow moon climbs: the deep / Moans round with many voices. [55]

10 My purpose holds / To sail beyond the sunset, and the baths / Of all the western stars, until I die. / It may be that the gulfs will wash us down; / It may be we shall touch the Happy Isles / And see the great Achilles. [59]

11 Tho' / We are not now that strength that in old days / Moved earth and heaven: that which we are, we are; / One equal temper of heroic hearts, / Made weak by time and fate, but strong in will / To strive, to seek, to find, and not to yield. [65]

12 An' I thowt 'twur the will o' the Lord, but Miss Annie she said it wur draäins. [The Village Wife, 2]

13 God made Himself an awful rose of dawn. [The Village of Sin, 3; also last line]

14 Let us hob-and-nob with Death. [4]

15 Every moment dies a man, / Every moment one is born.

16 Drink to lofty hopes that cool – / Visions of a perfect State.

17 Sea-king's daughter from over the sea, Alexandra! [A Welcome to Alexandra]

18 O plump head-waiter at The Cock, / To which I most resort / How goes the time? 'Tis five o'clock. / Go fetch a pint of port. [Will Waterproof's Lyrical Monologue, 1]

19 Softly, thro' a vinous mist, / My college friendships glimmer. [5]

20 That eternal want of pence / Which vexes public men. [6]

21 As on this whirligig of Time / We circle with the seasons. [8]

22 High above roaring Temple-bar, / And set in Heaven's third storey, / I look at all things as they are, / But thro' a kind of glory. [9]

23 Carved cross-pipes, and, underneath, / A pint-pot neatly graven. [Last lines]

24 A land of settled government, / A land of just and old renown, / Where Freedom slowly broadens down / From precedent to predecent. [You ask me why]

25 A louse in the locks of literature. [Said of Churton Collins. Charteris, Life and Letters of Sir Edmund Gosse]

SHERPA TENZING NORGAY 1914–1986

26 We've done the bugger! [Attr., on conquering Mount Everest, 1953. Similar line from fellow climber, Sir Edmund Hilary: 'We knocked the bastard off!']

TERENCE c. 195–159 BC

27 Hinc illae lacrimae. – Hence these tears. [Andria, 126]

28 Amantium irae amoris integratio est. – Lover's quarrels are the renewal of love. [555]

29 Homo sum; humani nil a me alienum puto. – I am a man, and reckon nothing human alien to me. [Heauton Timoroumenos, 25]

30 Fortis fortuna adiuvat. – Fortune favours the brave. [Phormio, 203]

31 Quot homines tot sententiae: suo quoque mos. – As many opinions as there are men; each a law to himself. [454]

TERTULLIAN c. 160–c. 220

32 O testimonium animae naturaliter Christianae. – O witness of the soul Christian by nature. [Apologeticus, 17]

33 See how these Christians love one another. [39]

34 The blood of the martyrs is the seed of the Church. [50]

35 Credo quia impossibile. – I believe because it

is impossible. [(Usual adapt. of: *Certum est quia impossibile est.' – It is certain . . .*) *De Carne Christi*, 5]

EDWARD TESCHEMACHER 19 Cent.

1 Where my caravan has rested, / Flowers I leave you on the grass. [*Where my Caravan has Rested*]

W. M. THACKERAY 1811–1863

2 It is impossible, in our condition of society, not to be sometimes a snob. [*The Book of Snobs*, Ch. 3]

3 'Tis strange what a man may do, and a woman yet think him an angel. [*Henry Esmond*, Bk i. Ch. 7]

4 We love being in love, that's the truth on't. [ii. 15]

5 Why do they always put mud into coffee on board steamers? Why does the tea generally taste of boiled boots? [*The Kickleburys on the Rhine*]

6 Kind, cheerful, merry Dr Brighton. [*The Newcomes*, Ch. 9]

7 What money is better bestowed than that of a schoolboy's tip? [16]

8 As the last bell struck, a peculiar sweet smile shone over his face, and he lifted up his head a little, and quickly said, 'Adsum!' and fell back. It was the word we used at school, when names were called; and lo, he, whose heart was as that of a little child, had answered to his name, and stood in the presence of The Master. [80]

9 Yes, I am a fatal man, Madame Fribsbi. To inspire hopeless passion is my destiny. [(Mirobolant) *Pendennis*, Ch. 23]

10 Remember, it is as easy to marry a rich woman as a poor woman. [28]

11 For a slashing article, sir, there's nobody like the Capting. [32]

12 The *Pall Mall Gazette* is written by gentlemen for gentlemen. [The

13 Runs not a river by my palace wall? Have I not sacks to sew up wives withal? [*The Rose and the Ring*, Ch. 9]

14 'No business before breakfast, Glum!' says the King. 'Breakfast first, business next.' [11]

15 There are some meannesses which are too mean even for man – woman, lovely woman alone, can venture to commit them. [*A Shabby-Genteel Story*, Ch. 3]

16 This I set down as a positive truth. A woman with fair opportunities and without a positive hump, may marry whom she likes. [*Vanity Fair*, Ch. 4]

17 Whenever he met a great man he grovelled before him, and my-lorded him as only a freeborn Briton can do. [13]

18 Them's my sentiments. [(Fred Bullock) 21]

19 Darkness came down on the field and city: and Amelia was praying for George, who was lying on his face, dead, with a bullet through his heart. [32]

20 Nothing like blood, sir, in hosses, dawgs, and men. [(James Crawley) 35]

21 I think I could be a good woman if I had five thousand a year. [(Becky Sharp) 36]

22 Come, children, let us shut up the box and the puppets, for our play is played out. [67]

23 There's no sweeter tobacco comes from Virginia, and no better brand than the Three Castles. [*The Virginians*, Ch. 1]

24 Fashnable fax and polite annygoats. [*The Yellowplush Papers*, Pt I, title]

25 There were three sailors of Bristol City / Who took a boat and went to sea. [*Little Billee*]

26 There was gorging Jack and guzzling Jimmy, / And the youngest he was little Billee.

27 Little we fear / Weather without, / Sheltered about / The Mahogany Tree. [*The Mahogany Tree*]

28 Werther had a love for Charlotte, / Such as words could never utter; / Would you know how first he met her? / She was cutting bread and butter. [*The Sorrows of Werther*]

MARGARET THATCHER 1925–

29 I stand before you tonight in my green chiffon evening gown . . . the Iron Lady of the Western World. Me? [Taking up term used of her by Soviet newspaper *Red Star*. She had earlier been called the Iron Maiden in Britain. Speech in Dorking, Surrey, 31 Jan. 1976]

30 You turn if you want to – the lady's not for turning. [In denying the possibility of her making a U-turn over economic policy. Closing speech at Conservative Party Conference, Brighton, 11 Oct. 1980. Phrase ascr. to Ronald Millar as her speech-writer]

W. M. THAYER 1820–1898

1 Log-cabin to White House. [Title of biography of President Garfield]

ADOLPHE THIERS 1797–1877

2 *Il faut tout prendre au sérieux, mais rien au tragique.* – Everything must be taken seriously, nothing tragically. [Speech in National Assembly, 24 May 1873]

BRANDON THOMAS 1857–1914

3 I am Charley's aunt from Brazil, where the nuts come from. [*Charley's Aunt*, I]

DYLAN THOMAS 1914–1953

4 Where blew a flower may a flower no more / Lift its head to the blows of the rain; / Though they be mad and dead as nails, / Heads of the characters hammer through daisies; / Break in the sun till the sun breaks down, / And death shall have no dominion. [*And death shall have no dominion*]

5 Do not go gentle into that good night. / Rage, rage against the dying of the light. [*Do Not go gentle into that good night*]

6 Oh as I was young and easy in the mercy of his means, / Time held me green and dying / Though I sang in my chains like the sea. [*Fern Hill*]

7 The force that through the green fuse drives the flower / Drives my green age. [*The force that through the green fuse*]

8 The hand that signed the treaty bred a fever, / And famine grew, and locusts came; / Great is the hand that holds dominion over / Man by a scribbled name. [*The hand that signed the paper*]

9 Light breaks where no sun shines; / Where no sea runs, the waters of the heart / Push in their tides. [*Light breaks where no sun shines*]

10 My birthday began with the water- / Birds and the birds of the winged trees flying my name. [*Poem in October*]

11 And I rose / In rainy autumn / And walked abroad in a shower of all my days.

12 It was my thirtieth / Year to heaven stood there then in the summer noon.

13 And I must enter again the round / Zion of the water bead / And the synagogue of the ear of corn. [*A refusal to mourn the death, by fire, of a child in London*]

14 Deep with the first dead lies London's daughter, / Robed in the long friends, / The grains beyond age, the dark veins of her mother, / Secret by the unmourning water / Of the riding Thames. / After the first death, there is no other.

15 Shall gods be said to thump the clouds / When clouds are cursed by thunder? [*Shall gods be said to thump the clouds?*]

16 This bread I break was once the oat, / This wine upon a foreign tree / Plunged in its fruit; / Man in the day or wind at night / Laid the crops low, broke the grape's joy. [*This bread I break*]

17 It is a winter's tale / That the snow blind twilight ferries over the lakes / And floating fields from the farm in the cup of the vales. [*A Winter's Tale*]

18 It is spring, moonless night in the small town, starless and bible-black. [*Under Milk Wood*]

19 The boys are dreaming wicked or of the bucking ranches of the night and the jolly-rodgered sea.

20 Straightfaced in his cunning sleep he pulls the legs of his dreams.

21 ... kissed her once by the pigsty when she wasn't looking and never kissed her again although she was looking all the time.

22 Nothing grows in our garden, only washing. And babies.

23 The ship's clock in the bar says half past eleven. Half past eleven is opening time. The hands of the clock have stayed still at half past eleven for fifty years. It is always opening time in the Sailors Arms.

24 I see you got a mermaid in your lap he said and he lifted his hat. He is a proper Christian.

25 Johann Sebastian mighty Bach. Oh Bach fach.

EDWARD THOMAS 1878–1917

26 Yes. I remember Adlestrop – / The name, because one afternoon / Of heat the express-train drew up there / Unwontedly. It was late June. [*Adlestrop*]

27 I have come to the borders of sleep, / The

unfathomable deep / Forest where all must lose / Their way. [*Lights Out*]

1 Out in the dark over the snow / The fallow fawns invisible go / With the fallow doe; / And the winds blow / Fast as the stars are slow. [*Out in the Dark*]

2 The new moon hangs like an ivory bugle / In the naked frosty blue. [*The Penny Whistle*]

3 I love roads: / The goddesses that dwell / Far along them invisible / Are my favourite gods. [*Roads*]

4 Open your eyes to the air / That has washed the eyes of the stars / Through all the dewy night: / Up with the light, / To the old wars: / Arise, arise. [*The Trumpet*]

5 When these woods were young / The thrushes' ancestors / As sweetly sung / In the old years. [*Under the Woods*]

6 Out of us all / That make rhymes, / Will you choose / Sometimes – / As the winds use / A crack in a wall / Or a drain, / Their joy or their pain / To whistle through – / Choose me, / You English words? [*Words*]

R. S. THOMAS 1913–

7 We will listen instead to the wind's text / Blown through the roof, or the thrush's song / In the thick bush that proved him wrong, / Wrong from the start, for nature's truth / Is primary and her changing seasons / Correct out of a vaster reason / The vague errors of the flesh. [*Song at the Year's Turning*, 'The Minister', end]

8 We were a people taut for war; the hills / Were no harder, the thin grass / Clothed them more warmly than the coarse / Shirts our small bones. [*Welsh History*]

DOUGLAS THOMPSON 19 Cent.

9 And fearful the death of the diver must be, / Sleeping alone, sleeping alone, sleeping alone in the depths of the sea! [Song: *The Diver*]

FRANCIS THOMPSON 1859–1907

10 And I look through my tears on a soundless-clapping host / As the run-stealers flicker to and fro, / To and fro:– / O my Hornby and my Barlow long ago! [*At Lord's*]

11 Nothing begins, and nothing ends, / That is not paid with moan; / For we are born in other's pain, / And perish in our own. [*Daisy*]

12 I fled Him, down the nights and down the days; / I fled Him, down the arches of the years; / I fled him, down the labyrinthine ways / Of my own mind; and in the midst of tears / I hid from Him, and under running laughter. [*The Hound of Heaven*, 1]

13 But with unhurrying chase, / And unperturbèd pace, / Deliberate speed, majestic instancy, / They beat – and a Voice beat / More instant than the Feet – / 'All things betray thee, who betrayest Me.' [10]

14 I said to Dawn: Be sudden – to Eve: Be soon. [30]

15 My days have crackled and gone up in smoke, / Have puffed and burst as sun-starts on a stream. / Yea, faileth now even dream / The dreamer, and the lute the lutanist. [122]

16 I dimly guess what Time in mists confounds; / Yet ever and anon a trumpet sounds / From the hid battlements of Eternity. [143]

17 O world invisible, we view thee, / O world intangible, we touch thee, / O world unknowable, we know thee. [*The Kingdom of God*]

18 Not where the wheeling systems darken, / And our benumbed conceiving soars!– / The drift of pinions, would we harken, / Beats at our own clay-shuttered doors. / The angels keep their ancient places;– / Turn but a stone, and start a wing!

19 Shall shine the traffic of Jacob's ladder / Pitched between Heaven and Charing Cross.

20 Secret was the garden; / Set i' the pathless awe/ Where no star its breath can draw. / Life, that is its warden, / Sat behind the fosse of death. Mine eyes saw not, and I saw. [*The Mistress of Vision*, 1]

21 When thy seeing blindeth thee / To what thy fellow-mortals see; / When thy sight to thee is sightless; / Their living, death; their light, most lightless; / Search no more – / Pass the gates of Luthany, tread the region Elenore. [20]

22 When to the new eyes of thee / All things by immortal power, / Near or far, / Hiddenly / To each other linkèd are, / That thou canst not stir a flower / Without troubling of a star. [22]

23 Summer set lip to earth's bosom bare, / And left the flushed print in a poppy there. [*The Poppy*]

24 I hang 'mid men my needless head, / And my fruit is dreams, as theirs is bread: the goodly

men and the sun-hazed sleeper / Time shall reap, but after the reaper / The world shall glean of me, me the sleeper.

1 What heart could have thought you?– / Past our devisal. (O filigree petal) / Fashioned so purely? [*To a Snowflake*]

2 His hammer of wind, / And His graver of frost.

3 Look for me in the nurseries of Heaven. [*To my Godchild*]

W. H. THOMPSON 1810–1886

4 We're none of us infallible – not even the youngest among us. [Remark to a junior fellow, when Master of Trinity College, Cambridge. Quoted in G. W. E. Russell, *Collections and Recollections*, Ch. 18]

JAMES THOMSON 1700–1748

5 When Britain first, at heaven's command, / Arose from out the azure main, / This was the charter of the land, / And guardian angels sung this strain: / 'Rule, Britannia, rule the waves; / Britons never will be slaves. ' [*Alfred: a Masque*, II. v]

6 Delightful task! to rear the tender thought, / To teach the young idea how to shoot. [*The Seasons*, 'Spring', 1152]

7 An elegant sufficiency, content, / Retirement, rural quiet, friendship, books, / Ease and alternate labour, useful life, / Progressive virtue, and approving Heaven! [1161]

8 The meek-eyed Morn appears, mother of dews. ['Summer', 47]

9 Falsely luxurious! will not man awake? [67]

10 Or sighed and looked unutterable things. [1188]

11 While listening senates hang upon thy tongue. ['Autumn', 15]

12 For loveliness / Needs not the foreign aid of ornament, / But is, when unadorned, adorned the most. [204]

13 Welcome, kindred glooms! / Congenial horrors, hail! ['Winter', 5]

14 There studious let me sit, / And hold high converse with the mighty dead. [431]

15 Oh! Sophonisba! Sophonisba! Oh! [*Sophonisba*, III, ii]

JAMES THOMSON 1834–1882

16 The City is of Night; perchance of Death, / But certainly of Night. [*The City of Dreadful Night*, 1]

17 For life is but a dream whose shapes return, / Some frequently, some seldom, some by night / And some by day.

18 The chambers of the mansion of my heart, / In every one whereof thine image dwells, / Are black with grief eternal for thy sake. [10]

19 I find no hint throughout the universe / Of good or ill, of blessing or of curse; / I find alone Necessity Supreme. [14]

20 As we rush, as we rush in the train, / The trees and the houses go wheeling back, / But the starry heavens above the plain / Come flying on our track. [*Sunday at Hampstead*, 10]

21 A little straw hat with the streaming blue ribbons / Is soon to come dancing over the bridge. [*Sunday up the River*, 1]

22 Give a man a horse he can ride, / Give a man a boat he can sail. [15]

ROY THOMSON, later LORD THOMSON OF FLEET 1894–1976

23 A stake in commercial television is the equivalent of having a licence to print money. [On the profit in commercial TV in Britain, Aug. 1957. Quoted in R. Braddon, *Roy Thomson*, Ch.32]

H. D. THOREAU 1817–1862

24 The mass of men lead lives of quiet desperation. [*Walden*, 'Economy']

25 I have lived some thirty years on this planet, and I have yet to hear the first syllable of valuable or even earnest advice from my seniors.

26 As if you could kill time without injuring eternity.

27 Beware of all enterprises that require new clothes.

28 Our life is frittered away by detail ... Simplify, simplify. ['Where I Lived, and What I Lived For']

29 Time is but the stream I go a-fishing in.

30 I never found the companion that was so companionable as solitude. ['Solitude']

31 I had three chairs in my house: one for

solitude, two for friendship, three for society. ['Visitors']

1 I frequently tramped eight or ten miles through the deepest snow to keep an appointment with a beech-tree, or a yellow birch, or an old acquaintance among the pines. ['Winter Visitors']

2 It takes two to speak the truth,– one to speak, and another to hear. [*A Week on the Concord and Merrimack Rivers*, 'Wednesday']

3 Some circumstantial evidence is very strong, as when you find a trout in the milk. [*Journal*, 11 Nov. 1854]

JEREMY THORPE 1929–

4 Greater love hath no man than this, that he lay down his friends for his life. [Of Macmillan's swingeing Cabinet reshuffle on 13 July 1962. Quoted in Bernard Levin, *The Pendulum Years*, Ch. 12]

ROSE H. THORPE 1850–1939

5 As she climbed the dusty ladder on which fell no ray of light,– / Up and up, her white lips saying, 'Curfew shall not ring tonight.']*Curfew Must not Ring Tonight*]

REV. GODFREY THRING 1823–1903

6 Fierce raged the tempest o'er the deep. [Hymn]

THUCYDIDES *c.* 471–*c.* 400 BC

7 To famous men all the earth is a sepulchre. [*History*, II. 43, iii]

8 It is great glory in a woman to show no more weakness than is natural to her sex, and not be talked of, either for good or evil by men. [II. 45, ii]

9 That war is an evil is something that we all know, and it would be pointless to go on cataloguing all the disadvantages involved in it. No one is forced into war by ignorance, nor, if he thinks he will gain from it, is he kept out of it by fear. The fact is that one side thinks that the profits to be won outweigh the risks to be incurred, and the other side is ready to face danger rather than accept an immediate loss. [IV. 4]

JAMES THURBER 1894–1961

10 Why don't you get dressed, then, and go to pieces like a man? [*Alarms and Diversions*, cartoon caption]

11 It is better to have loafed and lost than never to have loafed at all. [*Fables of Our Time*, 'The Courtship of Arthur and Al']

12 You can fool too many of the people too much of the time. ['The Owl Who Was God']

13 It's a naïve domestic Burgundy without any breeding, but I think you'll be amused by its presumption. [*Men, Women and Dogs*, cartoon caption]

14 You wait here and I'll bring the etchings down.

15 I said the hounds of Spring are on Winter's traces – but let it pass, let it pass!

16 Well, if I called the wrong number, why did you answer the phone?

17 I suppose that the high-water mark of my youth in Columbus, Ohio, was the night the bed fell on my father. [*My Life and Hard Times*, Ch. 1]

18 Her own mother lived the latter years of her life in the horrible suspicion that electricity was dripping invisibly all over the house. [2]

19 When the dam broke, or, to be more exact, when everybody in town *thought* that the dam broke. [3]

20 The ghost that got into our house on the night of November 17, 1915, raised such a hullabaloo of misunderstandings that I am sorry I didn't just let it keep on walking, and go to bed. [4]

21 Q. We have cats the way most people have mice. [Signed] Mrs C. L. FOOTLOOSE.

A. I see you have. I can't tell from your communication whether you wish advice or are just boasting. [*The Owl in the Attic*]

22 All right, have it your way – you heard a seal bark. [*The Seal in the Bedroom*, cartoon caption]

23 'We all have flaws,' he said, 'and mine is being wicked.' [*The 13 Clocks*, Ch. 8]

24 It had only one fault. It was kind of lousy. [When asked his opinion of a play. Quoted in P. G. Wodehouse, *Performing Flea*, 25 Sept. 1950]

EDWARD, FIRST BARON THURLOW
1731–1806

25 When I forget my sovereign, may God forget me! [Speech in House of Lords, 15 Dec. 1778]

1 As guardian of His Majesty's conscience. [Speech in House of Lords, 1779]

2 Corporations have neither bodies to be punished, nor souls to be condemned; they therefore do as they like. [(Usually quoted as: 'Did you ever expect a corporation to have a conscience, when it has no soul to be damned, and no body to be kicked?') Poynder, *Literary Extracts*, Vol. i]

PAUL W. TIBBETTS 20 Cent.

3 A mushroom of boiling dust up to 20,000 feet. [Description by the pilot of atomic bomb explosion]

TIBULLUS 54?–18? BC

4 *Te spectem, suprema mihi cum venerit hora, / Te teneam moriens deficiente manu.* – May I see you when my last hour comes, and hold you with my dying hand. [I. i, 59]

5 *Nile pater, quanam possim te dicere causa / Aut quibus in terris occuluisse caput? / Te propter nullos tellus tua postulat imbres, / Arida nec pluvio supplicat herba Iovi.* – Father Nile, why or in what lands can I say you have hidden your head? On your account your Egypt never sues for showers, nor does the dry grass bow to Jupiter the Rain-bringer. [I. vii. 23]

THOMAS TICKELL 1686–1740

6 I hear a voice you cannot hear, / Which says I must not stay; / I see a hand you cannot see, / Which beckons me away. [*Colin and Lucy*]

7 There taught us how to live; and (oh! too high / The price for knowledge) taught us how to die. [*On the Death of Mr Addison*, 81]

JOHN TILLOTSON 1630–1694

8 If God were not a necessary Being of himself, He might almost seem to be made for the use and benefit of mankind. [*Sermon* 93]

HARRY TILZER [ALBERT VON TILZER] 1878–1956

9 Come, Come, Come and have a drink with me / Down at the old 'Bull and Bush'. [Song]

THE TIMES

10 In my childhood it was said by all: 'A child of ten can go on the road of a town playing with a golden ball in perfect safety under British rule.' [Quoted in *The Times*]

MATTHEW TINDAL 1657–1733

11 Matters of fact, which as Mr Budgell somewhere observes, are very stubborn things. [*Will of Matthew Tindal*]

TITUS VESPASIANUS 40/41–81

12 Friends, I have lost a day. [Quoted in Suetonius, *Titus*, 8]

JOHN TOBIN 1770–1804

13 The man that lays his hand upon a woman, / Save in the way of kindness, is a wretch / Whom 'twere gross flattery to name a coward. [*The Honeymoon*, II. i]

ALEXIS DE TOCQUEVILLE 1805–1859

14 Experience shows that the most dangerous moment for a bad government is usually just as it's starting on reform. [*The Ancien Régime and the Revolution*, Bk iii. Ch. 4]

JACOPONE DA TODI ?–1306

15 *Stabat mater dolorosa / Iuxta crucem lacrimosa.* – At the cross her station keeping / Stood the mournful mother weeping. [*Stabat mater (English Hymnal* translation)]

ALVIN TOFFLER 1928–

16 Future Shock. [Title of book. Derived from term 'Culture Shock']

J. R. R. TOLKIEN 1892–1973

17 In a hole in the ground there lived a hobbit. [*The Hobbit*, Ch. 1]

18 One Ring to rule them all, One Ring to find them, / One Ring to bring them all and in the darkness bind then. [*The Lord of the Rings*, Part I: *The Fellowship of the Ring*, Ch. 2]

LEO TOLSTOY 1828–1910

19 All happy families resemble one another, each unhappy family is unhappy in its own way. [*Anna Karenina*, I. Ch. 1]

20 This new feeling has not changed me, has

not made me happy and enlightened all of a sudden, as I dreamed it would . . . Be it faith or not – I don't know what it is – through suffering this feeling has crept just as imperceptibly into my heart and has lodged itself firmly there. [VII. 19]

1 But my life now, my whole life, independently of anything that can happen to me, every minute of it is no longer meaningless as it was before, but has a positive meaning of goodness with which I have the power to invest it.

2 I am always with myself, and it is I who am my tormentor. [*Memoirs of a Madman*]

3 The highest wisdom has but one science – the science of the whole – the science explaining the whole creation and man's place in it. [*War and Peace*, V. Ch. 2]

4 The chief attraction of military service has consisted and will consist in this compulsory and irreproachable idleness. [VII. 1]

5 All, everything that I understand, I understand only because I love. [16]

6 Love is God, and to die means that I, a particle of love, shall return to the general and eternal source.

7 Pure and complete sorrow is as impossible as pure and complete joy. [XV. 1]

8 The most powerful weapon of ignorance – the diffusion of printed material. [Epilogue, Pt II Ch. 8]

9 How do peasants die? [Death-bed words. Attr. in Kenneth Clark, *Civilisation*, Ch. 13]

A. M. TOPLADY 1740–1778

10 Rock of ages cleft for me, / Let me hide myself in Thee. [Hymn]

CYRIL TOURNEUR 1575?–1626

11 Were't not for gold and women, there would be no damnation. [*The Revenger's Tragedy* II. i]

12 Does the silk-worm expend her yellow labours / For thee? For thee does she undo herself? / Are lordships sold to maintain ladyships, / For the poor benefit of a bewildering minute? [III. iv]

ARNOLD TOYNBEE 1889–1975

13 America is a large, friendly dog in a very small room. Every time it wags its tail it knocks over a chair. [Broadcast radio news summary, 14 July 1954]

THOMAS TRAHERNE 1637?–1674

14 You never enjoy the world aright, till the sea itself floweth in your veins, till you are clothed with the heavens, and crowned with the stars. [*Centuries of Meditations*, i.29]

15 The corn was orient and immortal wheat, which never should be reaped, nor was ever sown. I thought it had stood from everlasting to everlasting. [iii. 3]

16 The Men! O what venerable and reverend creatures did the aged seem! Immortal Cherubims! And young men glittering and sparkling angels, and maids strange seraphic pieces of life and beauty! Boys and girls tumbling in the street, and playing, were moving jewels.

H. D. TRAILL 1842–1900

17 Why do you wear your hair like a man, / Sister Helen? [*After Dilettante Concetti* (a parody of D. G. Rossetti)]

18 Look in my face. My name is Used-to-was; / I am also called Played-out and Done-to-death, / And It-will-wash-no-more.

REV. JOSEPH TRAPP 1679–1747

19 The King, observing with judicious eyes / The state of both his universities, / To Oxford sent a troop of horse, and why? / That learned body wanted loyalty; / To Cambridge books, as very well discerning / How much that loyal body wanted learning. [On George I's donation of a library to Cambridge. (For reply see Sir William Browne, 71:23)]

HERBERT TRENCH 1865–1923

20 O dreamy, gloomy, friendly trees. [*O Dreamy, Gloomy, Friendly Trees*]

21 Come, let us make love deathless, thou and I. [*To Arolilia*, 2]

ARCHBISHOP R. V. TRENCH 1807–1886

22 England, we love thee better than we know. [*Gibraltar*]

G. M. TREVELYAN 1876–1962

23 Education . . . has produced a vast popula-

tion able to read but unable to distinguish what is worth reading. [*English Social History*, Ch. 18]

TOMMY TRINDER 1909–1989

1 They're overpaid, overfed, oversexed and over here. [(Of the GIs) Attr. by Alan Brien in the *Sunday Times*, 4 Jan. 1976]

ANTHONY TROLLOPE 1815–1882

2 He must have known me if he had seen me and he was wont to see me, for he was in the habit of flogging me constantly. Perhaps he did not recognize me by my face. [*Autobiography*, Ch. 1]

3 Three hours a day will produce as much as a man ought to write. [15]

4 Among these Mr Quiverful, the rector of Puddingdale, whose wife still continued to present him from year to year with fresh pledges of her love. [*Barchester Towers*, Ch. 7]

5 The blood of Tiberius flows in her veins. She is the last of the Neros! [11]

6 Not only humble but umble, which I look upon to be the comparative, or, indeed, superlative degree. [*Doctor Thorne*, Ch. 4]

7 In these days a man is nobody unless his biography is kept so far posted up that it may be ready for the national breakfast-table on the morning after his demise. [25]

8 It's dogged as does it. It ain't thinking about it. [*The Last Chronicle of Barset*, Ch. 61]

9 Those who offend us are generally punished for the offence they give; but we so frequently miss the satisfaction of knowing that we are avenged! [*The Small House at Allington*, Ch. 50]

10 The tenth Muse, who now governs the periodical press. [*The Warden*, Ch. 14]

LEON TROTSKY 1874–1940

11 Old age is the most unexpected of all the things that happen to a man. [*Diary in Exile*, 8 May 1935]

12 The vengeance of history is more terrible than the vengeance of the most powerful Secretary General. [*Final Testament* (written 10 days before his murder)]

13 Insurrection is an art, and like all arts it has its laws. [*The History of the Russian Revolution*, III. 6]

14 There is a limit to the application of democratic methods. You can inquire of all the passengers as to what type of car they like to ride in, but it is impossible to question them as to whether to apply the brakes when the train is at full speed and accident threatens.

15 From being a patriotic myth, the Russian people have become an awful reality. [7]

16 It was the supreme expression of the mediocrity of the apparatus that Stalin himself rose to his position. [*My Life*, Ch. 40]

17 We only die when we fail to take root in others. [Quoted in Trevor Griffiths, *The Party*, II]

18 I myself took this job [Commissar for Foreign Relations] so I would have more time for Party work. All there is to do is to publish the secret treaties. Then I will close the shop. [Quoted in A. Ulam, *Expansion and Coexistence*]

19 An ally has to be watched just like an enemy.

PRESIDENT HARRY TRUMAN 1884–1972

20 The buck stops here. [Notice on his presidential desk]

21 An eight-ulcer man on a four-ulcer job, and all four ulcers working. [Letter to *Washington Post* on unflattering reviewer of his daughter's song recital, 5 Dec. 1950. Quoted in Frank Muir, *The Frank Muir Book*]

22 It's a recession when your neighbour loses his job; it's a depression when you lose your own. [*Observer*, 'Sayings of the Week', 6 Apr. 1958]

23 A politician is a man who understands government, and it takes a politician to run a government. A statesman is a politician who's been dead ten or fifteen years. [Impromptu speech, in Washington, 11 Apr.]

24 You don't set a fox to watching the chickens just because he has a lot of experience in the hen house. [On Vice-President Nixon's candidacy for the Presidency. Speech, 30 Oct. 1960]

25 I didn't fire him [General MacArthur] because he was a dumb son of a bitch, although he was, but that's not against the law for generals. If it was, half to three-quarters of them would be in gaol. [Said in an interview. Quoted in Merle Miller, *Plain Speaking*, 24]

26 I sit here all day trying to persuade people to do the things they ought to have sense

enough to do without my persuading them ...
That's all the powers of the President amount
to. [Quoted in R. E. Neustadt, *Presidential Power*]

1 If you can't stand the heat, get out of the
kitchen. [Proverbial saying adopted by him and
quoted in *Mr Citizen*, Ch. 15]

JOHN TRUMBULL 1750–1831

2 But optics sharp it needs, I ween, / To see
what is not to be seen. [*McFingal*, Canto 1. 67]

SOPHIE TUCKER 1884?–1966

3 I'm the last of the red-hot mommas. [Title of
song (written by Jack Yellen) which became
her sobriquet]

4 Life begins at forty. [Quoted in *The Times*,
21 Jan. 1978]

A. W. TUER 1838–1900

5 English as she is Spoke. [Title of
Portuguese–English conversational guide]

MARTIN TUPPER 1810–1889

6 A good book is the best of friends, the same
today and for ever. [*Proverbial Philosophy*, Series
I, 'Of Reading']

7 It is well to lie fallow for a while. ['Of
Recreation']

MARSHAL TURENNE 1611–1675

8 *Dieu est toujours pour les gros bataillons.*
– God is always on the side of the big battalions.
[Attr. See also 86:25, 443:1]

IVAN TURGENEV 1818–1883

9 I agree with no man's opinion. I have some
of my own. [*Fathers and Sons*, Ch. 13]

10 The temerity to believe in nothing. [14]

11 Go and try to disprove death. Death will
disprove you, and that's all! [27]

12 Whatever a man prays for, he prays for a
miracle. Every prayer reduces itself to this:
'Great God, grant that twice two be not four.'
[*Prayer*]

13 Diary of a Superfluous Man. [Title of story
(the phrase was taken from Pushkin's *Eugene
Onegin*)]

W. J. TURNER 1889–1946

14 When I was but thirteen or so / I went into
a golden land, / Chimborazo, Cotopaxi / Took
me by the hand. [*Romance*]

THOMAS TUSSER 1524?–1580

15 At Christmas play and make good cheer, /
For Christmas comes but once a year. [*Five
Hundred Points of Good Husbandry*, 'The Farmer's
Daily Diet']

16 Yet true it is, as cow chews cud, / And trees
at spring do yield forth bud, / Except wind stands
as never it stood, / It is an ill wind turns none to
good. ['A Description of the Properties of Winds']

17 'Tis merry in hall / When beards wag all.
['August's Abstract']

18 Who goeth a borrowing / Goeth a sorrow-
ing. / Few lend (but fools) / Their working
tools. ['September's Abstract']

19 In doing of either, let wit bear a stroke, /
For buying or selling of pig in a poke. ['September's Husbandry']

20 February, fill the dyke / With what thou
dost like. ['February's Husbandry']

21 Sweet April showers / Do spring May
flowers. ['April's Husbandry']

22 Some respite to husbands the weather may
send, / But housewives' affairs have never an
end. ['Preface to the Book of Housewifery']

23 Seek home for rest, / For home is best.
['Instructions to Housewifery']

24 The stone that is rolling can gather no
moss; / For master and servant oft changing is
loss. ['Housewifely Admonitions']

MARK TWAIN [S. L. CLEMENS]
1835–1910

25 There was things which he. stretched, but
mainly he told the truth. [*The Adventures of
Huckleberry Finn*, Ch. 1]

26 *Pilgrim's Progress*, about a man who left his
family, it didn't say why. The statements was
interesting, but tough. [17]

27 All kings is mostly rapscallions. [23]

28 If there was two birds sitting on a fence, he
would bet you which one would fly first. [*The
Celebrated Jumping Frog*]

29 Soap and education are not as sudden as a

massacre, but they are more deadly in the long run. [*The Facts concerning the Recent Resignation*]

1 I admire him [Cecil Rhodes], I frankly confess it; and when his time comes I shall buy a piece of the rope for a keepsake. [*Following the Equator*]

2 They spell it Vinci and pronounce it Vinchy; foreigners always spell better than they pronounce. [*Innocents Abroad*, Ch. 19]

3 Guides cannot master the subtleties of the American joke.

4 Lump the whole thing! say that the Creator made Italy from designs by Michael Angelo! [27]

5 Are you going to hang him *anyhow* – and try him afterward? [*Innocents at Home*, Ch. 5]

6 Whem I'm playful I use the meridians and parallels of latitude for a seine, and drag the Atlantic Ocean for whales! I scratch my head with the lightning and purr myself to sleep with the thunder! [*Life on the Mississippi*, Ch. 3]

7 All the modern inconveniences. [43]

8 At bottom he [Carlyle] was probably fond of them [the Americans], but he was always able to conceal it. [*My First Lie*]

9 An experienced, industrious, ambitious, and often quite picturesque liar. [*Private History of a Campaign that Failed*]

10 Cauliflower is nothing but cabbage with a college education. [*Pudd'nhead Wilson* epigraph to Ch. 5]

11 All say, 'How hard it is to die' – a strange complaint to come from the mouths of people who have had to live. [10]

12 It is difference of opinion that makes horse races. [19]

13 They make a mouth at you and say thank you 'most to death, but there ain't-a-going to be no core. [*Tom Sawyer Abroad*, Ch. 1]

14 The cross of the Legion of Honour has been conferred upon me. However, few escape that distinction. [*A Tramp Abroad*, Ch. 8]

15 Some of his words were not Sunday-school words. [20]

16 This poor little one-horse town. [*The Undertaker's Chat*]

17 There was worlds of reputation in it, but no money. [*A Yankee at the Court of King Arthur*, Ch. 9]

18 A classic is something that everybody wants to have read and nobody wants to read. [Speech: *The Disappearance of Literature*]

19 The report of my death is exaggerated. [Cable from London to the Associated Press, 1897. Slightly varying versions exist]

KENNETH TYNAN 1927–1980

20 A novel is a static thing that one moves through; a play is a dynamic thing that moves past one. [*Curtains*, Pt 1, 'Cards of Identity']

21 What, when drunk, one sees in other women, one sees in Garbo sober. [2 'Garbo']

22 A good drama critic is one who perceives what is happening in the theatre of his time. A great drama critic also perceives what is not happening. [*Tynan Right and Left*, Foreword]

23 A critic is a man who knows the way but can't drive the car. [Quoted in the *New York Times Magazine*, 9 Jan. 1966]

U

MIGUEL DE UNAMUNO 1864–1937

1 *La vida es duda, / y la fe sin la duda es sólo muerte.* – Life is doubt, and faith without doubt is nothing but death. [*Poesías*, 1907]

2 And killing time is perhaps the essence of comedy, just as the essence of tragedy is killing eternity. [*San Manuel Bueno*, prologue]

3 May God deny you peace but give you glory! [*The Tragic Sense of Life*, closing words]

4 They [the Franco rebels] will conquer, but they will not convince. [Said at the end of his life]

EDWARD SMITH UFFORD 1851–1928

5 Throw out the life-line, throw out the life-line, / Someone is sinking today. [Revivalist hymn]

LUDWIG UHLAND 1787–1862

6 *In gleichem Schritt und Tritt.* – Alike in step and tread. [*Ich hatt' einen Kameraden*]

UMBERTO I 1844–1900

7 It is one of the incidents of the profession. [After an attempt on his life]

UNESCO

8 Since wars begin in the minds of men, it is in the minds of men that the defences of peace must be constructed. [Constitution, adopted 16 Nov. 1945]

UPANISHADS 7 Cent. BC

9 This earth is the honey of all beings; all beings the honey of this earth. [*Famous Debates in the Forest*, V]

10 Death said: 'The good is one thing, the pleasant another; these two, having different objects, chain a man. It is well with him who clings to the good; he who chooses the pleasant misses his end.' [*Katha Upanishad*, ii]

11 I am this world and I eat this world. Who know this, knows. [*Taittireeya Upanishad*, III. 10]

JOHN UPDIKE 1932–

12 A healthy male adult bore consumes each year one and a half times his own weight in other people's patience. [*Assorted Prose*, 'Confessions of a Wild Bore']

13 The founding fathers in their wisdom decided that children were an unnatural strain on parents. So they provided jails called schools, equipped with tortures called education. School is where you go between when your parents can't take you and industry can't take you. [*The Centaur*, Ch. 4]

14 Americans have been conditioned to respect newness, whatever it costs them. [*A Month of Sundays*, Ch. 18]

RALPH R. UPTON Late 19 Cent.

15 Stop; look; listen. [Notice devised in 1912 for American railway crossings]

W. UPTON 18 Cent.

16 The lass so neat, with smile so sweet, / Has

Peter Ustinov

won my right good will, / I'd crowns resign to call thee mine, / Sweet lass of Richmond Hill. [*The Lass of Richmond Hill*]

PETER USTINOV 1921–

1 Sometimes I wish I could fall in love. Then at least you know who your opponent is! [*Romanoff and Juliet*, II]

2 I do not believe that friends are necessarily the people you like best, they are merely the people who got there first. [*Dear Me*, Ch. 5]

3 I sometimes wished he [his father] would realize that he was poor instead of being that most nerve-racking of phenomena, a rich man without money. [6]

V

AMANDA VAIL 1921–1966

1 Sometimes I think if there was a third sex men wouldn't get so much as a glance from me. [*Love Me Little*, Ch. 6]

VALERIUS MAXIMUS *fl. c.* AD 15

2 I appeal from Philip drunk to Philip sober. [*Facta et Dicta Memorabilia*, VI. ii]

PAUL VALÉRY 1871–1945

3 A man is more complex, infinitely more so than his thoughts. [*Analects*, 'Odds and Ends']

4 Cognition reigns but does not rule. [*Bad Thoughts and Not So Bad*, D]

5 The painter should not paint what he sees, but what will be seen. [S]

6 God made everything out of nothing. But the nothingness shows through. [T]

7 Man is only man at the surface. Remove his skin, dissect, and immediately you come to machinery. [Quoted in W. H. Auden, *A Certain World*]

8 A poem is never finished, only abandoned.

SIR JOHN VANBRUGH 1664–1726

9 The want of a thing is perplexing enough, but the possession of it is intolerable. [*The Confederacy*, I. ii]

10 As if a woman of education bought things because she wanted 'em. [II. i]

11 Much of a muchness. [*The Provoked Husband*, I. i]

12 BELINDA: Ay, but you know we must return good for evil.

LADY BRUTE: That may be a mistake in the translation. [*The Provoked Wife*, I. i]

13 No man worth having is true to his wife, or can be true to his wife, or ever was, or ever will be so. [*The Relapse*, I. ii]

VIVIEN VAN DAMM ?1889–1960.

14 We Never Closed. [Slogan of London's Windmill Threatre during the 1939–45 War, when he was its manager. [*Tonight and Every Night*, Ch. 18]

W. H. VANDERBILT 1821–1885

15 The public be damned! [Reply to a question whether the public should be consulted about luxury trains. [Quoted in A. W. Cole, Letter *The New York Times*, 25 Aug. 1918]

BARTOLOMEO VANZETTI 1888–1927

16 If it had not been for these things, I might have lived out my life talking at street corners to scorning men. I might have died, unmarked, unknown, a failure. Now we [Sacco and himself] are not a failure. This is our career and our triumph. Never in our full life could we hope to do such work for tolerance, for justice, for man's understanding of man as now we do by accident. Our words – our lives – our pains – nothing! The taking of our lives – lives of a good shoemaker and a poor fish-pedlar – all! That last moment belongs to us – that agony is our triumph. [On receiving the death sentence. Letter to his son, 9 Apr. 1927]

C. J. VAUGHAN 1816–1897

17 Must you go? Can't you stay? [Method of

breaking up awkward schoolboy breakfast parties, often quoted as: 'Can't you go? Must you stay?' Quoted in G. W. E. Russell, *Collections and Recollections*, Ch. 24]

HENRY VAUGHAN 1622–1695

1 I cannot reach it; and my striving eye / Dazzles at it, as at eternity. [*Childhood*]

2 Man is the shuttle, to whose winding quest / And passage through these looms / God ordered motion, but ordained no rest. [*Man*]

3 Men might look and live as glow-worms shine, / And face the moon: / Wise Nicodemus saw such light / As made him know his God by night. [*The Night*]

4 Dear night! this world's defeat; / The stop to busy fools; care's check and curb.

5 There is in God (some say) / A deep but dazzling darkness; as men here / Say it is late and dusky, because they / See not all clear; / O for that night! where I in him / Might live invisible and dim.

6 My soul, there is a country / Far beyond the stars, / Where stands a wingèd sentry / All skilful in the wars: / There, above noise and danger, / Sweet peace sits crowned with smiles, / And one born in a manger / Commands the beauteous files. [*Peace*]

7 For none can thee secure, / But one, who never changes, / Thy God, thy life, thy cure.

8 But life is, what none can express, / A quickness, which my God hath kissed. [*Quickness*]

9 Happy those early days! when I / Shined in my angel-infancy. / Before I understood this place / Appointed for my second race, / Or taught my soul to fancy aught / But a white celestial thought. [*The Retreat*]

10 And in those weaker glories spy / Some shadows of eternity.

11 But felt through all this fleshly dress / Bright shoots of everlastingness.

12 O how I long to travel back, / And tread again that ancient track! / That I might once more reach that plain, / Where first I left my glorious train; / From whence th' enlightened spirit sees / That shady city of palm-trees.

13 Some men a forward motion love, / But I by backward steps would move, / And when this dust falls to the urn, / In that state I came, return.

14 Search well another world; who studies this, / Travels in clouds, seeks manna, where none is. [*The Search*, last lines]

15 They are all gone into the world of light! / And I alone sit lingering here; / Their very memory is fair and bright, / And my sad thoughts doth clear. [*They Are All Gone*]

16 I see them walking in an air of glory, / Whose light doth trample on my days; / My days which are at best but dull and hoary, / Mere glimmering and decays.

17 Dear, beauteous death! the jewel of the just, / Shining no where, but in the dark.

18 Remove me hence unto that hill, / Where I shall need no glass.

19 I saw Eternity the other night / Like a great ring of pure and endless light, / All calm, as it was bright, / And round beneath it, Time in hours, days, years, / Driv'n by the spheres / Like a vast shadow moved; in which the world / And all her train were hurled. [*The World*]

20 This ring the Bride-groom did for none provide / But for his bride.

MARQUIS DE VAUVENARGUES 1715–1747

21 Great thoughts come from the heart. [*Réflexions et maximes*, 127]

22 In order to carry out great enterprises, one must live as if one will never have to die. [142]

THOMAS, LORD VAUX 1510–1556

23 For Age, with stealing steps, / Hath clawed me with his clutch. [*The Aged Lover Renounceth Love*]

THORSTEIN VEBLEN 1857–1929

24 Conspicuous consumption of valuable goods is a means of reputability to the gentleman of leisure. [*The Theory of the Leisure Class*, Ch. 4]

VEGETIUS 4th Cent. AD

25 *Qui desiderat pacem, praeparet bellum.* – Let him who desires peace prepare for war. [*De re mil.*, 3, Prologue]

PIERRE VERGNIAUD 1753–1793

26 There was reason to fear that, like Saturn, the Revolution might devour each of its chil-

dren in turn. [Lamartine, *Histoire des Girondins*, Bk xxxviii. Ch. 20]

PAUL VERLAINE 1844–1896

1 *De la musique avant toute chose, / Et pour cela préfère l'Impair, / Plus vague et plus soluble dans l'air, / Sans rien en lui qui pèse ou qui pose.* – Music before all else, and for that choose the irregular, which is vaguer and melts better into the air, having nothing in it that is heavy or emphatic. [*L'Art poétique*, 1]

2 *Prends l'éloquence et tords-lui son cou!* – Take eloquence and wring its neck. [21]

3 *Et tout le reste est littérature* – And everything else is just literature [36]

4 *Les sanglots longs / Des violons / De l'automne / Blessent mon cœur / D'une langueur / Monotone.* – The long sobs of the autumn violins infect my heart with a monotonous languor. [*Chanson d'automne*]

5 *Son regard est pareil au regard des statues, / Et pour sa voix, lointaine, et calme, et grave, elle a / L'inflexion des voix chères qui se sont tues.* – Her gaze is like the gaze of statues, and her voice, far-away, calm and grave, speaks with the accent of those who were dear and are now silent. [*Mon Rêve familier*]

6 *Il pleure dans mon cœur / Comme il pleut sur la ville.* – Tears fall in my heart like the rain on the town. [*Romances sans paroles*, 3]

'VICKY' 1913–1966

7 Introducing Super-Mac. [Caption to cartoon of Harold Macmillan as Superman, *Evening Standard*, 6 Nov. 1958]

QUEEN VICTORIA 1819–1901

8 I will be good. [Resolution on seeing she might become Queen, 11 Mar. 1830. Quoted in Elizabeth Longford, *Victoria R. I.*, Ch. 2]

9 He [Gladstone] speaks to Me as if I was a public meeting. [G. W. E. Russell, *Collections and Recollections*, Ch. 14]

10 We are not interested in the possibilities of defeat. [To A. J. Balfour, Dec. 1899]

11 We are not amused. [*Notebooks of a Spinster Lady*, 2 Jan. 1900]

GORE VIDAL 1925–

12 American writers want to be not good but great; and so are neither. [*Two Sisters*]

13 Whenever a friend succeeds, a little something in me dies. [Quoted in the *Sunday Times Magazine*, 16 Sept. 1973]

ALFRED DE VIGNY 1797–1863

14 *Le vrai Dieu, le Dieu fort, est le Dieu des idées.* – The true God, the mighty God, is the God of ideas. [*La Bouteille à la mer*]

15 *La femme, enfant malade et douze fois impur.* – Woman, a sick child and twelve times unclean. [*La Colère de Samson*]

16 *J'aime le son du cor, le soir, au fond des bois.* – I love the sound of the horn, at evening, from the depths of the woods. [*Le Cor*]

17 *J'aime la majesté des souffrances humaines.* – I love the majesty of human sufferings. [*La Maison du berger*]

18 *Hélas! je suis, Seigneur, puissant et solitaire, / Laissez-moi m'endormir du sommeil de la terre!* – Alas, Lord, I am powerful but alone. Let me sleep the sleep of the earth. [*Moïse*]

19 *Seul le silence est grand; tout le reste est faiblesse.* – Only silence is great; all else is weakness. [*La Mort du loup*]

20 *Fais énergiquement ta longue et lourde tâche! Dans la voie où le sort a voulu t'appeler, / Puis, après, comme moi, souffre et meurs sans parler.* – Perform your long and heavy task with energy, treading the path to which Fate has been pleased to call you. Then, afterwards, like me, suffer and die without a word.

21 An army is a nation within a nation; it is one of the vices of our age. [*Servitude et grandeur militaire*, 1. Ch. 2]

GEORGE VILLIERS *see* BUCKINGHAM, SECOND DUKE OF

PHILIPPE-AUGUSTE VILLIERS DE L'ISLE ADAM 1838–1889

22 *Vivre? les serviteurs feront cela pour nous.* – Live? Our servants will do that for us. [*Axel*, IV. ii]

FRANÇOIS VILLON 1431–1465?

23 *Mais où sont les neiges d'antan?* – Where are last year's snows? [*Ballade des dames du temps jadis*]

ST VINCENT OF LERINS 5 Cent.

1 *Quod semper, quod ubique, quod ab omnibus creditum est.* – What has been believed always, everywhere, and by everyone. [*Commonitorium*, ii]

VIRGIL 70–19 BC

2 *Arma virumque cano, Troiae qui primus ab oris / Italiam fato profugus Lavinaque venit / Litora.* – I sing of arms and of the hero who first came from the shores of Troy, exiled by Fate, to Italy and its Lavinian shore. [*Aeneid*, I, 1]

3 *Tantae molis erat Romanam condere gentem.* – Such a struggle was it to found the Roman race. [33]

4 *Furor arma ministrat.* – Anger supplies the arms. [150]

5 *O passi graviora, dabit deus his quoque finem.* – You have endured worse things, God will grant an end even to these. [199]

6 *Forsan et haec olim meminisse iuvabit.* – Perhaps one day this too will be pleasant to remember. [203]

7 *Durate, et vosmet rebus servate secundis.* – Endure, and preserve yourselves for better things. [207]

8 *Sunt lacrimae rerum et mentem mortalia tangunt.* – Human deeds have their tears, and mortality touches the heart. [462]

9 *Mens sibi conscia recti.* – A mind conscious of the right. [604]

10 *Conticuere omnes intentique ora tenebant.* – All were silent and kept their gaze fixed upon him. [II. 1]

11 *Quaeque ipse miserrima vidi / Et quorum pars magna fui.* – I have myself seen these sad events, and played no small part in them. [5]

12 *Timeo Danaos et dona ferentes.* – I fear the Greeks, even though they offer gifts. [49]

13 *In utrumque paratus, / Seu versare dolos seu certae occumbere morti.* – Prepared for either event, to set his traps or to meet with certain death. [61]

14 *Horrosco referens.* – I shudder at the word. [204]

15 *Tacitae per amica silentia lunae.* – Through the friendly silence of the quiet moon. [255]

16 *Quantum mutatus ab illo / Hectore qui redit exuvias indutus Achilli.* – How changed from that Hector who returned, clad in the spoils of Achilles. [274]

17 *Fuimus Troes, fuit Ilium et ingens / Gloria Teucrorum.* – We are Trojans no more, Ilium is destroyed, and the great glory of the Trojans has passed. [325]

18 *Una salus victis nullam sperare salutem.* – There is but one safe thing for the vanquished: not to hope for safety. [354]

19 *Dis aliter visum.* – The gods thought otherwise. [428]

20 *Quid non mortalia pectora cogis, / Auri sacra fames!* – To what cannot you compel the hearts of men, O cursed lust for gold! [III. 56]

21 *Agnosco veteris vestigia flammae.* – I feel again a spark of that ancient flame. [IV. 23]

22 *O luce magis dilecta sorore.* – O you, dearer than the light to your sister. [31]

23 *Nec me meminisse pigebit Elissae / Dum memor ipse mei, dum spiritus hos regit artus.* – Nor will the thought of Dido be bitter to me so long as I have memory and breath controls these limbs. [335]

24 *Varium et mutabile semper / Femina.* – Woman is always fickle and changing. [569]

25 *Hos successus alit: possunt, quia posse videntur.* – Success nourished them; they seemed to be able, and so they were able. [V. 231]

26 *Facilis descensus Averni: / Noctes atque dies patet atri ianua Ditis; / Sed revocare gradum superasque evadere ad auras, / Hoc opus, hic labor est.* – The way down to hell is easy. The gates of black Dis stand open night and day. But to retrace one's steps and escape to the upper air – that is toil, that is labour. [VI. 126]

27 *Procul, o procul este, profani.* – Hence, away, uninitiated ones. [258]

28 *Tendebantque manus ripae ulterioris amore.* – Their hands outstretched in yearning for the other shore. [314]

29 *Spiritus intus alit, totamque infusa per artus / Mens agitat molem et magno se corpore miscet.* – The spirit within nourishes, and the mind, diffused through all the members, sways the mass and mingles with the whole frame. [(Of the Universe) 726]

30 *Tu regere imperio populos, Romane, memento / (Hae tibi erunt artes), pacisque imponere morem, / Parcere subiectis et debellare superbos.* – O Romans, be it your care to rule the nations

with imperial sway; these shall be your arts: to impose the rule of peace, to spare the humbled and to crush the proud. [851]

1 *Sunt geminae Somni portae, quarum altera fertur / Cornea, qua veris facilis datur exitus umbris, / Altera candenti perfecta nitens elephanto, / Sed falsa ad caelum mittunt insomnia manes.* – There are two gates of Sleep, whereof one is said to be of horn, through which the spirits of truth find an easy passage, the other made of gleaming white ivory, through which the gods send up false dreams to the upper world. [893]

2 *Geniumque loci . . . precatur.* – Prayed to the Genius of the place. [VII. 136]

3 *Flectere si nequeo superos, Acheronta movebo.* – If I cannot bend the gods, I will let hell loose. [312]

4 *Pedibus timor addidit alas.* – Fear lent wings to his feet. [VIII. 224]

5 *Nox ruit et fuscis tellurem amplectitur alis.* – Night came down and wrapped the earth in its dusky wings. [369]

6 *Me, me adsum qui feci, in me convertite ferrum.* – Here am I who did the deed. Turn your sword on me. [IX. 427]

7 *Sic itur ad astra.* – Thus shall you go to the stars. [641]

8 *Experto credite.* – Trust one who has proved it. [XI. 283]

9 *Formosam resonare doces Amaryllida silvas.* – You teach the woods to echo back the charms of Amaryllis. [*Eclogue* I. 5]

10 *Deus nobis haec otia fecit.* – A god gave us this leisure. [6]

11 *Non equidem invideo, miror magis.* – Indeed I am not envious, rather I am amazed. [11]

12 *Et penitus toto divisos orbe Britannos.* – And the Britons completely isolated from the whole world. [66]

13 *Quem fugis, a, demens? Habitarunt di quoque silvas.* – Whom do you flee, madman? Even gods have lived in the woods. [II. 60]

14 *Latet anguis in herba.* – A snake lurks in the grass. [III. 93]

15 *Magnus ab integro saeclorum nascitur ordo. / Iam redit et virgo, redeunt Saturnia regna / Iam nova progenies caelo demittitur alto.* – The great march of the centuries begins anew. Now the maiden returns, now Saturn is king again, and a new race descends from on high. [IV. 5]

16 *Incipe, parve puer: qui non risere parenti, / Nec deus hunc mensa, dea nec dignata cubili est.* – Begin then, little boy: no one who has not given his mother a smile has ever been thought worthy of his table by a god, or by a goddess of her bed. [62]

17 *Arcades ambo, / Et cantare pares et respondere parati.* – Arcadians both, and each as ready as the other to lead off with a song, or to give an apt response. [VII. 4]

18 *Nunc scio quid sit Amor.* – At last I know what Love is really like. [VIII. 43]

19 *Non omnia possumus omnes.* – We are not all capable of everything. [63]

20 *Sunt et mihi carmina, me quoque dicunt / Vatem pastores; sed non ego credulus illis. / Nam neque adhuc Vario videor nec dicere Cinna / Digna, sed argutos inter strepere anser olores.* – I too have written songs. I too have heard the shepherds call me bard. But I am incredulous of them: I have the feeling that I cannot yet compare with Varius or Cinna, but cackle like a goose among melodious swans. [IX. 33]

21 *Omnia vincit Amor: et nos cedamus Amori.* – Love carries all before him: we too must yield to Love. [X. 69. See also 107:13]

22 *Ultima Thule.* – Farthest Thule. [*Georgics*, I. 30]

23 *Labor omnia vicit / Improbus et duris urgens in rebus egestas.* – Persistent work triumphed, and the stress of need in a hard life. [145]

24 *Imponere Pelio Ossam / Scilicet, atque Ossae frondosum involvere Olympum.* – Indeed, to pile Ossa on Pelion, and to roll leafy Olympus upon Ossa. [281]

25 *O fortunatos nimium, sua si bona norint, / Agricolas! Quibus ipsa procul discordibus armis / Fundit humo facilem victum iustissima tellus.* – How blest beyond all blessings are farmers, if they but knew their happiness! Far from the clash of arms, the most just earth brings forth from the soil an easy living for them. [II. 458]

26 *Felix qui potuit rerum cognoscere causas.* – Happy is he who has been able to learn the causes of things. [490]

27 *Fortunatus et ille deos qui novit agrestis.* – Happy is he who knows the country gods. [493]

28 *Sed fugit interea, fugit inreparabile tempus.* – Meanwhile time is flying – flying never to return. [III. 284]

1 *Agmine facto / Ignavum fucos pecus a praesepibus arcent.* – They form a line, and drive out the idle bands of drones from the hives. [IV. 167]

2 *Si parva licet componere magnis.* – If one may measure small things by great. [176]

3 *At genus immortale manet, multosque per annos / Stat fortuna domus, et avi numerantur avorum.* – But the race remains immortal, the star of their house is constant through many years, and the grandfather's grandfathers are numbered in the roll. [208]

FRANÇOIS-MARIE AROUET, called VOLTAIRE 1694–1778

4 *Si Dieu n'existait pas, il faudrait l'inventer.* – If God did not exist, it would be necessary to invent Him. [*À l'Auteur du livre des Trois Imposteurs*]

5 *Sachez que le secret des arts / Est de corriger la nature.* – Know that the secret of the arts is to correct nature. [*À M. de Verrière*]

6 *Tous les genres sont bons, hors le genre ennuyeux.* – All styles are good except the tiresome sort. [*L'Enfant prodigue*, Preface to edn. of 1738]

7 *Le superflu, chose très nécessaire.* – The superfluous, a very necessary thing. [*Le Mondain*, 22]

8 *Dans ce meilleur des mondes possibles.* – In this best of all possible worlds. [*Candide*, Ch. 1 and *passim*]

9 *Ceux qui ont avancé que tout est bien ont dit une sottise: il fallait dire que tout est au mieux.* – Those who maintain that all is right talk nonsense; they ought to say that all is for the best. [Ch. 1]

10 *Cunégonde . . . vit entre les broussailles le docteur Pangloss qui donnait une leçon de physique expérimentale à la femme de chambre de sa mère, petite brune très jolie et très docile.* – Cunégonde . . . saw Dr Pangloss behind some bushes giving a lesson in experimental philosophy to her mother's waiting-woman, a pretty little brunette who seemed eminently teachable.

11 *Dans ce pays-ci il est bon de tuer de temps en temps un amiral pour encourager les autres.* – In this country we find it pays to shoot an admiral from time to time to encourage the others. [23]

12 *Le travail éloigne de nous trois grands maux: l'ennui, le vice et le besoin.* – Work banishes those three great evils, boredom, vice, and poverty. [30]

13 *Cela est bien dit, répondit Candide, mais il faut cultiver notre jardin.* – That's true enough, said Candide, but we must go and work in the garden.

14 *Ils ne se servent de la pensée que pour autoriser leurs injustices et n'emploient lés paroles que pour déguiser leurs pensées.* – [Men] use thought only to justify their wrong-doings, and words only to conceal their thoughts. [*Dialogue du Chapon et de la Poularde*]

15 *Le mieux est l'ennemi du bien.* – The best is the enemy of the good. [*Dictionnaire philosophique*, 'Art dramatique']

16 *Ce corps qui s'appellait et qui s'appelle encore le saint empire romain n'était en aucune manière ni saint, ni romain, ni empire.* – This agglomeration which was called and still calls itself the Holy Roman Empire was neither holy, nor Roman, nor an empire in any way. [*Essai sur le mœurs et l'esprit des nations*, lxx]

17 *L'histoire n'est que le tableau des crimes et des malheurs.* – History is just the portrayal of crimes and misfortunes. [*L'Ingénu*, Ch. 10]

18 *Toutes les histoires anciennes, comme le disait un de nos beaux esprits, ne sont que des fables convenues.* – All our ancient history, as one of our wits remarked, is no more than accepted fiction. [*Jeannot et Colin*]

19 *On doit des égards aux vivants: on ne doit aux morts que la vérité.* – One owes respect to the living: but to the dead one owes nothing but the truth. [*Lettres sur Œdipe*, i, note]

20 *Si Dieu nous a fait à son image, nous le lui avons bien rendu.* – If God made us in His image, we have certainly returned the compliment. [*Le Sottisier*, xxxii]

21 *N'ayant jamais pu réussir dans le monde, il se vengeait par en médire.* – Never having been able to succeed in the world, he took his revenge by speaking ill of it. [*Zadig*, Ch. 4]

22 *On presse l'orange, et on jette l'écorce.* – They squeeze the orange and throw away the skin. [Letter to Mme Denis, about his quarrel with Frederick the Great, 2 Sept. 1751]

23 *Quoi que vous fassiez, écrasez l'infâme, et aimez qui vous aime.* – Whatever you do crush that infamous thing [superstition], and love those who love you. [Letter to M. d'Alembert, 28 Nov. 1762]

24 *Quand la populace se mêle de raisonner, tout*

est perdu. – Once the people begin to reason, all is lost. [Letter to Damilaville, 1 Apr. 1766]

1 *On dit que Dieu est toujours pour les gros bataillons.* – It is said that God is always on the side of the big battalions. [Letter to M. le Riche, 6 Feb. 1770. See also 86:25, 433:8)]

2 I disapprove of what you say, but I will defend to the death your right to say it. [Attr. to Voltaire in S. G. Tallentyre, *The Friends of Voltaire* (1906) Ch. 7]

DIANA VREELAND 1903?–1989

3 Pink is the navy blue of India. [Attr. Quoted in *Rolling Stone*, 11 Aug. 1977]

RICHARD WAGNER 1813–1883

1 *Frisch weht der Wind* / *Der Heimat zu:–* / *Mein irisch Kind,* / *Wo weilest du?* – The wind blows freshly towards the homeland: where do you linger, my Irish child? [*Tristan and Isolde,* I. i]

2 Now you have seen what we can do. Now want it! and if you do, we will achieve an art. [Speech after performance of *Die Götterdämmerung*]

ARTHUR WALEY 1889–1965

3 It is not difficult to censor foreign news, / What is hard today is to censor one's own thoughts, – / To sit by and see the blind man / On the sightless horse, riding into the bottomless abyss. [*Censorship*]

JAMES WALKER 1881–1946

4 Will you love me in December / As you did in May? [Song: *Will You Love Me In December?*]

JAMES J. WALKER 19 Cent.

5 A reformer is a guy who rides through a sewer in a glass-bottomed boat. [Speech as Mayor of New York, 1928. See also 283:7]

W. S. WALKER 1795–1846

6 Too solemn for day, too sweet for night, / Come not in darkness, come not in light; / But come in some twilight interim, / When the gloom is soft, and the light is dim. [*Too Solemn for Day*]

MAX WALL 1908–1990

7 Wall is the name – Max Wall. My father was the Great Wall of China. He was a brick. [Opening patter to variety act]

HENRY WALLACE 1888–1965

8 The century on which we are entering can be and must be the century of the common man. [Address, 8 May 1942]

W. R. WALLACE 1819–1881

9 The hand that rocks the cradle / Is the hand that rules the world. [*John o'London's Treasure Trove*]

GRAHAM WALLAS 1858–1932

10 The little girl had the makings of a poet in her who, being told to be sure of her meaning before she spoke, said: 'How can I know what I think till I see what I say?' [*The Art of Thought,* Ch. 4]

EDMUND WALLER 1606–1687

11 Poets that lasting marble seek / Must carve in Latin or in Greek. [*Of English Verse*]

12 The seas are quiet, when the winds give o'er: / So calm are we, when passions are no more. [*Of the Last Verses in the Book*]

13 The soul's dark cottage, battered and decayed, / Lets in new light thro' chinks that time has made. / Stronger by weakness, wiser men become / As they draw near to their eternal home: / Leaving the old, both worlds at once they view, / That stand upon the threshold of the new.

1 That which her slender waist confined / Shall now my joyful temples bind; / No monarch but would give his crown / His arms might do what this has done. [*On a Girdle*]

2 A narrow compass, and yet there / Dwells all that's good, and all that's fair: / Give me but what this ribbon tied, / Take all the sun goes round beside.

3 Go, lovely rose, / Tell her that wastes her time and me, / That now she knows, / When I resemble her to thee, / How sweet and fair she seems to be. [*Song*]

4 How small a part of time they share, / That are so wondrous sweet and fair.

5 Why came I so untimely forth / Into a world which, wanting thee, / Could entertain us with no worth / Or shadow of felicity? [*To a very young Lady*]

HORACE WALPOLE, FOURTH EARL OF ORFORD 1717–1797

6 Our supreme governors, the mob. [Letter to Horace Mann, 7 Sept. 1743]

7 Every drop of ink in my pen ran cold. [Letter to George Montagu, 3 July 1752]

8 It is charming to totter into vogue. [Letter to G. A. Selwyn, 2 Dec. 1765]

9 The next Augustan age will dawn on the other side of the Atlantic ... At last some curious traveller from Lima will visit England, and give a description of the ruins of St Paul's, like the editions of Balbec and Palmyra. [Letter to Horace Mann, 24 Nov. 1774]

10 The world is a comedy to those that think, a tragedy to those that feel. [Letter to the Countess of Upper Ossory, 16 Aug. 1776]

SIR ROBERT WALPOLE 1676–1745

11 Madam, there are fifty thousand men slain this year in Europe, and not one Englishman. [Remark to Queen Caroline, 1734]

12 They now *ring* the bells, but they will soon *wring* their hands. [Remark on the declaration of war with Spain, 1739]

13 The balance of power. [Speech in House of Commons, 13 Feb. 1741]

14 Sir Robert Walpole's definition of the gratitude of place-expectants, 'That it is a lively sense of *future* favours'. [W. Hazlitt, *Lectures on the English Comic Writers*, 'Wit and Humour']

15 Anything but history, for history must be false. [Remark to his son, who offered to read to him. *Walpoliana*, Vol. i. p. 60]

16 All those men have their price. [(Reference to pretended patriots) 88]

WILLIAM WALSH 1663–1708

17 In love alone we hate to find / Companions of our woe. [Song: *Of all the Torments*]

18 I can endure my own despair, / But not another's hope.

IZAAK WALTON 1593–1683

19 As no man is born an artist, so no man is born an angler. [*The Compleat Angler*, 'Epistle to the Reader']

20 I am, Sir, a Brother of the Angle. [Pt I. Ch. 1]

21 I remember that a wise friend of mine did usually say, 'that which is everybody's business is nobody's business'. [2]

22 An excellent angler, and now with God. [4]

23 I love such mirth as does not make friends ashamed to look upon one another next morning. [5]

24 No man can lose what he never had.

25 Use him [your frog] as though you loved him. [8]

26 This dish of meat is too good for any but anglers, or very honest men.

27 I love any discourse of rivers, and fish and fishing. [18]

28 Look to your health; and if you have it, praise God, and value it next to a good conscience; for health is the second blessing that we mortals are capable of; a blessing that money cannot buy. [21]

29 The great Secretary of Nature and all learning, Sir Francis Bacon. [*Life of Herbert*]

30 Of this blest man, let his just praise be given, / Heaven was in him before he was in heaven. [Written in Dr Richard Sibbes, *Returning Backslider*]

JOHN WANAMAKER 20 Cent.

31 Half the money I spend on advertising is wasted, and the trouble is I don't know which half. [Paraphrasing the first Lord Leverhulme.

Quoted in David Ogilvy, *Confessions of an Advertising Man*, Ch. 3]

BISHOP WILLIAM WARBURTON
1698–1779

1 Orthodoxy is my doxy; heterodoxy is another man's doxy. [Remark to Lord Sandwich]

ARTEMUS WARD [CHARLES FARRAR BROWN] 1834–1867

2 I now bid you a welcome adoo. [*Artemus Ward His Book*, 'The Shakers']

3 I wish thar was winders to my Sole, sed I, so that you could see some of my feelins. ['The Showman's Courtship']

4 If you mean gettin hitched, I'M IN!

5 My pollertics, like my religion, being of an exceedin accommodatin character. ['The Crisis']

6 Shall we sell our birthrite for a mess of potash?

7 N.B. This is rote Sarcasticul. ['A Visit to Brigham Young']

8 I girdid up my Lions & fled the Seen.

9 Did you ever hav the measels, and if so how many? ['The Census']

10 'Fair youth, do you know what I'd do with you if you was my sun?' 'No,' sez he. 'Wall,' sez I, 'I'd appint your funeral tomorrow arternoon & the *korps should be ready*! You're too smart to live on this yearth.' ['Edwin Forrest as Othello']

11 Before he retired to his virtuous couch.

12 The female woman is one of the greatest institooshuns of which this land can boste. ['Woman's Rights']

13 Do me eyes deceive me earsight? Is it some dreams? ['Moses, the Sassy']

14 I'm not a politician and my other habits are good. ['Fourth of July Oration']

15 The ground flew up and hit me in the hed. ['Thrilling Scenes in Dixie']

16 I presunted myself at Betty's bedside late at nite, with considerbul licker koncealed about my persun. ['Betsy-Jain Reorgunised']

17 Why these weeps? [*Artemus Ward's Lecture*]

18 I prefer temperance hotels – although they sell worse liquor than any other kind of hotels.

19 He [Brigham Young] is dreadfully married.

He's the most married man I ever saw in my life.

20 Why is this thus? What is the reason of this thusness?

21 Let us be happy and live within our means, even if we have to borrer the money to do it with. [*Science and Natural History*]

THOMAS WARD 1577–1639

22 Where to elect there is but one, / 'Tis Hobson's choice, – take that or none. [*England's Reformation*, Ch. 4. p. 326]

E. F. WARE 1841–1911

23 O Dewey was the morning / Upon the first of May, / And Dewey was the Admiral / Down in Manila Bay; / And Dewey were the Regent's eyes, / Them orbs of royal blue! / And Dewey feel discouraged? / I Dew not think we Dew. [*Manila*]

GEORGE WARE 19 Cent.

24 The boy I love is up in the gallery. / The boy I love is looking now at me. [Song: *The Boy in the Gallery*, sung my Marie Lloyd]

ANDY WARHOL 1927–1987

25 It's the place where my prediction from the sixties finally came true: 'In the future everyone will be famous for fifteen minutes.' [*Andy Warhol's Exposures*, 'Studio 54']

SUSAN WARNER 1819–1885

26 Jesus loves me – this I know, / For the Bible tells me so. [*The Love of Jesus*]

SAMUEL WARREN 1807–1877

27 There is probably no man living, though ever so great a fool, that cannot do *something* or other well. [*Ten Thousand a Year*, xxviii]

H. S. WASHBURN 1813–1903

28 We shall meet, but we shall miss him, / There will be one vacant chair. [*The Vacant Chair*]

GEORGE WASHINGTON 1732–1799

29 Father, I cannot tell a lie. I did it with my little hatchet. [Attr.]

1 We must consult Brother Jonathan. [Jonathan Trumble, Governor of Connecticut. Frequent remark during American Revolution]

2 It is our true policy to steer clear of permanent alliance with any portion of the foreign world. [Farewell address, 17 Sept. 1796]

ROWLAND WATKYNS 17 Cent.

3 I love him not, but show no reason can / Wherefore, but this, I *do not love* the man. [*Flamma sine Fumo*, 'Antipathy']

SIR WILLIAM WATSON 1858–1936

4 April, April, / Laugh thy girlish laughter; / Then, the moment after, / Weep thy girlish tears! [*April*]

5 The staid, conservative, / Came-over-with-the-Conqueror type of mind. [*A Study in Contrasts*, I. i. 42]

ISAAC WATTS 1674–1748

6 When'er I take my walks abroad, / How many poor I see! / What shall I render to my God / For all his gifts to me? [*Divine Songs for Children*, 4, 'Praise for Mercies']

7 While others early learn to swear, / And curse and lie and steal.

8 Lord, I ascribe it to Thy grace, / And not to chance, as others do, / That I was born of Christian race, / And not a Heathen or a Jew. [6, 'Praise for the Gospel']

9 There is a dreadful Hell, / And everlasting pains; / There sinners must with devils dwell / In darkness, fire, and chains. [11, 'Heaven and Hell']

10 Let dogs delight to bark and bite, / For God has made them so, / Let bears and lions growl and fight, / For 'tis their nature to.

But, children, you should never let / Such angry passions rise; / Your little hands were never made / To tear each other's eyes. [16, 'Against Quarrelling and Fighting']

11 Birds in their little nests agree; / And 'tis a shameful sight, / When children of one family / Fall out, and chide, and fight. [17, 'Love between Brothers and Sisters']

12 How doth the little busy bee / Improve each shining hour, / And gather honey all the day / From every opening flower!

How skilfully she builds her cell! / How neat she spreads the wax; / And labours hard to store it well / With the sweet food she makes. [20, 'Against Idleness and Mischief']

13 For Satan finds some mischief still / For idle hands to do.

14 The tulip and the butterfly / Appear in gayer coats that I: / Let me be dressed fine as I will, / Flies, worms, and flowers exceed me still. [22, 'Against Pride in Clothes']

15 Hush! my dear, lie still and slumber, / Holy angels guard thy bed! [35, 'Cradle Hymn']

16 Hark! from the tombs a doleful sound. [Hymn]

17 There is a land of pure delight / Where saints immortal reign; / Infinite day excludes the night, / And pleasures banish pain. [Hymn]

18 Could we but climb where Moses stood, / And view the landskip o'er, / Nor Jordan's stream, nor death's cold flood, / Should fright us from the shore.

19 When I can read my title clear / To mansions in the skies, / I bid farewell to every fear, And wipe my weeping eyes. [Hymn]

20 When I survey the wondrous Cross, / On which the Prince of Glory died, / My richest gain I count but loss / And pour contempt on all my pride. [Hymn]

21 Were the whole realm of nature mine, / That were a present far too small; / Love so amazing, so divine / Demands my soul, my life, my all.

22 'Tis the voice of the sluggard: I heard him complain, / 'You have waked me too soon, I must slumber again.' [*Moral Songs*, 1, 'The Sluggard']

23 Our God, our help in ages past, / Our hope for years to come, / Our shelter from the stormy blast, / And our eternal home.

Under the shadow of Thy Throne / Thy saints have dwelt secure; / Sufficient is Thine Arm alone, / And our defence is sure.

Before the hills in order stood, / Or earth received her frame, / From everlasting Thou art God, / To endless years the same.

A thousand ages in Thy sight / Are like an evening gone; / Short as the watch that ends the night / Before the rising sun.

Time like an ever-rolling stream / Bears all its sons away; / They fly forgotten as a dream /

Dies at the opening day. [*Psalms*, xc. First line altered by John Wesley to 'O God . . .']

EVELYN WAUGH 1903–1966

1 I expect you'll be becoming a schoolmaster, sir. That's what most of the gentlemen does, sir, that gets sent down for indecent behaviour. [*Decline and Fall*, Prelude]

2 We class schools, you see, into four grades: Leading School, First-rate School, Good School, and School. [I. 1]

3 That's the public-school system all over. They may kick you out, but they never let you down. [3]

4 I'm one of the blind alleys off the main road of procreation. [12]

5 Anyone who has been to an English public school will always feel comparatively at home in prison. [III. 4]

6 What did your Loved One pass on from? [*The Loved One*]

7 You never find an Englishman among the underdogs – except in England of course.

8 Enclosing every thin man, there's a fat man demanding elbow-room. [*Officers and Gentlemen*, Interlude. (See also 121:19, 300:17, 453:10)]

9 'The Beast stands for strong mutually antagonistic governments everywhere,' he said. 'Self-sufficiency at home, self-assertion abroad.' [*Scoop*, Bk i. Ch. 1. 3]

10 Up to a point, Lord Copper.

11 Feather-footed through the plashy fen passes the questing vole. [Ch. 2.1]

12 Personally I can't see that foreign stories are ever news – not *real* news. [5.1]

13 Creative Endeavour lost her wings, Mrs Ape. [*Vile Bodies*, Ch. 1]

14 Particularly against books the Home Secretary is. If we can't stamp out literature in the country, we can at least stop it being brought in from outside. [21]

15 I feel my full income when that young man is mentioned. [6]

16 All this fuss about sleeping together. For physical pleasure I'd sooner go to my dentist any day.

F. E. WEATHERLY 1848–1929

17 Where are the boys of the Old Brigade? [*The Old Brigade*]

18 Roses are flowering in Picardy, / But there's never a rose like you. [*Roses of Picardy*]

BEATRICE WEBB 1858–1943

19 If I ever felt inclined to be timid as I was going into a room full of people, I would say to myself, 'You're the cleverest member of one of the cleverest families in the cleverest class of the cleverest nation in the world, why should you be frightened?' [Quoted in Bertrand Russell, *Portraits from Memory*, VIII]

SIDNEY WEBB, LORD PASSFIELD 1859–1947

20 The inevitability of gradualness. [Presidential address to the Labour Party Conference, 1920]

MAX WEBER 1864–1920

21 The Protestant Ethic and the Spirit of Capitalism. [Title of book]

DANIEL WEBSTER 1782–1852

22 There is always room at the top. [When advised not to become a lawyer, since the profession was overcrowded]

23 The past, at least, is secure. [Second speech on Foot's Resolution, 25 Jan. 1830]

24 Fearful concatenation of circumstances. [*Argument on the Murder of Captain White*, 6 Apr.]

25 He touched the dead corpse of the Public Credit, and it sprang upon its feet. [Speech in praise of Alexander Hamilton, made in New York, 10 Mar. 1831]

JOHN WEBSTER 1580?–1625?

26 Glories like glow-worms, afar off shine bright, / But looked to near, have neither heat nor light. [*The Duchess of Malfi*, IV. ii. 148]

27 I know death hath ten thousand several doors / For men to take their exits. [222]

28 Cover her face; mine eyes dazzle: she died young. [267]

29 We are merely the stars' tennis-balls, struck and bandied / Which way please them. [V. iv. 52]

30 When I look into the fish-ponds in my

garden, / Methinks I see a thing armed with a rake, / That seems to strike at me. [v. 5]

1 Is not old wine wholesomest, old pippins toothsomest, old wood burn brightest, old linen wash whitest? Old soldiers, sweethearts, are surest, and old lovers are soundest. [*Westward Hoe*, II. ii]

2 'Tis just like a summer bird-cage in a garden; the birds that are without despair to get in, and the birds that are within despair and are in a consumption for fear they shall never get out. [*The White Devil*, I. ii. 47]

3 Call for the robin redbreast and the wren, / Since o'er shady groves they hover, / And with leaves and flowers do cover / The friendless bodies of unburied men. [V. iv. 100]

4 But keep the wolf far thence, that's foe to men, / For with his nails he'll dig them up again. [108]

5 My soul, like to a ship in a black storm, / Is driven, I know not whither. [vi. 248]

6 I have caught / An everlasting cold; I have lost my voice / Most irrecoverably. [270]

JOSIAH WEDGWOOD 1730–1795

7 Am I not a man and a brother? [Inscription on a medal, afterwards the motto of the Anti-Slavery Society]

SIMONE WEIL 1909–1943

8 All sins are attempts to fill voids. [*Gravity and Grace*, p. 27]

MAX WEINREICH 20 Cent.

9 A language is a dialect that has an army and a navy. [Quoted in Leo Rosten, *The Joys of Yiddish*, Preface]

ORSON WELLES 1915–1985
[*see also under* H. J. MANKIEWICZ]

10 In Italy for thirty years under the Borgias they had warfare, terror, murder, bloodshed – they produced Michelangelo, Leonardo da Vinci and the Renaissance. In Switzerland they had brotherly love, five hundred years of democracy and peace, and what did they produce . . .? The cuckoo clock. [Harry Lime's parting speech in film *The Third Man*. Script by Graham Greene, but Welles contributed this himself]

11 I started at the top and worked my way down. [Quoted in Leslie Halliwell, *The Filmgoer's Book of Quotes*]

ARTHUR WELLESLEY, DUKE OF WELLINGTON 1769–1852

12 Ours [our army] is composed of the scum of the earth. [4 Nov. 1831]

13 I don't know what effect these men will have upon the enemy, but, by God, they terrify me [On a draft sent out to him in Spain, 1809]

14 Up Guards and at them again! [Attr. words at Waterloo. He himself said that his words probably were 'Stand up, Guards!' and that he then gave the order to attack]

15 Nothing except a battle lost can be half so melancholy as a battle won. [Dispatch from the field of Waterloo]

16 A battle of giants. [Referring in conversation with Samuel Rogers to the Battle of Waterloo]

17 The battle of Waterloo was won on the playing fields of Eton. [Attr. by Montalembert, *De l'avenir politique de l'Angleterre*]

18 I don't care a twopenny damn what becomes of the ashes of Napoleon Bonaparte. [Attr.]

19 I used to say of him [Napoleon] that his presence on the field made the difference of forty thousand men. [Stanhope, *Notes on Conversations with the Duke of Wellington*, 2 Nov. 1831]

20 All the business of war, and indeed all the business of life, is to endeavour to find out what you don't know from what you do; that's what I called 'guessing what was at the other side of the hill'. [*Croker Papers*, Vol. iii]

21 I never saw so many shocking bad hats in my life. [On seeing the first Reformed Parliament]

22 Don't quote Latin; say what you have to say, and then sit down. [Advice to a new MP]

23 Publish and be damned. [Of Harriette Wilson's *Autobiography*. Attr.]

24 Sparrowhawks, Ma'am. [Alleged answer to Queen Victoria's question as to how the sparrows could be got out of the trees that were to be enclosed in Paxton's glass pavilion for the 1851 Exhibition]

1 Possible? Is anything impossible? Read the newspapers. [Quoted in *Words of Wellington*]

2 There is no mistake; there has been no mistake; and there shall be no mistake. [*Wellingtoniana*, 1852]

3 Educate men without religion and you make them but clever devils. [Attr.]

H. G. WELLS 1866–1946

4 Roöötten Beëëastly Silly Hole! [*The History of Mr Polly*, Ch. 1. 2]

5 And then came the glorious revelation of that great Frenchman whom Mr Polly called Raboo-loose.

6 'Sesquippledan,' he would say. 'Sesquippledan verboojuice. [5]

7 'Smart Juniors,' said Polly to himself, 'full of Smart Juniosity. The Shoveacious Cult.' [3.1]

8 I'll make a gory mess of you. I'll cut bits orf you. [9.6]

9 'I'm a Norfan, both sides,' he would explain, with the air of one who had seen trouble. [*Kipps*, Bk i. Ch. 6. 1]

10 'It's giving girls names like that [Euphemia],' said Buggins, 'that nine times out of ten makes 'em go wrong. It unsettles 'em. If ever I was to have a girl, if ever I was to have a dozen girls, I'd call 'em all Jane.' [6. 2]

11 You can't have money like that and not swell out. [ii. 4. 2]

12 I was thinking jest what a Rum Go everything is. [iii. 3.8]

13 The Social Contract is nothing more nor less than a vast conspiracy of human beings to lie to and humbug themselves and one another for the general Good. Lies are the mortar that binds the savage individual man into the social masonry. [*Love and Mr Lewisham*, Ch. 23]

14 Human history becomes more and more a race between education and catastrophe. [*The Outline of History*, Ch. 15]

15 The War to End War. [Title of book published in 1914]

16 The Shape of Things to Come. [Title of book (1933)]

17 It seems to me that I am more to the left than you, Mr Stalin. [In an interview with Stalin, *New Statesman*, 27 Oct. 1934]

ARNOLD WESKER 1932–

18 You breed babies and you eat chips with everything. [*Chips with Everything*, I. ii]

CHARLES WESLEY 1707–1788

19 Gentle Jesus, meek and mild, / Look upon a little child, / Pity my simplicity, / Suffer me to come to thee. [Hymn]

20 Hark now all the welkin rings, / 'Glory to the King of Kings, / Peace on earth, and mercy mild, / God and sinners reconciled.' [Christmas hymn. First two lines altered by George Whitefield to: 'Hark! the herald-angels sing / Glory to the new-born king']

21 Jesu, lover of my soul, / Let me to thy bosom fly, / While the nearer waters roll, / While the tempest still is high; / Hide me, O my Saviour, hide, / Till the storm of life is past: / Safe into the haven guide, / O receive my soul at last. [Hymn]

22 Other refuge have I none, / Hangs my helpless soul on Thee.

23 Cover my defenceless head / With the shadow of thy wing.

24 Lo! He comes with clouds descending, / Once for favoured sinners slain. [Hymn]

JOHN WESLEY 1703–1791

25 I look upon all the world as my parish. [*Journal*, 11 June 1739]

26 If justice and truth take place, if he is rewarded according to his desert, his name will stink to all generations. [(Of Lord Chesterfield) *Diary*, 11 Oct. 1775]

27 Though I am always in haste, I am never in a hurry. [Letter to a member of the Society, 10 Dec. 1777]

28 Let it be observed, that slovenliness is no part of religion; that neither this nor any text of Scripture, condemns neatness of apparel. Certainly this is a duty, not a sin. 'Cleanliness is, indeed, next to godliness.'* [*Sermon* XCIII, 'On Dress'. *This phrase is probably Hebrew in origin]

REV. SAMUEL WESLEY 1662–1735

29 Style is the dress of thought; a modest dress, / Neat, but not gaudy, will true critics please. [*An Epistle to a Friend concerning Poetry*]

MAE WEST 1892?–1980

1 Keep cool and collect. [In film, *Belle of the Nineteen*]

2 She's the kind of girl who climbed the ladder of success, wrong by wrong. [In film *I'm no Angel*]

3 When I'm good I'm very good; when I'm bad I'm better.

4 Beulah, peel me a grape.

5 Between two evils, I always pick the one I never tried before. [In film *Klondike Annie*]

6 Goodness, what beautiful diamonds! M.W. Goodness had nothing to do with it, dearie! [In film *Night After Night*, script by Vincent Lawrence]

7 Why don't you come up some time, see me? [In film *She Done Him Wrong*, script by Harvey Thew and John Bright. (Usually misquoted as 'Come up and see me sometime')]

8 I'm tired, send one of them home. [On being told that ten men were waiting to meet her at home. Quoted in J. Weintraub, *Peel Me a Grape*]

9 I used to be Snow White . . . but I drifted.

10 You can say what you like about long dresses, but they cover a multitude of shins.

11 Everything. [When asked what she wanted to be remembered for. Quoted in the *Observer Weekend Review*, 30 Nov. 1969]

12 Is that a pistol in your pocket or are you just glad to see me? [Quoted in the *Guardian*, 13 Nov. 1974. Variant version: 'your sword']

13 She's one of the finest women who ever walked the streets. [Quoted in Leslie Halliwell, *The Filmgoer's Book of Quotes*]

NATHANAEL WEST 1903–1940

14 Are-you-in-trouble? – Do-you-need-advice? – Write-to-Miss-Lonelyhearts-and-she-will-help-you. [*Miss Lonelyhearts*]

15 When they ask for bread don't give them crackers as does the Church, and don't, like the State, tell them to eat cake. Explain that man cannot live by bread alone, and give them stones. ['Miss Lonelyhearts and the dead pan']

DAME REBECCA WEST 1892–1983

16 Our four uncles. [(Wells and Bennett, Shaw

and Galsworthy) Quoted in Stephen Potter, *The Sense of Humour*, Ch. 1]

17 There is of course no reason for the existence of the male sex except that one sometimes needs help moving the piano. [Quoted in review of Victoria Glendinning, *Rebecca West*, in the *Sunday Telegraph*, 28 June 1970]

LORD WESTBURY 1800–1873

18 Then, sir, you will turn it over once more in what you are pleased to call your mind. [T. A. Nash, *Life of Lord Westbury*, Bk ii. Ch. 12]

R. P. WESTON ?–1936

19 Some soldiers send epistles, say they'd sooner sleep in thistles / Than the saucy, soft, short shirts for soldiers, sister Susie sews. [Song: *Sister Susie's Sewing Shirts for Soldiers*. Music by Herman E. Darewski. Sung by Jack Norworth]

R. P. WESTON,
    F. J. BARNES ?–1917
    and MAURICE SCOTT 20 Cent.

20 Hush! Here comes a Whizz-Bang! [Title of song]

R. P. WESTON and BERT LEE 1880–1946

21 Good-bye-ee! good-bye-ee! / Wipe the tear, baby dear, from your eye-ee. / Tho' it's hard to part, I know, / I'll be tickled to death to go. / Don't cry-ee! – don't sigh-ee! – / There's a silver lining in the sky-ee! – / Bonsoir, old thing! cheerio! chin-chin! /Nahpoo! Toodle-oo! Good – bye-ee! [Song: *Good-bye-ee!*]

GENERAL WEYGAND 1867–1965

22 In three weeks England will have her neck wrung like a chicken. [At the fall of France, Apr. 1940. Quoted in Winston S. Churchill, *Their Finest Hour*, Ch. 10; Churchill answered, 'Some chicken, some neck!' (see 113:4)]

EDITH WHARTON 1862–1937

23 Blessed are the pure in heart for they have so much more to talk about. [*John O'London's Weekly*, 10 Apr. 1932]

24 An unalterable and unquestioned law of

the musical world required that the German text of French operas sung by Swedish artists should be translated into Italian for the clearer understanding of English speaking audiences. [*The Age of Innocence*, Bk i. Ch. 1]

1 She was like a disembodied spirit who took up a great deal of room. [*The House of Mirth*, Bk i. Ch. 2]

2 No *divorcées* were included, except those who had shown signs of penitence by being remarried to the very wealthy. [5]

3 Miss Farish, who was accustomed, in the way of happiness, to such scant light as shone through the cracks of other people's lives. [14]

ARCHBISHOP WHATELY OF DUBLIN 1787–1863

4 Happiness is no laughing matter. [*Apothegms*]

J. A. McNEILL WHISTLER 1834–1903

5 I am not arguing with you – I am telling you. [*The Gentle Art of Making Enemies*]

6 'I only know of two painters in the world,' said a newly introduced feminine enthusiast to Whistler, 'yourself and Velazquez.' 'Why,' answered Whistler in dulcet tones, 'why drag in Velazquez?' [D. C. Seitz, *Whistler Stories*]

7 Yes, madam, Nature is creeping up. [Answer to a lady who said that a certain landscape reminded her of his pictures]

8 No, I ask it for the knowledge of a lifetime. [Answer to counsel in his case against Ruskin, who had asked, 'For two days' labour you ask two hundred guineas?']

9 I'm lonesome. They are all dying. I have hardly a warm personal enemy left.

10 OSCAR WILDE: I wish I had said that. WHISTLER: You will, Oscar, you will. [L. C. Ingleby, *Oscar Wilde*]

E. B. WHITE 1899–1985

11 Commuter – one who spends his life / In riding to and from his wife; / A man who shaves and takes a train, / And then rides back to shave again. [*The Commuter*]

12 To perceive Christmas through its wrapping becomes more difficult with every year. [*The Second Tree from the Corner*, 'Time Present']

13 All poets who, when reading from their own works, experience a choked feeling, are major. For that matter, all poets who read from their own works are major, whether they choke or not. [*How to Tell a Major Poet from a Minor Poet*]

14 It is easier for a man to be loyal to his club than to his planet; the by-laws are shorter, and he is personally acquainted with the other members. [*One Man's Meat*]

15 MOTHER: It's broccoli, dear.
CHILD: I say it's spinach, and I say the hell with it. [Caption to cartoon by Carl Rose in the *New Yorker*, 28 Dec. 1928]

HENRY KIRKE WHITE 1785–1806

16 Much in sorrow, oft in woe, / Onward, Christians, onward go. [Hymn. Altered by Dr W. B. Collyer to 'Oft in danger, oft in woe']

JOSEPH BLANCO WHITE 1775–1841

17 Mysterious Night! when our first parent knew / Thee from report divine, and heard thy name, / Did he not tremble for this lovely frame, / This glorious canopy of light and blue? [*To Night*]

PATRICK WHITE 1912–1990

18 'I dunno,' Arthur said. 'I forget what I was taught. I only remember what I've learnt.' [*The Solid Mandala*, Ch. 2]

19 Conversation is imperative if gaps are to be filled, and old age, it is the last gap but one.

T. H. WHITE 1906–1964

20 Seventeen years ago, come Michaelmas, and been after the Questing Beast ever since. Boring, very. [*The Sword in the Stone*, Ch. 2]

21 But I unfortunately was born at the wrong end of time, and I have to live *backwards* from in front. [3]

WILLIAM ALLEN WHITE 1868–1944

22 All dressed up, with nowhere to go. [On the Progressive Party in 1916, after Theodore Roosevelt retired from the Presidential campaign]

W. L. WHITE 1900–

23 They Were Expendable. [Title of book (1942)]

GEORGE WHITEFIELD 1714–1770

1 I had rather wear out than rust out. [Attr. by Robert Southey]

A. N. WHITEHEAD 1861–1947

2 It is more important that a proposition be interesting than that it be true. [*Adventures of Ideas*, Ch. 16]

3 The deliberate aim at Peace very easily passes into its bastard substitute, Anaesthesia. [20]

4 Civilization advances by extending the number of important operations which we can perform without thinking about them. [*An Introduction to Mathematics*, Ch. 5]

5 An instant of time, without duration, is an imaginative logical construction. Also each duration of time mirrors in itself all temporal durations. [*Science and the Modern World*, Ch. 4]

6 A science which hesitates to forget its founders is lost. [Attr.]

7 The history of Western philosophy is, after all, no more than a series of footnotes to Plato's philosophy. [Attr.]

WILLIAM WHITEHEAD 1715–1785

8 Yes, I'm in love, I feel it now, / And Caelia has undone me; / And yet I'll swear I can't tell how / The pleasing plague stole on me. [*The Je ne sçay quoi*, song]

9 Say, can you listen to the artless woes / Of an old tale, which every schoolboy knows. [*The Roman Father*, Prologue]

KATHARINE WHITEHORN 1926–

10 In answer to: Inside every thin woman there's a fat woman trying to get out. I always think it's: Outside every thin woman there's a fat man trying to get in. [BBC Radio 4 programme *Quote, Unquote*, quoted in *Picking on Men Again*, compiled by Judy Allen and Dyan Sheldon. See also 121:19, 300:17, 448:8]

WILLIAM [later VISCOUNT] WHITELAW 1918–

11 I have always said it is a great mistake to prejudge the past. [At his first press conference after being appointed Ulster Secretary]

12 They [Labour Ministers] are going about the country stirring up complacency. [(The last word frequently misquoted as 'apathy') During 1974 election, quoted by Simon Hoggart, *On the House*, p.38]

WILLIAM WHITING 1825–1878

13 O hear us when we cry to Thee / For those in peril on the sea. [Hymn: *Eternal Father, Strong to Save*]

WALT WHITMAN 1819–1892

14 I hear it was charged against me that I sought to destroy institutions, / But really I am neither for nor against institutions. [*I Hear It was Charged against Me*]

15 If any thing is sacred the human body is sacred. [*I Sing the Body Electric*, 125]

16 O Captain! my Captain! our fearful trip is done, / The ship has weathered every rack, the prize we sought is won, / The port is near, the bells I hear, the people all exulting. [*O Captain! my Captain!*]

17 But O heart! heart! heart! / O the bleeding drops of red, / Where on the deck my Captain lies, / Fallen cold and dead.

18 Out of the cradle endlessly rocking, / Out of the mocking-bird's throat, the musical shuttle. [*Out of the Cradle endlessly Rocking*]

19 Have you your pistols? have you your sharp-edged axes? / Pioneers! O pioneers! [*Pioneers! O Pioneers!*]

20 Camerado, this is no book, / Who touches this touches a man. [*So Long!*, 53]

21 A great city is that which has the greatest men and women. [*Song of the Broad-Axe*, 108]

22 Where the populace rise at once against the never-ending audacity of elected persons. [121]

23 I celebrate myself, and sing myself. [*Song of Myself*, 1. 1]

24 I loafe and invite my soul. [4]

25 Always the procreant urge of the world. [3. 45]

26 I believe a leaf of grass is no less than the journey-work of the stars. [31. 663]

27 I think I could turn and live with animals, they're so placid and self-contained, / I stand and look at them long and long. / They do not sweat and whine about their condition, / They

do not lie awake in the dark and weep for their sins, / They do not make me sick discussing their duty to God, / Not one is dissatisfied, not one is demented with the mania of owning things, / Not one kneels to another, nor to his kind that lived thousands of years ago, / Not one is respectable or unhappy over the whole earth. [32. 684]

1 Behold, I do not give lectures or a little charity, / When I give I give myself. [40. 994]

2 Do I contradict myself? / Very well then I contradict myself, / (I am large, I contain multitudes). [51. 1324]

3 I sound my barbaric yawp over the roofs of the world. [52, 1333]

4 Afoot and light-hearted I take to the open road, / Healthy, free, the world before me. [*Song of the Open Road*, 1. 1]

5 When lilacs last in the dooryard bloomed, / And the great star early drooped in the western sky in the night, / I mourned, and yet shall mourn with ever-returning spring. [*When Lilacs last in the Dooryard Bloomed*, 1. 1]

JOHN GREENLEAF WHITTIER 1807–1892

6 'Shoot, if you must, this old gray head, / But spare your country's flag,' she said. [*Barbara Frietchie*, 35]

7 For all sad words of tongue or pen, / The saddest are these: 'It might have been!' [*Maud Muller*,105]

8 The Indian Summer of the heart. [*Memories*, 9]

9 Dinna ye hear it?– Dinna ye hear it? / The pipes o' Havelock sound. [*The Pipes at Lucknow*, 4]

ROBERT WHITTINGTON *c.* 1480–*c.* 1530

10 A man of marvellous mirth and pastimes; and sometime of as sad a gravity; a man for all seasons. [(Of Sir Thomas More) *Vulgaria: Exercise in School Latin*]

REV. CORNELIUS WHUR 1782–1853

11 But lasting joys the man attend / Who has a polished female friend! [*The Accomplished Female Friend*]

G. J. WHYTE-MELVILLE 1821–1878

12 Then drink, puppy, drink, and let every puppy drink. [*Drink, Puppy, Drink*]

13 The swallows are making them ready to fly, / Wheeling out on a windy sky: / Goodbye, Summer, goodbye, goodbye. [*Goodbye, Summer*]

14 Wrap me up in my tarpaulin jacket, / And say a poor buffer lies low, / And six stalwart lancers shall carry me / With steps solemn, mournful, and slow. [*The Tarpaulin Jacket*]

NORBERT WIENER 1894–1964

15 We have decided to call the entire field of control and communication theory, whether in the machine or in the animal, by the name of Cybernetics, which we form from the Greek [for] steersman. [*Cybernetics*]

BISHOP SAMUEL WILBERFORCE 1805–1873

16 If I were a cassowary / On the plains of Timbuctoo, / I would eat a missionary, / Cassock, bands, and hymn-book too. [Impromptu verse]

ELLA WHEELER WILCOX 1855–1919

17 No question is ever settled / Until it is settled right. [*Settle the Question Right*]

18 Laugh and the world laughs with you; / Weep, and you weep alone; / For the sad old earth must borrow its mirth, / But has trouble enough of its own. [*Solitude*]

19 So many gods, so many creeds, / So many paths that wind and wind, / While just the art of being kind / Is all the sad world needs. [*The World's Need*]

OSCAR WILDE 1854–1900

20 I never saw a man who looked / With such a wistful eye / Upon that little tent of blue / Which prisoners call the sky. [*The Ballad of Reading Gaol*, Pt I. 3]

21 Yet each man kills the thing he loves, / By each let this be heard, / Some do it with a bitter look, / Some with a flattering word. / The coward does it with a kiss, / The brave man with a sword! [7]

22 I know not whether Laws be right, / Or whether Laws be wrong; / All that we know who lie in gaol / Is that the wall is strong; / And that each day is like a year, / A year whose days are long. [V. 1]

1 The vilest deeds like poison-weeds / Bloom well in prison-air; / It is only what is good in Man / That wastes and withers there: / Pale Anguish keeps the heavy gate / And the warder is Despair. [5]

2 Down the long and silent street, / The dawn, with silver-sandalled feet, / Crept like a frightened girl. [*The Harlot's House*]

3 Tread lightly, she is near / Under the snow, / Speak gently, she can hear / The daisies grow. [*Requiescat*]

4 And yet, and yet, / These Christs that die upon the barricades, / God knows it I am with them, in some ways. [*Sonnet to Liberty*]

5 Other people are quite dreadful. The only possible society is oneself. [*An Ideal Husband*, III]

6 Really, if the lower orders don't set us a good example, what on earth is the use of them? [*The Importance of Being Earnest*, I]

7 Truth is rarely pure, and never simple.

8 I have invented an invaluable permanent invalid called Bunbury, in order that I may be able to go down into the country whenever I choose.

9 The amount of women in London who flirt with their own husbands is perfectly scandalous. It looks so bad. It is simply washing one's clean linen in public.

10 In married life three is company and two is none.

11 LANE: There were no cucumbers in the market this morning, sir. I went down twice.
ALGERNON: No cucumbers!
LANE: No, Sir. Not even for ready money.

12 Rise sir, from this semi-recumbent posture.

13 To lose one parent, Mr Worthing, may be regarded as a misfortune; to lose both looks like carelessness. [Abbreviated in some edns.]

14 All women become like their mothers. That is their tragedy. No man does. That's his.

15 The old-fashioned respect for the young is fast dying out.

16 The good ended happily, and the bad unhappily. That is what Fiction means. [II]

17 Charity, dear Miss Prism, charity! None of us are perfect. I myself am peculiarly susceptible to draughts.

18 I never travel without my diary. One should always have something sensational to read in the train.

19 On an occasion of this kind it becomes more than a moral duty to speak one's mind. It becomes a pleasure.

20 CECILY: When I see a spade I call it a spade.
GWENDOLEN: I am glad to say I have never seen a spade. It is obvious that our social spheres have been widely different.

21 In matters of grave importance, style, not sincerity, is the vital thing. [III]

22 Three addresses always inspire confidence, even in tradesmen.

23 Never speak disrespectfully of Society, Algernon. Only people who can't get into it do that.

24 No woman should ever be quite accurate about her age. It looks so calculating.

25 Prism! Where is that baby?

26 This suspense is terrible. I hope it will last.

27 It is a terrible thing for a man to find out suddenly that all his life he has been speaking nothing but the truth.

28 I can resist everything except temptation. [*Lady Windermere's Fan*, 1]

29 I am the only person in the world I should like to know thoroughly. [II]

30 We are all in the gutter, but some of us are looking at the stars.

31 In this world there are only two tragedies. One is not getting what one wants, and the other is getting it. [III. See also 388:22]

32 What is a cynic? A man who knows the price of everything and the value of nothing.

33 Experience is the name every one gives to their mistakes.

34 The English country gentleman galloping after a fox – the unspeakable in full pursuit of the uneatable. [*A Woman of No Importance*, I]

35 One should never trust a woman who tells one her real age. A woman who would tell one that would tell one anything.

36 LORD ILLINGWORTH: The Book of Life begins with a man and a woman in a garden.
MRS ALLONBY: It ends with Revelations.

37 Children begin by loving their parents. After a time they judge them. Rarely, if ever, do they forgive them. [II]

38 GERALD: I suppose society is wonderfully delightful!
LORD ILLINGWORTH: To be in it is merely a bore. But to be out of it simply a tragedy. [III]

1 You should study the Peerage, Gerald . . . It is the best thing in fiction the English have ever done.

2 There is no such thing as a moral or an immoral book. Books are well written, or badly written. [*The Portrait of Dorian Gray*, Preface]

3 All art is quite useless.

4 There is only one thing in the world worse than being talked about, and that is not being talked about. [Ch. II]

5 A man cannot be too careful in the choice of his enemies.

6 It is only shallow people who do not judge by appearances. [2]

7 When good Americans die they go to Paris. [3]

8 I can sympathize with everything, except suffering.

9 Women represent the triumph of matter over mind, just as men represent the triumph of mind over morals. [4]

10 Meredith is a prose Browning, and so is Browning. [*The Critic as Artist*, Pt I, 'Intentions']

11 A little sincerity is a dangerous thing, and a great deal of it is absolutely fatal. [II]

12 Ah! don't say you agree with me. When people agree with me I always feel that I must be wrong.

13 As long as war is regarded as wicked, it will always have its fascination. When it is looked upon as vulgar, it will cease to be popular.

14 There is no sin except stupidity.

15 Art never expresses anything but itself. [*The Decay of Lying*]

16 Please do not shoot the pianist. He is doing his best. [*Impressions of America*, 'Leadville']

17 As for the virtuous poor, one can pity them, of course, but one cannot possibly admire them. [*The Soul of Man under Socialism*]

18 With our James vulgarity begins at home, and should be allowed to stay there. [Letter to the *World*, on the subject of Whistler]

19 The man who can dominate a London dinner-table can dominate the world. [Quoted by R. Aldington in his edn. of Wilde]

20 The gods bestowed on Max the gift of perpetual old age. [Max Beerbohm]

21 I have nothing to declare except my genius. [At the New York Customs House, 1882. Quoted in F. Harris, *Oscar Wilde*]

22 He [Bernard Shaw] hasn't an enemy in the world, and none of his friends like him. [Quoted in Shaw, *Sixteen Self Sketches*, Ch. 17]

23 'Ah, well then,' said Oscar, 'I suppose that I shall have to die beyond my means.' [(When asked a very large sum for an operation) Sherard, *Life of Wilde*]

24 I have put my genius into my life; all I've put into my works is my talent. [In conversation with André Gide, who quotes it in his *Oscar Wilde: In Memoriam*]

25 Work is the curse of the drinking classes. [Quoted in Hesketh Pearson, *Life of Oscar Wilde*, Ch. 12]

BILLY WILDER 1906–

26 I've met a lot of hardboiled eggs in my time, but you're twenty minutes. [Film *Ace in the Hole*, script by Billy Wilder, Lesser Samuels and Walter Newman]

27 HOLDEN: You used to be in pictures, you used to be big.

SWANSON: I *am* big. It's the pictures that got small. [Film *Sunset Boulevard*, script by Billy Wilder, Charles Brackett and D. M. Marshman]

28 Why don't you slip out of those wet clothes and into a dry Martini. [Film *The Major and the Minor*, script by Billy Wilder and Charles Brackett. Line spoken by Robert Benchley, who sometimes is given credit; ascr. also to Alexander Woollcott]

29 Well, nobody's perfect. [In film *Some Like It Hot*, last lines, as Joe E. Brown is told by his bride-to-be Jack Lemmon, that he is not a woman. Screenplay by Wilder and I. A. L. Diamond]

30 You have Van Gogh's ear for music. [Attr. remark to Cliff Osmond]

31 Hindsight is always twenty-twenty. [Quoted in J. R. Colombo, *Colombo's Hollywood*]

THORNTON WILDER 1897–1975

32 My advice to you is not to inquire why or whither, but just enjoy your ice-cream while it's on your plate, – that's my philosophy. [*The Skin of our Teeth*, I]

33 Ninety-nine per cent of the people in the world are fools and the rest of us are in great danger of contagion. [*The Matchmaker*, I]

34 The best part of married life is the fights. The rest is merely so-so. [II]

1 AMBROSE: That old man with one foot in the grave!
MRS LEVI: And the other three in the cash box. [III]

EMPEROR WILHELM I 1797–1888

2 I haven't got time to be tired. [Answer during his last illness]

EMPEROR WILHELM II 1859–1941

3 You will be home before the leaves have fallen from the trees. [To troops leaving for the Front, Aug. 1914. Quoted in B. Tuchman, *The Guns of August*, Ch. 9]

4 A contemptible little army. [Description of British Expeditionary Force. Order at Aix-la-Chapelle HQ, 19 Aug. 1914]

JOHN WILKES 1727–1797

5 The chapter of accidents is the longest chapter in the book. [Attr. by R. Southey, in *The Doctor*, Vol. iv. p. 166]

EMMA WILLARD 1787–1870

6 Rocked in the cradle of the deep. [Song]

WILLIAM III 1650–1702

7 There is one certain means by which I can be sure never to see my country's ruin: I will die in the last ditch. [Quoted in Hume, *History of England*]

8 He [Professor Dodwell] has set his heart on being a martyr, and I have set mine on disappointing hm. [Attr. remark on a Jacobite]

9 Every bullet has its billet. [Quoted by John Wesley, *Journal*, 6 June 1765]

HARRY WILLIAMS 1874–1924
and JACK JUDGE 1878–1938

10 Good-bye Piccadilly, Farewell Leicester Square; / It's a long, long way to Tipperary, but my heart's right there! [*It's a Long Way to Tipperary*]

11 I'm Afraid to Go Home in the Dark. [Title of song]

12 In the Shade of the Old Apple Tree. [Title of song]

TENNESSEE WILLIAMS 1911–1983

13 We're all of us guinea pigs in the laboratory of God. Humanity is just a work in progress. [*Camino Real*, Block 12]

14 Cat on a Hot Tin Roof. [Title of play]

15 I'm not living with you. We occupy the same cage. [I]

16 That Europe's nothin' on earth but a great big auction, that's all it is.

17 A Streetcar Named Desire. [Title of play]

18 I have always depended on the kindness of strangers. [Blanche's final words in II xi]

WILLIAM CARLOS WILLIAMS 1883–1963

19 so much depends / upon / a red wheel / barrow / glazed with rain / water / beside the white / chickens. [*Spring and Fall*, 21, 'The Red Wheelbarrow']

20 This is just to say / I have eaten / the plums / that were in / the icebox / and which / you were probably / saving / for breakfast. / Forgive me / they were delicious / so sweet / and so cold. [*This is just to say*]

N. P. WILLIS 1806–1867

21 At present there is no distinction among the upper ten thousand of the city. [*The Necessity for a Promenade Drive*]

WENDELL WILLKIE 1892–1944

22 The constitution does not provide for first and second class citizens. [*An American Programme*, Ch. 2]

23 There exists in the world today a gigantic reservoir of good will toward us, the American people. [*One World*, Ch. 10]

W. G. WILLS 1828–1891

24 I'll sing thee songs of Araby, / And tales of fair Cashmere. [*Lalla Rookh*]

D. EARDLEY WILMOT 19 Cent.

25 But with love brooding there, why, no place can compare / With my little grey home in the west. [*My Little Grey Home*]

CHARLES E. WILSON 1890–1961

26 For years I thought what was good for the

country was good for General Motors, and vice versa. [To a Congressional Committee, 15 Jan. 1953. Often misquoted as: 'What's good for General Motors is good for the country']

1 A bigger bang for a buck. [Of the H-Bomb tested at Bikini in 1954. Quoted in W. Safire, *Political Dictionary*]

EDMUND WILSON 1895–1972

2 No two people read the same book. [Quoted by John Russell in the *Sunday Times*, 25 July 1971]

HAROLD [later LORD] WILSON 1916–

3 All these financiers, all the little gnomes of Zürich and the other financial centres, about whom we keep on hearing. [Speech in House of Commons, 12 Nov. 1956]

4 This party is a moral crusade, or it is nothing. [At Labour Party Conference, 1 Oct. 1962]

5 The Britain that is going to be forged in the white heat of this revolution will be no place for restrictive practices or out-dated methods on either side of industry. [Speech at Labour Party Conference, 1 Oct. 1963]

6 A week is a long time in politics. [Probably said in 1964 at parliamentary lobby after sterling crisis. Quoted in N. Rees, *Quote . . . Unquote*]

7 It does not mean, of course, that the pound here in Britain in your pocket or purse or in your bank has been devalued. [In prime-ministerial broadcast on TV announcing devaluation, 19 Nov. 1967]

8 I believe the greatest asset a head of state can have is the ability to get a good night's sleep. [In BBC Radio interview, *The World Tonight*, 16 Apr. 1975]

HARRIETTE WILSON 1789–1846

9 I shall not say why and how I became, at the age of fifteen, the mistress of the Earl of Craven. [*Memoirs*, first sentence]

JOHN WILSON *see* NORTH, CHRISTOPHER

JOHN WILSON ?–1889

10 O for a book and a shady nook, / Either in door or out; / With the green leaves whispering overhead, / Or the street cries all about, / Where I may read all at my ease, / Both of the new and old; / For a jolly good book whereon to look, / Is better to me than gold. [Motto to secondhand book catalogue, quoted in Percy Lubbock, *Pleasures of Life*]

SANDY WILSON 1924–

11 But it's nicer, much nicer in Nice. [*The Boy Friend*, II]

T. WOODROW WILSON 1856–1924

12 There is such a thing as a man being too proud to fight. [Address at Philadelphia, 10 May 1915]

13 Armed neutrality. [Message to Congress, 26 Feb. 1917]

14 The world must be made safe for democracy. [Address to Congress, 2 Apr.]

15 It [D. W. Griffith's film *Birth of a Nation*] is like writing history with lightning and my only regret is that it is all so terribly true. [Quoted in D. J. Boorstin, *The Image*, Ch. 4]

ARTHUR WIMPERIS 1874–1953

16 Gilbert the Filbert, / The Colonel of the Knuts. [*Gilbert the Filbert*]

17 On Sunday I walk out with a soldier, / On Monday I'm taken by a tar, / On Tuesday I'm out with a baby Boy Scout, / On Wednesday an Hussar. [Song: *I'll Make a Man of You*]

18 And on Saturday I'm willing, / If you'll only take the shilling, / To make a man of every one of you.

19 I've gotter motter – / Always merry and bright! ['My Motter', from *The Arcadians*, III]

ANNE FINCH, COUNTESS OF WINCHILSEA 1661–1720

20 We faint beneath the aromatic pain. [*The Spleen*]

WILLIAM WINDHAM 1750–1810

21 Those entrusted with arms . . . should be persons of some substance and stake in the country. [Speech in House of Commons, 22 July 1807]

DUCHESS OF WINDSOR 1896–1986

22 One can never be too thin or too rich. [Attr.]

JOHN WINTHROP 1588–1649

1 For we must consider that we shall be as a City upon a hill. The eyes of all people are upon us. So that if we shall deal falsely with our God in this work we have undertaken, and so cause him to withdraw his present help from us, we shall be made a story and a byword throughout the world. [*Discourse written on board the Arbella, 1630, as the Pilgrim Fathers approached America*]

GEORGE WITHER 1588–1667

2 I loved a lass, a fair one, / As fair as e'er was seen; / She was indeed a rare one, / Another Sheba queen. [*A Love Sonnet*]

3 'Twas I that beat the bush, / The bird to others flew, / For she, alas, hath left me, / Falero, lero, loo.

4 Shall I, wasting in despair, / Die because a woman's fair? [*Sonnet*]

5 For, if she be not for me, / What care I how fair she be.

LUDWIG WITTGENSTEIN 1889–1951

6 The world is everything that is the case. [*Tractatus Logico-Philosophicus*, 1. 1]

7 Everything that can be said can be said clearly. [4.116]

8 Whereof one cannot speak, thereof one must be silent. [7]

P. G. WODEHOUSE 1881–1975

9 Chumps always make the best husbands. When you marry, Sally, grab a chump. Tap his forehead first, and if it rings solid, don't hesitate. All the unhappy marriages come from the husbands having brains. What good are brains to a man? They only unsettle him. [*The Adventures of Sally*, Ch. 10]

10 He spoke with a certain what-is-it in his voice, and I could see that, if not actually disgruntled, he was far from being gruntled. [*The Code of the Woosters*, Ch. 1]

11 It is no use telling me that there are bad aunts and good aunts. At the core they are all alike. Sooner or later, out pops the cloven hoof. [2]

12 I turned to Aunt Agatha, whose demeanour was now rather like that of one who, picking daisies on the railway, has just caught the down express in the small of the back. [*The Inimitable Jeeves*, Ch. 4]

13 Jeeves coughed one soft, low, gentle cough like a sheep with a blade of grass stuck in its throat. [13]

14 It was my Uncle George who discovered that alcohol was a food well in advance of modern medical thought. [16]

15 There was another ring at the front door. Jeeves shimmered out and came back with a telegram. [*Jeeves Takes Charge*]

16 In this matter of shimmering into rooms the chappie [Jeeves] is rummy to a degree. [*My Man Jeeves*, 'The Hard-Boiled Egg']

17 She fitted into my biggest armchair as if it had been built round her by someone who knew they were wearing armchairs tight about the hips that season. ['Jeeves and the Unbidden Guest']

18 I was so darned sorry for poor old Corky that I hadn't the heart to touch my breakfast. I told Jeeves to drink it himself. ['Leave it to Jeeves']

19 I can honestly say that I always look on Pauline as one of the nicest girls I was ever engaged to. [*Thank You Jeeves*, Ch. 6]

20 'Alf Todd', said Ukridge, soaring to an impressive burst of imagery, 'has about as much chance as a one-armed blind man in a dark room trying to shove a pound of melted butter into a wild cat's left ear with a red-hot needle.' [*Ukridge*, Ch. 6]

21 The Right Hon. was a tubby little chap who looked as if he had been poured into his clothes and had forgotten to say 'When!'. [*Very Good Jeeves*, 'Jeeves and the Impending Doom']

22 He felt like a man who, chasing rainbows, has had one of them suddenly turn and bite him in the leg. [Quoted in R. Usborne, *Wodehouse at Work to the End*, Ch. 4]

23 He groaned slightly and winced, like Prometheus watching his vulture dropping in for lunch. [10]

JOHN WOLCOT *see* PINDAR, PETER

CHARLES WOLFE 1791–1823

24 Not a drum was heard, not a funeral note,

/ As his corse to the rampart we hurried. [*The Burial of Sir John Moore*, 1]

1 We buried him darkly at dead of night, / The sods with our bayonets turning [2]

2 But he lay like a warrior taking his rest, / With his martial cloak around him.[3]

3 We carved not a line, and we raised not a stone – / But we left him alone with his glory. [8]

HUMBERT WOLFE 1886–1940

4 You cannot hope / To bribe or twist, / Thank God! The British journalist. / But seeing what / That man will do / Unbribed, there's no occasion to. [*The Uncelestial City*, 'Over the Fire']

JAMES WOLFE 1727–1759

5 I would rather have written those lines [Gray's *Elegy*] than take Quebec. [On the night before the storming of Quebec.]

6 Now God be praised, I will die in peace. [Dying words]

THOMAS WOLFE 1900–1938

7 Most of the time we think we're sick, it's all in the mind. [*Look Homeward, Angel*, Pt I. Ch. 1]

8 Making the world safe for hypocrisy. [III. 36]

TOM WOLFE 1931–

9 Radical chic. [Title of essay]

MARY WOLLSTONECRAFT 1759–1797

10 I do not wish them to have power over men; but over themselves. [(Of women) *A Vindication of the Rights of Women*, 4]

11 When a man seduces a woman, it should, I think, be termed a *left-handed* marriage.

CARDINAL WOLSEY 1475?–1530

12 Had I but served God as diligently as I have served the King, he would not have given me over in my gray hairs. [To Sir William Kingston]

13 Father abbot, I am come to lay my weary bones among you. [Said to the Abbot of Leicester Abbey, 26 Nov. 1529]

MRS HENRY WOOD 1814–1887

14 Dead! and . . . never called me mother. [*East Lynne* (dramatized version)]

J. T. WOOD 19 Cent.

15 Wait till the clouds roll by, Jenny, / Wait till the clouds roll by. [Song: *Wait Till the Clouds Roll By*]

LIEUTENANT-COMMANDER 'TOMMY' WOODROOFFE 1899–1978

16 The Fleet's lit up. It is like fairyland; the ships are covered with fairy lights. [BBC Radio commentary at the Coronation Review of the Royal Navy at Spithead, 20 May 1937]

VIRGINIA WOOLF 1882–1941

17 The poet gives us his essence, but prose takes the mould of the body and mind entire. [*The Captain's Death Bed*]

18 Life is not a series of gig lamps symmetrically arranged: life is a luminous halo, a semitransparent envelope surrounding us from the beginning of consciousness to the end. [*The Common Reader*, First Series, 'Modern Fiction']

19 *Middlemarch*, the magnificant book which with all its imperfections is one of the few English novels for grown up people. ['George Eliot']

20 In or about December, *1910*, human *character* changed. ['Mr Bennett and Mrs Brown']

21 Those comfortably padded lunatic asylums which are known euphemistically as the stately homes of England. ['Lady Dorothy Nevill']

22 A good essay must have this permanent quality about it; it must draw its curtain round us, but it must be a curtain that shuts us in not out. ['The Modern Essay']

23 A Room of One's Own. [Title of book]

24 'The guns?' said Betty Flanders, half asleep . . . Again, far away, she heard the dull sound, as if nocturnal women were beating great carpets. [*Jacob's Room*, Ch. 13]

25 Life itself, every moment of it, every drop of it, here, this instant, now, in the sun, in Regent's Park, was enough. Too much, indeed. [*Mrs Dalloway*]

26 So that is marriage, Lily thought, a man and a woman looking at a girl throwing a ball. [*To the Lighthouse*, Ch. 13]

1 I have lost friends, some by death ... others through sheer inability to cross the street. [*The Waves*]

ALEXANDER WOOLLCOTT 1887–1943

2 All the things I really like to do are either illegal, immoral, or fattening. [*The Knock at the Stage Door*]

3 I am in no need of your God-damned sympathy. I ask only to be entertained by some of your grosser reminiscences. [*Letter to a Rex O'Malley*, 1942]

4 A broker is a man who runs your fortune into a shoestring. [Quoted in R. E. Drennan, *Wit's End*]

ELIZABETH WORDSWORTH 1840–1932

5 If all the good people were clever, / And all clever people were good, / The world would be nicer than ever / We thought that it possibly could.

But somehow, 'tis seldom or never / The two hit it off as they should; / The good are so harsh to the clever, / The clever so rude to the good! [*Good and Clever*]

WILLIAM WORDSWORTH 1770–1850

6 Where art thou, worse to me than dead? [*The Affliction of Margaret*]

7 My apprehensions come in crowds; / I dread the rustling of the grass; / The very shadows of the clouds / Have power to shake me as they pass.

8 Three times to the child I said, / 'Why, Edward, tell me why?' [*Anecdote for Fathers*]

9 Action is transitory – a step, a blow. / The motion of a muscle – this way or that – / 'Tis done, and in the after-vacancy / We wonder at ourselves like men betrayed: / Suffering is permanent, obscure and dark, / And shares the nature of infinity. [*The Borderers*, III. 1539]

10 Who is the happy warrior? Who is he / That every man in arms should wish to be? [*Character of the Happy Warrior*]

11 Who doomed to go in company with pain, / And fear, and bloodshed, miserable train! / Turns his necessity to glorious gain.

12 More skilful in self-knowledge, even more pure, / As tempted more; more able to endure, / As more exposed to suffering and distress.

13 From low to high doth dissolution climb. [*Ecclesiastical Sonnets*, III. 34, 'Mutability']

14 Tax not the royal Saint with vain expense. [43,'Inside of King's College Chapel, Cambridge']

15 Give all thou canst; high Heaven rejects the lore / Of nicely-calculated less or more.

16 The light that never was, on sea or land, / The consecration, and the poet's dream. [*Elegiac Stanzas, suggested by a Picture of Peele Castle*]

17 I have submitted to a new control: / A power is gone, which nothing can restore; / A deep distress hath humanised my soul.

18 Farewell, farewell the heart that lives alone, / Housed in a dream, at distance from the kind!

19 Not without hope we suffer and we mourn.

20 Oh! many are the poets that are sown / By Nature; men endowed with highest gifts, / The vision and the faculty divine; / Yet wanting the accomplishment of verse. [*The Excursion*, I. 77]

21 Strongest minds / Are often those of whom the noisy world / Hears least. [91]

22 Rapt into still communion that transcends / The imperfect offices of prayer and praise. [215]

23 The good die first, / And they whose hearts are dry as summer dust / Burn to the socket. [500]

24 Thus was I reconverted to the world; / Society became my glittering bride, / And airy hopes my children. [III. 734]

25 One in whom persuasion and belief / Had ripened into faith, and faith become / A passionate intuition. [IV. 1293]

26 Spires whose 'silent fingers point to heaven'. [VI. 19 (echoing Coleridge's *The Friend*, No. 14)]

27 A man of hope and forward-looking mind / Even to the last! [VII. 276]

28 Nor less I deem that there are powers / Which of themselves our minds impress; / That we can feed this mind of ours / In a wise passiveness. [*Expostulation and Reply*]

29 Think you, 'mid all this mighty sum / Of things forever speaking. / That nothing of itself will come, / But we must still be seeking?

30 The rapt one, of the godlike forehead, / The heaven-eyed creature sleeps in earth: / And Lamb, the frolic and the gentle, / Has vanished from his lonely hearth. [*Extempore Effusion upon the Death of James Hogg*]

William Wordsworth

1 How fast has brother followed brother, / From sunshine to the sunless land!

2 I travelled among unknown men, / In lands beyond the sea: / Nor, England! did I know till then / What love I bore to thee. [*I travelled among unknown Men*]

3 I wandered lonely as a cloud / That floats on high o'er vales and hills, / When all at once I saw a crowd, / A host, of golden daffodils. [*I wandered lonely as a Cloud*]

4 Continuous as the stars that shine / And twinkle on the milky way.

5 Ten thousand saw I at a glance / Tossing their heads in sprightly dance.

6 The waves beside them danced; but they / Out-did the sparkling waves in glee: / A poet could not but be gay, / In such a jocund company.

7 They flash upon that inward eye / Which is the bliss of solitude.

8 Him whom she loves, her Idiot Boy. [*The Idiot Boy*, 41]

9 The gods approve / The depth, and not the tumult, of the soul. [*Laodamia*, 74]

10 He spake of love, such love as spirits feel / In worlds whose course is equable and pure; / No fears to beat away – no strife to heal, – / The past unsighed for, and the future sure. [97]

11 More pellucid streams, / An ampler ether, a diviner air, / And fields invested with purpureal gleams. [104]

12 These waters, rolling from their mountain-springs / With a soft inland murmur. [*Lines composed a few miles above Tintern Abbey*, 3]

13 That best portion of a good man's life, / His little, nameless, unremembered acts / Of kindness and of love. [33]

14 That blessed mood, / In which the burthen of the mystery, / In which the heavy and the weary weight, / Of all this unintelligible world, / Is lightened. [37]

15 We are laid asleep / In body, and become a living soul: / While with an eye made quiet by the power / Of harmony, and the deep power of joy, / We see into the life of things. [45]

16 More like a man / Flying from something that he dreads than one / Who sought the thing he loved. [70]

17 For Nature then . . . / To me was all in all. [72]

18 The sounding cataract / Haunted me like a passion; the tall rock, / The mountain, and the deep and gloomy wood, / Their colours and their forms, were then to me / An appetite. [76]

19 I have learned / To look on nature, not as in the hour / Of thoughtless youth: but hearing oftentimes / The still, sad music of humanity. [88]

20 I have felt / A presence that disturbs me with the joy / Of elevated thoughts; a sense sublime / Of something far more deeply inter-fused, / Whose dwelling is the light of setting suns, / And the round ocean and the living air, / And the blue sky, and in the mind of man. [93]

21 All the mighty world / Of eye, and ear,– both what they half create, / And what perceive. [105]

22 Nature never did betray / The heart that loved her. [122]

23 Nor greetings where no kindness is, nor all / The dreary intercourse of daily life, / Shall e'er prevail against us, or disturb / Our cheerful faith, that all which we behold / Is full of blessings. [130]

24 I heard a thousand blended notes / While in a grove I sate reclined, / In that sweet mood when pleasant thoughts / Bring sad thoughts to the mind. [*Lines written in Early Spring*]

25 If this belief from heaven be sent, / If such be Nature's holy plan, / Have I not reason to lament / What man has made of man?

26 The sweetest thing that ever grew / Beside a human door! [*Lucy Gray*]

27 O'er rough and smooth she trips along, / And never looks behind; / And sings a solitary song / That whistles in the wind.

28 The cottage which was named the Evening Star / Is gone. [*Michael*, 476]

29 Nuns fret not at their convent's narrow room; / And hermits are contented with their cells. [*Miscellaneous Sonnets*, I. 1]

30 'Twas pastime to be bound / Within the sonnet's scanty plot of ground; / Pleased if some souls (for such there needs must be) / Who have felt the weight of too much liberty, / Should find brief solace there, as I have found.

31 A flock of sheep that leisurely pass by, / One after one; the sound of rain and bees /

Murmuring; the fall of rivers, winds and seas, / Smooth fields, white sheets of water, and pure sky; / I have thought of all by turns, and yet do lie / Sleepless! [14, 'To Sleep']

1 The first cuckoo's melancholy cry.

2 Blessed barrier between day and day.

3 Surprised by joy – impatient as the wind / I turned to share the transport. [27]

4 The holy time is quiet as a nun / Breathless with adoration. [30]

5 Where lies the land to which yon ship must go? [31]

6 The world is too much with us; late and soon, / Getting and spending, we lay waste our powers: / Little we see in Nature that is ours; / We have given our hearts away, a sordid boon! / The sea that bares her bosom to the moon; / The winds that will be howling at all hours, / And are up-gathered now like sleeping flowers; / For this, for everything, we are out of tune. [33]

7 Great God! I'd rather be / A pagan suckled in a creed outworn; / So might I, standing on this pleasant lea, / Have glimpses that would make me less forlorn; / Have sight of Proteus rising from the sea; / Or hear old Triton blow his wreathèd horn.

8 Scorn not the Sonnet; Critic, you have frowned, / Mindless of its just honours; with this key / Shakespeare unlocked his heart. [II, 1]

9 When a damp / Fell round the path of Milton, in his hand / The thing became a trumpet; whence he blew / Soul-animating strains – alas, too few!

10 Earth has not anything to show more fair: / Dull would he be of soul who could pass by / A sight so touching in its majesty: / This city now doth, like a garment, wear / The beauty of the morning; silent, bare, / Ships, towers, domes, theatres, and temples lie / Open unto the fields, and to the sky; / All bright and glittering in the smokeless air. [36, 'Upon Westminster Bridge']

11 Ne'er saw I, never felt, a calm so deep! / The river glideth at his own sweet will: / Dear God! the very houses seem asleep; / And all that mighty heart is lying still!

12 Why art thou silent! Is thy love a plant / Of such weak fibre that the treacherous air / Of absence withers what was once so fair? [III. 25]

13 A Poet! – He hath put his heart to school. [27]

14 My heart leaps up when I behold / A rainbow in the sky. [My heart leaps up]

15 The child is father of the man; / And I could wish my days to be / Bound each to each by natural piety.

16 Once did she hold the gorgeous east in fee; / And was the safeguard of the west. [National Independence and Liberty, I. 6, 'On the Extinction of the Venetian Republic']

17 Venice, the eldest child of Liberty.

18 When she took unto herself a mate, / She must espouse the everlasting sea.

19 Men are we, and must grieve when even the shade / Of that which once was great is passed away.

20 Thou hast great allies; / Thy friends are exultations, agonies, / And love, and man's unconquerable mind. [8, 'To Toussaint l'Ouverture']

21 Two voices are there; one is of the sea, / One of the mountains; each a mighty voice: / In both from age to age thou didst rejoice, / They were thy chosen music, Liberty! [12, 'On the Subjugation of Switzerland']

22 Plain living and high thinking are no more. [13, 'Written in London, Sept. 1802']

23 Milton! thou shouldst be living at this hour: / England hath need of thee: she is a fen / Of stagnant waters. [14, 'London, 1802']

24 Thy soul was like a star, and dwelt apart.

25 We must be free or die, who speak the tongue / That Shakespeare spake; the faith and morals hold / Which Milton held. [16]

26 Another year! – another deadly blow! / Another mighty empire overthrown! / And we are left, or shall be left, alone. [27, 'Nov. 1806']

27 With gentle hand / Touch – for there is a spirit in the woods. [Nutting]

28 O Nightingale, thou surely art / A creature of a 'fiery heart'. [O Nightingale]

29 That was the song – the song for me!

30 There was a time when meadow, grove, and stream, / The earth, and every common sight, / To me did seem / Apparelled in celestial light, / The glory and the freshness of a dream. / It is not now as it hath been of yore; – / Turn wheresoe'er I may, / By night or day, / The

William Wordsworth

things which I have seen I now can see no more. [*Ode, Intimations of Immortality*, 1]

1 The rainbow comes and goes, / And lovely is the rose, / The moon doth with delight / Look round her when the heavens are bare. / Waters on a starry night / Are beautiful and fair; / The sunshine is a glorious birth; / But yet I know, where'er I go, / That there hath past away a glory from the earth. [2]

2 While the young lambs bound / As to the tabor's sound. [3]

3 A timely utterance gave that thought relief, / And I again am strong.

4 The winds come to me from the fields of sleep.

5 The babe leaps up on his mother's arm. [4]

6 Whither is fled the visionary gleam? / Where is it now, the glory and the dream?

7 Our birth is but a sleep and a forgetting: / The soul that rises with us, our life's star, / Hath had elsewhere its setting, / And cometh from afar: / Not in entire forgetfulness, / And not in utter nakedness, / But trailing clouds of glory do we come / From God who is our home: / Heaven lies around us in our infancy!/ Shades of the prison-house begin to close. / Upon the growing boy. [5]

8 The youth who daily farther from the east / Must travel, still is Nature's priest, / And by the vision splendid / Is on his way attended: / At length the man perceives it die away, / And fade into the light of common day.

9 Earth fills her lap with pleasures of her own: / Yearnings she hath in her own natural kind. [6]

10 Behold the child among his new-born blisses, / A six-years' darling of a pigmy size! [7]

11 Thou best philosopher, who yet dost keep / Thy heritage, thou eye among the blind. [8]

12 Provoke / The years to bring the inevitable yoke.

13 O joy! that in our embers / Is something that doth live, / That nature yet remembers / What was so fugitive! / The thought of our past years in me doth breed / Perpetual benediction. [9]

14 Those obstinate questionings / Of sense and outward things, / Fallings from us, vanishings; / Blank misgivings of a Creature / Moving about in worlds not realised, / High instincts before which our mortal nature / Did tremble like a guilty thing surprised.

15 Hence in a season of calm weather / Though inland far we be, / Our souls have sight of that immortal sea / Which brought us hither, / Can in a moment travel thither, / And see the children sport upon the shore, / And hear the mighty waters rolling evermore.

16 Though nothing can bring back the hour / Of splendour in the grass, of glory in the flower. [10]

17 In the faith that looks through death, / In years that bring the philosophic mind.

18 And O, ye fountains, meadows, hills and groves, / Forebode not any severing of our loves! / Yet in my heart of hearts I feel your might. [11]

19 The clouds that gather round the setting sun / Do take a sober colouring from an eye / That hath kept watch o'er man's mortality.

20 To me the meanest flower that blows can give / Thoughts that do often lie too deep for tears.

21 Stern Daughter of the Voice of God! / O Duty! if that name thou love / Who art a light to guide, a rod / To check the erring and reprove. [*Ode to Duty*]

22 Me this unchartered freedom tires; / I feel the weight of chance-desires; / My hopes no more must change their name, / I long for a repose that ever is the same.

23 Thou dost preserve the stars from wrong.

24 Give unto me, made lowly wise, / The spirit of self-sacrifice.

25 The dew was falling fast, the stars began to blink; / I heard a voice; it said 'Drink, pretty creature, drink!' [*The Pet-Lamb*]

26 There's something in a flying horse, / There's something in a huge balloon; / But through the clouds I'll never float / Until I have a little boat, / Shaped like the crescent-moon. [*Peter Bell*, Prologue, 1]

27 A primrose by a river's brim / A yellow primrose was to him, / And it was nothing more. [I. 248]

28 Some sipping punch, some sipping tea, / But, as you by their faces see, / All silent and all damned! [518 (later omitted)]

29 After ten months' melancholy, / Became a good and honest man. [III, 1134]

1 One that would peep and botanize / Upon his mother's grave. [*A Poet's Epitaph*]

2 A reasoning, self-sufficing thing, / An intellectual all-in-all.

3 You must love him, ere to you / He will seem worthy of your love.

4 The harvest of a quiet eye, / That broods and sleeps on his own heart.

5 Dust as we are, the immortal spirit grows / Like harmony in music; there is a dark / Inscrutable workmanship that reconciles / Discordant elements. [*The Prelude*, I. 340]

6 Small circles glittering idly in the moon, / Until they melted all into one track / Of sparkling light. [365]

7 A huge peak, black and huge, / As if with voluntary power instinct / Upreared its head. [378]

8 The grim shape / Towered up between me and the stars, and still, / For so it seemed, with purpose of its own / And measured motion like a living thing, / Strode after me. [381]

9 My brain / Worked with a dim and undetermined sense / Of unknown modes of being. [391]

10 Huge and mighty forms, that do not live / Like living men, moved slowly through the mind / By day, and were a trouble to my dreams. [398]

11 The leafless trees and every icy crag / Tinkled like iron. [441]

12 Science appears but what in truth she is, / Not as our glory and our absolute boast, / But as a succedaneum, and a prop / To our infirmity. [II. 212]

13 Where the statue stood / Of Newton with his prism and silent face, / The marble index of a mind for ever / Voyaging through strange seas of thought, alone. [III. 60]

14 I made no vows, but vows / Were then made for me; bond unknown to me / Was given, that I should be, else sinning greatly, / A dedicated spirit. [IV. 334]

15 When from our better selves we have too long / Been parted by the hurrying world, and droop, / Sick of its business, of its pleasures tired, / How gracious, how benign, is solitude. [354]

16 Spirits overwrought / Were making night do penance for a day / Spent in a round of strenuous idleness. [IV. 376]

17 There was a boy: ye knew him well, ye cliffs / And islands of Winander! [V. 364 (cf. *There Was a Boy*)]

18 When the earliest stars began / To move along the edges of the hills. [366 (cf. as above)]

19 A gentle shock of mild surprise / Has carried far into his heart the voice / Of mountain torrents. [382 (cf. as above)]

20 Visionary power / Attends the motions of the viewless winds, / Embodied in the mystery of words. [595]

21 Through the turnings intricate of verse, / Present themselves as objects recognised, / In flashes, and with glory not their own. [603]

22 Whether we be young or old, / Our destiny, our being's heart and home, / Is with infinitude, and only there; / With hope it is, hope that can never die, / Effort, and expectation, and desire, / And something evermore about to be. [VI. 603]

23 The brook and road / Were fellow-travellers in this gloomy strait. [621 (cf. *The Simplon Pass*)]

24 The immeasurable height / Of woods decaying, never to be decayed, / The stationary blasts of waterfalls. [624 (cf. as above)]

25 Characters of the great Apocalypse, / The types and symbols of Eternity, / Of first, and last, and midst, and without end. [638 (cf. as above)]

26 Brothers all / In honour, as in one community, / Scholars and gentlemen. [IX. 227]

27 Bliss was it in that dawn to be alive, / But to be young was very heaven! [XI. 108 (cf. *French Revolution*)]

28 That which sets . . . The budding rose above the rose full blown. [118 (cf. as above)]

29 Not in Utopia, – subterranean fields, – / Or some secreted island, Heaven knows where! / But in the very world, which is the world / Of all of us, – the place where, in the end, / We find our happiness, or not at all! [140 (cf. as above)]

30 There is / One great society alone on earth: / The noble living and the noble dead. [393]

31 The pious bird with the scarlet breast, / Our little English robin. [*The Redbreast chasing the Butterfly*]

32 There was a roaring in the wind all night; / The rain came heavily and fell in floods. [*Resolution and Independence*, 1]

William Wordsworth

1 Fears and fancies thick upon me came. [4]

2 I thought of Chatterton, the marvellous boy, / The sleepless soul that perished in his pride. [7]

3 By our own spirits are we deified: / We poets in our youth begin in gladness; / But thereof come in the end despondency and madness.

4 The oldest man he seemed that ever wore grey hairs. [8]

5 As a huge stone is sometimes seen to lie / Couched on the bald top of an eminence. [9]

6 Like a sea-beast crawled forth, that on a shelf / Of rock or sand reposeth, there to sun itself.

7 Upon the margin of that moorish flood / Motionless as a cloud the old man stood, / That heareth not the loud winds when they call; / And moveth all together, if it move at all. [11]

8 Mighty poets in their misery dead. [17]

9 Still glides the stream, and shall for ever glide; / The form remains, the function never dies. [*The River Duddon*, 34, 'After-Thought']

10 Enough, if something from our hands have power / To live, and act, and serve the future hour; / And if, as toward the silent tomb we go, / Through love, through hope, and faith's transcendent dower, / We feel that we are greater than we know.

11 The good old rule / Sufficeth them, the simple plan, / That they should take, who have the power, / And they should keep who can. [*Rob Roy's Grave*, 37]

12 A youth to whom was given / So much of earth – so much of heaven, / And such impetuous blood. [*Ruth*, 124]

13 She dwelt among the untrodden ways / Beside the springs of Dove, / A maid whom there were none to praise / And very few to love:

A violet by a mossy stone / Half hidden from the eye! / – Fair as a star, when only one / Is shining in the sky.

She lived alone, and few could know / When Lucy ceased to be; / But she is in her grave, and oh, / The difference to me! [*She Dwelt among the untrodden Ways*]

14 She was a phantom of delight / When first she gleamed upon my sight; / A lovely apparition, sent / To be a moment's ornament. [*She Was a Phantom of Delight*]

15 I saw her upon nearer view, / A spirit, yet a woman too! / Her household motions light and free, / And steps of virgin-liberty.

16 And now I see with eye serene / The very pulse of the machine; / A being breathing thoughtful breath, / A traveller between life and death.

17 A perfect woman, nobly planned, / To warn, to comfort, and command.

18 For still, the more he works, the more / Do his weak ankles swell. [*Simon Lee*, 59]

19 A slumber did my spirit seal; / I had no human fears: / She seemed a thing that could not feel / The touch of earthly years.

No motion has she now, no force; / She neither hears nor sees; / Rolled round in earth's diurnal course, / With rocks, and stones, and trees. [*A Slumber did my Spirit Seal*]

20 To be a prodigal's favourite – then, worse truth, / A miser's pensioner – behold our lot! / O man, that from thy fair and shining youth / Age might but take the things youth needed not! [*The Small Celandine*]

21 Behold her, single in the field, / Yon solitary Highland lass! [*The Solitary Reaper*]

22 A voice so thrilling ne'er was heard / In spring-time from the cuckoo-bird, / Breaking the silence of the seas / Among the farthest Hebrides.

23 Will no one tell me what she sings?– / Perhaps the plaintive numbers flow / For old, unhappy, far-off things / And battles long ago.

24 The silence that is in the starry sky, / The sleep that is among the lonely hills. [*Song at the Feast of Brougham Castle*, 163]

25 Degenerate Douglas! oh, the unworthy lord! [*Sonnet, composed at — Castle*]

26 Stepping westward seemed to be / A kind of *heavenly* destiny. [*Stepping Westward*]

27 Strange fits of passion have I known: / And I will dare to tell, / But in the lover's ear alone, / What once to me befell. [*Strange Fits of Passion*]

28 What fond and wayward thoughts will slide / Into a lover's head / 'O mercy!' to myself I cried, / 'If Lucy should be dead!'

29 One impulse from a vernal wood / May teach you more of man, / Of moral evil and of good, / Than all the sages can. [*The Tables Turned*]

1 I've measured it from side to side: / 'Tis three feet long, and two feet wide. [*The Thorn* (early version)]

2 Three years she grew in sun and shower, / Then Nature said, 'A lovelier flower / On earth was never sown; / This child I to myself will take: / She shall be mine, and I will make / A Lady of my own. [*Three Years she Grew*]

3 The stars of midnight shall be dear / To her; and she shall lean her ear / In many a secret place.

4 'Tis said that some have died for love. [*'Tis Said that some have Died*]

5 Sweet childish days, that were as long / As twenty days are now. [*To a Butterfly, I've Watched you now*]

6 Small service is true service, while it lasts. [*To a Child, Written in her Album*]

7 O blithe new-comer! I have heard, / I hear thee and rejoice. / O cuckoo, shall I call thee bird, / Or but a wandering voice? [*To the Cuckoo*]

8 Thrice welcome, darling of the spring! / Even yet thou art to me / No bird, but an invisible thing, / A voice, a mystery.

9 Still longed for, never seen.

10 Thou unassuming common-place / Of Nature. [*To the Daisy, 'With little here to do'*]

11 Oft on the dappled turf at ease / I sit, and play with similes, / Loose types of things through all degrees.

12 Ethereal minstrel! pilgrim of the sky! / Dost thou despise the earth where cares abound? [*To a Skylark, 'Ethereal Minstrel!'*]

13 Type of the wise who soar, but never roam; / True to the kindred points of heaven and home!

14 Up with me! up with me into the clouds! [*To a Skylark, 'Up with me!'*]

15 Pleasures newly found are sweet / When they lie about our feet. [*To the Small Celandine, 'Pleasures newly Found'*]

16 – A simple child, / That lightly draws its breath, / And feels its life in every limb, / What should it know of death? [*We Are Seven*]

17 Still / The little maid would have her will, / And said, 'Nay, we are seven!'

18 Like an army defeated / The snow hath retreated. [*Written in March*]

19 There's not a nook within this solemn pass / But were an apt confessional for one / Taught by his summer spent, his autumn gone, / That life is but a tale of morning grass / Withered at eve. [*Yarrow Revisited*, 6, 'The Trossachs']

20 Let . . . / The swan on still St Mary's Lake / Float double, swan and shadow! [*Yarrow Unvisited*]

21 Like – but oh, how different! [*Yes, it was the mountain Echo*]

22 There neither is, nor can be, any *essential* difference between the language of prose and metrical composition. [*Lyrical Ballads*, Preface]

23 Poetry is the breath and finer spirit of all knowledge; it is the impassioned expression which is in the countenance of all Science.

24 Poetry is the spontaneous overflow of powerful feelings: it takes its origin from emotion recollected in tranquillity.

25 Every great and original writer, in proportion as he is great and original, must himself create the taste by which he is to be relished.

H. C. WORK 1832–1884

26 Father, dear father, come home with me now, / The clock in the steeple strikes one. [*Come Home, Father* (Temperance song)]

27 My grandfather's clock was too large for the shelf. / So it stood ninety years on the floor. [*Grandfather's Clock*]

28 But it stopped short – never to go again – / When the old man died.

29 It mus' be now de kingdom coming, / An' de year ob Jubilo! [*Kingdom Coming*]

30 'Hurrah! hurrah! we bring the Jubilee! / Hurrah! hurrah! the flag that makes you free!' / So we sang the chorus from Atlanta to the sea / As we were marching through Georgia. [*Marching Through Georgia*]

31 There's a good time coming, it's almost here, /'Twas a long, long time on the way. [*Wake Nicodemus*]

SIR HENRY WOTTON 1568–1639

32 How happy is he born and taught, / That serveth not another's will; / Whose armour is his honest thought, / And simple truth his utmost skill! [*The Character of a Happy Life*]

33 And entertains the harmless day / With a religious book, or friend.

1 Lord of himself, though not of lands, / And having nothing, yet hath all.

2 He first deceased; she for a little tried / To live without him: liked it not, and died. [*Upon the Death of Sir Albert Morton's Wife*]

3 You meaner beauties of the night, / That poorly satisfy our eyes, / More by your number than your light; / You common people of the skies, / What are you when the sun shall rise? [*Upon his Mistress, the Queen of Bohemia*]

4 Virtue is the roughest way, / But proves at night a bed of down. [*Upon the sudden Restraint of the Earl of Somerset*]

5 An ambassador is an honest man sent to lie abroad for the good of his country. [Written in a friend's album. Quoted in Izaak Walton, *Life*]

SIR CHRISTOPHER WREN 1632–1723

6 *Si monumentum requiris, circumspice.* – If you seek his monument, look round. [Inscription in St Paul's Cathedral (written by his son)]

FRANK LLOYD WRIGHT 1869–1959

7 The physician can bury his mistakes, but the architect can only advise his client to plant vines. [*New York Times Magazine*, 4 Oct. 1953]

SIR THOMAS WYATT 1503?–1542

8 And wilt thou leave me thus? / Say nay, say nay, for shame! [*And wilt thou leave me thus?*]

9 Forget not yet the tried intent / Of such a truth as I have meant, / My great travail so gladly spent / Forget not yet. [*Forget not yet*]

10 They flee from me that sometime did me seek / With naked foot stalking in my chamber. [*They flee from me*]

11 Whoso list to hunt, I know where is an hind, / But as for me, alas, I may no more. [*Whoso list to hunt*]

12 There is written her fair neck round about: / *Noli me tangere*, for Caesar's I am; / And wild for to hold, though I seem tame.

WILLIAM WYCHERLEY 1640?–1716

13 Go to your business, I say, pleasure, whilst I go to my pleasure, business. [*The Country Wife*, II]

14 I have been toiling and moiling for the prettiest piece of china, my dear. [IV. iii]

15 Well, a widow, I see, is a kind of sinecure. [*The Plain Dealer*, V. iii]

JOHN WYCLIFFE c. 1320–1384

16 I believe that in the end the truth will conquer. [To the Duke of Lancaster, 1381. Quoted in J. R. Green, *Short History of the English People*]

P. WYNDHAM LEWIS 1884–1957

17 The root of the comic is to be sought in the sensations resulting from the observations of a thing behaving like a person. But from that point of view all men are necessarily comic; for they are all things, or physical bodies, behaving as persons. [*The Wild Body*]

XENOPHON *c.* 430–*c.* 359 BC

1 The sea! The sea! [*Anabasis*, IV. vii]

Y

ADMIRAL ISOROKU YAMAMOTO
  1884–1943

1 I fear we have only awakened a sleeping giant, and his reaction will be terrible. [After Japanese attack on Pearl Harbor, 1941. Quoted by A. J. P. Taylor, in the *Listener*, 9 Sept. 1976]

W. B. YEATS 1865–1939

2 I said, 'A line will take us hours maybe; / Yet if it does not seem a moment's thought, / Our stitching and unstitching has been naught.' [*Adam's Curse*]

3 Better go down upon your marrow-bones / And scrub a kitchen pavement, or break stones / Like an old pauper, in all kinds of weather; / For to articulate sweet sounds together/ Is to work harder than all these.

4 His element is so fine / Being sharpened by his death, / To drink from the wine-breath / While our gross palates drink from the whole wine. [*All Souls' Night*]

5 When I was young, / I had not given a penny for a song / Did not the poet sing it with such airs / That one believed he had a sword upstairs. [*All Things can Tempt me*]

6 O body swayed to music, O brightening glance, / How can we know the dancer from the dance? [*Among School Children*, 8]

7 Bring the balloon of the mind / That bellies and drags in the wind / Into its narrow shed. [*The Balloon of the Mind*]

8 That dolphin-torn, that gong-tormented sea. [*Byzantium*]

9 Now that my ladder's gone, / I must lie down where all the ladders start, / In the foul rag-and-bone shop of the heart. [*The Circus Animals' Desertion*]

10 There's more enterprise / In walking naked. [*A Coat*]

11 Suddenly I saw the cold and rook-delighting heaven / That seemed as though ice burned and was but the more ice. [*The Cold Heaven*]

12 The years like great black oxen tread the world, / And God the herdsman goads them on behind, / And I am broken by their passing feet. [*The Countess Cathleen*, IV]

13 I would be ignorant as the dawn / That has looked down / On that old queen measuring a town / With the pin of a brooch. [*The Dawn*]

14 Down by the salley gardens my love and I did meet; / She passed the salley gardens with little snow-white feet. / She bid me take love easy, as the leaves grow on the tree; / But I, being young and foolish, with her would not agree. [*Down by the Salley Gardens*]

15 I have met them at close of day / Coming with vivid faces / From counter or desk among grey / Eighteenth-century houses. / I have passed with a nod of the head / Or polite meaningless words. [*Easter 1916*]

16 All changed, changed utterly: / A terrible beauty is born.

17 One that is ever kind said yesterday: / 'Your well-belovèd's hair has threads of grey, / And little shadows come about her eyes.' [*The Folly of Being Comforted*]

18 Time can but make her beauty over again.

19 O heart! O heart! if she'd but turn her head, / You'd know the folly of being comforted.

1 The little fox he murmured, / 'O what of the world's bane?' / The sun was laughing sweetly, / The moon plucked at my rein; / But the little red fox murmured, / 'O do not pluck at his rein, / He is riding to the townland / That is the world's bane.' [*The Happy Townland*]

2 I have spread my dreams under your feet; / Tread softly because you tread on my dreams. [*He wishes for the Cloths of Heaven*]

3 Processions that lack high stilts have nothing that catches the eye. [*High Talk*]

4 Out-worn heart, in a time out-worn, / Come clear of the nets of wrong and right. [*Into the Twilight*]

5 Nor law, nor duty bade me fight, / Nor public men, nor cheering crowds, / A lonely impulse of delight / Drove to this tumult in the clouds. [*An Irish Airman Forsees his Death*]

6 I will arise and go now, and go to Innisfree, / And a small cabin build there, of clay and wattles made: / Nine beanrows will I have there, a hive for the honey-bee, / And live alone in the bee-loud glade. [*The Lake Isle of Innisfree*]

7 And I shall have some peace there, for peace comes dropping slow, / Dropping from the veils of the morning to where the cricket sings.

8 And evening full of the linnet's wings.

9 The wind blows out of the gates of the day, / The wind blows over the lonely of heart, / And the lonely of heart is withered away. [*The Land of Heart's Desire*]

10 The land of faery, / Where nobody gets old and godly and grave, / Where nobody gets old and crafty and wise, / Where nobody gets old and bitter of tongue.

11 All things uncomely and broken, all things worn out and old, / The cry of a child by the roadway, the creak of a lumbering cart, / The heavy steps of the ploughman, splashing the wintry mould, / Are wronging your image that blossoms a rose in the deeps of my heart. [*The Lover tells of the Rose in his Heart*]

12 I shudder and I sigh to think / That even Cicero / And many-minded Homer were / Mad as the mist and snow. [*Mad as the Mist and Snow*]

13 Time drops in decay, / Like a candle burnt out. [*The Moods*]

14 Why, what could she have done, being what she is? / Was there another Troy for her to burn? [*No Second Troy*]

15 A pity beyond all telling / Is hid in the heart of love. [*The Pity of Love*]

16 Rose of all Roses, Rose of all the World! [*The Rose of Battle*]

17 Who dreamed that beauty passes like a dream? [*The Rose of the World*]

18 Under the passing stars, foam of the sky, / Lives on this lonely face.

19 An aged man is but a paltry thing, / A tattered coat upon a stick, unless / Soul clap its hands and sing, and louder sing / For every tatter in its mortal dress. [*Sailing to Byzantium*]

20 Turning and turning in the widening gyre / The falcon cannot hear the falconer; / Things fall apart; the centre cannot hold; / Mere anarchy is loosed upon the world, / The blood-dimmed tide is loosed, and everywhere / The ceremony of innocence is drowned; / The best lack all conviction, while the worst / Are full of passionate intensity. [*The Second Coming*]

21 And what rough beast its hour come round at last, / Slouches towards Bethlehem to be born?

22 Far-off, most secret and inviolate Rose, / Enfold me in my hour of hours. [*The Secret Rose*]

23 A woman of so shining loveliness / That men threshed corn at midnight by a tress, / A little stolen tress.

24 When shall the stars be blown about the sky, / Like the sparks blown out of a smithy, and die?

25 Romantic Ireland's dead and gone, / It's with O'Leary in the grave. [*September 1913*]

26 We have gone round and round / In the narrow theme of love / Like an old horse in a pound. [*Solomon to Sheba*]

27 And pluck till time and times are done / The silver apples of the moon, / The golden apples of the sun. [*The Song of Wandering Aengus*]

28 The brawling of a sparrow in the eaves, / The brilliant moon and all the milky sky, / And all that famous harmony of leaves, / Had blotted out man's image and his cry. [*The Sorrow of Love*]

29 Civilisation is hooped together, brought / under a rule, under the semblance of peace /

By manifold illusion. [*Supernatural Songs*, 'Meru']

1 Unwearied still, lover by lover, / They paddle in the cold / Companionable streams or climb the air. [*The Wild Swans at Coole*]

2 What shall I do with this absurdity – / O heart, O troubled heart – this caricature, / Decrepit age that has been tied to me / As to a dog's tail? [*The Tower*, 1]

3 Death and life were not / Till man made up the whole, / Made lock, stock and barrel / Out of his bitter soul. [3]

4 When you are old and grey and full of sleep, / And nodding by the fire, take down this book. [*When you are old*]

5 But one man loved the pilgrim soul in you, / And loved the sorrows of your changing face.

6 Love fled / And paced upon the mountains overhead / And hid his face amid a crowd of stars.

7 Out of the quarrel with others we make rhetoric; out of the quarrel with ourselves we make poetry. [*Essay*]

8 He [Wilfred Owen] is all blood, dirt and sucked sugar stick. [*Letters on Poetry to Dorothy Wellesley*, Letter, 21 Dec. 1936]

JACK YELLEN 1892–1991

9 Happy Days Are Here Again. [Title of song]

YEVGENY YEVTUSHENKO 1933–

10 The hell with it. Who never knew / the price of happiness will not be happy. [*Lies*]

FREDERICK AUGUSTUS, DUKE OF YORK 1763–1827

11 Then the little man [Walpole] wears a shocking bad hat. [Attr. remark at Newmarket]

ANDREW YOUNG 1807–1889

12 There is a happy land, / Far, far away, / Where saints in glory stand, / Bright, bright as day. [Hymn]

EDWARD YOUNG 1683–1765

13 Some for renown, on scraps of learning dote, / And think they grow immortal as they quote. [*Love of Fame*, Satire I. 89]

14 Be wise with speed; / A fool at forty is a fool indeed. [II. 281]

15 With skill she vibrates her eternal tongue, / For ever most divinely in the wrong. [VI. 105]

16 One to destroy, is murder by the law; / And gibbets keep the lifted hand in awe; / To murder thousands takes a specious name, / War's glorious art, and gives immortal fame. [VII. 55]

17 How commentators each dark passage shun, / And hold their farthing candle to the sun. [97]

18 Tired Nature's sweet restorer, balmy sleep! / He, like the world, his ready visit pays / Where fortune smiles; the wretched he forsakes. [*Night Thoughts*, 'Night I', 1]

19 Night, sable goddess! from her ebon throne, / In rayless majesty, now stretches forth / Her leaden sceptre o'er a slumb'ring world. [18]

20 Creation sleeps. 'Tis as the general pulse / Of life stood still, and Nature made a pause; / An awful pause! prophetic of her end. [23]

21 The bell strikes one. We take no note of time / But from its loss. [55]

22 Be wise today: 'tis madness to defer. [390]

23 Procrastination is the thief of time. [393]

24 Time flies, death urges, knells call, heaven invites, / Hell threatens. ['Night 2', 292]

25 Man wants but little, nor that little long. ['Night 4', 118]

26 A God all mercy is a God unjust. [233]

27 By night an atheist half believes a God. ['Night 5', 176]

GEORGE W. YOUNG 1846–1919

28 Though in silence, with blighted affection, I pine, / Yet the lips that touch liquor must never touch mine! [*The Lips That Touch Liquor*]

MICHAEL [later LORD] YOUNG 1915–

29 The Rise of the Meritocracy. [Title of book]

Z

JAN ZAMOYSKI 1541–1605

1 The king reigns, but does not govern. [Speech in Polish Parliament, 1605]

ISRAEL ZANGWILL 1864–1926

2 Scratch the Christian and you find the pagan – spoiled. [*Children of the Ghetto*, II. Ch. 6]

3 America is God's Crucible, the great Melting Pot where all the races of Europe are melting and re-forming. [*The Melting Pot*, I]

RONALD L. ZIEGLER [Press Secretary to President Nixon] 1939–

4 This is an operative statement. The others are inoperative. [Statement to White House press corps, 17 Aug. 1973, admitting the untruth of earlier denials of government involvement in Watergate affair]

ÉMILE ZOLA 1840–1902

5 *Une œuvre d'art est un coin de la création vu à travers un tempérament.* – A work of art is a corner of creation seen through a temperament. [*Mes Haines, 'M. H. Taine, Artiste'*]

6 *La vérité est en marche; et rien ne l'arrêtera.* – Truth is on the march; nothing will stop it now. [*La Vérité en Marche*, [article on the Dreyfus case]

7 *Les documents humains.* – Human documents. [Title of an article]

8 *J'accuse.* – I accuse. [Title of an open letter to the French President concerning the Dreyfus case in *L'Aurore*, 13 Jan. 1898]

Index

Academe: olive-grove of A. 281:8
Academi: inter silvas A. quaerere verum 207:27
Academus: seek the truth in the groves of A. 207:27
Academy: Squeer's A., Dotheboys Hall 139:6
Accents: follow with a. sweet 97:25
  Loved a. are soon forgot 391:21
Acceptable: a. in thy sight, O Lord 37:38
  must say a. things 239:16
Accident: A.s will occur 137:23
  By many a happy a. 273:3
  chapter of a.s 109:18 457:5
  have it found out by a. 246:17
  he runs into a.s 267:30
  moving a.s by flood and field 374:3
  There's been an a.! 184:7
*Accipe: A. fraterno multum manantia fletu*104:6
Accommodating: most a. are the cleverest 244:17
Accommodement: on trouve . . . des a.s 284:15
Accomodants: plus a., ce sont les plus habiles 244:17
Account: a. . . . in the day of judgement 50:7
exhaustive a. of that period 29:3
  in making up the main a. 77:20
Accursed: A. be he that first invented war 267:15
  think themselves a. they were not here 357:19
Accuse: J'a. 473:8
Accused: grown a. . . . to her face 253:22
Ace: a. of trumps up his sleeve 243:1
Acheronta: A. movebo 441:3
Achieve: to a. that I have done 265:15
Achieving: Still a., still pursuing 257:6
Achilles: A.' wrath 316:10
  clad in the spoils of A. 440:16
  stood upon A.' tomb 91:34
  what name A. assumed 71:17
Achitophel: false A. was first 149:9
Acid: She drank prussic a. 25:1
Acquaintance: a.s are all very common-place 196:16
  hope our a. may be a long 'un 140:36
  If a man does not make new a. 221:1
  I love good creditable a. 411:6
  Should auld a. be forgot 83:26
  What! old a.! 355:7
Acquainted: Love and I were well a. 178:14
Acres: few paternal a. bound 315:6
  Three a. and a cow 119:4
Acroceraunian: In the A. mountains 390:11
Act: a. of thy life as if it were the last 16:9
  A. upon it, if you can 176:23
  both a. and know 268:26
  coach and six through the A. of Settlement 327:6
  Familiar a.s are beautiful 393:17
  His a.s being seven ages 345:11
  Into a narrow a. 77:21
  last a. crowns the play 323:2
  little, nameless, unremembered a.s 462:13
  sleep an a. or two 359:8
  so second a.s in American lives 165:10
  within the meaning of the A. 7:2
Acte: a. gratuite 176:2
Acting: A. is . . . the lowest of the arts 286:19
  Between the a. of a dreadful thing 359:27
  when he was off, he was a. 181:21
Action: A. is transitory 461:9
  a.s are what they are 86:28
  A. will furnish belief 115:9
  In a. faithful 315:5
  lose the name of a. 350:14

Makes that and th' a. fine 199:13
my a.s are my ministers' 106:21
only the a.s of the just 396:5
pious a. we do sugar o'er 350:13
represented an a. as objectively necessary 229:9
Spheres of a. 184:22
Suit the a. to the word 350:26
Their dearest a. in the tented field 373:41
Activities: All men's a. 227:16
Actor: After a well-graced a. leaves the stage 377:16
  best a.s in the world 350:2
  fault and not the a. of it 368:10
  our a.s . . . were all spirits 381:10
  they didn't act like a.s 336:14
Ads: He watched the a. 292:9
Adair: fled with thee, Robin A. 236:3
Adam: A., called 'the happiest of men' 92:16
  A. Had 'em 178:25
  A. lay I-bowndyn 5:15
  A. the goodliest man 279:28
  A. was a gardener 239:7
  As in A. all die 55:32
  gardener A. and his wife 419:5
  grave man, nicknamed A. 115:11
  old A. in this Child 319:25
  Old A., the carrion crow 28:21
  son of A. and Eve 320:20
  sought A. and accused him 59:4
  When A. delved 22:2
  whipped the offending A. out of him 356:21
Adamant: a. for drift 112:15
Adder: bright day that brings forth the a. 359:25
  like the deaf a. 39:2
Addington: Pitt is to A. 98:17
Addison, Joseph 312:22,312:23
Addresses: A. are given to us 335:13
  Three a. always inspire confidence 455:22
Adhem: Abou Ben A. . . . Awoke one night 212:10
  Ben A.'s name led all the rest 212:12
Adieu: A., a., kind friends 8:21
  A., a.! my native shore 89:12
  A.! she cries 174:27
  bid you a welcome a. 446:2
  With a. for evermore 84:30
Adlestrop: Yes, I remember A. 426:26
Admiral: A.s all, for England's sake 293:13
  it pays to shoot an a. 442:11
Admiralty: If blood be the price of a. 240:23
Admiration: As great in a. as herself 359:7
  Season your a. for a while 348:11
Admire: Not to a. is all the art 91:41, 316:13
  Where none a. 260:15
Admired: all who understood a. 318:9
Admit: I . . . Labour to a. you 145:23
Admittance: No a. till the week after next 102:20
Ado: Much a. there was, God wot 67:22
Adonais: I weep for A. 389:23
  soul of A., like a star 390:9
Adonis: This A. in loveliness 212:17
Adoration: All a., duty and observance 346:11
  Breathless with a. 463:4
  For a. all the ranks Of angels 398:7
Adore: he a.s his maker 68:19
  youth, I do a. thee 385:5
Adored: I was a. once too 383:8
Adorn: touched nothing that he did not a. 222:24
Adsum: quickly said, 'A.!' 425:8

Adullam: political Cave of A. 68:15
Adulescens: A. moritur 310:6
Adultère: Mélange a. de tout 122:11
Adulteries: all the a. of art 225:4
Adultery: a. Is much more common 91:2
    rather be taken in a. 212:23
    Tasmanians, who never committed a. 270:16
Advance: retrograde if it does not a. 175:23
  Advantage: a. of doing one's praising 88:21
    It's them that take a. 155:9
Adventure: I first a., follow me 191:1
    most beautiful a. in life 169:16
    awfully big a. 25:24
Adversary: Agree with thine a. quickly 49:2
    mine a. had written a book 37:8
    never sallies out and sees her a. 282:18
    your a. the devil 57:36
Adversitee: of fortunes sharp a. 108:25
Adversity: a. doth best discover virtue 19:5
    a. is not without comforts 19:4
    a. is the blessing of the New 19:3
    A.'s sweet milk, philosophy 380:1
    bread of a. 45:21
    hundred that will stand a. 99:34
    in all a. of fortune 64:2
    In his a. I ever prayed 225:31
    in the day of a. consider 43:30
    Sweet are the uses of a. 344:25
Advertising: A. . . . . the science of arresting 250:10
    Half the money I spend on a. 445:31
Advertisement: special a. to impart 306:11
Advice: A. is seldom welcome 109:9
    A. to persons about to marry 322:3
    earnest a. from my seniors 428:25
    gives nothing so freely as a. 248:8
    We may give a. 248:17
Advise: Death! whom none could a. 325:9
Advising: to go round a. people 67:12
Aegean: Isles that crown th' A. deep 187:11
Aeneas: A. would not come 316:20
Aequam: A. memento rebus in arduis 208:16
Aeroplane: it wasn't the a. 129:4
Aeson: herbs That did renew old A. 370:18
Aesop: prettily devised of A. 20:37
Affairs: for the ordering your a. 384:30
    in which our a. prosper 59:12
    misleading guide to current a. 236:15
Affection: a. beaming in one eye 138:25
    history of the a.s 215:17
    Or thy a. cannot hold the bent 383:11
    some idea what unrequited a. is 137:37
    to me-wards your a.'s strong 200:8
    young a.s run to waste 90:11
Affinity: betray a secret a. 196:15
Affliction: furnace of a. 46:2
    widows in their a. 57:22
Afford: Can't a. them, Governor 389:5
Affright: bad a., afflict the best 186:19
Afraid: a., because I was naked 34:1
    a. to die 4:17
    be not a. 50:15
    Men not a. of God 316:6
    they were sore a. 52:1
    Who's A. of the Big Bad Wolf? 142:19
    Who's A. of Virginia Woolf? 3:32
Africa: A. and her prodigies 70:25
    always something new out of A. 310:10

I speak of A. and golden joys 356:16
    looking far away into A. 136:29
    more familiar with A. 300:9
    silent over A. 75:2
Africa: Ex A. semper aliquid novi 310:10
Afterlife: a. will be any less exasperating 123:10
Afternoon: it seemèd always a. 420:8
    rude multitude call the a. 364:2
    slant of light, On winter a.s 142:9
Agag: A. came unto him 35:45
Again: country of A. 289:18
    Why, I do it a. and a. 100:33
Against: not with me is a. me 50:5 52:16·
    said he was a. it 122:6
    somewhat a. thee 58:6
    who can be a. us? 54:30
Agas: Quidquid a., prudenter a. 9:11
Agate-stone: no bigger than an a. 378:30
Age: accurate about her a. 455:24
    a., ache, penury and imprisonment 368:23
    a. and stability 285:19
    A. cannot wither her 343:30
    A. shall not weary them 59:18
    A.s of hopeless end 278:36
    As our different a.s move 320:30
    a. that will her pride deflower 403:1
    A. will not be defied 20:18
    a. without a name 287:18
    A., with stealing steps 438:23
    bring forth fruit in old a. 40:5
    buried in a good old a. 34:21
    childhood, youth and old a. 33:9
    choice and master spirits of this a. 360:9
    Crabbed a. and youth cannot live together 385:4
    Damn the a. 246:15
    Decrepit a. that has been tied to me 472:2
    Do you think at your a. 100:33
    each a. is a dream 301:17
    fetch the a. of gold 277:24
    first sign of a. 201:5
    gift of perpetual old a. 456:20
    Hear this, thou a. unbred 386:23
    He hath not forgotten my a. 401:23
    Here an a. 'tis resting 74:1
    How many a.s hence Shall this . . . scene 360:7
    in every a. and clime we see 174:20
    invention of a barbarous a. 277:30
    I summon a. 77:17
    lady of a 'certain a.' 92:1
    Let a. approve of youth 77:22
    Like the old a. 383:12
    my a. is as the lusty winter 344:30
    never remembers her a. 170:17
    not of an a., but for all time 225:24
    old a., and experience 328:11
    outworn buried a. 386:2
    sixth a. shifts 345:11
    that is a pitiless a. 244:20
    That men call a. 69:6
    Though a. from folly 343:21
    thousand a.s in Thy sight 447:23
    Through every unborn a. 186:24
    Till a. snow white hairs on thee 146:8
    to all succeeding a.s curst 149:9
    We have passed a.'s icy caves 393:13
    we live in such an a. 151:27
    well an old a. is out 151:28

when a., Disease, or sorrows strike 115:18
when a. is in 373:12
when Mozart was my a. 252:4
when thou comest to a. 378:28
While unending a.s run 292:26
who tells one her real a. 455:35
world's great a. begins anew 391:2
worst of woes that wait on a. 89:20
Wrinkled with a., and drenched with dew 134:24
Years hence . . . may dawn an a. 11:9
Ye unborn a.s 185:26
Age: â. amènera tout 284:9
   cet â. est sans pitié 244:20
Aged: a. man is but a paltry thing 471:19
Agent: prime a. of all human perception 118:17
Agincourt: affright the air at A. 356:20
A-gipsying: to go a. through the world 246:16
A-gley: Gang aft a. 85:28
Aggravate: a. your choler 355:27
Aggressors: Quarantine the a. 329:20
Agnostic: appropriate title of 'a.' 213:14
Agonies: Where small talk dies in a. 392:18
Agony: conquers a. 90:14
   that a. is our triumph 437:16
Agree: busy world and I shall ne'er a. 124:13
   except to those who a. 248:16
   in one fact we all a. 115:19
   though all things differ, all a. 316:9
   When people a. with me 456:12
   you and I shall never a. 7:6
Agreeable: do not want people to be very a. 17:18
Agreed: except they be a. 47:14
Agri: modus a. non ita magnus 209:17
Agricolas: O fortunatos nimium . . . A.! 441:25
Agriculture: taxes . . . fall upon a. 175:18
Agrippa: Now tall A. lived close by 203:3
Ague: war, dearth, age, a.s 145:16
Ahome: Are you not gone a.? 226:10
A-hunting: a. we will go 163:5
Aid: Alliteration's artful a. 111:23
   Lend us Thine aid! 196:22
   summoned the immediate a. 30:16
Ailes: Ses ailes de géant 26:11
Ailment: because our a.s are the same 411:5
Aim: a.s his heart had learned to prize 180:24
   two things to a. at in life 399:6
   You ask: 'What is our a.?' 112:19
Aimé: je l'ai trop a. 324:23
Aimless: Feckless and A. 175:25
Ain't: to know what a. so 389:17
Air: a., a chartered libertine 356:22
   a. bites shrewdly 348:27
   a. is delicate 365:4
   a. like a draught of wine 123:16
   a. nimbly and sweetly recommends itself 365:3
   a.s from heaven or blasts from hell 348:29
   a.; which, but for vacancy 343:29
   as one that beateth the a. 55:12
   both feet firmly planted in the a. 330:3
   breathe his native a. 315:6
   bright and glittering in the smokeless a. 463:10
   carcasses . . . That do corrupt my a. 346:29
   do not saw the a. too much 350:23
   drag us from the a. 236:8
   fairer than the evening a. 267:1
   flies through the a. 254:11
   forming in the a. and darkening the sky 328:5

I eat the a. promise-crammed 351:6
Into my heart an a. that kills 210:25
I' the a., and catch again 77:23
Make the cold a. fire 393:11
melted into a., into thin a. 381:10
methinks I scent the morning a. 349:7
mock the a. with idle state 185:19
No stir of a. was there 230:27
Only to kiss that a. 200:17
Open your eyes to the a. 427:4
Receive our a. 126:36
Sounds and sweet a.s 381:8
To a. the ditty 210:3
to the Germans that of the a. 327:9
viewless forms of a. 339:25
which way the hot a. blows 198:20
Airly: A. Beacon; Oh the pleasant sight 237:12
Airship: looks down on a.s when stimulated 198:17
Airt: a.s the wind can blaw 85:5
Aisle: long-drawn a. and fretted vault 186:7
Aitches: nothing to lose but our a. 301:1
Ajax: Thersites' body is as good as A.' 347:14
Akond: A. of Swat 250:15
Alabama: I've come from A. 168:7
Alabaster: grandsire cut in a. 369:2
   smooth as monumental a. 375:21
Alacrity: I have not that a. of spirit 378:17
   kind of a. in sinking 371:12
   strange a. in sinking 146:25
Alamein: Before A. we never had a victory 113:2
Alan: don't worry about A. 304:16
Alarms: dwell in the midst of a. 127:37
   Swept with confused a. 10:22
Alarums: stern a. changed to merry meetings 377:21
Alcestis: Brought to me like A. 282:5
Alcohol: discovered that a. was a food 459:14
Aldershot: burnish'd by the A. shot 32:24
Ale: A., man, a.'s the stuff to drink 210:31
   bring us in good a.! 7:8
   drank a pint of English a. 110:6
   fed purely upon a. 161:14
   give us some a. 62:1
   I should prefer mild a. 409:22
   jolly good a. and old 408:2
   no more cakes and a. 383:6
   quart of a. is a dish for a king 384:22
   Shoulder the sky, my lad, and drink your a. 209:25
   size of pots of a. 87:5
   spicy nut-brown a. 276:29
   twopenny a. and cheese 110:7
Alea: Iacta a. est 95:7
Aleppo: in A. once 375:26
Alexander: She's gane, like A. 84:1
   Some talk of A. 8:17
Alexandrine: needless A. ends the song 313:13
Alfred: Truth-teller was . . . A. named 421:21
Alibi: He always has an a. 156:27
   If your governor don't prove a a. 141:7
   vy worn't there a a. 141:14
Alice: A., where art thou? 80:10
Alienum: humani nil a me a. puto 424:29
Alive: he is no longer a. 31:26
   lucky if he gets out of it a. 163:9
   never knew Lord Jones was a. 111:7
   shall all be made a. 55:32

show that one's a. 83:14
wish they were the only one a. 15:22
All: After a., I . . . will not hang myself 109:31
A. for one, one for a. 152:9
a.'s love, yet a.'s law 78:16
A.'s over, then 75:20
Cared not to be at a. 278:31
make that, which was nothing, A. 146:18
Allah: A. created the English mad 239:22
Allegiance: To hell, a.! 352:12
Allegory: as headstrong as an a. 395:28
man's life . . . is a continual a. 234:11
Shakespeare led a life of a. 234:12
Which things are an a. 56:10
Alley: lowest and vilest a.s of London 147:17
she lives in our a. 99:6
Alliance: entangling a.s with none 217:22
steer clear of permanent a. 447:2
Allies: Thou hast great a. 463:20
All-in-all: intellectual a. 465:2
Alliteration: A.'s artful aid 111:23
Allonging: couldn't exist without a. 138:10
Ally: a. has to be watched 432:19
Her faithful a. and our sneaking foe 397:22
Alma: A. Mater all dissolved in port 311:21
Alma: Con el a. de charol 173:2
Almanack: Look in the a. 372:1
Almighty: A.! thy power hath founded 184:17
pleased the A.'s orders to perform 1:9
Almond-tree: a. shall flourish 44:11
Alms: a. for oblivion 382:12
a. of thy superfluous praise 148:19
so give a.; Pray so 384:30
Aloft: now he's gone a. 136:12
Alone: All we ask is to be let a. 133:3
A., a., about the dreadful wood 14:8
A., a., all, all a. 117:4
A. and palely loitering 231:7
A. I did it 347:1
a. in the midst of the earth 44:35
a. when he falleth 43:21
be a. on earth 89:20
I feel I am a. 246:26
I want to be a. 172:16
leaving home after living a. 253:13
man who stands most a. 214:9
Never less a. than when a. 328:25
nor less a. than when without company 339:8
not good that the man should be a. 33:20
To be a. is the fate 339:1
We are left a. with our day 15:16
Alp: A.s on A.s arise! 313:5
many a fiery A. 279:4
O'er the white A.s alone 144:24
Sun-smitten A.s before me lay 416:6
Alph: Where A., the sacred river 117:35
Alpha: I am A. and Omega 58:38
Alphabet: remaining . . . letters of the a. 300:14
ven he got to the end of the a. 140:38
Altar: a. with its inscription 53:54
self-slain on his own strange a. 412:16
thy sad floor an a. 93:23
To what green a. 231:23
Upon death's purple a. 396:5
Alteration: alters when it a. finds 386:32
Alternative: when you consider the a. 111:16
Altitudo: pursue my reason to an O a.! 70:24

Alway: Rejoice in the Lord a. 56:27
Alysoun: lyht on A. 5:10
Am: I A. That I A. 34:43
I a.: yet what I a. 114:26
in the infinite I A. 118:17
Amalgamation: Heaven and Hell A. Society 100:21
Amaranth: like fields of a. 134:8
no fields of a. 247:5
Amaranthus: Bid a. all his beauty shed 277:16
Amari: Surgit a. aliquid 259:24
Amaryllida: Formosam resonare doces A. silvas 441:9
Amaryllis: To sport with A. 277:8
Amateur: disease that afflicts a.s 110:29
Hell is full of musical a.s 388:20
nation of a.s 330:17
Amavit: Cras amet qui nunquam a. 9:8
Amazed: not envious, rather I am a. 441:11
Ambassador: a. is an honest man 468:5
a.s for Christ 55:47
Ambiguity: Seven Types of A. 159:24
Ambition: A., Distraction, Uglification 101:14
A. first sprung from your bless'd abodes 312:4
A. should be made of sterner stuff 360:16
A., The soldier's virtue 343:35
a. thick-sighted 230:5
Cromwell . . . fling away a. 358:24
Ill-weaved a. 355:6
Let not a. mock their useful toil 186:5
low a., and the pride of kings 313:25
not with a. joined 120:29
Restless A., never at an end! 131:8
That lowliness is young a.'s ladder 359:26
That make a. virtue 375:5
Vaulting a., which o'erleaps itself 365:8
virtue in a. is violent 19:21
Who doth a. shun 344:39
Ambitious: as he was a., I slew him 360:13
Amboss: A. oder Hammer 179:25
Ame: donner le vice aux â. vertueuses 284:2
Amelia: author of 'A.' 65:7
Amen: 'A.' Stuck in my throat 365:24
sound of a great A. 321:3
Will no man say, a.? 377:10
America: A. became top nation 342:23
A. is a country of young men 159:14
A. is a large, friendly dog 431:13
A. is God's Crucible 473:3
England and A. are two countries separated 389:15
good will toward us, the A. people 457:23
Greening of A. 326:14
huntsmen are up in A. 70:19
If you're going to A. 251:15
moral climate of A. 329:19
next to of course god a. 130:2
O my A.,! my new-found-land 144:26
American: A. nation in th' Sixth Ward 152:17
A.s have been conditioned 435:14
A.s have taken umbrage 322:10
A. writers want to be not good but great 439:12
business of the A. people 122:5
Carlyle was probably fond of the A.s 434:9
Europeans and A.s are like men and women 217:17
Good A.s, when they die 9:22
love all mankind, *except an A.* 223:2
new deal for the A. people 329:13

new generation of A.s 235:15
no second acts in A. lives 165:10
process whereby A. girls turn into A. women
191:16
silent majority of my fellow A.s 295:7
This generation of A.s 329:16
When good A.s die 456:7
Americanism: Hyphenated A. 330:6
no fifty–fifty A. in this country 330:8
Ami: a. du genre humain 284:1
Chacun se dit a. 244:12
choix fait les a.s 134:32
Nos a.s, les ennemis 32:3
Amicably: separation, a. if they can 323:5
A-milking: I'm going a., sir 298:15
Amiss: Nothing comes a. 380:17
Ammunition: and pass the a. 167:14
Among: A. them, but not of them 90:4
Amo: A., amas, I love a lass 299:13
Amongst: Be a. you and remain with you 319:23
Amor: a. che move il sole 132:2
A. vincit omnia 107:13
Nunc scio quid sit A. 441:18
Omnia vincit A. 441:21
Amorem: longum subito deponere a. 104:3
Amoris: Amantium irae a. integratio est 424:28
Amorous: Still a., and fond, and billing 87:25
Amour: a. de ma mie 284:6
a. en tout temps 27:15
a. qui ôtait l'esprit 142:13
a., tel qu'il existe 106:3
jealous because of his *a. propre* 188:4
On ne badine pas avec l'a. 290:14
peu d'a., Un peu de haine 285:26
Amurath: Not A. an A. succeeds 356:15
Amuse: talent to a. 123:9
Amused: We are not a. 439:11
Amusement: were it not for its a.s 254:7
Amusing: a. herself with me 285:16
Anaesthesia: bastard substitute, A. 453:3
Analogy: a. is often misleading 88:3
Anarch: So A. became a good crier 324:8
Thy hand, great A.! 311:29
Anarchy: do not even get a. 111:9
Mere a. is loosed upon the world 471:20
shapeless lump, like A. 149:13
Anathema: Let him be A. 55:42
Ancestor: I am my own a. 227:14
wisdom of our a.s 82:27
Ancestry: I can trace my a. back 177:18
Anchor: firm a. in nonsense 172:4
Wedges of gold, great a.s 378:1
Ancient: A. of days did sit 47:6
Ancientry: wronging the a. 384:19
Ancre: levons l'a. 26:18
Ane: plus â. des trois 244:8
Anecdotage: fell into his a. 143:22
And: including 'and' and 'the' 263:5
Anders: ich kamm nicht a. 260:2
Andromache: as smiling through her tears 204:12
in the margin opposite 'A.' 330:25
Angel: a. and archangel join 315:31
a. appear to each lover beside 304:26
a. dropped down from the clouds 354:36
a. girt with golden wings 275:12
a. of death has been abroad 68:12
A. of Death spread his wings 93:5

a. of the Lord came down 414:18
a. of the Lord came upon them 52:1
A.s affect us oft 144:14
a.s all were singing out of tune 93:29
A.s and ministers of grace 348:29
a.s are all Tories 94:3
A.s are bright still 367:6
A.s are painted fair 301:20
a.s keep their ancient places 427:18
A.s may be familiar 305:21
A. that presided o'er my birth 60:30
a. whose muscles developed no more 190:5
As far as a.s' ken 278:4
as if a.s were pushing 172:7
As pure in thought as a.s are 328:26
band of A.s coming after me 8:18
band Of glorious a.s 292:23
beautiful and ineffectual a. 12:23
better a. is a man right fair 387:7
clip an a.'s wings 231:16
Curse his better a. from his side 375:23
drew an a. down 150:9
Drew one a. 76:13
drive an a. from your door 62:13
faces of a.s 188:5
feet of a.s bright 62:20
flights of a.s sing thee to thy rest! 353:14
Four a.s to my bed 3:16
From A.s bending near the earth 341:16
give his a.s charge over thee 40:2
glittering and sparkling a.s 431:16
glorious fault of a.s 312:4
God and a.s to be lookers-on 18:5
guardian a.s sung this strain 428:5
Hear thy guardian a. say 158:2
Holy a.s guard thy bed 447:15
If an a. out of heaven 110:23
in action how like an a! 349:36
in comparison . . . I am an A. 138:2
in his motion like an a. sings 370:20
Let a.s prostrate fall 308:2
Like A.s' visits, short and bright 295:15
Like those of a.s 60:5
little lower than the a.s 37:26
make the a.s weep 368:15
Man did eat a.s' food 39:23
Milton wrote . . . of A.s and God 63:8
ministering a. shall my sister be 352:31
ministering a. thou 340:19
Neither death, nor life, nor a.s 54:31
No other than the a. of this life 77:26
Now walk the a.s 267:18
on the side of the a.s 143:5
Praise Him, A. in the height! 235:7
ranks Of a.s yield eternal thanks 398:7
Recording A., as he wrote it down 405:29
some have entertained a.s 57:17
story Which a. voices tell 273:27
Tears such as a.s weep 278:23
to domesticate the Recording A. 406:30
where a.s fear to tread 313:24
Where a.s tremble while they gaze 187:14
wrote like an a. 173:6
You may not be an a. 152:4
Angel-duck: A., a., winged and silly 245:5
Angelicam: nam et a. habent faciem 188:5
Angel-visits: Like a., few and far between 97:17

Anger: A. is a brief madness 207:17
  A. is one of the sinews 171:3
  A. makes dull men witty 18:10
  A. supplies the arms 440:4
  grievous words stir up a. 42:11
  In holy a., and pious grief 24:11
  take care that you strike it in a. 388:29
Angle: Brother of the A. 445:20
  reply was that they were A.s 188:5
  Themselves in every a. greet 268:16
Angler: excellent a., and now with God 445:22
  no man is born an a. 445:19
  too good for any but a.s 445:26
Angleterre: ah! la perfide A. 65:17
Angli: quod A. vocarentur 188:5
Anglo-Saxon: those are A. attitudes 102:14
Angry: a. and poor and happy 110:19
  a. with my friend 62:2
  A. Young Man 306:8
  Be ye a. and sin not 56:18
Anguis: Latet a. in herba 441:14
Anguish: A. keeps the heavy gate 455:1
  that divinest a. 69:4
  With a. moist and fever dew 231:8
Angusta: Res a. domi 227:21
Animal: All a.s are equal 300:15
  A.s are such agreeable friends 155:19
  a.s went in one by one 7:4
  anything but that vain a. 328:9
  Be a good a. 249:21
  committee is an a. with four back legs 251:19
  distinguish us for the other a.s 27:15
  I could turn and live with a.s 453:27
  if we stop loving a.s 400:26
  Man is a gaming a. 245:25
  Man is a noble a. 71:20
  Man is . . . a religious a. 82:19
  Man is a tool-making a. 168:26
  monstrous a. a husband and wife 163:1
  poor, bare, forked a. 362:23
  Wild a.s never kill for sport 170:18
Animal: Cet a. est très méchant 9:14
  homme est . . . un méchant a. 284:17
Animosity: full fervour of sisterly a. 409:25
Animula: A. vagula blandula 190:2
Animus: a. si te non deficit aequus 207:21
Ankle: the more Do his weak a.s swell 466:18
Ann: A.!, A.! Come! quick as you can! 134:5
Anna: great A.! whom three realms obey 315:19
Annabel: I and my A. Lee 310:16
Annal: If you have writ your a.s true 347:1
  short and simple a.s of the poor 186:5
  War's a.s will cloud into night 193:1
  whose a.s are blank 99:24
Anne: O sweet A. Page! 371:9
  Sister A., can you see nothing 308:1
  Tell 'em Queen A.'s dead 119:23
Annie: for bonnie A. Laurie 147:6
Annihilating: A. all that's made 268:21
Annihilation: One Moment in A.'s Waste 164:16
Anno Domini: A. – that's the most fatal 201:14
  you shall taste my A.161:13
Annoy: only does it to a. 101:3
Annoyance: To his extreme a., tempted him 30:28
Annuity: a. is a very serious business 17:14
  But an a. cheap 138:29
Anointed: Rail on the Lord's a. 378:11

touch the Lord's A. 7:29
Anomalies: How to achieve such a. 180:15
Anser: sed argutos inter strepere a. olores 441:20
Answer: a. came there none 339:14
  a. . . . is blowin' in the wind 153:6
  But a. came there none 102:9
  give me your a., do 131:1
  I ask, and cannot a. 389:19
  I'll not a. that 370:6
  Just for lack Of a. 205:21
  sent an a. back to me 102:12
  soft a. turneth away wrath 42:11
  Take, if you must have a. 110:1
  what a dusty a. gets the soul 272:12
  What *is* the a.? 404:18
  would not stay for an a. 18:17
Ant: a. is no lender 243:16
  cry famine at her neighbour's, the a.'s 243:15
  Go to the a., thou sluggard 41:26
Antagonist: Our a. is our helper 82:23
Anthem: grand old Puritan a. 256:16
  here followeth the a. 318:29
  hollaing, and singing of a.s 355:17
  pealing a. swells the note of praise 186:7
  plaintive a. fades 232:8
Anthropophagi: A., and men whose heads 374:5
Antic: put an a. disposition on 349:17
Antick: there the a. sits 377:2
Antidote: a. to desire 121:3
  some sweet oblivious a. 367:19
Antipathies: God knows what a. 330:20
  Violent a. are always suspicious 196:15
Antipathy: Dread is a sympathetic a. 237:2
  strong a. of good to bad 316:5
Antipodes: like A. in shoes 269:5
Antique: constant service of the a. world 344:31
Antiquity: I will write for A.! 246:15
  little skill in a. 171:1
Antithesis: himself one vile a. 312:27
  proper a. to prose 118:24
Antony: My A. is away 343:23
Antres: A. vast and desarts idle 374:4
Anulus: consumitur a. usu 301:24
Anvil: a. or hammer 179:25
Anybody: Is there a. there? 134:20
  Then no one's a. 176:25
Anything: a. goes 316:24
Ape: a.s and peacocks 269:24
  A.s are a.s 225:8
  blue-behinded a. 408:1
  Is man an a. or an angel? 143:5
  lead a.s in hell 380:18
  naked a. self-named *Homo sapiens* 288:8
  played the sedulous a. 406:20
Aphorism: a. never coincides with the truth 242:14
Aphrodisiac: circumambulatory a. 170:24
  Power is the ultimate a. 242:1
Apocalypse: Characters of the great A. 465:25
Apollo: A., with hair and harpstring 412:26
  bards in fealty to A. 233:2
  harsh after the songs of A. 364:9
  Not here, O A.! 10:24
  'Tis A. comes leading 11:1
Apollos: A. watered 54:51
Apollyon: A. straddled quite over 80:22
Apologize: I never a. 387:20
Apology: a. for the Devil 88:10

Never make a defence of a. 106:17
Apostate: characteristic of a.s 262:16
Apostle: all the A.s would have done 91:3
  Cristes lore and his a.s twelve 107:27
Apothecary: ointment of the a. 43:39
Apparel: a. oft proclaims the man 348:22
  Every true man's a. 368:27
  gay a. for an almsman's gown 377:4
Apparition: lovely a. 466:14
Appearance: according to the a. 53:16
  who do not judge by a.s 456:6
Appeased: Wilt be a. or no? 75:8
Appeasement: limitation . . . by political a. 258:1
Appendice: d'un pareil a. 332:5
Appétit: a. vient en mangeant 324:2
Appetite: And not their a.s 375:1
  A. comes with eating 324:2
  a. may sicken, and so die 382:23
  As if increase of a. had grown 348:2
  cloy The a.s they feed 343:30
  cloy the hungry edge of a. 376:15
  good digestion wait on a. 366:24
  Subdue your a.s, my dears 139:8
  were then to me An a. 462:18
Applause: A., n. The echo of a platitude 59:5
  attentive to his own a. 312:23
  in the sunshine and with a. 80:27
Apple: all was for an a. 5:15
  a. of his eye 35:17
  a.s, cherries, hops and women 140:23
  a.s were gathered and stored 157:14
  a. wood of Hereford 110:1
  candied a., quince, and plum 230:18
  comfort me with a.s 44:19
  golden a.s of the sun 471:27
  goodly a. rotten at the heart 369:15
  Keep me as the a. of the e. 37:34
  millionaires love a baked a. 163:17
  moon-washed a.s of wonder 148:24
  mossy a. tree 117:31
  My a. trees will never get across 170:9
  My heart is like an a. 331:1
  putting a.s wondrous ripe 76:27
  small choice in rotten a.s 380:15
  Where the a. reddens 79:12
Apple-dumpling: who refuse a.s 245:17
Apple-john: withered like an old a. 354:31
Apple Tree: In the Shade of the old A. 457:12
Appliance: all a.s and means to boot 355:32
  By desperate a. are relieved 351:38
Application: bearings . . . lays in the a. on it 137:34
Appointment: a. by the corrupt few 388:26
  to keep an a. with a beech-tree 429:1
Apprehension: My a.s come in crowds 461:7
Appris: Ils n'ont rien a. 414:8
  sans avoir rien a. 284:11
Approach: Beats my a. 237:8
Approbation: A. from Sir Hubert Stanley 289:7
Apricock: bind thou up yon dangling a.s 377:6
April: after A., when May follows 74:36
  A., A., Laugh thy girlish laughter 447:4
  A. is the cruellest month 156:33
  A., June, and November 6:17
  hides the green hill in an A. shroud 231:28
  lovely A. of her prime 385:13
  Men are A. when they woo 346:4
  Now that A.'s there 74:34

Of A., May, of June 200:2
proud-pied A. 386:20
Since A., January, June or July 295:24
'Twas A., as the bumpkins say 125:2
uncertain glory of an A. day 384:4
well-apparelled A. 378:26
April-fools: One of love's A. 120:17
Aprille: Whan that A. with his shoures soote 107:7
Aprons: made themselves a. 33:25
Aqua: rapida scribere oportet a. 104:1
Aquarius: How is your trade, A. 185:12
Aquitaine: *prince d'A. à la tour abolie* 293:9
Arab: A.'s Farewell to his Steed 295:21
Arabia: all A. breathes from yonder box 315:14
  all the perfumes of A. 367:14
  Far are the shades of A. 134:9
Araby: A. the blest 279:21
Aral: shine upon the A. Sea 11:35
Araminta: My own A. 318:8
Arbiter: A. of taste 414:6
Arbitrate: Now, who shall a.? 77:19
Arcades: A. ambo 91:33 441:17
Arcadia: Et in A. ego 9:9
Arch: o' night's black a. 85:19
Archangel: A. a little damaged 246:13
  Less than a. ruined 278:20
Archbishop: one illusion left . . . the A. 399:29
Archer: A.s stand there on every side 289:18
  busy a. his sharp arrows tries 396:12
  mark the a. little meant 340:5
Archer: Qui . . . se rit de l'a. 26:11
Arches: Underneath the a. 165:17
Archibald: A., certainly not 328:1 335:8
Architect: a. can only advise his client 468:7
  a. of his own fate 9:21
Architectooralooral: drawd too a. 138:7
Architecture: is music in space 338:6
  I call a. frozen music 180:13
  New styles of a. 15:13
Arch-Mediocrity: A. who presided 143:13
Arcum: Neque semper arcum 208:19
Arden: now am I in A. 344:32
Ardeur: Ce n'est plus une a. 325:1
Are: tell you what you a. 68:20 333:20
  We know what we a. 352:6
Arena: a. swims around him 90:15
Arethusa: A. arose From her couch 390:11
  saucy A. 202:1
Argifying: What's the good of a.? 241:22
Argo: loftier A. cleaves the main 391:3
Arguing: I am not a. with you 452:5
Argument: All a. is against it 222:28
  a. for a week 353:36
  by a. alone 408:4
  furnish you with a. 182:27
  heard great A. 164:11
  height of this great a. 278:2
  I have found you an a. 223:19
  not to stir without great a. 352:2
  only a. available 259:5
  Racks, gibbets, halters, were their a.s 299:18
  sheathed their swords for lack of a. 357:4
  stronger man's a. 244:1
  when blood is their a. 357:10
Ariel: Caliban casts out A. 317:22
Ariosto: A. of the North 90:7
Arise: A., shine 46:17

profuse strains of unpremeditated a. 394:17
progress of the a.s and the sciences 266:11
secret of the a.s is to correct nature 442:5
sooner than work at anything but his a. 388:17
that is where the a. resides 338:20
Venerate a. as a. 196:13
we will achieve an a. 444:2
when a. Is too precise 200:6
work of a. is a corner of creation 473:5
you are only interested in a. 389:14
Art: a. pour l'a. 123:7
Arthur: He's in A.'s bosom 356:30
Article: For a slashing a. 425:11
  have the art rather than the a. 114:4
  snuffed out by an a. 92:7
  These a.s subscribed 120:35
Artifex: Qualis a. pereo.! 293:8
Artificer: Another lean unwashed a. 361:23
Artificial: All things are a. 70:26
Artist: a. cannot deny art 106:2
  A.s are not engineers of the soul 236:1
  a. will be judged 121:10
  a. will betray himself 110:30
  As an a., a man has no home 294:19
  Every a. writes his own autobiography 158:6
  Every good a. paints what he is 311:2
  God is really only another a. 308:20
  grant the a. his subject 217:2
  Great a.s have no country 290:12
  no man is born an a. 445:19
  one lucky bastard who's the a. 408:8
  Portrait of the A. as a Young Man 226:17
  too difficult for a.s 338:21
  true a. will let his wife starve 388:17
  What an a. dies in me! 293:8
Artiste: grands a.s n'ont pas de patrie 290:12
Ash: A. on an old man's sleeve 156:8
Ashamed: a. of confessing 83:15
  Hope maketh not a. 54:21
  more things a man is a. of 388:16
  Nor ever be a. 10:17
Ashes: All a. to the taste 89:26
  a. to a. 320:5
  beauty for a. 46:19
  E'en in our a. live their wonted fires 186:16
  Fell in the fire and was burnt to a. 184:8
  For the a. of his fathers 261:13
  handful of grey a. 123:3
  Her a. new-create another heir 359:7
  into a. all my lust 269:2
  little monograph on the a. 147:15
  splendid in a. 71:20
  turn to a. on the lips 287:12
  Worldly Hope . . . Turns A. 164:4
Ashlar: My new-cut a. 240:10
Ask: A., and it shall be given 49:22
  Do not a. Such knowledge is not for us 208:9
  not a dinner to *ask* a man to 221:19
Askelon: streets of A. 35:47
Asking: first time of a. 319:37
Asleep: Half a. as they stalk 192:25
  see now that I am a. 95:12
  We are laid a. In body 462:15
Aspect: With grave A. he rose 278:38
Aspen: light quivering a. 340:19
Aspersion: a. upon my parts of speech! 395:27
Aspidistra: biggest a. in the world 163:6

Asquith: A. is good and immoral 114:2
  calling Margot A. by her first name 13:23
Ass: a. his master's crib 44:30
  Egregiously an a. 374:17
  every a. thinks he may kick at him 305:1
  Get out, you blazing a.! 96:2
  greatest a. of the three 244:8
  great Hunter – the Wild A. 164:6
  law is a a. – a idiot 140:4
  write me down an a. 373:20
Assassin: copperheads and the a. 336:27
Assassins: que MM. les a. commencent 229:10
Assassination: absolutism moderated by a. 6:23
  Absolutism tempered by a. 290:1
  A. is the extreme form of censorship 389:11
  Despotism tempered by a. 326:15
  if the a. Could trammel up 365:5
Assay: a. so hard, so sharp the conquering 108:21
Assemblies: calling of a. 44:31
Asses: Mankind are the a. who pull 92:33
Assurance: a. of a man 351:27
  I'll make a. double sure 366:41
  on whom a. sits As a silk hat 157:7
Assure: a. you she's the dearest girl 137:22
Assyrian: A. came down like the wolf 93:4
  doted upon the A.s 46:35
Asthmatic: Freemason, and an a. 147:26
Astonish: A. me! 136:3
Astonished: a. at my own moderation 115:5
Astra: Sic itur ad a. 441:7
Astronomer: Confounding her a.s 202:14
Astronomy: A. teaches the correct use 250:7
Asunder: let no man put a. 319:45
  let not man put a. 50:34
Asylum: lunatics have taken over the a. 332:18
  padded lunatic a.s 460:21
Atahualpa: who strangled A. 262:7
Atheism: inclineth man's mind to a. 19:36
  never wrought miracle to convince a. 19:35
Atheist: a. . . . has no invisible means 79:20, 167:24
  a. under an atheistic king 243:7
  a. who finds creation so perfect 321:15
  By night an a. half believes a God 472:27
  female a. talks you dead 218:25
  I was a sacrilegious a. 336:16
  Rebel and A. too 145:31
  sort of village a. brooding 111:4
Athena: A.'s wisest son 89:15
Athenian: all the A.s and strangers 53:53
Athens: Another A. shall arise 391:6
  A., the eye of Greece 281:7
  Maid of A., ere we part 93:13
A-tishoo: A.! A.! We all fall down 297:27
Atlantic: drag the A. Ocean for whales 434:6
  on the other side of the A. 445:9
Atlas: immense, improbable a. 14:4
Atom: A.s or systems into ruin 313:27
  concurrence of a.s 303:11
  no evil in the a. 406:11
  Nor a. that his might 69:1
Atomic bomb 430:3
Atomies: team of little a. 378:30
Atom-stream: I saw the flaring a.s 420:21
Atrophy: poetry begins to a. 317:27
ATS: As beefy A. 32:16
Attached: a. to what is called the Tory 129:6
Attack: by his plan of a. 338:2

enemy tires, we a. 266:8
Attempt: a. and not the deed Confounds us 365:22
  a. to impose upon man 81:6
  By fearing to a. 368:6
Attendance: dance a. on their lordships 359:6
Attendre: J'ai failli a.! 258:6
Attends: Ne t'a. qu'à toi seul 244:13
Attention: cannot give their entire a. 31:19
  So a. must be paid 273:24
  Thank him for his kind a.s 110:23
  would wish to draw my a. 148:1
Attic: A. salt 310:12
  glory of the A. stage 12:8
Atticus: if A. were he 312:23
Attlee, Clement: 113:26
Attorney: rich a.'s . . . daughter 178:16
Attracted: a. by God or by nature 215:3
Attractions: A. for their coming week 14:27
Attribute: greatest moral a. of a Scotsman 26:2
Auburn: Sweet A.! loveliest village 180:16
Audace: De l'a., encore de l'a. 132:3
Audacity: a. of elected persons 453:22
Audience: a. takes him serious 329:4
  fit a. find 280:19
  understanding of English-speaking a.s 451:24
Augenblicke: Werd ich zum A. sagen 179:19
Auger: He bored with his a. 22:20
Augury: we defy a. 353:8
August: A. for the people 14:1
  sicklemen, of A. weary 381:9
Augustan: next A. age will dawn 445:9
Auguste: Lorsque A. buvait 169:2
Augustus: A. was a chubby lad 202:22
Aunt: a. was off to the theatre 30:17
  bad a.s and good a.s 459:11
  I had an a. in Yucatan
  maiden A. Took this fair day 421:32
  My a. died of influenza 389:6
Aurae: Quem mulcent a. 103:21
Auream: A. quisquis mediocritatem 208:18
Auri: A. sacra fames 440:20
Austen, Jane: 283:2 283:3 341:9
Austerity: Changing their high a. to delight 169:6
Austerlitz: Pile the bodies high at A. 337:2
  sun of A. 291:15
Austria: Don John of A. is going to the war 110:9
Austrian: A. army, awfully arrayed 5:23
Author: All the physicians and a.s 105:17
  a. and giver of all good things 319:16
  a. ought to write for the youth 165:15
  a.s could not endure being wrong 98:3
  a. who speaks about his own books 143:9
  Choose an a. as you choose a friend 330:12
  faults of great a.s 118:27
  go to the a. to get at *his* meaning 333:11
  like a distinguished a. 291:2
  shrimp of an a. 187:19
  They damn those a.s 111:20
  truth about its a. 110:28
  We a.s, Ma'am 143:36
  where is any a. in the world 363:29
  where one expected to see an a. 305:5
Authority: A. forgets a dying king 417:15
  Drest in a little brief a. 368:15
  faith that stands on a. 158:30
  in a. settled and calm 19:21
  reproofs from a. 19:20

tongue-tied by a. 386:6
  wilful defiance of military a. 338:3
Autobiography: artist writes his own a. 158:6
Autograph: a. as a souvenir 201:20
Autumn: a. always get me badly 249:26
  a. 'twas That grew the more by reaping 344:6
  breath of A.'s being 392:4
  I rose In rainy a. 426:11
  old A. in the misty morn 205:1
Autumnal: seen in one a. face 144:21
Autumn-evening: When the long, dark a.s come 73:14
Avalanche: Beware the awful a.! 256:25
Avarice: A., the spur of industry 212:4
  beyond the dreams of a. 286:16
  take up with a. 91:8
Avaunt: Hence, a.! ('tis holy ground) 186:22
Ave: a. atque vale 104:6
Ave Marie: Their songs were A.s 122:10
Avenger: Time, the a.! 90:13
Averni: Facilis descensus A. 440:26
Aversion: begin with a little a. 395:19
  indifference closely bordering on a. 406:21
Avi: a. numerantur avorum 442:3
Avis: Rara a. in terris 227:24
Avon: Sweet swan of A.! 225:26
Avow: a. to God made he 22:10
Awake: As one who a.s 78:33
  At last a. 74:12
  A., arise, or be for ever fall'n! 278:14
  A., my heart 67:23
  He will a. no more 389:26
  We're very wide a. 177:25
A-watering: a. the last year's crop 155:7
Away: a. with him! he speaks Latin 358:5
Awe: ever-increasing wonder and a. 229:8
  In a. of such a thing as I myself 359:13
  Make this bed with a. 141:31
  Stand in a. and sin not 37:21
  strike an a. into the beholders 410:22
Aweary: I am a., a. 420:23
Awful: Anything a. makes me laugh 246:12
Awl: All that I live by is with the a. 359:9
Awoke: a., and . . . it was a dream 80:31
Axe: a. is laid unto the root 48:38
  a.'s edge did try 268:25
  have you your sharp-edged a.s? 453:19
Axiom: long been an a. of mine 147:16
Axis: a. of the earth sticks out 203:32
Ay: it stinted and said 'A.' 378:27
Aye: A., and what then? 118:16
  no question makes of A.s and Noes 164:19
Ayr: Auld A., wham ne'er a town 85:14
Azure: With a., white, and red 149:2

B

B: B. bit it 296:4
Babblative: arts b. 401:25
Babe: as newborn b.s 57:30
  b. leaps up on his mother's arm 464:5
  Behold, a silly tender B. 402:2
  like a testy b. 384:3
  mouth of b.s and sucklings 37:25
  pretty B. all burning bright 401:28
  Sleep, Holy B. 103:6

to love the b. that milks me 365:12
Babel: stir Of the great B. 127:13
Babie: O hush thee, my b. 340:7
Babies: B. are bit 298:12
    B. haven't any hair 202:19
    but the b. in the cradles 76:23
    hates dogs and b. 332:7
    Other people's b. 198:30
    putting milk into b. 113:7
Baby: a bachelor's b. 14:9
    B. in an ox's stall 32:14
    B., sleep a little longer 423:13
    Dost thou not see my b. at my breast 344:12
    Down will come b. 296:24
    Prism! Where is that b.? 455:25
    Rock-a-bye b. 60:6
    when the first b. laughed 25:22
    Yes sir, That's my B. 229:6
    You must have been a beautiful b. 271:24
Babylon: B. is fallen 58:23
    Ere B. was dust 392:24
    How many miles to B.? 296:22
    I was a King in B. 198:2
    king of B. stood 46:34
    London is a modern B. 143:27
Bacchus: B. ever fair 149:35
    charioted by B. and his pards 232:4
Baccy: B. for the Clerk 240:21
Bach: If B. wriggles 88:5
    Johann Sebastian mighty B. 426:25
Bachelor: All reformers are b.s 286:17
    b., a solicitor, a Freemason 147:26
    b. of three-score 372:25
    B.'s fare; bread and cheese 411:10
    said I would die a b. 372:39
    Two old b.s were living in one house 251:8
Back: hath borne me on his b. 352:25
    little fleas upon their b.s 288:2
    one glance at the lettered b. 77:24
    One who never turned his b. 74:16
    Our b.s is easy ris 138:36
    to the b. o' beyont 340:25
    turn your b. upon the world 256:29
    With our b.s to the wall 190:4
Backgammon: sport I ever mastered was b. 218:15
Backward: o b. to comply 125:25
    Thou wilt fall b. 378:28
Backwards: walking b. for Christmas 274:4
Bacon: b.'s not the only thing 238:4
    people expect to find b. 104:24
Bacon, Francis: 225:30 225:31
    great Secretary of Nature . . . B. 445:29
    think how B. shined 314:10
    wise and large-browed Verulam 421:28
Bad: altogether irreclaimably b. 100:7
    and the b. unhappily 455:16
    antipathy of good to b. 316:5
    b. die late 133:16
    b. end unhappily 408:7
    B. men live to eat and drink 400:22
    B.'s the best of us 27:19
    being a little b. 368:31
    If we believe a thing to be b. 274:35
    nothing either good or b. 349:33
    so much b. in the best of us 202:11
    things that are b. for me 387:17
    When b. men combine 82:28

when I'm b. I'm better 451:3
    when she was b. she was horrid 257:18
Badness: b. of her b. 25:25
Baffled b., get up and begin again 75:15
    Though b. oft is ever won 93:2
Bag: one and all, b. and baggage 178:32
    steal the b.s to hold the crumbs 215:21
    though not with b. and baggage 345:20
    Three b.s full 296:6
    What did you take out of the b. 322:13
Baggage: I believe the b. loves me 120:16
Baghdad: B.-on-the-Subway 198:15
Bah: Sing 'B. to you' 177:43
Bailey: remember poor Miss B. 119:29
    Say the bells at Old B. 297:18
Bailiff: b.'s daughter of Islington 22:3
Baker: B. Street irregulars 148:5
Balance: redress the b. of the Old 98:21
    sitting in the b. 229:3
    small dust of the b. 45:35
    weighed in the b.s 47:4
    weighed the stars in the b. 110:11
Bald: b. as the bare mountain tops 12:29
Baldheaded: Go into it b. 258:26
Bale: undid his corded b.s 11:29
Balfour: Arthur is wicked and moral 114:2
    Mr B.'s Poodle 255:13
Ball: b. For them to play upon 376:5
    B. no question makes 164:19
    elliptical billiard b.s 177:29
    hopes have vanished, after the b. 194:7
    On a round b. 146:18
    Only wind it into a b. 61:4
    Three high b.s, and I think I'm St Francis 304:4
    Urge the flying b. 187:4
Ballad: grand old b. of Sir Patrick Spence 117:25
    permitted to make all the b.s 166:16
Ballad-monger: these same metre b.s 354:24
Ballast: our b. is old wine 306:18
Ballet: b. dance of bloodless categories 66:11
Balloon: Bring the b. of the mind 470:7
    if the moon's a b. 129:21
    There's something in a huge b. 464:26
Ballot: b. is stronger than the bullet 254:14
Balm: B. of hurt minds 365:26
    general b. th' hydroptic earth 146:1
    I wash away my b. 377:12
    no b. in Gilead 46:27
    wash the b. from an anointed king 376:27
Banality: b. of evil 9:27
Bananas: Yes, we have no b. 397:7
Band: brake their b.s in sunder 40:15
    Lonely Hearts Club B. 253:12
    strong as iron b.s 257:19
    when the b. begins to play 240:30
    when the wearied B. Swoons 213:8
    with b.s of love 47:9
    With b.s of rosy hue 212:19
Bandersnatch: shun The frumious B. 101:25
Bandusiae: O fons B. 209:2
Bane: Deserve the precious b. 278:25
    O'er his white b.s 23:20
    O what of the world's b.? 471:1
    Willie Michie's b.s 84:18
Bang: bigger b. for a buck 458:1
    Not with a b. but a whimper 156:17
Banish: B. plump Jack 354:19

Banished: Alone, a b. man 23:4
Banishment: bitter bread of b. 376:26
Banister: shape twisted on the b. 155:26
Banjo: wid my b. on my knee 168:7
Bank: As I sat on a sunny b. 7:5
  cashiers of the Musical B.s 87:31
  cried all the way to the b. 254:12
  Happiness: a good b. account 332:14
  I know a b. whereon thw wild thyme 371:38
  pregnant b. swelled up 145:1
  tyrannize over his b. balance 236:13
  What is robbing a b. 67:17
  Ye b.s and braes o' bonnie Doon 85:35
Banknotes: fill old bottles with b. 236:12
Bankrupt: B. of life 149:11
Banner: b. with the strange device 256:23
  Hang out the b.s 367:22
  royal b., and all quality 375:5
  star-spangled b. 236:6
  yet thy b., torn, but flying 90:10
Banquet: trifling foolish b. 379:5
Banquet-hall: Some b. deserted 287:15
Banqueting-hall: lonc sparrow through the b. 28:23
Bar: Back of the b., in a solo game 342:26
  Between their silver b.s 166:11
  gold b. of heaven 331:15
  look out through the same b.s 247:10
  no moaning of the B. 416:2
  Nor iron b.s a cage 258:13
  Stare out between b.s 335:2
  Till clomb above the eastern b. 117:2
  When I have crost the b. 416:4
  When I went to the B. 177:10
Barabbas: B. was a robber 53:33
  Now B. was a publisher 97:23
Barbarian: B.s, Philistines, and Populace 12:13
  become of us without b.s 104:8
  He is a b. 387:22
  young b.s all at play 90:16
Barbarousness: confess mine own b. 396:21
Barber: b. kept on shaving 163:7
  imprudently married the b. 166:24
Barco: b. sobre el mar 173:4
Bard: B.s of Passion and of Mirth 230:4
  b.s sublime 256:18
  blame not the b. 287:3
  Hail, B. triumphant! 124:10
  Hear the voice of the B.! 61:17
  If the B. was weather-wise 117:25
  place me among the lyric b.s 208:2
  To feed a b. 127:32
Bargain: Here's the rule for b.s 138:28
Barge: b. she sat in 343:28
Bark: dumb dogs, they cannot b. 46:15
  fatal and perfidious b. 277:11
  Like those Nicean b.s of yore 310:28
Barley: among the bearded b. 419:9
Barley-sheaves: He rode between the b. 419:12
Barn: He'll sit in a b. 297:11
Barncocks: Ere the b. say 193:4
Baron: While the Norman B. lay 5:21
Baronet: All b.s are bad 178:10
  b.s by dozens 176:10
  No little lily-handed B. he 422:24
Barracks: single men in b. 240:31
Barren: and cry, 'Tis all b. 405:10
  Most b. with best using 131:7

Barricade: At some disputed b. 341:23
  pile her b.s with dead 418:38
  These Christs that die upon the b.s 455:4
Barrier: Blessed b. between day and day 463:2
Barrow: grassy b.s of the happier dead 423:25
  so much depends upon a red wheel-b. 457:19
Barty: Vhere ish dat b. now? 252:17
Base: Why brand they us With b.? 361:32
Baseness: no b. we would hide 418:5
Bashan: String bulls of B. 37:43
Bashful: he wore a b. look 63:30
Bashfulness: a particular b. 2:13
Basia: Da mi basia mille 103:12
Basilisk: b. is sure to kill 174:12
Basil-pot: To steal my B. away from me 231:6
Basingstoke: hidden meaning – like 'B.' 178:13
Bastards: gods stand up for b.! 361:32
  I wish the b. dead 378:6
Bastardizing: twinkled on my b. 362:1
Bat: As b.s with baby faces 157:9
  b.s in the belfry 308:19
  Do b.s eat cats? 100:28
  flittering b.s 226:10
  On the b.'s back I do fly 381:17
  save where the weak-eye b. 119:11
  Suspicions . . . are like b.s 20:19
  Wool of b. and tongue of dog 366:36
Bataillons: pâle mort mêlait les sombres b. 211:18
Bate: Do I not b.? 354:31
Baths: Two walking b. 128:24
Bathing-machine: something between a large b. 177:14
Baton: b. of a marshal of France 291:19
Batsman: I am the b. and the bat 247:7
Battalions: not single spies, But in b. 352:9
  on the side of the big b. 433:8 443:1
Batte: Je veux qu'il b., moi 283:21
Battell: b. on the dragon blak 152:15
Batter: B. my heart 145:22
Batteries: b. of alluring sense 268:17
Battle: Agreed to have a b. 101:31
  b. and the breeze 97:20
  b. of giants 449:16
  b. rages loud and long 97:21
  b. to the strong 43:38
  Ben B. was a soldier bold 204:21
  drunk delight of b. with my peers 424:3
  far-off things And b.s long ago 466:23
  first blow is half the b. 182:19
  Fought all his b.s o'er again 150:2
  France has lost the b. 173:16
  in the midst of the b. 36:2
  It was not in the b. 125:35
  Lord mighty in b. 38:5
  Marriage is like . . . a field of b. 406:29
  Money is the sinews of b. 324:4
  noise of b. rolled 417:9
  Nor war, or b.'s sound 277:23
  Nothing except a b. lost 449:15
  openings b.s of all subsequent wars 300:18
  Our life was but a b. and a march 338:14
  smelleth the b. afar off 37:13
  souls of the brave that die in b. 115:10
  strife is o'er, the b. done 317:4
  was ever a b. like this 422:33
  When the b.'s lost and won 364:10
  Your b.s inspired me 226:30

Battle-day: Now the b. is past 158:1
Battledore: B. and shuttlecock 140:28
Battlefield: grass grows green on the b. 112:11
Battle-flags: b. were furled 419:31
Battle-line: far-flung b. 240:16
Battlements: Under my b. 364:30
Bauble: do with this b. 129:15
  Pleased with this b. still 314:5
Baukunst: B. eine erstarrte Musik nenne 180:13
Bawd: when a b. was carted 320:24
Bawdy-house: *pretence of keeping a b.* 223:10
Bay: Here, in this little b. 306:3
  In the B. of Biscay 109:2
  Somebody bet on the b. 168:3
Bayonets: build . . . a throne of b. 215:7
  opinion backed by b. 291:18
Bay-tree: flourishing like a green b. 38:16
Be: poem should not mean But b. 263:20
  To b. at all is to be religious 88:14
  To b. or not to b. 350:14
Beach: kick a pebble? On the b. 110:32
  only pebble on the b. 66:16
Beaches: we shall fight on the b. 112:20
Beachy Head: Birmingham by way of B. 110:13
Bead: b.s and prayer-books are the toys 314:5
  Venomous B. 342:16
Beadle: A b.! A parish b. 140:2
  'cept a b. on boxin' day 141:3
  very b. to a humorous sigh 363:26
Beadsman: To be your b. now 307:2
Beak: can take in his b. 272:27
  Take thy b. from out my heart 310:27
Beaker: b. full of the warm South 232:2
Be-all: b. and end-all 365:5
Beam: b. in the countenances 245:11
  b. . . . . in thine own eye 49:20
  Eternal co-eternal b. 279:10
Beamish: Come to my arms, my b. boy! 101:27
Bean: Full o' b.s and benevolence 409:19
  home of the b. and the cod 65:16
  way he eats jelly b.s 326:8
Bean-flowers: With the b.' boon 74:3
Beanrows: Nine b. will I have there 471:6
Bear: B. of Very Little Brain 274:23 274:27
  b. robbed of her whelps 42:18
  b. with a sore head 268:3
  Every hair of the b. reproduced 212:25
  Exit, pursued by a bear 189:6 384:18
  For every b. that ever there was 235:13
  funny How a b. likes honey 274:24
  Grizzly B. is huge and wild 209:21
  herds Of wandering b.s 215:21
  Let b.s and lions growl and fight 447:10
  never to sell the b.'s skin 244:15
  no dancing b. was so genteel 125:21
  Said Mr Wagg like a b. 397:14
  tunes for b.s to dance to 165:23
Bear-baiting: Puritan hated b. 262:17
Beard: built their nest in my b. 250:13
  endure a husband with a b. 372:28
  His b. was grizzled, no? 348:15
  King of Spain's b. 148:10
  long b.s and stinking armpits 185:6
  precious ointment . . . upon the b. 41:7
  until your b.s be grown 36:5
  When b.s wag all 433:17
Bearings: b. of this observation 137:34

Beast: after the Questing B. 452:20
  b., but a just b. 6:18
  b. is laid down in his lair 128:2
  b., no more 351:41
  b. that wants discourse of reason 348:5
  b. went to the well and drank 265:10
  b. With many heads 346:30
  b. with two backs 373:35
Beauty killed the B. 129:4
Both man and bird and b. 117:15
Brute b.s that have no understanding 319:38
chase had a b. in view 151:28
Cocoa is a vulgar b. 110:24
Either a b. or a god 10:8
  either a wild b. or a god 20:12
every b. of the forest 38:29
followed the questing b. 265:11
Four b.s full of eyes 58:12
Frets doubt the maw-crammed b.? 77:12
How like a b. was I! 125:25
like the b.s that perish 38:28
many-headed b. 423:27
more subtil than any b. 33:23
multitude . . . make one great b. 71:6
No b. so fierce 377:26
number of the b. 58:22
O judgment! thou art fled to brutish b.s 360:17
righteous man regardeth . . . his b. 42:3
subtlest b. of all the field 280:31
That Man is an UNGRATEFUL B. 31:2
The B. stands for 448:9
what he had figured as the b. in the jungle
  216:14
what rough b., its hour come round at last
  471:21
When people call this b. to mind 30:2
which the Blatant B. men call 403:5
Beastie: long-leggety b.s 6:21
  Wee, sleekit, cow'rin', tim'rous b. 85:27
Beastly: Don't let's be b. to the Germans 123:14
Beateth: as one that b. the air 55:12
Beating: hear the b. of his wings 68:12
Beatitude: ninth b. 316:16
Beatius: O quid solutis est b. curis? 103:16
Beatles: And the B.' first LP 247:19
Beatus: B. ille, qui procul negotiis 208:1
Beaumont: learned Chaucer, and rare B. 26:9
Beauties: saved for b. not his own 311:12
  You meaner b. of the night 468:3
Beautiful: b. . . . . as all truly great swindles 198:18
  b. and therefore to be wooed 357:30
  B. must be the mountains 68:5
  believe to be b. 289:1
  bid them own that thou art b. 390:21
  both were young, and one was b. 92:20
  good as thou art b. 416:36
  How b. . . . . are the feet 46:4
  most b. things in the world 333:14
  name of which was B. 80:20
  one of the b. people 253:5
  see, not feel, how b. they are 117:26
  Small is B. 339:7
  to find the b. 158:19
  told them how b. you are 332:11
  Too b. to last 27:5
Beauty: After the wildest b. in the world 302:17
  As I b., I'm not a great star 160:2

As much b. as could die 225:15
b. and length of days 412:5
b. and power 262:33
b. cold and austere 333:22
B. crieth in an attic 88:24
b. draws us with a single hair 315:18
b. faded has no second spring 308:12
B. for some provides escape 213:10
B. in distress is much the most 82:8
B. in things exists in the mind 212:5
B. is but a flower 292:20
B. is in the eye of the beholder 212:8
B. is momentary in the mind 406:8
B. is Nature's brag 275:32
B. is Nature's coin 275:31
b. is only sin deep 336:8
B. is truth, truth b. 231:25
B. itself doth of itself persuade 385:6
B. killed the B. 129:4
b. making beautiful old rhyme 386:24
B. provoketh thieves 344:23
B. sat bathing by a spring 289:20
B. sat with me 67:26
B.'s ensign yet Is crimson 380:10
B. stands In the admiration 281:3
b., though injurious 281:25
B. took from those who loved them 134:14
bereft of b. 380:23
breast that b. cannot tame 23:26
Coming in solemn b. 269:22
Could I come near your b. 357:31
daily b. in his life 375:19
dreamed that life was b. 6:5, 205:9
England, home, and b. 13:6, 66:14
For b. being the best 67:25
friend of B. in distress 93:27
give unto them b. for ashes 46:19
grew in b., side by side 197:14
Helen, thy b. is to me 310:28
her b. made The bright world dim 394:25
in your b.'s orient deep 98:29
Isle of B., fare thee well! 27:4
looked on B. bare 273:17
Look not thou on b.'s charming 340:26
Maybe she warn't a b. 421:10
maketh his b. to consume away 38:18
none of B.'s daughters 93:25
poetic truth and poetic b. 12:27
principle of b. in all things 234:16
She dwells with B. 231:29
she walks in b., like the night 93:8
simple b. and nought else 74:25
Such seems your b. still 386:21
swear that B. lives 166:2
terrible b. is born 470:16
thing of b. is a joy for ever 230:6
This is that Lady B. 331:23
Thy b. shall no more be found 269:2
'Tisn't b., so to speak 241:33
To B., Common Sense 272:10
What the imagination seizes as b. 233:23
Who dreamed that b. passes like a dream? 471:17
whose b. is past change 206:13
yet doth b., like a dial-hand 386:22
Beaux: Where none are b. 260:15
Bechstein: pawn the B. grand 123:17
Becket, Thomas: 198:6

Bed: Ample make this b. 141:31
And so to b. 307:8
As to a lover's b. 344:2
at night a b. of down 468:4
b. be blest 3:16
b. by night 181:9
Creep into thy narrow b. 11:10
drunk to b. 343:19
Each within our narrow b. 103:4
four of us about that b. 288:17
grave as little as my b. 235:10
Grief . . . Lies in his b. 361:17
he cursed him in b. 24:11
his b., the hard, cold ground 146:23
I haste me to my b. 385:21
I have to go to b. by day 407:12
I should of stood in b. 216:3
I toward thy b., Yasmin 166:4
keeping open b. 212:24
Lying in bed . . . altogether perfect 111:3
Must we to b. indeed? 407:21
my second best b. 387:13
never got out of one b. and bedstead 139:30
nicer to stay in b. 248:29
night the b. fell on my father 429:17
on her pensive b. 315:25
pendent b. and procreant cradle 365:4
remember thee upon my b. 39:8
Rose-leaves . . . for the belovèd's b. 394:6
sand in the porridge and sand in the b. 123:24
spare b. for my friends 307:21
take up thy b. 53:12
This b. thy centre is 146:13
Welcome to your gory b. 85:10
Who chariotest to their dark wintry b. 392:4
Will there be b.s for me 331:14
woman who goes to b. with a man 285:9
Beddes: lever have at his b. heed 107:19
Bedeuten: was soll es b. 197:2
Bed-fellow: acquaints a man with strange b.s 380:41
Bedonebyasyoudid: Mrs B. is coming 237:24
Bedpost: on the B. Overnight 330:15
Bedroom: what you do in the b. 96:20
Bedspring: triumphant twang of a b. 307:30
Bed-staff: twinkling of a b. 343:1
Bed-time: I would it were b., Hal 355:1
Bee: b. has quit the clover 239:31
b.'s kiss, now 75:7
b. with honied thigh 276:14
brisk as a b. in conversation 220:14
helmet now shall make a hive for b.s 307:1
How doth the little busy b. 447:12
I am the b. 163:21
later flowers for the b.s 233:17
Love . . . like a b. 256:1
Murmured like a noontide b. 394:15
murmuring of innumerable b.s 422:20
Some b. had stung it newly 409:8
that bringest home the b. 97:19
Where the b. sucks 381:17
Beechen: spare the b. tree 97:3
Beech-tree: appointment with a b. 429:1
Under yonder b. 272:2
Beef: English an article as a b. 195:7
great eater of b. 382:27
roast b. of England 162:19
stole a piece of b. 298:2

Beer: all b. and skittles 96:3
   chronicle small b. 374:15
   Come, my lad, and drink some b. 224:2
   felony to drink small b. 358:3
   foost-rate lager b. 252:16
   goned afay mit de lager b. 252:18
   more inseparable than B. and Britannia 400:11
   O B.! O Hodgson 95:17
   other b.s cannot reach 3:3
   your justice would freeze b. 273:21
Beerbohm, Max 456:20
Beer-sheba: From Dan even to B. 35:36
   travel from Dan to B. 405:10
Beethoven: B.'s Fifth Symphony 167:19
Beetle: b. and the bat detract 221:26
   intolerable . . . to a black b. 271:7
   poor b., that we tread upon 368:20
   Save where the b. wheels 186:1
   scarce so gross as b.s 362:36
   shard-borne b. with his drowsy hums 366:17
   Where the b. winds 119:11
Before: Gone b. 245:4
   When she has walked b. 181:16
Beg: Better . . . to die than to b. 48:26
   to b. I am ashamed 52:28
Begetter: only b. of these insuing sonnets 385:10
Beggar: Bare-footed came the b. maid 415:18
   B. that I am 349:35
   Be not made a b. 48:12
   Stiff-necked Glasgow b.! 240:8
   When b.s die, there are no comets seen 360:1
   whiles I am a b., I will rail 161:13
Beggar-maid: King Cophetua loved the b. 379:7
Beggary: no vice but b. 361:13
   There's b. in the love 343:15
Begin: anything That other men b. 359:28
   Then I'll b. 247:9
Beginning: As it was in the b. 318:17
   Begin at the b. 101:21
   b., a middle, and an end 10:4
   b. and the end 58:38
   b. of the end 414:9
   Better is the end . . . than the b. 43:28
   end of Job . . . more than his b. 37:17
   In my b. is my end 155:33
   In the b. God created 33:13
   In the b. was the Word 52:48
   mighty things from small b.s grow 150:11
   not even the b. of the end 113:5
   Nothing so difficult as a b. 91:29
   told you from the b. 45:36
   true b. of our end 372:17
Begot: How b., how nourishèd 370:1
   thing b. Within a pair of minutes 242:22
Begotten: B. not made 319:21
Begriffe: Denn eben, wo B. fehlen 179:20
Beguiled: Thou sleep'st too long, thou art b. 397:24
Beguine: begin the b. 316:25
Begun: He who has b. has half done 207:16
   I have not yet b. to fight 224:18
Behave: can never prompt b. 248:17
   Now mind . . . you b. yourself! 138:4
Behaviour: gets sent down for indecent b. 448:1
   immediate check to loose b. 404:9
   upon his good b. 91:38
   With so much sweet b. 121:7
Behind: Get thee b. me 50:24

thy tail hangs down b. 240:19
Behold: B. the man! 53:34
Beholder: in the eye of the b. 212:8
Being: b., breathing thoughtful breath 466:16
   B., erect upon two legs 141:10
   darkness of mere b. 227:2
   dignity of thinking b.s 219:18
   If God were not a necessary B. 430:8
   move, and have our b. 53:55
   odd fork in B.'s road 142:4
   Thou art B. and Breath 69:1
   Thou hadst a b. 328:14
Belfry: bats in the b. 308:19
Belgrade: by battery besieged B. 5:23
Belgrave: Hearts . . . May beat in B. Square 177:9
Belial: Hand and foot in B.'s gripe 78:24
   sons of B. had a glorious time 149:24
   thou man of B. 36:8
   wander forth the sons Of B. 278:16
Belief: It is my b., Watson 147:17
   Let me assert my firm b. 329:14
   One in whom persuasion and b. 461:25
   various modes of man's b. 73:31
   will that b. be the true one? 115:9
   within the prospect of b. 364:17
Believe: B. it or not 327:22
   I do not b. . . . . I know 227:6
   I don't b. there's no sich a person 139:2
   Lord, I b. 51:37
   not b. it though himself 99:3
   temerity to b. in nothing 433:10
   They didn't b. me! 332:11
   to b. and take for granted 20:31
Believed: b. . . . . that there are witches 71:1
   What has been b. always 440:1
Believer: In a b.'s ear 294:11
Believing: B. where we cannot prove 417:23
Bell: B., book and candle 361:16
   b. invites me 365:20
   B.s are profane 224:22
   b.s of hell 7:7
   b. strikes one 472:21
   by battery besieged B. 5:23
   cost a passing b. 28:22
   Forlorn! the very word is like a b. 232:7
   for whom the b. tolls 146:21
   From the b., b., b., b. 310:17
   I'll b. the cat 147:2
   Like sweet b.s jangled 350:22
   matched in mouth like b.s 372:10
   merry as a marriage b. 89:21
   Oh, noisy b.s, be dumb 210:16
   Ring out, wild b.s, to the wild sky 418:22
   ring the b.s of Heaven 202:12
   sexton toll'd the b. 204:24
   Silence the dreadful b.! 374:21
   Sounds ever after as a sullen b. 355:12
   surly sullen b. 386:8
   They now *ring* the b.s 445:12
   'Tis the b.s of Shandon 321:21
   Twilight and evening b. 416:4
   Unto the B. at Edmonton 125:7
   Who will b. the cat? 135:14
   with a tower and b.s 128:4
   With silver b.s, and cockle shells 297:9
Belles: b.s ringeth to evensonge 195:2
Bellman: owl that shrieked, the fatal b. 365:21

Belly: Embrace me, b. 15:5
filled his b. with the husks 52:26
he who does not mind his b. 221:18
noise was in the b.'s belly 265:10
something a round b. 355:17
Thy b. is like an heap of wheat 44:26
Upon thy b. shalt thou go 34:2
Whose God is their b. 56:26
Bellyful: not by cups, but by the b. 402:22
Rumble thy b.! 362:15
Belong: devils . . . b. to us 249:19
where do they all b. 253:7
Beloved: never be b. by men 60:13
Only b., and loving me 124:14
she b. knows nought that knows not this 381:34
Belt: see a b. without hitting below it 13:21
Bend: b. but do not break 244:4
Though she b.s him 257:14
Benedick: B. the married man 372:27
Benediction: Perpetual b. 464:13
Benefacta: Siqua recordanti b. 104:2
Benefice: dreams he of another b. 379:1
Beneficium: Inopi b. bis dat 413:12
Benevolence: b. which extends 132:7
lazy glow of b. 73:31
Benison: For a b. to fall 200:22
Bennett, Arnold 451:16
Bent: follow his natural b. 241:3
They are not our b. 178:7
to the top of my b. 351:19
Beoplesh: I tont dink mooch of b. 252:12
Beresford, Charles: 112:9
Berkeley: Nightingale sang in B. Square 269:20
When Bishop B. said 92:4
Berliner: Ich bin ein b. 235:23
Bermoothes: still-vexed B. 380:31
Bermuda: Where the remote B.s ride 268:12
Berries: pluck your b. harsh and crude 276:36
Two lovely b. moulded on one stem 372:5
Berry: God could have made a better b. 88:25
Berth: death which happened in his b. 204:24
Berye: as broun as is a b. 107:15
Beschrankung: In der B. zeigt sich erst 180:4
Beset: Who so b. him round 81:1
Beside: Like to be B. the Seaside 179:7
Besoin: b. d'un plus petit que soi 244:5
Best: all b. things are thus confused with ill 392:26
All is b. though we oft doubt 281:30
all is for the b. 442:9
all that's b. of dark and bright 93:8
any other person's b. 195:15
Bad's the b. of us 27:19
B. and brightest, come away! 394:9
B. be yourself 72:28
b. is the enemy of the good 442:15
b. is yet to be 77:11
b. that has been known and said 12:30
b. thing God invents 74:25
b. things carried to excess 112:3
b. thing to be up and go 159:20
b. which has been thought and said 12:12
Fear not to touch the b. 325:7
feels the noblest – acts the b. 21:10
He . . . that knew it b. 19:22
how much the b. 168:11
it is not looking at its b. 148:11
It was the b. of times 141:26

Sat we two, one another's b. 145:1
we will do our b. 113:2
what began b. can't end worst 72:22
Best-humoured: Thou b. man 181:23
Bestial: what remains is b. 374:25
Bestowed: Divinely b. upon man 128:1
Best-seller: b. . . . somehow sold well 65:2
Bet: bet you which one would fly first 433:28
You b. I would! 1:5
Bête: qui nous distingue des autres b.s 27:15
Bethel: O God of B. 144:10
Bethlehem: O come ye to B. 299:1
O little town of B. 70:2
Slouches towards B. to be born 471:21
Betray: All things b. thee 427:13
b.s instead of serving 81:12
Betrogen: die will b. sein 66:20
Better: always trying to get the b. 245:25
b. to have fought and lost 115:24
doth make men b. be 225:16
far, far b. thing that I do 141:30
far, far b. thing to have a firm anchor 172:4
for b. for worse 319:42
Gad! she'd b.! 100:22
getting b. and b. 123:6
got to admit it's getting b. 253:9
He is no b., he is much the same 17:20
if way to the B. there be 192:24
I see b. things and approve 302:2
nae b. than he should be 84:9
no b. than you should be 27:20
Striving to b., oft we mar 362:4
Who rises from prayer a b. man 272:23
Betwixt: So I fall b. and between 211:1
Beware: And all should cry, B.! B.! 118:6
both false and friendly be, B.! 256:10
Bewitched: B., Bothered and Bewildered 194:21
Bewrapt: B. past knowing to what he was going
193:5
Beyond: to the back of b. 340:25
Bezonian: Under which king, B.? 356:17
Bias: Commodity, the b. of the world 361:12
Bibendum: nunc est b. 208:14
Bibble-babble: Leave thy vain b. 383:31
Bible: B. is literature 337:9
B.s laid open 199:24
English B. 262:33
gentle B. beast 289:19
Just knows . . . her B. true 127:36
No man . . . knows even his B. 12:17
reads the B, day and night 60:23
studie was but litel on the B. 107:23
that book is the B. 13:4
To read in de B. 175:6
Bicycle: b. made for two 131:1
Bid: do as you're b. 154:6
Bidding: To her b. she could bow 339:25
Bier: bore him barefaced on the b. 352:13
Borne on the b. 385:14
Big: you used to be b. 456:27
Bigamist: appealed to all the instinctive b. 213:5
Bigamy: b., sir, is a crime 284:18
Big-endian: B.s and small-endians 410:23
Bigger: b. they come, the harder 165:16
Bike: He got on his b. 415:13
Bill: b. will hold more than his belican 272:27
god mustn't pay hotel b.s 67:3

Half a crown in the b. 140:21
inflammation of his weekly b.s 91:18
likeness in the red b.s 138:7
On the same b. 250:5
Roaring B. (who killed him) 30:29
wife and children but as b.s of charges 19:11
Billabong: camped by a b. 305:19
Bill Bailey: Won't you come home, B. 98:22
Billboard: b. lovely as a tree 292:16
Billee: youngest he was little B. 425:26
Billet-doux: patches, bibles, b. 315:15
Billiards: Let's to b. 343:32
to play b. was the sign 402:12
Billow: b.s smooth and bright 101:33
falling shower, A breaking b. 390:2
Who take the ruffian b.s by the top 355:31
Billy: heart to poke poor B. 184:8
waited till his b. boiled 305:19
way for B. and me 203:14
Binnorie: *bonnie milldams o' B.* 22:6
Biographers: first of b. 262:21
poets, historians, b., etc. 118:26
Biographies: essence of innumerable b. 99:16
Biography: B. . . . can never be wholly true 318:2
B. is about chaps 31:25
b. . . . life without theory 143:16
history . . . but the b. of great men 99:31
man is nobody unless his b. 432:7
no history; only b. 158:26
Birches: swinger of b. 169:21
Bird: Attic b. Trills 281:8
B. in a Gilded Cage 245:1
b. of the air shall carry 44:3
b. of wonder dies 359:7
b.s began to sing 297:31
B.s build 206:18
B.s in the high Hall-garden 420:30
B.s in their little nests agree 447:11
b.s of the air have nests 49:31
b.s of the winged trees 426:10
b.s outside desperate to get in 285:21
b.s sit brooding in the snow 364:8
B. thou never wert 394:17
b. to others flew 459:3
b. with broad wings flying 249:22
chant, ye little b.s 85:35
eagle suffers little b.s to sing 381:30
fine feathers . . . fine b.s 3:22
full of b.s' cries 270:5
household b., with the red stomacher 144:27
If b.s confabulate or no 126:10
I heard a b. at dawn 405:4
Irks care the crop-full b.? 77:12
I see all the b.s are flown 106:18
like a b. on the wing 65:20
listen to the b.s and winds 176:1
Lo! the B. is on the Wing 163:26
My heart is like a singing b. 331:1
nest of singing b.s 220:12
No b., but an invisible thing 467:8
No b. can contradict 15:17
no b.s sing 231:7
No b.s were flying overhead 102:2
no further than a wanton's b. 379:20
O cuckoo, shall I call thee b. 467:7
one of the early b.s 121:21
perceive a young b. in this bush 250:12

pious b. with the scarlet breast 465:31
prophet still, if b. or devil 310:26
rare b. on earth 227:24
self-begotten b. 281:28
She is alone the Arabian b. 347:3
sing like b.s i' the cage 363:9
spray the B. clung to 75:30
spread in the sight of the b. 41:21
Sweet b., that shunn'st the noise 276:6
time of singing b.s 44:20
Two fairer b.s I yet did never see 403:13
wast not born for death, immortal B. 232:7
We think no B.s so happy as we 251:4
What b. so sings 260:9
When b.s do sing 346:12
When thou my b. untwined 398:1
widow b. sate mourning for her love 390:12
With this her solemn b. 279:34
Yesterday the b. of night did sit 359:23
Bird-cage: like a summer b. 449:2
Birdie: What does little b. say 423:12
Bird-song: Of b. at morning 407:24
Birkenhead: Lord B. is very clever 13:22
Birmingham: no great hopes from B. 16:29
to B. by way of Beachy Head 110:13
wanted to go to B. 255:12
When Jesus came to B. 409:4
Birnam: Great B. wood to high Dunsinane hill 367:1
Birth: at the hour of our b. 155:22
B., and copulation, and death 156:32
b. is certain 33:11
had some thought of dying at b. 337:25
no cure for b. and death 337:13
one that is coming to b. 301:17
Our b. is but a sleep 464:7
presided o'er my b. 60:30
subject to his b. 348:18
three events . . . : b., life, and death 243:5
time draws near the b. of Christ 417:35
Birthday: Because the b. of my life 331:2
B.s? yes, in a general way 405:1
Happy b. to you 201:11
My b. began with the water-Birds 426:10
remembers a woman's b. 170:17
Birth-rate: provoke the world Into a rising b. 170:24
Birthright: Esau selleth his b. 34:25
sell our b. for a mess of potash 446:6
Biscuit: as dry as the remainder b. 345:7
hyacinths and b.s 337:5
Bishop: B. and abbot and prior 24:8
contradicting a b. 223:16
How can a b. marry? 399:28
without hitting the niece of a b. 300:29
No b., no king 216:10
Bisier: semed b. than he was 107:21
Bison: walls with heads of b. 264:11
Bisy: No-wher so b. a man 107:21
Bit: growled and b. him till he bled 202:26
I'll cut b.s orf you 450:8
Went mad and b. the man 182:36
Bitch: called John a Impudent B. 166:14
Mr Wild, why b.? 162:22
old b. gone in the teeth 317:24
son and heir of a mongrel b. 362:6
Bite: b. the hand that fed them 82:26
man recovered of the b. 182:37
wish he would *bite* . . . my generals 174:32

Biting: His b. is immortal
Bitterness: b. of death is past 35:45
  b. of my soul 45:28
  I realize . . . the b. of life 102:28
Black: as b. as b. might be 23:18
  b., but O! my soul is white 62:18
  b. men fought on the coast 262:4
  B.'s not so b. 98:15
  for the b. man there is only one destiny 161:8
  Half b. half white 317:17
  I am b., but comely 44:17
  looking for a b. hat 66:1
  not so b. as they are painted 256:2
  so long as it's b. 167:5
  thou read'st b. 60:23
  too b. for heav'n 150:21
  Why do you always wear b.? 108:34
Blackberries: as plentiful as b. 354:13
Blackbird: down came a b. 297:31
  b.'s tune, And May, and June 74:3
  Four and twenty b.s 297:31
  full of b.s 2:19
  O b., what a boy 70:11
Blackguard: b.s both 91:33
  Whatever brute and b. made the world 209:24
Blackness: b. of darkness for ever 58:2
Bladder: blows a man up like a b. 354:16
  swim on b.s 358:21
Blade: B. on the feather 122:22
  vorpal b. went snicker-snack 101:26
  with b., with bloody blameful b. 372:18
Blake: B. is damned good to steal from 171:12
Blame: Alike reserved to b. 312:23
  b. not the bard 287:3
  In part to b. is she 301:21
  murderous, bloody, full of b. 387:4
  neither is most to b. 412:31
  Whatever you b. 188:15
Blank: b., my lord. She never told her love 383:14
Blanket: this b. round you fold 102:30
  tossed in the b. yesterday 104:19
Blasphemies: All great truths begin as b. 387:14
Blasphemy: b. against the Holy Ghost 50:6
  B. itself could not survive 111:8
  in the soldier is flat b. 368:16
Blast: Bleak blows the b. 98:11
  Me howling b.s drive devious 126:9
  only in trances of the b. 117:32
  spread his wings on the b. 93:5
  wert thou in the cauld b. 85:7
Blazon: this eternal b. 349:1
Bless: except thou b. me 34:28
  God b. us every one! 137:2
Blessed: be the name of the Lord 36:34
  B. is he that considereth the poor 38:19
  b. them unaware 117:6
  b. you, bear onward b. me 396:16
  Her children . . . call her b. 43:11
  I *have been* b. 93:3
  it is twice b. 370:9
  Judge none b. 48:9
Blessedness: gazing on b. 306:6
  in single b. 371:18
  let him ask no other b. 100:3
Blessing: all the b.s of his life 319:10
  b.s in disguise 200:23
  continual dew of thy b. 318:31

full of b.s 462:23
  glass of b.s standing by 199:20
  I had most need of b. 365:24
  Lord, dismiss us with Thy b. 80:2
  Praise God from whom all b.s flow 235:11
  When thou dost ask me b. 363:9
Blind: accompany my being b. 307:26
  b. man in a dark room 66:1
  both extremely b. 94:1
  drawing-down of b.s 302:9
  eyes to the b. 37:7
  halt, and the b. 52:21
  If the b. lead the b. 50:19
  I have a right to be b. 293:4
  one-armed b. man in a dark room 459:20
  Painting is a b. man's profession 308:21
Blinded: B. ere yet a-wing 192:13
Blindness: triple sight in b. keen 233:6
Bliss: B. in our brows 343:20
  b. in proof 387:5
  B. was it in that dawn to be alive 465:27
  deep, deep b. of the double-bed 96:21
  dream of perfect b. 27:5
  excels all other b. 153:1
  farewell earth's b. 292:19
  my wingèd hours of b. 97:17
  promise of pneumatic b. 157:11
  sum of earthly b. 280:25
  Thou source of all my b. 181:15
  What is b., and which the way? 224:2
Blitz: b. of a boy is Timothy Winters 104:7
Bloaters: If you were queen of b. 205:5
Block: each b. cut smooth 317:18
  old b. itself 81:24
  You b.s, you stones 359:11
Blockhead: bookful b., ignorantly read 313:23
  hear his death, ye b.s! 219:7
  I call thee b. 62:24
Blood: b. and iron 59:25
  b. and judgement are so well co-mingled 351:3
  B. and soil 132:5
  b. creeps, and the nerves prick 418:3
  b. of the martyrs is the seed 424:34
  b. of this just person 51:24
  b. she has spilt 124:18
  b., toil, tears and sweat 112:18
  cant all be of the Blood royal can we 13:13
  Christ's b. streams in the firmament 267:3
  haste to shed innocent b. 46:16
  he today that sheds his b. with me 357:19
  He walks again on the Seas of B. 397:18
  His b. be on us 51:25
  His b. upon the rose 310:15
  Hot and rebellious liquors to the b. 344:29
  If b. be the price of admiralty 240:23
  in b. Stepped in so far 366:34
  Inhabits our frail b. 383:29
  I smell the b. of a British man 362:28
  I smell the b. of an Englishman 296:14
  kiss the b. From these pale feet 392:23
  nothing like b., sir 425:20
  O! the b. more stirs 353:31
  pure and eloquent b. 146:5
  rather have b. on my hands 187:23
  red b. reigns in the winter's pale 384:21
  shed his b. for his country 330:4
  smell of the b. still 367:14

summon up the b. 357:3
They waded thro' red b. 23:16
Tiber foaming with much b. 318:5
to have had so much b. in him 367:12
voice of thy brother's b. 34:8
washed in the b. of the Lamb 202:20
We be of one b. 241:16
welt'ring in his b. 150:3
When b. is nipped 364:7
when b. is their argument 357:10
white in the b. of the Lamb 58:16
Whose b. is fet from fathers 357:4
Whoso sheddeth man's b. 34:18
Who thicks man's b. with cold 116:30
Will all great Neptune's ocean wash this b.
   365:28
Yet I'll not shed her b. 375:21
Yet still the b. is strong 341:11
Young b. must have its course 237:17
Bloody: Be b., bold, and resolute 366:40
   come out, thou b. man 36:8
   Not b. likely 389:8
Bloom: b. is gone, and with the b. go I 12:4
   b. sae fresh and fair 85:35
   Each opening sweet, of earliest b. 119:8
   hung with b. along the bough 210:5
   sight of vernal b. 279:13
   snatched away in beauty's b. 93:7
   sort of b. on a woman 25:28
Blossom: b. and with briddes roune 5:11
   Cut off even in the b.s of my sin 349:9
   It b.s through the year! 395:21
   Love's perfect b. only blows 305:21
   Under the b. that hangs on the bough 381:17
   With here a b. sailing 415:22
Blot: art to b. 316:1
   b. out his name 58:9 75:19
   bright b. Upon this gloomy scene 393:32
   does the sun and moon b. out 60:24
   inky b.s, and rotten parchment bonds 376:18
Blow: apostolic b.s and knocks 87:10
   bless the hand that gave the b. 151:30
   b. hot and cold 3:24
   b. in cold blood 388:29
   first b. is half the battle 182:19
   he who gets his b. in fust 389:16
   Remember thy swashing b. 378:24
   vile b.s and buffets of the world 366:12
   will you never b. again 389:9
   word and a b. 379:31
Bludgeoning: Under the b.s of chance 197:25
Blue: darkly, deeply, beautifully b. 91:35
   drink till all look b. 167:10
   Eyes of most unholy b.! 286:24
   Floating in the B. 274:25
   grappling in the central b. 419:30
   one of Nature's agreeable b.s 124:16
   Presbyterian true b. 87:8
   too expressive to be b. 11:2
   way out there in the b. 273:25
Blume: Du bist wie eine Blume 197:3
Blunder: frae mony a b. free us 85:25
   it is a b. 65:19
   so grotesque a b. 31:27
Blunderbuss: b. against religion and morality
   220:26
Blundered: Someone had b. 415:26
Blush: beautiful as a woman's b. 246:21

bring a b. into the cheek 140:11
To make man b. 93:16
with a b. retire 137:38
Blushes: turn off the light to spare my b. 217:6
Blut: B. und Boden 132:5
Board: Love and the B. school 29:19
   struck the b., and cried 199:7
Boarding-house: landlady of a b. 250:4
Boasteth: buyer . . . then he b.
Boat: beautiful pea-green b. 250:24
   b.s against the current 165:9
   Give a man a b. he can sail 428:22
   if men are together in a b. 190:9
   leathern b.s begin to hoist 269:5
   messing about in b.s 184:12
   slow b. to China 256:4
   Speed, bonny b. 65:20
   they were there to meet the b. 329:7
   through a sewer in a glass-bottomed b. 283:7
   to see no b.s upon the River 307:17
   Until I have a little b. 464:26
Boaters: water, dropped by b. 205:5
Boatman: B., do not tarry! 97:9
Bob: thirty b. a week to keep a bride 132:16
Boche: well-killed B. 326:4
Bodies: b. are buried in peace 48:30
   friendless b. of unburied men 449:3
   Pile the b. high at Austerlitz 337:2
Bodkin: With a bare b. 350:14
Body: As a b. everyone is single 200:25
   as stout a b. as the best 105:9
   beneficial for the b. 321:20
   b. gets its sop 72:27
   b. of a weak and feeble woman 157:26
   Casting the b.'s vest aside 268:22
   commit his b. to the deep 320:6
   commit his b. to the ground 320:5
   demd, moist, unpleasant b. 139:20
   Find thy b. by the wall 11:12
   Gave His b. to that pleasant country's earth
      377:8
   Gin a b. meet a b. 84:2
   her b. thought 146:5
   Here in the b. pent 286:3
   human b. is sacred 453:15
   informing and filling some other b. 234:9
   in this b. the embodied soul 33:9
   keep under my b. 55:13
   more familiar with Africa than my own b. 300:9
   no B. distinct from his Soul 63:5
   of the mind, as well as of the b. 196:1
   Our b. why do we forbear? 145:4
   sound mind in a sound b. 228:7
   Still carry his b. around 170:21
   Upon my buried b. lie 27:25
   What this tumultuous b. now denies 69:23
   When that this b. did contain a spirit 355:6
   Whether in the b. 56:4
   Whose b. nature is 313:33
   with a b. filled and vacant mind 357:13
   with my b. I thee worship 319:44
   Your b. is the temple 55:6
Boehme: Another B. with a tougher book 79:5
Bog: To an admiring b. 142:3
   to its bottom shook the b. 311:15
Bognor: Bugger B.! 175:4
Boil: b. at different degrees 159:13
Boire: B. sans soif 27:15

Bois: *Nous n'irons plus aux b.* 24:3
Bois Bou-long: As I walk along the B. 176:7
Bokes: As olde b. maken us memorie 108:8
   Twenty b. clad in blak or reed 107:19
Bold: Be b., be b. 403:3
   b. bad man! 402:27
   Here's to the b. and free! 293:12
Boldest: b. held his breath 97:1
Boldness: B. be my friend! 347:4
   b. is a child of ignorance 19:24
   b. is an ill-keeper of promise 19:25
Bolingbroke, Viscount: 220:26
Bolt: like the b., And the breech 326:11
Bomb: art of making b.s 114:4
   b. them back into the Stone Age 252:19
   Come, friendly b.s 32:23
Bombazine: B. would have shown 173:14
Bombing: Learn to get used to it 112:21
   We begin b. in five minutes 326:9
Bond: b. unknown to me 465:14
   Let him look to his b. 369:31
   'Tis not in the b. 370:12
Bondage: disguise our b. as we will 287:16
   modern b. of rhyming 277:31
   in a b.'s key 369:19
Bondman: So every b. . . . bears The power 359:24
   Who is there so base that would be a b.? 360:13
Bondsmen: Hereditary b.! 89:18
Bone: as curs mouth a b. 111:25
   B. and Skin, two millers thin 88:27
   b. of my b.s 33:21
   bracelet of bright hair about the b. 146:4
   can these b.s live? 46:37
   come to lay his weary b.s 358:27
   curst be he that moves my b.s 387:12
   full of dead men's b.s 51:8
   Give the dog a b. 264:14
   Grief never mended no broken b.s 141:24
   grind his b.s to make my bread 296:14
   I am come to lay my weary b.s among you
      460:13
   I may tell all my b.s 38:1
   mocked the dead b.s 378:1
   no b. to pick with graveyards 28:11
   Rattle his b.s over the stones 295:13
   valley . . . full of b.s 46:36
   When rattling b.s together fly 151:8
   your b.s are very brittle 407:20
Bonfire: primrose way to the everlasting b. 366:1
Bong-Tree: land where the B. grows 251:1
Bonjour: *Et puis – b.!* 285:26
Bono: *Cui b.?* 114:22
Bononcini: Signor B., Compared to Handel 88:26
Bon soir: *Et puis – b.!* 285:26
Bonum: *Summum b.* 114:15
Boobies: only good for b. 244:11
Booby: give her b. for another 174:19
Boojum: Snark *was* a B., you see 102:27
Book: adversary had written a b. 37:8
   against b.s the Home Secretary is 448:14
   all b.s else appear so mean 79:26
   and a few friends and many b.s 124:14
   Another damned, thick, square b.! 179:6
   author in his b. 165:24
   base authority from others' b.s 363:19
   b. in question 147:3
   b. may be amusing with numerous errors 182:23
   b. of knowledge fair 279:14

B. of Life begins with a man and a woman
   455:36
b. of Moons defend ye! 5:17
b.'s a b. 92:23
B.s are good enough in their own way 407:4
B.s are not absolutely dead things 282:15
B.s cannot always please 128:6
b.s, the arts, the academes 363:32
B.s think for me 246:2
b.s will speak plain 20:1
b. that furnishes no quotation 306:12
b. that is not a year old 159:11
b. to kill time 261:4
borrowers of b.s – those mutilators 245:29
but his b.s were read 30:27
Camerado, this is no b. 453:20
dainties that are bred in a b. 363:28
Deep versed in b.s 281:10
disease of writing b.s 286:2
do most by B.s 70:15
do not throw this b. about 30:20
do you read b.s *through?* 222:8
Even bad b.s are b.s 184:23
genius I had when I wrote that b. 411:28
gets at the substance of a b.. directly 242:7
God has written all the b.s 88:10
Go, litel b. 108:30
Go, little b., and wish to all 407:29
good b. is the best of friends 433:6
good b. is the precious life-blood 282:17
her b.s have grown fewer 121:28
Hers of the B. 323:4
If my b.s had been any worse 106:9
I'll burn my b.s! 267:6
I'll drown my b. 381:16
I never read a b. before reviewing it 400:7
I never read b.s 322:14
jolly good b. whereon to look 458:10
kill a good b. 282:16
Kiss the b.'s outside 125:1
Knowing I loved my b.s 380:30
let my b.s be then the eloquence 385:19
making b.s is a skilled trade 243:9
man behind the b. 159:8
moral or an immoral b. 456:2
Nature's infinite b. of secrecy 343:17
needed not the spectacles of b.s 151:33
nodding by the fire, take down this b. 472:4
No furniture so charming as b.s 399:27
Not on his picture, but his b. 225:18
No two people read the same b. 458:2
Of making many b.s 44:14
O moral Gower, this b. I directe 108:31
one discovers in writing a b. 305:4
one English b. and one only 13:4
out of the b. of life 58:9
poring over miserable b.s 420:3
read any good b.s recently? 327:19
reading of all good b.s 135:11
Read of in b.s 24:8
sat down to write a b. 222:1
Some b.s are to be tasted 20:32
Some b.s are undeservedly forgotten 15:21
this square old yellow B. 77:23
to make one b. 222:13
true University . . . collection of b.s 99:32
unbent her mind . . . over a b. 245:24
What's the use of a b. 100:27

moves the b. 92:34
Out of the b. of the harmless earth 353:30
Bower: b. we shrined to Tennyson 192:11
my skiey b.s 390:15
Bowl: golden b. be broken 44:12
inverted B. we call The Sky 164:21
Let onion atoms lurk within the b. 400:3
Love in a golden b. 60:21
Morning in the B. of Night 163:22
my friendly b. 315:28
Went to sea in a b. 298:9
Whither in your b. so free? 306:18
Bowler: *I* am the b. and the ball 247:7
Bowling: Here . . . lies poor Tom B. 136:11
Bowling-green: Some recommend the b. 187:22
Bowndyn: Adam lay I-b. 5:15
Bow-shot: b. from her bower-eaves 419:12
Bowsprit: Then the b. got mixed 102:24
Bow-wow: Big B. strain I can do 341:9
Daddy wouldn't buy me a b. 414:1
gone to the demnition b.s 139:24
most atrocious b. public park manner 26:4
were it not for his *b. way* 307:5
Box: breathes from yonder b. 315:14
guinea a b. 3:15
Boxes: Herring b. without topses 286:9
Boy: And I were the only b. 188:20
Being read to by a b. 156:10
b. I love is up in the gallery 446:24
B.s and girls come out to play 296:8
B.s and girls tumbling in the street 431:16
B.s are capital fellows 245:26
b.s are dreaming wicked 426:19
B.'s Best Friend is His Mother 273:28
b.s in the back room 256:5
B.s of the Old Brigade 253:29
b.s That fear no noise 182:20
b. stood on the burning deck 197:13
B.s will be b.s 205:13
b.'s will is the wind's will 256:31
by office b.s for office b.s 336:22
can't expect a b. to be depraved 335:11
Chatterton, the marvellous b. 466:2
Cheer! B.s, c.! 263:16
fifteen-year-old b., and will remain 332:8
horrid wicked b. was he 202:24
if they like a b. 336:15
I haf von funny leedle b. 1:3
In the third-class seat sat the journeying b. 193:5
I only know two sorts of b. 140:1
Kill the b.s and the luggage! 357:20
lad of mettle, a good b. 354:4
Let the b. win his spurs 154:9
like a b. playing on the sea-shore 294:8
Like little wanton b.s that swim 358:21
Little b. blue 297:2
Love is a b. 87:19
Mad about the b. 123:29
men that were b.s when I was a b. 31:4
nice little b. had a nice cake of soap 24:10
Oh! where is my wandering b. to-night? 8:9
plump and hearty healthy b. 202:22
poor blind b. 114:6
pretty large experience of b.s 138:4
Quo' the wee b. 22:16
silly twisted b. 274:3
Speak roughly to your little b. 101:3

speak to your little b. 62:19
Tell the b.s to follow 217:8
tell the other girls and b.s 407:14
There was a b.: ye knew him well 465:17
There was a naughty B. 232:17
thing of duty is a b. for ever 299:4
Thou lily-livered b. 367:17
till the b.s come home 167:12
to be b. eternal 384:11
what a b. you are! 70:11
What a good b. am I! 297:3
What are little b.s made of? 298:14
When that I was and a little tiny b. 383:33
When the b.s came out to play 296:16
who would not be a b. 89:16
young b.s and girls Are level now with men 344:4
your b.s will not be sent 329:21
Boyhood: If even I were as in my b. 392:9
Braces: Damn b. 63:20
Bracelet: b. of bright hair 146:4
diamond and safire b. 257:26
Bradford: there goes John B. 66:9
Bradshaw: vocabulary of 'B.' 148:7
Brae: waly, waly, down the b. 23:23
Brahmin: hymn the B. sings 158:10
Braids: twisted b. of lilies 275:34
Brain: Bear of Very Little B. 274:23, 274:27
B., n. An apparatus 59:7
b. of feathers 311:16
b.s enough to make a fool of himself 407:3
Cudgel thy b.s no more 352:21
dashed the b.s out 365:12
feeble wanderings of her fading b. 394:24
girl with b.s 257:25
gleaned my teeming b. 233:10
heat-oppressèd b. 365:19
his b.s go to his head 13:22
I mix them with b.s, sir 300:2
just fluffy, with no b.s at all 198:28
leave the naked b. 230:7
memory, the warder of the b. 365:14
might injure the b. 100:33
My b. Worked with a dim . . . sense 465:9
nourish a blind life within the b. 417:20
physical occurrences of the b. 271:4
poor and unhappy b.s for drinking 374:18
Raze out the written troubles of the b. 367:19
shallow draughts intoxicate the b. 313:4
should possess a poet's b. 148:16
steal away their b.s 374:26
very coinage of your b. 351:32
What good are b.s to a man? 459:9
when the b.s were out 366:27
Brain-work: Conception . . . *fundamental b.* 332:2
Brakes: whether to apply the b. 432:14
Branch: b. of one of your antediluvian 120:11
B. shall grow out of his roots 45:9
Cut is the b. 267:7
Brandy: B. for the Parson 240:21
hero . . : must drink b. 223:6
music is the b. of the damned 388:20
some are fou o' b. 84:27
Bras: deux b. croisés 284:7
Brass: Men's evil manners live in b. 359:3
Since b., nor stone, nor earth 386:4
sounding b., or a tinkling cymbal 55:21

thighs of b. 46:40
Were b. impregnable 377:2
Brattle: Wi' bickering b. 85:27
Bravado: roaring boys' b. 5:18
Brave: clime of the unforgotten b.! 93:1
  Fortune favours the b. 424:30
  home of the b. 236:6
  How sleep the b. 119:15
  None but the b. 149:33
  not too late tomorrow to be b. 10:11
  O Mr Hodgitts! . . . you are b.! 184:10
  souls of the b. that die in battle 115:10
  Toll for the b. 125:33
Braver: I have done one b. thing 146:15
Bravery: With all her b. on 281:24
Brawling: b. woman in a wide house 42:27
Brazil: Charley's aunt from B. 426:3
Breach: i' the imminent deadly b. 374:3
  More honoured in the b. 348:28
  Once more unto the b. 357:3
Bread: bitter b. of banishment 376:26
  b. and games 228:6
  b. and work for all 60:3
  b. of adversity 45:21
  b. in secret 41:31
  b. of tears 39:25
  b. which strengtheneth 40:11
  Bring us in no browne b. 7:8
  Cast thy b. upon the waters 44:4
  crammed with distressful b. 357:13
  cutting b. and butter 425:28
  daily b. 49:8
  did eat b. to the full 34:50
  don't bother about the b., please 274:26
  don't give b. with one fish-ball 247:6
  Explain that man cannot live by b. alone 451:15
  his seed begging b. 38:15
  if his son ask b. 49:23
  look to government for b. 82:26
  not live by b. only 35:12
  one half-pennyworth of b. 354:20
  Royal slice of b. 274:16
  seeking better b. than is made of wheat 104:15
  shall not live by b. alone 48:39
  shalt thou eat b. 34:4
  smell of b. and butter 89:6
  Some gave them white b. 296:32
  spoiled the b. and spilled the wine 305:20
  take the children's b. 50:20
  This b. I break was once the oat 426:16
  trees were b. and cheese 5:20
  which did eat of my b. 38:20
  White b. and butter 297:6
Bread-sauce: b. of the happy ending 217:3
Breadth: Apollyon straddled . . . the whole b. 80:22
Break: John Peel at the b. of the day 185:2
  Never Give a Sucker an Even B. 163:11
Breakages: B. Limited 387:16
Breakers: wantoned with thy b. 90:24
Breakfalls: rolls and throws and b. 326:12
Breakfast: B. first, business next 425:14
  B., supper, dinner, luncheon 76:28
  counted them at b. of day 91:25
  critical period in matrimony is b. time 199:1
  free b. table 68:16
  hadn't the heart to touch my b. 459:18
  Hope is a good b. 18:11

probably saving for b. 457:20
Where shall we our b. take? 23:18
Breakfast-table: ready for the national b. 432:7
Breast: b. high amid the corn 205:2
  broached his boiling bloody b. 372:18
  Come to my woman's b.s 364:33
  deeply implanted in the human b. 139:35
  eternal in the human b. 313:28
  lie lightly on thy b. 312:6
  Miss Twye was soaping her b.s 160:8
  On some fond b. the parting soul relies 186:16
  Rugged the b. that beauty 23:26
  she hath no b.s 44:29
  soothe a savage b. 120:13
  Thy two b.s are like two young roes 44:26
  Upon thy mother's b. 103:6
  within his own clear b. 275:18
  would require a b. projecting 190:5
Breastie: what a panic's in thy b. 85:27
Breastplate: What stronger b. 358:2
Breath: Although thy b. be rude 345:12
  as fleeting as a b. 324:4
  borne away with every b. 93:20
  b. can make them 180:18
  b. goes now, and some say no 146:16
  B.'s a ware that will not keep 210:8
  b. thou art, Servile 368:18
  call the fleeting b. 186:8
  draw thy b. in pain 353:12
  Fail, sun and b.! 333:19
  flattered its rank b. 90:3
  Fly away, fly away, b. 383:13
  healthy b. of morn 230:26
  heaven's b. Smells wooingly here 365:4
  hot and cold with the same b. 3:24
  How sweet the b. beneath the hill 196:23
  love thee with the b. 72:8
  My b. to heaven like vapour goes 423:7
  still to hear her tender-taken b. 232:19
  Suck my last b. 312:12
  sweetness of man's b. 216:7
  take into the air my quiet b. 232:7
  thou set b. in steel 128:15
  With bated b., and whispering humbleness 369:19
  With their love the b. between them 393:11
Breathers: When all the b. of this world 386:11
Breathing: Closer is He than b. 416:25
Breathless: B., we flung us 69:9
Brede: With b. ethereal wove 119:11
Bredon: In summertime on B. 210:14
Breeches: His b. cost him but a crown 8:5
  So have your b. 98:11
  to put its hand in its b. pocket 233:28
Breed: happy b. of men 376:17
  lesser b.s with the Law 240:18
Breeding: to show your b. 395:39
Breeks: ill taking the b. aff 340:27
Breeze: b. of morning moves 420:33
  b.s and the sunshine 96:18
  cooling western b. 313:13
  fair b. blew 116:26
  hay harvest b. 122:22
  Little b.s dusk and shiver 419:8
  though the spicy b.s 196:25
Breezy: B., Sneezy, Freezy 158:5
Breitmann: Hans B. gife a barty 252:14
Brethren: b. to dwell together in unity 41:7

great Twin B. 261:11
thy b. of the slimy fin 127:32
Brevis: B. esse laboro 206:29
Brevity: B. is the soul of wit 349:21
Brewery: Oh, take me to a b. 7:26
Briars: binding with b. my joys 61:21
Bribe: hope To b. or twist 460:4
  Too poor for a b. 187:16
Brick: carried a piece of b. in his pocket 410:21
  'Eave 'arf a b. at 'im 322:6
  not even red b., but white tile 301:12
  straw to make b. 34:45
  throw a b. without hitting 300:29
Bridal: Against the b. day 403:12
  b. of the earth and sky 199:25
Bride: b. hath paced into the hall 116:23
  B.s of Enderby 215:8
  encounter darkness as a b. 368:21
  My b. to be he murmered several times 13:18
  never a blushing b. 252:7
  Over his feet lay the b. 288:17
  prepared as a b. 58:32
  Sat like a blooming Eastern b. 149:32
  still unravished b. of quietness 231:18
Bride-bed: I thought thy b. to have decked 352:33
Bridegroom: b. all night through 210:20
  b. in my death 344:2
  B. with his bride 423:9
  Fresh as a b. 353:28
  Of b.s, brides 200:2
  This ring the B. 438:20
Bridesmaid: always a b. 252:7
  happy b. makes a happy bride 415:19
Bridge: B., and Women, and Champagne 30:26
  broken arch of London B. 262:11
  drive the road and b. the ford 240:24
  keep the b. with me 261:14
  Like a b. over troubled water 397:8
  over the B. of Sighs into eternity 237:1
  promise to build a b. 236:20
  golden b. Is for a flying enemy 90:30
  great B., our Myth 128:15
  London b. is broken down 297:7
  on the b. at midnight 256:11
  Standing on the b. at midnight 8:15
  Venice, on the B. of Sighs 90:5
Bridle: b. for the ass 42:37
Bridle-reins: gae his b. a shake 84:30
Brief: when I struggle to be b. 206:28
Brier: grows a bonny b. bush 203:12
  how full of b.s is this working-day world! 344:22
Brier-patch: Bred en bawn in a b. 194:14
Brigade: Forward the Light B.! 415:25
  London's noble Fire B. 30:16
  Where are the boys of the Old B.? 448:17
Brigands: B. demand money or your life 88:16
Bright: b. in the fruitful valleys 68:5
  Dark with excessive b. 279:15
  Such a b. little, tight little 178:12
  young lady named B. 80:9
Brightest: Best and b., come away! 394:9
Brightness: B. falls from the air 292:20
Brighton: Kind, cheerful, merry Dr B. 425:6
Brilliant: b. to the top of his army boots 255:20
Brillig: 'Twas b., and the slithy toves 101:24
Brink: scared to go to the b. 152:7
Brioche: Qu'ils mangent de la b. 266:15

Britain: B. is A world by itself 347:8
  coal and fish in Great B. 33:5
  Great B. is going to make war 32:13
  I expect the Battle of B. 112:22
  limits of B. are laid bare 414:3
  make B. a fit country 255:16
Britannia: B. needs no bulwarks 97:22
  more inseparable than Beer and B. 400:11
  Rule B., rule the waves 428:5
  shouted 'Rule, B.' 238:6
  Singing, Rule B. 8:23
Britannos: Et penitus toto divisos orbe B. 441:12
British: in perfect safety under B. rule 430:10
  less known by the B. 65:9
  maxim of the B people 112:10
Briton: as only a free-born B. 425:17
  B.s completely isolated 441:12
  B.s never . . . shall be marr-i-ed 8:23
  I glory in the name of B. 174:33
Broad: B. before and b. behind 33:3
  come into the b. 47:31
  She's a smart old b. 333:3
  She's the B. and I'm the High 403:25
Broadcloth: B. without 124:33
Broken: healeth the b. in heart 41:16
  Is it not b.? 390:2
Broken-hearted: bind up the b. 46:18
  In silence and tears, Half b. 94:8
  ne'er been b. 83:25
  You hoped we were both b. 412:30
Broker: b. is a man who runs your fortune 461:4
  honest b. 59:24
Brooch: With the pin of a b. 470:13
Brooches: I will make you b. and toys 407:24
Brook: b. and road Were fellow-travellers 465:23
  I sing of b.s, of blossoms 200:2
  noise like of a hidden b. 117:9
  Shall be my b.; be he ne'er so vile 357:19
  Shallow b.s and rivers wide 276:26
  where the b. is deep 358:1
  wholesome salad from the b. 127:27
  with b.s taken otherwhere in song 170:7
Brooks: Only B. of Sheffield 137:3
Brot: Wer nie sein B. mit Tranen ass 180:7
Brothel: b.s with bricks of Religion 63:16
  metaphysical b. for the emotions 242:10
Brother: All men are b.s 318:1
  all the b.s too 383:15
  Am I my b.'s keeper? 34:7
  Am I not a man and a b.? 449:7
  Bear . . . no b. near the throne 312:22
  Big B. is watching you 300:20
  B.s all In honour 465:26
  B.s and Sisters, I bid you beware 240:14
  For all the B.s were valiant 293:23
  Forty thousand b.s Could not 352:34
  grew so like my b. 252:10
  Had it been his b. 6:2
  He that loveth not his b. 58:1
  How fast has b. followed b. 462:1
  lo'ed him like a vera b. 85:16
  make b.s and sisters hate each other 220:10
  Men, my b.s, men the workers 419:29
  Night, B. to Death 131:10
  noble pair of b.s 209:16
  occasion to fall in his b.'s way 54:48
  Oh! little brown b. 293:10

Romans were like b.s 261:16
scan your b. man 83:21
Sleep . . . B. to Death 28:7
sticketh closer than a b. 42:22
thou elder b. ev'n to shade 328:14
two b.s and their murdered man 231:5
Ye are b.s, ye are men 97:2
Brotherhood: Love the b. 57:32
Brothers-in-law: they aren't all b. 318:1
Brow: Gathering her b.s like gathering storm 85:13
Her b. shades frowns 131:9
manly b. Consents to death 90:14
not seen in either of our b.s 148:21
That great b. 73:16
Your bonnie b. was brent 84:31
Brown: in some b. study 260:11
John B.'s body lies a-mouldering 190:12
so uncommonly b. 24:7
Browning: B.! Since Chaucer was alive 247:2
Hang it all, Robert B. 317:15
Robert B., you writer of plays 75:16
Tennyson and B. are poets 157:21
Bruce: Scots, wham B. has aften led 85:10
Brüder: Alle Menschen werden B. 338:8
Bruises: One mask of b. 139:14
Bruit: b. lointain des chars gémissant 244:24
Brunck: most learn'd professor, B. 316:21
Brush: work with so fine a b. 17:19
Brute: As we to the b.s 272:18
b. I hated so 73:27
b. I might have been 77:14
'Gainst a woman that was a b. 391:1
made b.s men and men divine 305:20
simple race of b.s 417:7
such a cross-grained b. 182:21
we had been b.s without you 301:20
Brute: Et tu, B.? 95:10 360:5
Brutish: nasty, b., and short 202:7
Brutus: B. makes mine greater 360:31
For B. is an honourable man 360:15
Bubble: beaded b.s winking at the brim 232:2
earth hath b.s 364:18
Life's troubled b. broken 134:30
Like the b. on the fountain 339:21
now a b. burst and now a world 313:27
world's a b. 21:3
Buccaneer: Very haughty! . . . the wild B. 172:9
Bücher: wo man B. verbrennt 197:6
Buck: b. stops here 432:20
Bucket: as a drop of a b. 45:35
dropping b.s into empty wells 127:7
Buckingham: High-reaching B. 378:7
so much for B. 114:9
Buckles: Silver b. at his knee 296:7
Buckram: eleven b. men grown out of two 354:11
two rogues in b. suits 354:10
Bud: b. may have a bitter taste 125:32
Make boot upon the summer's velvet b.s 356:24
nip him in the b. 328:5
On each b. and blossom 62:20
spare the b.s 268:30
Buddhism: nothing in Christianity or B. 336:5
Buddhist: some sort of B. 270:13
Buffs: drunken private of the B. 148:8
Steady the B. 241:29
Buffalo: where the b. roam 201:7
Buffer: say a poor b. lies low 454:14

Buffets: fortune's b. and rewards 351:3
Buffoon: statesman, and b. 149:20
Bug: b. with gilded wings 312:25
like an industrious b. 311:11
snug As a b. in a rug 168:18
Bugaboo-baby: Don't b. *me*! 96:2
Bugger: We've done the b.! 424:26
Bugle: Blow, b., blow 421:39
Blow out, you b.s 69:6
b.s calling for them 302:8
Our b.s sang truce 97:18
There came a wind like a b. 142:7
Build: B. me straight 256:12
When we b., let us think 333:13
Builders: stone which the b. refused 40:26
stone which the b. rejected 50:46
Builded: b. better than he knew 158:14
Building: altered in the b. trade 241:2
it's a very old b. 301:9
life o' the b. 366:3
plenty of ruined b.s 263:9
principal beauty in a b. 171:2
tall b., with a tower 128:4
Bull: bumping b. of the Cassidys 226:5
Down at the old B. and Bush 430:9
Edward B. The curate 416:13
savage b. doth bear the yoke 372:26
savage b. sustains the yoke 242:19
See an old unhappy b. 202:13
String b.s of Bashan 37:43
taking the b. by both horns he kissed her 13:18
to milk the b. 221:13
Bulldog: boys of the b. breed 263:13
Bullet: b. that is to kill me 291:17
Each b. has got its commission 136:6
Every b. has its billet 457:9
paper b.s of the brain 372:38
stronger than the b. 254:14
with a b. through his heart 425:19
Bullocks: good yoke of b. 356:3
whose talk is of b. 48:24
Bulrush: With b. and watercresses 79:14
Bumbast: well able to b. out a blank verse 188:3
Bump: go b. in the night 6:21
Buns: Hot cross b.! 296:21
Bunbury: permanent invalid called B. 455:8
Buncombe: Parliament speaking . . . to B. 99:36
Bung-hole: stopping a b. 352:28
Bunk: History is more or less b. 167:4
Bunting: Bye, baby b. 296:9
Burden: Borne the b. and heat 50:41
b. of his song 59:2
Burg: feste B. ist unser Gott 260:3
Burglar: enterprising b.'s not a-burgling 178:6
many a b. I've restored 178:18
Burglary: Flat b. as ever 373:18
Burgundy: naïve domestic B. 429:13
Burial: in one red b. blent 89:25
Buried: b. in a good old age 34:21
We b. him darkly at dead of night 460:1
Burke, Edmund: 181:17 181:18 224:8 303:4 303:5
like B., who winds into a subject 183:3
Burlap: B. walked home 213:4
Burlington: I'm B. Bertie 194:1
Burn: Better to marry than to b. 55:7
You'll b. me to death 203:2
Burning: b. and a shining light 53:13

Cabin: average c. of a life 72:29
  he mounted to the c. 7:11
  Make me a willow c. at your gate 382:36
  small c. build there 471:6
Cabined: I am c., cribbed, confined 366:23
Cabinet: C. of Mediocrities 143:13
Cabman: c. dances 289:3
Cabots: C. talk only to God 65:16
Cadence: harsh c. of a rugged line 151:6
Cadiz: reeking into C. bay 75:1
Caelum: C. non animum mutant 207:20
Café: laughter . . . in every street c. 191:9
Cage: Bird in a Gilded C. 245:1
  in making nets, not in making c.s 411:20
  marriage is like a c. 285:21
  We occupy the same c. 457:15
Cain: and the first city, C. 124:3
  cruel sons of C. 251:26
  Had C. been Scot 115:4
  Lord set a mark upon C. 34:10
Cake: Bake me a c. 297:20
  Hear, Land o' C.s 85:6
  highly geological home-made c. 138:24
  Let them eat c. 266:15
  no more c.s and ale 383:6
  Some gave them plum c. 296:32
Calais: 'C.' lying in my heart 269:19
  shew a light at C. 221:16
Calamities: C. are of two kinds 59:8
  c. of life were shared 133:13
Calamity: makes c. of so long life 350:14
  wedded to c. 379:38
Calculation: c. out of the other 138:25
Calculus: C. racked him 74:29
Caledonia: O C.! stern and wild 340:2
Caledonian: indirect expressions before a C. 245:20
Calf: Bring hither the fatted c. 52:27
  c. and the young lion 45:10
Calf's-skin: c. on those recreant limbs! 361:15
Caliban: 'Ban, 'Ban, Ca-C. 381:2
  C. casts out Ariel 317:22
California: C., Here I Come 413:7
Call: But will they come when you do c. 354:22
  Just c. on me 253:8
  obey th' important c. 127:19
  wild c. and a clear c. 270:3
Caller: who calls it be the c. 99:2
Calm: All our c. is in that balm 295:23
  c. reigned in Warsaw 341:17
  it is c. and classical 139:29
  Ne'er saw I, never felt, a c. so deep! 463:11
  no joy but c. 420:13
Calumny: thou shalt not escape c. 350:18
Calypso: Ulysses leaves once more C. 391:3
Cambria: since C.'s fatal day 185:20
Cambridge: C. has seen many strange sights 211:1
  C. people rarely smile 69:14
  nonsense . . . put gently back . . . at C. 29:5
  To C. books, as very well discerning 431:19
  to C. books he sent 71:23
Cambridgeshire: C., of all England 69:13
Cambuscan: story of C. bold 276:12
Cambyses: In King C.' vein 354:17
Came: But soon c. down again 125:10
  I c., and no-one answered 134:21
  I c., I saw, I conquered 95:8
  I c., saw and overcame 356:9

Cameelious: get the Hump – C. Hump 239:20
Camel: c. has a single hump 292:6
  c. to go through the eye of a needle 50:38
  in the shape of a c. 351:18
  swallow a c. 51:7
  Take my c., dear 261:3
Camelot: many-towered C. 419:7
  To look down to C. 419:10
Came-over-with-the-Conqueror: C. type of mind
  447:5
Camera: I am a c. with its shutter open 215:20
Cammin: Nel mezzo del c. di nostra vita 131:14
Camp: c.s had taught him 400:27
  Courts and c.s are the only places 109:6
  From c. to c. 357:9
Campbell: The C.s are comin' 7:10
Camphire: all c. and frankincense 121:2
Cam-u-el: C., that primal Desert Ship 189:5
Can: crams with c.s of poisoned meat 110:17
  cry *I can no more* 205:22
  He who c., does 388:27
  millions of tin c.s 264:14
  Pass me the c., lad 209:22
Canakin: let me the c. clink 374:20
Canaries: song of c. Never varies 292:7
Canary: mine host's C. wine 231:17
Cancel: debt which c.s all others 120:1
Cancers: because women have c. 234:4
Candidate: c. of heaven 151:7
Candle: c. of understanding 47:32
  c. . . . under a bushel 48:44
  Here comes a c. to light you to bed 297:19
  hold their farthing c. to the sun 472:17
  How far that little c. throws his beams! 370:23
  Latin for a c. 162:15
  light such a c. 248:25
  must I hold a c. to my shames 369:28
  My c. burns at both ends 273:18
  Night's c.s are burnt out 380:3
  Out, out, brief c.! 367:24
  set a c. in the sun 86:18
  Their c.s are all out 365:16
Candle-ends: called him 'C.' 102:23
Candle-light: Can I get there by c.? 296:22
  Fire and fleet and c. 23:1
Candlestick-maker: C. much acquaints 78:20
Candy: C. is dandy 292:13
  what a c. deal of courtesy 353:33
Cane: nice conduct of a clouded c. 315:26
Canker: As killing as the c. 277:6
  c.s of a calm world 354:38
Cannibal: better sleep with a sober c. 271:17
  C.s that each other eat 374:5
  if a c. uses knife and fork 251:16
Cannibalism: permissible, even c. 146:26
Cannon: c.'s opening roar 89:23
  C. to the right of them 415:27
  if we could carry c. by our sides 353:7
  Where the thundering c.s roar 182:20
Cannon-ball: c. took off his legs 204:21
Canoe: paddle his own c. 268:7
  shod their heads in their c.s 269:5
Canon: c. 'gainst self-slaughter 347:36
Canopy: glorious c. of light and blue 452:17
  rich embroidered c. To kings 358:8
  this most excellent c., the air 349:36
  Under the c. 346:31

Canossa: We shall not go to C. 59:23
Cant: c. of hypocrites 405:25
   clear your *mind* of c. 223:14
   It is all c. 224:10
   rest of that nauseous c. 120:33
Can't: If you don't think you c. 215:1
Can't-help-it: holy c. touch 249:2
Cantie: c. wi' mair 84:3
Canton: Write loyal c.s of contemnèd love 382:36
Caps: They threw their c. 346:21
Capability: Negative C. 233:26
Capacity: c. of taking trouble 99:23
   notwithstanding thy c. 382:24
Cap-a-pe: Armed at points exactly, c. 348:13
Caparisons: No c., miss 395:30
Cape: Nobly, nobly C. Saint Vincent 75:1
   Round the c. of a sudden 76:19
Capers: run into strange c. 344:34
Capital: fowl and mushrooms – c. thing! 140:22
   to that high c. 389:25
Capitalism: definition of C. 191:16
   monopoly stage of c. 252:21
   unacceptable face of c. 196:21
Capricorn: Lady C. . . . still keeping open bed 212:24
Capster: Ancient C. of this Hostel 134:16
Captain: C. is a good travelling name 161:19
   C. of the Gate 261:13
   C., or colonel, or knight in arms 282:13
   C.s and the Kings depart 240:17
   c.s by the hundred 176:10
   c.s . . . clothed most gorgeously 46:35
   C.s of Industry 100:4
   Foremost c. of his time 421:15
   his C.'s hand on his shoulder 293:21
   I am the c. of my soul 197:26
   plain russet-coated c. 129:10
   train-band c. eke was he 125:6
   When c.s courageous 23:2
   Where on the deck my C. lies 453:17
Captive: c. good attending captain ill 386:7
Captivity: power to cancel his c. 359:24
   thou hast led c. captive 39:16
   Turn again our c. 40:35
Car: c. rattling o'er the stony street 89:22
   drive the rapid c. 132:11
   Would you buy a second-hand c. 335:4
Caravan: Put up your c. 202:18
   Where my c. has rested 425:1
Caravanserai: C. Starts 164:16
   This battered C. 164:5
Caravelle: à l'avant des blanches c.s 199:31
Carbon: my theme is c. 249:24
Carcase: Wheresoever the c. is 51:12
Carcass: rotten c. of a boat 380:29
Carcasse: As the dead c.s of unburied men 346:29
Card: He's a cheery old c. 338:2
   learnt to play at c.s 223:34
   old age of c.s 314:27
   patience and shuffle the c.s 105:19
   that can pack the c.s 20:2
   They do not play at c.s 245:22
   we must speak by the c. 352:24
   wicked pack of c.s 156:36
   you may cut it on his c. 240:27
   your c., the drowned Phoenician 156:37
Cardboard: Sailing over a c. sea 192:5
Care: against eating c.s 276:33

Begone, dull c.! 7:6
Black C., at the horseman's back 96:7
Black C. takes her seat 208:23
Can a woman's tender c. 125:28
Careless she is with artful c. 121:5
c. not whether a man is good 61:7
c.'s an enemy to life 382:25
C. Sat on his faded cheek 278:22
c.s that infest the day 256:19
C. to our coffin adds a nail 309:4
If no one c.s for me 59:2
Irks c. the crop-full bird? 77:12
Let us have no c. 65:6
my help is past my c. 27:21
O polished perturbation! golden c.! 356:11
past redress are . . . past c. 376:25
pleasures are their only c. 126:16
ravelled sleave of c. 365:26
sae weary fu' o' care 85:35
so wan with c. 353:15
Sport that wrinkled C. derides 276:20
teach us to c. and not to c. 155:24
then the c. is over 415:14
this life if, full of c. 133:1
to-night so full of c. 67:24
to throw c.s aside 103:16
weep away the life of c. 394:4
Whose c. is lest men see 77:26
Yet what I am none c.s 114:26
Career: bright and brief c. 340:4
   c. open to talents 292:1
   might damage his c. 26:2
   points clearly to a political c. 388:11
   suspend your mad c. 126:28
   This is our c. and our triumph 437:16
Careful: it makes him c. 270:19
Carelessness: to lose both looks like c. 455:13
Carew: grave of 'Mad C.' 195:10
Caricature: c. of a face 177:34
Carl: c. spak oo thing 107:32
Carlyle: best men are dead! C., Tennyson 322:17
   was probably fond of the Americans 434:8
Carmina: nec vivere c. possunt 207:26
   Sunt et mihi c. 441:20
Carnage: where his c. and conquests cease 89:9
Carnally: To be c. minded is death 54:27
Carol: It was the c. of a bird 93:18
Caroling: So little cause for c.s 192:15
Carpe: C. diem, quam minimum credula postero 208:10
Carpenter: At his c.'s tray 397:20
   nocturnal women were beating great c.s 460:24
   Walrus and the C. 102:3
   You may scold a c. 221:8
Carpet: figure in the c. 216:15
   long c.s rose along the dusty floor 230:20
   quality of the c. 218:3
Carriage: can't afford a c. 131:1
   c. held but just ourselves 142:1
   very small second-class c. 177:14
Carrière: c. ouverte aux talents 99:20 292:1
Carry: c. it with us or we find it not 158:19
Cart: C.s to good drivers 67:2
   creak of a lumbering c. 471:11
Carthage: To C. I came 15:31
   To come again to C. 370:18
Carthago: Delenda est C. 103:8
Cartridges: What use are c. in battle? 387:18

Casca: See what a rent the envious C. made 360:20

Case: c. is concluded 16:7
  hardly a c. in which the dispute 227:26
  lady in the c. 91:37
  knows only his own side of the c. 273:12
  nothing to do with the c. 177:33
  when a lady's in the c. 174:22
  Which in our c. we have not got 326:11
  Woman in the C. 163:20
  world is everything that is the c. 459:6

Casement: Charmed magic c.s 232:7
  on this c. shone the wintry moon 230:17

Casey: C. Jones, he mounted 7:11

Cash: c. over the counter 216:13
  In epochs when c. payment 99:11
  take the C., and let the Credit go 164:3

Cash box: other three in the c. 457:1

Cashmere: tales of fair C. 457:24

Casket: seal the hushèd C. of my Soul 233:9

Casques: O the very c. That did affright 356:20

Cassia: Heap c., sandal-buds 76:17

Cassio: C., I love thee 374:24

Cassius: Yond C. has a lean and hungry look 359:18

Cassowary: If I were a c. 454:16

Castilian: as might an old C. 94:5

Castle: c., called Doubting C. 80:28
  c. hath a pleasant seat 365:3
  I'm the king of the c. 296:28
  man's house is his c. 116:9
  mistletoe hung in the c. hall 27:6
  our c.'s strength Will laugh 367:22
  rich man in his c. 4:4

Castlereagh: mask like C. 392:1

Castle-wall: little pin Bores through his c. 377:2

Castum: Nam c. esse decet plum poetam 103:14

Casualty: Crass C. obstructs the sun and rain 192:20
  first c. when war comes 218:16

Cat: as a c. laps milk 380:38
  c. and the fiddle 296:19
  C. He walked by himself 241:17
  C. on a Hot Tin Roof 457:14
  C.s and monkeys, monkeys and c.s 216:16
  C.s may have had their goose 96:10
  c. will mew 353:2
  Do c.s eat bats? 100:28
  don't want to swing a c. 137:25
  endow a college or a c. 314:32
  greater c.s with golden eyes 335:2
  Hanging of his c. on Monday 66:21
  harmless necessary c. 370:7
  I will consider my C. Jeoffry 398:6
  Like the poor c. i' the adage 365:10
  little black c. with bright green eyes 284:20
  melodious c.s under the moon 212:28
  More ways of killing a c. 238:1
  O c. of churlish kind 398:1
  on little c. feet 337:1
  part to tear a c. in 371:25
  Runcible C. with crimson whiskers 251:6
  see how the c. jumps 341:10
  We have c.s the way most people 429:21
  What c.'s averse to fish? 186:27
  When c.s run home 423:19
  When I play with my c. 285:16
  would have made a c. laugh 309:25

Catalogue: c. was so large 120:22

in the c. ye go for men 366:11

Cataract: sounding c. Haunted me 462:18
  wild c. leaps in glory 421:39
  You c.s and hurricanoes spout 362:14

Catastrophe: I'll tickle your c. 355:22
  like the c. of the old comedy 362:2

Catch: fell to playing the game of c. 166:26
  Fifteen fingers on the safety c. 264:9
  hard to c. and conquer 272:3
  only one c. and that was Catch-22 197:9

Catechism: so ends my c. 355:2

Categories: ballet dance of bloodless c. 66:11

Caterpillar: c.s of the commonwealth 376:24
  c. on the leaf 60:14

Cathay: cycle of C. 420:6

Catholic: C. and grown-up 301:8
  C. and the Communist are alike 301:5
  C.s and Communists have committed 187:23
  myself a C. will be 124:10

Cato: Like C., give his little senate laws 312:23

Cattle: also much c. 47:17
  c. upon a thousand hills 38:29
  go and call the c. home 237:15
  women are mostly troublesome c. 258:19

Catoni: sed victa C. 259:12

Cattes: c. wild and tame 397:25

Caucasus: thinking on the frosty C. 376:15

Cauldron:c. of unholy loves 15:31
  Fire burn and c. bubble 366:35

Cauliflower: C. in nothing but cabbage 434:10

Causa: Nulla fere c. est 227:26

Causas: Felix qui potuit rerum cognoscere c. 441:26

Cause: c. . . . . I searched out 37:7
  C. of Freedom 66:5
  c., or just impediment 319:36
  c. that perishes with them 115:10
  c. that the former days were better 43:29
  do it without c. 105:1
  Home of lost c.s 12:19
  I'll try the whole c. 100:31
  in the heart Of all right c.s 170:19
  It is the c., it is the c., my soul 375:21
  not ever jealous for the c. 375:11
  Report me and my c. aright 353:11
  Ring out a slowly dying c. 418:25
  tenacious of purpose in a rightful c. 208:25
  To set the c. above renown 293:14
  victorious c. pleased the Gods 259:12
  What great c. 31:17
  Who can foretell for what high c. 268:29

Causeway: Giant's C. worth seeing 223:7

Cavaliero: he was a perfect c. 89:4

Cave: dark unfathomed c, of ocean 186:10
  her vacant, interlunar c. 281:17
  Out of the misty eastern c. 394:12

Cavern: c.s measureless to man 117:35
  In a c., in a canyon 286:8

Caviare: 'twas c. to the general 350:4

Cease: C.! must men kill and die? 391:8
  fears that I may c. to be 233:10
  happy, and c. to be so 273:10

Ceasing: Pray without c. 56:36
  Without c. I make mention 54:13

Cecil: No, after you, C. 229:13

Cedar: c. tall and slender 299:13
  grow like a c. in Lebanon 40:4

Ceiling: to draw on the c. 111:3

Celebrated: c. . . . for his Deportment 136:26
Celebrities: they knew they were c. 336:14
Celerity: C. is never more admired 343:36
Celia: Come, my C., let us prove 225:11
  Not, C., that I juster am 341:19
Celibacy: c. has no pleasures 220:7
Cell: Each in his narrow c. 186:3
  for cloistered c. 234:20
  o'erbrimmed their clammy c.s 233:17
Cellar: born in a c. 120:6 166:23
Cellarer: Old Simon the C. 30:1
Celt: blind hysterics of the C. 418:29
Cemetery: c. is an open space 389:22
Censor: to c. one's own thoughts 444:3
Censorship: extreme form of c. 389:11
Censure: All c. of a man's self 223:3
  No man can justly c. 71:8
  Take each man's c. 348:22
Cent: elegant simplicity of the three per c.s 341:12
Centaur: moral c., man and wife 91:42
Centipede: C. was happy quite 129:1
  That loathsome c., Remorse 252:8
Centre: c. cannot hold 471:20
  c. of each and every town or city 203:32
  From the c. all round to the sea 127:37
  My c. is giving way 166:22
Centuries: forty c. look down upon you 291:13
  I shall lie through c. 73:12
  Through what wild c. 134:6
Century: born this c., tempered by war 235:15
  c. of the common man 444:8
Cerberus: like C., three gentlemen at once 395:31
  Of C. and blackest Midnight born 276:17
Cerebration: deep well of unconscious c. 216:11
Ceremony: It useth an enforcèd c.! 360:26
  No c. that to great ones 'longs 368:11
  Save c., save general c. 357:12
Certain: nothing can be said to be c. 168:20
Certainties: better than most people's c. 192:7
  hot for c. 272:12
  If a man will begin with c. 18:2
Certainty: last one is a c. 155:5
  not knowledge but c. 333:25
Cervantes: Whether you choose C.' serious air 311:7
Cervicem: *unam c. haberet* 95:14
Cesse: Grand roi, c. de vaincre 64:18
Cetera: Permitte divis c. 208:8
Ceux: c. qui en avaient en donnait 142:13
Ceylon: Blow soft o'er C.'s isle 196:25
Chaffinch: While the c. sings 74:35
Chain: adamantine c.s and penal fire 278:3
  bind their kings with c. 41:18
  Bound by gold c.s about the feet of God 417:20
  bright c.s Eat with their burning cold 392:22
  c. of events which shall be the formula 157:18
  everywhere he is in c.s 332:12
  flesh to feel the c. 69:2
  nothing to lose but their c.s 269:14
  safer to be in c.s 229:2
  Servitude that hugs her c. 186:23
  Shake your c.s to earth like dew 392:2
  Though I sang in my c.s like the sea 426:6
  Untwisting all the c.s that tie 276:34
Chair: c.s are being brought in 14:15
  C. she sat in, like a burnished throne 156:40
  Give Dayrolles a c. 109:23
  He fills a c. 223:12

I had three c.s in my house 428:31
Is the c. empty? 378:14
rack of a too easy c. 311:28
Seated in thy silver c. 224:27
tavern c. was the throne 224:11
There will be one vacant c. 446:28
tilts up his c. 203:1
Two old c.s, and half a candle 250:16
Chair: c. est triste, hélas 265:5
Chaise: All in a c. and pair 125:7
Chalice: c. of the grapes of God 417:30
Challenge: c. to his end 128:27
Cham: great C. of literature 400:14
Chamber: capers nimbly to a lady's c. 377:22
  c.s of the mansion of my heart 428:18
  in his c., weak and dying 5:21
  in my lady's c. 296:17
  Now get you to my lady's c. 352:27
  stalking in my c. 468:10
Chamberlain: c. had carried with him 327:11
Chamberlain, Neville: 201:20 255:18
Chamber-melody: More oft than to a c. 396:16
Chameleon: c.'s dish: I eat the air 351:6
  C.s feed on light and air 390:28
Champagne: C. certainly gives one . . . ideas 409:22
  C., dice, music 92:29
  Drinking the c. she sends them 8:14
  ice of his Lordship's c. 318:7
  not a c. teetotaller 387:26
Champion: to his faithful c. 281:31
Champs: c. n'étaient point noirs 211:21
Chance: Against ill c.s men are ever merry 356:7
  All c., direction 313:34
  c.s change by course 402:3
  every c. brought out a noble knight 417:16
  I am so sometimes by c. 385:2
  most disastrous c.s 374:3
  Nor now to prove our c. 148:13
  Which erring men call C. 275:26
Chancellor: rather susceptible C.! 177:8
Change: C. and decay in all around 260:13
  C. is not made without inconvenience 205:8
  Each c. of many-coloured life 219:3
  far from consisting in c. 337:10
  How will the c. strike me 73:12
  I c. but I cannot die 390:16
  more things c. 229:11
  Neither to c., nor falter, nor repent 393:19
  No c., though you lie under 210:19
  O the heavy c. 277:4
  preferable to c. and disturbance 285:19
  state without the means of some c. 82:11
  Think you that I would c. with him? 1:5
  Times c., and we c. with them 9:12
  When c. itself can give no more 341:20
  world's a scene of c.s 124:4
Change: Plus ça change 229:11
Changé: nous avons c. tout cela 283:22
Changed: All c., c. utterly 470:16
  But we have c. all that 283:22
Chankly: Hills of the C. Bore 250:18
Channel: brush the C. with his sleeve 338:18
  Butting through the C. 269:25
  dream you are crossing the C. 177:14
  drum them up the C. 293:16
Chant: c.s les plus beaux 290:11
  quand le c. a cessé 335:9

Chante: la peine d'être dit, on le c. 27:13
Chanticleer: to crow like c. 345:5
Chantiez: Vous c.? J'en suis fort aise 243:17
Chaos: C. is come again 374:29
    C. of thought and passion 314:2
    Not c.-like 316:9
    reign of C. and old Night 278:18
    thy dread empire, C.! 311:29
Chap: Biography is about c.s 31:25
    clean, upstanding c. like you 238:3
    from the nave to the c.s 364:13
    good c. for not liking myself 5:3
Chapel: c.s had been churches 369:8
    Devil always builds a c. there 133:18
    gates of this C. were shut 61:20
    Who lied in the c. 92:35
Chaplain: as Blue Beard's domestic c. said 140:31
Chappie: c. is rummy to a degree 459:16
Chapter: c. of accidents 109:18
    first c. of Guinness'es 226:23
Character: capable of being not only the c.s 104:14
    c. dead at every word 395:35
    c. is destiny 155:17
    c. of hell to trace 185:22
    c. undecided, the way of life uncertain 230:5
    content of their c. 237:9
    formation of c. 402:10
    gave me a good c. 101:22
    human *c.* changed 460:20
    I leave my c. behind me 395:36
    Man of wit, bad c. 305:7
    Most women have no c.s at all 314:22
    tell a lot about a fellow's c. 326:8
    true index of a man's c. 121:20
    various parts of my c. 271:3
    Who have c.s to lose 84:33
Characteristic: c. of the present age 143:3
Charakter: C. in dem Strom der Welt 180:2
Charge: c. is prepared 174:17
    die to save c.s 86:9
    two c.s for the same thing 250:5
Charing Cross: between Heaven and C. 427:19
Chariot: Bring me my c. of fire! 61:9
    flying c. through the field of air 132:11
    he burneth the c. 38:25
    Her c. is an empty hazel-nut 378:30
    Some trust in c.s 37:39
    Swing low, sweet c. 8:18
    tarry the wheels of his c.s 35:28
Charioteer: C. Of the patient year 230:25
Chariot-wheel: axle-tree of the c. 20:37
Charity: and have not c. 55:21
    C. begins at home 71:9
    C., dear Miss Prism, c.! 455:17
    c. edifieth 55:9
    c. never faileth 55:23
    C. shall cover . . . sins 57:35
    c. suffereth long 55:22
    excellent gift of c. 319:14
    Give him a little earth for c. 358:27
    greatest of these is c. 55:26
    In c. there is no excess 19:27
    in love and c. with your neighbours 319:20
    in order to practice c. 98:6
    living need c. 10:18
    mankind's concern is c. 314:6
    man's mind to move in c. 18:20

O! the c. of the penny cord 347:16
    organized c., scrimped and iced 300:6
Charity-boy: learn so little, as the c. said 140:38
Charles: By headless C. see heartless Henry 94:10
    colour of a C. the Fifth 134:11
    In good King C.'s golden days 7:28
    King C. the First walked and talked 6:6
    out of King C.'s head 137:13
Charles II 328:13
Charles-his-Wain: running after C. 304:19
Charlie: C. is my darling 291:7
    Good Grief, C. Brown 339:6
    live or die wi' C. 203:11
    live or die with C. 341:1
Charlotte: Werther had a love for C. 425:28
Charm: acres o' c.s 84:24
    all those endearing young c.s 286:22
    C.s by accepting 314:28
    C.s strike the sight 315:27
    Despair thy c. 367:30
    issue of their c. depended 14:14
    till life can c. no more 119:9
    What c. can soothe her melancholy 182:38
    You know what c. is 98:4
Charmer: hearken to the voice of c.s 39:2
    Were t'other dear c. away 174:15
Charming: Ever c., ever new 153:3
Charon: C., seeing, may forget 246:23
Charter: as large a c. as the wind 345:8
Chartreuse: system that produced green C. 336:7
Chase: c., the sport of kings 401:1
Chassis: worl's in a state o' c. 299:7
Chaste: be amorous, but be c. 92:28
    ever c., except you ravish me 145:24
    godly poet must be c. himself 103:14
Chasteneth: Whom the Lord loveth he c. 57:15
Chastised: little c. . . . . greatly rewarded 47:39
Chastity: all c. and odour 121:2
    c. of honour 82:14
    clothed on with c. 416:21
    Give me c. and continency 16:2
    'Tis C., my brother 275:20
Chat: couldn't c. together 176:9
Chatham: Great C. with his sabre 5:24
Chatter: c. of a transcendental kind 177:39
Chatterley: end of the C. ban 247:19
Chatterton: C., the marvellous boy 466:2
Chaucer: 12:28 151:34 151:35 260:7
    Dan C., the first warbler 416:10
    Dan C., well of English undefiled 403:4
    learned C., and rare Beaumont 26:9
Chavender: fine stuffed c. 335:10
Cheap: c., it costs . . . nothing 86:13
    Hold them c. 206:9
Cheat: And c. you yet 83:19
    detecting what I think a c. 222:11
    sweet c. gone 134:15
Cheating: period of c. 59:15
Check: Oh! dreadful is the c. 69:2
Checkmate: Cheating c. by painting 185:3
Cheek: blood Spoke in her c.s 146:5
    Care Sat on his fadd c. 278:22
    c.s of sorry grain 275:33
    c. that doth not fade 230:23
    crack your c.s! rage! 362:14
    Fat ruddy c.s Augustus had 202:22
    Feed of her damask c. 383:14

give this c. a little red 314:20
He that loves a rosy c. 98:25
His withered c. and tresses grey 339:23
My c. is cold and white, alas! 391:13
Pale grew thy c. and cold 94:8
smite thee on thy right c. 49:4
That I might touch that c. 379:9
warm wet c. 246:27
Cheer: Be of good c. 50:15
C.! Boys, c.! 263:16
C. up, the worst is yet to come 218:24
Don't c., boys 308:11
Nor c. of mind 378:17
scarce forbear to c. 262:1
silence sounds no worse than c.s 210:13
Two c.s are quite enough 167:23
Cheerful: so c. as keeps me going 230:1
Cheerfulness: c. was always breaking in 154:14
Cheering: great c. of cheering us all up 31:17
Cheerio: its c. my deario 267:29
Cheerioh: 'c.' and 'cheeri-bye' 32:16
Cheerly: But c. c., She loves me dearly 230:10
Cheese: ate the c.s out of the vats 76:23
dreamed of c. – toasted, mostly 406:27
Hellish dark, and smells of c. 409:20
I do not like green c. 110:26
when the c. is gone 67:8
Chefs-d'oeuvre: au milieu des c. 168:15
Chemist: c., fiddler, statesman, and buffoon 149:20
Cheque: political blank c. 183:18
Chequer-board: C. of Nights and Days 164:18
Cherish: love, c. and to obey 319:43
to love and to c. 319:42
Cherries: Just a Bowl of C. 70:10
There c. grow which none may buy 97:30
Cherry: C. ripe, ripe, ripe, I cry 200:4
Like to a double c. 372:5
Loveliest of trees, the c. now 210:5
ruddier than the c. 173:24
That a c. Was as red 232:17
There c.s grow 4:11
To see the c. hung with snow 210:7
Cherry-isle: There's the land, or c. 200:4
Cherry-ripe: Till c. themselves do cry 4:11 97:30
Cherry-stone: carve heads upon c.s 223:17
Cherry-tree: Bow down good c. 22:9
Cherubim: C. and seraphim falling down 196:27
c. does cease to sing 60:11
heaven's c., horsed 365:7
Cherubin: quiring to the young-eyed c.s 370:20
Cherubinnes: fyr-reed c. face 107:28
Cheshire: C. Cat vanished quite slowly 101:4
Chess: devil played at c. with me 70:27
Life's too short for c. 94:15
Chessboard: called the c. white 73:3
Chest: c. contrived a double debt 181:9
Fifteen men on the dead man's c. 406:24
Chester: Charge, C., c.! 340:20
Chesterfield, Earl of 220:24 220:25 540:26
Chesterton: dared attack my C. 30:31
Chestnut: Under the spreading c. tree 257:19
Chevalier: young C. 291:7
Chevalier: c. sans peur et sans reproche 27:2
Chevaux: c. du roi de France 191:20
Chewed: some few to be c. and digested 20:32
Chic: Radical c. 460:9
Chicken: all my pretty c.s and their dam 367:9

c. in his pot 198:3
count their c.s ere they're hatched 87:24
don't count your c.s 3:25
have her neck wrung like a c. 451:22
Some c.; some neck! 113:4
Chid: you'll never be c. 154:6
Chide: c. me for loving 122:3
Chief: c. of Ulva's isle 97:10
Hail to the c. 339:20
will be c. among you 50:43
Chieftain: c. to the Highlands bound 97:9
Great c. o' the puddin'-race 85:24
Child: all any reasonable c. can expect 300:10
as . . . with a sprightly and forward c. 109:12
As yet a c., not yet a fool 312:19
at least one delicate c. 337:25
Beheld the c. 314:5
brought to bed . . . of a dead c. 17:17
Cease towards the c. she bare 125:28
c. imposes on the man 150:24
c. is afraid of being whipped 220:10
c. is father of the man 463:15
c. is known by his doings 42:25
c. of a day 246:22
c. of ten can go on the road 430:10
c.'s a plaything 246:18
c. should always say what's true 407:13
c. that is not clean and neat 407:17
cry of a c. by the roadway 471:11
Dupe . . . even from a c. 126:6
flourish in a c. of six 30:5
for the mother's sake, the c. was dear 118:11
happy English c. 415:4
He became a little c. 62:16
Here a little c. I stand 200:22
I could lie down like a tired c. 394:4
If you strike a c. 388:29
I heard one calling, 'C.' 199:8
I'm nobody's c. 103:2
infant c. is not aware 209:21
Inside the smithy the c. has closed his eyes 173:3
Is it well with the c.? 36:24
I was a c. and she was a c. 310:16
Like a c. at play 271:22
Like a c. from the womb 390:17
little c. shall lead them 45:10
nicest c. I ever knew 30:4
old Adam in this C. 319:25
painted c. of dirt 312:25
simple c., That lightly draws its breath 467:16
speak like a c. 291:2
spoil the c. 87:19
teach the c. to doubt 60:17
This c. I to myself will take 467:2
To have a thankless c. 362:3
Train up a c. 42:30
unto us a c. is born 45:8
When I was a c., I spake 55:25
wise father that knows his own c. 369:24
young healthy c. well nursed 411:8
Childhood: C. is measured out 33:1
c. shows the man 281:6
c., youth and old age 33:9
In my days of c. 245:6
sleep as I in c. 114:27
'tis the eye of c. 365:27
Where once my careless c. strayed 187:2

White c. moving like a sigh 14:23
Childish: C., but very Natural 118:10
  put away c. things 55:25
Childishness: It does from c. 343:21
  second c. and mere oblivion 345:11
Childless: proceeded from c. man 19:9
Children: and on our c. 51:25
  Anyone who hates c. and dogs 163:13
  become as little c. 50:28
  best understood by c. and animals 409:2
  borne him three c. 214:6
  Bring forth men c. only 365:15
  but c. of a larger growth 151:18
  But, c., you should never let 447:10
  called the c. of God 48:42
  C. aren't happy with nothing to ignore 292:11
  c. are true judges 14:29
  C. begin by loving their parents 455:37
  C. dear, was it yesterday 11:6
  c. followed with endearing wile 181:4
  c. of the kingdom 49:30
  C. of the Ritz 123:26
  c. of this world are . . . wiser 52:29
  C. sweeten labours 19:8
  C. to the motherly 67:2
  c. walking two and two 62:12
  c. were an unnatural strain on parents 435:13
  C. with Hyacinth's temperament 335:16
  C., you are very little 407:20
  Come, dear c., let us away 11:3
  comes after c. when they won't go to bed 202:21
  Do you hear the c. weeping 71:26
  For c. at the gate 155:28
  Her c. arise up 43:11
  He that hath wife and c. 19:10
  his c. go barefoot 388:17
  In sorrow thou shalt bring forth c. 34:3
  little c. died in the streets 14:6
  justified of her c. 50:3
  kept me from c. who were rough 402:15
  known as the C.'s Hour 256:14
  little c. cried in the streets 289:11
  Madonna of the Slums with her pallid c. 255:16
  many men, many women, and many c. 221:5
  more careful . . . than of their c. 307:7
  neither c. nor gods 238:28
  opponent of . . . the c. of light 12:21
  procreation of c. 319:39
  Rachel weeping for her c. 48:34
  see the c. sport upon the shore 464:15
  so many c. she didn't know what to do 298:5
  Suffer the little c. 51:39
  tale which holdeth c. from play 396:20
  Thy c. like the olive-branches 41:4
  till her c. came from school 86:19
  tiresome for c. 335:7
  too easy for c. 338:21
  to the farmer's c. you beckon 14:2
  When c. of one family Fall out 447:11
  wife and c. but as bills of charges 19:11
  your c. all gone 296:31
Child-wife: Only my c. 137:26
Chill: Ah, bitter c. it was! 230:13
Chime: heard the c.s at midnight 356:4
  Higher than the sphery c. 275:35
Chimeras: dire c. and enchanted isles 275:22
Chimney: c. shudders to the blast 68:2
  old men from the c. corner 396:20

Sixty Horses Wedged in a Chimney 289:4
So your c.s I sweep 62:9
Chimney-sweepers: As c., come to dust 347:15
Chimpanzees: Brainless as c.s 96:9
Chin: C. upon hand 73:28
  close-buttoned to the c. 124:33
  his c. new-reaped 353:28
  pillows his c. upon an orient wave 277:27
China: moiling for the prettiest piece of c. 468:14
  slow boat to C. 256:4
  surrounded by cows – and c. 137:33
  though C. fall 314:29
Chinee: heathen C. is peculiar 194:23
Chinese Wall: erection of the C. of Milton 157:19
Chink: c. in the floor 413:9
  fill hup the c.s wi' cheese 409:18
  their importunate c. 82:17
Chip: c. off the old 'block' 81:24
  c.s with everything 450:18
Chit: bit of a c. of a boy 95:19
Chit-chat: divine c. of Cowper 246:6
Chivalry: age of c. is gone 82:13
  age of c. is past 238:2
  charge with all thy c. 97:7
  Christian service and true c. 376:17
  swear by all the orders of c. 104:13
Chloe: Say, what can C. want? 314:25
Chocolate: c. cream soldier 387:19
  I always carry c. instead 387:18
Choice: Each to his c., and I rejoice 240:28
  just the terrible c. 78:10
  small c. in rotten apples 380:15
  you takes your c. 322:4
Choir: Bare ruined c.s 386:10
  c.s and places where they sing 318:29
  in a wailful c. 233:20
  join the c. invisible 155:21
Choler: aggravate your c. 355:27
Choose: do not c. to have it known 109:20
Choosing: long c., and beginning late 280:30
Chopcherry: And c., c. ripe within 306:22
Chopper: Here comes a c. 297:19
Chopping-block: Who wants a doctrine for a c. 76:3
Chorasmian: lone C. shore 390:10
Chord: c. in the human mind 136:28
  struck one c. of music 321:3
Chorus: c. of indolent reviewers 416:18
  sang the c. from Atlanta to the sea 467:30
Chose: c.s sont contre nous 218:4
  plus c'est la même c. 229:11
Chosen: few are c. 51:2
Christ: ambassadors for C. 55:47
  Behold a man raised up by C. 417:36
  Came C. the tiger 156:11
  cautious, statistical C. 300:6
  C. have mercy upon us 318:26
  C. his only Son 318:24
  C. is thy strength 284:22
  C. of his gentleness 185:4
  C. the same yesterday 57:18
  If Jesus C. were to come 100:18
  in C. shall be made alive 55:32
  one foundation Is Jesus Christ her Lord 408:3
  Our campioun C. 152:15
  Our fair father C. 416:33
  These C.s that die upon the barricades 455:4
  time draws near the birth of C. 417:35
  to live is C. 56:23

unsearchable riches of C. 56:14
unto his captain C. 377:8
Who dreamed that C. has died in vain? 397:18
Why did you kill C.? 79:16
Christendom: wisest fool in C. 198:5
Christian: as I am a C. faithful man 377:30
better . . . than a drunken C. 271:17
C.! dost thou see them 292:25
C. ideal . . . has been found difficult 111:6
C.s awake, salute 88:29
C., seek not yet repose 158:2
C.s have burnt each other 91:3
Fled with a C.! O my C. ducats! 369:29
forgive them, as a C. 17:13
hard it is To be a C. 74:11
He is a proper C. 426:24
honourable style of a C. 70:21
I hate him for he is a C. 369:13
in what peace a C. can die 2:23
I was born of C. race 447:8
O father Abram! what these C.s are 369:20
Onward, C. soldiers 25:4
Onward, C.s, onward go 452:16
O witness of the soul C. by nature 424:32
perfectly like a C. 316:14
persuadest me to be a C. 54:12
render the C. life intensely difficult 254:6
Scratch the C. and you find the pagan 473:2
See how these C.s love one another 424:33
Some C.s have a comfortable creed 91:10
souls of C. peoples 109:25
tiger that *hadn't got* a C. 322:12
you were a C. slave 198:2
Christ Church: I am the Dean of C. 403:25
Christianity: C. naturally, but why journalism? 21:23
C. promises to make men free 215:5
decay of C. 336:7
local c., called C. 193:15
loving C. better than Truth 118:15
Muscular C. 7:1
nothing in C. or Buddhism 336:5
Rock and roll or C. 253:4
where C. was the religion 411:18
Christmas: At C. I no more desire a rose 363:20
born on C. Day 7:18
callèd unto mind that it was C. Day 402:1
C. comes but once a year 433:15
C. Day in the workhouse 397:11
C. Eve, and twelve of the clock 193:7
C. should fall out in . . . winter 2:9
counted loss for C. 56:25
dreaming of a white C. 32:10
If someone said on C. Eve 193:8
insulting C. card I received this morning 188:18
keep our C. merry still 340:14
Old C. brought his sports again 340:15
On C. Day in the morning 7:5
perceive C. through its wrapping 452:12
walking backwards for C. 274:4
Christopher: C. Robin is saying his prayers 274:18
C. Robin went down with Alice 274:13
Chronic: Do not weep for me. It is c. 138:26
Chronicle: abstracts and brief c.s 350:6
Look in the c.s 380:12
make your c. as rich with praise 356:23
Scandalous C. 332:20
When in the c. of wasted time 386:24

Chronique: *C. scandaleuse* 332:20
Chub: chavender, or c. 335:10
Chump: C.s always make the best husbands 459:9
Sally, grab a c. 459:9
Church: As some to c. repair 313:11
Broad of C. 33:3
Built God a c. 126:22
C. and no steeple! 410:18
C. of England . . . a compromise 396:7
C.'s one foundation 408:3
Come all to c., good people 210:16
from the C. to stray 62:1
get me to the c. on time 253:20
Halloa! Here's a c.! 138:8
Here is the c. 296:18
holy Catholic C. 318:25
I can see a c. by daylight 372:29
I like the silent c. 159:5
I will build my c. 50:23
nearer the C. 5:7
no salvation outside the C. 16:4
not been in the inside of a c. 221:9
not so wide as a c. door 379:32
plain as way to parish c. 345:9
Saint Praxed's ever was the c. 73:10
seed of the C. 424:34
some new and great period in His C. 282:20
To c.; and with my mourning 307:23
too close in c. and mart 72:10
waiting at the c. 252:5
What is a c.? 128:4
what no other c. has ever understood 262:12
Churches: keep silence in the c. 55:27
Churchyard: C. abounds with images 219:25
When c.s yawn 351:20
Churn: Attract a silver c. 177:42
Cibus Ut quod ali c. 259:23
Cider-press: Into a c.'s gripe 76:27
Ciel: *c. défend* 284:15
c. t'aidera 244:16
*en un c. ignoré*199:31
Cieux: *c. n'étaient pas mornes* 211:21
Cigar: good c. is a smoke 238:14
He smokes a fifty-cent c. 1:4
really good five-cent c. 268:8
Cinarae: *Sub regno C.* 209:7
Cincinnatus: C. of the West 93:16
Cinco: *A las c. de la tarde* 172:17
Cinders: Love forgive us! – c., ashes, dust 231:15
Sat among the c. 297:5
Cinema: c. is truth twenty-four times a second 179:8
Circe: elegance of C.'s hair 317:21
Circenses: *Panem et c.* 228:6
Circle: All things . . . come round in a c. 16:11
Describe a c., stroke its back 215:14
Small c.s glittering idly in the moon 465:6
weave a c. round him thrice 118:6
within this c. of flesh 71:3
Circuit: C. of the All 310:14
Circumference: whose c. is nowhere 159:19
Circumlocution: C. Office was beforehand 138:11
Circumscribed: no limits, nor is c. 266:20
Circumspect: Buckingham grows c. 378:7
Circumstance: C.s beyond my individual control 137:27
every conceivable c. 318:2
Fearful concatenation of c.s 448:24

Unsifted in such perilous c. 348:24
very slave of c. 93:20
Citadel: mountain-built with peaceful c. 231:23
vain c.s that are not walled 302:18
Cité: Fourmillante c. 26:16
Cities: He saw the c. of many peoples 204:13
Seven c. warred for Homer 201:3
sung women in three c. 317:19
Towered c. please us 276:30
Citizen: All free men . . . are c.s of Berlin 235:23
c. of no mean city 54:5
c. of the world 19:28 400:21
c.s of death's grey land 337:29
civil c.s kneading up the honey 356:24
first and second class c.s 457:22
John Gilpin was a c. 125:6
tyrannize . . . over his fellow c.s 236:13
you fat and greasy c.s 344:28
Citoyen: Aux armes, c.s! 332:10
City: as a C. upon a hill 459:1
Babylon . . . that great c. 58:23
beautiful c. of Prague 321:22
C. is of Night 428:16
c. now doth, like a garment, wear 463:10
c. of Destruction 80:18
c. with no more personality 106:7
coming out of a keen c. 129:21
first c., Cain 124:3
great c. is that which 453:21
holy c., new Jerusalem 58:32
in this c. at the feet of Gamaliel 54:6
long in c. pent 233:7
No c. should be too large 121:17
no continuing c. 57:19
populous and a smoky c. 392:17
rose-red c. – 'half as old as time' 81:9
run about through the c. 39:3
Seventy-two suburbs in search of a c. 304:13
shady c. of palm-trees 438:12
Sun-girt C. 391:25
sweet c. with her dreaming spires 12:2
Unreal C., Under the brown fog 156:38
Up and down the C. Road 266:2
wander o'er c., and sea, and land 394:13
wealth is his strong c. 41:33
City-square: house for me . . . in the c. 79:7
Civet: Give me an ounce of c. 362:40
Civil: too c. by half 395:29
Civilian: For a botched c. 317:24
mushroom rich c. 94:5
Civilities: bandy c. with my Sovereign 221:23
Civility: c. of my knee 70:22
see a wild c. 200:6
Civilization: As c. advances 262:26
C. advances by extending 453:4
C. is hooped together 471:29
degree of a nation's c. 270:20
elements of modern c. 99:21
resources of c. 179:2
Clad: never venture thinly c. 102:31
Claes: some upo' their c. 84:26
Claim: last territorial c. 201:19
Clamour: c. of the crowded street 257:1
C. rings in his sad ear 185:5
Clan: great verse unto a little c. 231:26
Clap: Don't c. too hard 301:9
Clapper-clawing: one another c. 87:21

Clara: Lady C. Vere de Vere 419:2
Clarence: Duke of C. . . . put to death 161:6
Claret: C. is the liquor for boys 223:6
Clarion: Great winds Thy c.s 111:18
Her c. o'er the dreaming earth 392:4
Sound, sound the c. 287:18
Clarté: Cette obscure c. qui tombe 122:12
Clash: E'en let them c. 85:9
Clasp: I shall c. thee again 77:10
Class: sinking middle c. 301:1
While there is a lower c. 133:8
without distinction of c. 388:4
Classes: back the masses against the c. 179:4
Bow, bow, ye lower middle c.! 177:5
Comfort came in with the middle c. 29:29
responsible and the irresponsible c. 249:10
reviewers . . . fall into two c. 29:11
You may tempt the upper c. 398:19
Classic: c. is something that everybody 434:18
high seriousness of the great c.s 12:28
Classical: it is calm and c. 139:29
Classicism: C. . . . presents them 404:20
Claude: After you, C. 229:13
Claver'se: 'twas C. who spoke 339:11
Claw: pair of ragged c.s 156:23
red in tooth and c. 418:10
Clay: C. lies still 210:8
dead and turned to c. 352:29
I perhaps compounded am with c. 386:9
o'er-informed the tenement of c. 149:10
part of iron and part of c. 46:40
porcelain c. of humankind 151:23
power over the c. 54:33
Shall the c. say 46:1
Clean: Be c., be tidy 15:20
C-l-e-a-n, c., verb active 139:10
only one more thing to keep c. 170:22
pleasant and c. work 333:12
Then I was c. and brave 210:12
You have to c. your plate 330:19
Cleaning: We had daily c. 326:10
Cleanliness: C. is . . . next to godliness 450:28
Clear: c. as a whistle 88:28
C. the air! clean the sky! 157:17
That they could get it c. 102:3
Clearing: c. the world of its . . . problems 140:10
Clearing-house: London . . . the c. of the world 105:22
Cleave: delight to c. . . . . thy glassy wave 187:3
Clemenceau, Georges: 236:15
Clementine: Oh, my darling C.! 286:8
Clerc: Trahison des c.s 31:14
Cleopatra: gone to gaze on C. too 343:29
If C.'s nose had been shorter 305:9
in the bed of C. 70:18
Some squeaking C. boy my greatness 344:8
Your C.; Dolabella's C. 151:19
Clergy: For c. are men 162:23
never been a virtue with the Romish c. 237:21
that the c. were beloved 411:18
We have . . . an Armenian c. 309:17
Clergyman: Mr Wilkinson, a c. 165:4
Clergymen: men, women, and c. 399:30
Cleric: C. before, and Lay behind 87:17
Clerk: city c. but gently born and bred 423:11
c. foredoomed his father's soul 312:15
C. Saunders and May Margaret 22:11

give me indifference and a c. 119:21
Go call a c. 99:2
rattling of a c. 146:22
Coaches: Slow c. and immaculate contraceptives 226:4
Coach-maker: fairies' c.s 378:30
Coal: cargo of Tyne c. 269:25
 diamond may be c. or soot 249:24
 Heap c.s of fire 42:35
 island almost made of c. 33:5
 I sleep on the c.s 137:8
 like a c. His eyeball 398:8
 though the whole world turn to c. 199:27
 With England's own c. 238:15
Coalition: England does not love c.s 142:28
 You may call it a c. 303:11
Coalmine: at suitable depths in disused c.s 236:12
Coarse: one of them is rather c. 6:4
Coaster: Dirty British c. 269:25
Coat: As I take . . . my c. from the tailor 183:1
 c. of many colours 34:29
 for the sake of a ribboned c. 293:21
 Her c. is so warm 296:26
 loves a scarlet c. 204:23
 tattered c. upon a stick 471:19
Coats-of-arms: worth a hundred c. 419:3
Cobham: you, brave C.! 314:21
Cobweb: laws were like c.s 18:13
Cocaine: C. isn't habit-forming 24:1
Cock: Before the c. crow 51:20
 Can this c. hold The vasty fields 356:20
 C. a doodle doo! 296:10
 'C. and a Bull,' said Yorick 406:2
 c.'s shrill clarion 186:4
 c. that crowed in the morn 298:6
 c. who thought the sun had risen 155:10
 drenched our steeples, drowned the c.s 362:14
 offer a c. to Asclepius 400:23
 tall anchoring bark Diminished to her c. 362:36
 While the c. with lively din 276:23
Cock-horse: Ride a c. 297:26
Cocking-piece: And the breech, and the c. 326:11
Cockle: C.s and mussels! 7:27
Cocklicrane: coming of the c.s 324:5
Cockloft: Often the c. is empty 171:8
Cockpen: refuse the Laird o' C. 291:9
Cockroaches: huge laughing c. on his top lip 266:3
Cocksure: as c. of anything as Tom Macaulay 271:13
Cockyolybird: All the butterflies and c.s 237:26
Cocoa: C. is a cad and a coward 110:24
Cocquecigrue: A la venue des c.s 324:5
Codlin: C.'s the friend, not Short 139:28
Cœur: blessent mon c. 439:4
 c. est du côté gauche283:22
 fond de mon c. 325:3
 Il pleure dans mon c. 439:6
Coffee: always put mud into c. 425:5
 C., which makes the politician wise 315:23
 if this is c., I want tea 322:19
Coffin: becomes his c. prodigiously 182:10
Cogito: C., ergo sum 135:13
Cognition: C. reigns but does not rule 437:4
Cohort: c. of the damned 239:5
 his c.s were gleaming 93:4
Coil: shuffled off this mortal c. 350:14
Coin: c.s in my pocket reddened 196:20

like to c.s, Some true, some light 416:35
silver c.s sob in the pocket 172:18
Coinage: very c. of your brain 351:32
Coincidence: long arm of c. 105:29
 'strange c.', to use a phrase 92:2
Cold: banners of the ancient C. 397:17
 called a c. a c. 31:16
 catch your death of c. 102:30
 caught a c. in the park 226:24
 caught An everlasting c. 449:6
 C. doth not sting 292:21
 C. in the earth 69:3
 c. war 26:8
 Goodbye and keep c. 170:6
 Keep cool and c. 451:1
 Madame Sosostris . . . Had a bad c. 156:36
 only a little c. I have 299:8
 Out o' the c. an' the rain 238:10
 Spy Who Came in from the C. 251:18
Coldness: faithless c. of the times 418:26
Coleridge, Samuel Taylor: 90:31 195:18 246:13
 brother C. lull the babe 92:31
 You will see C. 391:18
Coliseum: While stands the C. 90:17
Collar: His lockèd, letter'd, braw brass c. 85:31
Collective: layer I call the c. unconscious 227:1
College: endow a c. or a cat 314:32
Collins, Churton 424:25
Colonel: C. of the Knuts 458:16
 C.'s Lady an' Judy O'Grady 239:26
Colonnade: whispering sound of the cool c. 126:11
Coloquintida: as bitter as c. 374:11
Colosse: c. puissant 26:16
Colossus: bestride the narrow world Like a C. 359:16
 cut a C. from a rock 223:17
Colour: All c.s will agree 18:24
 Any c., so long as it's black 167:5
 coat of many c.s 34:29
 Her c. comes and goes 144:6
 which love c. the most 333:15
Colouring: take a sober c. from an eye 464:19
Colour-Serjeant: C. of the Nonpareil battalion 136:34
Columbas: vexat censura 227:17
Columbia: Hail, C.! happy land! 206:26
Columbus: C. sailed the ocean blue 335:1
Column: At first it was a gianty c. 248:31
 enormous fluted Ionic c.s 264:13
 fifth c. will arise 283:8
 firm and unmoved as that c. 220:15
 fountain's silvery c. 118:9
 Throws up a steamy c. 127:12
Combat: c. deepens 97:7
 Et le c. cessa 122:13
Combatant: dust Involves the c.s 127:6
 faute de c.s 122:13
Combination: c. and a form indeed 351:27
Combray: Sunday mornings at C. 321:6
Come: c. he slow, or come he fast 340:10
 C. what may, Time and the hour 364:24
 C. when you're called 154:6
 Do you c. here often? 274:2
 it c.s to me sometimes 274:21
 Let 'em all come! 242:6
 possible that it may not c. 141:29
 She c.s unlooked for 316:7
 taught him NEVER TO c. 124:26

That have c., that have gone 325:6
therefore I cannot c. 52:20
to Hollywood . . . I should not have c. 106:9
until the day that one c.s along 152:2
Where did you c. from, baby dear? 263:10
Why don't you c. up some time 451:7
Will ye no c. back again? 291:5
Will you no c. back again? 203:13
won't c. back till it's over 116:6
Comedian: c. can only last 329:4
Comedies: All c.s are ended by a marriage 91:17
Come-down: scandal, the incredible c.! 29:10
Comedy: c. in long-shot 106:11
  C. . . . is society protecting itself 320:13
  dressed for this short c. 9:1
  killing time is . . . the essence of c. 435:2
  most lamentable c. 371:23
  world is a c. to those that think 445:10
Comer: grasps in the c. 382:14
Comet: there are no c.s seen 360:1
  Ye country c.s, that portend 268:27
Comfit: to be deceived with c.s 18:9
Comfort: a' the c. we're to get 85:30
  Be of good c., Master Ridley 248:25
  carry their c. about with them 155:15
  C. came in with the middle classes 29:29
  C. ye, c. ye my people 45:29
  I beg cold c. 361:27
  naught for your c. 109:27
  Now I, to c. him 356:33
  receives c. like cold porridge 380:37
  so will I c. you 46:23
  This must my c. be 376:11
  thy rod and thy staff they c. me 38:3
  Well, here's my c. 380:42
Comfortable: baith grand and c. 25:20
Comforted: would not be c. 48:34
Comforter: C., where, where is your comforting?
  206:8
  Miserable c.s are ye all 37:2
Comic: root of the c. 468:17
Coming: as their c. hither 363:8
  cold c. we had of it 156:18
  meet thee at thy c. 45:11
Command: Less used to sue than to c. 339:18
  not born to sue, but to c. 376:9
  wide as his c. 149:5
Commandment: Fear God, and keep his c.s 44:15
  I'd set my ten c.s in your face 357:31
  new c. I give unto you 53:26
  Where there aren't no Ten C.s 240:6
Commence: Let wealth and c. . . . die 266:7
Comment: C. is free 339:9
Commentary: snivelling c. 185:7
Commentator: As learned c.s view 410:13
  give me c.s plain 128:9
  How c.s each dark passage shun 472:17
Commission: Each bullet has got its c. 136:6
Commodity: smooth-faced gentleman, tickling C.
  361:12
Common: century of the c. man 444:8
  C. sense is the most widely distributed 135:10
  morality of the c. man 294:21
  nothing c. did 268:25
  to make it too c. 355:18
  word of a c. man 110:11
Commonplace: c.s are the great poetic truths 407:9

provided his c. book be full 411:17
  Thou unassuming c. 467:10
Commons: C., faithful to their system 263:19
  speak very well in the House of C. 143:31
Commonwealth: caterpillars of the c. 376:24
C. of Nations 330:16
  if the British Empire and its C. 112:23
  raise up c.s, and ruin kings 149:8
  wider vision of the C. 264:6
Commune: Look at the Paris C. 159:27
Communication: Evil c.s corrupt 55:35
Communion: rapt into still c. 461:22
Communism: C. is Soviet power plus 252:25
  spectre of C. 269:13
Communist: Catholic and the C. are alike 301:5
  Catholics and C.s have committed 187:23
  Nazis came for the C.s 294:17
  We C.s are dead men 254:3
  What is a c.? 158:3
Community: carry conviction to our whole c. 310:3
  part of the c. of Europe 336:21
Commuter: C. – one who spends his life 452:11
Companion: All her lovely c.s 287:8
  best c.s, innocence and health 180:19
  c.s for middle age 19:12
  hate to find C.s of our woe 445:17
  only fit c. is his horse 124:32
  that such c.s thou'dst unfold 375:16
  think of those c.s true 98:19
  unwholesome c.s for grown people 245:26
Company: c. that pleased me mightily 307:25
  C., villanous c. 354:32
  conversation in a mixed c. 109:19
  except the present c. 299:15
  hell for c. 25:19
  In married life three is c. 455:10
  in the climate or the c. 224:6
  I love to be the worst of the c. 411:6
  little love and good c. 161:20
  Live always in the best c. 399:32
  one part of the c. would weigh it down 190:9
  pleasure of your c. 246:8
  take the tone of the c. 109:7
  time to spare From c. 192:23
  United Metropolitan . . . Punctual Delivery C.
    139:5
  when without c. 339:8
Companye: Allone, withouten any c. 108:5
  Withouten other c. in youthe 107:24
Compare: doesn't compare to what it was 148:11
Comparison: c.s are odious 144:20
  C.s are odorous 373:10
Compass: faithful c. that still points to thee 174:26
  narrow c., and yet there Dwells 445:2
  seams, opening wide, and c. lost 126:9
  Though a wide c. round be fetched 72:22
  Through all the c. of the notes 150:33
  to the top of my c. 351:17
  Truth lies within a . . . c. 64:22
Compassed: we also are c. about 57:14
Compasses: As stiff twin c. are two 146:17
Compassion: bowels of c. 57:39
Competency: c. lives longer 369:7
Competition: Approves all forms of c. 115:23
Complacency: entire c. and satisfaction 245:11
  stirring up c. 453:12
Complaint: C.s is many and various 185:12

most fatal c. 201:14
Completion: time available for its c. 304:21
Complexion: c.s And Cheeks of sorry grain 275:33
  Mislike me not for my c. 369:22
  often is his gold c. dimmed 385:17
  That schoolgirl c. 3:9
Compliance: by a timely c., prevented him 162:21
Complice: *come un c. à pas de loup* 26:14
Compliment: returned the c. 442:20
  your c.s reaching the proper ears 241:24
Composer: good c. does not imitate 409:1
  Soviet c.'s reply 396:8
Composition: Movement and Space c. 32:4
  Read over your c.s 222:9
Compound: C. for sins 87:11
Comprendre: Tout c. c'est tout pardonner 403:29
Compressing: c. the largest amount of words 112:14
Compromise: Church of England . . . no doubt a c.
  396:7
  founded on c. and barter 81:21
Compt: when we shall meet at c. 375:25
Compulsion: Give you a reason on c.! 354:13
  Such sweet c. 275:1
Comrade: bring his c.s home 204:13
  c. of thy wanderings over heaven 392:9
  stepping where his c. stood 340:21
Comus: C. all allows 92:29
Concealment: let c. like a worm i' the bud 383:14
Conceit: curst c. o' bein' richt 263:7
  force his soul so to his own c. 350:8
  Infusing him with self and vain c. 377:2
  wise in his own c. 42:39 42:41
  wise in your own c.s 54:37
Conceited: never any pity for c. people 155:15
Concentration: seventh degree of c. 387:33
Conception: C. . . . *fundamental brain-work* 332:2
  present at the c. 300:10
Concern: Conduct . . . its largest c. 13:1
  power narrows the areas of man's c. 235:24
Concertina: I've a head like a c. 238:18
Concessions: c. of the weak 81:14
Conclave: In stately c. met 110:3
Conclusion: art of drawing sufficient c.s 87:38
  comin' to c.s 263:8
  denoted a foregone c. 375:9
  men hasten to a c. 20:9
  most lame and impotent c. 374:16
Concord: Unity, peace, and c. 319:6
Concordia: C. discors 207:22
Concubine: Twenty-two acknowledged c.s 175:17
Concurrence: fortuitous c. of atoms 303:11
Condamner: c. les gens 284:8
Condemning: before thinking of c. others 284:8
Condition: All sorts and c.s of men 319:9
  c. of man . . . is a c. of war 202:4
  stars . . . govern our c.s 362:35
  that can speak to thy c. 168:12
Conduct: c. isn't all your fancy paints 240:31
  C. is three-fourths of our life 13:1
  I consider your c. 10:14
  secondly, gentlemanly c. 13:7
Cones: eat the c. under his pines 170:9
Conference: c. a ready man 20:33
  naked into the c. chamber 33:8
Confess: confessing that I have nothing to c. 83:15
Confessional: apt c. for one 467:19
Confidant: her c. stark mad in white linen 395:12

Confine: on the very verge Of her c. 362:11
Confirmation: to the jealous c.s strong 375:2
Conflict: Never in the field of human c. 112:24
  We are in armed c. 154:1
Conform: either c., or be more wise 307:15
Confound: do but themselves c. 81:1
  to c. the wise 54:50
Confusion: big, booming, buzzing c. 217:14
  C. now hath made his masterpiece! 366:3
  C. on thy banners wait 185:19
  C. worse confounded 279:9
  from a couch in some c. 120:31
  in the last c. 94:7
  mazes of metaphorical c. 227:9
  quick bright things come to c. 371:21
Confute: C., change hands, and still c. 87:4
Congs: Kinquering C. 403:19
Congo: Then I saw the C. 255:3
Congratulation: C.s; we all knew 304:13
Congregation: latter has the largest c. 133:18
Congrès: c. ne marche pas 254:13
Congress: C. makes no progress 254:13
Conjecture: not beyond all c. 71:17
  Now entertain c. of a time 357:9
Conjunction: c. of the mind 268:16
Connect: Only c.! 167:18
Connecting-rod: stride o' you c. 239:35
Connoisseur: ruins, preserved by the c. 321:1
Connubiality: wictim of c. 140:31
Conquer: c. but to save 97:2
  conquering, and to c. 58:13
  will c., but they will not convince 435:4
Conquered: Thou hast c., O Galilean 226:31
Conquering: so sharp the c. 108:21
Conqueror: came in with the C. 68:21
  Lie at the proud foot of a c. 361:28
Conquest: Are all thy c.s . . . Shrunk 360:8
  fanned by C.'s crimson wing 185:19
  peace is of the nature of a c. 356:8
  Roman C. was . . . a *Good Thing* 342:15
  shameful c. of itself 376:18
  To spread her c.s farther 84:1
Conscience: catch the c. of the king 350:12
  C. and grace to the profoundest pit! 352:12
  c. as their King 416:31
  C. avaunt, Richard's himself 114:10
  c. void of offence 54:7
  c. with injustice is corrupted 358:2
  guardian of His Majesty's c. 430:1
  My c. hath a thousand several tongues 378:19
  O coward c. 378:18
  still and quiet c. 358:23
  uncreated c. of my race 226:19
  will not cut my c. to fit 197:10
Consciousness: attitude peculiar to a c. 227:3
  growth of national c. 264:8
  highest activities of c. 271:4
  world of our present c. 217:11
Consecration: c., and the poet's dream 461:16
Consent: hath without c. been only tried 301:21
  whispering 'I will ne'er c.' 91:4
Consequence: c.s . . . will be what they will be 86:28
  damn the c.s 274:35
  In nature . . . there are c.s 215:12
  to betray's In deepest c. 364:20
Conservation: without the means of its c. 82:11
Conservative: C. government is . . . hypocrisy 142:26

C. is only a Tory who is ashamed 169:10
c.s when they are least vigorous 158:28
or else a little C. 177:11
sound C. government 142:14
staid, c. . . . type of mind 447:5
with more propriety be called the C. party 129:6
would make me c. when old 170:10
Conservatism: What is c.? 254:15
Consideration: C. like an angel came 356:21
In war, moral c.s 291:14
primary c. . . . to take care of ourselves 222:20
Consolation: one c., as they always say 140:34
With peace and c. 281:32
Conspicuous: c. by its presence 334:2
Conspiracy: Open-eyed c. 380:39
Conspirator: All the c.s save only he 361:4
Constable: fit man for the c. of the watch 373:5
Outrun the c. at last 87:18
Constabulary: When c. duty's to be done 178:5
Constancy: Hope c. in wind 92:25
infernal c. of the women who love me 389:2
no object worth its c. 394:11
Constant: But c., he were perfect 384:10
C. you are 354:3
if thou wilt be c. then 286:7
She is so c. to me 230:10
To one thing c. never 372:36
Constellations: foreign c. west 192:16
Constitution: c. does not provide for 457:22
fundamental principle of the English c. 59:30
higher law than the C. 342:28
principles of a free c. 175:14
Constraint: All c. . . . is evil 127:24
Consubstantial: C., co-eternal 292:26
Consule: fortunatam natam me c. Romam 114:24
Consume: creature that c.s without producing
300:11
Consummation: c. Devoutly to be wished 350:14
Consummatum: C. est 53:38
Consumption: Conspicuous c. 438:24
very profitable c. 395:5
Contagion: C. to this world 351:20
foul c. spread 277:14
From the c. of the world's slow stain 390:5
great danger of c. 456:33
Contemneth: He that c. small things 48:13
Contemplation: Cherub C. 276:5
C.'s sober eye 187:9
For c. he and valour formed 279:26
Has left for c. 32:18
Contempt: for c. too high 124:5
Contend: Let's c. no more, Love 79:11
Content: He that wants money, means, and c.
345:16
In measureless c. 365:18
land of lost c. 210:26
O sweet c.! 133:21
range with humble livers in c. 358:16
That c. surpassing wealth 394:3
therewith to be c. 56:30
Contented: C. wi' little 84:3
Contention: Let the long c. cease! 11:11
Contentment: Preaches c. to that toad 240:13
Contest: Great c. follows 127:6
What mighty c.s rise 315:11
Contiguity: boundless c. of shade 126:34
Continent: C. will not suffer England 142:23

every man is a piece of the C. 146:20
iron curtain . . . across the C. 113:10
many nations and three separate c.s 148:3
wind of change blowing through this C. 264:8
Contract: nothing but a civil c. 342:7
Social C. is . . . a vast conspiracy 450:13
verbal c. isn't worth the paper 183:13
Contradict: Do I c. myself? 454:2
Contradicting: c. a bishop 223:16
Contradiction: at best a c. still 314:30
C. for its own dear sake 124:28
It is a c. in terms 389:10
Military intelligence is a c. in terms 269:10
Contraries: Without c. is no progression 63:4
Contrariwise: C. . . . if it was so 101:32
Contrary: everythink goes c. with me 137:4
Contrast: derive intense enjoyment from a c. 169:11
Contree: Know thy c. 107:6
Contrive: c. to write so even 17:4
Control: beyond my individual c. 137:27
I have submitted to a new c. 461:17
Controlled: claim not to have c. events 254:22
Contumely: proud man's c. 350:14
Convent: To happy c.s, bosomed deep in vines
311:27
Conventicle: being at a c. 307:15
Convention: To the Lords of C. 339:11
Converser: c. avec ceux des autres siècles 135:12
Conversation: C. is imperative 452:19
different name for c. 405:20
His c. usually threatened 221:30
make his c. perfectly delightful 400:2
proper subject of c. 109:19
Converse: Formed by thy c. 314:12
hold high c. with the mighty dead 428:14
Spend in pure c. 69:23
Conversing: With thee c. I forget all time 279:33
Convert: can true c.s make 162:1
perfectly qualified for making c.s 182:28
Convey: 'Convey' the wise it call 371:4
Conveyance: marriage . . . not a public c. 290:3
Conviction: best lack all c. 471:20
Convince: conquer, but they will not c. 435:4
Convincing: less c. than one 213:1
Conviviality: kindled at the taper of c. 139:26
Convocation: c. of politic worms 351:39
Cooing: no one cares for matrimonial c.s 91:16
Cook: can't c. them unless you have them 270:21
c. and a captain bold 176:14
C. is a little unnerved 32:17
c. was a good c. 336:6
Every c. has to learn how 252:24
good c., and a good digestion 332:14
ill c. that cannot lick 380:5
very uncommon c. 335:12
Cookery: Kissing don't last; c. do! 272:24
Cool: c. of the day 33:26 155:25
Coot: haunts of c. and hern 415:20
Cope: starry c. of heaven 280:4
Cophetua: Before the king C. 415:18
When King C. loved 379:7
Copier: mere c. of nature 327:1
Copia: Inopem me c. fecit 302:1
Copperheads: c. and the assassin 336:27
Copulation: Let c. thrive 362:39
Cor: J'aime le son du c. 439:16
Coral: India's c. strand 196:24

Of his bones are c. made 380:35
Corbie: I heard twa c.s 23:19
Cord: charity of the penny c. 347:16
    drew them with c.s of a man 47:9
    silver c. be loosed 44:12
    threefold c. 43:22
Core: ain't-a-going to *be* no c. 434:13
    In my heart's c. 351:4
Corinth: not everyone that can get to C. 207:23
Corinthian: C., a lad of mettle 354:4
Corinthum: Non cuivis homini contingit adire C.
    207:23
Cormorant: common c. or shag 215:21
    Sat like a c. 279:22
    Spite of c. devouring Time 363:17
Corn: bowed locks of the c. 288:20
    breast high amid the c. 205:2
    c. is as high as an elephant's eye 191:11
    c. was orient and immortal wheat 431:15
    Kansas had better stop raising c. 251:12
    men threshed c. at midnight 471:23
    raise the price of c. 89:2
    stood in tears amid the alien c. 232:7
    treadeth out the c. 35:15
    two ears of c. or two blades of grass 410:27
    yellow like ripe c. 331:16
    your shooting c.s presage 410:5
Cornea: quarum altera fertur C. 441:1
Corneille, Pierre: 243:11
Cornfield: That o'er the green c. did pass 346:12
Corner: bad times just around the c. 123:22
    become the head of the c. 50:46
    Come the three c.s of the world in arms 361:28
    from the four c.s of the sky 151:8
    head stone of the c. 40:26
    in every c. sing 199:2
    keep a c. in the thing I love 375:1
    not done in a c. 54:11
    round earth's imagined c.s 145:15
    Sat in the c. 297:3
    Sits the wind in that c.? 372:37
    some c. of a foreign field 69:20
    turn a c. jinkin' 83:19
Cornet: sound of the c., flute, harp 47:1
Cornfield-side: By a c. a-flutter with poppies 74:2
Cornish: twenty thousand C. men 195:3
Coromandel: On the coast of C. 250:16 262:4
Coronation: reject a petrarchal c. 234:4
Coronet: Kind hearts are more than c.s 419:6
Corporation: biggest industrial c. 387:16
    cannot commit treason 116:11
    C.s have neither bodies 430:2
Corpore: mens sana in c. sano 228:7
Corpse: c. you planted last year 156:39
    Each like a c. within its grave 392:4
    frozen c. was he 257:23
    funeral . . . & the *c. should be ready* 446:10
    He'd make a lovely c. 138:34
    he makes a very handsome c. 182:10
    mock the riddled c.s 337:28
    She made a ravishing c. 163:14
    slovenly unhandsome c. 353:29
    this c. which is man 412:29
Correction: c. of the world 284:5
Correlative: finding an 'objective c.' 157:18
Correspondent: c. to command 380:32
Corridor: c.s of power 400:16

c.s of Time 256:18
Corriger: c. le monde 284:5
Corruptible: my fate, 'mongst things c. 273:2
Corruption: C., the most infallible symptom 175:19
    C. wins not more than honesty 358:25
    sown in c. 55:37
    turned into c. 320:6
Corsair: left a C.'s name 90:29
Corse: As his c. to the rampart we hurried 459:24
    thou, dead c. 348:31
Cortez: like stout C. 233:3
Corvis: Dat veniam c. 227:17
Cosmos: God plays dice with the c. 155:4
    too much Ego in your C. 241:21
Cost: But at what c.? 28:9
    not to count the c. 259:11
Cotopaxi: C. Took me by the hand 433:14
Cottage: About your c. eaves 75:20
    c. homes of England! 197:17
    c. which was named the Evening Star 462:28
    c. with a double coach-house 401:15
    Hides not his visage from our c. 384:33
    Love and a c.! 119:21
    Make me a c. in the vale 421:29
    poor men's c.s princes' palaces 369:8
    soul's dark c. 444:13
    Wherever there's a c. small 304:20
Couch: levee from a c. in some confusion 120:31
    retired to his virtuous c. 446:11
Cough: cure the whooping c. 6:8
    one soft, low, gentle c. 459:13
Couldn't: its not 'cause I c. 317:1
Council: Great in c. and great in war 421:15
Counsel: cannot give good c. 86:13
    darkeneth c. by words 37:9
    dost sometimes c. take 315:19
    hard . . . for women to keep c. 360:3
    His c.s guide, uphold you 325:18
    intention to keep my own c. 179:3
    Lord bringeth the c. of the heathen 38:13
    princely c. in his face 278:38
    Sic c.s ye gave to me, O 22:15
    Take my c., happy man 176:23
    To think how mony c.s sweet 85:15
    We took sweet c. together 38:33
    Where no c. is 41:34
Counsellor: in the multitude of c.s 41:34
    when c.s blanch 20:1
    Wonderful, C. 45:8
Counted: c. them all out 191:21
Countenance: c. of his friend 42:48
    c. more in sorrow than in anger 348:14
    damned disinheriting c. 395:38
    did the C. Divine 61:9
    dismal grew his c. 22:12
    journey into a far c. 52:25
    Knight of the Sad C. 104:20
    light of thy c. upon us 37:22
    maketh a cheerful c. 42:12
    shew us the light of his c. 39:12
Counter: All things c.,original 206:13
    Words are wise men's c.s 202:5
Countercheck: c. quarrelsome 346:14
Counterpane: pleasant land of c. 407:15
Counties: Across two c. he can hear 185:5
    Forget six c. overhung with smoke 288:12
    see the coloured c. 210:15

Counting-house: king was in his c. 297:31
Countree: hame to my ain c. 130:7
Countries: no c. in the world less known 65:9
Country: Ask not what your c. can do for you 235:18
  billion dollar c. 167:25
  Born and educated in this c. 174:33
  But that was in an other c. 267:11
  c. in the town 268:11
  died to save their c. 30:22
  dying for their c. 334:1
  Every c. as its own constitution 6:23
  Every c. has the Jews 169:1
  for the good of my c. 161:18
  God made the c. 126:33
  good for the c. was good for General Motors 457:26
  grow up with the c. 187:20
  guts to betray my *country* 167:22
  I have no relish for the c. 399:22
  I loathe the c. 120:32
  I love thee still – My c.! 126:37
  in the c. I wish to vegetate 196:4
  I tremble for my c. 217:25
  I vow to thee, my c. 403:23
  left our c. for our c.'s good 26:7
  Let all the ends . . . be thy c.'s 358:25
  man should know something of his own c. 406:1
  My c. is the world 303:6
  My c., right or wrong 110:27
  My c., 'tis of thee 399:13
  My soul, there is a c. 438:6
  nothing good to be had in the c. 195:20
  Now your c. calls you 194:5
  O my c.! how I leave my c. 309:23
  our c., right or wrong 133:10
  past is a foreign c. 194:29
  prepare the mind of the c. 143:6
  right to say to his c. 304:23
  save in his own c. 50:14
  she is my c. still 111:21
  ship I have got in the North C. 22:19
  'Tis your c. bids! 127:19
  to die for one's c. 208:24
  To do our c. loss 357:15
  undiscovered c. from whose bourn 350:14
  What this c. needs 268:8
  with a place in the c. 172:10
Countrymen: in the hearts of his fellow c. 251:22
  very great many of your c. cannot help 221:3
Countryside: smiling and beautiful c. 147:17
Couplet: at the last and only c. 313:13
  bawl His creaking c.s 92:21
Courage: bear his c. up 60:4
  C., brother! do not stumble 264:1
  'C.!' he said, and pointed 420:8
  C. in your own trouble 183:17
  c. mounteth with occasion 361:8
  c. never to submit or yield 278:7
  c. to change things I can 294:15
  C. was mine 302:18
  One man with c. 216:2
  screw your c. to the sticking place 365:13
  Spontaneous c. 291:20
  With c. love and joy 174:9
Courage: c. de l'improviste 291:20
  C., l'ami, le diable est mort 326:5

Courier: sightless c.s of the air 365:7
Course: cannot steer A middle c. 270:10
  great nature's second c. 365:26
  I have finished my c. 57:7
  I must fight the c. 367:27
  what c. others may take 198:23
Court: at the kinges c. 108:1
  case is still before the c.s 207:1
  C.s and camps are the only places 109:6
  c.s of everlasting day 277:21
  day in thy c.s 39:27
  Death Keeps his pale c. 389:25
  Fresh from brawling c.s 418:19
  In c.s, at feasts, and high solemnities 275:32
  in the c.s of the sun 110:8
  in this supreme c. of yours 324:13
Courtesies: trade in c. and wit 199:14
Courtesy: mirror of all c. 358:14
  very pink of c. 379:25
  what a candy deal of c. 353:33
Courtier: c.'s. soldier's, scholar's eye 350:21
  gallops o'er a c.'s nose 379:1
  O'er c.s' knees 378:30
Courting: Are you c.? 309:1
Courtisan: C.s qui l'entourent 152:12
Courtship: C. to marriage 120:20
Covenant: c. between me and the earth 34:19
Covet: shalt not c., but tradition 115:23
Coveting: C. other men's property 336:23
Cow: cheaper . . . than to keep a c. 88:13
  couple-colour as a brindled c. 206:11
  c. is of the bovine ilk 292:8
  c. jumped over the moon 296:19
  C.s are my passion 137:33
  c.'s in the corn 297:2
  c. with the crumpled horn 298:6
  friendly c., all red and white 407:18
  I wrote the 'Purple C.' 81:8
  Kiss till the c. come home 28:4
  never saw a Purple C. 81:7
  Thank you, pretty c. 415:5
  Three acres and a c. 119:4
  two dun c.s under a walnut tree 336:9
  when she kissed her c. 411:12
Coward: As many other mannish c.s 344:24
  conscience does make c.s of us all 350:14
  count myself the c. 422:27
  c. does it with a kiss 454:21
  C.s die many times before their deaths 360:2
  c.s insult dying majesty 3:27
  c.'s weapon, poison 166:19
  gross flattery to name a c. 430:13
  hero wid c.'s legs 274:7
  Most men are c. 328:12
  No c. soul is mine 68:24
  plague of all c.s 354:6
  Public . . . is greatest of c.s 196:10
  Though c.s flinch 121:9
Cowslip: bottom of a c. 347:5
  c. wan that hang the pensive head 277:16
  In a c.'s bell I lie 381:17
  Sweet c.'s grace 299:13
Coxcomb: hear a c. ask two hundred guineas 333:8
Coy: Sometimes coming, sometimes c. 341:21
Coyness: This c., lady, were no crime 268:31
Cozenage: greatest c. that men can put upon 129:17

517

Crabs: roasted c. hiss in the bowl 364:8
Cracked: It c. and growled 116:25
Cracked-up: We must be c. 138:36
Cradle: Between the c. and the grave 153:4
  c. will rock 60:6
  hand that rocks the c. 444:9
  high mountain c. in Pamere 11:34
  I will c. you 214:18
  our c. stands in the grave 190:13
  Out of the c. endlessly rocking 453:18
  your c., your home, and your bier 391:22
Craft: c. so long to learn 108:21 201:15
  gentlemen of the gentle c. 134:4
  Trim little, prim little c. 178:12
  work of their c. 48:25
Crag: leafless trees and every icy c. 465:11
  water lapping on the c. 417:14
Crambe: Occidit miseros c. repetita magistros 228:3
Cramoisie: sails o' c. 22:24
Cranberry: pound of Rice, and a C. Tart 250:23
Crane: Tall as a c. 397:12
Cranmer, Thomas: 198:7
Cranny: In every c. but the right 126:19
Cras: C. amet qui nunquam amavit 9:8
  C. ingens iterabimus aequor 208:7
Crazy: Checkin' the c. ones 185:1
  half c., all for the love of you 131:1
Cream: choking her with c. 238:1
  Quite the c. of the thing 295:4
  She gives me c. with all her might 407:18
Created: Thou hast c. us for Thyself 15:30
Create: we were tempted to c. 192:19
Creation: acts his own c.s 76:16
  appropriate to a mechanical c. 81:6
  as c.'s dawn beheld 90:22
  C. purged o' the miscreate 78:2
  C. sleeps 472:20
  eternal act of c. 118:17
  fear that c. will expire 400:8
  fevers into false c. 90:12
  finds c. so perfect 321:15
  greatest week . . . since the c. 295:6
  His c.'s approval or censure 78:16
  O fairest of c.! 280:36
  Our c., preservation 319:10
  present at the c. 4:9
  since the c. of the world 222:28
  To which the whole c. moves 418:41
  up and down de whole c. 168:8
  whole c. groaneth 54:28
  whole round of c. 78:16
Creator: abide with my C., God 114:27
  can dispense with a c. 321:15
  creature more than the C. 54:15
  law of our C. 82:3
  Remember now thy C. 44:9
  storehouse for the glory of the C. 18:3
  when it leaves the C.'s hands 332:13
Creature: All c.s great and small 4:3
  All men become good c.s 75:24
  call these delicate c.s ours 375:1
  c. native and indued Unto that element 352:20
  c. of the moment 196:7
  C. in whom excelled 280:36
  c.'s at his dirty work again 312:18
  C.s that by a rule in nature teach 356:24
  Every c. of God 56:42

every c. shall be purified 266:21
From fairest c.s we desire increase 385:11
Good wine is a good familiar c. 374:27
heaven-eyed c. sleeps in earth 461:30
lone, lorn 137:4
meanest of his c.s 76:12
most perverse c.s 2:10
No c. smarts so little 312:17
O what venerable and reverend c.s 431:16
Praise him all c.s here below 235:11
reasonable c.s of God 71:6
Served the c. 54:15
Several poor c.s carried by 307:15
sleek and shining c.s of the chase 422:10
through c.s you dissect 314:17
Credence: so slight it would surpass C. 185:5
Credit: an't much c. in that 138:22
  dead corpse of the Public C. 448:25
  done my c. in this World much wrong 164:27
  greatly to his c. 177:3
  let the C. go 164:3
  Not to thy c. 96:8
  Pass the hat for your c.'s sake 238:9
  some c. in being jolly 138:23
Creditor: c.s who keep pestering us 214:23
  not everyone who wishes makes c.s 324:10
Creditum: quod ab omnibus c. est 440:1
Credo: C. quia impossibile 424:35
Credulity: characteristic . . . is a craving c. 143:3
  C. is the man's weakness 245:31
Creed: comfortable c. 91:10
  c. is a rod 412:22
  dust of c.s outworn 393:2
  It is a modest c. 393:25
  more faith . . . than in half the c.s 418:20
  So many gods, so many c.s 454:19
  Vain are the thousand c.s 68:25
  We have a Calvinistic c. 309:17
  wrought With human hands the c. of c.s 418:1
Creep: C. into thy narrow bed 11:10
Crème: you would have been the c. de la c. 402:4
Crescent: blunt their c.s on the edge of day 150:10
Cressid: Where C. lay that night 370:18
Crete: people of C. . . . make more history 336:3
Crew: c. of the captain's gig 176:14
  Set the c. laughing 166:9
  We were a ghastly c. 117:8
  With all her c. complete 125:34
Cricket: 211:16
  c. on the hearth 276:9
  for the really keen c. fan 295:14
  Her whip, of c.'s bone 378:30
Cricklewood: Midland, bound for C. 32:21
Cried: c. all the way to the bank 254:12
  suddenly c. and turned away 69:10
Crier: C. cried, 'O Yes!' 24:20
Crime: atrocious c. of being a young man 309:15
  bigamy, sir, is a c. 284:18
  c. to love too well 312:2
  c. you haven't committed 318:4
  How many c.s committed 98:3
  man's greatest c. 95:11
  melt into c. 89:7
  more featureless and commonplace a c. 147:13
  one virtue, and a thousand c.s 90:29
  worst of all c.s 388:13
Crime: C'est pire qu'un c. 65:19

c. a ses degrés 325:2
que de c.s on commet en ton nom 329:8
tableau des c.s et des malheurs 442:17
Criminal: punishment of a c. 243:12
   while there is a c. element 133:8
Cripps, Stafford: 113:27
Crisis: Poetry . . . is a c. 336:18
Crispian: This day is called the feast of C. 357:17
Cristes: C. lore and his apostles twelve 107:27
Criterion: only infallible c. of wisdom 82:31
Critic: c. is a man who knows the way 434:23
   c.s all are ready made 92:24
   c.s of the next generation 165:15
   first attribute of a good c. 259:4
   good c. is one who narrates 168:15
   good drama c. is one who perceives 434:22
   Nor in the c. let the man be lost 313:18
   Sir C., good day! 163:7
   therefore they turn c.s 118:26
   writer what he thinks about c.s 191:17
Critical: nothing if not c. 374:13
Criticism: because it permits c. 167:23
   cant of c. is the most tormenting 405:25
   c.: a disinterested endeavour 12:20
   c. is applied only to what he makes of it 217:2
   c. of life under the conditions fixed 12:27
   c. reads to me like a man saying 110:26
   every wind of c. 223:20
   father of English c. 219:24
   most penetrating of c.s 213:2
   People ask you for c. 270:23
   reply to just c. 396:8
   Stealthy School of C. 332:3
   they pass no c.s 155:19
Critique: bon c. est celui qui raconte 168:15
Criticize: don't c. What you can't understand 153:10
Criticizing: pleasure of c. 243:10
Croce: signe triumphall rasit is of the c. 152:15
Crocodile: How doth the little c. 100:30
   What manner o' thing is your c.? 343:34
   wisdom of the c.s 20:7
Cromwell: C. . . . . fling away ambition 358:24
Cromwell, Oliver: 13:26
   C. damned to everlasting fame 314:10
   Some C. guiltless of his country's blood 186:11
   that C. knocked about a bit 255:11
Crony: government by c. 214:25
   His ancient, trusty, drouthy c. 85:16
Crooked: c. shall be made straight 45:31
   strive to set the c. straight 288:11
   There was a c. man 298:4
Crop: a-watering the last year's c. 155:7
   Who said, 'C.s are ripe'? 134:27
Cross: Blind as the . . . nails Upon the C. 397:19
   For our advantage on the bitter c. 353:16
   little marble c. below the town 195:10
   merit Of the Holy C.! 292:25
   no c., no crown 307:6
   on his breast a bloody c. he bore 402:26
   orgasm has replaced the C. 289:14
   take up his c. 50:25
   upon a c. of gold 79:19
   sparkling c. she wore 315:16
   When I survey the wondrous C. 447:20
   With the C. of Jesus 25:4
Crossed: girl likes to be c. in love 17:11
Crosses: Between the c., row on row 264:18

clinging to their c. 109:24
   c. from his sov'reign hand 200:23
Cross-gartered: wished to see thee ever c. 383:17
Crotchet: some c.s in thy head 371:7
Crow: c. Makes wing to the rooky wood 366:20
   c.s and choughs that wing the midway air 362:36
   many-wintered c. 419:23
   upstart c., beautified with our feathers 188:3
   wars of kites and c.s 282:22
Crowd: all at once I saw a c. 462:3
   All c., who foremost shall be damned 311:18
   c. is not company 20:13
   C.s without company 175:11
   far from the madding c.'s ignoble strife 186:14
   If you can talk with c.s 239:13
   I hate the uninitiated c. 208:22
   Lonely C. 327:9
   not feel the c. 127:13
   not preached to the c. 238:13
   Out of the c. a mistress or a friend 390:24
   We met, 'twas in a c. 27:9
Crown: And broke his c. 296:29
   Casting down their golden c.s 196:27
   c. ourselves with rosebuds 47:36
   c.s resign to call thee mine 435:16
   fighting for the c. 296:32
   Give c.s and pounds and guineas 210:11
   give thee a c. of life 58:7
   go forth and conquer a c. 301:16
   hairy gold c. on 'er 'ead 241:11
   hath worn the c. 48:8
   I give away my c. 377:12
   Life's fresh c. 28:22
   Not the king's c. 368:11
   obtain a corruptible c. 55:11
   power of the C. has increased 13:9
   tripled C. 323:4
   Uneasy lies the head that wears a c. 356:1
   walked the earth with c. and palm 78:3
   within the hollow c. 377:2
Crowned: C., and again discrowned 218:17
   fate . . . doth seem To have thee c. 364:29
Crow-toe: tufted c. and pale jessamine 277:16
Crucified: dear Lord was c. 4:7
   Was c., dead. and buried 318:24
Crucify: wouldn't even c. him 100:18
Crude: think me lamentably c. 29:16
Cruel: c. as she's fair 131:9
   c. only to be kind 351:1
   Let me be c., not unnatural 351:21
Cruelties: neither the c. nor the enchantments
   321:18
Cruelty: C. has a human heart 62:23
   O c., To steal my Basil-pot 231:6
   top full Of direst c. 364:31
Cruise: we are all on our last c. 407:2
Crumb: c.s which fell 52:32
   dogs eat of the c.s 50:21
Crumble: curled up like Lord Olofa C. 226:3
Crusade: This party is a moral c. 458:4
Cruse: As my small c. best fits 200:12
Crust: all upper c. here 190:8
Cry: I c. in the daytime 37:41
   I heard a sudden c. of pain! 405:5
   Make 'em laugh; make 'em c. 326:6
   monstrous Head and sickening c. 110:4
   no language but a c. 418:8

still should c, Not to be born 21:6
Crystal: clear as c. 123:22
   moon-freezing c.s 392:22
Cubit: add one c. unto his stature 49:15
Cuckold: great year for c.s 324:11
Cuckoo: as the c. is in June 354:30
   C., jug-jug, pu-we 292:21
   c. then, on every tree 364:6
   first c.'s melancholy cry 463:1
   hear the pleasant c. 132:19
   Lhude sing c. 5:13
   merry c., messenger of spring 402:16
   O c., shall I call thee b. 467:7
   responsive to the c.'s note 187:8
   weather the c. likes 193:12
   Who can hedge in the c.? 104:24
Cuckoo-buds: c. of yellow hue 364:6
Cuckoo clock: what did they produce . . .? The c.
   449:10
Cucumber: c. should be well sliced 223:29
   There were no c.s in the market 455:11
Cudgel: C. thy brains no more 352:21
Cue: Lightly we follow our c. 189:6
   With a twisted c. 177:29
Culpa: O felix c. 283:1
Cult: abolish the c. of the individual 236:17
   local c., called Christianity 193:15
   Shoveacious C. 450:7
Culture: C. being a pursuit of . . . perfection 12:12
   c. is no better than its woods 15:19
   C., the acquainting ourselves 12:30
   highest possible stage in moral c. 132:6
   lead a whore to c. 304:14
   man of c. rare 177:38
   Two C.s 400:15
   two half-cultures do not make a c. 242:11
   universal c. for the crowd 421:32
   When I hear anyone talk of c. 224:16
   When I hear the word C. 179:14
Cumnor: Silvered the walls of C. Hall 272:33
Cunning: c. is the weapon 237:21
   c. men pass for wise 20:4
   more c. to be strange 379:14
   right hand forget her c. 41:10
Cup: Ah, fill the C. 164:15
   Awake . . . and fill the C. 163:23
   Come, fill the C. 163:26
   Come fill up my c. 339:12
   c., and the wine is red 39:21
   c.s That cheer but not inebriate 127:12
   Fill high the c. with Samian wine! 91:27
   his c., the bare Of his palm closed 146:23
   in their flowing c.s freshly remembered 357:18
   Let this c. pass from me 51:21
   no more personality than a paper c. 106:7
   tak a c. o' kindness yet 83:27
Cupboard: c. was bare 297:15
   her c.s opened 193:21
   No! She went to the c. 135:9
   wicked man in the bathroom c. 160:8
Cupid: C. and my Campaspe played 260:8
   C.'s darts do not feel 6:10
   In C.'s net had caught her 7:15
   silent note which C. strikes 71:11
   therefore is winged C. painted blind 371:22
   There's death in the c. 84:28
   where the bolt of C. fell 371:36

Young Adam C. 379:7
Cur: already cur-tailed c. 95:19
   round the ears of the old c. 87:16
   You common cry of c.s! 346:29
Cura: Post equitem sedet atra C. 208:23
Curate: C.s, long dust 69:12
   Edward Bull, the c. 416:13
   feel like a shabby c. 15:23
   I was then a pale young c. 178:15
   mildest c. going 176:12
   preached to death by wild c.s 400:5
Curd: Eating her c.s and whey 297:4
   queen of c.s and cream 384:31
Cure: labour against our own c. 71:12
   no c. for this disease 30:7
   only one c. for the evils 263:1
   Show me a sane man and I will c. him 227:4
   Thy God, thy life, thy c. 438:7
Curfew: C. shall not ring tonight 429:5
   c. tolls the knell of parting day 185:27
   I hear the far-off c. sound 276:8
Curious: Be not c. in unnecessary matters 48:2
Curiouser: C. and c.! 100:29
Curl: had a little c. 257:18
   sable c.s all silvered o'er with white 385:14
Currency: Debasing the moral c. 155:20
Current: Time . . . its c. is strong 16:16
Curse: C. God, and die 36:36
   c. is come upon me 419:14
   c. is on her if she stay 419:10
   c. of hell frae me 22:15
   C.s are like young chickens 401:12
   c.s heaped on each gashed head 401:5
   C.s, not loud but deep 367:18
   rigged with c.s dark 277:11
   such a terrible c. 24:12
Curtain: adverse conditions – the c. was up 269:9
   all the neat c.s are drawn 284:20
   behind the 'iron c.' at last 400:17
   forever slamming down his silly c. 336:20
   fringèd c.s of thine eye 380:36
   it must draw its c. round us 460:22
   Let fall the c.s 127:12
   Mrs Caudle's C. Lectures 218:10
   Ring down the c. 324:21
   rung down the c. 286:12
   tape-tied c.s, never meant to draw 315:3
Curtiosity: full of 'satiable c. 241:18
Curtsey: C. while you're thinking 101:28
Curtsied: C. when you have 380:34
Cusha: 'C.! C.! C.!' calling 215:9
Cushion: I cannon off the c. 108:33
   To rest, the c. and soft dean invite 315:4
Custodes: Quis custodiet ipsos C.? 228:1
Custom: C. . . . . is the great guide 212:6
   C. reconciles us 82:9
   c.s of his tribe and island Britain 387:22
   C.s, politics, and tongue 305:23
   C., that is before all law 131:13
   C., that unwritten law 132:12
   c. to whom c. 54:42
   it is a c. More honoured 348:28
   Lest one good c. should corrupt 417:18
   Nice c.s curtsey to great kings 357:25
   nor c. stale Her infinite variety 343:30
Customer: c. is always right 342:13
   raising up a people of c.s 398:17

tough c. in argeyment 136:14
Cut: c. off out of the land 46:10
  most unkindest c. of all 360:21
  name, that shall not be c. off 46:14
  short c. to everything 223:25
Cut-purse: c. of the empire 351:30
  c. sworn 5:18
Cybernetics: by the name of C. 454:15
Cymbal: high-sounding c.s 41:19
  sounding brass, or a tinkling c. 55:21
Cynara: C! in my fashion 147:10
Cynic: What is a c.? 455:32
Cynicism: C. is intellectual dandyism 272:19
Cynosure: c. of neighbouring eyes 276:26
Cypress: in sad c. let me be laid 383:13
  Nor shady c. tree 331:11
  Nor waves the c. in the palace walk 422:15
  outside the cc. groves 248:32
  where the c. and myrtle are emblems 89:7
Cypresses: Along the avenue of c. 248:34
Cytherea: lids of Juno's eyes Or C.'s breath 384:29
Cythère: cette île triste et noir . . . C. 26:19

D

D: I never use a big, big D. 176:27
Dacian: their D. mother 90:16
Dad: if the d. is present at the conception 300:10
  Since I first called my brother's father d. 361:10
Daddy: D.'s gone a-hunting 296:9
  D. wouldn't buy me a bow-wow 414:1
  in the Great War, d.? 3:13
  My heart belongs to D. 317:3
Daemon: Some d. stole my pen 311:13
Daffadillies: d. fill their cups with tears 277:16
Daffadowndilly: Diaphenia, like the d. 111:12
Daffed: That d. the world aside 354:35
Daffodil: d.s, That come before the swallow 384:29
  Fair d.s, we weep to see 200:15
  host, of golden d.s 462:3
  When d.s begin to peer 384:21
Daffy-down-dilly: D. is new come to town 296:12
Dagger: air-drawn d. 366:26
  Give me the d.s 365:27
  Is this a d. which I see before me 365:19
  speak d.s to her but use none 351:21
Daggers-drawing: Have always been at d. 87:21
Dainties: d. that are bred in a book 363:28
Daintiest: d. last to make the end most sweet 376:10
Dairymaid: Queen asked The D. 274:16
Daisies: D. smell-less, yet most quaint 28:6
  D., those pearled Arcturi of the earth 393:21
  picking d. on the railway 459:12
  she can hear The d. grow 455:3
  When d. pied and violets blue 364:6
Daisy: D., D., give me your answer 131:1
Dalliance: primrose path of d. 348:20
  silken d. in the wardrobe lies 356:26
Dam: did not give a singel d. 166:13
  When the d. broke 429:19
Dame: belle d. sans merci 230:19 231:13
  Call me the Squire of D.s 403:2
  My d. has lost her shoe 296:10
  sits our sulky sullen d. 85:13

Stoutly struts his d.s before 276:23
Damn: d. the consequences 274:35
  D. with faint praise 312:22
  not true that life is one d. thing 273:20
  once was a man who said, 'D.!' 193:31
Damnation: deep d. of his taking-off 365:7
  I dare d. 352:12
  liquid fire and distilled d. 191:3
  there would be no d. 431:11
  Twenty-nine distinct d.s 78:23
Damned: Better be d. than mentioned not at all
    309:6
  d. are those who dare resist 7:29
  d. if you do 147:8
  d. like an ill-roasted egg 345:17
  d. long, dark, boggy, dirty 182:17
  for ever d. with Lucifer 266:19
  just one d. thing after another 211:13
  thou must be d. perpetually 267:2
Damning: d. those they have no mind to 87:11
Damozel: blessed d. leaned out 331:15
Damp: d.s there drip upon Sagged seats 192:11
Damsel: d. lay deploring 174:28
  d. with a dulcimer 118:5
  Fairy d.s met in forest wide 281:4
  to every man a d. or two 35:29
Dan: From D. even to Beer-sheba 35:36
Danaë: all D. to the stars 422:16
Dance: D., and Provençal song 232:2
  D., d., d. little lady 123:25
  Each d. the other would 134:25
  On with the d.! 89:22
  spectral d., before the dawn 69:12
  That d.s as often as d. it can 117:19
  Their d.s were procession 122:10
  too far from the d. 317:27
  Well, d. now 243:17
  when you do d. I wish you A wave 384:30
  won't you, will you join the d. 101:18
Danced: d. with a man, who's d. with a girl 161:11
  move easiest who have learned to d. 313:14
  Where once we d., where once we sang 192:10
Dancer: d.s are all gone under the hill 155:35
  know the d. from the dance 470:6
Dancing: d. on a volcano 336:25
  past our d. days 379:3
Dancing-master: manners of a d. 220:25
Dandin: *Vous l'avez voulu, George D.* 283:19
Dandyism: Cynicism is intellectual d. 272:19
Dane: never get rid of the D. 238:24
Dane-geld: once you have paid him the D. 238:24
Danger: appalling d.s of family life 212:26
  D.s by being despised grow 82:2
  d.s of the seas 304:18
  d.s that were real and immediate 197:9
  loved me for the d.s I had passed 374:6
  only real d. .. is man himself 227:7
  other side is ready to face d. 429:9
  Out of this nettle, d. 354:2
  Pleased with the d. 149:10
  run into any kind of d. 318:28
  Security is the mother of d. 171:7
  She feared no d. 150:17
  There's d. on the deep 27:7
  What d.s thou canst make us scorn! 85:20
Danger: tire-moi de d. 244:3
Dangerous: All generalizations are d. 152:10

Into the d. world 61:23
Mad, bad, and d. to know 245:2
Daniel: D. come to judgement! 370:11
    second D., a D., Jew! 370:14
Danny: hangin' D. Deever 238:25
Danse: ne marche pas, il d. 254:13
Dansez: Eh bien, d. maintenant 243:17
Dante: D. of the dread Inferno 76:13
    D.'s one of those that one can only just hope
        157:20
    D., who loved well 76:11
Dappled: Glory be to God for d. things 206:11
Dare: D. to be true 199:5
    I d. do all that may become a man 365:11
    Letting 'I d. not' wait upon 'I would' 365:10
    never d. to write As funny as I can 203:24
    What man d., I dare 366:29
    You who d. 272:15
Dared: I have d. and done 72:15
    what none hath d., thou hast done 325:9
Darien: Silent, upon a peak in D. 233:3
Daring: essential tact in d. 116:3
Dark: Are you awake in the d.? 293:10
    as children fear to go in the d. 18:21
    as good i' th' d. 200:10
    At one stride comes the d. 117:1
    between the d. and the daylight 265:14
    colours will agree in the d. 18:24
    D. with excessive bright 279:15
    Death could drop from the d. 330:21
    feel the fell of the d. 206:3
    from the d. and doubtful 128:9
    hunt it in the d. 126:23
    I'm Afraid to Go Home in the D. 457:11
    never to refuse a drink after d. 271:21
    O d., d., d., amid the blaze of noon 281:16
    plotting in the d. 126:32
    we are for the d. 344:7
    What in me is d. Illumine 278:2
    With darkness ridge the riven d. 169:7
Darkness: awful d. and silence reign 250:17
    between his D. and his Brightness 94:4
    Cast him into outer d. 51:1
    cast out into outer d. 49:30
    d. again and a silence 257:17
    D. came down on the field and city 425:19
    d. from light 74:7
    D. more clear than noonday 331:8
    d. silvers away 67:23
    d. was upon the face of the deep 33:13
    d. which may be felt 34:47
    Dawn on our d. 196:22
    deep but dazzling d. 438:5
    Deep into the d. peering 310:25
    head-foremost in the jaws Of vacant d. 417:38
    In d., and with dangers compassed round 280:18
    instruments of d. tell us truths 364:20
    jaws of d. 371:21
    leaves the world to d. 185:27
    Lighten our d. 318:32
    light shineth in d. 52:49
    light to them that sit in d. 51:43
    May not the d. hide it 331:13
    Men loved d. 53:9
    No light, but rather d. visible 278:5
    out of d. and the shadow of death 40:15
    people that walked in d. 45:7

Scatters the rear of d. thin 276:23
separate d. of man's love 249:11
universal d. buries all 311:29
What of the D.? 252:2
year Of now done d. 205:23
Darling: Charlie is my d. 291:7
    d. of our crew 136:11
    d. of the Gods 268:29
    he's a d. man 299:6
    In thy green lap was Nature's d. laid 187:12
    Oh, my d., Oh, my d. 286:8
    poor d.s, I'm awfully fond 31:10
    She is the d. of my heart 99:6
    six-years' d. of a pigmy size 464:10
    wealthy curlèd d.s of our nation 373:38
Dart: sharp d. of longing love 115:6
    shook a dreadful d. 279:6
    Time shall throw a d. 71:21
Daughter: D. am I in my mother's house 240:12
    d. of Earth and Water 390:16
    D. of Jove, relentless power 186:19
    d. of the gods, divinely tall 416:11
    d.s are the thing 25:17
    d.s crying, Give, give 43:7
    d.s of men 34:12
    d.s shall prophesy 47:12
    Don't put your d. on the stage 123:15
    Duke-and-a-Duchess's d. 25:1
    Elderly ugly d. 178:16
    harping on my d. 349:28
    I am all the d.s of my father's house 383:15
    King of Spain's d. 296:25
    king's d. o' Noroway 23:10
    lest the d.s of the uncircumcised 35:47
    lies London's d. 426:14
    Lord Ullin's d. 97:10
    My d.! O my ducats! 369:29
    my love among the d.s 44:18
    'O d., dear,' her mother said 102:30
    O fairer d. 208:11
    preaching down a d.'s heart 419:27
    Sea-king's d. from over the sea 424:17
    Sole d. of his voice 280:34
    sweet her artless d.s 232:20
    trust not your d.s' minds 373:36
    two d.s of one race 423:18
    undaunted d. of desires 128:17
    will ever rear a d. 174:3
Dauphin: kingdom of daylight's d. 206:21
David: D. his ten thousands 35:46
    D. in the midst 398:7
    D.'s word with Sibyl's blending 104:11
    in royal D.'s city 4:6
    King D. and King Solomon 292:22
Daw: For d.s to peck at 373:32
Dawn: awful rose of d. 424:13
    brown fog of a winter d. 156:38
    d. comes up like thunder 240:2
    D. with her rose-tinted hands 204:14
    d., with silver-sandalled feet 455:2
    Dreaming when D.'s Left Hand 163:23
    From dewy d. to dewy night 288:15
    grey d. is breaking 129:2
    I said to D.: Be sudden 427:14
    mistaken for a d. 133:9
    No d. – no dusk 204:31
    sighed for the d. and thee 420:35

Starts for the D. of Nothing 164:16
When I arose and saw the d. 394:14
Dawning: Somebody in the d. passing through
193:14
Day: all the d.s of thy life 34:2
Ancient of D.s 184:16
another for working d.s 372:33
as general as the d. 111:24
As it fell upon a d. 25:10
As thy d.s, so shall thy strength 35:19
behold these present d.s 386:25
benight our happiest d. 144:28
brave d. sunk in hideous night 385:14
bright d. is done 344:7
bright d. that brings forth the adder 359:25
courts of everlasting d. 277:21
d. begins to droop 68:10
d. break not, it is my heart 144:17
d. brought back my night 282:6
d. is at hand 54:44
D. It Rained Forever 66:8
d. of death 43:26
d. of small things 47:21
D. of wrath and doom impending 104:11
d. of wrath, that dreadful d. 340:3
d. returns too soon 93:21
D.s and moments quickly flying 103:4
d.s darken round me 417:17
d.s dividing lover and lover 412:1
d.'s march nearer home 286:3
d.s of wine and roses 147:12 271:22
d. unto d. uttereth speech 37:36
death of each d.'s life 365:26
death will have his d. 376:29
dim light of this immortal d. 393:18
Does d. close his eyes? 128:25
Each d. dies with sleep 206:10
each d. is like a year 454:22
end of this d.'s business 360:36
enjoy bright d. 275:18
entertains the harmless d. 467:33
Every d., in every way 123:6
Everything is only for a d. 16:15
first, last, everlasting d. 144:15
former d.s were better 43:29
Friends, I have lost a d. 430:12
from noon to dewy eve, A summer's d. 278:27
Go not, happy d. 420:32
Good things of d. begin to droop 366:20
Happy D.s Are Here Again 472:9
hard d.'s night 253:10
He that outlives this d. 357:17
How many d.s will finish up the year 358:7
how many ways and d.s! 331:23
idle singer of an empty d. 288:10
I have met them at close of d. 470:15
It was Thy d., sweet! 128:19
I love the garish d. 294:4
jocund d. Stands tiptoe 380:3
latter d. upon the earth 37:4
lengthen our d.s 287:9
length of d.s 285:8
let the d. be time enough to mourn 131:10
Little Man, You've Had a Busy D. 397:6
Live this d., as if 'twere thy last 235:9
long d.'s task is done 344:1
long d. wanes 424:9

looked on better d.s 345:10
look, the gentle d. 373:27
love o' life's young d. 289:10
most wasted of all d.s 106:2
My d.s are swifter 36:41
My d.s have crackled 427:15
My d.s, which are at best but dull 438:16
My salad d.s 343:26
no d. for me to look upon 384:6
not to me returns D. 279:13
Now the d. is over 25:3
Of all the d.s that's in the week 99:7
On evil d.s though fall'n 280:18
On the bald street breaks the blank d. 417:29
pause in the d.'s occupations 256:14
runs through the roughest d. 364:24
Sabbath . . . poor man's d. 184:9
shineth . . . unto the perfect d. 41:25
so foul and fair a d. 364:15
spend a single d. really well 235:6
stand a tip-toe when this d. is named 357:17
Sweet childish d.s 467:5
Sweet d., so cool, so calm 199:25
teach us to number our d.s 39:34
tender eye of pitiful d. 366:19
Ten D.s that Shook the World 326:13
Think . . . every d. is your last 207:18
think warm d.s will never cease 233:17
this d. may be the last 293:3
This d. shall gentle his condition 357:19
though the d. be never so longe 195:2
to a diviner d. 393:13
to buy a world of happy d.s 377:30
to have known a better d. 339:23
Underneath D.'s azure eyes 391:24
Until the d. break 44:22
up by break of d. 199:11
We have seen better d.s 381:25
what a d. may bring forth 42:45
when will this long weary d. have end 402:23
yield d. to night 357:26
Day-labour: Doth God exact d. 282:4
Daylight: all the long and lone d. 394:12
In the broad d. Thou art unseen 394:19
We burn d. 371:6
When d. comes 115:26
Dayrolles: Give D. a chair 109:23
Daysies: Swiche as men callen d. 108:19
Day-star: Does the d. rise? 128:25
So sinks the d. in the ocean bed 277:17
Daytime: I cry in the d. 37:41
Dead: all the d. lie down 142:2
apples on the D. Sea's shore 89:26
as a d. man out of mind 38:10
between two worlds, one d. 11:8
Blessed are the d. 58:24
bury the d. 293:20
cold and pure and very d. 254:9
D.! and . . . never called me mother 460:14
d. and then restored to life 74:18
d. ar-re always pop'lar 152:16
d., but in the Elysian fields 143:33
d. have no consciousness of anything 400:19
d. men on leave 254:3
d. shall live, the living die 151:4
deal to be said For being d. 31:26
Do we indeed desire the d. 418:5

England mourns for her d. 59:17
few are wholly d. 185:15
frightful when one's d. 314:20
Ha! D.! Impossible! 99:3
He is d. and gone, lady 352:5
he is d. who will not fight 188:8
high talk with the departed d. 391:10
How fares it with the happy d.? 418:2
I have been d. these two years 109:20
In the long run we are all d. 236:15
I praised the d. 43:20
lane to the land of the d. 14:25
Let the d. bury 49:32
liveth and was d. 58:5
living among the d. 52:46
Mistah Kurtz – he d. 121:22
My days among the d. are past 401:20
not d. – but gone before 328:25
Now he is d.! 11:15
O he is d. then? 205:24
sea gave up the d. 58:30
sheeted d. Did squeak and gibber 347:24
She's d., sir, long ago 22:3
simplify me when I'm d. 147:4
There are no d. 264:19
they may say when I am d. 23:7
Trust that those we call the d. 418:35
What, d. at last 120:15
When I am d. and opened 269:19
When I am d., I hope 30:27
When I am d., my dearest 331:11
when we are d. 321:16
worse to me than d. 461:6
Deadlock: Holy D. 198:32
Deaf: d. and does not hear 315:7
I'm d. in one year 194:16
Why seemed you so d. to my prayers? 235:1
Deafanddumb: In every language even d. 130:3
Deafness: Your tale . . . would cure d. 380:27
Deal: given a square d. 330:4
new d. for the American people 329:13
Dealing: Whose own hard d. teaches them 369:20
Dean: and soft d. invite 315:4
Let us drink to the queer old D. 403:21
no dogma, no D. 143:35
sly shade of a Rural D. 69:12
Dear: D. as the light that visits 185:21
Dearest: throw away the d. thing he owed 364:25
Dearth: pine within and suffer d. 387:8
weak with sweats of d. 302:14
Death: Absence . . . is worse than d. 125:5
absolute for d.; either d. or life 368:18
After d. has stopped the e.s 210:13
After the first d. 426:14
Against the hour of d. 320:1
and from sudden d. 319:4
and his name . . . was D. 58:14
Any man's d. diminishes me 146:21
Because I could not stop for D. 142:1
Better be killed than frightened to d. 409:23
bitterness of d. is past 35:45
Black Widow, d. 259:9
blessed before his d. 48:9
by feigned d.s to die 146:6
Come away, come away, d. 383:13
conception of d. which decides 191:8
D. and life were not 472:3

D., as the Psalmist said, is certain 356:3
D. be not proud 145:18
D. borders upon our birth 190:13
D. cometh soon or late 261:13
D. could drop from the dark 330:21
D., ere thou hast slain another 71:21
D. has done all d. can 72:16
d. had undone so many 156:38
D. hath a thousand doors 270:12
D. hath no more dominion 54:23
d. hath ten thousand several doors 448:27
d. in the pot 36:25
d. is certain 33:11
D. is Life's high meed 233:13
D. is still working like a mole 199:15
d. is the cure of all diseases 71:12
[d.] is the only disease 266:5
D. is the only pure, beautiful conclusion 249:9
D. is the veil 393:14
d. itself must be . . . a mockery 393:25
D. lays his icy hand on kings 396:4
D. lies dead 412:16
d. makes equal 201:1
d. shall be no more 145:19
d. shall have no dominion 426:4
d. so noble 281:29
d., whene'er he call 178:20
d. will have his day 376:29
deliver me from the body of this d. 54:26
dens, and shades of d. 279:4
die the d. of the righteous 35:10
direful d. indeed they had 166:13
Done to d. by slanderous tongues 373:26
eloquent, just, and mighty D.! 325:9
enormously improved by d. 335:15
Fear d.? – to feel the fog 77:6
fed on the fullness of d. 412:27
For D., he taketh all away 123:4
For I say, this is d. 74:7
foretaste of d. 339:3
for restful d. I cry 386:5
friend and enemy is but D. 69:18
Go and try to disprove d. 433:11
half-dead, a living d. 281:18
half in love with easeful d. 232:7
How wonderful is D. 390:18
if ought but d. part
in that sleep of d. 350:14
In the hour of d. 319:5
in their d. they were not divided 36:1
In the midst of life we are in d. 320:4
Into the jaws of D. 416:1
I signed my d. warrant 119:5
It is but D., who comes at last 340:10
It might make one in love with d. 389:22
Keeps D. his court 377:2
last enemy . . . is d. 55:33
Lead him to d. 328:11
Let us hob-and-nob with D. 424:14
Life is . . . the shadow of d. 70:16
look on d. itself 366:4
love thee better after d. 72:8
make d. proud to take us 344:5
Meetest for d. 370:8
Men fear d. 18:21
My soul looked down . . . with D. 302:14
Neither d., nor life 54:31

Not d. the poet sees 11:18
Rocked in the cradle of the d. 457:6
There rolls the d. where grew the tree 418:37
Though d., yet clear 134:33
very singularly d. young man 177:40
Deer: a-chasing the d. 85:3 341:7
I was stricken d. 127:4
let the stricken d. go weep 351:14
Poor d. . . . thou makest a testament 344:27
running of the d. 7:25
Time's d. is slain 289:18
Where the d. and the antelope play 201:7
Deeth: D. is an ende of every worldly sore 108:6
Défaut: défauts de leurs qualités 23:25
Defeat: d. is an orphan 235:19
d. without a war 112:16
In d.: defiance 113:18
In d. unbeatable 114:1
not interested in the possibilities of d. 439:10
snatching glory out of d. 320:14
we never had a d. 113:22
Defect: chief d. of Henry King 30:6
Fine by d. 314:23
Defence: admit of no d. 330:13
d. of England 21:16
D. of philosophic doubt 21:20
He is my d. 39:6
Never make a d. of apology 106:17
our d. is sure 447:23
Defend: I will d. to the death your right 443:2
Défend: Quand on l'attaque il se d. 9:14
Defender: I mean the Faith's D. 88:30
Defiance: wilful d. of military authority 338:3
Deficiency: industry will supply their d. 326:20
Defiled: toucheth pitch . . . d. therewith
Defileth: this d. a man 50:18
Deformed: D., unfinished, sent before my time
377:23
Dégagé: Or half so *d.* 125:21
Degeneration: fatty d. of his moral being 406:28
Degrade: not to d. the human being 301:2
Degree: Changed not in kind but in d. 75:13
Observe d., priority, and place 381:35
scorning the base d.s 359:26
Stand, each in our d. 193:11
Take but d. away 382:1
thou's but of low d. 7:22
y-fallen out of heigh d. 108:8
Dei: Estne D. sedes nist terra 259:16
Deified: one more day I am d. 75:11
Deities: d. of his own invention 310:2
never found the d. so kindly 324:9
Deity: D. and the Drains 408:16
Delay: D.s have dangerous ends 357:28
In d. there lies no plenty 383:3
reproved each dull d. 181:2
sweet reluctant amorous d. 279:27
think not much of my d. 237:7
Delectable: came to the D. Mountains 80:29
Delectando: Lectorem d. pariterque monendo 207:8
Delenda: D. est Carthago 103:8
Deliberation: on his front engraven D. 278:38
Délice: Laissez-nous savourer les rapides d.s
244:23
Delicta: D. maiorum immeritus lues 208:30
Delight: Ah, Moon of my D. 165:1
all d.s are vain 363:18

d. in simple things 238:19
fine d. that fathers thought 206:19
lonely impulse of d. 471:5
My d. and thy d. 68:4
never too late for d. 287:9
Oh, 'tis my d. 8:8
other aims than my d. 193:2
Spirit of D. 393:26
turn d. into a sacrifice 199:3
violent d.s have violent ends 379:27
we have a degree of d. 82:6
yet I hear thy shrill d. 394:19
Delighted: d. us long enough 17:6
Delightful: It's d., it's delicious 316:27
Delirious: It's delectable, It's d. 316:27
Delito: Pues el d. mayor 95:11
Deliver: d. me from the body of this death 54:26
Delos: Where D. rose 91:23
Delphi: Woods that wave o'er D.'s steep 187:11
Delude: Whom God d.s is well deluded 115:20
Deluge: After us the d. 311:3
Déluge: Après nous le d. 311:3
Delusion: displeased with those harmless d.s 182:26
Hence, dear d. 398:20
Trial by jury . . . a d. 134:34
Demagogue: vilest specimens . . . among d.s
262:20
Demarcation: criterion of d. 316:18
Demeaning: So womanly, Her d. 398:4
*Demens: Quem fugis, a, d.?*441:13
Demented: not one is d. 453:27
Demi-tasses: you villainous d. 398:19
Democracy: D. is on trial 144:12
D. means government by the uneducated 111:11
D. passes into despotism 310:5
D. resumed her reign 30:26
D. substitutes election by the incompetent 388:26
five hundred years of d. and peace 449:10
great arsenal of d. 329:22
made safe for d. 458:14
makes d. necessary 294:16
our d. was . . . the most aristocratic 262:15
pretends that d. is perfect 113:11
perfect d. is . . . the most shameless 82:20
Two Cheers for D. 167:23
we can't save d. 123:22
Democrat: not to tell the truth about the D.s 135:2
Democratic: application of d. methods 432:14
thoroughly d. and patronize everybody 388:4
Demon: wailing for her d. lover 117:36
Demonstrandum: Quod erat d. 159:33
Demonstration: called a Spontaneous D. 300:13
Demure: Sober, steadfast, and d. 276:3
Den: beard the lion in his d. 340:16
d. of thieves 50:44
in the seven sleepers' d. 145:8
to think upo' yon d. 83:20
Denied: He . . . that comes to be d. 301:21
Denmark: All the might of D.'s crown 96:24
I'm sure it may be so in D. 349:13
Prince of D. being left out 341:6
Something is rotten in the state of D. 348:34
Dentist: I'd sooner go to my d. 448:16
Deny: Let him d. himself 50:25
Still why d. its use 96:10
Deoch-an-duoris: Just a wee d. 248:27
Depart: D., – be off, – excede 204:2

D., I say 4:23 129:16
time for you to d. 207:30
Departed: He d., withdrew, rushed off 114:18
Lord was d. from him 35:35
Department: fair sex is your d. 148:2
Depict: I d. men as they ought to be 401:4
Deportment: beforehand with all the public d.s 138:11
celebrated . . . for his D. 136:26
Deposed: must he be d.? 377:4
Depravity: total d. of inanimate things 191:4
Depression: d. when you lose your own 432:22
Depth: drowned in the d. of the sea 50:29
far beyond my d. 358:21
I love thee to the d. 72:7
Out of the d.s have I cried 41:5
Plunge it in the d.s 209:8
Deputy: d. elected by the Lord 376:27
Derision: clothed with d. 412:6
Time turns the old days to d. 412:11
Derogatory: nothing d. wrong with me 299:8
Descant: her amorous d. sung 279:31
Descartes: I cannot forgive D. 305:8
Descent: claims of long d. 419:5
Describe: d. the indescribable 90:8
Description: It beggared all d. 343:28
truth of the d. 341:9
Desert: Cam-u-el, that primal D. Ship 189:5
d. shall rejoice 45:24
d. sighs in the bed 14:25
d. were a paradise 85:8
ebbing to the d.s of the east 249:16
High-Park's a d. to you 159:31
hies to the d.s wild 149:1
his d.s are small 286:6
In a dry d. 315:33
I never will d. Mr Micawber 137:11
in this d. inaccessible 345:10
legs of stone Stand in the d. 392:13
Nothing went unrewarded but d. 149:22
that the D. were my dwelling-place 90:18
water but the d. 90:11
Desert-folk: spoke Unto lost d. 185:4
Deserve: She d.s More worlds 151:15
success in war . . . but only d. it 113:21
success . . . we'll d. it 1:10
you somehow haven't to d. 170:2
Design: His d.s were strictly honourable 162:33
I see the whole d. 77:15
not my d. to drink or to sleep 129:18
not that you do wrong by d. 227:10
palpable d. upon us 233:28
virtue of d., pattern, or inscape 206:24
Desipere: Dulce est d. in loco 209:10
Desirable: d. shall fail 44:11
d. to be praised twice over 248:10
establishment . . . any other than highly d. 17:7
Desire: all their d. is in the work 48:25
antidote to d. 121:3
d. accomplished is sweet 42:6
D. of Man being Infinite 63:26
doing what one d.s 273:15
He who d.s but acts not 63:11
hours and times of your d. 385:31
If country loves such sweet d.s gain 188:2
kindle soft d. 150:8
Man's D.s are limited 63:25

my joys and d.s 61:21
naught for your d. 109:27
nearer to the Heart's D. 164:30
other than for the d. of the man 118:32
starting-point for further d.s 321:9
strange d. to seek power 19:18
strange that d. should so . . . outlive 355:29
this fond d. 1:13
Those who restrain D. 63:7
what I've tasted of d. 170:4
winged with vain d.s 150:19
wonder and a wild d. 77:29
Your heart's d.s be with you! 344:18
Dèsirer: coutume d'en d. plus qu-ils en ont 135:10
Desirous: aught else on earth d. 174:9
Desolate: d. and sick of an old passion 147:9
Desolation: abomination of d. 51:11
d., and despair of Nature 188:11
Despair: begotten by d. 268:15
depth of some divine d. 422:3
D., law, chance 145:16
hurried question of D. 89:10
I can endure my own d. 445:18
I'll not, carrion comfort, D. 205:22
leaden-eyed d.s 232:3
look forward to d. 123:22
minor form of d. 59:14
owner was . . . Giant D. 80:28
quality of his d. 121:10
too near neighbour to d. 11:25
under Teucer's star, never d. 208:6
warder is D. 455:1
wasting in d. 459:4
Yet did she d.? 135:9
Yet now d. itself is mild 394:4
Despairer: Too quick d. 12:5
Desperandum: Nil d. Teucro duce 208:6
Desperate: not as d. as that 67:7
Tempt not a d. man 380:8
Desperation: lives of quiet d. 428:24
Despise: you d. me, Mr Gigadibs 72:26
Despond: name of the slough was D. 80:16
Despondency: in the end d. and madness 466:3
Despot: d.'s heel is on thy shore 325:17
once a d. and a slave 393:18
Despotism: Democracy passes into d. 310:5
D. tempered by assassination 326:15
d. tempered by epigrams 99:25
Destin: pire d. 265:4
Destiny: as if I were walking with d. 113:20
character is d. 155:17
Hanging and marriage . . . go by D. 162:3
in shady leaves of d. 128:26
only one d. And it is white 161:8
rendezvous with d. 329:16
what, if I may ask, is your d.? 214:24
Where D. with Men for Pieces plays 164:18
Destroy: water the one, and d. the other 20:24
Whom God wishes to d. 160:1
Whom the gods wish to d. 121:14
Destroyed: d. but not defeated 197:20
Destroyer: D. and preserver; hear, oh, hear! 392:5
Destruction: d. that wasteth at noonday 40:1
for d. ice Is also great 170:4
grandmother of d. 171:7
I come from the city of D. 80:18

leadeth to d. 49:25
Pride goeth before d. 42:15
Destructive: D., damnable, deceitful woman! 301:19
Detail: Merely corroborative d. 177:32
Our life is frittered away by d. 428:28
Deteriora: D. sequor 302:2
Determined: d. to some particular direction 219:20
D., dared, and done 398:10
Detraction: D. will not suffer it 355:2
Deutschland: D., D. über alles 203:10
Developed: instinct for being unhappy highly d. 336:4
Device: ingenious d. for avoiding thought 197:11
Devil: abashed the d. stood 280:2
apology for the D. 88:10
as you hate the d. 292:32
A walking the D. is gone 401:13
clever d.s he'll mak them 84:18
d. can cite Scripture 369:14
d. damn thee black 367:16
D., having nothing else to do 30:28
D. is a gentleman 392:16
d. is asleep 306:20
d. is come down unto you 58:21
d. is dead 326:5
D.s are not so black 256:2
D.'s awa' wi' the Exciseman 84:10
d.'s leavings 316:15
D. take me 324:15
d. turned precisian 270:11
d. was sick 289:13
D. whispered behind the leaves 238:23
D. whoops. as he whooped of old 238:22
envy of the d. 47:37
every man . . . was God or D. 149:21
fears a painted d. 365:27
find a poor d. 75:26
first Whig was the D. 223:4
Half d. and half child 241:9
Here's the d. to pay! 24:7
He should dream of the d. 24:11
How then was the D. dressed 401:14
if the d. doesn't exist 146:27
no good casting out d.s 249:19
not serve God if the d. bid you 373:34
of the D.'s party 63:8
Or who cleft the D.'s foot 146:7
Renounce the d. 319:26
Resist the d. 57:26
serpent, which is the d. 58:29
sugar o'er The d. himself 350:13
tell truth, and shame the d. 354:23
those poor d.s are dying 308:11
What a mischievous d. Love is 88:11
What a surly d. that is 162:5
Why the d. should have 201:12
world, the flesh and the d. 319:3
you make them but clever d.s 450:3
Devil's-triumph: One more d. and sorrow   75:19
Devocioun: Farwel my book and my d.! 108:18
Devoir: Faire son d. tellement quellement 142:11
Faites votre d. 122:15
Dévot: pour être d. 284:14
Devotee: great d. of the Gospel of Getting On 389:1
to have no genuine d.s 215:19
Devotion: d.'s visage And pious action 350:13
d. to something afar 394:8

great object of universal d. 215:19
Devour: seeking whom he may d. 57:36
Devourer: be become so great d.s 287:19
Dew: Brushing with hasty steps the d.s away 186:17
continual d. of thy blessing 318:31
d. is cold upon the ground 423:19
d. shall weep thy fall to-night 199:25
d.s of summer night 272:33
d. was falling fast 464:25
d. was on the lawn 405:4
Ere the early d.s were falling 215:9
for the d. will rust them 373:37
Into a sea of d. 162:14
Like the d. on the mountain 339:21
ne'er brushed d. from lawn 93:30
On whom the d. of heaven drops 167:6
resolve itself into a d. 347:36
Walks o'er the d. 347:27
which fades like d. 114:28
Dew-drop: fragile d. on its perilous way 232:13
ge seek some d.s here 371:32
With showers and d.s wet 331:11
women like a d. 73:13
Dewey: D. was the Admiral 446:23
Dexterity: Your d. seems a happy compound 144:3
Di: Habitarunt d. quoque silvas 441:13
Quem d. diligunt 310:6
Diable: d. est mort 326:5
Diadem: precious d. stole 351:30
Dial: as the d. to the sun 65:3
drew a d. from his poke 345:3
lowly air Of Seven D.s 177:9
To carve out d.s, quaintly 358:7
Dialect: in a d. I understand very little 307:14
Dial-hand: beauty, like a d. 386:22
Dialogue: To hear the wooden d. 382:3
Diamond: d.s are trumps 298:12
D., what! This is carbon 249:24
Goodness, what beautiful d.! 451:6
Like a d. in the sky 415:6
O D.! D.! thou little knowest 294:9
Dian: hangs on D.'s temple 346:33
Diana: Great is D. of the Ephesians 54:3
Let us be D.'s foresters 353:17
Diapason: d. closing full in Man 150:33
Diaries: Let d. . . . be brought in use 19:41
Diary: I never travel without my d. 455:18
Dice: God plays d. with the cosmos 155:4
same a. as you gentlemen use 324:13
some were playing d. 22:20
Dicers: false as d.' oaths 351:26
Dich: as digne as water in a d. 108:10
Dichten: Lord Byron is nur gross, wenn er d. 180:11
Dick: D. the shepherd blows his nail 364:7
Dickens: what the d. his name is 371:10
Dictators: D. ride to and fro 113:25
Dictatorship: d. of the proletariat 269:18
Dictionary: but a walking d. 106:16
Dictum: Ventre's stark d. 218:4
Did: he danced his d. 129:22
Diddle: Hey d., d. 296:19
Didn't: he sang his d. 129:22
Dido: D. with a willow in her hand 370:18
thought of D. be bitter to me 440:23
When D. found Aeneas 316:20
widow D. on the floors below 213:5
Die: all shall d. 356:3

All that live must d. 347:33
argue that I shall some day d. 250:6
As in Adam all d. 55:32
as natural to d. as to be born 18:23
Ay, but to d., and go we know not where 368:22
being born, to die 21:6
Better . . . to d. than to beg 48:26
Call no man happy till he d.s 400:24
Curse God, and d. 36:36
Dear, I d. As often as from thee I go 145:28
d. all, d. merrily 354:37
d. is cast 95:7
D. . . . that's the last thing 303:12
d. not, poor death 145:18
d. without ever laughing 243:3
dare to d. 314:7
For thou must d. 199:25
for thou shalt d. 45:27
for to morrow we d. 55:34
greatly think, or bravely d. 312:3
have to d. beyond my means 456:23
He did not d. in the night 288:18
He that d.s pays all debts 381:7
How hard it is to d. 434:11
I d., – but first 93:3
I d.! I faint! I fail! 391:13
If d. I must 266:13
If I should d. before I wake 6:13
If I should d., think only 69:20
If we are marked to d. 357:15
I'm sorry – but we all must d.! 410:11
in what peace a Christian can d. 2:23
I shall d. at the top 411:27
I shall not altogether d. 209:6
it was sure to d. 287:11
king never d.s 59:28
Let us do or d.! 85:11
man can d. but once 356:5
Not d. here in a rage 411:26
not difficult to d. 271:9
not that I'm afraid to d. 4:17
Now that I come to d. 73:34
No young man believes he shall ever d. 196:2
One only d.s once 283:11
possess our soul Before we d. 11:36
since I needs must d. 325:7
sooner d. that think 333:26
taught us how to d. 430:7
Theirs but to do and d. 415:26
those about to d. salute you 409:12
time to d. 43:19
To d. . . . awfully big adventure 25:24
to d. is gain 56:23
To d.; to sleep 350:14
Tomorrow let us do or d.! 97:4
try . . . what it is to d. 71:15
We d. – does it matter when? 423:1
We only d. when we fail to take root 432:17
Who did not wish to d. 389:19
who would wish to d.? 65:11
without Thee I dare not d. 234:24
Died: liked it not, and d. 468:2
who have d. for thee 74:19
Diem: Omnem crede diem tibi diluxisse supremem 207:18
Dienen: Oder d. und verlieren 179:25
Dies: D. irae, d. illa 104:11

Diet: Be . . . sober in your d. 285:1
Dieu: D., a-t-il donc oublié 258:3
D. est d'ordinaire 86:25
Si D. n'existait pas 442:4
vrai D., le D. fort 439:14
Dieux: laisser faire aux d. 122:15
Differ: d. as Heaven and Earth 417:6
Difference: as much d. between us 285:13
end our d.s 235:22
more d. within the sexes 120:2
not . . . find much d. 224:6
that has made all the d. 170:11
Different: found d. and left untried 111:6
How d., how very d. 6:22
Like – but oh, how d.! 467:21
something completely d. 286:14
They are d. from you and me 165:14
Difficile: Ne soyons pas si d.s 244:17
Difficult: D. do you call it, Sir? 224:12
d. is what takes a little time 291:11
d. to speak 82:1
Difficulties: little local d. 264:6
Difficulty: d. for every solution 336:26
Dig: I cannot d. 52:28
Digest: learn, and inwardly d. 319:13
Digestion: d. is the great secret of life 399:21
Few radicals have good d.s 88:2
good cook, and a good d. 332:14
good d. wait on appetite 366:24
prove in d. sour 376:13
Digne: as d. as water in a dich 108:10
Dignities: peace above all earthly d. 358:23
Dignity: d. of history 64:21
In every gesture d. and love 280:23
left the room with silent d. 188:17
Dilly: Don't d. dally on the way 252:6
Dime: Brother, Can You Spare a D.? 192:4
efery d. she gife a shoomp 252:15
Dimidium: D. facti qui coepit habet 207:16
Diminished: power of the C . . . ought to be d. 13:9
Din: May'st hear the merry d. 116:19
Dine: I am in haste to d. 125:19
Where sall we gang and d. to-day? 23:19
Dîner: d. réchauffé ne valut jamais rien 64:17
Diner-out: philosophic d. 76:3
Diners-out: Ye d. from whom we guard our spoons 262:2
Ding: Always d., dinging Dame Grundy 289:8
D., dong, bell 296:13
D. dong! the bells are gonna chime 253:20
Dingle: D., or bushy dell 275:15
Dinner: ask him to d., and hear 100:18
conservatives after d. 158:28
d. lubricates business 341:13
d. waits, and we are tired 125:15
good d., and company that pleased 307:25
good d. enough, to be sure 221:19
may mak our d. sweet 23:19
three hours' march to d. 196:5
Dinner-bell: tocsin of the soul – the d. 91:39
Dinner-table: dominate a London d. 456:19
Dip: I am a kind of farthing d. 408:1
Diplomat: d. is a man who always remembers 170:17
Dirce: With D. in one boat conveyed 246:23
Direct: To be d. and honest is not safe 375:8

Direction: By indirections find d.s out 349:20
  often moving in opposite d.s 400:1
Direness: D., familiar to my . . . thoughts 367:23
Dirge: By forms unseen their d. is sung 119:16
  d. for her, the doubly dead 310:23
  sad d. of her certain ending 385:9
  Thou d. Of the dying year 392:6
  with d. in marriage 347:29
Dirt: d. doesn't get any worse 129:5
Dirty: At D. Dick's and Sloppy Joe's 15:6
  hard and d. work 333:12
Dis: *D. aliter visum* 440:19
Disappointed: he shall never be d. 316:16
Disappointing: d. them, I should not . . . mind
    182:14
Disappointment: constant succession of d. 221:32
  feeling of d. 246:3
  why must D. all I endeavour end? 206:17
Disaster: day's d.s in his morning face 181:6
  laugh at all d. 256:12
  make guilty of our d.s the sun, the moon 361:34
  middle station had the fewest d.s 133:13
  primeval d. in the heart of Man 397:17
  sense of . . . a d. 249:25
Disbelief: willing suspension of d. 118:19
Discharge: no d. in that war 43:34
  no d. in the war 238:17
Discipline: D. must be maintained 136:31
  I know the d.s of the wars 357:8
Discobolus: D. standeth and turneth his face 88:24
Discontent: divine d. 237:20
  Nor is d. to keep the mind 89:28
  winter of our d. 377:20
Discontented: everyone that was d. 68:15
Discord: All d., harmony not understood 313:34
  from civil d. flow 1:15
  hark what d. follows 382:1
Discouragement: There's no d. 80:35
Discourse: d. of the elders 48:5
  fittest for d. and nearest prose 150:32
  he that made us with such large d. 351:41
  rather hear thy d. 86:17
Discoverers: d. that think there is no land 18:4
Discovery: D. consists of seeing 413:16
  given . . . of his d. to the world 336:12
Discretion: better part of valour is d. 355:8
  woman . . . without d. 42:1
  years of d. 319:35
Discussion: Rupert of parliamentary d. 142:24
Disdain: more love or more d. 98:28
  What! my dear Lady D. 372:24
Disease: appropriate for extreme d.s 201:16
  Cured yesterday of my d. 320:26
  Cure the d. and kill 20:14
  death is the cure of all d.s 71:12
  th is the only d. 266:5
  desperate d. requires a dangerous remedy 162:7
  d. is incurable 355:19
  d. of writing books 286:2
  D.s desperate grown 351:38
  find her d., And purge it 367:21
  his favourite d. 162:29
  Life is an incurable d. 124:12
  long d., my life 312:20
  Meet the d. on its first appearance 308:4
  no cure for this d. 30:7
  remedy is worse than the d. 19:34

strange d. of modern life 11:26
  those in the last stage of d. 14:29
Disfigures: D. earth 126:32
Disgrace: Intellectual d. 14:12
  O the d. of it! 29:10
  When in d. with fortune and men's eyes 385:22
Dish: butter in a lordly d. 35:26
  carve him as a d. fit for the gods 359:30
  d. ran away with the spoon 296:19
  Serve up in a clean d. 251:10
  Was that not a dainty d. 297:31
Dished: we have d. the Whigs 135:8
Dishonour: another unto d. 54:33
Dislike: strong d.s that vice should inspire 284:2
Dismiss: Lord, d. us with Thy blessing 80:2
Disobedience: children of d. 56:19
  Man's first d. 277:32
Disorder: meet him in a pretty d. 120:31
  sweet d. in the dress 200:5
Disposal: Headmasters have powers at their d.
    113:15
Dispose: charitably d. of anything 357:10
Disposition: d. is not the sole qualification 112:12
  put an antic d. on 349:17
  truant d., good my lord 348:7
Disputants: Our d. put me in mind 2:18
Disputation: that's a feeling d. 354:27
  to doubtful d.s 54:45
Dispute: D. it like a man 367:10
  knew better to live than d. 320:22
Disputed: Facts . . . downa be d. 84:11
Disquiet: deep d. of Man's passion 188:11
Disraeli: 68:19
  wave her wand for Disraeli alone 408:19
Dissemble: d. in their double heart 37:30
  right to dissemble your love 235:1
Dissimilar: For one another, though d. 390:23
Dissimulation: Let love be without d. 54:35
Dissipation: d. without pleasure 175:11
Dissociation: d. of sensibility set in 157:22
Dissolution: From low to high doth d. climb 461:13
Dissonance: filled the air with barbarous d. 275:24
Distance: despite the d. and the dark 77:30
  d. lends enchantment 97:13
Distance: *distance n'y fait rien* 133:12
Distemperature: Thorough this d. we see 371:34
Distempered: questions the d. part 155:36
Distinction: few escape that d. 434:15
  pedantic d.s of *meum* and *tuum* 245:28
Distinctiveness: vice of d. 206:24
Distingue: *Je veux qu'on me d.* 284:1
Distinguish: could d. and divide 87:4
Distinguished: at last, the d. thing! 217:5
Distress: All pray in their d. 62:10
  Beauty in d. is much the most 82:8
  deep d. hath humanised my soul 461:17
  everyone that was in d. 68:15
  friend of Beauty in d. 93:27
  incapable of her own d. 352:20
  not affected by the reality of d. 303:5
Distressed: Art thou sore d.? 292:24
Distrust: D. yourself, and sleep 10:11
Dit: *peine d'être d.* 27:13
Ditch: both shall fall into the d. 50:19
  die in the last d. 83:8
  I will die in the last d. 457:7
  lay distracted in the d. 129:1

Ditties: spirit d. of no tone 231:19
Ditty: ancient d. long since mute 230:19
  Let me set my mournful d. 393:27
Diver: d. in deep seas 305:16
  Don't forget the d. 229:15
  fearful the death of the d. 427:9
Diverb: as the d. goes 86:20
Diversion: walking: 'tis a country d. 120:32
Diversities: there are d. of gifts 55:20
Diversity: make the world safe for d. 235:22
  richness and d. of his existence 235:24
Divided: if a house be d. 51:29
Dividend: no d. from time's tomorrows 337:29
Dividing: d. asunder of soul and spirit 57:10
Divine: Ah, what the form d.! 246:28
  all, save the spirit of man, is d. 89:8
  But all are d. 11:1
  fou o' love d. 84:27
  Hand that made us is d. 2:16
  to forgive, d. 313:19
Divinely: d. tall, And most d. fair 416:11
Diviner: glad d.'s theme 149:16
Diving: D. deeper than anyone else 213:6
Divinity: believe the d. of – another Jew 197:8
  d. that shapes our ends 353:3
  piece of d. in us 71:14
  such d. doth hedge a king 352:11
Division: D. is as bad 6:11
  equal d. of unequal earnings 158:3
  How many d.s has he got? 404:1
  Never come such d. 'tween our souls! 360:34
Divorceée: No d.s were included 452:2
Dixerunt: qui ante nos nostra d. 144:13
Do: and d. thou likewise 52:12
  Can I d. you now, sir? 229:14
  D. as I say, not as I do 342:11
  D. not d. unto others 388:23
  D. what you will 324:6
  I can – I ought – I do 395:9
  If to d. were as easy as to know 369:8
  Let us d. or die! 85:11
  luckiest of mortals . . . must d. 15:26
  man's gotta d. 243:14
  often discover what will do 398:12
  rule for bargains: D. other men 138:28
  that men should d. to you 49:24
  that write what men d. 18:6
  This will never d. 218:1
  what I d. in anything 199:12
  what men daily d. 373:14
  what you can do for your c. 235:18
  What you d. Still betters 384:30
  while aught remains to d. 328:24
Doasyouwouldbedoneby: her name is Mrs D. 237:25
Doc: What's up D.? 80:12
Doctor: Dear D., I have read your play 92:34
  d. understood the call 320:25
  frequent D. and Saint 164:11
  Illness is the most heeded of d.s 321:17
  Those budge d.s of the Stoic fur 275:29
  when d.s disagree 314:31
Doctrine: d. could be held 73:33
  d. of ignoble ease 330:2
  d. of the enclitic De 74:30
  every wind of d. 56:16
  Not for the d. 313:11
  prove their d. orthodox 87:10

Document: Human d.s 473:7
Dodger: dodgerest of the d.s 140:17
  soubriquet of 'The artful D.' 139:33
Dodo: D. never had a chance 130:11
Doeg: D., though without knowing how 149:29
Dog: All the d.s in the town 298:3
  All the d.s of Europe 14:11
  And every d. his day 237:17
  Anyone who hates children and d.s 163:13
  as a d. that shakes his ears 422:31
  beaten d. beneath the hail 317:17
  cast it to d.s 50:20
  comely d. is he 134:11
  d. did nothing in the night-time 148:1
  D. in the Manger 3:18
  d. is turned to his own vomit 57:37
  d. it was that died 182:37
  d. knows he is miserable 224:10
  d. returneth to his vomit 42:40
  d.s bark at me as I halt by them 377:23
  d.s did bark, the children screamed 125:13
  d.s eat of the crumbs 50:21
  d.s go on with their doggy life 14:22
  d.'s life without a d.'s decencies 241:14
  d. starved at his master's gate 60:10
  d., to gain some private ends 182:36
  d. will have his day 353:2
  Don't let's go to the d.s tonight 198:27
  dumb d.s, they cannot bark 46:15
  Dumb's a sly d. 114:7
  every d. has his day 65:13
  fought the d.s and killed the cats 76:23
  Franklyn's D. leped over a style 24:17
  Give the dog a b. 264:14
  giving your heart to the d. to tear 240:14
  grin like a d. 39:3
  hates d.s and babies 332:7
  Helping . . . Lame d.s over stiles 237:14
  I'd be a d., a monkey 328:9
  I do honour the very flea of his d. 225:7
  If you call a dog Hervey 220:13
  Is thy servant a d. 36:37
  Leave Now for d.s and apes 74:28
  Let d.s delight to bark and bite 447:10
  let slip the d.s of war 360:12
  like a d.'s walking on his hind legs 221:17
  little d. laughed 296:19
  living d. is better 43:36
  love will make a d. howl 28:3
  Mad d.s and Englishmen 123:27
  Mine enemy's d. 363:4
  more I admire d.s 342:27
  poor d. Tray 97:5
  rather be a d. and bay the moon 360:28
  really kind to d.s 29:15
  Something better than his d. 419:21
  That tossed the d. 298:6
  Throw physic to the d.s 367:20
  To get her poor d. a bone 297:15
  took by the throat the circumcisèd d. 375:26
  treat the myriad creatures as straw d.s 247:18
  Unmissed but by his d.s 126:12
  what could he not d.? 26:1
  When a d. bites a man 131:5
  whose d. are you? 315:8
  young man's d. with them 47:33
Dogged: It's d. as does it 432:8

Doggedly: set himself d. to it 220:17
Dogma: Any stigma will . . . beat a d. 189:2
   literature, not d. 337:9
   no d., no Dean 143:35
   teach an old d. new tricks 304:7
Dog-star: d. rages! 312:14
Doing: child is known by his d.s 42:25
   D. or suffering 278:8
   one way of *doing* things rightly 333:17
   see what she's d. 322:11
   weary in well d. 56:13
Doll: called me Baby D. a year ago 194:8
   I once had a sweet little d. 237:16
Dollar: almighty d. 215:19
   billion d. country 167:25
   d. in another man's hands 198:19
   on th' back iv a d. 152:17
Dolly: Little D. Daydream 408:21
Dolores: O sanguine and subtle D. 412:10
Dolos: Seu versare d. 440:13
Dolphin-chamber: sitting in my D. 355:24
Dombey: I positively adore Miss D. 137:36
Dome: d. of many-coloured glass 390:8
Dominate: d. a London dinner-table 456:19
Dominion: Death hath no more d. 54:23
   death shall have no d. 426:4
   Great is the hand that holds d. 426:8
   His Majesty's d.s 295:16
   sun does not set in my d.s 338:12
   Tired of his dark d. 272:6
Dominoes: You have a row of d. set up 155:5
Don: D.s admirable! 30:32
   If the D.s sight Devon 293:16
   never turned my back upon D. or devil 422:30
   Oxford D.: I don't feel 14:28
   Remote and ineffectual D. 30:31
Done: been and gone and d. 176:11
   d. those things which we ought not 318:13
   If it were d. when 'tis d. 365:5
   not my will, but thine, be d. 52:43
   thank God I have d. with him 220:27
   that you have d. yourself 188:15
   What have I d. for you, England 197:23
   what's d. is d. 366:13
   What's d. we partly may compute 83:22
   When thou hast d., thou hast not d. 145:26
Done-to-death: Played-out and D. 431:18
Dong: D. with a luminous Nose 250:19
Donkey: d. wot wouldn't go 33:4
   lions led by d.s 203:9
   that's a dead d. 141:22
Donne: 98:26
   D. . . . found no substitute for sense 157:12
   Dr D.'s verses are like the peace of God 216:9
   thought to D. was an experience 157:21
   To read D. you must measure *time* 118:25
   With D. whose muse 118:8
Donné: grant the artist . . . his *d.* 217:2
Doodah: Oh! d. day! 168:3
Doom: God would have changed his d. 115:4
   purpose of God and the d. assigned 421:3
   slow, sure d. falls pitiless and dark 333:21
   wrath and d. impending 104:11
Doomsday: crack of d. 367:2
   D. is near 354:37
Doomster: These purblind D.s 192:20
Doon: o' bonnie D. 85:35

Door: Beside a human d. 462:26
   Came out by the same D. 164:11
   Death hath a thousand d.s 270:12
   D. must be either Open or Shut 290:13
   d.s of the rest being as yet shut 234:3
   d. stood open at our feast 116:17
   D. to which I found no Key 164:14
   d. we never opened 155:30
   even hard at death's d. 40:16
   every d. is shut but one 125:29
   For barring of the d. 22:17
   Get up and bar the d. 22:18
   I slew him at the d. 124:26
   I stand at the d., and knock 58:11
   knocked laughing at the d. 72:25
   knocking at Death's d. 146:24
   Knocking on the moonlit d. 134:20
   ladies leave their d.s ajar 74:22
   Men shut their d.s against a setting sun 381:24
   O for d.s to be open 15:14
   Open the d. and here are the people 296:18
   sat at her ivied d. 95:15
   Shut the d. after you 154:6
   shut the d., good John! 312:14
   take thy form from off my d. 310:27
   'Thou shalt not' writ over the d. 61:20
   Three, four, Knock at the d. 297:16
   thunder on my d. 214:13
   trick everyone abhors . . . is slamming d.s 30:19
   What . . . is the wind in that d.? 265:13
   whining of a d. 146:22
   ye everlasting d.s 38:5
Doorkeeper: I had rather be a d. 39:27
Dope: proper share, man, of D. and drink 15:15
Dorian: D. mood Of flutes 278:19
   To whom the D.s pray 261:11
Dots: what those damn d. meant 112:6
Dotes: she, sweet lady, d., Devoutly d. 371:19
Doth: all it hath a mind to do, d. 73:23
Double: D., d., toil and trouble 366:35
Double-entendre: But the horrible d. 6:16
Doublethink: Newspeak word *doublethink* 300:25
Doubt: Defence of philosophic d. 21:20
   d. diversified by faith 73:3
   D. thou the stars are fire 349:25
   Frets d. the maw-crammed beast? 77:12
   he shall end in d.s 18:2
   His d.s are better 192:7
   Humility is only d. 60:24
   let us never, never d. 30:33
   lives more faith in honest d. 418:20
   no manner of d. 176:17
   Our d. is our passion 216:17
   our d.s of today 330:2
   saucy d.s and fears 366:23
   state of philosophical d. 119:1
   sunnier side of d. 415:15
   When in d., win the trick 211:12
   wherefore didst thou d.? 50:16
Doubter: d. and the doubt 158:10
Douglas: Degenerate D! 466:25
   doughty D. bound him to ride 22:5
   D., D., tender and true 128:14
   D. in his hall 340:16
   Like D. conquer 204:7
   maugre of doughty D. 22:10
   O D., O D., tendir and trewe! 203:18

Dove: Beside the springs of D. 466:13
By all the eagle . . . all the d. 128:17
came in a d. at a window 265:14
d. descending breaks the air 156:9
d. found no rest 34:16
gently as any sucking d. 371:29
had I the wings of a d. 128:1
harmless as d.s 49:39
hawk at eagles with a d. 199:23
moan of d.s in immemorial elms 422:20
that I had wings like a d. 38:32
Dovecot: d. doors of sleep 272:29
Dover: burning a farthing candle at D. 221:16
milestones on the D. Road 138:17
Dowel: D., Dobet and Dobest 247:13
Dower: all thy d. of lights and fires 128:17
faith's transcendent d. 466:10
Down: All in the D.s the fleet was moored 174:25
danced away with d. upon your feet 151:17
D. and away below 11:3
D., Sir! Put it d.! 30:9
never go d. to the end of the town 274:15
when they were d., they were d. 6:12
Down-hearted: Are we d.? No! 242:6
Downstairs: Be off, or I'll kick you d.! 101:1
many kicked d. 83:9
Doxy: With heigh! the d., over the dale 384:21
Drachenfels: castle crag of D. 89:27
Dragon: before he killed the d. 110:6
habitation of d.s 45:23
laid hold on the d. 58:29
Saint George, that swinged the d. 361:9
Dragon-fly: With the d. on the river 72:1
Dragon-green: d., the luminous . . . sea 166:1
Drain: between the Deity and the D.s 408:16
leave Oxford by the next town d. 403:22
Miss Annie she said it wur the d.s 424:12
pale owing to the d.s 13:12
Drainpipe: wrong end of a municipal d. 255:18
Drake: D. he's in his hammock 293:17
Drama: close the d. with the day 32:6
d.'s laws, the d.'s patrons give 219:4
what this wild d. means 421:30
Dramatist: d. only wants more liberties 216:12
d. who had discovered himself 336:12
Draught: fee the doctor for a nauseous d. 150:14
large d.s of intellectual day 128:17
peculiarly susceptible to d.s 455:17
shallow d.s intoxicate the brain 313:4
Draughty: Monet's pictures . . . too d. for me 133:19
Draw: let me try and d. you 77:2
Drawback: being royal has many painfull d.s 13:16
Drawer: d.s of water 35:22
Drawing: back to the old d. board 10:15
Drawing room: flowing through my d. 154:2
Drawling: D., Stretching and Fainting 101:15
Drayhorse: Didst fettle for the great grey d. 205:25
Dread: close your eyes with holy d. 118:6
d. and fear of kings 370:9
D. is a sympathetic antipathy 237:2
mighty d. Had seized their troubled mind 414:18
walk in fear and d. 117:10
Dreadnought: as much to keep up as two D.s 255:15
Dream: All men d. 249:29
as a d. doth flatter 386:15
awakened from the d. of life 390:4

behind, a d. 387:5
behold it was a d. 80:31
beyond the d.s of avarice 286:16
broke this happy d. 144:19
closes Within a d. 147:12
d. we not live in d.s 416:24
d. all night without a stir 230:29
dreamed a dreary d. 22:4
dreaming d.s no mortal ever dared 310:25
d. our d.s away 165:17
d. when I am awake 95:12
d. within a d. 310:20
each age is a d. that is dying 301:17
even in d.s a good deed 95:13
faileth now even d. 427:15
fly forgotten as a d. Dies 447:23
from a deep d. of peace 212:10
glory and freshness of a d. 463:30
he pulls the legs of his d.s 426:20
hope is but the d. 320:28
Housed in a d. 461:18
I arise from d.s of thee 391:11
If I d. I have you 144:22
If there were d.s to sell 28:22
I have a d. 237:9
I have bad d.s 349:34
It shall be called Bottom's D. 372:12
keep a d. or grave apart 72:10
Land of D.s is better far 61:8
Large d.s from little fountains flow 160:7
latest d. I ever dreamed 231:12
Life is a d. 285:17
life is but a d. whose shapes return 428:17
Life is but an empty d. 257:2
Like wrecks of a dissolving d. 391:2
love's young d. 287:1
Made holy by their d.s 176:1
my fruit is d.s 427:24
no need for cheering d.s 113:20
old men shall d. d.s 47:12
our d.s are tales 134:7
Out of a misty d. 147:12
perceived they had dreamed a d. 78:35
perchance to d. 350:14
Real are the d.s of Gods 231:14
Soft! I did but d. 378:18
such stuff As d.s are made on 381:10
that insane d. we take For waking 74:12
Thou wovest d.s of joy and fear 394:12
Tread softly because you tread on my d.s 471:2
trouble to my d.s 465:10
waken from his summer d.s 392:7
what my d. was 372:11
Writing is . . . a guided d. 65:5
Dreamer: Beautiful d., wake 168:2
Behold, this d. cometh 34:30
d. of dreams 35:13 288:11 301:15
d.s of the day are dangerous 249:29
Dreaming: I'm d. of a white Christmas 32:10
Dregs: drain not to the d. of the urn 391:8
Dress: always d. aright 102:31
Be plain in d. 285:1
make their d. a principal part 195:21
modest d., Neat, but not gaudy 450:29
tha mun d. thysen 249:14
Dressed: all d. up and no place to go 86:3
All d. up, with nowhere to go 452:22

good spirits . . . when he's well d. 138:22
Drink: A little in d. 404:12
  Another little d. wouldn't do us any harm 188:19
  brings you other things to d. 110:23
  Come and have a d. with me 430:9
  d., and leave the world unseen 232:2
  D., pretty creature, d.! 464:25
  d. till all look blue 167:10
  D. to me only with thine eyes 225:20
  D. with me, and d. as I 299:19
  every creature d. but I 124:1
  First you take a d. 165:13
  five reasons we should d. 4:1
  gapes for d. again 123:31
  Have ye tippled d. more fine 231:17
  he has taken to d. 414:14
  His d., the running stream 146:23
  I can d. With him that wears a hood 408:2
  I d. for the thirst to come 324:1
  Let us eat and d. 55:34
  long time between d.s 287:26
  Man wants but little d. below 203:29
  never taste who always d. 320:31
  never to d. by daylight 271:21
  One more d. and I'd have been 304:6
  Shall sit and d. with me 31:4
  taste any d. once 95:1
  taste for d., combined with gout 176:18
  told Jeeves to d. it himself 459:18
  What should we do for d.? 5:20
  Without the power to d. or rise 306:14
Drinking: D. is the soldier's pleasure 149:36
  D. when we are not thirsty 27:15
  next to d. and sabbath-breaking 135:6
  Now is the time for d. 208:14
  Once d. deep 69:4
  poor and unhappy brains for d. 374:18
  there's nothing like d. 136:8
  'tis not the d., that is to be blamed 342:2
  With constant d. fresh and fair 123:31
Drive: d. it away, and remember 48:23
Driving: d. is like the d. of Jehu 36:28
  you are d. rapidly from something 222:19
Droghte: d. of March hath perced 107:7
Drôle: C'est un d. de guerre 131:3
Dromedary: d., two 292:6
  muse on d. trots 118:8
Drone: idle bands of d.s 442:1
  lazy yawning d. 356:24
Drop: Dear as the ruddy d.s 185:21
  Like kindred d., been mingled 126:35
  Nor any d. to drink 116:28
  One d. would save my soul 267:3
  people whom one should have . . . to d. 223:11
  Some pious d.s the closing eye requires 186:16
  turn on, tune in, and d. out 251:11
Dropping: continual d. in a very rainy day 42:47
Dropsy: twice tapped for a d. 395:5
Dross: all is d. that is not Helena 266:22
  Who . . . can separate thy d.? 89:17
Drown: Duffers won't d. 325:21
  methought what pain it was to d. 378:1
Drowned: But he'll be d. 295:3
Drudge: harmless d. 219:14
Drug: D.s are a delusion 387:30
  Everything is a dangerous d. 121:18
  Literature is a d. 65:12

most powerful d. used by mankind 241:34
Poetry's a mere d., Sir 162:2
Drum: Bang-whang-whang goes the d. 79:8
  Dumb as a d. with a hole in it 140:35
  My pulse like a soft d. 237:8
  Not a d. was heard 459:24
  Of guns, and d.s, and wounds 353:30
  plays the kettle d.s in the orchestra 336:16
  rumble of a distant D.! 164:3
  spirit-stirring d. 375:5
  Take my d. to England 293:16
  Thy voice is heard thro' rolling d.s 422:9
Drumlie: drumlie grew his ee 22:12
Drunk: Gloriously d. 127:19
  Man . . . must get d. 91:13
  man should always be d. 299:10
  never happy . . . but when he is d. 222:19
  Not d. is he 306:14
  not so think as you d. I am 403:27
  this meeting is d. 141:9
Drunkard: d.s, liars and adulterers 361:34
  rolling English d. 110:12
Drunken: d., but not with wine 45:16
  stagger like a d. man 40:18
Drunkenness: branch of the sin of d. 216:6
Dry: Thoughts of a d. brain 156:13
  what shall be done in the d? 52:44
Dryad: light-winged D. of the trees 232:1
Dryden, John: 187:15 219:24
  D. calls 'the fairy way' 2:11
  D. taught to join 315:34
  Ev'n copious D. wanted 316:1
  poetry of D., Pope, and all their school 12:26
  Read all the prefaces of D. 410:14
  To read D., Pope, etc. 118:25
Dublin: In D.'s fair city 7:27
Dubuque: old lady from D. 330:24
Ducat: Dead for a d. 351:25
  My daughter! O my d.s! 369:29
Duchess: D.! The D.! Oh my dear paws! 100:32
Duck: Always do that, wild d. 214:21
  D. and the Kangaroo 250:20
  Four d.s on a pond 4:20
  Oh, your precious 'lame d.s'! 172:11
Dudgeon: civil d. first grew high 87:2
Dues: Render . . . to all their d. 54:42
Duffers: Better drowned than d. 325:21
Duke: Bury the Great D. 421:12
  drawing room full of d.s 15:23
  D. of Plaza-Toro 176:16
  D. returned from the wars 266:16
  D.s were three a penny 176:24
  everybody praised the D. 401:10
  fully equipped D. 255:15
Dukedom: My library Was d. large enough 380:28
Dulce: D. et decorum est 208:24 302:10
Dulcimer: d., and all kinds of music 47:1
  on her d. she played 118:5
Dull: D. – beyond all conception 392:20
  D. would he be of soul 463:10
  not only d. in himself 167:2
  part of this paper appears d. 404:8
  so smoothly d. 311:19
  Tell them that they are d. 390:21
  Though it's d. at whiles 237:14
  thou wast not wont to be so d. 378:6
  Why, Sir, Sherry is d. 221:15

Dullard: d.'s envy of brilliant men 29:14
Dullness: cause of d. in others 167:2
  Still with this d. was he cursed 392:20
Dumas, Alexandre 272:32
Dumb: because he was a d. son of a bitch 432:25
  D. as a drum with a hole in it 140:35
  D.'s a sly dog 114:7
Dummheit: Mit der D. kampfen Götter 338:13
Dumps: in such doleful d. 399:4
  We are all in the d. 298:12
Duncan: D. is in his grave 366:15
  this D. Hath borne his faculties so meek 365:7
Dunce: calls you a d. 79:15
  Pooh! . . . you great d.! 24:6
  Satan, thou art but a d. 60:28
Dundee: bonnets of Bonny D. 339:12
Dunfermline: king sits in D. 23:8
Dungeon: This D., that I'm rotting in 98:19
  What other d. is so dark 195:5
Dunghill: needy out of the d. 40:21
Dunkirk: 320:14
Dunn: Miss J. Hunter D. 32:24
Dunsinane: to high D. hill 367:1
Dupe: d. and a deceiver; a decay 393:18
  D. of to-morrow 126:6
  sharper once played with a d. 129:7
Durance: In d. vile 235:12
Dusk: each slow d. 302:9
  In the d. with a light behind her 178:17
Dust: Bezide the red d. o' the ridges 25:9
  blossom in their d. 396:5
  But what is D. 397:22
  but writes in d. 21:4
  come to d. 347:15
  d. alone remains of thee 312:7
  d. and silence of the upper shelf 262:25
  d. beneath thy chariot wheel 205:18
  D. hath closed Helen's eye 292:20
  d. in the air suspended 156:8
  d. of creeds outworn 393:2
  D. are our frames; and gilded d. 415:17
  d. return to the earth 44:12
  d. shalt thou eat 34:2
  D. thou art, to d. returneth 257:2
  d. to d. 320:5
  D. to the d.! 390:3
  enemies shall lick the d. 39:19
  Excuse my d. 304:17
  forbear To dig the d. enclosèd here 387:12
  For d. thou art 34:5
  give to d. that is a little gilt 382:17
  Guilty of d. and sin 199:18
  light in the d. lies dead 391:21
  much learned d. 127:6
  noble d. of Alexander 352:28
  not without d. and heat 282:18
  of the d. of the ground 33:19
  our proud and angry d. 209:25
  pinch of unseen, unguarded d. 193:9
  poor out of the d. 40:21
  richer d. concealed 69:20
  shake off the d. of your feet 49:38
  To stir a little praise of d. 418:17
  vile d. from whence he sprung 340:1
  What a d. do I raise 20:37
Dust-heap: great d. called 'history' 59:20
Dustman: Golden D. 140:18

Dutch: fault of the D. 98:20
  for my dear old D. 111:14
Dutchman: like an icicle on a D.'s beard 383:21
Duties: brace ourselves to our d. 112:23
  If . . . I had no d. 222:25
  Property has its d. 148:25
Duty: daily stage of d. run 235:8
  discussing their d. to God 453:27
  done my d.. and I've done no more 163:4
  D. and dereliction guide thee 394:2
  d. that lies nearest thee 100:14
  D. whispers low 158:16
  every man will do his d. 293:5
  Every subject's d. is the king's 357:11
  Faithful, below, he did his d. 136:12
  found that life was d. 6:5 205:9
  he always declares that it is his d. 387:23
  little d. and less love 357:29
  moral d. to speak one's mind 455:19
  no duty we so much underrate 407:6
  O D.! if that name thou love 464:21
  only done my d. 423:5
  path of d. was the way to glory 421:22
  right of all . . . d. of some 323:5
  Such d. as the subject owes the prince 380:24
  Thank God, I have done my d. 293:6
  that which was our d. to do 52:34
  thing of d. is a boy for ever 299:4
  To do my d. 319:31
  toppling crags of D. scaled 421:23
  when love and d. clash 421:35
  whole d. of man 44:15
Duvetyne: Mind my d. dress 226:6
Dwarf: d. sees farther 118:23
  number of anxious d.s 320:12
Dwelling: Where and what his d.? 292:28
  Whose d. is the light of setting suns 462:20
Dwelt: too long have d. on thee 145:32
Dwindle: Shall he d., peak and pine 364:14
Dwyer: John Richard William Alexander D. 399:5
Dyck: though the Van D.s have to go 123:17
Dyer: like the d.'s hand 386:31
Dying: act of d. is not of importance 221:29
  as a d. man to d. men 27:1
  bliss of d. 311:30
  can't stay d. here all night 395:11
  d. for their country 334:1
  D. Is an art 309:26
  D. when fair things are fading 27:3
  d. with the help of . . . physicians 4:2
  I am d., Egypt, d. 344:3
  If this is d., I don't think much of it 408:20
  I'm d. now and done for 33:2
  there's no more d. then 387:9
  to behold you again in d. 407:28
  unconscionable time d. 107:1
  We thought her d. when she slept 204:20
Dyingness: sort of d. 120:28
Dyke: February, fill the d. 433:20

E

E: E = mc superior 2
Eagle: By all the e. in thee 128:17
  Does the E. know 60:21

e. or the snake 239:34
e.s be gathered together 51:12
e. suffers little birds to sing 381:30
hawk at e.s with a dove 199:23
hooded e. among blinking owls 391:18
imperial e. of the house of Austria 175:7
In and out the E. 266:2
I see her as an e. 282:21
like an e. in a dovecote 347:1
mount up with wings as e.s 45:37
upon my e.'s wings 151:16
They love th' e. 152:17
way of an e. in the air 43:8
Eagle-feather: A moulted feather, an e.! 75:29
Ear: beat upon my whorlèd e. 205:27
    buzzing in my e.s 73:34
    came o'er my e. like the sweet sound 382:23
    close at the e. of Eve 279:37
    e. filled with hearing 43:14
    e. of jealousy 47:35
    e. of man hath not seen 372:11
    e.s like bombs 104:7
    e.s like errant wings 110:4
    e.s of flesh and blood 349:1
    e.s that sweep away the morning dew 372:10
    ever penetrated into the e. of man 167:19
    fearful hollow of thine e. 380:2
    flea that I have in my e. 324:12
    Give e. unto my song 182:33
    Give every man thine e. 348:22
    Hark in thine e.; change places 362:42
    have e.s, but they hear not 40:23
    hearing of the e. 37:16
    He that hath e.s to hear 51:30
    He that planteth the e. 40:6
    I had no human e.s 466:19
    I have no e. 245:12
    I was all e. 275:25
    I will enchant thine e. 387:11
    jest's prosperity lies in the e. 364:5
    'Jug jug' to dirty e.s 157:2
    lend me your e.s 360:14
    like was in the Eternal. 187:24
    lover's e. will hear the lowest sound 363:30
    mentions hell to e.s polite 315:4
    mighty world of eye, and e. 462:21
    more is meant than meets the e. 276:13
    my great, long, furry e.s 31:24
    not to the sensual e. 231:19
    plucked the ripened e.s 421:34
    porches of mine e.s 349:8
    she shall lean her e. 467:3
    split the e.s of the groundlings 350:24
    stillness first invades the e. 150:12
    Stop thine e. against the singer 340:26
    that stoppeth her e. 39:2
    to soothe thy modest e. 119:10
    Unpleasing to a married e. 364:6
    Vexing the dull e. of a drowsy man 361:18
    went and shouted in his e. 102:13
    When the e. begins to hear 69:2
    With ravished e.s 149:34
Earl: As far as the 14th E. is concerned 147:7
    bonny E. of Murray 22:8
    E. of Fitzdotterel 70:5
    slain the E. of Murray 22:7
Early: E. one morning 7:13

Earnest: e. of the things that they shall do 419:29
    I am in a. 173:8
    Intermingle . . . jest with e. 20:21
    Only we die in e. 9:2
Earning: equal division of unequal e.s 158:3
Earth: all e. to love 240:28
    All people that on e. do dwell 236:5
    all the e. is a sepulchre 429:7
    As low as where this e. Spins 331:17
    aware that the e. revolves 321:7
    clothe the general e. 117:31
    Didst tread on e. unguessed at 11:31
    did thee feel the e. move? 197:18
    Dost thou despise the e. 467:12
    e. and every common sight 463:30
    E. and Ocean seem To sleep 390:27
    E. cannot show so brave a sight 268:17
    e. doth like a snake renew 391:2
    E. felt the wound 280:35
    E. fills her lap with pleasures 464:9
    E. has not anything to show more fair 463:10
    e. hath bubbles 364:18
    e. in fast thick pants 118:1
    E. is but a star 166:3
    e. is the honey of all beings 435:9
    e. is the Lord's 38:4 55:17
    e.'s about five thousand million years old 309:10
    e. shall be filled 3:30
    E.'s last picture is painted 241:6
    E.'s the right place for love 169:20
    e., tideless and inert 21:21
    e. to e. 320:5
    e. was without form 33:13
    e. which is sometimes so pretty 320:11
    E. will grow worse 110:18
    e. with its store of wonders 184:17
    fell to e., I know not where 256:8
    Greatest Show on E. 25:14
    Her all on e. 90:28
    I'll put a girdle round about the e. 371:37
    in the deep delvèd e. 232:2
    it is e. with me 72:14
    kindly e. shall slumber 419:32
    kindly fruits of the e. 319:7
    Lay her i' the e. 352:30
    Leaves this peopled e. a solitude 393:6
    Let me enjoy the e. no less 193:2
    Lie heavy on him, E.! 160:4
    lightly, gentle e. 27:25
    listening. e. 2:15
    Meantime, there is our e. here 79:2
    new heaven and a new e. 58:31
    new heavens and a new e. 46:22
    Now lies the E. all Danaë 422:16
    of the e., earthy 55:38
    Or e. received her frame 447:23
    replenish the e. 33:17
    Rolled round in e.'s diurnal course 466:19
    smile o' the brown old e. 75:9
    Things learned on e. 76:9
    thirsty e. soaks up the rain 123:31
    this goodly frame, the e. 349:36
    thou bleeding piece of e. 360:11
    Though e. and man were gone 68:26
    thou hast formed the e. 39:29
    thou upon e. 43:23
    to and fro in the e. 36:33

Travel . . . a part of e. 19:40
Edward: sons of E. sleep 378:10
   Why, E., tell me why? 461:8
Edward VIII 226:26
Edwin: let me always call you E. 162:4
Eels: as e. are to be flayed 91:36
   e. get used to skinning 112:21
Effect: did not believe in wasting her e.s 129:8
   name for an e. 127:26
   What dire e.s from civil discord 1:15
   worst e. is banishing for hours 124:30
Efficiency: e. and inefficiency 388:6
Efficient: e. and the inefficient 388:6
Effort: e. very nearly killed her 30:15
Egard: On doit des é. aux vivants 442:19
Egg: as an e. is full of meat 379:30
   as a weasel sucks e.s 344:38
   boil e.s in your shoes 251:9
   but to roast their e.s 20:6
   cook himself a couple of e.s 106:1
   damned like an ill-roasted e. 345:17
   eating an e. without salt 241:28
   e. boiled very soft 16:21
   e.'s way of making another e. 87:36
   from fresh e.s to rotten boroughs 262:8
   Go to work on an e. 3:1
   Hard-boiled as a picnic e. 303:13
   I'm afraid you've got a bad e. 322:18
   I've met a lot of hardboiled e.s 456:26
   Lays e.s inside a paper bag 215:21
   learned roast an e. 316:3
   like an e. without salt 104:10
   radish and an e. 127:15
   Remorse, the fatal e. 126:15
   When a weasel sucks e.s 320:7
   when the e.s are fried 105:5
   white and hairless as an e. 200:11
Ego: Chairman of E., Inc. 15:15
   too much E. in your Cosmos 241:21
Egypt: E., when we sat by the flesh pots 34:50
   I am dying, E., dying 344:3
   new king over E. 34:39
   not at war with E. 154:1
   rail against all the first-born of E. 344:40
   there was corn in E. 34:32
   wonders in the land of E. 34:46
Egyptians: E. worshipped an insect 143:34
   spoiled the E. 34:49
Eighteen: E. in the attics 213:5
Einstein: Ho! Let E. be! 403:26
Eld: Palsied e. 368:19
Elders: discourse of the e. 48:5
Elderly: e. man of 42 13:10
Eldorado: E. banal 26:19
Election: e. by the incompetent 388:26
Electricity: E. is of two kinds 250:8
   suspicion that e. was dripping 429:18
Electrification: e. of the whole country 252:25
Elegance: endearing e. of female friendship 220:9
Elements: e. So mixed in him 361:5
   I tax you not, you e. 362:15
   something that was before the e. 71:14
   Weak and beggarly e. 56:8
Elementary: 'E.,' said he 147:24
Elenore: tread the region E. 427:21
Elephant: E.'s Child 241:18
   high as an e.'s eye 191:11
   Nature's great masterpiece, an e. 146:2

thought he saw an E. 102:28
woman is like an e. 163:8
Elephanto: Altera candenti perfecta nitens e. 441:1
Elf: not a modest maiden e. 193:3
Elf-locks: bakes the e. in foul sluttish hairs 379:2
Elginbrodde: Here lie I, Martin E. 263:12
Elijah: E. . . . cast his mantle 36:19
*Elissae: Nec me meminisse pigebit E.*440:23
Elizabeth: my sonne's wife E. 215:10
   No scandal about Queen E., I hope? 395:7
   spacious times of great E. 416:10
Elm-tops: It tore the e. down for spite 77:4
Eloquence: Take e. and wring its neck 439:2
Elsewhere: I would not be e. 293:3
Eludes: While the one e. 75:14
Elves: Fairy e., Whose midnight revels 278:29
   Ye e. of hills, brooks, standing lakes 381:15
Elysian: dead, but in the E. fields 143:33
Elysium: What E. have ye known 231:17
Elysium: Tochter aus E. 338:7
Emanation: its fallen E. 61:1
   My E. far within 61:12
Embalmer: O soft e. of the still midnight 233:8
Embarras: L'e. des richesses 4:12
Embers: Blow on a dead man's e. 185:15
   O joy! that in our e.s 464:13
Embrace: as to e. me she inclined 282:6
   none, I think, do there e. 269:2
   spirit-like, eludes e. 305:24
Embroidery: every flower that sad e. wears 277:16
Embryos: E. and idiots, eremites and friars 279:16
Emelye: up roos E. 108:4
Emendation: e. wrong 219:32
Emerald: as green as e. 116:24
   men of the E. Isle 148:23
   road to the City of E.s 26:20
Emerson: There comes E. first 259:2
Emily: put 'E., I love you' on the . . . bill 269:6
Eminence: bald top of an e. 466:5
   Satan exalted . . . To that bad e. 278:30
Eminent: all e. men in their way 307:25
Emotion: e. recollected in tranquillity 467:24
   expressing e. in the form of art 157:18
   metaphysical brothel for e.s 242:10
   Undisciplined squads of e. 156:2
   whole gamut of her e.s 304:10
Empêche: Cela n'e. pas 174:31
Emperor: E. has nothing on 5:5
   e. of ice-cream 406:5
   E.? You old fake! 214:16
   I am the Roman E. 397:5
   makes you e. 300:1
   To the tent-royal of their e. 356:24
Empire: All e. is no more 149:18
   Another mighty e. overthrown! 463:26
   course of e. takes its way 32:6
   day of E.s has come 105:24
   e. founded by war 285:27
   e. of the future are the e.s of the mind 113:8
   e. unpossessed 378:14
   Ghost of the deceased Roman E. 202:8
   great e. and little minds 81:23
   Holy Roman E. was neither holy 442:16
   How is the E.? 175:3
   if the British E. . . . last 112:23
   liquidation of the British E. 113:6
   may make us an E. yet 239:30
   Mother E. stands splendidly isolated 168:1

to found a great e. 398:17
to the French the e. of the land 327:9
vaster than e.s and more slow 269:1
wide arch Of the ranged e. fall! 343:16
Empire: saint e. romain 442:16
Employed: more innocently e. 222:12
Employment: hand of little e. 352:23
  How various his e.s 127:10
  pleasantness of an e. 17:15
Empty: e., swept, and garnished 50:9
  seek the e. world again 69:4
Emulation: pale and bloodless e. 382:2
  Shouting their e. 346:21
Enchanter: like ghosts from an e. fleeing
  392:4
Enchantment: sole source of life e.s 32:4
Encourager: pour e. les autres 442:11
End: all the e.s thou aim'st at 358:25
  best e.s by the best means 212:21
  Better is the e. of a thing 43:28
  chief e. of man 396:6
  come from the e.s of the earth 238:11
  come to a bad e. 29:14
  cruelties not the e.s 321:19
  Delays have dangerous e.s 357:28
  e. crowns all 382:20
  e. is not yet 51:10
  e. was still far, far off 108:37
  God will grant an e. 440:5
  go on till you come to the e. 101:21
  he made a good e. 352:16
  In my e. is my beginning 156:3
  latter e. of Job 37:17
  lest he should make an e. 225:30
  let my last e. be like his 35:10
  Let the e. try the man 355:25
  look to the e. 9:11
  make the e. most sweet 376:10
  may make an e. the sooner 20:9
  one must consider the e. 244:10
  Out to the undiscovered e.s 30:21
  regarded as an e. 236:11
  there's an e. on't 221:25
  This is not the e. 113:5
  unless perhaps the e. 91:29
  Vich likeways is the e. of all things 138:35
  violent delights have violent e.s 379:27
  Waiting for the e., boys 159:22
  wish it all at an e. 83:12
Endeavour: advantage of my honest e.s 70:27
  armed against all death's e. 69:19
  Creative E. lost her sings 448:13
  criticism: a disinterested e. 12:20
Ending: bread-sauce of the happy e. 217:3
  quickest way of e. a war 301:6
Endowed: thinks himself so well e. 135:10
Endurance: patient e. is godlike 256:22
Endure: continue to e. you 120:35
  E., and preserve yourselves 440:7
  first e., then pity 314:4
Endured: Intolerable, not to be e. 380:22
  much is to be e. 220:6
Endureth: He that e. to the end 49:40
Enemies: His e. shall lick the dust 39:19
  let his e. be scattered 39:13
  Love your e. 49:5
  mortal e. ever since 253:24
  naked to mine e. 358:26

one of my most intimate e. 331:19
paranoid can have e. 242:2
smote his e. in the hinder parts 39:24
too careful in the choice of his e. 456:5
Enemy: any sense of an e. 249:25
  better class of e. 274:9
  care's an e. to life 382:25
  Do be my e. 62:25
  e. advances, we retreat 266:8
  e. faints not, nor faileth 115:25
  e. hath done this 50:12
  for a flying e. 90:30
  found me, O mine e. 36:20
  great e. of clear language 301:3
  hardly a warm personal e. left 452:9
  Here shall he see No e. 344:37
  How goes the e.? 326:19
  last e. that shall be destroyed 55:33
  my vision's greatest e. 60:22
  No e. can match a friend 410:10
  no e. to learning 120:30
  no more sombre e. of good art 121:15
  Our friends, the e. 32:3
  put an e. in their mouths 374:26
  She did not recognise her e. 397:22
  spoils of the e. 266:14
  That sweet e., France 396:15
  We have met the e. 234:28
  what effect these men will have upon the e.
    449:13
  with the wrong e. 66:13
Energies: e. of our system will decay 21:21
Energy: E. equals mass times the speed of light
  154:15
  E. is eternal delight! 63:6
  take the e. process seriously 251:11
Enfant: Allons, e.s de la patrie 332:9
  e.s terribles 173:21
  e. terrible of literature 88:8
  fripon d'e. 244:20
  Lorsque l'e. parait 211:19
Engaged: nicest girls I was ever e. to 459:19
Engagement: loose from every honourable e.
  82:29
Engine: cannot be amiss for the e.s to play 82:10
  e. that moves In predestinate grooves 193:31
  two-handed e. at the door 277:15
Engineer: Artists are not e.s of the soul 236:1
  e. Hoist with his own petard 351:36
  glorified sanitary e. 408:16
England: Admirals all, for E.'s sake 293:13
  Be E. what she will 111:21
  bores for E. 289:15
  describing E. in a phrase 300:19
  E. and America are two countries 389:15
  E.! awake! 61:5
  E., bound in with the triumphant sea 376:18
  E. does not love coalitions 142:28
  E. expects every man 293:5
  E. has saved herself 309:21
  E. hath need of thee 463:23
  E., home, and beauty 13:6 66:14 194:5
  E. is a paradise for women 86:20
  E. is the mother of Parliaments 68:14
  E. is the paradise of individuality 337:11
  E. is the paradise of women 166:21
  E. keep my bones 361:25
  E. mourns for her dead 59:17

Envy: dullard's e. of brilliant men 29:14
  E. and calumny and hate and pain 390:5
  e. and wrath shorten the life 48:17
  E., hatred, and malice 319:2
  e. of the devil 47:37
  in e. of great Caesar 361:4
  Too low for e. 124:5
  Whom e. dared not hate 93:16
Ephesian: Great is Diana of the E.s 54:3
Epicure: Serenely full, the e. would say 400:4
Epicurus: fattest hog in E.' sty 270:7
Epiderme: contact de deux é.s 106:3
Epidermis: contact of one e. with another 106:3
Epigram: despotism tempered by e.s 99:25
  purrs like an e. 267:32
Epilogue: good play needs no e. 346:17
Epitaph: Believe a woman or an e. 92:25
  better have a bad e. 350:6
  nice derangement of e.s 395:27
Epitome: all mankind's e. 149:20
Equal: disinterested commerce between e.s 182:7
  E., unclassed, tribeless and nationless 393:15
  least of all between e.s 20:28
  more e. than others 300:15
  which is e. to anything 250:4
Equality: never be e. in the servants' hall 25:16
  Were we all upon an e. 221:12
Equanimity: e. bordering on indifference 178:22
  if you have but e. 207:21
Equator: speak disrespectfully of the E. 399:25
Equinox: who knows when was the e.? 71:19
Equivocate: I will not e. 173:8
Equivocation: or e. will undo us 352:24
Ercles: This is E.' vein 371:26
Erde: kriegbewegte E. 338:14
Erebus: his affections dark as E. 370:22
Erect: above himself he can E. himself 131:11
  grows e., as that comes home 146:17
Eremite: e.s and friars 279:16
  Like Nature's patient, sleepless E. 232:18
Eric: call me E. 162:4
Erlösen: Den können wir e. 179:22
Eros: Unarm, E. 344:1
Err: most may e. as grossly 149:27
Errand: in thy joyous E. 165:2
  What thy e. here below? 245:7
Error: amusing with numerous e.s 182:23
  By e.s and perversities 73:30
  destruction of e. 14:15
  e. is immense 64:22
  e. is ineradicable 271:2
  E.s, like straws 151:14
  e. to imagine the loudest 82:5
  few e.s they have ever avoided 113:9
  gross e., held in schools 174:23
  If this be e., and upon me proved 387:2
  liable to e. 255:22
  more harmful than reasoned e.s 213:12
  Pray correct that e. 245:10
  some female e.s 315:17
  stalking-horse to e. 64:19
Erump: excede, – evade, – e.! 204:2
Erupit: Abiit, excessit, evasit, e. 114:18
Eruption: bodes some strange e. 347:21
Es: je te dirai ce que tu e. 68:20
Esau: E. selleth his birthright 34:25
  hands are the hands of E. 34:26

Escadron: pour les gros e.s contre les petits 86:25
Escalier: esprit de l'e. 142:12
Escape: E. me? Never 75:14
  hair-breadth e.s 374:3
  No e., No such thing 185:3
  whilst that I withal e. 41:14
Escurial: outlive the palace of the E. 175:7
Esmé: For E., With Love and Squalor 336:17
Espoir: peu d'e., Un peu de rêve 285:26
Esprits: Reprenez vos e. 64:17
Essay: good e. . . . must draw its curtain 460:22
  My e.s . . . come home 18:16
  Of seeming arms to make a short e. 150:13
Essence: glassy e., like an angry ape 368:15
Establish: e. oneself in the world 248:2
Establishment: e. . . . highly desirable 17:7
  single gentlemen to come into this e. 139:30
Estando: Pues veo e. dormido 95:12
Estate: fallen from his high e. 150:3
  fourth e. of the realm 262:6
  good e. with any man 120:9
  his town e. 1:4
  ordered their e. 4:4
  relief of man's e. 18:3
  steals your whole e. 174:5
  there sat a *Fourth E.* 99:33
  they had his e. 149:22
Estimate: thou know'st thy e. 386:14
Etat: E. c'est moi 258:4
Etching: I'll bring the e.s down 429:14
Eternal: portion of the e. 390:3
  We feel and know that we are e. 403:17
Eternally: we wake e. 145:19
Eternity: All things from e. 16:11
  babe in E. 60:16
  Damned from here to E. 239:6
  Dazzles at it, as at e. 438:1
  Deserts of vast e. 269:2
  e. and a heaven to throne in 346:34
  E. by term 142:4
  e.: Cold Pastoral 231:24
  E. in an hour 60:8
  E. is in love 63:14
  E.'s a terrible thought 408:6
  E.'s too short 2:12
  E.! thou pleasing, dreadful thought! 1:14
  E. was in our lips and eyes 343:20
  From the hid battlements of E. 427:16
  image of e. 90:23
  instant made e. 75:13
  I saw E. the other night 438:19
  kill time without injuring e. 428:26
  Lives in E.'s sunrise 60:31
  lovers' hours be full e. 145:28
  mighty ages of e. 100:24
  over the Bridge of Sighs into e. 237:1
  Passing through nature to e. 347:33
  prepared for you from all e. 16:20
  Silence is deep as E. 99:19
  Some shadows of e. 438:10
  thou thyself to all e. 331:24
  types and symbols of E. 465:25
  white radiance of e. 390:8
Ether: ampler e., a diviner air 462:11
Ethic: Good are the E.s, I wis 115:13
  Grub first, then e.s 67:16
  Protestant E. 448:21

Ethiop: rich jewel in an E.'s ear 379:4
Ethiopian: Can the E. change his skin 46:29
Etoile: *qui tombe des é.*122:12
Eton: in the holidays from E. 397:23
   playing-fields of E. 300:18 449:17
*Etonne: E.-moi!*136:3
Etranger: Plus je vis d'é. 31:12
Etre: Je le suis, je veux l'ê. 122:14
Etruscan: secret of the long-nosed E.s 248:32
Eunuch: kind of moral e. 392:19
   prerogative of the e. 408:10
   strain, Time's e. 206:18
Euphelia: borrowed name: E. 320:23
Euphemism: inflated style is . . . a kind of e. 301:3
Eureka: E.! 9:25
Euridice: half-regained E. 276:35
Euripides: chorus-ending from E. 73:1
   E. portrays them as they are 401:4
   Our E., the human 72:11
Europe: Better fifty years of E. 420:6
   ebbing away from . . . western E. 249:16
   E., Afrique and an Asia 146:18
   glory of E. is extinguished 82:13
   last territorial claim . . . in E. 201:19
   never . . . spoken of l'E. *des patries* 173:17
   part of the community of E. 336:21
   splendidly isolated in E. 168:1
   That E.'s nothin' on earth 457:16
Europeans: E. and Americans are like 217:17
   very common expression among the E. 181:35
Evanescent: As e. too 246:21
Eve: and E. span 22:2
   E. saw her reflection 59:4
   fairest of her daughters E. 279:28
   fallen sons of E. 110:21
   May hope, chaste E., to soothe 119:10
   meekest E.! 119:13
   our grandmother E., a female 363:21
   to Eve: Be soon 427:14
   vanquished e., as night prevails 210:21
Eve-jar: spins the brown e. 272:4
Even: grey-hooded e. 275:10
   Would God it were e.! 35:16
Evening: Come in the e. 133:4
   coming on Of grateful e. 279:34
   e. full of the linnet's wings 471:8
   e. shades prevail 2:15
   e. spread out against the sky 156:19
   e. star is just raising 103:20
   in the e. it is cut down 39:32
   quiet-coloured end of e. 75:22
   Softly along the road of e. 134:24
   Some enchanted e. 191:14
   Soup of the e., beautiful Soup! 101:20
   welcome peaceful e. in 127:12
   when e. shuts 77:18
   your shadow at e. rising to meet you 156:35
Event: e. has happened 82:1
   e.s have controlled me 254:22
   great e.s . . . in world history 269:17
   How much the greatest e. it is 168:11
   I have myself seen these sad e.s 440:11
   One e. happeneth 43:18
   thinking too precisely on the e. 352:1
   third e. to me 142:5
Eventide: Fast falls the e. 260:12
Ever: But I go on for e. 415:21

Christ the same . . . for e. 57:18
Hardly e.! 176:27
He is mine for e. 21:12
Still for e., fare thee well 92:37
Everlasting: but have e. life 53:8
   even from e. to e. 39:29
   stood from e. to e. 431:15
   that the E. had not fixed 347:36
Everlastingness: Bright shoots of e. 438:11
Evermore: Which wert, and art, and e. shalt be
     196:27
Everyman: E., I will go with thee 5:9
Everyone: E. . . . comes round by Rome 78:1
Everything: E. 451:11
   E. has been said 243:8
   God made e. out of nothing 437:6
   he thinks he knows e. 388:11
   place for e. 398:13
   responsible for e. 337:19
   wanting that have wanted e. 195:19
Everywhere: Out of the e. into here 263:10
Evidence: Belief without e. 59:11
   e. of things not seen 57:12
   it's not e. 141:12
   Some circumstantial e. is very strong 429:3
Evil: All constraint . . . is e. 127:24
   all e. shed away 69:21
   because the days are e. 56:20
   because their deeds were e. 53:9
   Be not overcome of e. 54:39
   Between two e.s, I always pick 451:5
   call e. good 44:36
   deliver us from e. 49:10
   Don't let's make imaginary e.s 182:8
   dreadful wood Of conscious e. 14:8
   Eschew e., and do good 38:14
   e. and adulterous generation 50:8
   E. be thou my Good 279:20
   e. that men do lives after them 360:14
   E., what is e.? 248:33
   e. which I would not 54:25
   expect new e.s 20:8
   feared God, and eschewed e. 36:32
   Few and e. have the days 34:37
   From e.s which never arrived 158:15
   Government . . . is but a necessary e. 303:3
   gracious voice, Obscures the show of e. 370:2
   I will fear no e. 38:3
   justified in doing e. 330:10
   knowing good and e. 33:24
   least of all e.s 18:15
   less grievous of two e.s 339:1
   Let us do e. 54:18
   Man's capacity for e. 294:16
   necessary e.s 220:1
   no e. in the atom 406:11
   Of moral e. and of good 466:29
   origin of all coming e. 227:7
   punishment in itself is e. 31:23
   Resist not e. 49:4
   root of all e. 57:2
   Speechless E. 14:3
   Sufficient . . . is the e. thereof 49:18
   sun rise on the e. 49:6
   that serve things e. 393:9
   to find means of e. 278:9
   Two e.s, monstrous either one apart 325:20

unmitigated e. 249:7
unruly e. 57:25
we must return good for e. 437:12
what all the blessed e.'s for 73:5
wrangling with e. 289:16
Ewe: milk my e.s and weep 385:1
My e.s breed not 25:12
tupping you white e. 373:33
Ewigkeit: Afay in de e. 252:18
Ewig-Weibliche: *E. Zieht uns hinan* 179:24
Exactitude: E. is not truth 270:14
Exactitude: e. est la politesse des rois 258:8
Exactness: with e. grinds He all 257:8
Exactly: I do not think so, e. 115:8
Exalt: Whosoever shall e. himself 51:6
Examinations: E. are formidable 119:32
Example: E. is always more efficacious 220:8
E. is the school of mankind 83:5
If the lower orders don't set us a good e. 455:6
My great e., as it is my theme! 134:33
philosophy drawn from e.s 142:17
save Europe by her e. 309:21
Exasperating: afterlife any less e. 123:10
Excel: thou shalt not e. 34:38
Excellences: e. carried to an excess 118:27
Excellent: 'E.!' I cried 147:24
most e. gift of charity 319:14
Exception: make an e. in your case 269:11
Exceptional: mistakes the e. for the important 215:2
Excess: best things carried to e. 112:3
blasted with e. of light 187:14
Give me e. of it 382:23
In charity there is no e. 19:27
Nothing to e. 9:5
road of e. 63:10
surprise by a fine e. 233:29
'Tis not the eating . . . but the e. 342:2
wasteful and ridiculous e. 361:21
Exchange: By just e. one for another given 396:10
Exchequer: e. of the poor 376:22
Exciting: found it less e. 176:15
Exclamation: sort of e. not right out 193:18
Excommunicate: nor e., for they have no souls
116:11
Excrucior: sed fieri sentio et e. 104:5
Excuse: E. my dust 304:17
hoped that they would e. it 107:1
if you'll e. my having such a thing 389:12
make the fault worse by the e. 361:22
several e.s are always less convincing 213:1
'tis an e. every man will plead 342:5
Two wrongs . . . make a good e. 413:14
Execution: daily led to e. 325:11
will is infinite and the e. confined 382:9
Executioner: I am mine own E. 146:19
Revenge proves its own e. 167:7
Executive: power is nominated by the e. 175:14
Executors: Let's choose e. 377:1
Exemplaria: Vos e. Graeca 207:6
Exercise: for cure, on e. depend 150:14
Some, hilly walks; all, e. 187:22
what e. is to the body 404:11
women should talk . . . 'Tis their e. 28:1
Exertion: e. is too much for me 306:17
saved herself by her e.s 309:21
Exhalation: Like a bright e. in the evening 358:20
Rose like an e. 278:26

Exile: Long as my e. 346:32
Not abrupt e. 14:16
therefore I die in e. 188:6
Exist: all springs, and all must e. 143:28
Existed: not that I have never e. before 33:9
Existence: bare e. is no better 87:32
disregard for the necessities of e. 270:20
Every e. would exist in Thee 68:26
E. saw him spurn her bounded reign 219:3
God who let us prove his e. 65:1
Let us contemplate e. 138:27
put behind him . . . out of e. 140:10
struggle for e. 132:9
when e. or when hope is gone 16:33
Exit: Exit, pursued by a bear 384:18
look on every e. being an entrance 408:5
They have their e.s and their entrances 345:11
Expatiate: E. free o'er all this scene 313:25
Expects: man who c. nothing 316:16
Expectancy: e. and rose of the fair state 350:21
Expectation: e. whirls me round 382:8
For now sits E. in the air 356:26
indeed better bettered e. 372:21
Expediency: justified . . . on the ground of e. 330:10
Expedient: all thing are not e. 55:16
to pursue *expedient* 181:18
Expendable: They Were E. 452:23
Expenditure: annual e. nineteen nineteen six 137:12
Expensive: I love fruit, when it is e. 309:8
little more e., but is more durable 250:8
Experience: All e. is an arch wherethro' 424:4
altogether perfect and supreme e. 111:3
Barbarous e., barbarous hexameters 416:16
E. isn't interesting 66:3
E. is the name everyone gives 455:33
e. of life . . . drawn from life 29:16
e. to make me sad 346:2
Expert beyond e. 157:12
so . . . that we don't have to e. it 169:15
tested by e. 316:18
Till old e. do attain 276:16
Travel . . . a part of e. 19:40
triumph of hope over e. 222:3
true e. from this great event 281:32
we all learn by e. 136:2
worth a life's e. 204:3
Experientia: E. does it 137:9
Experiment: desist from the e. in despair 245:19
Expert: e. . . . has made all the mistakes 64:6
e. is one who knows more 86:30
Experto: E. credite 441:8
Explanation: he would explain his e. 90:31
I do loathe e.s 25:21
Expletive: While e. their feeble aid 313:12
Exploit: Honour is flashed off e. 206:14
Exploitation: E. without work 159:25
Export: Fascism is not an article for e. 290:16
Exposition: I have an e. of sleep 372:9
Exposure: unseemly e. of the mind 196:1
Expotition: E. to the North Pole 274:34
Express: down e. in the small of the back 459:12
Hull e. goes off line 123:16
Expression: His e. may often be called bald 12:29
his favourite e. 137:10
vulgar e. of the passion 120:3
Express-train: e. drew up there Unwontedly 426:26
Extenuate: nothing e. 375:26

543

Extinct: sole purpose of becoming e. 130:11
Extinguished: sometimes overcome; seldom e. 20:23
Extol: How shall we e. thee 31:21
Extra: add some e., just for you 247:22
Extremes: E. meet 205:4 263:7 272:1
Extrèmes: e. se touchent 272:1
Extremism: e. in the defence of liberty 183:5
Exultations: Thy friends are e. 463:20
Eye: adds a precious seeing to the e. 363:30
   although her e.s are sunny 131:9
   apple of his e. 35:17
   before my wery e.s 141:8
   but with his keener e. 268:25
   catch his e.s through the helmet-slit 288:14
   dizzy 'tis to cast one's e. so low 362:36
   Do me e.s deceive me earsight? 446:13
   dress her beauty at your e.s 132:13
   dry one's e.s and laugh 75:15
   ever changing, like a joyless e. 394:11
   E. for e., tooth for tooth 35:1
   e. is not satisfied 43:14
   e. of man hath not heard 372:11
   e.s have they, but they see not 40:23
   E.s look your last! 380:11
   E.s of most unholy blue! 286:24
   e.s that shone, Now dimmed and gone 287:14
   E.s too expressive to be blue 11:2
   e.s were as a flame of fire 58:3
   e. was white 307:28
   flash upon that inward e. 462:7
   Four beasts full of e.s 58:12
   fringèd curtains of thine e. 380:36
   From women's e.s this doctrine I derive 363:32
   Get thee glass e.s 363:2
   gloom-pleased e.s 233:8
   great Task-Master's e. 282:1
   He had but one e. 139:7
   Her e.s are homes of silent prayer 417:37
   Her e.s were deeper 331:15
   her e.s were wild 231:8
   he that formed the e. 40:6
   Hide me from day's garish e. 276:14
   his e.s Were with his heart 90:16
   his e. was backward cast 402:29
   holds him with his glittering e. 116:20
   hundred e.s were fixed on her 29:12
   If I could write the beauty of your e.s 385:15
   If thine e. offend thee 50:31
   I have a good e., uncle 372:29
   In a dark time the e. begins to see 328:17
   In my mind's e., Horatio 348:9
   in the twinkling of an e. 55:39
   In woman's e.s 287:7
   I shut her wild, wild e.s 231:11
   Is thine e. evil 50:42
   kindling her undazzled e.s 282:21
   left me with the jaundiced e. 419:33
   less of this than meets the e. 24:2
   lifting up a fearful e. 401:28
   lift up my mine e.s unto the hills 40:30
   light that visits these sad e.s 185:21
   Locked and frozen in each e. 14:12
   Lockt up from mortal e. 128:26
   looking on it with lack-lustre e. 345:3
   Love-darting e.s 275:33
   Make thy two e.s, like stars 349:1
   may act their dream with open e.s 249:29

meet in her aspect and her e.s 93:8
microscopic e. 313:30
mighty world Of e., and ear 462:21
mine e.s dazzle 448:28
mine e. seeth thee 37:16
Mine e.s have seen the glory 211:4
Mine e.s saw not, and I saw 427:20
Mine e.s smell onions 343:13
mote . . . in thy brother's e. 49:20
My e.s were blind with stars 202:17
My mistress' e.s are nothing like the sun 387:6
my ravished e.s 1:16
my striving e. Dazzles at it 438:1
no longer blinded by our e.s 69:23
no more assail mine e.s 134:12
no speculation in those e.s 366:28
Not from the East, but from Thine e.s 128:19
Oh e.s, no e.s, but fountains 242:20
one auspicious and one dropping e. 347:29
Open your e.s to the air 427:4
piteous recognition in fixed e.s 302:16
quaint enamelled e.s 277:16
Right well mine e.s arede 311:20
sail, with unshut e. 11:5
scholar's e., tongue, sword 350:21
see e. to e. 46:5
seek the beauteous e. of heaven to garnish 361:21
sees with equal e. 313:27
see with, not thro', the e. 60:25
Send home my long strayed e.s 145:32
Smoke Gets in Your E.s 192:2
soft e.s looked love 89:21
Sometimes too hot the e. of heaven shines 385:17
stars the glory of His e.s 310:15
still-soliciting e. 361:31
Store of ladies, whose bright e.s 276:31
such beauty as a woman's e. 363:29
Take a pair of sparkling e.s 176:22
tempts your wand'ring e.s 186:29
That poorly satisfy our e.s 468:3
Then can I drown an e. 385:24
They strike mine e.s 225:4
those e.s, the break of day 368:26
thou e. among the blind 464:11
through another man's e.s 346:9
thy dying e.s were closed 312:5
turn thine e.s And pause awhile 219:6
Two grey e.s with lids to them 382:35
two lovely black e.s 116:1
unforgiving e. 395:38
until you see the whites of their e.s 322:20
we . . . Have e.s to wonder 386:25
when first your e. I eyed 386:21
Where did you get your e.s so blue? 263:11
where you turn your e.s 315:9
Which e.s not yet created shall o'er-read 386:11
While I have e.s to see 200:14
wipe my weeping e.s 447:19
with an e. made quiet 462:15
with a threatening e. 361:19
With e.s upraised 119:18
with his half-shut e.s 315:23
With its soft black e. 287:11
With my little e. 298:19
with scornful, yet with jealous e.s 312:22
With such a wistful e. 454:20
yellow to the jaundiced e. 313:21

Yes I have a pair of e.s 141:13
Eyeball: scaled e. owns the mystic rod 78:30
  We're e. to e. 333:6
Eye-consciousness: e. is on fire 80:6
Eye-lids: opening e. of the morn 277:3
  tinged the e. and the hands 305:16
  tired e. upon tired eyes 420:11
  weigh mine e. down 355:30
Eyesight: Not with blinded e. 420:3

F

Fable: Neither give heed to f.s 56:39
  profane and old wives' f.s 56:43
Fable: ne sont que des f.s convenues 442:18
Fabric: f. huge Rose like an exhalation 278:26
  like the baseless f. of this vision 381:10
Fabrum: F. esse suae quemque fortunae 9:21
Face: Accustomed to her f. 253:22
  apparition of these f.s in the crowd 317:25
  Before I knew thy f. or name 144:14
  Bid them wash their f.s 346:24
  born with a different f. 63:3
  Cover her f.; mine eyes dazzle 448:28
  did not recognize me by my f. 432:2
  discover everybody's f. but their own 410:19
  F. of Man Is blackened 164:24
  f. One would meet in every place 230:24
  f.s are but a gallery 20:13
  f. that launched a thousand ships 266:22
  f. when he repeats his verses 246:13
  familiar with her f. 314:4
  Give me them that will f. me 354:8
  God hath given you one f. 350:19
  hawk-like foreign f.s 264:13
  Her angel's f. 402:28
  hides a smiling f. 125:31
  hid his f. amid a crowd 472:6
  Honest labour bears a lovely f. 134:2
  how blubbered is that pretty f. 320:15
  How my f., your flower 75:6
  human f. divine 279:13
  human f. is . . . a whole cluster of f.s 321:12
  I know the f.s I shall see 331:24
  I never forget a f. 269:11
  In nice clear f.s 24:9
  I will pass nor turn my f. 79:13
  I wish I loved its silly f. 325:14
  Just such a f. 74:23
  Kissing with golden f. 385:27
  Lives on this lonely f. 471:18
  Look on her f., and you'll forget 315:17
  Looks the whole world in the f. 257:20
  make his f. shine upon thee 35:7
  make the f. of heaven so fine 379:37
  mind's construction in the f. 364:26
  my f. – I don't mind it 160:2
  My f. is my fortune 298:16
  never f. so pleased my mind 167:13
  never looked upon a f. 148:3
  noo mwore do zee your f. 25:8
  Oft he seems to hide his f. 281:31
  old familiar f.s 245:6
  old plain men have rosy f.s 407:25
  open f. of heaven 233:7

Private f.s in public places 14:19
sea of upturned f.s 341:2
She has a lovely f. 419:15
so many millions of f.s 71:7
tenth transmitter of a foolish f. 338:4
those angel f.s smile 294:5
Visit her f. too roughly 348:1
When two strong men stand f. to f. 238:11
whole f. of the earth 305:9
with how wan a f. 396:12
With white f.s like town children 212:3
ye have a singing f. 28:8
Your f., my thane, is as a book 365:1
Facility: fatal f. of the octosyllabic verse 90:25
Fact: But F.s are chiels 84:11
  complete possession of the f.s 270:21
  F.s are better than dreams 113:20
  f.s are sacred 339:9
  falls upon the f.s like soft snow 301:3
  Fashnable f.s and polite annygoats 425:24
  heat of religious f. 175:20
  Matters of f. . . . are very stubborn 430:11
  Now, what I want is F.s 138:9
  shilling life . . . all the f.s 15:18
  When the legend becomes f. 29:30
Faction: To die for f. is a common evil 149:31
Faculties: T'affections, and to f. 145:5
Faculty: try the edge of his f. 76:3
Fade: cheek that doth not f. 230:23
  F. far away, dissolve 232:2
  She cannot f. 231:20
  They only f. away! 8:12
  Whatever f.s, but fading pleasure brings 396:17
Faery: Full beautiful, a f.'s child 231:8
  in f. lands forlorn 232:7
  land of f. Where nobody gets old 471:10
Fafafather: He was f. of all schemes 226:4
Faiblesse: tout le reste est f. 439:19
Fail: If we should f. – 365:13
  I was sure I should not f. 113:20
  I would sooner f. 234:6
  no such word As – f. 260:18
Failed: Light that F. 241:23
Failings: e'en his f. leaned to Virtue's side 181:1
  sifted her, and separated her f. 120:22
Failure: Half the f.s in life arise 193:29
  might have died, unmarked, unknown, a f.
    437:16
Faint: F., yet pursuing 35:30
  so f., so spiritless, So dull 355:11
Fainted: I should utterly have f. 38:7
Fainting: Stretching and Fainting in Coils 101:15
Fair: all so excellently f. 117:26
  deserve the f. 149:33
  divinely f., fit love for Gods 280:33
  every f. from f. sometime declines 385:17
  F. is foul, and foul is f. 364:11
  F. is my love, and cruel 131:9
  F. is too foul an epithet 267:17
  F. stood the wind for France 148:13
  fifty times as f. 60:3
  For ever wilt thou love and she be f. 231:20
  Is it very f.? 252:2
  never yet was foolish that was f. 374:14
  not f. to outward view 116:15
  What care I how f. she be 459:5
Fairest: My f., my espoused 280:7

I am the f. face 192:22
in a f. one man is appointed 342:4
refined f. had to include 337:25
refuse to help his f. 152:16
Famine: f. grew, and locusts came 426:8
She went to cry f. 243:15
Famine: Elle alla crier f. 243:15
Famous: f. for fifteen minutes 446:25
found myself f. 94:12
now praise f. men 48:27
Fan: with her f. spread 120:24
Fanatics: F. have their dreams 230:21
Fancies: f. that broke through language 77:21
Fears and f. thick upon me came 466:1
high region of his f. 282:24
host of furious f. 5:19
Our f. are more giddy 383:10
set your f. free 74:14
then f. flee away 81:2
Fancy: all my f. painted her 271:12
All the gardener F. e'er could feign 232:11
Ever let the fancy roam 230:22
f. from a flower-bell 73:1
F. is indeed no other 118:18
f. to see my own funeral 154:5
food of sweet and bitter f. 346:6
little of what you f. 255:10
makes f. lame 126:24
not expressed in f. 348:22
of most excellent f. 352:25
so full of shapes is f. 382:24
Tell me where is f. bred 370:1
young man's f. lightly turns 419:19
Fanny: F. by Gaslight 335:3
only pretty F.'s way 304:24
Fantaisie: échange de deux f.s 106:3
laisser aller le monde à sa f. 142:11
Fantastic: On the light f. toe 276:20
Fantastical: it alone is high f. 382:24
Fantasy: all made of f. 346:11
much too strong for f. 144:19
Far: F. and few, f. and few 250:22
How f. one can go too f. 116:3
thus f. shalt thou go 304:23
Farce: second as f. 269:17
Farce: f. est jouée 324:21
Fardeau: pénible f. 64:16
Fare: F. thee well! and if for ever 92:37
last of all the Romans, f. thee well! 361:2
Not f. well, but f. forward 156:7
Farewel: f.! he is gon! 107:30
Farewell: Everlasting f.s! and again 135:4
F.! a long f., to all my greatness! 358:21
F. and adieu 7:14
f. goes out sighing 382:14
F., green fields 62:20
F. house, and f. home! 128:21
F. the tranquil mind 375:5
F.! thou art too dear 386:14
F. to Lochaber 325:16
F., too little and too lately known 151:5
For ever, and for ever, f., Cassius! 360:35
may there be no sadness of f. 416:4
Farm: lass wi' the weel-stockit f.s 84:24
little snug f. of the World 401:13
to retreat to a Swiss f. 137:33
Farmer: better f. ne'er brushed dew 93:30

blest beyond all blessings are f.s 441:25
embattled f.s stood 158:12
f. sowing his corn 298:6
Like a red-faced f. 212:3
They all ran after the f.'s wife 298:8
Three jolly F.s 134:25
Farrago: Gaudia discursus nostri f. libelli est 227:16
Farrier: Some f. should prescribe 124:32
Farrow: old sow that eats her f. 226:18
Farthing: Latin word for three f.s 363:25
never pay a f. for it 129:14
paid the uttermost f. 49:3
two sparrows sold for a f. 49:41
You owe me five f.s 297:18
Fascination: war . . . will always have its f. 456:13
Fascism: F. is not an article for export 290:16
Fashion: f. of this world passeth away 55:8
f.'s brightest arts 181:11
high-flyer at F. 140:8
not for the f. of these times 344:31
nothing else holds f. 382:21
out of the world, as out of the f. 114:8
Quite out of f. 382:13
tell you the leading f. 333:7
to fit this year's f.s 197:10
true to you, darlin', in my f. 316:23
Fast: grew f. and furious 85:21
hold f. that which is good 56:37
Fasting: between a fou man and a f. 340:36
will die f. 168:23
Fat: could eat no f. 296:30
eat the f. of the land 34:35
f. and flourishing 40:5
F., fair and forty 299:14
f. man demanding elbow-room 448:8
f. man trying to get in 453:10
f. of others' works 86:5
first seven f. kine 34:31
I'm f., but I'm thin inside 300:17
Imprisoned in every f. man 121:19
Let me have men about me that are f. 359:18
one of them is f. and grows old 354:7
till the f. lady sings 122:2
waxed f., and kicked 35:18
Who drives f. oxen 223:18
Who's your f. friend? 79:18
Fate: architect of his own f. 9:21
Beyond the limits of a vulgar f. 187:15
cannot suspend their f. 133:16
Could thou and I with F. conspire 164:30
f. and metaphysical aid 364:29
F. cannot harm me 400:4
F. so enviously debars 268:16
F. wrote her a . . . tragedy 29:8
fears his f. too much 286:6
hanging breathless on thy f. 256:13
hold f. Clasped in my list 167:11
jeers at F. 1:4
master of his f. 417:3
take a bond of f. 366:41
Their f. . . . the same as yours 15:12
thy f. and mine are sealed 422:14
when f. summons 150:27
would f. but mend it! 320:30
Father: about my F.'s business 52:4
all one f. 47:25
But not an angry f. 97:11

child is f. of the man 463:15
Dreading to find its F. 14:8
everlasting F. 45:8
f. answered never a word 257:23
F., dear f., come home with me now 467:26
F.! f.! where are you going? 62:19
F., forgive them 52:45
F., O f.! what do we here 61:8
f. of English criticism 219:24
f. of the fatherless 39:14
F.s, from hence trust not 373:36
f.s have eaten sour grapes 46:33
F.'s sorrow, f.'s joy 187:29
F.s that, like so many Alexanders 357:4
Had it been his f. 6:2
his f. was before him 411:16
I had it from my f. 358:13
leave f. and mother 50:33
leave his f. and his mother 33:22
My f. argued sair 25:6
my f. wept 61:23
Neither f. nor lover 328:16
no man cometh unto the F. 53:28
nothing more than an exalted f. 169:13
Old f. antick the law 353:20
Old f., old artificer 226:19
only f. . . . might expect 182:9
Our F. that art in heaven 320:11
our f.s that begat us 48:27
rather Have a turnip than a f. 224:3
slept with his f.s 36:14
this is my true-begotten f. 369:23
wise f. that knows his own child 369:24
wise son maketh a glad f. 41:32
without your F. 49:41
Fathom: certain f.s in the earth 381:16
fifty f. deep 23:13
Full f. five thy father lies 380:35
Fathom-line: Where f. could never touch 353:32
Fattening: illegal, immoral, or f. 461:2
Fauces: misplace his f. 226:16
Fault: All his f.s, observed 360:32
best men are moulded out of f.s 368:31
Be to her f.s a little blind 320:18
but it's their own silly f. 31:10
Condemn the f. 368:10
England . . . with all her f.s 111:21
England, with all thy f.s 126:37
Every one f. seeming monstrous 345:25
excusing of a f. Doth make the f. the worse
    361:22
f., dear Brutus, is not in our stars 359:16
f. . . . grows two thereby 199:5
faultless to a f. 78:6
f.s of great authors 118:27
fill you with the f.s they had 247:22
Has she no f.s then 315:7
his f.s lie gently on him 359:1
if the f. were on only one side 248:19
If we had no f.s 247:26
Just hint a f. 312:22
no kind of f. or flaw 177:6
not for thy f.s, but mine 90:9
O happy f. 283:1
only confess our little f.s 248:15
only f.'s with time 75:24
only one f. It was kind of lousy 429:24

Sailor men 'ave their f.s 216:5
To hide the f. I see 316:8
without f. or stain 68:6
world of vile ill-favoured f.s 371:11
Faultless: Faultily f., icily regular 420:27
Faustus: F. must be damned 267:3
Faute: c'est un f. 65:19
Favour: accepts a smaller as a f. 99:8
almost like a f. 121:7
lively sense of *future* f.s 445:14
nor for her f.s call 316:7
to this f. she must come 352:27
Favourite: f. has no friend 186:28
To be a prodigal's f. 466:20
Fawns: fallow f. invisible go 427:1
Fear: Arch F. in a visible form 77:7
As if his f. still followed him 402:29
concessions of f. 81:14
craven f.s of being great 416:23
f. first in the world made gods 225:9
F. God 57:32
F. has many eyes 104:21
F. lent wings to his feet 441:4
f. not what men say 81:2
f. of every man that heard him 225:30
f. of some divine and supreme powers 86:22
f. of the Lord 40:20 41:40
F.s thick upon me came 466:1
F.s of the brave 219:10
f. thou not at all 412:23
f. to whom f. 54:42
freedom from f. 329:23
grown from sudden f.s 93:17
He is F., O Little Hunter 240:25
imagining some f. 372:15
men as had the f. of God 129:10
natural f. in children 18:21
never f. to negotiate 235:17
no f. in love 57:41
No passion so effectually robs . . . as f. 82:7
Not mine own f.s 386:26
only thing we have to f. is f. itself 329:14
Present f's Are less than . . . imaginings 364:23
suffering from what he f.s 285:25
when f.s attack 96:7
with f. and trembling 56:24
Fearfully: f. and wonderfully made 41:12
Feast: As you were going to a f. 225:2
beginning of a f. 354:40
great f. of languages 364:1
guests are met, the f. is set 116:19
Paris is a moveable f. 197:19
public f.s, where meet a public rout 132:17
someone disturbed the f. 243:20
Spare f.! a radish and an egg 127:15
Table of Moveable F.s 318:10
Feasting: house of f. 43:26
Feats: 'Twas one of my f. 93:12
What f. he did that day 357:18
Feather: f. to tickle the intellect 246:5
fine f.s that make fine birds 3:22
I am a f. for each wind 384:16
Stuck a f. in his cap 23:27
Features: for homely f. to keep home 275:33
February: F., fill the dyke 433:20
F. hath twenty-eight 184:6
Excepting F. alone 6:17

Fire: after the f. a still small voice 36:18
Against my f. 363:4
at the round table, by a sea-coal f. 355:24
bush burned with f. 34:41
clean f., a clean hearth 245:21
every time she shouted 'Fire!' 30:18
eye is on f. 80:6
f. is not quenched 51:38
f.s out of the Grand Duke's wood 391:20
f. which in the heart resides 11:14
frighted with false f. 351:13
'gins to pale his uneffectual f. 349:11
I am warm, I have seen the f. 45:40
I pray it be f. to me 68:9
Keep the home f.s burning 167:12
little f. is quickly trodden out 358:10
Love is a spirit all compact of f. 387:11
Now stir the f. 127:12
one whose f.s True genius kindles 312:22
our brother F. 264:14
pleasant f. our souls to regale 62:1
quickened now with f. 188:10
sparkle still the right Promethean f. 363:32
Spit, f.! spout, rain! 362:15
take f. in his bosom 41:28
they will set an house on f. 20:6
till the f. is dying 272:8
Upon a wheel of f. 363:5
who can hold a f. in his hand 376:15
world will end in f. 170:4
Firebrand: f. plucked out of the burning 47:15
Fire-fly: f. wakens: waken thou with me 422:15
Fire-folk: all the f. sitting in the air 206:15
Fireman: f. and afraid of bumps! 399:4
Fireside: glass of wine *by his own f.* 396:1
make a happy f. clime 85:29
winter talk by the f. 20:22
Firing: what to do after f. 326:10
Firmament: brave o'erhanging f. 349:36
f. sheweth his handiwork 37:36
no fellow in the f. 360:4
pillared f. is rottenness 275:28
spacious f. on high 2:14
Firmness: f. in the right 254:19
First: Be not the f. 313:10
f. and the last 58:38
f. and wisest of them all 281:9
F. in war, f. in peace 251:22
f. man is of the earth 55:38
f. shall be last 50:40
f. that ever burst 116:26
In the f. is the last 78:17
left thy f. love 58:6
one discovers . . . what to put f. 305:4
First-born: rail against the f. of Egypt 344:40
Fish: bonnie f. and halesome farin' 291:6
F. fiddle de-dee 251:5
F. fuck in it 163:10
f. of the sea 37:27
f. that *talks* 134:5
have my own f. to fry 104:24
like a f. without a bicycle 184:5
man may f. with the worm 351:40
no more land, say f. 69:8
surrounded by f. 33:5
Thou deboshed f. thou 381:5
Fishers: make you f. of men 48:40

Three f. went sailing 237:18
Fishermen: bite every time for f. 289:5
f. that walk upon the beach 362:36
Fishes: F. . . . know no such liberty 258:12
I marvel how the f. live in the sea 376:4
little f. of the sea 102:12
make little f. talk 183:2
thousand men that f. gnawed upon 378:1
Fishing: discourse of rivers, and fish and f. 445:27
Fish-knives: Phone for the f., Norman 32:17
Fishmonger: Excellent well; you are a f. 349:26
Fish-ponds: look into the f. in my garden 448:30
Fishy: something f. about the French 123:13
Fist: His withered f. still knocking 146:24
Fit: become f. for this world 233:22
not f. with them to stir and toil 89:28
only the F. survive 342:25
pleasing f. of melancholy 275:23
Why then, I'll f. you 242:21
Fittest: Survival of the F. 132:10 402:8
Fitzgerald: shall hoarse F. bawl 92:21
Five: all life is six to f. against 333:2
At f. in the afternoon 172:17
F. Towns 28:28
full of the strength of f. 32:20
Five-and-twenty: count f., Tattycoram 138:14
Flabbiness: moral f. born of . . . Success 217:12
Flag: death's pale f. 380:10
f. of morn in conqueror's state 210:21
f. that makes you free 467:30
Keep the Red F. flying 121:9
old f. flyin' 293:18
red f. in front of the steam-roller 216:13
spare your country's f. 454:6
Under great yellow f.s 397:17
Whose f. has braved 97:20
Flagon: Out of an English f. 110:6
Stay me with f.s 44:19
Flail: f. of the lashing hail 390:14
smitten as with a f. 68:2
Flakes: In large white f. 67:30
Flame: eyes were as a f. of fire 58:3
feed his sacred f. 118:7
hard, gem-like f. 305:18
live f. will start 185:15
mutual f. is fanned 119:7
Nor public f., nor private 311:29
plays about the f. 174:2
roof-lamp's oily f. 193:5
so full of subtle f. 27:17
So his f.s must waste away 98:25
spark of that ancient f. 440:21
Though absence seemed my f. to qualify 386:29
Went by her like thin f.s 331:18
Flanders: In F. fields the poppies blow 264:18
Flank: silken f.s with garlands drest 231:23
Flash: One F. of It within the Tavern 164:22
Thought is only a f. 311:1
Flashes: In f., and with glory not their own 465:21
Flask: F. of Wine, a Book of Verse 164:1
Flat: Very f., Norfolk 123:18
Flatter: f. with their lips 37:30
he will never f. his country 162:9
lie that f.s 126:26 .
Some men fawn and f. 303:14
What really f.s a man 388:5
Flatterer: all f.s live at the expense 243:18

arch-f. . . . is a man's self 19:15
when I tell him he hates f.s 359:31
Flattering: talent of f. with delicacy 17:5
you think him worth f. 388:5
Flattery: Everyone likes f. 143:32
F. is all right – if you don't inhale 406:13
F. is false coin 248:11
f. soothe the dull cold ear of death 186:8
f.'s the food of fools 410:3
gained by every sort of f. 109:17
paid with f. 219:16
Was f. lost on poet's ear 339:28
Flatteur: tout f. Vit aux dépens 243:18
Flavour: That gives it all its f. 127:2
Wich wanity do you like the f. on 141:20
Flaw: break into a hundred thousand f.s 362:13
We all have f.s 429:23
Flax: smoking f. shall he not quench 45:38
Flea: all the f.s in my bed 105:3
f. Hath smaller f.s that on him prey 410:16
f.s that tease 31:6
f. that I have in my ear 324:12
Great f.s have little f.s 288:2
literature's performing f. 299:11
must do as the f.s do 329:3
obvious to a f. 311:25
very f. of his dog 225:7
Fled: all f. with thee, Robin Adair 236:3
I f. him, down the nights 427:12
Flee: devil . . . with f. from you 57:26
f. from me that sometime did me seek 468:10
Fleece: His f. was white as snow 297:8
Fleet: F.'s lit up 460:16
Spanish f. thou canst not see 395:8
Ten thousand f.s sweep over thee 90:20
Where the f. of stars is anchored 165:26
who can be dull in F. Street 246:9
Fler: Far better hand wrong f. 136:35
Flesche: f. is brukle 152:13
Flesh: according to the f. 54:32
All f. is grass 45:32
could not all this f. Keep in a little life? 355:7
F. and Blood can't bear it 88:27
f. is weak 51:22
f. of my f. 33:21
F. perishes, I live on 192:22
hair of my f. stood up 36:38
her fair and unpolluted f. 352:30
I have more f. than another man 354:34
I wants to make your f. creep 140:24
Leave the f. to the fate 78:15
little f. and breath 16:8
O f., f., how art thou fishified! 379:24
shall be one f. 33:22
since f. must live 78:20
soul to feel the f. 69:2
spite of this f. today 77:16
take off my f. and sit in my bones 399:31
that this too too solid f. would melt 347:36
this f. which walls about our life 377:2
thorn in the f. 56:5
twain shall be one f. 50:33
unto thee shall all f. come 39:10
vague errors of the f. 427:7
What a change of f. 27:18
Whilst my gross f. sinks downward 377:19
Word was made f. 53:2

world, the f., and the devil 319:3
world-wearied f. 380:11
Fleshly: F. School of Poetry 79:21
Fleshy: f. tables of the heart 55:43
Flies: As f. to wanton boys 362:33
Dead f. cause the ointment 43:39
fills the butchers' shops with large blue f. 399:1
where the small f.s were caught 18:13
Flight: His f. was madness 367:4
In what fond f. 331:23
not attained by sudden f. 256:29
Swift be thine approaching f. 394:16
vulgar f. of common souls 290:4
winged his roving f. 315:29
Flim-flam: pretty f. 27:23
Flint: in time the f. is pierced 242:19
wear out the everlasting f. 379:29
Flock: fleecy f.s of light 68:8
f.s of the memories 272:29
My f.s feed not 25:12
not armies . . . but f.s of sheep 104:18
shepherd that leaveth the f. 47:23
Flock-bed: once a f., but repaired with straw 315:3
Flogging: habit of f. me constantly 432:2
Flood: All whom the f. did 145:16
bathe in fiery f.s 368:22
beachèd verge of the salt f. 381:26
fellows that f. could not wash away 120:11
f. may bear me far 416:4
giant race, before the f. 150:15
Land of the mountain and the f. 340:2
Let the f.s clap their hands 40:8
mergin of that moorish f. 466:7
neither can the f.s drown it 44:28
taken at the f. leads – God knows 91:43
taken at the f., leads on to fortune 360:33
ten years before the f. 269:1
Thorough f., thorough fire 371:31
Floor: across the f.s of silent seas 156:23
f. lay paved with broken hearts 258:10
f.s are shrunken 192:10
f.s of plaster 315:3
just waxed the f. 292:18
spit on a well-scrubbed f. 170:23
Flora: Tasting of f. and the country green 232:2
Florence: lily of F. blossoming in stone 256:27
Rode past fair F. 231:5
Flos: Ut f. in saeptis secretus 103:21
Flour: f. of cities all 152:14
Floures: alle the f. in the mede 108:19
f. ginnen for to springe 108:18
Flourish: f. set on youth 386:1
peculiar f. of his right arm 140:10
Flout: F. 'em, and scout 'em 381:6
Flow: What need you f. so fast? 8:26
Flower: As a f. springs up secretly 103:21
As midsummer f. 398:3
blushing f.s shall rise 315:9
breeding f.s will never breed the same 232:11
bunch of other men's f.s 285:24
constellated f. that never sets 393:21
Ensnared with f.s 268:20
fell upon a little western f. 371:36
f. is born to blush unseen 186:10
f. of kings of knights 265:21
f. of the field 40:10 45:32
f. o' the broom 74:24

f. presented to him as a pledge 118:16
f.s anew, returning seasons bring! 308:12
f.s appear on the earth 44:20
F.s I leave you on the grass 425:1
F.s of all hue 279:24
f.s o' the forest 158:4
f.s that bloom in the spring 177:33
F. that once has blown 164:10
For the f.s now that . . . thou let'st fall 384:29
for the f.s of the forest 116:2
fosters the droop-headed f.s 231:28
fresh showers for the thirsting f.s 390:13
gathered f.s are dead, Yasmin 166:5
Gather the f.s 268:30
glory in the f. 464:16
got Thee f.s to strew Thy way 199:11
Heaven in a wild f. 60:8
Here's f.s for you 384:28
I sipped each f. 174:7
Letting a hundred f.s blossom 266:11
Look like the innocent f. 365:2
lovelier f. On earth was never sown 467:2
No f. upon the ground 390:12
no stronger than a f. 386:4
O fairest f., no sooner blown 277:19
paints the wayside f. 96:19
Say it with f.s 299:16
summer's f. is to the summer sweet 386:18
sweet will be the f. 125:32
These f.s . . . sleep 98:29
this same f. that smiles to-day 200:19
thou canst not stir a f. 427:22
through the green use drives the f. 426:7
To me the meanest f. that blows 464:20
up-gathered now like sleeping f.s 463:6
Wee modest crimson-tippèd f. 85:26
what f.s are at my feet 232:5
Where blew a f. 426:4
Where have all the f.s gone? 341:24
with the f.s she comes again 252:1
You seize the f. 85:18
Flower-de-luce: lilies . . . f. being one 384:29
Flower-pots: Water your damned f. 78:21
Flowret: meanest f. of the vale 187:7
Flue: broth of goldish f. 205:28
Fluidity: solid for f. 112:15
Fluke: parson . . . who knows a f. 127:30
Flummoxed: what the Italians call reg'larly f. 141:7
Flung: f. himself from the room 250:9
Flush: wings of gentle f. 231:1
Flute: Blows out his brains upon the f. 78:20
   soft complaining f. 151:3
   To fairy f.s 289:3
Flux: All is f. 198:24
Fly: blue f. sung in the pane 420:26
   Busy, curious, thirsty f. 299:19
   f. . . . may sting a stately horse 220:23
   f. that sips treacle 174:13
   I, said the F. 298:19
   man is not a f. 313:30
   noise of a f. 146:22
   small gilded f. Does lecher 362:39
   Then f. betimes 99:1
   then would I f. away 38:32
   those that f., may fight 87:27
   to let it. escape 405:21
   you cannot f. 159:21

Flying-fishes: Where the f. play 240:2
Foam: Like the f. on the river 339:21
Foe: ah, my f.s, and oh, my friends 273:18
   angry with my f. 62:2
   fear no f. in shining armour 302:19
   f. that comes with fearless eyes 293:14
   f.! they come! 89:24
   From the f.s they captive make 106:4
   furnace for your f. so hot 358:12
   He makes no friend who never made a f. 417:1
   His c. against the f.s 398:8
   His f. was folly and his weapon wit 205:17
   in the midst of f.s 158:2
   I wish my deadly f. no worse 67:20
   make one worthy man my f. 312:24
   sternest knight to thy mortal f. 265:23
   thrice he routed all his f.s 150:2
   tim'rous f. 312:23
   to let in the f. 281:22
   When we go to meet the f. 179:9
Foeman: When the f. bares his steel 178:4
Foemen: f. worthy of their steel 339:22
Fog: f. comes on little cat feet 337:1
   His rising f.s prevail 150:28
   London particular . . . A f., miss 136:18
   to feel the f. in my throat 77:6
   yellow f. that rubs its back 156:21
Foible: ha, F.? A swimmingness in the eyes 120:28
Foie: *f. du côté droit* 283:22
Fold: We are all driven into the same f. 208:17
Folding: little f. of the hands to sleep 41:27
Folk: Dere's where de old f.s stay 168:8
   hand f.s over to God's mercy 155:11
   It's the f. out in front 160:2
   men as well as other f.s 162:23
   My f.s didn't come over on the *Mayflower* 329:7
   Some f.s rail against other f.s 162:27
Follies: f. of the town crept slowly 182:12
   pretty f. that themselves commit 369:27
Follow: he will never f. anything 359:28
   I f. but myself 373:31
Folly: brood of F. without father bred 275:36
   f. of being comforted 470:19
   f. of the wise 224:13
   f. to be wise 187:6
   fool according to his f. 42:38 42:39
   fool returneth to his f. 42:40
   fool would persist in his f. 63:15
   forts of f. fall 11:12
   He knew human f. 14:6
   If thou remember'st not the slightest f. 344:33
   lovely woman stoops to f. 157:8
   Mingle some brief f. 209:10
   shoot f. as it flies 313:26
   shunn'st the noise of f. 276:6
   Though age from f. 343:21
   uses his f. like a stalking-horse 346:16
Folwed: first he f. it himselve 107:27
Fond: fair and yet not f. 302:21
   F. thing vainly invented 320:8
   I love the f., The faithful 114:28
Fons: *tecto vicinus iugis aquae f.* 209:17
Fonte: *Medio de f. leporum* 259:24
Food: ever craving for their f. 128:6
   f. convenient for me 43:6
   f. of sweet and bitter fancy 346:6
   f. that cures all hunger 105:21

f. that to him now is as luscious 374:11
homely was their f. 173:9
Man did eat angels' f. 39:23
man who swallows his f. 245:16
most delicious, nourishing, and wholesome f.
    411:8
Music, moody f. Of us that trade in love 343:31
perpetual struggle for room and f. 266:1
Seeking the f. he eats 344:39
What is f. to one man 259:23
Fool: amongst f.s a judge 124:31
Beggared by f.s 149:22
brains enough to make a f. of himself 407:3
cannot f. all the people 254:20
Dreading e'en f.s 312:23
flannelled f.s at the wicket 239:17
flattery's the food of f.s 410:3
f. according to his folly 42:38 42:39
f., a f.! I met a f. i' the forest 345:1
f. at forty is a f. indeed 472:14
f. hath said . . . There is no God 37:31
f. his whole life long 260:5
f. lies here who tried to hustle 240:11
F., . . . look in thy heart 396:11
f. me to the top of my bent 351:19
f. must follow his natural bent 241:3
f. must now and then be right 124:27
f. returneth to his folly 42:40
F.s are my theme 92:22
f.s by heavenly compulsion 361:34
f. sees not the same tree 63:13
f. shall be in danger 49:1
f.s make a mock at sin 42:8
f.s! 'od rot 'em! 399:4
f.s rush in 313:24
f.s, who came to scoff 181:3
f. to make me merry 346:2
f. to the correction of the stocks 41:29
f. uttereth all his mind 43:4
f. will be meddling 42:24
f. would persist in his folly 63:15
For f.s admire 313:15
Fortune, that favours f.s 224:20
greatest f. may ask more 119:32
Hated by f.s, and f.s to hate 410:17
He hated a f., and he hated a rogue 224:4
He that begetteth a f. 42:19
human bodies are sic f.s 85:32
I am two f.s, I know 146:14
If honest nature made you f.s 84:12
I hate a f.! 138:13
learned f. is more foolish 283:17
let f.s contest 314:6
life of the f. is worse 48:14
life's time's f. 355:5
Lord, what f.s these mortals be! 372:4
lose a thing That none but f.s would keep 368:18
Love's not Time's f. 387:1
more hope of a f. 42:41
more of the f. than of the wise 19:23
needs a very clever woman to manage a f. 241:25
Ninety-nine per cent . . . are f.s 456:33
no rest for the sole of her f. 34:16
poor f.s decoyed into our condition 307:18
Pretty f., it stinted 378:27
rather than a f. in his folly 42:18
resolved to live a f. 27:17

shame the f.s 312:16
smarts so little as a f. 312:17
So true a f. is love 385:32
straitened forehead of a f. 419:22
suckle f.s and chronicle small beer 374:15
That f.s should be so deep-contemplative 345:5
Th' athletic f. 10:10
this great stage of f.s 363:3
Thou f., this night thy soul 52:17
through excess of wisdom is made a f. 158:22
twenty-seven millions mostly f.s 99:36
Why should I play the Roman f. 367:28
wisest f. in Christendom 198:5
world is made up . . . of f.s and knaves 79:23
ye suffer f.s gladly 56:3
You can f. too many of the people 429:12
You will always be f.s! 163:18
Foolery: hateful form of f. 76:3
Foolish: f. things of the world 54:50
He never said a f. thing 328:7
never yet was f. that was fair 374:14
These f. things 269:21
very f., fond old man 363:6
You f. man, you do not even know 109:21
Foolishness: f. depart from him 43:1
wisdom of the world is f. 55:2
Foonf: F. speaking 229:16
Foot: always one f. on the ground 324:14
dash thy f. against a stone 40:2
from the sole of his f. 24:11
Here at the fountain's sliding f. 268:22
her f. speaks 382:19
leave . . . the Forty-second F. 204:22
madly squeeze a right-hand f. 102:19
make crouch beneath his f. 78:9
man's naked f. on the shore 133:14
not suffer thy f. to be moved 40:31
One f. in sea, and one on shore 372:36
one f. in the grave 457:1
O! so light of f. 379:29
Thy soul the fixt f. 146:17
with shining F. shall pass 165:2
Footfalls: F. echo in the memory 155:30
Foot-in-the-grave: F. young man 178:2
Footman: eternal F. hold my coat 156:24
Foot-path: Jog on, jog on, the f. way 384:26
Footprint: F.s on the sands of time 257:5
    looking for a man's f. 29:13
Footsteps: plants his f. in the sea 125:30
Footstool: make thine enemies thy f. 40:19
Fop: six-foot column of f. 204:29
Foppery: excellent f. of the world 361:34
Forbearance: f. ceases to be a virtue 82:4
Forbid: they said, God f. 52:41
Forbidden: hinting at the f. 14:2
Force: achieve more than our f. 82:24
    balance of actual f.s 291:14
Brute f. without wisdom 208:29
brute male f. of the wicked world 237:21
Ev'ry member of the f. 328:19
F. is not a remedy 68:17
f. that through the green fuse 426:7
not only love but every living f. 146:26
one of the f.s of nature 272:32
should be thrown with great f. 304:9
Surprised by unjust f. 275:27
use of f. alone is . . . *temporary* 81:16

Fat, fair and f. 299:14
F. years on 66:2
From f. to fifty a man 309:7
gave her mother f. whacks 6:9
hopeful than to be f. years old 204:4
Life begins at f. 433:4
Forward: fare f., voyagers 156:7
Fossils: Like f. of the rock 415:16
Foster-child: f. of silence and slow time 231:18
Fou: between a f. man and a fasting 340:36
I wasna f. 84:8
Fought: what they f. each other for 401:9
Foul: Fair is f., and f. is fair 364:11
I thank the gods I am f. 345:27
most f., strange, and unnatural 349:2
too f. an epithet 267:17
Foules: here the f. singe 108:18
Found: if one is promptly f. out 236:10
Foundation: f. of all our hopes 86:26
Good order is the f. 82:25
hour when earth's f.s fled 210:2
Founder: enjoyed the gifts of the f. 175:9
forgotten the names of their f.s 171:4
which hesitates to forget its f. 453:6
Fount: Slow, slow, fresh f. 224:26
White f.s falling in the courts 110:8
Fountain: Afric's sunny f.s 196:24
Back to the burning f. 390:3
Deep in its f. 89:28
f. filled with blood 125:26
f. of all goodness 318:30
f. of gardens 44:23
f.s mingle with the river 391:27
f.s of the great deep 34:15
from the heart of the f. of delight 259:24
My mind is troubled, like a f. stirred 382:18
passion and the life, whose f.s 117:27
perpetual f. of good sense 151:35
silver f.s mud 385:29
Still the f. weeps for all 128:25
Weep you no more, sad f.s 8:26
woman moved is like a f. troubled 380:23
ye f.s, meadows, hills and groves 464:18
Four: F. things greater than all things 238:12
Fourfold: I see the F. Man 61:1
Four-footed: parody On all f. things 110:4
Fourmi: Chez la f. sa voisine 243:15
f. n'est pas prêteuse 243:16
Fourscore: F. and upward 363:6
f. Was as eighty 232:17
Fourteen: In f. hundred and ninety-two 335:1
Foutra: f. for the world 356:16
Fowl: broiled f. and mushrooms 140:22
f. of the air 37:27
You elegant f.! 251:1
Fowles: smale f. maken melodye 107:8
Fowler: net of an inhuman f. 236:8
Fox: f. from his lair 185:2
f. may steal your hens 174:5
gentleman galloping after a f. 455:34
hunting . . . of the f. 64:1
little f. he murmured 471:1
set a f. to watching the chickens 432:24
Foxes: f. have holes 49:31
f. stunk and littered 186:21
portion for f. 39:9
Take us the f., the little f. 44:21

Frabjous: O f. day: Callooh! Callay! 101:27
Fraction: pitifullest infinitesimal f. 100:15
Thou wretched f. 99:14
Frailest: Why choose you the f. 391:22
Frailties: draw his f. from their dread abode 186:18
Frailty: f. of all things here 391:22
F., thy name is woman! 348:3
Love's but the f. of the mind 120:29
love's the noblest f. of the mind 151:24
more flesh . . . therefore more f. 354:34
wit's the noblest f. of the mind 342:31
Frame: calm and heavenly f. 125:22
man's whole f. is obvious to a flea 311:25
quit this mortal f. 311:30
tremble for this lovely f. 452:17
universal f. began 150:33
Whatever stirs this mortal f. 118:7
Français: Ce qui n'est pas clair n'est pas f.
327:23
France: Anything may happen in F. 248:22
'Battle of F.' is over 112:22
Fair stood the wind for F. 148:13
F., famed in all great arts 12:11
F. has lost the battle 173:16
F. was long a despotism 99:25
garden of F. 324:7
nearer is to F. 101:19
one illusion – F. 236:9
order . . . this matter better in F. 405:6
That sweet enemy, F. 396:15
thought of F. in a certain way 173:15
France: F., mère des arts 152:1
Francesca: F. di Rimini, miminy, piminy 178:1
Franglais: Parlez-vous F.? 159:32
Frankfort: I went to F. 316:21
Frankie: F. and Johnny were lovers 7:17
Fratrum: Par nobile f. 209:16
Frau: in lofe mit a Merican f. 252:14
Fray: Fought was this noble f. 148:14
latter end of a f. 354:40
Freckles: Love, curiosity, f., and doubt 303:15
Fred: Here lies F. 6:2
Frederick: Here is cruel F., see! 202:24
Free: All f. men . . . are citizens of Berlin 235:23
all men everywhere could be f. 254:21
as f. as nature first made man 151:21
Before they're allowed to be f. 153:6
definition of a f. society 406:12
freedom to the f. 254:16
here we may be f. 131:12
I only ask to be f. 136:22
land of the f. 236:6
let us die to make men f. 211:6
Man is condemned to be f. 337:22
none the less f. than you were 16:19
No one can be perfectly f. 402:11
safer . . . than to be f. 229:2
Thou art f. 11:30
truth shall make you f. 53:18
Who would be f. themselves 89:18
Freed: thousands He hath f. 106:4
Freedom: A! f. is a noble thing! 24:5
battle for f. and truth 214:8
Cause of F. 66:5
every infringement of human f. 309:20
evils which newly acquired f. produces 263:1
four essential f.s 329:23

F. is a disinterested commerce 182:7
F. is almost always the union 337:12
F. is constant in all other things 372:31
F. is Love without his wings! 93:10
F. may . . . grow into love 94:13
indeed true f. 336:24
keep his f. *in constant repair* 221:1
little f. in the world 20:28
may bring money, but f. hardly ever does 16:28
Most f. is feigning 345:13
My college f.s glimmer 424:19
pious f.s of the female sex 120:23
Thy f. oft has made my heart to ache 62:25
true f.'s laws 316:12
two for f. 428:31
wing of f. never moults a feather 139:26
Fright: bad one in a hell of a f. 102:32
Frighted: f. with false fire 351:13
Fringe: lunatic f. 330:9
Frisson: Vous créez un f. nouveau 212:2
Fritter: F. my wig! 102:22
Frivolity: gay without f. 11:9
Frog: he would a wooing go 296:15
F.s and snails And puppy-dogs' tails 298:14
How public, like a f. 142:3
On a log, Expiring f. 140:26
Use your f. as though you loved him 445:25
Frolics: youth of f. 314:27
Front: All Quiet on the Western F. 326:16
Frontier: on the edge of a new f. 235:14
Frontier-grave: f. is far away 293:15
Frost: f. from purest snow 346:33
f. is over and done 77:27
F. performs its secret ministry 117:30
hoary headed f.s 371:34
secret ministry of f. 117:32
Thaw not the f. 389:23
third day comes a f., a killing f. 358:21
Froth: mostly f. and bubble 183:17
with his embossèd f. 381:26
Froude: F. believes Kingsley a divine 409:3
Frown: Fear no more the f. o' the great 347:15
he cried, with an angry f. 30:9
her very f.s are fairer far 116:16
Phyllis, without f. or smile 341:22
Fruit: As a globed f., Dumb 263:20
boughs are bent with thick-set f. 331:1
bring forth f. in old age 40:5
By their f.s ye shall know them 49:28
f. for their songs 2:19
I love f., when it is expensive 309:8
kindly f.s of the earth 319:7
Like Dead Sea f.s 287:12
Much f. of sense 313:8
No f.s, no flowers 204:32
to bring forth f. 265:16
weakest kind of f. Drops earliest 370:8
Wherein all pleasant f.s do flow 97:30
Frye: in his owene grece I made him f. 108:14
Fucking: cold-hearted f. 249:12
f. for chastity 183:21
Fudge: two fifths sheer f. 259:3
Fuel: adding f. to the flame 281:26
F. to maintain his fires 98:25
Gathering f. in vacant lots 156:31
Fulfilment: image of f. 289:14
Fulmen: Brutum f. 310:8

Fulness: earth . . . and the f. thereof 38:4 55:17
Fume: memory . . . Shall be a f. 365:14
Fun: Ain't we got f. 229:7
hear . . . and make f. of it 100:18
I wish I thought *What Jolly Fun!* 325:14
most f. I ever had 4:15
People must not do things for f. 198:33
taken my f. where I've found it 239:25
To come and spoil the f. 102:1
We've missed all the f.! 24:7
What . . . was all the f. for? 33:2
Function: f. never dies 466:9
own no other f. 384:30
Fundament: so frigid upon the f. 292:15
Funeral: as if you were off to a f. supper 67:1
fancy to see my own f. 154:5
f. baked meats Did coldly furnish 348:8
I'd appint your f. tomorrow 446:10
misbehaved once at a f. 246:12
not a f. note 459:24
No war nor prince's f. 268:27
seldom seen a costlier f. 416:15
sound of f. or of marriage bells 416:19
Funny: As f. as I can 203:24
Everything is f. as long as 329:6
F. peculiar, or f. ha-ha? 195:9
F. without being vulgar 178:24
Fur: f. side inside 5:22
make the f. Fly 87:16
Oh my f. and whiskers! 100:32
Furies: Fierce as ten f. 279:6
See the F. arise! 150:6
Furiously: green ideas sleep f. 111:17
Furnace: burning fiery f. 47:2
f. of affliction 46:2
Heat not a f. for your foe 358:12
Furniture: don't bump into the f. 123:30
No f. so charming as books 399:27
Furor: F. arma ministrat 440:4
Furrow: f. followed free 116:26
On a half-reapèd f. 233:18
plough my own f. alone 330:18
Fury: blind F. with th' abhorred shears 277:9
cunning old F. 100:31
f. of a patient man 149:28
Nor hell a f. 120:14
Furze: blossomed f. unprofitably gay 181:5
Fuse: through the green f. drives the flower 426:7
Fusee: How they who use f.s 96:9
Fussy: call me A f. man 274:17
Fust: To f. in us unused 351:41
Fustian: whose f.'s so sublimely bad 312:21
Fustilarian: You f.! 355:22
Future: cannot fight against the f. 178:31
empires of the f. 113:8
F., n. That period of time 59:12
I mean a F. Life 86:26
orgastic f. that year by year recedes 165:9
Past, Present, and F. existing 61:1
past unsighed for, and the f. sure 462:10
plan the f. by the past 82:32
seen the f. and it works 404:13
time f. contained in time past 155:29
Trust no f. 257:4
vast, vamped f. 311:14
Who controls the past controls the f. 300:23
Futurity: seeks perpetuity by way of f. 310:14

iron g. ground its teeth 78:19
lift up your heads, O ye g.s 38:5
matters not how strait the g. 197:26
no latch ter de golden g. 194:20
poor man at his g. 4:4
right against the eastern g. 276:24
Saint Peter sat by the celestial g. 93:28
sprouting despondently at area g.s 156:28
strait is the g. 49:26
what boots it at one g. 281:22
wide is the g. 49:25
Gath: tell it not in G. 35:47
Gather: knoweth not who shall g. them 38:17
Gatling: g.'s jammed 293:22
Gaudeamus: g. igitur 9:10
Gaudy: neat, not g. 246:10
Gaul: G. is at her gates! 124:19
  G. is divided into three parts 95:6
  to G., to Greece 126:23
Gave: the Lord g. 36:34
  never g. away anything 70:1
Gay: g. in the mazy 115:14
Gay, John 307:31
Gaza: eyeless in G. 281:15
Gaze: coldly she turns from their g. 287:6
  show and g. o' the time 368:1
  which I g. on so fondly 286:22
Gazelle: I never nursed a dear g. 205:6, 287:11
Geboren: nie g. sein 197:5
Gedanken: G. sind zollfrei 260:4
Geese: g. are swans 11:11
Geist: G., der stets verneint! 179:17
Gem: g. of purest ray serene 186:10
  reflecting g.s, that wooed 378:1
  rich and rare were the g.s she wore 287:5
  song is considered a perfect g. 95:16
Genealogies: fables and endless g. 56:39
General: *bite* some other of my g.s 174:32
  G. . . . most immoral man 238:21
  G.s Janvier and Février 294:13
  too important . . . to be left to the g.s 115:2
  not against the law for g.s 432:25
General Motors: good for G. 457:26
Generalization: all g.s are dangerous 152:10
Generalize: to g. is to be an idiot 63:27
Generation: evil and adulterous g. 50:8
  fleeting g.s of mankind 394:26
  g.s of living things 259:22
  had it been the whole g. 6:2
  honoured in their g. 48:28
  knowledge is transmitted from g. to g. 63:24
  no hungry g.s tread thee down 232:7
  one g. passeth away 43:12
  stubborn and rebellious g. 39:22
  write for the youth of his own g. 165:14
  ye are a chosen g. 57:31
  you are a lost g. 404:17
Generosity: do without g. 98:6
Génie: g. n'est qu'une grande aptitude 80:8
  vous vous croyez un grand g. 27:16
Genius: country full of g. 253:19
  eccentricities of g. 141:1
  few, whom g. gave to shine 186:24
  g. and the mortal instruments 359:27
  g. . . . capacity of taking trouble 99:23
  g. does what it must 272:26
  g. is formed in quiet 180:2
  g. is of no country 111:24

g. is one per cent inspiration 154:8
g . . . man who has *two* great ideas 68:22
g.s are the luckiest of mortals 15:26
German and a g. 411:29
gives g. a better discerning 182:16
I have put my g. into my life 456:24
I think like a g. 291:2
most singular g. 65:7
nothing to declare except my g. 456:21
organizing g. could produce a shortage 33:5
prayed to the G. of the place 441:2
since when was g. found respectable? 71:24
three fifths of him g. 259:3
true g. is a mind 219:20
true g. kindles 312:22
unless one is a g. 205:12
what a g. I had 411:28
Genre: tous les g.s sont bons 442:6
Gens: plus honnêtes g. des siècles passés 135:11
  g. de qualité 284:11
Gentes: G. and laitymen 226:7
Gentile: might of the G. 93:6
  such boastings as the G.s use 240:18
Gentle: do not go g. into that good night 426:5
  g. mind by g. deeds is known 403:6
Gentleman: always talking about being a g. 409:17
  bears not alive so stout a g. 355:6
  cannot make a g. 83:3
  Chamberlain seemed such a nice old g. 201:20
  country g. galloping after a fox 455:34
  definition of a g. 294:2
  fine old English g. 8:5
  finished g. from top to toe 92:9
  first true g. that ever breathed 133:20
  G. in the Parlour! 196:7
  g. is indebted to his memory 396:2
  g. is not in your books 372:23
  g.: look at his boots 389:4
  g. on whom I built an absolute trust 364:26
  grand old name of g. 418:30
  I am a g. 68:21
  it's only if a man's a g. 270:19
  little too pedantic for a g. 120:12
  most loving, kissing, kind-hearted g. 128:3
  not quite a g. 13:11
  once a g. 138:20
  prince of darkness is a g. 362:26
  shew'd him the g. and scholar 85:31
  since every Jack became a g. 377:28
  smooth-faced g. 361:12
  sometimes the Devil is a g. 392:16
  tea . . . is a g. at least 110:24
  very gallant g. 13:24
  who was then the g.? 22:2
Gentleman-Ranker: G.s out on the spree 239:6
Gentlemen: all g. of the gentle craft 134:4
  g. in England now a-bed 357:19
  G. of the French Guard 195:8
  g. of the shade 353:17
  g. were not seamen 262:18
  God Almighty's g. 149:25
  God rest you merry g. 7:18
  like Cerberus, three g. at once 395:31
  mob of g. 315:32
  not a religion for g. 106:22
  not to forget that we are g. 82:30
  one of Nature's G. 255:7
  single g. . . . sleep like double g. 139:30

three jolly g. 134:17
two single g. rolled into one 119:26
we shall never be g. 163:18
while the G. go by! 240:21
written by g. for g. 425:12
you g. of England 304:18
you g.'s g. are so hasty 395:23
Genus: hoc g. omne 209:12
  ut placem g. irritabile vatum 207:29
Geography: g. is about maps 31:25
Geological: highly g. home-made cake 138:24
Geometry: as exact a science as g. 165:21
George: down went the Royal G. 125:34
  G. the First was always reckoned 246:24
  G. the Third ought never to have occurred
    31:27
  God be praised, the G.s ended! 246:24
  King G. slipped into heaven 94:7
George III 93:30
Georgia: marching through G. 467:30
Germ: to be discontented . . . is the very g. 237:20
German: don't let's be beastly to the G.s 123:14
  G. and a genius 411:29
  G.s in Greek 316:22
  given . . . to the G.s of the air 327:9
  how appallingly thorough these G.s 213:6
  how the G.s would admire them 229:5
  I speak . . . G. to my horse 107:2
  phrase would be more g. 353:7
Germanic: G. life were slowly ebbing away 249:16
Germany: offering G. too little 293:11
Gesang: das ist der ewige G. 179:18
Gesanges: Auf Flügeln des G. 197:1
Gespenst: es gibt ein G. 288:3
Get: an' you've gut to g. up airly 258:20
  g. what you want 399:6
Ghost: blasphemy against the Holy G. 50:6
  conceived by the Holy G. 318:24
  G. in the Machine 334:5
  g. that eats handkerchiefs 288:3
  g. that got into our house 429:20
  haunted by the g.s they have deposed 377:2
  I'll make a g. of him 348:33
  impute to each frustrate g. 79:1
  like a g. from the tomb 390:17
  move among a world of g.s 421:33
  murmur of the mourning g. 144:4
  talk with some old lover's g. 145:30
  temple of the Holy G. 55:6
  that affable familiar g. 386:13
  turn thou g. that way 144:28
  vex not his g. 363:15
  what beck'ning g. 312:1
  your g. will walk 74:2
Ghoulie: g.s and ghosties 6:21
Giant: as when a g. dies 368:20
  awakened a sleeping g. 470:1
  dwarf sees farther than the g. 118:23
  g.s in the earth in those days 34:13
  he sleeps with the primeval g.s 99:15
  not g.s but windmills 104:16
  standing on the shoulders of g. 294:7
  to have a g.'s strength 368:14
Gibbet: g.s keep the lifted hand in awe 472:16
Gibes: where be your g. now? 352:26
Gift: crave of thee a g. 90:13
  diversities of g.s 55:20
  every good g. 57:20

g.s of God are strown 196:25
given for nought her priceless g. 305:20
God's g.s put man's best g.s to shame 72:6
Gods themselves cannot recall their g.s 423:24
great contempt of God's good g.s 216:7
Heaven's last best g. 280:7
her g.s may henceforth be bestowed equally
  344:15
men endowed with highest g.s 461:20
rarer g.s than gold 69:6
rich g.s wax poor 350:16
suffered in order to bestow their g.s 321:14
taught song by g. of thee 77:30
they have the g. to know it 345:7
Gift-horse: look a g. in the mouth 87:12
Gigadibs: G. the literary man 73:7
  you despise me, Mr G. 72:26
Gilbert: G. the Filbert 458:16
Gilbert, W.S. 205:17
Gilding: pill . . . swallow without g. 224:5
Gilpin: and G., long live he 125:20
  away went G., neck or naught 125:12
  John G. was a citizen 125:6
Gilt: dust that is a little g. 382:17
Gin: g. was mother's milk to her 389:7
  has to drink worse g. 271:20
Ginger: all 'ot sand an' g. 239:4
  g. shall be hot i' the mouth too 383:6
Giotto: G.'s tower 256:27
Gipsy: G. snap and Pedro 5:18
  time, you old g. man 202:18
  vagrant g. life 270:4
Giraffe: He invented the g. 308:20
Gird: g. up now thy loins 37:10
Girder: rumbling under blackened g.s 32:21
Girdle: bright g. furled 10:21
  I'll put a g. round about the earth 371:37
Girl: of all the g.s that are so smart 99:6
  All the Nice G.s Love a Sailor 274:10
  g. with brains 257:25
  g.s who wear glasses 303:15
  great big mountainous sports g. 32:20
  Heaven will protect the Working G. 398:19
  if you were the only g. in the world 188:20
  it's giving g.s names like that 450:10
  it's my old g. that advises 136:31
  kissed the g.s and made them cry 296:16
  not for little g.s 173:18
  Oh, she's a splendid g. 212:27
  one of the nicest g.s I was ever engaged to
    459:19
  pretty g. once said to me 29:9
  prevent g.s from being g.s 205:13
  scores of lovely, gifted g.s 185:11
  she's the dearest g. 137:22
  slit your g.'s throat 238:3
  speak like a green g. 348:24
  there was a little g. 257:18
  think of this fair g. 102:31
  trick that everyone abhors in little g.s 30:19
  trouble with g.s is 336:15
  unlessoned g., unschooled 370:4
  we all love a pretty g. 59:3
  what are little g.s made of? 298:14
  wretched *un-idea'd* g.s 220:19
  young g.s picked them every one 341:24
Give: more blessed to g. 54:4
Giver: g. of all good things 319:16

561

God loveth a cheerful g. 56:2
good received, the g. is forgot 121:6
when g.s prove unkind 350:16
Giving: g. it up for ever 183:6
Gizzard: something in her g. 307:24
Glacier: crawling g.s pierce me 392:22
   g. knocks in the cupboard 14:25
Glad: great things . . . whereof we are glad 40:35
   right g. to find 125:17
   some folks would be g. of 162:27
Glade: alone in the bee-loud g. 471:6
   points to yonder g. 312:1
Gladiator: I see before me the G. lie 90:14
Gladness: g. of her g. 25:25
   snatch g. from the days that are 271:9
Gladsome: g. light of jurisprudence 116:8
Gladstone, W.E., 143:11, 295:20, 439:9
   Mr G. was in his shirt-sleeves 408:18
Glance: g., and nod, and bustle by 11:36
   melted like snow in the g. of the Lord! 93:6
   wouldn't get so much as a g. from me 437:1
Glass: double g. o' the inwariable 141:2
   drink not the third g. 199:4
   fill ev'ry g. 174:9
   g. is falling hour by hour 264:12
   g. of fashion 350:21
   he is a brittle crazy g. 199:28
   he was indeed the g. 355:26
   hill where I shall need no g. 438:18
   over the g.s' edge 72:27
   prove an excuse for the g. 395:37
   through a g., darkly 55:25
   turn down an empty G.! 165:2
Glasses: girls who wear g. 303:16
   Shakespeare, and the musical g. 182:31
   there were two g. and two chairs 264:16
Gleam: follow The G. 421:5
   whither is fled the visionary g. 464:6
Glee: filled one home with g. 197:14
   filled to the brim with girlish g. 177:21
   forward and frolic g. was there 339:17
   laughed with counterfeited g. 181:6
   piping songs of pleasant g. 62:6
Gleichnis: ist nur ein G. 179:23
Glen: down the rushy g. 4:19
Glendoveer: I am a blessed G. 399:3
Glimmering: mere g. and decays 438:16
Glittering: holds him with his g. eye 116:20
Gloaming: in the g., O my darling! 300:7
   late in the g. Kilmeny came hame! 203:15
Gloat: I g.! Hear me g.! 241:31
Global: my wars were g. from the start 326:12
Globe: in this distracted g. 349:12
   solemn temples, the great g. itself 381:10
   wears the turning g. 209:29
Globule: protoplasmal primordial atomic g. 177:18
Gloire: c'est la g. en gros sous 212:1
Gloom: inspissated g. 221:26
   should go with him in the g. 193:8
   welcome, kindred g.s! 428:13
Gloria: o quam cito transit g. mundi 235:2
Glories: g. like glow-worms 448:26
   g. of our blood and state 396:4
   in those weaker g. spy 438:10
   you may my g. . . . . depose 377:11
Glorious: g. things of thee are spoken 294:10
   more g. as more hacked and torn 311:23

'tis a g. thing, I ween 176:21
Glory: be thine the g. 150:19
   calls the g. from the grey 77:18
   crowned with g. now 234:27
   do all to the g. of God 55:18
   excess of g. obscured 278:20
   for the hope of g. 319:11
   Freedom's home or G.'s grave! 93:1
   g. and the dream 464:6
   g. and the good of Art 78:13
   g. dropped from their youth 78:35
   g. is departed from Israel 35:42
   g. of God 3:30
   g. of the coming of the Lord 211:4
   g. of the Lord shone round about 52:1
   g. of the world passes away 235:2
   g. shone around 414:18
   g. that was Greece 310:29
   g. to God in the highest 52:2
   g. to Man in the highest! 412:24
   g. to the new-born king 450:20
   heavens declare the g. of God 37:36
   hoary head is a crown of g. 42:16
   Land of Hope and G. 31:21
   like thy g., Titan 393:19
   may God . . . give you g.! 435:3
   mellow g. of the Attic stage 12:8
   our g. and our absolute boast 465:12
   past away a g. from the earth 464:1
   path of duty was the way to g. 421:22
   sudden g. is the passion 202:6
   thro' a kind of g. 424:22
   'tis to g. we steer 173:5, 331:3
   trailing clouds of g. 464:7
   uncertain g. of an April day 384:4
   we left him alone with his g. 460:3
   who is this King of g.? 38:5
   whose g. is in their shame 56:26
   why in the name of G. 231:4
   with a g. in his bosom 211:6
   with inward g. crowned 394:3
Gloss: so fine a g. on things 76:4
Gloucestershire: stranger here in G. 376:20
Glove: and he played at the g. 22:8
   as hand for g. 76:2
   hand and g. 126:27
   O! that I were a g. upon that hand 379:9
   walk through the fields in g.s 122:19
   with my g.s on my hand 194:1
Glow: her g. has warmed the world 406:14
Glow-worm: g. in the grass 93:14
   g. shows the matin to be near 349:11
   her eyes the g. lend thee 200:9
   men might look and live as g.s shine 438:3
Glued: knees and elbows are only g. together 61:10
Gluttony: g. is an emotional escape 135:17
Gnashing: weeping and g. of teeth 51:1
Gnat: g. that dances in the ray 306:6
   small g.s mourn 233:20
   small grey-coated g. 378:30
   strain at a g. 51:7
Gnome: g.s of Zürich 458:3
Go: as cooks g. she went 336:6
   how fast do you think you'll g. 250:3
   I like to g. by myself 196:3
   I will not let thee g. 34:28, 67:29
   if some of us g. to him 307:4

I'm going to 'g. it' a bit 94:14
in the name of God, g.! 4:23, 129:16
it's no g., my honey love 264:12
must you g.? 437:17
ready to g. 285:7
We Think You Ought To G. 332:21
Whither thou goest, I will g. 35:38
Goad: words of the wise are as g.s 44:13
Goal: g. stands up 210:20
  moving freely, without g. 242:3
Goat: divideth his sheep from the g.s 51:16
  lust of the g. 63:17
  paddling with hoofs of a g. 72:1
Goat-feet: their g. dance an antic hay 267:8
Gobble-uns: an' the g.'ll git you 327:10
Goblet: my figured g.s for a dish of wood 377:4
  swear to upon a parcel-gilt g. 355:24
Goblin: hag and hungry g. 5:17
  spirit of health or g. 348:29
God: abode of G. 259:16
  afraid of nothing but his nagging g.s 236:7
  as flies . . . are we to the g.s 362:33
  assumes the g. 149:34
  attribute of G. himself 370:9
  beast or a g. 10:8
  before the g.s that made the g.s 109:26
  bid him a' should not think of G. 356:33
  bitter G. to follow 412:26
  blends itself with G. 390:22
  bosom of his Father and his G. 186:18
  by the Nine G.s he swore it 261:12
  canst thou by searching find out G.? 36:43
  conspired against our G. 266:19
  counsel of her country's g.s 124:17
  cry 'G. for Harry!' 357:6
  dead limbs of gibbeted G.s 412:28
  did his best to dispense with G. 305:8
  dish fit for the g.s 359:30
  doubtless G. could have made a better berry 88:25
  ef you want to take in G. 258:20
  effect whose cause is G. 127:26
  eternal G. is thy refuge 35:20
  even g.s have lived in the woods 441:13
  every g. did seem to set his seal 351:27
  fear first in the world made g.s 225:9
  feeble G. has stabbed me 173:22
  first prompting of what I call G. 78:8
  for G.'s sake look after our people 339:10
  for the dear G. who loveth us 117:16
  further from G. 5:7
  glorious the song, when G.'s the theme 398:9
  G. all mercy 472:26
  G. Almighty first planted a garden 20:27
  G. Almighty made 'em to match the men 155:12
  G. alone knows 242:5
  G. be with you 325:18
  G. bless the King 88:30
  'G. bless the Prince of Wales!' 255:5
  G. cannot change the past 3:29
  G. changes, and man 412:21
  G. created man 33:16
  G. disposes 235:5
  G. doth not need 282:4
  G. fulfills Himself in many ways 417:18
  G. has written all the books 88:10
  G. in the whizzing of a pleasant wind 306:21
  G. is a circle 159:19

G. is a righteous Judge 37:24
G. is a Spirit 53:10
G. is always on the side of the big battalions 443:1
G. is dead 169:19
G. is decreeing 282:20
G. is faithful 55:15
G. is gone up with a merry n. 38:27
G. is love 57:40
G. is love but get it in writing 251:21
G. is Love – I dare say 88:11
G. is no respecter of persons 53:49
G. is not Dead 183:22
G. is nothing more than an exalted father 169:13
G. is our refuge 38:24
G. is really only another artist 308:20
G. is the perfect poet 76:16
G. is thy law 279:32
G. is working his purpose out 3:30
G. knoweth 56:4
G. lets loose a thinker 158:20
G. made him 369:9
G. made Himself an awful rose of dawn 424:13
G. moves in a mysterious way 125:30
G. must be glad 76:30
G. must find it exceedingly odd 242:9
g. mustn't pay hotel bills 67:3
G. never wrought miracle 19:35
G. of ideas 439:14
G. of my idolatry 379:16
G. of our fathers 240:16
g. of the golden bow 230:25
G. save the king! 99:4, 377:10
G. saw everything that he had made 33:18
G. so commanded 280:34
G. so loved the world 53:8
G. the All-Terrible King 111:18
G. the Father turns a school divine 315:31
G. the first garden made 124:3
G. we both adore 310:26
G. who let us prove his existence 65:1
G. who made thee mighty 31:21
G. works his own 124:34
G.'s in his heaven 76:29
g.s and men, we are all deluded 391:9
g.s approve 462:9
g.s are just 363:11
g.s arrive 158:11
g.s help them that help themselves 3:21
g.s recognized by the State 310:2
G.s themselves cannot recall their gifts 423:24
g.s thought otherwise 440:19
good to them that love G. 54:29
has G. then forgotten what I have done 258:3
hath not one G. created us? 47:25
he for G. only 279:26
highest praise of G. 321:15
how can he love G. 58:1
how like a g.! 349:36
how odd of G. 160:9
I am a G. 393:1
I don't know whether I believe in G. 270:13
if G. be for us 54:30
if G. did not exist 442:4
if G. made us in His image 442:20
if G. were not a necessary Being 430:8
if triangles invented a g. 286:1

563

if you talk to G. 413:15
I'll leap up to my G.! 267:3
inclines to think there is a G. 115:18
it's not G. that I don't accept 146:28
just are the ways of G. 281:21
justify the ways of G. 278:2
kings it makes g.s 378:15
know that I am G. 38:25
large utterance of the early G.s 230:28
let G. be true 54:17
'Let us worship G.!' 84:6
Little Tin G.s on Wheels 240:15
live with the g.s 16:18
Lord G. give you the joy of it 288:14
Lord G. is subtle 155:2
Lord G. of Hosts 240:17
Lord G. of Sabaoth 318:18
man whose g. is in the skies 388:31
man's love for the present, unknowable G. 249:11
many are afraid of G. 255:24
my G. and King 199:2
My G., how wonderful Thou art 161:2
My G., I love Thee 103:5
'My G. my King' 199:17
my G., why hast thou forsaken me? 37:40, 51:27
Nearer, my G. to Thee 1:8
next to of course g. america 130:2
no G. could please 149:7
none deny there is a G. 19:37
not spoken of these things save . . . unto G. 218:19
not three G.s: but one G. 318:34
Now, G. be thanked 69:17
on G.'s side, is a majority 308:17
one G., one law 418:41
one that feared G. 36:32
only excuse for G. 404:24
ought to have let G. alone 31:10
our G. is marching on 211:5
Polite Society believed in G. 337:26
praise G. from whom all blessings flow 235:11
presume not G. to scan 314:1
put your trust in G. 59:26
render unto G. 51:3
reserved only for G. and angels 18:5
see G. made and eaten all day long 73:12
sees G. in clouds 313:29
served my G. with half the zeal 358:26
shall g.s be said to thump the clouds 426:15
so near is G. to man 158:16
strong brown g. 156:4
sun-flower turns on her g. 286:23
thanks G. for anything 220:27
there, but for the grace of G., goes G. 113:27
there G. to aggrändise 205:21
there is no G. 37:31
they shall see G. 48:42
this man is now become a g. 359:14
those whom G. hath joined together 319:45
thou art G. from everlasting 39:30
thou shalt have one G. only 115:21
thy G. my G. 35:38
to glorify G. and to enjoy him for ever 396:6
to the unknown g. 53:54
to which our G. Himself is moon and sun 421:23
trust G.: see all nor be afraid! 77:11
trust in G. 264:1
Very G. of Very G. 319:21

vindicate the ways of G. to man 313:26
voice of G. 315:30
wants nothing of a g. 346:34
we owe G. a death 356:5
were better to have no opinion of G. 19:38
were I Lord G. 263:12
we're in G.'s hands now! 67:7
what G. abandoned 210:2
what G. hath joined together 387:32
what the Lord G. thinks of money 25:2
what will G. say to us 307:4
when G. created man 184:4
when I reflect that G. is just 217:25
whom the g.s favour dies young 310:6
whom the g.s love die young 91:32
whom the g.s wish to destroy 121:14
whose G. is their belly 56:26
wild beast, or a g. 20:12
will not serve G. if the devil bid you 373:34
with G. all things are possible 50:39
with G. he passed the days 304:25
Word was G. 52:48
would G. I had died for thee 36:9
would the g.s had made thee poetical 345:26
ye shall be as g.s 33:24
yellow g. forever gazes down 195:10
God-intoxicated: G. man 296:1
Goddamm, lhude sing G. 317:14
Goddess: g. and maiden and queen 412:25
    G., excellently bright 224:27
    heavenly g. sing! 316:10
    she moves a g. 316:11
Goddesses: g. that dwell far along 427:3
Godot: waiting for G. 28:15
Goers-between: let all pitiful g. 382:11
Goethe: open thy G. 100:13
Gog: set thy face against G. 46:39
Going: I think I'm g. fast 250:3
    learn by g. where I have to go 328:18
    men must endure their g. hence 363:8
    stand not upon the order of your g. 366:32
Gold: better to me than g. 458:10
    cursed be the g. 419:22
    from the red g. keep thy finger 340:26
    g.? a transient, shining trouble 184:14
    g. and silver becks me to come on 361:16
    g. by bronze heard iron steel 226:25
    g. is the touchstone 171:6
    g. that the goose could give 3:20
    good morning to . . . my g.! 225:10
    hadde he put litel g. in cofre 107:19
    heav'n, as its purest g. 313:1
    if g. ruste, what shall iren do? 107:26
    image's head was of fine g. 46:40
    is she not pure g., my mistress? 78:26
    little censer of g. 265:14
    mast was o' beaten g. 22:24
    more to be desired . . . than g. 37:37
    nor all that glisters, g. 186:29
    O cursed lust for g. 440:20
    O delvèd g. 72:2
    ring . . . is yet of g. 128:7
    saint-seducing g. 378:25
    silver and g. have I none 53:43
    silver threads among the g. 326:18
    street of the city was pure g. 58:36
    this is fairy g. 384:20

thrice their weight in g. 162:11
to gild refinèd g. 91:21, 361:21
to a shower of g. 99:26
were't not for g. and women 431:11
what female heart can g. despise? 186:27
what's become of all the g. 79:4
Gold-fish: might have been a g. 336:2
Golden: god of the g. bow 230:25
g. opes, the iron shuts amain 277:12
Golden Vanity: goes by the name of the G. 22:19
Goldsmith: here lies Nolly G. 173:6
to Oliver G., poet, naturalist and historian
222:24
Gondola: g. of London 143:21
Gone: been and g. and done 176:11
g., and for ever 339:21
g. is g. 81:5
I would have thee g. 379:20
make what haste I can to be g. 129:18
not dead – but g. before 328:25
now thou art g. 277:4
often welcomed when they are g. 357:27
remember me when I am g. away 331:6
Gong: strong g.s groaning 110:9
struck regularly, like g.s 123:20
Good: all g. and no badness 398:4
all g. things which exist 273:14
all partial evil, universal g. 313:34
and when she was g. 257:18
any g. thing come out of Nazareth? 53:4
apprehension of the g. 376:15
behold, it was very g. 33:18
borrowed the language of the G. 14:3
cannot come to g. 348:6
do g. by stealth 316:4
every creature of God is g. 56:42
evil, that g. may come 54:18
g. are so harsh to the clever 461:5
g., but not religious-g. 193:25
g., but they were *too* g. 336:14
g. die early 133:16
g. die first 461:23
g. ended happily 455:16
g. is oft interred 360:14
g. must associate 82:28
g. news baits 281:27
g., pleasure, ease, content! 314:7
g. received, the giver is forgot 121:6
g. still to find means of evil 278:9
g. that I would do not 54:25
g. want power 392:26
g. when it leaves the Creator's hands 332:13
g. will be the final goal of ill 418:7
hanging is too g. for him 80:25
he was very g. to me 136:25
highest g. 114:15
hold thou the g. 418:6
I will be g. 439:8
if . . . all clever people were g. 461:5
if you can't say anything g. 257:24
is to be g., great and joyous 393:19
know their own g. 151:10
knowing g. and evil 33:24
little of what you fancy does you g. 255:10
lose the g. we oft might win 368:6
luxury of doing g. 128:12, 181:26
man's capacity for g. 294:16

music, the greatest g. 1:17
must return g. for evil 437:12
never had it so g. 264:5
nor g. compensate bad in man 78:10
not g. that man should be alone 33:20
nothing can harm a g. man 400:20
nothing either g. or bad 349:33
nothing g. to be had in the country 195:20
nothing left for you . . . but to be g. 406:30
portend no g. to us 361:33
sat too long here for any g. 129:16
shall go to those who are g. for it 67:2
she was g. as she was fair 328:26
so great and g.! 124:7
so much g. in the worst of us 202:11
some said, 'It might do g.' 80:13
they love the G. 69:15
well with him who clings to the g. 435:10
wiser being g. than bad 72:22
woe unto them that call . . . g. evil 44:36
you was a g. man 193:28
Good day: g. to you 177:43
Good will: g. to man 341:16
Goodbeare: do you remember Mr G. 397:20
Good-bye: G., I've barely said a word to you 321:16
G. to All That 185:17
g.-ee! 451:21
Goodliness: all the g. thereof 45:32
Good-morning: bid me 'G.' 24:4
Goodness: felt how awful g. is 280:2
fountain of all g. 318:30
g. had nothing to do with it 451:6
g. never fearful 368:24
g. of the Lord 38:7
g. only knowses 110:22
I thank the g. and the grace 415:4
thou crowneth the year with thy g. 39:11
whose g. faileth never 21:12
Good-night: bid the world g. 200:7
gives the stern'st g. 365:21
G., ladies 352:8
g.! parting is such sweet sorrow 379:21
my native Land – G.! 89:13
said 'G.' and gone to rest 30:25
Goods: all his worldly g. 250:16
g. and services 295:12
half so precious as the G. they sell 164:28
he's got the g. 198:21
his g. are in peace 52:14
Man Who Delivers the G. 270:6
she isn't a bad bit of g. 105:3
with all my worldly g. 319:44
Goose: cackle like a g. 441:20
every g. a swan 237:17
gabble o' the g. 96:2
gold that the g. could give 3:20
royal game of g. 181:10
steels the g. from off the common 6:7
where gott'st thou that g. look? 367:16
Gooseberry-pie: help your mother to make the g.
182:28
Goose-feather: in which a great g. grew 203:3
Goose-pen: though thou write with a g. 383:22
Goosey: G., g. gander 296:17
Gore: I hope it mayn't be human g. 136:15
Gored: tossed and g. several persons 221:24
Gorge: my g. rises at it 352:25

Gorgon: great G. prince of darkness 402:27
Gorgonised: g. me from head to foot 420:31
Gormed: I'm G. 137:28
Gospel: g. according to Jean Jacques Rousseau 99:28
  G. of Getting On 389:1
  music of the G. 161:3
Gossip: make the babbling g. of the air 382:36
Gost: lat thy g. thee lede 107:6
Got: I've G. You Under My Skin 316:28
Gotham: G.'s three Wise Men 306:18
  three wise men of G. 298:9
Gothic: more than G. ignorance 162:31
Gott: was wirst du tun, G. 327:20
Gott-betrunkener: G. Mensch 296:1
Götter: G. selbst vergebens 338:13
Göttingen: -niversity of G. 98:19
Goujat: bon pour des g.s 244:11
Gout: combined with g. 176:18
Govern: *all* will g. in turn 252:23
  he that would g. others 270:8
Governesses: tremendous lot for her old g. 321:13
Government: against g. by crony 214:25
  all g. . . . is founded on compromise 81:21
  democracy is the worst form of g. 113:11
  every nation has the g. it deserves 265:2
  for forms of g. let fools contest 314:6
  four pillars of g. 19:31
  g. is a contrivance of human wisdom 82:12
  g. . . . is but a necessary evil 303:3
  g. of the people 254:17
  g. shall be upon his shoulder 45:8
  g.s never have learnt anything 196:28
  land of settled g. 424:24
  live under a g. of men 308:15
  looked to g. for bread 82:26
  monarchy . . . is an intelligible g. 21:8
  most dangerous moment for a bad g. 430:14
  negation of God . . . system of g. 179:5
  no G. can be long secure 143:12
  only good g. . . . is a bad one 102:32
  opinion of His Majesty's G. 112:8
  strongly mutually antagonistic g.s 448:9
  sun never sets on G. House 123:28
  they the G. go on in strange paradox 112:15
  virtue of paper g. 81:13
  what a free g. is 82:36
Governor: g.s, teachers, spiritual pastors 319:29
  t'other g. 140:16
Governorship: without a g. you came 105:11
Gower: O moral G. 108:31
Gown: ease the heart like a satin g. 304:2
  fellow . . . that hath two g.s 373:21
  like an old lady's loose g. 354:31
  my g. of glory 325:8
  plucked his g. 181:4
Grace: but for the g. of God 66:9
  ends of Being and ideal G. 72:7
  fallen from g. 56:11
  for the means of g. 319:11
  God in his mercy lend her g. 419:15
  g. did much more abound 54:22
  g. is given of God 115:15
  g. me no g. 376:23
  g. of God which was with me 55:30
  g. under pressure 197:21
  g. was in all her steps 280:23

gracious, graceful, graceless G. 92:18
grow old with a good g. 404:6
he does it with a better g. 383:4
inward and spiritual g. 319:32
liken his G. to an acorned hog 74:32
Lord, I ascribe it to Thy g. 447:8
number all your g.s 385:15
petitionary g. of sweet seventeen 415:23
Sacrifice to the G.s 109:10
sermons, psalms, and g.s 320:21
shame which is glory and g. 48:3
such g. had kings 76:32
there, but for the g. of God 113:27
with their courtly foreign g. 423:4
your G. is too costly 372:33
Gracehoper: G. was always jigging 226:15
Graceless: G., Pointless, Feckless 175:25
Gracing: sweetly g. 97:26
Gracious: if a man be g. 19:28
  Lord . . . be g. unto thee 35:7
Gradient: altered g. at another rate 14:16
Gradualness: inevitability of g. 448:20
Graeculus: G. esuriens 227:19
Grail: G. when they found it 29:20
  until I find the holy G. 423:17
Grain: faith as a g. of mustard seed 50:27
  reaps the bearded g. 257:7
  say which g. will grow 364:16
  warmth to swell the g. 96:18
Grais: g. ingenium 207:7
Grammaire: g. qui sait régenter jusqu'aux rois 283:14
Grammar: g. and nonsense 182:16
  g., which can govern even kings 283:14
  heedless of g. 24:13
  Roman Emperor . . . above g. 397:5
  what sairs your g.s? 84:12
Grammarian: g.s dispute 207:1
Grand: baith g. and comfortable 25:20
  that g. old man 295:20
Grandam: soul of our g. 383:30
Grandeur: baldness full of g. 12:29
  charged with the g. of God 205:26
  g. hear, with a disdainful smile 186:5
  g. is a dream 127:8
  g. that was Rome 310:29
  g. to our dust 158:16
Grandfather: g.'s g.s are numbered 442:3
  my g.'s rule was safer 258:29
  my great g. was but a waterman 80:26
Grandmother: Man may not marry his G. 320:10
Grandsire: like his g. cut in alabaster 369:2
  proverbed with a g. phrase 378:29
Grange: at the moated g. 368:25
  upon the lonely moated g. 420:22
Granite: g.s which titanic wars had groined 302:15
Grape: burst Joy's g. against his palate fine 231:29
  fathers have eaten sour g.s 46:33
  first from out the purple g. 275:6
  G. that can with Logic absolute 164:17
  g.s are sour 3:19
  g.s of the wine-press 261:8
  g.s of wrath 211:4
  peel me a g. 451:4
  sour g.s and ashes 13:17
Grapeshot: whiff of g. 99:27
Grasp: man's reach should exceed his g. 72:18
Grass: be the green g. above me 331:11

dread the rustling of the g. 461:7
g. below – above the vaulted sky 114:27
g. growing green 308:1
g. grows green on the battlefield 112:11
g., it grew as scant as hair 73:25
g. withereth 45:33
I am the g. 337:2
it quivered through the g. 142:7
kissed the lovely g. 69:9
know the g. beyond the door 332:1
leaf of g. is no less 453:26
like g. which groweth up 39:32
make . . . two blades of g. to grow 410:27
man, his days are as g. 40:10
Oh lift me from the g. 391:13
presage the g.'s fall 268:27
splendour in the g. 464:16
tale of morning g. 467:19
thin g. clothed them more warmly 427:8
White Horse . . . cut out of the g. 109:26
Grass-bank: g. beyond 4:20
Grasshopper: cover, of the wings of g.s 378:30
g. shall be a burden 44:11
half a dozen g.s under a fern 82:17
is this a g! 395:13
Gratiano: G. speaks an infinite deal 369:5
Gratitude: g. of place-expectants 445:14
Grave: comfort . . . ayont the g. 85:30
country . . . kind of healthy g. 399:22
dark inn, the g.! 340:6
dig the g. and let me die 407:31
dread the g. 235:10
e'er I descend to th' g. 124:14
find ourselves dishonourable g.s 359:16
fretted us a pair of g.s 377:5
from g. to gay 314:12
g. hides all things beautiful and good 393:1
g. with rising flow'rs be dressed 312:6
g.'s a fine and private place 269:2
g.s have yawned 359:33
g.s stood tenantless 347:24
her heart in his g. is lying 287:6
in cold g. she was lain 23:21
in his g. rained many a tear 352:13
on his g., with shining eyes 11:15
let's talk of g.s 377:1
lies a-mouldering in the g. 190:12
lies silent in the g. 125:27
little little g., an obscure g. 377:4
on my g., as now my bed 71:15
no work, nor device . . . in the g. 43:37
not have strewed thy g. 352:33
nothing . . . so pleasant on this side the g. 136:8
now in his colde g. allone 108:5
O g.! where is thy victory? 55:40, 311:31
over this damp g. 328:16
paths of glory lead but to the g. 186:6
pompous in the g. 71:20
rotting g. shall ne'er get out 60:17
see myself go into my g. 307:26
she is in her g. 466:13
their g.s are severed 197:14
they have no g.s as yet 110:3
they have their g.s at home 110:2
thy humble g. adorned 312:5
'tis I, my love, sits on your g. 23:22
when my g. is broke up again 146:3

with sorrow to the g. 34:34
without a g., unknelled 90:21
without a governorship . . . to the g. 105:11
Gravel: cold in the dreary g. 69:3
Gravender: pub, wherein I eat my g. 335:10
Graver: wherein the g. had a strife 225:17
Graveyard: no bone to pick with g.s 28:11
Gray, Thomas: 219:25
G., a born poet 12:25
Great: dangers by being despised grow g. 82:2
even g. men have their poor relations 136:33
far above the g. 187:15
forgive Thy g. big one on me 170:1
g. man helped the poor 261:15
g. ones eat up the little ones 376:4
g. scholars not commonly g. men 204:1
g. things are done when men 60:29
it's g. to be g. 329:5
little things are g. 181:27
no g. man lives in vain 99:31
nothing g. was ever achieved 158:21
rightly to be g. 352:2
that he is grown so g. 359:17
those who were truly g. 402:14
to be g. is to be misunderstood 159:4
whatever was g. seemed to him little 262:22
Greater: we are g. than we know 466:10
Greatest: life to live as the g. he 325:5
than not be among the g. 234:6
Great-grandchildren: our g., when they learn 320:14
Great-grandfather: greatest possible pleasure to
their g.s 404:20
Great-heart: one G. 80:32
Greatness: all the far-stretched g. 325:9
fear his g. weighed 348:18
for g. he could not want 225:31
highest point of all my g. 358:20
long farewell, to all my g. 358:21
man's unhappiness . . . comes of his g. 100:12
pray God our g. may not fail 416:23
some have g. thrust upon them 383:16
some squeaking Cleopatra boy my g. 344:8
Greaves: brazen g. of bold Sir Lancelot 419:12
Grece: in his owene g. I made him frye 108:14
Greece: glory that was G. 310:29
G., Italy and England, did adorn 150:26
I dreamed that G. might yet be free 91:24
isles of G., the isles of G. 91:23
Greek: G., Sir . . . is like lace 223:9
I fear the G.s 440:12
it was G. to me 359:22
Muse gave the G.s genius 207:7
she's a merry G. indeed 381:33
small Latin and less G. 225:23
tell the hungry little G. 227:19
'tis known he could speak G. 87:3
turn over the pages of the G.s 207:6
what is the G. name for Swine's Snout? 78:22
when G.s joined G.s 251:24
Green: but not quite so g. 241:27
for the wearin' o' the g. 7:16
g. how I love you g. 173:4
summer's g. all girded up 385:14
they laid him on the g. 22:7
walked o'er yon gravelled g. 22:11
Greenery: enfolding sunny spots of g. 117:35
Greenhouse: who loves a garden loves a g. 127:11

Greening: G. of America 326:14
Greenland: from G.'s icy mountains 196:24
Greenly: we have done but g. 352:10
Greensleeves: G. was all my joy 7:19
Greenwood: I ha' been at the g. 22:25
  I must to the g. go 23:4
Greet: how should I g. thee? 94:9
Greeting: nor g.s where no kindness is 462:23
Grenadier: British G. 8:17
Grenville: at Flores in the Azores Sir Richard G.
  lay 422:26
Grey: too lovely to be g. 11:2
  when you are old and g. 472:4
Greyhound: fawning g. then did proffer me! 353:33
  stand like g.s in the slips 357:6
Grief: acquainted with g. 46:7
  antheming a lonely g. 230:30
  black with g. eternal 428:18
  every one can master a g. 373:2
  Good G., Charlie Brown 339:6
  g. develops the powers of the mind 321:20
  g. enough for thee 187:29
  g. fills the room 361:17
  g. flieth to it 18:22
  g. for a while is blind 392:25
  g. is itself a med'cine 124:23
  g. itself be mortal! 389:29
  g. never mended no broken bones 141:24
  g. returns with the revolving year 389:28
  g. that does not speak 367:8
  g. with a glass that ran 412:3
  g.s that harass the distressed 218:26
  hopeless g. is passionless 72:3
  my g.s: still am I king of those 377:11
  parents' g.s and fears 19:7
  patch g. with proverbs 373:22
  perked up in a glistering g. 358:16
  plague of sighing and g.! 354:16
  should be past g. 384:17
  silent g.s which cut the heart-strings 167:9
  silent manliness of g. 181:14
  thy mother's g. 60:14
Grieve: g. not over that which is unavoidable 33:11
Grimace: g.s called laughter 202:6
Grin: all Nature wears one universal g. 163:2
  ev'ry g., so merry 309:4
  vanished . . . ending with the g. 101:4
Grind: g. exceeding small 257:8
  my life is one demd g.! 139:23
Grinder: g., who serenely grindest 96:4
  g.s cease because they are few 44:10
Groan: hear each other g. 232:2
  sinks into thy depths with bubbling g. 90:21
Grocer: God made the wicked G. 110:16
Grolle: Ich g. nicht 197:4
Gromboolian: over the great G. plain 250:17
Groom: unmissed but by his . . . groom 126:12
Groove: down the ringing g.s of change 420:5
  moves in predestinate g.s 193:31
Gross: not g. to sink 387:11
Grossness: losing all its g. 82:15
Grosvenor: G. Gallery, Foot-in-the-grave young man!
  178:2
Ground: content . . . in his own ground 315:6
  in a fair g. 240:28
  free walk on firm g. 338:19
  gardener of the untoward g. 78:7

g. flew up and hit me 446:15
g. upon which one treads 321:7
g. was as hard 232:17
haunted, holy g. 89:19
let us sit upon the g. 377:2
one foot on the g. 324:14
we shall fight on the landing g.s 112:20
Grove: green fields and happy g.s 62:20
  o'er shady g.s they hover 449:3
  wandering in many a coral g. 63:1
Growed: 'I 'spect I g. 408:13
Grown-up: Catholic and g. 301:8
  G.s never understand anything 335:7
  novels for g. people 460:19
  spoke in quiet g. wise 306:2
Grub: g. first, then ethics 67:16
  my gravender or g. 335:10
Grudge: ancient g. I bear him 369:13
  took it as a personal g. 198:19
Gruel: basin of nice smooth g. 16:23
Grumbling: g. grew to a mighty rumbling 76:26
Grundy: more are afraid of Mrs G. 255:24
  Solomon G., born on a Monday 298:1
  what will Mrs G. say? 289:8
Grunt: g. and sweat under a weary life 350:14
Guarantee: no reliable g. that the afterlife 123:10
Guard: changing g. at Buckingham Palace 274:13
  Gentlemen of the French G. 195:8
  gone on business to the Horse G.s 139:21
  G.s die, but do not surrender 96:15
  up G.s and at them again! 449:14
  who is to g. the g.s themselves? 228:1
Guardian: constitutional g. 177:7
Guardian-angel: good as g.s are 124:14
Gudgeon: swallow g.s ere they're catched 87:24
Guenille: g., si l'on vent 283:16
Guerdon: g. when we hope to find 277:9
Guerre: c'est un drôle de g.131:3
  magnifique, mais ce n'est pas la g. 65:15
  years of l'entre deux g.s 156:1
Guerrilla: g. wins if he does not lose 241:36
Guess: g. now who holds thee? 72:4
Guesses: boys and girls gave g. 79:14
Guessing: 'g. what was at the other side of the
  hill' 449:20
Guest: among the G.s Star-scattered 165:2
  fits a . . . keen g. 354:40
  go, Soul, the body's g. 325:7
  g.s are met 116:19
  new admirèd g. 97:31
  slightly shakes his passing g. by the hand 382:14
  sombre g. on the sorry earth 180:3
  some second g. to entertain 146:3
  speed the parting g. 316:12
  unbidden g.s often welcomed 357:27
Guide: blind g.s which strain at a gnat 51:7
  great g. of human life 212:6
  g., philosopher and friend 314:13
  probability is the very g. of life 86:27
  with thee and be thy g. 5:9
Guiding-star: g. of a whole brave nation 289:11
Guile: urban, squat, and packed with g. 69:14
Guilt: all g. is punished on earth 180:8
  so full of artless jealousy is g. 352:3
  unstained by g. 208:12
  wash her g. away 182:38
Guilty: but I am not g. 229:4

no g. man is acquitted 228:8
started like a g. thing 347:26
ten g. persons escape 59:31
Guinea: jingling of the g. 419:28
worth a g. a box 3:15
Guinea pig: g.s in the laboratory of God 457:13
Guinness: G. is good for you 3:2
My Goodness, My G. 3:6
Guinness'es: first chapter of G. 226:23
Guitar: touched his g. 27:10
Gules: threw warm g. on Madeline's fair breast
230:17
Gulf: beyond the glassy g.s we flee 393:13
great g. fixed 52:33
g.s will wash us down 424:10
into the g. of death 389:24
whelmed in deeper g.s than he 124:22
Gull: to the g.'s way 270:4
Gulled: would not willingly be g. 224:21
Gum: can't fart and chew g. 218:23
our poesy is as a g. 381:21
their med'cinable g. 375:26
Gun: beggarly son of a g. 96:1
but for these vile g.s 353:30
g.s aren't lawful 304:1
g.s boom far 110:9
g.s? said Betty Flanders 460:24
g.s will make us powerful 179:12
in order to get rid of the g. 266:10
monstrous anger of the g.s 302:7
nor ever lost an English g. 421:17
political power grows out of . . . a g. 266:9
they got the g.s 289:2
Gunga Din: better man than I am, G.! 239:10
Gunner: g. and his mate 381:1
Gunpowder: G., Printing, and the Protestant Religion
99:21
g. ran out . . . of their boots 166:26
G. Treason and Plot 6:14
Gut: I'll lug the g.s into the neighbour room
351:37
Gutta: g. cavat lapidem 301:24
Gutter: we are all in the g. 455:30
yearning for the g. 15:29
Guy: nice g.s finish last 152:19
Gwynne, Nell 307:16
Gym: flare was up in the g. 32:22
Gyre: did g. and gimble in the wabe 101:24
turning in the widening g. 471:20

H

H.: to drop thy 'H.s' 96:11
Habit: cocaine isn't h.-forming 24:1
costly thy h. as thy purse can buy 348:22
h. is a second nature 321:18
h. with him was all the test of truth 128:5
use doth breed a h. in a man! 384:9
Habitation: God in his holy h. 39:14
Hack: do not h. me 284:19
Hag: black and midnight h.s! 366:38
Haggard: H.s ride no more 405:3
if I do prove her h. 374:33
Haig, Lord 255:19
Hail: h. and farewell 104:6

sharp and sided h. 206:1
unless God send his h. 76:14
where falls not h. 417:21
Haine: ces h.s vigoureuses 284:2
Hair: beauty draws us with a single h. 315:18
bring down my grey h.s 34:34
by flying h. and fluttering hem 331:23
covered with h. 288:8
distinguish and divide a h. 87:4
draw you to her with a single h. 151:13
each particular h. to stand on end 349:1
h. of my flesh stood up 36:38
h.s of your head are all numbered 49:42
her h. that lay along her back 331:16
her h. was long 231:8
his floating h.! 118:6
his head and his h.s were white 58:3
how ill white h.s become a fool 356:18
if a woman have long h. 55:19
Jeanie with the light brown h. 168:4
loose train of thy amber-dropping h. 275:34
make your h. curl 178:11
my fell of h. 367:23
my h. is grey 93:17
my mother bids me bind my h. 212:19
oldest man . . . that ever wore grey h.s 466:4
serve one to pin up one's h. 120:25
she has braided her yellow h. 23:14
she has brown h. 371:1
smoothes her h. with automatic hand 157:8
to tie up my bonny brown h. 297:13
Wash That Man Right Out of My H. 191:15
whose h.s grow hoary 92:30
why do you wear your h. like a man 431:17
wipes from out her h. 76:17
with such h. too 79:4
your h. has become very white 100:33
your well-belovèd's h. has threads of grey
470:17
Haïr: pour ne le point h.! 324:22
Haircut: lies a h. and a shave 202:19
Halcyon: h.s brood around the foamless isles 390:26
Half: best image of myself and dearer h. 280:8
created h. to rise 314:2
h. of one order, h. another 87:17
h. was not told me 36:11
horrid image doth unfix my h. 364:23
one h. of the world cannot understand 16:22
only h. way up 6:12
rather less than h. o' that be'ind 239:8
scarce h. made up 377:23
send me the h. that's got my keys 184:7
Half-a-dozen: six of one and h. of the other 268:6
Half-and-half-affair: no h. 176:21
Half-god: when h.s go 158:11
Half-truth: either a h. or one-and-a-half truths
242:14
two h.s do not make a truth 242:11
Half-workers: women must be h. 347:7
Hall: I dreamt that I dwelt in marble h.s 80:11
puts you in de H. o' Fame 300:1
Hallow: Christ . . . and all his h.s 206:16
Halo: life is a luminous h. 460:18
what after all is a h.? 170:22
Halt: h., and the blind 52:21
how long h. ye between two opinions? 36:15
Halter: now fitted the h. 320:29

talk of h.s in the hanged man's house 105:2
Halves: I'll go h. with him 324:15
Hame: it's h. and it's h. 130:7
Hamelin: H. Town's in Brunswick 76:22
Hamlet: *H.* . . . equally rooted in . . . incest-complex
    169:12
  h.s brown, and dim-discovered spires 119:12
  I am not Prince H. 156:25
  I saw H., Prince of Denmark played 160:6
  playbill . . . announced the tragedy of H. 341:6
  where the kneeling h. drains 417:30
Hammer: h., h. along the 'ard 'igh road 322:7
Hampden: some village H. 186:11
Ha'nacker: Sally is gone from H. Hill 30:30
Hand: and then take h.s 380:34
  as bald as the palm of your h. 24:13
  bear thee up in their h.s 40:2
  before rude h.s have touched it 225:13
  bless the h. that gave the blow 151:30
  by foreign h.s thy dying eyes were closed 312:5
  children could warm their h.s at 25:18
  cloud . . . like a man's h. 36:17
  cursed be the h. 22:22
  degenerates in the h.s of man 332:13
  do not saw the air . . . with your h. 350:23
  fall into the h.s of God 423:2
  fed and watered by God's Almighty h. 96:18
  go into his h. and pierce it 45:26
  h. in h., on the edge of the sand 251:3
  H. that made us is divine 2:16
  h. that rocks the cradle 444:9
  h. that signed the treaty 426:8
  h., the head, and the heart of man 333:16
  h. to execute 175:21, 227:12
  h.s of the living God 57:11
  hat was in his h. 219:2
  he hath shook h.s with time 167:8
  her h. on her bosom 375:17
  her prentice h. she tried on man 84:23
  here's my h. 381:4
  his h. will be against every man 34:22
  hold you with my dying h. 430:4
  house not made with h.s 55:45
  I fear thy skinny h.! 117:3
  I see a h. you cannot see 430:6
  I will hold your h. 75:21
  if you want to win her h. 66:16
  in the h. of God 47:38
  in the h. of the Lord 39:21
  into thy h.s I commend my spirit 38:9
  keep my h.s from picking and stealing 319:30
  knit h.s, and beat the ground 275:9
  know the sweet Roman h. 383:23
  laid our groping h.s away 69:23
  lay violent h.s upon themselves 320:2
  Laying on of H.s 319:34
  leans her cheek upon her h. 379:9
  lend thy guiding h. 281:14
  let me kiss that h.! 362:41
  let not man have the upper h. 37:29
  let not thy left h. know 49:7
  let the floods clap their h.s 40:8
  lifting distressful h.s 302:16
  man's h. is not able to taste 372:11
  mischief still for idle h.s to do 447:13
  my h. is unworthy your acceptance 17:7
  nearer than h.s and feet 416:25

on ev'ry h. it will allow'd be 84:9
our times are in His h. 77:11
put your h. into the h. of God 194:30
queen that caught the world's great h.s 212:14
red right h. 278:35
shake h.s for ever 148:21
signed it wi' his h. 23:9
sit thou at my right h. 40:19
spirit-small h. propping it 73:16
spits on its h.s and goes to work 337:6
ten thousand at my right h. 40:1
their h.s upon their hearts 209:26
there shall thy h. lead me 41:11
there's a h., my trusty fiere 83:28
they pierced my h.s 38:1
they will soon *wring* their h.s 445:12
this h. hath offended 128:16
this my h. will rather 365:28
time on her h.s 326:2
warmed both h.s before the fire of life 246:25
washes his h.s 354:5
we are in God's h. 72:17
what coarse h.s he has! 138:3
whatsoever thy h. findeth to do 43:37
will not sweeten this little h. 367:14
will these h.s ne'er be clean? 367:13
with cold immortal h.s 412:18
with gentle h. touch 463:27
with my own fair h.s 411:4
with your h.s . . . all red 261:8
your little h.s were never made 447:10
Handel, George Frideric 411:29
  H. is scarcely fit to hold a candle 88:26
Handful: fear in a h. of dust 156:35
  h. of grey ashes 123:3
Handiwork: firmament sheweth his h. 37:36
Handkerchief: drenches h.s like towels 92:34
  moral pocket h.s 140:37
  no little h. to wipe his little nose 24:18
Handle: h. toward my hand 365:19
  polished up the h. 176:29
Handmaiden: riches are a good h. 18:14
Handsome: everything h. about him 373:21
  I am a h. man 119:28
  my h. young man 22:25
Handwork: pronounced on the rest of his h. 78:16
Handy-dandy: h., which is the justice 362:42
Hang: all h. together 168:25
  are you going to h. him *anyhow* 434:5
  h. a man first 284:10
  I will not h. myself today 109:31
  something in them to h. him 327:8
  we will h. you 178:8
  why, she would h. on him 348:2
  would cry to a sailor 'Go h.!' 381:1
Hanged: halters in the h. man's house 105:2
  knows he is to be h. in a fortnight 222:26
  men are not h. for stealing horses 190:11
  they would be h. forthwith 86:9
Hanging: good h. prevents a bad marriage 382:30
  h. and wiving goes by destiny 369:30
  h. is too good for him 80:25
  h. men . . . for the wearin' o' the Green 7:16
  h. so light 117:19
Hangman: seen me with these h.'s hands 365:23
Hanner: lost our little H. 2:24
Hanover: by famous H. city 76:22

Hanyfink: wot's the good of H.? 111:13
Happen: everything that h.s 16:13
    formula for describing what h.s 333:24
    thing that was to h. to him 216:14
Happened: 'Nothing has h.' 327:12
Happier: h. than I know 280:22
Happiest: 'h. of men' 92:16
Happiness: greatest h. of the greatest number 31:22
    greatest h. for the greatest numbers 212:22
    h.: a good bank account 332:14
    H. is a Warm Puppy 339:5
    h. is beneficial 321:20
    h. is like coke 213:3
    h. is no laughing matter 452:4
    h. too swiftly flies 187:6
    lifetime of h. 388:15
    look into h. through another man's eyes 346:9
    makes the h. she does not find 219:13
    miseries of the world . . . necessary to h. 220:3
    no h. within this circle of flesh 71:3
    no more right to consume h. 387:24
    O h.! our being's end 314:7
    our h. is assured 59:12
    price of h. will not be happy 472:10
    recall a time of h. 131:17
    rob him of his h. 214:22
    ruin of all h.! 83:11
    so much h. is produced . . . by a good tavern
       222:18
    something curiously boring about . . . h. 212:29
    we find our h., or not at all! 465:29
Happy: all be as h. as kings 407:19
    ask yourself whether you are h. 273:10
    call no man h. 400:24
    count myself in nothing else so h. 376:21
    delusions . . . make us more h. 182:26
    duty of being h. 407:6
    h. is he who . . . learn the causes of things 441:26
    h. is the man 41:3
    h. life be these 409:15
    h. men that have the power to die 423:25
    h. the man 151:9, 208:1, 315:6
    H. Though Married 192:8
    help to make the earth h. 100:25
    how h. could I be with either 174:15
    if all were as h. as we 61:22
    little h. if I could say how much 372:32
    no one can be perfectly h. 402:11
    to make men h. 316:13
    wanted only one thing to make me h. 195:19
Harangue: tu feras après ta h. 244:3
Harbinger: amber scent . . . her h. 281:24
    evening star, love's h. 280:41
    merry Spring-time's h. 28:6
    morning star, day's h. 281:33
Harbour: ship was cheered, the h. cleared 116:21
Hard: h. . . . . as nails 139:34
    h. for him that spake it 20:12
    how very h. it is 74:11
Hard-boiled: h. as a picnic egg 303:13
Harder: borne a yet h. thing 204:16
    h. they fall 165:16
Hard-faced: lot of h. men 21:14
Hardship: many h.s on the high seas 204:13
Hardy: H. went down to botanize in the swamp
    111:4
    kiss me, H. 293:7

Hare: h. limped trembling 230:13
    h. sits snug 203:7
    I like the hunting of the h. 64:1
    thou woldest find an h. 108:13
Harebell: azured h., like thy veins 347:13
Harlot: h.'s cry from street to street 60:20
    Portia is Brutus' h. 359:32
    prerogative of the h. 21:15, 241:35
Harlow: *t* is silent as in H. 13:23
Harm: nothing can h. a good man 400:20
    win us to our h. 364:20
    wouldn't do us any h. 188:19
Harmless: elephant . . . the only h. great thing 146:2
Harmonies: O mighty-mouthed inventor of h.
    416:17
Harmony: from h., from heavenly h. 150:33
    h. in discord 207:22
    hidden soul of h. 276:34
    makes heaven drowsy with the h. 363:31
    music where ever there is a h. 71:11
    sentimentally I am disposed to h. 245:12
    such h. is in immortal souls 370:20
    touches of sweet h. 370:19
Harness: die with h. on our back 367:26
    Nicanor lay dead in his h. 48:33
Haroun: golden prime of good H. Alraschid 422:25
Harp: hang my h. on a weeping willow-tree 8:21
    h. not on that string 378:13
    h. that once through Tara's halls 286:26
    high-born Hoel's h. 185:20
    to touch their h.s of gold 341:16
    we hanged our h.s upon the willows 41:9
    wild h. slung behind him 287:2
Harping: still h. on my daughter 349:28
Harrow: h. the house of the dead 15:13
Harry: but H., H. 356:15
    H. the King 357:18
    I saw young H. with his beaver on 354:36
    such a King H.? 148:14
Harshness: no h. gives offence 313:14
Hart: as pants the h. 414:16
    h. panteth after the water brooks 38:21
    h. ungallèd play 351:14
    to start a h. 353:31
Hart: sentant la h. 267:26
Harumfrodite: kind of giddy h. 240:22
Harvest: h. is past 46:26
    h. of a quiet eye 465:4
    h. truly is plenteous 49:36
    in h. teach 63:9
    she laughs with a h. 218:12
    white already to h. 53:11
Harwich: tossing about in a steamer from H. 177:14
Has: one of the *h.* beens 204:17
Haste: h. still pays h. 368:30
    men love in h. 92:10
    this sweaty h. 347:23
    though I am always in h. 450:27
    why such h.? 174:21
Hastings, Warren 262:13
Hat: away with h. and wig! 125:12
    by his cockle h. 352:4
    civility of my knee, my h. 70:22
    complete with h. and gloves 95:20
    forbade me to put off my h. 168:13
    little straw h. 428:21
    my h. and wig will soon be here 125:16

never passes a church without pulling off his h. 221:9
pass the h. 238:9
put my h. upon my head 219:2
so many shocking bad h.s 449:21
where did you get that h.? 329:9
Hatched: chickens before they are h. 3:25
couldna be h. o'er again 155:8
Hatchet: forgets where he buried a h. 211:14
Hate: dowered with the h. of h. 421:31
each sequestered in its h. 14:11
h. the man one has injured 414:5
H. Week 300:28
I h. and detest that animal called man 411:25
I h. and love 104:5
I know enough of h. 170:4
if h. killed men 78:21
if you h. a person 200:24
immortal h. 278:7
just enough religion to make us h. 411:19
let them also that h. him flee 39:13
let them h. 1:1
must h. and death return? 391:8
my only love sprung from my only h. 379:6
no h. lost between us 273:5
not without hopes . . . to h. her heartily 120:22
scarcely h. anyone that we know 196:17
Two Minutes H. 300:26
Hateful: I. is h. 305:12
Hater: h. he came and sat by a ditch 391:1
he was a very good h. 224:4
Hatred: bound up with h. 301:7
deep burning h. for the Tory Party 33:6
h. and cark and care 72:23
h. is by far the longest pleasure 92:10
healthy h. of scoundrels 100:1
more like h. than friendship 248:3
no h. or bitterness towards anyone 104:9
stalled ox and h. therewith 42:13
Hatta: other Messenger's called H. 102:15
Haunches: no keeping one's h. still 79:8
Haunt: murmurous h. of flies 232:6
Haunted: h. house. Tenants unknown 68:3
Have: H.s and the Have-nots 105:18
to h. and to hold 319:42
Have-not: Haves and the H.s 105:18
Havoc: cry 'H.!' 360:12
Hawk: all haggard h.s will stoop to lure 242:19
but his h., his hound 23:19
dark h.s near us 226:11
I know a h. from a handsaw 350:1
Hawthorn: give not the h. bush 358:8
under the h. in the dale 276:25
Hay: dance an antic h. 267:8
lie tumbling in the h. 384:23
live on h. 201:9
when husbands win their h. 22:5
world is a bundle of h. 92:33
Haycock: under a h. fast asleep 297:2
Hazlitt: we cannot write like H. 407:8
He: because it was h. 285:11
every h. has got him a she 7:12
poorest h. that is in England 325:5
Head: bear with a sore h. 268:3
beast with many h.s 346:30
cover my defenceless h. 450:23
curling their monstrous h.s 355:31

cuts the wrong man's h. off 140:34
go up, thou bald h. 36:23
Hampden had a h. to contrive 114:31
he seems no bigger than his h. 362:36
h. is not more native to the heart 347:30
H. that once was crowned with thorns 234:27
h. was as bald as the palm of your hand 24:13
h. was cut off 6:6
h.s do grow beneath their shoulders 374:5
'H.s I win, tails you lose' 129:7
heart runs away with his h. 119:25
hide his h. under his wing 297:11
his h. and his hairs were white 58:3
hoary h. is a crown of glory 42:16
how many times can a man turn his h. 153:6
I hang 'mid men my needless h. 427:24
if she'd but turn her h. 470:19
if you can keep your h. 239:11
I'll eat my h.! 140:2
incessantly stand on your h. 100:33
lay your sleeping h. 14:17
lift up your h.s 38:5
my h. is bloody, but unbowed 197:25
my object gather to a h. 381:10
no matter which way the h. lieth 325:13
no wool on de top of his h. 168:9
off with her h.! 101:9
off with his h.! 114:9, 378:5
old men's h.s are just as bare 202:19
one small h. could carry 181:7
ought to have his h. examined 183:10
reasons . . . quite unknown to the h. 305:10
shorter by a h. 157:23
shot . . . this old gray h. 454:6
so empty was each h. 111:26
stars hide their diminished h.s 279:18
their h.s are green 250:22
tossing their h.s in sprightly dance 462:5
trouble out of King Charles' h. into my h. 137:13
turns no more his h. 117:10
uneasy lies the h. 356:1
very h. and front of my offending 373:40
with a white h. 355:17
with bent h. and beseeching hand 77:30
Head-waiter: O plump h. at The Cock 424:18
Headache: lying awake with a dismal h. 177:13
Headmaster: h.s have powers at their disposal 113:15
Headstone: h.s yield their names 414:15
Heal: physician, h. thyself 52:6
Healing: arise with h. in his wings 47:27
h. of the nations 58:37
Health: and h. on both! 366:24
he that will this h. deny 153:2
h. is the second blessing 445:28
h. of his wife 121:20
his h., his honour and his quality taken 63:33
in my state of h.! 230:2
life is . . . being in h. 268:10
no h. in us 318:13
purge it to a sound and pristine h. 367:21
Heap: in h.s they run 151:11
struck all on a h. 395:16
unsunned h.s of miser's treasure 275:19
Hear: come on and h. 32:7
let him h. 51:30
time will come when you will h. me 142:22

what they h., they repeat! 397:13
Hearer: attentive and favourable h.s 205:7
Hearing: h., thinking, writing 195:19
  make passionate my sense of h. 363:24
Hearse: strew the laureate h. 277:16
  underneath this sable h. 71:21
Heart: absence makes the h. grow fonder 27:4
  all that human h.s endure 181:31
  all that mighty h. is lying still 463:11
  aye a h. aboon them a' 85:23
  bear, O my h. 204:16
  betray the h. that loved her 462:22
  blessed are the pure in h. 451:23
  blossoms a rose in the deeps of my h. 471:11
  borrow H.'s lightness 230:9
  broken and a contrite h. 38:31
  broken h. lies here 261:9
  broods and sleeps on his own h. 465:4
  bury my h. at Wounded Knee 31:15
  call home the h. you gave me 148:18
  chambers of the mansion of my h. 428:18
  cheerful h.s now broken! 287:14
  cherish those h.s that hate thee 358:25
  cold untroubled h. of stone 97:14
  commune with your h. 37:21
  cursed be the h. 22:22
  day breaks not, it is my h. 144:17
  dere's where my h. is turning ebber 168:8
  eat thy h. through comfortless despairs 403:10
  ensanguined h.s 127:16
  enthronèd in the h.s of kings 370:9
  every lusty h. beginneth to blossom 265:16
  farewell the h. that lives alone 461:18
  floor lay paved with broken h.s 258:10
  following her daily of thy h. 331:23
  give a loving h. to thee 200:13
  give me back my h. 93:13
  Greensleeves was my h. of gold 7:19
  half as many h.s lost to her 29:12
  has a h. and gets his speeches by it 328:23
  has been my h.'s undoing 287:7
  have wound themselves about this h. 127:35
  he tears the h. out of it 242:7
  head, and the h. of man 333:16
  head is not more native to the h. 347:30
  h. as sound as a bell 373:1
  h. and stomach of a king 157:26
  h. grow fonder 7:3
  h. has its reasons 305:10
  h. is deceitful above all things 46:30
  h. is sick 418:3
  h. less bounding at emotion new 12:6
  h. may think it knows better 66:4
  h. must pause to breathe 93:21
  h. of a man is depressed 174:10
  h. of lead 311:16
  h. of oak 173:5
  h. runs away with his head 119:25
  h. the Queen leant on 75:31
  h. to resolve 175:21
  h. . . . too easily impressed 76:6
  h. treads on h. 72:10
  h. untainted 358:2
  h. whose love is innocent! 93:9
  h. within, and God o'erhead 257:4
  h.s are in the right place 143:19
  h.'s denying 25:12

h.s that we broke long ago 15:7
h.s were her favourite suit 245:23
his h. was mailed with oak 208:3
his h. was one of those which most enamour us 89:5
hold me in thy h. 353:12
hope deferred maketh the h. sick 42:4
humble and a contrite h. 240:17
I am sick at h. 347:19
I feel my h. new opened 358:22
I said to H. 30:23
if thou wilt ease thine h. 28:20
in h.s at peace 69:22
in my h. of h. 351:4
in my h. of h.s 464:18
in the h. or in the head 370:1
Indian Summer of the h. 454:8
intellect is always fooled by the h. 248:7
it dies upon her h. 391:12
kind h.s are more than coronets 419:6
King of H.s the only one that hasn't a moustache
  95:2
leaves a h. high-sorrowful 231:22
locked my h. in a case o' gowd 23:24
look in thy h. and write 396:11
lose your h.'s desire 388:22
make my seated h. knock at my ribs 364:23
man after his own h. 35:44
man's . . . h. is not able to report 372:11
many a h. is aching 194:7
merry h. goes all the day 384:26
merry h. maketh a cheerful countenance 42:12
mine h. will not serve now 265:21
mine with my h. in't 381:4
more knowledge of the h. 222:6
moving toyshop of their h. 315:13
my h. aches 231:30
my h. at some noonday 75:7
my h. beats loud and fast 391:13
my h. belongs to Daddy 317:3
my h. did leap for joy 168:12
my h. is a lonely hunter 263:22
my h. is at rest 62:21
my h. is inditing a great matter 38:23
my h. is like a singing bird 331:1
my h. leaps up 463:14
my h., safe left, shall meet 396:16
my h. untravelled 181:25
my h. waketh 44:24
my h. was in the sea 25:6
my h. was like to break 25:6
my h.'s in the Highlands 85:3, 341:7
my true love hath my h. 396:10
neither have the h.s to stay 87:26
no longer tear his h. 411:30
now cracks a noble h. 353:14
O troubled h. 472:2
of finite h.s that yearn 79:6
open my h. and you will see 74:4
open not thine h. to every man 48:6
our h. is not quiet 15:30
our h.s are great 417:2
out-worn h. 471:4
poor h. would fain deny 367:18
pourest thy full h. 394:17
return, my roving h. 144:11
set not your h. upon them 39:7
shall command my h. and me 128:26

she wants a h. 314:25
since man's h. is small 240:28
sink h. and voice opprest 292:30
so the h. be right 325:13
some men break your h. in two 303:14
soothe or wound a h. that's broken! 340:5
Splendid H.s may go 69:13
steal away your h.s 360:23
sudden heat which made my h. to glow 401:28
there will your h. be also 49:12
this h. shall break 362:13
thou hast my h. 320:17
though the h. be still as loving 93:21
two h.s beating each to each 75:27
two h.s that beat as one 258:16
unto whom all h.s be open 319:19
vacant h. and hand 340:26
warm h. within 124:33
watched my foolish h. expand 73:31
wear my h. upon my sleeve 373:32
what h. could have thought you? 428:1
what hast thou found in thine h. to sing? 413:1
whether it be the h. to conceive 227:12
while your h.s are yearning 167:12
whispers the o'er-fraught h. 367:8
words, no matter from the h. 382:22
you thought to break a country h. 419:2
your h.'s desires be with you! 344:18
your h.'s supreme ambition 260:14
Heart-ache: h. and the thousand natural shocks
    350:14
Heart-break: feel the h. in the heart of things
    176:1
Heartburn: I am h. 206:5
Heart-easing: tell the most h. things 232:16
Hearth: scatter, as from an unextinguished h.
    392:12
    though they sweep their h.s no less 122:9
Heart-strings: silent griefs which cut the h. 167:9
Heart-throb: count time by h.s 21:10
Heat: h. . . . concentrate in the Hons' cupboard
    283:4
    h., ma'am! it was so dreadful 399:31
    h. of the day 50:41
    know not where is that Promethean h. 375:22
    surprised I was with sudden h. 401:28
    thinking on fantastic summer's h. 376:15
    white h. of this revolution 458:5
Heath: foot is on my native h. 341:5
    land of brown h. 340:2
    quite open to the h. 193:22
    stormed across the war-convulsèd h. 338:14
Heathen: counsel of the h. 38:13
    h. in his blindness 196:25, 238:26
    pore benighted h. 239:3
    why do the h. rage 37:19
Heather: I know how the h. looks 142:10
    over the h. the west wind blows 15:4
Heaven: all I seek, the h. above 407:22
    all of h. we have below 1:17
    all places are distant from h. alike 86:15
    all that h. allows 328:8
    all the way to h. is h. 103:7
    all this and h. too 198:12
    as near to h. by sea 176:8
    as nigh h. as my own 287:22
    ascribe to h. 343:6

battering the gates of h. 423:10
builds a H. in Hell's despair 61:19
can make a h. of hell 278:11
catch larks if the h.s fell 324:3
clothed with the h.s 431:14
cold and rook-delighting h. 470:11
distorts the H.s from pole to pole 60:25
even from the gates of h. 80:30
floor of h. is thick inlaid 370:20
flowerless fields of h. 411:31
gave . . . his blessed part to h. 358:28
give the jolly h. above 407:22
glance from h. to earth 372:14
God creating the h. and the earth 33:13
God is in h. 43:23
heard the h.s fill with shouting 419:30
h. and earth are ruthless 247:18
H. and earth in ashes ending 104:11
h. be in these lips 266:22
h. commences ere the world be past! 180:21
h. has no rage like love to hatred turned 120:14
h. held his hand 124:25
H. in a wild flower 60:8
h. in her eye 280:23
h. itself, that points out 1:14
h. itself would stoop to her 275:35
h. knows, anything goes 316:24
h. lies around us in our infancy 464:7
h. on earth 279:23
h. smiles, and faiths and empires gleam 391:2
h. take my soul 361:25
h. that bends above us 310:26
h. to throne in 346:34
h. upon earth 18:20
H. views it with delight 268:17
h. was in him before he was in h. 445:30
h.'s light forever shines 390:8
h.s look bright 287:9
h.s themselves blaze forth 360:1
h.s themselves, the planets 381:35
hell I suffer seems a h. 279:19
hell that is not h. 266:21
help yourself, and h. will help you 244:16
high H. rejects the lore 461:15
hills of H. 22:13
how art thou fallen from h. 45:12
how long or short permit to h. 280:40
hung be the h.s with black 357:26
I create new h.s 46:22
I see H.'s glories shine 68:24
in that H. of all their wish 69:8
in the blue h.'s height 272:30
in the day when h. was falling 210:2
is he in h.? 300:5
lead you in at H.'s gate 61:4
leave her to h. 349:10
leave to H. the measure 219:12
light from H. 85:33
love is h. 339:27
men . . . differ as H. and Earth 417:6
more than all in h. 90:28
more things in h. and earth 349:16
new h. and a new earth 58:31
not because I hope for h. thereby 103:5
not scorned in H. 126:8
nothing under H. so blue 407:30
order is h.'s first law 314:8

parting is all we know of h. 142:6
Pennies from H. 83:6
pitched between H. and Charing Cross 427:19
serve in h. 278:12
shun the h. that leads men to this hell 387:5
so much of h. 466:12
some call it the road to h. 23:17
starry cope of h. 280:4
starry h.s above me 229:8
starry h.s above the plain 428:20
steep and thorny way to h. 348:20
there may be h. 79:2
there's h. above 75:10
three days today, between Hell and H. 331:26
through the h.'s wide pathless way 276:7
treasure in h. 50:36
we know the way to h. 158:7
we shall practise in h. 76:9
we suddenly know, what h. we're in 316:25
weariness of climbing h. 394:11
what's a h. for? 72:18
when h. and earth shall pass away 340:3
whether in H. ye wander fair 62:26
ye h.s adore Him 235:7
Heaviness: h. foreruns the good event 356:7
take no. h. to heart 48:23
Heavy: little h., but no less divine 91:28
makes it much more h. 382:6
Hebraism: H. strictness of conscience 12:16
Hebrew: called in the H. tongue Armageddon 58:26
I said it in H. 102:26
Hebrides: among the farthest H. 466:22
colder than the H. 165:26
in dreams behold the H.! 341:11
Hector: how changed from that H. who returned 440:16
Hecuba: what's H. to him 350:9
Hedge: green-ruddy, in h.s 25:9
out into the highways and h.s 52:22
unkempt about those h.s blows 69:11
Hedgehog: if you start throwing h.s at me 236:21
thorny h.s, be not seen 371:39
Heel: hath lifted up his h. against me 38:20
one woe doth tread upon another's h. 352:18
thou who on the boldest h. 128:15
Heffalump: decided to catch a H. 274:28
Heifer: h. lowing at the skies 231:23
plowed with my h. 35:32
Heigh ho: h., h., it's off to work we go 142:21
H., how I do love thee! 111:12
'H.' says Rowley 296:15
H., would she were mine 256:3
then h.! the holly! 345:13
Height: h.s by great men reached 256:29
nor h., nor depth 54:31
what pleasure lives in h. 422:18
Heine: H. for songs 74:10
Heineken: H. refreshes the parts 3:3
Heinz: Beanz Meanz H. 2:26
Heir: I the h. of all the ages 420:4
Heiresses: all h. are beautiful 151:25
Held: wunderlich nah ist der H. 327:13
Helen: H., thy beauty is to me 310:28
I wish I were where H. lies 22:21
like another H. 150:7
sees H.'s beauty in a brow of Egypt 372:14
Helican: darned if I know how the h. 272:27

Helicon: watered our horses in H. 106:14
where H. breaks down 10:24
Hell: all h. broke loose 280:3
better to reign in h. 278:12
builds a Heaven in H.'s despair 61:19
danger of h. fire 49:1
down, down to h. 358:11
England is . . . h. for horses 86:20
England is . . . the h. of horses 166:21
excursion to h. 320:14
gates of h. shall not prevail 50:23
half so wicked as Lord George H. 29:6
h. on earth 388:15
h. from beneath is moved 45:11
H. hath no limits 266:20
h. is a city much like London 392:17
h. is full of musical amateurs 388:20
h. is murky! 367:11
h. is other people 337:23
h. that is not heaven 266:21
if there is a h. upon earth 86:11
in h. they'll roast thee like a herring 85:22
influence hath alloted death and h. 267:4
into the mouth of H. 416:1
Kansas . . . begin raising h. 251:12
long is the way . . . out of h. 279:2
h. of heav'n 278:11
make a h. of this world 28:17
married, and that's his h. 86:10
mocking laughter from H. 253:26
myself am h. 279:19
never mentions h. to ears polite 315:4
nor h. a fury, like a woman scorned 120:14
of Devils and H. 63:8
parting is . . . all we need of h. 142:6
raises from H. a human soul 60:12
there is a dreadful H. 447:9
there must be h. 79:2
there was a way to H. 80:30
they go to h. like lambs 110:10
three days today, between H. and Heaven 331:26
ugly h., gape not! 267:6
walked eye-deep in h. 317:23
war is h. 396:3
way down to h. is easy 440:26
willing to go through h. to get it 268:2
Hellenism: H. is spontaneity of consciousness 12:16
Hellespont: he could . . . have passed the H. 91:11
to the Propontic and the H. 375:10
Helmet: h. now shall make a hive 307:1
she saw the h. and the plume 419:14
Help: encumbers him with h. 220:21
from whence cometh my h. 40:30
hath not another to h. him up 43:21
h. of the helpless 260:12
in whom there is no h. 41:15
little h. from my friends 253:17
make haste to h. us 318:16
our God, our h. in ages past 447:23
people must h. one another 244:19
sometimes needs h. moving the piano 451:17
vain is the h. of man 39:5
very present h. in trouble 38:24, 406:9
what is past my h. 27:21
what's past h. 384:17
without the h. of anything on earth 60:30
you can't h. it 59:19

Helped: we shall have h. it 141:29

Helper: our antagonist is our h. 82:23
  when other h.s fail 260:12

Hem: touch the h. of his garment 50:17

Hemisphere: find two better h.s 145:11

Hemlock: as though of h. I had drunk 231:30

Hen: h. . . . . egg's way of making another egg 87:36
  not of that text a pulled h. 107:14

Hen-pecked: have they not h. you all? 90:33

Henry: abdicated in favour of H. IV, part II 342:20
  heartless H. lies 94:10
  Hoorah H. 333:5
  I'm H. the Eight 290:8

Henry I 197:15

Hepburn, James, Earl of Bothwell 304:10

Heraclitus: H., they told me you were dead 123:1

Herald: last and greatest h. of Heaven's King 149:1

Herald-angel: hark! the h.s sing 450:20

Heraldry: boast of h. 186:6

Herb: better is a dinner of h.s 42:13
  Medea gathered the enchanted h.s 370:18
  of h.s and other country messes 276:27

Hercules: let H. himself do what he may 353:2

Herd: from heat did canopy the h. 385:14
  h. of such, who think too little 149:19
  lowing h. winds slowly 185:27
  stricken deer, that left the h. 127:4

Herde: oon ere it h. 108:26

Here: H. or There as strikes the Player 164:19
  h. we are! 242:6
  I have gone h. and there 386:30
  I've been h. before 332:1
  'tis neither h. nor there 375:18
  we're h. because we're h. 8:25

Hereafter: cease to exist h. 33:9
  points out an h. 1:14
  she should have died h. 367:24

Hereditas: Damnosa h. 172:2

Hereford: road from heaven to H. 110:1

Heresies: new truths . . . begin as h. 213:13

Heresy: Englishman believes be h. 389:10

Heretic: Jews, Turks, Infidels, and H.s 319:15

Heritage: I have a goodly h. 37:33
  we have come into our h. 69:7

Hermann: H.'s a German 316:22

Hermit: h. hoar, in solemn cell 224:2
  h.s are contented with their cells 462:29

Hermitage: take that for an h. 258:13

Hero: conquering h. comes 288:1
  every h. becomes a bore 159:9
  good novel . . . truth about its h. 110:28
  he came with h.'s arms 236:7
  h. from the waist up 274:7
  land where her young h. sleeps 287:6
  no h. is mortal till he dies 15:11
  no man is a h. to his valet 122:20
  show me a h. 165:11
  very valet seemed a h. 89:4
  who sees . . . a h. perish 313:27

Héro: il n'y a pas de h.s pour son valet de chambre 122:20

Herod: it out-herods H. 350:25

Heroes: all the world's brave h.s 8:17
  fit country for h. 255:15
  hail, ye h.! 206:26
  land that has no h. 67:4
  my peers the h. of old 77:9
  speed glum h. up the line to death 337:27

we aren't no thin red h. 240:31

Heroic: h. times have passed away 172:14

Herring: Neighbours o'er the H. Pond 152:18
  plague o' these pickled h.! 382:32
  roast thee like a h. 85:22
  wha'll buy my caller h.? 291:6

Herring-pond: h. is wide 76:5

Herrschen: Du musst h. und gewinnen 179:25

Hervey, Lord 12:25

Hervey: world consists of . . . H.s 285:3

Herz: mein H. ist schwer 179:21
  wenn das H. auch bricht 197:4

Hésite: elle flotte, elle h. 324:27

Hesper: slippered H. 69:11

Hesperus: H. entreats thy light 224:27
  it was the schooner's H. 257:22

Heterodoxy: h. is another man's doxy 446:1

Heure: et vous, h.s propices! 244:23

Hewer: h.s of wood 35:22

Hexameter: barbarous h.s 416:16
  in the h. rises 118:9
  long roll of the H. 420:20

Hey: h.! then up go we! 323:3
  with a h. and a ho 346:12
  with h., ho, the wind and the rain 383:33

Hey-day: h. in the blood is tame 351:29

Hi: he would answer to H.! 102:22

Hickory: h., dickory, dock 296:20

Hid: one braver thing . . . to keep that h. 146:15
  wherefore are these things h.? 382:28

Hide: gazelle . . . with its dappled h. 205:6
  his h. is sure to flatten 'em 30:3

Hie: away we both must h. 210:3

Hierarchy: in a H. Every Employee 308:7
  Olympus' faded h. 232:9

Hierusalem: H., my happie home 7:24

Hiesiger: ist er ein H.? 327:17

Higginbottom: last words of H. 399:4

High: h. that proved too h. 72:12
  thou has ascended on h. 39:16

High-Churchman: furious h. I was 7:28

Highest: needs must love the h. 416:34

High-flyer: h. at fashion 140:8
  no h. 307:13

Highland: heart is H. 341:11
  in the h.s in the country places 407:25
  my heart's in the H.s 85:3, 341:7
  was my sweet H. Mary 84:25
  where is your H. laddie gone? 225:33
  ye H.s and ye Lawlands 22:7

Highlandman: taking the breeks aff a wild H. 340:27

Highly: what thou wouldst h. 364:28

High-mindedness: odour of . . . honourable h. 66:18

High-Park: all beyond H.'s a desert to you 159:31

Highway: broad h. of the world 390:25
  h., since you my chief Parnassus be 396:16
  happy h.s where I went 210:26
  out into the h.s and hedges 52:22

Hill: a-dried at Woak H. 25:9
  as immutable as the h.s 241:27
  before the h.s in order stood 447:23
  blue remembered h.s 210:25
  dwell . . . in the hollow h.s 263:21
  green h. far away 4:7
  'guessing what was at the other side of the h.' 449:20
  h. will not come to Mahomet 19:26

Hollow: dwell . . . in the h. hills 263:21
    we are the h. men 156:14
Holly: h. and the ivy 7:25
    h. branch shone on the old oak wall 27:6
Hollywood: I should not have been invited to H. 106:9
Holocaust: lay ere while a h. 281:28
Holy: ears have heard the H. Word 61:17
    everything that lives is h. 60:7
    h., divine, good, amiable, or sweet! 280:36
    h., h., h., Lord God Almighty! 196:26
    he died to make men h. 211:6
    'tis h. ground 186:22
Homage: owes no h. unto the sun 71:14
Home: any more at h. like you? 66:6, 191:2
    best country ever is at h. 181:28
    better to stay peacefully at h. 104:15
    came h., h. to a lie 317:23
    comin' for to carry me h. 8:18
    confined him h. 115:4
    draw near to their eternal h. 444:13
    English h. – gray twilight 421:27
    for h. is best 433:23
    from quiet h.s 30:21
    gae h., gae h. 22:23
    he that . . . comes safe h. 357:17
    her h. is on the deep 97:22
    h. is the girl's prison 388:32
    h., James 201:13
    h. life ceases to be free 214:4
    h. on the rolling deep 337:16
    h. . . . they have to take you in 170:2
    how I wish him safe at h. 225:33
    I don't want to go h. in the dark 198:22
    I'm Afraid to Go H. in the Dark 457:11
    little grey h. in the west 457:25
    man goeth to his long h. 44:11
    many a man who thinks to found a h. 147:5
    more difficult is it to bring it h. 147:13
    never is at h. 124:31
    no place like h. 306:10
    old folks at h. 168:8
    return h. and rest on the couch 103:16
    returns h. to find it 286:18
    sated with h. 398:22
    shall never more go h. 261:10
    she's leaving h. 253:13
    stately h.s of England 123:17, 197:16, 249:14, 460:21
    take it h. with you 217:16
    that makes her loved at h. 84:7
    there's nobody at h. 312:13
    this little pig stayed at h. 298:7
    'tis thou must bring her h. 23:10
    travel to their h. among the dead 390:25
    we won't go h. till morning 80:3
    what's the good of a h. 188:16
    when I was at h. 344:32
    who live at h. at ease 304:18
    won't you come h., Bill Bailey 98:22
Homer: Greece, sound thy H.'s . . . name 127:33
    H. . . . nods for a moment 207:9
    many-minded H. 471:12
    our poets steal from H. 86:6
    read H. once 79:26
    single exception of H. 389:13
    view in H. more than H. knew 410:13

    when H. smote 'is bloomin' lyre 241:8
    you must not call it H. 32:1
Homerus: *bonus dormitat H.* 207:9
Homespun: what hempen h.s 372:2
Homines: quidquid agunt h. 227:16
Homme: h. affable, bon, courtois, spirituel 332:5
    h. est né libre 332:12
    h. est . . . un méchant animal 284:17
    je n'en suis pas moins h.! 284:14
    pauvre h.! 284:12
    style est l'h. même 80:7
Homo: ecce h.! 53:34
    naked ape self-named *H. sapiens* 288:8
Honest: as h. as any man living 373:9
    cannot be both h. and intelligent 301:5
    few h. men are better than numbers 129:9
    for h. men and bonnie lasses 85:14
    h. and true 8:3
    h. God's the noblest work of man 88:15, 215:11
    h. man, close-buttoned to the chin 124:33
    h. man's the noblest work of God 84:7, 314:9
    h. woman and a broken leg 105:13
    I am not naturally h. 385:2
    if h. nature made you fools 84:12
    made h. by an act of parliament 225:1
    pay for it like an h. man 295:19
    poor but h. 343:7
    six lines written by the most h. man 327:8
    though I be poor, I'm h. 273:4
    though it be h., it is never good 343:33
    to be h., as this world goes 349:27
    twelve h. men have decided the cause 322:2
    Whig to pretend to be h. 223:31
Honesty: armed so strong in h. 360:30
    h. is praised and starves 227:15
    neither h., manhood or good fellowship 353:24
    thy h. and love doth mince this matter 374:23
Honey: all beings the h. of this earth 435:9
    chosen to fill our hives with h. 410:20
    eating bread and h. 297:31
    gather h. all the day 447:12
    h. or condensed milk with your bread? 274:26
    is there h. still for tea? 69:16
    land flowing with milk and h. 34:42
    meat was locusts and wild h. 48:36
    sweeter also than h. 37:37
    they took some h. 250:24
    Tiggers don't like h. 274:20
Honey-bee: for so work the h.s 356:24
Honey-dew: he on h. hath fed 118:6
Honeysuckle: you are my honey, h. 163:21
Honi: 'h. soie qui mal y pense' 342:19
Honneur: tout est perdu fors l'h. 168:16
Honour: all is lost save h. 168:16
    as h., love, obedience 367:18
    blushing h.s thick upon him 358:21
    book of h. razèd quite 385:20
    can h.'s voice provoke the silent dust 186:8
    drowned my H. in a Shallow Cup 164:27
    gave his h.s to the world again 358:28
    greater share of h. 357:15
    helps the hurt that H. feels 419:28
    his h. rooted in dishonour stood 416:37
    h. a physician 48:22
    h. all men 57:32
    h. aspireth to it 18:22
    h. but an empty bubble 150:4

great lies about his wooden h. 166:9
he delighteth not in the strength of the h. 41:17
h. is drawn by the cart 238:22
h. of that colour 383:7
h.s and dorgs is some men's fancy 137:16
h.s for ye 73:11
h.s of instruction 63:19
king of France's h.s 191:20
like an old h. in a pound 471:26
little dearer than his h. 419:21
more careful of the breed of their h.s 307:7
my h., my wife, and my name 409:21
my h.s understand me tolerably well 411:3
my kingdom for a h.! 378:20
no secret so close . . . between a rider and his h. 410:2
not best to swap h.s 254:18
not hanged for stealing h.s 190:11
nothing like blood, sir, in h.s 425:20
O! for a h. with wings 347:9
old h. that stumbles and nods 192:25
one h. was blind 398:21
one stiff blind h. 73:26
other is a h. still 220:23
plaits the manes of h.s in the night 379:2
pulling in one's h. as he is leaping 193:29
ride the tallest h. 'e can 238:16
rode their h.s up to bed 134:17
Saint George . . . sits on his h. 361:9
SIXTY H.S WEDGED IN A CHIMNEY 289:4
some will trust . . . in h.s 37:39
something in a flying h. 464:26
soon expect the white h. at Rosmersholm 214:19
tempers her words to trampling h.s' feet 396:16
turning to his h., he said 125:19
two things about the h. 6:4
watered our h.s in Helicon 106:14
where's the bloody h.? 96:23
White H. of the White H. Vale 109:26
wild white h.s play 11:4
Horse race: difference of opinion that makes h.s 434:12
Horseback: you must ride on h. after we 125:8
Horseleach: h. hath two daughters 43:7
Horseman: drumming the plain, the h. is coming 173:3
Horsemanship: witch the world with noble h. 354:36
Horsemen: h. riding upon horses 46:35
Hose: I dream of wellfilled h. 226:27
youthful h. well saved 345:11
Hospital: not an inn, but a h. 71:13
Host: I'd have been under the h. 304:6
soundless-clapping h. 427:10
time is like a fashionable h. 382:14
Hostage: h.s to fortune 19:10
Hostess: h. of the tavern 353:18
H. with the Mostes' 32:9
Hostility: Graduated H. of Things 218:3
Hotel: I prefer temperance h.s 446:18
Mr Reilly who owns the h.? 8:2
strode rapidly across . . . the h. 321:11
Hoti: he settled H.'s business 74:30
Hottentot: consider him as a respectable H. 109:16
Hound: cry of his h.s 185:2
h.s all join in glorious cry 163:5
h.s are bred out of the Spartan kind 372:10

h.s of spring 411:32
questing of thirty couple h.s 265:10
traveller, by the faithful h. 256:26
with his h.s and his horn 185:2
Hour: against the h. of death 320:1
awaits alike th'inevitable h. 186:6
changed ev'ry h. 174:7
chase the glowing h.s 89:22
for a dark h. or twain 366:9
enfold me in my h. of h.s 471:22
from h. to h. we ripe and ripe 345:4
golden h.s on angel wings 84:25
had na' been the-erre abune twa h.s 322:8
heavy weight of h.s has chained 392:10
h. is come 340:33
h. of my death 234:14
h. to play and the last man in 293:21
h.s I spent with thee 328:22
h.s, that danced away 151:17
h.s . . . which are the rags of time 146:11
how many make the h. full complete 358:7
I also had my h. 110:5
I can sit and look at it for h.s 218:8
lighting a little H. or two 164:4
mine h. is not yet come 53:5
neglect the creeping h.s of time 345:10
nothing can bring back the h. 464:16
one bare h. to live 267:2
one crowded h. of glorious life 287:18
one dead deathless h. 331:20
pore by the h., o'er a weed 24:15
seven h.s to law 224:19
shorter h.s and better pay 5:21
some people can stay longer in an h. 211:9
space of half an hour 58:17
steal a few h.s from the night 287:9
take what this sweet h. yields 394:10
tell of sunny h.s 211:10
their finest h. 112:23
think down h.s to moments 127:25
though it be but an h. ago 145:28
truly that h. foretold 94:8
what h.s, O what black h.s 206:3
what h.s were thine and mine 416:5
what peaceful h.s once enjoyed! 125:23
when my last h. comes 430:4
who has matched us with His h. 69:17
winged h. is dropped 331:21
wingless, crawling h.s 392:23
Hour-glass: silence, still as the h. 331:21
Housbond: have sovereyntee . . . over hir h. 108:17
Housbondes: H. at chirche-dore she hadde fyve 107:24
House: build his h. in the woods 159:16
build the h. of death 285:6
dark h., by which once more I stand 417:28
eaten me out of h. and home 355:23
except the Lord build the h. 41:1
falling h.s thunder on your head 218:25
fired that the h. reject him 312:16
had a mind to sell his h. 410:21
handsome h. to lodge a friend 410:6
he would burn your h. down 106:1
home to his mother's h. 281:12
h. for me, no doubt 79:7
h. is a machine for living in 251:20
h. not made with hands 55:45, 73:17

h. that Jack built 298:6
h. with lawns enclosing it 407:29
h.s are all gone under the sea 155:35
h.s are built to live in 20:26
h.s are built without walls 298:12
I will hold my h. in the high wood 31:4
I would say to the H. 112:18
if it wasn't for the h.s in between 26:10
in my Father's h. 53:27
man . . . in the way in the h. 173:12
man's h. is his castle 116:9
mere lodger in my own h. 182:6
my h. has been broken open 306:13
no man a h. of good stone 317:18
nothing in your h.s . . . know to be useful 289:1
palace is more than a h. 119:2
peace be to this h. 319:47
plague o' both your h.s! 379:33
return no more to his h. 36:42
sell the H. 108:36
set thine h. in order 45:27
small h. and large garden 124:14
talent . . . at the White H. 235:20
that h. cannot stand 51:29
their h.s shall continue for ever 38:28
this h. . . . as nigh heaven 287:22
very h.s seem asleep 463:11
walked unto the h. of God 38:33
we two kept h. 192:18
when h. and land are gone 167:1
when ye depart out of that h. 49:38
woe unto them that join h. to h. 44:35
wounded in the h. of my friends 47:24
you take my h. when you do take the prop
    370:16
your h. is on fire 296:31
House of Lords: fail very completely in the H.
    143:31
    H., an illusion 408:10
Household: familiar . . . as h. words 357:18
Housemaid: damp souls of h.s 156:28
    I had not got . . . h.'s knee 218:7
    tho' I walks with fifty h.s 240:5
House-top: dwell in a corner of the h. 42:27
Housewife: here's to the h. that's thrifty 395:37
    honest h. would sort them out 185:8
    mock the good h. 344:15
Housewives: h.' affairs have never an end 433:22
Housework: no need to do any h. 129:5
How: H. and Where and Who 239:19
How-de-doo: here's a h.! 177:26
Hubbard: Mother H., you see, was old 135:9
    old Mother H. 297:15
Hue: left thee all her lovely h.s 132:21
Huée: au milieu des h.s 26:11
Huffy: not h. or stuffy 198:28
Hug: still we h. the dear deceit 123:5
Hugger-mugger: in h. to inter him 352:10
Hugo: H. – alas! 176:3
    H. was a madman 116:4
Hum: busy h. of men 276:30
    h. of human cities torture 89:29
    smell and hideous h. 179:10
Human: all h. life is there 216:16, 294:6
    all h. things are subject to decay 150:27
    all that is h. must be retrograde 175:23
    but he's a h. being 273:24

compare h. life to a large mansion 234:3
contrivance of h. wisdom 82:12
exquisite picture of h. manners 175:7
greater to be human 329:5
history of the h. spirit 12:30
h. being . . . assembly of . . . plumbing 288:4
h. beings are . . . ivy-covered ruins 321:1
h. bodies are sic fools 85:32
h. life is everywhere a state 220:6
h. nature is finer 234:1
h. nature is so well disposed 16:25
h. on my faithless arm 14:17
h. passions now no more 186:25
h. race, to which so many of my readers belong
    110:33
h. reason won 236:19
it isn't fit for h.s now 32:23
more understanding of h. nature 227:7
most thorough knowledge of h. nature 16:30
new edition of h. nature 195:16
no more miserable h. being 217:10
not to degrade the h. being 301:2
outgrows . . . majority of h. passions 157:20
proles are not h. beings 300:27
reckon nothing h. alien to me 424:29
Socialism with a H. Face 151:38
sole purpose of h. existence 227:2
there is in h. nature 19:23
to err is h. 313:19
to step aside is h. 83:21
Treatise of H. Nature 212:7
true pathos and sublime of h. life 85:29
vilest specimens of h. nature 262:20
wish I loved the H. Race 325:14
you've conquered h. natur 139:8
Humanity: H. in deadly sleep 61:1
    h. is just a work in progress 457:13
    h. with all its fears 256:13
    imitated h. so abominably 351:2
    law of h. 82:3
    Oh wearisome condition of h.! 188:12
    religion of h. 303:7
Humankind: h. cannot bear very much reality
    155:31
    Lord of h. 151:31
    porcelain clay of h. 151:23
Humble: he that shall h. himself 51:6
    not only h. but umble 432:6
Humbleness: all h., all patience and impatience
    346:11
Humbug: style of most artists and all h.s 121:11
Humiliation: valley of H. 80:21
Humility: h. is only doubt 60:24
    pride that apes h. 401:15
    thank God for my h. 378:2
Humour: career of his h. 372:38
    has her h. most when she obeys 314:28
    h.s and flatters them 109:12
    I have a h. 224:21
    in all thy h.s 2:5
    in this h. wooed 377:27
    own up to a lack of h. 116:13
    say it is my h. 370:6
    'unconscious h.' 88:7
    unyoked h. of your idleness 353:26
Hump: h. helmet and all 226:3
    H. that is black and blue! 239:20

Humpty: H., Dumpty sat on a wall 296:23
   have you heard of one H. Dumpty 226:3
Hun: H. is at the gate 239:1
Huncamunca: sun myself in H.'s eyes 163:3
Hundred: all the same a h. years hence 139:12
   how it will tell a h. years hence 88:4
   ran a h. years to a day 203:22
   rode the six h. 415:24
Hundred-horse-power: Winston with his h. mind
   21:18
Hunger: h. allows no choice 15:9
   h. is the best sauce 105:12
   war against h. 235:21
Hungered: h., and ye gave me meat 51:17
Hungry: h. as a hunter 246:7
   tigers are getting h. 113:25
   we ate when we were not h. 411:2
Hunt: he h.s in dreams 419:25
   H. – one of those happy souls 391:18
   to h., and vote 89:2
Hunter: heart is a lonely h. 263:22
   hungry as a h. 246:7
   h. home from the hill 407:31
   H. of the East 163:22
   man is the h. 422:10
   Nimrod the mighty h. 34:20
   seith that h.s been nat holy men 107:14
Hunting: discourse was about h. 307:14
   good h.! 241:15
   h. he loved 387:10
   his hound is to the h. gane 23:19
   I like the h. of the hare 64:1
   I'm wearied with h. 22:25
   passion for h. 139:35
   wet and dirty from h. 409:26
Huntsman: cassocked h. 126:13
   h. winds his horn 163:5
Huntsmen: h. are up in America 70:19
Hurler: on apprend à h.325:4
Hurly-burly: h. of the chaise-longue 96:21
   when the h.'s done 364:10
Hurry: H. up please, it's time 157:4
Hurt: if I don't h. her 296:26
   that doth the h. 18:19
   not h. a hair of thy head 405:21
   nothing doth more h. in a state 20:4
   some of your h.s you have cured 158:15
   sweareth to his own h. 37:32
   they that have power to h. 386:17
Husband: as the h. is, the wife is 419:20
   at all times yr faithful h. 404:12
   being a h. is a whole-time job 31:19
   bride adorned for her h. 58:32
   chumps always make the best h.s 459:9
   could not endure a h. with a beard 372:28
   flirt with their own h.s 455:9
   happened unawares to look at her h. 17:17
   h. frae the wife despises 85:15
   h. provides the landscape 67:19
   h.s, love your wives 56:32
   light wife doth make a heavy h. 370:25
   monstrous animal a h. and wife 163:1
   'My h. and I' 157:28
   ne'er answers till a h. cools 314:28
   no worse a h. 343:27
   so sways she level in her h.'s heart 383:10
   virtuous woman is a crown to her h. 42:2

when h.s . . . breathe their last 315:24
when Lil's h. got demobbed 157:4
woman oweth to her h. 380:24
Husbandry: borrowing dulls the edge of h. 348:23
   there's h. in heaven 365:16
Hush: H.! H.! Whisper who dares! 274:18
   h. with the setting moon 420:34
Hush-a-bye: h., baby, on the tree top 296:24
Husk: h.s that the swine did eat 52:26
Hussy: little intricate h. for you! 395:20
Hut: I Wouldn't Leave My Little Wooden H. 271:15
   rude h. by the Danube lay 90:16
Hyacinth: children with H.'s temperament 335:16
   every H. the Garden wears 164:7
   poetry is . . . h.s and biscuits 337:5
Hyades: rainy H. vext the dim sea 424:2
Hybla: as the honey of H. 353:18
Hybrid: h.s and lubberds! 226:7
Hydra: monstrosity more hideous than H. 71:6
Hydrostatics: it gives me the h. 395:25
Hyeste: trouthe is the h. thing 107:31
Hymn: chanting faint h.s 371:17
   hushed was the evening h. 83:16
   sing h.s at heaven's gate 385:23
   singing h.s unbidden 394:20
Hyperbole: speaking in a perpetual h. 19:14
   three-piled h.s 364:3
Hyperion: H. to a satyr 348:1
   H.'s curls 351:27
Hypocrisy: h. is the homage paid by vice 248:12
   making the world safe for h. 460:8
   notorious; we call it h. 88:19
   organized h. 142:26
Hypothetics: taken the highest degree in h. 87:30
Hyssop: purge me with h. 38:30
Hysterica: h. passio! 362:10

           I

I: I is hateful 305:12
Iberian: dark I.s come 11:29
Ibykus: Kraniche des I.! 338:10
Ice: as chaste as i. 350:18
   i., mast-high 116:24
   i. of her Ladyship's manners 318:7
   i. was here, the i. was there 116:25
seemed as though i. burned 470:11
   some say in i. 170:4
   thrilling region of thick-ribbèd i. 368:22
to smooth the i. 361:21
Ice-cream: enjoy your i. while it's on your plate
   456:32
Ichor: his perspiration was but i. 94:2
Icicle: chaste as the i. 346:33
   hang them up in silent i.s 117:32
   like an i. on a Dutchman's beard 383:21
   when i.s hang by the wall 364:7
Ida: O mother I. 421:25
   whether on I.'s shady brow 62:26
Idea: better to entertain an i. 217:16
   between the i. and the reality 156:16
   colourless green i.s sleep 111:17
   entertain such inhuman i.s 410:26
   he had only one i. 143:25
   i. isn't responsible 268:1

i.s above her station 326:1
i.s are events l65:20
i.s of economists . . . are more powerful 236:14
i.s simply pass through him 66:12
man who has *two* great i.s 68:22
most heterogenous i.s 219:23
nice man is a man of nasty i.s 411:21
possess but one i. 222:2
powerful i. communicates 321:8
teach the young i. how to shooot 428:6
would be a good i. 172:15
Ideal: Christian i. . . . found difficult 111:5
if you believe in an i. 106:8
pestering us with the demands of their i.s 214:23
Idée: certaine i. de France 173:15
Identity: his i. presses upon me 234:5
poet . . . has no i. 234:9
Ides: beware the i. of March 359:12
Idiocy: cold-hearted fucking that is death and i.
249:12
Idiot: blaspheming over the village i. 111:4
him whom she loves, her I. Boy 462:8
to generalize is to be an i. 63:27
Idle: every i. word that men shall speak 50:7
if you are i., be not solitary 223:8
never less i. 339:8
whom the world calls i. 127:10
words seemed to them as i. 52:47
Idleness: arms and i. 175:16
blow away all this i. and indifference 108:35
compulsory and irreproachable i. 431:4
i. is only the refuge of weak minds 109:14
love in i. 380:16
round of strenuous i. 465:16
unyoked humour of your i. 353:26
Idling: impossible to enjoy i. thoroughly 218:5
Idol: I., saint, virgin, prophet 89:17
I.s I have loved so long 164:27
kisses on an 'eathen i.'s foot 240:3
one-eyed yellow i. 195:10
would be an i., 65:1
Idolatries: to its i. a patient knee 90:3
Idolatry: dotes in i. 371:19
God of my i. 379:16
god of our i., the Press 126:17
on this side i. 225:28
'tis mad i. 382:5
If: your 'i.' is the only peace-maker 346:15
Ignis: i. fatuus of the mind 328:10
Ignorance: boldness is a child of i. 19:24
distinguished for i. 143:25
from knowledge i. 74:7
helpless man, in i. sedate 219:11
I pity his i. 139:15
i. alone makes monsters 196:16
i. is bliss 187:6
I. is Strength 300:22
i., Madam, pure i. 220:29
i. of the law 342:5
man's i. of the gods 87:35
more than Gothic i. 162:31
most powerful weapon of i. 431:8
no sin but i. 267:9
our i. must necessarily be infinite 316:17
putting us to i. again 73:32
Ignorant: i. as the dawn 470:13
i. man always adores 256:7

most i. of what he's most assured 368:15
Ignorer: i. les choses qu'elle sait 283:13
île: cette i. triste et noir 26:19
Iliad: I. itself, perfect plainness of speech 13:4
Ilion: cloud-kissing I. 385:8
Ilium: burnt the topless towers of I. 266:22
Ilium: fuit I. 440:17
Ill: bear those i.s we have 350:14
good will be the final goal of i. 418:7
he thinks no i. 385:32
makes i. deeds done! 361:24
nae real i.s perplex them 85:32
nought shall go i. 372:7
some i. a-brewing 369:25
supernatural soliciting cannot be i. 364:22
sure remedy for all i.s 325:12
Ill-doing: doctrine of i. 384:12
Ill-favoured: i. thing . . . but mine own 346:13
Ill-housed: one-third of a nation i. 329:18
Illa: laudant i. sed ista legunt 268:9
Illegal: either i., immoral, or fattening 461:2
means it is not i. 295:10
Illiterate: i. him . . . from your memory 395:18
Illness: i. is the most heeded of doctors 321:17
verse was a special i. of the ear 15:2
Illusion: fond i. mock me 208:27
Great I. 5:8
indulgin' in i.s 263:8
modern man lives under the i. 169:17
only one i. left 399:29
Ilsley: looks on I. downs 12:1
Image: best i. of myself 280:8
blotted out man's i. 471:28
in the i. of God 33:16
if God made us in His i. 442:20
kills the i. of God 282:16
man . . . created him the devil in his own i. 146:27
met his own i. 392:24
stamped with the i. of the King 416:35
this i.'s head was of fine gold 46:40
Imaginary: exchange of two i. pictures 106:3
make i. evils 182:8
Imagination: how abhorred in my i. 352:25
if i. amend them 372:19
i. bodies forth 372:14
i. droops her pinion 91:30
i. . . . living power and prime agent 118:17
i. of a boy is healthy 230:5
in ages of i. 63:22
lady's i. is very rapid 17:3
my i.s are as foul 351:5
of i. all compact 372:13
perish through their own i.s 37:23
striking his i. 303:5
sweeten my i. 362:40
things that concern the i. 404:22
truth of the i. 233:23
Imagined: was once only i. 63:18
Immanuel: shall call his name I. 45:4
Immensum: omne i. peragravit 259:17
Immoral: Asquith is good and i. 114:2
'that most i. man' 238:21
Immorality: most rigid code of i. in the world 66:7
nurseries of all vice and i. 162:26
Immortal: grew i. in his own despite 315:29
his biting is i. 344:9
i. dead who live again 155:21

Indus: from I. to the Pole 312:8
Industry: avarice, the spur of i. 212:4
    Captains of I. 100:4
    i. will improve them 326:20
    nobility . . . commonly abateth i. 19:30
    war is Prussia's national i. 282:27
Inelegance: continual state of i. 17:16
Ineptire: miser Catulle, desinas i. 103:13
Inevitable: no good in arguing with the i. 259:5
Inexactitude: risk of terminological i. 112:8
Inexorable: more fierce and more i. far 380:7
Infallible: we're none of us i. 428:4
Infâme: écrasez l'i. 442:23
Infamous: rich, quiet, and i. 262:13
Infancy: initiate her very i. 121:4
    nations . . . have their i. 64:20
    of shadow-peopled i. 393:13
Infant: i. crying in the night 418:8
    i., mewling and puking 345:11
    i.s question in such wise 331:19
    more than the i. that is born tonight 378:2
    should be on every i.'s tongue! 95:17
    to a little i . . . one is as painful as the other
        18:23
Infected: i. that th' i. spy 313:21
Inferiority: always conscious of an i. 222:22
    they'll say he has an i. complex 336:15
Infidel: cross . . . i.s adore 315:16
    Jews, Turks, I.s, and Heretics 319:15
    worse than an i. 56:44
Infidelity: accused him of i. 59:4
    indifference . . . half i. 83:2
Infini: i. me tourmente 290:10
Infinite: appear to man as it is, i. 63:23
    possession is I., and himself i. 63:26
    there is an I. in him 100:12
Infinities: numberless i. of souls 145:15
Infinitive: when I split an i. 106:10
Infinitude: give both the i.s their due 74:31
    our destiny . . . is with i. 465:22
Infinitum: and so proceed *ad i.* 410:16
Infinity: hold I. in the palm of your hand 60:8
    shares the nature of i. 461:9
Infirmities: bear the i. of the weak 54:49
    friend should bear his friend's i. 360:31
    thine often i. 56:45
Infirmity: last i. of noble mind 277:9
Inflammation: i. of his weekly bills 91:18
Influence: enforced obedience of planetary i. 361:34
    servile to all the skyey i.s 368:18
Influenza: call it i. if you like 31:16
Information: I only ask for i. 137:17
    know where we can find i. 222:15
Infortune: worst kind of i. is this 108:25
Infusion: i. of a China plant 2:6
Ingratitude: hate i. more in a man 383:29
    kind of i. 248:13
    not so unkind as man's i. 345:12
Ingres: I.'s the modern man that paints 74:10
Ingress: our i. into the world 257:16
Inhabitant: only i.s of the field 82:17
Inherit: to-night it doth i. 11:17
Inheritance: ruinous i. 172:2
Inhibition: cultivate a few i.s 257:27
Inhumanity: essence of i. 387:27
    man's i. to man 85:2
Iniquities: If thou, Lord, shouldest mark i. 41:6

reward us after our i. 319:8
Iniquity: that grey i. 354:18
    ye have reaped i. 47:8
Injured: hate the man one has i. 414:5
    know that he hath i. you 162:20
Injuries: adding insult to i. 286:15
Injury: i. is much sooner forgotten 109:5
    if on bad, an i. 388:25
Injustice: conscience with i. is corrupted 358:2
    fear of suffering i. 248:4
    i. . . . sometimes of service to the public 227:13
    threatened with a great i. 99:8
Ink: all the sea were i. 5:20
    every drop of i. in my pen 445:7
    he hath not drunk i. 363:28
Ink-horn: sage left nothing in his i. 105:10
Inkstand: he had a mighty i. too 203:3
Inlet: chief i.s of Soul 63:5
Inn: and go to i.s to dine 110:16
    die drinking in an i. 266:13
    do you rememember an i. 31:5
    earth his sober i. 97:27
    I count it not an i. 71:13
    in the worst i.'s worst room 315:3
    incognito of an i. 196:6
    life at best is but an i. 211:8
    no room for them in the i. 51:44
    so much happiness is produced . . . by a good i.
        222:18
    take mine ease at mine i. 354:33
    that dark i., the grave! 340:6
    warmest welcome, at an i. 395:3
    when you have lost your i.s 31:9
    'You cannot miss that i.' 331:13
Inner: his Spirit in the i. man 56:15
Innisfree: go to I. 471:6
Innocence: ceremony of i. is drowned 471:20
    dallies with the i. of love 383:12
    i. for i. 384:12
    i. is closing up his eyes 148:22
    i. thy sister dear 268:19
    silence often of pure i. 384:15
Innocence: mon i. enfin commence à me peser
    324:24
Innocent: i. of the blood of this just person 51:24
    one i. suffer 59:31
    rich shall not be i. 43:3
Innovate: to i. is not to reform 82:33
Innovator: time is the greatest i. 20:8
Inops: magnas inter opes i. 209:3
Inquest: greatest i. of the nation 81:26
    they come together like the coroner's i. 120:21
Inquiry: world is . . . school of i. 285:22
Inquisition: if I left them . . . to these I. dogs
    422:27
Insania: auditis an me ludit amabilis I.? 208:27
Insaniae: i. proxima est 3:33
Insanity: close to i. 3:33
Inscription: in lapidary i.s 222:16
Insect: Egyptians worshipped an i. 143:34
    loud and troublesome *i.* 82:18
    so impotent and grovelling an i. as I 410:26
Insensibility: preserved from a state of such i. 17:10
    stark i. 220:11
Insensible: it is i. then 355:2
Inside: those i. equally desperate to get out
    285:20

Insight: moment's i. worth a life's experience 204:3

Insincerity: great enemy . . . is i. 301:3

Insisture: i., course, proportion, season 381:35

Insolence: flown with i. and wine 278:16
she once used me with that i. 120:22
wretch who supports with i. 219:16

Inspiration: find no more i. in her 388:19
genius is one per cent i. 154:8

Instant: be i. in season 57:6

Instinct: all healthy i. for it 88:12
i. for being unhappy 336:4
true to your animal i.s 249:21
what we believe upon i. 66:10

Institute: gas was on in the I. 32:22

Institution: i. is the . . . shadow of one man 159:6
it's an i. 211:16
neither for nor against i.s 453:14

Instruction: I will better the i. 369:34
no i. book came with it 170:26
read . . . for the purpose of i. 165:22

Instrument: he made an i. to know 87:23
make i.s to plague us 363:11
players on i.s followed after 39:17
tune the i. here at the door 145:27

Insularum: paene i., Sirmio 103:15

Insult: adding i. to injuries 286:15
sooner forgotten than an i. 109:5

Insurrection: i. is an art 432:13

nature of an i. 359:27

Integer: i. vitae scelerisque purus 208:12

Integrity: i. was not enough 15:2

Intellect: furnish you with argument and i.s 182:27
i. is always fooled by the heart 248:7
i. is invisible 339:2
man . . . with his god-like i. 132:7
march of i. 401:26
put on i. 61:7
strengthening one's i. 234:15

Intellectual: being i., was amongst the noblest of
mankind 96:14
fear is an i. thing 61:3
full of pain, this i. being 278:34
i. is someone whose mind watches itself 98:9
'I.' suggests straight away 14:26
lords of ladies i. 90:33
North-west passage to the i. world 405:27

Intelligence: arresting the human i. 250:10
military i. is a contradiction 269:10
more i. one has 305:3
nightly gulls him with i. 386:13
we are the i.s 145:4

Intelligent: is there i. life on earth? 184:1
on the whole we are not i. 178:7

Intelligible: best to aim at being i. 205:12

Intensity: full of passionate i. 471:20

Intent: forget not the tried i. 468:9
his first avowed i. 80:35
i.s wicked or charitable 348:29
my i.s are savage-wild 380:7

Intercourse: dreary i. of daily life 462:23
sexual i. began in nineteen sixty-three 247:19

Interdependence: new electronic i. 264:2

Interea: nunc tamen i. 104:6

Interest: common i. always will prevail 149:26
I du believe in i. 258:25
natural i. of money 262:32

Interfere: dying religion always i.s more 111:10

Interfolds: ev'n the leaden i. are bright 169:6

Intérieur: shouting: 'Vive l'I.!' 342:22

Interim: i. is like a phantasma 359:27

Intermission: I did laugh sans i. 345:5

Interpretation: i. is a free walk on firm ground 338:19

Interval: enjoy the i. 337:13
fill the i. between dinner and supper 222:4
full of lucid i.s 105:17
lucid i.s and happy pauses 20:39
make a lucid i. 150:28

Interview: strange and fatal i. 144:23

Intestine: product of the smaller i.s 99:18

Intoxication: best of life is but i. 91:13

Intrigue: i. of a Greek of the lower empire 144:3

Introduced: had not been i. 176:9

Introduction: buy back my i. to you 269:7

Introspection: how much i. there is going on 28:28

Intrude: I hope I don't i. 311:4

Invariable: double glass o' the i. 141:2

Invasion: waiting for the long-promised i. 112:25

Invented: fond thing vainly i. 320:8

Invention: all one's i.s are true 165:21
beggars i. 126:24
brightest heaven of i. 356:19
my own i. 102:17
sought out many i.s 43:33
whoring with their own i.s 40:14

Inventor: God bless the i. of sleep 105:21

Investment: no finer i. for any community 113:7

Invideo: non equidem i. 441:11

Invisible: atheist . . . no i. means of support 167:24
fingers . . . are . . . often i. to him 28:26
intellect is i. 339:2
throne of the I. 90:23
till he becomes i. 2:18

Invitation: her mien carries much more i. 404:9

Invite: i. with gilded edges 15:14

Involuntary: it was i. 236:2

Inwards: he looked i. 151:33

Iope: white I., blithe Helen 97:31

Ipse: i. dixit 114:14

Ipswich: twins of learning . . . I. and Oxford 359:5

Ira: ça i. 9:13
i. furor brevis est 207:17

Ire: where slept thine i.? 230:25

Ireland: called I. for short 226:29
I'll not forget old I. 60:3
I. gives England her soldiers 272:16
I. is the old sow 226:18
problem with I. 253:19
rhymed to death as . . . in I. 397:1
romantic I.'s dead and gone 471:25

Iren: if gold ruste, what shall i. do? 107:26

Irish: I. . . . . have a psychosis 29:22

Iron: behind the 'i. curtain' at last! 400:17
blood and i. 59:25
heat me these i.s hot 361:20
his legs of i. 46:40
hold out mine i 356:27
i. curtain has descended 113:10
i. curtain would at once descend 179:11
i. has entered his soul 255:19
i. sharpeneth i. 42:48
man that meddles with cold i. 87:15
rod of i. 37:20, 58:8

whim of i. 200:1
Ironies: Life's Little I. 193:20
Irony: clap an extinguisher on your i. 245:20
Irradiation: intense i. of a mind 391:18
Irregular: Baker Street i.s 148:5
   choose the i. 439:1
Irresponsible: better to be i. and right 113:12
Iser: of I., rolling rapidly 97:6
Ishmael: call me I. 271:16
Island: August for . . . their favourite i.s 14:1
   i. is almost made of coal 33:5
   it's a snug little i. 136:13
   look, stranger, at this i. now 14:18
   no man is an i. 146:20
   our i. home 420:10
   round many western i.s 233:2
   some secreted i. 465:29
   we shall defend our i. 112:20
   Zuleika, on a desert i. 29:13
Island-story: not once or twice in our rough i.
   421:22
Isle: beside a pumice i. in Baiae's bay 392:7
   frights the i. from her propriety 374:21
   i. is full of noises 381:8
   Kelly from the I. of Man 290:5
   many a green i. needs must be 391:23
   matted rushy i.s 11:34
   Men of the Emerald I. 148:23
   this sceptered i. 376:17
   throned on her hundred i.s! 90:6
   touch the Happy I.s 424:10
   touched on this same i. 73:33
Islington: fields from I. to Marylebone 61:2
Isn't: as it i., it ain't 101:32
Isolation: our splendid i. 183:19
Israel: again in his border see I. set 74:33
   all I. scattered upon the hills 36:21
   glory is departed from I. 35:42
   I arose a mother in I. 35:24
   no, not in I. 49:29
   outcasts of I. 41:16
   smote the king of I. 36:22
   there is a prophet in I. 36:26
   to your tents, O I. 36:13
Israelite: who seem like I.s to be 269:4
Issue: but to fine i.s 368:3
   personal i. of adipose tissue 123:12
It: it's just I. 241:33
   lift not thy hands to I. 164:21
Italian: I speak . . . I. to women 107:2
   writ in very choice I. 351:12
Italy: graved inside of it, 'I.' 74:4
   in I. . . . they had warfare 449:10
   I. is a geographical expression 272:28
   I. a paradise for horses 86:20
   made I. from designs by Michael Angelo 434:4
   man who has not been in I. 222:22
   no looking at a building here after seeing I. 83:11
   Paradise of exiles, I.! 391:14
   some jay of I. 347:10
Itch: insatiate i. of scribbling 176:5
   rubbing the poor i. of your opinion 346:20
Itchez: when Ah i., Ah scratchez 292:14
Iter: per i. tenebricosum 103:10
Iteration: prone to an i. of nuptials 121:1
   thou hast damnable i. 353:21
Iustum: i. et tenacem propositi virum 208:25

Iuvenes: i. dum sumus 9:10
Ivory: bit (two inches wide) of i. 17:19
   dreams of the i. gate 70:20
   other made of gleaming white i. 441:1
   with a cargo of i. 269:24
Ivy: just like the i. I'll cling to you 274:11
   pluck an i. branch for me 331:10
Ivy-tod: when the i. is heavy with snow 117:12

J

Jabberwock: beware the J. 101:25
Jack: banish plump J. 354:19
   'Damn you J. – I'm all right!' 64:23
   he calls the knaves, J.s 138:3
   house that Jack built 298:6
   J. fell down 296:29
   J. shall have Jill 372:7
   J. Sprat could eat no fat 296:30
   keep watch for the life of poor J.! 136:9
   lamented J.! 118:12
   little J. Horner 297:3
   poor J., farewell 355:7
   since every J. became a gentleman 377:28
   there was gorging J. 425:26
Jack-knife: just a j. has Macheath 67:18
Jackdaw: j. sat in the Cardinal's chair 24:8
Jacket: day has put on his j. 203:23
   wrap me up in my tarpaulin j. 454:14
Jackson: J. standing like a stone wall 28:24
Jacky: J. shall have a new master 297:29
Jacob: J. saw that there was corn 34:32
   Lord will have mercy on J. 74:33
Jade: arrant j. on a journey 182:5
   'Go spin, you j., go spin!' 341:8
   let the galled j. wince 351:11
   pampered j.s of Asia 267:20, 355:28
Jail: gits you in j. soon or late 300:1
   man in a j. has more room 221:2
Jailor: what j. so inexorable 195:5
Jam: j. to-morrow and j. yesterday 102:10
James: J. J., Morrison Morrison 274:14
   my name is Truthful J. 194:27
   work of Henry J. . . . divisible . . . three reigns 189:1
James I, King of England 198:5
Jamshy'd: Courts where J. gloried and drank deep
   164:6
Jane: I'd call 'em all J. 450:10
   J., J., tall as a crane 397:12
   John Thomas marryin' Lady J. 249:13
Japanese: reconcile J. action with prudence 113:3
Jardin: il faut cultiver notre j. 442:13
Jaw: j.s that bite 101:25
   oped his ponderous and marble j.s 348:30
Jaw-jaw: j. is always better than war-war 113:13
   j. is better than war-war 264:7
Jay: some j. of Italy 347:10
Jazz: J. Age 165:6
Je-ne-sais-quoi: 'j.' young man! 178:1
Jealous: j. for they are j. 375:11
   man is j. 188:4
   one not easily j. 375:26
Jealousy: ear of j. heareth all things 47:35
   j. a human face 62:23
   j. is cruel as the grave 44:27

j.; it is the green-eyed monster 374:32
so full of artless j. is guilt 352:3
Jeanie: J. with the light brown hair 168:4
Jeeves: J. coughed one soft, low, gentle cough
    459:13
    J. shimmered out 459:15
Jefferson: when Thomas J. dined alone 235:20
Jehovah: of Jesus and J. thou art still 60:28
Jehu: like the driving of J. 36:28
Jellies: j. soother than the creamy curd 230:18
Jelly: meaty j. . . . is mellering to the organ 140:9
    out, vile j. 362:30
Jellyby: Mrs J. was looking far away 136:29
Jem: J. is joky for Jacob 226:8
Jenny: J. kissed me 212:16
Jericho: tarry at J. 36:5
Jerusalem: built in J.'s wall 61:4
    four great walls in the New J. 72:19
    holy city, new J. 58:32
    if I forget thee, O J. 41:10
    J. the golden 292:30
    J. thy sister calls! 61:5
    O ye daughters of J. 44:17
    there J.'s pillars stood 61:2
    was J. builded here 61:9
Jeshurun: J. waxed fat 35:18
Jessamine: all night has the casement j. stirred
    420:34
Jesse: rod out of the stem of J. 45:9
Jesses: j. were my dear heart-strings 374:33
Jest: fellow of infinite j. 352:25
    good j. for ever 353:36
    he had his j. 149:22
    his whole wit in a j. 27:17
    j. with earnest 20:21
    j.'s prosperity lies in the ear 364:5
    life is a j. 174:24
    most bitter is a scornful j. 218:26
    rueful j. 126:13
    that's no j. 9:2
    to use myself in j. 146:6
Jester: fool and j. 356:18
Jesu: J., by a nobler deed 106:4
    thy name, O J., be for ever blest 211:2
Jesus: foundation is J. Christ her Lord 408:3
    gentle J., meek and mild 450:19
    how sweet the name of J. sounds 294:11
    J., lover of my soul 450:21
    J. calls us 4:5
    J. Christ her little Child 4:6
    J. from the Ground suspires 163:24
    J. loves me – this I know 446:26
    J. loves you more than you will know 397:9
    J. wept 53:24
    more popular than J. Christ 253:4
    of J. and Jehovah thou art still 60:28
    power of J.' name! 308:2
    stand up for J.! 152:5
    there is one, even Christ J. 168:12
    thing J. really would've liked 336:16
    this J. will not do 60:26
    when J. came to Birmingham 409:4
    whether you think J. was God 387:15
Jeunesse: si j. savait 159:30
Jew: cross . . . which J.s might kiss 315:16
    difficult for a J. to be converted 197:8
    every country has the J.s that it deserves 169:1

hath not a J. eyes? 369:32
I am a J. else 354:9
I decide who is a J. 259:25
I thank thee, J. 370:15
J.s have a psychosis 29:22
J.s, Turks, Infidels and Heretics 319:15
let Apella the J. believe that 209:15
then they came for the J.s 294:17
till the conversion of the J.s 269:1
to choose the J. 160:9
Jewel: boys and girls . . . were moving j.s 431:16
    capital bosom to hang j.s upon 138:16
    children . . . are my j.s 86:19
    give my j.s for a set of beads 377:4
    immediate j. of their souls 374:31
    j. . . . and the rest of that nauseous cant 120:33
    j. in a ten-times-barred-up chest 376:8
    j. of gold in a swine's snout 42:1
    j. of the just 438:17
    j.s five-words long 421:36
    precious j. in his head 344:25
Jewellery: rattle your j. 253:3
Jewish: j. man with parents alive 332:8
    not really a Jew; just J. 273:29
    total solution of the J. question 179:13
Jigsaw: piece in a j. puzzle 266:6
Jill: Jack and J. 296:29
Jim: moisten poor J.'s lips once more 161:12
    poor J. Jay 134:19
    was a boy whose name was J. 30:8
Jinete: j. se acercaba 173:3
Jingle: J. worn't a doin' something 141:21
Jingo: by J., if we do 212:9
    by the living j. 182:30
Jinks: forgotten pastime of high j. 340:32
Joan: greasy J. doth keel the pot 364:7
Job: as poor as J. 355:15
    being a husband is a whole-time j. 31:19
    Lord blessed the latter end of J. 37:17
    patience of J. 57:27
    we will finish the j. 113:1
Jobiska: Aunt J.'s Runcible Cat 251:6
Jog: might j. on with 246:19
Johannes: absolute J. fac totum 188:3
John: J. Thomas marryin' Lady Jane 249:13
    O, no J.! 8:6
    old J. of Gaunt 376:7
    to J. I owed great obligation 320:19
    whose name was J. 52:50
John Anderson: J., my jo 84:31
John Barleycorn: inspiring bold J. 85:20
    J. should die 84:32
John Bull: greatest of all is J. 92:33
Johnny: do not despair for J. Head-in-Air 322:1
    J.'s so long at the fair 297:12
    little J. Green 296:13
    little J. Head-in-Air 203:4
Johnson, Dr 109:16, 242:7, 305:1
    Dr J. condemns whatever he disapproves 83:13
    Dr J.'s morality 195:7
    Dr J.'s sayings 307:5
    great Cham of literature, Samuel J. 400:14
    J. is dead 191:7
    no arguing with J. 182:39
    you are a philosopher, Dr J. 154:14
Johnsonese: sort of broken J. 262:24
Joined: God hath j. together 50:34

Joint: every j. and motive of her body 382:19
   time is out of j. 349:19
Joint-labourer: make the night j. with the day
   347:23
Joke: aim of a j. 301:2
   get a j. well into a Scotch understanding 399:24
   hackneyed j.s from Miller 92:24
   laughed . . . at all his j.s 181:6
   life is a j. 177:22
   my little j.s on Thee 170:1
   rich man's j. is always funny 70:12
Joles: catch our heedless j. 205:5
Jollity: all now was turned to j. 280:42
   jest and youthful j. 276:19
Jolly: some credit in being j. 138:23
Jonah: belly j. hunting the polly joans 226:13
   lot fell upon J. 47:16
Jonathan: Saul and J. were lovely 36:1
   we must consult Brother J. 447:1
Joneses: Keeping Up With the J. 287:17
Jonson: if J.'s learnèd sock be on 276:32
   O rare Ben J. 225:32
Jordan: do not take a bath in J. 397:16
   I looked over J. 8:18
   nor J.'s stream 447:18
Joseph: new king . . . which knew not J. 34:39
Josephine: not tonight, J. 130:13
Joss-stick: permeated with the odour of j.s 66:18
Jostling: not done by j. in the street 60:29
Jot: one j. of former love retain 148:21
Jour: j. de gloire est arrivé 332:9
   j. n'est pas plus pur 325:3
   tous les j.s, à tous points de vue 123:6
Journalism: but why j.? 21:23
   j. what will be grasped at once 121:13
   j. largely consists in saying 111:6
Journalist: bribe . . . the British j. 460:4
   j.s . . . have nothing to say 242:15
   j.s say a thing that they know isn't true 31:20
Journée: plus perdue de toutes les j.s 106:2
Journey: dreariest and the longest j. go 390:25
   here is my j.'s end 375:24
   is your j. really necessary? 3:4
   j. into a far country 52:25
   j.s end in lovers meeting 383:2
   life's j. just begun 126:4
   love to begin a j. on Sundays 411:15
   or he is in a j. 36:16
   our j. has advanced 142:4
   pleasantest things . . . going a j. 196:3
   traveller's j. is done 61:18
   when the j.'s over 210:8
   'Will the day's j. take the whole long day?' 331:12
   wondering j. from the East 289:19
   worst time of the year for a j. 156:18
Journeymen: some of nature's j. 351:2
Jove: ask me no more where J. bestows 98:29
   at love's perjuries . . . J. laughs 379:13
   flatter J. for's power to thunder 346:28
Joy: all my j.s to this are folly 86:4
   all our j.s are but fantastical 144:22
   all the sons of God shouted for j. 37:11
   asks, if this be j. 181:11
   bed of crimson j. 62:3
   before, a j. proposed 387:5
   formed of j. and mirth 60:30
   former j.s recurring ever 181:24

homely j.s and destiny obscure 186:5
j. cometh in the morning 38:8
j. is my name 62:14
j. shall be in heaven 52:24
j. was never sure 412:19
J., whose hand is ever at his lips 231:29
j.'s soul lies in the doing 381:34
lasting j.s the man attend 454:11
must not express great j. or sorrow 167:15
not a j. the world can give 93:26
perfect herald of j. 372:32
shall reap in j. 40:35
snatch a fearful j. 187:5
such present j.s therein I find 153:1
surprised by j. 463:3
thing of beauty is a j. 230:6
thy j. and crown eternally 284:22
unfriendly to society's chief j.s 124:30
vain, deluding j.s 275:36
who bends to himself a J. 60:31
wild j.s of living! 78:14
writhed not at passed J. 233:15
Joyicity: on akkant of his j. 226:15
Jubilee: first day of our j. is death 71:3
   we bring the J.! 467:30
Jubilo: year of J.! 467:29
Jubjub: beware the J. bird 101:25
Judaeus: credat J. Apella 209:15
Judas: J. to a tittle 74:23
Juden: Jedes Land hat die J. 169:1
Judge: fool with j.s 124:31
   God is a righteous J. 37:24
   God is the j. 39:20
   hungry j.s soon the sentence sign 315:21
   I'll be j., I'll be jury 100:31
   indifferent j. between the high and low 396:14
   j. not according to the appearance 53:16
   j. not, that ye be not judged 49:19
   j. of all the earth 34:23
   j. you as you are 368:12
   j.s all ranged 174:17
   j.s of fact 322:2
   justice or injustice . . . decided by the j. 223:21
   now I am a J. 178:19
   O wise young j. 370:11
   out of thine own mouth will I j. thee 52:39
   sober as a j. 162:18
   sole j. of truth 314:2
   ye that be j.s of the earth 47:34
Judgement: account thereof in the day of j. 50:7
   Daniel come to j. 370:11
   dice of j. 324:13
   diff'ring j.s serve 125:4
   don't wait for the Last J. 98:5
   except by the legal j. of his equals 264:20
   God's great J. Seat 238:11
   green in j. 343:26
   He, which is the top of j. 368:12
   I expect a j., Shortly 136:19
   if some of my j.s were wrong 295:9
   in the day of j. 319:5
   j. falls on a man 342:3
   j. of the great whore 58:27
   Last J.'s fire must cure this place 73:24
   leaves of the J. Book 415:7
   no one complains of his j. 248:6
   nor is the people's j. always true 149:27

O. j.! thou art fled 360:17
representative owes you . . . but his j. 81:12
reserve thy j. 348:22
'tis with our j.s as our watches 313:2
vulgarize the day of j. 218:11
wait till j. break 141:31
waits upon the j. 351:29
would not give his j. rashly 2:8
Judice: adhuc sub j. lis est 207:1
   j. nemo nocens absolvitur 228:8
Judicium: per legale j. parium suorum 264:20
Jug: j., j., j., j., tereu 260:9
   'J. j.' to dirty ears 157:2
   little brown j. 7:21
Juggler: threadbare j. 346:19
Juliet: J. is the sun 379:8
Julius: ere the mightiest J. fell 347:24
July: English winter – ending in J. 92:12
Jumblies: lands where the J. live 250:22
June: as the cuckoo is in J. 354:30
   ice in J. 92:25
   in the leafy month of J. 117:9
   newly sprung in J. 85:4
   when J. is past 98:29
Jungle: cutting through the j. 255:3
   down in the j. 109:3
   Law of the J. 239:29
   Mumbo-Jumbo is dead in the j. 255:4
   never get out of the j. that way 273:23
   through the J. very softly 240:25
Junior: smart J.s . . . full of Smart Juniosity 450:7
Juniper: sat under a j. tree 155:25
Junket: constructing a Gothic arch out of j. 408:4
Juno: J. when she walks 225:14
Jupiter: dry grass bow to J. 430:5
   J. est quodcumque vides 259:16
   whatever you see . . . that is J. 259:16
   whom J. has destined to be cabbage-planters
     324:14
Jurisprudence: gladsome light of j. 116:8
Jury: j., passing on the prisoner's life 368:7
Jurymen: wretches hang that j. may dine 315:21
Just: be j., and fear not 358:25
   j. are the ways of God 281:21
   j. shall live by faith 54:14
   nine j. persons 52:24
   path of the j. 41:25
   rain on the j. and on the unjust 49:6
   rain it raineth on the j. 65:22
   spirits of j. men 57:16
   thou art indeed j. 206:17
Juster: not, Celia, that I j. am 341:19
Justice: as infinite a j. too 74:31
   as thou urgest j. 370:13
   believing in the j. of our cause 190:4
   Chief J. was rich, quiet, and infamous 262:13
   handy-dandy, which is the j. 362:42
   I have loved j. 188:6
   j., but do you want to pay for it 67:1
   j., in fair round belly 345:11
   j. is such a fine thing 253:23
   j. or injustice of the cause 223:21
   j. should not only be done 200:26
   'J.' was done 193:24
   let j. be done 162:10
   love of j. in most men 248:4
   no sense of j. 339:4

place of j. 20:38
poetic j., with her lifted scale 311:8
revenge is a kind of wild j. 19:1
sad-eyed j. 356:24
see how yond j. rails 362:42
temper j. with mercy 280:38
this even-handed j. 365:6
though j. be thy plea 370:9
your j. would freeze beer! 273:21
Justification: carry its j. in every line 121:23
Justify: j. God's ways to man 210:30
   j. the ways of God 278:2
Justitia: fiat j. 162:10
Jutty: no j., frieze, buttress 365:4
Juvescence: in the j. of the year 156:11
Juxtaposition: J., in short, and what is j.? 115:7

K

Kaiser: Kibosh on the K. 157:29
Kalendas: ad k. Graecas soluturos 95:5
Kanga: K. and Baby Roo 274:32
Kangaroo: Duck and the K. 250:20
Kansas: K. had better stop raising corn 251:12
Karshish: K., the picker-up of learning's crumbs
   74:17
Kaspar: old K.'s work was done 401:7
Kate: change K. into Nan 60:28
   none of us cared for K. 381:1
Keats, John 92:7
   what porridge had John K.? 77:3
   who killed John K.? 93:12
Keck: seven k.s of foost-rate lager beer 252:16
Keel: k. ploughs air 106:13
   no k. has ever ploughed that path before 390:26
Keep: still k. something to yoursel 84:16
   you k. out of this 330:25
Keeper: am I my brother's k.? 34:7
   k. is only a poacher turned outside in 237:22
   k. stands up to keep the goal 210:20
   Lord is thy k. 40:32
Keeping: K. Up With the Joneses 287:17
Keith: O K. of Ravelston 144:4
Kelly: has anybody here seen K.? 290:5
Kempenfelt: when K. went down 125:35
Ken: as far as angel's k. 278:4
Kendal: misbegotten k.s in K. Green 354:12
Kennedy: kind of nation . . . President K. died for
   218:21
Kensal Green: go to Paradise by way of K. 110:14
Kent: everybody knows K. 140:23
   knocked 'em in the Old K. Road 111:15
Kentucky: old K. home far away 168:5
   sun shines bright in the old K. home 168:6
Kept: nor k. it without wishing 70:1
Kettle: how agree the k. and the earthen pot 48:11
   language is a cracked k. 165:23
Kew: go down to K. in lilac-time 296:3
   his Highness' dog at K. 315:8
Key: all her shining k.s 193:21
   all k.s must resign 134:16
   fingers wandered idly over the noisy k.s 321:2
   he pattered with his k.s at a great rate 94:2
   his k.s were rusty 93:13
   k. is Russian national interest 112:17

think the K. sees thee still 199:6
till the K. enjoys his own again 304:19
till those we now call k.s 310:4
to be k. stands not 364:17
to reverence the K. 416:31
under which k., Bezonian? 356:17
walk with k.s 239:13
wash the balm from an anointed k. 376:27
wha the deil hae we got for a k. 130:8
what have k.s that privates have not 357:12
what must the k. do now? 377:4
whilst thus I sing, I am a K. 114:6
with half the zeal I served my k. 358:26
worm that hath eat of a k. 351:40
worse k. never left a realm undone! 93:30
Kingdom: act of order to a peopled k. 356:24
advantage on the k. of the shore 386:3
all the k.s of the world 52:5
best walls of this k. 123:8
deny the existence of an unseen k. 87:32
enter into the k. of heaven 50:28
in this k. by the sea 310:16
it mus' be now de k. coming 467:29
k. for it was too small 355:6
k. of God is within you 52:35
k. of heaven 48:41
k. of heaven suffereth violence 50:2
k.s are clay 343:16
k.s are less by three 413:4
kissed away k.s 343:37
like to a little k. suffers then 359:27
my large k. for a little grave 377:4
my mind to me a k. is 153:1
rich man to enter into the k. of God 50:38
seek ye first the k. of God 49:17
such is the k. of heaven 51:39
thy k. is divided 47:5
trample a k. down 301:16
Kingfisher: as k.s catch fire 205:20
Kingsley, Charles 293:25
Kinsmen: my k. according to the flesh 54:32
Kirkconnel: on fair K. lea! 22:21
Kirtle: Janet has kilted her green k. 23:14
Kiss: ae fond k. 83:23
full kingdom of that final k. 128:18
I dare not ask a k. 200:16
I saw you take his k.! 305:22
if you want to k. me 165:7
k. and part 148:20
k. her until she be wearied out 394:13
k. long as my exile 346:32
k. me, and be quiet 285:1
k. me as if you entered gay 75:7
k. me as if you made believe 75:6
k. me, Hardy 293:7
k. me, Kate 380:19
k. of the sun for pardon 189:8
k. till the cow come home 28:4
k. without a moustache 104:10
last lamenting k. 144:28
leave a k. but in the cup 225:20
make me immortal with a k.! 266:22
must not k. and tell 120:7
none k. each other but the men 405:12
nothing wrong in a connubial k. 91:16
part at last without a k. 288:13
swear to never k. the girls 74:26

though they did not k. 94:4
Kissed: air that lately k. thee 200:17
I k. thee ere I killed thee 376:1
k. her once by the pigsty 426:21
Kisses: aëreal k. of shapes that haunt 393:4
a-wastin' Christian k. 240:3
bachelor's fare; bread . . . and k. 411:10
but my k. bring again 368:26
dear as remembered k. after death 422:5
give me a thousand k. 103:12
I fear thy k. 394:5
I understand thy k. 354:27
if you have forgotten my k. 412:31
k. of his mouth 44:16
let thy love and k. rain 391:13
played at cards for k. 260:8
reaps a thousand k. there 124:2
with k. four 231:11
Kissing: die with k. of my lord 267:19
k. don't last 272:24
k. your hand 257:26
when the k. had to stop 79:3
Kit-bag: pack up your troubles in your old k. 13:8
Kitchen: get out of the k. 433:1
Kite: fatted all the region k.s 350:11
Kitten: ez shoshubble ez a baskit er k.s 194:13
I had rather be a k. 354:24
k.s are gone to St Paul's 298:12
Klug: bin so k. als wie zuvor 179:16
Knave: all men should be k.s 328:12
called them untaught k.s 353:29
he's an arrant k. 349:14
how absolute the k. is! 352:24
K. of Hearts 297:24
k.s, thieves and treachers 361:34
little better than false k.s 373:16
rascally yea-forsooth k. 355:14
thank God you are rid of a k. 373:6
they are lying k.s 373:24
three misbegotten k.s 354:12
to feed the titled k. 85:30
world is . . . fools and k.s 79:23
Knee: better to die . . . than to live on your k.s 214:1
bury my heart at Wounded K. 31:15
climb upon my k. 70:9
down on your k.s 345:28
gardener's work is done upon his k.s 239:7
her k.s and elbows are only glued together 61:10
kirtle a little aboon her k. 23:14
k.s and tresses folded 272:2
now they are all on their k.s 193:7
upon what were once k.s 130:6
Kneel: not one k.s to another 453:27
Knell: all-softening, overpowering k. 91:39
k. that summons thee to heaven or to hell 365:20
strikes like a rising k.! 89:21
their k. is rung 119:16
thy k. who shall survive? 192:19
Knew: we all k. you had it in you 304:11
Knicker: their k.s are made of crêpe-de-chine 264:11
Knife: cannibal uses a k. and fork 251:16
cheese with a pocket k. 110:7
cut off their tails with a carving k. 298:8
death ending all with a k. 75:25
k. is lost in it 391:19
strike with our spirit's k. 390:4
'War even to the k.!' 89:14

war to the k. 303:8
wind's like a whetted k. 270:4
Knife-grinder: needy k.! whither are you going?
98:11
Knight: chance brought out a noble k. 417:16
death of the most noblest k.s of the world 265:20
false k. upon the road 22:16
gentle k. was pricking on the plain 402:25
goodliest fellowship of famous k.s 417:11
impossible to say who was top k. 342:17
k. came riding by 288:21
k. errant who turns mad 105:1
k. in arms 282:13
k. of ghosts and shadows 5:19
K. of the Sad Countenance 104:20
k. without fear 27:2
K.'s bones are dust 117:33
maiden k. 423:16
many a k. and many a squire 24:8
never matched of earthly k.s hand 265:23
never was k. like the young Lochinvar 340:12
sorrier for my good k.'s loss 265:18
that was your k. 307:2
there came a k. to be their wooer 22:6
there lies a new-slain k. 23:19
verray parfit gentil k. 107:10
Knock: as yet but k. 145:22
don't k. it 4:16
exceed in interest a k. at the door 245:30
k., and it shall be opened unto you 49:22
k. as you please 312:13
should k. him down first 222:20
stand at the door, and k. 58:11
Knocker: tie up the k. 312:14
Knot: certain k. of peace 396:14
wreathe iron pokers into true-love k.s 118:8
Knotted: sat and k. all the while 341:22
Know: all this the world well k.s 387:5
don't k. better as they grow older 335:16
dost thou k. who made thee? 62:15
God alone k.s 242:5
I am he that aspired to k. 76:15
I do not believe . . . I k. 227:6
I k. not what to call you 157:24
I k. what I like 29:18
I k. what I mean to do 73:14
I k. who I am 104:14
It's Been Good to K. Yuh 189:9
k. then thyself 314:1
k. thyself 9:4
like the ones I used to k. 32:10
love what he k.s 129:10
not to k. me 280:1
now I k. it 174:24
people don't k. what they want 268:2
saying you want to k. 138:12
tell me what you k. 159:18
they k. not what they do 52:45
to k. her was to love her 328:26
to k. is everlasting life 319:18
we k. in part 55:24
we k. what we are 352:6
what do I k.? 285:18
what you don't k. would make a great book
400:6
why need the other women k. so much? 72:21
ye k. on earth 231:25

you k. more than you think you do 403:18
Know-All: Ole man K. died las' year 194:17
Knowing: greater than their k. 240:26
Knowledge: all k. to be my province 21:7
close the five ports of k. 70:17
desire more love and k. of you 344:21
fear of the Lord is the beginning of k. 41:20
follow k. like a sinking star 424:6
he that hath k. 42:20
he that increaseth k. increaseth sorrow 43:16
I ask it for the k. of a lifetime 452:8
if it rained k. 223:5
k. comes, but wisdom lingers 419:35
k. is born in the market 115:15
k. is of two kinds 222:15
k. is transmitted from generation 63:24
k. itself is power 21:2
k. of nothing 141:25
k. puffeth up 55:9
k. which they cannot lose 300:4
night unto night sheweth k. 37:36
not according to k. 54:34
not k. but certainty 333:25
one who speaks without k. 59:11
our k. can only be finite 316:17
out-topping k. 11:30
science is organized k. 402:7
time of which we have no k. 28:23
woman's happiest k. 279:32
words without k. 37:9
Known: apart from the k. and the unknown 309:11
have ye not k.? 45:36
till I am k. 220:22
Knyf: smyler with the k. 108:3
Kopje-crest: his landmark is a k. 192:16
Kosciusko: as K. fell! 97:15
Kraft: K. durch Freude 254:10
Kremlin: turns to the K. mountaineer 266:3
Krug: Ich bin dein K. 327:20
Kruger: finished killing K. 238:6
Kunst: in der K. ist das Beste gut genug 180:6
Kurtz: Mistah K. - he dead 121:22
Kyd: sporting K. 225:22

L

Labdanum: stripes of l. 76:17
Labor: l. omnia vincit 441:23
Laborem: alterius spectare l. 259:21
Laboribus: quod unum est pro l. tantis 103:16
Labour: all things are full of l. 43:14
all ye that l. 50:4
bound as to the l.'s sound 464:2
continuous l. of your life 285:6
endless l. all along 224:1
had my l. for my travail 381:32
honest l. bears a lovely face 134:2
I'll l. night and day 81:2
in all l. there is profit 42:9
insupportable l. of doing nothing 404:10
l. and the wounds are vain 115:25
l. in vain 41:1, 56:9
l. of an age 277:28
l. of love 56:34
l. we delight in physics pain 366:2

learn to l. and to wait 257:6
light l. spread her wholesome store 180:19
little effect after much l. 17:19
man goeth . . . to his l. until the evening 40:13
many still must l. for the one! 90:26
no sin for a man to l. in his vocation 353:23
political leader for the L. Party 33:7
press down upon the brow of l. 79:19
rest from their l.s 58:24
ruined by Chinese cheap l. 194:26
that long day's l. lost 402:24
their incessant l.s see 268:18
this alone is worth all that l. 103:16
we l. soon, we l. late 85:30
what profit hath a man of all his l. 43:12
youth of l. 180:20
Laboured: I l. more abundantly 55:30
Labourer: l. is worthy of his hire 52:9
l.s are few 49:36
settest the weary l. free! 97:19
Labyrinth: dreamt I was in the l. 289:17
peopled l. of walls 391:24
Labyrinthine: still more l. buds the rose 78:29
Lace: Arsenic and Old L. 236:4
Greek, Sir . . . is like l. 223:9
Lächeln: stand er am Ende der L. 327:14
Lack: l. of many a thing I sought 385:24
Lacrimae: Hinc illae l. 424:27
sunt l. rerum 440:8
Lad: best l. in the world 267:26
cheer up my l.s 331:3
golden l.s and girls all must 347:15
I'll come to you, my l. 85:34
l. that's born to be king 65:20
l.s that thought there was no more 384:11
l.s that will die in their glory 210:17
many a lightfoot l. 210:29
thinking lays l.s underground 210:28
though your l.s are far away 167:12
Ladder: climbed the l. of success 451:2
Jacob's l. pitched between Heaven and Charing
Cross 427:19
l., if we will but tread 256:28
now that my l.'s gone 470:9
she climbed the dusty l. 429:5
unto the l. turns his back 359:26
wiv a l. and some glasses 26:10
Ladies: calls these over-offended l. 404:7
Good-night, l. 352:8
I am parshial to l. 13:11
if l. be but young and fair 345:7
in praise of l. dead 386:24
l., whose bright eyes 276:31
l. of Spain 7:14
lang may the l. stand 23:12
o'er l.' lips 378:30
rhyme themselves into l.' favours 357:24
several other old l. of both sexes 138:15
sportive l. leave their doors ajar 74:22
what would ye, l.? 166:7
worth any number of old l. 162:6
young l. spend their time 411:20
Ladle: go into my casting l. 214:17
Lady: ain't a l. living in the land 111:14
cheerio . . . that pulls a l. through 267:29
dance little l. 123:25
dying l., lean and pale 394:24

heard that l. sing at the noon 288:21
I met a l. in the meads 231:8
I will make a L. of my own 467:2
Iron L. of the Western World 425:29
l. doth protest too much 351:10
L. Jane was tall and slim 24:14
l. of a 'certain age' 92:1
l. of Christ's College 13:25
l. of my delight 272:31
l. sweet and kind 167:13
L. with a Lamp 257:9
L.'s not for Burning 170:20
l.'s not for turning 425:30
like a l. as thou art 354:28
longing to be a lazy l. 397:15
look to the l. 366:7
middle-aged maiden l. 326:2
my l. sweet, arise 347:6
old l. from Dubuque 330:24
Old L. of Threadneedle Street 178:26
see a fine l. upon a white horse 297:26
sighed for the love of a l. 178:21
there had been a l. in the case 91:37
they have belied a l. 373:24
when a l.'s in the case 174:22
Lady-smocks: l. all silver-white 364:6
Ladybird: l., l., fly away home 296:31
Ladyship: ice of her L.'s manners 318:7
saving her l.'s presence 105:6
Lafayette: L., we are here! 404:3
Lairdie: wee, wee German l. 130:8
Laissez: l. faire 183:20
Laissez-faire: well-tried principles of *l.* 236:12
Lait: l. tombe 244:18
Laity: conspiracies against the l. 387:31
Lake: by the Great L.s of North America 262:4
did its worst to vex the l. 77:4
rose up from . . . the l. 417:12
they rode till they came to a l. 265:12
Lalagen: dulce ridentem L. amabo 208:13
Lamb: as a l. to the slaughter 46:9
behold the bleeding L. of God 144:9
being flattered, is a l. 106:12
did he who made the lamb make thee? 62:5
God tempers the wind . . . to the shorn l. 405:14
holy L. of God 61:9
L., the frolic and the gentle 461:30
l.s could not forgive 139:3
like a l. . . . brought to the slaughter 46:28
lion lie down with the l. 249:15
little hills skipped like l. 40:22
little L., God bless thee! 62:16
little L., who made thee? 62:15
Mary had a little l. 190:7, 297:8
nothing, save one little ewe l. 36:6
pipe a song about a L.! 62:7
receive the L. of God 61:6
road that leads me to the L.! 125:22
shall gather the l.s with his arm 45:34
were as twinned l.s 384:12
while the young l.s bound 464:2
white in the blood of the L. 58:16
Lamb, Charles 195:14
Lambeth: doin' the L. walk 171:11
Lame: feet was I to the l. 37:7
Lamely: so l. and unfashionable 377:23
Lament: l. not the days that are gone 401:22

my l. is cries countless 206:4
Lamenting: he was left l. 97:12
Lammas: it fell about the L. tide 22:5
Lamp: dying l., a falling shower 390:2
 filled their l.s with everlasting oil 275:11
 golden l.s in a green night 268:13
 Lady with a L. 257:9
 l. burns low and dim 1:5
 l.s are going out all over Europe 188:13
 l.s shone o'er fair women 89:21
 life is not a series of gig l.s 460:18
 old l.s for new 9:23
 thy word is a l. 40:27
 unlit l. and the ungirt loin 79:1
 when the l. is shattered 391:21
Lamp-post: as a drunken man uses l.s 247:8
 asking a l. how it feels about dogs 191:17
Lampada: vitai l. tradunt 259:22
Lamprey: surfeit by eating of a l. 161:5
Lancaster: time-honoured L. 376:7
Lancelot: by the river sang Sir L. 419:13
 L. or Pelleas, or Pellenore 281:4
 Sir L. saw her visage 265:22
Lancer: six stalwart l.s shall carry me 454:14
Land: as I went to the holy l. 325:6
 clear the l. of evil 240:24
 eat the fat of the l. 34:35
 far away into the silent l. 331:6
 I went into a golden l. 433:14
 ill fares the l. 180:18
 into the l. of my dreams 237:11
 l. flowing with milk and honey 34:42
 l. laid waste 14:14
 l. of Hope and Glory 31:21
 l. of pure delight 447:17
 l. of the mountain 340:2
 l. to which yon ship must go 463:5
 l. was ours 170:5
 l. you used to plough 210:19
 marching to the Promised L. 25:5
 near to heaven by sea as by l. 176:8
 no l. beside 361:6
 one still strong man in a blatant l. 420:28
 ploughs and reploughs his ancestral l. 208:1
 pointed toward the l. 420:8
 saw a sad l. 302:14
 search the l. of living men 340:9
 splendid and an happy l. 181:12
 spy out the l. 35:8
 stranger in a strange l. 34:40
 there is a happy l. 472:12
 this dear, dear l. 376:17
 This L. is Your L. 189:10
 thro' the l. at eve we went 421:34
 to the l. of the leal 291:10
 westward, look, the l. is bright 115:26
 woman is a foreign l. 305:23
Land: Jedes L. hat die Juden 169:1
Land-breeze, l. shook the shrouds 125:34
Landmark, remove not the ancient l. 42:31
Land-rat: there be l.s and water-rats 369:12
Landscape: fades the glimmering l. 186:1
 if l.s were sold 406:23
 l. is a condition of the spirit 5:1
 when will the l. tire the view? 153:3
Landscape-painter: he is but a l. 420:7
Land-thieves: l. and water-thieves 369:12

Lane: in an English l. 74:2
 while there's a country l. 304:20
Langage: non de beau l. 283:15
Language: conveyed . . . in the best chosen l. 16:30
 how many people speak the same l. 202:3
 I don't think anything of that l. 139:17
 instructed in all l.s 139:6
 knowledge of the ancient l.s 68:18
 l. all nations understand 29:27
 l. charged with meaning 317:29
 l. is a cracked kettle 165:23
 l. is a dialect 449:9
 l. is fossil poetry 159:1
 l. of prose and metrical composition 467:22
 l. of the age 187:18
 l. of the unheard 237:10
 l. that would make your hair curl 178:11
 l. was not powerful enough 139:18
 life is a foreign l. 288:5
 make their l. convey more than they mean 121:11
 my l. fails! 30:14
 my l. is plain 194:23
 no l., but the l. of the heart 312:29
 noble simplification of l.! 245:28
 poetical l. of an age 206:25
 sarcasm . . . the l. of the devil 100:10
 silent in seven l.s 338:17
 sithe of our l. he was the lodesterre 260:7
 sorry when any l. is lost 223:26
 speaks three or four l.s 382:26
 sure in l. strange she said 231:10
 that dear l. 261:9
 there's l. in her eye 382:19
 two countries separated by the same l. 389:15
 two most beautiful words in the English l. 217:4
 use any l. you choose 177:13
 wit in all l.s 151:32
 you taught me l. 380:33
Languish: relieve my l. and restore the light 131:10
Laodameia: L. died 247:4
Lap: every Hyacinth . . . dropt in her L. 164:7
 in thy green l. 187:12
 upon the l. of Earth 186:18
Lap-dog: l.s give themselves the rousing shake 315:12
 when l.s breathe their last 315:24
Lapidem: stilicidi casus l. cavat 259:20
Lapse: liquid l. of murmuring streams 280:21
Lard: l.s the lean earth 354:1
 they l. their lean books 86:5
Larem: fessi venimus l. ad nostrum 103:16
Lark: hear the l. begin his flight 276:22
 hear the l.s so high 210:15
 hope to catch l.s 324:3
 l. at break of day arising 385:23
 l. at heaven's gate sings 347:6
 l. becomes a sightless song 418:33
 l. now leaves his watery nest 132:13
 l. so shrill and clear 260:10
 l.'s on the wing 76:29
 no l. more blithe than he 59:1
Larke: bisy l., messager of day 108:2
Larved: *he l. and he l.* 226:16
Lashes: teary round the l. 258:28
Lass: come l.s and lads 7:12
 I loved a l. 459:2

it was a lover and his l. 346:12
l. that loves a sailor 136:10
l. that were to go a-gipsying 246:16
l. unparalleled 344:13
O, gie me the l. 84:24
on Richmond Hill there lives a l. 264:10
sweet l. of Richmond Hill 435:16
yon solitary Highland l.! 466:21
Lasses: an' then she made the l. O 84:23
l. a' lilting 158:4
spent among the l. O! 84:21
'twere na for the l. O 84:22
Lassie: I love a l. 248:26
my love she's but a l. yet 203:16
Last: after L. returns the First 72:22
die . . . l. thing I shall do! 303:12
l. is commonly best 86:6
l., not least in love 360:10
l. of life 77:11
L. of the Mohicans 122:8
l. shall be first 50:40
l. to lay the old aside 313:10
loneliness and mire of the l. land! 69:24
look thy l. on all things lovely 134:13
no l. or first 77:1
would that this might be the l.! 127:34
Latchet: shoe's l. I am not worthy to unloose 53:3
Late: five minutes too l. all my life-time! 124:15
three o'clock is always too late 337:24
Later: l. than you think 342:24
Latin: don't quote L. 449:22
he speaks L. 358:5
must carve in L. or in Greek 444:11
small L. and less Greek 225:23
Latitude: l.'s rather uncertain 321:22
Laud: more l. than gilt o'er-dusted 382:17
Laudanum: some fell by l. 173:11
Laudator: l. temporis acti se puero 207:5
Laugh: force myself to l. at everything 27:14
he l.s like anything 110:17
l. and be merry 269:26
l. and be well 187:21
l. and the world l.s with you 454:18
l. before one is happy 243:3
l. broke into a thousand pieces 25:22
L.! I thought I should 'ave died 111:15
l. where we must 313:26
loud l. that spake 180:22
make 'em l. 326:6
nobody has ever heard me l. 109:11
nothing more unbecoming . . . than to laugh 120:3
nothing sillier than a silly l. 103:17
solitary l. 187:25
will have your proper laugh 77:25
would have made a cat l. 309:25
Laughed: on which one has not l. 106:2
once heartily and wholly l. 100:7
Laughing: cannot be always l. at a man 17:12
cannot forbear l. 307:11
most fun . . . without l. 4:15
Laughter: laugh thy girlish l. 447:4
l. and the love of friends 30:21
l. for a month 353:36
l. holding both his sides 276:20
l. is pleasant 306:17
l. of the fool 43:27
mocking l. from Hell 253:26

sincerest l. with some pain is fraught 394:21
Laundries: Land of L. stood 32:21
Laundry: in any first-class l. 250:11
Laundry-list: l. and I'll set it to music 332:4
Laura: rose-cheeked L., come 97:26
Laurea: concedant l. laudi 114:16
Laurel: from Caesar's l. crown 60:18
yet once more, O ye l.s 276:36
Laurel-bough: burnèd is Apollo's l. 267:7
Laurier: l.s sont coupés 24:3
Lave: let the l. go by me 407:22
Lavender: l., mints, savory, marjoram 384:28
Lavinia: she is L. 381:28
Law: army of unalterable l. 272:7
born under one l. 188:12
broke the l.s of God and man 255:25
dusty purlieus of the l. 418:19
everything which the l.s allow 285:28
God is thy l. 279:32
good of the people is the chief l. 114:13
he is always breaking the l. 388:7
higher l. than the Constitution 342:28
I know not whether L.s be right 454:22
ignorance of the l. 342:5
in l.'s grave study 116:12
keep ye the L. 240:24
lapt in universal l. 419:32
l. doth punish man or woman 6:7
l. hath not been dead 368:13
l. is a ass 140:4
L. is the true embodiment 177:6
l. of the land 264:20
l. to ourselves 280:34
l. unto themselves 54:16
l.'s delay 350:14
l.'s made to take care o' raskills 155:14
l.s are dumb in time of war 114:21
l.s grind the poor 181:30
l.s of the Persians and the Medes 36:30
l.s or kings can cause or cure 181:31
l.s were like cobwebs 18:13
l.s were made to be broken 295:17
love is the fulfilling of the l. 54:43
moral l. within me 229:8
my l. the seventh time disobeyed 306:2
necessity gives the l. 413:13
necessity hath no l. 129:17
not judges of l.s 322:2
obedient to their l.s we lie 397:10
of no force in l. 116:7
old father antick the l. 353:20
one l. for all 82:3
prisons are built with stones of L. 63:16
progress is the l. of life 76:18
this is the l. and the prophets 49:24
unequal l.s unto a savage race 423:35
very good l. for all that 340:30
when you break the big l.s 111:9
where l.s end 309:16
where no l. is 54:19
who should make the l.s of a nation 166:16
windward of the l. 111:22
windy side of the l. 383:27
wrest once the l. to your authority 370:10
Law-court: l.s of England are open to all men 132:4
Lawful: all things are l. for me 55:16
l. for me to do what I will 50:42

Lawn: l. as white as driven snow 384:32
  leave the printed l. 209:30
  meet the sun upon the upland l. 186:17
Lawyer: as a l. knows how 126:18
  if l.'s hand is fee'd 174:5
  l. has no business 223:21
  l.s are met 174:17
  let's kill all the l.s 358:4
  o'er l.s' fingers 378:30
  two l.s the battledores 140:28
Laxative: Lumbago and the L. Islands 342:21
Lay: constructing tribal l.s 239:15
  from her melodious l. 352:20
  he fell, he l. down 35:27
  little do we know wot l.s afore us! 139:1
  there she l. in the Bay of Biscay 109:2
  unpremeditated l. 339:24
Laying: L. on of Hands 319:34
L.B.J.: Hey, hey, L. 183:23
Lea: up the river and o'er the l. 203:14
Lead: all thy friends are lapped in l. 25:11
  eyes grew dross of l. 74:29
  go down like lumps of l. 202:17
  l. and I follow 416:29
  L., Kindly Light 294:3
  owes all its weight . . . to l. 124:31
Leader: found favour with the l.s of men 207:23
  four-and-twenty l.s of revolts 78:32
  l. is fairest 11:1
  right kind of political l. 33:7
  true l. is always led 227:5
Leaf: if I were a dead l. 392:8
  last red l. is whirled away 417:31
  no l. upon the forest bare 390:12
  November's l. is red and sear 340:8
  one red l. 117:19
  sear, the yellow l. 367:18
  we all do fade as a l. 46:21
  where does a wise man hide a l.? 110:32
  where the dead l. fell 230:27
League: half a l. onward 415:24
  keep a l. till death 377:15
  she had not sailed a l. 22:12
  ten l.s beyond the wild world's end 5:19
  though thy soul sail l.s 331:22
Leak: she sprang no fatal l. 125:35
Lean: his wife could eat no l. 296:30
  it l.s, and hearkens after it 146:17
  l. and the ill-favoured kine 34:31
  out of my l. and low ability 383:28
Leander: L., Mr Ekenhead, and I did 91:11
Leap: great l. in the dark 202:9
  it were an easy l. 353:32
  l. over the hedge 104:22
  one giant l. for mankind 10:12
Leap-year: twenty-nine in each l. 6:17
Lear: how pleasant to know Mr L. 250:14
Learn: but she may l. 370:4
  l. all we lacked before 69:23
Learned: I have l. . . . to be content 56:30
  l. roast an egg 316:3
  make the l. smile 313:9
Learning: a' the l. I desire 84:13
  cry both arts and l. down 323:3
  just enough of l. to misquote 92:24
  l. hath gained most 171:5
  l. is but an adjunct to ourself 363:29

l. is most excellent 167:1
l. of a sort 30:32
L. wiser grow without his books 127:25
l.'s triumph o'er her barb'rous foes 219:3
little l. is a dang'rous thing 313:4
little l. was painfully beaten into him 306:16
love he bore to l. 181:6
men of polite l. 198:11
much l. doth make thee mad 54:10
no enemy to l. 120:30
on scraps of l. dote 472:13
progeny of l. 395:22
shocking passion for acquiring l. 283:13
so well with her l. did suit 320:22
those twins of l. 359:5
university should be a place of . . . l. 143:8
wearing all that weight of l. 418:40
without l. anything 284:11
Learnt: I only remember what I've l. 452:18
  when what has been l. has been forgotten 398:5
Lease: summer's l. hath all too short a date 385:17
Leave: and often took l. 320:29
  I pray thee l. 148:18
  I Wouldn't L. My Little Wooden Hut 271:15
  l. off first for manners' sake 48:18
Leaven: little l. leaveneth the whole lump 55:5
Leaves: all that famous harmony of l. 471:28
  as naturally as the l. to a tree 233:30
  as the l. grow on the tree 470:14
  before the l. have fallen from the trees 457:3
  behold when yellow l. 386:10
  burning of the l. 59:16
  crowned with calm l. 412:18
  hid, where the l. drip with sweet 397:13
  l. dead are driven, like ghosts 392:4
  L. of Life keep falling 163:27
  l. of the tree were for the healing of the
  nations 58:37
  l. they were crispèd and sere 310:30
  my l. are falling like its own! 392:11
  one year's l. are scattered 204:11
  other half with green l. on it 261:1
  shows his hoar l. 352:19
  thick as autumnal l. 278:13
  words are like l. 313:8
Leaving: nothing in his life became him like the l. it
  364:25
Lebanon: streams from L. 44:23
Leben: L. geht hin mit Verwandlung 327:15
  so l. wir 327:17
  unnütz L. ist ein früher Tod 180:1
Lechery: wars and l. 382:21
Leçon: cette l. vaut bien un fromage 243:19
Lecteur: Hypocrite l.! 26:12
Lecture: I do not give l.s 454:1
  Mrs Caudle's Curtain L.s 218:10
Leda: L., was the mother of Helen 305:16
  L . . . went before 247:4
Lee: pleasant waters of the River L. 321:21
Leef: right as an aspes l. 108:24
Leek: by this l. 357:23
Leer: assent with civil l. 312:22
Lees: mere l. is left this vault to brag of 366:5
Left: I am more to the l. than you 450:17
  if you keep to the l. 159:28
  my position was on the l. 289:9
  we only, are l.! 11:19

Leg: can honour set-to a l.? 355:2
    four l.s good, two l.s bad 300:12
    here I leave my second l. 204:22
    honest woman and a broken l. 105:13
    I took him by the left l. 296:17
    if you could see my l.s 137:37
    is those things arms, or is they l.s? 292:10
    kiss my Julia's dainty l. 200:11
    literary man – *with* a wooden l. 140:5
    'Pray which l. goes after which?' 129:1
    run your l.s off 67:15
    short, fat, hairy l.s 287:25
    slimy things did crawl with l.s 116:29
    sturdy l.s were flannel-slack'd 32:19
    taketh not pleasure in the l.s of a man 41:17
    two vast and trunkless l.s of stone 392:13
    walk under his huge l.s 359:16
    when his l.s were smitten off 389:20
Legem: necessitas non habet l. 413:13
    per l. terrae 264:20
Legend: when the l. becomes fact 29:30
Leges: silent enim l. inter arma 114:21
Legion: give me back my l.s 95:4
    l. of the lost ones 239:5
    my name is L. 51:32
Legiones: Quintili Vari, l. redde 95:4
Legislation: foundation of morals and l. 31:22
Legislator: unacknowledged l.s of the world 395:2
Legislature: l. called it May 125:2
Legitimate: Edmund . . . shall top the l. 361:32
Leisure: god gave us this l. 441:10
    l. answers l. 368:30
    l. to be good 186:20
Lemon: squeeze out of a l. 174:29
Lemon-tree: land where the l.s flower 180:9
Lend: few l. but fools 433:18
Lender: neither a borrower, nor a l. be 348:23
Length: l. and breadth enough 23:7
Lenten: L. ys come with love 5:11
    what l. entertainment 349:37
Leonard: for L., Rafael, Agnolo and me 72:19
Leopard: can the . . . l. change his spots? 46:29
    l. shall lie down with the kid 45:10
    three white l.s sat under a juniper tree 155:25
Leprosy: scant as hair in l. 73:25
Lergy: dreaded l. 274:5
Lerne: gladly wolde he l. 107:20
Less: l. is more 273:8
    l. of this than meets the eye 24:2
    little l., and what worlds away! 73:19
    nicely-calculated l. or more 461:15
    rather than be l. 278:31
Lesson: l. . . . worth a cheese 243:19
    l. you should heed 201:6
    reason they're called l.s 101:16
    should preach a high moral l. 408:17
    this is that other l. 271:18
    useful l. to the head 127:25
    we have had an Imperial l. 239:30
Lethe: go not to L. 231:27
    in ease on L. wharf 349:4
    wait upon the tedious shores of L. 245:15
Letter: copied all the l.s 176:30
    cries like dead l.s sent 206:4
    elegantly engraved in capital l.s 324:18
    great art o' l. writin' 141:5
    I am persecuted with l.s 120:25

king has written a braid l. 23:9
    l. from his wife 102:28
    l. killeth 55:44
    l.s ten feet high 216:13
    pause awhile from l.s to be wise 219:6
    remaining twenty-two l.s of the alphabet 300:14
    republic of l.s 2:1, 181:35
    thou unnecessary l.! 362:7
    when he wrote a l. 20:3
Lettre: nought the l.s space 108:29
Lettuce: too much l. is 'soporific' 317:9
Level: bring to one dead l. 311:26
Leveller: l.s wish to level *down* 221:14
Leven: lies across yon lilly l.? 23:17
Leviathan: draw out l. with an hook 37:14
Levity: nothing like a little judicious l. 407:10
Lewd: certain l. fellows of the baser sort 53:52
Lexicographer: L.. A writer of dictionaries 219:14
Liar: all men are l.s 40:24
    ambitious, and often quite picturesque l. 434:9
    every man a l. 54:17
    I am the Club L. 335:14
    l. and the father of it 53:20
    l. of the first magnitude 120:5
    l.s find ready-made for lies 76:2
    l.s ought to have good memories 396:9
    they only answered 'Little l.!' 30:18
Libel: convey a l. in a frown 410:7
Liberal: either a little L. 177:11
    watchword of the great L. party 68:13
Liberality: l. lies less in giving liberally 243:2
    yon blue l. of heaven 72:23
Liberation: mankind's war of l. 235:21
Liberté: L.! égalité! Fraternité! 9:17
    L.! que de crimes on commet en ton nom 329:8
Liberties: extending the l. of his country 70:6
Libertine: air, a chartered l., is still 356:22
    like a puffed and reckless l. 348:20
Liberty: abstract l. . . . is not to be found 81:17
    brightest in dungeons, L.! thou art 93:22
    eldest child of L. 463:17
    give me l. 198:23
    God hath given l. to man 130:12
    he that commands the sea is at great l. 20:17
    I must have l. 345:8
    know no such l. 258:12
    l. consists in doing what one desires 273:15
    l. is precious 253:2
    l. is the right to do everything 285:28
    l. of the individual 273:13
    l., too, must be limited 83:1
    L., what crimes are committed 329:8
    l.'s a kind o'thing 258:23
    l.'s in every blow! 85:11
    mountain nymph, sweet L. 276:21
    proclaim l. to the captives 46:18
    so loving-jealous of his l. 379:20
    strange desire . . . to lose l. 19:18
    sweet land of l. 399:13
    symptom of constitutional l. 175:19
    they were thy chosen music, L.! 463:21
    tree of l. 217:24
    university should be a place of . . . l. 143:8
    vigilance is the price of l. 308:16
    weight of too much l. 462:30
    when they cry l. 282:2
    you do not get l. 111:9

l.'s time's fool 355:5
l.'s too short for chess 94:15
live a l. half-dead 281:18
long disease, my l. 312:20
love o' l.'s young day 289:10
make L. . . . one grand sweet song 237:13
man's l. of any worth 234:11
may be l., but ain't it slow? 198:29
measured out my l. 156:22
methinks it were a happy l. 358:7
most loathèd worldly l. 368:23
much too far out all my l. 399:15
my l. is done 376:8
no man loses any other l. 16:10
no wealth but L. 333:18
nor love thy l. 280:40
nothing in his l. became him 364:25
O l., no l. 242:20
people say that l. is the thing 399:10
present l. of man 28:23
reason thus with l. 368:18
resurrection and the l. 53:23
sech is l. 138:35
seen as much of l. as the world can show
  223:30
set my l. at a pin's fee 348:32
such is L.! 138:5
take my l. 161:21
then, what is l. 394:23
this l. is most jolly 345:13
time of l. is short 355:3
time of this mortal l. 319:12
tired of l. 222:27
to deny l. 248:33
to know is everlasting l. 319:18
to make l. is more difficult by far 271:9
treasured up on purpose to a l. beyond l. 282:17
troubled with her lonely l. 307:12
useless l. is an early death 180:1
value of l. 285:8
veil which those who live call l. 393:14
way, the truth and the l. 53:28
we see into the l. of things 462:15
well-written L. is almost as rare 99:17
went for the Simple L. 110:7
what is our l.? 9:1
which leadeth unto l. 49:26
which those who live call l. 393:31
white flower of a blameless l. 416:26
who saw l. steadily 12:8
why should l. all labour be? 420:14
you take my l. 370:16
young l.'s before us 9:10
Life-blood: good book . . . precious l. 282:17
Life-in-Death: Nightmare L. was she 116:30
Life-insurance: I detest l. agents 250:6
Life-lie: deprive the average human being of his l.
  214:22
Life-line: throw out the l. 435:5
Lifemanship: first murmured. . .'L.' 317:12
Lifetime: not see them lit again in our l. 188:13
Light: apparelled in celestial l. 463:30
  armour of l. 319:12
  as far as l. excelleth darkness 43:17
  be near me when my l. is low 418:3
  burning and a shining l. 53:13
  by her own radiant l. 275:17

coastwise l.s of England 238:20
common as l. is love 393:10
consider how my l. is spent 282:3
dearer than the l. to your sister 440:22
disdaineth every other vulgar l. 396:18
followed false l.s 150:19
glorious the northern l.s astream 398:9
God stooping shows sufficient of his l. 78:5
hail holy l. 279:10
have seen a great l. 45:7
he was not that L. 52:51
if once we lose this l. 225:12
infant crying for the l. 418:8
it gives a lovely l. 273:18
kindle a l. in the darkness 227:2
Lead, Kindly L. 294:3
leaping l. for your delight 14:18
let there be l. 33:14
l. at the end of the tunnel 259:7
l. breaks where no sun shines 426:9
l. broke in upon my brain 93:18
l. but the shadow of God 70:16
l. dies before thy uncreating word 311:29
l. enough for what I've got to do 140:3
l. (God's eldest daughter!) 171:2
l. of Terewth 136:30
l. of the bright world dies 65:21
l. of thy countenance 37:22
l. shall be spread 416:22
l. shineth in darkness 52:49
L. that Failed 241:23
l. that led astray 85:33
l. that loses 412:1
l. that never was 461:16
l. thickens 366:20
l. to them that sit in darkness 51:43
l. we sought is shining 12:7
lived l. in the spring 10:23
long l. shakes across the lakes 421:39
long levelled rule of streaming l. 275:16
men loved darkness rather than l. 53:9
more l.! 180:14
morning l. creaks down again 397:12
one track of sparkling l. 465:6
out of hell leads up to l. 279:2
put out the l. 375:22
seek it, ere it come to l. 126:19
send thy l. and brilliancy 247:16
shall be to you better than l. 194:30
speed of l. squared 154:15
such scant l. as shone through the cracks 452:3
they are all gone into the world of l.! 438:15
they are but broken l.s of thee 417:26
things l. and swollen 20:36
thy l. is come 46:17
thy word is. . .a l. 40:27
truly the l. is sweet 44:7
turn off the l. to spare my blushes 217:6
turn up the l.s 198:22
we all know what l. is 222:23
what l. through yonder window breaks? 379:8
when the brief l. has once set 103:11
when the l.s are dim and low 300:7
who art a l. to guide 464:21
whose l.s are fled 287:15
your l.s burning 52:18
Lighten: l. our darkness 318:32

Lighthouse: l. without any light atop 204:29
  sitivation at the l. 141:19
Lightning: brief as the l. in the collied night 371:21
  I scratch my head with the l. 434:6
  l., my pilot sits 390:15
  mind . . . with its own internal l. blind 391:18
  to keep the l. out 215:21
  too like the l. 379:17
Like: find their l. agen! 340:9
  I know she l.s me 408:22
  l. doth quit l. 368:30
  nothing says we have to l. each other 136:1
  shall not look upon his l. again 348:10
  tell me what you l. 333:20
  to l. and dislike the same things 336:24
  why every one as they l. 411:12
Liked: he's l., but not well l. 273:22
  how I like to be l. 246:14
Likelihood: no mark, nor l. 354:29
Likeness: l. must be true 124:25
  they four had one l. 46:32
Likewise: canst thou do l.? 137:38
  do thou l. 52:12
Liking: made up of l.s and dislikings 245:18
  not l. myself much 5:3
Lilac: l.s out of the dead land 156:33
  when l.s last in the dooryard bloomed 454:5
Lilac-time: go down to Kew in l. 296:3
Lilies: consider the l. of the field 49:16
  had three l. in her hand 331:15
  in the beauty of the l. 211:6
  like an heap of wheat set about with l. 44:26
  l. and languors of virtue 412:9
  l. of all kinds 384:29
  l. that fester 386:19
  l. without, roses within 268:28
Lillabulero: whistling half a dozen bars of L.
  405:19
Lilting: I've heard them l. 158:4
Lily: as the l. among thorns 44:18
  fair as the l. 111:12
  how sweet the l. grows! 196:23
  I see a l. on thy brow 231:8
  L. O'Grady, silly and shady 397:15
  paint the l. 91:21
  seen but a bright l. grow 225:13
  set thick with l. 288:15
  to paint the l. 361:21
  trembles to a l. 144:6
  waved her l. hand 174:27
Lily-seed: l. to find 288:22
Limb: consent to have a l. amputated 221:22
  dispersed l.s are those of a poet 209:13
  great smooth marbly l.s 73:11
  hang a calf's-skin on those recreant l.s 361:15
  if these poor l.s die 69:19
  so wasted each l. 74:13
  thy decent l.s composed 312:5
  tired pilgrim's l.s affected slumber 97:28
  well compensated in l.s 10:10
  yeomen whose l.s were made in England 357:5
Limbo: L. large and broad 279:17
Lime: you have *got* to give her l. 239:27
Lime-tree: l. bower my prison! 118:13
Limestone: what I see is a l. landscape 14:13
Limit: how wide the l.s stand 181:12
  stony l.s cannot hold love out 379:12

Limited: liberty, too, must be l. 83:1
Limousine: all we want is a l. 264:11
  one perfect l. 303:17
Limpopo: great grey-green, greasy L. River 241:19
Lincoln: at the back o' merry L. 22:23
  Ford, not a L. 167:3
  when Abraham L. was shovelled into the tombs
    336:27
Linden: on L., when the sun was low 97:6
Line: *active* l. on a walk 242:3
  as l.s, so love oblique 268:16
  creep in one dull l. 313:12
  dry desert of a thousand l.s 315:33
  following a l. with left and right 14:16
  he never blotted out a l. 225:27
  high aesthetic l. 177:38
  I would rather have written those l.s 460:5
  if in my lagging l.s you miss 206:20
  learn the l.s 123:30
  l. stretch out to the crack of doom 367:2
  l. upon l. 45:15
  l. will take us hours maybe 470:2
  l.s are fallen unto me 37:33
  my l.s and life are free 199:7
  never has six l.s together 221:27
  not a day without a l. 310:13
  six l.s written by the most honest man 327:8
  thin red l. 334:4
  we carved not a l. 460:3
  wit . . . in the very first l. 181:20
Linea: *nulla dies sine* l. 310:13
Lineage: poets of the proud old l. 166:2
Lineament: moulded the changing l.s 305:16
Linen: clothed in . . . fine l. 52:31
  did not love clean l. 221:7
  her confidant stark mad in white l. 395:12
  love is like l. often changed 166:18
  old l. wash whitest 449:1
  washing one's clean l. in public 455:9
Lingered: I l. round them 69:5
Lingering: something l. with boiling oil 177:31
Lining: silver l. through the dark cloud shining
    167:12
  turn forth her silver l. on the night 275:13
Linnet: I heard a l. courting 67:28
  l. born within the cage 417:33
  pipe but as the l.s sing 417:32
Linsey-wolsey: lawless l. brother 87:17
  piebald, l. brothers 311:17
Lion: beard the l. in his den 340:16
  being . . . threatened, a l. 106:12
  hind that would be mated by the l. 343:4
  I hear the l. roar 125:29
  l. among ladies 371:40
  l. and the unicorn 296:32
  l. lie down with the lamb 249:15
  l. on your old stone gates 419:4
  living dog is better than a dead l. 43:36
  nation . . . that had the l. heart 113:14
  now that the old l. is dead 305:1
  rise like l.s after slumber 392:2
  roaring of the young l.s 12:18
  saw the l.'s shadow ere himself 370:18
  strong is the l. 398:8
  there is a l. in the way 42:42
  they say the L. and the Lizard keep 164:6
  thou wear a l.'s hide 361:15

teach me to l. 235:10
there taught us how to l. 430:7
to itself it only l. and die 386:18
to know how to l. is my trade 285:14
to l. is like to love 88:12
to l. more nearly as we pray 234:22
you might as well l. 304:1
Lived: I have l. long enough 367:18
I have l. today 124:6
Livelihood: must slave for l. 1:5
Liver: getting at a boy and at . . . his l. 138:2
Liverpool: folk that live in L. 110:10
Livery: shadowed l. of the burnished sun 369:22
Lives: he most l. who thinks most 21:10
how a man dies, but how he l. 221:29
if two l. join 73:20
music of men's l. 377:18
ninety l. have been taken away 263:14
we can make our l. sublime 257:5
Liveth: I am he that l. 58:5
none of us l. to himself 54:47
Livia: O tell me all about Anna L.! 226:9
Living: blend the l. with the dead 103:4
cut off out of the land of the l. 46:10
earning a precarious l. 6:19
fever called 'L.' 310:21
getting ready to live, but never l. 159:17
land of the l. 38:7
l. and partly l. 157:15
l. are getting rarer 215:16
more than the l. which are yet alive 43:20
no l. with thee 2:5
plain l. and high thinking 463:22
set to earn their l.s 184:11
why seek ye the l. among the dead? 52:46
will it not live with the l.? 355:2
Living-dead: l. man 346:19
Livingstone: Dr L. I presume 404:2
Livre: j'ai lu tous les l.s 265:5
lecture de tous les bons l.s 135:11
Lizzie: L. Borden took an axe 6:9
Llewellyn: soft L.'s lay 185:20
Lloyd George, David 13:21
Load: laid many heavy l.s on thee! 160:4
Loaf: L. of Bread – and Thou 164:2
L. of Bread beneath the Bough 164:1
of a cut l. to steal a shive 381:28
who makes the quartern l. 399:1
Loafed: better to have l. and lost 429:11
Loan: l. oft loses both itself and friend 348:23
Loaning: moaning on ilka green l. 158:4
Loath: l. to look a gift-horse in the mouth 87:12
Lob: nothing but a l. 333:5
Lobby: go into the L. against us 21:17
Lobcock: dine with Lord L. 15:14
Lobster: like a l. boiled the morn 87:20
Loca: quae nunc abibis in l. 190:2
Localism: genuine spirit of l. 65:8
Loch: bonnie banks of L. Lomon' 8:10
Lochaber: farewell to L. 325:16
Lochiel: L., L.! beware of the day 97:8
Lochinvar: never was knight like the young L. 340:12
young L. is come out of the west 340:11
Loci: geniumque l. . . . precatur 441:2
Lock: golden l.s time hath to silver turned 306:23
knotted and combinèd l.s 349:1

l., stock and barrel 472:3
l. was dull 93:28
never shake thy gory l.s at me 366:25
oil the l. 15:20
open l.s, whoever knocks 366:37
pluck up drowned honour by the l.s 353:32
shaking her invincible l.s 282:21
your l.s were like the raven 84:31
Locust: as luscious as l.s 374:11
meat was l.s and wild honey 48:36
palmerworm . . . hath the l. eaten 47:11
Lodesterre: of our language he was the l. 260:7
Lodge: l. in some vast wilderness 126:34
Lodger: mere l. in my own house 182:6
Queer Street is full of l.s 140:14
Lodging: hard was their l. 173:9
Lodore: water come down at L. 401:11
Lofty: l. and sour 359:4
Log: 'God save King L.!' 311:15
see the dying on a l. 140:26
Log-cabin: L. to White House 426:1
Logic: as it isn't, it ain't. That's l. 101:32
l. . . . but not in fine weather 115:13
l. . . . makes men able to contend 20:34
Oriel Common Room stank of L. 294:1
Logres: by knights of L. 281:4
Loin: fire of my l.s 291:1
gird up now thy l.s 37:10
I girdid up my l.s 446:8
let your l.s be girded about 52:18
unlit lamp and the ungirt l. 79:1
with your l. girded 34:48
Lois: France, mère . . . des l. 152:3
Loitered: l. my life away 195:19
Lolita: L., light of my life 291:1
London 115:28
anything deserving . . . to be found out of L. 195:22
as L. is to Paddington 98:17
best club in L. 140:13
by seeing L. 223:30
crowd flowed over L. Bridge 156:38
deep with the first dead lies L.'s daughter 426:14
dream of L. 288:12
in L. all that life can afford 222:27
in L. poetry only is a trade 150:31
I've been up to L. 297:23
L. doesn't love the latent 216:13
L. is a modern Babylon 143:27
L., thou art the flour of cities 152:14
L. . . . the clearing-house of the world 105:22
L.'s noble Fire Brigade 30:16
of famous L. town 125:6
one road leads to L. 270:1
Sam Weller's knowledge of L. 140:29
Sir, he lived in L. 220:18
something very shocking . . . in L. 16:31
this is a L. particular 136:18
to merry L. 403:14
we didn't find that it [L.] come up to its likeness 138:7
Loneliness: if you are afraid of l. 109:1
Lonely: l. of heart is withered away 471:9
so l. 'twas that God himself 117:14
Lonelyhearts: write-to-Miss-L. 451:14
Long: it cannot hold you l. 182:33
Lord, how l.? 45:3

So L., It's Been Good to Know Yuh 189:9
Longed: still l. for, never seen 467:9
Longer: anything written . . . wished l. 224:9
  or so very little l.! 75:21
Longing: I have immortal l.s in me 344:11
  l. to be at 'em 5:24
  more l., wavering 383:10
Longitude: l. also is vague 321:22
Long-shot: life is a comedy in l. 106:11
Look: baby just l. at you now 271:24
  don't l. at me, Sir 322:16
  how sweet are l.s that ladies bend 423:15
  lean and hungry l. 359:18
  longing ling'ring l. behind 186:15
  l.s commercing with the skies 276:4
  not be deep-searched with saucy l.s 363:19
  only a l. and a voice 257:17
  only loveless l. 306:1
  puts on his pretty l.s 361:17
  screen them in those l.s 393:11
  some do it with a bitter l. 454:21
  we l. before and after 394:21
  whom to l. at was to love 419:24
Looked: no sooner l. but they loved 346:8
Looker-on: sit thou a patient l. 323:2
Lookers-on: only for God and angels to be l. 18:5
Looking: here's l. at you, kid 64:3
  l. forward to the past 301:13
Loon: thou cream-faced l.! 367:16
Loophole: from her cabined l. peep 275:8
  through the l.s of retreat 127:13
Loose: all hell broke l. 280:3
  let l. upon the world 26:1
Lord: am an attendant l. 156:25
  and I replied, 'My L.' 199:8
  bless ye the L. 318:21
  certain l., neat, and trimly dressed 353:28
  fail very completely in the House of L.s 143:31
  great L. of all things 314:2
  I am l. of the fowl 127:37
  let a l. once own the happy lines 313:16
  let me kiss my l. before I die 267:19
  l. among wits 220:24
  L. bless thee 35:7
  L. do so to me 35:39
  L. God made them all 4:3
  L. hath done great things 40:35
  L. hath spared our lives 423:3
  L. have mercy upon us 318:24
  L. High Everything Else 177:15
  L. is my shepherd 38:2
  L. is the maker of them all 42:29
  L. is thy keeper 40:32
  l. of fat prize-oxen 422:24
  l. of himself 468:1
  l. of thy presence 361:6
  L. prefers common-looking people 255:2
  L. sent me forth into the world 168:13
  L. shall preserve thy going out 40:33
  L. strong and mighty 38:5
  L. survives the rainbow 259:10
  L. was departed from him 35:35
  love, thou art absolute sole L. 128:20
  my most noble l. slain 265:20
  out of the depths have I cried unto thee, O L.
    41:5
  plough for the l.s who lay ye low 393:28

praise the L.! 235:7
praise the L., for he is kind 281:13
seek ye the L. 46:12
speak, L.; for thy servant heareth 35:40
waiting for their ain dear l.s 23:12
what doth the L. require of thee 47:19
whom the L. loveth 57:15
Lordly: l. ones who dwell in the hills 263:21
Lordship: dance attendance on their l.s' pleasures
  359:6
  his l. may compel us 25:16
Lore: curious volume of forgotten l. 310:24
  follow not her l. 281:2
Lorenzo: L., a young palmer 231:2
Lorraine: wine . . . they make in Haute L. 109:32
Los Angeles 304:12
Lose: for whatever we l. 130:1
  no man can l. what he never had 445:24
  take care not to l. the next war 114:3
  this which he now l.s 16:10
  We Don't Want To L. You 332:21
Loser: all are l.s 105:25
  neither party l. 356:8
Loses: who l. and who wins 363:9
Loseth: he that l. his life for my sake 49:44
Losing: when all about you are l. theirs 239:11
Loss: black as our l. 397:19
  bombazine . . . deeper sense of her l. 173:14
  for l. of time 125:11
  man's l. comes to him from his gain 74:7
  suffer the l. they were afraid of 15:12
  those I counted l. for Christ 56:25
Losses: all l. are restored 385:25
  fellow that hath l. 373:21
  God bless all our l. 71:27
Lost: being lacked and l. 373:15
  better to have fought and l. 115:24
  better to have loved and l. 417:34
  game . . . is never l. till won 128:13
  give up for l. what you see is l. 103:13
  l. and waiting for you 238:30
  never to have l. at all 88:23
  not l. but gone before 295:23
  praising what is l. 343:12
  sheep which was l. 52:23
  thou art l. 286:8
  whatsoever thing is l. 126:19
  your cause is l. 170:19
Lot: cast l.s upon my vesture 38:1
  l. has fallen to me 240:28
  no l. is in all respects happy 208:21
  our loving l. was cast 204:18
  remember L.'s wife 52:36
  weary l. is thine 340:24
Loth: me the loving and you the l. 75:14
Lothario: gay L. 332:17
Lots: so they cast l. 47:16
Lottery: won first prize in the l. of life 327:3
Lou: lady that's known as L. 342:26
Loud: I said it very l. and clear 102:13
Lounging: l. 'round' en suffer'n 194:15
Loup: hurler . . . avec les l.s 325:4
Louse: l. in the locks of literature 424:25
Lousy: conduct unethical and l. 10:14
Love: al for l. 5:12
  alas my l.! 7:20
  all are but ministers of L. 118:7

all l. is sweet 393:10
all she loves is l. 91:15
and all for l. 402:31
as swift as . . . thoughts of l. 349:3
beautiful through l. 393:17
because my l. is come to me 331:1
before the god of l. was born 145:30
brief . . . as woman's l. 351:9
brief is life, but l. is long 422:8
but I do l. thee 374:29
but l. I gave thee 74:19
comely in nothing but in l. 19:14
conquer L. that run away 99:1
course of true l. never did run smooth 371:20
crime to l. too well 312:2
died . . . but not for l. 346:3
do they above l. to be loved 396:13
except for l.'s sake only 72:5
farewell, blighted l. 8:15
fit l. for Gods 280:33
fitter L. for me 146:6
Go, my L. 72:20
God is l. 57:40
God is L. – I dare say 88:11
greater l. hath no man 53:29, 429:4
hail wedded l. 279:35
he fell in l. with himself 317:30
he was all for l. 136:5
he will seem worthy of your l. 465:3
he would l. and she would not 67:22
how do I l. thee? 72:7
how should I your true l. know 352:4
how wayward is this foolish l. 384:3
I am in l., you say 115:8
I am sick of l. 44:19
I could not l. thee, Dear, so much 258:15
I *do not l.* the man 447:3
I do not l. thee! 295:22
I heartily l. John, Peter, Thomas 411:25
I know what L. is really like 441:18
I l. but you alone 23:3
I l. her till I die 167:13
I l. thee true 231:10
I l. thee with a l. 72:8
I shall be past making l. 320:30
I understand only because I l. 431:5
I would *l.* infinitely 76:15
if music be the food of l. 382:23
if my l. were in my arms 5:16
if of herself she will not l. 409:6
if one judges l. 248:3
if yet I have not all thy l. 145:29
I'm tired of l. 30:24
imagine a faultless l. 14:13
in l. alone we hate to find 445:17
in the narrow theme of l. 471:26
is thy l. a plant 463:12
it was l. for me 214:20
lack of l. from l. made manifest 74:7
last, not least in l. 360:10
leave me, O L. 396:17
leave to come unto my l. 402:23
let brotherly l. continue 57:17
let thy l. be younger than thyself 383:11
let us make l. deathless 431:21
let your l. even with my life decay 386:9
lies my young l. sleeping 272:2

lightly turn to thoughts of l. 419:19
little duty and less l. 357:29
l. all alike 146:11
l., an abject intercourse 182:7
l. and a cottage 119:21
l., and do what you will 16:6
L. and I were well acquainted 178:14
l. and murder will out 120:4
l. but her, and l. for ever 83:24
l. ceases to be a pleasure 29:23
l., curiosity, freckles, and doubt 303:15
l. fled 472:6
l. for sale 316:29
l. goes toward l. 379:18
l. had been sae ill to win 23:24
l. hath an end 412:25
l. he laughed to scorn 387:10
L. in a golden bowl 60:21
l. in a hut 231:15
l. in her sunny eyes 124:2
l. in her train 67:26
l. in idleness 380:16
l., in present-day society 106:3
l. is a boy 87:19
l. is a sickness full of woes 131:7
l. is a spirit all compact 387:11
l. is a universal migraine 185:13
l. is best 75:23
l. is blind 369:27
l. is dying 25:12
l. is enough 288:16
l. is God 431:6
l. is like linen often changed 166:18
l. is like the measles 218:6, 218:14
l. is not l. which alters 386:32
l. is not the dying moan 307:30
l. is strong as death 44:27
l. is swift of foot 199:10
l. is the fulfilling of the law 54:43
l. is the wisdom of the fool 224:13
l. is then our duty 174:11
l. itself have rest 93:21
l. itself shall slumber on 394:6
l. levels all 29:19
l. lies beyond the tomb 114:28
l. . . . like a bee 256:1
l. looks not with eyes 371:22
l. makes the world go round 8:4
l. means never having to say you're sorry 341:26
l. never subsides into friendship 94:13
l. once pleads admission to our hearts 1:12
l. one another 53:26
l. rules the court 339:27
l. seeketh not itself to please 61:19
l. set you going 310:1
l. slights it 18:22
l. so amazing, so divine 447:21
l. sought is good 383:20
l. still has something of the sea 341:18
l. that can be reckoned 343:15
L. that dare not speak its name 147:1
l. that moves the sun 132:2
l. that never told can be 61:13
l. that so desires 272:5
l. that time was not as l. is nowadays 265:17
l. that was more than l. 310:16
L., the human form divine 62:11

l., thou art absolute sole Lord 128:20
l. thy neighbour 35:6, 50:35
l. thyself last 358:25
l. we swore would last for an age 133:6
l. which doth us bind 268:16
l. . . . whole concern of everyone's life 292:4
l. will make a dog howl in rhyme 28:3
L. without his wings! 93:10
l. wol nat ben constreyned by maistrye 107:30
l. your enemies 49:5
l.'s but the frailty of the mind 120:29
l.'s long since cancelled woe 385:24
l.'s not Time's fool 387:1
l.'s perfect blossom 305:21
l.'s planet rises yonder 75:2
l.'s proper hue 280:28
l.'s the noblest frailty of the mind 151:24
l.'s tongue is in his eyes 166:20
l.'s young dream 287:1
making l. at all seasons 27:15
man's l. for an animal 400:26
man's ultimate l. for man 249:11
many waters cannot quench l. 44:28
met you not with my true l. 325:6
mie l. ys dedde 107:5
money can't buy me l. 253:6
more of l. than matrimony 182:32
must l. one another or die 15:9
my l. is of a birth as rare 268:15
my l. is the maid ov all maïdens 25:7
my l.'s like a red red rose 85:4
my only l. sprung from my only hate 379:6
my true l. sits him down 8:19
my true l. will never meet again 8:10
my vegetable l. should grow 269:1
my whole course of l. 374:1
ne'er ebb to humble l. 375:10
never doubt I l. 349:25
new every morning is the l. 234:19
no l. lost between us 182:22
no peace of mind in l. 321:9
not Death, but L. 72:4
not enough religion to make us l. 411:19
O lyric L., half angel 77:29
O spirit of l.! 382:24
off with the old l. 8:3
One Must Not Trifle with L. 290:14
only our l. hath no decay 144:15
Our l. shall live 402:19
oyster may be crossed in l. 395:14
pangs of disprized l. 350:14
perfect l. casteth out fear 57:41
possible to l. such a man? 109:16
pray l. me little 200:8
prize of learning l. 74:6
put aside a long-standing l. 104:3
regain l. once possessed 281:25
renewing is of l. 154:13
right place for l. 169:20
right true end of l. 144:25
sad and heavy was the l. 22:11
save in the office and affairs of l. 372:31
she l.s you 253:14
some have died for l. 467:4
sometimes I wish I could fall in l. 436:1
speak low if you speak l. 372:30
such l. as spirits feel 462:10

sweet l. remembered 385:23
thank heaven, fasting, for a good man's l. 345:28
that ever l. did make thee run into 344:33
though L. and all his pleasures 97:29
through our l. that we have loved together
    265:20
thy l. is better than wine 44:16
thy l. prove likewise variable 379:15
thy l. to me was wonderful 36:3
to let the warm L. in 232:12
to l. and to cherish 319:42
to l., cherish and to obey 319:43
to l. her is a liberal education 404:9
to l. or not 280:12
to l. so, be so loved 74:15
tomorrow may he l. 9:8
true l.'s the gift 339:30
trust thou thy L. 333:19
two l.s have I of comfort and despair 387:7
two passions, vanity and l. 109:15
we l. being in l. 425:4
we l. the things we l. 170:7
we must l. one another 136:1
when I was in l. with you 210:12
when l. and duty clash! 421:35
when l. begins to sicken 360:26
when L. speaks 363:31
when no man dies for l. 151:27
where L. is throned 383:9
whose l. will never die 273:7
with l. from me to you 253:8
you cannot call it l. 351:29
you learn to l. by loving 213:7
you made me l. you 263:3
your true l.'s coming 383:2
Love-adept: dreaming like a l. 393:3
Loved: all we l. of him should be 389:29
    and the l. one all together! 76:8
    better l. ye canna be 291:5
    better l. you'll never be 203:13
    better to have l. and lost 88:23, 417:34
    first he l. her 8:13
    had we never l. sae kindly 83:25
    I l. him for himself alone 395:15
    I l. him not 246:26
    l. not wisely but too well 375:26
    never l. has never lived 174:18
    no sooner l. but they sighed 346:8
    out upon it, I have l. 409:9
    pressed to say why I l. him 285:11
    shamed . . . to have l. so slight a thing 420:1
    than never to have l. at all 417:34
    those whom he l. so long 328:25
    to be l. needs only to be seen 150:18
    to have l. 10:23
    who ever l., that l. not at first sight 267:22
    who sought the thing he l. 462:16
Loved One: what did your L. pass on from? 448:6
Love-in-idleness: maidens call it L. 371:36
Love-light: l. in your eye 60:2
Loveliness: bathed in eve's l. 134:28
    enough their simple l. for me 232:20
    her l. I never knew 116:15
    its l. increases 230:6
    l. needs not the foreign aid of ornament 428:12
    luxuries . . . your l. 234:14
    portion of the l. 390:7

woman of so shining l. 471:23
Lovely: Is it l., and gentle 136:27
  l. and a fearful thing 91:14
  look thy last on all things l. 134:13
  love the l. that are not beloved 305:25
  once he made more l. 390:7
  she's l., she's divine 271:12
  thou art more l. and more temperate 385:17
Love-match: l. was the only thing for happiness 154:4
Lover: all mankind love a l. 158:27
  came two l.s lately wed 419:11
  Frankie and Johnny were l.s 7:17
  it was a l. and his lass 346:12
  l., all as frantic 372:14
  l., sighing like furnace 345:11
  l.'s eyes will gaze an eagle blind 363:30
  l.'s quarrels are the renewal of love 424:28
  l.s cannot see the pretty follies 369:27
  l.s find their peace at last 166:3
  l.s lying two by two 210:10
  l.s scorn whom that love doth possess 396:13
  l.s to bed 372:20
  make two l.s happy 311:5
  must pure l.s' souls descend 145:5
  my fause l. stole my rose 86:1
  O l. of my life 78:4
  old l.s are soundest 449:1
  pair of star-crossed l.s 378:21
  sighed as a l. 175:10
  sleepless l.s . . . awake 315:12
  such a constant l. 409:9
  suppose they were l.s 104:24
  through l.s' brains 378:30
  thy l.s were all untrue 151:28
  true l.s run into strange capers 344:34
  truest l. of a sinful man 265:23
Love-sick: l. all against our will 177:36
Lovest: an thou l. me 354:15
Loveth: whosoever l. and maketh a lie 58:39
Loving: end by l. himself better than all 118:15
  l. not, hating not 73:22
  me the l. and you the loth 75:14
  most l. mere folly 345:13
  privilege . . . of l. longest 16:33
  they talks a lot o' l. 240:5
Low: speak l. if you speak love 372:30
Lower: a little l. than the angels 37:26
Lowlands: as she sails by the L. 22:19
  L. shall meet thee in battle array 97:8
Loyal: easier for a man to be l. 452:14
  l. and neutral 366:6
Loyalty: impossible l.s! 12:19
  l. no harm meant 7:28
Lucifer: he falls like L. 358:22
  L., son of the morning! 45:12
  on a starred night Prince L. uprose 272:6
  unhappy spirits that fell with L. 266:19
Lucis: l. tuae radium 247:16
Luck: amazed at one's l. 290:2
  as good l. would have it 371:13
  generally have great l. with my Glubjullas 148:12
  l. in odd numbers 258:18
Lucky: L. Jim 5:2
Lucre: filthy l. 56:41

Lucy: 'If L. should be dead!' 466:28
  when L. ceased to be 466:13
Luddites: who makes L. rise? 399:1
Lugete: l., o Veneres Cupidinesque 103:9
Luggage: kill the poys and the l.! 357:20
Lugger: forcing her on board the l. 224:15
Lukewarm: because thou art l. 58:10
Lullaby: I will sing a l. 134:3
  once in a l. 192:6
Lullay: with l., l., like a child 397:24
Lully: Good Master Raymund L. 245:10
Lumbago: L. and the Laxative Islands 342:21
Lumber: loads of learned l. in his head 313:23
Lumberjack: I'm a l. 286:11
Lumina: exspectata diu vix tandem l. tollit 103:20
Lump: born a shapeless l. 149:13
  l. bred up in darkness 242:22
  little leaven leaveneth the whole l. 55:5
Luna: cuando sale la l. 172:18
Lunatic: l., the lover, and the poet 372:13
  l.s have taken over the asylum 332:18
Lunch: unable to l. today 317:2
Lundy: Lord L. from his earliest years 30:11
Lung: my l.s began to crow 345:5
  parks were the l.s of London 309:19
Lurch: he'd left me in the l. 252:5
Lurcher: half l. and half cur 127:20
Lust: for l. of knowing 166:6
  l. is perjured 387:4
  that own no l. 417:7
Lustre: shine . . . with such a l. 127:29
  sits obscure in the exceeding l. 391:18
  where is thy l. now? 362:30
Lute: lascivious pleasing of a l. 377:22
  little rift within the l. 417:4
  musical as is Apollo's l. 275:21
  took an old cracked l. 391:1
  when the l. is broken 391:21
Luthany: pass the gates of L. 427:21
Luther, Martin 286:4
Lux: cum semel occidit brevis l. 103:11
  fiat l. 33:15
Luxuries: give us the l. of life 289:12
  l. not for him who went for the Simple Life 110:7
  two l. to brood over 234:14
Luxurious: falsly l.! will not man awake? 428:9
Luxury: all their l. was doing good 173:9
  knowledge of the ancient languages . . . a l. 68:18
  l. of doing good 128:12, 181:26
  to l. and riot 280:42
Lyf: l. so short 108:21
Lying: how this world is given to l.! 355:9
  l., vainness, babbling drunkenness 383:29
  let me have no l. 385:3
  one of you is l. 304:3
  this vice of l.! 356:6
Lyme: was an old party of L. 284:18
Lyon: known as Richard Gare de L. 342:18
Lyonnesse: when I set out for L. 193:13
Lyre: l. with other strings 126:25
  make me thy l. 392:11
  sound of l.s and flutes 305:16
  waked to ecstasy the living l. 186:9
Lyricis: quodsi me l. vatibus inseres 208:2
Lyttelton, Lord 109:16

M

Mab: Queen M. hath been with you 378:30
   this is that very M. 379:2
Macaroni: and called it M. 23:27
MacArthur, General 432:25
Macassar: 'incomparable oil', M.! 90:32
Macaulay, Thomas Babington 400:1
   as cocksure of anything as Tom M. is 271:13
   M. is well for a while 100:20
Macavity: M. wasn't there! 156:27
Macbeth: M. does murder sleep 365:26
   M. shall never vanquished be 367:1
McCarthyism: M. is Americanism 263:4
MacDonald, Ramsay 112:13 112:14
Macduff: lay on, M. 368:2
   M. was from his mother's womb 367:30
Macedonia: come over into M. 53:51
McGregor: don't go into Mr M.'s garden 317:6
   my name is M.! 341:5
McGrew: Dangerous Dan M. 342:26
Machiavelli: much beholden to M. 18:6
Machine: desiccated calculating m. 33:7
   Ghost in the M. 334:5
   man . . . an ingenious m. 142:14
   more like a great thought than a great m. 217:19
   you're a m. 387:21
Machine-à-habiter: maison est une m. 251:20
Machinery: immediately you come to m. 437:7
Machte: ihr himmlischen M. 180:7
Mackerel: not so the m. 169:9
Macmillan, Harold 429:4, 439:7
Maçon: soyez plutôt m. 64:14
Mad: he first makes m. 160:1
   he is m., 'tis true 349:24
   he made me m. 353:30
   heroically m. 149:29
   it will make us m. 365:25
   let me not be m. 362:5
   m. about the boy 123:29
   m. as the mist and snow 471:12
   m., bad, and dangerous to know 245:2
   m. in pursuit 387:5
   M. World, My Masters 67:21
   men that God made m. 109:28
   much learning doth make thee m. 54:10
   nothing else but m. 349:22
   O fool! I shall go m. 362:13
   pleasure sure in being m. 151:29
   we are all born m. 28:16
Madam: M., I may not call you 157:24
Made: fearfully and wonderfully m. 41:12
   thou hast m. me 145:12
Madeleine: little crumb of m. 321:6
Madilda: her name vas M. Yane 252:14
Madman: Hugo was a m. 116:4
   if a m. were to come into this room 222:20
   m. saith He said so 74:19
   whom do you flee, m.? 441:13
Madmen: none but m. know 151:29
Madness: best minds . . . destroyed by m. 178:27
   clear account of his m. 105:17
   fine m. still he did retain 148:16
   m. of art 216:17
   midsummer m. 383:24
   moon-struck m. 280:39
   such harmonious m. 394:22

though this be m. 349:30
   'tis m. to defer 472:22
   to define true m. 349:22
   work like m. in the brain 117:23
Madonna: M. of the Slums 255:17
Madrid: columns advancing on M. 283:8
Madrigal: melodious birds sing m.s 267:24
Maenalus: singing how down the vale of M. 391:9
Maeonides: old M. the blind 166:12
Magazine: by the butt of the M. Wall 226:3
Magdalen: fourteen months at M. College 175:8
Magic: all thy threads with m. art 127:35
   like m. in a pint bottle 138:18
   old black m. 271:23
   with a m. like thee 93:25
Magistrate: considered . . . by the m. as equally
   useful 175:13
   like m.s correct at home 356:24
Magna Carta: M. is such a fellow 116:10
Magnanimity: curb your m. 234:17
   m. in politics 81:23
Magnet: m. ever attract a silver churn! 177:42
Magnifique: m., mais ce n'est pas la guerre 65:15
Magnify: doth m. the Lord 51:42
Magnitude: liar of the first m. 120:5
Magnus: vivit post proelia M. 259:14
Magpie: swollen m. in a fitful sun 317:17
Mahogany: sheltered about The M. Tree 425:27
Mahomet: M. will go to the hill 19:26
Maid: be good, sweet m. 237:13
   chariest m. is prodigal enough 348:19
   could not live a m. 306:22
   free m.s that weave their thread 383:12
   he kissed likewise the m. in the kitchen 128:3
   I am a m. at your window 352:7
   if seven m.s with seven mops 102:3
   little m. would have her will 467:17
   m. famous for all time 209:1
   m. is not dead 49:35
   m. singing in the valley below 7:13
   m. was in the garden 297:31
   m.s are May when they are m.s 346:4
   m.s dance in a ring 292:21
   m.s strange seraphic pieces of life 431:16
   my pretty m. 298:15
   O Music! sphere-descended m. 119:20
   pretty m.s all in a row 297:9
   slain by a fair cruel m. 383:13
   though all m. be comely 25:7
   three little m.s from school 177:21
   three little m.s who, all unwary 177:23
   way of a man with a m. 239:34
   weary lot is thine, fair m. 340:24
   welcome m.s of honour 200:18
   yonder a m. 193:1
Maiden: and a village m. she 420:7
   archly the m. smiled 256:17
   de m. mit nodings on 252:13
   here's to the m. of bashful fifteen 395:37
   I know a m. fair to see 256:10
   I pursued a m. 391:9
   kissed the m. all forlorn 298:6
   m. and mistress of the months 411:31
   m. in the mor lay 5:14
   m. never bold 374:2
   m.s, like moths 89:11
   many a rose-lipt m. 210:29

scanter of your m. presence 348:26
simple m. in her flower 419:3
still fit for the m.s 209:4
tell me, pretty m. 66:6, 191:2
to love one m. only 416:32
twenty love-sick m.s 177:36
use a poor m. so 7:13
Mail: quite out of fashion, like a rusty m. 382:13
Main: every man is . . . part of the m. 146:20
Maisie: proud M. is in the wood 340:34
Maison: il brûlerait votre m. 106:1
    m. est une machine-à-habiter 251:20
Maistrye: love wol nat ben constreyned by m. 107:30
Maître: je suis m. de moi 122:14
Maîtresse: j'aurai des m.s 174:31
Majesty: attribute to awe and m. 370:9
    busied in his m. 356:24
    I love the m. of human sufferings 439:17
    insult dying m. 3:27
    next in m. 150:26
    of an infinite M. 318:20
    ride on in m.! 274:12
    thy m. how bright 161:2
Major: live with scarlet M.s at the Base 337:27
Major-General: very model of a modern M. 178:3
Majority: great silent m. 295:7
    he has gone over to the m. 99:15
    joined the great m. 308:8
    on God's side, is a m. 308:17
    one man with courage makes a m. 216:2
Make-up: two types of mental m. 217:9
Maker: gone to meet its m. 286:12
    he adores his m. 68:19
    man be more pure than his m.? 36:39
    Our M., Defender, Redeemer and Friend! 184:18
    scattered his M.'s image through the land 149:5
    t' abhor the m.s 150:25
Makest: what m. thou? 46:1
Mal: sors d'un m. pour tomber dans un pire 122:16
    souvent la peur d'un m. 64:9
Maladies: work is the grand cure of all the m. 100:5
Malady: m. most incident to maids 384:29
    only m. I . . . had not got 218:7
Male: beastly . . . m. of the species 249:1
    female . . . more deadly than the m. 238:31
    m. and female created he them 33:16
    no reason for the existence of the m. sex 451:17
Malherbe: enfin M. vint 64:10
Malice: m. domestic, foreign levy 366:15
    m. never was his aim 410:12
    much m. mingles with a little wit 150:22
    nor set down aught in m. 375:26
    with m. toward none 254:19
Malicious: he is not m. 155:2
Malign: one had rather m. oneself 248:9
Malignity: m. . . . characteristic of apostates 262:16
Mall: loved M., Meg and Marian 381:1
Mallecho: this is miching m. 351:8
Malmesey: drowned in a barrel of M. wine 161:6
Malmsey: rare store of m. 30:1
Malt: m. does more than Milton can 210:30
    rat that ate the m. 298:6
Mammalia: we are m.! 271:7
Mammon: cannot serve God and m. 49:14
    m. of iniquity 196:20
    m. of unrighteousness 52:30
    M. wins his way 89:11

Man: Angry Young M. 306:8
    any m. with a good estate 120:9
    as a grown m. 67:12
    away, slight m.! 360:29
    behold the m.! 53:34
    best good m. 328:6
    better m. than I am 239:10
    bold bad m. 358:15
    brief and powerless is M.'s life 333:21
    busiest m. who has time to spare 304:21
    do all things like a m. 199:6
    each m. as he really is 217:15
    ech m. for him-self 108:1
    every m.'s the son of his own deeds 105:7
    fit m. for the constable of the watch 373:5
    fury of a patient m. 149:28
    give me that m. 351:4
    give the world assurance of a m. 351:27
    God created m. 33:16
    he was a m. 348:10
    hour is come, but not the m. 340:33
    how many roads must a m. walk down 153:5
    I love not m. the less 90:19
    I met a m. who wasn't there 271:10
    I must also feel it like a m. 367:10
    I think the m. was I 22:4
    inner m. 319:48
    is the old m. agreeable? 139:25
    is the substantial m. 70:15
    large-hearted m. 72:9
    laughs to see the green m. pass 203:7
    let him pass for a m. 369:9
    let not m. have the upper hand 37:29
    let the m. be lost 313:18
    Little M., You've Had a Busy Day 397:6
    looked from pig to m. 300:16
    M. after his own heart 35:44
    m. all tattered and torn 298:6
    m. alone beneath the heaven 339:30
    m. always dies 169:18
    m. appears on earth for a little while 28:23
    m. be more pure than his maker? 36:39
    m., being reasonable, must get drunk 91:13
    m. doth not live by bread alone 35:12
    m. dreaming I was a butterfly 111:19
    m., false m. 251:25
    m. for all seasons 454:10
    m. for the field 422:11
    m. from the Pru 3:5
    m. goeth to his long home 44:11
    m. has his will 203:30
    m. he was, to all the country dear 180:23
    m., his days are as grass 40:10
    m. I am may cease to be! 420:29
    m. . . . is a being born to believe 143:4
    m. is a gaming animal 245:25
    m. is a history-making creature 15:24
    m. is a noble animal 71:20
    m. is . . . a political animal 10:7
    m. is . . . a religious animal 82:19
    m. is a social animal 403:16
    m. is a tool-making animal 168:26
    m. is a tool-using animal 100:8
    m. is a useless passion 337:20
    m. is an ungrateful beast 31:2
    m. is born unto trouble 36:40
    m. is condemned to be free 337:22

m. is dead 169:19
m. is more complex 437:3
m. is no more than a reed 305:11
m. is not m. as yet 76:18
m. is only m. at the surface 437:7
m. is something that is to be surpassed 294:18
m. is the hunter 422:10
m. is the measure of all things 321:4
m. is the only creature that consumes 300:11
m. is the whole world 71:10
m. is what he eats 162:12
m. marks the earth with ruin 90:20
m. must think o' things 239:36
m. never found the deities so kindly 324:9
m. never is, but always to be blessed 313:28
m. not old 308:14
m. of an unbounded stomach 359:2
M. of Feeling 263:17
m. partly is 74:8
m. proposes 235:5
m. remains sceptreless, free 393:15
m. severe he was 181:6
m. shall not live by bread alone 48:39
m. so various 149:20
m. that is born of a woman 37:1, 320:3
m. wants but little 182:29
m. was born free 332:12
m. was formed for society 59:27
m. was made to mourn 85:1
M. Who Delivers the Goods 270:6
m. who does not lose his reason 253:25
m. who makes no mistake 308:10
m. who used to notice such things 192:9
m. whom the king delighteth to honour 36:31
m.'s a m. for a' that 84:19
m.'s desire is for the woman 118:32
m.'s gotta do 243:14
m.'s inhumanity to m. 85:2
m.'s love is of m.'s life 91:7
m.'s ultimate love for m. 249:11
m.'s understanding of m. 437:16
many a m. has been a wonder 285:20
mildest mannered m. 91:19
modest little m. 113:26
new m. may be raised up in him 319:25
no bad m. can be a good poet 305:14
no m. . . . . hath lived better than I have done
    265:15
no m. is an island 146:20
no m. is entitled to 330:6
no m. see me more 358:20
no m. shall ever put asunder 387:32
no m. truly knows 71:8
no m. worth having 437:13
not a m., you're a machine 387:21
not m. for the sabbath 51:28
nothing great but m. 191:6
of M.'s first disobedience 277:32
old m. and no honester than I 373:9
old m., broken 358:27
one m. among a thousand 43:32
one m. with a dream 301:16
only m. is vile 196:25
people arose as one m. 35:37
play is the tragedy 'M.' 310:19
ready now to call a m. *a good m.* 223:15
right m. to fill the right place 250:1

sadder and a wiser m. 117:17
she knows her m. 151:13
so much one m. can do 268:26
so soon as the m. overtook me 80:24
so unto the m. is woman 257:14
social, friendly, honest m. 84:14
spared a better m. 355:7
standing with the greatest m. 224:8
strongest m. upon earth 214:9
there shall no m. see me 35:4
there was an old M. who said 250:12
there was an Old M. with a beard 250:13
thin m. inside every fat m. 300:17
this is the state of m. 358:21
this m. is now become a god 359:14
'This m. loved *me*!' 246:27
this was a m.! 361:5
thou art the m. 36:7
thou madest m. 417:25
thou wert the meekest m. 265:23
thought the old m. to have had so much blood in
    him 367:12
to be a well-favoured m. 373:4
use every m. after his desert 350:7
way of a m. with a maid 43:8
we know nothing of m. 227:7
weak, and despised old m. 362:16
what a piece of work is a m.! 349:36
what bloody m. is that? 364:12
what is a m. 351:41
what m. has made of m.? 462:25
what should a m. be? 214:15
when a m. bites a dog 131:5
when God at first made m. 199:20
when I became a m. 55:25
where's the m. could ease a heart 304:2
wilt scarce be a m. 27:24
wished that heaven had made her such a m.
    374:6
wonderful all-round m. 29:21
wondrous necessary m. 273:1
you'll be a M., my son! 239:14
young m. not yet 19:13
Management: not all under same m. 202:2
Man-at-alms: m. must now serve on his knees 307:1
Mandalay: no buses runnin' from the Bank to M.
    240:4
    road to M. 240:2
Mandarin: christen this style M. 121:11
Manderlay: I dreamt I went to M. again 152:11
Mandragora: give me to drink m. 343:22
Mandrake: get with child a m. root 146:7
Manet: M. and the Post-Impressionists 170:25
Manger: dog in the m. 3:18
    in a m. for His bed 4:6
    in the rude m. lies 277:22
Manges: dis-moi ce que tu m. 68:20
Mangle: turning an immense pecuniary M. 141:27
Mangler: mother and a m. 140:15
Manhood: for a bright m. 260:18
    hold their m.s cheap 357:19
    m. a struggle 143:15
    m.'s dark and tossing waves 393:13
    my m., long misled by wandering fires 150:19
    neither honesty, m. or good fellowship 353:24
Manifest: work shall be made m. 55:1
Manifesto: first powerful m. 402:13

Man-in-the-street: m. . . . keen observer of life 14:26
Mankind: all m. love a lover 158:27
  as I know more of m. 223:15
  fleeting generations of m. 394:26
  how beauteous m. is! 381:18
  I am involved in M. 146:21
  maddest of all m.! 239:22
  made for the use and benefit of m. 430:8
  m. are the asses who pull 92:33
  m. in conscious virtue bold 315:10
  m. moves so slowly 178:30
  m. won 236:19
  mass of m. understand monarchy 21:8
  need not be to hate, m. 89:28
  not unlike the great ones of m. 126:32
  nuptial love maketh m. 19:16
  of all m. I love but you alone 23:3
  one disillusion – m. 236:9
  only the wisest of m. 399:6
  proper study of m. is man 314:1
  ride m. 158:13
  survey m. from China to Peru 219:5
  upper and lower part of m. 133:13
  willing to love all m. 223:2
  wisest, brightest, meanest of m. 314:10
  woman that seduces all m. 174:1
  you shall not crucify m. 79:19
Manliness: silent m. of grief 181:14
Man-milliner: respectable architectural m. 333:7
Mann: Kleiner Mann, was nun? 161:7
Manner: bewrayed as by his m.s 403:6
  bow-wow public park m. 26:4
  catch the m.s living as they rise 313:26
  cease to think about the m. of doing it 196:14
  describe not men, but m.s 162:25
  evil communications corrupt good m.s 55:35
  graced with polished m.s 127:28
  I know their tricks and their m.s 140:12
  leave off first for m.s' sake 48:18
  men's evil m.s live in brass 359:3
  particular m.s can be known to few 219:30
  prose . . . affair of good m.s 270:25
  to the m. born 348:28
  where noble m.s veil defect 305:21
  with sweeter m.s, purer laws 418:25
Mansion: before the starry threshold . . . my m. is
    275:3
  build thee more stately m.s 203:31
  compare human life to a large m. 234:3
  in my Father's house are many m.s 53:27
  made his everlasting m. 381:26
  title clear to m.s in the skies 447:19
Mantle: cast his m. upon him 36:19
  cast like a m. the sea 184:17
  green m. of the standing pool 362:25
  twitched his m. blue 277:18
Manu: te teanam . . . deficiente m. 430:4
Manure: blood . . . is its natural m. 217:24
Manuscript: brown Greek m.s 73:11
  Youth's sweet-scented M. 164:29
Many: done because we are too m. 193:19
  for we are m. 51:32
  m. are called 51:2
  m. fail, the one succeeds 416:8
  mutable, rank-scented m. 346:26
  through the unheeding m. 393:32
  ye are m. – they are few 392:2

Map: geography is about m.s 31:25
  roll up that m. 309:22
Maran-atha: let him be Anathema, M. 55:42
Marathon: M. looks on the sea 91:24
Marble: but this in m. 28:2
  Chair . . . glowed on the m. 156:40
  found it brick and left it m. 409:11
  I dreamt that I dwelt in m. halls 80:11
  in thy m. vaults 269:2
  life is made up of m. and mud 195:4
  not m., nor the gilded monuments 385:30
Marbre: vers, m., onyx, émail 173:19
March: her m. is o'er the mountain waves 97:22
  long majestic m. 315:34
  m. of the human mind 81:20
  m. of the retreating world 302:17
  take the winds of M. with beauty 384:29
Machen: M. aus alten Zeiten 197:2
Marches: our dreadful m. to delight measures
    377:21
Marching: while God is m. on 211:6
Mere: lend me your grey m. 8:22
  man shall have his m. again 372:7
  patience be a tired m. 356:28
Margaret: merry M., as midsummer flower 398:3
Margery: some went upstairs with M. 15:6
Mariana: resides this dejected M. 368:25
Maries: Queen had four M. 23:5
Marigold: m., that goes to bed wi' the sun 384:28
Marin: combien de m.s 211:20
Mariner: I fear thee, ancient M.! 117:3
  it is an ancient m. 116:18
  merry m.s are bold and free 390:26
  Oh rest ye, brother m.s 420:19
  we be three poor m.s 326:3
  ye M.s of England 97:20
Mariposas: barba llena de m. 173:1
Mark: God save the m.! 353:30
  it is an ever-fixèd m. 386:32
  Lord set a m. upon Cain 34:10
  may none these m.s efface! 93:24
  no drowning m. upon him 380:25
  nobody m.s you 372:24
  three quarks for Muster M.! 226:14
Market: at noon-day upon the m. place 359:23
  chief good and m. of his time 351:41
  fellow in a m. town 309:5
  great m.s by the sea 166:3
  knowledge is born in the m. 115:15
  this little pig went to m. 298:7
Marlborough: from M.'s eyes 219:10
Marlowe, Christopher 148:15
  M.'s mighty line 225:22
Marmion: last words of M. 340:20
Marmorean: sit gloriatus m. se relinquere 409:11
Marred: man that's m. 343:9
Marriage 400:11
  all the unhappy m.s 459:9
  coldly furnish forth the m. tables 348:8
  doesn't have to get anywhere in a m. 290:3
  exclaim loudly against second marriage 162:16
  far from being natural . . . to live in a state of m.
    222:5
  good hanging prevents a bad m. 382:30
  hanging and m. 162:3
  I'll frighten her into m. 224:15
  in a happy m. it is the wife 67:19

who slew his m.? 36:29
who's m., who's man 410:8
Master-passion: m. is the love of news 128:8
one m. in the breast 314:3
Masterpiece: adventures of his mind among m.s
168:15
Nature's great m., an elephant 146:2
Masters: m.s at the moment 389:18
Mastery: m. of the thing! 206:22
Mastiff: what can ail the m. bitch? 117:20
Masturbation 4:16
Mat: caught my foot in the m. 188:17
Match: blue spurt of a lighted m. 75:27
ear and eyes m. me 77:19
ten to make and the m. to win 293:21
Mate: his lady's ta'en anither m. 23:19
m. of the *Nancy* brig 176:14
one of them said to his m. 23:18
when she took unto herself a m. 463:18
Matelot: entends le chant des m.s 265:6
Mater: dulcium m. saeva Cupidinum 209:7
stabat m. dolorosa 430:15
Mathematics: m. make men subtle 20:34
m. may be defined 333:23
m. possess not only truth 333:22
Matilda: a-waltzing, M. with me 305:19
M. told such dreadful lies 30:15
Matin: glow-worm shows the m. to be near 349:11
Mating: only in the m. season 274:2
Matrimony: critical period in m. 199:1
from love to m. in a moment 17:3
m. to begin with a little aversion 395:19
more of love than m. 182:32
Matron: m.'s glance 180:17
night, thou sober-suited m. 379:36
Matter: Bishop Berkeley said 'there was no m.' 92:4
consults them about . . . serious m.s 109:12
doesn't much m. what else you have 25:28
he that repeateth a m. 42:17
how great a m. a little fire kindleth! 57:24
m. . . . a convenient formula 333:24
meaning, however, is no great m. 96:5
more m. with less art 349:23
much m. decocted 171:9
root of the m. 37:5
take away the m. of them 19:32
thy honesty and love doth mince this m. 374:23
triumph of m. over mind 456:9
what can the m. be? 297:12
Matthew: M., Mark, Luke and John 3:16
Maud: come into the garden, M. 420:33
Maunder: let her m. and mumble 100:16
Maupassant: I beat Mr de M. 197:22
Maux: raconter ses m. 122:17
Mawkish: so sweetly m. 311:19
Mawkishness: thence proceeds m. 230:5
Max: M. und Moritz ihrerseits 86:24
Maxim: it is a m. with me 32:2
it was a m. with Foxey 139:31
m. of the British people 112:10
'twas a m. he had often tried 128:11
with a little hoard of m.s 419:27
May: ac on a M. morwenyng 247:14
and M., and June 74:3
blotted the pleasant M. 67:27
crowned with milk-white m. 68:8
fair as is the rose in M. 108:20

fresh as is the month of M. 107:11
I'm to be Queen o' the M. 421:4
M. month flaps its glad green leaves 192:9
M. when they are maids 346:4
M. will be fine next year 209:23
merriment of M. 230:9
merry month of M. 23:6, 25:10
mid-M.'s eldest child 232:6
month of M. is comen 108:18
month of M. was come 265:16
more matter for a M. morning 383:26
nuts in M. 6:3
shake the darling buds of M. 385:17
there's an end of M. 209:22
we frolic while 'tis M. 187:10
wish a snow in M.'s new-fangled mirth 363:19
Maybe: definite m. 183:11
No sir, don't mean m. 229:6
Mayde: as meke as is a m. 107:9
Mayflower: my folks didn't come over on the *M.*
329:7
Maypole: away to the m. hie 7:12
I sing of m.s 200:2
Maze: faints, entangled in their m.s 393:11
m.s of metaphorical confusion 227:9
mighty m.! but not without a plan 313:25
pleasant m.s of her hair 124:2
Me: you would not be seeking M. 305:13
Me-ow: 'M.', they said, 'm., m.' 203:2
Meadow: infinite m.s of heaven 256:21
m.s trim with daisies pied 276:26
meander through a m. of margin 395:34
paint the m.s with delight 364:6
time when m., grove and stream 463:30
Mean: citizen of no m. city 54:5
down these m. streets 106:6
I m. what I say 101:5
not a more m., stupid . . . animal 196:10
place and m.s for every man alive 343:11
Private M.s is dead 399:16
thwarted by narrow m.s at home 227:21
whoever prizes the golden m. 208:18
Meander: by slow M.'s margent green 275:14
Meaning: as to the m., it's what you please 95:16
charge his mind with m.s 127:5
free from all m. 149:29
go to the author to get at *his* m. 333:11
language charged with m. 317:29
m. doesn't matter 177:39
m., however, is no great matter 96:5
subtler m.s of what roses say 79:5
to some faint m. make pretence 150:28
wrestle with words and m.s 155:34
Meannesses: some m. which are too mean 425:15
Means: as a m. the businessman is tolerable 236:11
die beyond my m. 456:23
live within our m. 446:21
my m. may lie too low for envy 124:5
war is . . . continuation of politics by other m.
114:32
you do take the m. whereby I live 370:16
Measles: did you ever hav the m. 446:9
love is like the m. 218:6, 218:14
Measure: man is the m. of all things 321:4
m. small things by great 442:2
M. still for M. 368:30
'not men but m.s' 82:29

our dreadful marches to delight m.s 377:21
shrunk to this little m. 360:8
wielder of the stateliest m. 423:28
with what m. ye mete 51:31
Meat: dined upon cold m. 307:20
gall for my m. 39:18
I can not eat but little m. 408:2
I can't abide his m. 134:18
m. and drink to me 346:7
one man is appointed to buy the m. 342:4
out of the eater came forth m. 35:31
some hae m., and canna eat 85:12
taste my m. 199:19
this dish of m. is too good 445:26
upon what m. doth this our Caesar feed 359:17
young lions . . . seek their m. from God 40:12
Mecca: some to M. turn to pray 166:4
Medal: m. inscribed 'For Vaguery in the Field'
    301:10
Medallion: dumb as old m.s to the thumb 263:20
Medea: M. gathered the enchanted herbs 370:18
Medes: given to the M. and Persians 47:5
laws of the Persians and the M. 36:30
Medias: in m. res 207:4
Medicine: faithful friend is the m. of life 48:4
given me m.s to make me love him 353:35
grief is itself a m. 124:23
m. for the soul 142:15
miserable hath no other m. 368:17
Medio: m. tutissimus ibis 301:26
Mediocrity: supreme expression of the m. of the
    apparatus 432:16
Meditate: strictly m. the thankless Muse 277:7
Meditation: in maiden m., fancy free 371:36
m. here may think down hours 127:25
m. of my heart 37:38
wings as swift as m. 349:3
Mediterranean: blue M., where he lay 392:7
set out again immediately for the M. 342:18
Medium: m. is the message 264:3
m. . . . neither rare nor well done 242:13
Meed: Death is Life's high m. 233:13
without the m. of some melodious tear 277:2
Meek: He is m. and He is mild 62:16
ornament of a m. and quiet spirit 57:33
safer being m. than fierce 72:22
Meet: if I should m. thee 94:9
if we do m. again 360:35
we shall m. 446:28
Meeter: therefore deemed it m. 306:15
Meeting: changed to merry m.s 377:21
m.s are indispensable 172:5
this m. is drunk 141:9
Megrim: M. at her head 315:25
Meister: zeigt sich erst der M. 180:4
Meistersinger: our M., thou set breath in steel
    128:15
Melancholy: after ten months' m. 464:29
charm can soothe her m. 182:38
cue is villainous m. 362:2
hail divine m. 276:2
hence loathèd M. 276:17
I can suck m. out of a song 344:38
in a m. man's heart 86:11
inherited a vile m. 223:24
it is a m. of mine own 346:1
m. fit shall fall 231:28

M. marked him for her own 186:18
moral (like all morals) m. 91:40
naught so sweet as m. 86:4
pale M. sat retired 119:18
pleasing fit of m. 275:23
rare recipe for m. 246:9
stool there to be m. upon 225:5
sweet as lovely m. 27:26
veiled M. has her sovran shrine 231:29
with a green and yellow m. 383:14
Mélange: m. adultère de tout 122:11
Meliora: video m. proboque 302:2
Melodies: heard m. are sweet 231:19
loveliest m. are not too sublime 271:4
Melody: blundering kind of m. 149:29
falling in m. back 118:9
from ancient m. ceased 62:26
m. lingers on 32:11
Melon: stumbling on m.s 268:20
Melrose: view fair M. aright 339:26
Member: club that will accept me as a m. 269:12
hundredth part of its m.s 175:16
m. of the most ancient profession 241:30
personally acquainted with the other m.s 452:14
we are m.s one of another 56:17
when she saw the sign 'M.s only' 274:8
Membra: invenias etiam disiecti m. poetae 209:13
Memoir: m.s can never be wholly true 318:2
Memorial: m. from the Soul's eternity 331:20
their m. is perished with them 37:28
Memories: liars ought to have good m. 396:9
Memory: dear son of m. 277:29
everyone complains of his m. 248:6
Fancy is . . . mode of m. emancipated 118:18
fond M. brings the light 287:14
from the table of my m. 349:12
good enough m. 285:5
honour his m. 225:28
how sweet their m. still 125:23
illiterate him . . . from your m. 395:18
indebted to his m. 396:2
make friends proud of my m. 234:16
m. be green 347:28
m. of man runneth not to the contrary 59:29
m., the warder of the brain 365:15
O M.! thou fond deceiver 181:24
Thanks for the M. 328:3
their very m. is fair and bright 438:15
tho' lost to sight to m. dear 255:6
thoughts to m. dear 340:23
vibrates in the m. 394:6
while m. holds a seat 349:12
Men: all m. are created equal 217:20
all m. become good creatures 75:24
all m. everywhere could be free 254:21
all m. would be tyrants 133:17
all of them desirable young m. 46:35
all sorts and conditions of m. 319:9
all the m. and women merely players 345:11
all things to all m. 55:10
as m. do a-land 376:4
aversion to the very sight of m. 121:4
best m. are moulded out of faults 368:31
by keeping m. off 174:4
Corneille paints m. as they should be 243:11
decent easy m. 175:9
despised and rejected of m. 46:7

down among the dead m. 153:2
good m. and true 373:3
great m. are almost always bad m. 1:2
how vainly m. themselves amaze 268:18
lives of great m. all remind us 257:5
made brutes m. 305:20
many m., many women and many children 221:5
m. and sea interpenetrate 121:24
m. are but children 151:18
m. are m.; the best sometime forget 374:22
m. are so honest 253:21
m. are unwise 166:7
m. devote the greater part of their lives 243:6
m. . . . differ as Heaven and Earth 417:6
m. have an extremely erroneous opinion 271:2
m. have died from time to time 346:3
m. in a world of m. 238:28
m. in their generations 204:11
m. may come and m. may go 415:21
m. must work 237:19
m. of England 82:21
m. of few words 357:7
m. of sense 343:2
m. seldom make passes 303:16
m. should be what they seem 374:30
m. that worked for England 110:2
m. . . . triumph of mind over morals 456:9
m. were deceivers ever 372:36
m. who borrow 245:27
m. will confess to reason 116:13
M.'s m. 155:13
mighty m. which were of old 34:14
more I see of m. 342:27
most m. are cowards 328:12
nearly all our best m. are dead 322:17
no two m. can be half an hour together 224:14
not three good m. unhanged 354:7
O! what men dare do! 373:14
of alle manner of m. 247:12
quit yourselves like m. 35:41
roll of common m. 354:21
some m. are born great 383:16
some m. break your heart in two 303:14
such m. are dangerous 359:18
thus we are m. 71:2
truth acceptable to lying m. 15:3
we are m., my liege 366:11
we petty m. 359:16
we, who are m. of the world 141:18
why don't the m. propose 27:11
wisest m. have erred 281:20
women . . . either better or worse than m. 243:4
wonder m. dare trust themselves with m. 381:23
Mend: we can't m. it 115:19
Mene: m., m., tekel, upharsin 47:3
Menial: pampered m. 183:4
Mens: cum m. onus reponit 103:16
  m. sana in corpore sano 228:7
  m. sibi conscia recti 440:9
Mensa: nec deus hunc m.441:16
Mensch: es irrt der M. 179:15
  M. ist, was er isst 162:12
Mental: psychoanalysis is that m. illness 242:16
Mer: toute une m. immense 199:30
Mercenary: followed their m. calling 210:2
Merchant: like m.s, venture trade abroad 356:24
  m. to secure his treasure 320:23

there where m.s most do congregate 369:13
whose m.s are princes 45:14
Mercies: for his m. ay endure 281:13
thanks for m. past received 80:2
thy m. how tender 184:18
Merciful: God, be m. to me 52:38
God be m. unto us 39:12
Mercuries: wingèd heels, as English M. 356:26
Mercury: licked the m. right off 6:8
like feathered M. 354:36
station like the herald M. 351:27
words of M. are harsh 364:9
Mercy: crowning m. 129:13
for M. has a human heart 62:11
half so good a grace as m. does 368:11
hand folks over to God's m. 155:11
have m. on us worms 161:1
have m. upon us miserable sinners 319:1
his m. endureth for ever 41:8
leaving m. to heaven 162:30
Lord have m. upon us 318:26
Lord will have m. on Jacob 74:33
m. and truth are met together 39:28
M. I asked for 96:16
m. is above the sceptred sway 370:9
M. no more could be 61:22
peace on earth, and m. mild 450:20
quality of m. is not strained 370:9
render the deeds of m. 370:9
shut the gates of m. 186:13
temper justice with m. 280:38
that is M.'s door 125:29
that m. I to others show 316:8
to love m. 47:19
to M., Pity, Peace and Love 62:10
when m. seasons justice 370:9
young and easy in the m. of his means 426:6
Mercy-seat: how beautiful thy m. 161:2
Meredith: M. climbed towards the sun 111:4
M. is a prose Browning 456:10
Meridian: full m. of my glory 358:20
Merit: deserves neither m. nor thanks 105:1
he esteems your m. 125:3
m. wins the soul 315:27
m.'s all his own 112:2
no farther seek his m.s 186:18
sense of injured m. 278:6
Meritocracy: Rise of the M. 472:29
Mermaid: choicer than the M. Tavern 231:17
done at the M. 27:17
heard a m. on a dolphin's back 371:35
I see you got a m. in your lap 426:24
m.-like, awhile they bore her up 352:20
oyster shop for m.s 203:21
until he came to a m. 8:23
Merriment: flashes of m. 352:26
source of innocent m. 177:28
Merry: always m. and bright! 458:19
have they been m.! 380:9
m. and wise 8:3
never m. when I hear sweet music 370:21
to drink and to be m. 43:35
Merrygoround: it's no go the m. 264:11
Merryman: song of a m. 178:21
Merses: m. profundo209:8
Mesech: I sojourn in M. 40:28
Mess: I'll make a gory m. of you 450:8

in every m. I find a friend 136:7
Message: across the wires the electric m. came
   17:20
   medium is the m. 264:3
Messager: bisy larke, m. of day 108:2
Messenger: bade his m.s ride forth 261:12
   dusk misfeatured m. 77:26
   he's an Anglo-Saxon M. 102:14
Messes: of herbs and other country m. 276:27
Messiah: they found the new M. 150:23
Messing: m. about in boats 184:12
Messmaker: pioneers . . . invariably . . . m.s 309:12
Met: no sooner m. 346:8
Metal: here's m. more attractive 351:7
Metaphor: terrific m.s of speed 96:22
Metaphysical: writers that may be termed the *m.*
   poets 219:21
Metaphysician: m.: a blind man in a dark room 66:1
Metaphysics: explaining m. to the nation 90:31
   m. is the finding of bad reasons 66:10
Mete: snewed in his hous of m. and drinke 107:22
Metempsychosis: had the artistic m. 198:17
Meteor: cloud-encircled m. of the air 391:18
   m. on the grave 93:14
   now slides the silent m. on 422:17
   shone like a m. 278:17
   upon yon m. 273:2
Method: madness, yet there is m. in't 349:30
   traditional scientific m. 309:13
   you know my m. 147:14
   you know my m.s 147:23
Métier: c'est son m. 197:7
Metre: God and man and m. 255:25
   prose is opposed to m. 118:24
   stretchèd m. of an antique song 385:16
   when I think of m. 249:22
   wretched matter with lame m. 277:30
Metropolis: gray m. of the North 416:7
Mettle: m. of your pasture 357:5
Meurt: on ne m. qu'une fois 283:11
Mexico: poor M., so far from God 136:4
Mexique: echo beyond the M. Bay 268:14
Micawber: I never will desert Mr M. 137:11
Mice: best laid schemes o' m. and men 85:28
   feet . . . like little m. 409:7
   three blind m. 298:8
Michelangelo: Borgias . . . produced M. 449:10
   made Italy from designs by M. 434:4
   talking of M. 156:20
Microscope: gas m.s of hextra power 141:13
Mid-course: in the m. of our life 131:14
Middle: dead vast and m. of the night 348:12
   honeyed m. of the night 230:15
   most safely in the m. 301:26
Middle Age: last enchantments of the M. 12:19
Middle-aged: m. life is merry 292:12
Middle-class: specially suits our m. 12:15
Middlemarch: M., the magnificent book 460:19
Middlesex: acre in M. 262:23
Midge: spins like a fretful m. 331:17
Midlands: when I am living in the M. 31:3
Midnight: cease upon the m. 232:7
   chimes at m. 356:4
   during a clear m. such as this 193:16
   iron tongue of m. 372:20
   it came upon the m. clear 341:16
   m. in the silence of the sleep-time 74:14

m. never come 267:2
moan upon the m. hours 232:10
not to be a-bed after m. 383:1
once upon a m. dreary 310:24
profoundest m. shroud 394:1
stroke of m. ceases 210:4
'tis the year's m. 145:33
visions before m. 70:20
Midst: in the m. of the word 102:27
Midsummer: high m. pomps come on 12:5
   m. madness 383:24
Midwife: she is the fairies' m. 378:30
Mid-winter: in the bleak m. 331:5
Mien: truth hath . . . such a m. 150:18
   with an indignant m. 124:17
Mieux: je vais de m. en m. 123:6
   m. est l'ennemi du bien 442:15
tout est au m. 442:9
Might: all-enacting M. 193:2
   do it with thy m. 43:37
   exceeds man's m. 382:10
   'It m. have been!' 454:7
   m. half slumbering 232:15
   shining with all his m. 101:33
   strengthened with m. by his Spirit 56:15
   times when you know that you m. 239:23
Might-have-been: my name is M. 331:25
Mightiest: 'tis m. in the m. 370:9
Mightn't: times when you'll think that you m.
   239:23
Mighty: called thee M. and dreadful 145:18
   how are the m. fallen 36:2
Migraine: love is a universal m. 185:13
Migration: began the huge m.s 397:17
   m. of the soul 400:19
Milan: retire me to my M. 381:20
Milbanke, Annabella 94:11
Mile: as men do walk a m. 28:1
   draw but twenty m.s a day 267:20
   draw out our m.s 376:20
   evening smiles, m.s and m.s 75:22
   five m.s meandering 118:2
   he be many m.s asunder 380:4
   m.s to go before I sleep 170:14
   twice five m.s of fertile ground 117:35
   walked a crooked m. 298:4
Mile-a: your sad tires in a m. 384:26
Miles: M. Gloriosus 310:7
   sed m., sed pro patria 293:15
Milestone: m.s on the Dover Road 138:17
Military: chief attraction of m. service 431:4
   too serious . . . to be left to m. men 414:13
Military-industrial: m. complex 155:6
Milk: gin was mother's m. to her 389:7
   his mother's m. were scarce out of him 382:33
   land flowing with m. and honey 34:42
   m. comes frozen home in pail 364:7
   m. falls 244:18
   m. is more likely to be watered 88:13
   m. of human kindness 82:34, 364:27
   m. to soak my bread 415:5
   one end is moo, the other, m. 292:8
   putting m. into babies 113:7
   shalt not seethe a kid in his mother's m. 35:2
   sincere m. of the word 57:30
   skim m. masquerades as cream 177:1
   take my m. for gall 364:33

white curd of ass's m. 312:25
with m. and honey blest 292:30
Milky way: twinkle on the m. 462:4
Mill: m.s of God grind slowly 257:8
Mille: si j'avais m. ans 26:17
Miller: m. sees not all the water 86:21
than wots the m. of 381:28
there was a jolly m. 59:1
Milliner: perfumèd like a m. 353:28
Million: play . . . pleased not the m. 350:4
we mortal m.s live *alone* 12:9
Millionaire: all m.s love a baked apple 163:17
he must be a m. 176:7
I am a M. That is my religion 388:8
silk hat on a Bradford m. 157:7
Millionen: Seid umschlungen, M.! 338:9
Mill-race: love . . . drove her into the m. 214:20
Millstone: m. were hanged about his neck 50:29
Mill-wheel: except the m.'s sound 390:12
Milton, John 13:25 187:14
Chinese Wall of M. 157:19
England's M. equals both in fame 127:33
fell round the path of M. 463:9
go to the making of . . . a M. 119:3
M., a name to resound for ages 416:17
M.! thou shouldst be living at this hour 463:23
M. . . . was a genius 223:17
M. was for us 75:18
M.'s the prince of poets 91:28
morals which M. held 463:25
read not M. 96:13
reason M. wrote in fetters 63:8
some mute inglorious M. 186:11
Mince: they dined on m. 251:3
Mind: admiration only of weak m.s 281:3
among new men . . . other m.s 417:17
as many sorts of m. as moss 314:16
beauty in things exists in the m. 212:5
best m.s of my generation 178:27
certain unsoundness of m. 262:27
charge his m. with meanings 127:5
clear your *m.* of cant 223:14
concentrates his m. wonderfully 222:26
dagger of the m. 365:19
dividing the swift m. 417:13
education forms the common m. 314:18
empires of the m. 113:8
Eternal Spirit of the chainless M.! 93:22
extend thy m. o'er all the world 281:6
farewell the tranquil m. 375:5
fate of all great m.s 339:1
find the m.'s construction in the face 364:26
four seasons in the m. of man 233:1
fruitful ground, the quiet m. 409:15
grief develops the powers of the m. 321:20
guilty of corrupting the m.s of the young 310:2
happiest and best m.s 395:1
his m. is open 66:12
I don't m. if I do 229:17
I will ease your m. 397:8
in m.s made better by their presence 155:21
in my m.'s eye 348:9
in the m. of man 462:20
it's all in the m. 274:6, 460:7
let the m. be a thoroughfare 234:15
lie that passeth throuth the m. 18:19
little things affect little m.s 143:24

lose myself in other men's m.s 246:2
love looks . . . with the m. 371:22
man cannot have a pure m. 245:17
man of hope and forward-looking m. 461:27
man's unconquerable m. 463:20
march of the human m. 81:20
mighty m.s of old 401:20
m. at peace with all below 93:9
m. conscious of the right 440:9
m., diffused through all the members 440:29
m. . . . fetched up with a bump 300:25
m. is in a state of philosophical doubt 119:1
m. is its own place 278:11
m. puts down its burden 103:16
m. quite vacant 126:21
m. that maketh good or ill 403:7
m., that ocean 268:21
m. which feeds this verse 391:26
m.s are not ever craving for their food 128:6
m.s innocent and quiet 258:13
minister to a m. diseased 367:19
my m., aspire to higher things 396:17
my m. is troubled 382:18
my m. to me a kingdom is 153:1
nakedness is uncomely . . . in m. 19:6
never brought to m. 83:26
no m. to do what nobody can do for you 105:8
noble m. is here o'erthrown 350:21
nothing great but m. 191:6
of its own beauty is the m. diseased 90:12
pity the state of his m. 222:20
process of a rational m. 197:9
purest and most thoughtful m.s 333:15
refuge of weak m.s 109:14
religion of feeble m.s 82:22
serve thee with a quiet m. 319:17
she had a frugal m. 125:9
she unbent her m. afterwards 245:24
should not m. anything at all 17:10
someone whose m. watches itself 98:9
sound m. in a sound body 228:7
speaking truth, to m.s like mine 78:13
straight m.s grown crooked 289:16
strongest m.s are often those 461:21
that can feed this m. of ours 461:28
there *are* chords in the human m. 136:28
'tis strange the m. 92:7
to change your m. 16:19
to one dead level ev'ry m. 311:26
to the noble m. 350:16
triumph of m. over morals 456:9
union of a part of one m. 337:12
vulgar m. always mistakes the exceptional 215:2
wars begin in the m.s of men 435:8
what you are pleased to call your m. 451:18
will hardly m. anything else 221:18
worked her m. to such a pitch 129:1
years that bring the philosophic m. 464:17
yet is thy m. perplexed? 133:21
Mindfulness: right m., right contemplation 80:4
Mine: love's undiscovered m.s 71:22
what's m. is yours 368:32
would she were m. 256:3
Miner: dwelt a m., Forty-niner 286:8
Minerva: M. when she talks 225:14
Mingle: m., m., m., you that m. may! 273:6
Minion: this morning morning's m. 206:21

m.s of the moon 353:17
Minister: designated as a 'stickit m.' 340:29
  I have not become the King's First M. 113:6
  if I quench thee, thou flaming m. 375:22
  my actions are my m.s 106:21
  one fair Spirit for my m. 90:18
  powers . . . which Prime M.s have never yet been
    invested 113:15
  Prime M. of Mirth 327:24
  that grand old man, the Prime M. 295:20
Ministry: Frost performs its secret m. 117:30
Minnehaha: named her, M., Laughing Water 257:13
Minnow: Triton of the m.s 346:27
Minority: m. is always right 214:7
Minstrel: ethereal m.! 467:12
  M. Boy to the war is gone 287:2
  M. was infirm and old 339:23
  wandering m. I 177:16
Mintage: coiner the m. of man 210:17
Minute: fill the unforgiving m. 239:14
  five m.s on even the nicest mountain 14:20
  five m.s too late all my life-time! 124:15
  girdle round about the earth in forty m.s 371:37
  little m.s, humble though they be 100:24
  our m.s hasten to their end 385:33
  sucker born every m. 25:15
  this live-long m. true to thee 328:8
  to see the m.s, how they run 358:7
  Two M.s Hate 300:26
Mirabeau: this M.'s work 99:15
Miracle: God never wrought m. 19:35
  he prays for a m. 433:12
  Life, Death, M.s of Saint Somebody 77:24
  m. of rare device 118:4
  m.s are past 343:8
  m.s do not happen 12:31
  there will have to be m.s 187:27
Mire: wallowing in the m. 57:37
Mirror: as m.s are lonely 15:8
  find a m. in every mind 219:25
  following the m. of all Christian kings 356:26
  hold . . . m. up to nature 351:1
  m. cracked from side to side 419:14
  m. of all courtesy 358:14
  m.s of the sea are strewn 166:11
  novel is a m. 404:23
Mirth: Bards of Passion and M. 230:4
  far from all resort of m. 276:9
  I love such m. 445:23
  m. and fun grew fast 85:21
  m. that has no bitter springs 238:19
  m. the music of derision 9:1
  m. . . . with her enticing parts 7:9
  much m. and no madness 398:4
  Prime Minister of M. 327:24
  sad old earth must borrow its m. 454:18
  very tragical m. 372:16
  with m. in funeral 347:29
Misanthropy: compounded of m. and voluptuousness
    262:31
Misbeliever: you call me m. 369:18
Mischief: all punishment is m. 31:23
  foundation of lasting m. 220:10
  great enterprises, either of virtue, or m. 19:10
  hand to execute any m. 114:31
  in every deed of m. 175:21
  it means m. 351:8

little knowest the m. done 294:9
  record the m.s she has done 126:32
  Satan finds some m. still 447:13
  to mourn a m. 374:7
  wait on nature's m. 364:33
Miscreate: creation purged o' the m. 78:2
Miserable: me m.! 279:19
  of all men most m. 55:31
Miseria: ricordarsi del tempo felice nella m.
    131:17
Miserie: y-fallen out of heigh degree into m. 108:8
Miseries: bound in shallows and in m. 360:33
  long to see the m. of the world 220:3
Miserrima: quaeque ipse m. vidi 440:11
Misery: gave to M. all he had 186:18
  in the deep wide sea of M. 391:23
  man . . . is full of m. 320:3
  m. acquaints a man with strange bedfellows
    380:41
  m. still delights to trace 124:21
  relation of distant m. 175:22
  result m. 137:12
  thou art so full of m. 423:29
  worst sort of m. 64:2
Misfortune: calamities are . . . m. to ourselves 59:8
  children make m.s more bitter 19:8
  could not bear another's m.s 316:14
  follies and m.s of mankind 175:15
  m.s . . . from the wrong notions 404:19
  m.s great and sma' 85:23
  m.s hardest to bear 259:6
  once untangled much m. bodes 379:2
  real m.s and pains of others 82:6
  some great m. to portend 410:10
Misleading: least m. thing we have 88:3
Missed: never would be m. 177:20
  we m. it, lost it for ever 79:15
Missionary: I would eat a m. 454:16
Mist: draw up Faustus, like a foggy m. 267:4
  grey m. on the sea's face 270:2
  m. and hum of that low land 11:33
  m. in my face 77:6
  m. is dispelled 174:10
  rank m. they draw 277:14
Mistake: all the m.s which can be made 64:6
  he who never made a m. 398:12
  man who makes no m. 308:10
  may be a m. in the translation 437:12
  name every one gives to their m.s 455:33
  never do right by m. 227:10
  there is no m. 450:2
  when she made any such m. 139:12
Mistaken: loved, yet so m.! 74:15
  think it possible you may be m. 129:12
  unless I am m. 147:21
Mistletoe: m. hung in the castle hall 27:6
Mistress: art is a jealous m. 158:17
  is she not pure gold, my m.? 78:26
  master, a m. and two slaves 59:13
  m. I am ashamed to call you 157:24
  m. in my own [house] 240:12
  m. moderately fair 124:14
  m. of herself 314:29
  m. of the Earl of Craven 458:9
  O m. mine! where are you roaming? 383:2
  riches are . . . the worst m. 18:14
  so court a m. 225:19

Monk: devil a m. he'd be 289:13
  many a m. and many a friar 24:8
  solitary m. who shook the world 286:4
Monkey: m.s . . . refrain from speech 184:11
  purple m. climbing on a yellow stick 2:25
  species of m.s and apes 288:8
  wilderness of m.s 369:35
Monocle: seeming to be in pursuit of his m. 321:11
Monograph: little m. on the ashes 147:15
Monopoly: m. stage of capitalism 252:21
Monotony: bleats articulate m. 405:2
Monster: faultless m. 80:1
  great-sized m. of ingratitudes 382:12
  jealousy . . . green-eyed m. 374:32
  man, and not of a m. 141:10
  many-headed m. of the pit 316:2
  m., which the Blatant Beast men call 403:5
  vice is a m. 314:4
Monstruosity: this is the m. in love 382:9
Montagne: m. en mal d'enfant 244:14
Monte Carlo: broke the bank at M. 176:7
Montes: parturient m. 207:3
Montezuma: every schoolboy knows who imprisoned
    M. 262:7
  mechanical America M. still 248:33
Montgomery, Viscount 114:1
Month: for m.s and m.s and m.s 414:2
  fourteen m.s the most idle 175:8
  merriest m. in all the year 23:6
  mother of m.s in meadow 411:32
  old man in a dry m. 156:10
  propose two m.s 137:21
  this is the m. 277:20
Montmorenci: monstrous steep of M. 232:13
Montreal: O God! O M.! 88:24
Monument: as Mr Levi did from off the M.
    24:19
  early, but enduring m. 390:1
  felt . . . like the M. 220:15
  gilded m.s of princes 385:30
  if you seek his m. 468:6
  in this shalt find thy m. 386:28
  m. more lasting than brass 209:5
  m. without a tomb 225:21
  sonnet is a moment's m. 331:20
  wanst to vote a m. to a man 152:16
  when smashing m.s 251:17
  your m. shall be my gentle verse 386:11
Monumentum: exegi m. aere perennius 209:5
Moo: you silly m. 402:5
Mood: in listening m. 339:16
Mookse: M. and the Gripes 226:7
Moon: and he astride the m. 413:10
  and the m. be still as bright 93:21
  bay at the m. 360:28
  behold the wandering m. 276:7
  beneath a waning m. was haunted 117:36
  beneath the visiting m. 344:4
  cold fruitless m. 371:17
  danced by the light of the m. 251:3
  danced the m. on Monan's rill 339:15
  dwelleth i' the cold o' the m. 73:21
  ebb and flow by the m. 363:9
  fair as the m. 44:25
  friendly silence of the quiet m. 440:15
  glimpses of the m. 348:31
  hang them on the horns o' the m. 346:21

hornèd m., with one bright star 117:2
I had an affair with the m. 405:7
I saw the new m. 23:11
if the m. shine at full or no 87:23
if the Sun and M. should doubt 60:19
in the course of one revolving m. 149:20
inconstant m. 379:15
Man in the M. 304:19
m. arose up in the murky east 394:24
m. doth shine as bright as day 296:8
m. doth with delight 464:1
m. is nothing 170:24
m. of a hundred identical faces 172:18
M. of Heav'n is rising 165:1
m. of m.s 136:30
m. plucked at my rein 471:1
m. sits arbitress 278:29
m., sweet regent of the sky 272:33
m. takes up the wondrous tale 2:15
m. under her feet 58:20
m. walks the night in her silver shoon 134:26
m.'s a balloon 129:21
M.'s in a fit 298:12
m.s . . . lie mirror'd on her sea 202:14
moving m. went up the sky 117:5
new m. hangs like an ivory bugle 427:2
new m.s and sabbaths 44:31
nor the m. by night 40:32
O the m. shone bright on Mrs Porter 157:6
pale-faced m. 353:32
quietly shining to the quiet m. 117:32
rake the m. from out the sea 306:18
saw the ruddy m. 212:3
shine on, harvest m. 295:24
ship, an isle, a sickle m. 166:11
silent as the m. 281:17
slow m. climbs 424:9
so sicken waning m.s 150:10
some nine m.s wasted 373:41
under the solitary m. 11:33
unmask her beauty to the m. 348:19
what do you think of it, M. 193:10
when the m. is on the wave 93:14
white in the m. 210:24
white saucer like some full m. 284:21
wind whistles – the m. rises 395:13
with how sad steps, O M. 396:12
Moonlight: how sweet the m. sleeps 370:19
  ill met by m. 371:33
  visit it by the pale m. 339:26
Moonshine: find out m. 372:1
  its glory is all m. 396:3
  transcendental m. 100:2
Moor: batten on this m. 351:28
  I never saw a m. 142:10
  maiden in the m. lay 5:14
  m. is dark beneath the moon 394:1
  she's for the M.s 128:21
  your daughter and the M. 373:35
Mopser: has anybody seen my M.? 134:11
Moral: all reform except a m. one 99:12
  and is there any m. shut 416:9
  Arthur Balfour is wicked and m. 114:2
  Englishman thinks he is m. 388:21
  everything's got a m. 101:10
  foundation of m.s and legislation 31:22
  have you no m.s 389:5

m. that is in thy brother's eye 49:20
Moth: desire of the m. for the star 394:8
  like a m., the simple maid 174:2
  m. fretting a garment 38:18
  m.'s kiss, first! 75:6
  m.s get into it 250:8
  unfading m.s, immortal flies 69:8
  watched the m.s fluttering among the heath 69:5
  where m. and rust doth corrupt 49:11
Mother: all women become like their m.s 455:14
  Athens . . . m. of arts 281:7
  Boy's Best Friend is His M. 273:28
  come m.s and fathers 153:10
  cruel m. of sweet loves 209:7
  dearer was the m. for the child 118:11
  disclaim her for a m. 175:8
  does your m. know that you are out? 24:22
  foolish son is the heaviness of his m. 41:32
  go back to the great sweet m. 413:5
  happy he with such a m.! 422:22
  Her M. Came Too 296:2
  his m. drudge for his living 388:17
  I arose a m. in Israel 35:24
  m. and a mangler 140:15
  M. cried, baby lept 188:1
  m., do not cry! 161:12
  m., give me the sun 214:10
  m. of all living 34:6
  M. of the Free 31:21
  m. to dozens 198:30
  m., who talks about her own children 143:9
  m., who was patient, being dead 306:2
  m., who'd give her booby 174:19
  m. wi' her needle 84:4
  m. will be there 198:27
  my m. bore me in the southern wild 62:18
  my m. didna speak 25:6
  my m., drunk or sober 110:27
  my m. groaned 61:23
  never called me m. 460:14
  never had no father, nor m. 408:12
  obey, were she ten times our m. 351:15
  Oedipus . . . took his m. to wife 169:12
  one whom his m. comforteth 46:23
  rolled m. with infant down the rocks 282:8
  scarce be a man before thy m. 27:24
  sea from whence his m. rose 341:18
  send out my M. 253:29
  shall a man leave father and m. 50:33
  so loving to my m. 348:1
  thou art thy m.'s glass 385:13
  thy m. a lady 340:7
  took great care of his M. 274:14
  what will ye leave to your ain m. dear 22:15
Motion: between the m. and the act 156:16
  God ordained m. 438:2
  her m. blushed at herself 374:2
  little m. in the air 390:12
  meandering with a mazy m. 118:2
  measured m. like a living thing 465:8
  must to thy m.s lovers' seasons run? 146:10
  no m. has she now 466:19
  time's eternal m. 167:11
  two weeping m.s 128:24
Motive: m.s meaner than your own 26:6
Motley: made myself a m. to the view 386:30
  m. fool 345:1

m.'s the only wear 345:6
Motto: be that my m. and my fate 410:17
  I've gotter m. 458:19
  rather suffer than die is man's m. 244:2
  that is my m. 267:31
Mottoes: m. on sundials 317:21
Mould: if you cannot m. yourself 235:4
  m. of form 350:21
  then broke the m. 10:2
Moulded: bullet . . . has not yet been m. 291:17
Mouldy: m. from over-keeping 104:17
Moulmein: by the old M. Pagoda 240:6
Moulting: when they're m. they're pretty revolting 292:7
Mountain: before the m.s were brought forth 39:29
  come down, O maid, from yonder m. height 422:18
  Delectable M.s 80:29
  don't much care if I never see another m. 246:8
  every m. and hill shall be made low 45:31
  five minutes on even the nicest m. 14:20
  flatter the m. tops 385:27
  high m.s are a feeling 89:29
  look how the snowy m.s 8:26
  mind has m.s 206:9
  m. in labour 244:14
  m. tops that freeze 358:18
  m.s are the beginning 333:10
  m.s divide us 341:11
  m.s interposed 126:35
  m.s look on Marathon 91:24
  m.s of Mourne 169:8
  m.s skipped like rams 40:22
  m.s will be in labour 207:3
  on this fair m. leave to feed 351:28
  one of the m.s 463:21
  paced upon the m.s overhead 472:6
  robes the m. in its azure hue 97:13
  scattered on the Alpine m.s cold 282:7
  stands tiptoe on the misty m. tops 380:3
  steepy m. yields 267:23
  this firm persuasion removed m.s 63:22
  up the airy m. 4:19
  when men and m.s meet 60:29
Mountebank: impudent m. who sold pills 2:21
  m., a threadbare juggler 346:19
Mounted: ere he m., kissed his horse 126:20
Mourir: c'est m. à ce qu'on aime 192:1
Mourn: comfort all that m. 46:18
  in summer skies to m. 230:12
  makes countless thousands m.! 85:2
  man was made to m. 85:1
  no longer m. for me 386:8
Mourne: mountains of M. 169:8
Mourned: I m.; and yet shall mourn 454:5
Mourner: be every m.'s sleep tonight 234:25
Mourning: don't waste any time m. 201:10
  go to the house of m. 43:26
  in m. for my life 108:34
Mouse: absurd little m. 207:3
  always leave room for the m. 336:1
  brought forth a m. 244:14
  good my m. of virtue 382:31
  I frightened a little m. 297:23
  killing of a m. on Sunday 66:21
  m. behind the mouldering wainscot shrieked 420:26

m. even in the beauty 71:11
m. hath charms 120:13
m. is immediate 15:25
m. is the best means we have 15:27
m. is the brandy of the damned 388:20
m., moody food 343:31
m. of the Gospel 161:3
m. of the spheres 71:11
m. sent up to God 72:12
m. shall untune the sky 151:4
m. . . . such is the force of habit 29:18
m. that gentlier on the spirit lies 420:11
m., the greatest good 1:17
m., when soft voices die 394:6
m. wherever she goes 297:26
my m. is best understood by children 409:2
never merry when I hear sweet m. 370:21
not for the doctrine, but the m. 313:11
not formed, as notes of m. 390:23
O M.! sphere-descended maid 119:20
reasonable good ear in m. 372:8
sound of m. 191:13
sounds of m. creep in our ears 370:19
still, sad m. of humanity 462:19
swan-like end, fading in m. 369:36
sweet compulsion doth in m. lie 275:1
take this slave of m. 394:27
thou hast thy m. too 233:31
Van Gogh's ear for m. 456:30
well set to m. 2:3
what m. is more enchanting 399:8
what passion cannot m. raise and quell 151:1
when M. . . . was young 119:17
will make the m. mute 417:4
with thy beauty's silent m. 97:26
Musical: most m., most melancholy! 276:6
none of us m. 173:13
Music-hall: no more jokes in M.s 337:28
Musician: 'tis we m.s know 72:13
Music-maker: we are the m.s 301:15
Musicologist: m. . . . can't hear it 28:25
Musk-rose: m. and the well-attired woodbine 277:16
m., full of dewy wine 232:6
with sweet m.s, and with eglantine 371:38
Must: I m. – I will 395:9
Mustard: faith as a grain of m. seed 50:27
Mustn't: tell her she m. 322:11
Musty: proverb is something m. 351:16
Mutability: from chance, and death, and m. 393:16
nought may endure but M. 392:3
Mutamur: nos m. in illis 9:12
Mute: if she be m. 333:19
Mutilator: those m.s of collections 245:29
Mutter: blessed m. of the mass 73:12
Mutter: O M., M.! 81:5
Muttering: m. grew to a grumbling 76:26
Mutton: boiled leg of m. 141:15
joint of m. 356:14
Muzzle: thou shalt not m. the ox 35:15
Myriad: there died a m. 317:24
Myriad-minded: our *m.* Shakespeare 118:21
Myrtle: m. mixed in my path like mad 76:20
once more ye m.s brown 276:36
Myself: I celebrate m. 453:23
when I give I give m. 454:1
Mystère: m.s partout coulent comme des sèves 26:16
Mysterious: God moves in a m. way 125:30

Mystery: burthen of the m. 462:14
comprehend its m.! 257:10
for a m. and a sign 110:16
in m. our soul abides 11:14
lose myself in a m. 70:24
pluck out the heart of my m. 351:17
riddle wrapped in a m. 112:17
see the m. of his life 234:11
take upon's the m. of things 363:9
Myth: from being a patriotic m. 432:15
some magnificent m. 310:3
Mythology: what counted was m. of self 406:4

N

Nachte: wer nie die kummervollen N. 180:7
Nag: bet my money on the bobtail n. 168:3
Naiad: guardian N. of the strand 339:16
thy N. airs have brought me home 310:29
Nail: care to our coffin adds a n. 309:4
come near your beauty with my n.s 357:31
for want of a n. 168:21
hard . . . as n.s 139:34
nineteen hundred and forty n.s upon the Cross, 397:19
with his n.s he'll dig them up again 449:4
Naître: donné la peine de n. 27:16
Naked: afraid, because I was n. 34:1
I was born n. 104:24
n. came I out of my mother's womb 36:34
n. every day he clad 182:35
Nakedness: n. is uncomely 19:6
n. of woman is the work of God 63:17
to see the n. of the land ye are come 34:33
Namby-pamby: n. madrigals of love 176:6
Name: allow their n.s to be mentioned 17:13
breathe not his n. 287:4
call their lands after their own n.s 38:28
change the n. 209:11
ere I called her n. 320:27
filches from me my good n. 374:31
give them an everlasting n. 46:14
good n. in man and woman 374:31
good n. is better than precious ointment 43:26
good n. is rather to be chosen 42:28
he left the n. 219:8
his n. shall be called Wonderful 45:8
his n. will stink to all generations 450:26
I have forgotten your n. 412:31
I have lost all the n.s 223:13
I have no n. 62:14
I wrote her n. upon the strand 402:18
illustrious n., revered by the nations 259:15
in the n. of God, go!, 4:23, 129:16
just mention my n. 165:7
leaving here a n. I trust 401:21
left a n. behind them 48:29
local habitation and a n. 372:14
lost her honest n. 8:13
Love that dare not speak its n. 147:1
millions of ages before we have . . . a name 245:15
must he lose the n. of king? 377:4
my n. is a dirty word 301:11
my n. is Used-to-was 431:18
my poor n. rehearse 386:9

n. to all succeeding ages curst 149:9
n. was writ in water 234:18
n.s familiar in his mouth 357:18
new-made honour doth forget men's n.s 361:7
nothing is commoner than the n. 244:12
only a friend in n. 48:21
our n. will be joined with these 301:23
play so nicely with their n.s 376:19
ravished with the whistling of a n. 314:10
remember the n. of the Lord 37:39
set down my n., Sir 80:19
shadow of a glorious n. 259:13
their n. liveth for evermore 48:30
there is no n. 247:5
to see one's n. in print 92:23
to write against your n. 327:5
twenty more such n.s 380:13
what's in a n.? 379:11
you mentioned your n. 147:26
Naming: n. of parts 326:10
Nan: put on the pan, says Greedy N. 296:11
Napoleon 99:20, 449:19
  ashes of N. Bonaparte 449:18
  N. of crime 147:25
  N.'s armies . . . march on their stomachs 342:22
Narcissa: last words that poor N. spoke 314:19
Nard: smeared with dull n. 76:17
Narr: bleibt ein N. sein Lebe lang 260:5
Narrative: bald and unconvincing n. 177:32
  whole n. is permeated with . . . joss-sticks 66:18
Narrow: if he went not through the n. 47:31
  in a very n. field 64:6
Narrowness: with the grave's n. 185:10
Nasty: how n. the n. people are 318:3
  something n. in the woodshed 175:24
Nathan: N. said to David 36:7
Nation: all n.s in the world 21:9
  America became top n. 342:23
  Commonwealth of N.s 330:16
  day of small n.s has long passed 105:24
  dedicate this n. to the policy of the good neighbour
    329:15
  English . . . foul-mouthed n. 195:23
  every n. has the government it deserves 265:2
  fierce contending n.s 1:15
  great deal of *ruin* in a n. 398:16
  great multitude . . . of all n.s 58:15
  he hates our sacred n. 369:13
  he shall subdue . . . the n.s under our feet 38:26
  healing of the n.s 58:37
  hoarse n. croaked 311:15
  honest friendship with all n.s 217:22
  in the best interest of the n. 295:9
  intercourse with foreign n.s 133:10
  language all n.s understand 29:27
  law of . . . n.s 82:3
  living n.s wait 14:11
  make enemies of n.s 126:35
  march of a n. 304:23
  n. and race dwelling all around the globe 113:14
  n. is not governed 81:16
  n. ne'er would thrive 320:24
  n. . . . . not judged by the colour of their skin 237:9
  n. of amateurs 330:17
  n. of pure philosophers 21:9
  n. of shopkeepers 1:7, 291:21, 398:17
  n. shall not lift up sword against n. 44:33

n. shall speak peace unto n. 326:17
n. talking to itself 273:26
n.s are as a drop of a bucket 45:35
n.s . . . have their infancy 64:20
n.s tend towards stupidity 178:30
noble and puissant n. 282:21
old, and haughty n. 275:5
one-third of a n. ill-housed 329:18
Privileged and the People formed Two N.s 143:26
publish it to all the n. 320:19
read their history in a n.'s eyes 186:12
righteousness exalteth a n. 42:10
sherry . . . which will transform a n. 65:14
temptations to belong to other n.s 177:4
trick of our English n. 355:18
twilight sheds on half the n.s 278:21
wealthy curled darlings of our n. 373:38
ye are . . . an holy n. 57:31
Nationality: other people have a n. 29:22
Nationalliterature: N. will jetzt nicht viel sagen
  180:12
Native: my n. Land – Good Night! 89:13
  my own, my n. land 339:31
  though I am n. here 348:28
Nativity: in n., chance or death 371:16
Natur: aus beiden Reichen erwuchs seine . . . N. 327:17
Natura: n. il fece 10:2
Natural: Childish but very N. 118:10
  far from being n. for a man 222:5
  I do it more n. 383:4
  large as life, and twice as n.! 102:16
  n., wholesome, contented . . . people 388:3
  nothing prevents us from being n. 248:18
  thoughts . . . seldom n. 219:22
Naturam: n. expellas furca 207:19
Nature 310:9
  accuse not N. 280:27
  against the use of n. 364:23
  all n. is but art 313:34
  all N. was degraded 61:15
  all N. wears one universal grin 163:2
  at two with n. 4:18
  auld n. swears 84:23
  Beauty is N.'s brag 275:32
  Beauty is N.'s coin 275:31
  constant, in N. were inconstancy 124:4
  customs of his tribe . . . laws of n. 387:22
  disguise fair n. with hard-favoured rage 357:3
  drive N. out with a pitchfork 207:19
  erroneous opinion of their position in n. 271:2
  eye N.'s walks 313:26
  fools call N. 78:8
  force of n. could no further go 150:26
  formed by n. to bear 16:17
  generous n. has been suffered 81:15
  habit is a second n. 321:18
  his n. is too noble for the world 346:28
  hold . . . mirror up to n. 351:1
  I have learned to look on n. 462:19
  I love . . . N. more 90:19
  if such be N.'s holy plan 462:25
  if you want to change her n. 239:27
  in n. things move violently 19:21
  in N.'s infinite book of secrecy 343:17
  in our life alone does N. live 117:28
  little we see in N. 463:6
  looks through n. up to n.'s God 314:11

N.s o'er the Herring Pond 152:18
need not bid . . . our n. . . . farewell 234:20
our n.'s house is on fire 82:10
policy of the good n. 329:15
to hate your n. 262:31
when your n.'s wall is on fire 207:25
Neighing: pleasure from the n. of my horse 169:4
Nell: poor witty N. 307:16
Nelly: let not poor N. starve 106:23
Nelson: Good Lord N. had a swollen gland 152:20
N. touch 292:31
of N. and the North 96:24
of N. only a touch 76:7
Neptune: chase the ebbing N. 381:15
envious siege of watery N. 376:18
star upon whose influence N.'s empire stands
347:25
will all great N.'s oceans wash this blood 365:28
would not flatter N. for his trident 346:28
Nero: she is the last of the N.s 432:5
Nerve: blood creeps, and the n.s prick 418:3
is weakness to expredge my n.s 139:4
my n.s are bad tonight 157:3
nobody feels for my poor n.s 17:9
Nest: n. is in a watered shoot 331:1
n. of singing birds 220:12
Nestor: though N. swear the jest be laughable
368:33
Net: fain would fling the n. 272:5
n. is spread in the sight of the bird 41:21
wicked fall into their own n.s 41:14
Nettle: tender-handed stroke a n. 201:8
Neues: Im Westen nichts N. 326:16
Neumann, John von 68:22
Neurotic: everything . . . great has come to us from
n.s 321:14
n. . . . builds a castle in the air 249:27
Neutrality: armed n. 458:13
'n.', a word . . . often been disregarded 32:13
Never: lay down my arms – n., n., n. 309:18
n. met – or n. parted 83:25
n., n., n., n., n.! 363:14
thinks what n. was 313:6
thou shalt hear the 'N., n.' 419:26
what n.? 176:27
Nevermore: quoth the Raven, 'N.' 310:27
New: against the n. and untried 254:15
first by whom the n. are tried 313:10
hear some n. thing 53:53
I make all things n. 58:34
n. things are made familiar 219:26
no n. thing under the sun 43:14
piping songs for ever n. 231:21
New South Wales: go out and govern N. 30:14
New World: I called the N. into existence 98:21
New York 198:15
little old N. 198:14
New Yorker: N. will not be edited 330:24
New-comer: O blithe n.! 467:7
New-found-land: O my America! my n. 144:26
Newgate: in the condemned cells of N. 88:17
Newness: conditioned to respect n. 435:14
News: all the n. that's fit to print 299:12
bringer of unwelcome n. 355:12
brought from Heaven the n. 166:17
brought me bitter n. to hear 123:1
can't see that foreign stories are ever n. 448:12

evil n. rides post 281:27
good n. from a far country 42:36
good n. yet to hear 110:14
literature is n. 317:28
master-passion is the love of n. 128:8
never good to bring bad n. 343:33
n. from the humming city 416:19
n. much older than their ale 181:8
n. value 325:15
talk of court n. 363:9
when a dog bites a man that is not n. 131:5
Newspaper: art of n. paragraphing 267:32
good n. . . . is a nation talking to itself 273:26
government of morning n.s 308:15
n.s always excite curiosity 246:3
read the n.s 450:1
Newspeak: N. was the official language 300:24
Newstatesmanship: *mention* in N. 317:13
Newt: eye of n. 366:36
Newton: God said 'Let N. be!' 312:30
N. with his prism and silent face 465:13
souls of five hundred N.s 119:3
New-year: happiest time of all the glad N. 421:4
Nexus: sole n. of man to man 99:11
Nez: énorme, mon n.! 332:5
ne voyait pas plus loin que son n. 244:9
Niagara 113:24
one wouldn't *live* under N. 100:20
Nicanor: N. lay dead in his harness 48:33
Nice: be n. to people on your way up 283:5
how nasty the n. people can be 318:3
n. man is a man of nasty ideas 411:21
nicer, much nicer in N. 458:11
Nicely-Nicely: what N. dies of 333:4
Nickle-ben: fare you weel, auld N. 83:20
Nickname: n. is the heaviest stone 196:12
Nicodemus: wise N. saw such light 438:3
Niger: on the left bank of the N. 136:20
Nigger: gone whar de good n.s go 168:10
libbaty . . . don't agree with n.s 258:23
Night: abide with me when n. is nigh 234:24
all the world will be in love with n. 379:37
black it stood as n. 279:6
borrower of the n. 366:9
closed his eyes in endless n. 187:14
closing n. will be the dome 392:6
come, civil n. 379:36
come, seeling n. 366:19
dark n. of the soul 165:2
dear n.! this world's defeat 438:4
desire . . . of the n. for the morrow 394:8
do not go gentle into that good n. 426:5
flash between two long n.s 311:1
for one n. or the other n. 166:5
God makes sech n.s 258:27
gwine to run all n.! 168:3
hangs upon the cheek of n. 379:4
hard day's n. 253:10
have one other gaudy n. 343:39
heaven above, and n. by n. 75:10
hitherand-thithering waters of N.! 226:12
I ask of thee, belovèd N. 394:16
I cry . . . in the n. season 37:41
I sleep all n. 286:11
in hoary winter's n. 401:28
in such a n. 370:18
it was mirk, mirk n. 23:16

it was not n. 142:2
let n. or day do what they will 128:25
making n. do penance for a day 465:16
making n. hideous 348:31
many a watchful n.! 356:11
middle of the n. 101:33, 348:12
moonless n. in the small town 426:18
must follow, as the n. the day 348:23
mysterious N.! 452:17
naughty n. to swim in 362:24
n. and day on me she cries 22:21
n. and sleep in the n. 412:5
n. came down 441:5
n. cometh, when no man can work 53:21
n. has a thousand eyes 65:21
n. is dark 294:3
n. is drawing nigh 25:3
n. is far spent 54:44
'n. is fine', the Walrus said 102:6
n. makes no difference 200:10
N.! N.! My ho head halls 226:11
n. of time 71:19
n., sable goddess! 472:19
n. that first we met 27:8
n. unto n. sheweth knowledge 37:36
n. was made for loving 93:21
n. with her train of stars 198:1
n.'s black agents 366:20
n.'s starred face 233:11
not n. if thou be near 234:23
now n. descending 311:9
now welcome, n. 402:24
O n.s and feasts of the gods! 209:18
out of the n. that covers me 197:24
pass, like n., from land to land 117:13
passed a miserable n. 377:30
returned home the previous n. 80:9
rung n.'s yawning peal 366:17
sable-vested N. 279:8
shades of n. 280:5
Shadwell's genuine n. 150:28
shorten tedious n.s 97:29
some n. you'll fail us 77:2
son of the sable N. 131:10
spirit of N.! 394:12
there's n. and day, brother 65:11
this ae n. 23:1
this is the n. 375:20
this present were the world's last n. 145:21
through the foul womb of n. 357:9
'tis a fearful n. 27:7
'tis with us perpetual n. 225:12
very witching time of n. 351:20
watchman, what of the n.? 45:13
we must sleep one endless n. 103:11
weary N.'s decline 60:28
what hath n. to do with sleep? 275:7
what is the n.? 366:33
when n. darkens the streets 278:16
when n.s are longest there 368:9
who is it that this dark n. 396:18
windy n. a rainy morrow 386:16
Night-cap: n. decked his brows 182:1
Night-cloud: n. had lowered 97:18
Night-fowl: waking she heard the n. crow 420:25
Night-gown: upstairs and downstairs in his n. 274:1, 298:13

Nightingale: abandoned for the sake of Miss N. 408:15
brown bright n. amorous 411:32
I envy no man's n. 199:17
I will roar you as 'twere any n. 371:29
n. and not the lark 380:2
n. in the sycamore 407:29
N. Sang in Berkeley Square 269:20
n.'s complaint 391:12
n.s are sobbing 15:7
no music in the n. 384:6
O n., that on yon bloomy spray 282:12
O N., thou surely art 463:28
spoils the singing of the n. 230:12
thy n.s, awake 123:4
'tis the ravished n. 260:9
told in dim Eden by Eve's n.s 134:7
wakeful n. 279:31
Night-lamp: where the dying n. flickers 419:25
Nightmare: history . . . is a n. 226:22
n. of the dark 14:11
Night-shriek: to hear a n. 367:23
Night-time: dog did nothing in the n. 148:1
Nihil: n. est ab omni 208:21
Nil: nil posse creari de nilo 259:19
Nile: allegory on the banks of the N. 395:28
Father N. 430:5
pour the waters of the N. 100:30
serpent of Old N. 343:24
Nimini-pimini: pronouncing to yourself n. 81:10
Nimrod: N. the mighty hunter 34:20
Nimshi: Jehu, the son of N. 36:28
Nine: Fair N., forsaking Poetry! 63:1
Nine-fifteen: Romance brought up the n. 239:21
Ninepence: n. in ready money 2:22
1910: in . . . *1910* human *character* changed 460:20
Niño: n. tiene los ojos cerrados 173:3
Niobe: like N., all tears 348:4
Nipping: n. and an eager air 348:27
Nipple: plucked my n. from his boneless gums 365:12
Nives: diffugere n. 209:9
Nixon, Richard 335:4, 432:24
won't have N. to kick around 295:5
No: everlasting N. 100:11
my own Araminta, say 'N.!' 318:8
others said, 'N.' 80:13
rebel . . . a man who says n. 98:10
No-encouragement: expression of n. 66:17
No-man-fathomed: frightful, sheer, n. 206:9
No-more: also called N. 331:25
Noah: N. he often said to his wife 110:25
one poor N. dare hope to survive 213:9
Nobilitas: n. sola est atque unica virtus 228:4
Nobility: betwixt the wind and his n. 353:29
leave us still our old n. 266:7
n. carries its obligations 254:4
n. of birth commonly abateth industry 19:30
new n. is but the act of power 19:29
Noble: do n. things 237:13
eternally n. 253:21
n. living and the n. dead 465:30
n.s and heralds, by your leave 320:20
n.s by the right of an earlier creation 262:28
n.s-with-links-of-iron 261:7
'tis only n. to be good 419:6
Nobleman: cultivated, underrated n. 176:16

king may make a n. 83:3
live cleanly, as a n. should do 355:10
Nobleness: allied with perfect n. 13:4
N. walks in our ways again 69:7
Nobler: whether 'tis n. in the mind 350:14
Noblesse: n. oblige 254:4
Noblest: amongst the n. of mankind 96:14
Nobody: business of n. 262:5
give a war and n. will come 337:3
I care for n. 59:2
n. asked you 298:17
n. is on my side 17:9
n. tells me anything 172:8
one whom n. can imitate 107:4
there is n. . . . to put you in mind of Johnson
191:7
what n. can do for you 105:8
Noctes: O n. cenaeque deum! 209:18
Noctis: lente currite n. equi! 267:3
Nod: affects to n. 149:34
land of N. 34:11
n.s and becks, and wreathèd smiles 276:19
Old N., the shepherd, goes 134:24
Wynken, Blynken and N. 162:14
Noe: honest kersey n.s 364:4
Noise: boys that fear no n. 182:20
full of dreary n.s! 72:2
God is gone up with a merry n. 38:27
happy n. to hear 210:14
I heard a ragged n. 199:22
isle is full of n.s 381:8
like n.s in a swound! 116:25
most sublime n. 167:19
n.s at dawn 15:17
play . . . with a loud n. 38:12
reduced it to n. 14:3
Noisy: n. man is always in the right 124:29
Noli: n. me tangere 53:40
Nom: rien n'est plus commun que le n. 244:12
Nomen: clarum et venerabile n. Gentibus 259:15
nostrum n. miscebitur istis 301:23
Nomine: mutato n. de te 209:11
Nominis: stat magni n. umbra 259:13
Non-Commissioned: N. Man! 238:27
Non-U: U and N. 330:22
Nonconformist: must be a n. 159:2
None: I have n. to tell, Sir 98:12
some believe they've n. at all 87:29
who dares do more is n. 365:11
Nonny: hey n, n., hey n. 352:13
Nonpareil: she's Colour-Serjeant of the N.
battalion 136:34
Nonsense: all time and n. scorning 80:3
n. of the old women 405:26
n. which was knocked out of them at school 29:5
nothing . . . that is not n. 2:3
sounds like n. 340:30
to be hanged for n. 149:31
Nook: not a n. within this solemn pass 467:19
O for a book and a shady n. 458:10
Noon: far from the fiery n. 230:26
has not attained his n. 200:15
lying till n. 223:23
riding near her highest n. 276:7
stood there then in the summer n. 426:12
where the Princes ride at n. 134:9
Noonday: at n. upon the market place 359:23

darkness more clear than n. 331:8
Noontide: 'N. Peace', a study of two dun cows 336:9
Noose: n.s give 304:1
Sultan's Turret in a N. of Light 163:22
Norfolk: bear him up the N. sky 32:15
very flat, N. 123:18
North: heart of the N. is dead 249:26
of Nelson and the N. 96:24
without sharp N. 145:11
North, Lord 223:12
North-north-west: I am but mad n. 350:1
Northcliffe, Lord 415:1
Norval: my name is N. 204:5
Norway: to N., to N. 23:10
Nose: cannot see beyond his own n. 28:26
courses one another down his innocent n. 344:26
did not see further than his own n. 244:9
Dong with a luminous N. 250:19
entuned in hir n. ful semely 107:12
having a n. for fish 185:8
he gave his n. 353:28
how haughtily he cocks his n. 410:4
keep a clean n. 153:8
let's cut off our n.s 70:4
Marian's n. looks red and raw 364:8
my n. is huge 332:5
n., n., jolly red n. 27:22
n. was as sharp as a pen 356:32
n.s have they, but they smell not 40:23
nothing pay for wearing our own n.s 347:8
pecked off her n. 297:31
Pimple on her n. 328:2
they haven't got no n.s 110:21
to wipe his little n. 24:18
with a little red n. 290:7
Noselessness: N. of Man 110:22
Nostalgie: n. de la boue 15:29
Nostril: breathed into his n.s 33:19
smell that ever offended n. 371:14
Not: HOW N. TO DO IT 138:11
Note: as the gen'l'm'n said to the fi' pun' n. 140:36
deed of dreadful 366:18
I heard a thousand blended n.s 462:24
not too sublime to be expressed by n.s 271:4
n.s are often necessary 220:1
n.s by distance made more sweet 119:18
n.s i handle no better 338:20
n.s with many a winding bout 276:33
sad n.s, fall at her flying feet 97:25
simple bird that thinks two n.s a song 132:19
simplest n. that swells the gale 187:7
soul of Orpheus sing such n.s 276:11
sound is forced, the n.s are few! 63:2
sound me from my lowest n. 351:17
take no n. of him 373:6
take n., take n., O world! 375:8
turn his merry n. 344:37
when found, make a n. of 137:31
wrapped up in a five-pound n. 250:24
Nothing: better to know n. 389:17
brought n. into this world 57:1
cucumber . . . good for n. 223:29
did n. in particular 177:12
does – n. at all 161:16
Emperor has n. on at all! 5:5
for n. less than thee 144:19
foreign policy is 'N. for N.' 290:15

gives to airy n. 372:14
having n. and yet possessing all things 56:1
he knows n. 388:11
he n. knew 281:9
I do n. upon myself 146:19
I got plenty o' n. 175:5
I have n. to do today 147:19
I n. lack if I am His 21:12
insupportable labour of doing n. 404:10
invulnerable n.s 390:4
is it n. to you 46:31
learnt n. and forgotten n. 414:8
n. a-year, paid quarterly 410:1
n. begins, and n. ends 427:11
n. can be created out of n. 259:19
n. can be known 89:15
n. for n. 'ere 322:9
n. happens to any man 16:17
'N. has happened' 327:12
n. is ever done in this world 388:12
n. is had for n. 115:16
n. is wasted 198:31
n. makes a man suspect much 20:20
n. matters very much 22:1
N. scrawled on a five-foot page 110:20
n. to do but work 237:5
n. to do with a man 3:24
n. to what I could say if I chose 101:12
n. will come of n. 361:29
signifying n. 367:24
such laboured n.s 313:9
think n. done while aught remains to do 328:24
to whom n. is given 162:24
we are n. 245:15
we said n. all the day 145:3
when one does n. 337:19
when you have n. to say 119:31
who knows n. else 12:17
worked . . . from n. to . . . poverty 269:8
you ain't heard n. yet 224:17
Nothingness: love and fame to n. do sink 233:12
never pass into n. 230:6
n. shows through 437:6
Notice: n. which you have been pleased to take 220:22
Noticing: it is our n. . . . . things 321:10
Not-incurious: n. in God's handiwork 74:17
Notion: and foolish n. 85:25
n. be doctrinally correct or not 237:21
Nought: n. is worth a thought 318:6
n. shall make us rue 361:28
n. . . . . so much the spirit calms 91:9
Nourished: chief n. in life's feast 365:26
n. during his whole life 327:11
Noveca: tristior n. fuerit 310:9
Novel: because a n.'s invented 318:2
good n. tells us the truth 110:28
I can't think of a single Russian n. 271:5
it is only a n. 16:30
last fashionable n. 262:34
more entertaining than half the n.s 270:26
my scrofulous French n. 78:24
not a n. to be tossed aside 304:9
n. is a mirror 404:23
n. is a static thing 434:20
n. tells a story 167:16
n.s for grown up people 460:19

ordinary n. would trace the history 249:24
read a n., or wring her hands 135:9
when I want to read a n. 144:1
November: N.'s sky is chill and drear 340:8
no fruits, no flowers . . . N.! 204:32
remember the Fifth of N. 6:14
than these N. skies 169:6
thirty days hath N. 184:6
Now: if it be n. 353:8
Nowadays: not as love is n. 265:17
Nowhere: n. to fall but off 237:6
real N. Man 253:11
Nox: n. est perpetua una dormienda 103:11
n. ruit et fuscis 441:5
Nudge: n., n., wink, wink 286:13
Nuée: prince des n.s 26:11
Nuffink: Why – N.! 111:13
Nuisance: make himself a n. to other people 273:13
Nuit: entends la douce n. 26:15
horreur d'une profonde n. 324:26
Number: divinity in odd n.s 371:16
few honest men are better than n.s 129:9
greatest happiness for the greatest n.s 212:22
harmonious n.s 279:12
his n. is Six hundred threescore and six 58:22
I lisped in n.s 312:19
if I called the wrong n. 429:16
in fresh n.s n. all your graces 385:15
in unvanquishable n. 392:2
luck in odd n.s 258:18
to add to golden n.s 134:1
Numbered: hairs of your head are all n. 49:42
Numbness: drowsy n. pains my senses 231:30
Numinosum: altered by the experience of the *n.* 227:3
Numskull: she married a n. 388:2
Nun: ejected n. of Wilton 341:8
holy time is quiet as a n. 463:4
if you become a n., dear 212:15
n.s fret not 462:29
upbringing a n. would envy 300:9
Nunnery: get thee to a n. 350:17
n. of thy chaste breast 258:14
Nuptial: n. love maketh mankind 19:16
prone to an iteration of n.s 121:1
Nurse: always keep a hold of N. 30:10
meet n. for a poetic child 340:2
my most kindly n. 403:14
nature's soft n. 355:30
n. of arms 181:29
n. sleeps sweetly 126:31
old men's n.s 19:12
priest continues what the n. began 150:24
that sucks the n. asleep 344:12
will scratch the n. 384:3
Nurseries: look for me in the n. of Heaven 428:3
n. of all vice and immorality 162:26
Nursery: n. still lisps out 89:6
Nursling: n. of the sky 390:16
Nut: Brazil, where the n.s come from 426:3
I had a little n. tree 296:25
N.s! 263:2
n.s in May 6:3
Nutmeg: n.s and ginger 27:22
silver n. and a golden pear 296:25
Nutshell: I could be bounded in a n. 349:34
Nymph: haste thee, n. 276:19

mountain n., sweet Liberty 276:21
n., with long dishevelled hair 387:11
O n. more bright 173:24
Nympha: n. pudica Deum vidit 128:23

O

O.K.-people: *O. to mention* in Newstatesmanship 317:13
O.K.-words: O. in conversationship 317:13
Oaf: muddied o.s at the goals 239:17
Oak: bend a knotted o. 120:13
  heart of o. are our ships 173:5
  many an o. that grew thereby 272:33
  O. and Ash and Thorn 241:1
  tall o.s, branch-charmèd 230:29
  tall o.s from little acorns grow 160:7
Oar: o.s were silver 343:28
Oat: *O.s. A grain . . . given to horses* 219:15
Oath: good mouth-filling o. 354:28
  in lapidary inscriptions a man is not upon o. 222:16
  men deceived with o.s 18:9
  o.s are but words 87:22
  o.s are straws 357:2
  swore a solemn o. 84:32
Oatmeal: cultivate literature on a little o. 399:17
Obadiah: O. Bind-their-kings 261:7
Obedience: be swift in all o. 240:24
  keeps men in o. 86:22
  reluctant o. of distant provinces 262:9
Obey: has her humour most when she o.s 314:28
  safer to o. than to rule 235:3
  to love, cherish and to o. 319:43
  we shall o. 351:15
Object: my o. all sublime 177:27
  my o. gather to a head 381:10
  you don't o. to an aged parent 138:6
Oblation: bring no more vain o.s 44:31
Obligation: accept the o. laid on thee 78:8
  haste to repay an o. 248:13
  to John I owed great o. 320:19
Oblige: one should o. everyone 244:5
Obliger: o. tout le monde 244:5
Obliging: so o. that he ne'er obliged 312:23
Oblivion: commend to cold o. 390:24
  drink o. of a day 272:9
  iniquity of o. 71:18
  leaping from place to place over o. 192:22
Obscure: through the palpable o. 279:1
Obscurity: decent o. of a learned language 175:12
Obsequies: celebrates his o. 339:29
Observance: more honoured in the breach than the o. 348:28
Observation: let o. with extensive view 219:5
  o.s which ourselves we make 314:15
  strange places crammed with o. 345:7
Observe: thou o.s not 45:39
Observer: he is a great o. 359:19
  keen o. of life 14:26
  o. of human nature 140:20
  observed of all o.s 350:21
  strict o. 243:7
Obstinacy: o. in a bad one 405:18

Obstruction: to lie in cold o. 368:22
Occasion: all o.s do inform against me 351:41
  courage mounteth with o. 361:8
  on such an o. as this 80:3
  there is o.s 357:22
Occupation: absence of o. is not rest 126:21
  let us love our o.s 136:36
  pleasant o. for . . . Chancellor 177:8
  worse o.s . . . than feeling a woman's pulse 405:11
Ocean: Columbus sailed the o. blue 335:1
  cross the o. of this world 72:29
  deep and dark blue O. 90:20
  fall into the o. 267:5
  glad o. comes and goes 306:3
  great o. of truth 294:8
  I have loved thee, O. 90:24
  in the o.'s bosom unespied 268:12
  life on the o. wave 337:16
  make the mighty o. 100:24
  on one side lay the O. 417:10
  on the o. of life we pass 257:17
  portable, and compendious o.s 128:24
  round o. and the living air 462:20
  seen the hungry o. gain 386:3
  thou hast been O.'s child 391:25
  treacherous o. has forsworn its wiles 390:26
  upon a painted o. 116:27
  watched the o. and the sky 391:17
Oceania: official language of O. 300:24
October: funny kind of month, O. 295:14
  night in the lonesome O. 310:30
  since golden O. declined 157:14
Octopus: tell me, O Octopus 292:10
Odd: how o. of God 160:9
  it's a very o. thing 134:23
  nothing o. will do long 222:17
  this was scarcely o. 102:9
Odds: facing fearful o. 261:13
  my soul is any jot at o. 378:2
  o. is gone 344:4
Ode: I intended an O. 144:7
Oderint: o., dum metuant 1:1
Odi: o. et amo 104:5
Odin: let him try to blaspheme O. 111:8
Odious: comparisons are o. 144:20
Odium: young o. and aversion to the very sight of men 121:4
Odour: Body O. 2:27
  o.s from the spicy shore 279:21
  o.s when sweet violets sicken 394:6
  stealing and giving o.! 382:23
Oedipus: myth of King O. 169:12
Oeuf: pour se faire cuire deux o.s 106:1
Oeuvre: o. sort plus belle 173:19
Offal: with this slave's o. 350:11
Offence: conscience void of o. 54:7
  generally punished for the o. they give 432:9
  love th' offender, yet detest th' o. 312:9
  my o. is rank 351:22
  needs be that o.s come 50:30
  what dire o. 315:11
Offended: for him have I o. 360:13
  hath not o. the king 287:20
  this hand hath o. 128:16
Offender: list of society o.s 177:20
  love th' o., yet detest th' offence 312:9
  most notorious o. 400:12

Offending: very head and front of my o. 373:40

Offensive: You are o., sir 59:19

Offer: make him an o. he can't refuse 322:21

Offering: o. Germany too little 293:11

Office: by o. boys for o. boys 336:22
  insolence of o. 350:14
  o., and custom 381:35
  so clear in his great o. 365:7

Office-boy: o. to an Attorney's firm 176:29

Officer: God rest his soul, o.s . . . said 399:16
  never more be o. of mine 374:24

Offspring: of human o. sole propriety 279:35
  Time's noblest o. 32:6

O'Flynn: Father O., you've the wonderful way wid
  you 184:24

Ogre: famous men of old, the O.s 185:6

Oil: I shall be anointed with fresh o. 40:3
  o. to make his face to shine 40:11
  something lingering with boiling o. 177:31
  words were softer than o. 38:34

Ointment: good name is better than precious o.
  43:26
  like the precious o. 41:7

Old: adherence to the o. and tried 254:15
  being o. is having lighted rooms 247:20
  Darling, I am growing o. 326:18
  for I'm o. and ill 33:2
  grow o. along with me! 77:11
  grow o. always learning many things 400:25
  grow o. with a good grace 404:6
  growing o. in drawing nothing up 127:7
  growing o. is like being penalized 318:4
  grown o. before my time 331:10
  how subject we o. men are to this vice of lying!
    356:6
  I am too o. to learn 362:8
  I grow o. 156:26
  I have been young, and now am o. 38:15
  I know thee not, o. man 356:18
  I love everything that's o. 182:13
  last to lay the o. aside 313:10
  man is as o. as he's feeling 119:6
  motionless as a cloud the o. man stood 466:7
  needs not make new songs, but say the o. 124:8
  o. age, it is the last gap but one 452:19
  O. Age a regret 143:15
  o. age is the most unexpected 432:11
  o. age isn't so bad 111:16
  o. and young . . . all on our last cruise 407:2
  o. get o. 289:2
  o. man in a dry month 156:10
  o. man with an o. soul 94:1
  o. men forget 357:18
  read an o. one 329:2
  she's been thinking of the o. 'un! 137:6
  some day before I'm o.! 239:18
  that which should accompany o. age 367:18
  they shall not grow o. 59:18
  times when o. are good 89:1
  too o. to go again to my travels 106:24
  when he is o. he will not depart from it 42:30
  when it [wine] is o. 48:7
  when the o. man died 467:28
  when they get to feeling o. 69:15
  where nobody gets o. 471:10
  why wasn't I born o. and ugly? 136:17
  you are o. 362:11

you never can be o. 386:21

Older: make way for an o. man 270:15

Oldest: o. hath borne most 363:16

O'Leary: with O. in the grave 471:25

Olive: peace proclaims o.s 386:27
  ranged the o. stones about its edge 73:7

Olive-branches: thy children like the o. 41:4

Olive-leaf: in her mouth was an o. 34:17

Olivia: cry out 'O.' 382:36

Olympo: Pelion imposuisse O. 208:28

Olympum: frondosum involvere O. 441:24

Ombrifuge: o. (Lord love you!) 95:20

Omega: Alpha and O. 58:38

Omen: quod di o. avertant 114:20

Omnes: non omnia possumus o. 441:19
  o. eodem cogimur 208:17

Omnipotent: to be O. but friendless 393:7

Omniscience: his specialism is o. 147:20

On: this is o. me 304:15

Once: journalism what will be grasped at o.
  121:13

Onde: comme une o. quit bout 211:18

One: but the O. was Me 213:9
  God . . . putteth down o. 39:20
  he stoppeth o. of three 116:18
  how to be o. up 317:11
  like the splendour of the Mighty O. 33:12
  my Dear O. is mine 15:8
  o. of us two, Herminius 261:10
  o. remains, the many change 390:8
  o. to come, and o. to go 102:15
  o. to watch 3:16
  o., two, buckle my shoe 297:16
  o., two! O., two! 101:26
  pay for o. by o. 240:29
  than O. who rose 391:7
  they are o. and o. 73:20

One-and-twenty: when I was o. 210:11

One-armed: busy as a o. man 198:13

One-eyed: little o., blinking sort o' place 193:23

Onion: lot o. atoms lurk within the bowl 400:3
  mine eyes smell o.s 343:13
  you're just an o. 214:16

Onward: he o. came 280:17

Ooze: o. and bottom of the sea 356:23
  to o. juicily 81:6

Open: no fear of the movement into the o. 65:6
  so o. that nothing is retained 66:12

Opening: always o. time in the Sailors Arms 426:23

Opera: German text of French o.s 451:24
  o. ain't over till the fat lady sings 122:2

Operatic: sunsets . . . so o. 321:19

Operation: important o.s which we can perform
  453:4
  requires a surgical o. 399:24

Operative: this is an o. statement 473:4

Opinion: always think the last o. right 313:17
  as many o.s as there are men 424:31
  error of o. may be tolerated 217:21
  give him my o. 136:32
  how long halt ye between two o.s? 36:15
  I agree with no man's o. 433:9
  I have bought golden o.s 365:9
  in the gross and scope of my o. 347:21
  new o.s are always suspected 255:21
  no very exalted o. 81:13
  now but a climate of o. 14:10

of his own o. still 87:28
public buys its o.s 88:13
stiff in o.s 149:20
such an o. as is unworthy of 19:38
takes no notice of their o.s 129:11
wish to spread those o.s 87:33
Opium: o. of the people 269:16
Opponent: at least you know who your o. is! 436:1
   never ascribe to an o. 26:6
   o. cannot be both honest and intelligent 301:5
   strong, dogged, unenlightened o. 12:21
Opportunities: wise man will make more o. 20:35
Opportunity: maximum of o. 388:28
Opposed: new opinions are . . . usually o. 255:21
Opposite: o. is also a profound truth 64:5
Opposition: duty of an O. was very simple 135:7
   his Majesty's loyal o. 328:15
   His Majesty's O. 202:10
   no government . . . secure without . . . O. 143:12
   o.s of science 57:5
Oppressed: he was o. 46:9
Oppressor: bear . . . o.'s wrong 350:14
Oppugnancy: meets in mere o. 382:1
Optics: o. sharp it needs 433:2
Optimism: o. of the will 184:15
   pessimism . . . as agreeable as o. 31:18
Optimist: o. proclaims that we live 95:3
Opus: hoc o., hic labor est 440:26
Oracle: I am Sir O. 369:4
   it speaks o.s 324:20
   o.s are dumb 277:25
Orange: clockwork o. 81:6
   hangs in shades the o. bright 268:13
   o.s and lemons 297:17
   squeeze the o. and throw away the skin 442:22
Orator: eyes of men without an o. 385:6
   I am no o. 360:23
   one of those o.s 112:9
   swords shall play the o.s 267:14
Oratory: object of our o. 262:3
Orb: monthly changes in her circled o. 379:15
   not the smallest o. which thou behold'st 370:20
Orbis: si fractus illabitur o. 208:26
Orchard: in the pleasant o. closes 71:27
   keep cold, young o. 170:6
   o.s of our mothers 15:7
Ordained: powers that are o. of God 54:41
Order: 'e don't obey no o.s 238:26
   good o. is the foundation 82:25
   in all line of o. 381:35
   let all things be . . . in order 55:28
   lower o.s don't set us a good example 455:6
   old o. changeth 417:18
   o. in variety we see 316:9
   o. is heaven's first law 314:8
   right words in the right o. 63:29
   stand not upon the o. of your going 366:32
Ordo: ab integro saeclorum nascitur o. 441:15
Ore: load every rift of your subject with o. 234:17
   with new-spangled o. 277:17
Organ: hath not a Jew . . . o.s 369:32
   let the pealing o. blow 276:15
   meaty jelly . . . is mellering to the o. 140:9
   playing of the merry o. 7:25
   remorse invaded . . . my nasal o. 252:8
   seated one day at the o. 321:2
Organism: desire . . . of every o. to live beyond its

income 88:1
Organization: trouble with peace . . . no o. 67:5
Organize: don't waste any time mourning – o.!
   201:10
Orgasm: o. has replaced the Cross 289:14
Oriel: O. Common Room stank of Logic 294:1
Oriental: then you are an O. 167:21
Original: more people one finds o. 305:3
   their great O. proclaim 2:14
Originality: fruits of o. 273:14
Orion: loose the bands of O. 37:12
   O. plunges prone 210:4
Orison: nymph, in thy o.s 350:15
   patter out their hasty o.s 302:7
Ornament: needs not the foreign aid of o. 428:12
   o. of a meek and quiet spirit 57:33
   studies serve . . . for o. 20:29
   this o. is but the guilèd shore 370:3
   world is still deceived with o. 370:2
Ornamental: not merely be useful and o. 408:17
Orphan: I'm a o. both sides 450:9
   listeneth to the sighs of o.s 135:3
   Little O. Annie 185:18
Orpheus: another O. sings again 391:3
   bid the soul of O. sing 276:11
   O. with his lute 358:18
Orthodoxy: o. is my doxy 446:1
Ortolan: die eating o.s 143:29
Ossa: pile O. on Pelion 441:24
Ostentation: designed for use rather than o. 175:17
Other: I have used no o. 322:15
   not as o. men are 52:37
   passed by on the o. side 52:11
Otherwise: some are o. 168:22
Otia: deus nobis haec o. fecit 441:10
Otis: Miss O. regrets 317:2
Oublié: courtisans . . . n'ont rien oublié 152:12
Ours: vendre la peau de l'o.244:15
Ourselves: eternal not o. 13:2
Outcast: he gathereth together the o.s of Israel
   41:16
   spiritless o.! 98:13
Outrun: o. the constable at last 87:18
Outside: I am just going o. 299:2
Ouvrage: mais les o.s les plus courts 244:22
   remettez votre o. 64:11
Over: till it's o. o. there 116:6
Overcoat: his o. for ever 209:29
   to put on your o. 259:5
Overcome: o. evil with good 54:39
   We Shall O. 209:20
Over-feeding: what Nicely-Nicely dies of will be o.
   333:4
Over-keeping: mouldy from o. 104:17
Oversexed: o. and over here 432:1
Overthrow: linger out a purposed o. 386:16
   thou dost o. 145:18
Over-violent: so o., or over-civil 149:21
Owe: he o.s not any man 257:20
Owen, Wilfred 472:8
Owl: answered o.s are hooting 93:14
   by a mousing o. hawked at 366:8
   court for o.s 45:23
   curves of the white o. sweeping 272:4
   he respects O. 274:22
   I'm an o. 163:7
   it was the o. that shrieked 365:21

like an o. in an ivy-bush 411:11
like an o. of the desert 40:9
moping o. does to the moon complain 186:2
nightly sings the staring o. 364:7
o., for all his feathers, was a-cold 230:13
O. and the Pussy-Cat 250:24
o.s would have hooted 186:21
there I couch when o.s do cry 381:17
they bought an O. 250:23
two o.s and a hen 250:13
white o. in the belfry sits 423:20
Owlet: o. whoops to the wolf below 117:12
Owl-song: sadder than o.s 92:15
Own: he came unto his o. 53:1
I never o. to it before her 136:31
think and call my o. 151:5
you don't o. it an ideal 106:8
Ox: as an o. goeth to the slaughter 41:29
better . . . than a stalled o. 42:13
o. knoweth his owner 44:30
thou shalt not muzzle the o. 35:15
Oxen: come see the o. kneel 193:8
who drives fat o. 223:18
Oxenford: Clerk there was of O. also 107:17
Oxford 12:2
clever men at O. 184:13
King to O. sent 71:23
nonsense . . . put gently back at O. 29:5
O. Street, stony-hearted stepmother 135:3
poetry, which is in O. made an art 150:31
to O. sent a troop of horse 431:19
University of O. . . . no obligation 175:8
Oxlip: bold o.s and the crown imperial 384:29
faint o.s 393:21
where o.s and the nodding violet grows 371:38
Oxus: shorn and parcelled O. 11:34
Oyster: man who first swallowed an o. 216:8
o. may be crossed in love 395:14
o. shop for mermaids 203:21
poverty and o.s 140:32
sympathetic unselfishness of an o. 336:5
world's mine o. 371:8
you'd ha' made an uncommon fine o. 140:33
Oysterman: tall young o. lived by the riverside
203:20
Ozymandias: my name is O., king of kings 392:15

P

P.C.: P.C.49 194:3
Pace: creeps in this petty p. 367:24
p. is too good to inquire 295:3
she made three p.s thro' the room 419:14
time travels in divers p.s 345:24
two p.s of the vilest earth 355:6
Pacisque: p. imponere morem 440:30
Pack: p.s and sets of great ones 363:9
Pack-horse: p. on the down 288:12
Paddington: as London is to P. 98:17
Paddle: p. his own canoe 268:7
Paddock: cold as p.s 200:22
Padlock: clap your p. – on her mind 320:18
Pagan: p. suckled in a creed outworn 463:7
you find the p. 473:2
Page: blotted from life's p. 89:20

hither, p., and stand by me 292:28
Nothing scrawled on a five-foot p. 110:20
see them on a beautiful quarto p. 395:34
you find it in his wisest p. 115:20
Pageant: like this insubstantial p. faded 381:10
Paid: well p. that is well satisfied 370:17
Pail: to fetch a p. of water 296:29
Pain: die of a rose in aromatic p.? 313:31
doomed to go in company with p. 461:11
faint beneath the aromatic p. 458:20
I feel no p. 7:26
I have no p. 161:12
labour we delight in physics p. 366:2
neither shall there be any more p. 58:33
no gains without p.s 406:10
no p. felt she 77:5
no p., no palm 307:6
of p., darkness and cold 77:9
one who never inflicts p. 294:2
Our Lady of P. 412:10, 412:12
owes its pleasures to another's p.s 127:9
p. and anguish wring the brow 340:19
p. at her side 315:25
p. clings cruelly to us 230:8
p. rises up 423:32
p. we obey 321:17
pleasure in poetic p.s 127:1
pleasure is . . . intermission of p. 342:9
sweet is pleasure after p. 150:1
sympathize with people's p.s 212:29
threats of p. 186:12
travaileth in p. together 54:28
we are born in other's p. 427:11
wicked to deserve such p. 73:27
wilt thou find passion, p., or pride? 423:33
wish no living thing to suffer p. 392:25
with p. purchased 363:18
Paint: flinging a pot of p. in the public's face 333:8
fresh as p. 398:11
he p.s not what he sees 308:21
I takes and p.s 70:3
let her p. an inch thick 352:27
p.s men as they should be 243:11
Painter: hate all Boets and Bainters [p.s] 174:30
I am a p. too! 122:21
I only know of two p.s 452:6
p. should not paint what he sees 437:5
some great p. dips his pencil 393:23
Painting: as in p., so in poetry 207:10
difference between p. a face 170:27
figure p., the type of all p. 32:4
I have heard of your p.s too 350:19
p. is a blind man's profession 308:21
p. is self-discovery 311:2
Pair: blest p. 279:36
Palace: my gorgeous p. for a hermitage 377:4
p. and a prison on each hand 90:5
p. is more than a house 119:2
prosperity within thy p.s 40:34
saw in sleep old p.s and towers 392:7
spider . . . is in kings' p.s 43:9
strong man armed keepeth his p. 52:14
very stately p. before him 80:20
Paladin: Sidney's self, the starry p. 78:28
Palate: our gross p.s drink 470:4
Pale: art thou p. for weariness 394:11
turn not p., beloved snail 101:19

why so p. and wan 409:5
Palestine: haven in sunny P. 269:24
Palfrey: his p. was as broun as is a berye 107:15
Paling: piece-bright p. shuts the spouse 206:16
Pall Mall: *P. Gazette* is written by gentlemen 425:12
   shady side of P. 288:7
Palladium: liberty of the Press is the *P.* 227:8
Palm: bear the p. alone 359:15
   condemned to have an itching p. 360:27
   Infinity in the p. of your hand 60:8
   lands of p. and southern pine 416:5
   oozing out . . . at the p.s of my hands! 395:32
   p.s before my feet 110:5
   pudding p.s and pinching fingers 384:13
   quietly sweating p. to p. 213:8
   to win the p. 268:18
Palm-tree: righteous shall flourish like the p.
   40:4
Palmer: Lorenzo, a young p. 231:2
Palmerston, Lord 144:3
Palmerworm: p. hath . . . locust eaten 47:11
Pam: P., I adore you 32:20
Pan: fish that *talks* in the frying p. 134:5
   great God P. 72:1
Panacea: far beyond all their p.s 86:16
Pandars: call them all P. 382:11
Pandemonium: P., the high capital of Satan 278:28
Pandion: King P., he is dead 25:11
Panem: p. et circenses 228:6
Pang: corporal sufferance finds a p. as great 368:20
   more p.s and fears 358:22
   more p.s will . . . wilder wring 206:8
Pangloss: saw Dr P. behind some bushes 442:10
Panjandrum: great P. himself 166:25
Panomphaean: *trink* is a p. word 324:20
Pansies: p., that's for thoughts 352:14
Pant: in fast thick p.s were breathing 118:1
Pantaloon: lean and slippered p. 345:11
Pantoufle: apportez moi mes p.s 283:9
Papa: as p. used to say 137:9
   or else his dear p. is poor 407:17
Papacy: P. . . . . Ghost of . . . Roman Empire 202:8
Paper: he fornicated and read the p.s 98:2
   he hath not eat p. 363:28
   he's got my p.s 309:9
   his name was never in the p. 273:24
   if all the world were p. 5:20
   isn't worth the p. its written on 183:13
   make dust our p. 377:1
   only a p. moon 192:5
   when any part of this p. appears dull 404:8
   words that ever blotted p.! 370:5
Parable: troubled to invent p.s 193:26
Paraclete: come, thou holy P. 247:16
Paradis: but in P. if we meet 79:13
   p. to what we fear of death 368:23
Paradise: all P. opens! 143:29
   desert were a p. 85:8
   drunk the milk of P. 118:6
   England is a p. for women 86:20
   England is the p. of women 166:21
   enjoy p. in the next [world] 28:17
   go to P. by way of Kensal Green 110:14
   heavenly p. is that place 97:30
   how has she cheapened p. 305:20
   in P. of all things common else 279:35
   p. of fools 279:17

pass through P. in a dream 118:16
same old glimpse of P. 246:20
such are the Gates of P. 60:27
thou P. of exiles 391:14
to him are opening p. 187:7
two p.s 'twere in one 268:23
upon the trees of P. 408:1
Wilderness is P. enow 164:1
wine they drink in P. 109:32
Paradox: Government go on in strange p. 112:15
   p. which comforts while it mocks 77:14
Paradys: P. stood formed in hir yën 108:27
Paragon: P. of animals! 349:36
Parallel: but ours so truly p. 268:16
   delves the p.s in beauty's brow 386:1
   of things without p. 59:11
Parallelogram: landlady . . . is a p. 250:4
   My Princess of P.s 94:11
Paranoid: p. can have enemies 242:2
Parchment: mysterious virtue of wax and p. 81:18
Pard: bearded like the p. 345:11
Pardon: they ne'er p. 151:22
Pardoned: more in him to be praised than to be p.
   225:29
Pardonner: Tout comprendre c'est tout p. 403:29
Pardoun: bretful of p. comen from Rome 107:29
Parens: p. melior homini 310:9
Parent: aged p.s live 8:14
   children begin by loving their p.s 455:37
   his p.s were not married 388:7
   Jewish man with p.s alive 332:8
   joys of p.s are secret 19:7
   P. of good! 280:9
   proved a kind p. to man 310:9
   that's what p.s were created for 292:11
   to lose one p. 455:13
   would put any p. mad 166:13
   you don't object to an aged p. 138:6
Parent: sort fait les p.s 134:32
Parenti: qui non risere p. 441:16
Parfit: verray p. gentil knight 107:10
Paries: p. cum proximus ardet 207:25
Paris: Frensh of P. was to hir unknowe 107:12
   good Americans . . . go to P. 9:22
   I love P. in the springtime 316:26
   in P. as none kiss each other 405:12
   is P. burning? 201:21
   last time I saw P. 191:9
   lucky enough to have lived in P. 197:19
   no home in Europe save in P. 294:19
   P. is well worth a mass 198:4
   si le roi m'avait donné P. 284:6
   when good Americans die they go to P. 456:7
Parish: look upon all the world as my p. 450:25
Park: over p., over pale 371:31
   p.s were the lungs of London 309:19
Parkinson: P.'s Law 304:22
Parley-voo: hinky pinky p. 332:19
Parliament: England is the mother of P.s 68:14
   made honest by an act of p. 225:1
   no reference to fun in any Act of P. 198:33
   P. speaking through reporters to Buncombe 99:36
   Three Estates in P. 99:33
Parliamentary: as an old P. hand 179:3
Parlour: will you walk into my p.? 211:11
Parmaceti: was p. for an inward bruise 353:30
Parnassus: not a sapling upon P. 223:20

sick of an old p. 147:9
so I triumphed ere my p. 419:33
strange fits of p. 466:27
tear a p. to tatters 350:24
to inspire hopeless p. is my destiny 425:9
vows his p. is infinite 304:3
vulgar expression of the p.! 120:3
what p. cannot music raise and quell 151:1
when p.s are no more 444:12
win the p. and the life 117:27
Passionless: hopeless grief is p. 72:3
Passiveness: in a wise p. 461:28
Past: absurd about the p. 29:2
    borne back ceaselessly into the p. 165:9
    dead P. bury its dead! 257:4
    every race . . . in the p. has perished 249:8
    God cannot change the p. 3:29
    great mistake to prejudge the p. 453:11
    neither repeat his p. 15:24
    p. and to come seems best 355:20
    p., at least, is secure 448:23
    p. is a foreign country 194:29
    P., Present and Future existing all at once 61:1
    p. unsighed for 462:10
    p. was a sleep 78:33
    plan the future by the p. 82:32
    portions and parcels of the dreadful P. 420:15
    those who do not remember the p. 337:10
    turning all the p. to pain! 181:24
    we two kept house, the P. and I 192:18
    whatever makes the p. 219:18
    who can afford to live in the p.? 309:10
    who controls the p. 300:23
    world is weary of the p. 391:8
Pastime: forgotten p. of high jinks 340:32
Pastor: as some ungracious p.s do 348:20
Pastoral: cold P.! 231:24
Pasture: fresh woods, and p.s new 277:18
    lie down in green p.s 38:2
    on England's pleasant p.s seen 61:9
    sell the p. now 356:26
Pasty: p. costly made 415:16
Pat: now might I do it p. 351:23
    There's P. and Mac and Tommy 242:6
Pat-a-cake: p., p., baker's man 297:20
Patch: purple p. or two 206:28
Patches: mad in p. 105:17
Pate: feather p. of folly 210:27
    you beat your p. 312:13
Pâté: heaven is, eating p.s de foie gras 400:9
Patent-leather: with their p. souls 173:2
Paterna: p. rura bubus exercet suis 208:1
Paternité: recherche de p. est interdite 116:5
Path: all her p.s are peace 403:24
    light unto my p. 40:27
    make a beaten p. to his door 159:16
    out of a misty dream our p. emerges 147:12
    p. of the just 41:25
    p. on the sea's azure floor 390:26
    p.s of love are rougher 192:17
    shine by the side of every p. we tread 127:29
    so many p.s that wind and wind 454:19
    straight was a p. of gold for him 76:19
    take the gentle p. 199:9
    This Ariyan Eightfold P. 80:4
    though thy p. be dark as night 264:1
    through the p.s of the seas 37:27

thy p.s drop fatness 39:11
    when life's p. is steep 208:16
Pathetic: 'P. . . . that's what it is. P.' 274:30
Pathos: true p. and sublime of human life 85:29
Patience: in your p. possess ye your souls 52:42
    old abusing of God's p. 371:5
    our p. will achieve more 82:24
    P., a minor form of despair 59:14
    p. and passage of time 244:6
    p. and shuffle the cards 105:19
    p. be a tired mare 356:28
    p. of Job 57:27
    p. to prevent 282:4
    pattern of all p. 362:18
    poor are they that have not p. 374:28
    sad P., too near neighbour to despair 11:25
    sat like P. on a monument 383:14
Patience: grande aptitude à la p. 80:8
    p. et longeur de temps 244:6
Patient: I will be p. and proud 72:14
    kill the p. 20:14
    not so p. as Job 355:15
    p. etherised upon a table 156:19
Patines: thick inlaid with p. of bright gold 370:20
Patois: I write in a sort of broken-down p. 106:10
Patria: pro p. mori 302:10
    sed miles, sed pro p. 293:15
Patriarch: lived like the wives in the p.s' days 193:6
Patrick: grand old ballad of Sir P. Spence 117:25
Patrie: grands artistes n'ont pas de p. 290:12
    plus j'aimai ma p. 31:12
Patriot: although he is a p. 162:9
    blood of p.s 217:24
    for what were all these country p.s born? 89:2
    p.s always talk of dying for their country 334:1
    so to be p.s 82:30
    steady p. of the world alone 98:14
    such is the p.'s boast 181:28
    sunshine p. 303:2
    thing no p. would think of saying 110:27
    true p.s we 26:7
Patriotism: p. is not enough 104:9
    p. is the last refuge of a scoundrel 222:14
Patron: best of all p.s 103:19
    P. . . . Commonly a wretch 219:16
    p. . . . looks with unconcern 220:21
    p. of some thirty charities 422:24
Patronage: office he'll hold and p. sway 70:5
Patronize: p. everybody without distinction of class 388:4
Patronus: quanto tu optimus omnium's p. 103:19
Patter: p. of little feet 256:15
Pattern: cunning'st p. of excelling nature 375:22
    p. of all patience 362:18
Paul: P., thou art beside thyself 54:10
Paunch: his p. grew mutinous 76:25
Pauper: break stones like an old p. 470:3
    only a p. 295:13
    p. in the midst of wealth 209:3
Paupertas: nil habet . . . p. durius in se 227:20
Paupertate: hic vivimus ambitiosa p. omnes 227:22
Pause: lucid intervals and happy p.s 20:39
    Nature made a p. 472:20
    p.s between the notes 338:20
Pavement: scrub a kitchen p. 470:3
Pavender: decks the rural p. 335:10
Paviour: p.s cry 'God bless you, Sir!' 160:3

pursuit of p. 12:14
take her own way to p. 81:15
to know what p. is 396:22
to their right praise and true p.! 370:24
what's come to p. perishes 76:9
Performance: desire should . . . outlive p. 355:29
value . . . observed in the p. of every act 16:14
Perfume: as a p. doth remain 413:8
to throw a p. on the violet 361:21
Perfumed: p. into the bargain 104:13
Perhaps: grand P.! 73:2
in search of a great p. 324:22
Peril: smile at p.s past 339:13
through p.s both of wind and limb 87:14
what p.s do environ 87:15
Perish: better to p. than to continue schoolmastering
100:17
p. the thought! 114:11
p. through their own imaginations 37:23
p. with the sword 51:23
should not p., but have everlasting life 53:8
thy money p. with thee 53:44
Perished: their memorial is p. with them 37:28
we p. each alone 124:22
Perisse: *quod vides p. perditum ducas* 103:13
Periwig: new p., make a great show 307:23
Perjuries: at love's p. . . . Jove laughs 379:13
Perpendicular: p., precise and taciturn 283:3
Perpetuity: seeks p. by way of futurity 310:14
without distinction to merit of p. 71:18
Perplexed: p. in the extreme 375:26
Persecution: religious p. may shield itself 81:27
some degree of p. 411:18
Persepolis: ride in triumph through P. 267:16
Perseverance: p. in a good cause 405:18
p. . . . keeps honour bright 382:13
Persia: past their first sleep in P. 70:19
Persian: given to the Medes and P.s 47:5
I loathe P. luxury 208:15
laws of the P.s and the Medes 36:30
Persicos: P. odi, puer, apparatus 208:15
Person: comprehended two aspicious p.s 373:13
conversation with the finest p.s of past centuries
135:11
did certain p.s die before they sing 117:29
God is no respecter of p.s 53:49
I am made up of several p.s 271:3
if an innocent p. is condemned 243:12
many a gentle p. made a Jack 377:28
neither confounding the P.s 318:33
no more a p. 14:10
no respect of . . . p.s, nor time in you 383:5
only p. . . . I should like to know thoroughly
455:29
there's no sich a p.! 139:2
thou wert the goodliest p. 265:23
when a p. dies 195:17
young p., who either marries or dies 16:25
Personal: call it the p. unconscious 227:1
Personalities: all great events and p. in world history
269:17
Personality: no more p. than a paper cup 106:7
Perspiration: genius is . . . ninety-nine per cent p.
154:8
Persuade: trying to p. people to do 432:26
Persuaded: fully p. in his own mind 54:46
Persuadest: thou p. me to be a Christian 54:12

Persuading: by p. others, we convince ourselves
227:11
Persuasion: firm p. that a thing is so 63:22
not truth but p. 262:3
Perturbation: O polished p.! 356:11
Pessimism: p. . . . as agreeable as optimism 31:18
p. of the spirit 184:15
Pessimist: p. fears this is so 95:3
p. is a man who looks both ways 308:6
Pestilence: deliver thee . . . from the noisome p.
39:35
he who . . . acts not breeds p. 63:11
p. that walketh in darkness 40:1
Pet: kept it for a p. 31:1
Petal: now sleeps the crimson p. 422:15
O filigree p. fashioned so purely 428:1
p.s on a wet black bough 317:25
pursed its p.s up 75:6
Petar: hoist with his own p. 351:36
Peter: Shock-headed P. 203:8
thou art P. 50:23
Petrarch: if Laura had been P.'s wife 91:16
Petronius 414:6
Petticoat: in the tempestuous p. 200:6
put it on again with her p. 285:9
venerate a p. 92:14
with a yellow p. 296:12
Peut-être: chercher un grand p. 324:22
Phagocyte: stimulate the p.s 387:30
Phalanx: perfect p. to the Dorian mood 278:19
Phallusy: always thought men were a p. 184:4
Phantasma: interim is like a p. 359:27
Phantom: she was a p. of delight 466:14
with p.s an unprofitable strife 390:4
Phebe: so am I for P. 346:10
Phenomenon: describe the infant p. 139:18
Phil: Fidgety P. 203:1
Philadelphia: rather be in P. 163:12
Philip: I appeal from P. drunk to P. sober 437:2
Philistine: lest the daughters of the P.s rejoice
35:47
P. must have originally meant 12:21
P. . . . something particularly stiff-necked 12:15
P.s be upon thee 35:34
Philistinism: P.! – We have not the expression
12:22
Philologist: p.s who chase 126:23
Philomel: change of P. 157:1
Philosopher: at the same time a profound p. 118:22
considered . . . by the p. as equally false 175:13
nation of pure p.s 21:9
never was yet p. 373:23
that some p. has not said it 114:12
thou best p. 464:11
till p.s become kings 310:4
to be a true p. 305:2
too much of a p. 334:6
tried . . . to be a p. 154:14
Philosophorum: non dicatur ab aliquo p. 114:12
Philosophre: but albe that he was a p. 107:19
Philosophy: adversity's sweet milk, p. 380:1
dreamt of in your p. 349:16
false p. 279:3
fear divine p. 418:6
great advantage for a system of p. 337:14
hast any p. in thee, shepherd? 345:15
history of Western p. 453:7

how charming is divine p.! 275:21
lesson in experimental p. 442:10
natural p. [makes men] deep 20:34
not faith, but mere p. 71:4
not to care for p. 305:2
p. inclineth man's mind to atheism 19:36
p. is a good horse in the stable 182:5
p. . . . the handmaid to religion 18:7
p., the lumber of schools 410:9
p. will clip an angel's wings 231:16
superstition to enslave a p. 215:4
Phoebus: before the wheels of P. 373:27
bright P. in his strength 384:29
P. arise 149:2
P.' gins arise 347:6
rose from the hindmost wheels of P.' wain 275:10
towards P.' lodging 379:35
Phoenix: maiden p. 359:7
Phone: happy to hear that the p. is for you 251:14
why did you answer the p.? 429:16
Photography: p. is truth 179:8
Phrase: I'll tell you in a p. 130:13
p. would be more german 353:7
portentous p., 'I told you so' 92:15
proverbed with a grandsire p. 378:29
Phyllis: neat-handed P. dresses 276:27
P. is my only joy 341:21
P. without frown or smile 341:22
Physic: take p., pomp 362:20
throw p. to the dogs 367:20
Physician: all the p.s and authors in the world
105:17
died last night of my p. 320:26
every p. almost hath his favourite disease 162:29
help of too many p.s 4:2
honour a p. 48:22
is there no p. there? 46:27
Nazarene p. of his tribe 74:18
p. can bury his mistakes 468:7
p., heal thyself 52:6
they that be whole need not a p. 49:33
time is the great p. 143:18
Physicist: p.s have known sin 300:4
Physique: donnait une leçon de p. expérimentale
442:10
Pianist: do not shoot the p. 456:16
no better than many p.s 338:20
Piano: when I sat down at the p. 98:23
Picardy: roses are flowering in P. 448:18
Piccadilly: good-bye P. 457:10
Pickle: how camest thou in this p.? 381:19
Pickwick: P., the Owl, and the Waverley pen 3:11
Pickwickian: used the word in its P. sense 140:19
Picnic: teddy bears have their p. 235:13
Pictoribus: P. atque poetis 206:27
Pictura: ut p. poesis 207:10
Picture: all his p.s faded 61:15
book . . . without p.s or conversations 100:27
cutting all the p.s out 30:20
every p. tells a story 2:32
it's the p.s that got small 456:27
look here upon this p. 351:27
look not on his p. 225:18
p . . . something between a thing and a thought
303:10
p.s for the page atone 311:12
p.s in our eyes 145:2

sleeping and the dead are but as p.s 365:27
Pie: baked in a p. 297:31
eat one of Bellamy's veal p.s 309:24
p. in the sky 201:9
Piece: all of a p. throughout 151:28
dash them in p.s 37:20
go to p.s like a man 429:10
I took her to p.s 120:22
old, revived new p. 311:14
peace is broken into p.s 204:27
p. in a jigsaw . . . missing p. 266:6
p.s of eight 406:26
thinks a faultless p. to see 313:6
Pie-crust: promises and p. 411:9
Piedmontese: bloody P. that rolled 282:8
Pieman: Simple Simon met a p. 297:30
Pier: effusive welcome of the p. 14:1
from this here p. it is my fixed intent 24:19
Pierce: p. my side 145:20
Pierian: drunk deep of the P. spring 148:17
Pietate: reddite mi hoc pro p. mea 104:4
Piety: bound to each by natural p. 463:15
grant me this in return for my p. 104:4
mistaken and over-zealous p. 81:27
nor all thy P. nor Wit 164:20
to p. more prone 4:8
Piffle: p. before the wind 13:14
Pig: as naturally as p.s squeak 87:3
dear P., are you willing 251:2
looked from p. to man 300:16
selling of p. in a poke 433:19
stole a p. and away he run 298:11
this little p. went to market 298:7
whether p.s have wings 102:5
Pigeon: p.s on the grass alas 404:15
Piggy-wig: there in a wood a P. stood 251:1
Pigmy-body: fretted the p. to decay 149:10
Pilate: P. saith unto him 53:32
rather have blood on my hands than water like P.
187:23
suffered under Pontius P. 318:24
Pile: earn a monumental p. 126:32
Pilgrim: came forth with p. steps 281:11
forth, p., forth! 107:6
land of the p.s 130:2
one man loved the p. soul in you 472:5
onward goes the p. band 25:5
p. of eternity 390:1
P.'s Progress, about a man 433:26
strangers and p.s on the earth 57:13
to be a p. 80:35 81:2
wished longer . . . excepting . . . P.'s Progress 224:9
Pilgrimage: and quiet p. 97:27
he overtaketh in his p. 384:5
longen folk to goon on p.s 107:8
my p.'s last mile 145:14
songs beguile your p. 166:2
strown blisses about my p. 192:20
thus I'll take my p. 325:8
Pilgrimes: p., passinge to and fro 108:6
Pill: death in ambush lay in every p. 173:11
Dr Williams' pink p.s 2:29
life is a p. 224:5
out-lived the doctor's p. 174:12
Pillage: p. they with merry march 356:24
Pillar: builded over with p.s of gold 61:2
four p.s of government 19:31

p. of state 278:38
triple p. of the world 343:14
with antique p.s massy proof 276:15
Pillicock: P. sat on P.-hill 362:21
Pillow: like a p. on a bed 145:1
Pilot: daring p. in extremity 149:10
here's to the P. that weathered the storm 98:18
I hope to see my P. face to face 416:4
P. of the Galilean lake 277:12
woe to that p. of the living God 271:18
Pimpernel: that demmed, elusive P. 300:5
Pimple: P. on her nose 328:2
Pin: friend in merry p. 125:17
might have heard a p. drop 328:27
pinned it wi' a siller p. 23:24
p.s extend their shining rows 315:15
set my life at a p.'s fee 348:32
with a little p. bores through his castle-wall
377:2
Pinch: necessity's sharp p. 362:12
P., a hungry lean-faced villain 346:19
p. of unseen, unguarded dust 193:9
Pine: hill p.s were sighing 67:27
old acquaintance among the p.s 429:1
p. for what is not 394:21
p.s are gossip p.s 165:25
steer, your winged p.s 71:22
Pine-tree: beware the p.'s withered branch 256:25
Pineapple: very p. of politeness! 395:24
Pining: it's not p. 286:12
Pinion: drift of p.s 427:18
imagination droops her p. 91:30
Pink: p. is the navy blue of India 443:3
p. of perfection 182:15
Pinta: drinka p. milka day 2:30
Pint-pot: underneath, a p. neatly graven 424:23
Pioneer: one thing about p.s 309:12
p.s! O p.s 453:19
Pip: hear the p.s squeak 174:29
Pipe: he called for his p. 297:14
his p. might fall out 167:15
not a p. for fortune's finger 351:3
p. for my capacious mouth 173:23
p.s o' Havelock sound 454:9
ye soft p.s, play on 231:19
Piper: five-and-thirty p.s 17:22
Peter P. picked a peck 297:22
wi' a hundred p.s 291:8
Pipeur: p., larron, jureur 267:26
Piping: helpless, naked, p. loud 61:23
his p. took a troubled sound 12:3
p. down the valleys wild 62:6
p. songs for ever new 231:21
weak p. time of peace 377:24
Pippin: right as a Ribstone P.! 30:23
Pire: tomber dans un p. 122:16
Pirt: knows some touch of p. 377:26
Pissing: outside my tent p. in 218:22
Pistol: have you your p.s? 453:19
is that a p. in your pocket 451:12
It [a pun] is a p. 246:5
when his p. misses fire 182:39
Pit: fill a p. as well as better 354:39
he that diggeth a p. 44:1
man will go down into the p. 21:21
many-headed monster of the p. 316:2
they have digged a p. before me 39:1

to the profoundest p. 352:12
whoso diggeth a p. shall fall therein 42:44
Pitch: bumping p. and a blinding light 293:21
he that toucheth p. 48:10
pitched past p. of grief 206:8
Pitcher: p. be broken at the fountain 44:12
Pitfall: with P. and with Gin 164:23
Pith: all the p. is in the postscript 195:14
Pitié: il regarde en p. 284:7
Pitiful: 'twas p., 'twas wondrous p. 374:6
Pitt, William 92:35, 98:18
P. is to Addington 98:17
Pittore: anch-io sono p.! 122:21
Pity: arousing p. and terror 10:3
attempted your p. to move 235:1
but yet the p. of it 375:13
p. beyond all telling 471:15
P. a human face 62:11
p., like a naked new-born babe 365:7
p. of War 302:6
p. those they torture not 392:27
p. would be no more 61:22
then cherish p. 62:13
thou wilt never come for p. 393:27
till P.'s self be dead 119:9
Place: all other things give p. 174:22
all p.s are distant from heaven alike 86:15
all p.s that the eye of heaven visits 376:14
buried in so sweet a p. 389:22
calmly in their p. 19:21
doubled down the useful p.s 320:21
everything in its p. 398:13
I did not know the p. 289:17
in pleasant p.s 37:33
it the Last Judgement takes p. every day 98:5
little one-eyed, blinking sort o' p. 193:23
men in great p. are thrice servants 19:17
mustn't come into the p. 138:12
neither shall his p. know him 36:42
never the time and the p. 76:8
no p. to go 86:3
nor wished to change his p. 180:23
p. and means for every man alive 343:11
p. appointed for my second race 438:9
p. not to live but to die in 71:13
p. of justice is a hallowed 20:38
p. where woman never smiled or wept 114:27
p. within the meaning of the Act 7:2
public faces in private p.s 14:19
reign in this horrible p. 127:37
right man to fill the right p. 250:1
savage p.! as holy and enchanted 117:36
to know their p. 30:12
what a p. to plunder! 63:31
Plagiarism: steal from one author it's p. 283:6
Plague: all the p.s with which the world is cursed
184:21
married . . . and that's his p. 86:10
of all p.s, good Heaven, thy wrath can send 98:16
p. o' both your houses! 379:33
p. o' these pickled herring! 382:32
p. of all cowards 354:6
p. upon such backing! 354:8
pleasing p. stole on me 453:8
red p. rid you 380:33
'tis a p., a mischief 86:16
Plaidie: my p. to the angry airt 85:7

Plain: darkling p. 10:22
  old p. men have rosy faces 407:25
  p., blunt man 360:23
  that I might once more reach that p. 438:12
  thousands on her p.s 197:17
  whiten the green p.s 390:14
Plan: commends a most practical p. 215:1
  fulfils great Nature's p. 84:14
  hurled their hopeful p.s to emptiness 209:24
  making all his nowhere p.s 253:11
  mighty maze! but not without a p. 313:25
  p. to dye one's whiskers green 102:18
Plane: face . . . juxtaposed on different p.s 321:12
  not allowed to say how many p.s 191:21
Planet: new p. swims into his ken 233:3
  not born under a rhyming p. 373:25
  our p. is poorly equipped 271:9
  p. of Love is on high 420:33
Plant: old p.s left over from the Edwardian
    Wilderness 301:14
  p. that with most cutting grows 131:7
  p.s suck in the earth 123:31
  sensitive p. in a garden grew 393:24
  time to p. 43:19
Plantation: still longing for de old p. 168:8
Planted: I have p. 54:51
Plate: clean your p. 330:19
Platinum: bullets made of p. 30:3
Platitude: echo of a p. 59:5
  stroke a p. until it purrs 267:32
Plato: attachment à la P. 177:41
  footnotes to P.'s philosophy 453:7
  P. is dear to me 10:9
  P. the wise 421:28
  P., thou reason'st well 1:13
  P. was . . . very unreliable Platonist 334:6
  P.'s retirement 281:8
  rather be wrong with P. 114:23
Platone: errare . . . malo cum P. 114:23
Platonist: very unreliable P. 334:6
Platter: they licked the p. clean 296:30
Play: better than a p.! 106:20
  but when I started to p.! 98:23
  good p. needs no epilogue 346:17
  he that hears p.s 342:10
  I didn't like the p. 269:9
  I doubt some foul p. 348:17
  I have read your p. 92:34
  judge not the p. 132:18, 323:2
  life's poor p. is o'er 314:5
  nothing to do with fair p. 301:7
  old p.s begin to disgust this refined age 160:6
  only p. at playing 245:22
  our p. is done 383:34
  pack the cards and yet cannot p. well 20:1
  p. is a dynamic thing 434:20
  p. is the tragedy 'Man' 310:19
  p. it, Sam 32:5
  p. . . . pleased not the million 350:4
  'P. up! p. up! and p. the game!' 293:21
  p.'s the thing 350:12
  rather hear thy discourse than see a p. 86:17
  they will not let my p. run 135:1
  this may be p. to you 254:2
  why . . . do you come to the p. 83:14
  you would p. upon me 351:17
Play-actor: never meddle with p.s 105:16

Play-bill: no time to read p.s 83:14
  p. . . . announced the tragedy of Hamlet 341:6
Playboy: P. of the Western World 413:11
Player: all the men and women merely p.s 345:11
  lenten entertainment the p.s shall receive 349:37
  monstrous that this p. here 350:8
  poor p. that struts 367:24
  some p.s upon plaintive strings 218:19
Playing: ever amid our p. 100:26
  purpose of p. 351:1
Playmate: I have had p.s 245:6
Plaything: child's a p. for an hour 246:18
  great princes have great p.s 127:21
  no book – it is a p. 306:12
  some livelier p. 314:5
Playwright: our P. may show 421:30
  some p. . . . slamming down his silly curtain
    336:20
Plea: tyrant's p. 279:29
  what p. so tainted 370:2
Pleasant: all that was p. in man 181:19
  but a few think him p. enough 250:14
  England's green and p. land 61:9
  he who chooses the p. misses his end 435:10
  how p. it is to have money 115:17
Please: books cannot always p. 128:6
  hard to p. 340:19
  if you p., ma'am 268:4
  nothing can permanently p. 118:20
  she never fails to p. 341:21
  strive to p. you every day 383:34
  'twas natural to p. 149:6
  we that live to p. 219:4
Pleased: all seemed well p. 280:14
Pleasing: art of p. 196:11
Pleasure: aching p. nigh 231:29
  English take their p.s sadly 409:14
  friend of P. 119:20
  I don't feel quite happy about p. 14:28
  I go to my p. 468:13
  I have no p. in them 44:9
  if this is p. we'd rather be dead 123:24
  it's the greatest p. in life 79:8
  lie doth ever add p. 18:18
  love ceases to be a p. 29:23
  mere animal p. 221:12
  'mid p.s and palaces 306:10
  no profit grows where there is no p. 380:14
  no sterner moralist than P. 91:20
  on p. she was bent 125:9
  p. after all is a safer guide 88:20
  p. in poetic pains 127:1
  p. is . . . intermission of pain 342:9
  p. is oft a visitant 230:8
  p. never is at home 230:22
  p. of having it over 204:30
  p. was his business 154:7
  p.'s a sin 91:6
  p.s are all alike 342:10
  p.s are like poppies spread 85:18
  p.s in a long immortal dream 231:14
  p.s newly found are sweet 467:15
  p.s with youth pass away 401:22
  should not take so much p. 247:26
  so earnestly pursued p. 59:9
  sucked on country p.s 145:8
  sweet is p. after pain 150:1

thou wilt come for p. 393:27
'twas for your p. 125:19
unholy p. of cutting all the pictures out 30:20
variety is the soul of p. 29:25
we will all the p.s prove 267:23
we will some new p.s prove 144:16
Pleasure-dome: stately p. decree 117:35
sunny p. with caves of ice! 118:4
Pleasure-house: I built my soul a lordly p. 421:26
Pledge: fair p.s of a fruitful tree 200:3
fresh p.s of her love 432:4
Pleiades: sweet influences of the P. 37:12
Pleiads: rainy P. wester 210:4
Plenty: but just had p. 84:8
fear that p. should attain the poor 89:3
here is God's p. 151:34
p. makes me poor 302:1
scatter p. o'er a smiling land 186:12
Pleurer: peur d'être obligé d'en p. 27:14
Plie: je p. et ne romps pas 244:4
Plodder: small have continuous p.s ever won 363:19
Ploffskin: P., Pluffskin, Pelican jee! 251:4
Plot: her p. hath many changes 323:2
melodious p. of beechen green 232:1
p. of land not too large 209:17
p. thickens 79:25
p.s, true or false 149:8
this blessed p. 376:17
what . . . does the p. signify 79:24
Plough: cut worm forgives the p. 63:12
p. my own furrow 330:18
tested his first p. 73:9
Ploughman: heavy steps of the p. 471:11
p. homeward plods 185:27
Ploy: one p. of Gattling's 317:12
Pluck: p. it [thine eye] out 50:31
Plum: biscuit or confectionary p. 126:7
p.s that were in the icebox 457:20
pulled out a p. 297:3
Plumage: he pities the p. 303:5
Plumbing: ingenious assembly of portable p. 288:4
Plummet: deeper than did ever p. sound 381:16
Plunder: take your ill-got p. 293:20
what a place to p.! 63:31
Plunge: p. in a pool's living water 78:14
Plures: abiit ad p. 99:15 308:8
Pluto: drew iron tears down P.'s cheek 276:11
Pneumatic: wonderfully p. 212:27
Pneumonia: never anything small like p. 333:4
Poacher: p. a keeper turned inside out 237:22
Pobble: P. who has no toes 251:5
P.s are happier without their toes 251:7
Pocket: and put it in his p. 351:30
do I carry the moon in my p.? 75:26
I pot into the middle p. 108:33
pound . . . in your p. 458:7
smile I could feel in my hip p. 106:5
traveller with empty p.s 228:5
would not scruple to pick a p. 134:36
young man feels his p.s 210:1
Pocket-handkerchief: holding his p. before his
streaming eyes 102:8
Pocket-money: furnished with p. 139:6
Pod: when the p.s went pop on the broom 132:14
Poe: There comes P. 259:3
Poem: it is a pretty p. 32:1
majority of p.s one outgrows 157:20

no p.s can please for long 207:26
ought himself to be a true p. 282:14
p. is never finished 437:8
p. lovely as a tree 237:3
p. should be palpable and mute 263:20
p. unlimited 350:2
p.s are made by fools like me 237:4
true ornament of p. 277:30
Poesy: drainless shower of light is p. 232:15
force of heaven-bred p. 384:7
nothing so difficult as a beginning in p. 91:29
our p. is as a gum 381:21
overwhelm myself in p. 232:14
viewless wings of P. 232:4
with Nature, Hope and P. 118:14
Poet: all p.s are mad 86:8
all p.s believe that it does 63:22
all p.s who read from their own works 452:13
allowed p.s to be mediocre 207:11
because he was a true p. 63:8
brave translunary things that the first p.s had
148:15
business of a p. 220:5
Catullus, the worst of all p.s 103:19
certain also of our own p.s 54:1
did not the p. sing it with such airs 470:5
God is the perfect p. 76:16
good p.'s made as well as born 225:25
hate all Boets [p.s.] and Bainters 174:30
I shall be among the English p.s 234:7
like a p. hidden 394:20
like a p. woo the moon 96:22
many are the p.s that are sown 461:20
many most excellent p.s 396:19
mighty p.s in their misery dead 466:8
Milton's the prince of p.s 91:28
muse on Nature with a p.'s eye 97:16
no bad man can be a good p. 305:14
no man was ever yet a great p. 118:22
no p. . . . wishes he were the only one who ever
lived 15:22
no person can be a p. 262:27
of all modern, and perhaps ancient p.s 151:33
on a p.'s lips I slept 393:3
our p.s steal from Homer 86:6
pensive p.s painful vigils keep 311:10
p. could not but be gay 462:6
p. gives us his essence 460:17
P.! – He hath put his heart to school 463:13
p. is the most unpoetical of anything 234:9
p. soaring in the high region 282:24
p. without love 99:9
p.s are the unacknowledged legislators 395:2
p.s better prove 385:26
p.'s eye, in a fine frenzy rolling 372:14
p.s' food is love and fame 390:28
P.s militant below 124:10
p.s that lasting marble seek 444:11
reviewers . . . would have been p.s 118:26
sage and serious p. Spenser 282:19
stand still, true p. 77:2
three p.s, in three distant ages born 150:26
to a p. nothing can be useless 220:4
we p.s in our youth 466:3
when the P. dies 339:29
which only p.s know 127:1
you will never be a p. 151:37

Pomp: in lowly p. ride on to die 274:12
  p.s and vanity of this wicked world 319:28
  puts all the p. to flight 312:11
  vain p. and glory 358:22
Pompey: P. lives after his battles 259:14
Pompilia: P., faultless to a fault 78:6
  P., will you let them murder me? 78:12
Pond: cream and mantle like a standing p. 369:3
Ponderous: oped his p. and marble jaws 348:30
Pontefract: licorice fields at P. 32:19
Pontic: like to the P. sea 375:10
Ponto: 'P.!' he cried 30:9
Pony: riding on a p. 23:27
Poodle: Mr Balfour's P. 255:14
Pooh-Bah: P. (Lord High Everything Else) 177:15
Pool: green mantle of the standing p. 362:25
  where the p.s are bright and deep 203:14
Poop: p. was beaten gold 343:28
Poor: anger . . . keeps them p. 18:10
  as for the virtuous p. 456:17
  blessed are the p. in spirit 48:41
  Blessed is he that considereth the p. 38:19
  destruction of the p. is their poverty 41:33
  even p. in thanks 349:35
  exchequer of the p. 376:22
  foundst me p. at first 181:15
  gives the p. twice as much good 413:12
  good to the p. 98:27
  grind the faces of the p. 44:34
  he raiseth up the p. out of the dust 40:21
  how apt the p. are to be proud 383:18
  how p. a thing is man 131:11
  I was a father to the p. 37:7
  if we did not make somebody p. 61:22
  if you was as p. as me 389:5
  inconvenient to be p. 124:24
  makes me p. indeed 374:31
  p. always ye have with you 53:25
  p., and the maimed 52:21
  p. get poorer 229:7
  p. have become poorer 394:28
  p. in a loomp is bad 421:11
  p. man at his gate 4:4
  p. man had nothing 36:6
  p. man loved the great 261:15
  p. what gets the blame 8:16
  she was p., but she was honest 8:13
  though I be p., I'm honest 273:4
  we are p. indeed 83:4
  would realize that he was p. 436:3
Pope, Alexander 219:26 219:27
  better to err with P. 92:26
  Dryden, P. and all their school 12:26
  I can become p. 105:7
  if P. be not a poet 219:27
  it is a pretty poem, Mr P. 32:1
  P.! How many divisions has he got? 404:1
  to read Dryden, P. etc. 118:25
  worthy of washing the hands of the P. 24:10
Popery: inclines a man to P. 171:1
Poplar: p.s are felled 126:11
Poppies: drowsed with the fume of p. 233:18
  in Flanders fields the p. blow 264:18
Poppy: left the flushed print in a p. there 427:23
  not p., nor mandragora 375:3
  oblivion blindly scattereth her p. 71:18
Populace: where the p. rise at once 453:22

Popularité: p.? c'est la gloire en gros sous 212:1
Popularity: p. is a crime 190:10
Population: only talked of p. 182:24
Populi: salus p. suprema est lex 114:13
Porch: beyond p. and portal 412:18
Porches: in the p. of mine ears 349:8
Porcum: Epicuri de grege p. 207:18
Porcupine: I shall throw two p.s 236:21
Pore: pass through the p.s of the ocean 390:16
Porgie: Georgie P., pudding and pie 296:16
Porlock: person on business from P. 117:34
Pornography: p. is the attempt to insult sex 249:18
Porpentine: quills upon the fretful p. 349:1
Porpoise: p. close behind us 101:17
Porridge: comfort like cold p. 380:37
  pease p. hot 297:21
Porsena: Lars P. of Clusium 261:12
Porson: Cambridge . . . has seen P. sober 211:1
Port: Alma Mater all dissolved in p. 311:21
  come open the West P. 339:12
  compact of ancient tales, and p. 30:32
  go fetch a pint of p. 424:18
  in every p. a wife 136:7
  little p. had seldom seen a costlier funeral 416:15
  of his p. as meke as is a mayde 107:9
  p. for men 223:6
  p. is near 453:16
  to a wise man p.s and happy havens 376:14
Portal: P.s are alternate Night and Day 164:5
Portcullis: let the p. fall 340:17
Porte: p. soit ouverte ou fermée 290:13
Porter: O the moon shone bright on Mrs P. 157:6
  Oh, mister p. 255:12
  poor mechanic p.s 356:24
Portion: become P. of that around me 89:29
  best p. of a good man's life 462:13
  he wales a p. with judicious care 84:6
  they have no p. in us 147:11
Portrait: always a p. of himself 88:18
  every time I paint a p. 337:18
  p. . . . something not quite right 337:17
  P. of the Artist as a Young Man 226:17
  two styles of p. painting 139:13
Posies: pocket full of p. 297:27
  thousand fragrant p. 267:25
Position: every p. must be held to the last man
    190:4
  holders of one p. 15:12
Possess: no desire to p. more of it than they have
    135:10
Possessing: having nothing and yet p. all things
    56:1
  too dear for my p. 386:14
Possession: all my p.s for a moment of time 157:27
  for he had great p.s 50:37
  p. is infinite 63:26
  p. of it is intolerable 437:9
  p. of them both in the same minute 234:14
Possibilities: sum-total of our vital p. 300:8
Possibility: unconvincing p. 10:6
Possible: if politics is the art of the p. 271:11
  in two words: im-p. 183:12
  politics is the art of the p. 59:22
  with God all things are p. 50:39
Possunt: p., quia posse videntur 440:25
Post: only one p. fit for you 100:21
  place with only one p. a day 400:8

high p.s of God be in their mouth 41:18
if there be any p. 56:29
'let us now p. famous men' 240:26
our mouth shall shew forth thy p. 318:16
p. him upon the loud cymbals 41:19
p. the Lord and pass the ammunition 167:14
since that all things thou wouldst p. 134:14
some p. at morning 313:17
they only want p. 270:23
those they p. 268:9
to refuse p. 248:10
to utter all Thy p. 2:12
were no small p. 281:5
Praised: more in him to be p. than to be pardoned 225:29
Praising: doing one's p. for oneself 88:21
p. the way things were when he was a boy 207:5
Pram: p. in the hall 121:15
Prattle: thinking his p. to be tedious 377:16
Pray: fools . . . remained to p. 181:3
I'd as lief p. with Kit Smart 221:6
p. for us now 155:22
p. without ceasing 56:36
to live more nearly as we p. 234:22
watch and p. 158:2
whene'er he went to p. 182:34
who . . . cannot pray 155:28
Prayer: better than good men's p.s 104:22
called the house of p. 50:44
Christopher Robin is saying his p.s 274:18
fall to thy p.s 356:18
feed on p.s 307:1
for a pretence make long p.s 51:40
four [hours] spend in p. 116:12
frame of mind . . . close to . . . p. 270:13
her eyes are homes of silent p. 417:37
his p. is answered 272:23
imperfect offices of p. 461:22
knowing God, they lift not hands of p. 417:20
man who would not say his p.s 296:17
mention of you always in my p.s 54:13
more things are wrought by p. 417:19
most perfect p. 253:27
p. all his business 304:25
p.s remained unanswered 187:24
people's p. 149:16
pray but one p. for me 288:19
thou that hearest p. 39:10
wherever God erects a house of p. 133:18
Prayeth: he p. best 117:16
he p. well 117:15
Praying: if you talk to God you are p. 413:15
now he is p. 351:23
Preach: never sure to p. again 27:1
Preached: deserves to be p. to death 400:5
Preacher: like the p. found it not 393:32
p.s say Do as I say 342:11
Preaching: better than any p. 159:5
woman's p. 221:17
Precedence: believe I take p. 335:14
Precedent: create good p.s as to follow them 19:19
p. embalms a principle 142:27, 341:14
Precept: example . . . more efficacious than p. 220:8
love the p.s for the teacher's sake 162:1, 203:28
p. must be upon p. 45:15
Precinct: warm p.s of the cheerful day 186:15
Precious: liberty is p. 253:2

p. in the sight of the Lord 40:25
that were most p. to me 367:10
Precisian: devil turned p.! 270:11
Predecessor: one of my illustrious p.s 162:17
Predestination: p. in the stride o' yon connectin'-rod 239:35
with P. round enmesh me 164:23
Predicament: life is . . . a p. 337:15
Prefab: better than a p. 109:3
Preferment: knocking at P.'s door 11:22
so I gained p. 7:28
Prejudice: blow away all this . . . p. against work 108:35
bundle of p.s 245:18
merely rearranging their p.s 217:13
popular p. runs in favour of two 139:7
Prelude: transmit the P.s through his hair 156:29
Prematur: nonumque p. in annum 207:12
Premise: based upon licensed p.s 299:3
Preparation: politics . . . no p. is thought necessary, 406:17
p. for this hour 113:20
p.s were not sufficiently complete 105:28
Prepared: formidable even to the best p. 119:32
Prerogative: last p. 150:20
p. of the harlot 21:15
Presager: dumb p.s of my speaking breast 385:19
Presbyter: new P. is but old Priest 282:9
Presbyterian: 'twas P. true blue 87:8
Presbyterianism 106:22
Presence: conspicuous by its p. 334:2
depths of the ocean its p. confessed 161:10
Present: act in the living P.! 257:4
nor things p., nor things to come 54:31
predominate over the p. 219:18
p. has latched its postern 192:9
p. in spirit 55:4
p. were the world's last night 145:21
'P.s . . . endear absents' 245:14
that I might there p. it! 393:22
things p., [seem] worst 355:20
who controls the p. 300:28
who p., past and future sees 61:17
Presentment: counterfeit p. of two brothers 351:27
Preservation: p. of life, and liberty 217:20
Preserve: p. me from unseasonable . . . sleep 219:28
President: all the powers of the P. amount to 432:26
all the P.'s men 241:37
rather be right than be P. 115:1
when the P. does it 295:10
Press: flee fro the p. 107:6
gentleman of the P. 143:2
god of our idolatry, the P. 126:17
it fell *dead-born from the p.* 212:7
liberty of the P. 227:8
my last P. Conference 295:5
p. it to thine own again 391:13
who now governs the periodical p. 432:10
Press-men: so we be named P. 10:17
Pressure: grace under p. 197:21
Presumption: you'll be amused by its p. 429:13
Pretence: p. that God put it there 243:1
Pretender: no harm in blessing – the P. 88:30
Old P. 189:1
Pretio: omnia Romae cum p. 227:23
Pretty: comes along and does it p. 308:22

'it's p., but is it Art?' 238:23
not so p. anyone would want to ruin her 67:10
Prevaricate: thou dost p. 87:13
Prevent: that won't p. you! 174:31
Prey: expects his evening p. 185:24
greater p. upon the less 187:21
have they not divided the p.? 35:29
young lions roar after their p. 40:12
Priam: drew P.'s curtain 355:11
Price: all things can be had at a p. 227:23
all those men have their p. 445:16
at a stroke . . . reduce the rise in p.s 121:25
King should have bought it at any p. 114:30
no good lying about the p. 104:24
'Pearl', as being of great p. 195:6
pearl of great p. 50:13
raised the p. of literature 220:28
set her own p. 305:20
some contrivance to raise p.s 398:14
Prick: if you p. us, do we not bleed? 369:33
kick against the p.s 53:46
Pride: family p. is something inconceivable 177:18
gilded dust our p. 415:17
he that is low needs fear no p. 80:33
my p. fell with my fortunes 344:20
my p. struck out new sparkles 150:19
p., cruelty, and ambition of man 325:9
p. goeth before destruction 42:15
p. of kings 313:25
p., pomp and circumstance of glorious war! 375:5
p. ruled my will 294:4
p. that apes humility 401:15
p. that licks the dust 312:28
p. that puts this country down 7:22
p., the never failing vice 313:3
ring out false p. 418:27
spite of p. 313:34
towering in her p. of place 366:8
what argufies p. and ambition? 136:6
writer's p. in having given up his p. 336:19
Priest: fiddling p.! 126:13
inspires the pale-eyed p. 277:26
Muses' p. sing for girls and boys 208:22
new Presbyter is but old P. 282:9
p., a piece of mere church furniture 127:31
p. all shaven and shorn 298:6
p. continues what the nurse began 150:24
p. hales the reluctant victim 392:23
p.s are only men 77:28
p.s by the imposition of a mightier hand 262:28
p.s in black gowns 61:21
p.s in gold and black 248:34
p.s, tapers, temples 312:11
rid me of this turbulent p. 198:6
robin redbreast, he shall be the p. 398:2
that whisky p. 187:26
unbelieving p.s reformed the nation 313:20
Priestcraft: pious times, ere p. did begin 149:4
Priesthood: literary men are . . . a perpetual p. 99:22
ye are . . . a royal p. 57:31
Prieur: dire du bien de M. le p. 142:11
Primate: served the Lord P. on bended knee 24:8
Prime: return the glory of your p. 391:16
Prime Minister: best P. we have 87:1
next P. but three 30:13
three groups that no British P. should provoke 21:19

Primer: armed with his p. 70:6
Primrose: like thy face, pale p. 347:13
pale p.s that die unmarried 384:29
p. by a river's brim 464:27
P., first born child of Ver 28:6
p. path of dalliance 348:20
p. that forsaken dies 277:16
p. way to the everlasting bonfire 366:1
soft silken p. fading timelessly 277:19
sweet as the p. 181:13
to P. Hill and Saint John's Wood 61:2
wan as p.s gathered at midnight 230:11
Prince: affirm it before any p. in Europe 225:6
danced with the P. of Wales 161:11
death of p.s 360:1
for every folly of their p.s 207:15
'God bless the P. of Wales!' 255:5
good-night, sweet p. 353:14
great P. in prison lies 145:5
great p.s have great playthings 127:21
her p.s are come home again 361:28
man that hangs on p.s' favours! 358:22
p. of darkness 362:26
P. of Peace 45:8
p.s and lords are but the breath of kings 84:7
p.s and lords may flourish 180:18
P.s do but play us 146:12
p.s in this case 131:6
put not your trust in p.s 41:15
such duty as the subject owes the p. 380:24
writ . . . to foreign p.s 358:19
Princedom: thrones, dominations, p.s, virtues 280:13
Principalities: nor p., nor powers 54:31
we wrestle . . . against p. 56:22
Principibus: p. placuisse viris 207:23
Principle: broken open on the most scientific p.s 306:13
called this p . . . by the term of Natural Selection 132:8
fundamental p. of the English constitution 59:30
he does everything on p. 388:34
I don't believe in p. 258:25
other p. of Lysander 18:9
p. in life with me 389:12
p. seems the same 113:24
precedent embalms a p. 142:27, 341:14
religious and moral p.s 13:7
shows that he has good p.s 221:9
sincere in good p.s 223:32
we might our p.s swaller 258:22
Print: all the news that's fit to p. 299:12
p. of a man's naked foot 133:14
proud of seeing our names in p. 110:19
'sdeath I'll p. it 312:16
some said, 'John, p. it' 80:13
to see one's name in p. 92:23
Printed: diffusion of p. material 431:8
Printer: books by which the p.s have lost 171:5
Printing: Gunpowder, P., and the Protestant Religion 99:21
Printing-house: p. in Hell 63:24
Prior: here lies what once was Matthew P. 320:20
Priscian: P. a little scratched 363:33
Prison: compare the p. where I live unto the world 377:17

feel comparatively at home in p. 448:5
home is the girl's p. 388:32
let's away to p. 363:9
lime-tree bower my p.! 118:13
opening of the p. to them that are bound 46:18
p. is a holy place 93:23
p.s are built with stones of Law 63:16
stone walls do not a p. make 258:13
what is a ship but a p.? 86:14
while there is a soul in p. 133:8
world itself is but a large p. 325:11
Prison-air: bloom well in p. 455:1
Prison-house: tell the secrets of my p. 349:1
Prisoner: insane root that takes the reason p.
    364:19
poor p. in his twisted gyres 379:20
p.s call the sky 454:20
set my p.s free 73:24
ye p.s of hope 47:22
Privacy: for all the p. I got 336:2
Private: convartin' public trusts to very p. uses
    258:24
drunken p. of the Buffs 148:8
faith, her p.s we 349:32
invade the sphere of p. life 271:14
what have kings that p.s have not 357:12
Privilege: accursed power which stands on p. 30:26
p. I claim for my own sex 16:33
Privileged: not p. to see a saint 78:3
P. and the People formed Two Nations 143:26
Prize: fraught with a later p. 391:3
is lawful p. 186:29
judge the p. 276:31
just the one p. vouchsafed unworthy me 78:7
p. of all too precious you 386:12
p. of learning love 74:6
p. we sought is won 453:16
won first p. in the lottery of life 327:3
Probability: p. is the very guide of life 86:27
Probationer: young p., and candidate of heaven
    151:7
Probitas: p. laudatur et alget 227:15
Problem: three-pipe p. 147:18
Proceeding: subsequent p.s interested him no more
    194:28
Procès: puis ils lui font son p. 284:10
Procession: p.s that lack high stilts 471:3
Proconsul: great P. 262:14
Procrastination: incivility and p. 135:6
p. . . . art of keeping up with yesterday 267:28
p. is the thief of time 472:23
Procreation: blind alleys off the main road of p.
    448:4
ordained for the p. of children 319:39
Procul: p. hinc, p. este, severae! 301:22
'qui p. hinc' 293:15
Procuress: P. to the Lords of Hell 418:6
Prodigal: p. of ease 149:11
Prodigies: all Africa and her p. 70:25
what p. surprise 219:10
Prodigious: 'P.!' exclaimed Dominie Sampson 340:31
Produce: P.! P.! 100:15
Production: attempts to read all the new p.s 329:3
in love with the p.s of time 63:14
perfect tragedy is the noblest p. 2:4
Productivity: at a stroke . . . increase p. 121:25
Profani: procul este, p. 440:27

Profession: all p.s are conspiracies 387:31
fairies were of the old p. 122:10
most ancient p. 241:30
one of the incidents of the p. 435:7
Professor: become a p. of the fact that another
    suffered 236:22
p. is one who talks in someone else's sleep 15:28
respectable P.s of the Dismal Science 99:35
Profit: he p.s most who serves best 389:21
mingles p. with pleasure 207:8
no p. grows where there is no pleasure 380:14
what p. hath a man of all his labour 43:12
what shall it p. a man 51:36
winds will blow the p. 264:12
Progenies: iam nova p. caelo demittitur 441:15
Progeny: p. of learning 395:22
whose p. they are 282:15
Progress: all p. based upon a universal innate desire
    88:1
history of England . . . history of p. 262:10
our p. through the world 257:16
p. depends on the unreasonable man 388:30
p. far from consisting in change 337:10
p. is the law of life 76:18
p. therefore, is not an accident 402:9
p. would be wonderful 290:9
Progression: without contraries is no. p. 63:4
Project: working on a Much Less Ambitious P.
    183:22
Prole: p.s are not human beings 300:27
Proletariat: dictatorship of the p. 159:27 269:18
whatever crimes the P. commits 123:26
Prologue: as happy p.s to the swelling act 364:21
courtship . . . a very witty p. 120:20
foolish thing to make a long p. 48:31
Prolonged: War is being deliberately p. 338:3
Prometheus: like P. watching his vulture 459:23
Promise: boldness is an ill-keeper of p. 19:25
I have p.s to keep 170:14
keep the word of p. to our ear 367:31
p.s . . . made to be broken 411:9
who broke no p. 315:5
whose p. none relies on 328:7
Promising: emphatically a p. politician 111:2
they first call p. 121:14
Promontory: earth seems to me a sterile p. 349:36
once I sat upon a p. 371:35
Promotion: none will sweat but for p. 344:31
Proof: dost thou ask p.? 12:7
give me the ocular p. 375:6
how I would correct the p.s 114:29
Prop: as a succedaneum, and a p. 465:12
p. that doth sustain my house 370:16
Propagation: was all our p. 145:2
Propensities: excite my amorous p. 220:16
Propensity: p. . . . venture to christen Boswellism
    262:29
Proper: as p. men as ever trod 359:10
never does a p. thing 388:10
Properties: remark general p. 220:5
Property: coveting other men's p. 336:23
give me a little snug p. 154:3
man of p. 172:10
mortgaging of his extensive p. 226:28
p. has its duties 148:25
p. is theft 321:5
p. owns them rich men 215:13

p., p., p., that's what I 'ears 'em saay 421:8
Prophecies: whether there be p., they shall fail
55:23
Prophecy: urn of bitter p. 391:8
Prophesy: don't never p. 258:29
I will eat exceedingly, and p. 224:23
p. unto the wind 46:38
we p. in part 55:24
Prophet: arise among you a p. 35:13
beware of false p.s 49:27
historian is a p. in reverse 338:15
in the name of the P. 398:23
is Saul among the p.s? 35:43
p. is not without honour 50:14
p. new inspired 376:16
'P.! . . . thing of evil 310:26
sole qualification to be a prophet 112:12
there is a p. in Israel 36:26
Propose: duty of an Opposition . . . to p. nothing
135:7
why don't the men p.? 27:11
Proposition: more important that a p. be interesting
453:2
Propriété: p. c'est le vol 321:5
Proprietorship: p. of these papers is aiming at
21:15
Propriety: employment . . . evince its p. 17:15
study first P. 96:12
Prose: all my p. and verse were much the same
311:13
differs in nothing from p. 187:18
fittest for discourse and nearest p. 150:32
he had written much . . . blanker p. 94:6
I love thee in p. 320:17
I never pin up my hair with p. 120:26
in p., the worst thing one can do with words
301:4
language of p. and metrical composition
467:22
not poetry, but p. run mad 312:21
not verse now, only p.! 73:15
poétry is not the proper antithesis to p. 118:24
p. = words in their best order 118:31
p. takes the mould of the body 460:17
talking p. for the last forty years 283:9
that p. is verse 92:27
to write good p. 270:25
unattempted yet in p. 278:1
verse will seem p. 79:26
whose p. is grand verse 259:2
write a page of living p. 106:8
Prose: c'est de la p. 283:9
je dis de la p. sans que j'en susse rien 283:9
Proserpina: O. P.! For the flowers now that frighted
384:29
Prospect: p.s brightening to the last 180:21
shining p.s rise 1:16
though every p. pleases 196:25
Prosper: for if it treason prosper 194:4
Prosperitee: him that stood in greet p. 108:8
man to have ben in p. 108:25
Prosperity: in the day of p. 43:30
one man that can stand p. 99:34
p. doth best discover vice 19:5
p. is not without many fears 19:4
p. is the blessing of the Old Testament 19:3
p. within thy palaces 40:34

Prostrate: drunk is he, who p. lies 306:14
Protest: lady doth p. too much 351:10
Protestant: Gunpowder, Printing, and the P.
Religion 99:21
I was a P. so I didn't speak up 294:17
thy P. to be 200:13
Proteus: have sight of P. 463:7
Proud: all the p. and mighty have 153:4
all the p. shall be! 312:7
how apt the poor are to be p. 383:18
I might be p. the while 200:16
if she be p. 333:19
p. of seeing our names in print 110:19
we ain't p. 139:16
why were they p.? 231:4
yes, I am p. 316:6
Prove: believing where we cannot p. 417:23
p. all things 56:37
Proved: what is now p. 63:18
Proverb: patch grief with p.s 373:22
p. and a byword 36:10
p. is one man's wit 334:3
p. is something musty 351:16
p.s provide them with wisdom 271:1
Providence: assert eternal P. 278:2
behind a frowning p. 125:31
marciful P. fashioned us holler 258:22
P. had sent a few men into the world 262:19
P. has given to the French 306:7
P. their guide 281:1
put upon the P. of God 129:17
rest in p. 18:20
special p. in the fall of a sparrow 353:8
there's a P. in it all 141:23
they say there's a P. sits up aloft 136:9
way that P. dictates 201:18
Province: all knowledge to be my p. 21:7
kissed away kingdoms and p.s 343:37
p. they have desolated and profaned 178:32
reluctant obedience of distant p.s 262:9
Provincialism: rather . . . adultery than . . . p. 212:23
Provocation: ask you what p. I have had? 316:5
Provoked: God is p. every day 37:24
Pru: man from the P. 3:5
Prude: no age to be a p. 284:9
*Prude: d'être p. à vingt ans*284:9
Prudence: reconcile Japanese action with p. 113:3
Prudent: p. in their own sight! 45:1
Prune: p.s and prism 138:19
Prussian: others may be P.s 138:31
Prussic: rather . . . p. acid in the hands 147:3
Psalm: at my door the Hundredth P. 96:4
left him practising the hundredth p. 94:7
singing the Hundredth P. 256:16
Psyche: his p. should be studied 227:7
Psychiatrist: anyone who goes to see a p. 183:10
p. . . . collects the rent 249:27
Psychoanalysis: p. is that mental illness 242:16
Psychosis: Irish and the Jews have a p. 29:22
Psychotic: p. . . . lives in it [castle in the air]
249:27
Pub: p., wherein I eat my gravender 335:10
will some-one take me to a p.? 109:29
Public: conspiracy against the p. 398:14
fashion to abuse in p. 65:7
flinging a pot of paint in the p.'s face 333:8
if they've kept a p. house 140:30

Radical: few r.s have good digestions 88:2
  r. is a man with both feet . . . in the air 330:1
  r. when young 170:10
Rafael: R. of the dead Madonnas 76:13
Rag: for religion when in r.s 80:27
  passion to tatters, to very r.s 350:24
  r.s of time 146:11
  r.s they may be, but I love my r.s 283:16
Rage: all heaven in a r. 60:9
  hard-favoured r. 357:3
  heaven has no r. 120:14
  I r., I melt, I burn 173:22
  r. of the vulture 89:7
  r., r. against the dying of the light 426:5
  swell the soul to r. 150:8
  with this r. shall beauty hold a plea 386:4
Rage: plus que force ni que r. 244:6
Raging: r. of the skies 97:11
Ragtime: Alexander's R. Band 32:7
Rail: narrowing r.s slide together 156:6
  suffers anybody else to r. 120:16
Railway: R. Bridge of the Silv'ry Tay! 263:14
  Sunday morning . . . takes this r. by surprise
    178:23
Railway-share: threaten its life with a r.
    102:25
Rain: cloud which had outwept its r. 389:27
  comes in the terrible R. 397:18
  dissolve it in r. 390:14
  few small drops of r. 23:21
  gentle r. from heaven 370:9
  Hard R's. A-Gonna Fall 153:7
  in winter, . . . r. came down in slanting lines
    398:18
  It is not raining r. to me 258:17
  r. came heavily 465:32
  r. comes pattering out of the sky 15:4
  r. is over and gone 44:20
  r. it raineth every day 383:33
  r. it raineth on the just 65:22
  r., r., go away 297:25
  r. set in early tonight 77:4
  sendest r. on the dust 49:6
  singing in the r. 169:5
  small r. down can rain 5:16
  soaks up the r. 123:31
  soft refreshing r. 96:18
  still falls the R. 397:19
  sun and the r. are flying 407:27
  tears are in the falling r. 252:1
  thresh of the deep-sea r. 239:32
Rainbow: add another hue unto the r. 361:21
  behold a r. in the sky 463:14
  like a man . . . chasing r.s 359:22
  my heart is like a r. shell 331:1
  r. and a cuckoo's song 132:20
  r. comes and goes 464:1
  r. gave thee birth 132:21
  r. of His will 259:10
  r's. glory is shed 391:21
  somewhere over the r. 192:6
Raineth: r. drop and staineth slop 317:14
Raison: parfaite r. fuit tout extremité 284:4
  r. du plus fort 244:1
*Raisonner: Quand la populace se mèle de r., tout est
  perdu* 442:24
Rake: every woman is at heart a r. 314:26

excuse for thus playing the r. 287:10
  man's a r. 178:9
  Regency R.s 123:12
  thing armed with a r. 448:30
Rakehell: tremendous r. 5:3
Ralph: Sir R. the Rover tore his hair 401:18
Ram: behind him a r. caught in the thicket
    34:24
  mountains skipped like r.s 40:22
  old black r. is tupping 373:33
  r.s speed not 25:12
Rammer: lay their r.s by 160:3
Rampage: on the R., Pip, and off the R. 138:5
Randal: R. the farrier 205:24
  where ha you been, Lord R., my son? 22:25
Range: r. of exhausted volcanoes 143:7
  r. of practical politics 179:1
  something lost behind the r.s 238:30
Rank: my offence is r. 351:22
  r.s of death 287:2
Ransom: world's r., blessed Mary's son 376:17
Rant: I'll r. as well as thou 353:1
Rapacious: r. and licentious soldiery 81:25
Raphael: talked of their R.s 181:22
Rapid: r.s are near 286:21
Rapidly: not so r. 28:14
Rapport: aussitôt qu'on me fait un r. 152:8
Rapscallion: kings is mostly r.s 433:27
Rapture: first fine careless r. 74:37
  modified r! 177:24
  r. on the lonely shore 90:19
  r.s and roses of vice 412:9
Rare: as r. things will 76:10
  neither r. nor well done 242:13
Rarely: r., r., comest thou 393:26
Rascal: get down you dirty r. 296:28
  if the r. have not given me medicines 353:35
  law's made to take care of r.s 155:14
  muddy-metalled r. 350:10
  ragged r. ran 297:28
  whip to lash the r.s naked 375:16
Rash: be not r. 90:30
  do not be r. 184:10
  too r., too unadvised, too sudden 379:17
Rashes: green grow the r. 84:21
Raspberry: r. time in Runcorn 123:16
Rat: droll r., they would shoot you 330:20
  great r. of Sumatra 147:22
  how now! a r.? 351:25
  Mr Speaker I smell a r. 328:5
  r.s came tumbling 76:26
  r.s instinctively have quit it 380:29
  R.s! They fought the dogs 76:23
  smell a r. 87:13
Ratcatcher: putty little r's. daughter 7:15
Raths: mome r. outgrabe 101:24
Ration: live upon our daily r.s 136:36
Rational: so proud of being r. 328:9
Rattle: nice new r. 101:31
  pleased with a r. 314:5
Rattle-note: r. unvaried 272:4
Raven: censure acquits the r. 227:17
  quoth the R., 'Nevermore' 310:27
  r. himself is hoarse 364:30
  three r.s sat on a tree 23:18
Ravish: except you r. me 145:24
Ravished: r. this fair creature 162:21

Red: in r. and blue and green 62:12
  never blows so r. the Rose 164:7
  r. it never dies 144:6
  r. men scalped each other 262:4
  r. was on your lip 60:2
  seas incarnadine, making the green one r. 365:28
  wine when it is r. 42:33
Redaction: r. known as the Sayings Attributed 226:2
Redbreast: call for the robin r. 449:3
  r, sit and sing 117:31
  r. whistles from a garden-croft 233:21
  robin r. in a cage 60:9
Rede: recks not his own r. 348:20
Redeem: r. the time. R. 155:27
  till men r. it 110:18
Redeemer: I know that my r. liveth 37:4
Redeeming: r. the time 56:20
Redemption: everlasting r. 373:19
  married past r. 151:26
Redemptorem: *talem ac tantum meruit habere R.* 283:1
Redire: negant r. quemquam 103: 10
Redress: r. to all mankind 418:24
  things past r. are now . . . past care 376:25
  what hope of answer or r.? 418:11
Reed: broken r., on Egypt 45:26
  bruised r. shall he not break 45:38
  hundred r.s of decent growth 173:23
  man is no more than a r. 305:11
  r. is as the oak 347:15
  r. shaken with the wind 50:1
Reel: r. to and fro 40:18
  threesome r.s and foursome r.s 84:10
Reeling: r. and writhing 101:14
Reference: verify your r.s 332:15
  without r. to any other purpose 229:9
Reflection: r. dwells on them 229:8
  r., you may come tomorrow 394:10
  when Eve saw her r. 59:4
Reform: all r. except a moral one 99:12
  fringe in all r. movements 330:9
  innovate is not to r. 82:33
  peace, retrenchment and r. 68:13
  starting on r. 430:14
  stop the progress of R. 399:18
Reformation: reforming of the R. itself 282:20
Reformer: all r.s are bachelors 286:17
  r. is a guy who rides through a sewer 444:5
Refuge: eternal God is thy r. 35:20
  God is our r. 38:24
  other r. have I none 450:22
Refugees: sorrow of the r.s 264:13
Refusal: great r. 131:16
  r. . . . looks like a favour 121:7
Refuse: daft to r. the Laird o' Cockpen 291:9
  offer he can't refuse 322:21
Refute: I r. it *thus* 221:20
  r. a sneer 303:9
Regard: r. for religion 299:9
  things without all remedy should be without r.
  366:13
Regard: avec des r.s familiers 26:13
  son r. est pareil au r. des statues 439:5
Regarder: se r. soi-meme un fort long temps 284:8
Regent: God bless the R. 398:24
  r. of love rhymes 363:27
  revelled with the R. 29:6
Reges: quidquid delirant r. 207:15

Regime: no r. has ever loved great writers 400:28
Regiment: led his r. from behind 176:15
  r. blind with the dust and smoke 293:22
Region: blue r.s of the air 62:26
Register: r. of the crimes . . . of mankind 175:15
Regret: my r. becomes an April violet 418:34
Regular: require it to be brought r. 138:32
Reigle: en leur r. n'estoit que ceste clause 324:6
Reign: dynastic arrangement into three r.s 189:1
  his r. is marked 175:15
Reilly: Mr R. who owns this hotel 8:2
Reiz: fanden darin keinen R. 86:24
Rejoice: r. in the Lord alway 56:27
  R., O man, in thy youth 44:8
  r. with them that do r. 54:36
Relation: fate chooses your r.s 134:32
  friends and his r.s 178:18
  God's apology for r.s 238:5
  great men have their poor r.s 136:33
  poor r. . . . most irrelevant thing 246:4
  r.s between them are not important 167:20
Relative: in a r. way 80:9
  when our r.s are at home 388:1
Relaxes: bless r.s 63:20
Reliance: virtue now in blind r. 236:8
Relic: cold and unhonoured his r.s are laid 287:4
Relief: for this r. much thanks 347:19
  give thyself r. 16:9
Religio: tantum r. potuit suadere malorum 259:18
Religion: all of the same r. 143:17
  bashfulness . . . in r. 2:13
  blasphemy . . . could not survive r. 111:8
  bringeth men's minds to religion 19:36
  brings him about again to our r. 171:1
  dying r. 111:10
  educate men without r. 450:3
  enough r. to make us hate 411:19
  handmaid to r. 18:7
  her r. so well with her learning did suit 320:22
  impossibilities enough in r. 70:23
  men are driven by r. 259:18
  Millionaire. That is my r. 388:8
  my r. is to do good 303:6
  no reason to bring r. into it 299:9
  not a r. for gentleman 106:22
  nothing is so fatal to r. 83:2
  one r. is as true as another 86:23
  one's r. is whatever he is most interested in 25:27
  only one r. 389:3
  pure r. and undefiled 57:22
  really but of one r. 343:2
  r. . . . a product of the smaller intestines 99:18
  r. . . . attitude peculiar to a consciousness
  227:3
  r. blushing veils 311:29
  r. but a childish toy 267:9
  r. is allowed to invade . . . private life 271:14
  R. is by no means a proper subject of conversation
  109:19
  r. is powerless to bestow 159:10
  r. is the frozen thought 242:18
  r. . . . is the opium of the people 269:16
  r., justice, counsel, and treasure 19:31
  r. of humanity 303:7
  r. when in rags 80:27
  r. without science 155:1
  rum and true r. 91:9

take my r. from the priest 183:1
they alone neurotics who found r. 321:14
true meaning of r. 12:32
wrangle for r. 119:30
Religion: r. pour la r. 123:7
Religious: r. more or less 88:14
Religious-good: good but not r. 193:25
Relish: imaginary r. is so sweet 382:8
Rely: r. only on yourself 244:13
Remain: amongst you and r. with you always
    319:23
  all things leave me: you r. 413:8
  some r. so 28:16
Remark: men who have made our r.s before us
    144:13
Remedies: all r. refusing 131:7
  extreme r. for extreme diseases 201:16
  new r. must expect new evils 20:8
  r. oft in ourselves do lie 343:6
Remedy: dangerous r. 162:7
  force is not a r. 68:17
  no r. against this consumption 355:19
  one r. for all 423:32
  r. for everything 105:15
  r. is worse than the disease 19:34
  sharp r. executioner's axe 325:12
  sought the r. 346:8
  sovereign r. to all diseases 86:16
  things without all r. should be without regard
    366:13
  this story . . . suggests no r. 336:10
Remember: can't r. how they go 95:18
  I r., I r., the house where I was born 204:26
  I r. your name perfectly 403:20
  if thou wilt, r. 331:11
  pleasant to r. 440:6
   please to r. the fifth of November 6:14
  r. and understand 74:20
  r. for years 4:20
  r. me when I am gone 331:6
  r. the last end 48:23
  r. while the light lives yet 412:13
  should r. and be sad 331:7
  that which r.s 16:15
  we will r. them 59:18
  yet will I r. thee 125:28
Remembered: made myself r. 234:16
  none are undeservedly r. 15:21
Remembrance: dear r. of his dying Lord 402:26
  makes the r. dear 343:12
  poetry should . . . appear almost a r. 233:29
  r. of things past 385:24
Remind: these foolish things r. me of you
    269:21
Reminiscences: grosser r. 461:3
Remorse: farewell r! all good to me is lost 279:20
  r., the fatal egg 126:15
Remorseless: r., treacherous lecherous 350:11
Remove: r. hence to yonder place 50:27
Remover: tends with the r. to remove 386:32
Remuneration: r.! . . . Latin word for three farthings
    363:25
Render: r. therefore unto Caesar 51:3
Rendezvous: generation of Americans has a r. with
    destiny 329:16
  r. with Death 341:23
Renovation: continual r. of hope 221:30

Renown: glorious day's r. 96:24
  living, shall forfeit fair r. 340:1
  mighty men . . . men of r. 34:14
Rent: no r.! 109:3
Repeat: till it begins to r. itself 66:3
Repelled: r. by man 215:3
Repentance: which need no r. 52:24
Repine: do not r., my friends 138:26
Repletion: others are merely r. 113:17
Reply: third, 'the r. churlish' 346:14
Report: false r. 373:24
  ill r. while you live 350:6
  of good r. 56:29
  r. me . . . aright 363:11
Reporter: R's. Gallery yonder 99:33
Repose: earned a night's r. 257:21
  r. is tabooed by anxiety 177:13
  r. that ever is the same 464:22
  thoughts that nature gives way to in r. 365:17
  tumultuous life and great r. 306:3
Reprehend: if I r. anything in this world 395:27
Representation: just r.s of a general nature
    219:30
Representative: r. owes you . . . his judgement
    81:12
Reproach: r. of being 387:3
  r. of men 37:42
  without fear and without r. 27:2
Reprobation: fall to r. 375:23
Reproche: sans r. 27:2
Reproof: fourth, 'the r. valiant' 346:14
Republic: Love the Beloved R. 167:23
  'R. of Letters' 181:35
Republican: telling lies about the R. Party 135:2
Reputation: ev'ry word a r. dies 315:20
  murdered r.s 120:21
  r., r., r.! 374:25
  seeking the bubble r. 345:11
  sold my R. for a Song 164:27
  wink a r. down 410:7
  worlds of r. 434:17
  written out of r. 32:2
Requiem: thy high r. become a sod 232:7
Require: I do r. it . . . to be brought reg'lar 138:32
  thought 'e might r. 241:8
Research: r. is . . . the art of the soluble 271:11
  steal from two it's r. 283:6
Researches: no deep r. vex the brain 128:9
Resemblance: straight its own r. find 268:21
Resent: r. someone who can do it better 106:8
Residence: forted r. 'gainst the tooth of time
    368:29
Resist: nothing to r. at all 249:5
Resistance: r. to light and its children 12:15
Resisted: we know what's r. 83:22
Resistentialism: r. is concerned with what Things
    think 218:2
Resolution: had not r. to fire it 220:26
  if you carry this r. 33:8
  native hue of r. 350:14
  our present r. 328:15
Resolved: r. to be irresolute 112:15
Resonance: r. of his solitude 121:10
Resource: few people had intellectual r.s 222:4
  r.s of civilization 179:2
Respect: no r. of place, persons, nor time 383:5
  old-fashioned r. for the young 455:15

one owes r. to the living 442:19
Respectable: more r. he is 388:16
  not one is r. 453:27
  since when was genius found r.? 71:24
Respecter: God is no r. of persons 53:49
Responsibility: heavy burden of r. . . . as King
    154:12
  power without r. 21:15
  r. without power 408:10
Responsible: idea isn't r. 268:1
Rest: crept silently to R. 164:9
  die or r. at last! 391:8
  far better r. 141:30
  gets him to r. 357:13
  I will give you r. 50:4
  leave the r. to the gods 208:8
  r. may reason and welcome 72:13
  r. of your life 133:11
  set up my everlasting r. 380:11
  she's at r. and so am I 150:16
  shortly be with them that r. 281:23
  sing thee to thy r. 353:14
  so may he r. 359:1
  talk about the r. of us 202:11
  toil and not to seek for r. 259:11
Reste: j'y suis, j'y r. 264:4
Resting-place: my r. is found 72:15
Restoration: Church's R. 32:18
Restorer: tired Nature's sweet r. 472:18
Restrained: weak enough to be r. 63:7
Restraint: firm r. with which they write 96:23
Result: r. happiness 137:12
Resumption: way to r. is to resume 107:3
Resurrection: foretaste of the r. 339:3
  in the r. they neither marry 51:4
  looking for the r. of the body 320:6
  r. and the life 53:23
  R. of the body 318:25
  sure and certain hope of the R. 320:5
Retainer: Old R. night and day 30:12
Retentiveness: change depends on r. 337:10
Retire: r. from the world 143:22
Retirement: r. urges sweet return 280:32
Retort: first, 'the r. courteous' 346:14
Retreat: enemy advances, we r. 266:8
  it never r.s 141:28
  let us make honourable r. 345:20
Retrogression: blank verse has suffered . . . r. 157:19
Return: I shall r. 261:2
  r. my roving heart, r. 144:11
Returning: r. were as tedious as go o'er
    366:34
Rêve: peu de r. 285:26
Revelation: ends with R.s 455:37
  extraordinary r.s and gifts of the Holy Ghost
    86:29
  r.s of the Eichmann trial 9:27
Revelry: sound of r. by night 89:21
Revels: midnight r., by a forest side 278:29
  r. now are ended 381:10
Revenge: capable and wide r. 375:10
  man that studieth r. 19:2
  most horribly r. 357:23
  R. is a kind of wild justice 19:1
  r. proves its own executioner 167:7
  r., r., Timotheus cries 150:6
  R. triumphs over death 18:22

spur my dull r. 351:41
sweet as my r.! 346:32
sweet is r. 91:5
Reverence: none so poor to do him r. 360:18
Reverie: r.s so airy 127:7
Reversion: no bright r. in the sky 312:3
Reviewer: chorus of indolent r.s 416:18
  r.s are . . . poets, historians 118:26
  r.s would have to say 29:11
Reviewing: read a book before r. 400:7
Revivals: history of r. 88:6
Revolt: four and twenty leaders of r.s 78:32
  it r.s me, but I do it! 177:19
Révolte: c'est une r.? 248:23
Revolution: revolts, republics, r.s 422:23
  r. from above 338:16
  r. is an opinion 291:18
  R. might devour each of its children 438:26
  r.s are not made with rosewater 260:16
  Social R. will be moral 307:3
  white heat of this r. 458:5
Révolution: Non, Sire, c'est une r. 248:23
Revolver: reach for my r. 179:14, 224:16
Reward: farewell r.s and fairies 122:9
  labour and not ask for any r. 259:11
  neither r.s nor punishments 215:12
  nothing for r. 402:31
  reap his old r. 241:10
  r. him according to his works 57:8
Rewarded: greatly r. 47:39
Rex: Ego et R. meus 358:19
Reynolds: when Sir Joshua R. died 61:15
Rheims: Lord Archbishop of R. 24:8
Rhein: Wacht am R. 338:22
Rhetoric: out of the quarrel . . . we make r. 472:7
  r. . . . . to which poetry would be made subsequent
    282:23
Rhetorician: sophisticated r. 143:11
Rhine: think of the R. 21:16
  Watch on the R. 338:22
  wide and winding R. 89:27
Rhodes: I admire him [Cecil R.] 434:1
Rhyme: build the lofty r. 277:1
  make a dog howl in r. 28:3
  many a musèd r. 232:7
  more fivet of R. 30:24
  murmuring r. beats with light 288:11
  neither r. nor reason 287:21
  out of us all that make r.s 427:6
  outlive this powerful r. 385:30
  petty fools of r. 419:16
  punish me with loss of r. 199:17
  random r. 144:5
  received nor r. nor reason 403:8
  r. being no necessary adjunct 277:30
  r.s are so scarce 96:6
  r.s grow worse 92:30
  sort of Runic r. 310:17
  unattempted yet in prose or r. 278:1
Rhymed: r. to death 397:1
Rhymesters: rival r.s frown 92:32
Rhyming: modern bondage of r. 277:31
Rhythm: some in sprung r. 206:23
  take away the r. 209:13
Ri: celle où l'on n'a pas r. 106:2
Rialto: in the R. you have rated me 369:16
Rib: under the r.s of Death 275:25

Ribald: man's a r. 178:9
Riband: r. to stick in his coat 75:17
  very r. in the cap of youth 352:17
Ribbon: blue r. of the turf 143:20
  bunch of blue r.s 297:13
  give me but what this r. tied 445:2
Rice: beside the ungathered r. he lay 257:11
Rich: being r., my virtue then shall be 361:13
  curse not the r. 44:3
  few r. men own their own property 215:13
  greater part of r. people 398:15
  it is easier . . . for a rich man to enter 50:38
  it's the r. what gets the pleasure 8:16
  let him be r. and weary 199:21
  maketh haste to be r. 43:3
  marry a r. woman as a poor woman 425:10
  never be too . . . r. 458:22
  r. and free 83:4
  r. and the poor meet together 42:29
  r. get r. 229:7
  r. have become richer 394:28
  r. in good works 57:4
  r. man has his motor car 1:4
  r. man in his castle 4:4
  r. man's joke 70:12
  r. men rule the law 181:30
  So friendly, and so r. 14:24
  very r.. They are different from you and me
    165:14
  wretchedness of being r. 399:9
Richard: came in with R. Conqueror 380:12
  R. Gare de Lyon 342:18
  R's. himself again 114:10
Richardson: one letter of R's. 222:6
Riche: qu'il ait tué bien des gens pour s'etre si r.
  283:20
Richer: for r. for poorer 319:42
Riches: enjoyment of r. consists in the parade of r.
  398:15
  good name is rather to be chosen than great r.
    42:28
  he heapeth up r. 38:17
  his best r., ignorance of wealth 180:19
  if r. increase 39:7
  infinite r. in a little room 267:10
  looked upon r. to be a valuable thing 411:24
  r. are a good handmaiden 18:14
  r. are for spending 20:15
  r. certainly make themselves wings 42:32
  r. grow in hell 278:25
  r. have wings 127:8   r. left not got with pain
    409:15
  unsearchable r. of Christ 56:14
  world's r. . . . . contract into a span 199:20
Richesses: l'embarras des r. 4:12
Richmond: on R. Hill there lives a lass 264:10
Richness: here's r. [Mr Squeers] 139:9
Ricks: r. stand grey to the sun 239:31
Rid: purely to be r. of thee 120:19
Riddle: found out my r. 35:32
  I'm bad at r.s 252:9
  r. of destiny 245:7
  r. of the world 314:2
  r. wrapped in a mystery 112:17
Ride: in haste to r. 125:10
  r. on! r. on in majesty! 274:12
  r. r. together 75:13

  you must ride on horseback 125:8
Rideau: tirez le r. 324:21
Rider: r. and horse 89:25
Ridiculous: from the sublime to the r. 291:16
  one step above the sublime makes the r. 303:1
Riding: here we are r. 75:12
Rien: de n'avoir r. à faire 64:16
Riff-raff: epithet which r. apply 205:14
Rifiuto: gran r. 131:16
Rifle: stuttering r's rapid rattle 302:7
Riflemen: R., R., R. form 423:6
Rift: load every r. of your subject 234:17
  r. within the lute 417:4
Riga: there was a young lady of R. 6:15
Right: all's r. with the world 76:29
  anything but what's r. 211:15
  customer is always r. 342:13
  do a great r. 370:10
  every-single-one-of-them-is-r. 239:15
  I am not . . . a man of the r. 289:9
  if it's done r. 4:14
  I'm all r.! 64:23
  in his r. mind 51:33
  irresponsible and r. 113:12
  keep to the r. you are wrong 159:28
  life . . . always in the r. 124:9
  mind conscious of the r. 440:9
  no r.s in this matter 328:16
  noisy man is always in the r. 124:29
  now and then be r. 124:27
  public . . . commonly attains to think r. 219:19
  rather be r. than be President 115:1
  r. as r. can be! 177:17
  r. divine of kings 311:24
  r. hands of fellowship 56:7
  r. is in retreat 166:22
  r. people stay at home 123:21
  r. that these wants should be provided for 82:12
  r. there is none to dispute 127:37
  r. view, r. aim, r. speech 80:4
  r. was r. 128:11
  r. words in the r. order 63:29
  r.s inherent and inalienable 217:20
  r.s of a man 72:16
  safer guide than either r. or duty 88:20
  though r. were worsted 74:16
  to be decorative and to do r. 163:17
  too fond of the *r.* 181:18
  Ulster will be r. 112:5
  Whatever is, is r. 313:34
  whose life is in the r. 314:6
Righteous: be not r. over much 43:31
  death of the r. 35:10
  godly, r., and sober life 318:14
  have I not seen the r. forsaken 38:15
  leave r. ways behind 80:5
  r. are bold as a lion 43:2
  r. forsaken 63:33
  r. man regardeth the life of his beasts 42:3
  r. shall flourish like the palm tree 40:4
  souls of the r. 47:38
Righteousness: love r., ye that be judges of the earth
  47:34
  makes for r. 13:2
  r. and peace have kissed each other 39:28
  r. exalteth a nation 42:10
  r. readable 64:24

r.s whose entrance leads to Hell 275:22
round the rugged r. 297:28
she ran upon no r. 125:35
soften r.s 120:13
upon this r. 50:23
walled round with r.s 412:14
with r.s, and stones, and trees 466:19
Rocket: rose like a r. 303:4
Rod: all humbled kiss the r. 384:3
bleeding from the Roman r.s 124:17
he that spareth his r. spoileth his son 42:7
r. for the fool's back 42:37
r. of empire might have swayed 186:9
r. of iron 37:20, 58:8
r. out of the stem of Jesse 45:9
r. produces an effect which terminates 220:10
scaled eyeball owns the mystic r. 78:30
spare thr r. and spoil the child 87:19
throw away thy r. 199:9
thy r. and thy staff they comfort me 38:3
Roes: two young r. that are twins 44:26
Rogue: bewitched with the r's. company 353:35
der createst r. 1:3
four r.s in buckram 354:10
that is not fool is r. 149:30
you r.s, do you want to live for ever? 169:3
Roi: plus royaliste que le r. 9:15
r. est mort 9:19
si je n'etais pas r. 258:2
Roll: fell with a r. and a rumble 226:3
mouldy r.s of Noah's ark 149:17
r. of common men 354:21
r. of the world eastward 193:16
r., the rise, the carol, the creation 206:20
r. up that map 309:22
Roller: r., pitch and stumps, and all 247:7
Rolling: just keeps r. 191:12
Romae: si fueris R. 4:21
Romam: natan me consule R. 114:24
Roman: before the R. came to Rye 110:12
high R. fashion 344:5
last of all the R.s 361:2
live as the R.s 4:21
no R. ever was able to say 29:7
noblest R. of them all 361:4
rather be a dog . . . than such a R. 360:28
R. and his trouble are ashes 210:22
R. for that 161:18
R. holiday 90:16
R's. life, a R's. arms 261:17
R.s were like brothers 261:16
Romanam: tantae molis erat R. condere gentem 440:3
Romance: 'Confound R!' 239:21
spirit of r. is dead 238:2
symbols of a high r. 233:11
Romanciers: r. des raconteurs du présent 183:15
Romane: tu regere imperio populos, R., memento 440:30
Romano: R. vivito more 4:21
Romanticism: r. . . . . greatest possible pleasure 404:20
Romanus: civis R. sum 114:19
populus R. unam cervicem haberet I95:14
Rome: all you writ to R. 358:19
Bishop of R. 320:9
comes round by R. 78:1
grandeur that was R. 310:29

high and palmy state of R. 347:24
lay thou on for R! 261:10
let R. in Tiber melt 343:16
R. has spoken 16:7
R. lies gold and glad 77:27
R. shall perish 124:18
R.'s. gross yoke 73:30
time will doubt of R. 91:35
when in R. 4:21
when R. falls – the World 90:17
Romeo: O R., R.! wherefore art thou R.? 379:10
Ronsard: R. me célébrait 329:11
Roo: Baby R. 274:32
Roof: climbed the r.s at break of day 416:6
had no r. to shroud his head 201:3
r. fretted with golden fire 349:36
right through its gorgeous r. 75:10
Rook: r.s are blown about the skies 417:31
r.s came home in scramble sort 202:15
Rookery: leads the clanging r. home 419:23
Room: boys in the back r. 256:5
'cross a crowded r. 191:14
from my lonely r. 17:21
in the r. the women come and go 156:20
into the neighbour r. 351:37
lighted r.s inside your head 247:20
no r. for them in the inn 51:44
noticing them puts things in a r. 321:10
one little r., an everywhere 145:10
R. at the Top 66:15
R. of One's Own 460:23
r. to deny ourselves 234:21
r. with a view 123:23
r.s at college was beastly 240:7
sit down in the lowest r. 52:19
that holy r. 145:27
who sweeps a r. 199:13
who's in the next r.? 193:14
Roosevelt: kind of nation that President R. hoped for 218:21
she Eleanor R. would rather light candles 406:14
Root: burning from its r. to its tip 261:1
drunkenness . . . the r. of all sins 216:6
eaten of the insane r. 364:19
fail to take r. in others 432:17
fruit tree's mossy r. 268:22
laid unto the r. of the trees 48:38
nips his r. 358:21
r. of all evil 57:2, 87:34
r. of the matter 37:5
send my r.s rain 206:18
Rope: buy a piece of r. for a keepsake 434:1
escape from r. and gun 174:12
r. that hangs my dear 174:6
Rosaleen: My Dark R.! 266:4
Rosary: every one apart, my r. 328:22
Rose: all night have the r.s heard 420:34
ash the burnt r.s leave 156:8
beauty's r. might never die 385:11
blood upon the r. 310:15
blossom as the r. 45:24
budding r. above the r. full blown 465:28
canker to the r. 277:6
days of wine and r.s 271:22
die of a r. 313:31
each Morn a thousand R.s brings 163:28
English unofficial r. 69:11

good old r. sufficeth 466:11
in their r.s there was only one clause 324:6
little r., a little sway 153:4
long levelled r. of streaming light 275:16
pretences to break known r.s by 129:17
r. of three 6:11
r. them with a rod of iron 58:8
safer to obey than to r. 235:3
she r.s him, never shows she r.s 341:28
these simple little r.s 31:1
twelve good r.s 181:10
Ruler: R. of the Queen's Navee! 176:29
r.s of the darkness 56:22
Rum: r. and true religion 91:9
what a R. Go 450:12
yo-ho-ho, and a bottle of r.! 406:24
Rumour: r. of oppression and deceit 126:34
Run: *long r.* is a misleading guide 236:15
r. at least twice as fast 101:29
yet we will make him r. 269:3
Run-stealer: r.s flicker to and fro 427:10
Runcorn: raspberry time in R. 123:16
Running: all the r. you can do 101:29
Rupert: R. of parliamentary discussion 142:24
Rus: r. in urbe 268:11
Ruskin: savage R. 70:3
Russell, Lord John 143:34
do not hack me as you did Lord R. 284:19
Russia: action of R. 112:17
last out a night in R. 368:9
outlaw R. for ever 326:9
R. has two generals 294:13
Russian: intelligent R. 6:23
might have been a R. 177:4
R. people have become an awful reality 432:15
some people may be R.s 138:31
Rust: better to wear out than to r. out 129:20
r. to the harrow 134:27
Sunday clears away the r. of the whole week 2:7
that which never taketh r. 396:17
to r. unburnished 424:5
Rustic: amazed the gazing r.s 181:7
Ruth: sad heart of R. 232:7
Rutland: R. blue's got out of passion 226:6
Rye: coming through the r. 84:2
pocket full of r. 297:31
r. reach to the chin 306:22
Roman came to R. 110:12

S

Sábana: niño trajo la blanca s. 172:17
Sabaoth: Lord God of S. 318:18
Sabbath: hail, S. thee I hail 184:9
last S. day of 1879 263:14
never broke the S. but for gain 149:23
on the holy S., on the peaceful day! 397:16
s. was made for man 51:28
S.s of Eternity 423:9
Sable: a s. shivered 348:15
Sabre: great Chatham with his s. drawn 5:24
Sabrina: S. fair 275:34
Sacerdos: Musarum s. virginibus puerisque canto 208:22

Sack: addict themselves to s. 356:10
intolerable deal of s. 354:20
purge and leave s. 355:10
s. the lot! 163:19
s.s to sew up wives withal 425:13
Sacred: books are books and therefore s. 184:23
keep nothing s. 423:27
Sacrifice: our spotless s. 1449
pay thy morning s. 235:8
s. to God of the devil's leavings 316:15
s. to the Graces 109:10
s.s of God are a broken spirit 38:31
still stands thine ancient s. 240:17
unpitied s. 82:28
upon such s.s, . . . the gods themselves throw incense! 363:10
Sacrificer: let us be s.s 359:29
Sad: how s. and bad and mad 73:35
Saddle: strangers to bridle or s 411:3
things are in the s. 158:13
Saddled: millions ready s. . . . to be ridden 262:19
Sadness: farewell s. 158:8
s. of her s. 25:25
shady s. of a vale 230:26
taste the s. of her might 231:29
wraps me in most humorous s. 346:1
Saecla: inque brevi spatio mutantur s. animantum 259:22
Saeclum: solvet s. in favilla 104:11
Safe: s. because you can watch 59:10
s. shall be my going 69:19
see me s. up 287:23
Safeguard: s. of the west 463:16
Safety: in a multitude of counsellors there is s. 41:34
pluck this flower, s. 354:2
safe though all s's. lost 69:19
Sage: content . . . s. in meditation found 394:3
German s. 115:20
hoary s. replied 224:2
lengthen'd s. advices 85:15
s. left nothing in his ink-horn 105:10
sit the sainted s. 186:24
s.s may pour out their wisdom's treasure 91:20
without hardness will be s. 11:9
Said: as well s. as if I had s. it 411:14
everything that can be s. 459:7
I wish I had s. that 452:10
s. I to myself, s. I 177:10
so very little s. 111:26
Sail: full s. 120:24
never weather-beaten s. 97:28
purple the s.s, and so perfumed 343:28
s. and s. with unshut eye 11:5
sea-mark of my utmost s. 375:24
s.s filled with a lusty wind 106:13
s.s ripped, seams opening 126:9
when we our s.s advance 148:13
white and rustling s. 130:9
white dipping s.s 270:1
Sail-yards: till his s. tremble 106:13
Sailor: All the Nice Girls Love a S. 274:10
drowned Phoenician S. 156:37
home is the s. 407:31
lass that loves a s. 136:10
no man will be a s. 221:2
s. men have their faults 216:5
s.s but men 369:12

Satan: get thee behind me, S. 50:24
 Lord said unto S. 36:33
 S. and his peers 278:28
 S. exalted sat 278:30
 S. thou art but a dunce 60:28
 S. met his ancient friend 94:5
Satanic: called the S. School 401:27
 S. mills 61:9
Satchel: schoolboy with his s. 60:4
Satin: stark mad in white s. 395:12
Satire: let s. be my son 92:22
 s. . . . closes on Saturday night 229:12
 s. is a lesson 291:3
 s. is a sort of glass 410:19
 s. or sense 312:25
 s. should . . . wound with a touch 285:2
Satirist: second English s. 191:1
Satis: lusisti s. 207:30
Satisfaction: miss the s. of knowing we are avenged
  432:9
 s. . . . depends . . . on your will 285:8
Satisfied: well paid that is well s. 370:17
Satisfies: that s. 129:11
Saturday: day . . . betwixt a S. and Monday 99:7
 satire . . . closes on S. night 229:12
Saturn: S. and Love their long repose shall burst
  391:7
 sat gray-haired S. 230:26
Saturnia: iam . . . redeunt S. regna 441:15
Satyr: either a stoic or a s. 309:7
 like s.s grazing on the lawns 267:8
Sauce: best s. in the world 105:12
 crier of green s. 324:8
 only one s. 98:24
Saucer: white s. like some full moon 284:21
Saul: is S. among the prophets? 35:43
 S. and Jonathan were lovely and pleasant 36:1
 S. hath slain his thousands 35:46
Sausen: wie des Windes S., heimatlos 338:14
Savage: lust is . . . s., extreme 387:4
 noble s. 151:21
 take some s. woman 420:2
Savaged: s. by a dead sheep 196:19
Savante: passion choquante de se rendre s. 283:13
Save: can, but will not, s. me 148:18
 himself he cannot s. 51:26
 O God, make speed to s. us 318:16
 s. me, oh, s. me, from the candid friend 98:16
 whenever you s. 5s 236:16
 you would s. none of me 145:7
Saved: we are not s. 46:26
Saviour: hide me, O my S., hide 450:21
 rejoiced in God my S. 51:42
 S. dear 234:23
 S. of the world was born 88:29
 then bespoke our S. 22:9
Savoir: belle chose que de s. quelquechose 283:10
Savour: s. as all the spicery of the world 265:14
 salt hath lost his s. 48:43
 seeming and s. all the winter long 384:27
 send forth a stinking s. 43:39
Saw: full of wise s.s 345:11
Sawdust: S. Caesar 342:12
Say: if you can't s. anything good 257:24
 know what they are going to s. 112:9
 never s. the things we would like to 321:16
 nothing to s. 242:15

people who s. nothing carry something 400:27
 s. nothing 119:31
 s. nothing but what has been said 86:6
 s. what you mean 101:5
 thinking what to s. 101:28
 want to know what it s.s 137:30
Saying: as I was s. the other day 253:18
 s.s are . . . like women's letters 195:14
Sbuddikins: 's.! on my own ten toes 95:20
Scab: make yourself s.s 346:20
Scaffold: never on the s. 112:11
Scale: equal s. weighing delight and dole 347:29
 every golden s. 100:30
 geometric s. 87:5
 more colossal s. than ever before 144:12
 result from the new s. 264:3
 sink i' the s. 77:14
Scallop-shell: s. of quiet 325:8
Scandal: greatest s. waits on greatest state 385:7
 love and s. are the best sweeteners 162:28
 no s. about Queen Elizabeth 395:7
 s. the incredible come-down 29:10
Scandale: s. du monde est ce qui fait l'offense
  284:16
Scandalous: merry monarch, s. and poor 328:13
Scanter: somewhat s. of your maiden presence
  348:26
Scapegoat: go for a s. into the wilderness 35:5
Scar: jests at s.s, that never felt a wound 379:8
 there is oft a s. 73:20
Scarce: good people's wery s. 141:24
Scarf: beauteous s. 370:3
 s.s, garters, gold 314:5
Scarlet: arrayed in purple and s. 58:28
 clothed in s. 225:8
 his sins were s. 30:27
Scene: all the changing s.s of life 414:17
 come no more behind your s.s, David
  220:16
 gay gilded s.s 1:16
 in his tragic s.s there is . . . something wanting
  219:31
 live o'er each s. 315:10
 lofty s. be acted over 360:7
 my lady's last s. 145:14
 s.s where man has never trod 114:27
Scenery: end of all natural s. 333:10
 s. is fine 234:1
Scent: amber s. of odorous perfume 281:24
Sceptic: will yield such people no more milk 221:13
Scepticism: s. is the first attribute of a good critic
  259:4
Sceptre: I'll give . . . my s. for a palmer's walking staff
  377:4
 leaden s. o'er a slumb'ring world 472:19
 s. and crown must tumble down 396:4
 s., learning, physic must 347:15
 s. shows the force of temporal power 370:9
Sceptreless: s., free, uncircumscribed 393:15
Scheme: best laid s.s 85:28
 sorry S. of Things 164:30
 s.s of political improvement 221:28
Scherzando: 'S.! ma non troppo' 176:13
Schiller: S. has the material sublime 118:29
Schilling: prize on s.s postlots free 226:2
Schizophrenia: if God talks to you, you have s.
  413:15

always ourselves we find in the s. 130:1
among the mountains by the winter s.
   417:9
beneath a rougher s. 124:22
s. of glory 358:21
English that of the s. 327:9
espouse the everlasting s. 463:18
goes to s. for nothing 144:25
gong-tormented s. 470:8
guard our native s.s 97:20
he that commands the s. 20:17
I must go down to the s.s again 270:2
in the flat s. sunk 275:17
jolly-rodgered s. 426:19
little cloud out of the s. 36:17
love still has something of the s. 341:18
men and s. interpenetrate 121:24
more steady than an ebbing s. 167:11
most dangerous s. 370:3
mother and lover of men, the s. 413:5
multitudinous s.s incarnadine 365:28
newly come from the s.s 326:3
no more s. 58:31
not having been at s. 223:1
nothing but s. 18:4
one [voice] is of the s. 463:21
out of the s. came he 116:22
paddles in a halcyon s. 331:1
precious stone set in the silver s. 376:17
rainy Hyades vext the dim s. 424:2
receiveth as the s., nought enters there 382:24
rude s. grew civil 371:35
sail on the salt s. 22:24
sang in my chains like the s. 426:6
scattered in the bottom of the s. 378:1
s., Floy, what it . . . keeps on saying 137:30
s. gave up the dead 58:30
s. is all about us 156:5
s. is boiling hot 102:5
s. rises higher 109:27
s. that bares her bosom 463:6
s. where it goes 10:20
s.s were roaring 174:28
secret of the s. 257:10
serpent-haunted s. 166:1
shore of the sounding s. 204:8
sight of that immortal s. 464:15
silence of the s.s 466:22
silent s. 116:26
sleeping alone in the depths of the s. 427:9
slimy s. 116:29
snotgreen s. 226:20
sunless s. 117:35
take mine honour . . . if Ye take away the s.
   239:28
there is more s. 331:22
those in peril on the s. 453:13
tideless midland s. 413:6
till the s. itself floweth in your veins 431:14
triumphant s. 376:18
troubled s.s of thought 172:4
unplumbed, salt, estranging s. 12:10
used to 'ave faults myself when I was at s. 216:5
uttermost parts of the s. 41:11
walking on foot through a green s. 269:4
what thing of s. or land? 281:24
when I put out to s. 416:2

when the S. shall give up her dead 320:6
wine-dark s. 204:10
within a walk of the s. 31:4
wrinkled s. beneath him 416:12
yet the s. is not full 43:13
Sea-bank: stood Dido . . . upon the wild s.s 370:18
Sea-beast: s. crawled forth 466:6
Sea-change: doth suffer a s. 380:35
Sea-flower: quiet s. moulded by the sea 412:7
Sea-fowl: s. has gone to her nest 128:2
Sea-king: s.'s daughter from over the sea 424:17
Sea-maid: hear the s.'s music 371:35
Sea-shell: she sells s.s 409:13
Sea-shore: like a boy playing on the s. 294:8
Seal: heard a s. bark 429:22
   s. of God 58:18
   s. upon thine heart 44:27
   s.! The s.! 469:1
   seventh s. 58:17
   s.s of love 368:26
Seamen: s. three! what men be ye? 306:18
   s. were not gentlemen 262:18
Search: after a s. so painful 328:11
   not worth the s. 369:5
   s. the scriptures 53:14
Searching: by s. find out God 36:43
Seaside: Beside the S. 179:7
Season: all s.s shall be sweet 117:31
   circle with the s.s 424:21
   envious s.s roll 203:27
   four s.s fill . . . the year 233:1
   love . . . no s. knows 146:11
   out of s. 57:6
   s. of mists and mellow fruitfulness 233:16
   s. of snows and sins 412:1
   s. of the year 8:8
   s. your admiration for a while 348:11
   soote s. 409:16
   swift s.s roll 203:31
   there is a s., and a time to every purpose 43:19
   things by s. seasoned 370:24
   with the year S.s return 279:13
   word spoken in due s. 42:14
Seat: mount my soul! thy s. is up on high 377:19
   s. of a bicycle made for two 131:1
   s. of the scornful 37:18
   sagged s.s, the creeper-nails are rust 192:11
   people in the cheaper s.s clap your hands 253:3
   vaulted with such ease into his s. 354:36
   wild sequestered s. 119:18
Second: not a s. on the day 122:1
   twenty-four times a s. 179:8
Second-hand: buy a s. car 335:4
Secrecy: infinite book of s. 343:17
Secret: dark s. love 62:3
   digestion is the great s. of life 399:21
   from whom no s.s are hid 319:19
   s. none can utter 323:4
   s. of the sea 257:10
   that is our s. 74:20
   that's a s. 120:8
   when it ceases to be a s. 29:23
Secretary: send a Foreign S . . . naked into the
   conference chamber 33:8
Sect: loving his own s. 118:15
   paradise for a s. 230:21
   sixty different religious s.s 98:24

slave to no s. 314:11

that great s. 390:24

Two-and-Seventy jarring S.s confute 164:17

Security: s. is the mother of danger 171:7

Sedge: giving a gentle kiss to every s. 384:5

   s. is withered from the lake 231:7

Sedition: surest way to prevent s.s 19:32

Seduction: no attempt at ethical or social s.
   33:6

See: each man as he s.s himself 217:15

   I now can s. no more 463:30

   may I be there to s. it 125:20

   rather s. than be one 81:6

   s. oursels as others s. us 85:25

   that we s. or seem 310:20

   to s., and eke for to be seye 108:15

   to s. her is to love her 84:1

   to s. her was to love her 83:24

See-saw: S. Margery Daw 297:29

Seed: good s. on the land 96:18

   groweth s. and bloweth med 5:13

   in s. time learn 63:9

   look into the s.s of time 364:16

   s. from the feathered grass 230:27

   seed ye sow, another reaps 393:29

   some s.s fell by the way side 50:11

   wingèd s.s, where they lie cold 392:4

Seeing: one way of s. them 333:17

Seeing: s. many things 45:39

   when thy s. blindeth thee 427:21

   worth s.? yes 223:7

Seek: All who s. you tempt you 327:19

   beds for me and all who s.? 331:14

   never s. to tell thy love 61:13

   s. all the day ere you find them 369:5

   s. and ye shall find 49:22

   s. one to come 57:19

   we s. him here, we s. him there 300:5

Seeking: we must still be s. 461:29

   you would not be s. Me if you had not found Me
     305:13

Seem: I know not 's.s' 347:34

Seemed: all s. but were not all 280:14

Seen: justice should . . . be s. to be done 200:26

Seigneur: un grand s. 27:16

Sein: couvrez ce s. que je ne saurais voir 284:13

Seine: red fool-fury of the S. 418:38

Seize: s. today 208:10

Selection: Natural S. 132:8

Self: each one a murdered s. 331:24

   man's s. to himself 246:1

   never agreed with my other s. 175:27

   toll me back . . . to my sole s. 232:7

Self-discovery: painting is s. 311:2

Self-indulgence: favourite form of s. 270:17

Self-interest: heedless s. was bad morals 329:17

Self-limitation: in s. a master first shows himself
   180:4

Self-love: s. seems so often unrequited 317:30

   true s. and social 314:14

Self-lover: nature of extreme s.s 20:6

Self-sacrifice: spirit of s. 464:24

Self-schooled: s., self-scanned, self-honoured 11:31

Self-sufficiency: s. at home 448:9

Self-sufficient: know how to be s. 285:12

Seligkeit: nur aushalten den Anblick der S. 306:6

Selling: book . . . s. well 65:2

every one lives by s. something 406:16

Selves: drown your empty s. 31:9

   from our better s. 465:15

   their dead s. to higher things 417:27

Semblance: outface it with their s.s 344:24

   outward s. of a man 141:10

   s. in another's case 124:21

Seminary: ladies' s. 177:23

Senate: applause of listening s.s 186:12

   listening s.s hang upon thy tongue 428:11

Senator: green-robed s.s of mighty woods 230:29

   s.s burst with laughter 14:6

Send: for God's sake don't s. me 253:29

Senior: s's. ceaseless verse 92:30

Senior-junior: s., giant-dwarf, Dan Cupid 363:27

Se'nnight: weary s.s nine times nine shall he dwindle
   364:14

Sens: bon s. est la chose du monde la mieux partagée
   135:10

   bon s. s'accorde avec la rime 64:7

   s. plus pur aux mots de la tribu 265:7

Sensation: life of s.s 233:25

   s. is s. 223:22

   uncomfortable s. now and then 136:21

Sensational: something s. to read 455:18

Sense: betrayed me into common s. 311:13

   decency is want of s. 330:13

   devoid of s. and motion 278:34

   discerned by the five s.s 63:5

   fountain of good s. 151:35

   gift to Beauty, Common S. 272:10

   hath the daintier s. 352:23

   learned without s. 111:27

   man of s. and his books 109:13

   men of s. approve 313:15

   men of s. never tell it 343:2

   money is like a sixth s. 270:24

   no substitute for s. 157:12

   odours . . . live within the s. they quicken 394:6

   palter with us in a double s. 367:31

   poetry is more than good s. 119:2

   relish . . . enchants my s. 382:8

   seldom attribute common s. 248:16

   s. aches at thee 375:15

   s. and feeling beneath it 115:11

   s. may reach and apprehend 145:5

   s. or nonsense, never out nor in 149:28

   s. sublime 462:20

   s.s know that absence blots people out 66:4

   s.s would have cooled 367:23

   take care of s. 101:11

   trained and organized common s. 213:11

   withdraws us from the power of our s.s 219:18

Sensibility: dissociation of s. 157:22

   modified his s. 157:21

   wanting s. 127:28

Sensible: s. men never tell 143:17

Sentence: judges soon the s. sign 315:21

   mouths a s. 111:25

   s. first 101:23

   s. is for open war 278:32

   single s. will suffice 98:2

   speak after s. 218:18

Sententiae: quot homines tot s. 424:31

Sentiment: s. is what I am not acquainted with
   166:15

   sentimentality is only s. 271:6

them's my s.s 425:18
Sentimentalism: s. is the working off . . . of feelings 249:17
Sentimentality: s. is only sentiment 271:6
s. . . . the sentiment we don't share 187:28
Sentiments: s. sont toujours les plus naturels 258:7
Sentinel: s. on Whitehall gate 261:6
s.s to warn th' immortal souls 267:18
Sentry: where stands a wingèd s. 438:6
Separate: s. them one from another 51:16
s. us from the love of God 54:31
Separation: restraints . . . to prevent s. 222:5
s., amicably if they can 323:5
September: thirty days hath S. 6:17
Sepulchre: dome of a vast s. 392:6
s. in stubborn Jewry 376:17
wilted s.s 51:8
Sequel: s. of today unsolders all 417:11
Seraph: where S.s might despair 89:11
Seraphim: above it stood the s.s 45:2
sister of the S. 128:18
Serene: breaks the s. of heaven 401:24
s. and joyful 136:27
Serenity: s. to accept things 294:15
Serf: s. in the house of some landless man 204:15
Sergeant: fell s., death 353:10
Seriously: everything must be taken s. 426:2
Seriousness: he (Chaucer) lacks the high s. 12:28
Sermon: brought her s.s 320:21
good honest and painful s. 307:10
him who a s. flies 199:3
s.s and soda-water 91:12
s.s in stones 344:25
takes pleasure to hear s.s 342:10
turn out a s. 84:15
Serpent: charming s. draws 417:38
like Aaron's s. 314:3
like the innocent flower, . . . the s. under't 365:2
s. of Old Nile 343:24
s. subtlest beast of all the field 280:31
s. was more subtil than any beast 33:23
subject like a s. 183:3
that old s. 58:29
trail of the s. 287:13
way of a s. upon a rock 43:8
wise as s.s 49:39
Serpentine: dignify the S. 144:8
Servant: few men have been admired by their s.s 285:20
good and faithful s. 51:14
good s.s, but bad masters 254:1
let him be your s. 50:43
Lord, now lettest thou thy s. depart in peace 52:3
our s.s will do that 439:22
reveal Himself to His s.s 282:20
said by the s. girls in the kitchen 413:9
s. of God, well done 280:16
s. of the Living God 398:6
s. to be bred at an university 120:12
s.s of the sovereign 19:17
thy s. a dog 36:27
thy s. heareth 35:40
to s.s kind 98:27
unprofitable s.s 52:34
when ye hae a gude s. 341:3
'your s.'s cut in half' 184:7
Serve: come to s. the Lord 48:1

little scratched: 'twill s. 363:33
profits most who s.s best 389:21
s. thee with a quiet mind 319:17
they also s. who only stand and wait 282:4
'tis enough, 'twill s. 379:32
Served: had I but s. God 460:12
Service: all s. ranks the same 77:1
goods and s.s can be paid for 295:12
make the s. greater than the god 382:5
out on active s. 238:7
pressed into s. 170:12
s. is perfect freedom 318:27
s. sweat for duty 344:31
shrink from the s. of his country 303:2
small s. is true s. 467:6
song the s. divyne 107:12
Serviette: crumpled the s.s 32:17
Serving-men: six honest s. 239:19
Servitude: base laws of s. 151:21
s. that hugs her chain 186:23
Sesame: open S. 9:24
Seson: in somer s. whan soft was the sonne 247:11
Set: here is the whole s.! 395:35
Setebos: S., S., and S.! 73:21
Setter: proud s. up 358:9
Setting: haste now to my s. 358:20
Settle: lived in S's. numbers 311:9
Settled: such things are s. nowadays 92:2
Seven: 'Nay, we are s.' 467:17
one of the S. 18:13
seventy times s. 50:32
Seventeen: grace of sweet s. 415:23
Seventy: s. times seven 50:32
s. years young 204:4
Sever: then we s. 83:23
Severe: nothing but herself s. 98:27
Severing: s. of our loves 464:18
Severity: S. breedeth fear 19:20
usual s. 118:28
Seville: dogs of S. 422:30
Sewer: life is like a s. 252:3
rides through a s. in a glass-bottomed boat 444:5
trip through a s. 283:7
Sewing: Ah Bottomley, s.? 65:18
Sex: continental people have s. life 273:9
country where men despise s. 249:20
fair s. is your department 148:2
if s. were all 406:7
insult s, to do dirt on it 249:18
is s. dirty? 4:14
literature is . . . about having s. 255:26
ruin of our s. 400:13
s. by themselves 29:9
s. is something I really don't understand 336:13
s. war ended with slaughter 14:9
s. whose presence civilizes 124:30
s. with someone you love 4:16
weaker s. 4:8
your s's. earliest, latest care 260:14
Sexes: difference within the s. 120:2
old ladies of both s. 138:15
there are three s. 399:30
Sexophones: s. wailed like melodious cats 212:28
Sexton: went and told the s. 204:24
Sextones: newest s. with princess effect 226:6
Seye: to see and eke for to be s. 108:15
Shackle: s.s fall 126:36

Shade: beneath its s. 121:9
  clutching the inviolable s. 11:27
  crowns in s.s like these 180:20
  dancing in the chequered s. 276:28
  fleeting image of a s. 394:25
  he is old and she is a s. 246:23
  I lie where s.s of darkness 134:12
  no s., no shine 204:32
  pillared s. 280:37
  sit under the shade of it 137:32
  s. and loneliness and mire 69:24
  s. of that which once was great 463:19
  s. off the trees 122:22
  s. upon thy right hand 40:32
  s.s of night were falling fast 256:23
  th'Etrurian s.s, high overarched imbower 278:13
  under the s. of melancholy 345:10
Shadow: are s.s not substantial things 396:4
  best . . . are but s.s 372:19
  falls the S. 156:16
  follow a s. 225:19
  grasping at the S. 3:17
  half sick of s.s 419:11
  hence horrible s. 366:30
  land of the s. of death 45:7
  lengthened s. of one man 159:6
  little s. that goes in and out 407:16
  outsoared the s. of our night 390:5
  possible s. of doubt 176:17
  quiet s.s falling 300:7
  s. at morning striding behind you 156:35
  s. of a dream 421:33
  s. of death 40:15, 51:43
  s. of three dead men 417:22
  s. of turning 57:20
  s.s. of the living 70:16
  s.s come out of her eyes 470:17
  s.s flee away 44:22
  s.s numberless 232:1
  s.s of the evening 25:3
  swift as a s. 371:21
  unhappy s. 97:24
  white-haired s. roaming like a dream 423:23
Shadwell: S. never deviates into sense 150:28
Shady: s. in Latin 115:12
Shaft: many a s. at random sent 340:5
Shafting: s. broken 133:7
Shaftoe: Bobby S's. gone to sea 296:7
Shaggy: s., and lean, and shrewd 127:20
Shake-scene: only S. in a country 188:3
Shaken: so s. as we are 353:15
Shakespeare, William: 151:33 187:12 219:31
    225:28 225:29
  great part of S. 175:1
  honour to S. 225:27
  I despise S. 389:13
  immortal S. rose 219:3
  making up of a S. 119:3
  might have chanced to be S. 213:9
  myriad-minded S. 118:21
  out-topping knowledge 11:31
  S. . . . grew immortal in his own despite 315:29
  S. . . . wrote of common life 96:13
  S. in your threefold 26:9
  S. led a life of allegory 234:12
  S. made use of it first 395:10
  S. never has six lines . . . without a fault 221:27

S. unlocked his heart 75:3, 463:8
S. was with us 75:18
soul of the Age! . . . my S. 225:19
sweetest S., Fancy's child 276:32
thou smilest and art still 11:31
tongue that S. spake 463:25
what needs my S. 277:28
Shalimar: pale hands I loved beside the S. 205:19
Shall: mark you his absolute 's.'? 346:27
Shallow: by s. rivers to whose falls 267:24
  s. in himself 281:10
  s. people who do not judge by appearances 456:6
Shalot: Lady of S. 419:12
Shame: ashamed with the noble s. 237:20
  bound in with s. 376:18
  each deed of s. 256:28
  glory is their s. 56:26
  God send them sorrow and s.! 397:25
  hold a candle to my s.s? 369:28
  isn't it a blooming s.? 8:16
  mine the s. 150:19
  put man's best gifts to s. 72:6
  s. that bringeth sin 48:3
  s. to their love pure 302:12
  waste of s. 387:4
Shameless: most s. thing in the world 82:20
Shamming: s. when 'e's dead 239:4
Shandon: 'tis the bell of S. 321:21
Shape: pressed out of s. 170:12
  S. of Things to Come 450:16
  such a questionable s. 348:29
  what art thou, execrable s? 279:7
Share: take your proper s. 15:15
Shark: s. has pretty teeth 67:18
Sharon: S.'s. dewy rose 196:23
Sharp: fifty different s.s and flats 76:24
  somebody's s. 137:3
Shaw, George Bernard 28:26 336:12 451:16,
    456:22
  Mr S. . . . only man . . . never written poetry
    111:1
Shay: wonderful one-hoss s. 203:22
She: chaste and unexpressive s. 345:14
  s. that shall command 128:26
  s.-who-must-be-obeyed 190:3
  you are the cruell'st s. alive 382:34
She-bear: great s., coming up the street 166:24
She-dragon: old weather-beaten s. 395:26
Shear: blind Fury with th'abhorred s.s 277:9
  mother with her . . . s.s 84:4
  pair of s.s 400:1
Sheba: another S. queen 459:2
Shed: into its narrow s. 470:7
  lowly cattle s. 4:6
  stand . . . beneath a s. while it rained 224:8
Sheep: better than s. or goats 417:20
  Bo-Peep has lost her s. 297:1
  feed my s. 53:41
  flock of s. that . . . passes by 462:31
  giveth his life for the s. 53:22
  hungry s. look up 277:14
  like lost s. 318:12
  mountain s. are sweeter 307:15
  old half-witted s. 405:2
  savaged by a dead s. 196:19
  s. before her shearers is dumb 46:9
  s. have gone astray 46:8

s. that have not a shepherd 36:21
s., that were wont to be so meek 287:19
s. which was lost 52:23
s.'s guts should hale souls 372:35
s.'s in the meadow 297:2
silly s. 126:14
with His s. securely fold you 325:18
Sheep-herding: rest is mere s. 317:26
Sheep-hook: how to hold a s. 277:13
Sheet: boy brought the white s. 172:17
  fornicate between clean s.s 170:23
  if we the s.s and leaves could turn 149:3
  prepare my winding s. 22:23
  wet s. and a flowing sea 130:9
Shelf: silence of the upper s. 262:25
Shell: that's S., that was 3:10
Shelley-Percy Bysshe 12:2 76:21
  Burns, S. were with us 75:18
  did you once see S. plain 75:28
Shelter: I'd s. thee 85:7
  s. from the stormy blast 447:23
Shelves: huddled up on the slatted s. 283:4
Shem: S. . . . short for Shemus 226:8
Shenandoah: oh, S. I long to hear you 8:7
Shepherd: every s. tells his tale 276:25
  gentle S., tell me where 211:3
  good s. giveth his life for the sheep 53:22
  King of love my S. is 21:12
  Lord is my s. 38:2
  sheep that have not a s. 36:21
  s. divideth his sheep 51:16
  s., from the hill 11:20
  s.s looking on their silly sheep 358:8
  what lady would not love a s. swain? 188:2
  while s.s watched their flocks 414:18
  woe to the idle s. 47:23
Shepherdess: s. of sheep 272:31
Sheridan: S. was listened to 328:27
Sherry: fond of brown s. 110:26
  s. . . . a sickly compound 65:14
Shield: our S. and Defender 184:16
  trusty s. and weapon 260:3
Shieling: lone s. of the misty island 341:11
Shift: coming down let me s. for myself 287:23
  they put you on the day s. 153:9
Shilling: gladly give ten s.s 188:18
  if you'll only take the s. 458:18
  Philip and Mary on a s. 87:25
  rather than forty s.s 371:3
  s. a day 240:20
  s. life will give you all the facts 15:18
  Splendid S. 308:13
Shimmering: s. into rooms 459:16
Shimmy: put thy s. on 249:14
Shin: cover a mutitude of s.s 451:10
  till I break my s.s against it 344:36
Shine: not s. in use 424:5
  s. by the side of every path 127:29
  s. here to us 146:13
Shingle: naked s.s of the world 10:21
Ship: all I ask is a tall s. 270:2
  being in a s. is being in a jail 221:2
  born in a s. 11:7
  build a bonny s. 22:24
  down to the sea in s.s 40:17
  gallant s. in twain 22:14
  I spied three s.s come sailing by 7:5

idle as a painted s. 116:27
land to which your s. must go 463:5
like a stately s. 281:24
mighty s.s ten thousand ton 202:16
old s.s sail like swans asleep 166:8
rapt s. run on her side 106:13
s. I have got in the North Country 22:19
s. is floating in the harbour 390:26
S. of State 256:13
s. on the sea 173:4
s. was cheered 116:21
s. was still as she could be 401:16
s.s and stars and isles 166:2
s.s are but boards 369:12
s.s are covered with fairy lights 460:16
s.s that pass in the night 257:17
sink me the s., Master Gunner 423:2
so old a s. 166:9
something wrong with our bloody s.s today 27:12
stately s.s are twirled and spun 202:16
that ever scuttled s. 91:19
they may build their s.s 263:13
Thracian s.s 411:32
watch the s.s of England go! 238:20
way of a s. in the midst of the sea 43:8
we've got the s.s 212:9
whale s. was my Yale College 271:19
what is a s. but a prison? 86:14
whither, O splendid s. 68:7
Ship-boy: seal up the s.' eyes 355:31
Shipwreck: s. of my ill-adventured youth 131:10
Shire: calling for them from sad s.s 302:8
  round both the s.s they ring them 210:14
  s.s and towns from Airly Beacon 237:12
Shirt: no s. or collar ever comes back twice 250:11
Shit: some s. I will not eat 130:6
Shoal: s. of fools 120:24
Shock: Future S. 430:16
  thousand natural s.s 350:14
Shocking: something very s. indeed 16:31
Shoe: buckle my s. 297:16
  call for his old s.s 342:1
  he stood in his s.s 232:17
  her s.s were number nine 286:9
  left-hand s. 102:19
  old woman who lived in a s. 298:5
  over Edom will I cast my s. 39:4
  sailed off in a wooden s. 162:14
  s.s and ships and sealing-wax 102:5
  s.s were on their feet 398:21
  take my s.s from the shoemaker 183:1
  want of a s. 168:21
  wear wooden s.s 182:3
  your s.s on your feet 34:48
Shoemaker: brave s.s 134:4
Shoeshine: riding on a smile and a s. 273:25
Shone: far off his coming s. 280:17
  he s. bright 116:22
Shoon: silver s. 134:26
Shoot: up and s. themselves 69:15
Shooting-star: s.s attend thee 200:9
Shop: because a man has s. to mind 78:20
  rag-and-bone s. of the heart 470:9
  shun the awful s. 110:16
  then I will close the s. 432:18
Shopkeepers: nation of s. 1:7, 291:21 398:17
Shore: adieu! my native s. 89:12

control stops with the s. 90:20
desolate s.s 233:4
England . . . whose rocky s. beats back 376:18
fast by their native s. 125:33
meet on that beautiful s. 337:8
on the s. . . . I stand alone 233:12
over some wide-watered s. 276:8
possess these s.s with me 131:12
round earth's s. lay 10:21
s. of the sounding sea 204:8
that peaceful s. 126:5
unknown and silent s. 245:4
when many leave these s.s 302:13
yearning for the other s. 440:28
Shoreditch: say the bells of S. 297:18
Short: but a s. time 58:21
  find it my song wondrous s. 182:33
  where he falls s. 112:2
Shorter: s. by a head 157:23
Shortest: s. works are always the best 244:22
Shortness: spend that s. basely 355:3
Shot: long s., Watson 147:27
  s. heard round the world 158:12
Shoulder: borne on our s.s 74:27
  giant's s. to mount on 118:23
  one tapped my s. 14:7
  reading over my s. 185:9
  standing on the s.s of giants 294:7
  their s.s held the skies suspended 210:2
Shouldn't: it's not 'cause I s. 317:1
Shoures: after sharpest s. 247:15
Shout: ceased the inhuman s. 90:15
  s. about my ears 110:5
  s. that tore hell's concave 278:18
  s. with the largest 140:25
  s.s and plaudits of the throng 257:1
Shovel: two boys that S. 25:26
Show: greatest S. on Earth 25:14
  I think of it . . . as a s. 193:10
  No Business Like S. Business 32:8
  s. and gaze o' the time 368:1
  what do you think of the s. so far? 287:24
  within which passeth s. 347:35
Shower: coming s. 410:5
  drainless s. of light 232:15
  fresh s.s for the thirsting flowers 390:13
  small s.s last long 376:16
  sweet April s.s 433:21
  walked abroad in a s. of all my days 426:11
Showery: S., Flowery, Bowery 158:5
Shred: king of s.s and patches 351:31
  thing of s.s and patches 177:16
Shriek: not louder s.s 315:24
Shrieking: s. and squeaking 76:24
Shrimp: s. of an author 187:19
Shrine: honour the s. where you alone are placed 188:9
  open the s. . . . see my saint 225:10
  silence of the s. 83:16
Shriving-time: not s. allowed 353:5
Shroud: comes to s. me 145:6
  my s. of white, stuck all with yew 383:13
Shun: s. what I follow 77:19
  thought he would s. me 27:9
Shuttle: each throwing his s. 75:25
  man is the s. 438:2
  swifter than a weaver's s. 36:41

Shy: we are not s. 177:25
Sick: created s., commanded to be sound 188:12
  hired to watch the s. 126:31
  I am s., I must die 292:20
  made him deathly s. 2:25
  more than a little s. 238:18
  most of the time we think we're s. 460:7
  nothing but to make him s. 144:25
  s. in soul and body both 202:13
  s. man – a seriously s. man on our hands 294:12
  s. men play so nicely 376:19
  they that are s. 49:33
Sickle: bending s's. compass 387:1
  s. in his hand 257:11
  with his s. keen 257:7
Sicklemen: sun-burned s. 381:9
Sickness: falling s. 359:21
  in s. and in health 319:42
  love is a s. full of woes 131:7
  s. enlarges the dimensions 246:1
  stand convicted of s. 400:12
Sidcup: get down to S. 309:9
Side: fell upon the buttered s. 205:6
  hear the other s. 16:5
  measured it from s. to s. 467:1
  much might be said on both s.s 2:8
  only his own s. of the case 273:12
  sat, s. by s. 60:1
  shifting his side 126:18
  to go by thy s. 5:9
  washes its wall on the southern s. 76:22
  windy s. of the law 383:27
Sidera: sublimi feriam s. vertice 208:2
Sidney: S.'s. self, the starry paladin 78:28
Siege: will laughs a s. to scorn 367:22
Sieve: in a s. they went to sea 250:21
  went to sea in a s. 250:22
Sigh: all made of s.s and tears 346:10
  freedom with a s. 93:19
  hear them s. and wish to die 175:7
  perhaps 'twill cost a s. 24:4
  prompts th'eternal s. 314:7
  s. is the sword of an angel king 61:3
  s. no more, ladies 372:36
  s.s . . . the natural language of the heart 342:30
  some a light s. 28:22
  telling this with a s. 170:11
  took her with a s. 61:14
  world of s.s 374:6
Sighed: no sooner s. but they asked 346:8
  s. and looked and s. again 150:5
  when I . . . saw the dawn, I s. for thee 394:14
Sighing: sorrow and s. shall flee away 45:25
Sight: few more impressive s.s 26:3
  full of ugly s.s 377:30
  hide them from my aching s. 17:21
  keen discriminating s. 98:15
  lost to s., to mem'ry dear 255:6
  love of other s.s controls 145:10
  loved not at first s. 267:22
  many a vanished s. 385:24
  never admit to your s. 17:13
  one who from thy s., being, ah! exiled 396:18
  s. so touching in its majesty 463:10
  s. to dream of 117:21
  s. to make an old man young 416:20
  s.s before the dark of reason grows 33:1

when you s., I'd have you buy and sell so 384:30
whilst thus I s. 114:6
Singeing: s. of the King of Spain's beard 148:10
Singer: German s.! 169:4
idle s. of an empty day 288:10
none hear beside the s. 247:1
s.s went before 39:17
there lived a s. in France 413:6
Singing: delight in s. 247:1
everyone suddenly burst out s. 337:30
s. in the rain 169:5
s. still dost soar 394:18
s. will never be done 338:1
sweet s. in the choir 7:25
Singing-boys: six little s. 24:9
Single: continued s. 182:24
nothing in the world is s. 391:27
Singularity: s. is . . . a clue 147:13
Sink: it s.s and I am ready to depart 246:25
pour them down the s. 110:23
Sinking: alacrity in s. 371:12
someone is s. today 435:5
Sinner: be a s. and strong in your sins 260:1
be merciful to me a s. 52:38
God and s.s reconciled 450:20
make . . . I of her a s. 121:8
miserable s.s 319:1
once for favoured s.s slain 450:24
one s. that repenteth 52:24
po' s.s'll be kotched out 194:20
s.s must with devils dwell 447:9
s.s plunged beneath that flood 125:26
why do s.'s ways prosper? 206:17
Sinning: man more sinned against than s. 362:19
Sipped: how here he s. 311:11
Sire: bequeathed by bleeding S. to Son 93:2
land of my s.s 340:2
thy s. was a knight 340:7
Siren: blest pair of S.s 275:2
S. waits thee 247:3
Sisera: fought against S. 35:25
Sister: all the S.s virtuous 293:23
barren s. all your life 371:17
had it been his s. 6:2
his s.s, and his cousins, and his aunts! 176:28
I kissed her little s. 286:10
ministering angel shall my s. be 352:31
never praise a s. to a s. 241:24
no friend like a s. 331:4
say, my heart's s. 390:26
s.s under their skins 239:26
sphere-born harmonious s.s 275:2
still gentler s. woman 83:21
twa s.s sat in a bour 22:6
we have a little s. 44:29
weird s.s 367:3
will the veiled s. pray 155:28
Sisyphus: imagine S. happy 98:8
Sit: s. down, man 271:8
s. down, says love 199:19
though I s. down now 142:22
when they s. down 112:9
Sitting: are you s. comfortably? 247:9
Situation: interesting s.s 16:25
s. excellent 166:22
Six: life is s. to five against 333:2
s. of one and half-a-dozen of another 268:6

Sixpence: *bang* – went s. 322:9
could have saved s. 28:9
found a crooked s. 298:4
he'll give him s. 67:14
I love s. 296:27
I only got s. 322:13
precious little for s. 322:8
sing a song of s. 297:31
s. in her shoe 122:9
S.! I will see thee damned first 98:13
Sixteen: no age between s. and three-and-twenty 384:19
Sixty-four: when I'm s. 253:16
Skein: life's tangled s. 176:19
Sketcher: race of s.s 65:14
Skies: change their s. but not their souls 207:20
man whose god is the s. 388:31
paint the sable s. 149:2
s. are not cloudy all day 201:7
s. they were ashen and sober 310:30
Skill: sharpens our s. 82:23
Thy Power brings all s. to naught 239:36
Skimble-skamble: s. stuff 354:26
Skin: apostolic s. 94:2
be it known to s. and bone 88:27
beauty of their s.s 422:10
girt with rough s.s 149:1
Got You Under My S. 316:28
judged by the colour of their s. 237:9
made them with the s. side outside 5:22
my s. bristles 210:35
scar that whiter s. of hers 375:21
s. for s. 36:35
s. hangs about me 354:31
s. of my teeth 37:3
Skin-deep: colours, that are but s. 198:8
Skinning: eels get used to s. 112:21
Skipper: s. had taken his daughter 257:22
Skirt: lay aside her modesty with her s. 285:9
Skittles: beer and s. 96:3
Skugg: S. lies snug 168:18
Skull: empty s. 111:27
s. beneath the skin 157:10
s. which thou hast made 417:24
some lay in dead men's s.s 378:1
Skuttle fish: put me in mind of the s. 2:18
Sky: bed of daffodil s. 420:33
blue s. bends over all 117:22
clear blue s. above my head 196:5
inverted Bowl we call the S. 164:21
lonely sea and the s. 270:2
out of the s. 263:11
ring out, wild bells, to the wild s. 418:22
sent him down the s. 123:2
s. grows darker yet 109:27
since first our s. was overcast 127:34
sings about the s. 91:35
stared into the s. 202:17
true as the s. 239:29
twelve-winded s. 210:23
vaulted s. 114:28
Skye: beyond the Isle of S. 22:4
over the sea to S. 65:20, 407:26
Skylark: s. wounded in the wing 60:11
Slab: beneath the cold s. 92:35
beneath this s. 292:9
Slain: he can never do that's s. 87:27

my love is s., I saw him go 144:24
s. thinks he is s. 158:9
thrice he slew the s. 150:2
Slander: civic s. 418:27
secondarily, they are s.s 373:24
speak no s. 416:31
Slang: s. . . . rolls up its sleeves 337:6
Slant: certain s. of light 142:9
Slaughter: as an ox goeth to the s. 41:29
brought to the s. 46:28
threatenings and s. 53:45
Slave: at the mill with s.s 281:15
base is the s. that pays 356:29
being your s. 385:31
Britons never will be s.s 428:5
certain s.s . . . preached him and Christ 73:33
creed of s.s 309:20
freedom to the s. 254:16
here I stand, your s. 362:16
him who is the s. of thee 394:27
rogue and peasant s. am I 350:8
ruling them like s.s 393:16
s. of words 100:9
s. to thousands 374:31
s.s cannot breathe 126:36
s.s of some defunct economist 236:14
s.s of the lamp 10:17
sleep so soundly as the wretched s. 357:13
those poor s.s 390:25
two s.s making in all two 59:14
Slavery: classified as s. 112:8
s. of the tea and coffee 115:27
s. they can have anywhere 81:22
Slayer: red s. thinks he slays 158:9
who considers this is a s. 33:10
Sleek-headed: s. men and such as sleep 359:18
Sleep: all be as before, Love, – only s. 79:11
as one out of s. 39:24
balmy s. 472:18
be but to s. and feed 351:41
birth is but a s. 464:7
care-charmed s. 131:10
care-charming S. 28:7
come s.! O s. 396:14
come to the borders of s. 426:27
Death and his brother S.! 390:18
deep and dreamless s. 70:2
exposition of s. 372:9
fields of s. 464:5
first sweet s. of night 391:11
full of s. 472:4
get some s. 257:27
giveth his beloved s. 41:2, 72:2
good night's s. 458:8
great gift of s. 198:1
heard a voice cry, 'S. no more!' 365:26
I s. but my heart waketh 44:24
in s. a king 386:15
in s. had fallen on you 392:2
let them s. 145:17
little s., a little slumber 41:27
medicine thee to that sweet s. 375:3
now I lay me down to s. 6:13
O gentle s.! 355:30
oh s.! it is a gentle thing 117:7
shake off this downy s. 366:4
short s. past 145:19

six hours in s. 116:12
s. after toil 402:30
S., Death's twin brother 418:14
s. is a death 71:15
s. is good 197:5
s, my pretty one 421:38
s., O s., my dearest boy 214:18
s. of a labouring man is sweet 43:25
s. of death 61:5
s. shall neither night nor day 364:14
s. that is is among the lonely hills 466:24
s. the s. of the earth 439:18
s. the s. that knows not breaking 339:19
s. to wake 74:16
someone else's s. 15:28
straightfaced in his cunning s. 426:20
then s. dear 28:20
they s. and it is lifted 393:14
thy sweet child S. 394:15
to s.; perchance to dream 350:14
unseasonable and immoderate s. 219:28
vision between a s. and a s. 412:6
wake to s. 328:18
weighs heavily . . . like unwilling s. 233:5
what has night to do with s.? 275:7
when we s. we are awake, and when we wake we
s. 285:17
where s.s she now? 134:28
will not let you s. 23:22
your little life is rounded with a s. 381:10
Sleeper: goodly men and the sun-hazed s. 427:24
s.s in that quiet earth 69:5
Sleeping: all this fuss about s. together 448:16
s. when she died 204:20
wakened us from s. 69:17
Sleepless: yet do lie S.! 462:31
Sleepwalker: assurance of a s. 201:18
Sleepy-head: let's to bed, says S. 296:11
Sleet: through s. and snow 192:23
Sleeve: Americanism with it s.s rolled 263:4
brush the Channel with his s. 338:18
slang . . . rolls up its s.s 337:6
wear my heart upon my s. 373:32
Slenderly: fashioned so s. 204:19
Slept: he s. with his fathers 36:14
Slides: s. . . . will now be shown 226:28
Slimy: s. things did crawl 116:29
Sling: s.s and arrows of outrageous fortune 350:14
Slipper: golden s.s in the sunshine 80:27
same old s.s 246:20
Slop-kettle: other s. 115:27
Sloth: s. finds the down pillow hard 347:12
shake off dull s. 235:8
time in studies is s. 20:30
Slothful: s. man saith 42:42
Slough: come, friendly bombs, and fall on S. 32:23
name of the s. was Despond 80:16
Slovenliness: s. is no part of religion 4450:28
Slow: ain't it s.? 198:29
s. and steady wins the race 255:13
s. to speak 57:21
tarry a while, says S. 296:11
too swift arrives as tardy as too s. 379:28
were he reckoned s. 67:29
wisely and s. 379:23
Slug: s.s that come crawling out after a shower
24:15

Slug-horn: s. to my lips I set 73:29
Sluggard: foul s's. comfort 99:13
  go to the ant, thou s. 41:26
  s. is wiser in his own conceit 42:43
  voice of the s. 447:22
Slum: swear-word in a rustic s. 29:4
Slumber: affected s. more 97:28
  equal quantity of s. 139:30
  ere s's. chain has bound me 287:14
  golden s.s kiss your eyes 134:3
  hast thou golden s.s? 133:21
  he that keepeth thee will not s. 40:31
  infant's s.s, pure and light 234:25
  lie still and s. 447:15
  ports of s. 356:11
  s. did my spirit seal 466:19
  s. is more sweet than toil 420:19
  soothing s. seven 224:19
Slut: foul s.s in dairies 122:9
  I am not a s. 345:27
Sly: devilish s. 137:29
Small: day of s. things 47:21
  is it so s. a thing 10:23
  S. is Beautiful 339:7
  s. laws 111:9
Smart: as lief pray with Kit S. 221:6
  love and all its s. 28:20
Smartness: s. of an attorney's clerk 144:3
Smattering: s. of everything 141:25
Smelfungus: the learned S. 405:9
Smell: measured out by sounds and s.s 33:1
  rankest compound of villanous s. 371:14
  sweet keen s. 332:1
  very ancient and fish-like s. 380:40
Smile: charm it with s.s 102:25
  coined my cheek to s.s 90:3
  eternal s.s his emptiness betray 312:26
  good gigantic s. 75:9
  kind of sickly s. 194:28
  one very substantial s. 137:1
  peculiar sweet s. 425:8
  robbed that s.s steals something 374:8
  same kind, beaming s. 25:18
  seldom he s.s 359:20
  should forget and s. 331:7
  s. at perils past 339:13
  s. at us 110:15
  s. I could feel in my hip pocket 106:5
  s. on her lips 340:13
  s. on the face of the tiger 6:15
  s. out; but still suffer 192:17
  s. s. s. 13:8
  s. that glowed 280:28
  s. that was childlike and bland 194:24
  s. we would aspire to 358:22
  s.s awake you 134:3
  s.s before they dwindle 393:11
  s.s of other maidens 116:16
  s.s, the tears of boyhood's years 287:14
  society protecting itself with a s. 320:13
  vain tribute of a s. 339:28
Smiled: Never S. Again 197:15
  until she s. on me 116:15
Smiling: when you're s. the whole world 183:16
Smirk: serious and the s. 139:13
Smite: Christian up and s. them 292:25
  stands ready to s. 277:15

Smith: chuck it, S.! 109:25
  first s. 127:23
  s. a mighty man is he 257:19
  Wicked Captain S. 119:29
Smithy: s. of my soul 226:19
  village s. stands 257:19
Smitten: one be s. against the other 48:11
Smock: pale as thy s. 375:25
Smok: whan she cast of her s. 108:16
Smoke: as s. is driven away 39:13
  little s., in pallid moonshine 230:16
  s. and stir of this dim plot 275:4
  S. Gets in Your Eyes 192:2
  that stinking s. 216:7
Smooth: so large, and s., and round 401:8
  speak unto us s. things 45:18
Smoothness: turns earth's s. rough 77:13
Smote: s. him with the edge of the sword 35:9
Smyler: s. with the knyf under the cloke 108:3
Snaffle: use the s. and the bit 96:23
Snail: creeping like s. 345:11
Snake: like a wounded s. 313:13
  s. came to my water-trough 249:3
  s. is living yet 31:1
  s. lurks in the grass 441:14
  scotched the s. 366:14
  spotted s.s with double tongue 371:39
Snapper-up: s. of unconsidered trifles 384:24
Snare: deliver thee from the s. 39:35
  mockery, and a s. 134:34
Snark: S. was a Boojum 102:27
Sneer: teach the rest to s. 312:22
Sneering: born s. 177:18
Sneeze: beat him when he s.s 101:3
  like having a good s. 249:23
Sneezed: not to be s. at 119:24
Snewed: s. in his house of mete and drinke 107:22
Snicker: hold my coat and s. 156:24
Snickersnee: drew my s.! 177:30
Snip: S.! Snap! S.! 203:6
Snob: not to be sometimes a s. 425:2
Snow: deep s. piled above thee 69:3
  fall o' the s. 225:13
  farewel al the s. 108:28
  half-buried in the s. 256:26
  Hollywood money . . . congealed s. 304:12
  like S. upon the Desert's dusty face 164:4
  like the s. falls 85:18
  long last streak of s. 418:32
  mockery king of s. 377:13
  near under the s. 455:3
  pure as s. 350:18
  s. came flying 67:30
  s. had fallen, s. on s. 331:5
  s. hath retreated 467:18
  s. in winter 96:18
  s. lay round about 292:27
  s.s are sparkling to the moon 423:7
  s.s have fled 209:9
  stifling s. 76:14
  untrodden s. 97:6
  wallow naked in December s. 376:15
  we shall have s. 297:11
  where are last year's s.s? 439:23
  where the s. lay dinted 292:30
  white as driven s. 384:32
  whiter than s. 38:30

Somebody: everyone is s. 176:25
   happening to s. else 329:6
   how dreary to be s.! 142:3
Someone: next morning . . . it was s. else 329:1
Someres: mery s. day: 108:23
Something: do s. or other well 446:27
   now for s. completely different 286:14
   s. attempted, s. done 257:21
   s. in us that can be without us 71:2
   s. must be done 154:11
   s. very like him 115:18
   s. will come of this 136:15
   time for a little s. 274:31
   you do s. . . . then somebody else . . . does it
      pretty 308:22
Sommeil: s. de la terre 439:18
Somni: sunt geminae S. 441:1
Son: duke's s. 238:8
   every wise man's s. doth know 383:2
   he that spareth his rod spoileth his s. 42:7
   horny-handed s.s of toil 230:3
   if his s. ask bread 49:23
   if I had a thousand s.s 356:10
   Jesus Christ his only S. our Lord 318:24
   my father's s. 104:19
   my little s., who looked from thoughtful eyes
      306:2
   my s. – and what's a s.? 242:22
   O Absalom, my s. my s. 36:9
   obeyed as a s. 175:10
   only begotten S. 53:8
   only s. . . . might expect more indulgence 182:9
   only son of his mother 52:8
   renounce me as a s. 175:8
   s. and heir of a mongrel bitch 362:6
   s. of a gun 96:1
   s. of man, can these bones live? 46:37
   S. of man hath not where to lay his head 49:31
   s. of man, set thy face against Gog 46:39
   s.s of bitches 131:4
   s.s of God shouted for joy 37:11
   third among the s.s of light 389:24
   this is my s. 424:7
   thy s.s acclaim your glorious name 130:3
   two-legged thing, a s. 149:12
   unto us a s. is given 45:8
   virgin shall conceive, and bear a s. 45:4
   wise s. maketh a glad father 41:32
   your s.s and your daughters 47:12
Song: all their s.s are sad 109:28
   all this for a s.? 83:7
   any little old s. 192:12
   better the world with a s. 269:26
   breeze of s. 418:17
   cannot sing the old s.s 95:18
   death could drop . . . easily as a s. 330:21
   frame my s. 109:22
   glorious s. of old 341:16
   it may turn out a s. 84:15
   joyful s. I'll raise 2.12
   lark becomes a sightless s. 418:33
   lean and flashy s.s 277:14
   let the s. of praise be sung 317:4
   listen . . . to the wind's text, . . . or the thrush's s.
      427:7
   Lord's s. in a strange land 41:10
   low lone s. 100:26

make new s.s 124:8
may I commence my s. 77:30
metre of an antique s. 385:16
mother of immortal s. 206:19
music-hall s.s provide the dull with wit
   271:1
my s.s she will not hear 413:3
never heard the old s. of Percy and Douglas
   396:21
new s.'s measure 301:16
On Wings of S. 197:1
one grand sweet s. 237:13
one s. for the old Kentucky home 168:5
perhaps the self-same s. 232:7
sing no sad s.s for me 331:11
sing unto the Lord a new s. 40:7
singing s. for s. 247:3
sings a solitary s. 462:27
s., from beginning to end 256:9
s. is ended 32:11
s. of a lad that is gone 407:26
s. was wordless 338:1
sing unto him a new s. 38:12
s.s of Araby 457:24
still govern thou my s. 280:19
subject for heroic s. 280:30
summer s.s for me and my aunts 384:23
sweet Thames! run softly, till I end my s.
   403:12
sweetest s. ever heard 93:18
sweetest s.s are those . . . of saddest thought
   394:21
teach in s. 391:15
that was the s. – the s. for me 463:29
to make s.s 31:7
with the s.s they have sung 191:13
wrote my happy s.s 62:8
wrote one s. 76:13
ye learn your s. 68:5
Song-bird: my own sweet little s. 214:5
Sonne: up roos the s. 108:4
   whan soft was the s. 247:11
Sonne: S. geht in meinem Staat nicht unter 338:12
Sonnet: Book of Songs and S.s 371:3
   lovers' s.s turned to holy psalms 307:1
   only begetter of these insuing s.s 385:10
   scorn not the S. 463:8
   s. is a moment's monument 331:20
   s's. scanty plot of ground 462:30
   turned to a s. 144:7
   written s.s all his life 91:16
Sonnette: qui pendra la s. au chat? 135:14
Sonny: S. Boy 70:9
Sooner: s. it's over, the s. to sleep 237:19
Sooth: it is silly s. 383:12
Sophisters: s. economists and calculators 82:13
Sophocles: 12:8
Sophonisba: Oh! S.! S.! Oh! 428:15
Soporific: effect of eating too much lettuce is s.
   317:9
Sordello: can be but one 'S.' 317:15
   has heard S.'s story told 78:31
   may hear S.'s story told 78:27
Sore: s. with loving her 137:36
Sorrel: growth of meadow-sweet or s. 412:7
Sorrow: bear the s. of this world 306:6
   beguile thy s. 381:29

doubt and s. 25:5
eat the bread of s.s 41:2
ere the s. comes with years 71:26
few s.s, however poignant 399:7
give s. words 367:8
glut thy s. on a morning rose 231:28
guttural s. of the refugees 264:13
he that begetteth a fool doeth it to his s.
    42:19
I and s. sit 361:14
in s. thou shalt bring forth children 34:3
losses are restored and s.s end 385:25
man of s.s 46:7
more in s. than in anger 348:14
mused on s. 97:14
my heart hath 'scaped this s. 386:16
no s. in thy song 256:6
not sure of s. 412:19
nought but vast s. 134:15
O S. why dost borrow 230:9
O S., wilt thou live with me 418:13
parting is such sweet s. 379:21
pine with fear and s. 403:9
pure and complete s. 431:7
regions of s. 278:5
rooted s. 367:19
sit by the fireside with S. 394:10
solitary s. best befits 230:30
s. and sighing shall flee away 45:25
s. and silence are strong 256:22
s. in thy song 79:17
s. like unto my sorrow 46:31
s. makes us wise 418:31
s. never comes too late 187:6
s. of your changing face 472:5
s.'s most detested fruit 89:26
sphere of our s. 394:8
text for s. 133:7
thou climbing s.! 362:10
to S. I bade good-morrow 230:10
travail and s. 412:4
wear a golden s. 358:16
whatever crazy s. saith 423:34
when s.s come 352:9
write s. on the bosom of the earth 377:1
Sorrowful: he went away s. 50:37
Sorry: having to say you're s. 341:26
Sort: people who like this s. of thing 255:1
Sosostris: Madame S., famous clairvoyante
    156:36
Sot: s. savant est s. plus qu'un s. ignorant 283:17
s. trouve toujours un plus s. 64:12
Souffrances: majesté des s. humaines 439:17
Souffrir: plutôt s. que mourir 244:2
Soul: ages past the s. existed 74:1
    awake, my s. 235:8
    be swift, my s. 211:5
    breadth and height my s. can reach 72:7
    call upon my s. within the house 382:36
    catch my flying s. 312:12
    conceived and composed in the s. 12:26
    desire accomplished is sweet to the s. 42:6
    distinct from his s. 63:5
    division 'tween our s.s 360:34
    do the deed that my own s. . . . itself decreed
    232:14
    embodied s. passes through childhood 33:9

everyone is single, as a s. never 200:25
fiery s. 149:10
flow of s. 315:28
force his s. so to his own conceit 350:8
gave . . . his pure s. unto his captain Christ 377:8
Go, S., the body's guest 325:7
hale s.s out of men's bodies 372:35
hang there like fruit, my s. 347:18
harrow up thy s. 349:1
have ye s.s in heaven too? 230:4
he that hides a dark s. 275:18
hurl my s. from heaven 375:25
I am positive I have a s. 405:13
I pray the Lord my s. to keep 6:13
invite my s. 453:24
large a s. as the next man 105:9
largest and most comprehensive s. 151:33
lay thou thy s. full in her hands 333:19
leaves s. free a little 72:27
let every s. be subject unto the higher powers
    54:40
lie in the S. is a true lie 225:34
little s. . . . companion of the body 190:2
little s. for a little bears up 412:29
lose his own s. 50:26, 51:36
man, with s. so dead 339:31
man became a living s. 33:19
merry old s. 297:14
most offending s. alive 357:16
mount, mount my s. 377:19
my s. doth magnify the Lord 51:42
my s. into the boughs does glide 26:22
my s. is an enchanted boat 393:12
my s., revolving hopeless strife 67:24
never once possess our s. 11:36
nor s. helps flesh more 77:16
O my prophetic s.! 349:5
out of his bitter s. 472:3
parting s. 128:18
poetry . . . enters into one's s. 233:28
poor s., the centre of my . . . earth 387:8
possess ye your s.s 52:42
poverty of s., impossible 285:23
prepare thy s. for temptation 48:1
prophetic s. of the wide world 386:26
rapt s. sitting in thine eyes 276:4
repent it from my very s. 381:31
restless s. is driven abroad to roam 398:22
single s. does fence 268:17
sleepless s. that perished 466:2
so panteth my s. after thee 38:21
soft intercourse from s. to s. 312:8
s. clap its hands 471:19
s. hath been alone 117:14
s. is dead that slumbers 257:2
s. is in a ferment, the character undecided 230:5
s. is marching on 190:12
s. is satisfied with what is assigned to him 16:18
s., like to a ship 449:5
s. looked down from a vague height 302:14
s. of my s. 77:10
s. of the Age! 225:21
s. wears out the breast 93:21
s.s exult 61:6
s.s mounting up to God 331:18
s.s of poets dead and gone 231:17
sucks two s.s 144:28

this night thy s. shall be required 52:17
thou art a s. in bliss 363:5
through such s.s alone 78:5
thy s. sail leagues and leagues 331:22
thy s. was like a star 463:24
tumult of the s. 462:9
two s.s with but a single thought 258:16
unconquerable s. 197:24
unction to your s. 351:33
virtuous s.s for life 91:42
vulgar flight of common s.s 290:4
waking s.s 145:9
what of s. was left 79:3
whither goest the s. 64:4
whom shall my s. believe? 77:19
whose s. was sad 178:21
will to do, s. to dare 339:17
winders to my s. 446:3
windows of the s. 60:25
Soul-making: 'The Vale of S.' 234:13
Soul-sides: boasts two s. 76:12
Soulage: souvent on les s. 122:17
Sound: articulate sweet s.s together 470:3
concord of sweet s.s 370:22
from the tombs a doleful s. 447:16
full of s. and fury 367:24
heal the blows of s. 203:26
measured out by s.s 33:1
not many s.s in life 245:30
o'er my ear like the sweet s. 382:23
s. must seem an echo 313:14
sighing s., the lights around the shore
   332:1
something direful in the s. 16:29
s.s will take care of themselves 101:11
Soup: s of the evening, beautiful s. 101:20
take the s. away 202:23
Soupe: je vis de bonne s. 283:15
Sour: grapes are s. 3:19
Source: sacred s. of sympathetic tears 187:13
Souris! elle accoucha d'une s. 244:14
South: Alas! for the S. 121:28
fierce and fickle is the S. 422:7
go s. in winter 156:34
heard the S. sing 132:15
South-wind: s. strengthens to a gale 68:2
Southey, Robert 94:6
Souvenirs: j'ai plus de s. 26:17
Sovereign: Anointed s. of sighs and groans 363:27
bandy civilities with my S. 221:23
change for a s. 139:20
Magna Charta . . . will have no s. 116:10
when I forget my s., 429:25
Sovereyntee: wommen desyren to have s. 108:17
Sow: s. by the right ear 198:7
s. that was washed 57:37
walk before thee like a s. 355:13
Soweth: whatsoever a man s. 56:12
Space: between dark and dark – a shining s.
   185:10
clears a s. for us 321:10
here is my s. 343:16
more s. where nobody is than where anybody is
   404:16
mourn a s. 145:17
myself a king of infinite s. 349:34
order of time and s. 118:18

s. and time 311:5
s. of life between 230:5
s.s in your togetherness 175:26
Spaceship: S. Earth 170:26
Spade: 'let S.s be trumps!' 315:22
never seen a s. 455:20
s.s, the emblem of untimely graves 127:16
Spain: devildoms of S. 422:27
not left to S. 422:28
slow old tunes of S. 269:22
Span: flung the s. on even wing 128:15
less than a s. 21:3
skies in a s. 110:11
world's riches contract into a s. 199:20
Spaniards: S. seem wiser than they are 20:11
thrash the S. too 148:9
Spanish: fair S. ladies 7:14:
speak S. to God 107:2
taken by a S. Ga-la-lee 22:19
Spare: s. all I have 161:21
Spark: as the s.s. fly upward 36:40
nor human s. is left 311:29
oh! illustrious s. 126:1
s. from heaven 11:24
s. o' Nature's fire 84:13
s.s blown out of a smithy 471:24
s.s of fire befriend thee 200:9
vital s. of heav'nly flame! 311:30
Sparrer-grass: hit look like s. 194:10
Sparrow: brawling of a s. 471:28
I, said the Sparrow 298:18
mistress's s. is dead 103:9
old king to the s. 134:27
providence in the fall of a s. 353:8
s. alone upon the house-top 40:9
s.s' good-night twitter 75:20
swift flight of a lone s. 28:23
two s.s sold for a farthing 49:41
Sparrowhawks: s. Ma'am 449:24
Spartans: go, tell the S. 397:10
Speak: all men shall s. well of you 52:7
did he s. to you again? 75:28
let him now s. 319:40
never s.s well of me 120:16
not s. of oneself at all 248:9
now s., or be for ever silent 270:9
s. for England 4:22
s. for yourself, John 256:17
s. one moment before they think 243:13
s. softly and carry a big stick 330:3
'tis mine to s., and yours to hear 399:3
whereof one cannot s. 459:8
will s. more in a minute 379:26
Speaking: pure innocence persuades when s. fails
   384:15
when they are s. 112:9
Spear: burning s. 5:19
cutteth the s. in sunder 38:25
ever put s. in the rest 265:23
hinder end of the s. 36:4
sheen of their s.s 93:4
they shall beat . . . their s.s into pruning-hooks
   44:33
Spear-men: stubborn s. still made good 340:21
Spearmint: Does the S. Lose Its Flavour 330:15
Specatcle: s. unto the world 55:3
Specialist: other men are s.s 147:20

Specializing: s. in the Universe 122:4
Species: examine, not the individual but the s. 220:5
    human s. . . . is composed of two . . . races 245:27
    not an individual, but a s. 162:25
    than as one of the s. 2:2
Specimen: s.s of both 143:31
Spectacle: not a s. or a feast 337:15
    s.s lay on her aproned knees 95:15
Spectator: as a s. of mankind 2:2
    bear-baiting . . . gave pleasure to the s.s 262:17
Spectre: my S. round me night and day 61:12
    s. is haunting Europe 269:13
Spectre: où le s. . . . raccroche la passant! 26.16
Speculation: everybody else that watches a s. 138:29
    fine subject for s.! 95:13
    no s. in those eyes 366:28
Speculator: raised by a s. 408:12
Speech: day unto day uttereth s. 37:36
    freedom of s. and expression 329:23
    he gave man s. 393:8
    I am slow of s. 34:44
    let thy s. be short 48:19
    let your s. be alway with grace 56:33
    make your s. afterwards 244:3
    perfect plainness of s. 13:4
    rude am I in my s. 373:41
    s. is shallow as time 99:19
    s. is the small change of silence 272:25
    s. was given to man 414:12
    speak the s., I pray you 350:23
    strange power of s. 117:13
Speeches: gets his s. by it [heart] 328:23
Speed: s. was far faster than light 80:9
Spell: a name which . . . no one can spell 401:19
    old black magic has me in its s. 271:23
    s. of far Arabia 134:10
    who lies beneath your s.? 205:19
Speller: taste and fancy of the s. 141:11
Spend: s. a single day 235:6
    s., s., s. 294:14
Spenser: renowned S. 26:9
    sage and serious poet S. 282:18
Speranza: lasciate ogni s. vol ch'entrate 131:15
Spermatozoa: million million s. 213:9
Sphere: ever-moving s.s of heaven 267:2
    motion in one s. 355:4
    music of the s.s 71:11
    rose to touch the s.s 72:11
    shake the s.s 149:34
    s.s of action 184:22
    these walls, thy s. 146:14
    they the s. 145:4
Sphinx: subtler s. renew 391:5
Spice: s. of life 127:2
    sugar and s. 298:14
    woodbine s.s are wafted abroad 420:33
Spider: s. is sole denizen 192:11
    s. taketh hold with her hands 43:9
    said a s. to a fly 211:11
    s.'s touch 313:32
    there came a big s. 297:4
    traces, of the smallest s.'s web 378:30
Spies: as if we were God's s. 363:9
    subtle s. of colour 169:6
    they come not single s. 352:9
    ye are s. 34:33
Spiflicate: while I s. Johnny 24:6

Spill: it [guilt] s.s itself in fearing to be split 352:3
Spin: they toil not, neither do they s. 49:16
Spinach: I say it's s. 452:15
    world of gammon and s. 137:19
Spinoza, Benedict 296:1
Spinsters: s. and the knitters in the sun 383:12
Spire: dim-discovered s.s 119:12
    dreaming s.s 12:2
    s.s whose 'silent fingers point' 461:26
    what s.s, what farms are those 210:25
    ye distant s.s! 187:1
Spirit: all s.s are enslaved 393:9
    all things . . . in one s. meet 391:27
    beauteous s.s do engirt 97:31
    black s.s and white 273:6
    bold s. in a loyal breast 376:8
    break a man's s. 387:25
    broken s. 38:31
    by our own s.s are we deified 466:3
    dedicated s. 465:14
    disembodied s. 452:1
    expense of s. 387:4
    follow your s. 357:6
    God is a S. 53:10
    hail to thee, blithe s.! 394:17
    his s. passed away 288:18
    holiday-rejoicing s. 245:8
    holy s. of man 412:4
    immortal s. grows 465:5
    instance of the s. . . . after death 222:28
    into thy hands I commend my s. 38:9
    like two s.s do suggest 387:7
    make thou my s. pure 423:8
    master s.s of this age 360:9
    motions of his s. are dull 370:22
    my s. hath rejoiced in God 51:42
    pure s. shall flow 390:3
    recover my s.s 221:22
    rest, perturbèd s. 349:18
    scorned his s. 359:20
    s. . . . that loves t'have his sails filled 106:13
    s. be thine 78:15
    s. bloweth and is still 11:14
    s. burning but unbent 90:27
    s. giveth life 55:44
    s. of the chainless mind 93:22
    s. of the Lord bloweth upon it 45:33
    s. shall return unto God 44:12
    s. so still and quiet 374:2
    s. that quickeneth 53:15
    s. that stands by the naked man 5:17
    s. walks abroad 361:1
    s., yet a woman too! 466:15
    s.'s vestal grace 305:24
    s.s are not finely touched 368:3
    s.s from the vasty deep 354:22
    straight in the strength of thy s. 412:22
    tranquil s. 133:20
    unhappy s.s that fell with Lucifer 266:19
    wild S. which art moving everywhere 392:5
    worser s. a woman 387:7
    wounded s. 42:21
Spiriting: do my s. gently 380:32
Spiritualist: if the dead talk to you, you are a s.
    413:15
Spiritus: dum s. hos regit artus 440:23
    s. intus alit 440:29

s. where every man must play a part
369:1

this were played upon a s. now 383:25

two hours' traffic of our s. 378:22

we do on the s. 408:5

well-trod s. anon 276:32

where'er his s.s may have been 395:3

wonder of our s.! 225:21

Stage-coach: on the outside of a s. 196:9

travel faster than a s. 182:12

Stagirite: staggered that stout S. 245:9

Stain: bright s. on the vision 185:13

leave not a s. in thine honour 48:20

lose all their guilty s.s 125:26

s. like a wound 82:14

Stair: as I was going up the s. 271:10

first turning of the second s. 155:26

follow me and climb the s.s 316:29

rat-riddled s.s 75:26

structure in a winding s.? 199:16

up s.s or down below 25:8

see through a flight of s.s 141:13

Stake: I am tied to the s. 362:29

tied me to a s. 367:27

Stalin: more to the left than you, Mr S. 450:17

that S. himself rose 432:16

Stalking-horse: make truth serve as a s. 64:19

uses his folly like a s. 346:16

Stall: s.s in our street looked rare 79:14

Stallion: play the s. 324:17

Stamford: bullocks at S. Fair 356:3

Stamp: indelible s. of his lowly origin 132:7

Stampa: e poi ruppe la s. 10:2

Stand: here I s. 260:2

nowhere to s. 237:6

s. a little less between me and the sun 142:16

s. on either hand 261:14

s. up! s. up for Jesus! 152:5

who shall s.? 41:6

will s. to in a month 379:26

Standard: raise the scarlet s. high 121:9

Standard-authors: let s., thus, like trophies borne
311:23

Standeth: him that thinketh he s. take heed 55:14

Standfast: Mr S. 81:3

Standing: heart of s. 159:21

Stanley: on, S., on! 340:20

Stanza: who pens a s. 312:15

Star: all the s.s that round her burn 2:15

another s. gone out 93:32

blossomed the lovely s.s 256:21

bright morning s. 281:33

bright particular s. 343:3

bright s., would I were steadfast 232:18

but not the s.s 73:21

catch a falling s. 146:7

clad in the beauty of a thousand s.s 267:1

constant as the northern s. 360:4

continuous as the s.s that shine 462:4

cottage which was named the Evening S.
462:28

crown of twelve s.s 58:20

doubt thou the s.s are fire 349:25

each in his separate s. 241:7

earliest s.s began to move 465:18

evening s., love's harbinger 280:41

fair as a s. 466:13

falling s.s are shooting 93:14

great s. early dropped 454:5

in the s.s the glory 310:15

kinship with the s.s 272:8

lights the evening s. 96:19

like a s. of Heaven 394:19

loftiest s. of unascended heaven 393:16

look at the s.s! look 206:15

maidenliest s. in the firmament twinkled 362:1

moist s. upon whose influence 347:25

morning s.s sang together 37:11

move the s.s to pity 165:23

never s. was lost here 79:10

new-bathed s.s emerge 11:35

new Messiah by the s. 150:23

one s. differeth from another 55:36

opposition of the s.s 268:16

particular beauteous s. 230:31

preserve the s.s from wrong 464:23

runaway young s. or two 93:29

sentinel s.s 97:18

shining of the s.s 417:8

silent s.s go by 70:2

s. looks down at me 193:11

s. of midnight 467:3

s. or two beside 117:5

s. that bringest home the bee 97:19

s. threw down their spears 62:5

s. to guide the humble 264:1

s.s, the s.s above us, govern our conditions
362:35

s.s are dead 15:16

s.s are shining bright 391:11

s.s began to blink 464:25

s.s came out 422:32

s.s hide their diminished heads 279:18

s.s in her hair were seven 331:15

s.s in their courses 35:25

s.s move still 267:3

s.s shot madly from their spheres 371:35

s.s that have different birth 394:11

s.s that nature hung in heaven 275:11

s.s that reigned at my nativity 267:4

take him and cut him out in little s.s 379:37

there was a s. danced 372:34

thus shall you go to the s.s 441:7

till . . . the s.s are old 415:7

touch the s.s with my exalted head 208:2

twinkle, twinkle, little s. 415:6

two s.s keep not their motion 355:4

under the passing s.s 471:18

vague unpunctual s. 69:11

wandering s.s 58:2

when shall the s.s be blown about 471:24

where no s. its breath can draw 427:20

who didst the s.s and sunbeams know 11:31

Ye s.s . . . the poetry of heaven! 90:1

yoke of inauspicious s.s 380:11

you chaste s.s! 375:21

Star-captains: young s. glow 165:26

Star-chamber: make a s. matter of it 370:26

Star-shine: s. at night 407:24

Stare: all the world should s. 125:18

no time to stand and s. 133:1

stony British s. 420:31

upon the ground I see thee s. 108:13

Starlight: into the frosty s. 11:33

Start: everything by s.s 149:20
  named a s. 77:2
Starting-point: fresh s. for further desires 321:9
Starve: let not poor Nelly s. 106:23
  s. before he stole 240:8
  s. with nothing 369:6
State: all S.s and all Princes 146:12
  all were for the s. 261:15
  beweep my outcast s. 385:22
  done the s. some service 375:26
  goodly s.s and kingdoms seen 233:2
  greatest asset a s. can have 458:8
  greatest scandal waits on greatest s. 385:7
  hides from himself his s. 219:9
  last s. of that man 50:10
  learn how to govern the s. 252:24
  little enjoyment from a s. of things 169:11
  maintain the s. of the world 48:25
  no happier s. 279:36
  no s. so bad . . . not preferable to change 285:19
  no s., without being soon exhausted 175:16
  no such thing as the S. 15:9
  Northern S.s will manage somehow 68:11
  not taught by the S. 238:13
  nothing doth more hurt in a s. 20:4
  ruin of the s. 60:10
  rule the s. 149:14
  scoffing his s. and grinning at his pomp 377:2
  servants of the sovereign or s. 19:17
  Servile S. 31:8
  so long as the s. exists 252:22
  S., in choosing men to serve it 129:11
  s. is not 'abolished' 159:26
  s. of man. like to a little kingdom 359:27
  s. without the means of some change 82:11
  s.s unborn 360:7
  thou art in a parlous s. 345:18
  visions of a perfect S. 424:16
State-oracle: chief s. is mute 421:14
Stately: s. homes of England 460:21
Statesman: s. . . . politician who's been dead
    432:23
  s. all over 111:25
  too nice for a s. 181:17
  witty s. 99:10
Statesmen: adored by little s. 159:3
  s. talked with looks profound 181:8
  s., yet friend 315:5
Station: born in that s. o' life 140:33
  ideas above her s. 326:1
  know our proper s.s 136:36
  middle s. had the fewest disasters 133:13
Statistics: lies, damned lies and s. 144:2
  proved by s. 15:10
  uses s. as a drunken man 247:8
Statue: her gaze is like the gaze of s.s 439:5
  s. inside every block of stone 300:17
  stood among the silent s.s 416:6
Stature: one cubit unto his s. 49:15
  shorten I the s. of my soul 272:9
  yet of no taller s. 185:6
Stay: here I am and here I s. 264:4
  padded man – that wears the s.s 421:7
  s. for me there 237:7
Stay-at-Home: sweet S. 133:2
Steady: s., boys, s. 173:5
Steak: smell of s. in passage ways 156:30

Steal: Blake is damned good to s. from 171:12
  s. out of your company 373:8
  's.!' foh! a fico 371:4
Stealing: for de little s. they gets you in jail 300:1
  picking and s. 319:30
  s. from the many to the few 308:16
Stealth: do good by s. 316:4
  good action by s. 246:17
Steam: forget the snorting s. 288:12
  unconquered s. 132:11
Steam-roller: red flag in front of the s. 216:13
Steamer: all you Big S.s 238:15
  little holiday s.s 320:14
  s.s sidle up to meet 14:1
Steed: Arab's Farewell to his S. 295:21
  farewell the neighing s. 375:5
  gallon apace, you fiery-footed s.s 379:35
  milk-white s. 23:15
  noble s. 93:15
  right soon I'll mount my s. 130:10
Steel: bronze heard iron s. 226:25
  clad in complete s. 275:20
  grapple . . . with hoops of s. 348:21
  more than complete s. 267:12
  red line tipped with s. 334:4
  some fell . . . by s. 173:11
Steeple: drenched our s.s, drowned the cocks!
    362:14
  here is the s. 296:18
Stehe: hier s. ich 260:2
Stenches: two and twenty s. 117:24
Stendhal: two draws with Mr S. 197:22
Step: alike in s. and tread 435:6
  by backward s.s would move 438:13
  fearful s.s pursuing 391:10
  gone the same s.s as the author 234:2
  in his master's s.s he trod 292:29
  on whose last s.s I climb 391:16
  one small s. for man 10:12
  s. twice into the same river 198:26
  s.s solemn, mournful, and slow 454:14
  to these dark s.s 281:14
  with s. so active 247:2
Step-mother: merciless s. 310:9
  stony-hearted s. 135:3
Stephen: Feast of S. 292:27
  King S. was a worthy peer 8:5
Sthruttin': s. about . . . like a paycock 299:5
Stick: carry a big s. 330:3
  fell like a s. 303:4
  liftin' the lazy ones on wid the s. 185:1
  sucked sugar s.s 472:8
Stickit: designated as a s. minister 340:29
Stigma: s. . . . will serve to beat a dogma 189:2
Stile: against a crooked s. 298:4
  sitting on the s. 60:1
Stile-a: merrily hent the s. 384:26
Still: be s., and know that I am God 38:25
  commune with your heart . . . and be s. 37:21
  everything else is s. 62:21
  their strength is to sit s. 45:17
  thou smilest and art s. 11:30
Stillness: air a solemn s. holds 186:1
  horrid s. first invades the ear 150:12
  modest s. 357:3
  soft s. and the night 370:19
Stilts: legs . . . to be reduced to mere s. 190:5

let's all go down the S. 103:3
walk down the S. 194:2
walking on the s. 23:9
Strange: how s. it seems 75:28
how s. now, looks the life 72:17
jeering at everything that looks s. 307:11
living here these eight years with a s. man 214:6
Lord's song in a s. land 41:10
passing s. and wonderful 390:19
something rich and s. 380:35
s. and fatal interview 144:23
s. and well-bred 120:34
'twas s., 'twas passing s. 374:6
Stranger: be better s.s 345:23
by s.s honoured 312:5
courteous to s.s 19:28 entertain s.s 57:17
I, a s. and afraid 209:27
I have been a s. 34:40
I was a s., and ye took me in 51:17
never fight fair with a s. 273:23
s., pause and ask thyself the question 137:38
s. to one of your parents 17:8
s.! 'Eave 'arf a brick at 'im 322:6
s.s and pilgrims on the earth 57:13
surety for a s. 41:35
tell whether a s. is your friend 167:21
Stratagem: love likes s. 77:28
Stratford: scole of S. atte Bowe 107:12
Straw: find quarrel in a s. 352:2
give the people s. 34:45
pipes of wretched s. 277:14
take a s. and throw it 342:6
Strawberries: good s. in your garden there 378:4
s. swimming in the cream 306:22
Strawberry: like s. wives 18:12
Stray: with me you'll fondly s. 174:8
Stream: coil of his crystaline s.s 392:7
cold companionable s.s 472:1
freezing s. below 390:12
gilding pale s.s 385:27
land of s.s 420:9
lapse of murmuring s.s 280:21
large s.s from little fountains flow 160:7
more pellucid s.s 462:11
shallow s.s run dimpling 312:26
sitting by desolate s.s 301:15
still glides the s. 466:9
s. my great example 134:33
s. that flashest white 418:42
strove against the s. 422:14
swap horses when crossing a s. 254:18
trailing in the cool s. 11:23
Streamer: s.s waving in the wind 174:25
Strebend: wer immer s. sich bemüht 179:22
Street: at the end of the s. 264:15
bald s. 417:29
children cried in the s.s 289:11
crossing a one-way s. 308:6
don't do it in the s. and frighten the horses 96:20
down these mean s.s 106:6
long and silent s. 455:2
long unlovely s. 417:28
one of the finest women who ever walked the s.s
451:13
sheer inability to cross the s. 461:1
s. of the city was pure gold 58:36
s. which is called Straight 53:47

S.s FULL OF WATER 31:13
Streetcar: S. Named Desire 457:17
Strength: as thy days, so shall thy s. be 35:19
clock collected . . . its s. and struck 209:28
confidence shall be your s. 45:19
enough s. to bear other people's troubles 247:24
from s. to s. 39:26
hast thou ordained s. 37:25
his s. the more is 81:1
my s. is as the s. of ten 423:14
prayed, that God would give him s. 225:31
s. is made perfect in weakness 56:6
s. might endure for a span 412:4
s. through joy 254:10
their s. is to sit still 45:17
try the soul's s. on 75:5
yet is their s. labour and sorrow 39:33
Strenuous: doctrine of the s. life 330:4
Strife: ancient forms of party s. 418:25
crowd's ignoble s. 186:14
double s. 21:5
is it s.? 136:27
none was worth my s. 246:25
s. is o'er 317:4
Strike: s. it out 222:9
String: end of a golden s. 61:4
hanging from a s. 238:4
harp not on that s. 378:13
I'll s. along with you 152:4
little bits of s. 30:6
lyre with other s.s 126:25
nothing of my own but the string 285:24
strangling in a s. 210:9
there are s.s 136:16
untune that s. 382:1
whisper music on those s.s 157:9
Stripling: nor sword nor spear the s. took 125:24
Strive: love, s. nor weep 79:11
s. officiously to keep alive 115:22
s. to wind ourselves too high 234:20
to s., to seek, to find 424:11
Stroke: till I received thy s. 125:25
Strong: be s. and quit yourselves like men 35:41
little drink . . . but wants that little s. 203:29
only the S. shall thrive 342:25
out of the s. came forth sweetness 35:31
quit you like men, be s. 55:41
Still Going S. 2:28
s. man armed 52:14
s. man must go 77:7
s. men shall bow themselves 44:10
s. ought to bear the infirmities of the weak 54:49
s. without rage 134:33
Strongest: s. shall stand the most weak 78:18
Stronghold: safe s. our God is still 260:3
turn you to the s. 47:22
Strove: I s., made head 77:16
little still she s. 91:4
Struggle: contemptible s. 82:28
gaze . . . on another's s.s 259:21
perpetual s. for room and food 266:1
s. for existence 132:9
s. itself . . . is enough 98:8
s. naught availeth 115:25
Strumpet: sturdy s. 193:3
transformed into a s.'s fool 343:14
Stubble: earth's base built on s. 275:28

they'll take s. as a cat laps milk 380:38
Suicide: live for it . . . which is s. 249:20
Suing: in s. long and bide 403:9
Suit: customary s.s of solemn black 347:34
  dreams he of smelling out a s. 379:1
  out of s.s with fortune 344:19
  s. is granted 199:22
  silk s. which cost me much money 307:9
Sujet: quelque s. qu'on traite 64:7
Sulphur: puffed its s. 32:21
Sum: could not . . . make up my s. 352:34
  giving thy s. of more 344:27
  s. of earthly bliss 280:25
  saved the s. of things for pay 210:2
Summer: after s. merrily 381:17
  all-hallown s. 353:25
  all right in the s. time 290:7
  bears eternal s. in his soul 203:27
  beauty's s. dead 386:23
  compare thee to a s's. day 385:17
  discontent made glorious s. 377:20
  English s's. done 239:31
  eternal s. gilds them yet 91:23
  eternal s. shall not fade 385:18
  guest of s. 365:4
  if it takes all s. 184:19
  in s. quite the other way 407:12
  last rose of s. 287:8
  lips . . . in their s. beauty kissed each other 378:9
  live murmur of a s.'s day 11:21
  not so much life as on a s.'s day 230:27
  peak of s's. past 133:6
  proper man, as one shall see in a s's. day 371:30
  s. afternoon – . . . the two most beautiful words 217:4
  s. clothe the general earth 117:31
  s. has set in 118:28
  s. hath his joys 97:29
  s. is icumen in 5:13
  s. set lip to earth's bosom 427:23
  s's. flower is to the s. sweet 386:18
  sweet as s. 359:4
  taught by his s. spent 467:19
  thousand s.s are over 413:1
Summer-gale: far from the sun and s. 187:13
Summer-night: upon a trancèd s. 230:29
Summits: snowy s. old in story 421:19
Summon: upon a fearful s.s 347:26
Sun: against a setting s. 381:24
  all, except their s. is set 91:23
  all the s. goes round beside 445:2
  beneath the s. the many must labour 90:26
  benighted walks under the midday s. 275:18
  between me and the s. 142:16
  bright-haired s. 119:11
  cannot make the s. stand still 269:3
  clear as the s. 44:25
  clothed with the s. 58:20
  correct use of the s. 250:7
  cut off their s. 133:5
  dies with the dying s. 65:21
  doubt that the s. doth move 349:25
  eyes to behold the s. 44:7
  follow the fair s. 97:24
  give me the s. 214:10

glory of the s. 21:21
goes to bed wi' the s. 384:28
going down of the s. 59:18
grow aweary of the s. 367:25
had not the great s. seen 67:29
hold up to the s. 92:8
let my s. his beams display 124:6
let not the s. go down 56:18
light breaks where no s. shines 426:9
loves to live i' the s. 344:39
maketh his s. rise 49:6
midday s. 123:27
more the heat o' the s. 347:15
move him into the s. 302:11
my s. sets to rise again 72:24
no better thing under the s. 43:35
no s. – no moon! 204:31
nothing but the s. 308:1
nothing like the s. 387:6
on which the s. never sets 295:16
pay no worship to the garish s. 379:38
place of the setting s. 68:10
radiance of a thousand s.s 33:12
rising of the s. 7:25
self-same s. that shines upon his court 384:33
sing of the s. 317:19
s. and the moon should doubt 60:19
s. breaks through the darkest clouds 380:21
s. came peeping in at dawn 204:26
s. climbs slow 115:26
s. does not set 338:12
s. had risen to hear him crow 155:10
s. is set 187:10
s. itself is but the dark *simulacrum* 70:16
s., moon and stars, brother 65:11
s. never sets on Government House 123:28
s. of Austerlitz 291:15
s. shall not smite thee by day 40:32
s. shines bright 168:6
s. shines sweetly on 22:13
s. that warms you here 376:11
s., the air, and skies 187:7
s. to me is dark 281:17
s. was laughing sweetly 471:1
s. was shining on the sea 101:33
s. went down 422:32
s. will pierce the thickest cloud 72:22
s.'s rim dips 117:1
s.s and universes ceased to be 68:26
s.s may set 103:11
s.s that set may rise again 225:12
thank heaven, the s. has gone in 399:11
till the s. grows cold 415:7
tired the s. with talking 123:2
to feel the s. 71:25
to have enjoyed the s. 10:23
too much i' the s. 347:32
unregulated s. 69:11
unruly S. 146:10
when the s. in bed 277:27
when the s. set where were they? 91:25
when the s. shall rise 468:3
where the great s. begins his state 276:24
white as the s. 111:12
why the s. isn't shining 301:14
wind up the s. and moon 93:29

with the s. to match 73:21
with the setting s. 278:27
Sun-flower: s. turns on her god 286:23
    s. weary of time 61:18
Sun-start: s.s on a stream 427:15
Sun-treader: s., I believe in God and truth 76:21
Sunbeam: extracting s.s out of cucumbers 410:28
    motes that people the s.s 276:1
    s. in a winter's day 153:4
Sunday: begin a journey on S.s 411:15
    calm S. that goes on and on 166:3
    divide the S. from the week 347:22
    he was in his S. best 401:14
    S. clears away the dust of the whole week 2:7
    S. morning . . . takes this railway by surprise
        178:23
Sundial: mottoes on s.s 317:21
Sunlight: somewhere in the s. strong 252:1
Sunny: they called him S. Jim 191:18
Sunset: Autumn s.s exquisitely dying 213:10
    beautiful s. mistaken for dawn 133:9
    bequeath, like s. to the skies 391:6
    horror of s.s 321:18
    sail beyond the s. 424:10
    s. ran 75:1
Sunset-touch: when we are safest, there's a s.
        73:1
Sunshine: from s. to the sunless land 462:1
    made a s. in a shady place 402:28
Sup: who supped no s. 178:21
Super-Mac: introducing S. 439:7
Supercalifragilisticexpialidocious: 142:18
Supererogation: Works of S. 320:7
Superflu: s., chose très nécessaire 442:7
Superfluity: barren s. of words 173:10
    s. comes sooner by white hairs 369:7
Superfluous: diary of S. Man 433:13
Superior: s. people never make long visits 286:20
Superiority: acquire an evident s. 224:14
    comparisons of s. 220:10
    laugh of s. 187:25
Superman: I teach you the s. 294:18
Superos: flectere si nequeo s. 441:3
    s. quid quaerimus ultra? 259:16
Superstition: foul S.! howsoe'er disguised 89:17
    necessary for a s. to enslave a philosopher 215:4
    new truths . . . end as s.s 213:13
    s. in avoiding s. 19:39
    s. is the religion of feeble minds 82:22
    their blind side – their s.s 245:23
    vast S.! 188:11
Supper: between dinner and s. 222:4
    hope . . . is a bad s. 18:11
    sings for his s. 297:6
Support: but to s. him after 381:22
    invisible means of s. 79:20, 167:24
    s. rather than illumination 247:8
Suppose: that we . . . came to an end 133:7
Sure: be s. of it 375:6
    nobody is s. about! 30:33
    one s. if another fails 78:23
    perfectly s. I have none 100:33
    quite s. she felt no pain 77:5
    s. way never to see it lost 83:8
Surety: s. for a stranger 41:35
Surface: like straws, upon the s. flow 151:14
Surfeit: crude s. reigns 275:21

s. by eating of a lamprey 161:5
s. with too much 369:6
Surge: murmuring s. 362:36
    rude imperious s. 355:31
    turbulent s. shall cover 381:26
Surgeon: s. to old shoes 359:9
    wounded s. plies the steel 155:36
Surgery: honour hath no skill in s. 355:2
Surmise: looked . . . with a wild s. 233:3
Surprise: bibles laid open millions of s.s
        199:24
    gentle shock of mild s. 465:19
    oh, what a s.! 116:1
    sure of a big s. 235:13
Surrender: Guards die, but do not s. 96:15
    unconditional and immediate s. 184:20
    we shall never s. 112:20
Surrey: meet S. in a wilderness 377:7
Survival: s. of the fittest 132:10, 402:8
    there is no s. 112:19
Susan: black-eyed S. came aboard 174:25
Susanna: O, S. don't you cry for me 168:7
Susie: sister S. sews 451:19
Suspect: always s. everybody 139:31
Suspense: s. is terrible 455:26
Suspension: s. of disbelief 118:19
Suspicion: Caesar's wife must be above s. 95:9
    people under s. 229:3
    S.s amongst thoughts 20:19
Swagman: once a jolly s. camped 305:19
Swain: all our s.s commend her 384:8
    frugal s. 204:5
    homely s. 358:7
Swallow: hope . . . flies with s.'s wings 378:15
    O S., S., flying, flying South 422:6
    s., my sister, O sister s. 413:1
    s. twittering from the straw-built shed 186:4
    s.s are making them ready 454:13
    s.s twitter in the skies 233:21
Swallowed: others to be s. 20:32
Swamp: botanize in the s. 111:4
Swan: after many a summer dies the s. 423:22
    float double, s. and shadow 467:20
    like a sleeping s. 393:12
    pale s. in her watery nest 385:9
    s.-like end 369:36
    saw two s.s of goodly hue 403:13
    s.s are geese 11:11
    s.s sing before they die 117:29
    sweet s. of Avon! 225:26
Swanee: way down upon the S. Ribber 168:8
Swarm: s. that in thy noontide beam were born
        185:23
Swarry: friendly s. 141:15
Swashing: s. and a martial outside 344:24
Swath: spares the next s. 233:18
Swear: by the time you s. you're his 304:2
    first time I ever heard you s. 162:5
    others early learn to s. 447:7
Swear-word: s. in a rustic slum 29:4
Sweareth: s. to his own hurt 37:32
Sweat: blood, toil, tears and s. 112:18
    in the s. of thy face shalt thou eat bread 34:4
    she was all of a muck of s. 182:30
Sweeping: s. them difficult problems behind him
        140:10
Sweet: all is not s. 225:3

box where s.s compacted lie 199:26
brought'st Thy s.s along with Thee 199:11
get s.s into your list 212:16
how it was s. 73:35
nothing's so dainty s. 26:27
perpetual feast of nectared s.s 275:21
s. and low 421:37
s. when the morn is gray 96:7
s.s to the s. 352:32
smell so s. 353:30
things s. to taste 376:13
when you speak s. I'd have you do it ever 384:30
wilderness of s.s 280:11
Sweet-pea: s.s, on tip-toe 231:1
Sweetest: s. things turn sourest 386:19
Sweetheart: s., canst thou tell me 22:3
Sweeting: trip no further, pretty s. 383:2
Sweetness: linkèd s. long drawn out 276:33
out of the strong came forth s. 35:31
s. and light 410:20
waste its sweetness on the desert air 186:10
Swell: green s. is in the havens dumb 206:2
Swelling: s. visibly 141:8
Swept: no sooner does anything appear than it is s.
away 16:16
Swerve: s. to the left 288:14
Swift: cousin S., you will never be a poet 151:37
S. expires a driv'ller 219:10
s. to hear 57:21
too s. arrives as tardy as too slow 379:28
with s., slow; sweet, sour 206:13
Swiftness: O s. never ceasing 306:23
Swim: said I could not s. 101:22
Swimmingness: s. in the eyes 120:28
Swindle: as all truly great s.s are 198:18
Swine: Gadarene S. 241:32
gr-r-r – you s. 78:25
Greek name for S.'s Snout? 78:22
husks that the s. did eat 52:26
jewel of gold in a s.'s snout 42:1
pearls before s. 49:21
Swing: I never do s. a cat 137:25
s. of the sea 206:2
Swinger: s. of birches 169:21
Switzerland: in S. they had brotherly love 449:10
look upon S. as an inferior sort of Scotland
399:20
Swoon: s. to death 232:19
Swoop: at one fell s. 367:9
Sword: beat their s.s into plowshares 44:33
believed he had a s. upstairs 470:5
brave man with a s. 454:21
die on my own s. 367:28
fall by the s. 39:9
famous by my s. 286:7
father's s. he has girded on 287:2
good s. rust 117:33
held a fair s. in that hand 265:12
is the s. unswayed? 378:14
keep up your bright s.s 373:37
kindest man that ever struck with s. 265:23
lightnings thy s. 111:18
nor s. nor spear 125:24
not to send peace, but a s. 49:43
pen is mightier than the s. 260:17
s. outwears its sheath 93:21
s. sleep in my hand 61:9

s. was in the sheath 125:35
sheathed their s.s for lack of argument 357:4
smote him with the edge of the s. 35:9
s.s shall play the orators 267:14
they that take the s. 51:23
turns our s.s 361:1
two-edged s. 41:18, 57:10
which I with s. will open 371:8
whoso pulleth out this s. of this stone 265:9
words . . . were drawn s.s 38:34
Sword-light: s. in the sky 169:7
Sword-pen: against this I raise my s. 81:6
Swore: our armies s. terribly in Flanders 405:24
Sycamore: s. leaves wer a spreaden 25:9
sighing by a s. tree 375:17
Syllable: count s.s 118:25
last s. of recorded time 367:24
panting s. 126:23
Syllogism: conclusion of your s. . . . is fallacious
299:3
Sylph: only s. I ever saw 139:19
Symbol: cloudy s.s of high romance 233:11
Symboles: des forêts de s. 26:13
Symmetry: fearful s. 62:4
Sympathies: cosmopolitan s. 330:20
Sympathize: s. with everything 456:8
Sympathy: antipathetic s. 237:2
failed to inspire s. in men 29:15
God-damned s. 461:3
s. is cold 175:22
s. that feels for the most debased 132:7
wrought to s. 394:20
Synagogue: s. of the ear of corn 426:13
Syne: for auld lang s. 83:27
Syrens: song the S. sang 71:17
Syrian: S. stars look down 11:15
Syrop: lucent s.s tinct with cinnamon 230:18
Syrup: drowsy s.s of the world 375:3
System: constitution of the solar s. 132:7
create a S. 60:32
empirical scientific s. 316:18
our little s.s have their day 417:26
that's our s., Nickleby 139:11

T

Ta-ra-ra-boom-de-ay: T! 338:5
Tabac: rien d'égal au t. 283:12
Tabby: demurest of the t. kind 186:26
Table: behave mannerly at t. 407:13
carpenter . . . made a bad t. 221:8
I reside at T. Mountain 194:27
make it plain upon t.s 47:20
Memorable Round T. 342:17
my t.s, – meet it is 349:13
rich man's t. 52:32
set the t. in a roar 352:26
smiled as he sat by the t. 194:24
T. of the Moveable Feasts 318:10
t.s of young ladies 262:34
Table-lands: close upon the shining t. 421:23
Tace: T, . . . is Latin for a candle 162:15
Tâche: longue et lourde t. 439:20
Tack: all the facts when you come to brass t.s
156:32

Tackle: gear and t. and trim 206:12
   nor t., sail, nor mast 380:29
   try and t. him 136:14
Tadlow: when T. walks the streets 160:3
Taffeta: t. phrases, silken terms 364:3
Tail: beginning with the end of the t. 101:4
   bringing their t.s behind them 297:1
   cut off their t.s with a carving knife 298:8
   hole where his t. came through 401:14
   improve his shining t. 100:30
   puppy-dog's t.s 298:14
   stings in their t.s 58:19
   such a little t. 30:2
   t. cropped short 127:20
   t. you lose 129:7
   thy t. hangs down behind 240:19
   treading on my t. 101:17
   t.s of both hung down behind 398:21
Tailor: called the t. lown 8:5
   ninth part of a t. 99:14
Take: t. him as we find him 238:7
Taken: from him that hath not shall be t. away
      51:15
   when t., to be well shaken 119:27
Talcum: heavy fall of t. 307:28
Tale: by t. or history 371:20
   every t. condemns me for a villain 378:19
   honest t. speeds best being plainly told 378:12
   I could a t. unfold 349:1
   idle t.s 52:47
   it is a winter's t. 426:17
   plain t. shall put you down 354:14
   round unvarnished t. 374:1
   sad t.'s best for winter 384:14
   t. of woe 162:13
   t. told by an idiot 367:24
   telling a t. not too importunate 288:11
   thereby hangs a t. 345:4
   t.s marvellous t.s 166:2
   with a t., forsooth, he cometh unto you 396:20
   your t., . . . would cure deafness 380:27
Talent: all I've put into my works is my t. 456:24
   blest with each t. 312:22
   extraordinary collection of t. 235:20
   if you have great t.s 326:20
   Ireland is . . . a country . . . with . . . no talent
      253:19
   t. alone cannot make a writer 159:8
   T. does what it can 272:26
   t. for silence 212:18
   t. to amuse 123:9
   t. which is death to hide 282:3
   tried their t. 118:26
Talent: si c'est votre t. 64:14
Talk: after-dinner t. 421:6
   he will t., – . . . how he will t. 251:23
   loves to hear himself t. 379:26
   mair they t. I'm kent the better 85:9
   need to talk 105:4
   summer t. stopped 14:15
   t. a little wild 358:13
   t. and discourse 20:31
   t. too much 149:19
   then we'll t. 391:19
   they always t. who never think 320:31
   wish I liked the way it t.s 325:14
Talked: he [Coleridge] t. on for ever 195:18

t. of, either for good or evil 429:8
   worse than being t. about 456:4
Talker: professional t. 162:8
Talking: he is t. or he is pursuing 36:16
   t. with those of other centuries 135:12
   what we are t. about 333:23
Tall: adequately t. 109:30
Taller: t. by almost the breadth of my nail 410:22
Tam: ah, T.! ah, T.! thou'll get thy fairin'! 85:22
   T. loved him like a brither 85:16
   T was glorious 85:17
Tambourine: play the t. on her other knee 139:19
Tamburlaine: T. the scourge of God 267:21
Tame: glass which thou canst not t. 199:4
Tameless: t., and swift, and proud 392:10
Tamer: t. of the human breast 186:19
Tammie: T glowr'd, amaz'd and curious 85:21
Tangere: noli me t. 53:40
Tank: put a Tiger in Your T. 3:8
   see a T. come down the stalls 337:28
Tannenbaum: O T., O T. 338:23
Tanqueray: The Second Mrs T. 30:17
Tap: t. at the pane 75:27
Taper: gleaming t.'s light 182:4
   glimmering t.s 128:9
   out went the t. 230:16
Tapping: suddenly there came a t. 310:24
Tapster: ancient T. of this Hostel 134:16
   surly T. 164:26
Tar-Baby: contrapshun what he call a T. 194:11
   T. ain't sayin nuthin 194:12
Tara: mute as T's. walls 286:26
Taradiddle: sent for telling t.s 252:9
Tarantara: t., t! we uncomfortable feel 178:4
Tarquin: great house of T. 261:12
Tarry: she will t. there 192:23
Tarshish: from T. into Tyre 240:9
Tart: she made some t.s 297:24
   t.'s vote 135:16
Taschentücher: Gespenst das frisst T. 288:3
Task: common t. 234:21
   one t. more declined 75:19
   thou hast thy t. 128:25
   though hard be the t. 103:1
   thy worldly t. hast done 347:15
Task-Master: great T.'s eye 282:1
Tasmanian: T.s . . . are now extinct 270:16
Tassie: fill it in a silver t. 84:20
Taste: arbiter of t. 414:6
   disliked the killibeate t. 141:16
   matter o' t. 140:38
   suspect his t. in higher matters 245:16
   t. and taste of the speller 141:11
   t. any drink once 95:1
   t. by which he is to be relished 467:25
   t. not 56:31
   t. of your quality 350:3
   t. the whole of it 77:9
   t. you again 128:1
   t.s may not be the same 388:23
   they never t. who always drink 320:31
   various are the t.s of men 3:31
   whose mortal t. brought death 277:32
Tatter: t. in its mortal dress 471:19
Taught: I forget what I was t. 452:18
   men must be t. 313:22
   t. me all I knew 239:19

Taughte: afterward he t. 107:25
Tavern: sat in t.s while the tempest hurled 209:24
   t. for his friends 147:5
   there is a t. in the town 8:19
Tavernes: knew the t. well in every toun 107:16
Taxation: t. without representation 301:18
Taxes: as true . . . as t. 137:18
   nothing . . . certain except death and t. 168:20
   t. must . . . fall upon agriculture 175:18
Tea: cup of real or of lime-flower t. 321:6
   sometimes counsel . . . sometimes t. 315:19
   t. . . . is a gentleman 110:24
   T. for Two, and Two for T. 192:3
   t. generally taste of boiled boots 425:5
   t.s, where small talk dies 392:18
   when I makes t. I makes t. 226:21
   when the t. is brought at five o'clock 284:20
Tea-cup: crack in the t. opens 14:25
   Storm in a T. 32:12
Tea-time: creation will expire before t. 400:8
Tea-tray: like a t. in the sky 101:7
Teabag: woman is like a t. 326:7
Teach: t. me, my god and King 199:12
   t. us to care 155:24
Teacher: precepts for the t.'s sake 162:1, 203:28
Teaches: he who cannot, t. 388:27
Teaching: t. not so obscured 73:30
Team: is my t. ploughing 210:18
Tear: big round t.s 344:26
   bitter t.s to shed 123:1
   blood, toil, t.s and sweat 112:18
   bread of t.s 39:25
   crocodiles that shed t.s 20:7
   drop, slow t.s 166:17
   drop the brynie t. 107:5
   drop t.s fast 375:26
   dropped a t. upon the word 405:29
   droppings of warm t.s 72:11
   eternal reciprocity of t.s 302:13
   every t. from every eye 60:16
   fallen a splendid t. 421:1
   freely moved to t.s 30:11
   hence these t.s 424:27
   if you have t.s 360:19
   in the midst of t.s 427:12
   kissed again with t.s 421:34
   like Niobe, all t.s 348:4
   nor all thy T.s wash out 164:20
   nothing is here for t.s 281:29
   our t.s thaw not the frost 389:23
   remember with t.s 4:20
   shed a bitter t. 102:3
   smiling through her t.s 204:12
   some melodious t. 277:2
   some natural t.s they dropped 281:1
   some pretty match with shedding t.s? 377:5
   son of these t.s should perish 16:1
   source of sympathetic t.s 187:13
   t. in her eye 340:13
   t. is an intellectual thing 61:3
   t.s are pearl 385:28
   t.s fall in my heart like the rain 439:6
   t.s fell with the dew at even 420:24
   t.s, idle t.s 422:3
   t.s of children 135:3
   t.s such as angels weep 278:23
   they that sow in t.s 40:35

thoughts that . . . lie too deep for t.s 464:20
tired of t.s and laughter 412:17
wipe away all t.s 58:33
wipe the t., baby dear 451:21
with mine own t.s I wash away my balm 377:12
Tease: he knows it t.s 101:3
   t. us out of thought 231:24
   while ye thus t. me 174:15
Teche: gladly t. 107:20
Technology: t. . . . the knack of so arranging the
   world 169:15
Teddy: t. bears have their picnic 235:13
Teenager: as a t. you are at the last stage of your
   life 251:14
Teens: married in his t. 132:16
Teeth: blow in the t. of a wrong 270:1
   cast into my t. 360:32
   children's t. are set on edge 46:33
   iron gate ground its t. to let me pass 78:19
   keep their t. clean 346:24
   not show their t. in way of smile 368:33
   skin of my t. 37:3
   t. like ships at sea 134:11
   t. like splinters 104:7
   we shows our t. 138:36
   weeping and gnashing of t. 49:30, 51:1
Teetotaller: only a beer t. 387:26
Tehee: 'T.!' quod she 108:7
Teint: son t. au vôtre pareil 329:10
Telegram: Jeeves . . . came back with a t. 459:15
Telegraph: young lions of the *Daily T* 12:18
Telemachus: my son, mine own T. 424:7
Television: stake in commercial t. 428:23
   see bad t. for nothing 183:8
Tell: how could they t.? 304:8
   kiss and t. 120:7
   t. me all. t. me now 226:9
   you never can t. 389:12
Téméraire: Fighting T. 293:19
Temerity: have not the t. 183:18
Temper: any man may have good t. 138:22
   keep me in t. 362:5
   such feeble t. 359:15
   uncertain t. 17:2
Temperament: artistic t. 110:29
   corner of creation seen through a t. 473:5
Tempest: dark lowers the t. overhead 256:24
   fierce raged the t. o'er the deep 429:6
   we the t. fear 150:12
Temple: in the T. lost outright 164:22
   in thy T. thou dost him afford 199:28
   Lord's anointed t. 366:3
   out of which religion they build t.s 242:18
   t. of the Holy Ghost 55:6
   t.s of his Gods 261:13
Temple-bar: high above roaring T. 424:22
Temple-bells: t. are calling 240:6
Tempo: t. felice nella miseria 131:17
Tempora: O t., O mores 114:17
   t. certa modosque 209:13
   t. mutantur 9:12
Temps: O t.! suspends to vol 244:23
   t. heroïques sont passés 172:14
Tempt: all who seek you t. you 327:19
   t. not a desperate man 380:8
Temptation: enter not into t. 51:22
   everything except t. 455:28

last t. 157:16
lead us not into t. 49:10
maximum of t. 388:28
most men are . . . under t. 255:22
never resist t. 387:17
prepare thy soul for t. 48:1
t. comes . . . in gay, fine colours 198:8
to t. slow 386:17
why comes t. but for man to meet 78:9
Tempted: one thing to be t. 368:7
t. above that ye are able 55:15
Tempus: fugit inreparabile t. 441:28
t. abire tibi est 207:30
T. edax rerum 302:3
Ten: rise at t. thirty 194:1
t. o'clock 345:3
they are only t. 295:18
1066: 1066 and All That 342:14
Tenant: t.s of the house 156:13
Tender: fools for t.s 120:24
t. for another's pain 187:6
Tender-minded: titles t. and 'tough-minded' 217:9
Tenderly: take her up t. 204:19
Tenderness: t. becomes me best 120:28
Ténébreux: Je suis le t. 293:9
Tenet: in some nice t.s 124:9
Tennis: t. with the net down 170:15
Tennis-ball: stars' t.s 448:29
t.s, my liege 356:25
Tennis-court: that vast t. 376:5
Tennyson: as for T. – well, T. goes without saying 88:9
T. and Browning are poets 157:21
Tenor: noiseless t. of their way 186:14
Tent: fold their t.s like the Arabs 256:19
Grecian t.s where Cressid lay 370:18
inside my t. pissing out 218:22
little t. of blue 454:20
living in a tent 109:3
nightly pitch my moving t. 286:3
to your t.s, O Israel 36:13
t.s of Kedar 40:28
t.s of wickedness 39:27
yon western t. 119:11
Tenth: Submerged T. 65:4
Term: fair t.s and a villain's mind 369:21
good set t.s 345:2
Terminus: arrive at any t. 156:6
Terre: c'est une pauvre t. 26:19
nous resterons sur la t. 320:11
Terrestrial: written on t. things 192:15
Terrible: t. man with a t. name 401:19
Terrify: they t. me 449:13
Territory: descend on this t. 179:11
it comes with the t. 273:25
Terror: flame of incandescent t. 156:9
full of dismal t. 377:30
in spite of all t. 112:19
swift t. on the dark 169:7
t. by night 40:1
T. of St Trinian's 341:15
Test: life is a t. 174:24
t. of truth 128:4
Testament: blessing of the Old T. 19:3
purple t. of bleeding war 377:3
thou makest a t. 344:27
Testing: some strict T. of us 164:26

Text: English t. is chaste 175:12
holy t. of pike and gun 87:9
thundering t. 185:7
Thais: lovely T. by his side 149:32
Thames: clear T. bordered by its gardens green 288:12
drown myself in the T. 139:20
stripling T. 11:23
sweet T.! run softly 403:12
T. is liquid 'istory 83:17
unmourning water of the riding T. 426:14
Thane: T. of Fife had a wife 367:13
Thanked: not t. at all, I'm t. enough 163:4
Thanks: deserves the love and t. 303:2
hast ta'en with equal t. 351:3
Thanksgiving: proud t. 59:17
thank with brief t. 412:20
Thcream: I'll t., an' t., an' t. till I'm thick 129:8
Theatre: as in a t., the eyes of men 377:16
off to the t. 30:17
problems of the modern t. 326:2
quit going to the t. 336:20
t. of man's life 18:5
Thèâtre: jusqu'à la fin le t. rempli 64:13
Thebes: presenting T., or Pelop's line 276:10
riddles . . . T. never knew 391:5
Thee: without T. I cannot live 234:24
Them: Adam had t. 178:25
Theme: two truths . . . of the imperial t. 364:21
Themselves: law unto t. 54:16
Thence: go not t. 115:6
Theogony: God of some oriental t. 321:12
Theology: my t. . . . the universe was dictated 288:6
Theoric: bookish T. 373:29
Theory: life without t. 143:16
specious in t. 81:28
There: because it's t. 265:8
not t., not t., my child 197:12
Thermopylae: new T. 91:26
old man of T. 251:9
Thersites: T.' body is as good as Ajax 347:14
Thessalian: T. bulls 372:10
They: everyone else is T. 241:5
Thick: t. and exactly in the right places 88:21
t. and fast they came at last 102:4
thcream, an' thcream till I'm t. 129:8
through t. and thin 87:14
Thief: dwarfish t. 367:15
he that cries out stop t. 120:10
if you do take a t. 373:8
in the sworn twelve have a t. or two 368:7
pretty sneaking t. 61:16
rascally t. 24:11
steals something from the t. 374:8
t. and a liar 96:14
true man's apparel fits your t. 368:27
Thieves: beauty provoketh t. sooner than gold 344:23
den of t. 50:44
mirth of t. and murderers 199:22
one of the t. was saved 28:12
t. break through and steal 49:11
Thigh: bee with honied t. 276:14
cushes on his t.s 354:36
hip and t. 35:33
Thimble: seek it with t.s 102:25
silver t. lies cold and tarnished 397:21

Thin: enclosing every t. man 448:8
  never be too t. 458:22
  outside every t. woman 453:10
  t. man inside every fat man 300-17
  t. one is . . . signalling 121:19
  through thick and t. 87:14
Thing: all good t.s are ours 77:16
  all t.s . . . are on fire 80:6
  all t.s both great and small 117:16
  all t.s bright and beautiful 4:3
  all t.s to all men 55:10
  all t.s work together 54:29
  as t.s have been 115:25
  between a t. and a thought 303:10
  do this great t. 36:27
  draw the T. as he sees it 241:7
  how can these t.s be? 53:7
  if a t. is worth doing 111:5
  lot of little t.s behind him 238:7
  none of these t.s 54:2
  old, unhappy, far-off t.s 466:23
  people don't do such t.s 214:12
  Roman Conquest . . . a *Good T.* 342:15
  sighed and looked unutterable t.s 428:10
  sweetest t. that ever grew 462:26
  that is not the t. 234:10
  these t.s shall be added unto you 49:17
  t. behaving like a person 468:17
  t. that hath been 43:14
  T. which seemed very T.ish 274:23
  t. which was not 411:1
  t.s are not what they seem 257:2
  t.s are seldom what they seem 177:1
  t.s are shewed unto thee 48:2
  t.s fell apart 471:20
  t.s they didn't know 317:16
  T.s think about men 218:2
  three t.s I never lend 409:21
  very few t.s matter at all 22:1
Thing-um-a-jig: especially T.! 102:22
Think: before him I may t. aloud 158:24
  he t.s too much 359:18
  I must not t. of thee 272:30
  I t. therefore I am 135:13
  inclined to t. 148:6
  know what I t. 444:10
  not be bound to t. 150:30
  one who t.s differently 260:6
  sooner die than t. 333:26
  speak one moment before they t. 243:13
  they always talk who never t. 320:31
  t. continually of those who were truly great 402:14
  t. him so, because I t. him so 384:2
  t. that we t. 59:7
  t. too little 149:19
  those who greatly t. 312:3
  when I t. I must speak 345:22
  while I t. on thee 385:25
  ye are not paid to t. 240:1
Thinker: t. on this planet 158:20
Thinking: everybody is t. most often 330:11
  fool for t. 318:6
  little enough to get . . . without t. 136:23
  never thought of t. for myself 176:31
  plain living and high t. 463:22
  Power of Positive T. 306:19

solitary t.s 230:7
  think they are t. 217:13
  t. lays lads underground 210:28
  t. to have common thought 314:24
  t. what nobody has thought 413:16
Third: shadowy t. 73:20
  T. World 21:13
  to make a t. she joined the former two 150:26
  with never a t. 73:18
Thirst: in my t. they gave me vinegar 39:18
  provocation of t. 411:2
  t. to come 324:1
  water t. 105:20
Thirsty: I was t., and ye gave me drink 51:17
Thirteenth: t. at table 214:24
Thirty: t. pieces of silver 51:18
Thirty-one: all the rest have t. 184:6
Thisbe: T. fearfully o'erstrip the dew 370:18
Thistle: long live the t.s of the field 324:17
Thither: say I sent thee t. 358:11
Thoghte: spak oo thing, but he t. another 107:32
Thomas: took true T. up behind 23:16
Thorn: crackling of t.s under a pot 43:27
  fall upon the t.s of life 392:10
  he left the t. wi' me 86:1
  Head . . . crowned with t.s 234:27
  no pain, no t.s, no throne 307:6
  Oak and Ash and T. 241:1
  primrose peeps beneath the t. 181:13
  rose without a t. 264:10
  this crown of t.s 79:19
  t. in the flesh 56:5
  t. will blow in tufts 423:31
  t.s he spares 412:15
  t.s that in her bosom lodge 349:10
Thoroughfare: mind . . . t. for all thoughts 234:15
  t.s of stones 192:17
Thou: Loaf of Bread – and T. 164:2
  t. also 302:4
Thought: all t.s, all passions 118:7
  begin to have bloody t.s 381:11
  between a thing and a t. 303:10
  bloody t.s, with violent pace 375:10
  cursed t.s that nature gives way to in repose 365:17
  every third t. shall be my grave 381:20
  fond and wayward t.s 466:28
  good t.s his only friends 97:27
  great t.s come from the heart 438:21
  green t. in a green shade 268:21
  he t. I t. he t. I slept 305:22
  hidden in the light of t. 394:20
  hundred schools of t. contend 266:11
  in loftiness of t. surpassed 150:26
  indolent vacuity of t. 127:17
  life is what our t.s make it 16:12
  more strong than all poetic t. 418:1
  my t.s are not your t.s 46:13
  my t.s remain below 351:24
  no t. for the morrow 49:18
  nor any unproportioned t. 348:21
  original t. is like original sin 251:13
  pale cast of t. 350:14
  pansies, that's for t.s 352:14
  perish113:11
  rear the tender t. 428:6
  second and sober t.s 198:9

second t.s are good 26:5
sensations rather than t.s 233:25
shroud of t.s 90:4
single grateful t. raised to heaven 253:27
sleep out the t. of it 384:25
smallest amount of t. 112:14
so thy t.s when thou art gone 394:6
speech created t. 393:8
still are the t.s to memory dear 340:23
strange seas of t. 465:13
stray t.s, fancies fugitive 78:20
strike the reader as . . . his own highest t.s 233:29
sweet silent t. 385:24
t. does not become a young w. 395:17
t. is free 381:6
t. is only a flash 311:1
t. of you remaining 413:8
T. Police 300:21
t. that lurks in all delight 272:30
t. to justify . . . wrongdoings 442:14
t. would destroy their paradise 187:6
t.s, not breaths 21:10
t's. wildernesses 393:4
t.s are often new 219:22
t.s hardly to be packed 77:21
t.s of men are widened 419:34
t.s pay no duty 260:4
t.s that . . . lie too deep for tears 464:20
t.s that voluntary move 279:12
t.s that wander through eternity 278:34
t.'s the slave of life 355:5
two people . . . hit on the same t. 395:10
two souls with but a single t. 258:16
timely utterance gave that t. relief 464:3
trouble himself with any such t.s 356:33
was t. but ne'er so well expressed 313:7
we ought to control our t.s 132:6
white celestial t. 438:9
working-house of t. 357:21
ye t.? 240:1
Thousand: but one ten t. of those men 357:14
die by t.s 110:17
difference of forty t. men 449:19
fifty t. men slain . . . in Europe 445:11
he had ten t. men 6:12
I can draw for a t. pounds 2:22
Maconides . . . said it three t. years ago 166:12
one man among a t. have I found 43:32
one t. shall flee 45:20
picked out of ten t. 349:27
ride ten t. days and nights 146:8
ten t. saw I at a glance 462:5
t. shall fall at thy side 40:1
t. years in thy sight 39:31
t.s at his bidding speed 282:4
t.s careless of the damning sin 125:1
t.s die, without 314:32
t.s equally meant 410:12
upper ten t. 457:21
would he Shakespeare had blotted a t. 225:27
Thraldom: single t. 21:5
Thrall: hath thee in t.! 231:13
Thread: feels at each t. 313:32
line of scarlet t. 35:21
silk t. plucks it back again 379:20
silver t.s among the gold 326:18
spinning the t. of your being 16:20

t.s with magic art 127:35
where is the t. now? 79:6
Thread-paper: worn to a t. 317:8
Threadneedle: Old Lady of T. Street 178:26
Threatening: breathing out t.s and slaughter 53:45
Threats: no terror . . . in your t. 360:30
Three: born about t. of the clock 355:17
ever T. and ever One 292:26
t., four, knock at the door 297:16
t. o'clock is always too late 337:24
t. times is true 102:21
thou wast one of the t. 417:22
when shall we t. meet again 364:10
you're only t. Sonny Boy 70:9
Three hundred: of the t. grant but three 91:26
Three-pipe: t. problem 147:18
Three-score: bachelor of t. 372:25
t. and ten 296:22
t. years and ten 39:33
Threepenny: it'll only be a t. bit 67:14
Threshold: stand upon the t. of the new 444:13
starry t. of Jove's Court 275:3
Thrice: thou shalt deny me t. 51:20
Thrift: t., t., Horatio! 348:7
Throat: brazen t. of war 280:42
cut a t. 91:20
cutting foreign t.s 379:1
doesn't cut your t. 307:29
my sore t.s 16:32
taking life by the t. 170:16
t. of Old Time 138:1
your t. is hard to slit 238:3
Throne: around the t. of God 292:23
fiery-wheelèd t. 276:5
here is my t. 361:14
living t., the sapphire-blaze 187:14
river, that flows by the t. of God 337:7
royal t. of kings 376:17
t.s, dominations, princedoms 280:13
under the shadow of Thy T. 447:23
wade through slaughter to a t. 186:13
your t. is above the King's 239:16
Through: best way out is always t. 170:13
Thrush: wise t. 74:37
Thrushes: t.' ancestors as sweetly sung 427:5
Thucydides: 64:21
Thule: Ultima T. 441:22
Thumb: both his t.s are off 203:6
by the pricking of my t.s 366:37
coarse t. and finger 77:20
do not bite my t. 378:23
if you have any strength in your t. 326:11
put in his t. 297:3
with a flip of His t. 305:8
Thump: t.s upon your back 125:3
Thunder: dawn comes up like t. 240:2
fettered the t. 390:15
glorious the t.'s roar 398:9
laugh as I pass in t. 390:14
loud t. . . . shook the bog 311:15
steal my t. 135:1
t., lightning, or in rain 364:10
t. of the captains 37:13
Thunder-cloud: terrific t. advancing upon us 108:35
Thunder-harp: his t. of pines 398:18
Thunder-storm: t. against the wind 90:10
Thunderbolt: harmless t. 310:8

like a t. he falls 416:12
Thursday: I do not love you T. 273:19
  t'was on a Holy T. 62:12
Thus: 'tis in ourselves that we are t., or t. 374:9
  to be t. is nothing 366:10
Thusness: reason of this t.? 446:20
Thwackum: T. was for doing justice 162:30
Thyme: sweet t. true 28:6
Thyself: I am t. – what hast thou done 331:24
Tiber: Oh T.! father T.! 261:17
  River T. foaming with much blood 318:5
Tiberius: blood of T. flows in her veins 432:5
Ticket: got a t. to ride 253:15
  return him the t. 146:28
Tickle: if you t. us 369:33
Ticky-tacky: made out of t. 327:2
Tiddely: nobody knows (T. pom) 274:19
Tide: blood-dimmed t. is loosed 471:20
  call of the running t. 270:3
  drew these t.s of men 249:28
  going out with the t. 137:24
  salt t.s seaward flow 11:4
  t. in the affairs of men 360:33
  t. in the affairs of women 91:43
  t. of times 360:11
  turning o' the t. 356:31
Tidings: confirm the t. as they roll 2:15
  conveyed the dismal t. 181:6
  glad t. of great joy 414:18
  he that bringeth good t. 46:4
Tie: t. that only death can sever 270:18
Tier: T., das es nicht gibt 327:18
Tiers: le T. Monde 21:13
Tiger: imitate the action of a t. 357:3
  more fierce . . . than empty t.s 380:7
  paper t.s 266:12
  put a T. in Your Tank 3:8
  riding on the back of the t. 235:16
  rode with a smile on a t. 6:15
  T.! T.! burning bright 62:4
  t. that hadn't got a Christian 322:12
  t.s are getting hungry 113:25
  t.'s heart wrapped in a player's hide 188:3
  t.'s heart wrapped in a woman's hide 358:6
  t.s of wrath 63:19
Tiggers: T. don't like honey 274:20
Tight: t. little island 136:13
Tights: played it in t. 29:8
Tilburina: enter T. stark mad in white satin 395:12
Tile: not even red brick, but white t. 301:12
  t.s of each red roof 77:27
  where did you get that t.? 329:9
Tim: 'God bless us every one!' said Tiny T. 137:2
  poor tired T. 134:31
Timber: like seasoned t., never gives 199:27
Timbrel: damsels playing with 39:17
Timbuctoo: cassowary on the plains of T. 454:16
Time: A Good T. Was Had by All 399:14
  abysm of t. 380:26
  bank and shoal of t. 365:5
  bid t. return 376:28
  Bird of T. 163:26
  book to kill t. 261:4
  born out of due t. 55:29
  busiest man who has t. to spare 304:21
  by T.'s fell hand defaced 386:2
  conversing I forget all t. 279:33

corridors of T. 256:18
dicing T. for gladness 192:20
dimly guess what T. 427:16
envious and calumniating t. 382:15
fleet the t. carelessly 344:14
foremost files of t. 420:4
from this t. forth 40:33
give peace in our t. 318:23
good old t.s 89:1
hardest t. of all 146:29
haven't the t. to take our t. 215:15
holy t. is quiet 463:4
how long a t. lies in one little word! 376:12
how small a part of t. 445:4
in a dark t. the eye begins to see 328:17
instant of t. without duration 453:5
it will last my t. 99:13
keeping t., t., t. 310:17
loved the t. too well 114:25
many a t. and oft 369:16
may be some t. 299:2
means . . . of digesting t. 15:27
Miss Jenkyns beat t. 173:13
my t. has not yet come either 294:20
never the t. 76:8
new direction of T. 249:4
nobility is the act of t. 19:29
not of an age, but for all t. 225:24
nothing troubles me more than t. and space 246:11
now is the accepted t. 55:48
O t. too swift 306:23
old common arbitrator, T. 382:20
old T. is still a-flying 200:19
old t. makes these decay 98:25
olden T. long ago 310:22
panting T. toiled after him 219:3
passed the t. 28:14
pluck till t. and t.s are done 471:27
redeem thy mis-spent t. 235:9
river of T. 11:7
shallow as t. 99:19
shook hands with t. 167:8
short t. to live 320:3
so little t. 329:24
sour sweet music is when t. is broke 377:18
spend too much t. 20:30
spite of cormorant devouring T. 363:17
take no note of t. 472:21
tell her that wastes her t. 445:3
there's a good t. coming 263:15 467:31
there's a gude t. coming 341:4
throat of Old T. 138:1
t. . . . must have a stop 355:5
T. a maniac scattering dust 418:4
t. and the hour runs through 364:24
t. can but make her beauty 470:18
t. doth transfix 386:1
t. drops in decay 471:13
t. flies, death urges 472:24
't. has come,' the Walrus said 102:5
t. held me green and dying 426:6
t. in hours, days, years 438:19
T. in one's life 321:7
t. is but the stream I go a-fishing in 428:29
t. is drawing near 3:30
T. is fleeting 257:3

wish I could say T. was any better 234:5
Tom Jones: romance of T. 175:7
Tomb: come to the cold t. 396:5
Fidele's grassy t. 119:8
forgot . . . the assassin . . . in the cool t.s 336:27
fourfold t. 26:9
from the t. the voice of Nature cries 186:16
love lies beyond the t. 114:28
our earth is a t. 74:24
smell like what it is – a t. 391:18
this side the t. 132:20
toward the silent t. 466:10
t.s of brass 386:28
Tombstone: carve it on his t. 240:27
end of the fight is a t. 240:11
Tommy: little T. Tucker 297:6
T. knew other things 25:26
T. this, an' T. that 240:30
Tomnoddy: Lord T. is thirty-four 70:5
Tomorrow: boast not thyself of t. 42:45
dividend from time's t. 337:29
here today, and gone t. 29:24
leave t. behind 123:25
limit to our realization of t. 329:25
such a day t. as today 384:11
t., and t., and t. 367:24
t. do thy worst 151:9
t. 'ill the happiest time . . . the New-year 421:4
T. it may be Myself 164:8
t. let us do or die 97:4
t. we die 55:34
t. we will run faster 165:9
this, no t. hath 144:15
Tomtit: by a river a little t. 177:35
Tone: t. of the company you are in 109:7
Tongue: bells put out their t.s 142:2
cloven t.s 53:42
death by slanderous t.s 373:26
every t. brings in a several tale 378:19
fellows of infinite t. 357:24
finds t.s in trees 344:25
give thy thoughts no t. 348:21
his t. dropt manna 278:33
his t. the clapper 373:1
his t. to conceive 372:11
hold your t., and let me love 144:18
in their Mother T. 319:33
lack t.s to praise 386:25
lisping, stammering t. 125:27
love's t. in his eyes 166:20
my t. is the pen of a ready writer 38:23
of all people, and t.s 58:15
one t. is sufficient 282:26
prosperity lies in the ear . . . not in the t. 364:5
put a t. in every wound 360:24
rolls it under his t. as a sweet morsel 198:10
saying . . . what comes to my t. 105:4
senates hang upon thy t. 428:11
sharp t. . . . grows keener with . . . use 215:18
sharp t. in your head 307:29
she had a t. with a tang 381:1
silence envious t.s 358:25
silence is become his mother t. 182:11
silver-sweet sound lovers' t.s by night 379:19
so loud each t. 111:26
strife of t.s 38:11
stroke of the t. 48:16

t.; . . . a wery good thing when it ain't a woman's 140:27
t. can no man tame 57:25
t. shall be split 298:3
t. so varied in discourse 247:2
t. sounds . . . as a sullen bell 355:12
t. that Shakespeare spake 463:25
t. to persuade 114:31
t.s of men and of angels 55:21
t.s to be, your beings shall rehearse 386:11
trippingly on the t. 350:23
understanding but no t. 348:16
use of my oracular t. 395:27
vibrates her eternal t. 472:15
Tonight: not t., Josephine 130:13
Tool: give us the t.s 113:1
only edged t. that grows keener with . . . use 215:18
t.s to him that can handle them 99:21
without t.s he is nothing 100:8
Tooth: set my pugging t. on edge 384:22
sharper than a serpent's t. 362:3
t. of time 368:29
t. for t. 35:1
thy t. is not so keen 345:12
Tooth-point: exactly where each t. goes 240:13
Toothache: endure the t. patiently 373:23
feels not the t. 347:17
Top: always room at the t. 448:22
looking at the men at the t. 116:14
Room at the T. 66:15
spun like whipping t.s 202:16
started at the t. 449:11
Top-boots: pleasure me in his t. 266:16
Top-mast: strack the t. wi' his hand 22:14
Topic: other fashionable t.s 182:31
Topping: t. in Plays 115:12
Tor: ich armer Tor! 179:16
Torch: bright t. . . . ope at night 232:12
runners hand on the t. of life 259:22
t. has passed to a new generation 235:15
Torches: teach the t. to burn bright 379:4
Tories: angels are all T. 94:3
T. own no argument but force 71:23
Torment: delicious t. 158:23
I am in t. 104:5
shall no t. touch them 47:38
t.s of grief you endured 158:15
Tormentor: it is I who am my t. 431:2
Torpedo: pen . . . becomes a torpedo 220:14
Torrent: t. of his fate 219:11
voice of mountain t.s 465:19
Tortoise: we called him T. 101:13
Torture: t. . . . of his fellow-creatures is amusing 170:18
t. one poor word 150:29
Tory: deep burning hatred for the T. Party 33:6
T. men and Whig measures 143:14
T. who is ashamed of himself 169:10
what is called the T. 129:6
Tossed: t. and gored several persons 221:24
Total: t. of such moments 121:16
Toten: den jugendlich T. 327:13
Touch: exquisite t. 341:9
its t. awoke him once 302:11
lose the common T. 239:13
natural t. 367:5

t. came by 61:14
t. from an antique land 392:13
t. from the cradle to the grave 393:18
t.s must be content 344:32
Travelling: fairly worth the t. to 407:
  t. is . . . like talking 135:12
  t. is that the ruin of all happiness 83:11
Tray: faithful T. came out to drink 202:26
  my poor dog T. 97:5
Treachery: fear their subjects' t. 358:8
Treacle: fly that spits t. 174:13
  lived on t. 101:8
Tread: close behind him t. 117:10
Treason: bloody t. flourished 360:22
  fit for t.s 370:22
  men will confess to t. 116:13
  moderation, . . . is a sort of t. 82:35
  princes . . . love the t. 131:6
  they corporations cannot commit t. 116:11
  t. can but peep to what it would 352:11
  t. doth never prosper 194:4
  t. has done his worst 366:15
  t. of the intellectuals 31:14
  t. was no crime 149:24
  'twixt t. and convenience 115:3
Treasure: heaps of miser's t. 275:19
  merchant to secure his t. 320:23
  religion, justice, counsel and t. 19:31
  rich the t. 150:1
  stolen the t. 120:10
  thou shalt have t. 50:36
  what t., uncle? 356:25
  where your t. is 49:12
Treasuries: sumless t. 356:23
Treasury: sitting on the T. bench 112:13
  T. . . . fill old bottles with banknotes 236:12
  Vatican, the T. and the miners 21:19
Treaties: publish the secret t. 432:18
Treaty: hand that signed the t. bred a fever 426:8
Treble: turning again toward childish t. 345:11
Tree: ancient t.s 61:17
  bears down the pivotal t. 236:8
  billboard lovely as a t. 292:16
  bosomed high in tufted t.s 276:26
  die when t.s were green 114:25
  dreamy, gloomy, friendly t.s 431:20
  ever-green t. of diabolical knowledge 395:21
  filled the t.s and flapped 202:15
  fruit of that forbidden t. 277:32
  God can make a t. 237:4
  growing like a t. 225:16
  I see men as t.s, walking 51:35
  if they do these things in a green t. 52:44
  incense-bearing t. 117:35
  leafless t.s and every icy crag 465:11
  like that t. 411:27
  lofty t.s I see barren of leaves 385:14
  look at the t.s 68:1
  lover of t.s 74:2
  of all the t.s that are in the wood 7:25
  of all the t.s that grow so fair 241:1
  old patrician t.s 124:7
  Orpheus with his lute made t.s 358:18
  our t. yet crowns the hill 12:7
  pledges of a fruitful t. 200:3
  poem lovely as a t. 237:3
  procreate like t.s 71:10

rock-a-bye baby on the t. top 60:6
tall t. on the river bank 261:1
till the t. die 347:18
too happy, happy t. 233:14
t. continues to be 242:9
t. of Life 279:22
t. that a wise man sees 63:13
t.'s inclined 314:18
t.s as beauteous are 124:11
t.s bow down their heads 331:9
t.s burst into bud 204:11
t.s where you sit 315:9
under the greenwood t. 344:37
went on cutting down a t. 408:18
where the t. falleth 44:5
'whispers through the t.s' 313:13
Trelawny: shall T. die? 195:3
Trembler: boding t.s learned to trace 181:6
  no t. in the world's storm-troubled sphere 68:24
Trembling: t. at that where I had stood 391:16
Trencher: dead Caesar's t. 343:38
Trencherman: very valiant t. 372:22
Trenches: dig deep t. in thy beauty's field 385:12
  how horrible . . . that we should be digging t.
    105:26
Trespasses: forgive us our t. 318:15
Tress: little stolen t. 471:23
Tresses: breathing t. 119:13
  t. man's imperial race ensnare 315:18
Trial: democracy is on t. 144:12
  not a t. at all 229:1
  t. by jury . . . will be a delusion 134:34
Triangle: eternal t. 6:20
  if t.s invented a god 286:1
Tribe: all that t. 209:12
  badge of all our t. 369:17
  his t. were God Almighty's gentlemen 149:25
  richer than all his t. 375:26
  touchy t. of poets 207:29
Tribu: mots de la t. 265:7
Tribulation: came out of great t. 58:16
Tribunal: highest T. the House of Commons will
    accomplish 81:26
  there's a new t. now 78:11
Tribute: t. to whom t. is due 54:42
Trick: knavish t.s 99:5
  more t.s . . . than make a noise 105:6
  no t.s in plain and simple faith 360:26
  plays such fantastic t.s 368:15
  such affected t.s 30:5
  teach an old dogma new t.s 304:7
  their t.s and their manners 140:12
  t. that everyone abhors 30:19
  t. worth two of that 353:34
  when in doubt, win the t. 211:12
  when the long t.'s over 270:4
Trickster: trick the t. 244:7
Tried: t. and found wanting 111:6
Trifle: man of sense only t.s 109:12
  observance of t.s 147:14
  snapper-up of unconsidered t.s 384:24
  t.s light as air 375:2
  'twere a careless t. 364:25
  win us with honest t.s 364:20
Trifler: busy t. dreams 124:34
Trigger: draw the t. after his death 220:26
  whose finger on the t.? 131:2

Trim: gallant t. the gilded vessel 185:24
  t. little, prim little 178:12
Trimmer: T. signifies no more than this 190:9
Trink: one word was heard: T. 324:19
  T. is a panomphaean word 324:20
Trinket: returned to your t.s 239:17
Trip: farewell t. into the promised land 7:11
  fearful t. is done 453:16
Tripe: scraping t. 76:27
Triste: jamais t. archy jamais t. 267:31
Tristesse: bonjour t. 158:8
Tristram Shandy: T. did not last 222:17
Triton: old T. blow his wreathèd horn 463:7
  T. blowing loud his wreathèd horn 402:20
  T. of the minnows 346:27
Triumph: chief . . . in t. advances 339:20
  come ye forth in t. 261:8
  in ourselves are t. and defeat 257:1
  meet with T. and Disaster 239:12
  pedestaled in t. 78:9
  sure t. of her eye 67:26
  sweeping t. 143:30
  tears, their little t.s o'er 186:25
  t. of hope over experience 222:3
  we shall not see the t. 141:29
Trivial: contests rise from t. 315:11
Trivialities: t. where opposites are obviously absurd
  64:5
Troia: iam seges ubi T. fuit 301:25
Troilus: T. . . . mounted the the Troyan walls 370:18
 Trojan: we are T.s no more 440:17
Trompeur: tromper le t. 244:7
Troop: farewell the plumèd troop 375:5
  foreign t. was landed in my country 309:18
  t.s of Midian 292:25
Trophies: among her cloudy t. hung 231:29
  gold nails . . . to hang t. on 259:2
  standard-authors, thus, like t. borne 311:23
Troubadour: gaily the T. 27:10
Trouble: ain't see no t. yit 194:9
  full of t. 37:1
  give us help from t. 39:5
  in time of t. 38:13
  man is born unto t. 36:40
  no end to the t.s of state 310:4
  nothing t.s me less 246:11
  other people's t.s 247:24
  pack up your t.s 13:8
  saves me the t. 17:18
  take arms against a sea of t.s 350:14
  t. brewing 242:6
  t. him much more 125:11
  t.s over I would make a case 21:17
Trough: t. was full 202:25
Trousers: best t. to go out to battle 214:8
  hitched his t. up 24:21
  wear the bottoms of my t. rolled 156:26
Trout: find a t. in the milk 429:3
  grey t. lies asleep 203:14
  here and there a lusty t. 415:22
  stipple upon t. that swim 206:11
Trouthe: t. is the hyeste thing 107:31
  t. shall delivere 107:6
Trovato: è molto ben t. 9:20
Trowel: laid on with a t. 344:17
  lay it [flattery] on with a t. 143:32
Troy: another T. for her to burn? 471:14

fields where T. once was 301:25
fired another T. 150:7
half his T. was burned 355:11
heard T. doubted 91:34
ringing plains of windy T. 424:3
tale of T. divine 276:10
write no more the tale of T. 391:4
Truant: t. disposition, 348:7
True: as t. as another 86:23
  be so t. to thyself 20:5
  because a novel's invented, it isn't t. 318:2
  been t. to *one* party 258:21
  faithful and the t. 114:28
  good men and t. 373:3
  he said t. things 73:8
  how shall I know your t. love 325:6
  if all be t. 4:1
  I'll prove more t. 379:14
  is it T.? 32:14
  is it t. or is it not 274:33
  it *will* be t. 31:20
  let God be t. 54:17
  proposition be interesting than . . . t. 453:2
  so young, my lord, and t. 361:30
  substantially t. 337:14
  swore to be t. to each other 7:17
  tender and t. 128:14
  three times is t. 102:21
  'tis easy to be t. 341:20
  'tis t. 'tis pity 349:24
  t. to you, darlin', in my fashion 316:23
  t., very t., ma'am 83:12
  t. when you met her 146:9
  what we are saying is t. 333:23
  whatsoever things are t. 56:29
True-love: but one t. 23:21
Truman: kind of nation that President T. worked for
  218:21
Trump: at the last t. 55:39
  t.s they were 315:22
  with the sound of the t. 38:27
Trumpery: embryos and idiots . . . with all their t.
  279:16
Trumpet: blow your t.s, angels 145:15
  blowin' er de t.s 194:20
  dreads the final T. 193:3
  eating . . . to the sound of t.s 400:9
  First Blast of the T. 242:8
  he saith among the t.s, Ha Ha 37:13
  heart moved more than with a t. 396:21
  shifted his t. 181:22
  snarling t.s gan to chide 230:14
  sound the t.s, beat the drums 288:1
  t. of a prophecy 392:12
  t. shall be heard on high 151:4
  t. shrill hath thrice already sounded 402:16
  t. sounds from the hid battlements 427:16
  t. whence he [Milton] blew 463:9
  t.'s. loud clangour 151:2
  t.s sounded on the other side 81:4
Truncheon: marshal's t. 368:11
Trunk: so large a t. 30:2
Trust: betray the t. 423:27
  built an absolute t. 364:26
  convartin' public t.s 258:24
  men dare t. themselves with men 381:23
  never t. a woman 455:35

voice of the t. is heard in our land 44:20
Tuscany: even the ranks of T. 262:1
Tusculum: lay on for T. 261:10
Tusk: savage Ruskin sticks his t. in 70:3
Tussis: T. attacked him 74:29
Tutor: still more plain the T. 115:11
Twain: never the t. shall meet 238:11
   with t. he covered his face 45:2
Tweedledum: T. and Tweedledee agreed to have a
   battle 101:31
   'twixt T. and Tweedledee 88:26
Twelve: t. of the clock 193:7
Twenty: having had t. years 156:1
   kiss me, sweet and t. 383:3
   let t. pass 73:22
   long-expected one and t. 219:1
   t. more such names and men 380:13
   t. will not come again 210:6
Twenty-four: t. hour day 28:27
   then we shall be t. 209:23
Twenty-three: married, charming, chaste and t. 91:1
Twenty-two: still alive at t. 238:3
Twice: bored once and t. 22:20
   something that will be read t. 121:13
   t. or thrice had I loved thee 144:14
Twig: just as the t. is bent 314:18
   topmost t. 117:19
Twilight: come in some t. interim 444:6
   disastrous t. sheds 278:21
   fly by t. 20:19
   gray t. poured 421:27
   snow blind t. ferries over the lakes 426:17
   t. dim with rose 134:24
Twin: one of us was born a t. 252:11
Twining: slowly t. over one another 137:15
Twinkle: t. t. little bat 101:7
Twinkling: t. of a bed-staff 343:1
   t. of an eye 55:39
Twist: no more t. 317:8
   Oliver T. has asked for more 139:32
Two: at the expense of t. 115:21
   can t. walk together 47:14
   if they be t. 146:17
   remember the T.
   ride on, we t. 75:13
   t. to bear my soul away 3:16
   t. with nature 4:18
   we t. stood there 73:18
   we're number t. 3:12
Twopence: penny plain, t. coloured 3:7
Type: careful of the t. 418:9
   grey paper with blunt t. 78:24
Tyranny: appeal from t. to God 93:25
   where laws end, t. begins 309:16
Tyrant: argument of t.s 309:20
   intercourse between t.s and slaves 182:7
   kings will be t.s from policy 82:16
   past the t.'s stroke 347:15
   t.'s crests and tombs of brass 386:28
   t's. threatening face 208:25
   t.s if they could 133:17
Tyrawley: T. and I have been dead 109:20
Tyre: T., the crowning city 45:14
   village which men still call T. 166:8

U

U: U. and Non-U 330:22
Ugly: born old and u. 136:17
   makes me u. 375:19
Ulcer: eight-u. man on a four-u. job 432:21
Ulster: U. will fight 112:5
Ultio: prima est haec u. 228:8
Ulysse: heureux qui, comme U. 152:2
Ulysses: naked U. 106:15
   new U. 391:3
   U. come 131:12
Ulysses: U. . . . . attempt to cover the universe with
   mud 167:17
'Umble: so very 'u. 137:14
Umbrage: Americans have taken u. 322:10
Umbrella: steals the just's u. 65:22
Umpire: I am . . . the u., the pavilion cat 247:7
Un: tous pour u., u. pour tous 152:9
Unaccommodated: u. man is . . . a poor, bare, forked
   animal 362:23
Unaffected: to seem u. 121:5
Unattractive: u. old thing 177:34
Unawares: come u. 75:26
Unbelief: all we have gained then by our u. 73:3
   help thou mine u. 51:37
   ignorantly in u. 56:40
Un-birthday: u. present 102:11
Uncharitableness: all u. 319:2
Uncle: down went my U. Sol 130:4
   grace me no grace, nor u. me no u. 376:23
   old U. Tom Cobbleigh and all 8:22
   our four u.s 451:16
Unclubbable: very u. man 221:21
Uncomely: things u. and broken 471:11
Uncomfortable: moral when he is only u. 388:21
Unconcern: looks with u. on a man struggling
   220:21
Unconscionable: u. time dying 107:1
Unconscious: superficial layer of the u. 227:1
Unction: u. to your soul 351:33
Underdog: Englishman among the u.s 448:7
Undergraduate: u.s owe their happiness 29:5
Underground: Johnny U. 322:1
Undersold: never knowingly u. 254:8
Understand: adores what he cannot u. 256:7
   don't criticise what you can't u. 153:10
   Europeans and Americans . . . u. each other
   worse 217:17
   hardly anywhere in the world u. 21:8
   men who u. 69:13
   some who did not u. them 318:9
   thinks she u.s 74:9
Understanding: Donne's verses . . . pass all u. 216:9
   give it an u. 348:16
   him that hath u. 58:22
   light a candle of u. 47:32
   not likely to propagate u. 224:7
   not obliged to find you an u. 223:19
   passeth all u. 56:28
   Perfect u. will . . . extinguish pleasure 210:34
   u. . . . . between our two governments 258:9
   u. to direct 227:12
   with all thy getting get u. 41:24
Understood: I want to be better u. 284:1
Undertaker: u. cleans his sign 123:16
   wot 'ud become o' the u.s 141:23

Underwear: addiction to silk u. 98:1
Underwood: green u. and cover 412:2
Undevout: relished by the u. 210:33
Undo: some to u. 151:11
Undone: left u. those things which we ought to have done 318:13
Uneducated: government by the u. 111:11
  u. man to read books 113:16
Unemployment: at a stroke, . . . reduce u. 121:25
  no more u. 236:12
Unexamined: u. life is not worth living 400:18
Unfortunate: one more U. 204:19
Ungained: men prize the thing u. more than it is 381:34
Ungodly: u. in great power 38:16
Ungratefulness: do they call virtue there u.? 396:13
Unguem: ad u. factus homo 209:14
Unhand: u. me, gentlemen 348:33
Unhappiness: man's u. . . . comes of his greatness 100:12
Unhappy: each u. family is u. in its own way 430:19
  I am u. 108:34
  keeps the u. from thinking 136:8
  u. the land that has no heroes 67:4
Unhouseled: u. disappointed, unaneled 349:9
Unicorn: like the horn of an u. 40:3
  lion and the u. were fighting 296:32
  O U. among the cedars 14:23
Uniform: good u. must work its way with the women 141:11
  love . . . should be more u. 204:23
  put this u. on 177:37
  u. 'e wore 239:8
Uninitiated: hence, away, u. ones 440:27
Union: O U. strong and great 256:13
  u. in partition 372:5
  u. of hands and hearts 415:10
  vulgar way of u. 71:10
United States: in the U. there is more space 404:16
  in the U., there one feels free 217:18
  so near to the U.! 136:4
  U. might . . . make an agonising reappraisal 152:6
Unity: dwell together in u. 41:7
  u., peace, and concord 319:6
Univers: périsse l'U. 130:14
Universal: u characteristics 109:15
Universe: arrangement of the U. 4:9
  boundless u. 423:30
  God in his u. 165:24
  I accept the U. 213:4
  I accept the u. 100:22
  into this U. 164:13
  peopling the lone u. 391:26
  pretend to understand the u. 408:11
  torrents of her myriad u. 420:21
  traversed the boundless u. 259:17
  understand the u. 100:19
  u. . . . . queerer than we can suppose 190:6
  u. begins to look more like a great thought 217:19
  u. is not hostile 203:19
  u. is transformation 16:12
  u. was dictated but not signed 288:6
  very interested in the U. 122:4
  what is the measure of the u.? 393:8

wide vessel of the u. 357:9
Universities: state of both his u. 431:19
University: Jimmy's u. . . . . not even red brick 301:12
  to the u., where it learning was . . . taken out 306:16
  true U. of these days 99:32
  U. should be a place of light 143:8
  We are the U. 403:25
Unjust: u. steals the just's umbrella 65:22
Unkind: I am u. 258:14
Unknowe: u. unkist, and lost 108:22
Unknowing: thick clouds of u. 115:6
Unknown: TO THE U. GOD 53:54
  tread safely into the u. 194:30
Unloading: u. history 113:23
Unlucky: person born who is so unlucky 267:30
Unmarried: keep u. as long as he can 388:18
Unobserved: u. home to his mother's house . . .
  returned 281:12
Unparticular: nice u. man 193:17
Unpleasant: u. and unacceptable face of capitalism 196:21
Unpleasing: something that is not u. 248:20
Unpopular: free society . . . where it is safe to be u. 406:12
Unprepared: magnificently u. 122:18
Unreason: Colleges of U. 87:30
Unrespited: u., unpitied, unreprieved 278:36
Unrest: u. which men miscall delight 390:5
Unrighteousness: mammon of u. 52:30
Unruly: u. evil 57:25
Unsearchable: doubt what the u. dispose 281:30
  sums up the u. 67:25
Unselfishness: u. of an oyster 336:5
Unsex: u. me here 364:31
Unsought: lost that is u. 108:22
  love . . . giv'n u. is better 383:20
Unspeakable: u. in full pusuit of the uneatable 455:34
Unspotted: u. from the world 57:22
Unstoried: still u., artless 170:5
Unsubdued: than many u. 391:7
Untroubling: u. and untroubled 114:27
Untruth: spoken u.s 373:24
Unwashed: great U. 70:8
Unwept: u. unhonoured, and unsung 340:1
Up: levelling u. to themselves 221:14
  u. and doing 257:6
  u. and go 159:20
  way u. is the w. down 198:25
  when they were u. they were up 6:12
Upbringing: u. a nun would envy 300:9
Upright: God hath made man u. 43:33
Uprising: wakening and u. prove 234:19
Uproar: u's. your only music 233:27
Upstairs: came u. into the world 120:6
  his Lordship . . . to be equal u. 25:16
  u. and downstairs 296:17
Urban: u. squat and packed with guile 69:14
Uriah: U. with his long hands slowly twining 137:15
Uricon: ashes under U. 210:22
Urine: wine of Shiraz into u. 142:14
Urn: bubbling and loud-hissing u. 127:12
  storied u. or animated bust 186:8
  tears that overflow thy u. 246:22
Us: difference between us and ouselves 285:13
USA: God bless the U. 14:24

v. of history 432:12
v. upon the heathen 41:18
Veni: v., vidi, vici 95:8
Venice: ocean's nursling V. 391:24
  V., on the Bridge of Sighs 90:5
  V. sat in state 90:6
  V. the eldest child of Liberty 463:17
Ventre: v. affamé n'a point d'oreilles 244:21
Venus: in the absence of the planet V. 139:21
  she is V. when she smiles 225:14
  V. grown fat 212:13
Venus: V. toute entière à sa proie attachée
    325:1
Ver: first born child of V. 28:6
Ver: v. egelidos refert tepores 103:18
Vera: quam cum istis v. sentire 114:23
Veracity: no v. in me 120:27
Verba: sesquipedalia v. 207:2
Verbe: V. c'est Dieu 211:17
Verboojuice: sesquippledan v. 450:7
Verbosity: exuberance of his own v. 143:11
Verbum: semel emissum volat irrevocabile v. 207:24
Verde: v. que te quiero v. 173:4
Verdict: v. afterwards 101:23
  v. of his own heart 228:8
  v. of the world 16:3
Vergängliche: alles V. 179:23
Verge: v.s on the poetical 141:4
Verify: always . . . v. your references 332:15
Verisimilitude: give artistic v. 177:32
Veritas: magna est v. et praevalet 47:30
Vérité: on ne doit aux morts que la v. 442:19
  v. est en marche 473:6
Verloren: v. ist v.! 81:5
Vermin: pernicious race of little odious v. 410:25
  Tory Party . . . they are lower than v. 33:6
Vero: se non è v. 9:20
Vers: chantant mes v., en vous émerveillant
    329:11
  dans les v. une juste cadence 64:10
  mon v., bien ou mal 64:15
Verse: blank v. has suffered . . . retrogression 157:19
  Book of V. – and Thou 164:1
  Book of V.s underneath the bough 164:2
  court others in v. 320:17
  curst be the v. 312:24
  free v. is like playing tennis 170:15
  full sail of this great v. 386:12
  great v. unto a little clan 231:26
  high immortal v. 275:22
  his v., the Lord knows 259:2
  look upon this v. 386:9
  married to immortal v. 276:33
  not v. now 73:15
  octosyllabic v. 90:25
  only with those in v. 120:26
  praised in v. 127:32
  reads v. and thinks she understands 74:9
  subject of all v. 71:21
  turnings intricate of v. 465:21
  unpolished rugged v. 150:32
  varying v. 315:34
  v. . . . . differs in nothing from prose 187:18
  v., Fame and Beauty 233:13
  v. is merely prose 92:27
  V. was a special illness 15:2
  v. will seem prose 79:26

very false gallop of v.s 345:19
wanting the accomplishment of v. 461:20
writtem much blank v. 94:6
Versiculos: v. nihil necesse est 103:14
Versifier: now swarm many v.s 396:19
Version: hundred v.s of it [religion] 389:3
Versuchen: alle die dich suchen v. dich 327:19
Vertical: let us honour . . . the v. man 14:5
Vertu: v. traitable 284:3
Vertue: ainsi que la v. le crime a ses degrés 325:2
Verulam: large-browed V. 421:28
Verwandlung: leben geht hin mit V. 327:15
Vesper: v. adest 103:20
Vespers: 'st, there's V.! 78:25
Vessel: goodly v. 256:12
  one v. unto honour 54:33
  potter's v. 37:20
  v. strikes with a shivering shock 401:17
  weaker v. 57:34
Vestal: blameless v's. lot 312:10
Vestry: see you in the v. after service 399:28
Veteran: world its v.s rewards 314:27
Vex: make enow themselves to v. them 85:32
Vexation: all is vanity and v. of spirit 43:15
Vial: preserve as in a vial 282:15
Vicar: hundred v.s down the lawn 69:12
  I will be the V. of Bray, Sir! 7:29
Vice: distinction between virtue and v. 221:11
  dwelling on their v.s 388:1
  forgiveness of each v. 60:27
  good old-gentlemanly v. 91:8
  homage paid by v. to virtue 248:12
  lashed the v. 410:12
  liberty is no v. 183:5
  of our v.s we can frame a ladder 256:28
  pride . . . v. of fools 313:3
  raptures and roses of v. 412:9
  reverend v. 354:18
  through tattered clothes small v.s do appear 363:1
  to flee v. is a virtue 207:13
  v. and virtues are products 414:7
  v. is a monster 314:4
  v. itself lost half its evil 82:15
  v. pays homage to virtue 88:19
  v. sometime's by action dignified 379:22
  v. whose strong corruption 383:29
  virtues are only v.s in disguise 248:21
Vicious: stroke its back and it turns v. 215:14
Vicissitude: sad v. of things 176:4, 406:3
Victim: some day . . . a v. must be found 177:20
  v. of the squire's whim 8:13
  v.s to a great lie 201:17
Victis: una salis v. 440:18
Victor: let the v.s when they come 11:12
  to the v.s belong the spoils 266:14
  V.'s triumph won 317:4
  whichever side may call itself the v. 105:25
Victor-victim: where the v. bleeds 396:5
Victoria, Queen: 408:19
Victories: peace hath her v. 282:10
  thousand v. once foiled 385:20
Victorious: o'er the ills of life v. 85:17
Victory: aboard the V., V. O 152:20
  before Alamein we never had a v. 113:22
  'but 'twas a famous v.' 401:10
  'Dig for V' 399:12
  in v.: magnanimity 113:18

v. of wax and parchment 81:18
v. . . . one and only nobility 228:4
v., she alone is free 275:35
v. . . . should be malleable 284:3
v., unexercised and unbreathed 282:18
v. will have nothing to do with ease 285:15
v.! a fig! 374:9
v.s are only vices in disguise 248:21
v.s of sincerity and moderation 175:20
v.s we write in water 359:3
v.s will plead like angels 365:7
world to hide v.s in 382:29
Virtuous: outrageously v. 404:7
  v. men pass mildly away 146:16
  when men grow v. in their old age 316:15
Virtus: v. est vitium fugere 207:13
Virtutem: v. videant 308:3
Vis: v. consili maiorum immeritus lues 208:29
Visage: daub his V. with the Smoke of Hell 164:26
  hides not his v. from our cottage 384:33
  men whose v.s do cream 369:3
Vishnu-land: in V. what Avatar? 79:10
Vision: by the v. splendid 464:8
  fatal v., sensible to feeling as to sight 365:19
  lost in stormy v.s 390:4
  loveliest v. far 232:9
  multiplied v.s 47:10
  my v.'s limited 141:13
  unread v. 155:27
  v. and the faculty divine 461:20
  v. of Christ 60:22
  v. or a waking dream 232:8
  v.s of glory 185:26
  watch or a v. 412:6
  what stately v. mocks my waking sense? 398:20
  where there is no v., the people perish 43:5
  write the v. 47:20
  young men shall see v.s 47:12
  young men's v. 149:16
Visit: superior people never make long v.s 286:20
  v.s . . . short and far between 60:5
Visiting: compunctious v.s of nature 364:32
Vita: non est vivere, sed valere v. est 268:10
Vitae: v. summa brevis 208:5
Vivamus: V. mea Lesbia 103:11
Vive: il faut que je v. 10:1
Vivre: v.? les serviteurs feront cela 439:22
Vixen: v. when she went to school 372:6
Vocabulary: v. of Bradshaw 148:7
Vocation: 'tis my v. 353:23
Vogue: totter into v. 445:8
Voice: after the fire a still small v. 36:18
  aggravate my v. 371:29
  ancestral v.s 118:3
  but a wandering v.? 467:7
  familiar v. wearies not 393:10
  God-gifted organ v. of England 416:17
  heard the v. of the Lord God 33:26
  her v. was ever soft, gentle and low 363:13
  his v. in all her music 390:6
  hollow v. is all I have 204:25
  I hear a v. you cannot hear 430:6
  in that tone of v. 322:16
  lost my v. most irrecoverably 449:6
  loudest v. 330:11
  melting v. through mazes running 276:34
  monstrous little v. 371:27

my v., I have lost it 355:17
no v.; but oh! the silence sank 117:11
no v.s, O Rhodope! 247:5
people's v. is odd 315:30
pleasant v.s 123:4
raise for good the supplicating v. 219:12
seasoned with a gracious 370:2
sing . . . with cheerful v. 236:5
sing with mortal v. 280:18
so in a v. 144:14
still small v. spake unto me 423:29
such a tender v. 62:15
thank you for your v.s 346:25
they beat – and a V. beat 427:13
thy v. is on the rolling air 418:39
two v.s are there 463:21
v. as the sound of many waters 58:4
v. divine rang through . . . the shrine 83:16
v. I hear this passing night 232:7
v. in the streets 41:22
v. is full of money 165:8
v. is heard through rolling drums 422:9
v. less loud 75:27
v. of all the gods 363:31
v. of him that crieth 45:30
v. of my heart 129:3
v. of one crying in the wilderness 48:35
v. of the brother's blood 34:8
v. of the dead 419:1
v. of the people 3:33
v. of the world 71:9
v. so thrilling ne'er was heard 466:22
v. that breathed o'er Eden 234:26
v. without a face 15:10
v.s of children are heard 62:21
v.s of young people 399:8
wailing in your v.s 72:2
where's the v., however soft 230:24
woods have no v. 288:16
your v. is music 29:18
Void: aching v. 125:23
Voix: j'aimais les v. du soir 244:24
  pour sa v., lointaine, et calme 439:5
Volatile: ain't I v.? 137:20
Volcano: dancing on a v. 336:25
Vole: passes the questing v. 448:11
Volontade: e'n la sua v. è nostra pace 132:1
Volscian: fluttered your V.s in Corioli 347:1
Voltaire 126:22
  mock on, V. 61:11
Volume: all Earth's v. carry 106:16
  creators of odd v.s 245–29
  raise the v.'s price 410:14
  sixty-two thousand v.s 175:17
  such v.s of stuff 250:14
  this fair v. 149:3
  v.s that I prize above my dukedom 380:30
Voluntas: sit pro ratione v. 227:25
Voluptuousness: compounded of misanthropy and v.
  262:31
Vomit: dog is turned to his own v. 57:37
  dog returneth to his v. 42:40
Votaress: imperial v. passed on 371:36
Votarist: sad v. in palmer's weed 275:10
Vote: straw v. only shows 198:20
  tart's v. 135:16
Vow: cancel all our v.s 148:21

thou shouldst not v. 43:24
v.s can't change nature 77:28
v.s to the blackest devil 352:12
v.s were then made for me 465:14
Vowel: A black, E white . . . v.s 327:21
Vox: V. populi 3:33
Voyage: last v, a great leap in the dark 202:9
v. of their life 360:33
Voyage: un beau v. 152:2
Voyager: lands the v. at last 158:1
Voyager: ceux des autres siècles que de v. 135:12
Voyaging: v. after maidens 226:13
Voyelles: A noir, E blanc . . . v. 327:21
Vulcan: foul as V.'s stithy 351:5
Vulgar: funny without being v. 178:24
v. boil 316:3
when it is looked upon as v. 456:13
Vulgarity: v. begins at home 456:18
Vulgi: V. semper insaniae proxima est 3:33
Vulgus: odi profanum v. et arceo 208:22
Vulture: v. dropping in for lunch 459:23
Vultus: non v. instantis tyranni 208:25

W

Wag: mother's w., pretty boy 187:29
Wage: gone and ta'en thy w.s 347:15
oppress the hireling in his w.s 47:7
royal w. 69:7
took their w.s and are dead 210:2
w.s of sin is death 54:24
Waggon-spoke: w.s made of long spinners' legs
378:30
Wagner: W. writhes 88:5
Wagon: hitch your w. to a star 159:12
Wail: w., for the world's wrong 390:20
Waist: dead from the w. down 74:30
hero from the w. up 274:7
that which her slender w. confined 445:1
Waistcoat: antique square-cut w. 115:11
providing infant negroes . . . with flannel w.s
140:37
Wait: make 'em w. 326:6
nearly had to w. 258:6
they that w. upon the Lord 45:37
very well, I can w. 338:24
w. and see 13:20
Waiter: if you look at the w. 140:21
w. roars it through the hall 247:6
way in which a Swiss w. talks 106:10
Waiting: people you are w. for 178:29
w. at the church 252:5
W. for Godot 28:15
w. for the end 159:22
w. time . . . is the hardest 146:29
Waiting-gentlewoman: talk so like a w. 353:30
Wake: do I w. or sleep? 232:8
w. and call me early . . . mother dear 421:4
w. and remember 74:20
Waking: take my w. slow 328:18
w., no such matter 386:15
Walcum: bit of talcum is always w. 292:5
Waldo: W. . . . would be . . . improved by death
335:15
Wales: all the way to W. 110:1

bleeds upon the road to W. 210:21
Walet: w. lay biforn him 107:29
Walk: doin' the Lambeth w. 171:11
echoing w.s between 280:37
oh for a closer w. with God 125:22
this is the way, w. ye in it 45:22
w. for a w.'s sake 242:3
w. humbly with thy God 47:19
w. out of in a morning 121:17
when'er I take my w.s abroad 44&:6
will you w. a little faster 101:17
Walked: Cat. He w. by himself 241:17
Walking: craves wary w. 359:25
from w. up and down in it 36:33
I nauseate w. 120:32
men as trees, w. 51:35
w. round him has always tired me 29:21
when I am not w., I am reading 246:2
Wall: close the w. up with our English dead 357:3
doesn't love a w. 170:8
four great w.s in the New Jerusalem 72:19
Great W. of China 444:7
Humpty Dumpty sat on a w. 296:23
old oak w. 27:6
outward w.s so costly gay 387:8
standing like a stone w. 28:24
stone w.s do not a prison make 258:13
thy ancient w.s 61:5
watch the w. my darling 240:21
white-washed w. 181:9
without a city w. 4:7
wooden w.s 123:8
w.s and towers was girdled round 117:35
Wall-paper: one-armed man . . . pasting on w.
198:13
Wallace: wha hae wi' W. bled 85:10
Waller: W. was smooth 315:34
Wallet: time hath, . . . a w. at his back 382:12
Walnut: across the w.s and the wine 421:6
cows under a w. tree 336:9
Walpole, Sir Robert 472:11
Walrus: W. and the Carpenter 102:3
Walsinghame: holy land of W. 325:6
Waly: w. w. up the bank 23:23
Wand: touching all with thine opiate w. 394:13
Wander: how now, wit.! whither w. you.? 344:16
we will not w. more 420:19
Wanderer: foiled circuitous w. 11:34
w. from the narrow way 126:14
w. is a man from birth 11:7
Wandering: chid their w.s 180:24
have one with me w. 288:15
Want: anything that you w. 253:8
didn't w. to do it 263:3
everything that he w.s 211:15
freedom from w. 329:23
provide for human w.s 82:12
ring out the w. 418:26
things which he does not w. 205:15
w. something you . . . won't w. 205:11
w.s what he is supposed to w. 169:17
Wanting: always something w. 219:31
art found w. 47:4
tried and found w. 111:6
Wanton: sleep pretty w.s 134:3
w. love corrupteth 19:16
w. smiled, father wept 188:1

weep not, my w. 187:29
Wantonness: kindles in clothes a w. 200:5
Wapping: parted at W. 307:27
War: all their w.s are merry 109:28
  all this w. been wrought 265:20
  as long as w. is regarded as wicked 456:13
  blast of w. 357:3
  British W. Office 387:29
  came forth to w. 264:17
  cold war 26:8
  condition of w. of everyone against everyone
    202:4
  dauntless in w. 340:12
  defeat without a w. 112:16
  discipline of w.s 357:8
  done well out of the w. 21:14
  empire founded by w. 285:27
  first casualty when w. comes is truth 218:16
  France . . . has not lost the w. 173:16
  good w. 67:5
  Great Britain is going to make w. 32:13
  great God of W. 311:6
  he maketh w.s to cease 38:25
  he that first invented w. 267:15
  hear of w.s and rumours of w.s 51:9
  how we began this w. 320:14
  in w. . . . there are no winners 105:25
  in w. moral considerations account 291:13
  in w.: resolution 113:18
  little of the w. as he will 20:17
  lose the next w. 114:3
  love's a man of w. 199:10
  marching as to w. 25:4
  my subject is w. 302:6
  my w.s were global 326:12
  neither shall they learn w. any more 44:33
  never a good w. 168:19
  no less renowned than w. 282:10
  no less than w. to waste 280:
  nor w., or battle's sound 277:23
  pigmy w.s 419:16
  pomp and circumstance of glorious w. 375:5
  prophesying w. 118:3
  quickest way of ending a w. 301:6
  sent into any foreign w.s 329:21
  state of w. by nature 410:15
  still, w.s and lechery 382:21
  subsequent w.s have been lost there 300:18
  tempered by w. 235:15
  testament of bleeding w. 377:3
  that w. is an evil . . . we all know 429:9
  there is no discharge in that w. 43:34
  they are for w. 40:29
  they'll give a w. 337:3
  thousand w.s of old 418:28
  titanic w.s had groined 302:15
  to w. and arms I fly 258:14
  unconditional w. on poverty 218:20
  unsuccessful or successful w. 126:34
  w. . . . is toil and trouble 150:4
  w. against hunger 235:21
  w. can only be abolished through w. 266:10
  w. is . . . continuation of politics 114:32
  W. is being deliberately prolonged 338:3
  W. is hell 396:3
  w. is like love 67:9
  w. is much too important 115:2

  w. is much too serious a thing 414:13
  W. is Peace 300:22
  w. is Prussia's national industry 282:27
  w. knows no power 69:19
  w. minus the shooting 301:7
  W. to End W. 450:15
  w. to the knife 303:8
  w., w. is still the cry 89:14
  w. waged without monetary reserves 324:4
  w. was in his heart 38:34
  w.'s a game 127:22
  w.'s glorious art 472:16
  w.s begin in the minds of men 435:8
  w.s brought nothing about 151:28
  w.s more evil 110:18
  w.s of kites and crows 282:22
  w.s of the peoples 112:7
  what can w., but endless w. still breed? 282:11
  what did you do in the Great W. daddy? 3:13
  whom w. . . . . hath slain 145:16
  won the w. single-handed 66:19
  wrong w. at the wrong place 66:13
War-drum: w. throbbed no longer 419:31
War-war: jaw-jaw is always better than w. 113:13
  jaw-jaw is better than w. 264:7
Warble: w., child; make passionate my sense of
  hearing 363:24
Warbler: Attic w. pours her throat 187:8
  Chaucer, the first w. 416:10
  every w. has his tune by heart 126:29
Ward: pretty young W.s in Chancery 177:7
  thou knowest my old w. 354:10
  w. has no heart 328:23
Warder: what, w., ho! 340:17
Ware: I should dine at W. 125:18
Wares: if you want to buy my w. 316:29
Waring: what's become of W. 79:9
Warld: this fals w. is bot transitory 152:13
Warm: w. but pure 92:28
Warmeth: he w. himself 45:40
Warning: come without w. 133:4
  give little w. 24:4
  horrid w. gapèd wide 231:13
  my w.s . . . had been so numerous 113:20
Warp: weave the w. 185:22
Warrant: signed my death w. 119:5
Warrior: home they brought her w. dead 422:12
  painful w. famousèd for fight 385:20
  pale w.s, death-pale were they all 231:13
  stern joy which w.s feel 339:22
  this is the happy w. 326:4
  w. taking his rest 460:2
  who is the happy w.? 461:10
Warsaw: resigned in W. 341:17
Warts: w., and everything as you see me 129:14
Warwick: W. and Talbot 357:18
  W., peace 358:9
Wash: w. me in the water 8:24
  W. That Man right Out of My Hair 191:15
Wash-pot: Moab is my w. 39:4
Washing: difference between painting a face and not
  w. it 170:27
  taking in one another's w. 6:19
Washing-day: being w., dined upon cold meat
  307:20
Washington, George 251:22
  bequeathed the name of W. 93:16

with w. and whirlwind wrestle 256:12
Waving: not w. but drowning 399:15
Wax: as w. melteth before the fire 39:13
  how neat she spreads the w. 447:12
  w. in the eternal ear 187:24
  w. to receive 89:5
Wax-works: w. weren't made to be looked at for
    nothing 101:30
Way: adorns and cheers our w. 182:4
  already on the w. 237:7
  as I wandered by the w. 393:20
  be nice to people on your w. up 283:5
  best w. out 170:13
  broad is the w. 49:25
  cheerful w.s of men 279:14
  consider her w.s 41:26
  dirty, dangerous w. 182:17
  down the labyrinthine w.s 427:12
  dwelt among the untrodden w.s 466:13
  eftest w. 373:17
  erred and strayed from thy w.s 318:12
  her w.s are w.s of gentleness 403:24
  her w.s are w.s of pleasantness 41:23
  his uncouth w. 279:1
  in the w. with him 49:2
  let all her w.s be unconfined 320:18
  long is the w. and hard 279:2
  looking one w., and rowing another 80:26
  looks both w.s 308:6
  many are the w.s . . . to heaven 105:14
  narrow is the w. 49:26
  neither are your w.s my w.s 46:13
  nine and sixty w.s 239:15
  parochial w.s 193:6
  part of all the w. through 183:14
  point me out the w. 230:31
  prepare ye the w. of the Lord 45:30
  seeds fell by the w. side 50:11
  solar walk or milky w. 313:29
  subtle w.s I keep 158:9
  such ever was love's w. 74:5
  this is the w. 45:21
  to keep thee in all thy w.s 40:2
  Two W.s 236:22
  unrighteous w.s 80:5
  vindicate the w.s of God 313:26
  war . . . always finds a w. 67:9
  w. is empty yet 247:17
  w. of all the earth 35:23
  w., the truth, the life 53:28
  w. was long 339:23
  winning w. 120:18
  wonderful w. wid you 184:24
  world and its w. have a certain worth 78:34
  w.s that are dark 194:23
We: people like us are W. 241:5
  who, whom? W. or they? 253:1
Weak: bear the infirmities of the w. 54:49
  concessions of the w. 81:14
  delicately w. 314:23
  him that is w. in the faith 54:45
  refuge of w. minds 109:14
  surely the W. shall perish 342:25
  to be w. is miserable 278:8
  w. alone repent 90:27
  w. and beggarly elements 56:8
Weakness: all else is w. 439:19

amiable w. 162:32
  glorious style of w! 188:11
  no w., no contempt 281:29
  strength is made perfect in w. 56:6
  stronger by w. 444:13
Weal: come w., come woe 341:1
Wealth: as their w. increases 267:10
  consume w. without producing it 387:24
  if we command w. 83:4
  let w. and commerce . . . die 266:7
  no w. but Life 333:18
  poor man's w. 396:14
  rich man's w. is his strong city 41:33
  squandering w. 149:22
  w. a well-spent age 97:27
  w. I ask not 407:23
  w. ye find another keeps 393:29
  where w. accumulates 180:18
Weaned: were we not w. 145:8
Weapon: art, is not a w. 236:1
  his w. wit 205:17
  Time's most lethal w. 397:22
Wear: better to w. out 129:20
  rather w. out than rust out 453:1
  w. and weary out your days 131:8
Weariness: much study is a w. of the flesh 44:14
  w. can snore upon the flint 347:12
  w. may toss him to my breast 199:21
  w. of thee 146:6
  w., the fever, and the fret 232:2
Wearing: I'm w. awa' 291:10
Weary: art thou w., art thou languid 292:24
  he that is w., let him sit 199:14
  w. be at rest 36:37
  w. in well doing 56:13
  w., stale, flat, and unprofitable 347:36
Wearywide: within a space and a w. space 226:7
Weasel: pop goes the w.! 266:2
  w. sucks eggs 344:38
  when a w. sucks eggs 329:12
Weather: blue Italian w. 391:17
  calm or stormy w. 331:4
  come wind, come w. 80:34
  dreadful hot w. 17:16
  first talk is of the w. 219:17
  gorgeous w. 96:6
  hold up the w. 264:12
  if it prove fair w. 409:9
  jolly boating w. 122:22
  little we fear w. without 425:27
  not in fine w. 115:13
  respite to husbands the w. may send 433:22
  season of calm w. 464:15
  through cloudy w. 24:4
  waiting for the w. to break 309:9
  w. the cuckoo likes 193:12
  winter and rough w. 344:37
  you don't need a w. man 153:8
Weather-wise: some are w. 168:22
Web: out flew the w. 419:14
  trafficked for strange w.s 305:16
  w. of our life 343:10
  what a tangled w. we weave 340:18
Webster: W. was much posessed by death 157:10
Wed: think to w. it 343:3
Wedding: before she has bought her w. clothes 2:17
  earliest w. day 234:26

Whale: great w.s come sailing by 11:5
    talk like w.s 183:2
    trying to grill a w. 320:12
    ye W.s and all that move in the Waters 318:22
What: knew w.'s w. 87:7
    knows w.'s w. 141:17
    w. is which and which is w. 274:33
    w. was, again may be 77:30
    Who Gets W. When How 248:24
What-you-may-call-it: W. is his prophet 137:35
What-you-may-call-um: to W. 102:22
Whatever: w. thou has been 92:36
What's-his-name: there is no W. 137:35
Whaup: w.s are crying 407:27
Wheat: immortal w. which never should be reaped
    431:15
    thy belly is like a heap of w. 44:26
Wheedling: taught the w. arts 174:1
Wheel: butterfly upon a w. 312:25
    fortune, . . . turn thy w.! 362:9
    little Tin Gods on w.s 240:15
    want to shee the w.s go wound 190:1
    w. broken at the cistern 44:12
    w. . . . in the midst of a wheel 46:32
    w. is come full circle 363:12
    w.'s kick 270:2
    w.s of Being slow 418:3
    why tarry the w.s of his chariots 35:28
Wheel-barrow: red w. glazed with rain 457:19
    she wheeled her w. 7:27
When: forgotten to say 'W'. 459:21
Whence: canst not tell w. it cometh 53:6
Where: never know w. the hell you are 336:13
Whereabouts: conceal our w. 335:13
Wherefore: for every why he had a w. 87:6
Wherewithal: had not always w. 320:25
Whiff: w. of grapeshot 99:27
Whig: caught the W.s bathing 142:25
    dear Bathurst . . . hated a W. 224:4
    dished the W.s 135:8
    first W. was the Devil 223:4
    great W. authority 135:7
    not like much to see a W. in any dress 223:27
    ridiculous for a W. to pretend 223:31
    Tory men and W. measures 143:14
    whether I were a W. or a Tory 410:24
    W.s admit no force but argument 71:23
Whim: tempted by a private w. 30:28
    w., envy, or resentment 111:20
    w. of iron 200:1
Whimper: not with a bang but a w. 156:17
Whimsies: they have my w. 320:17
Whinger: out with your w. 24:6
Whip: bear the w.s and scorns of time 350:14
    chastised you with w.s 36:12
    stroke of the w. 48:16
    w. for the horse 42:37
    w. to lash the rascals 375:16
Whipping: who would 'scape w.? 350:7
Whirligig: w. of time brings in his revenges 383:32
Whirlwind: reap the w. 47:7
    regardless of the sweeping w.'s sway 185:24
    rides in the w. 1:9
Whisker: dye one's w.s green 102:18
Whiskerandos: ha! no, it is my W. .. 395:13
Whiskies: born below par to th'extent of two w.
    285:4

Whisky: freedom and w. gang thegither 83:29
    w. priest . . . never had him in the house 187:26
Whisper: busy w., circling round 181:6
    w. down the field 239:31
Whispered: w. in heaven 161:10
Whispering: keeps eternal w. around 233:4
Whist: loved a good game at w. 245:21
Whistle: clear as a w. 88:28
    Cousin's w.! Go my love 72:20
    joly whistle wel y-wet 108:12
    let it w. as it will 340:14
    pay too much for your w. 168:24
    w. and I'll come to you 85:34
    w. her off 374:33
    w, while you work 142:20
    w.s thrice 116:31
    you know how to w., don't you 18:1
Whistler, James McN. 456:18
Whistling: w. to keep myself from being afraid
    151:20
White: grew it w. in a single night 93:17
    moment w. then melts 85:18
    my soul is w. 62:18
    nor w. so very w. 98:15
    O so w.! 225:13
    only one destiny. And it is w. 161:8
    they'll 'elp you a lot with the W.s! 239:23
    too w. for hell 150:21
    w. already to harvest 53:11
    w. clear w. inside 239:9
    w. is not my favourite colour 247:21
    w. it stays for ever 144:6
    W. Man's burden 241:10
    w. shall not neutralise the black 78:10
    whiter than w. 3:14
    w.s of their eyes 322:20
White House: Log-cabin to W. 426:1
    no whitewash at the W. 295:8
Whitehall: grass grows all up and down W. Court
    307:17
    sentinel on W. gate looked forth 261:6
Whitest: W. Man I Know 195:11
    w. man I know 226:28, 247:21
Whitethroat: w. builds 74:36
Whitewash: no w. at the White House 295:8
    whiter than the w. on the wall 8:24
Whither: know not W., willy-nilly blowing 164:13
    w. goest thou? 53:30
    w. thou goest, I will go 35:38
Whiting: as the w. said 205:4
Whitman, Walt 128:15
    beautiful aged Walt W. 173:1
    daintily dressed Walt W. 111:4
Whizz-Bang: Here comes a W. 451:20
Who: w. or why, or which or what 250:15
    w., whom? We or they? 253:1
Whole: inspire the w. 119:14
    parts of one stupendous w. 313:33
    seeing the w. of them 333:17
    till the w. has been surveyed 220:2
    w. . . . has a beginning, a middle and an end
    10:4
Whooping: out of all w.! 345:21
Whore: great w. 58:27
    lead a w. to culture 304:14
    morals of a w. 220:25
    more like a w.'s than a man's 240:7

w. you, won't you . . . join the dance 101:18
with all my w. but much against my heart 306:5
wrote my w. across the sky 249:28
William: Father W. the young man cried 401:22
  you are old Father W. 100:33
William the Silent 289:11
Willie: little W. from his mirror 6:8
  Wee W. Winkie runs through the town 274:1,
  298:13
Willing: Barkis is w. 137:7
  spirit indeed is w. 51:22
  w. faithfully to serve 129:11
Willow: green w. in my garland 201:2
  hanged our harps upon the w.s 41:9
  sang 'W., titwillow, titwillow' 177:35
  sing all a green w. 375:17
  w. grows aslant a brook 352:19
Willow-tree: al under the w. 107:5
  I'll hang my harp on a weeping w. 8:21
Willy: humble W. wet-leg 249:2
  wouldn't have a W. or a Sam 290:8
Wilson: 14th Mr W. 146:7
Wimpled: w., whining, purblind, wayward boy
  363:27
Win: to w. or to lose it all 286:6
  yet wouldst wrongly w. 364:28
Wind: aloud the w. doth blow 364:8
  beat of the off-shore w. 239:32
  blow, w.! Come wrack 367:26
  blow, w.s and crack your cheeks! 362:14
  blowin' in the w. 153:6
  blows the w. on the moors 407:27
  change, as ye list, ye w.s 174:26
  come as the w.s come 340:22
  come w., come weather 80:34
  courted by all the w.s 281:24
  faithless as the w.s 341:21
  feather for each w. that blows 384:16
  for whom all w.s are quiet 412:8
  frozen w. crept on above 390:12
  gathering w.s will call the darkness 394:1
  gentle w. does move 61:13
  God tempers the w. 405:14
  great w.s shoreward blow 11:4
  he that observeth the w. shall not sow 44:6
  hear a voice in every w. 187:5
  heareth not the loud w.s 466:7
  his hammer of w. 428:2
  hollow blasts of w. 174:28
  how the w. doth ramm! 317:14
  impatient as the w. 463:3
  imprisoned in the viewless w.s 368:22
  large a charter as the w. 345:8
  like the w.'s blast 338:14
  like W. I go 164:12
  listen instead to the w.'s text 427:7
  melodious w.s have birth 62:26
  mild, even as the w.s and waters are 394:4
  motions of the viewless w.s 465:20
  nor ever w. blows loudly 417:21
  north w. doth blow 297:11
  O wild West W. 392:4
  pass me by as the idle w. 360:30
  prophesy unto the w. 46:38
  roaring in the w. all night 465:32
  sits the w. in that corner? 372:37
  still ailing, w.? 75:8

stormy w.s do blow 97:21, 290:7
sullen w. was soon awake 77:4
they have sown the w. 47:7
thou winter w. 345:12
'twas but the w. 89:22
unhelped by any w. 117:30
visitation of the w.s 355:31
warm w., the west w. 270:5
west w., wanton w. 389:9
western w., when wilt thou blow 516
when the w. is southerly 350:1
when the w. blows 296:24
when the w.s are breathing low 391:11
which way the w. blows 153:8
which way the w. is 342:6
whizzing of a pleasant w. 306:21
who has seen the w.? 331:9
why does the w. blow 103:2
w. about, and in and out 415:22
w. bloweth where it listeth 53:6
w. blows it back again 61:11
w. blows over the lonely of heart 471:9
w. doth blow today 23:21
w. in that door 265:13
w. is hovering o'er the mountain's brow 390:26
w. of change 264:8
w. of doctrine 56:16
w. passeth over it 40:10
w. shall blaw for evermair 23:20
w. that blows through me 249:4
w. that follows fast 130:9
W., that grand old harper 398:18
w., w.! thou art sad 288:22
w. whistles 395:13
w.s and seas are troublesome 131:12
w.s begin to rise 417:31
w.s blow fast as the stars are slow 427:1
w.s come to me from the fields of sleep 464:4
w.s of heaven mix for ever 391:27
w.s of the heavens 175:26
w.s of the World 238:29
wings of the w. 37:35
young w.s fed it 393:24
Wind: frisch weht der W der Heimat zu 444:1
Wind-flower: bare w.s and violets 393:21
Winding-sheet: old England's w. 60:20
  w. of Edward's race 185:22
Windmill: not giants but w.s 104:16
Window: clapt the w. to 108:7
  cleaned the w.s 176:29
  crimson-blank the w.s flare 240:10
  light through yonder w. 379:8
  not by eastern w.s only 115:26
  opening the w.s at Randalls 16:27
  seen in a stained-glass w.'s hue 32:14
  stars through the w. pane 234:8
  storied w. richly dight 276:15
  takes this w. for the east 132:13
  through w.s . . . call on us 146:10
  throw the whole out of the w. 251:10
  underneath my w. plaineth 396:18
  up flew the w.s all 125:13
  w-i-n, win, d-e-r, der, w. 139:10
  w. through thy grace 199:28
  w.s of heaven were opened 34:15
  w.s of the soul 60:25
Windowpane: rubs its back upon the w.s 156:21

Windward: w. of the law 111:22
Wine: aged and a great w. 272:20
  bin of w. 407:29
  cargo of . . . sweet white w. 269:24
  doesn't get into the w. 110:25
  drinking the blude-red w. 23:8
  fetch to me a pint o' w. 84:20
  good w. a friend, or being dry 4:1
  good w. is a good familiar 374:27
  'good w. needs no bush' 346:17
  I'll not look for w. 225:20
  ill w. turns none to good 433:16
  like good w. 308:14
  look not upon the w. when it is red 42:33
  misusèd w. 275:6
  Mr Weston's good w. 16:24
  new friend is as new w. 48:7
  new w. into old bottles 49:34
  old books, old w.s 182:13
  old w. wholesomest 449:1
  pass the rosy w. 139:27
  pour out the w. without restraint or stay 402:22
  purple as their w.s 311:27
  red w. of Shiraz 142:14
  shouteth by reason of w. 39:24
  some are fond of Spanish w. 269:23
  take a glass of w. 396:1
  they are drunken, but not, with w. 45:16
  truth comes out in w. 310:11
  use a little w. 45
  when the w. is in 28:19
  w. and women, mirth and laughter 91:12
  w. is a mocker 42:23
  w. maketh merry 44:2
  W. of Life 163:27
  w. of life is drawn 366:5
  w. that maketh glad the heart of man 40:11
  w. they drink in Paradise 109:32
  w. upon a foreign tree 426:16
  w., woman and song 260:5
  women and w. should life employ 174:9
Wine-breath: drink from the w. 470:4
Wine-cup: taste not when the w. glistens 340:26
Winepress: trodden the w. alone 46:20
Wing: horse with w.s 347:9
  luminous w.s in vain 12:23
  nor knowst 'ou w. from tail 317:17
  riches certainly make themselves w.s 42:32
  shadow of thy w.s 37:34
  soars on golden w. 276:5
  take under my w. 177:34
  that which hath w.s shall tell the matter 44:3
  the seraphims; each one had six w.s 45:2
  with w.s as swift 349:3
  w.s of the morning 41:11
  w.s of the wind 37:35
Winged: w. life destroy 60:31
Wink: first a start and then a w. 93:32
  not slept one w. 347:11
  nudge, nudge, w. w. 286:13
  w. and hold out mine iron 356:27
Winner: in war . . . there are no w.s 105:25
Winning: glory of the w. were she won 272:3
  w. way 120:18
Winston: W. is back 113:19
  W. with his hundred-horse-power mind 21:18
Winter: April on the heel of limping W. treads 378:26

bare w. was suddenly changed to spring 393:20
Christmas . . . in the middle of w. 2:9
English w. 92:12
forty w.s shall besiege thy brow 385:12
fowre thowsand w. 5:15
furious w. blowing 325:20
I., . . . of all the seasons, most love w. 305:25
if W. comes 392:12
in w. enjoy 63:9
in w. I get up at night 407:12
in w., when the dismal rain came 398:18
it was the w. wild 277:22
my age is as the lusty w. 344:30
no w. in thy year 256:6
nor the furious w.'s rage 347:15
O W., ruler of th' inverted year 127:14
six weeks' w. in our blood 391:20
there was no w. in't 344:6
w. evening settles down 156:30
w. his delights 97:29
w. in thy year 79:17
w. is come and gone 389:28
w. is icummen in 317:14
w. is past 44:20
w. of our discontent 377:20
w. talk by the fireside 20:22
w.'s rains and ruins 412:1
w.'s traces 411:32
Winter-time: in the w. it's another thing 290:7
Winters: blitz of a boy is Timothy W. 104:7
Wiped: should have w. it up 405:28
Wire: across the w.s 17:20
Wisdom: apply our hearts unto w. 39:34
  be famous then by w. 281:6
  beginning of w. is to be done with folly 207:13
  can w. be put in a silver rod 60:21
  celestial W. calms the mind 219:13
  fear of the Lord is the begining of w. 40:20
  highest w. has but one science 431:3
  how can he get w.? 48:24
  in much w. is much grief 43:16
  love is the w. of the fool 224:13
  palace of w. 63:10
  part of w. 127:18
  price of w. is above rubies 37:6
  proverb is . . . all men's w. 334:3
  vain w. all 279:3
  w. . . . . the pursuing of the best ends 212:21
  w. and goodness to the vile seem vile 362:34
  w. at one entrance 279:14
  w. crieth without 41:22
  w. excelleth folly 43:17
  w. is better than rubies 41:30
  w. is justified 50:3
  w. is the principal thing 41:24
  w. lays on evil men 127:24
  w. lingers 419:35
  w. of our ancestors 82:27
  w. of this world is foolishness 55:2
  w. shall die with you 36:44
  w. to know the difference 294:15
  w. was mine 302:18
  with how little w. the world is governed 302:20
  W.'s aid 119:20
Wise: be not righteous . . . neither make thyself over
  w. 43:31
  be w., and love 382:10

be w. today 472:23
cunning men pass for w. 20:4
each in each, immediately w. 69:23
exceeding w. 359:4
have the courage to be w. 207:16
more of the fool than of the w. 19:23
one of the w. men 19:13
pretend they ne'er so w. 281:20
seeing ye yourselves are w. 56:3
so w. so young, they say 378:3
type of the w. who soar 46713
very, very w. 116:17
w., amazed, temperate 366:6
w. are never deluded 33:9
w. in his own conceit 42:39 42:41
w. in your own conceits 54:37
w. man kick a pebble 110:32
w. man that had it for a by-word 20:9
w. man will make more opportunities 20:35
w. through excess of wisdom 158:22
w. want love 392:26
w. with speed 472:14
woe unto them that are w. in their own eyes 45:1
worldly but not worldly w. 323:1
Wiser: thou speakest w. than thou art ware of
    344:35
w. than other people 109:4
w. than we know 158:29
Wisest: more than the w. can answer 119:32
    W., virtuousest, discreetest, best 280:26
Wish: don't you w. you may get it? 24:16
I w., I w. he'd go away 271:10
their w. has been granted 15:22
w. was father . . . to that thought 356:12
w. you anything but just what you are 214:5
without a w., without a will 202:17
Wishes: all their country's w. blest 119:15
w. and ways will be as nothing 193:21
Wisp: w. on the morass 93:14
Wist: had I w. before I kissed 23:24
Wistfulness: publish their w. abroad 218:19
Wit: as high as metaphysic w. can fly 87:7
at their w.s end 40:18
baiting place of w. 396:14
beef, . . . does harm to my w. 382:27
cause that w. is in other men 355:13
dunce with w.s 311:22
erected w. maketh us to know . . . perfection
    396:22
great w.s are sure to madness 149:10
hast so much w. and mirth 2:5
home-keeping youth have ever homely w.s 384:1
how now, w.! whither wander you? 344:16
how the w. brightens! 313:16
impropriety is the soul of w. 270:22
in w. a man 312:31
little less than little w. 382:7
liveliest effusions of w. 16:30
loudest w. 92:19
malice mingles with a little w. 150:22
man of w., bad character 305:7
men of w. will condescend 410:3
monarchy of w. 98:26
no more w. than a Christian 382:27
poetry is conceived in their w.s 12:26
proverb is one man's w. 334:3
rhyming mother w.s 267:13

shoots his w. 346:16
some beams of w. 150:28
soul of w. 349:21
stolen his w.s away 134:10
too proud for a w. 181:17
true w. is nature 313:7
ware of mine own w. 344:36
warming his five w.s the white owl . . . sits
    423:20
wine is in, the w. is out 28:19
w. . . . in the very first line 181:20
w. among Lords 220:24
w. enough to run away 87:26
w. in all languages 151:32
w. invites you by his looks to come 124:31
w. is out 373:12
w. that can creep 312:28
w. will shine 151:6
w. with dunces 311:22
W's. End 304:5
w's. the noblest frailty of the mind 342:31
Witchcraft: this only is the w. I have used 374:6
Witches: there are w. 71:1
Withal: Time ambles w. 345:24
Wither: our w.s are unwrung 351:11
state . . . w.s away 159:26
Within: ne'er look w. 125:1
never went w. 124:2
they that are w. 132:17
Without: they that are w. 132:17
things I'd been better w. 303:15
Witness: bore w. gloriously 281:31
thou such weak w. 277:29
w. of that light 52:51
w. ye days and nights 151:17
Witnesses: cloud of w. 57:14
Wittles: I live on broken w.s 137:8
w. and drink to me 137:16
Witty: anger makes dull men witty 18:10
not only w. in myself 355:13
stumbling on something w. 17:12
tend to be w. 31:11
w. and it shan't be long 109:22
Wives: go mad and beat their w. 96:9
husbands, love your w. 56:32
man with seven w. 296:5
married three w. at a time 284:18
old w.'s fables 56:43
poisoned by their w. 377:2
sky changes when they are w. 346:4
w. are so fulsomely familiar 120:33
W. are young men's mistresses 19:12
Wiving: w. goes by destiny 369:30
Wizard: w.s that peep 45:6
Wodehouse, P.G. 299:11
Woe: another's w. 62:22
brought . . . w. with loss of Eden 277:32
discover sights of w. 278:5
easer of all w.s 28:7
feel another's w. 316:8
her works gave signs of w. 280:35
hideous notes of w. 92:15
life protracted is protracted w. 219:9
listen to the artless w.s 453:9
old w.s new wail 385:24
one w. doth tread upon another's heel 352:18
proved a very w. 387:5

rearward of a conquered w. 386:16
such a w. 7:9
suits of w. 347:35
tale of w. 162:13
w. is me 40:28
w. to that man by whom the offence cometh 50:30
w. to the vanquished 255:9
w. unto you 52:7
w.s unencumbered 316:10
w.s which hope thinks infinite 393:19
Woe-begone: man, . . . so w. 355:11
Wold: that clothe the w. and meet the sky 419:7
Wolf: every w.'s and lion's howl 60:12
keep the w. far hence 449:4
the boy cried 'w.' 3:26
w. also shall dwell with the lamb 45:10
w. in Sheep's Clothing 3:28
Who's Afraid of the Big bad W.? 142:19
Wolf's-bane: neither twist w. . . . for its poisonous wine 231:27
Wollop: d'ye think I'd w. him? 33:4
Wolves: inwardly they are ravening w. 49:27
w. have preyed 373:27
Woman: bad, ugly w. 93:31
bloom on a w. 25:28
body of a weak and feeble w. 157:26
brief. . . . as w.'s love 351:9
child or our grandmother Eve, . . . a w. 363:21
content to be a w. 409:24
contentious w. 42:47
destructive, damnable, deceitful w. 301:19
difference between one w. and another 388:14
dispute . . . not caused by a w. 227:26
done the old w. in 389:6
don't become a young w. 395:30
driving . . . with a pretty w. 222:25
eternal in w. draws on us 179:24
every w. is . . . to be gained by . . . flattery 109:17
every w. is at heart a rake 314:26
every w. should marry 143:23
fair w. . . . without discretion 42:1
fat white w. 122:19
frailty, thy name is w. 348:3
God made the w. for the man 416:14
great glory in a w. 429:8
her voice was ever soft, . . . an excellent thing in w. 363:13
I am a w.. When I think I must speak 345:22
if a w. have long hair 55:19
large-brained w. 72:9
let still the w. take an elder than herself 383:10
love and good company improves a w. 161:20
lovely w. stoops to folly 157:8, 182:38
man delights not me; nor w. neither 349:36
man that is born of w. 37:1, 320:3
man that lays his hand upon a w. 430:13
no other but a w.'s reason 384:2
no other purgatory but a woman 28:5
not yet a w. 354:3
O W! . . . a ministering angel thou 340:19
of every ill, a w. is the worst 184:21
old w. who lived in a shoe 298:5
one man . . . have I found; but a w. . . . have I not found 43:32
perfect w., nobly planned 466:17
poor lone w. 355:21

she is a w., therefore may be wooed 381:28
silliest w. can manage 241:25
so unto the man is w. 257:14
sort of w. . . . one would . . . bury for nothing 138:33
speaks small like a w. 371:1
still be a w. to you 304:26
sufficient for a w. 282:26
sweeter w. ne'er drew breath 215:10
the w.'s a whore 222:10
there was never yet fair w. 362:17
think I could be a good w. 425:21
to show a w. when he loves her 76:12
tranced w., bound and stark 169:7
virtuous w. is a crown to her husband 42:2
was ever w. in this humour wooed? 377:27
wasteful w. 305:20
what a w. says 104:1
what does a w. want? 169:14
what is a w.? 124:16
when it [tongue] ain't a w's. 140:27
who can find a virtuous w.? 43:10
who takes a w. must be undone 174:12
why can't a w. be more like a man? 253:21
wickedness of a w. 48:15
wilt thou have this w. 319:41
wisest w. in Europe 156:36
w., a sick child 439:15
w., . . . alone, can venture to commit them 425:15
w. as old as she looks 119:6
w. clothed with the sun 58:20
w. drew her long black hair 157:9
w. for the hearth 422:11
w. has her way 203:30
w. I love 154:12
w. in every case; . . . look for the w. 152:8
W. in the Case 163:20
w. is a foreign land 305:23
w. is always fickle and changing 440:24
w. is his game 422:10
w. is jealous because of her lack of it [amour propre] 188:4
w. is like a teabag 326:7
w. is like an elephant 163:8
w. is only a w. 238:14
w. is so hard upon the w. 422:13
W. Killed with Kindness 201:4
w. led him to the promised land 152:20
w. ! lovely w.! 301:20
w. loves her lover 91:15
w. . . . may marry whom she likes 425:16
w. moved is like a fountain troubled 380:23
w. of mean understanding 17:2
w. sat in unwomanly rags 205:3
w. seldom asks advice 2:17
w. that deliberates is lost 1:12
w. that seduces all mankind 174:1
W. . . . the last thing civilized by Man 272:22
w. the rib and crooked piece of man 71:10
w. therefore to be won 357:30
w., w., rules us still 287:16
w. was arrayed in purple and scarlet 58:28
w. was full of good works 53:48
w., what have I to do with thee? 53:5
w. who cannot be ugly 242:17
W. who Did 4:13

w. who does a . . . lot for her old governesses 321:13

w. who is really kind to dogs 29:15

w. whose dresses are made in Paris 336:11

w. will always sacrifice herself 270:17

w. without a man 184:5

w. yet think him an angel 425:3

w.'s at best a contradiction 314:30

w.'s business to get married 388:18

w.'s cause is man's 422:21

w.'s deaf and does not hear 315:7

w.'s desire 118:32

w.'s whole existence 91:7

w.'s whole life is a history of broken affections 215:17

Womanhood: good, heroic w. 257:9

Womankind: faith in w. 422:22

    thinks the worst he can of w. 204:6

Womb: from his mother' w. untimely ripped 367:30

    naked came I out of my mother's w. 36:34

    our mothers' w.s the tiring houses be 9:1

    Saviour, all in his mother's w. 22:9

    teeming w. of royal kings 376:17

    w. and bed of enormity 224:24

    wide w. of uncreated night 278:34

    without a governorship . . . out of your mother's w. 105:11

Women: are not w. . . . the shadows of us men? 225:19

    by bad w. been deceived 281:20

    charming w. can true converts make 162:1

    dear dead w. 79:4

    experience of w. 148:3

    far hence, forbidding w. 301:22

    for several virtues . . . like several w. 381:3

    framed to make w. false 374:12

    from alle wymmen [w.] my love is lent 5:10

    goes with W. and Champagne 30:26

    happiest w. . . . have no history 155:16

    hard it is for w. to keep counsel 360:3

    hear these tell-tale w. 378:11

    how w. pass the time 198:16

    if w. could be fair and yet not fond 302:21

    learned about w. from 'er 239:24

    love of w.! . . . a lovely and a fearful thing 91:14

    man of sense only trifles with them 109:12

    Monstrous Regiment of W. 242:8

    more pangs and fears than . . . w. have 358:22

    most w. are not so young 29:1

    music and w. 307:19

    nonsense of the old w. 405:26

    our fancies are . . . sooner lost and worn, than w.'s are 383:10

    passing the love of w. 36:3

    pleasing punishment that w. bear 346:18

    revolve like ancient w. 156:31

    souls of w. are so small 87:29

    sung w. in three cities 317:19

    sweet is revenge – especially to w. 91:5

    tide in the affairs of w. 91:43

    why need the other w. know so much 72:21

    W. and Horses and Power and War 238:12

    w. are a sex by themselves 29:9

    w. are angels, wooing 381:34

    w. are angels, yet wedlock's the devil 93:11

    w. are foolish 155:12

    w. are mostly troublesome cattle 258:19

w. are strongest 47:28

w. become like their mothers 455:14

w. cloy the appetites they feed 343:30

w., [differ] worst and best 417:6

w. have cancers 234:4

w. have no characters 314:22

w. in London who flirt 455:9

w. . . . more like each other 109:15

w. must be half-workers 347:7

w. must weep 237:19

w. never look so well 409:26

w. represent the triumph 456:9

w. require both 88:16

w. run to extremes 243:4

w. should be struck regularly 123:20

w. should talk an hour 28:1

w. who would render the Christian life . . . difficult 254:6

    young men slain, the w. weeping 14:14

Womman: w. cast hir shame away 108:16

    worthy w. al hir lyve 107:24

Wommen: w. desyren to have sovereyntee 108:17

Won: things w. are done 381:34

    who w. and who lost 236:19

Wonder: apples of w. 148:24

    Boneless W. 112:13

    common w. of all men 71:7

    his w.s to perform 125:30

    lost the w. of our age 188:10

    multiply my signs and my w.s 34:46

    transcendent w. 99:30

    without our special w. 366:31

    w.s are many 401:3

    w.s in the deep 40:17

    w.s we seek without us 70:25

Wonderful: O w., w., and most w. 345:21

    passing strange and w. 390:19

Wont: as ever they were w. to be 124:11

Woo: that would w. her 374:6

    why, having won her do I w.? 305:24

Wood: bows down to w. and stone 196:25, 238:26

    dark impenetrable w. 340:21

    enter these enchanted w.s 272:15

    go down to the w.s today 235:13

    heap on more w. 340:14

    house in the high w. 31:4

    immeasurable height of w.s decaying 465:24

    impulse from a vernal w. 466:29

    never knew the summer w.s 417:33

    old w. burn brightest 449:1

    pathless w.s 90:19

    spirit in the w.s 463:27

    teach the w.s to echo back 441:9

    through the green w.s 14:23

    when all the w.s are still 282:12

    when the green w.s laugh 62:17

    when these w.s were young 427:5

    wild in w.s the noble savage 151:21

    w.s against the world 63:32

    w.s are lovely, dark and deep 170:14

    w.s decay, the w.s decay and fall 423:22

    w.s shall to me answer 402:21

Wood-note: warble his native w.s wild 276:32

Woodbine: over-canopied with luscious w. 371:38

Woodcock: spirits of well-shot w. 32:15

    springes to catch w.s 348:25

Woodland: about the w.s I will go 210:7

her noblest w. she classes 84:23
honest God's the noblest w. of man 88:15
I, a w. of God's hand 78:16
I like w.: it fascinates me 218:8
I want w. 354:5
if any would not work 56:38
I'm going to w. 108:35
it's off to w. we go 142:21
left no immortal w. 234:16
let the toad w. 247:23
look on my w.s ye mighty 392:15
man goeth forth to his w. 40:13
men . . . that do no w. today 357:14
no more w. for poor old Ned 168:10
noblest w. of God 84:7, 314:9
noblest w.s and foundations 19:9
ordinary w.s convince 19:35
out of w. for a day 236:16
plenty of w. to do 218:5
rest from their . . . w.s 58:24
reward him according to his w.s 57:8
rich in good w.s 57:4
some w. of noble note 424:8
sport would be as tedious as to w. 353:27
their w. continueth 240:26
there is no w. . . . in the grave 43:37
thy glorious w.s 280:9
volume of w. were to increase . . . or disappear
    304:22
warm w.; and this day may be the last 293:3
when all its w. is done 306:4
when no man can w. 53:21
who first invented w. 245:8
woman . . . full of good w.s 53:48
w. banishes those three great evils 442:12
w. comes out more beautiful 173:19
w. expands so as to fill the time available 304:21
w. for all 60:3
w. for man to mend 150:14
w. in the dark 216:17
w. is the curse of the drinking classes 456:25
w. is the grand cure 100:5
w. that aspires . . . to . . . art 121:23
w. your hands from day to day 264:12
w.s done least rapidly 76:9
w.s of the Lord 40:17
Workers: w. of the world unite 269:14
Workhouse: Christmas Day in the w. 397:11
    woman's w. 388:32
Working: sink . . . into the w. class 301:1
Working-day: full of briers is this w. world.! 344:22
Workmanship: inscrutable w. 465:5
Workshop: w. of the world 142:23
World: adapt the w. to himself 388:30
    all the w.'s a stage 345:11
    allured to brighter w.s 181:2
    as good be out of the w. 114:8
    as they did in the golden w. 344:14
    best of all possible w.s 95:3, 442:8
    bestride the narrow w. 359:16
    better w. than this 344:21
    between two w.s 11:8
    bright and rolling w.s 392:21
    busy w. and I shall ne'er agree 124:13
    citizen, . . . of the w. 400:21
    contagion to this w. 351:20
    exhausted w.s 219:3

far other w.s and other seas 268:21
fashion of this w. passeth away 55:8
from this vile w., with vilest worms 386:8
gain the whole w. 50:26, 51:36
girdled with the gleaming w. 420:18
gleams that untravelled w. 424:4
God so loved the w. 53:8
great while ago the w. begun 383:34
habitable w. 151:10
had we but w. enough 268:31
half the w. in a fit of absence 341:25
heard the w. around 277:23
her beauty made the bright w. dim 394:25
hold the w. but as the w. 369:1
how the w. wags 345:3
I am this w. 435:11
I have not loved the w., nor the w. me 90:3
if the w. were good for nothing else 195:13
it's a funny old w. 163:9
it's love that makes the w. go round 8:4
let the great w. spin 420:5
let the w. sink 199:29
let the w. slide 201:1
little w. made cunningly 145:13
live unto the w. 377:17
lover's quarrel with the w. 170:3
Mad W., My Masters 67:21
mad w.! mad kings! 361:11
made up . . . of fools and knaves 79:23
man for whom the outside w. exists 173:20
many w.s of consciousness 217:11
may the w. go well with thee 8:21
more things wrought by prayer than this w.
    dreams of 417:19
more w.s than I can lose 151:15
noble w. . . . be governed by . . . purest monarchy
    286:5
noisy w. hears least 461:21
not a joy the w. can give 93:26
nothing into this w. 57:1
nourish all the w. 363:32
O brave new w. 381:18
O w. invisible, we view thee 427:17
O w.! O life! O time! 391:16
of this bad w. 30:25
oh w., no w. 242:20
one loves His w. so much 76:30
pass through this w. but once 188:7
pendant w. 368:22
pomp and glory of this w. 358:22
prophetic soul of the wide w. 386:26
quiet limit of the w. 423:23
reconverted to the w. 461:24
riddle of the w. 314:2
ringed with the azure w. 416:12
runs the w. away 351:14
search well another w. 438:14
sent before my time into this breathing w.
    377:23
set the w. in motion 305:8
so many w.s, so much to do 418:16
solitary monk who shook the w. 286:4
springth the w. nu 5:13
start of the majestic w. 359:15
still point of the turning w. 155:32
stood against the w. 360:18
Ten Days that Shook the W. 326:13

Wound: bind up my w.s! 378:18
   bindeth up their w.s 41:16
   every w. of Caesar 360:24
   faithful are the w.s of a friend 42:46
   fight and not to heed the w.s 259:11
   help to w. itself 361:28
   man . . . keeps his own w.s green 19:2
   purple with love's w. 371:36
   such a w., the knife is lost 391:19
   take away the grief of a w. 355:2
   what w. did ever heal but by degrees? 374:28
Wounded: went to tend the w. 239:9
Wrack: thousand fearful w.s 378:1
Wrangle: w. for religion 119:30
Wrath: envy and w. shorten the life 48:17
   flee from the w. 48:37
   having great w. 58:21
   I told my w. 62:2
   infinite w., and infinite despair 279:19
   nursing her w. 85:13
   slow to w. 57:21
   soft answer turneth away w. 42:11
   sun go down upon your w. 56:18
   that day of w. 340:3
   w. of God 56:19
Wreath: subtle w. of hair 145:6
Wreck: hope creates from its own w. 393:19
   my brother's w. 157:5
   sunken w. and sumless treasuries 356:23
   w. of a square that broke 293:22
Wren: hurt the little w. 60:13
   I bore this w. 151:16
   Sir Christopher W. said 31:28
   w. goes to 't, and the small gilded fly 362:39
Wrestle: he that w.s with us 82:23
   w. not against flesh and blood 56:22
   w. with words 155:34
Wrestling: lay w. with . . . my God 205:23
Wretch: excellent w.! 374:29
   sharp-looking w. 346:19
   w., concentred all in self 340:1
   w. even then 126:4
   w. who won 90:15
Wretched: more skilled to raise the w. 180:24
   w. he forsakes 472:18
Wretchedness: w. of being rich 399:9
Wretches: expose thyself to feel what w. feel
      362:20
   sentence sign and w. hang 315:21
Wriggles: w. and giggles 203:1
Wrinkle: flower which w.s will devour 292:20
   stamps the w. deeper 89:20
   w. on thy azure brow 90:22
Writ: I never w. 387:2
   proofs of holy w. 375:2
   stol'n forth of holy w. 377:29
Write: how to w. letters 120:25
   I w. them 322:14
   little more I have to w. 200:7
   man may w. at any time 220:17
   man ought to w. 432:3
   people read because they want to w. 337:21
   w. and read comes by nature 373:4
   w. me as one that loves his fellow men 212:11
   w. when I feel spiteful 249:23
Writer: great and original w. 467:25
   little bit of the w.'s pride 336:19

no regime has ever loved great w.s 400:28
original w. . . . one whom nobody can imitate
   107:4
race of w.s . . . termed the *metaphysical* poets
   219:21
talent alone cannot make a w. 159:8
w. has to rob his mother 162:6
w. whose tendency is to make their language
   convey 121:11
w.'s ambition 242:12
w.s become more numerous 181:34
Writhe: w. from the waist upwards 137:15
Writhed: w. not at passed joy 233:15
Writing: easy w.'s curst hard reading 395:39
   get it in w. 251:21
   good w. is *swimming under water*165:12
   historians left blanks in their w.s 317:16
   in doubt . . . in his w. 88:4
   incurable itch for w. 228:2
   left hardly any style of w. untouched 222:24
   true ease in w. 313:14
   w. . . . different name for conversation 405:20
   w. and exact man 20:33
   w. increaseth rage 188:10
   w. is like getting married 290:2
   w. is nothing more than a guided dream 65:5
   w. 'The Shadow of the Glen' 413:9
   w. without thinking 146:25
Written: what I have w., I have 53:36
Wroghte: first he w. and afterward he taughte
   107:25
Wrong: alas my love ye do me w. 7:20
   all his life . . . in the w. 328:11
   always seemed to put it in the w. place 326:12
   called them by w. names 73:8
   could not endure being w. 98:3
   divinely in the w. 472:15
   do a little w. 370:10
   do him w. to sing so wildly 418:12
   doing w. extenuates not w. 382:6
   forgive w.s darker than death 393:19
   he done her w. 7:17
   if you w. us 369:33
   mass of public w.s 242:20
   multitude is always in the w. 330:14
   my country, right or w. 110:27
   no harm in being sometimes w. 236:10
   one idea, and that is a w. one 222:2
   one w. more to man 75:19
   our country right or w. 133:10
   redressing human w.s 416:31
   right w. 416:28
   something has gone w., however slightly
      317:11
   something w. with our bloody ships 27:12
   telling a man he was w. 116:1
   two w.s don't make a right 413:14
   wail for the world's w. 390:20
   w. from the start 317:20
   w. I did them 76:1
   w. left unredressed on earth 238:2
   w. people travel 123:21
   w. war at the w. place 66:13
   w. way to do something 290:6
Wykehamist: rather dirty W. 33:3
Wynken: W., Blynken and Nod 162:14
Wysest: noght the w. 108:11

X

Xanadu: in X. did Kubla Khan 117:35
Xenophon: 64:21

Y

Y-wet: whistle wel y. 108:12
Yale: whale ship was my Y. College 271:19
Yankee: Y. Doodle came to town 23:27
Yard: he found . . . that a y. was as long 232:17
    posing in the old back y. 290:7
Yarn: merry y. from a laughing fellow-rover 270:4
    mingled y., good and ill together 343:10
Yawn: too tired to y. 134:31
Yawp: barbaric y. 454:3
Yë: slepen al the night with open y. 107:8
Yea: let your y. be y. 57:28
    russet y.s and honest kersey noes 364:4
Year: Ah! happy y.s.! 89:16
    another y.! – another deadly blow 463:26
    beginning of y.s 412:3
    book that is not a y. old 159:11
    cuts off twenty y.s of his life 360:6
    days of the y.s of my life 34:37
    down the arches of the y.s 427:12
    five thousand million y.s old 309:10
    fleeting y.s are slipping by 208:20
    go softly all my y.s 45:28
    golden y.s return 391:2
    how many y.s a mortal man may live 358:7
    how many y.s can some people exist 153:6
    impress upon her tender y.s 121:4
    it may be for y.s 129:3
    knightly y.s were gone 198:2
    leaves before the mellowing y. 276:36
    making their remaining y.s unhappy 243:6
    most immemorial y. 310:30
    my thirtieth y. to heaven 426:12
    New Y. reviving old Desires 163:24
    nine y.s a-killing 375:12
    now of my threescore y.s and ten 210:6
    out of me the y.s roll 412:21
    proclaim the acceptable y. 46:18
    provoke the y.s to bring the . . . yoke 464:12
    remember not the past y.s 294:4
    revolving y. 389:28
    ruler of th' inverted y. 127:14
    save the undone y.s 302:17
    season of the golden y. 416:22
    seven thousand y.s in which man existed 243:8
    seventy y.s ago 241:4
    stoln . . . my three and twentieth y. 281:34
    such as are of Riper Y.s 319:27
    that time of y. 386:10
    three y.s she grew 467:2
    touch of earthly y.s 466:19
    twentieth y. is well-nigh past 127:34
    vale of y.s 374:34
    we spend our y.s as a tale that is told 39:33
    where all past y.s are 146:7
    whispered by the phantom y.s 419:26
    y. has shot her yield 239:31
    y.s draw nigh 44:9
    y.s like great black oxen 470:12

y.s of discretion 319:35
Yearning: y. for the gutter 15:29
Yellow: tawdry y. strove with dirty red 315:3
    things you will learn from the Y. and Brown
        239:23
    y., and black, and pale 392:4
    y. to the jaundiced eye 313:21
Yën: paradys stood formed in hir y. 108:27
Yeoman: y.'s service 353:4
Yeomen: y., whose limbs were made in England
    357:5
Yere: snow of ferne y. 108:28
Yes: way of getting the answer y. 98:4
Yesterday: all our y.s 367:24
    art of keeping up with y. 267:28
    but as y. 39:31
    call back y. 376:28
    man's y. may never be like his tomorrow 392:3
    Rose of Y. 164:28
    same y. and today 57:18
    stuck fast in Y. 134:19
    was it y. 11:6
    Y.'s Sev'n Thousand Years 164:8
Yet: but not y. 16:2
Yettis: y. of hell ar brokin 152:15
Yew: never a spray of y. 11:16
Yield: to find, and not to y. 424:11
    y. of joy and woe 74:6
Yoke: bear his mild y. 282:4
    savage bull doth bear the y. 372:26
    unaccustomed to the y. 125:25
Yolk: pasty . . . with golden y.s 415:16
Yonghy-Bonghy-Bò: lived the Y. 250:16
Yorick: Alas! poor Y. 352:25
York: noble Duke of Y. 6:12
    this sun of Y. 377:20
Young, Brigham 446:19
Young: blush into the cheek of a y. person 140:11
    both were y. 92:20
    crime of being a y. man 309:15
    I have been y. 63:33
    I have been y. and am now old 38:15
    I was very y. 62:9
    in comparison with which y. man 138:2
    lead those that are with y. 45:34
    life went a-maying . . . when I was y. 118:14
    like all y. men you exaggerate 388:14
    no y. man believes he shall ever die 196:2
    not so y. as they are painted 29:1
    Scotchman, if he be caught y. 222:7
    she died so y. 310:23
    singularly deep y. man 177:40
    so wise so y., they say 378:3
    so y. and so untender 361:30
    that 'ere y. lady 141:17
    though there he settle y. 305:23
    thoughts of y. 256:31
    to be y. was very heaven 465:27
    we were y., we were merry 116:17
    when music, . . . was y. 119:17
    whom the gods love die y. 91:32
    y. get younger 289:2
    y. man married 343:9
    y. men glittering and sparkling 431:16
    y. shall never see so much 363:16
Youngest: not even the y. among us 428:4
Yours: what is y. is mine 368:32

Youth: affair of y. 165:6
   approve of y. 77:22
   caught our y. 69:17
   done it from my y. 128:5
   figure of blown y. 350:22
   from her earliest y. 30:15
   home-keeping y. have ever homely wits 384:1
   hour of thoughtless y. 462:19
   in my y., I never did apply . . . liquors to the blood
     344:29
   'In my y.,' Father William replied 100:33
   in the days of my y. 401:23
   in the days of thy y. 44:9
   in y. it sheltered me 288:9
   laugh uproariously in y. 69:15
   lexicon of y. 260:18
   many a y. and many a maid 276:28
   my thoughtless y. was winged 150:19
   nourishing a y. sublime 419:18
   Rejoice, O young man, in thy y. 44:8
   sign of an ill-spent y. 402:12
   sins of my y. 38:6
   spirit of y. in everything 386:20
   sweet wine of y. 69:6
   Time, the subtle thief of y. 281:34
   vaward of our y. 355:16
   very riband in the cap of y. 352:17
   wherein the noble y. did dress himself 355:26
   y. and pleasure meet 89:22
   y. are boarded, clothed, booked 139:6
   y., beauty, graceful action 149:26
   y. grows pale and spectre-thin 232:3
   y. is a blunder 143:15
   y. is full of pleasance 385:4
   y. is vain 117:23
   y. of England are on fire 356:26
   y. on the prow 185:24
   y. pined away with desire 61:18
   y. replies, *I can* 158:16
   y. shows but half 77:11

   y. who bore, 'mid snow and ice 256:23
   y. who daily farther from the east 464:8
   y. will be served 65:13
   y. will come here and thunder at my door
     214:13
   y. would sleep out the rest 384:19
   y.'s a stuff will not endure 383:3
   y.'s heritage 77:17
   y.'s smooth ocean 393:13
   Y.'s sweet-scented Manuscript 164:29
   y.'s the season made for joys 174:11
Yukon: law of the Y. 342:25

Z

Zeal: all z. Mr Easy 268:5
   mistaken z. in politics 227:11
   not too much z.! 414:11
   z. of God 54:34
Zed: thou whoreson z.! 362:7
Zenith: dropt from the z. like a falling star 278:27
Zenocrate: entertain divine Z. 267:18
   fair Z. – divine Z. 267:17
Zephuri: lucundis Z. silescit auris 103:18
Zephyr: roses by the z. blown apart 231:3
Zephyrus: sweet-breathing Z. did softly play 403:11
Zimri: had Z. peace 36:29
Zion: Lord shall bring again Z. 46:5
   one of the songs of Z. 41:10
   round Z. of the water bead 426:13
   we wept when we remembered Z. 41:9
   Z. city of our God 294:10
Zitronen: wo die Z. blühn 180:9
Zone: torrid or frozen z. 98:28
Zoo: Lord No Z. 138:21
Zoroaster: Magus Z., my dead child 392:24
Zuleika: Z. on a desert island 29:13
Zürich: gnomes of Z. 458:3